THE FOOD
OF THE
WESTERN
WORLD

ALSO BY THEODORA FITZGIBBON

Cosmopolitan Cookery in an English Kitchen
Weekend Cookery
The High Protein Diet and Cookery Book (with Dr. Michael Hemans)
Country House Cooking
The Young Cook's Book
Game Cooking
The Art of British Cooking
Eat Well and Live Longer (with Dr. Robert Wilson)
Theodora FitzGibbon's Cookery Book
A Taste of Ireland
A Taste of Scotland
A Taste of Wales
A Taste of England: The West Country
A Taste of London
A Taste of Paris
A Taste of Rome

FICTION

Flight of the Kingfisher

THE FOOD
OF THE
WESTERN
WORLD

*An encyclopedia of food from Europe
and North America*

THEODORA FITZGIBBON

Illustrations prepared by George Morrison

Hutchinson of London

Photographs courtesy of: Angel Studio, page 205; Austrian National Tourist Office, page 234; Belgian National Tourist Office, pages 157, 168, 215 (left), 231 (bottom right), 515 (top); Birds Eye Foods Ltd., pages 91, 316, 485; Bord Iscaigh Mhara, pages 3, 135, 181, 231, 506; British Egg Information Service, pages 376, 423 (bottom), 482, 495, 524, 527; Danish Food Centre, page 437; Dutch Dairy Bureau, pages 291, 450, 492; Food from France, pages 8, 18, 119, 286, 308, 416; Paul Kemp, pages 17, 112 (upper left), 140; Ministry of Tourism, Parma, page 368 (bottom); George Morrison, pages 4, 10, 15, 19, 21, 25, 50, 72, 151, 230, 337, 423 (top), 466; National Dairy Council, pages 313, 368 (top), 454; National Tourist Organization of Greece, pages 20, 111, 226, 238; Voula Papaïoannou, page 319; P.R. Visuals Ltd., page 417; RHM Foods Ltd., pages 247, 344; SOPEXA, pages 22, 165; Spanish National Tourist Office, pages 215 (right), 389, 409, 518; Swiss National Tourist Office, pages 249 (left), 379, 465; Turkish Tourism, page 228; USDA, pages 54, 293, 489 (bottom left).

HUTCHINSON & CO (Publishers) Ltd
3 Fitzroy Square, London W1

London Melbourne Sydney Auckland
Wellington Johannesburg and agencies
throughout the world

First published 1976

To my husband, George Morrison,
who gave me not only encouragement and understanding during
the 15 years of work, but also practical help on all scientific
subjects.

Acknowledgments

My sincerest thanks are due to the many friends who have lent me precious books and papers for long periods, and who have helped me in my research for this book, especially Elizabeth Foster-Melliar, Anna Sheehy, Fionnuala Cullen, and Bronaca Ryan. I am also indebted to Thorvaldur Gudmundsson of Reykjavik, Iceland; the members of the Kirk Michael Women's Institute, Isle of Man; the German and Italian Cultural Institutes; Dr. A. T. Lucas, Director of the National Museum, Dublin, Ireland; Lt.-Col. Brian Clark, M.C., G.M.; Mrs. Munkŏ Orbach; Dr. and Mrs. Michael Wray; Mr. Donald Ross; and Mr. Anthony Dent for their help and the use of many reference works.

I also wish to thank Professor David Greene, Senior Professor of the Dublin Institute for Advanced Studies, who has been exceedingly helpful to me in solving many linguistic problems.

A special mention must be given to my editors, Claire Carlton and Rebecca Sacks, who by their kindness, patience, and hard work have advanced the publication of this book by many months. And finally, my deepest thanks to Betty Vreeland for her immense help just when it was needed.

T.F.G.
Dalkey, County Dublin

Contents

Introduction

The culinary art is one of the most ancient forms of expression, and, although a great many regional studies have been conducted, no really widely ranging survey of Europe and North America as a whole has, heretofore, been carried out. The present work is an attempt toward such a survey. In this book some 34 countries have been examined from the point of view of their traditional food habits and the flora and fauna which have influenced them.

It is not only geographical, geological, and agricultural conditions which have decided the food of a nation, but also the climate and history. Invasions, oppressions, explorations, foreign alliances, and social changes such as the Industrial Revolution have in some cases radically altered the eating habits of the countries concerned.

What has interested me in the correlation and writing of this book is the gastromonic inter-relation of the whole western world. The Russian *forshmak* is not such a far cry from the humble shepherd's pie. Potato cakes, universally thought of as traditionally Irish, exist in many forms in Jewish cookery. The good, rich peasant stews of all countries differ but little from each other, and all maritime peoples have fish soups and stews in common.

As early as 1500 B.C., the Phoenicians were attracted to the copper mines of Cyprus, and later to the tin mines of Cornwall. Wherever they journeyed, they established trading settlements, and the indigenous peoples bartered their raw materials for cloth, tools, wine, oil, and spices. Saffron, still used in the traditional Cornish saffron cakes and buns, is said to have been brought by these early visitors.

By the middle of the 8th century B.C., the Greeks began to found small colonies along the shores of the Mediterranean and the Black seas, and they too exchanged goods for the food and raw materials of the colonised countries. The Greek colony was not merely a trading post, it was a centre of Greek life. The sacred fire was carried from the public hearth of the homeland to the new settlement. Cicero wrote in *De Republica,* "All the Greek colonies are washed by the waves of the sea, and, so to speak, a fringe of Greek earth is woven on to foreign lands." Their most important colony was Byzantium, now Istanbul, where Greek and Turkish food remains intermixed today. Naples (Neapolis), the "new city," was built by the Greeks, and that influence can be clearly seen in the features of the southern Italians, as well as in the food of that area.

The Macedonian king Alexander the Great (356–323 B.C.) successfully invaded Persia, Asia Minor, India, and Egypt. From the latter he brought back the onion, regarded as a sacred plant in Egypt. He observed the cultivation of the haricot bean in India, and brought back seeds to grow in Greece. He must have been extremely interested in food for he gave the Indians their first vines in exchange for the beans, but they did not flourish in India. Cabbage was another of his culinary conquests. Again the ancient Egyptians worshipped it, and both the Greeks and the Romans thought it a cure for hangover. Cabbage was also thought to help paralysed people, and it was cooked with cumin, onion, fresh coriander leaves, caraway, pepper, and salt.

The Romans, superseding the Etruscans, conquered and colonised large parts of Europe and Asia, and again the interchange of cultures and eating habits is apparent. The famous Roman general Lucullus (110–56 B.C.) is perhaps better known for his fantastic banquets than his military victories. Plutarch wrote, "The life of Lucullus was like an ancient comedy where first we see great actions, both political and military, and afterwards feasts, debauches, races by torchlight, and every kind of frivolous amusement." It was Lucullus who converted the slopes of the Pincio in Rome to a fine series of terraces on which he kept thrushes. Plutarch wrote that when Pompey was ill and his doctor ordered him a dish of thrushes, they could be found nowhere at that time of the year except in Lucullus's breeding pens.

The ancient Romans knew and loved their food, and pertinent comments are made on the subject, especially by Pliny the Elder, who writes in *Naturalis historia* of cabbage, the fattening of snails, the spaying of cows to make them fatter, and even the use of additives to food. "In bread they put saltpetre from Chalastra instead of salt. With horse-radishes they use saltpetre from Egypt. This makes them more tender, but it takes away the colour of other foods and spoils it." He also advised a pinch of baking soda to keep the colour in boiled greenstuffs, thus being the first to introduce the habit of sacrificing flavour and vitamin content to colour.

The Romans brought many foods, such as cherries, grapes, and snails to Britain and during their almost three-hundred-year visit they worked the mines, improved the making of pottery and cloth, and the cultivation of wheat, as well as introducing the system of weights and measures and the making of wine.

In Britain many other cultural influences were felt and aspects were incorporated into the civilization. The Saxons had a great knowledge of herbs and farming. The Vikings (Danes) brought methods for storing butter, cheese, and whey ferments. They also knew a lot about salting, curing, and smoking foods. We can thank them for our bacon, and smoked fishes such as kippers, bloaters, smoked salmon and trout, and the famous smoked haddock from Findon, Scotland. The Scandinavian ties with Scotland are still very close.

A marked French influence is also found in Scotland, both in the food itself and in names of certain Scottish dishes which can be traced to the succession of French queens. The Norman invasion brought many new ideas to the kitchen as well as new words for foods; the words *beef* (from boeuf) and *mutton* (mouton) supplanting the words ox and sheep. The word *sauce* comes from the Latin word *salsus,* salted, but the word *saucer* comes from the Norman practice of serving sauces on individual plates for each diner. The regular folds of table napkins stem from the water-lily and the fleur-de-lys of the Norman table.

England has always been a host to many oppressed peoples, so, much later, there were the Flemish weavers who introduced the cooking of prunes with poultry and meat as in Hindle Wakes chicken. Today the many Indian and Pakistani restaurants are exerting their influence on the eating habits and cooking of the younger generation. This of course is also true in the United States, where the influence can be traced to the European country of origin of the immigrants, as well as to the indigenous American Indian, and, in the south, to Mexico and the Spanish conquests.

We in Europe daily eat many foods which came from the New World. The potato, which originally came from Quito in South America, was first brought to Europe by the Spaniards; the turkey was brought to Europe by the Jesuits, and is still called *jésuite* in parts of France; the rainbow trout has now completely adapted to European waters; and the Jerusalem artichoke, a native of Canada, was first imported into France in the 17th century.

Russian cuisine still shows the influence of nomadic peoples by its sour milk products; the use of large skewers or twigs for cooking meats over open fires, as in the case of shashlyk; the grinding or mincing of meat, which is a sure way of tenderising freshly killed, unhung carcases. Steak Tartare is reputed to have stemmed from the days when the Cossacks hung their meat under their saddles, finding the long day's riding broke down the fibres and made the meat more tender.

Prominent Russians and noblemen of the 18th and 19th centuries left their mark on classical French cuisine with such dishes as Beef Stroganoff, named after a Russian general; Veal Orloff from Prince Orloff's chef; the famous Nesselrode Pudding, favourite of the Russian aristocrat; and the salad and soup Bagration, named after Prince Peter Bagration who defeated Napolean at Eylau. A dinner given in his honour is described in Tolstoy's *War and Peace*.

Fashion changes food as much as dress, therefore, whenever possible I have preserved the old form rather than the new, so that it will not be lost. Some may be puzzled by my choice of traditional American foods. My motive in this book has been to perpetuate tradition, and I have deliberately chosen foods that were eaten for at least a hundred years and possibly much longer. America is not such a "new world" anymore and many traditional dishes are still served especially in country districts. Therefore I felt that American dishes, even if no longer generally made, should be included as part of that country's culinary history. Where a recipe occurs in several old sources I have made sure to include it. It is interesting to note how many customs of the Old World, now perhaps forgotten there, are still kept up in the United States. To this day the Colorado Folk Lore Society holds a Cornish dinner, with traditional Cornish dishes such as Leeky pie and Cornish pasties, on the Eve of St. Piran's Day. St. Piran, the patron saint of "tinners," came from Ireland and died in 550 A.D.

Although I would like to think of this book as a broad history of food, it is also a cookery book. Cooking is undoubtedly one of the major arts, and although scientific methods can and are applied to it, the ultimate result is due to the unique sensibilities of each individual cook. If six cooks followed the same recipe, the finished dish would vary six times. This should not dismay but be a challenge. Intuition, experience, aptitude, and one might almost say affection, play their roles in the preparation of food. Many factors are involved that can change the taste: the age of the animal used, the soil on which the pasture or vegetables were grown, the freshness of the produce. All living organisms are modified by their physical and chemical environment, and small differences in their surroundings can, and often do, produce very marked differences in the many subtle compounds which incorporate that elusive element flavour. The perfect example of this is the apple. The apple likes a temperate climate; that is, a cold but not severe winter, and a warm but not too hot summer. It also dislikes growing at above 600 feet in altitude. Nowadays many of the popular varieties such as Golden Delicious and Pippin are grown all over Europe and the United States as well as in South Africa and Australia. However you have only to eat the apple grown in a Kent or Normandy orchard and compare it to one grown in South Africa to see what I mean. Size and colour are no sure guides to excellence of taste.

In the field of artificially produced foods, such as cheese, this differentiation is further influenced by the special bacterial and fungal flora which are an essential part of the processes involved. An example of this is the effect on cheddar of the salinity of the soil where the cows graze, and the true Cheshire cheese. The limestone caves where Roquefort cheese is slowly matured have an underground lake which creates the humid atmosphere that is uniquely favourable to the ripening process. All this becomes obvious when one tastes the many imitations now made all over the world. Although they might have a good flavour, it is not the same as the original cheese. It is for this reason that many of the world's finest foods continue to be made by traditional methods in spite of the great advances in chemical technology over the past century. This is all part of the art of cooking, and must be accepted and accounted for.

There are many days and many meals in a lifetime. The desire to achieve perfection, and to please family or friends, is the basis of all traditional cooking, and also the reason it is so difficult to extract a "traditional" recipe. Brothers, and brother chefs, will argue all night on whether thyme or marjoram should be used in a certain dish, and it is this interchange that keeps dishes alive. Many traditional recipes of small European countries are fragmentary, perhaps only consisting of a paragraph or two in an out-of-print book or manuscript. These I have included, along with recipes for all basic foods, although they may be difficult for any but the experienced cook to make. Do not be too worried by exactitudes. Remember the distinguished chef Marcel Boulestin's sage remark, "The dangerous person in the kitchen is the one who goes rigidly by weights, measurements, thermometers, and scales." However, wherever possible a full recipe has been given. In a book of one volume there will, of course, be omissions. For this I apologise, and ask your indulgence, especially when I find that earlier editions of that prodigious work of French cooking, *Larousse Gastronomique* omit, amongst other things, such typical dishes as *ratatouille* and *tian*.

As many traditional foods are an integral part of the national holidays of the countries concerned, I have wherever possible included these holidays, and given a sample of the dishes eaten.

Nowadays all foods can be transported all over the world in a matter of hours. Even so, it is perhaps better to perfect and carry on one's own traditions before embarking on the culinary holiday which I hope this book will give to my readers.

The difficulty of coordinating information from the many countries, involving over thirty languages, has been immense. At times it seemed that no two sources would ever agree, not only as to the correct ingredients for a recipe, but also to the spelling of that dish when the first problem had been solved. France is exceptional in having produced a firmly established classical cuisine. Nevertheless despite all the difficulties, this work has given me pleasure to write, as I hope it will give my readers to use.

Notes on Using This Book

Every effort has been made to make this book useful to both American and British readers. Though Britishisms abound in the text, assiduous copyediting has endeavoured to make clear any culinary expressions that may be ambiguous. The material has been arranged alphabetically and contains plentiful cross references to aid the reader.

Languages using the Greek, Cyrillic, or Chinese alphabets are extremely difficult to render into English as no standard transliterations for certain sounds exist in the Latin alphabet. There is, therefore, great diversity of spelling. The Russian word czar is a good example: it is equally well known in English as tzar, tsar, and csar. I have endeavored to cross-index such words throughout the book.

American equivalents are given in parentheses following the usual British term if any ambiguity was felt to exist. This is true both for measures and for specific terminology. In the case of measurements, the English quantities have been converted into convenient American equivalents. Although the metric system is not yet widely used in the U.S., it doubtless will be in the near future. A table of weights and measures appears on pages xvii–xix.

In common British usage, many words will be unfamiliar to an American audience. In these cases, the American common name is inserted in parentheses following the British. For example, aubergines, tunny-fish, and vegetable marrows are common British terms for eggplant, tuna, and zucchini.

In all countries the art of butchery has evolved according to local custom and history. In order to aid the reader a complete chart of the various cuts of beef, veal, pork, and lamb has been provided with the American, English, and French terms accompanied by clear cut diagrams. These appear on pages xxi–xxvii.

American and British cooks also have available slightly different ingredients. A word about these is in order.

FLOUR. Generally no specific flour has been specified in the recipes. In Britain and Europe only bread flour, plain, and self-raising flour can be bought. However, if cake or pastry flour is available, as is true in America, then by all means use it when making a cake or pastry. Also, if the hard durum flour is available, then that, too, should be used for making pasta. All flour measurements given are for unsifted flour unless otherwise indicated.

CORNSTARCH. Cornstarch is known as corn flour in Britain and Ireland. In America, it is used strictly as a thickening agent, but certain European recipes use cornstarch as a flour, so do not be alarmed when larger quantities than you are accustomed to using are called for in the text.

SUGAR. In Europe and Britain, there are many varieties of sugar available, some of which do not have direct American equivalents. Please see the entry for sugar for a complete description of the various products.

MILK. Pasteurized milk does not sour, it goes bad. When a recipe calls for sour milk, buttermilk can be used, and if buttermilk is not available, then it is possible to achieve a similar result by adding the juice of half a lemon to approximately 1 pint of milk and leaving it in a warm place for about 1 hour. In some cases yogourt may be used, but this is always specified in the text. Cream can also be soured by using the lemon method, but is only advised as a last resort; it is not nearly as good as real cultured sour cream.

Conversion Table for Weights and Measures

English and American measurements differ slightly as the following tables will show. However, all American measures given in the book are scaled accordingly. All spoons are measured level unless otherwise stated. The metric measurements are to the nearest round figure, to make for easy weighing.

LIQUID MEASURE

American

1 pint = 16 fluid oz.
1 cup = 16 tablespoons = 8 fluid oz.
1 tablespoon = 3 teaspoons

British

1 pint = 20 fluid oz.
1 cup = 20 tablespoons = 10 fluid oz.
1 tablespoon = ½ fluid oz.

Metric Capacity

1 litre = 1000 grammes
½ litre or demi-litre = 500 grammes
¼ litre = 250 grammes
1 décilitre = 100 grammes
1 centilitre = 10 grammes
1 chopine (old measurement)

British Capacity

35 fluid oz. = almost 2 pints
17½ fluid oz. = almost 1 pint
8¾ fluid oz. = almost ½ pint
3½ fluid oz. = 6 tablespoons
⅓ fluid oz. = 1 dessertspoon
½ pint approx.
4 gills = 1 pint

Spoon and Wine-Glass

1 cuillère à bouche, à soupe
1 cuillère à pot
1 cuillère à café
1 verre = 2 décilitres
1 verre à Bordeaux = 1 décilitre
1 verre à liqueur = 15 grammes
1 tasse à café

Approximate Measures

1 tablespoon = ½ oz.
1 small ladle = 2 oz.
1 small level teaspoon
7 fluid oz.
6 tablespoons
1 tablespoon
2½ oz.

SOLID MEASURES

Metric Weight		*Avoirdupois*
1 kilogramme =	1000 grammes	2 lb. 3 oz. approx.
1 livre =	500 grammes	1 lb. 1½ oz. approx.
½ livre =	250 grammes	9 oz. approx.
¼ livre =	125 grammes	4½ oz. approx.
	100 grammes	3½ oz. approx.
	12 grammes	1 tablespoon approx.

OVEN TEMPERATURES

°F	°C	GAS No.	OVEN HEAT
225°F	110°C	¼	very cool
250°F	130°C	½	very cool
275°F	140°C	1	cool
300°F	150°C	2	slow
325°F	170°C	3	moderately slow
350°F	180°C	4	moderate
375°F	190°C	5	moderately hot
400°F	200°C	6	hot
425°F	220°C	7	very hot
450°F	230°C	8	very hot

MEASURES OF SELECTED FOODS

	American	*British*	*Metric*
Almonds, whole	1 cup	5 oz.	155 grams
chopped	1 cup	4 oz.	125 grams
Apricots, dried	3 cups	1 lb.	500 grams
Baking powder	1 teaspoon	1 teaspoon	4 grams
Beans, dried	2 cups, scant	1 lb.	500 grams
Breadcrumbs, dry	1 cup	3¼ oz.	90 grams
fresh	1 cup	1½ oz.	45 grams
Butter	2 cups	1 lb.	500 grams
	1 tablespoon	½ oz.	15 grams
Cheese, hard, grated	4 cups	1 lb., generous	500 grams
fresh, grated	5½ cups	1 lb.	500 grams
cottage cheese	2 cups	1 lb.	500 grams
Chocolate	1 square	1 oz.	30 grams
Cocoa	1 cup	4 oz.	125 grams
Coconut, grated	5 cups	1 lb.	500 grams
Corn flour (cornstarch)	1 cup	4½ oz.	140 grams
	1 tablespoon	⅓ oz.	12 grams
Cornmeal	3 cups	1 lb.	500 grams
Currants	2½ cups	1 lb.	500 grams
Dates, pitted	2 cups	1 lb.	500 grams
Figs, dried, chopped	3 cups	1 lb.	500 grams

	American	*British*	*Metric*
Flour, unsifted,			
all purpose	4 cups, generous	1 lb.	500 grams
brown	4½ cups	1 lb.	500 grams
cake & pastry	1 cup	4 oz.	125 grams
graham	1 cup	5 oz.	145 grams
sifted, cake & pastry	4½ cups	1 lb.	500 grams
Gelatine	1 tablespoon	½ oz.	4–5 medium leaves
Hominy, raw	1 cup	6 oz.	170 grams
Lentils	2 cups	1 lb.	500 grams
Macaroni, raw	3 cups	1 lb.	500 grams
(1 cup raw equals 2 cups cooked)			
Margarine	1 cup	4 oz.	500 grams
Meat, diced	1 cup	8 oz.	250 grams
Noodles (1 cup raw equals 1½ cups cooked)			
Nuts, coarsely chopped	4 cups	1 lb.	500 grams
Oats, rolled (oatmeal)	1 cup, generous	4 oz.	125 grams
Polenta meal	3½ cups	1 lb.	500 grams
Prunes	2½ cups	1 lb.	500 grams
Raisins, with seeds	2½ cups	1 lb.	500 grams
seedless	3 cups, generous	1 lb.	500 grams
Rice	1 cup, generous	½ lb.	250 grams
(1 cup raw equals 3–4 cups cooked)			
Rye meal	1 cup	4½ oz.	131 grams
Sago	1 cup	6 oz.	170 grams
Split peas	2 cups, generous	1 lb.	500 grams
Sugar, granulated	2 cups, generous	1 lb.	500 grams
brown	2¾ cups firmly packed	1 lb.	500 grams
castor	1 cup, generous	6 oz.	170 grams
icing (confectioners')	3½ cups	1 lb.	500 grams
lump or loaf	60 lumps	1 lb. approx.	500 grams
Sultanas	3 cups	1 lb.	500 grams
Tapioca, pearl or quick	1 cup	6 oz.	170 grams
Treacle (molasses)	1 cup	12 oz.	375 grams
Yeast, dried	1 tablespoon	1 oz.	30 grams
	1 package	⅔ oz.	20 grams

Table of Cuts of Meat

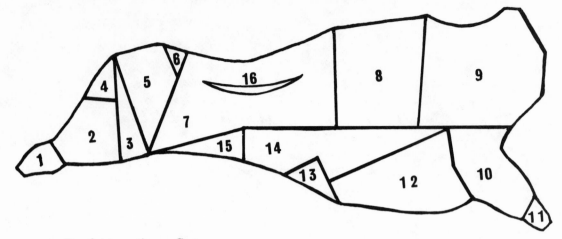

Beef: American Cuts

1. Butt end or knuckle bone
2. Top round; round steak
3. Aitchbone
4. Bottom round
5. Rump roast
6. Sirloin tip
7. Sirloin steak (tail end of section);
   rib or club steak (head end of section)
8. Rib roast

9. Chuck roast; stewing beef
10. Shank
11. Knuckle
12. Brisket
13. Rattleran
14. Shortribs; plate (tail end of section)
15. Flank
16. Tenderloin & Porterhouse (T-bone)

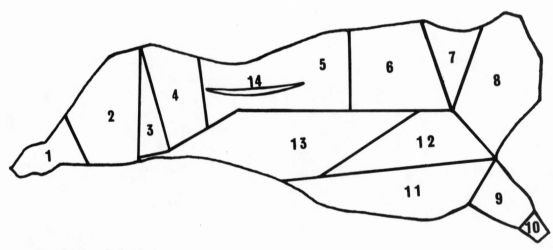

Beef: English Cuts

1. Shin
2. Round; round steak & topside;
   silverside and rump (tail end of section)
3. Aitchbone
4. Rump steak (tail end of section);
   sirloin steak (head end of section)
5. Baron (whole section both sides of back);
   this section is usually divided into either
   sirloin steak (head end of section)
6. Rib roast

7. Chuck
8. Neck
9. Shin
10. Knuckle
11. Brisket
12. Shoulder
13. Short or rolled ribs (head end of section);
    flank or skirt (tail end of section)
14. Fillet

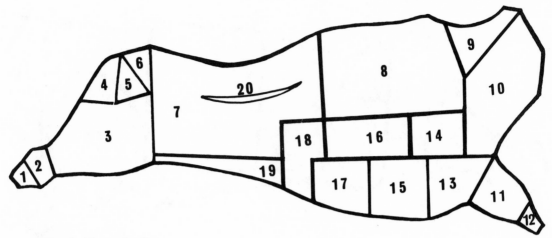

Beef: French Cuts

1. Crosse
2. Jarret or trumeau
3. Tende de tranche
4. Gite à la noix
5. Tranche grasse
6. Aiguillette & pointe de culotte
7. Entrecôte; contre filet; aloyau (in one piece)
8. Côte de boeuf (in one piece)
9. Paleron
10. Macreuse

11. Jarret or trumeau
12. Crosse
13, 15 & 17. Poitrine
14. Train de côtes (découvert)
15. Milieu de poitrine
16. Plat de côtes; entrecôte when boned
17. Milieu de tendron
18. Onglet
19. Flanchet
20. Filet; Chateaubriand

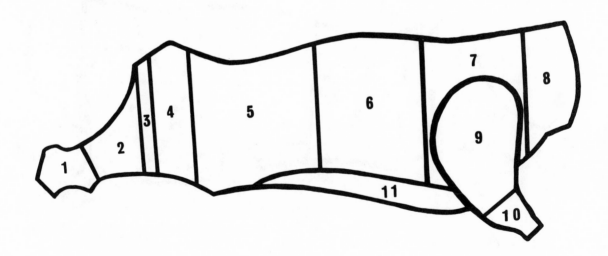

Veal: American Cuts

1. Knuckle
2. Leg from which veal birds are made; if boned, round roast
3. Round steaks (scallops)
4. Rump roast
5. Loin roast: loin chops; loin steaks (nearest to tail end)

6. Center rib chops or roast
7. Shoulder chops
8. City chicken, when cut into cubes
9. Shoulder
10. Shank
11. Breast

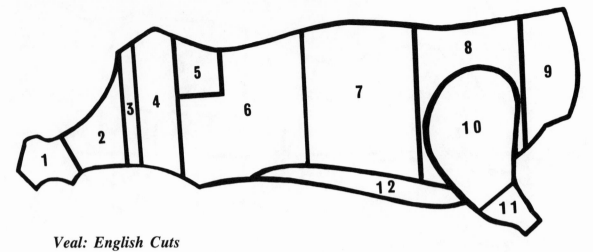

Veal: English Cuts

1. Knuckle or shin
2. Leg
3. Escallops or scallops
4. Fillet roast; escallops in slices
5. Rump end of loin
6. Saddle, if both sides of back are used; loin roast or loin cutlets
7. Best end of neck cutlets, or roast if boned
8. Middle neck cutlets, or roast if boned
9. Scrag end of neck
10. Shoulder
11. Knuckle and foot
12. Breast

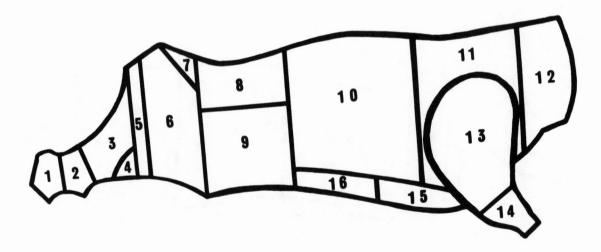

Veal: French Cuts

1. Crosse
2. Jarret
3. Noix (cuiseau): grenadins; rouelles, nearest to tail
4. Fricandeau
5. Escalopes; sous noix, at tail end
6. Quasi
7. Noix patissière
8. Selle; if both sides of back are used: filet; longe
9. Longe, rognon, and rognonnade
10. Carré, in one piece; côtelettes premières
11. Côtelettes découvertes
12. Collet
13. Épaule
14. Jarret
15. Poitrine (flanchet)
16. Tendron

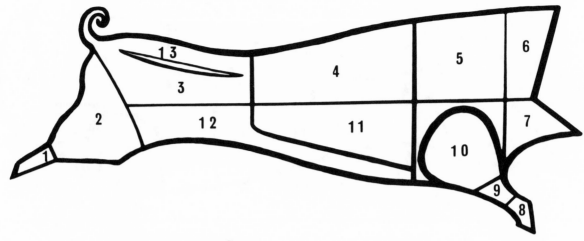

Pork: American Cuts

1. Shank
2. Ham or ham slices
3. Loin roast; butterfly chops if both sides of back are used
4. Loin chops; loin roast (in one piece)
5 & 6. Shoulder butt or shoulder slices
7. Jowl butt
8. Foot

9. Hock
10. Picnic shoulder
11. Spareribs
12. Bacon piece
13. Tenderloin

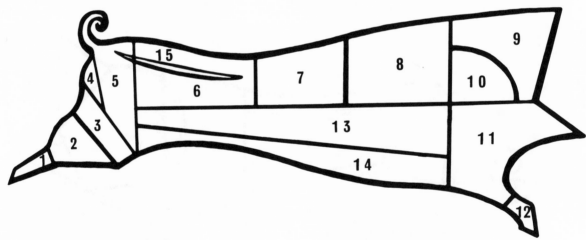

Pork: English Cuts

1. Trotter (foot)
2. Knuckle or hock
3. Leg or gammon slices
4. Slipper
4. & 5. Gammon
6. Hind loin (in one piece for roast); chump chops (near tail end); loin chops also called centreloin chops
7. Fore loin (in one piece for roast); fore loin chops

8. Shoulder cutlets; chine (in one piece)
9. Spareribs
10. Bladebone
11. Hand
12. Trotter (foot)
13. Streaky bacon
14. Belly
15. Fillet (pork steak in Ireland)

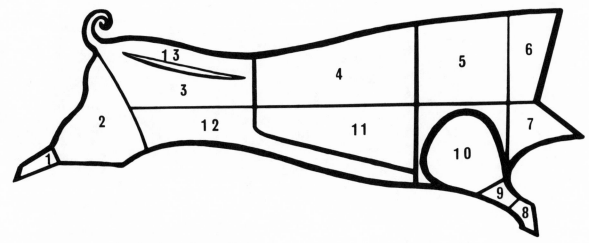

Pork: American Cuts

1. Shank
2. Ham or ham slices
3. Loin roast; butterfly chops if both sides of back are used
4. Loin chops; loin roast (in one piece)
5 & 6. Shoulder butt or shoulder slices
7. Jowl butt
8. Foot
9. Hock
10. Picnic shoulder
11. Spareribs
12. Bacon piece
13. Tenderloin

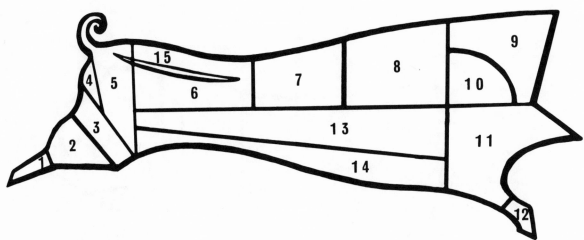

Pork: English Cuts

1. Trotter (foot)
2. Knuckle or hock
3. Leg or gammon slices
4. Slipper
4. & 5. Gammon
6. Hind loin (in one piece for roast);
   chump chops (near tail end); loin chops
   also called centreloin chops
7. Fore loin (in one piece for roast);
   fore loin chops
8. Shoulder cutlets; chine (in one piece)
9. Spareribs
10. Bladebone
11. Hand
12. Trotter (foot)
13. Streaky bacon
14. Belly
15. Fillet (pork steak in Ireland)

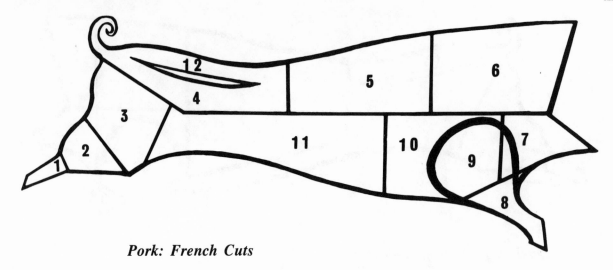

Pork: French Cuts

1. Pied
2. Jambonneau
3. Jambon
4. Pointe de filet; longe
5. Côtes (whole section); near head end, carré
6. Échine or palette

7. Gorge
8. Pied
9. Épaule or jambonneau
10. Plat de côtes
11. Poitrine
12. Filet

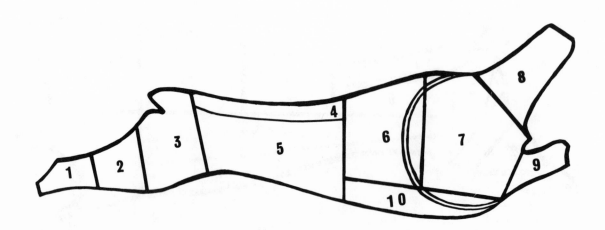

Lamb & Mutton: American Cuts

1. Shank end of leg
2. Leg steaks
2. & 3. French leg or gigot
4. & 5. Saddle, only when cut takes in both sides of back; centerloin chops
6. Whole cut is called a ''rack''; if cut, rib chops; crown roast

7. Shoulder; if boned, rolled shoulder
8. Neck
9. Shank
10. Breast

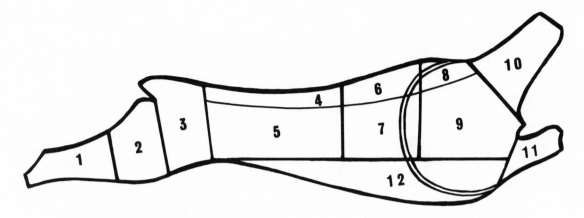

Lamb & Mutton: English Cuts

1. Shank end of leg
1. & 2. Leg (gigot in Scotland)
3. Fillet
4. & 5. Saddle, only when cut takes in both sides of back; loin or centreloin chops
6. Best end (fair end in Ireland) of neck roast; best end of neck chops if cut; Crown roast

7. Cutlets
8. Middle neck chops or cutlets (gigot chops in Ireland)
8. & 9. Shoulder
10. Scrag end of neck
11. Shank
12. Breast

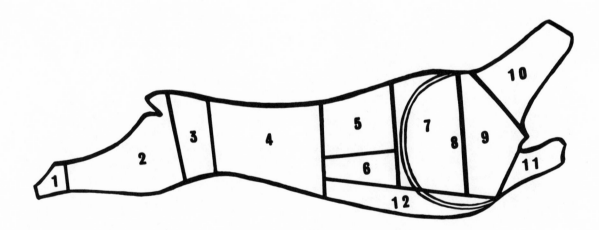

Lamb & Mutton: French Cuts

1. Pied
2. Gigot; Baron d'agneau if cut takes in both leg parts
3. Selle d'agneau, when cut takes in both sides of back
4. Filet (top half); côte de filet (bottom half)
5. Côtes or côtelettes première
6. Haute de côtelette

7. Carré
8. Côtes or côtelettes découvertes
7., 8. & 9. Épaule
10. Collet
11. Pied
12. Poitrine

Selected Bibliography

Some of the books consulted during the compilation of *The Food of the Western World:*

A Concise Encyclopedia of Gastronomy, Andre Simon, Wm. Collins & Sons, London, 1952

A Guide to Modern Cookery, Escoffier, 1907

Austrian Cookery, Gretel Beer, Andre Deutsch, Ltd., London, 1954

Buch der Kochkunst, Dr. Julius Bueb, Berlin, 1932

Cooking Wild Game, Fish and Wildlife Service, U.S. Department of the Interior, Orange Judd Publishing Co., New York, 1953

Cozinha Regional Portuguesa, Maria Odette Cortes Valente, Lisbon

Encyclopedia Britannica, 1797 & 1910 editions

Festival Menus Round the World, Sula Benet, Abelard Schuman, Ltd., New York, 1957

Finnish Food, Tolvanen, Helsinki & Deutsch, London, 1960

Food in England, Dorothy Hartley, Macdonald & Co., London, 1954

French Provincial Cooking, Elizabeth David, Herbert Joseph, Ltd., London, 1960

Gastronomic Hungaria, Kloeszer, Budapest, 1937

Gastronomie Pratique, Ali-Bab, Paris, 1919

German Cooking, N. Whitfield, Spring Books, 1957

Giant Fishes, Whales & Dolphins, John R. Norman & F.C. Fraser, Putnam, London, 1937

Good Food From Russia, K. Davydova, Frederick Muller, Ltd., London, 1960

Good Food From Sweden, Inga Norberg, Chatto & Windus, London, 1935

Greek Cooking, Robin Howe, Wm. Collins & Sons, Ltd., Toronto, 1960

Guide Gourmand, Brussels, 1938

Hortus Second: A Concise Dictionary of Gardening, General Horticulture & Cultivated Plants in North America, E. Z. Bailey & L. H. Bailey, Macmillan, New York, 1949

How America Eats, Clementine H. Paddleford, Charles Scribner's Sons, New York, 1960

Hungarian Cooking, Elizabeth de Biro, Andre Deutsch, Ltd., London, 1952

Il Talismano della Felicita, Ada Boni, Rome, 1947

Jewish Cookery, F. Greenburg, Jewish Chronicle, Ltd., London, 1947

Jewish Cookery, Leah W. Leonard, Andre Deutsch, Ltd., London, 1951

Kochbuechlein fuer Eizelgaenger, Paul Burckhardt, Zurich, 1936

L'Art Culinaire Moderne, Pellaprat, Paris, 1937

L'Arte di Mangiare Bene, Pellegino, Firenze, 1907

La Cucina Futurista, Filippo Tomaso Marinetti, Milan, 1932

La Cuisine et La Table Moderne, Paris, 1900

La Physiologie du Goût, Brillat Savarin, 1825

Larousse Gastronomique, Prosper Montagne, Larousse, Paris, 1938

Les Bons Plats Roumains, Bucharest, 1937

Lexikon der Küche, Hering, Giessen, 1950

Polish Cooking, Marja Ochorowicz-Monatowa, Andre Deutsch, Ltd., London, 1960

Portuguese Food, Wright, J. M. Dent & Sons, Ltd., 1969

Recipes From Scotland, F. M. McNeill, Blackie & Sons, London, 1947

Recipes of All Nations, Countess Marcelle Morphy, Herbert Joseph, Ltd., London, 1935

Spanish Cooking, E. Cass, Collins, Toronto, 1957

The Art of Cooking Made Plain and Easy, Glasse, London, 1758

The Art of Dutch Cooking, Countess van Limburg Stirum, Andre Deutsch, Ltd., London, 1962

The Art of Greek Cooking, Women of St. Paul's Greek Orthodox Church, Doubleday & Co., New York, 1961

The Art of Pennsylvania Dutch Cooking, Edna E. Heller, Doubleday & Co., New York, 1968

The Bulgarian Village Agricultural Household, Sofia, 1938

The Complete Herbal, Nicholas Culpeper, McKay, Stirling (Scotland), rev. ed. 1930, 1st ed. 1640

The Composition of Foods, McCance & Widdowson, H.M.S.O., 1960

The Cook's Oracle, Kitchiner, Edinburgh & London, 1822

The Englishman's Flora, G. Grigson, J. M. Dent & Sons, Ltd., London, 1958

The Field Guide to the Birds of Britain and Europe, Roger Tory Peterson and others, Collins, Toronto, 1954

The Fish of Britain and Europe, Wilkins, London, 1891

The Modern Housewife or Menagère, Soyer, London, 1850

The Natural History of Ireland, Robert Lloyd Praeger, Collins, Toronto, 1950

A

aal, Dutch for eel. See also PALING.

aalsoep, a Dutch soup, made from eels, capers, and parsley.

aal, German for eel.

aalsuppe, a German soup, made from eels, peas, white wine, shallots, and herbs. It is served in a tureen with pears steamed in red wine. See also HAMBURGER AALSUPPE.

aalsuppe

aalbes, Dutch for black, red, white currant.

aalraupe, German for eelpout.

aardappel, Dutch for potato. Like the herring, the potato is a national food in Holland. This is particularly true of the country districts and villages, where it is not uncommon to see families gathered round for a meal consisting solely of boiled potatoes. Each member, holding a mug filled with gravy or bacon fat, will, in order of seniority, pick a potato from a huge dish with his own fork, dip it into his mug, and eat. (Two lb. of potatoes per head is the usual amount allowed.) Throughout the country, potatoes are much relied on, and the Dutch housewife has a variety of ways of cooking them. Here are a few of the dishes.

aardappel gestoofd in peterselie saus, potatoes cooked in a parsley sauce, made from a roux composed of butter, flour, and milk (or stock or water). When blended, more butter is added, and lastly parsley. Sliced cold boiled potatoes are heated in the sauce.

aardappel purée met ham en uien, purée of potatoes with ham and onion. Alternate layers of potato purée, diced ham, and fried onions (ending with the purée) are topped with breadcrumbs and butter and baked in a moderate oven for about ½ hour.

aardappel purée met kaas, purée of potatoes with cheese. Two beaten eggs are mixed with ½ pint (1 cup) sour cream, salt, and 2 tablespoons grated Parmesan cheese. This is then mixed with a purée of mashed potatoes (made with 2 lb. potatoes), and poured into a baking dish, topped by more cheese mixed with breadcrumbs, and baked in a moderate oven for about ½ hour.

aardappel soufflé, potato soufflé. A potato purée is made by putting 2 lb. boiled potatoes through a sieve. Milk or cream previously heated with butter is added. Four egg yolks, salt, and nutmeg are next added, and lastly 4 stiffly beaten egg whites are folded in. The soufflé should not be disturbed while cooking, and should be baked for about 45 minutes in a slow oven.

aardbeien, Dutch for strawberry.

aarfugl, a small black Norwegian game bird. It is usually cooked by braising in sour cream.

abacate, Portuguese for avocado.

abaisse, a French culinary term generally used to describe a sheet of pastry rolled out to a certain thickness, depending on the use to be made of it. It can also mean a layer of sponge cake.

abalone (*Haliotis splendens; H. rufescens; H. cracherodii*), a large mollusc having an ear-shaped shell lined with mother-of-pearl. Much prized gastronomically, it is used in soups, chowders, and Chinese-American dishes. Abalone is found in warm coastal waters around Japan, Australia, and New Zealand. In the U.S. it can be bought in tins.

abatis de volaille, French for chicken giblets.

abats, French for offal (variety meats): *abats de boeuf,* beef offal; *abats de boucherie,* offal of all meats. In North America offal is referred to as variety meats, organ meats, and specialty cuts.

abatte, a colloquial French culinary term derived from *battre,*

3

to beat. An abatte is a rather thick, double-edged knife used for tenderizing and flattening meat.

abbachio al forno, an Italian dish consisting of roast baby lamb, usually cooked with rosemary. See also CACCIATORA, ABBACHIO ALLA.

Aberdeen crowdie, a soft cheese made in Aberdeen, Scotland. Its Gaelic name is *fuarog.* It can be made from either soured milk curds or buttermilk, drained, and then mixed with a little cream and salt. Sometimes caraway seeds are added. It can be eaten at once.

Aberdeen crulla, a Scottish plaited cake resembling a doughnut. It consists of ¼ lb. (½ cup) butter with the same quantity of sugar mixed together, with 4 eggs and enough flour to make a dough thick enough to roll. The dough is divided into 3 or 4 oblong strips about 5 inches long, which are plaited. The cakes are then deep fried in oil or fat until golden, and when drained, dredged with sugar. The *crule* means a small cake or bannock, from the Shetland Island *kril,* referring to anything very small.

Aberdeen sandwich, a Scottish sandwich made with curried chicken, ham, or tongue. The sandwich is cut into rounds about the size of a half-crown (1½ inches across) and fried in hot fat.

Aberdeen sausage, a Scottish sausage, about a foot in length and 4 or 5 inches in diameter. It is made from minced beef, bacon fat, oatmeal, and seasonings, put into a large skin, or boiled for several hours in a cloth.

Aberdeen softies, Scottish soft biscuits made from baker's (bread) dough with 3 oz. (⅓ cup) melted butter and 1 tablespoon sugar worked into every lb. The mixture is formed into flattened bun shapes, about 4 inches across, and baked in a moderate oven.

Aberfrau cake, a Welsh cake which comes from a seaside village in Anglesey. *Aber,* the ''mouth'' of the Frau River, is the derivation of the name. It is made from ¼ lb. (½ cup) butter, 4 oz. (½ cup) sugar, and 4 oz. (1 cup) flour mixed to a dough with milk. The dough is baked in a large scallop shell.

Abernethy biscuit, a Scottish biscuit made with butter, flour, sugar, eggs, milk, and caraway seeds. It is made and sold commercially, and named after Dr. John Abernethy (1764–1831) chief surgeon at Bart's Hospital, London. He suggested to a nearby baker that he add sugar and caraway to a plain biscuit, so the baker gave the new biscuit the patron's name.

abertam, a Czechoslovakian hard cheese made from ewe's milk. It comes from the region of Karlov Vary (Carlsbad), Bohemia.

abji l'amid, a Turkish soup, served cold and made from mashed potato, yogourt, and lemon juice.

ablette, French for bleak.

abóbora, Portuguese for pumpkin and squash.

abrestir, a rare Icelandic dish made from beestings' milk allowed to coagulate over hot water. It is served with thick cream, sugar, and cinnamon.

abricot, French for apricot.

abricoter, a French culinary term used in pastry-making, meaning to coat a cake or flan with apricot jam that has been boiled down to thicken, flavoured with a liqueur, and strained.

abrikoos, Dutch for apricot.

abruzzese, a method of cooking common to the Abruzzi region of Italy, in which large amounts of fiery red peppers are used in soups. Mozzarella cheeses are made in the Abruzzi. See SAETINA.

acacia, a pretty shrub (family *Leguminosae*), the yellow or white flowers of which are used for making fritters in France and Italy.

acacia

acajou, French for cashew nut.

acanthe, French for acanthus.

acanthus, a perennial plant (family *Acanthaceae*), with beautiful leaves; mostly native to the Mediterranean region. There are about twenty species, the young leaves of which are eaten as a salad in southern France.

acarne, local name in France for sea bream.

acave, a variety of edible snail in France.

acciughe, Italian for anchovy in northern Italy; in southern Italy it is known as *alice.*

acciughe, salsa d', anchovy sauce made from a roux, diluted with fish stock, and chopped green pepper, garlic, parsley, capers, and chopped anchovy fillets. It is served with hot poached fish.

accolade, en, an early French way of arranging meat, poultry, or fish on a dish. Whole birds or joints are arranged back to back.

accote-pot, an old French word that means a small piece of iron, put on the stove underneath a pot or saucepan to tilt it.

accoub (*Gundelia tournefortii*), an edible thistle growing widely in the Mediterranean area and parts of the Middle East. It is much prized gastronomically because of its interesting flavour—between that of an asparagus and a globe artichoke. The flower buds should be picked, well before flowering, lightly boiled in salted water, and tossed in seasoned butter. They may also be prepared as artichoke hearts. The shoots, while they are still 5 or 6 inches in length, may be treated like asparagus, and the roots in the same was as salsify. Altogether a most satisfactory plant, with no part wasted. Unfortunately it is not often found in European markets.

accuncciatu, a Corsican stew made with either goat, lamb, or mutton, with potatoes added toward the end of the cooking time.

aceite de oliva, Spanish for olive oil.

aceituna, Spanish for olive; also *oliva.*

acelga, Spanish for spinach beet or chard. This vegetable has a much larger, longer, and tougher leaf than the English-type spinach, and a long white stalk which is taken off and eaten separately, boiled and served with either vinaigrette sauce or melted butter. The leaves are used like spinach. It is a speciality of Málaga, where it is sometimes served with a sauce made by frying in oil, garlic, paprika, red pepper, breadcrumbs, salt, and pepper, pounding them in a mortar, and then mixing this with a little vinegar. The sauce is poured over the cooked spinach beet.

aceline, the French name for a European fish of the perch family. It is prepared like perch.

acepipes, Portuguese for hors d'oeuvre.

acepipes diversos, mixed hors d'oeuvre, containing clams, eggs, tomatoes, tunny (tuna), meat balls, sausage, potato salad, etc.

acetabula, a family of algae having broad cupola which resemble a mushroom. The two most valued for eating are: (1) *A. vulgaris,* whose appearance changes radically between spring and autumn, varying from bright red to orange-yellow, and (2) *A. sulcata,* which is dark brown.

aceto, Italian for vinegar.

acétomel, a sweet-sour syrup made of equal parts honey and vinegar. It is used in France to preserve fruit, such as pears, peaches, or grapes. In Italy, fruits so preserved are called *aceto-dolce.* See also AGRODOLCE.

acetosella, Italian for sorrel.

ache des marais, French for wild celery, used in cookery by the Romans and now replaced by cultivated celery. However, the leaves are still used in France for salad. It is known as *smallage* in English.

achicoria, Spanish for chicory.

achillée (*Achillea patarnica*), a wild herb like the milfoil, or goosetongue (and of the same family). Like chervil, a small amount, finely chopped, improves any green salad or sauce vert. See also YARROW.

achinoi or **ahinoi,** Greek for sea urchins, served usually as meze (Greek hors d'oeuvre) with lemon juice and bread.

acid drops, boiled sweets consisting of sugar flavoured with citric acid.

acini di pepe, Italian for small squares of pasta, used for garnishing soups.

açorda alantejana, a Portuguese thick bread and garlic soup, made by pouring boiling water over the bread and garlic. Often a poached egg is added.

açorda com amêijoas, a Portuguese thick clam bisque.

acorn barnacle (*Balanus eburneus*), a small unattractive-looking shellfish, much prized gastronomically. Also known as acorn shell or turban shell.

acorn coffee, a beverage at one time widely drunk in Germany and to some extent in England during World War I. It is prepared by cutting ripe acorns into pieces the size of coffee beans, drying them in an oven, roasting them to a cinnamon-brown colour, and then grinding them. After grinding, a little butter is added to the powder and it is ready for the preparation of coffee in the ordinary way. Medicinal properties have been claimed for the coffee.

acqua cotta (*cooked water*), an Italian soup from Tuscany, made with vegetables and sweet peppers. It is poured over bread brushed with beaten egg.

actinia, a sea anemone which is used as food in parts of southern France. The local name for one species is *rastègne,* which is said to taste like crab. Another less polite name is "mule's backside."

açúcar, Portuguese for sugar.

adana, a Turkish soup made from beef stock, and served with small pastry shapes filled with meat floating in it. It is garnished with yogourt, fresh thyme, and mint.

adèle, a French soup made from clear chicken broth or consommé with peas, cubed carrots, and chicken quenelles. See also CONSOMMÉ.

Adelina Patti, a French soup made from clear chicken broth or consommé garnished with tiny pieces of baked egg custard, carrots, and puréed chestnuts. It is named after the famous opera singer, who was very fond of it. See also CONSOMMÉ.

adeline, a French salad of chopped cooked salsify (oyster plant), with mayonnaise, garnished with sliced tomato and cucumber.

Adirondack bread, an American speciality, made from 2 oz. (4 heaped tablespoons) warm butter, 5 egg yolks beaten with 1 pint (2 cups) milk, and 5 oz. (1¼ cups) Indian cornmeal (ground maize), and 5 oz. (1¼ cups) wheat flour all beaten until smooth. Finally a heaped tablespoon of sugar, a heaped teaspoon of baking powder, and the 5 stiffly beaten egg whites are folded in. It is all put in a buttered tin and baked in a moderate oven for 45 minutes.

adlon salad, a mixed salad of raw celery hearts, cooked potatoes and beetroots, and raw apples, with an oil and vinegar dressing. Corn salad is served round the outside.

adobado, Spanish for marinated, which is essential to certain meat in Spain, such as beef, to make it tender.

adobo a la madrileña, a Spanish marinade for pork chops made from equal parts of vinegar and white wine; salt, pepper, a bay leaf, and marjoram are added.

adoucir, a French culinary word, which means to reduce the bitterness of a dish by prolonged cooking. It also applies to diluting a dish with milk, stock, or water to make it less salty.

adzuki (*Phaseolus angularis*), a bean grown in China and Japan and used like the french bean when young and fresh. The dried beans are ground and made into a flour which is used for pastry.

aeble, Danish for apple, a fruit which the Danish people put to many culinary uses.

æble bagt i dej, Danish for apple dumpling.

æbleflæsk, fried apple and bacon. Streaky bacon is fried or grilled, and garnished with sliced apples which have been fried in bacon dripping. The apples are sprinkled with sugar before serving.

æblegrød, apple sauce. This dish is sometimes eaten as a compote with whipped cream, but more often is used in the traditional Danish pudding *bondepige med slør.*

æblekage, apple cake, eaten traditionally in Denmark on Christmas Eve. It resembles the English apple charlotte, except that it is pressed flat before cooking. It is eaten cold, turned out onto a plate, and served with whipped cream.

æbleskiver, apple pancakes. A popular winter crêpe-like dessert which gives its name to the special iron pan set with hollows, known as the æbleskiver pan. A batter is made from ½ lb. (1¾ cups) flour, ⅔ pint (1½ cups) milk, 4 eggs, 6 oz. (⅔ cup) butter, salt, pepper, and 1 tablespoon beer. This is poured into the greased hollows in the pan and browned on top of the stove. When browned underneath, the cakes are turned over and browned on the other side. Served with sugar, they are accompanied by strawberry jam and *æblegrød.*

æblesuppe, apple soup. Sliced, unpeeled sour apples are cooked in water with cinnamon and lemon peel until reduced to a pulp. Then they are sieved and brought to a boil in fresh water. The soup is thickened with either sago or rice flour (both mixed to a paste with cold water). After cooking a few minutes longer, sugar is added to taste. Sometimes an apple cream soup is made by the addition of egg yolk and cream to the pulp. This soup is served with a little crumpled rusk and can be chilled, tepid, or hot, according to season.

aeble, Norwegian for apple.

æblepai, apple pie.

aeg, Danish for egg.

æggekage, bacon omelette. Four egg yolks are blended with 2 teaspoons cornflour; ¼ pint (½ cup) milk or cream and seasoning are added gradually. Then 4 beaten egg whites are folded into the mixture, which is cooked in butter in the usual way. It is garnished with chives, and rashers of grilled streaky bacon are laid on the top. *Aeggekage,* also spelt *aggekage,* can also mean a thick pancake, which is often served with fried pork fillets.

æggepynt, custard. Two eggs and ½ pint (1 cup) cream are beaten together and baked in a mould standing in water. When cold, the custard is cut into thin strips and used as a garnish for consommé.

aegir sauce, hollandaise sauce flavoured with a little mustard.

aeglé, French for ugli.

aerated flour, another name for self-raising flour.

aert, Danish and Norwegian for pea.

affriander, a French culinary term which means to tempt by making the dish of food look attractive.

africaine, à l', a method of French cooking, African style. It refers to garnishing all kinds of dishes in various ways, originally to imitate a style of cooking from parts of Africa. It consists of demi-glace, seasoned with cayenne pepper and Madeira, sliced onions, and truffles. A thick soup made from curried chicken pounded and mixed with cream and rice, garnished with artichoke bottoms and finely sliced aubergines (eggplant), is referred to as crème à l'africaine.

A sauce made from sliced fried bananas and chillies may garnish fried fish. A sauce made from cucumber, tomatoes, and aubergines (eggplant) fried in oil until they are a purée is served to garnish meat.

afronchemoyle, a Norman-French form of *haggis.* This form was made by one of Richard II's cooks. It is mentioned in his book *The Form of Cury* (The Art of Cookery) written in 1390. It appears to have been made from breadcrumbs, tripe, minced sheep's fat, eggs, and saffron.

agar-agar, the name given collectively to a number of edible seaweeds resembling somewhat the Irish carrageen. It is widely distributed along the Japanese and Chinese seaboards where it is used in the making of jellies and soups. In Europe and the U.S. it is used mainly as an emulsifying agent in foods, and in the preparation of bacterial cultures. By regurgitating seaweed of this sort the Chinese swallow builds its nest. See also BIRD'S NEST SOUP.

agerhøns, Danish for partridge. The most traditional Danish way of cooking this bird is to roast or casserole it, and serve it with a sour cream sauce.

ägg, Swedish for egg.

äggkrans, egg custard rings. Six beaten eggs are mixed with 1 pint (2 cups) milk and 1 heaped tablespoon parsley (or chives), and baked in a ring mould. When cooked, the centre is filled with a savoury filling such as stewed kidneys, meat, or poultry leftovers, mixed with cream.

aggekage, see AEG (AEGGEKAGE).

aglio, Italian for garlic.

agneau, French for lamb.

agneau de lait and *agnelet,* French for unweaned lamb, the most sought-after type being *Pauillac.* It is usually cooked quite simply—either brushed with melted butter and roasted on a spit and then served with watercress; or stuffed with half-cooked rice mixed with the chopped liver, heart, kidneys, and sweetbreads, rubbed with butter or oil, and roasted. See also MOUTON.

agnello, Italian for lamb. See also ABBACCHIO AL FORNO.

agnellino, Italian for suckling lamb, often served roasted whole at Easter in Italy.

Agnes Sorel, I. A French soup, named after the mistress of Charles VII of France. It is made from chicken stock, cream, and puréed mushrooms, and garnished with diced chicken and ox tongue. II. A garnish of small pastry tarts filled with chicken mousse, mushrooms, and diced ox tongue. It is served with chicken or turkey.

agneshka churba, a traditional Bulgarian Easter dish. It is a whole young spring lamb, stuffed with rice mixed with the lungs, heart, and sweetbreads chopped, and raisins; then roasted. See also VŬZKRESÈNIE.

agneshka soup, a Bulgarian soup eaten at Easter. It is made from lamb's liver, heart, sweetbreads, and kidneys, with onions, noodles, hot red pepper, eggs and yogourt.

agnolotti, an oblong-shaped Italian pasta filled with vegetable or meat stuffing, sealed, boiled, drained, and served with grated Parmesan cheese and melted butter. It is also used as a garnish for soups. Agnolotti is a regional name for *anolini.*

agoni, a small, flat, freshwater fish with a smoky flavour, found in Lake Como, Italy. It is usually cooked in oil and then marinated in a wild thyme-flavoured vinegar, and served as an hors d'oeuvre. It is also salted and dried, or can be cooked like fresh sardines. In parts of Italy it is known as *sardina.*

agoursi, French for ridge cucumber. It comes from the Russian *ogurki,* meaning "cucumber." In both Russia and France they are not only pickled, but braised, fried in batter, cooked au gratin, mornay, etc.

agrafa, a highly thought of Greek cheese, resembling gruyère. It is made from fresh ewe's milk.

agrimony (*Agrimonia eupatoria*), a very common perennial herb of the rose family growing widely on waste land in the British Isles, bearing spikes of small yellow flowers. It is used for making tea.

agrodolce, a favourite sweet-sour sauce of Italy which has been served since Roman times. I. Two oz. (¼ cup) sugar is steeped in ½ cup wine vinegar, and then cooked rapidly until it is a light caramel colour. Then 1 clove of crushed garlic, 2 bay leaves, and 2 oz. grated bitter chocolate are added. The mixture is stirred until the chocolate melts, then gravy is added to make it of pouring consistency—hare, wild boar, or venison stock, gravy, or the wine marinade is the most authentic. See Norman Douglas's recipe for CINGHIALE IN AGRODOLCE. II. An alternative method is to caramelize the sugar and vinegar as in I. and then add 1 cup white wine, about 1 tablespoon each chopped shallots, pignoli, raisins, mints, candied fruits. The mixture is boiled and thinned with stock, if desired. Chocolate can be added later. It is excellent with game. III. A fish sauce is made from 1 tablespoon each chopped parsley, basil, and 1 small onion fried in 1 tablespoon each olive oil and butter. The mixture is seasoned with salt, pepper, and a pinch of cinnamon. Then 2 chopped tomatoes, 1 cup white wine or wine vinegar, and a heaped teaspoon sugar are added, and all are cooked until the tomatoes are soft.

aguacate, Spanish for avocado.

aguglie, a variety of garfish found in Italian waters, and used for soup. It has a needle-like beak and bright green bones. It is one of the fishes Norman Douglas refers to in *Siren Land* (1911) as "floating pincushions." They are fried, or served in a tomato and onion sauce.

agurk, Norwegian for cucumber.

agurksalat, cucumber salad. The cucumber is cut into fine slices and sprinkled with a dressing of vinegar, lemon juice, castor sugar, and seasoning. In Norway this salad is garnished with parsley or lettuce, and is usually served in individual dishes. Another dressing sometimes used for cucumber is a mixture of sour cream, chives, dill, or parsley.

agurke, Danish for cucumber. The cucumbers which grow in Denmark are long and thin, and are almost without seeds.

agurkesalat, cucumber salad. If old, the cucumber should be peeled, otherwise just thinly sliced. It is left for about 1½ hours in a mixture of water and vinegar (lemon juice can be used instead of vinegar) to which have been added sugar and black pepper. Another method is to sprinkle the cucumber with salt and leave it to stand for ½ hour. Before serving, it is dredged with a mixture of oil, water, vinegar, and castor sugar, and garnished with minced parsley.

agurku salotas, Lithuanian for cucumber salad, which is eaten a lot in Lithuania. It is usually lightly salted.

ahinoi, see ACHINOI.

ahvenmuhennos, Finnish for stewed perch. The fish is cleaned, salted, and placed in a pan. It is sprinkled with pepper, salt, dill, chives, and parsley, and dotted with butter. It is then covered with water and cooked for 15–20 minutes. It is served with boiled potatoes.

aida salad, a salad of green peppers, tomatoes, artichoke hearts, curly endives (chicory), with an oil and vinegar dressing. Garnished with sliced hard-boiled eggs.

aiglefin, French for fresh haddock. See also ÉGLEFIN for alternative names.

aïgo bouïllido, a traditional Provençal soup, made from 2 large cloves garlic, 1 tablespoon olive oil, 1 bay leaf, salt, and 1 quart (4 cups) water. When this has boiled for 15 minutes, it is poured slowly over 2 raw eggs in a tureen, and beaten with a wooden spoon. The name means literally "boiling water," and it is served on Christmas Eve (which was a meatless day in Catholic countries) before a course of *cardons aux anchois,* followed by *cacalaus, anguilles en catigout,* a salad, and thirteen other traditional fruits and nuts consisting of dates, oranges, apples, pears, mandarins, almonds, walnuts, raisins, figs, chestnuts, black and white nougat, and *fougasse.* With the dessert a bottle of vin cuit, or unfermented wine, is served.

aïgo-sau, a Provençal fish and root vegetable soup. The soup is drunk poured over slices of garlic bread, and the fish is served on a separate dish.

aigre de cèdre (*Citrus medica*), the French name for a citron tree cultivated in Provence, Grasse, and Nice in France, and at San Remo and Genoa in Italy. The fruit has a refreshing taste on a hot summer's day.

aigre-doux, French for agrodolce and sweet-sour. See also AGRODOLCE.

aigrefin, French for fresh haddock. See also ÉGLEFIN for alternative names.

aigrette, a small and very light French biscuit, made like flaky pastry, which is fried quickly in hot fat. It is sometimes made with the addition of a little cheese.

aigroissade toulonnaise, a Toulon method of serving assorted warm fresh vegetables mixed with cooked dried beans or chick peas, with an *aïoli* sauce poured over them.

aiguillat, French for dogfish.

aiguille, French for needle.

aiguille à brider, a steel pin used for trussing; it is pierced at one end to thread twine in, and sew up a bird or meat.

aiguille à piquer, a small larding needle, pointed at one end and pronged at the other, used for larding meats with pieces of bacon, pork, or ham fat.

aiguillette, I. (*de boeuf*). A cut of beef in France, part of the hip or buttock piece of beef; in Britain part of the round, in the U.S. part of the rump. Also called in French *pièce de boeuf* and *pointe de culotte.* See also BOEUF. II. A French method of serving long strips of chicken breasts cold, with a brown chaud-froid sauce, aspic jelly, and hard-boiled egg whites cut into shapes. III. Duck breasts served with stock from the bones, thickened and reduced, with black cherries. Also called *rouennais aux cerises.* Or prepared in the same way, but with orange juice and finely cut orange peel strips, it is known as *rouennais a l'orange.* Rouen ducks are used for both dishes. IV. Raw shrimps.

aiguiser, a French culinary word meaning to sharpen a cream

or liquid by adding lemon juice or citric acid. It is also used for spicing a dish strongly.

aïl, French for garlic.

aïl beurre, see BEURRES COMPOSÉS.

aïle, French for wing.

aïle de poulet, wing of chicken. See AILERON.

aileron, French for the terminal segment of a bird's wing, also called a wing tip. In France, ailerons are classed as giblets, and used mainly for soup. However, turkey pinions are sometimes stuffed with forcemeat and braised with wine and vegetables.

aïllada, l', a French sauce for snails from Gascony and Bordeaus. See SNAIL.

aïllade, a word used in the south of France to denote that garlic is used in the preparation of the dish. Bread *à l'aïllade* means a slice of toast rubbed with garlic and sprinkled with olive oil. There is also a sauce aïllade made with garlic, shallots, chives, and other herbs, served with cold meat, fish, potatoes, and many dishes served à la vinaigrette.

aïllade de levraut, a French country method of roasting a young hare. It is served with a sauce made from bacon, shallots, garlic, and the liver and blood of the hare simmered in red wine vinegar.

aïllade toulousaine, a French sauce made from pounded, skinned walnuts and garlic. Olive oil is dripped in, and it is stirred until it is thick. It is served as an hors d'oeuvre, and also as a sauce with meat, particularly tongue.

aïoli, a sauce from Provence made from olive oil, garlic, and egg yolks. It is made like a mayonnaise, but contains a considerable quantity of pounded or pressed garlic, and is highly seasoned. It is served with salt cod, potatoes, snails, and in soups spread on bread. It is used in making other dishes such as *rouille sauce, algérienne,* and *bourride.* See also ALI-OLI (for origin).

aipo, Portuguese for celery.

airelle, French for a number of different berries, such as bilberry (huckleberry in the U.S.), whortleberry, blueberry, etc. *Airelle rouge* usually refers to cranberry or bilberry, both of which are red and used for jellies, jams, and sauces.

aish el sarya (*palace bread*), made from honey, sugar, butter, cream, and breadcrumbs, all melted together. It is eaten at the Muslim feast of Id-il-Fitr, which marks the end of the long fast of Ramadan. This Egyptian dish has been adopted by the Turks and is often eaten in Turkey as a sweet.

aisy cendré, a French cow's milk cheese from Burgundy. As the name cendré implies, the colour of the cheese is ashen. It is at its best from October to July.

aitch-bone or *edge-bone,* the terms used in England for the bone of the rump, or the cut of beef lying over it. It may be boiled, braised, or roasted. Also known as the "poor man's sirloin."

ajada, a Spanish sauce made from bread steeped in water and garlic, seasoned with salt. Also known as *ajolio.*

ajo, Spanish for garlic.

ajo blanco, a cold Spanish soup made from garlic and almonds pounded in a mortar with olive oil until it is a thick paste. Water and small slices of bread are added.

sopa de ajo, garlic soup, of which there are many varieties in the different provinces. The most basic is the one from Málaga which consists of 6 cloves of chopped garlic fried in a little oil, then 16 cups of boiling water are added, with salt to season. It is well stirred, then 1 cup of mayonnaise is added, drop by drop, stirring all the time until well mixed. The soup is garnished with 6 slices of bread fried in oil and cut into cubes. In Cádiz 3 tomatoes are boiled in 1 pint (2 cups) water, then 5 cloves garlic, 2 green peppers, 1 teaspoon paprika, salt, the drained tomatoes, and 2 tablespoons olive oil are pounded together and put into a saucepan. The tomato stock and 2 crustless slices of brown bread are added alternately, mixing well all the time until the bread is absorbed and it all becomes a thick purée. Nowadays it is often made in a blender and reheated.

sopa de ajo a la asmesnal, garlic soup from Salamanca. Six cloves garlic are browned in oil, then removed, and 6 small, crustless slices of bread are fried in oil in a saucepan before 3 pints (6 cups) of boiling water, 1 teaspoon chopped parsley, and salt are added. The garlic is well crushed and put into the soup with pieces of cubed cooked chicken and about 1 oz. of chopped *chorizo* is added. One poached egg is put into each soup plate, and the hot soup is poured over before serving.

ajolio, see AJADA.

ajonjoli, Spanish for sesame seed.

ål, Danish for eel.

ål gélé, jellied eel. After being skinned and cleaned the fish is cut crosswise into several pieces and covered with cold water which is brought to the boil and skimmed. Onions, peppercorns, bay leaves, parsley, lemon, and allspice berries are then added, and cooking is continued until the eel is tender, when it is placed in a wet mould. Gelatine and vinegar are dissolved in the strained stock and the liquid is then poured back over the fish. It is served chilled, either with creamed potatoes, or as a topping for *smørrebrød.*

ål stegt, fried eel. After cleaning and cutting, as in previous recipe, the fish is sprinkled with salt and left for 1 hour. It is rinsed and dipped in flour and egg, and breadcrumbed, then fried in butter. It is served with creamed potatoes and more butter.

al cuarto de hora, a Spanish soup made from mussels, onions, ham, rice, and parsley. It is garnished with finely chopped hard-boiled eggs.

ala, Spanish for wing; *ala de pollo,* wing of chicken

alacha, Spanish for a large fish like the sardine. See SARDINA.

alant, alternative German name, with *nerfling,* for chub.

alaska, baked, an American sweet consisting of ice cream standing on a sponge cake covered with stiffly beaten egg whites, and then baked quickly in a hot oven. The meringue and the cake prevent the ice cream from melting. It makes a very impressive sweet. It is thought to have been invented by an American physicist called Rumford (1753–1814), and in France is called *omelette à la norvégienne.*

alati, Greek for salt.

albacore (*Thynnus germo*), a long-finned species of tunny fish (tuna). The name comes from the Arabic al—the, *bukr*—young camel or heifer. See ATUN; TUNNY FISH.

albaricoque, Spanish for apricot.

alberchigo, Spanish for peach.

albert, a French name for an English hot horseradish sauce.

albertine, a French method of serving poached fish, with a white wine sauce made with mushrooms, truffles, and a little parsley.

albicocche, Italian for apricot.

albigensian soup, a French soup made from calf's foot, goose, sausage, root vegetables, and cabbage, served with thin slices of bread.

albigeoise, à l', a French garnish for meat consisting of stuffed tomatoes and potato croquettes.

albion, I. A French fish soup with lobster quenelles and truffles, slightly thickened with tapioca. II. A chicken broth with truffles, asparagus tips, chicken liver quenelles, and cock's combs.

albondigas, Spanish for meat balls or dumplings. Chopped ham, veal, and onion with *chorizo* and chopped parsley are well mixed together and formed into balls the size of walnuts.

albacore

These are dipped in flour and egg and are then fried in deep oil or butter. *Salsa de almendras con yema* is poured over the meat balls before serving.

albondiguillas, walnut-sized Spanish rissoles are made from 1 lb. minced meat or poultry, ¼ cup breadcrumbs, 2 eggs, 2 tablespoons white wine, 1 tablespoon chopped herbs, salt, and pepper, and then dipped in egg and breadcrumbs, fried, and served with tomato sauce. Also served *a criolla,* which is a creole sauce with sweet peppers simmered in butter, and served with saffron rice.

alboni, a brown Italian sauce for venison containing stock, grilled pine kernels, and red currant jelly.

albran, French name given to a very young wild duck before it becomes a duckling.

albuféra, d', I. A suprême sauce to which beurre pimenté is added, the whole being then flavoured with port. Often served with game and sometimes with roast pork in France. II. A stuffing for chicken, duck, goose, or turkey, of rice with chopped goose liver or chicken liver and truffles. The bird is then poached and garnished with pastry tartlets filled with mixed chicken mousse and mushrooms. III. A classic French garnish, consisting of small tartlets filled with small truffle balls and balls of the same size made from chicken forcemeat. On the top of each tartlet are placed *rognons de coq,* mushrooms, and either cock's combs or thin slices of pickled lamb's tongue cut in a serrated pattern. IV. Short pastry flavoured with arrack (a spirit made from coconut or rice and molasses), with chopped almonds on top. It is baked, and then cut into squares. V. *Duckling à la d'albuféra* is a roasted duckling with bayonne ham slices, herbs, butter, onion studded with cloves, and a small glass of Madeira wine. It is covered, and cooked in a moderate oven. Before serving, the herbs and onion are removed and 2 tablespoons of financière sauce and small mushrooms are added. Carême, the famous French chef, is thought to have invented the name.

albume, Italian for egg whites.

albur, see LISA.

alcachofas, Spanish for artichokes. Only globe artichokes are found in Spain. They are often boiled and served with a vinaigrette sauce.

alcachofas fritas, artichokes with the outer leaves removed and the hard tops on the remaining leaves broken off. They are quartered, dipped in beaten egg, and fried in oil.

alcachofras, Portuguese for artichokes.

alcaparras, Spanish for capers.

alcarab, Spanish for capon.

alcaravea, Spanish for caraway seed.

alcazar, a French pastry tart which consists of a 9-inch sponge tin lined with rich shortcrust pastry and filled with a mixture of ½ lb. (1 cup) icing sugar, 4 stiffly beaten egg whites, 4 tablespoons ground almonds, 4 tablespoons flour, and 2 tablespoons butter mixed with a little kirsch. It is baked in a moderate oven until browned and, when cool, garnished with marzipan, apricot jam, and either almonds or pistachio nuts.

alcide, French white wine sauce made with chopped shallots and grated horseradish, then thickened.

alcobaca, a local country name in Portugal for a farmhouse-made variety of serra cheese.

alderman's walk, the name given in London to the longest and finest cut sliced from a haunch of venison or lamb.

alec, an Old Latin word of Greek origin, meaning a herring or a number of herrings in brine. "Alec, the Heringe, is a Fisshe of the See and very many be taken betweene Bretayne and Germania and also in Denmarke about a place named Schonen. And he is best from the beginnynge of August to December, and when he is fresh taken he is very delicious to be eten. And also whan he has ben salted he is specyall fod unto man." (Lawerens Andrewe, in *Furnivall's Early English Meals and Manners.*)

alecost (*Tanecetum balsamita*), an aromatic herbaceous perennial plant with a flavour somewhat resembling mint, formerly used for the flavouring of ale, in salads, and as a medicinal herb. It is thought to be especially good for bee stings. The plant was introduced into England from Italy in 1568. It is found widely throughout the Middle East and in southern Europe.

alénois (family *Cruciferae*), French for a species of cress, known as "garden cress." It can be dwarf and curly or pale-yellowish green with a large leaf. It is eaten like watercress in salads and soup is made from it. However, it is the classic French garnish for roast meat or poultry. The name is thought to be a corruption of *orléanais* (the adjective from Orléans), where it grows wild in abundance though it is thought to be a native of Cyprus. It is called *tongue cress* in England.

alentejo, I. A Portuguese dish of partridges, braised in olive oil, onions, parsley, garlic, herbs, bay leaf, white wine, and 1 cup wine vinegar. It is served on slices of fried bread. II. A Portuguese soft cheese made from ewe's milk made into shapes which weigh about 6 lb.

ale soup, a German soup made from ale, lemon, and cinnamon, thickened with potato flour and semolina.

aletria, Portuguese for vermicelli.

alevin, see SALMON.

alewife (*Pomolobus pseudoharengus*), a fish of the herring family, much prized gastronomically. Plentiful off the Atlantic coast of North America.

alexander (*Smyrnium olusatrum*), at one time much used throughout Europe as a pot herb and in salads, this plant has now passed, undeservedly, into obscurity. A member of the cow-parsley (wild chervil) family, it has a character between that of celery and parsley. Like celery the stems can be blanched. The season is April and early May.

alexandra (French), I. A suprême sauce with truffles. It is served with chicken which has been sautéed with onion. II. A mayonnaise with mashed, hard-boiled egg yolks, a little English mustard, and chopped chervil added. III. A sauce for poached fish, made from Mornay (cheese) sauce with a garnish of poached truffles and asparagus. It is served cold. Also served with cold poultry. IV. A chicken broth or consommé slightly thickened. It is served with shredded lettuce, chicken

quenelles, and julienne of chicken. V. Cold poached eggs, served on pastry tarts filled with lobster mousse and glazed with aspic. Caviar is sometimes put round the base. VI. A salad of lettuce, artichoke hearts, beetroot, and celery, all sliced and covered with mayonnaise.

alface, Portuguese for lettuce.

alfajor, Spanish for gingerbread.

algérienne, I. A French garnish for steak (especially tournedos) consisting of tomatoes and green or red sweet peppers simmered in oil. It is served with croquettes of sweet potatoes. II. A method of serving fried eggs with a purée of tomatoes, peppers, and aubergines (eggplant) in fresh tomato sauce. III. A salad of courgettes (small marrows or zucchini), tomatoes, and sliced cooked sweet potatoes, all mixed with sauce *aïoli.* IV. Sautéed chicken and fried aubergine (eggplant), with a sauce of tomatoes, garlic, and onions. V. A cream soup made from puréed sweet potatoes flavoured with filbert nuts, and enriched with cream and butter.

alhambra, I. A French garnish for meat consisting of artichoke hearts, green or red sweet peppers, and tomatoes, all sautéed in oil or butter. II. A salad of beetroot, celery, artichoke hearts, and lettuce mixed with mayonnaise.

alho, Portuguese for garlic.

ali, Italian for wing; *ali di pollo,* wing of chicken.

alice, I. The name for anchovy in southern Italy. See also ACCIUGHE. II. A French cream potato and turnip soup, served with croûtons of fried bread. III. A mixed fruit and vegetable salad of orange, apple, grapefruit, nuts, black cherries, all stoned and sliced, mixed with diced sweet peppers, and covered with an oil and vinegar dressing. IV. Large eating apples, hollowed out and filled with diced apples, red currants, and walnuts, mixed with lemon juice and cream.

alicot, l', a ragoût made in southwestern France, consisting of giblets of turkey, duck, or goose, also wings and carcass. Garlic, herbs, onions, tomatoes, and 1 cup rich stock are also added. This ragoût (also called *alicuit*) is served with cooked, dried, white haricot (kidney) beans.

aligot, l', a French potato dish from southwestern France. Two lb. floury potatoes are boiled in their skins, peeled, and sieved to a dry purée, then seasoned. A cup of cream and 2 tablespoons butter are warmed and added to the potatoes with 1 crushed garlic clove and 8 oz. *tomme de cantal* (a soft, unfermented cheese) cut into small cubes. It is stirred briskly over low heat until it is quite smooth and the cheese just melted. It is served on its own as a first course.

ali-oli, a Spanish garlic sauce, the same as *aïoli.* The Valencian kind is said to be the original of the French *aïoli.* It is mentioned in Spanish literature of the 11th century and is thought to have been introduced into France via Provence. See AÏOLI.

alise, French for the fruit of the amelanchier tree, which is closely related to the rowan or mountain ash of Europe, and the shadbush (service-tree) of North America, the fruit of which is called juneberry.

alivenci, a delicious traditional Rumanian recipe, the main ingredient of which is cabbage. About 1 lb. (3½ cups) maize flour is scalded in 1 pint (2 cups) milk and left to cool. When it is cold, 1 pint (2 cups) sour milk (buttermilk), a little chopped dill, 1 tablespoon butter, and a pinch of salt are added. It is well mixed and set aside. Meanwhile the cabbage leaves, which have been washed and dried, are buttered on one side and a little of the maize mixture spread on each. Another leaf is placed on top to make a sandwich, and these are arranged in a baking dish and cooked until they are golden brown. This dish is at its best served very hot with sour cream.

alkanet (*Anchusa officinalis*), a small thick-leaved plant with bright blue star-shaped flowers. The leaves of this evergreen plant were once eaten as a vegetable in France and Germany, where it is called *buglosse* and *alkanna,* respectively. The roots of the alkanet were prized in Greece and Egypt, where a red dye was extracted from them and used for a cosmetic, no doubt it was the first lipstick. The name *anchusa* comes from a Greek word meaning "to paint" or "dye," and the dye is used today to colour wine and oils. Alkanet is used as a medicinal herb in the British Isles, but the flowers can be used like borage. It is also called "ox-tongue."

alkanet

alkekénge, French for the strawberry tomato, which grows well in France. It is used for jam and syrup, glacéed, and also as a compote. It is a variety of what is known as cape gooseberry in England. See also STRAWBERRY TOMATO.

all grenat, see BOUILLADE.

allemande, I. A classic French sauce which was so called by the famous chef Carême because it is light in colour, and to distinguish it from sauce espagnole, which is dark. It is made from velouté, blended with egg yolks and cream, with a touch of nutmeg. It is also sometimes called sauce blonde and sauce parisienne. When served with chicken, the dish is called *poulet d'allemande.* II. A garnish for meat made from sautéed sliced calf's kidney, chopped sweet peppers, and onions, with a little Madeira wine. III. In Germany, it is a clear beef broth flavoured with tarragon and garnished with quenelles which are also flavoured with tarragon and chervil. Cooked peas, asparagus, and french beans are sometimes added. IV. French beef consommé garnished with fine strips of cooked red cabbage and sliced frankfurter sausage. See also CONSOMMÉ.

allgäuer bergkäse, a German cow's milk cheese of the emmental type. It is made in large wheels and weighs between 50 and 100 lb.

allgäuer limburger, a mild limburger.

allgäuer rahmkase, a German full cream cow's milk cheese, not unlike a mild romadur.

alliance, I. A French sauce made from ½ pint (1 cup) reduced white wine and 1 tablespoon tarragon vinegar, then mixed with an egg yolk and beaten until thick. Seasoned with lemon juice and pepper. II. A garnish for meat made from demiglace, artichoke hearts, onions, and carrots.

allice shad, see SHAD.

alligator, a genus of saurian reptiles, of which the American species (*Alligator mississipiensis*) is eaten in North and South America, though very rarely, and on occasion may be served in London and Paris (also rare). It is not generally considered

edible. The edible portion however is cut from the tail, sautéed in butter, and served with sauce madère.

alligator pear, see AVOCADO.

allis, see SHAD.

allodola, Italian for lark. Often grilled in Italy with other small song birds.

alloro, Italian for bay leaf.

allspice (*Pimenta officinalis*), the dried berry of the allspice tree, sometimes called Jamaican pepper since it grows in abundance there. It is also known as pimenta or pimento. Some have imagined it to combine the flavour of cloves, cinnamon, and nutmeg, but in the author's opinion this is not a true description of its flavour. The term is sometimes applied to the seeds of other similar aromatic shrubs. It is used mainly for pickling, but also in some spicy stews, in mincemeat, and spiced cakes.

allspice

allumettes, I. French for potatoes cut as finely as matches and fried in oil or fat. II. Sticks of puff pastry spread either with sugar or royal icing and baked, or served as a savoury (hors d'oeuvre) with cheese or forcemeat spread on top.

Almacks preserve, a compote of fruit invented in the 19th century by a chef of Almacks Club, London. It consists of plums, apples, pears, and sugar, cooked until reduced to a very thick compote, cooled, and served in slices.

almejas, Spanish for small cockles. (Also called coquines.) In Spain almejas are usually served either with rice dishes or in soups. They must be well washed before being fried in oil, with parsley and chopped onion.

almejón, Spanish for scallop. See VIERAS. Also called morcillon.

almendra, Spanish for almond, used extensively in Spain in both sweet and savoury dishes. See also PASTAS DE ALMENDRAS MALLORQUINAS; SALSA DE ALMENDRAS CON YEMA.

almendrado, see MANTECADOS.

almibar, a basic syrup used in the preparation of Spanish puddings and sweets. There are five degrees of this syrup, but they are all made the same way and differ only in the proportion of sugar and water used.

almond, the kernel of a stone-fruit borne by two trees, one bitter (*Prunus amygdalus*), and the other sweet (*P. amygdalus dulcis*). The tree is allied to the plum and the peach, and is thought to be Moroccan in origin, but the plant was first brought to Britain by the Romans, who used it both for food and medicine. There is much legend attached to the almond: Aaron's rod is said to have been made of almond wood, and the Romans thought that almonds kept them sober if eaten while drinking alcohol. This could account for the origin of their accompaniment with drinks today. In the Balkans and Muslim countries generally, where alcohol is forbidden, almonds are used to make a drink. Elsewhere, they are used for sweetmeats, cakes, desserts, soups, and sauces. A valuable oil is extracted from them which is very high in protein and low in carbohydrates. Almond oil is excellent for frying fish or vegetables, and is used extensively in Portugal and Spain. See also ALMENDRA; AMANDE; AMÊNDOAS; AMYGDALIN; AMYGTHALA; TOURON.

almond

almond cake, see MACAROON.

almond fraze, an English 18th-century sweet or pudding made from ½ cup pounded blanched almonds, mixed with ½ pint (1 cup) cream, 3 egg yolks, 2 tablespoons sugar, and 1 tablespoon breadcrumbs, with 2 stiffly beaten egg whites added last. This is mixed to a paste and fried in foaming butter, and stirred until it fluffs up. It is eaten cold, sprinkled with castor sugar.

almond icing, used in the French cake called *condé.* It is made by beating 1 cup icing sugar with 2 egg whites, and when thick mixing in peeled, finely chopped almonds.

almond paste, see MARZIPAN.

almonds, ground, are sold commercially. They are used a lot for cakes and puddings, and 1 tablespoon added to ¼ lb. (1 cup) flour makes an excellent pastry for a sweet tart or flan. It was frequently used in the 18th century in the pastry for a fruit tart or pie.

almondegas, Portuguese for minced meat balls which are served in a tomato sauce.

almondija, a Spanish dish made from 1 lb. minced (ground) raw beef, 3 tomatoes, 1 onion, and 2 whole hard-boiled eggs. The ingredients are poached in the oven in a pan turned upside down in ½ another pan of water. The recipe is similar to a French terrine, except that it is served hot.

almorta, a flour used in Spain, made from the beans of the common vetch.

alondra, Spanish for lark, often prepared in Spain by grilling with other small song birds.

alosa, see SÁBALO.

alose, French for shad.

alouette, French for lark. For the past 200 years a famous lark pâté has been made at Pithiviers in Orléans, Franche, and lark pies at Étampes and Blois in the same region. The lark is also called *mauviette* in French.

alouette de mer, French for a kind of plover or sandpiper, which has a delicate flesh and is cooked like woodcock. It is known in English as summer-snipe or sea-lark, but is not eaten in Britain.

aloyau de boeuf, French for sirloin of beef.

alperches, Portuguese for apricots.

alphée, French name for a crustacean which resembles a crawfish and is common to all French sea coasts as well as the Mediterranean. It is not as good to eat as crawfish, but it is regularly fished for, and can be treated as such.

alphonse, a French garnish for meat made from sauce màdere with artichoke hearts and mushrooms.

alpkäse, see BERGKÄSE.

alsacienne, I. An Alsatian garnish for roast meats, chicken, and game, consisting of noodles with goose liver sautéed in butter, and slices of truffle with a little sauce madère. II. It also means sauerkraut with a slice of ham on top as a background for the main dish of choucroute which contains smoked meats and sausages. Sometimes the sauerkraut and ham are in small pastry tarts. III. There is also a cold sauce of this name made from pounded boiled calves' brains with cooked mashed onions, seasoned well with a little mustard, vinegar, and lemon juice, and then beaten until thick with a little olive oil. IV. A chicken broth garnished with small ravioli filled with goose liver and sauerkraut. Strasbourg sausages (saucisses de Strasbourg) are sometimes used in place of the ravioli.

alsen, German for shad.

alubia, Spanish for french bean.

alverde, a local name in Portugal for a farmhouse-made variety of serra cheese.

alverof (faki me pasta), Greek for mixed lentils and noodles. This recipe is from the Island of Rhodes. Lentils are put into cold water. When they are just soft half as much noodles (broken into squares) are added with salt and some more boiling water. Cooking is continued until the noodles are tender. This dish is garnished with chopped fried onion.

amande, French for almond. *Amande amère* is bitter almond; *amande douce* is sweet almond.

amande beurre, see BEURRES COMPOSÉS.

amandine, a word used in the U.S. to denote foods such as fish or poultry cooked with chopped almonds, generally fried or grilled (broiled).

amaretti, Italian for macaroons, first invented in Italy where there are many varieties, some being no larger than an unshelled almond. This small one is the speciality of Salsomaggiore, in the province of Parma, and is used in puddings. The crumbs from amaretti are mixed with breadcrumbs, spices, and cheese for stuffing, especially of onions and chicken. Another slightly larger variety is called *amaretti di saronna.* See also MACAROON; PINOCCATE.

amarettini, a variety of the amaretti, about 1 inch across and flavoured with apricot kernels.

amarilla, salsa, a Spanish "yellow sauce." Six hard-boiled egg whites are finely sieved. Their yolks are mixed with 2 tablespoons madeira wine, into which 2 tablespoons oil is very slowly beaten, and then seasoned with salt. One-half cup clarified stock and 1 tablespoon vinegar are stirred into this, then ½ teaspoon each of mustard and pepper, and finally the chopped egg whites.

amasette, French for palette knife.

amazone, a French garnish for meat. It is made of lentil fritters, the centres of which have been scooped out and stuffed with morels and chestnut purée.

ambassadeur, I. A French haute cuisine garnish served with meat, consisting of pommes duchesse and artichoke hearts filled with puréed mushrooms and grated horseradish. II. A clear strong chicken broth garnished with puréed truffles, chopped mushrooms, and slivers of chicken breast.

ambassadrice, I. A French sauce for chicken, consisting of a sauce suprême mixed with pounded chicken and whipped cream. II. A garnish for braised chicken with sauce suprême, buttered asparagus tips, and lamb's sweetbreads larded with truffles. Served with barquettes of pastry filled with chopped chicken livers, cock's combs, and truffles. III. A garnish for steaks consisting of pounded chicken livers and sautéed mushrooms, with pommes parisienne, kidneys, and braised lettuce. IV. A clear chicken soup garnished with small cubes of chicken, mushrooms, truffles, and peas. Chicken quenelles are sometimes used.

ambelopoùlia, a method of cooking a small bird called a figeater. In Cyprus they are boiled in salted water for 8 to 10 minutes, cooled, and preserved in wine vinegar to be eaten whole, bones and all. The feet are cut off, but they are not cleaned, and the heads are left on. See also FIGEATER.

amber fish, a good-eating tropical and sub-tropical fish of the *Seriolidae* family.

ambigu, a French word meaning a mixed cold collation, not eaten at a regular meal time. It probably relates to what in English would be a large "snack" meal, eaten either in between meals or after midnight. Meat, sweet courses, and fruit are all served at the same time.

amêijoas, Portuguese for a small clam or cockle. Although these two bivalves are of different families, they are closely related, and both varieties are used in Portugal. They are eaten in many different ways.

amêijoas à Bulhão pato, cockles or clams fried in olive oil in their shells with a lot of chopped garlic, sprinkled with pounded coriander, salt, and pepper, and served as soon as the shells open. They are called after the 18th century writer of that name.

amêijoas à espanhola, cockles and clams prepared like moules à la marinière.

amêijoas ao natural, clams or cockles gently steamed and served with lemon wedges. See also AÇORDA COM AMÊIJOAS; CARNE PORCO COM AMÊIJOAS.

ameixa, Portuguese for plum. At Elvas, Portugal, the delicious plums are dried in the sun, and taste like a less sweet crystallized fruit. They are packed in little round boxes and exported all over Europe.

amelanchier (*Amelanchier botryapium*), French for several types of shrubs, the fruits of which is called alise. See ALISE.

amélie, a French garnish for fish. It consists of a white wine sauce slightly coloured with tomato purée, and is served with diced truffles, mushrooms, and potato croquettes around.

amêndoas, Portuguese for almonds, which grow extensively in Portugal and are an important food source. The nuts are used in many ways. Grilled, or blanched and salted, they are often made into elaborate animal or fish shapes with dried figs. They are ground up, mixed with eggs and sugar for cakes, called *bôlo real do Algarve*, and the shells are used for fires, particularly in the Algarve. A delicious oil is also made, which is the best of all for frying fish or potatoes, as it is not at all greasy. It can also be used for salads or mayonnaise. In Portuguese it is called *oleo de amenoim*.

amêndoas croquetes, ½ lb. ground almonds mixed with 3 egg whites, sugar to taste, and grated orange peel moistened with port wine, and made into a thick paste with cakecrumbs. The mixture is shaped into small balls, rolled in egg yolk, and fried in hot almond oil.

américaine, I. A French sauce for sole and lobster, consisting of fish and velouté with pounded lobster, lobster coral, and butter, mixed with dry white wine and brandy. II. A cold sauce of mayonnaise with pounded lobster and a little mustard. III. A garnish of lobster tails and sliced truffles. IV. A garnish of corn fritters and sliced, fried sweet potatoes. V. A clear chicken soup with rice, crushed and peeled tomatoes, and diced chicken meat.

Some people think that the name américaine is a corruption of armoricaine, Armorica being a region of Brittany where lobsters and other fish are very good and plentiful. It is suggested that this corruption came about because of the American tourists' great liking for lobster armoricaine—but of course this may be an apocryphal story!

American cheddar, a cheese similar to English cheddar but made from pasteurized milk. It can be obtained in many different varieties of sharpness or mildness of flavour, flakiness or waxiness of texture, and also softness and hardness of the paste. All American cheddar belongs to the category of hard cheeses made from cow's milk. Americans tend to prefer the rindless variety of cheddar cheese, and progress in the production of a rindless cheese has vastly increased consumption. American cheddar is processed in its very young form (known as American cheese) and is much used for sandwiches.

Cheddar cheeses in different shapes and sizes—from a 14-inch-diameter cheese to large ones weighing over 70 lb.—are known as daisies, longhorns, flats, twins, and young America in the U.S. There is also a sharp black beauty cheddar cheese, made in Wisconsin, which has a coal-black outer covering and is matured for a year or more.

American cheeses. See AMERICAN CHEDDAR; AMERICAN MYSOST; AMERICAN SAGE; BAKER'S; BLACK BEAUTY CHEDDAR; BLUE MOLD (BLUE CHEESE); BRICK; BURMEISTER; CAMOSUN; CHANTELLE; COLBY; COON; CORNHUSKER; CREOLE; DAISIES; HAND; HERKIMER; HIGH MOISTURE JACK; LIEDERKRANZ; LONGHORN; MONTEREY (JACK); OLD HEIDELBERG; PINEAPPLE; POONA; SWISS; YOUNG AMERICA.

American cherry (*Prunus virginiana*), a bush-like tree which grows in North America. The fruit is tart, but used for pies and sauces.

American crab apple (*Malus coronaria*), a tasteless species of crab apple, admired mostly for its exquisite pink blossom.

American cress (*Barbarea praecox*), also known as land cress or Belle-isle cress in Europe; in America as watercress or garden cress; bank cress, upland cress, and hedge mustard are related species. It is a weed, but extremely useful as a winter salad. It is now cultivated in Europe and has a good peppery flavour. The great advantage is that it can be grown in garden soil, without the running water needed for watercress. See also WATERCRESS.

American mysost, a cheese made from the whey obtained from the manufacture of other cheeses. It is made chiefly in Wisconsin, New York, Michigan, and northern Illinois.

American partridge, a bird slightly larger than the quail, and of the same family. It is common in the U.S. See AMERICAN QUAIL.

American quail, sometimes called partridge in North America, where it is native. There are many varieties belonging to the *Odontophorinae* family, and the bobwhite (*Colinus virginianus*) is thought to be the best gastronomically. They are cooked as partridge.

American sage, a sage-flavoured cow's milk cheese made either by the granular or stirred curd process. The curd has a green and mottled appearance.

American short crust pastry, see PASTRY.

American woodcock (*Philohela minor*), a bird smaller than the British woodcock but highly prized as a food in North America. It is best in the winter, and it is cooked as snipe.

American widgeon, see BALDPATE WIDGEON.

amiral, I. A French sauce for boiled fish, consisting of 1 cup butter with 2 pounded anchovies, and 1 tablespoon each of chives, capers, and thin grated lemon peel. This mixture is simmered over a moderate heat until all ingredients are blended. A little lemon juice is added, and the sauce is served hot. II. Scrambled eggs, surrounded with lobster sauce with pieces of diced lobster in it. Sometimes it is made with anchovies in place of lobster. III. A garnish for fish made of oysters, mussels, mushrooms, and sauce normande with butter and pounded crayfish. IV. A fish consommé thickened with arrowroot; fish quenelles, diced lobster, sliced mushrooms, oysters, and julienne of truffles cooked in madeira, and sprinkled with chopped chervil.

ammocète, a fish somewhat like a cross between a lamprey and an eel, found in the mouth of the Seine River in France. It is prepared and cooked as lamprey or eel.

amoras, Portuguese for mulberries and blackberries.

amou, a cow's milk cheese from the Béarn district of France. It is at its best from October to May.

amourettes, French name for the marrow of calves' bones. It is usually taken out of the cracked bones, poached, seasoned, and used as a garnish for soups or for some meat dishes. Sometimes it is prepared as a single dish in the form of fritters or croquettes, or fried in batter.

amydon, Norman-English word for cornflour.

amygdalin, French word applied to all foods, cakes, or sweets, which contain almonds. See ALMOND.

amygthala, Greek for almond. They are very popular in Greece. See ALMOND; AMYGTHALOTA.

amygthalota, Greek for almond "pears," a sweet dish which is a speciality on the Island of Hydra. One lb. finely ground almonds are mixed with ½ lb. (1 cup) castor sugar, 1 teaspoon vanilla essence (extract), 3 egg whites, and ⅓ cup soft breadcrumbs. This mixture is kneaded to a dough and then moulded into pear-like shapes. A clove is inserted at the thin end to represent a stalk. They are baked in a moderate oven in a buttered tin for about 15 minutes. When cool, the "pears" are dipped in orange flower water and rolled in icing (confectioners') sugar.

anacard, a vinegar made from the fermented juice of the pulp surrounding the cashew nut. It is popular in Brazil.

ananas, Dutch, French, Norwegian, and German for pineapple.

ananaskrem, an unusual pineapple cream from Norway. It is made from tinned pineapple, the juice of which is mixed with gelatine and warmed (1 teaspoon gelatine to ½ pint [1 cup] juice). Two beaten egg yolks, sugar and vanilla to taste, a pinch salt are mixed together and the warm juice gradually is added and stirred well. Finally 2 stiffly beaten egg whites are folded into the still warm mixture, and poured over the pineapple chunks. It is served chilled.

ananasso, Italian for pineapple.

ananaz, Portuguese for pineapple.

anari, a Greek cheese made from goat's or ewe's milk. It is made in both square and round shapes.

anatto or *annatto* (*Bixa orellana*), a tree which grows in South America containing salmon-pink fruits which are quite tasteless. The dye extracted from them, however, is used to give cheese and confectionery an orange tone. The seeds are sometimes used for flavouring. In Argentina it is known as urucú.

anchoa, Spanish for anchovy.

anchoïade, both a Provençal and Corsican dish of anchovies, tomatoes, almonds, herbs, and olive oil pounded until they become a paste. Lemon juice is then added and the paste is put on large pieces of French bread and baked for not more than 20 minutes in a hot oven. In Corsica, figs and sweet red peppers are also added.

anchois, French for anchovy, used extensively for garnish in France, and for sauces. See also ANCHOÏADE.

anchois beurre, see BEURRES COMPOSÉS.

anchovy (*Engraulis encrasicholus*), a small herring-like fish of the *Engraulidae* family, found prolifically in the English Channel and the Mediterranean. Anchovies have been known to Europe for many centuries. They are caught only

anatto

when the moon is waning. Since we very seldom see fresh anchovies for sale in England, it is assumed that the catches go straight to canning or bottling factories. In Italy and the south of France, fresh anchovies are popular, either fried or grilled. When salted, or tinned in oil, they make an excellent garnish and salad, or are eaten with toast or bread. An essence (extract) and a paste are also made from them, and they are the basis for the well-known English relish called Gentleman's relish or *patum peperium*. See also ACCIUGHE; ANCHOIS; ANJOVIS.

ancien impérial, a French cheese of the Neufchâtel type, made from cow's milk. When eaten fresh, it is called *petit carré;* when fermented, it is *carré affiné*.

ancienne, à l', I. A classical French method of braising a fowl with a cream sauce flavoured with port, button onions, and mushrooms, garnished with puff pastry rosettes and truffles. II. Poached white fish cooked in a white wine sauce with button onions, mushrooms, and parsley. See CROÛTE-AU-POT À L'ANCIENNE.

and, Norwegian for duck. Ducks are extremely popular in Norway, where they are usually cooked with a stuffing of prunes. See SVISKEFYLLING.

andunge, duckling.

andalouse, I. A French sauce, consisting of a mayonnaise to which has been added a purée of tomatoes and some diced sweet peppers. II. A garnish for meat or poultry of halves of sweet peppers stuffed with rice à la grecque, slices of eggplant and tomatoes, both sautéed in olive oil and sprinkled with chopped parsley. III. A clear chicken soup garnished with peeled tomatoes, rice, ham, and a beaten egg and flour poured through a colander into the hot broth so that they form little balls. Beef broth is also sometimes used with vermicelli or rice, diced ham, and tomatoes.

andijvie, Dutch for endive.

andithia, Greek for endive (chicory).

andithia avgolémono, a popular way of serving endive (chicory) braised with butter, lemon juice, and stock for 30 minutes. Two eggs are then beaten with lemon juice and added to 1 pint (2 cups) hot stock, beating with a whisk all the time. The sauce is poured over the endive and the dish is served hot.

andouille, a large French sausage made from pork and pork intestines, or chitterlings, mixed with lardoons of pork fat. It is slightly salted and can be kept for some time. It is sold cooked, and often eaten for an hors d'oeuvre, thinly sliced. It can also be served hot, by poaching in boiling water, then grilling lightly and serving garnished with potatoes or other vegetables. The best andouille comes from Vire in Normandy. It is made with chitterlings, is slightly smoked, and is known as *andouille de Vire*. Strasbourg, Lyons, Nancy, and Paris are also well known for andouilles. Some are flavoured with shallots or spices.

andouillette, a smaller version of the *andouille*.

andruty, a Polish wafer, similar to a waffle or a *gaufre*, made from milk, flour, sugar, egg, and melted butter. This mixture is poured on to greased wafer irons and cooked for about 4 minutes, then served either flat or rolled.

andruty migdalowe, as above, but with grated almonds added. These wafers are sometimes filled and rolled up with a cream, or chocolate, nut, and cream mixture.

âne, Newfoundland word for haddock; also *anon*.

aneth, French for dill.

angel cake, a very light frothy cake made from 8–10 stiffly whipped egg whites, ½ lb. (1 cup) sugar, 4 oz. (1 cup) flour, and 1 teaspoon each cream of tartar and vanilla flavouring. It is put in a well-floured cake tin and baked in a slow to moderate oven. When cold, it is coated with icing.

angel fish, a variety of types of edible fish. I. The most common kind is a *squatina*, known in North America as monkfish, a ray-like shark. It is found in the Atlantic, and the fins are cooked the same way as skate. II. Another variety, also called butterfly fish (*Angelichthys ciliaris*), is a glorious blue and gold fish with long blue streamers and electric blue eyelids. It is about the size of a medium plaice and this tropical variety is prolific off the coast of Bermuda, the West Indies, and Florida. It is much prized gastronomically, but I have always found it too beautiful to eat. III. The black angel fish (*Pomocanthus arcuatus*) is found in the warmer waters of Bermuda, the West Indies, and the Gulf of Florida.

angelica (*Angelica archangelica*), an umbelliferous biennial aromatic herb, which grows to a height of 4 to 5 feet and prefers moist or swampy ground. It was known in ancient times as the "root of the Holy Ghost" and "an herbe of the sun," and was thought to be a remedy against witchcraft, poison, and plague, as well as an antidote against any disorder caused by lack of warmth or light. Even today, poets in Lapland are crowned with a wreath made from angelica.

In Britain only one species grows, namely *A. sylvestris*. Both the root and leaves are used, and the former produces an oil. It is found from Lapland to Spain. In Lapland and Norway the root is sometimes used as a substitute for bread, and the stalks are peeled and eaten as celery. In France the leaves are blanched and used in salads. Several liqueurs, including Benedictine, are also made from angelica; an angelica brandy used to be made in Britain, but is no longer made. The stalks are candied and used for flavouring, as well as decoration on cakes and biscuits. They are excellent added to rhubarb jam in the ratio of 4 parts rhubarb to 1 part angelica. It is simple to candy the stalks. They should be taken from second-year plants and dropped into boiling water. The outer skin is then peeled off and the stalks boiled again until green and transparent. A thick syrup of 4 oz. (½ cup) sugar and very little water (approximately 4 tablespoons) is made, and the stalks are boiled in this until they are clear. They are dried on a rack or oiled paper, sprinkled with more fine sugar, and left to dry in a warm place.

angelot, French for angel fish.

angels on horseback, an English savoury consisting of oysters wrapped in bacon, put on a skewer, and grilled. They are then served on buttered toast.

anginares, Greek for artichokes. When Greeks speak of artichokes they mean globe artichokes which are very tender in Greece. A Greek legend says that a beautiful girl called Cynara from the Island of Zinari was turned into a globe artichoke (*Cynara scolymus*) by a jealous goddess.

anginares à la polita, a recipe from Constantinople (Istan-

bul) but popular throughout Greece. The artichokes are well washed and their stems are cut off near the globe. The outer leaves are completely removed and 1 inch is cut from the remaining tips; they are then cut in half and the fuzz, or choke, is removed. (Baby artichokes may be left whole.) They are soaked for 15 minutes in salt water and lemon juice, and then well drained. When ready for cooking, they are placed in a pan with seasoning, dill, peeled and sliced potatoes, and other root vegetables (including onions and spring onions [scallions]) with water to cover. Six tablespoons olive oil, well blended into lemon juice, is added. The pan is covered and the contents slowly cooked until tender. The artichokes are served in the juice and garnished with the vegetables. In France, this method of cooking and serving vegetables in their juice is known as à la Grecque.

anginares me koykia, artichoke bottoms, mixed with cooked fresh broad beans in a sauce made from 1 tablespoon cornflour (cornstarch), 3 tablespoons olive oil, 1 pint (2 cups) bean stock, juice of 1 lemon, and 1 tablespoon chopped parsley, all heated and shirred until thick.

anginares tiyanites, boiled artichokes, which are then dipped in egg and breadcrumbs before frying in hot oil. They are served alone or with meat or poultry.

anginares yemistes, artichokes stuffed with minced onion, garlic, and herbs. Broad beans are also added. This dish is a popular Lenten meal in Greece and is eaten a lot during Holy Week.

anginarokardoules, Greek for artichoke hearts or bottoms.

anglaise, à l', I. A coating of eggs, salt, and pepper applied to foods that are breadcrumbed and then fried in oil. II. In France, this means a simple English method of cooking, such as boiling or steaming. III. A French garnish for boiled salted beef, consisting of boiled carrots, turnips, cauliflower, and potatoes, with no other sauce. IV. Crème à l'anglaise, see CRÈME.

anglerfish or **angler** (*Lophius piscatorius*), an ugly fish with a huge head, also known as the frogfish and monkfish, found in the Atlantic and the Mediterranean. Known in Italy as *Rana pescatrice*, and in France as *baudroie*. It is used invariably in fish soups, particularly zuppa de pesce and bouillabaisse. The tail is good to eat, firm and resembling lobster. It is called *coda di rospo* in Venice where it is a speciality, grilled, fried, or poached. See also RAPE.

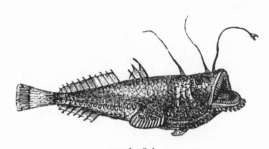

anglerfish

angoulême, a town in the Charente, France, famous for its partridge pâté called *pâté d'angoulême*.

angouria, Greek for cucumbers.

angouria yemista, cucumber stuffed with either chopped shellfish or feta cheese.

angourosalata, cucumber salad.

anguila, Spanish for a small eel, not conger eel.

salpicon de anguilas lara, a Valencian recipe. Before being cooked in boiling water, the eels are fried in oil. A scattering of ground almonds, parsley, and garlic are added later and cooked with the eel for a few minutes just before serving.

anguilla, Italian for eel. Comacchio, on the eastern Italian coast, is famous for its eels. They are very large and are most generally cut into thick slices, which are put between bay leaves and then roasted on a spit. They are also braised in white wine, and roasted with rosemary and bay leaves. In Lombardy, eel soup (*zuppa di ceci*) is traditionally eaten on All Souls' Night, November 2nd. Eel is cooked with a slice of pig's head, onion, garlic, carrots, celery, and herbs, and simmered for several hours. In Naples, eel is traditionally eaten on Christmas Eve, with a salad of cauliflower. See also INSALATA DI RINFORZ.

anguilla napoletana, a skinned filleted eel is cut into 3-inch pieces and flattened. Each piece is stuffed with a mixture of hard-boiled egg yolks, butter, parsley, onion, and a raw egg yolk. The fillets are tied up and cooked in melted butter with lemon juice for ½ hour. They are left to cool, the thread removed, then dipped in batter and fried in hot oil until golden.

anguille, French for eel.

anguille à la martégale, a classic and traditional dish served on Christmas Eve. A bed of finely sliced leeks is put in an ovenproof dish, then covered with chopped parsley and garlic. A few black olives, stoned, and then a skinned eel are added. A glass (approx. ½ cup) of dry white wine is poured over the dish, and then it is covered with breadcrumbs and baked for about 1½ hours.

anguilles en catigout, a Provençal dish of eels cooked with chopped bacon and mushrooms, barely covered with white wine. It is traditionally eaten on Christmas Eve. See also AïGO BOUïLLIDO.

anguille de haie, see GRASS SNAKE.

anguille de mer or *congre,* French for conger eel.

anho, Portuguese for lamb.

anice, Italian for aniseed.

anijs melk, Dutch for aniseed milk. In Holland aniseed milk is the traditional drink associated with ice skating. Wherever there is an ice rink, there will invariably be a ''Cook and Drink'' hut (*koek en zoopie*). These huts are really simple ''wind-break'' shelters, roofless and usually made of reeds. Inside there are benches and a small stove on which stands a large pot of hot anise milk. Cups of this refreshing drink and simple cakes or biscuits are sold, usually by an elderly man trying to eke out a meagre living. The Dutch people make this warming drink by scalding 2 pints (4 cups) milk with 1 tablespoon crushed aniseed, and adding 4 oz. (½ cup) sugar. The liquid is simmered for about 5 minutes; then 2 tablespoons cornflour (cornstarch), which has previously been dissolved in a small amount of water, is added, and the brew is stirred over a low fire for about another 5 minutes. It resembles a thin blancmange, and is very warming.

anijszaad, Dutch for aniseed.

animelle, Italian for sweetbreads. Both calves' and lambs' sweetbreads are used in Italy, and they are often cooked with cream, ham, vegetables, and wine.

animelle briache, sweetbreads first boiled in salted water, drained, and skinned, and then turned in butter and simmered in wine. Briache means ''drunken.''

animelle d'abbacchio al prosciutto, another Roman method for preparing lambs' sweetbreads, but using ham and Marsala wine instead of artichokes.

animelle d'abbacchio con carciofi, a Roman method of serving lambs' sweetbreads. The preliminary stages are as above, but when the sweetbreads are skinned, they are added to young globe artichokes which have been cooked in olive oil and basted with a little stock. Sometimes grated Parmesan or pecorino cheese is sprinkled over the finished dish and browned under the grill.

animelle di vitello con piselli, calves' sweetbreads cooked in butter with onion and marsala wine. In Bologna, 2 tablespoons cream are beaten into the sauce which is then sprinkled with basil and chives. The sweetbreads are served with young green peas mixed with mushrooms.

animelles, French culinary term for testicles of male animals, particularly rams. They are prepared and cooked as sweetbreads.

anis, French, German, and Spanish for aniseed.

anise, a French cow's milk cheese from Lorraine, flavoured with aniseed. It is made from scalded curd.

anisé, Greek for aniseed, which is much used in Balkan cooking. It is also popular as a pickling spice and, in hot weather, is made into a tisane. Greek herbalists prescribe a little in hot milk and honey as a cure for insomnia. In days gone by, a sprig of this plant was hung over the bed to prevent bad dreams.

aniseed (*Pimpinella anisum*), an umbelliferous plant with aromatic seeds, a member of the parsley family. Used for flavouring cakes, sauces, and for making a drink called anisette. It has a flavour resembling liquorice. It is used extensively in Balkan and oriental cookery. See also ANIJS MELK.

aniseed

anisette, a colorless sweet liqueur flavoured with aniseed.

anitho, Greek for fresh dill, often used with avgolémono sauce.

anitra, Italian for duck.

anitra arrosto alla genovese, a Genovese method of cooking duck. The duck is marinated in olive oil with a bay leaf and parsley for about 4 hours, turning it over a few times. It is drained and roasted in a moderate oven, the skin pricked to release the fat. When three quarters cooked ½ pint (1 cup) of stock and the juice of 1 lemon are poured over it and mixed with the pan juices; this is boiled up and served as the sauce.

anitra fredde alla genovese, Genovese cold duck. The duck is roasted as above and allowed to get cold before carving. It is served with a sauce rémoulade, made with chopped herbs, shallots, anchovy fillets, French mustard, hard-boiled egg yolks, capers, gherkins, raw egg yolk, wine vinegar, olive oil, the brown pan juices of the duck, salt, and pepper. The sauce is served separately.

anitra in salmi alla romana, Roman braised duck. Jointed duck is turned in hot oil, then put in a casserole with an onion stuck with cloves, sage, bay leaf, chopped heart, liver, and gizzard, 1 gill (½ cup) olive oil and 2 tablespoons wine vinegar, ½ pint (1 cup) stock, salt, and pepper. A tightly fitting lid is put on, and it is cooked for 1–2 hours. It is served with bread fried in butter. Green olives are sometimes added to the stock.

anitra selvatica, wild duck, roasted and basted with a hot mixture of olive oil, parsley, garlic, stock, juice and peel of orange, and marsala wine. The liquid is reduced on top of the stove. When the duck is cooked and put on a warm dish, a little more marsala is added to the sauce.

anjou, a French game consommé with asparagus tips, quenelles of game, and rice as a garnish. See also CONSOMMÉ.

anjovis, Swedish for anchovy.

anjovislåda, a Swedish dish of anchovies baked in layers with cooked sliced potatoes, butter, breadcrumbs, and parsley.

ankerstock, a Scottish loaf made of rye flour and seasoned with spice and currants. In the 19th century it was served as a gingerbread at New Year. Ankerstock gingerbread is still sold in Edinburgh. The name is thought to come from the Dutch ''anker,'' a measure. It is oblong in shape.

annatto, see ANATTO.

annona, the genus of the custard apple, which is fleshy tropical fruit with a smooth, yellowish-brown skin and a delicious white juicy interior. It can weigh up to 16 lb. Several varieties grow in South America. Another species is the Cherimoya, which comes from Central and South America. Custard apples are grown in Florida and California in the U.S. and are also exported to France and Germany. In France they are usually served raw, peeled, in slices, and sometimes steeped in a light white wine such as champagne. They are also served with the slices dipped in batter and deep fried. See also SOURSOP.

anodonta, a fresh-water genus of mollusc with a large thin shell. It is eaten like the mussel in Italy and the south of France. The shell of a large variety is used in northern France for skimming the cream off milk; they are called *ecalottes* when used for this purpose.

anodonte, French for anodonta.

anolini, form of Italian pasta, oval-shaped, and filled with either meat or vegetable stuffing. Used as a garnish for soups, and always served at Easter and Christmas in the province of Parma. See also AGNOLOTTI.

anon, a fish of the genus *gadus,* and a variety of haddock. It is very prolific in the English Channel. The flesh is white and flaky and it can be cooked in the same way as haddock, although it is not as good to eat. Similar varieties found in the U.S. are cusk and hake.

ânon, Newfoundland word for haddock; also *âne.*

anona, German for annona.

anone, French for annona.

ansjos, Norwegian for anchovy. It is usually served in smørgås or as a garnish.

antelope (family *Bovidae*), a collective name for a large number of deer-like ruminant mammals in Europe, Asia, and Africa. They are divided into 4 categories: the true, the bush, the bovine, and the capri form. The South African variety, known as eland, is almost as big as a bull, but there are many smaller, gazelle-like types. They are fast but shy animals, and therefore very difficult to stalk and shoot. The older animals are more prized gastronomically, as having more taste than the young ones. They need to be roasted with plenty of fat, otherwise they are dry. They can be prepared and cooked as venison.

antholyti, a round, yellow Greek cheese, with a thick mottled rind like a rhinoceros skin.

anthotyro, a goat's milk cheese made in Crete. It is delicate and firm to taste, and is eaten with grapes by the Cretans.

antiboise, a French sauce from Antibes of mayonnaise with a little tomato purée, anchovy essence (extract), and chopped tarragon added. It is served with fish.

antin, a French sauce made from a sauce madère, with shallots, chopped mushrooms, truffles, and parsley, cooked in reduced white wine.

antipasti (antipasto), Italian word meaning ''before the pasta'' for appetizers, or hors d'oeuvre, usually served as a start to the midday meal. It consists of many varieties of an Italian sausage called salame (salami), olives, ham (cooked and raw), raw and cooked vegetables served in oil and vinegar, tunny fish (tuna), sardines, anchovies, cold fish, and almost any shellfish, eggs, chicory, and all kinds of green salad. These are all served cold. There is also hot antipasti, consisting of rounds of fried or toasted bread with hot melted cheese with anchovies, also mashed cooked chicken liver or shellfish, and stuffed mushrooms and artichokes. See also CROSTINI.

antipasti

antoine, a French method of preparing scrambled eggs with chopped fried bacon, herbs, and capers, all covered in melted butter which has been heated until it is a dark-golden brown.

antoinette, a French method of poaching fish in an herb sauce, with anchovy essence (extract) mixed with butter, capers, and shrimps.

anversoise, à l', I. A French garnish for meat, of small pastry shells filled with creamed hop shoots (*jets de houblon*) and plain boiled potatoes. II. A method of preparing meat, calves' sweetbreads, or eggs, which are garnished with hop shoots sautéed in butter or cream, and potatoes fried in butter. III. A beef consommé, garnished with hop shoots and slightly thickened with tapioca. See also CONSOMMÉ.

anzio pie, an Italian flat pastry pie filled with underdone macaroni or spaghetti, and a layer of minced beef or veal mixed with grated orange peel. It is seasoned with salt, pepper, and cinnamon, moistened with a little good beef or veal stock, covered with more pastry, and baked in a slowish oven. When done, it is turned out of the dish and served with a meat sauce.

apfel, German for apple. See also APPLE.

apfel beignets regina, famous Swiss apple fritters. The apple rings are sprinkled with cinnamon, sugar, and brandy and left for 1 hour. The batter is made with 8 oz. (2 cups) flour, 3 egg yolks, 2 tablespoons olive oil, and mixed with ½ pint (1 cup) light beer. It is well beaten, and finally the stiffly beaten egg whites are added. The apple rings are dipped in this and fried in deep, hot fat.

apfelbrotsuppe, apple soup with slices of pumpernickel

bread soaked and simmered with the apples, water, currants, and lemon juice. See also OBST.

apfelkren, an Austrian sauce made from grated raw apples, horseradish, a little vinegar, sugar, and lemon juice, and a trace of white wine.

apfelstrudel, see STRUDEL.

apfelsuppe, a German soup made from apples with water, potato flour, and sugar.

apfelwähe, a large apple tart (about 18 inches across), baked with a custard around the apples. This is a common dish in Switzerland. Often eaten at *Sechsenläuten*.

apfelsine, German for orange.

aphie, a small fish found in the Mediterranean and prepared like whiting.

apio, Spanish for celeriac and for celery.

aplatir, a French culinary term meaning to flatten. It applies to beating meat with a mallet to make it more tender by breaking up the sinews.

apo aravosito, soupa, a Cretan village soup made from dried sweet corn. The corn is pounded and mixed with dried milk and kept for use in the winter. When needed, the dried corn and milk is mixed with water and simmered.

apogon, French for cardinal fish.

apokreo, a Greek word, the literal meaning of which is "fast from meat." It applies to the many days of fasting which the Greek Orthodox Church ordains.

apokries, has come to mean the two weeks of meat fasting, *kreatines*, and one week of cheese eating, *tyrini*. These three weeks constitute the Greek pre-Lenten carnival, which is enjoyed by Greeks and foreigners alike.

apostelkuchen, an Austrian bun which is very like a French brioche in taste and texture. It consists of 1 lb. (4 cups) flour, 1 oz. yeast, 4 oz. (½ cup) sugar, 2 oz. (¼ cup) butter, ½ pint (1 cup) milk, 6 egg yolks, and ¼ pint (½ cup) white wine. In Austria the mixture is often made into one large bun, not small ones as is usual in France.

appareil, a French word which, in culinary usage, means mixture, either savoury or sweet, of any ingredients used for a particular dish. These can be used in a number of ways. The savoury mixtures are usually for a hot hors d'oeuvre, and can be made into croquettes, put into pastry tarts, etc. They often consist of mixed cream cheese, egg yolks, and butter; a salpicon mixed with sauce velouté or demi-glace; finely sliced vegetables stewed in butter and flavoured with madeira wine; or mashed potatoes bound with egg and mixed with chou pastry. Sweet appareils are in the nature of custard, *bavaroise*, meringue, or creams.

appareil à soufflé, French for the basic roux of a soufflé, called *panada* in English.

appel, Dutch for apple. See also APPLE.

appelbeignets, apple fritters. All Dutch children eat apple fritters, accompanied by *slemp* and *oliebollen*, on the evening of St. Nicolas. The batter consists of approximately ½ lb. (2 cups) bread flour mixed with about ¾ pint (1½ cups) beer; salt is added. Sliced, cored apples are dipped in this, fried in deep fat or oil, and served with honey or sprinkled with icing sugar. See also SINT NICOLAAS AVOND.

appelschoteltje, a baked apple dish made by adding 3 egg yolks to 4 oz. (½ cup) creamed butter and ½ lb. (1 cup) sugar. Grated lemon peel is added to ½ pint (1 cup) boiling milk, together with a little salt. This mixture is thickened by the addition of 2 oz. (½ cup) flour that has been blended with 2 tablespoons butter; the resulting sauce is added to the egg mixture together with cooking apples (which have previously been simmered in butter and sugar). Next, the 3 stiffly beaten egg whites are folded in. This mixture is laid in a casserole with alternate layers of crumbled zwieback. The pudding is

appelbeignets

dotted with butter and baked for about 45 minutes in a slow oven.

äppel, Swedish for apple. See also APPLE.

äppel kaka, sweetened apple sauce, layered alternately in a baking dish with mixed butter and *limpa* crumbs. It is cooked for about 25 minutes and left to cool and served with whipped and sweetened cream.

appelsin, Norwegian for orange; also oransje.

appelsinfromasj, orange mousse. Sugar, to taste, is dissolved in ½ pint (1 cup) milk, and the juice of one orange is added; 1 pint (2 cups) whipped cream is gradually stirred in, and then 2 tablespoons gelatine which has previously been dissolved in hot water. Two beaten egg whites are folded in, and the mixture poured into a wet mould which has previously been sprinkled with castor sugar. The mousse should be chilled before serving.

appenzell cheese, a full-fat cheese which originated in the east Swiss canton of Appenzell, but today is made also in St. Gall, Zurich, and Thurgovia. It is made of whole cow's milk, and the curd is put into a liquid of cider or spiced white wine for a few days. It has a most delicate flavour, and is golden yellow in colour, with a few pea-sized holes in it.

appenzell räss cheese, a variant of appenzell but with a very pungent taste. It is made from skimmed milk and is put into a liquid of cider or spiced white wine for a month or more. The curd is grey in colour and full of holes the size of pin heads. It is not exported.

appétit, a common name for chives in France; also *ciboulette* and *civette*.

appetizer, a word used in North America for hot or cold hors d'oeuvre.

appigret, an old French word used by Rabelais to mean gravy, juice, or essence seasoning.

apple (*Malus pumila*; family *Rosaceae*), a round, firm, fleshy fruit of the rose family; a native of Europe. There are over 1,500 varieties, of which the best known British ones are Cox's Pippin, Golden Pippin, Golden Delicious, Blenheim Orange, Worcester Pearmain, Granny Smith, Russet, Kentish Codlin. These are the eating varieties, for dessert. The best known cooking varieties are Wellington, Colvilles, Rennet, Bramley Seedling, Newtown Wonder. A little known variety, and one now difficult to obtain, is the Irish Peach Apple. It is unsurpassed for flavour, having a taste like that of a peach. It is oval in shape, with a thin golden skin. No doubt one of the reasons for its disappearance is the fact that it must be pruned with great care, and in a way quite different from the usual apple tree pruning, since the fruit is borne, not at the trunk end of the branches, as with the other varieties of apple, but at the extremities of the new shoots. Another excellent variety is the Lebanon apple. In the U.S. the best known varieties for eating are Delicious, Golden Delicious, MacIntosh, Pippin, and Winesap; for cooking the crab apple is used in jams and preserves, and the Rome, Greening, and the Duchess are used in other recipes.

Golden Delicious apples

The better kinds of apple are invariably eaten raw. The coarser varieties are used for cooking in puddings or sauces. The Elizabethans used them in stews, and indeed I have found that any dish which takes onion will also take apple. Apples can be tinned or dried to advantage; the drink, cider, is made from fermented apples, and in Germany apple soup (*apfelbrotsuppe*) is popular. Apples are rich in pectin, so set easily as a jelly or jam, and are often added to other fruits, like blackberry, for that reason. See also AEBLE; APFEL; APPEL; ÄPPEL; JABŁKA; POMME; YABLOKO.

apple charlotte, an English pudding made from peeled, cored, and sliced apples, sugar, butter, and breadcrumbs. These are all put in a dish in layers, finishing with breadcrumbs, baked in a hot oven, and served hot with cream or custard. See also CHARLOTTE, DE FRUITS.

apple cider, a fermented drink made from apples. It is much used in cooking in Normandy and Brittany in France, also in the West Country of England. It can be used in many dishes instead of white wine.

apple dumpling, see DUMPLINGS.

apple relish, a relish served with pork or turkey. It is made from 1 lb. red apples, cored but not peeled, ground (minced) with 2 dill pickles and 1 medium onion, well mixed, and dressed with ½ lb. (½ cup) sugar and ½ gill (¼ cup) vinegar.

apple sauce, a classic English and American sauce made from peeled, cored, and sliced apples boiled with sugar to taste, a pinch of cinnamon, lemon juice (about 2 tablespoons to 1 lb. apples), and very little water. It is often served either hot or cold with pork, duck, and goose.

apple sugar, see BARLEY SUGAR.

apple mint (*Mentha rotundifolia*), see MINT.

apricot (*Prunus armeniaca*), an orange-coloured stone-fruit grown on a tree resembling a plum (of which it is the same family) but with a furry skin like a peach. Originally from the north of China, it was brought into Europe through Armenia around 400 B.C. but did not reach England until about 1500.

It is inferior to a good peach when eaten raw, but cans much better, having a stronger taste. Apricots are also dried extensively, which makes them a most valuable fruit both winter and summer. Dried apricots have a high food value,

being a good source of vitamin A and iron. They should be soaked for several hours before cooking, then they will purée easily and can be used for many puddings of the compote or fool variety, as well as for filling or topping cakes. They also make an excellent jam.

aprikos, Swedish for apricot.

aprikose, German for apricot.

apron, a small fresh water fish, of which only 2 species are known. One is found in the Rhône and its tributaries and called the "common apron," the other is found in the Danube. It is about 6 inches long and highly thought of gastronomically. It is prepared as perch.

arachide, French for peanut, when used for oil.

aragosta, or arigusta (*Palinurus vulgaris*), Italian for crawfish.

araignée de mer, French name for spider crab.

Aran isenach, a bannock made in the Outer Isles of Scotland from equal quantities of wheat flour and fine cornmeal, mixed with butter and buttermilk. The name means Indian bread, from the corn (maize) meal. See also BANNOCK.

araña, Spanish for weever or dragon fish. These fish are a lovely blue colour when fresh. The flesh is white, and they are good either grilled or fried; however, they are not often caught because of their poisonous sting.

arance, Italian for orange, often served in a syrup as a compote in Italy. They are also served with the pulp removed and mixed with strawberries, then put back in the skins. These stuffed oranges are called *arance ripiene*.

arancini alla Siciliana, a Sicilian speciality made from 1½ lb. minced veal, 1 lb. tomatoes, 1 teaspoon basil, and seasonings all cooked with water to cover, until the mixture becomes very thick. It is cooled; then 1 lb. (2 cups) rice is simmered in stock until done. A knob of butter, 2 egg yolks, and 4 tablespoons grated Parmesan cheese are added to the hot rice and carefully stirred. It is all chilled, and the rice mixture is made into little balls with some veal mixture in the middle. The balls are rolled in breadcrumbs and fried in hot oil.

arandano, Spanish for blueberry.

arapède, French name for a univalve shellfish found off Provence. It is cooked as cockles.

arbenne, French for a variety of grouse, also called snow partridge or Tibetan partridge in English. It is found in Savoy (France), Switzerland, and Piedmont (Italy), and is prepared and cooked as grouse or partridge.

arbouse, French for arbute, used in the making of a liqueur in France.

Arbroath smokie, a smoked haddock. Unlike a finnan haddock, it is not split and smoked to a golden yellow, but left closed and smoked to a dull copper colour. It originated in the fishing hamlet of Auchmithie, Scotland, and it was not until the end of the 19th century that the name Arbroath took over. The fish were smoked in pits sunk in the ground and hung over halved whisky barrels. Oak and silver birch were the wood chips most commonly used for smoking. The smokie is prepared for eating by being opened out and having the backbone removed; then it is spread with butter and black pepper. It is closed up and heated (it is already cooked by the long smoking process) under a grill. The smokie is a delicacy well worth trying.

arbute (*Arbutus unedo*), the fruit of the strawberry tree, which is native to southern Europe, and County Kerry, Ireland, especially in the Killarney district, and the U.S. The berries are an attractive scarlet colour, similar in appearance to a strawberry but the taste and graininess of their texture makes them disappointing to eat raw. In Spain and Italy they are used in confectionery, and in France a liqueur is made from them. This is probably the best idea of all, but a few raw arbute in a fresh fruit salad look delightful, and their texture does not obtrude.

arca, an edible bivalve mollusc found on all French sea coasts. Its shell is very dark in colour and it can be eaten raw or cooked, like clams or oysters. Its common name is arch in both French and English.

arcanette, French name given in Lorraine to a small local nonmigratory teal. It is a gastronomic delicacy and can be prepared and cooked as teal or wild duck.

arch, see ARCA.

archiduc, à l', a French garnish for steak and tournedos of small cakes of pommes duchesse, with croquettes made from puréed calves' brains. Each tournedo has a slice of sautéed truffle on top, and the pan juices are mixed with sherry, fresh cream, veal stock, in equal proportions, all reduced and seasoned with salt and paprika.

archiduc, sauce, sauce suprême to which reduced champagne has been added.

archiduchesse, à l', a French method of preparing hardboiled or scrambled eggs with diced ham, mushrooms, and paprika, garnished with mashed potato croquettes and asparagus tips.

Arctic flounder (*Liopsetta glacialis*), a small flounder found in the Bering Sea. It can be cooked in any way used for flounder and is highly thought of gastronomically.

Arctic loon, see BLACK-THROATED DIVER.

ardennaise, à l', I. A soup from the Ardennes region of France made from leeks, endives, and potatoes simmered in milk, thickened slightly with butter and flour (beurre manié), and served with slices of French bread. II. Soup made from pheasant, flavoured with port and kidney beans. III. A dish of small birds cooked in a cocotte with juniper berries. Usually the birds are thrush or blackbird. IV. Pork chops or cutlets grilled or sautéed with crushed juniper berries, served with sliced sautéed onion and potatoes; the pan juices moistened with white wine.

ardoise, a French word for slate. It refers to a bill sometimes presented on a slate. It has come to mean bill or check, but is considered slang and is only used in cheap French restaurants.

ardoise grillade à l', an Andorran method of cooking on a red-hot roof slate, heated over a wood fire.

aremberg, d', I. A French clear beef soup with peas, carrots, turnips, and truffles, all diced, and garnished with chervil. II. A clear chicken broth with diced carrots, turnips, truffles, and chicken quenelles.

arenque, Spanish for herring.

Argenteuil, a region in France which has a worldwide reputation for growing the finest asparagus. Argenteuil qualifying a food means it has asparagus either in the dish, or as a garnish. I. A French garnish for fish consisting of a white wine sauce with asparagus tips. II. A cream soup made from puréed asparagus, cream, and chervil.

Argentine marrow, see AVOCADELLA; ZAPALLITO DE TRONCO.

Argyll, the English name for a vessel or well in a carving dish which catches the juices from roasted meats, game, or poultry. It is used to serve the gravy and keep it hot. Owing to such dishes being difficult to find nowadays, its name has fallen into desuetude, but it was always used in the 19th century.

ariégeoise, a l', I. French name given to all dishes from the Ariège department of France, famous for its geese, pork, and ham. II. Various dishes, all of which are garnished with cooked green cabbage, pickled pork, and sometimes kidney beans.

aringa, Italian for herring.

arista fiorentina, a Florentine method of roasting pork. The rind is removed from a loin of pork, and the meat is then rubbed with salt and pepper. Cloves of garlic, rosemary, and a few whole cloves are pressed into the meat. It is roasted in about 2 inches of water, for somewhat longer than the usual roasting method so that it is very soft and succulent, but not dry. It is left to cool, removed from the liquid, and served cold. The fat is removed from the liquid, and if jellied, is diced, as a garnish.

arista perugina, a Perugian method of roasting pork with fennel leaves and garlic, otherwise the same as *arista fiorentina.*

Arles, saucisson d', a sausage made from lean pork and beef, pepper, garlic cloves, paprika, and a little saltpetre. This is all mixed, after chopping, with peppercorns and red wine. It is put into skins and smoked in a chimney for about a month. These sausages are eaten raw, and cooked in soups and stews. They are native to Arles, but are now seen all over the south of France. See also SAUCISSON.

arlésienne, I. A French garnish for tournedos, steaks, or noisettes. It consists of eggplants, onions, and tomatoes cooked in oil or butter. II. Scrambled eggs are also served arlésienne with the above garnish. III. A garnish of small whole tomatoes cooked in butter, with pickled chicory hearts fried in oil. IV. A garnish of tomatoes stuffed with rice, browned, and large olives stuffed with minced chicken, anchovy butter (*beurre anchois*), and new potatoes.

armadillo, a large family of mammals of which one variety, the three-banded armadillo (*Tolypeutes tricinctus*) is edible. It is a small mammal with body and head encased in small, bony scales like armour-plating. It is native to South America and highly thought of gastronomically in South America and in southwestern U.S. It is prepared in the same way as hedgehog.

armadillo

armadillo sausage, once popular in parts of Texas, U.S. Four lb. of armadillo meat is minced very finely and to it is added 1 lb. (4 cups) of brown breadcrumbs. It is very well mixed and a good pinch of ground allspice and ½ teaspoon chopped sage, some whole black peppercorns, and salt are added to taste. This mixture is put either in one large skin or several smaller ones, which are twisted to the size of the ordinary sausage, and firmly secured at the top. If the large skin is being used, it can be hung for some weeks over a gently smoking fire. The smaller ones can be fried or grilled like the usual sausages, or alternatively cooked in boiling salted water and served with cooked dried beans.

armand, d', a French garnish for meat made of soufflé potatoes, red wine sauce, with chopped sautéed goose liver and truffles.

arme riddere, a Danish sweet dish of sliced bread, soaked in a mixture of ¼ pint (½ cup) milk and 2 eggs and flavoured with salt and cinnamon; the bread is afterward fried on both sides in butter and spread with jam. Literally translated the name means "poor knights." The same dish in Germany is called *arme ritter*. See also PAIN PERDU.

Arménonville, I. A French garnish for joints made of pommes cocotte, with cooked artichoke hearts quartered, tomatoes, and french beans. II. A dish of *pommes anna* and morels. III. A thick soup made from puréed green peas and chervil.

armoise, French for mugwort.

armoricaine, à l', see AMÉRICAINE.

arnaki sti souvla, Greek for Easter lamb as eaten in the towns. Townspeople often find difficulty in roasting their lamb on the traditional spit, so a milk-fed lamb is cut into serving pieces and roasted in the oven, generously basted with butter. When half cooked, broad beans, onions, and sometimes potatoes are added, together with garlic and seasoning. In former days, before home ovens were popular, bakers used to allow their ovens to be used for roasting the Easter lamb after the day's baking was finished.

arnaki yemisto, a Dodecanese dish of young lamb, or kid, stuffed with the minced offal (variety meats) mixed with onions, rice, mint, cinnamon, and seasonings before roasting with a little water for about 3 hours.

arni, Greek for lamb roasted on a spit, one of the most traditional of Greek dishes, and always eaten at Easter and on St. George's Day, April 23. The young lamb is gutted and roasted whole over charcoal after being rubbed with lemon, salt, and pepper. The entrails are spiced and made into the Easter soup *mayieritsa*. The head is used for *arnissio kefalaki riyanato,* and other offal (variety meats) is made into *kokoretsi*. In fact, no part is wasted and a feast can be had by all members of the community.

arni

arni exochico, baked lamb wrapped in very thin phyllo pastry or paper; sometimes it is a joint, and at other times a whole baby lamb.

arni kokkinisto, literally meaning "red" lamb. The lamb is browned before braising with wine, onion, garlic, parsley, and bay leaf.

arni me domates, lamb braised in butter with tomatoes, and a pinch of cinnamon; it is usually served with rice or pasta.

arni me fassolia, lamb braised with large, dried, soaked, white beans, tomatoes, and garlic.

arni me maroulia, lamb braised with lettuce hearts, onions, and dill.

arni me spanaki avgolémono, lamb braised and served with spinach and egg and lemon sauce. See also AVGOLÉMONO.

arni souvlakia, chunks of lamb spiced and skewered before being grilled. This is now a familiar Greek dish, although it is

most certainly of Turkish origin. No doubt the Greeks do not always wish to admit this. These skewered pieces of lamb are also known as kebobs.

arni tis tihis, literally translated means "lamb of fortune." Thick slices or small joints are baked for several hours in parchment, with garlic, carrot, onion, celery, potato, salt, and pepper. Each piece of meat has a slice of feta cheese on top. Every guest has his own package, which is opened on the serving plate.

arni to fourno horiatiko, lamb baked with cubes of feta cheese on top, then covered with tomatoes, oil, and seasonings.

arni zoumo, lamb broth with root vegetables, celery, fine pasta, with avgolémono sauce stirred in finally.

arnissia paithakia riyanata, Greek for lamb cutlets in a marjoram (rigáni) sauce. For this dish, several cutlets are allowed for each person. They are seasoned and rubbed with lemon juice before being lightly browned, then covered in the marjoram sauce and baked. The sauce is made by mixing olive oil, seasoning, and a big handful of freshly chopped marjoram with lemon juice, stock, or water until it is a thick paste. (If liked, a little white wine can be included.) See also ARNI.

arnissio kefalaki riyanato, a traditional Greek Easter dish made from lamb's head. It is split and rubbed with lemon juice and seasonings, the brains removed and cleaned before baking. Meanwhile a sauce is made of chopped garlic, fresh marjoram, fresh tomato sauce, and seasonings. This is poured over the lamb's head and basted frequently. The meat, brains, and tongue are taken off before serving and served hot with watercress. It is essential to use the head of a young lamb; a sheep's head would be too fat and strong tasting.

arpenteur, common French name for plover.

arrigny, a French cow's milk cheese, in season from November to May. It comes from the Champagne district of France.

arroche, French for orach, cultivated in gardens in France and eaten as spinach.

arrostino annegato alla milanaise, an Italian method from Milan of cooking calf's liver cut lengthwise and rolled in a boned loin of veal. It is cut into thick slices, skewered, coated with herbs and flour, and fried in olive oil on both sides, then braised with white wine, lemon juice, and brown stock in the oven. It is served with rice, and the gravy poured over it.

arrosto di maiale, Italian for roast pork which is cooked with quite a lot of rosemary.

arrowhead (*Sagittaria sagittifolia*), a Chinese water-plant with leaves shaped like an arrow head. The starchy roots are grown and used in the U.S. by the Chinese population there. They are sliced thinly, lightly fried, and then used for the preparation of various Chinese dishes. The roots can also be used powdered like arrowroot. They are known by the Chinese of the San Joaquin and Sacramento districts of California as tule potato. Some American Indians also use the starchy tubers, called wappato by them. Arrowhead is found in ditches in England, Ireland, Europe, and Asia, and is used as an ornamental pond plant. I have not heard of its being used for food in England or Ireland.

arrowroot (*Maranta arundinacea*), a plant from which a nutritious gruel can be made. It is also used for biscuits, blancmanges, and for thickening sauces or soups. The root tubers of the plant are dried and then powdered. It is thought to be easily digested and therefore good for children and invalids. There are many other starchy preparations from the roots and tubers of a number of other plants that go by the name of arrowroot, but strictly speaking, this name should be given only to the genuine West Indian arrowroot prepared from the tubers of *M. arundinacea*. It is often suggested that

arrowhead

the English name of arrowroot arose because people thought that the Indians healed arrow wounds with the sap from the tubers of the plant. In fact it derives from the American Indian word for flour made from the root and called araruta.

arroz, Portuguese for rice.

arroz à valençana, a Portuguese traditional dish of rice with pork and clams (*amêijoas*) as the main ingredients. Diced pork and onions are browned in olive oil and small pieces of cooked chicken and lean, smoked ham are added. A little stock or water is poured over and it is all cooked for a few minutes. Uncooked rice and seasonings are added with twice the amount of stock or water as rice. The pan is covered and it is all simmered gently until the rice is half cooked; then a good quantity of both soft and hard shell clams are put in with strips of pimento and peeled tomatoes. The whole is then simmered until the rice and clams are cooked. The clams should be steamed gently first, so that they can be removed from the shells. It is all garnished with parsley and served hot.

arroz de lampreia, risotto as above with lampreys, *chouriço,* smoked ham, spices, and wine.

arroz de lulas, risotto as above, with squid, onions, garlic, and pimento.

arroz, Spanish for rice. Rice is one of the national dishes of Spain; it can vary from the peasants' simple midday meal of rice and vegetables to the most elaborate dishes. See also PAELLA.

arroz abanda, a Valencian dish of rice with rape, cockles, weever, *rata de mar,* deep sea prawns, and red gurnard. Onions are fried and a stock made by boiling the fish heads with tomatoes, garlic, parsley, and bay leaf. After straining, the fish and shellfish are cooked in the stock, when the liquid is once more drained and the rice boiled in it. Fish and rice are served on separate dishes.

arroz blanco, plain boiled rice.

arroz con leche, a sweet rice dish, served in Spain on feast days, made from ½ lb. (1 cup) rice boiled for 5 minutes, strained, washed in cold water and returned to heat with 2 pints (4 cups) of very hot milk, flavoured with lemon peel. The rice and milk are simmered slightly before adding sugar to taste, and cooking is continued for a further 20 minutes (or until all the milk has been absorbed). When cold, more sugar is sprinkled on, and the dish browned under the grill.

arroz con pollo, a traditional Spanish and Mexican dish made from jointed chicken simmered in water to cover with 1 sliced onion, ¼ teaspoon saffron, salt, and pepper, for 30 minutes. It is then strained and 2½ cups stock reserved. The chicken is dusted with seasoned flour and fried in hot oil until golden and tender. It is then kept warm. In the same oil 4 oz.

lean ham, 10 scallions, 2 pimentos, and 2 tablespoons chopped parsley are lightly fried. Then a bay leaf, 1 cup raw rice, and the boiling stock are added, brought to the boil and left uncovered over a moderate heat for 10 minutes. It is transferred to a casserole, the chicken put on top, covered, and left for 15 minutes. Then when all the liquid is absorbed it is put, uncovered, in a low to moderate over for about 20 minutes. This dish can also be made with chicken breasts or with lobster and large shrimp, cockles or clams, and squid. This last dish is called *arroz con mariscos y lomo.*

arselle, Italian for clams. See COZZE; VONGOLE.

ärt, Swedish for pea.

ärter med fläsk, split pea soup made with pork. Over the centuries this soup has been served on Thursdays in Swedish homes, often followed by pancakes. So it has become traditionally known as "Thursday Soup." It is made with 1 lb. yellow split peas soaked overnight, then brought to the boil in 2 quarts (8 cups) water. Then 1 lb. (chopped into pieces) pork, chopped marjoram, a pinch ground ginger, and 1 slice onion or leek are added. All are simmered until the peas are tender (about 1½ hours). Before being served, the soup is seasoned. The pork can either be served in the soup, or strained off and served as the main course. See also ÄTTER OCK FLÄSK.

Artagnan, d', I. A French soup made from clear beef broth with essence of game garnished with strips of heathcock or blackcock and peas. II. A garnish composed of cèpes à la béarnaise, small stuffed tomatoes, and potato croquettes, served with meat and poultry.

artésienne, à l', a French thick soup made from puréed, cooked, dried haricot (kidney) beans, white sauce, and tapioca.

artichaut, French for globe artichoke. A popular vegetable in France eaten after cooking in water with herbs, as an hors d'oeuvre, hot with melted butter or sauce hollandaise, or cold with vinaigrette sauce. The cooked bottoms are used extensively for garnishes. They are also served à la Grecque, and small ones can be eaten à la croque au sel. See also ARTICHOKE.

artichoke, I. (*Cynara scolymus*), the true artichoke, also known as globe artichoke. It is a thistle, and originated in Barbary, North Africa, although it is now a native of Europe and America. It is in season from June to September in Europe, and almost all the year in California. A delicious vegetable, it is usually cooked by boiling for about 20 minutes in salted water. Then the leaves are plucked singly, and if eaten hot are dipped in melted butter and the base of each leaf is sucked. If eaten cold, they are invariably dipped in a sauce vinaigrette. Fingers are used, as for asparagus. When all the leaves have been disposed of in this way, a heart, known as bottom, or in French fond, will be left, surmounted by a fuzzy, fringed, unfilled seed cap (the choke). This is cut off straight with a sharp knife, and the remaining sauce is poured over the bottom, and all of that is eaten with a knife and fork. Small, young artichokes which have been grown quickly in a hot climate can be eaten whole, and are often pickled, fried, braised, or boiled and used for salads. Artichoke hearts are excellent for garnish or hors d'oeuvre, fried in batter, or served with a variety of sauces. They are both bottled and canned commercially. See also ALCACHOFAS; ANGINARES; ARTICHAUT; CARCIOFI; KARCZOCHY. II. (*Helianthus tuberosus*), the Jerusalem artichoke. This is a tuber introduced into Europe from North America (Canada) in 1605. Much discussion has centred around the name, and the most popular theory is that it derives from the Italian girasole, which is a species of sunflower and of the same family. The edible roots are not unlike the globe artichoke in flavour, but resemble a rather knotted potato and can be prepared in any way as a potato. It is a winter vegetable, makes excellent soup, and is very good in salads, braised with a sauce, or simply used as a vegetable. See also JERUSALEM ARTICHOKE. III. (*Stachys sieboldii*), the Chinese artichoke, similar in taste and texture to the Jerusalem, but the tubers are smaller, more regular, and the taste finer and more like the globe variety. They are used as Jerusalem artichokes. See also JAPANESE ARTICHOKES. IV. A related species of the Chinese artichoke, having strong aperient properties, is known in Japan as "red artichoke" and is used there as a means of purging the house of "long bottoms," as guests who have overstayed their welcome are called. First, by way of warning, a maid enters the room bearing a broom, the head of which is wrapped in a duster. If this fails, a meal of them is served during which the unwanted guest is liberally helped, and thus leaves for very shame and necessity.

artichoke

artischocke, German for artichoke.

artois, d', I. A French garnish for steaks and noisettes of tart-shaped potato croquettes filled with green peas and covered with sauce madère. II. For poultry, the garnish is glazed carrots, onions, and artichoke hearts sautéed in butter with the jelly of a previous roast (*jus*) and a little madeira wine added.

arzavola, Italian for teal.

asado de cerdo, Spanish for roast pork.

asado de ternera, Spanish for roast veal.

äsche, German for grayling, a popular freshwater fish in Germany.

ash keys, the seeds of the ash tree, used in early English times for pickling. The keys were picked when young, boiled until soft, the first water being thrown away. After draining, they were covered immediately while still hot with a boiling, well-spiced vinegar.

ashberry jelly, a jelly made from the berries of the mountain ash tree, also known as a rowan tree. It is served with venison and mutton. The fruit should be gathered when it is red, but before the frost has touched it. See also ROWAN.

ashley bread, an American bread from the deep South. It is made from 1 cup (4 oz.) rice flour, 1 cup (½ pint) milk, 1½ teaspoons baking powder, 1 egg, 1 oz. melted butter, and salt. It is all mixed, baked in a shallow tin in a moderate oven for 45 minutes, and usually eaten hot. It is very good, and has a characteristic rice taste.

asiago, a cheese from the mountains of the Veneto, Italy, made from half-skimmed cow's milk. It is similar to *cantal,* and when stale can be grated.

asparago, Italian for asparagus. Often served in Italy, boiled, drained, and sprinkled with grated Parmesan cheese, and sometimes accompanied by a fried egg. See also ASPARAGUS.

asparagus (*Asparagus officinalis,* family *Liliaceae*), a highly prized plant of the lily family, originally called "sparrow-grass" in England. Almost every European country has its own variety. The finest is perhaps the French one, *argenteuil.* The belge, or Belgian kind, is, with the German one, thick, white, and of a good flavour. The anglaise, or English type, is smaller but has more flavour. The *lauris,* an improved kind of the English variety, is also grown in France and highly thought of. The Italian, or Genoese, type is also known as violet asparagus because of its colour, but the taste is not as fine as the foregoing varieties. Spain has a variety with long sharp thorns which is eaten when young—stalk as well as flower bud.

It is only the young green shoots which are eaten; if they are left to grow they produce a large, feathery, fern-like leaf which is decorative but inedible. There are countless ways of serving the asparagus "tips" but, in the opinion of the author, their taste is so delicate and delicious that the more simple methods are the best. One of the most usual ways of cooking them is to boil them in salted water in small bundles tied by string to prevent the delicate little heads from being thrown about. Cooking time is less than 20 minutes, but naturally varies according to the thickness and freshness of the shoots; a test at the root end of the shoot with a sharp, pronged fork is best with the thinner varieties. They are carefully drained and if eaten hot, accompanied by hot melted butter, sauce mousseline, or sauce hollandaise; if eaten cold, served with a sauce vinaigrette or mayonnaise, as in France. The traces of sulphur in asparagus are sufficient to make red wine taste metallic, and so in Italy, as in other countries where red wine is drunk more than white, asparagus tips are served with grated cheese to counteract this. To my taste, this spoils them completely, and one might just as well be eating broccoli or some other vegetable. I would prefer to forego the red wine and have them with butter. They are the perfect accompaniment for meat, chicken, fish, or eggs, and are also used extensively for garnishes. The liquid in which the tips are cooked—with older asparagus—makes an excellent soup. It is sieved, and cream is added. The tougher varieties are canned and exported all over the world. See also ASPARAGO; ASPARGO; ASPERGES; ESPÁRRAGO; SZPARAG.

asparagus bean (*Vigna catjang*), a South American bean which also grows in the Southern states of North America, where it is known as blackeye bean. The pods are from 1 to 2 feet long, and the beans resemble kidney beans in shape, but are reddish or yellowish-brown in colour. They are dried and soaked before cooking, and served with pork dishes in Texas. Another species, also called blackeyed bean, is grown widely in Italy, and cooked and used as for haricot bean.

asparagus lettuce (*Lactuca sativa, var. angustana*), a variety of cos lettuce (Romaine) which forms no head. Only the thick stems are used. They are boiled for about ½ hour and drained; then the outer cover is removed and the inside eaten with melted butter. It is also known as pamir lettuce.

asparagus pea (*Psophocarpus tetra gonolobus*), a decorative annual plant, native to southern Europe, with thin, green, rectangular pods, which are good to eat when no longer than 2 inches and simmered in very little water for 10 minutes. They are drained and served with butter.

asparges, Danish and Norwegian for asparagus.

aspargo, Portuguese for asparagus. The Portuguese generally use the wild variety, which is put into soups and stews and also used as a garnish. See also ASPARAGUS.

asperges, French for asparagus. Used extensively for haute cuisine garnish, as well as eaten hot or cold with a variety of sauces. See also ASPARAGUS.

asperges, Dutch for asparagus. The all-white asparagus and the white with purple heads are the two varieties usually grown in Holland, where the season is from the end of spring until early summer. This vegetable is popular with the Dutch, who (rightly) consider it a delicacy. A typical Dutch way of cooking it (green asparagus can be used equally well) is to scrape and remove the stalks, and cook the vegetable until tender in water, drain, and serve. Accompany with a dish of melted butter, hard-boiled eggs, and nutmeg. Each guest makes his own sauce of mashed eggs, mixed with the butter, and seasoned with salt and nutmeg. As in Britain, each stalk is dipped into this mixture before being eaten. Asperges is also served with melted butter mixed with finely chopped, toasted almonds and a sprinkling of grated nutmeg; and both hot and cold, with sauce hollandaise. See also ASPARAGUS.

asperges à la Flamande, Flemish asparagus. This vegetable is extremely popular in Belgium, and is served boiled, with a sauce made from 2 mashed, hard-boiled egg yolks mixed with 3 tablespoons melted butter, nutmeg, salt, and pepper. Another method is to serve each guest with a soft-boiled egg; melted butter and seasonings are on the table so that the sauce can be mixed to suit individual taste. Asparagus is used to garnish many dishes in Belgium.

asperula, Spanish for woodruff.

asperule, French for woodruff.

aspic, French and English for a savoury jelly made from fish or meat stock sometimes thickened with gelatine. The name comes from the herb espic or spikenard, the original word for aspic, which was put in with the knuckle of veal or calf's foot to make the jelly. The calf's foot is simmered with garlic, onions, carrots, meat trimmings, salt, pepper, and herbs in water for 2 or 3 hours. It is strained through a very fine sieve, then left to get quite cold, when any fat is removed from the top. It keeps well on ice. Aspic is also sold in powdered form in packets in most shops, but, needless to say, it is not nearly as good as the homemade variety; gelatine is a tasteless powdered and sheet form of aspic, made without the herbs and vegetables. Aspic is used for many cold dishes, using such foods as chicken, ham, tongue, eggs, sweetbreads, fish, and vegetables.

cucumber in aspic

   aspic mayonnaise, an American dressing sometimes squeezed through a "star" tube and bag to garnish salads or other cold dishes. It is made from 4 tablespoons of cool, but not congealed, aspic jelly added drop by drop to ½ cup thick mayonnaise, beating all the time. A little cream is sometimes also added. It is similar to the French *chaud-froid.*

   tomato aspic, an aspic made by adding tomato juice to the jelly when it is hot and liquid. This is of American origin.

aspik, German for aspic.

ass (*Equus asinus*), a quadruped of the horse family but usually much smaller than a horse, more commonly known today as donkey. Certain varieties of southern Italian salame (salami) are said to be made from the small Sicilian donkey, but this I have never proved. In times of siege it has been eaten with pleasure, notably during the siege of Paris in 1870. Labouchère, the famous Liberal politician, who was there at the time, said, "I never wish to taste a better dinner than a joint of donkey." It is said to resemble mutton and can be cooked as such. In China, the wild asses in ancient times used to provide food for troops in time of war.

assaisonnements, French for seasonings; also used for salad dressings.

assiette anglaise, the French name for a plate of cold, assorted meats. It usually consists of ham, beef, and tongue.

astako, Greek for lobster, often brushed with olive oil and grilled over charcoal, or served cold, after boiling, with olive oil, lemon juice, and herbs. An Athenian method given by Norman Douglas in *Birds and Beasts of the Greek Anthology* (Chapman and Hall, London, 1928) runs as follows: "For approximately a 1½ to 2 lb. lobster, slice 1 medium onion very fine, and colour (lightly brown) it in butter; then add ½ lb. skinned tomatoes, pulped, a glass of white wine and 1 of water, chopped parsley, salt, and pepper. When the sauce becomes thickish the lobster (raw) is added, and cooked quickly for about 20 minutes. If olive oil is used instead of butter, the dish can also be served cold. Lobster served in Greece often turns out to be spiny lobster or crawfish."

asticciole alla calabrese, traditional stuffed beef rolls from Calabria, Italy. The thin slices of beef are stuffed with mozzarella cheese and thin slices of pork sausage. They are rolled up, put on a skewer with a piece of bread and a bay leaf between each one, dipped in olive oil, and grilled on all sides.

astice, Italian for lobster.

astroderme, a curious-looking saltwater fish, found along the Mediterranean coast and known by Nice fishermen as *feï aermica.* It has black spots on a yellowish-pink coloured back and sides, with silver spots on the belly. It is mainly used in soup, particularly bouillabaisse.

athénienne, d', I. A French garnish for steaks and noisettes, made from thick slices of eggplant stuffed with duxelles, fried in oil, and covered with sauce madère. II. It also applies to various dishes flavoured with eggplant, lightly fried onion, tomatoes, and sweet peppers.

atherine (*Atherine presbyter*), a delicious small fish which resembles a smelt and can be cooked in the same way. Also known as a sand-smelt or silverside, they are called, in France, *prêtre* and *faux éperlan.*

attelet, a French word meaning a pin or a skewer with an ornamented top, which should be used solely, threaded with truffles, crayfish, and cock's combs, to decorate hot or cold dishes in the grand manner. It is often incorrectly used to describe a plain skewer such as used in kebab or shashlik, the word for which is *attereau.* See also CRÊTE DE COQ.

attendu, a French culinary word meaning to deliberately postpone eating to improve a dish or food, such as hanging a pheasant to improve its flavour.

ätter ock fläsk, a Swedish yellow split pea soup with pickled pork. See also ÄRT.

attereau, French word for a skewer threaded with various ingredients, dipped in a sauce, rolled in breadcrumbs, and deep fried. Sometimes the skewers are removed before serving, but in the old days they were often stuck into a thick piece of toast or fried bread and set in the middle of a dish. They can be savoury or sweet. See also ATTELET.

ättika, Swedish for vinegar.

atum, Portuguese for tunny fish (tuna). A salad is often made in Portugal with tunny (tuna) mixed with sliced hard-boiled eggs, celery, olives, and chopped, blanched almonds, all tossed in a mayonnaise. This is called *salada de atum com amêndoas*. When freshly caught, it is also cooked in a variety of ways, such as baking, grilling, or frying.

atun, Spanish for tunny fish (tuna) which is cooked in a variety of ways as for swordfish (*pez espada*), and also pickled as herrings in Britain, when it is served in salads.

albacora and *bacoreta* are two other forms of tunny (tuna) found in Spanish waters.

atun africano, African tunny (tuna) fish. It is slightly darker than other varieties.

atun con tomates, thick steaks of fresh tunny (tuna) are seasoned, and turned in very little oil on both sides. In another saucepan, 1 medium finely chopped onion and 3 garlic cloves are lightly browned in oil. Then 3 large skinned tomatoes are added with 1 gill (½ cup) white wine and 1 tablespoon chopped parsley, and well seasoned. It is covered and simmered gently for 1½ to 2 hours. The fish is put in a casserole, covered with the sieved sauce, and sprinkled with ½ cup breadcrumbs browned in oil. It is heated in a hot oven for 10 minutes before serving, and garnished with paprika.

atzem pilaf, a traditional Greek dish of ancient Turkish origin, as many Greek dishes are, consisting of meat or poultry, onions, herbs, and rice, cooked as *pilafi*.

auber, d', a French garnish for steaks and noisettes, made of artichoke hearts stuffed with pounded chicken and covered with sauce madère.

aubergine, French for eggplant.

auerhahn, German for black cock and capercaillie.

aufschnitt, German for cold meat, which usually consists of many kinds of sausage. See WÜRST.

augelot, *pont l'evêque* cheese made in the Vallée d'Auge, France.

augsburger würste, German sausages from Augsburg, made from coarsely chopped lean pork with diced bacon fat, seasoned with cloves, nutmeg, salt, saltpetre, and pepper. They are lightly smoked and served hot, after having been poached in water. See also WÜRST.

augusta, d', a French garnish for fish poached in white wine. It consists of sautéed sliced boletus and sautéed chopped shallots, covered with a sauce mornay.

aulagnier, d', a French clear beef soup garnished with peas and chopped cabbage.

aumale, d', a French method of scrambling eggs mixed with ox tongue and sliced truffles, served with grilled chopped veal kidneys, and a sauce madère.

auriol, Marseillaise name for mackerel.

aurone, French for southernwood.

aurora sauce, a Danish sauce, often served with fish, particularly turbot (*pighvarre*) or cod (*torsk*). It is composed of a sauce béchamel, flavoured with tomato purée. When cooked, a good pat of butter is added in small pieces and well stirred.

aurore, à l', I. A French sauce béchamel which can be made pink by either paprika or tomato purée. It is used with fish, chicken, and eggs. II. A clear beef soup with a little tomato juice, slightly thickened with tapioca, and garnished with thin chicken strips. III. A thick soup made from chicken, tomato, and cream, with chicken quenelles. IV. A good year-round double-cream cheese made in Normandy.

auster, German for oyster.

austern krabbe, German for oyster crab.

Austrian cheeses, according to Austrian federal laws, must have the percentage of butter fat to the total dry matter, corresponding to the descriptions given on the cheese. For example:

	butter fat content
doppelfett (double cream)	65%
ueverfett (extra cream)	55%
vollfett (full cream)	45%
dreiviertelfett (¾ cream)	35%
halbfett (half cream)	25%
viertelfett (quarter cream)	15%
mager (thin)	under 15%

An Austrian emmenthaler cheese is made in the Vorarlberg, and a port salut in the Steiermark. See also BERGKÄSE; BUTTERKÄSE; EDAMER; EDELPILZKÄSE; IMPERIAL FRISCHKÄSE; LIMBURGERKÄSE; MAINZER HANDKÄSE; MISCHLINGKÄSE; MONDSEER SCHLOSSKÄSE; QUARGEL; RAHMKÄSE; ROMADURKÄSE; SALAMIKÄSE; SCHLOSSKÄSE; STANGENKÄSE; TILSITERKÄSE; TRAPPISTENKÄSE.

auszpik, Polish for aspic. Sometimes in Poland a whole stuffed suckling pig is simmered and then put into aspic. Simmered and sliced goose or calf's liver is also used in this way. Otherwise it is used as a jellied soup.

auszug, German for essence or extract.

autocuiseur, French for pressure cooker. Alternative name is *marmite à pression*.

autrichienne, à l', a French term used to refer to preparations *à la hongroise* (Hungarian style). It applies to all dishes seasoned with paprika, fennel, and sour cream.

autun, a French cheese, made from cow's milk, which comes from Burgundy. It is in season year round.

auvergnate, à l', a French soup made from pig's head broth with lentils, leeks, and potatoes, garnished with thin strips of pig's head. It is served with rye bread. This dish comes from the Auvergne region of France, which is renowned for its cabbage and pork soup. See also POTÉE.

avefria, Spanish for plover.

aveline, French for filbert.

avellana, Spanish for hazelnut or filbert.

avena, Italian and Spanish for oats.

avern jelly, Scottish for jelly made from wild strawberries.

aves de corral, Spanish for fowls.

avga, Greek for egg.

avga me domates ke kremidia, sautéed tomatoes and onions put on top of lightly scrambled eggs and cooked until the eggs are set.

avgokalamara, see DIPLES.

avgolémono, a Greek sauce and soup. As a sauce it consists of 2 eggs and juice of 2 lemons beaten together, to which is added 1 pint (2 cups) hot stock from whatever it is to be served with. It is all beaten thoroughly until it froths up, and is served with meat, poultry, fish, or vegetables. Sometimes the eggs are separated, the stiffly beaten whites added just before serving.

avgolémono soupa, a soup made from the same ingredients as above, but with rice added and double the quantity of stock.

avgotaraho, Greek for purée of grey mullet roe or "red caviar," as it is sometimes called. The roe is mixed with bread (equal quantities of each) which has first been soaked in water, squeezed dry, and pounded. Olive oil is gradually added until the mixture has the consistency of a fairly soft purée. A trace of lemon juice is added to loosen it slightly. This is called *taramosalata*. Tunny (tuna) roe or cod's roe are sometimes used, but are not authentic. See also BOTARGO; CAVIAR.

avies koja, Lithuanian for roast leg of lamb which is first soaked in a marinade of vinegar, spices, and juniper berries, all boiled together, and when cool, buttermilk is added (1 cup to 1 pint marinade). The lactic acid in the buttermilk makes the meat tender. The meat is larded with fat pork and roasted in butter with cloves of garlic and onion wedges. The pan juices are sometimes thickened with sour cream.

avocadella, the popular name for a small (the size of a large grapefruit) vegetable marrow or squash, so called because of its resemblance in shape and taste to the avocado pear. It is cooked in the same way, though it is not a stone-fruit and is not in the same family as the avocado pear. It is also sometimes referred to as Argentine or South American marrow. Its correct name is *zapallito de tronco.*

avocado (*Persea americana gratissima*), a small bush-like fruited tree, native to the western hemisphere, from south Mexico to the Andes also called alligator pear. The name is thought to come from the Aztec word ahvacatl. It became known to Europeans from a description in the *Suma de Geografia* published in 1519 by de Enciso, who had seen these fruit trees on one of the first Spanish expeditions to the mainland of Colombia. It has been grown extensively in the West Indies and North America since about 1900.

The fruit varies in size, shape, and colour. Some Mexican varieties are the size of a hen's egg, while the largest known variety exceeds 3 lb. It is the shape of a pear and has a tough skin which can vary from greenish-brown to purple; the flesh too can vary in colour from acid-green to butter-yellow, and it has the consistency of butter when the fruit is ripe. Before serving, the large stone should be removed and the flesh loosened from the skin and cut; it is best to use a knife with a silver or stainless steel blade for this will not discolour the fruit, as carbon steel or aluminum are liable to do.

It is best served cut in half, with a little salt and fresh lime juice, but it is also acceptable with the large cavity made by the removal of the stone filled with an oil and wine vinegar or lemon juice dressing. The proportions should be about equal, that is, rather more lemon or vinegar than in a usual salad dressing. The cavity may be filled with shrimp, prawn, lobster, or chicken, but to savour the fruit properly, I think it is best to serve it as simply as possible.

In Mexico it is used for sauces and stuffings (see MOLE and GUACAMOLE), and, nowadays, with the increasing use of liquidisers, an excellent cold soup is made with a mixture of 1 medium avocado pear, ½ pint (1 cup) chicken broth, and ¼ pint (½ cup) cream. Also an avocado mousse is made as above, with the addition of 1 tablespoon gelatine or a good aspic powder.

It is also used as a sweet, filled with ice cream or guava jelly. Avocado ice cream with a little brandy added is sometimes found in the U.S., and the avocado is also sometimes peeled, cut into quarters, and cooked in a ginger-flavoured syrup.

The avocado also has medicinal uses. A ripe avocado rubbed onto the affected place is most soothing in cases of sunburn.

avocat, French for avocado.

avocatobirne, German for avocado.

avocette, French for avocet (family *Grallatores*), a beautiful wading bird with an upturned beak. It is eaten mainly in the Poitou region of France. It tastes a little fishy and is the size of a pigeon. It is cooked as teal.

avoine, French for oats.

axolotl (*Ambystoma*), a salamander found in the lakes of Mexico and the southern states of America, and sometimes eaten in those parts.

axolotl

axonge, French for a lard, which is of high quality when rendered down. It is made from the fat which surrounds pigs' kidneys. See also PANNE.

aydes, les, a French cow's milk cheese, in season from October to June. It comes from the Orléanais district of France.

Aylesbury duck, see DUCK.

ayran, an iced drink in Turkey, made from yogourt, iced water, and salt, all beaten together, and decorated with mint leaves.

Ayrshire shortbread, a traditional recipe for shortbread, which has rice flour in equal quantity with ordinary flour, castor sugar to taste, half the weight of the combined flours in butter, egg (1 egg equals approximately 3 oz.), and a little cream. This mixture is rolled out thinly, cut into shapes, and pricked on top with a fork before baking in a moderate oven until golden brown.

aythya, French for *pochard* duck, the flesh of which is greatly prized in France.

azafran, Spanish for saffron.

azarole (*Crataegus azarolus*), the berry of a kind of hawthorn bush, which grows prolifically in the Mediterranean regions, and, to a lesser extent, further north. In France it is mainly used in the making of confectionery and liqueurs, but in Italy, Spain, and Poland (głogu) it is used to make jam. It is also known as Neapolitan medlar.

azeitão, a variety of *serra* cheese, which is farmhouse-made. It is a white, soft cheese, made in the early spring. Unfortunately, although excellent, it is one of the rarest in Europe, for its season of production is short, and it does not keep. The top of this round, small cheese is cut off, and it is eaten with a spoon. It is made south of Lisbon, at Azeitão, which is under the northern slope of the Serra da Arrábida.

azeite, Portuguese for olive oil.

azeitonas, Portuguese for olives.

azerole, French for azarole.

azijn, Dutch for vinegar.

azúcar, Spanish for sugar, *azúcar cande,* powdered sugar.

A.1 sauce, a commercially bottled English sauce, which is semi-liquid and highly spiced. It is made from onions, spices, and a lot of vinegar. It is strong tasting, and used mostly with chops, steaks, and sausages. It is not to everyone's taste since it disguises flavour.

baba, a French cake made from 1 lb. (4 cups) flour, 1 oz. yeast, 1 gill (½ cup) milk, 1 heaped tablespoon sugar, 6 tablespoons raisins, 7 eggs, 4 tablespoons currants, 3 tablespoons sultanas, and a pinch of salt. After the yeast has proved the dough is put into special baba moulds and baked in a hot oven for about 15 minutes. When cool, the cakes are sprinkled with either kirsch or rum which has been mixed with a syrup made from boiled sugar and water. The cake is named according to the liqueur with which it is flavoured—baba au rhum or baba au kirsch. Various other cakes are made using the same mixture but a different mould.

King Stanislas I of Poland invented the baba in the 18th century and named it after Ali Baba, one of the characters in his favourite book, *A Thousand and One Nights.* The cake was not quite the same then as now, but it was perfected in the 19th century by a French pastry-cook in Paris called Sthorer, who had seen it in Lunéville, the town to which the Polish court had been moved. It became immensely popular and has remained so to this day. In Bordeaux the cake is called a *fribourg.*

About 1840 a *patissier* called Julien omitted the raisins, currants, and sultanas from the dough and soaked the *baba* in a syrup of his own invention, which was a secret for many years. This he called a *brillat-savarin,* and it is now called simply *savarin.* A friend of Julien's called Bourbonneux baked the mixture in hexagonal moulds and called the cake a *gorenflot,* after one of the characters in Alexandre Dumas's *La Dame de Monsoreau.* See also BABKA MIGDALOWA.

babeurre, French for buttermilk, often made into soup in France with the addition of flour and sugar. Sometimes rice is used instead of flour.

babi ketjap, a Dutch East Indian dish, consisting of pork strips simmered with onions in diluted soy sauce and served with rice as part of a *rijsttafel.*

babka, a Byelorussian vegetable dish using ½ lb. of either potatoes or carrots grated or puréed and mixed with 1 lb. (4 cups) flour, ½ oz. yeast, 3 heaped tablespoons butter, grated peel of 1 lemon, and a pinch of salt. It is left to rise and then baked in a greased dish for 1 hour. Sometimes 2 teaspoons baking powder is used in place of yeast.

babka, a Polish cake, similar to the French *baba,* but made without yeast. Babka is a national speciality of Poland, and there are many varieties, both sweet and savoury. Savoury babka often has minced and puréed chicken liver (*babka z watróbek*) or cream cheese added to the mixture.

babka migdalowa, almond babka made from 10 egg yolks beaten with 8 oz. (1 cup) sugar, and then combined with 2 cups potato flour. Flavouring of ¾ cup grated sweet almonds and ¼ cup grated bitter almonds or apricot kernels is added, and finally the stiffly beaten egg whites are folded in. The babka is baked in a greased dish for 30 minutes.

babovka, a Czechoslovak cake made from ½ lb. (1 cup) butter creamed with ½ lb. (1 cup) sugar. Six egg yolks are added, followed by 1 lb. (4 cups) flour, 1 teaspoon baking powder, 6 oz. (1 cup) chopped nuts, 4 tablespoons rum, and ½ pint (1 cup) milk. Finally, 6 stiffly beaten egg whites are folded in. The dough is divided in half and 4 oz. grated chocolate is added to one of the halves. A greased mould is filled with alternate layers of the light and dark dough and the *babovka* is baked in a moderate oven for about 45 minutes.

bacalao, Spanish for dried and salted cod. A traditional Lenten dish, it is eaten a great deal in Spain, especially inland. The following is a typical recipe.

bacalao à la vizcaína, dried cod, cut up and soaked overnight. It is then placed in cold water and parboiled, after which it is skinned and boned. The pieces are then fried in oil and removed from the pan. In the same oil an onion and peeled tomatoes are cooked, and in a separate pan, a purée of more tomatoes and cooked red peppers is heated in oil, and then added to the more firmly cooked vegetables. The sauce and fish are put in alternate layers in an ovenproof dish, finishing with a layer of thinly sliced red peppers, and then baked for about 30 minutes.

bacalao fresco, Spanish for fresh cod.

bacalhau, Portuguese for salt cod, which is a popular traditional dish.

bacalhau à brás, 1 lb. soaked salt cod cut into strips, fried in oil with 4 sliced onions. It is then mixed with fried potatoes and a flavouring of garlic. Finally 3 beaten eggs are poured over and cooked until just set.

bacalhau à gomes de sá, salt cod, cooked after soaking, flaked, and then baked in the oven with olive oil, garlic, onions, potatoes, hard-boiled eggs, parsley, and white wine.

bacalhau à Portuguesa, a traditional dish eaten on *Romania d'Agonia* consisting of soaked, dried salt cod, tomatoes, green peppers, onions, and potatoes cooked in a heavy closed pot with olive oil. It is garnished with a great deal of chopped parsley.

bacalhau cozido, steamed salt cod with cabbage, chard, and hard-boiled eggs.

bacalhau podre, a dish of pieces of soaked, salt cod fried in batter and served with a thick sauce with cheese and sautéed potatoes. About 2 lb. soaked salt cod is scalded in boiling water, then skinned, boned, and cut into small pieces. A batter is made from 8 oz. (2 cups) flour, 3 egg yolks, 3 stiffly beaten egg whites (added last), and 1 pint (2 cups) milk. The pieces of fish are coated with this and then fried in oil. A sauce is made by gradually adding to the pan juices 2 egg yolks well beaten with 2 tablespoons melted butter, stirring over a gentle heat to prevent curdling. One tablespoon grated hard ewe's milk cheese is also added. One lb. sliced raw potatoes are fried and put in a baking dish; the fish is placed on top followed by a layer of breadcrumbs and a sprinkling of cheese, and the sauce is finally poured over all. The dish is baked in a moderate oven until golden.

fofos de bacalhau, small balls of fried puréed salt cod.

bacalhau fresco, Portuguese for fresh cod.

baccalà fresco, Italian for haddock.

baccaliaros, see BAKALIAROS.

back rashers, see RASHER.

backerbsen, an Austrian and German garnish for soup consisting of a batter mixture which is poured through a colander into hot fat. When the "peas" are brown, they are ladled out and drained.

bäckerei, an Austrian biscuit (cookie) of which there are many varieties. A plain tea biscuit (cookie) is made from 10 oz. (2½ cups) flour, 4 oz. (½ cup) sugar, and a pinch of baking powder, with 2½ oz. (generous ¼ cup) butter rubbed in, 1 egg, and about 3 tablespoons cream or milk to make a smooth dough. It is kneaded, rolled, and left in a cold place for some hours, preferably overnight. Spice, nuts, chocolate, honey, etc., can be added as desired. The dough is rolled out to ¼-inch thickness, cut into shapes, brushed with egg, and baked on a greased sheet for about 7–10 minutes in a moderate oven. The biscuits are crisp when cold but soften during storage. A special batch of these biscuits, Weihnachtsbäckerei, is always made for Christmas.

backpulver, German for baking powder.

backpulverkrapfen, see KRAPFEN.

backsteinkäse, a German cheese made in Bavaria from whole cow's milk. It is not unlike a *limburgerkäse* but is smaller. It tastes somewhat like limburger cheese.

bacon, the smoked and cured meat product made from the back, sides, and belly of pigs. It was originally the old French word, of German origin, for pig. Bacon is a form of food used in many parts of the world not only because of its taste and protein content, but because if smoked in one piece and not cut, it will keep indefinitely. In a fresh piece of bacon the flesh is a deep pink and the fat a cream colour, but not dark. Bacon can be cooked in a variety of ways: fried, baked, grilled, braised, or boiled. The back and belly are often cut into thin slices and fried or grilled with eggs or tomatoes, a most popular British and American breakfast dish. In Ireland, a piece of bacon boiled in water with a good white cabbage cut into quarters is a national dish and highly thought of. Bacon cut from the belly or flank is used a great deal for barding as well as for frying, good streaky rashers having an almost even distribution of fat and lean meat. See also LARD.

bacoreta, a dark-meat variety of tunny (tuna) fish. See also ATUN.

Bácskai káposzta, a dish from Bácska in the south of Hungary, made with cabbage and pig's knuckles. Paprika, salt, a tomato, and a few caraway seeds are added to an onion which has been cut into rings and fried (sautéed) in butter. The knuckles are chopped and added, with a little water to cover, and are cooked until tender. A head of cabbage is then cut into 8 pieces, placed on top of the meat, and steamed for 20 minutes. About 4 potatoes are quartered and placed on top of the cabbage, basted, and all cooked until the potatoes are ready. The dish is best displayed on a large plate where the meat and cabbage can be placed in the centre and the potatoes arranged round them.

badderlocks, an edible seaweed (*Alaria esculenta*), found in the Faroe Islands and on the northern coasts of the British Isles. It is also known as *honeyware* in Scotland.

badger (*Meles meles*), a nocturnal hibernating quadruped with a grey coat and white head, sometimes weighing 40 lb. or more. The badger is not generally known to be edible, although it is eaten on occasion in England. The flesh is similar to that of a young pig, rich and full of flavour. It can be cured as bacon or used in any recipe calling for pork. A badger feast used to take place at a public house in Ilchester, Somerset, where a badger was roasted whole over an open fire.

bagels, small rolls shaped like a ring or a pretzel made from 1 lb. (4 cups) flour, 2 oz. (¼ cup) butter or oil, ½ pint (1 cup) milk, 1 oz. (1 heaped tablespoon) sugar, 1 egg yolk, 1 teaspoon salt, and 1 oz. yeast. All ingredients are mixed and then left to rise like bread dough in a warm place. They are shaped like a ring, poached in boiling salted water until they rise to the top, then sprinkled with poppy or caraway seeds, and baked until golden brown. They are a Jewish speciality.

bagna cauda, a hot, spicy sauce, a speciality of Piedmont in Italy. It is made from ½ pint (1 cup) olive oil and 3 tablespoons butter heated together, with 3 large pounded garlic cloves and 8 pounded anchovy fillets added. This is simmered for 10 minutes, then kept hot over a spirit lamp (alcohol lamp). Sliced raw vegetables cut into bite-sized pieces are dipped into the hot sauce. Vegetables like cardoons, cauliflower, cabbage, celery, endive, sweet peppers, etc., can be used. In Piedmont, sliced white truffles are sometimes added to the sauce. The name means literally "hot bath."

bagno-maria, Italian for *bain-marie*.

bagozzo, an Italian cheese, a variety of *caciotta*. Made in and around Brescia, it is a hard cheese, sharp and pungent in flavour, yellow inside but often red outside.

bagration, the name of a French salad and soup, named after a Russian general of that name who fought against Napoleon.

bagration salad, a salad of equal parts of cooked artichoke bottoms cut into thick strips and cooked sliced celeriac. Cooked macaroni is added, and it is all mixed with mayonnaise flavoured with tomato purée. The salad is arranged in a domelike fashion and garnished with chopped hard-boiled eggs, truffles, and tongue, then sprinkled with chopped parsley.

bagration soup, can be made with either meat or fish. In either case, it is prepared from velouté sauce. Then lean, diced veal or fillets of sole are cooked in butter and then pounded and egg yolks and cream added. The soup is garnished with macaroni, and grated cheese is served separately.

baguette, the name of a French bread. It is shaped like a long, thin wand, is about 2 feet in length, and weighs 9 oz.

bahmi, a Dutch-Indonesian dish of Chinese noodles (*mein*), which is extremely popular in Holland. Dry Chinese noodles are first soaked in warm water, then put into fresh boiling water; when the water has returned to the boil, the pan should be removed from the flame and the noodles left in it until they are tender but not too soft. Shredded leeks, chopped celery (stalks and leaves), and minced garlic, together with Chinese cabbage (*bok choy*), are fried in oil. Bean sprouts and a little water are added, and all are simmered until half cooked, when they are mixed with the drained noodles. Diced fried pork and either shrimps or prawns are now added, together with soy sauce to taste. The whole dish is then reheated in the oven and served. See RIJSTTAFEL.

baila, Spanish for salmon trout. The most usual method of cooking these fish in Spain is to bake them in butter with lemon juice or to poach them in water or wine and serve them cold with either mayonnaise or a sauce vinaigrette.

bain-marie, a French culinary term which applies to a vessel containing hot water in which dishes containing food can be kept hot. To cook in a bain-marie means to cook the food in one dish standing in the vessel of hot water. This prevents certain delicate sauces from "cracking," that is, prevents the oil and egg yolk from separating or drying up. In England and the U.S. a double boiler is often used instead for sauces, but a dish such as a pâté or a baked custard is baked in a bain-marie in the oven and not cooked on top of the stove.

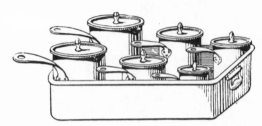

bain-marie

baiser, the French name given to two small meringues joined together with thick cream or jelly.

bajaina, the local name at Grasse, France, for the small garden snail (*Helix aspersa*) which is much prized gastronomically.

bakaliaros, Greek for salt cod; also spelt baccaliaros. It is usually cooked *plaki*, or is sometimes grilled after soaking.

bakaliaros me skorthalia, dried salt cod fried in batter and served with skorthalia sauce.

bakaliaros vrastos, boiled salt cod with onions, celery, potatoes, olive oil, lemon juice, and seasoning. Served with oil and lemon dressing.

baked alaska, see ALASKA, BAKED.

baked-apple berry, see CLOUDBERRY.

baker's cheese, a skimmed-milk cheese made in the U.S. It is similar to cottage cheese but contains less moisture and is finer-grained as farmer cheese. It has a high rennet content. The curd is not washed or cooked, as it is in the making of hard cheese, but hung up and drained in bags. It is used for such bakery products as cheesecake, cheese pie, and pastries. The curd is made both salted and unsalted and is packed in cans for shipping or in wooden tubs for storage.

Bakewell tart, an English tart from Bakewell in Derbyshire. A short-crust pastry case is spread with a red jam and a mixture is made of 2 heaped tablespoons ground almonds, 4 oz. (½ cup) butter, 4 oz. (½ cup) sugar, and 3 eggs, separated, the stiffly beaten whites being added last. This is poured over the jam and the tart is baked in a moderate oven until just set, about ½ hour. It is sometimes called Bakewell pudding.

baking powder, a mixture of various simple chemical substances, introduced in the 19th century as a substitute for yeast in bread and cake making. The formulas vary in a number of ways, but all depend upon the release of carbon dioxide gas from sodium bicarbonate by the action of an acid or an acid salt. The more usual acids used are tartaric or citric acid, and the acid salt, where used, is generally potassium acid tartarate. The chemical interaction which releases the car-

bon dioxide is initiated when the reagents dissolve in the moisture of the dough. In order to inhibit a premature reaction, the individual particles are often coated with a thin layer of starch. Care should always be taken to keep baking powder dry, and therefore it should be kept in an airtight container.

Baking powder is often used in scones and bread, particularly soda bread. It is essential to use only a small quantity since it can leave an unpleasant, salty, bitter taste if too much is used. It will also discolour the bread when it is cooked if not well mixed or if added too liberally. See also BICARBONATE OF SODA.

baking soda, an alternative culinary name for bicarbonate of soda.

baklava, a Greek and Turkish nut-filled pastry, popular throughout the Balkans. Whether it was invented by Greeks, Turks, or Russians is always a matter of argument between Hellenophiles and Turcophiles. In Turkey it is always eaten at the Spring festival *Hidrellez* on May 1st.

About 30 sheets of phyllo pastry are used in layers. The first, third, and fourth sheets should be brushed with unsalted, melted butter; the second should be sprinkled with cinnamon as well as butter; the fifth is spread with butter and chopped walnuts. The dish is continued in this way until only eight sheets remain. These are brushed only with butter. The last four should be scored through with a knife, making squares of serving size. Water is sprinkled on the top, and the dish is baked in a moderate oven for 1½ hours. A syrup is made from honey, sugar, lemon juice, and water. When the pastry is cool the boiling syrup is poured over it, and then the dish is allowed to cool again before serving.

baklażany, Polish for eggplant. In Poland eggplants are used as in French cuisine, that is, baked, fried, or stuffed and cooked in oil or butter.

baklazhany, Russian for eggplant.

ikra iz baklazhanov, "caviar" of eggplants, a dish which resembles caviar both in appearance and mildly in flavour. It is made with 1 lb. salted, baked eggplant, skinned, puréed, and mixed with 4 tablespoons olive oil and 1 tablespoon vinegar; the mixture is then seasoned and heated to reduce excess liquid. It is often served cold with bread for *zakuski*. Mushrooms and beetroot can be treated in a similar way, the latter being slightly sweetened with sugar.

marinovannye baklazhany, pickled eggplant. The fruits are cut in half, scalded and stuffed with grated carrot and garlic. The stuffed halves are then tied together again with strips of coarse celery, put into a jar, and covered with cold boiled vinegar flavoured with mixed spices. The jars are sealed and the pickled eggplants stored until required.

bakpoeder, Dutch for baking powder.

bakpulver, Swedish for baking powder.

balandėliai, Lithuanian cabbage rolls. White cabbage leaves are blanched and stuffed with a mixture of one pound each of minced mutton or lamb and boiled rice, with 2 medium chopped onions (which have been simmered in butter), chopped dill, and seasoning. They are rolled up and placed in a dish on top of sliced carrots and slices of lean bacon. A little stock mixed with tomato purée is added and the dish is then braised in the oven for 45 minutes. The stuffed cabbage is served with the bacon slice on top. The liquor is strained and heated up with sour cream, then poured over the rolls and dill is sprinkled on top.

balane, French for acorn barnacle.

baldpate widgeon (*Mareca americana*), also called American widgeon, and perhaps the best known bird in North America both for food and for sport. It is white and has a crown and a short narrow bill. It has been seen in the British Isles. Like other wild game birds in the U.S. it is given a number of names, according to the state in which it is found, wheat duck, green-headed widgeon, white-belly. All recipes for mallard or wild duck obtain for baldpate.

baleine, French for whale.

balik pilâki, a traditional fish dish among Turkish Jews. The fish (all but shellfish can be used) is prepared by cleaning and filleting and is rubbed with oil and lightly salted. It is first grilled under a low heat until brown on both sides, then placed on a long dish, covered with sliced onions and tomatoes, seasoned, and baked at a low temperature for 20 minutes. Then ½ pint (1 cup) boiling water is added and the fish is basted before being baked for 10 minutes more. It can be served hot or cold, garnished with chopped fresh mint and wedges of lemon.

baliste, French for triggerfish.

balka, a traditional Polish cake like the Italian *panettone,* usually eaten at Easter, New Year, or on other festive occasions. It is conical in shape and is made from 1 lb. (4 cups) flour, 1 oz. yeast, ½ pint (1 cup) milk, 4 oz. (½ cup) sugar, and 2 eggs, with various flavourings.

ballekes, a Belgian dish, eaten by both Flemings and Walloons. It consists of a mixture of 1 lb. freshly minced pork, 2 shallots, 1 cup breadcrumbs, and 2 raw eggs shaped into little cakes which are fried and then simmered in either white wine or beer with garlic, herbs, and potatoes.

ballotine, an early name for *galantine,* which is still used in France. The main difference between the two is that while a *galantine* is always cold, a *ballotine* is sometimes also served hot. Meat and fish are used, also chicken and eel. The meat, fowl, game, or fish is boned, stuffed, and rolled up like a bundle. See also VEAU, BALLOTTINE DE.

balm (*Melissa officinalis*), also called lemon balm, a lemon-flavoured perennial herb which grows abundantly in Europe. It will grow on any soil. If the soil is good the growth is almost too prolific and it has to be drastically thinned out. It is a favourite plant of bees, which is indicated by its Greek name *melissa* (honey); balm honey was always considered the best, many years ago. Balm was once used for making tea, with hyssop and blackberry leaves, and was thought to induce longevity. It is said that Llewelyn, Prince of Glamorgan and John Hussey, who were both regular balm tea drinkers, lived to be 108 and 116, respectively. Nowadays it is used, chopped, in salads, for fish sauces, and indeed for any dish in which a fragrant lemon taste is required.

balnamoon skink, an old Irish soup mentioned in Cassell's *Dictionay of Cookery* (1877), and probably still made in some country kitchens in present-day Ireland. It is prepared by boiling together chicken, sweet herbs, chives, onions, celery, lettuce, and green peas, thickened with egg yolks mixed with cream. Sometimes the trussed fowl was served in the middle of the soup. *Skink* is a Gaelic word which occurs also in Scotland and it means "essence," or a stew–soup, that is a soup containing a large quantity of meat, poultry, or fish, like a stew.

balorine, a Franco–Russian dish of 1 lb. minced beef mixed with 6 chopped spring onions (scallions), 1 chopped medium-sized beetroot, and 1 teaspoon caraway seeds. The ingredients are mixed well, then fried on both sides, and served with cooked sorrel or spinach.

bambelle, the French name for a small fish of the carp family, which is very prolific in some Swiss lakes. It is prepared and cooked as carp.

bamies, Greek for okra.

bamies me domates, okra soaked in vinegar for several hours, drained, then fried with onions, tomatoes, and parsley in olive oil. It is served as a separate course.

bamya, Turkish for okra.

banan, Danish for banana.

banana (*Musa sapientum*), a gigantic fruit-bearing herbaceous plant containing one of the most important fruits for food value. Over 100 varieties exist, and it has been known since the earliest times. The Arabs, Greeks, and Romans all mention it in their literature; Pliny says that the Greeks of Alexander's expedition saw it in India, where the wise men used to sit beneath the trees and eat the fruit—hence the botanical name *Musa sapientum*. It grows in most tropical climates, and can be eaten raw or cooked. It is high in vitamins A, B, C, and G (B_2). It is particularly good baked with sugar and orange juice, as a sweet course. Banana is served fried in oil or butter with some chicken dishes, especially chicken Maryland or stanley, and also with fried trout. In Bermuda, it is used with cooked dried cod, potato, and hard-boiled egg as a special breakfast dish. Banana is an African name. Generally what is sold as a banana in England is not the true one, but a plantain. These are bigger, straighter and firmer; they come from Mexico and Central America and do not have as good a flavour as the smaller, curved Canary bananas which are sweeter and more fragrant. See also PLANTAIN.

banana

banarut, see ESCARGOT.

Banbury cakes, oval cakes made from puff pastry filled with spices, cinnamon, currants, and chopped candied rind. They originated in Banbury in Oxfordshire, England, and used to be sold hot from a specially made chip-basket lined with flannel to keep the heat in.

bangers, a colloquial English name for sausages cooked in various ways and served with buttered mashed potatoes. When served in this manner, the dish is popularly referred to as bangers and mash.

banilia, Greek for vanilla. In Greece vanilla crystals, rather than the pods, are used for flavouring. The crystals no doubt come from what the French call *banilles,* the pods of a plant similar to vanilla which contain a sugary juice often used, dried, for confectionery, instead of vanilla.

banilles, French for the long, tapering, but small pods of a plant similar to vanilla. The pods are not used dried, as are vanilla pods, but the sugary juice is dried to crystals which are often used in confectionery.

bànitsa, a Bulgarian dish which is a type of tart made with layers of paper-thin pastry resembling the French *mille feuille* or the Greek phyllo. Fillings used are many and various, but the most noted are nuts and cream, cheese, and spinach. The bànitsa filled with spinach is said to have been the favourite dish of Ismet Inönü, President of Turkey from 1961 to 1965, who knew this dish through his Bulgarian mother. Ingredients

for the spinach filling are about 3 lb. spinach, 1 lb. onions,
1 lb. (2 cups) butter, a small bunch of spring onions (scallions), ¾ lb. (2 scant cups) soft cheese (such as ricotta or cottage), salt, and pepper. The spinach is washed and then
chopped and mixed with all the butter and scallions, but the
onions are fried and mixed with the cheese before being
added. The pastry is made with 1 lb. (4 cups) flour, 2–3 eggs,
1½ cups melted butter, salt, and a little water. The eggs,
flour, and water are beaten into a stiff dough; this is separated
into eight small pieces which are set aside for 30 minutes.
Each piece is then rolled out several times very thinly, brush-
ing each time with the melted butter. The sheets of pastry are
set aside to rest again, and then the rolling out process is
repeated. Four of the sheets are now placed on a greased
baking-dish, the filling mixture is spread on top of them in the
shape of a mound, and the remaining sheets are placed on top.
The edges are sealed and brushed again with melted butter,
and the bànitsa is baked for 45 minutes in a moderate oven
(350°F).

bank cress, an alternative American name for American
cress.

bankekød, a popular Danish dish of stewed beef, peppercorns, onions, and bay leaves.

banketletter, a puff pastry roll traditional in Holland, which is
filled with minced almonds, sugar, lemon juice, and beaten
egg, and then shaped into a letter, usually the family initial,
before being baked in a moderate to hot oven for 15–20 minutes. It is eaten on St. Nicholas's Day, December 5, and is
known as "St. Nicholas's Letter."

bannaan, Dutch for banana.

banneton, a receptacle with holes used in France to keep fish
in a tank. It can be pulled up when the fish is needed for
cooking. Also used to denote a baker's basket.

bannock, a Scottish and north of England homemade oatcake
or bread, made from 1 lb. (4 cups) oatmeal or barley flour,
1 pint (2 cups) buttermilk, 2 teaspoons bicarbonate of soda,
and a pinch of salt. The old Scottish name was *bannok* and
derives from the Latin *panicum,* probably through church influence for it may originally have been Communion bread.
There is an old druidical belief, still popular in the Highlands,
that in kneading bannocks or stirring porridge, the movement
must be a right-hand turn. Widdershins, or the left-hand turn,
is unlucky.

Bannocks are made from a variety of flours, barley or oatmeal being popular; but pease-meal, meal made from dried
peas, is also used. Bannocks made from a mixture of oats,
barley, and rye are known as mashlum bannocks. Until the
present century, there used to be bannocks made for any festive occasion. They are usually oval in shape and are cooked
on a griddle, first on one side and then on the other. A *Selkirk
bannock* is a fruit loaf. See also ARAN ISENACH; BROONIE;
PITCAITHLY BANNOCK; SCONE; STRUAN MICHEIL.

bano de azúcar, Spanish for icing.

baño maria, Spanish for *bain-marie.*

banon, a Provençal cheese made from ewe's milk, wrapped
in chestnut leaves or flavoured with a variety of wild savory
called *poivre d'âne.* It is in season from May to December.

banquière, à la, I. A French sauce which is a form of sauce
suprême coloured with tomato purée and blended with butter
and veal glaze, to which a little madeira wine is added. It is
used with poultry, white meats, sweetbreads, or *vol-au-vents.*
II. A French garnish of braised quenelles and truffles for noisettes and tournedos, chicken, or sweetbreads, and for haute
cuisine dishes, boned and stuffed larks.

bantam, a small, highly decorative, brightly coloured fowl,
named after the town in Java where it originated. It has very
fine, delicate flavour and can be prepared and cooked as

chicken. The eggs are indistinguishable from hen's eggs in
flavour, but are half the size.

bar (*Galeichthys marinus*), a good-eating, white-fleshed sea
fish popularly known in England as dogfish and in the U.S. as
catfish. In the South, it is very highly regarded gastronomically. In France, however, the bar is very much liked
and is prepared for the table as salmon, where it is also called
poisson-chat.

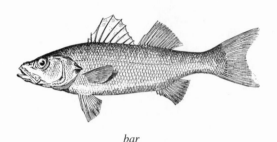

bar

bär, German for bear. The fillets are often cooked in red wine
in Germany as is venison, but the meat must be hung for
some days before cooking.

Bar-le-Duc, a town in Lorraine, France, famous for its red
currant preserve. A preserve is also made there of white currants but this is much more rare.

bara brith, a loaf-shaped Welsh cake made from 1 lb.
(4 cups) flour, 3 tablespoons sugar, 1 oz. yeast (or 2 teaspoons baking soda), 3 heaped tablespoons butter, 1 egg, 1
teaspoon caraway seeds, 6 oz. (1 cup) currants, 1 teaspoon
mixed spice, 2 tablespoons molasses, 1 tablespoon lemon
juice, and ½ pint (1 cup) buttermilk, all well mixed and left to
rise if using yeast, and baked in a moderate oven for 1 hour.
It is very like the Irish *barm brack.*

baranina, Polish for lamb, usually roasted in the oven or on a
spit and sprinkled first with ground ginger or thyme and
pulped garlic. While it browns, it is dredged with flour and
basted with melted butter. (The Polish taste is for rather rare
lamb, as in France.) Sometimes it is wrapped in a muslin
soaked in wine vinegar and left overnight before cooking. The
pan juices are often mixed with 1 teaspoon flour and 1 pint
(2 cups) sour cream, brought to the boil, and served as a
sauce.

baranina pieczeń, Polish for roast lamb. Often in Poland a
leg of lamb, pork, or veal is cooked on a spit and basted with
warm wine or sour cream.

baranina pieczeń à la moscovite, a Russian method used in
Poland for preparing lamb. The lamb is blanched in boiling
wine marinade before roasting with butter. Root vegetables
are sliced and cooked in the marinade and it is all poured over
the joint while cooking. See also MOSTEK.

baranina, Russian for mutton. See CHANAKHI; SHASHLIK;
SOLYANKA.

baranina novorssiyskaya, mutton cutlets braised with root
vegetables, stock, and seasonings, and covered with a paste
made of rye bread and water. It is baked in the oven for several hours.

baranka, a Russian cake like a round, unsalted, and unsweetened doughnut, which is baked and sprinkled with poppy
seed.

bárány, Hungarian for lamb. Lamb is not as popular in
Hungary as beef, pork, or veal, and is usually served as either
paprikás or *pörkölt.*

baraquilles, a hot French hors d'oeuvre, made from triangular
pastry shells filled with a *salpicon* of game birds, sweetbreads, foie gras, and mushrooms, bound with sauce alle-

mande flavoured with Madeira wine. They are not seen much nowadays.

barashek iz masla, a traditional symbolic lamb used in Russia for the ritual Easter table. It is made from butter modeled to make a lamb, with a piece of wood as a foundation. The outside is brushed with a coarse cloth to make it resemble the fleece, and the eyes are marked by either raisins or mushrooms; a small green branch is put in the mouth. It is chilled until very firm.

barbabietola, Italian for beetroot.

barbada, Spanish for dab.

barbadine, French for the edible fruit of the passionflower or granadilla tree. It is eaten as a dessert.

Barbados sugar, see SUGAR.

barbarin, the French name for a fish of the mullet family, called surmullet in English.

barbarine (*Cucurbitaceae*), a variety of American squash which comes in various shapes. The most common is long, like a cucumber, and usually yellow with green stripes or splashes. The plain yellow ones are the best, and are prepared and cooked as marrow (zucchini) or cucumber. It is grown in France, where it is popular.

barbe, German for barbel.

barbe-de-capucin, a wild, straight endive (chicory), which grows in France.

barbeau or ***barbillon,*** French for barbel.

barbecue, a Caribbean name for the wooden frame hung above a slow, smoky fire, where the human flesh they ate was dried. Much later, beef was dried in the same way. The whole hearth was known as a *boucan,* and so was the finished product; so at first the hunters were called, in French, *boucaniers.* It was these men who also put to sea as pirates, hence "buccaneers." In this way the terminology of cannibal cooking has come to denote, particularly in North and South America, a way of serving quite a lavish outdoor meal. However, in the cattle belt of the Midwest, to hold a barbecue means to dig a pit and light a fire in it; then that is covered with rocks which are left until they are hot through. A whole animal is wrapped in a sack, laid on the rocks and covered with leaves or corn husks before having earth and a tarpaulin put over the top. It is all left for 3–4 hours, when the earth and stones are shoveled away, and the most delicious meat is ready to eat. By the coast this is often done on the seashore, with clams, lobsters, corn on the cob, and large potatoes. Seaweed is used in place of leaves. Barbecue is in fact a primitive form of pressure cooking wherein everything tastes superb because none of the good juices have escaped. Barbecue also means cooking out-of-doors over a charcoal fire. Various small stoves are made for this purpose, easily transportable, and of differing designs. This constitutes a popular form of entertainment in the U.S.; a party of people are served a variety of foods such as steaks, cutlets, shellfish, etc., cooked in suburban gardens, on beaches, and in fields. A far cry from the cannibal beginning!

barbecue sauce, the name given to a variety of sharp sauces for serving with grilled meat and usually consisting of tomato pulp or purée mixed and cooked with meat gravy, chutney, grated horseradish, onion juice, mustard, garlic, paprika, chilli powder, sugar flavoured with worcestershire sauce, and tarragon vinegar.

barbecue spice, see POUDER FORT.

barbel (*Barbus barbus*), a fish of the carp family found in many European rivers, and also in Africa and Asia where it attains about three times the usual European weight. It is not thought much of in England since the flesh is coarse and flannelly, but it is eaten in France, cooked usually in white wine or butter, fried, or grilled. An alternative name is barbillon

barbecue

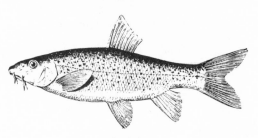

barbel

which usually refers to the smaller barbels. The soft roe is quite delicate and good to eat but the hard roe is said to be poisonous.

Barberey or ***Troyes,*** a soft cheese of the camembert type from the village of Barberey, near Troyes. It is made from fresh, warm cow's milk coagulated with rennet. In summer this cheese is often sold without ripening. It is in season from November to May.

barberon, the name used in the south of France for salsify.

barberry (*Berberis vulgaris*), a spiny stemmed shrub, originally from Asia but now naturalized in Great Britain, Europe, and the eastern U.S. The red berries were popular with 18th-century cooks, and a jelly was made from them and served with mutton. They are also candied for decoration on sweet dishes. They are tart in flavour. See also ÉPINE-VINETTE.

barbillon, see BARBEL.

barbo de mar, see SALMONETE.

barbotine, French for *tansy* or *mugwort,* used in France for flavouring some cakes.

barbounia, Greek for red mullet (family *Mullidae*), one of the most popular fish in Greece and served there in a great variety of ways. See also MULLET.

barbounia savore, red mullet fried in olive oil with tomato sauce, garlic, rosemary, and bay leaves. White wine is added to the oil left in the pan after frying, heated up, and reduced. The fish is served cold in the sauce.

barbounia sti shara, grilled mullet, basted with olive oil and lemon. Also served with lemon and oil.

barbounia sto harti, red mullet baked in parchment, each fish separately wrapped with olive oil, lemon, marjoram, and seasonings. The paper is brushed with oil before cooking.

barbounia tiganita, fried mullet, which is almost a national dish in Greece. After cleaning, the mullet are lightly coated with flour, sprinkled with salt and lemon juice, and left standing for 15 minutes; then they are fried in oil.

barbue, French for brill.

barbuta, Italian for brill.

barcelonesa, a Spanish regional soup from Barcelona, consisting of mutton broth flavoured with tomato purée and thickened with white breadcrumbs fried in butter. It is garnished with very small dumplings made from minced mutton, parsley, egg, flour, and seasonings. The dumplings are fried in oil and added to the soup before serving. Chopped parsley and chervil are sometimes sprinkled on top.

barding, the covering before cooking of a piece of meat, poultry, game, and occasionally a large fish, with thin slivers of fat from either bacon or fresh or salt pork, which are kept in place by being tied up with string. It is done to protect the delicate parts of the meat from drying or cooking too fast. Usually the fat is removed before serving, but in the case of game birds the bacon is often served with the dish. See also LARDING; PIQUAGE.

barding fat, is the name for the slices of fat bacon or fresh or salt pork cut very thin and of a length to enclose the pieces of food. They are also used for lining dishes for pâtés or *terrines*.

barge, French for godwit, which is prepared like woodcock in France.

barigoule, French name for a highly regarded mushroom found in the south of France.

barigoule, à la, a French method of stuffing globe artichokes with mushrooms. The word comes from the name of the mushroom which is used in the south of France for this dish.

bärkräm, Swedish for a fruit cream. Raspberries, gooseberries, currants, or strawberries are suitable for this traditional Scandinavian cream dessert. Fruit is cooked with castor sugar to taste in boiling water barely to cover, after which it is put through a sieve. Then 2 tablespoons of creamed cornflour (cornstarch) is added for every 1 pint (2 cups) fruit, and the purée is brought to the boil once more. It is served cold with cream.

barley (*Hordeum sativum vulgare*), a member of the grass family and one of the most important cereals. It is used for animal food, but large quantities are also made into malt. Its origin is obscure, but it is believed to derive from *Hordeum spontaneum,* a wild, annual species found in southwest Asia. Barley is grown in temperate regions all over the world. In India and Tibet it is a valuable food, and in Japan it is second in importance only to rice. In Latvia and other Baltic countries it is the chief farinaceous food; see MIEŽU PUTRA. A porous loaf cannot be made from it, but in the 15th century it was baked into round flat loaves for use as plates. Barley meal makes good bannocks and porridge; barley water and a wine are also made from it. In Europe and the U.S. it is used mainly for making malt liquors and spirits such as beer and whisky. See also MIEŽU PUTRA; PEARL BARLEY; POT BARLEY.

barley meal, a wholemeal flour made from ground barley. It is darker in colour than wheat meal, and is used for breads and bannocks in many parts of Europe, and for gruel and porridge in Scotland.

barley sugar, a sweetmeat (confection) made from boiled sugar flavoured originally with lemon juice and barley water, when finished having the form of an amber-coloured twisted stick. Nowadays it is almost impossible to obtain in its original form, since synthetic flavouring and colouring have replaced the original ingredients; only the sugar remains. In former times apple juice was added in place of lemon, giving a most delicious sugar well worth reviving, known as apple sugar.

barley water, a liquid made from barley, lemon juice, and water. It is both refreshing and nourishing, and is given to invalids. It is made by first boiling the peel of 2 lemons with 1 oz. (1 heaped tablespoon) sugar and 1 pint (2 cups) water, and then letting it simmer. Then 2 pints (4 cups) water and 1 oz. pearl barley are boiled in another saucepan, strained, and the

water thrown away; 2 more pints (4 cups) water are added to the barley, boiled, and again the water is strained and thrown away. The lemon liquid is now added to the barley with 2 pints (4 cups) water, and it is all boiled and simmered for 30 minutes. It is carefully strained and is now ready for use.

barm (from Old English *beorma*), the yeast formed on the top of malt liquor when fermenting. Also a form of yeast used in bread making.

barm brack, a traditional Irish yeast cake, made with ½ lb. (1¼ cups) raisins, 2 heaped tablespoons butter, 1 lb. (4 cups) flour, 4 oz. (1 cup) currants, 1 teaspoon mixed spices, 1 egg, 6 oz. (¾ cup) sugar, 2 oz. (½ cup) chopped candied peel, with 1 oz. (1 cake) yeast. It is made like bread but with fruit and spices added, the dried fruits being first soaked overnight in cold tea to make them swell. (My grandmother always used to add a small glass of Irish whisky to the tea, which greatly contributed to the flavour.) Barm brack is very good for tea in the winter, and is always eaten in Ireland at Halloween, when a ring is baked in the cake, and whoever gets it will be the next to marry. "Brack" comes from the Gaelic *brec* which means speckled (i.e., with fruit). Unyeasted brack, made from the above ingredients with 3 level teaspoons baking powder, is known as tea brack. See also BARA BRITH.

barnacle, a species of marine animal of the order *Cirripedia,* one of the crustacea, with a valved shell attached to other bodies, and legs like a curl of hair. Many varieties are edible, and there is a particularly delicious variety, the goose barnacle, which is eaten in Portugal. See also BERNACLE; PERÇEBAS.

goose barnacle

barnacle goose (*Branta leucopsis*), a wild goose which breeds in Arctic regions and visits the British Isles and Ireland in the winter. It is related to the brant, or brent, goose. A persistent medieval legend expounded the theory that the goose was hatched from the shell-like fruit of a tree growing by the seashore, which resembled a barnacle. Even after its nesting place was known, this theory was believed. Another legend has it that the goose was hatched from a shell of the genus *Cirripedia,* and shells of this genus have been named barnacles. Barnacle goose can be prepared in any way as for goose, but the wild varieties are not as fat or succulent as the domesticated goose.

baron, I. The most magnificent of all English joints of beef. It consists of both the sirloins, cooked and carved as a single joint and not divided at the backbone. It is usually roasted upon a spit and is used only for banquets, being too large for any other occasion. For many years it was the traditional dish at the Guildhall in the city of London. II. In France and the U.S., baron is the word generally used for a joint of lamb or mutton comprising the two hind legs and the saddle.

barquettes, small boat-shaped pastry shells which are filled with savoury mixtures of mushrooms, shellfish, or chicken. Fruit can also be used.

barracuda (*Sphyraena barracuda*), a vicious pike-like sea fish, with long pointed jaws filled with razor-like teeth. It is native to the warmer seas of Florida, the West Indies, Califor-

barnacle goose

nia, and Australia. It is thought to be more of a menace to swimmers than the shark. However, it makes delicious eating, and a grilled barracuda steak with melted butter and lemon juice is a meal that will not easily be forgotten. It is eaten in many tropical areas and in California, U.S., the California barracuda is popular.

barrot, a French word for a small barrel containing anchovies. It does not apply to other barrels.

barščiai, Lithuanian beetroot soup; see ŠALTI BARŠČIAI.

barse, an old English name for perch. It is the derivation of the word "bass," and a variety of perch is still known as black bass. (See BASS.)

barszcz, a traditional Polish soup, of which there are many varieties. The basic ingredient in many of them is fermented pickled beetroot. See also BEETROOT.

   barszcz kwaszony z buraków, soup consisting of large, diced and peeled beetroots covered with water, and a slice of rye bread placed on top. It is covered with muslin and left in a warm place for 4 days. Any mould is skimmed off. The bread is thrown away, and a little sugar, salt, and pepper are added to the beetroot. The soup is usually topped with sour cream and sometimes *pierogi,* and is served cold. Without the cream, and put into an air-tight jar, it will keep some time in a refrigerator and is used in other barszcz recipes. See also BORSCH.

   barszcz z uszkami, a vegetable soup, made from mushrooms, celery, onions, and beetroot juice, and served with little poached pastry squares filled with minced mushrooms. It is usually eaten on *Wigilia,* the Christmas Eve supper. Christmas Eve was a fast day until recent years, but the meal of soup and fish was on a grand scale.

   barszcz zimny, czyli chłodnik, a traditional Polish cold soup, made by boiling the juice of pickled red beetroot and pickled cucumbers, and thickening it with semolina, egg yolks, and sour cream. Seasonings are added. The soup is then chilled by stirring over broken ice. Quartered hard-boiled eggs are added before serving.

bartavelle, French for rock-partridge.

bartlett pear, the American name for the William pear.

Baseler art, "Basel-style," a Swiss sauce and garnish for fried fish. The butter the fish is fried in has ¼ pint (½ cup) hot water and a dash of worcestershire sauce added to it; it is brought to the boil, reduced, and then poured over the fish. Onion rings are fried in butter until soft and golden, and the fish is garnished with them; a little more water (about 4 tablespoons) is added to this butter, also the juice of 1 lemon, then all is boiled and poured over the fish. The dish is sprinkled with paprika and garnished with watercress or parsley.

Baseler leckerli, small biscuits (cookies) from Basel, Switzerland. They are made by heating 1 lb. (2 cups) honey with

¾ lb. (1½ cups) sugar; gradually 1½ lbs. (5 cups) flour is added, also 4 oz. (½ cup) chopped almonds, 2 tablespoons chopped candied peel, juice of 1 lemon, 1 teaspoon cinnamon, 1 teaspoon baking powder and 6 tablespoons kirsch or other liqueur. It is all well stirred and blended thoroughly, then put onto a floured board, rolled out to ½-inch thickness, and cut into shapes. This must be done while the mixture is warm, otherwise it is impossible to roll. The biscuits (cookies) should be left overnight and dried out in a low oven the next day. While warm, they are glazed with a mixture of icing sugar, lemon juice, and an egg white.

baselle, the French name for *basella* or Indian spinach, native to tropical countries but cultivated in certain parts of France, and prepared and cooked as spinach.

basil (*Ocymum basilicum*), a mainly tropical or subtropical genus of the family *Labiatae,* characterized by its pleasant, slightly clovey flavour and smell. Bush basil is the holy basil, or *tulsi,* of the Hindus, who plant it round their temples and make rosaries of 108 beads cut from its wood. Many superstitions are attached to basil; the ancients thought it had the power of propagating scorpions even in the brains of men. In the Middle Ages the roots of basil were chopped finely and mixed with pig's food to keep the animals free from disease. Sweet basil is an Indian annual, now cultivated in Europe and the U.S.

   Fresh basil is a fine culinary herb and is extremely complementary to tomatoes and should be cooked with them if possible. It dries very well, retaining its flavour for some months if kept in an air-tight container. It is always used in the making of turtle soup, *vasiliko, pesto alla genovese,* and *pistou.*

basilic, French for basil, an herb used extensively in France, and especially in Provence, for flavouring (together with garlic) the well-known *pistou soup.*

basilico, Spanish for basil.

basilico, Italian for basil, used extensively in Italy, but especially for the Genoese pesto sauce. *Basilico a foglie di lattughe* is a giant variety of basil, the lettuce-leaved basil.

basilico, Spanish for basil.

basilikum, German for basil.

basquaise, à la, I. A French garnish for large pieces of meat, consisting of fried *cèpes* and small *dariole* moulds of *pommes anna,* all sprinkled with chopped Bayonne ham. II. A French consommé of beef, garnished with a julienne of sweet peppers and diced tomatoes, both cooked in stock, cooked rice, and chopped chervil. See CONSOMMÉ. III. A French method of serving potatoes. See POMME DE TERRE.

bass, a collective name for many spiny-finned river and sea fish, resembling the common perch (*Perca fluviatilis*) and including the sea-bass (*Morone labrax*). It is an excellent fish to eat, whether from river or sea, and can be prepared as salmon; however, it does not resemble salmon in flavour, and is usually about one-tenth the price. The most common forms of bass are described here.

   bayou bass (*Huro floridiana; Micropterus salmoides*), can weigh up to 20 lb. and is distinguished by its large mouth.

   black sea bass (*Centropristes striatus*), one of the finest of the sea-basses for eating, found abundantly off the eastern seaboard of the U.S.

   calico or strawberry bass (*Pomoxis sparoides*), the finest river bass in America, variegated in colour, found in the Mississippi Valley lakes and also in fresh water in the east of North America.

   fresh-water black bass (*Micropterus dolomieu*), found off the eastern seaboard of the U. S. It has a small mouth and never weighs more than 5 lb.

   Kentucky black bass (*Micropterus pseudoplites*), a fresh water fish of medium size found from West Virginia to Texas.

rock bass (*Amploplites rupestris*), found in the Mississippi Valley. It has soft flesh and a muddy taste.

sea bass (*Morone labrax*), the European species of the bass family, and a firm white fish which makes excellent eating. It is found in the Mediterranean and also off the coast of the British Isles. It has the firmness and milky taste of a halibut, and can be cooked in similar ways. Its French name is *loup de mer*. See also SERRANO; SPIGOLA.

stone bass (*Polyprion cernium*) and in the U.S. (*P. americanum*), a deep-water sea perch found in the Mediterranean and in the warmer waters off the U.S.

striped bass (*Roccus saxitilis*), see ROCKFISH.

white bass (*Lepibema chrysops*), a river bass found in the Great Lakes and the Mississippi Valley. Not as good eating as the calico bass, it looks much the same as rock bass and has a finer flavour.

basse venaison, French for the meat of hare or wild rabbit.

bassine, a French hemispherical untinned copper bowl for beating egg whites. It makes them lighter, yet creamier, than the ordinary mixing bowl. A *bassine à friture* is a deep fryer.

bassine

bastable oven, an iron pot about 18 to 20 inches in diameter, with a lid, handles, and three short legs. It was, and still is, used in Ireland for cooking over a turf fire. It is suspended by chains over the fire and, for baking, burning turf sods are put on top to ensure an even heat. It is used for stews, roasts, or for baking bread. The bread cooked in such a pot is called bastable cake. See also SODA BREAD.

bastardau, French for bustard, also called *outarde*. This delicious bird comes to the Berry district of France in April. It is usually roasted, and can be served in the same way as goose or duck.

baste, to spoon either hot fat or other liquid over roasts or braised foods to keep them moist during cooking.

bastion, the name for a French method of arranging cold dishes in aspic, applied mainly to fish and especially to eel.

bastourma, a heavily spiced ham of Armenian origin, eaten in Turkey and Egypt. Garlic and red pepper (cayenne) are the main spices used.

basturma, a Russian dish consisting of marinated beef fillets threaded onto skewers and grilled on all sides. All the meat is removed from the skewers before serving, and garnished with tomatoes, spring onion (scallion), and lemon.

bat, a French culinary term meaning the tail of a fish.

ba-ta-clan, a French pastry invented by Lacam, a well-known Parisian pastry-cook of the 19th century. It consists of ½ lb. (2 cups) of pounded almonds to which 8 eggs are added one by one. When well mixed, nearly 1 lb. (2 cups) castor sugar is added and 1 gill (½ cup) rum. Finally 4 oz. (1 cup) flour is stirred in and the mixture is poured into a greased, fluted pan and baked in a moderate oven. When cool, it is sprinkled with vanilla sugar.

batalia pye, an old traditional English dish, now seldom found. The name is derived from the French *béatilles*, and the dish consists of a large pie of young chickens or pigeons, cock's combs, sweetbreads, lamb's stones (testicles), oysters, gizzards, tongues, spices, and butter. It is then covered with a pastry crust and baked slowly for some hours.

bâtard, the name of a French loaf which is more than a foot long and about 3 inches wide.

bâtarde, a French butter sauce, made from a roux to which boiling salt water and the yolk of an egg is added. When the mixture has thickened, a considerable quantity of butter (2 tablespoons to ½ pint) is added, and the whole is then flavoured with lemon juice. It is served with boiled poultry or white meat.

bâtarde blonde, a bâtarde sauce made with fish fumet. It is served with white fish.

batata, Portuguese for potato, which is used a great deal in Portuguese cooking, both as a vegetable, and for making a sweet course. For the latter, 4 cups cooked potato are pounded with 4 eggs and sugar, added to taste, before either rolling into small balls and frying in deep oil, or baking in the oven. It is served sprinkled with chopped almonds.

batatas (*Batatas edulis*), Spanish yellow sweet potatoes, which are used as a vegetable, and also to make a sweet course and a jam. They are a speciality of the province of Málaga. See also YEMAS.

bateaux, the French name for small boat-shaped containers of china or glass, used for serving cold hors d'oeuvre.

batelière, à la, I. A French garnish for fish, consisting of mushrooms, silver onions, fried eggs, and crayfish. II. Fish fillets served on small pastry tarts filled with shrimps and mussels in white wine sauce, with chopped herbs and gudgeon, which has been coated with egg and breadcrumbs and fried.

Bath bun, a small English cake made with 1 lb. (4 cups) flour, 1 oz. yeast, 4 oz. (½ cup) butter, 3 eggs, and ½ pint (1 cup) tepid milk, brushed over with sugar and decorated with candied peel before being baked in a moderate oven for 30 minutes. It was created by Dr. W. Oliver of Bath, *c.* 1750.

Bath chap, the lower half of a pig's head (that is, the bottom cheek and the tongue), which is cured like bacon, cooked, and eaten cold. It makes excellent eating, and is inclined to be sweetish since sugar as well as salt is included in the curing. The type of pig used is important, flat-headed pigs being unsuitable. The long-jawed Tamworth, Gloucester, Berkshire, and the local breed found outside Bath in Somerset, England, where the Bath chap originated, are the best.

Bath cheese, an English cheese made from cow's milk, which is, alas, no longer made. It was made in a mould 4 inches in diameter and about 2 inches high. It was slightly salted, and frequently had one-sixth cream added.

Bath Oliver, a flat biscuit (cracker) made from flour, butter, yeast, and milk, created by Dr. W. Oliver of Bath, *c.* 1750. It is usually served with cheese and butter, and has a good and characteristic flavour. It is pricked all over with a fork before cooking, and true Bath Olivers have an imprint of Dr. Oliver in the middle of the biscuit.

bâton, a French loaf made in the form of a long stick.

bâtonnets, the name given to various French biscuits (cookies) and pastries made in the form of small sticks.

bâtonnets royaux, an old-fashioned French hot hors d'oeuvre made from rectangular pastry pieces filled with minced chicken and partridge, rolled into little sticks, sealed well, and then fried in hot oil.

battelmatt, an Italian cheese that is a copy of the Swiss cheese of the same name. It is made in and around Piedmont.

battelmatt käse, a Swiss cheese made from cow's milk; it is a speciality of the St. Gothard district.

batter, a mixture of eggs, flour, and milk, beaten so that it is a smooth paste, and then fried spoonful by spoonful as pancakes, or baked in fat in the oven, or used as a coating for fish, meat, fruits, or vegetables before they are fried in deep fat or oil. These last are known as fritters. A usual batter recipe is 4 oz. (1 cup) flour to 1 egg, ½ pint (1 cup) milk, and a pinch of salt, all beaten until smooth. The recipe of the French chef, Carême, is 12 oz. (3 cups) flour, diluted with 2 oz. (4 heaped tablespoons) melted butter, with a little warm water added. Add a pinch of salt, 2 tablespoons brandy, and 2 stiffly beaten egg whites. Beer is often used instead of brandy. The recipe is called *pâte à foires*. In the U.S. batter also means the mixture, either liquid or doughy, prepared for making cakes and biscuits (cookies). See also LANE CIASTO; PASTELLA; YORKSHIRE PUDDING.

battuto, an Italian, and particularly a Roman, recipe for the first preparation of a soup or stew. It consists of browning 1 chopped onion, 1 carrot, 1 stalk celery, 2 tablespoons parsley, and 1 clove garlic in oil or butter. On top of this mixture go the broth and vegetables for the soup, or the meat or fish in the case of a stew. Sometimes chopped ham is added to the battuto. It is also called *soffritto*.

bauden, see KOPPEN.

baudroie, French for angler fish.

bauernfrühstück, German for "peasant's breakfast." This is a gargantuan meal consisting of scrambled eggs, cooked meats reheated, bacon, mixed vegetables, fried potatoes, and fried tomatoes. In some parts of Germany *bauernfrühstück* can also mean a plate of mixed garlic sausages.

bauernklösse, German farmhouse dumplings (see KLÖSSE) made from oatmeal, potato, bacon, onion, herbs, and seasoning, mixed with milk to a stiff paste which is then made into balls and baked in a dish until brown. These are served with gravy and mixed vegetables.

bauernschmaus, an Austrian speciality which consists of pork loin chops, bacon and various sausages all cooked in beer with sauerkraut, cumin seeds, garlic, grated raw potatoes, onions, and seasonings. Dumplings made from breadcrumbs are cooked separately and served with this massive dish (see KLÖSSE).

baume, the French name given to various plants of the mint variety.

baume de coq, French for *alecost*.

bavarois, also called crème bavarois or bavarois à la crème, a French cold sweet dish made from 1 pint (2 cups) custard whisked with 1 tablespoon gelatine, with ½ pint (1 cup) whipped cream added. It is not known whether it originated in Bavaria, or was simply devised by a French cook working in that country. It is often served with various fruit, nut, or chocolate flavourings and garnishes.

bavaroise, I. A form of sauce hollandaise flavoured with crayfish butter and chopped crayfish tails. II. A French garnish for fish consisting of crayfish tails. III. A hot beverage formerly served in France at evening parties, made from strong tea which is whisked with an egg yolk, sugar, and syrup until it becomes frothy, then has hot milk and kirsch added to it. It can also be flavoured with orange, lemon, vanilla, rum, brandy, calvados, or whatever is preferred.

bay leaf (*Lauris nobilis*), the leaf of the sweet bay or bay laurel, an evergreen tree native to Europe. The leaves of the sweet bay tree, used in Greek and Roman times for the wreaths given to victors in the games and worn by those awarded triumphs, have been in use as a pot herb for many thousands of years. They are an essential ingredient in many curries, and should always be included in a bouquet garni. They are extremely good in many meat dishes too, particularly those containing beef, are necessary for many marinades, game pies, fish sauces, and soups, and are also used in

many sweet milk puddings (see HASTY PUDDING). Since the sweet bay is an evergreen, fresh bay leaves are available all the year round, but the leaves dry well, preserving their flavour for a considerable time.

bay

bay salt, another name for rock salt. See SALT.

bayonnaise, à la, a French garnish for meat of cooked macaroni in sauce crème with julienne of Bayonne ham; or of macaroni croquettes with Bayonne ham and tomato-flavoured sauce madère. See also PORC (CÔTES DE PORC À LA BAYONNAISE).

Bayonne, a town in the Basses-Pyrénées which gives its name to the famous wine-cured Bayonne ham (although in fact, this is made at a nearby town called Orthez). It has a delicious and unusual flavour, and is usually eaten in thin slices, raw. It is also used to garnish eggs, and in sauces and ragoûts. Bayonne is also well known for its soup, *garbure à la Bayonne*, made from cabbage, bacon, goosefat, and rye bread, and for its black puddings and preserved goose and pork. Its sweet speciality is a citron preserve called *pâté de cédrat*. Some writers say that mayonnaise was created in Bayonne and should be called "bayonnaise"; the Irish, however, favour the legend of the Irish General Mahon and his invention of the sauce, which many people think bears his name, "mahonnaise," now corrupted to "mayonnaise." See also BAYONNAISE.

bayrische griesklösse, Bavarian soup dumplings made from 1 pint (2 cups) milk, 3 oz. semolina, 1 tablespoon parsley, 1 finely chopped shallot, 2 eggs, and seasonings. They are shaped into small balls and poached in hot stock or water.

bayrisches kraut, a Bavarian method of cooking cabbage by braising it with chopped bacon, 1 teaspoon caraway seeds, 4 tablespoons vinegar, ½ pint (1 cup) white wine, 2 tablespoons sugar, and a little flour to thicken.

bażant, Polish for pheasant. Traditionally in Poland the roasted bird is reassembled after being carved, and decorated with its own feathers. It is often stuffed with minced pork, veal, breadcrumbs, onion, chestnuts, and truffles, before being roasted and served with truffle sauce.

bean, the smooth seed of various annual leguminous plants cultivated for food all over the world. Perhaps the earliest bean known to civilization was the broad bean. It has been cultivated since prehistoric times and was grown in ancient Egypt, where it was regarded as unclean by the priests and thought to induce dreams because beans were supposed to contain dead men's souls. It was the only vegetable known as bean in Europe until the 16th century. Then, during the reign of Queen Elizabeth I, French Huguenot refugees are thought to have introduced the cultivation of the french (string) bean into England. About 1633, the runner bean was introduced from Mexico, first of all as a decorative climber, for its scarlet flowers. Since then a large number of other plants from the East and the Americas have been called beans. A notable and delicately flavoured variety, not grown in Europe but very popular in the Americas, is the lima bean.

The bean is extremely high in protein and is as nutritious as wheat. Many varieties can be eaten whole in their pods when young, as well as being allowed to age, when only the seed is extracted, dried, and stored for the winter. If fresh, they can be used as a vegetable, or for soups and salads. If dried, they are soaked overnight, boiled, and then used for salads, soups, stews, and certain well-known dishes such as Boston baked beans and *cassoulet*. The main varieties found over the world are described here.

adzuki bean (*Phaseolus angularis*).

broad bean (*Vicia faba*), also called field or horse bean. See BROAD BEAN.

coco bean (*P. vulgaris*), a blue-coloured variety of french bean, which turns green in cooking. It has a good flavour.

french bean (*Phaseolus vulgaris*), also called kidney bean, snap bean (U.S.), string bean (U.S.), and also wax bean and wax-pod bean.

haricot bean (*P. vulgaris*), also called butter bean, navy bean (U.S.), and flageolet.

kidney bean, also called french bean.

lima bean (*P. lunatus;* var. *macrocarpus;* also *P. limensis*).

mung bean (*P. mungo;* var. *radiatus*).

runner bean (*P. multiflorus, P. coccineus*), also called scarlet runner.

soya bean (*Glycine soja*).

tepary bean (*P. acutifolius;* var. *latifolius*).

See also BOHNEN; BONNER; BØNNER; BÖNOR; BRUINE BONEN.

bean sprouts, the sprouts from either soya bean or mung bean, popular in Chinese food all over the world. The beans are soaked in warm water and germinated under a damp cloth for several days until they sprout. They are used in many Chinese dishes and can be bought canned; the tiny beans are also sold for sprouting at home.

bear (*Ursidae*), a large, heavy-furred, partly carnivorous quadruped which inhabits parts of Europe (*Ursus arctos*), America (*U. americanus*), and the Arctic regions (*Thalarctos maritimus*). Bear steak is often eaten, and should be prepared and cooked like beef, but since it is somewhat tougher than beef it should first be marinated for about two days in oil and vinegar or wine. (See also BÄR.) Bear steaks are popular in North America and are enjoyed by the trappers and hunters. Smoked bear hams were available in London and New York until the outbreak of the World War II. Bear paws are the delicacy, however, and are usually cooked in the ashes of an open fire by the hunter. The Arctic explorer Nansen and his colleagues ate them every day for many months without tiring of them. They also found the breast of polar bear cubs to be extremely delicious. In Russia bear is braised and served with sour cream.

béarnaise, a French sauce classically served with fillet of beef or grilled red meat, but often nowadays served with fish, chicken, or eggs. The name derives from the name of the chef of the Pavillon Henri IV at St. Germain in Paris, who invented the sauce in about 1835. Some references attribute this sauce to the Béarn district, but this is unlikely since olive oil is more prevalent than butter in the cooking in that part of France. The sauce is made with 2 chopped shallots and 1 sprig chervil simmered in 4 tablespoons wine vinegar or white wine, with pepper and fresh tarragon leaves, until the vinegar has evaporated to about 2 teaspoonfuls. It is strained and allowed to cool. Then 2 egg yolks are placed in a double boiler, and the wine and herb mixture whisked with them; 3 oz. (¼ cup) butter is added in little pieces, one by one, also with a whisk, and this must be done slowly, over the boiling water, until the sauce is as thick as mayonnaise. Should the sauce curdle, a teaspoon of cold water should be whipped vigorously into it and the sauce must be removed from the stove. It is served warm, either on the meat or in a sauce-boat.

béatilles, the French name, meaning "titbits," for a dish consisting of small ingredients such as cock's comb, cock's kidneys (cock's testicles), sweetbreads, gizzards, livers, and mushrooms, all cooked in a little madeira and butter. Sometimes a velouté or sauce suprême is added to bind it. See also BATALIA PYE.

béatrix, a French garnish for a joint of meat, particularly beef, consisting of morel mushrooms sautéed in butter, or artichoke bottoms quartered with small young carrots and *pommes fondantes*.

beaufort, a hard French cow's milk cheese, made in the highlands of the Jura and Savoy mountains on the French side of the Franco–Swiss border. It is made from whole milk, rennetted, and pressed before and after being cooked. It is in season all the year round.

beauharnais, à la, I. A sauce béarnaise blended with tarragon purée, and without the chopped chervil. Served with small cuts of meat, mainly tournedos. II. A garnish for steaks and noisettes of stuffed mushrooms and quartered artichoke hearts, served with small cuts of meat, mainly tournedos. III. Chicken consommé thickened with arrowroot, garnished with paupiettes of lettuce, poached in stock and chopped, asparagus tips, and julienne of truffles, all sprinkled with chopped chervil. See also CONSOMMÉ.

beaumont, a French cheese made with cow's milk. It is in season from October to June, and Savoy is the main producing district.

beaupré de roybon, a French cow's milk cheese which comes from Dauphiné. It is in season from November to April.

beauvilliers, I. A French garnish for braised meat served in one large piece. It consists of tomatoes stuffed with a purée of brains, salsify sautéed in butter, and spinach kromeskies. It is named after A. Beauvilliers who opened the first restaurant in Paris, *circa* 1784, and wrote a standard work, *L'Art du Cuisinier* (1814). II. A French cake almost identical to *bonvalet*, and contemporary with it, but created by a different person.

beaver (*Castor fiber*), a large semiaquatic animal of the rodent family, about 4 feet long, one third of which is tail and the best part to eat. Formerly common in the British Isles, it is now found only in Germany, France, and Scandinavia. It is seldom used for food in Europe nowadays, except in Germany. The American beaver, *C. canadensis,* was once relished by the Indians of North America and also by trappers. Care has to be taken in skinning to avoid cutting into the musk glands, which will permeate the entire flesh if severed. It is not eaten much in the U.S. anymore. See also BIBERSCHWANZ.

becada, Spanish for woodcock and snipe.

bécard, French for "hooked nose." The term is used for old salmon when its nose begins to protrude like a beak.

bécasse, French for woodcock, which is highly esteemed as food in France. The finest French methods of cooking it are the simplest, such as roasting or sautéeing it in butter, the pan juices diluted with scorched brandy, armagnac, calvados, or other spirit. See also WOODCOCK FLAMBÉE.

bécasse à la perigourdine, as above, but the trail is added to the stuffing, and armagnac is used with the game fumet. Pies (pâtés) are made with boned bécasse and game forcemeat enclosed in *pâté moulée*. It is also used in salmis and soufflés.

bécasse en daube à l'ancienne, woodcock with backbone removed, and the bird stuffed with foie gras studded with truffle, barded with lean bacon, and cooked in butter with mushrooms, truffle, and a mixture of half red wine and half game fumet. Brandy is added to the cooked trail, with butter for the sauce.

bécasse de mer, a local name in the south of France for red mullet. This fish is often cooked undrawn, like a woodcock, hence the name "woodcock of the sea."

bécasseau, the French name for young woodcock until they are 8 months old. They are usually cooked on a spit.

bécassin, French for great snipe, which is usually roasted.

bécassine, French for snipe (common).

bécassine en casserole, snipe covered with bacon and cooked in butter for 12 minutes. Brandy and game fumet are added, and the birds are served on croûtons. Sometimes the cooked livers are pounded and mixed with the pan juices, with a little lemon juice, salt, and pepper heated up and served separately. Bécassines are often boned and stuffed and made into pâté with chopped truffle.

bécassine la sourde, French for jacksnipe, possibly so-called because it is slow to rise and no doubt thought to be deaf. The *bécassine* comes to France twice a year. It is about half the size of woodcock and can be prepared in the same way, but cooking time will be half as long.

becatses, Greek for woodcock.

beccabunga, French for brooklime.

beccaccia, Italian for woodcock and snipe.

beccafico, Italian for figeater or figpecker. The Latin name for this little bird is *ficedula,* and it is still called fucetola in the south of Italy. It does not live on figs or grapes, but on the insects which cluster round them when they are ripe. In Italy it is usually cooked over charcoal, on a skewer with other birds, the whole being consumed. In Liguria it is roasted on one of the large red mushrooms, which grow wild in that region, with a little salt and olive oil. See also TÀCCULA; UCCELLETTI.

bec-figue, French for figeater or figpecker.

béchamel, sauce, one of the basic French sauces, named after Louis de Béchamel, Marquis de Nointel, Lord Steward at the court of Louis XIV.

béchamel maigre, the sauce which is usually known simply as béchamel. It is made with ½ pint (1 cup) milk heated and 1½ oz. (2 level tablespoons) butter heated in another saucepan. When the butter starts to foam it is removed from the fire and 2 level tablespoons plain flour are stirred in. Now a little of the warm (not boiling) milk is added and stirred until a thick smooth paste is obtained. Then the rest of the milk is gradually added, on the fire, stirring to keep it well mixed. Finally it should be seasoned, and simmered for not less than 10 minutes. It can be kept hot in a double saucepan or *bain-marie* and used as required. This sauce is often known in Great Britain and the U.S. as white sauce. With the addition of grated cheese it becomes sauce mornay; with cream and egg yolks, sauce à la crème; and so on.

béchamel grasse, made in just the same way as béchamel maigre, but meat or chicken stock is used, with the addition of a little milk. The quantities are also the same; those given above will make about 1½–2 cups of sauce.

bechamel, saltsa, Greek for sauce béchamel, used in a great number of Greek dishes.

beckenoff, a country dish from Alsace, consisting of layers of mixed, sliced lean and fat pork, lamb, onions, and potatoes, moistened with white wine. It is cooked very slowly in butter in a closed ovenproof dish for 3–4 hours. The lid is removed for the last 30 minutes to allow the top potatoes to brown.

bec-plat, the common French name for spoonbill, a reference to its flat beak.

bec-pointu, the French name for a small white skate found in the Atlantic, and so named because its head is more elongated than that of the common skate.

bécsiszelet, a Hungarian dish of fried veal fillets. The fillets are cleaned, scored, and beaten. They are then soaked for about 10 minutes in milk. When removed, they are dried, salted, and dipped first in flour, then in beaten egg, and finally in breadcrumbs. They are fried in hot fat on both sides until golden brown. See also BORJÚ.

bedstraw, a plant of the *Rubiaceae* family. The yellow flowers are used to curdle milk, and the plant is also used in the preparation of Cheshire cheese.

beech leaves, noyau of, literally "fruit kernel," is an old speciality of Buckingham England. Young beech leaves are steeped in gin for 6 days. The gin is strained and the leaves are cooked with sugar and brandy in ½ pint water. Some bitter almonds in their skins are sometimes added before and all are bottled together.

beef, a Norman-French name from boeuf for the flesh of bovine quadrupeds, the bull, the cow, and also the castrated bull, the ox. The first two make very poor eating, but the latter is what is used when prime quality beef is wanted. There are many different breeds all over the world. The best known for quality in France is the Charollais; in the British Isles the Aberdeen Angus, the Hereford, the Belted Galloway, and the Shorthorn are considered excellent eating, to name only a few.

There are many different cuts, and the cutting varies in all countries; but in England the main and best joints are known by the original French word "beef," while the lesser cuts and parts of the animal have kept the Anglo-Saxon "ox" used as a prefix, as for example ox palate, ox cheek, ox heart, oxtail, ox tongue, etc. The finest joint is called a baron of beef, and that is followed by the sirloin, and the fillet, which is used for steak. The following is a table aligning as accurately as possible the different English, French, and American cuts, although it is rare that one corresponds exactly to another. Those in italics have an article to themselves in their alphabetical order in the book. Cuts that originate in France are: filet mignon, noisette, tournedos; and in England, topside.

Beef is eaten roasted, boiled, braised, and fried (sautéed), depending on the part of the animal used. It is also salted, when it is known as corned beef in Ireland and the U.S., and as salt beef in Great Britain; when dried, it is called pemmican and in Switzerland *binden fleisch*.

See also BIFE; BIFF; BIFSHTEK; BIFTECK; BISTECCA; BOEUF; CARNE DE VACA; COLLARED BEEF; GOVYADINA; HOVĚZI MASO; LIHA; MANZO; OKSE; OSSENHAAS; RINDFLEISCH; SPICED BEEF; VĂCUTĂ; VODINO.

beef olives, a British dish of thin slices of lean beef filled with a savoury stuffing of breadcrumbs, herbs, and onion, bound with an egg, rolled up, secured, and braised with root vegetables in good stock. Bacon rashers are sometimes used outside the beef. See also PAUPIETTES.

beef steak fungus (*Fistulina hepatica*), a large liver-coloured fungus found on the trunks of oak and ash trees, causing a dark-red discolouration of the wood. The edible flesh is reddish, red-streaked like a beetroot, and best for eating as a mushroom when mature.

beef stroganoff, an excellent Russian beef dish, made with 2 lb. fillet (tenderloin) of beef cut into thin strips which are seared in hot butter, care being taken that the meat remains

BRITISH	FRENCH	AMERICAN
brisket	*poitrine* de boeuf	*brisket* and fancy brisket
fillet or *undercut*	*filet*	*tenderloin*
flank	*flanchet*	*flank*
forequarter flank	*plat de côtes*	short ribs
marrow	*moelle*	*marrow*
spinal marrow	*amourettes*	spinal marrow
ox cheek or muzzle	*museau* de boeuf	muzzle
Porterhouse steak	*chateaubriand*	*center cut* or T-bone steak
rib	*côte* de boeuf	rib roast
rump	See *aiguillette*	*rump*
top rump [1]	*tranche grasse*	*sirloin* tip
rump steak	*entrecôte* or *romsteck*	rib steak [2]
end of *loin* toward hip-bone, part of *rump*	*culotte* de boeuf	end of *sirloin* toward hip-bone
shin	*jarret* or *trumeau* de boeuf	shank
Shoulder blade only, *neck* (shoulder) [3]	*paleron* (*épaule* for pork, mutton, etc.)	*chuck* roast/steak
silverside/round	*gîte à la noix* or *côte rond*	bottom *round*
sirloin	*aloyau* de boeuf	*sirloin*
skirt	*onglet* de boeuf	plate
steak	*bifteck*	*steak*
topside	*tende de tranche*	top round

[1] Not a true rump; it is a wedge-shaped piece from the round.

[2] A near equivalent is a club or Delmonico steak.

[3] There is really no cut ''shoulder of beef''; the term refers generally to the neck, with a bit of the blade bone. ''Shoulder'' is used for smaller animals, and the direct translation, *épaule*, is used in France for mutton, pork, and veal.

pink inside. The beef is combined with 4 finely sliced onions that also have been browned in butter, with ½ cup demi-glace, a squeeze of lemon juice, ½ teaspoon mustard, and ½ pint (1 cup) thick sour cream. The sauce is allowed to bubble up and reduce slightly, and all should be served at once, with mashed potatoes. Yogourt can be used in place of sour cream. In some parts of Russia mushrooms cooked in butter are added to the onions and beef, and this addition is also usual in France and Britain. In restaurants, tomato purée is sometimes added, but this completely destroys the true flavour of a superb and original dish. See also STROGANOFF.

beef tea, a concentrated meat broth made from beef scraped into very little water and put in a covered pot in a hot oven until all the juice is extracted. It is then put through a sieve, and is an invaluable form of protein for invalids unable to take solid food. Florence Nightingale lived on it almost exclusively in her latter years.

beefburgers, a modern American term for hamburgers.

beestings or **beistyn,** the first liquid a cow gives after she has calved. It has a thick yellow consistency, similar to the yolk of an egg. By law, beestings must not be sold, but most cows have too much and so some is taken away. In country districts the custom used to be that a jugful was given to friends; but it was important that the jug should never be returned empty, since an empty beistyn jug boded bad luck for the calf. It is thinned down with 3 or 4 times its quantity of plain milk, and made into custards, curds, cakes, puddings, and tarts. See also ABRESTIR.

beetroot or **beet** (family *Chenopodiaceae*), the name applied to several species of *Beta*, a biennial vegetable with a thick fleshy root and a leafy flowering stem. Beetroot is the name common to Great Britain; in the U.S. the name is beet. The beetroot is native to Europe, North Africa, and Asia. The Romans cultivated it, and used the leaves as a vegetable as well as the root. There are 3 main kinds which are of culinary interest. *Beta rubra* has a deep red root which is baked or boiled; then the skin is rubbed off, and the beet is used as a hot vegetable, a salad, or for a pickle. In Poland and the western states of Russia, a national soup is made from beets, called *borsch*. The leaves can also be used as a green vegetable. *Beta vulgaris* is a white-rooted beet which is used to make sugar; some varieties of it (*mangel wurzel*) are used as cattle food. *Beta cicla* is also known as chard, which is cultivated for the leaves and stalks. The leaves are used as spinach, and the stalks and midriffs as sea kale. See also BARSZCZ; BIEŠU SAKŅU SALÁTI; BIETEN; BORSCH; BURAKI; ROSSEL; SVEKLA.

béhague, a French consommé of chicken, garnished with poached egg and chopped chervil. See also CONSOMMÉ.

beigli, a special cake which is traditionally eaten in Hungary at Christmas time. A pastry is made from ½ lb. (2 cups) flour, 3 oz. (½ scant cup) butter, 1 egg yolk, 2 tablespoons rum, ½ oz. yeast, and 1 gill (½ cup) sour milk or buttermilk. The pastry is divided into two parts and set aside to rest. A filling is now made from 4 oz. (1 cup) ground almonds, which are added to a syrup made of 4 oz. (½ cup) sugar and 3 tablespoons milk and gently cooked for a few minutes. The filling is removed from the heat and 1 tablespoon butter and 3 tablespoons sultanas are added. The pastry is rolled out very thinly and half the filling spread over each half of it. The pastry is then rolled up, and the two rolls are brushed with egg white and left to stand for 30 minutes in a greased tin; then they are baked in a moderate oven for 40 minutes.

beignet, I. A very light French doughnut, made from ½ lb. (2 cups) flour, ½ lb. (1 cup) butter, 1 tablespoon sugar, a pinch of salt, and flavouring. The butter and sugar mixture is boiled with about ½ pint (1 cup) water or milk until thick, the flour being added gradually. Then, 4 eggs are added one by one and mixed in well. The mixture is made into little balls and cooked in deep, hot fat. They are rolled in sugar and eaten hot with melted jam or *sabayon* sauce. II. Beignet can also mean fritter, made from batter containing either fruit or vegetables, chopped meats, poultry, brains, sweetbreads, and fish. III. A paste, made as I, with the addition of pounded almonds, which is the basis for petits fours.

beistyn, see BEESTINGS.

bekasy, Polish for snipe. In Poland snipe feed on juniper berries, which give them an exclusive flavour of very aromatic gin. They are often grilled over charcoal.

bekasy lub kwiczoły duszone, snipe wrapped in bacon and casseroled with game stock, juniper berries, and dry white wine barely to cover.

bekkasin, Danish and Norwegian for snipe, which is a popular game-bird in Denmark, and often cooked by braising with sour cream.

bel paese, a soft Italian cheese made in Lombardy. It has a mild flavour, and is also good for cooking. It is made from cow's milk. Pastorella is a smaller version of bel paese.

belegte brote, German for open sandwiches, usually consisting of rye bread and wurst.

Belgian cheeses, see CASSETTE; FROMAGE DE BRUXELLES; HARZÉ; HERVÉ; LIMBURGER; MAQUÉE; REMOUDOU.

Belgian endive, see ENDIVE.

beli sir, a popular Yugoslavian cheese which is pickled in brine.

belle-alliance, a variety of winter pear popular in France. The skin is yellowish on one side and red on the other. It is a good dessert fruit and is at its best in December and January.

belle-angevine, a French winter dessert pear, which is very large. It is decorative, but does not make such good eating as the belle-alliance.

belle-chevreuse, a bright-red variety of peach popular in France. It ripens suddenly and care must be taken to ensure that it does not get overripe.

belle-de-berry, a French variety of pear, also called *poire de curé.*

belle-et-bonne, a French variety of cooking pear, usually cooked in red wine or syrup, or used in a compote.

belle-garde, a French peach which ripens in September or October. It has a firm flesh and so is often used for cooking in compotes or flans.

belle hélène, I. A French garnish for meat joints, made from grilled mushrooms stuffed with cooked tomato, or green peas, young carrots, and potato croquettes. II. Pears poached in vanilla-flavoured syrup, drained, and served on vanilla ice cream, with hot chocolate sauce served separately. In France this is called *poires belle hélène* or simply *poires hélène.*

belle-isle cress, see AMERICAN CRESS.

Bellelay cheese, originally made only in the Abbey of Bellelay in the Bernese Jura, but today is produced in dairies of the district. It is made from whole cow's milk, is very delicate in flavour, and takes almost a year to cure. It is a comparatively small cheese, weighing between 10 and 15 lb. It is not exported and is also known as *tête de moine.*

bellona, a variety of very large fig grown in Provence, France, and used for preserves and drying.

beluga, the Russian name for the white sturgeon (*Acipenser huro*) of the Black and Caspian Seas and other Russian waters. Its roe is the beluga caviar and is thought to be the best. Beluga sturgeons have the largest eggs, though some people prefer the smaller ones of the sevruga du ostrine sturgeon. See also CAVIAR; STURGEON.

belyashi, Russian meat tarts from Siberia. The dough is made from 1 lb. (4 cups) flour, ½ pint (1 cup) milk, and ½ oz. yeast, like bread, and is cut into rounds. The rounds are stuffed with minced meat, finely chopped onions and season-

ings, and pinched up. They are then fried in hot fat, pinched side first.

ben cotto, Italian for ''well-cooked,'' pertaining mostly to meat, particularly steak.

bénari, local French name for a kind of ortolan found in the Languedoc district.

bénédictin, a French almond-flavoured sponge cake, sprinkled with Bénédictine liqueur when cooked, then iced and scattered with chopped roasted almonds.

bénédictine, à la, I. A French garnish for fish or eggs, made from *brandade de morue* and truffles. II. A French method of serving potatoes, see POMMES DE TERRE (POMMES BÉNÉDICTINE). III. Bénédictine is also the name for a French liqueur made from honey, brandy, various herbs, and dried fruit skins. It is reputed to have been first made by Dom Bernardo Vincelli in 1510 at the Benedictine Abbey at Fécamp, but has been made since 1863 by the family of M. Alexandre le Grand. The taste of angelica and hyssop is prominent and the liqueur imparts an interesting flavour to fruit salads, or when flambéed over pancakes.

benløse fugler, a Norwegian dish of stuffed steak olives. The 6 rump steaks used should each be thinly sliced, about 3 inches by 1½ inches; they are stuffed with 6 oz. forcemeat, or sausage meat, and 2 oz. lean pork (each piece of the latter having just been dipped in a mixture of grated nutmeg and 1 teaspoon each of crushed herbs and minced parsley). After seasoning, each steak is rolled and secured. Onions are fried in butter, and the olives are added and browned; boiling stock is poured over to cover. The pan is covered and is simmered for 2 hours, when the steaks are untied and served in their own sauce.

beolas, a Jewish fritter made from 4 tablespoons matzo meal, the same of flour, and 4 eggs, all beaten until frothy; then spoonfuls of the mixture are fried on both sides in hot oil. When cooked, the fritters are sometimes sprinkled with ground cinnamon and a combination of sugar, lemon peel, and water, boiled and left until cold.

berce, French for cow parsnip.

Berchoux, I. A sauce allemande with herb butter and cream beaten into it. It is used to accompany meat or poultry, and is named after Joseph Berchoux (1765–1839), a French poet who also wrote on gastronomy. II. A French game consommé garnished with cubes of quail, chestnut royal garnish, sliced mushrooms, and truffles. See also CONSOMMÉ.

bercy, I. A fish sauce made from ½ pint (1 cup) white wine with 2 chopped shallots (which have been sweated in butter), 1 tablespoon parsley, and ½ pint (1 cup) fish velouté. II. A meat sauce also made from white wine, butter, and chopped shallots, as above, but with the addition of diced, blanched beef marrow and meat glaze.

bercy, beurre, see BEURRES COMPOSÉS.

berenjena, Spanish for eggplant.

berenjena rellena, Spanish stuffed eggplant. The eggplant is cut in half and the seeds are removed; it is then partially cooked in boiling salted water, and drained. Fried chopped mushrooms are mixed with grated cheese, seasoning, and beaten egg. The eggplants are filled with this mixture, sprinkled with breadcrumbs and dabbed with butter before being baked in the oven.

bergamot, the name for three quite distinct plants. I. *Monarda didyma*, an ornamental herb, native to North America and brought to Britain in 1656. The leaves can be dried and brewed as a tea called Oswego tea. The fresh leaves are good in a salad. This plant likes damp ground, and grows easily from seed. The blooms are red and very attractive. II. *Pyrus persica*, one of the oldest pears in England, also known by the name of bergamot, which in this case is said to be a corruption of the Turkish word beg-armudi—"prince's pear." It was probably introduced into England by the Romans. III. *Citrus bergamia*, a pear-shaped orange which is grown in Calabria, Italy, for the oil obtained from its peel. The peel itself is also used in confectionery and cookery as a flavouring agent.

bergamotte orange (*Citrus bergamia*), see BERGAMOT (III); ORANGE.

bergkäse, an Austrian hard cheese made in the mountainous parts of western Austria, whence the name "mountain" cheese. It is a large cheese sometimes weighing as much as 60 lb. The paste is firm and varies in colour from pale to deep yellow. It is full of eyes, which also vary in size from one farm to another. According to the making and the length of time allowed for maturing, the flavour starts by being quite mild but gets sharper with maturity. A smaller variety of bergkäse weighing about 20 lb. is known as alpkäse or alpine cheese.

berinjela, Portuguese for eggplant, used extensively in Portugal during August and September.

Berliner kranser, small glazed Norwegian pastry rings known as "Berlin crowns." They are made from 2 sieved, hardboiled egg yolks mixed with 2 raw yolks, together with 4 oz. (½ cup) sugar, all well beaten. Then ½ lb. (2 cups) flour and ½ lb. (1 cup) butter are put in, alternately in small amounts, until a smooth paste is formed. This is left in a cold place for up to 2 hours, then divided into small equal portions. The rings are made by rolling out the dough into thin strips, which are joined into circles. These are dipped into beaten egg white and sprinkled with icing sugar. They are baked for about 15 minutes in a moderate oven, or until a pale golden colour. When cold, they are stored in a tin until needed.

berlingot, a hard, sweet French toffee. It is usually flavoured with peppermint, but other flavours are used in the different regions of France.

Bermuda chub, see CHOPA BLANCA.

Bermuda onion, see ONION.

bernacle, French for barnacle, a mollusc with a conical-shaped shell. The flesh is rather tough, but it is usually eaten raw, either plain or with a vinaigrette dressing. Small ones are sometimes cooked like mussels or grilled with butter. Other local names in various regions are *flie*, *bassin*, *jamble*, and *arapède*. The term is also used to mean barnacle goose.

bernard-l'ermite, French for hermit crab.

Berner platte, a Swiss national dish from Berne, consisting of thin slices of beef and sauerkraut layered in a deep pan with chopped pig's trotter (foot), with a layer of chopped fried bacon and onion on top. A glass of white wine and water is added to two-thirds the depth, and it is covered and simmered for several hours. Finally sliced wurst is added, and all is cooked without a lid for 20 minutes. The dish is served with potatoes.

berny, I. A French method of serving potatoes. Mashed potatoes are mixed with chopped truffle, then made into apricot-shaped balls which are dipped in egg, rubbed in finely chopped almonds, and fried in hot oil. II. A French garnish for game consisting of croquettes of berny potatoes and little pastry tarts filled with puréed chestnuts and lentils, and garnished with sliced truffles. III. A French beef consommé, slightly thickened with tapioca and garnished with *pommes dauphine* mixed with chopped almonds and fried cubes of truffle. See also CONSOMMÉ.

berrichonne, à la, I. A French garnish for meat consisting of glazed button onions, cooked chestnuts, pieces of grilled bacon, and balls of braised cabbage. II. A French method of serving potatoes, see POMME DE TERRE (POMMES À LA BERRICHONNE).

berro, Spanish for watercress.

berry, any small, roundish fruit without a stone, the seeds enclosed in a juicy pulp. Almost all berries except those known to be poisonous, are used in cooking. All cereal foodgrains are technically berries.

berry, in, a term applied to fish eggs in roe, and to a hen lobster carrying eggs.

bertiche, Italian for perch.

bertines mandelbunn, a very rich Norwegian apple meringue pie. A pie case is made from ½ lb. pounded almonds mixed with ½ lb. (1 cup) castor sugar and 5 stiffly beaten egg whites. This is baked like a meringue in a slow oven for about 2 hours. The casing is then turned out and allowed to cool, when it is sprinkled with madeira and covered with large, cold, baked dessert apples. A cold sauce, made with 5 egg yolks beaten gradually into ¼ lb. (½ cup) sugar and vanilla essence (extract) to taste, to which ½ pint (1 cup) cream is added. This sauce is thickened by being brought almost to boiling point in a double saucepan. It is poured over the apples and when cold, the pie is topped with whipped cream.

besciamella, Italian for sauce béchamel.

besi, I. French generic term for several varieties of pear. *Besi de caissoy* is a winter pear of quite good quality; *besi d'héry*, a winter pear which gets its name from the forest in Brittany where it was first grown; and *besi de la motte* is an autumn pear with white, juicy flesh. II. A word used in the Jura region for salted and fried cow's meat.

bessensoep, a traditional Belgian soup. It consists of vermicelli cooked in water, to which is added salt, potato flour mixed with a little cold water to thicken slightly, red currant juice, and a little sugar.

besugo, the Portuguese name for a small bream with a pink head and a pinkish body. It is inclined to be bony and is not nearly as good as the larger *pargo*. It is best served in the typical Portuguese style known as *cozido*, or boiled. The fish is first rubbed with coarse salt, and left with 2 cloves for about 1 hour. It is then lightly poached in water or fish stock and usually served with boiled potatoes and boiled green runner beans (*feijão verde*).

besugo, Spanish for sea bream, also known as *chopa*. Besugo is also the Spanish name for another member of the *Sparides* family, the red gilthead, which makes excellent eating. See also SALPA.

betasuppe, a Norwegian mutton soup. It is thicker than ordinary soup and is like a cross between Scotch broth and pot-au-feu.

bête de campagne, the French term for a wild boar between one and two years old.

bête de campagne rousse, as above, except that this term describes a young boar between six months and one year old.

beterraba, Portuguese for beetroot.

betony (*Stachys officinalis* and *S. betonica*), also known in Great Britain as purple or wood betony. The word comes from Vettonica, the name of a Gaulish tribe, and the plant used also to be known as vervain. It is a weed, and was once thought to have magical properties. A tea was made from the dried leaves and flowers. In the U.S. the name betony is given to a quite different plant, the American germander *Teucrium canadense* (not to be confused with the European germander, *Veronica chamoedrys*).

betterave, French for beetroot.

beurecks, see BÖREK.

beurre, French for butter. See also BEURRES COMPOSÉS.

beurre à la broche, as *beurre frit* but left in a block and grilled.

beurre à l'Anglaise, French for melted butter.

beurre arachides, peanut butter.

beurre, au, French for meat, fish, or vegetables served with butter on top.

beurre blanc, a French sauce of 6 oz. (⅔ cup) soft butter, 3 finely chopped shallots gently cooked in 3 tablespoons each of wine and wine vinegar until the liquid is almost evaporated, salt, and pepper, all beaten vigorously until white. The butter should not be oily, but soft. Usually served with fish, particularly pike and shad, in the region of the Loire.

beurre de cacao, the fatty substance obtained from cocoa beans.

beurre de coco, a vegetable fat used in France, made from coconut.

beurre de Gascogne, a sauce from Gascony, France, consisting of 6 boiled garlic cloves pounded and added to ¼ lb. (½ cup) good pork dripping. When these are well mixed, chopped parsley is added. This sauce is stirred into cooked fried beans, lentils, or mushrooms, or is added to soups before serving.

beurre de Marseilles, a French slang name for olive oil.

beurre de Montpellier, a French dressing for cold dishes, particularly fish. It is made from 4 oz. fresh green herbs (a mixture of tarragon, parsley, chervil, etc.) and 4 oz. spinach poached in water with a sliced shallot for 2 minutes. All are drained and pounded well in a mortar. Then 6 anchovies, 2 tablespoons capers, 1 clove garlic, 4 small gherkins are also pounded, and 5 tablespoons butter, 3 hard-boiled egg yolks, and 2 raw yolks added to the combined mixtures. Finally, still pounding, ½ pint (1 cup) olive oil, salt, and cayenne are added little by little. The sauce is then sieved and whisked until very smooth. When used for spreading on croûtons, the raw egg is omitted.

beurre de muscade, a fatty substance obtained from nutmeg.

beurre fondu, a French garnish of melted butter, with seasoning and lemon juice added. Served with poached fish or boiled vegetables.

beurre frit, pats of butter mixed with herbs and well chilled, then rolled very thickly in breadcrumbs and fried quickly in smoking oil. It is served with poached fish.

beurre manié, a piece of butter about the size of a walnut, rolled and "squashed" in flour. It is used when a sauce or stew needs only slight thickening, and it is cooked for a few minutes before the dish is served. It is sometimes used to thicken a sauce bordelaise.

beurre marchand de vin, a sauce made of finely chopped shallots simmered in ½ pint (1 cup) red wine until reduced by half. To this is added 3 tablespoons meat glaze or jelly worked into 6 oz. (⅔ cup) soft butter. Finally 1 tablespoon parsley and 1 tablespoon lemon juice are added, the whole is then seasoned, and served with steak.

beurre meunière, butter melted to a light brown, to which lemon juice is then added.

beurre nantais, a French sauce served with fish or poultry. It consists of ½ pint (1 cup) dry white wine with 1 very finely chopped shallot and seasoning boiled until it is reduced to 2 tablespoons. It is removed from the heat and about ½ lb. (1 cup) butter cut into small cubes is beaten in. It must be very thoroughly beaten over very low heat, and not allowed to get oily.

beurre noir, French for black butter. It is made from ¼ lb. (½ cup) butter melted until it is brown but not burnt, and mixed with 2 tablespoons wine vinegar. Sometimes capers, with a little of the juice instead of vinegar, and parsley are also added. It is used chiefly with skate, brains, and eggs cocotte.

beurre noisette, butter heated until it is a light nut-colour, with juice of 1 lemon then added. It is served with fish and

veal. It can also be butter made from the oil obtained from hazelnuts.

beurre noix, walnut butter, made from oil obtained from the nuts.

beurré, a French dessert pear, of which there are several varieties.

beurré d'Angleterre (ripens September) is olive green with russet patches. It can overripen quickly.

beurré d'aremberg (ripens October–November) is bulbous in shape, and has a yellow skin with russet patches. Sweet and juicy, but it is inclined to be gritty in texture.

beurré clairgeau (ripens October) is a bright yellow colour with a red flush. It has firm flesh but is mediocre to eat.

beurré diel (ripens October) is yellow with a brown flush and a rough skin. Juicy, but it is inclined to be gritty in texture.

beurré giffard (ripens July) has a bulbous shape and is yellow with russet patches.

beurré hardy (ripens September) has a fragrant rose-water flavour. It is a large russet-coloured pear with a red flush, and the flesh is pinkish. It makes excellent eating.

beurrek, see BÖREK.

beurres composés, the French term for knobs of cold fresh butter worked with herbs or other foods and used as a garnish for fish or meat. They are known by the name of the principal ingredient used with the butter. The best known are included here.

beurre aïl, garlic butter.

beurre amande, sweet almond butter.

beurre anchois, anchovy butter.

beurre bercy, shallot butter.

beurre caviar, caviar butter.

beurre chivry, butter worked with shallot, tarragon, chives, and burnet.

beurre colbert, as *beurre maître d'hôtel,* made with tarragon and dissolved meat jelly (glaze).

beurre crevettes, shrimp butter.

beurre de noisettes, butter mixed with pounded and grilled filberts or hazelnuts. It is used to garnish fish and hors d'oeuvre, and also as a final liaison for soups and some white sauces.

beurre de thon, tunny (tuna) fish butter.

beurre de truffes, truffle butter.

beurre écrevisses, freshwater crayfish butter.

beurre estragon, tarragon butter.

beurre hareng, fresh herring butter.

beurre homard, lobster butter.

beurre maître d'hôtel, butter mixed with chopped parsley, pepper, salt, and a little lemon juice. It is used to garnish grilled meat and fish. Sometimes chives are added. When a little tarragon and dissolved meat jelly (glaze) are added, it is known as *beurre colbert.*

beurre moutarde, French mustard and lemon butter.

beurre paprika, paprika and chopped onion butter.

beurre pimenté, butter mixed with finely chopped pimento, salt, and pepper.

beurre printanier, butter mixed with cooked green puréed vegetables.

beurre raifort, horseradish butter.

beurre ravigote, as *beurre chivry.*

beurre rouge, shellfish coral butter.

beurre sardines, sardine butter.

beurre saumon, salmon butter.

beuschel, German for lights (lungs). These are used for a delicious stew in Austria, with root vegetables, grated lemon peel, onion, herbs, and spices. The sauce is thickened with flour, and then 1 tablespoon each of capers and anchovies, 1 teaspoon prepared mustard, sugar, and a squeeze of lemon juice are added. Sour cream is stirred in before serving, and the stew is garnished with dumplings.

bianchetti, a small white fish found especially off the Tuscan coast of Italy, and eaten either fried in *pastella* in a *fritto misto* or sometimes boiled. They resemble whitebait.

biberschwanz, German for beaver's tail, considered a delicacy in Germany. It is usually simmered after skinning and washing, and then dipped in egg and breadcrumbs before frying in hot fat. Thick slices of lemon accompany it. See also BEAVER.

bicarbonate of soda, acid sodium carbonate, $NaHCO_3$, a white powder which is in fact a salt formed when one of the two hydrogen atoms of carbonic acid is replaced by an atom of the metal sodium. Its gentle alkaline action promotes the retention of colour in some green vegetables during cooking, but only a pinch should be added, lest an unpleasant flavour be imparted. It is an important ingredient in Irish soda bread, where the lactic acid in sour milk or buttermilk interacts with it to release carbon dioxide in the dough.

biche, French for female deer.

biefstuk, Dutch for rump steak, which is very popular in Holland. The steak, which should be 2 inches thick, is rubbed with butter and seared on both sides in a very hot pan. It is then seasoned and cooked in more butter over a lower heat, 5 minutes on each side. Gravy is made by pouring a little milk or water into the middle of the pan with the pan juices. When the resulting foam has dispersed, the gravy is poured over the steak and it is served. See also OSSENHAAS.

bien cuit, French culinary term meaning well-cooked. It applies particularly to steak. *Bien asado* is the equivalent Spanish term.

bien me sabe, I. A Puerto Rican pudding made from freshly grated coconut and its milk, 4 egg yolks, 6 oz. (⅔ cup) sugar, and 4 tablespoons water. These are all cooked slowly over hot water, and are served over squares of sponge cake. II. A Spanish pudding, made from 3 egg yolks, ½ lb. (1 cup) sugar, ¼ lb. (1 cup) ground almonds, juice of 1 lemon, 1 teaspoon cinnamon, and 1 pint (2 cups) water. It is all cooked gently over hot water and eaten cold.

bierkaltsuppe, an Austrian and German soup speciality. It is made from light beers cooked with currants, brown breadcrumbs (to thicken), cinnamon, and lemon juice. It is served cold.

bierkäse, see STANGENKÄSE.

bierplinse, German for batter made with dark beer instead of milk; it is used for both sweet and savoury fritters.

biersuppe, a German soup made from 1 quart (4 cups) mild beer thickened with 1 tablespoon potato flour, with a pinch of powdered cinnamon or a ½-inch stick, spices, peel of ½ lemon, salt, and sugar. It is garnished with small pieces of fried bread.

bieslook, Dutch for chive.

biešu sakņu saláti, a Latvian beetroot salad, made from cooked beets skinned and sliced, with caraway seed extract poured over, also sugar, vinegar, or lemon juice. Caraway seed extract is made by pouring boiling water over the seeds and leaving it to stand, covered, until cool. It is then strained for use. This salad is served with hot or cold meats. See also BEETROOT.

bieten, Dutch for beetroot. In Holland this vegetable is commonly sold cooked; otherwise the Dutch housewife will boil it in water until the skin can be easily pulled off. The time taken varies according to the season. It may take up to 2 hours in winter and only about half as long in summer. After cooking, the beet is thinly sliced and stewed with chopped, sliced onions, cloves, and salt in a white sauce (made with part milk and part water). After about 20 minutes, when the dish is ready, the cloves are removed and a dash of vinegar added. See also BEETROOT.

bieten met appelen, a Dutch dish of sliced cooked beetroot, onion, apples, butter, and nutmeg. All are cooked together until reduced to a pulp, and served with hot or cold meats.

bietole, Italian for leaves of the beetroot, which are used for stuffing ravioli and soups in Italy.

bife, Portuguese for beef. *Bifes* is beefsteak.

bifes com ovos, a national dish which consists of thin slices of beefsteak fried very slowly in garlic butter and served with heaped scrambled eggs mixed with chives and added salt on top.

bifes de cebolada, braised steak and onions with a sauce of tomato, garlic, and white wine.

bifes de fígado, "liver steaks," calf's liver cooked in butter with smoked ham, onion, garlic, and eggs on top.

biff, Norwegian for beefsteak. Minced steak is much used in Norway in the preparation of meatballs. See also KJØTT; MEDISTERKAKER; OKSE.

biffkaker med saus, one of the various methods of cooking meatballs with gravy. Dried breadcrumbs (½ cup for every 1 lb. of meat) are soaked for 10 minutes in cream, when minced steak and pork, together with a beaten egg and seasoning, are stirred in. Minced onions are fried in butter, and all are well blended together. Small balls are shaped and fried in butter until evenly brown, but only half cooked. A gravy is made from a roux of flour and the pan juices mixed with boiling water and seasoning. The balls are simmered slowly in this gravy for 15 minutes.

biff, Swedish for beefsteak.

hackad biff med lök, beef cakes with onions. Well minced chuck steak is mixed with minced onion and seasoning, and the mixture is shaped into cakes which are fried in butter.

bifinhos de vitela, a Portuguese dish of slices of veal cooked in butter with a little port wine added to the pan juices.

bifshtek, Russian for beefsteak. Perhaps the Russian beef dish best known all over the world is stroganoff, in which only the best steak is used, with mushrooms, onions, and sour cream. See also BEEF STROGANOFF; BITKI.

bifteck, I. A French word taken from the English beefsteak, which means a slice of beef taken from either the fillet, sirloin, or *contre-filet.* It is usually grilled or fried, and can be cooked as Chateaubriand, *contre-filet,* or *entrecôte,* and served with garnishes appropriate to them. II. The word also applies to minced beef served raw or cooked.

bifteck à cheval, beef seasoned and sautéed in hot butter. It does not mean horsemeat. This dish is served with pan juices and garnished with 1 or 2 fried eggs on top.

bifteck à l'Américaine, finely chopped or minced lean beefsteak (no fat at all can be left), seasoned and shaped into a circle. A small well is made in the middle, and a raw egg yolk put in. The plate is garnished with chopped raw onion, parsley, and capers; a little worcestershire sauce is sprinkled on top. The egg is mixed into the raw beef, and the dish is eaten raw. This is also known as steak tartare in France, Britain, and the U.S., although the classic bifteck à la tartare omits the egg yolk, and serves *sauce tartare* separately.

bifteck à l'Andalouse, minced beefsteak, with a little chopped onion lightly fried in butter and garlic. Shaped into flat cakes, rolled in flour and fried in oil. Garnished with pilaf of rice mixed with pan juices diluted with sherry, and a sautéed tomato on each cake.

bifteck à la Russe, as above, but pan juices are diluted with demi-glace and sour cream. The cakes are garnished with pale fried onion. Sometimes a fried egg replaces the onion. See also BITKI.

bifteck à la tartare, see BIFTECK À L'AMÉRICAINE.

bigarade, French for Seville orange. See ORANGE.

bigarade, sauce, a French orange sauce made with the peel of 2 Seville oranges (*Citrus aurantium*) together with 1 table-spoon sugar, ½ pint (1 cup) duck stock, 2 tablespoons demi-glace, 1 tablespoon each butter and flour made into a roux, and a squeeze of lemon juice. It is served with duck.

bigarreau, a French variety of hard-fleshed cherry. There are red and white varieties. It is excellent to eat, and varieties are extensively grown in both the United Kingdom and the U.S.

bighorn (*Ovis canadensis*), a wild sheep found in the Rocky Mountains, U.S. It is best when eaten in the autumn; at other times of the year it is tough and tasteless. It is not eaten too much in the U.S. any season. It can be prepared and cooked in all ways that are suitable for mutton.

bigné, a kind of fritter eaten in Rome on St. Joseph's Day, March 19. They are made by heating ½ pint (1 cup) water, 3 heaped tablespoons butter, and a pinch of salt. When it boils 6 oz. (1½ cups) flour is added altogether, stirring well with a wooden spoon until the dough leaves the side of the saucepan. It is cooled a little, then three beaten egg yolks are added one by one. Then 1 teaspoon each grated lemon and orange peel are added and finally the beaten egg whites. They can either be fried in small balls in oil or baked on a greased baking sheet in a hot oven for about 10 minutes. They are eaten hot sprinkled with vanilla sugar.

bigoli in salsa, see PASTA ASCIUTTA; VERMICELLI.

bigorneaux, French for periwinkles.

bigos, a national Polish dish, which is a great favourite on shooting expeditions, since it will keep for weeks and can be heated up easily over a wood fire. It consists of sauerkraut, cooked meat, game, pork sausages, apples, ham, lard, flour, tomato essence, onions, vodka, and red or white wine. All these ingredients are put in layers into a casserole, covered with the wine and spirit, then simmered gently. It is said to improve with reheating.

bijane, a cold soup, popular in the Anjou region of France. It consists of crumbled bread steeped in sweetened red wine.

biksemad, a Danish method of using up leftover meat by fry-ing it up with sliced onions, potatoes, and gravy. The word means "useful mixture."

bilberry (*Vaccinium myrtillus*), a low-growing shrub, found in woods and heaths, chiefly in hilly districts in Great Britain, Ireland, northern continental Europe, and Asia. The berries, ripening in July and August, are dark blue with a waxy bloom. They are also known as blaeberry, whortleberry, and hurtleberry. They are a delicious fruit, and can be eaten raw with cream and sugar, or made into pies and tarts.

The Irish weave a special rush basket called *fruog* in prepa-ration for picking the fruit on Fraughan Sunday; brooms and whisks are made from the branches. In parts of County Down, and in the Clogher Valley, Tyrone, Northern Ireland, the first Sunday in August is known as "bilberry or blaeberry Sun-day," and a pilgrimage is made to Slieve Bloom with pipe music to pick the fruit. In the Hebrides dried bilberry leaves were sometimes used for making tea. See also BLÅBÆR; BLÅBÄR; JAGODOWA.

bindenfleisch, a Swiss method of serving air-dried (not sun-dried) beef, scraped into very thin wafers and dressed with oil and vinegar. It is eaten as an hors d'oeuvre. Sometimes called *bündnerfleisch* or *bündnerteller.*

bird's nest soup, a soup which, although it originated in China, is now drunk a great deal in Europe. It is made from the dried nests of the Salangane swallow. This bird feeds on a very gelatinous seaweed like agar-agar or goémon which is regurgitated to make the nests, and these are dried, and ex-ported all over the world. They make a wonderful strong clear soup and are usually added to a rich beef consommé flavoured with basil and madeira wine.

Birdseye, Clarence, a American scientist and explorer who,

bilberry

while trapping in Labrador in 1924, noted that fish caught from holes in the ice tasted very fresh, although they might have been trapped there for several months. This discovery led him to make experiments, and finally to pioneer quick deep freezing as we know it today. His name is given to a large concern dealing in frozen foods. See also DEEP FREEZ-ING.

bird's-foot trefoil (*Lotus corniculatus*), a small plant with a yellow spiky flower which grows wild in Britain and Europe. It has over 70 nicknames in Britain alone, and a very sweet smell. The seed-pods, four to six per head, resemble claws, and this acquired magical properties for the little plant in ear-lier times. It is still used as an herb in France. See also LO-TIER.

birne, German for pear, often used for soup in Germany as well as for a dessert.

bischofsbrot, "bishop's bread," an Austrian biscuit (cake) made in various ways but usually consisting of 3 separated eggs, 8 oz. (1 cup) sugar, and 8 oz. (1¾ cups) flour mixed together, with the stiffly beaten whites added last; then 2 oz. (½ cup) each of chopped dried figs, walnuts, dates, almonds, hazelnuts and candied peel are included, and juice and peel of ½ lemon. Sometimes chocolate and glacé cherries are also added. The mixture is put into an oblong tin and baked in a moderate oven for about 45 minutes; when cold it is sliced.

biscotte, French for rusk.

biscuit, I. From the Old French *bescoit,* a flat cake of unlea-vened bread, made from flour, fats, and eggs. Biscuits can be sweet, in which case they contain sugar and spices, or what are known as "dry" biscuits, which are savoury and are sometimes eaten with cheese. In the U.S. they are also called crackers when unsweetened. II. In France biscuit also means an iced sweet cut to resemble a biscuit.

biset, I. French name for a rock pigeon, which is a wild pigeon, smaller than the wood pigeon and slate grey in co-lour. It is prepared and cooked as pigeon. See also SQUAB. II. It is also the name given in France to a wading bird not unlike a wild duck.

biskuitschöberi-suppe, Austrian biscuit soup made with very rich beef broth. The biscuit, which is used as a garnish, is made by mixing 1 oz. (1 heaped tablespoon) butter, 1 egg yolk, 1 oz. (1 heaped tablespoon) flour, 2 tablespoons milk, a pinch of nutmeg and salt; the stiffly beaten egg white is folded in last. The mixture is baked in a flat, well-greased tin, and when cooked is cut into lozenge shapes which are served with the broth.

bismarckheringe, German for bismarck herrings, which are also eaten extensively in Great Britain and the U.S. The her-rings are scaled, cleaned, and soaked overnight in vinegar.

The next day they are filleted, topped, and tailed, and arranged in a deep dish. They are seasoned and a little sliced onion is added. These layers are repeated until all the herrings are used up. They are left for 24 hours before eating.

bismarck herrings, see BISMARCKHERINGE.

bismarck-schnitzel, see SCHNITZEL.

bismarck-suppe, a strong consommé slightly thickened with arrowroot and flavoured with port. It is garnished with diced mushrooms and grated cheese.

bison (*Bison bonasus*), the European bison, and (*B. bison*), the American bison, commonly called buffalo. They are both large, shaggy ox-like quadrupeds with short horns and low, heavy forequarters. They used to roam in large herds over Europe and North America; now there are only a very few in Europe, confined to Lithuania and the Polish plains, and in North America there are only about 5,000, most of which are found on the National Wildlife Refuges.

Buffalo steak is comparable to beef, but perhaps not the very best beef. The hump and tongue are also considered good. It is found profitable to raise buffalo for the market in the U.S. because of the universal desire to taste the once staple diet of the American Indians. It is best cooked in the same manner as reindeer, and the use of sour cream and wine for the sauces or gravies enhances the flavour. *Pemmican* was made from strips of sun-dried bison rump.

bisque, nowadays the French name for a thick soup made from any kind of shellfish. It consists of 1 quart (4 cups) white stock flavoured with ¼ pint (½ cup) white wine or sherry, 2 fresh tomatoes, 1 lb. (2 cups) pounded cooked shellfish, 2 egg yolks to thicken, ¼ pint (½ cup) cream, and 2 tablespoons brandy. The most famous are those made from lobster (bisque de homard), shrimps (bisque de crevettes), and crabs (bisque de crabes). In the 18th century this soup was not made exclusively from shellfish but also from game, such as pigeon, quail, or poultry, and not puréed, but cooked with crusty bread boiled to a pulp and served with it. In 1758, in *Dons de Comus*, it is described as a quail soup garnished with puréed crayfish. A note says: "All that is bisque must settle on the bottom of the plate, and form a gratin." Therefore it is thought that the bisque meant the puréed meat or bird, and breadcrumbs.

bistec, Spanish for beefsteak.

bistecca, Italian for beefsteak. The finest beef in Italy comes from Tuscany, especially the area around Florence. See also VITELLONE.

bistecca alla Siciliana, a Sicilian method of serving a beefsteak, which is cooked quickly in a hot pan and served with stoned black olives, pickled green peppers, tomato, capers, and a finely chopped heart of celery which has been fried lightly in olive oil, all seasoned with marjoram, fennel, salt, and pepper.

bistecca Fiorentina, Florentine beefsteak. It is very large, and the cut resembles a porterhouse. It is rubbed on both sides with black pepper and a little olive oil, and left to marinate for about 1 hour. It is then, ideally, grilled to taste over charcoal; if charcoal is not available, gas or electricity will do, but the flavour will not be the same. It is served with wedges of lemon, and salt to taste.

bistecchine, see VITELLONE.

bístola de roca, a Spanish fish called forkbread in English, belonging to the cod family (*Gadidae*), although it also lives in fresh water. It is like the French *lotte* and is good to eat, the liver being particularly esteemed. See also BURBOT.

bistort (*Polygonum bistorta*), a perennial plant with astringent properties, so named from its twisted roots. It is also called snakeweed and adderwort. It has pink flowers, and is used in traditional Easter puddings in Britain. In continental alpine regions, the young leaves are eaten as spinach.

bita śmietana, sour cream whipped with sugar flavoured with vanilla pods, and used in Poland with rice and soft fruit.

bitki, traditional Russian and Polish meatballs, usually made from raw minced beef with fried onions, butter, salt, pepper, and milk-soaked breadcrumbs (approximately 1 lb. meat to ½ cup breadcrumbs). They are shaped into balls, floured, then grilled or fried, and served with sour cream and potatoes. Sometimes they are made with minced veal or lamb inside the minced beef or with a little pounded salt herring or anchovy added as a flavouring. They are sometimes used as a garnish for *borsch*.

bitki carnot, veal forcemeat mixed with butter, eggs, and bread which has been soaked in water and shaped into flat, round cakes. (The proportion of bread to meat is as given above.) These are then indented in the centres and filled with purée of goose liver covered with forcemeat. They are poached, and when cool, are coated with thick sauce mornay, then dipped in egg and breadcrumbs and deep fried. They are served with pommes pailles (potato straws) and buttered green peas. Tomato sauce is served separately.

bitki novgorodskie, a Russian regional dish. The cakes are prepared as for *carnot*, but filled with raw chopped beef. They are fried in butter and served covered in fried onion rings, in a sauce madère. Thick fried potatoes are served separately.

bitki po kazatski, indented round cakes are prepared as for *carnot*, but are filled with scrambled eggs flavoured with chopped truffle. They are lightly poached, and when cool are dipped in egg and breadcrumbs, then fried. They are served on oval croûtons, smothered in tomato sauce, with thin slices of truffle on top.

bitki po russki, raw chopped beef is mixed with chopped fried onions and soaked white bread. Salt and pepper are added, and the mixture is shaped into small flat cakes and fried in butter. These are placed in a baking dish with a border of sliced boiled potatoes, and the whole is covered with thick sour cream sauce sprinkled with breadcrumbs and grated Parmesan cheese. It is placed in the oven to brown. This dish is sometimes made with veal.

bitki skobelev, flattish indented cakes, as for *carnot*. The stuffing is made with salpicon of ham, ox tongue, mushrooms, and truffle. They are deep fried, covered with truffle sauce, and served with a separate dish of braised shredded lettuce mixed with buttered peas, surrounded with mashed potatoes.

bitki tatarskie, chopped raw beef is mixed with egg yolks (1 lb. beef to 2 egg yolks), a little butter, and seasonings. This is formed into very small flat cakes which are fried very quickly on both sides in butter, taking care that the insides remain rare. They are served in the pan in which they are cooked, with separate dishes of boiled potatoes and lettuce salad.

bits, the local name for a common herb believed to be found only in North Cornwall. It is found in the hedges and on the cliffs, and often used in an herb, bacon, and onion Cornish pasty. Gypsies in those parts use it for medicinal purposes.

bitterballen, sharp-flavoured Dutch meatballs. Worcestershire sauce to taste, 1 minced onion, 1 tablespoon chopped parsley, and a pinch of grated nutmeg are mixed with 1 lb. cooked, chopped meat and salt, and all cooked together in a thick white sauce. When the mixture is cool, small balls are formed, rolled in breadcrumbs, then dipped in egg yolk mixed with 2 tablespoons water before being once more rolled in the crumbs. The balls are then deep fried in fat, and are eaten hot, with mustard, as appetizers with drinks.

bittern (*Botaurus stellaris*), a nocturnal water-bird highly prized as food in England during the 16th and 17th centuries;

they used to cost three times as much as chicken. The long claw of the spur was thought to preserve the teeth, and was much sought after as a toothpick. Its flesh is said to have resembled hare, and they were roasted with ginger and pepper. The bittern migrates in winter to India and tropical Africa, and there is a relative bird (*B. poiciloptilus*) in Australia and (*B. lentiginosus*) in North America.

bitto, an Italian cheese from Lombardy, made from a mixture of cow's and goat's milk.

bizcocho, a Spanish spongecake, made from 3 separated eggs, 2 tablespoons sugar, 4 heaped tablespoons flour, a pinch of baking powder, and 1 heaped tablespoon butter. The yolks are beaten with the sugar, then the flour and baking powder alternately with the melted butter. Finally the stiffly beaten egg whites are folded in and the mixture is poured into a flat greased tin and baked for 15 minutes in a hot oven.

bizet, a French chicken consommé, thickened with tapioca and garnished with tiny chicken quenelles mixed with chopped tarragon. It is sprinkled with chopped chervil and served with small *profiteroles* filled with a *brunoise* of vegetables. See also CONSOMMÉ.

bjørnebaer, Norwegian for blackberry.

blåbaer, Norwegian for bilberry or blaeberry.

blåbaerpannekake, bilberry pancake. These pancakes are made as in *pannenkake* (using a little less milk). Fresh or tinned bilberries are stirred into the batter. Castor sugar is sprinkled on each pancake, and they are served in layers, one on top of another, to form one cake.

blåbaersuppe, Norwegian bilberry soup. Bilberries, cold water, castor sugar, and lemon peel are brought to boiling point and simmered. A little of this mixture is mixed with cornflour (cornstarch) which has previously been blended with cold water (proportions are 1 tablespoon to 1 pint of the juice); salt is added, and all ingredients brought to the boil together. This soup needs to be well stirred until slightly thick, when it is ready to serve.

blåbär, Swedish for bilberry or blaeberry.

blåbärsglass, bilberry ice cream. Crushed bilberries are rubbed through a sieve and heated slightly. Then sugar is added to taste, and when the latter is dissolved, a little vanilla essence (extract) is added. The whole is chilled, and twice the quantity of sweetened whipped cream is stirred in. After flavouring to taste, the mixture is part frozen before being well beaten and returned to the freezing compartment.

black bass, see BASS; PERCH.

black bryony (*Tamus communis*), a climbing weed of the gourd family, common in England and native to Europe and western Asia. The young shoots are edible, but must be soaked for a few hours before boiling in salted water. They are then served hot with hot melted butter sauce, or cold with an oil and vinegar dressing. The bright red berries are poisonous, but are used for making certain drugs.

black bun, see SCOTCH CURRANT BUN.

black cumin (*Nigella sativa*), a plant grown in the East and also in the Mediterranean region. The seeds are used as spice and can also be used instead of pepper. It grows freely in Britain where it is used solely for decorative purposes and is known as "love-in-a-mist." The bright blue flowers and feathery fennel-like foliage are common in most herbaceous borders. It is also known as fennel flower. (This plant is not to be confused with cumin, which it does not resemble.)

black currant (*Ribes nigrum*), a small fruit-bearing shrub native to northern Europe and northern and central Asia. The small, black, juicy fruit is much esteemed for pies, tarts, jams, and jellies. It is also good for sore throats and is used in pastilles and lozenges. It is high in vitamins C and B. The best-known English varieties are Baldwin, Laxton, Seabrook, and Boskoop. It is also cultivated to a lesser extent in Canada

and the U.S. The white currant and red currant are of the same family, and are more popular in the U.S.

black currant

black diamond, see CANADIAN CHEDDAR.

black duck (*Anas rubripes*), also a name given in the U.S. to the mallard duck (*A. platyrhynchos*).

black game, see BLACKCOCK.

black grouse, see BLACKCOCK.

black jack damsons, see DAMASCENES.

black pepper, see PEPPER.

black pots, see GERTY MEAT PUDDINGS.

black pudding, also known as blood pudding, is one of the earliest puddings ever made and exists all over Europe and in the British Isles in only slightly varying forms. Old manuscripts depict the winter pigkilling and the making of black pudding from the pig's blood. It is about 1½ inches wide and 18 inches long. Originally it was made not only from pig's blood and suet, as it is today, but also with oatmeal, liver, and herbs, mixed with the cooled blood of either sheep or pig. The mixture was put in casings of membrane and shaped like a horseshoe. It still exists in that form, but with the increased use of plastic casings the sausage is often straight. In England and Ireland it is usually served fried with bacon and potatoes, but in France, Italy, and Spain it is often simmered with stock and served with cooked dried beans. In Germany, hot potato salad sometimes accompanies it. In Ireland it is still served traditionally for Sunday breakfast with bacon. See also BOUDIN; DRISHEEN; MORCILLA; PALTEN; VERIPALTTU.

black radish, see RADISH.

black radish preserve (Russian style), a traditional Jewish jam eaten during Passover. Although eaten particularly in Russia, it is also popular with Jews of all nationalities. It consists of black radishes, water, honey, sugar, slivered almonds, and ginger. It is made with 3 lb. of cleaned radishes cut into strips like julienne potatoes, covered with water, brought to the boil, and cooked for 10 minutes. Then they are drained and covered with fresh water. They are brought to the boil again, cooked for 10 minutes, and drained well. Then 1 lb. (2 cups) each of honey and sugar are added while the mixture is hot, and the pan is shaken well to distribute the sugar. The contents are cooked for a further 10 minutes till honey and sugar are dissolved; the cooking is continued till the whole is absorbed, and the mass is a heavy preserve with a rich brown colour. Then 1 cup slivered almonds and 3 tablespoons ground ginger are added a little at a time. The preserve is turned into glasses, or stored in an earthenware jar until wanted.

black raspberry (*Rubus occidentalis*), a species of raspberry native to the eastern U.S., especially New England. The fruit is quite black when ripe, and highly thought of. Locally it is known as blackcap.

black treacle, see MOLASSES.

blackberry (family *Rosaceae*), also called bramble, a prickly stemmed, wild fruit-bearing bush, a native of the temperate regions all over the world. The berry ripens in September and October, and in Ireland it is thought bad to eat them after Halloween (October 31), owing to the witches having done something unmentionable to them. They are one of the few fruits better wild than cultivated, for the latter are acid. The best cultivated blackberry is the Himalaya giant, which is good for preserving. They are good eaten raw with cream and sugar and also are used extensively for pies, tarts, jams, and jellies. Blackberry wine is also made. In earlier days they were used for dyes; navy blue and indigo originally came from blackberry juice, and when black was needed, the berries were mixed with ivy leaves and boiled. The ''pale lavender ribbons'' of the girls of the 18th century came from blackberry juice. During the Industrial Revolution in England they were used instead of currants in cakes and buns, and the very poor cooked them with parsnips or sugar beets to sweeten them. A ''tea'' was also made from the tips of the dried young leaves. See also BROMBAER.

blackbird (*Turdus merula*), a song bird of the thrush family, known in Old English as ousel and in French as *merle*. In France and Corsica they are a well-known food speciality, being usually served in a pâté or a terrine. They were highly thought of as food in England until the late 19th century. They are also served grilled in France. Mrs. Beeton has a recipe for blackbird pie made with chopped steak and hard-boiled eggs, the little birds having first been stuffed with minced veal.

blackcap, see BLACK RASPBERRY.

blackcock (*Lyrurus tetrix*), also known as heathcock, black game, and black grouse, a bird of the *Tetraonidae* family related to the capercaillie and the red grouse. The plumage of the male bird is a deep glossy black, with white patches on the wing, and curved tail feathers. The female is known as the grey-hen. In France it is known as coq de bruyère. It is distributed over the highland districts of north and central Europe, and also central and northern Asia. An allied species, *L. mlokosiewiczi*, inhabits the Caucasian Mountains. In England they are at their best for eating from October to December when adult male birds weigh about 4 lb.; the hen is about half that weight. They are roasted, casseroled, or made into pies, as for grouse, which they resemble in taste, but do not equal in popularity as a food. See also CIETRZEW.

black-eye(d) bean, another name for asparagus bean, used in the southern U.S.

black-eye(d) pea, another name for cow pea, used in the southern U.S.

blackfin, American name for chub.

blackfish, a collective name given to various dark or black fishes. In England it is *Centrolophus niger*, a perch-like fish. In the U.S. it is usually a fish called also tautog (*Tautaga onitis*), which is good for eating. It is found on the eastern seaboard. In Alaska it is *Dallia pectoralis*, a small freshwater fish which can live after having been frozen in rivers for a long time. In Australia it is the name given to *Girella simplex*.

blackman, see YELLOWMAN.

black-throated diver (*Colymbus arcticus*), a fish-eating bird which breeds in Scotland and also in the U.S. It is inferior to the wild duck but can be prepared for the table in the same way. It is also known as arctic loon.

bladder, a membranous bag from animals (usually pigs) after slaughter. Well washed, it is often used to cook certain dishes in, especially in France. See also CANETON (CANETON ROUENNAIS EN CHEMISE).

bladsalat, Norwegian for lettuce; also *hodesalat*.

bladselleir, Danish for celery.

blaeberry, see BILBERRY.

blanc, French culinary word for several preparations and methods of cooking. I. A mixture of flour and water used to cook brains, sweetbreads, or certain vegetables. II. A court-bouillon, especially one with cultivated mushrooms added. III. A white stock based on veal or chicken. IV. To define the breast of poultry on a menu, as blanc de volaille, etc. V. To describe a light (not necessarily white) colour, as blanc de Dijon, for a light-coloured mustard.

blanch, to prepare various foods by plunging them into boiling water. (It is a preliminary process used each with a specific function depending on the food.) I. To skin nuts by pouring boiling water over the shelled nuts in order to soften the husk. II. To boil in salted water some green vegetables in order to par-cook them. III. To bring to the boil in salted water certain offal (variety meats), such as brains or sweetbreads, in order to cleanse and harden the membranous skin so that removal is easier. Also applies to tomatoes, peaches, etc., to make them easy to peel. IV. To bring to the boil in water, pork fat, cut in large dice, in order to extract the salt before frying.

blanchaille, French for whitebait.

blanchir, French verb meaning to blanch.

blancmange, from Old French *blancmanger* (white food), an opaque jelly made from isinglass, gelatine, or cornflour and milk. It can be flavoured with fruit essences, chocolate, or coffee. It can also be made with carrageen moss. In the 17th century blancmange could mean calf's foot jelly or other jellies made from white meat, and they were decorated with bright scarlet geraniums or maidenhair fern. See also BLAUN-DESORYE.

blandet geitost, see GEITOST.

blandita(s), see TORTILLA.

blanquet, a variety of French pear. There are two kinds, the large and the small, and they both ripen in late July. They are not very highly prized, and are used mainly for compotes.

blanquette, a French method of cooking veal in particular, but also used for young lamb, chicken, or sweetbreads. The meat is diced, and simmered with an onion stuck with cloves, carrot, leek, bouquet garni, salt, pepper, and white stock or water to cover. This is cooked for 1½ hours. The strained stock is then thickened with a roux or sauce velouté and slightly reduced. The meat is sautéed with cooked button onions and mushrooms for 15 minutes and combined with the hot sauce, which has been thickened with 2 egg yolks mixed with ¼ pint (½ cup) cream. The whole is finally seasoned with a pinch of nutmeg and a squeeze of lemon juice, heated, but not allowed to reboil lest it curdle, and served with croûtons of bread fried in butter, or boiled rice.

Fricassee is made in the same way, but the meat or poultry is first slightly sautéed in butter. Vegetables such as celeriac, cucumber, lettuce, leeks, etc., are served as a garnish.

Blarney cheese, a comparatively new Irish cheese made from cow's milk. It is a good cheese for both eating and cooking. It is made in a large round shape and has a bright red rind similar to an Edam cheese. In taste it is like a cross between a good Edam and an emmentaler. The paste is a pale yellow, with occasional holes scattered throughout. It deserves to be better known in Europe. See also CÁIS.

blåskjell, Norwegian for mussels, often marinated in vinegar with dill.

blätterteig, German for puff pastry, which is used extensively in Germany for many elaborate cream pastries, as well as for savoury dishes.

blaufisch, ''blue fish,'' a German method of cooking almost any freshwater fish, which gives it a blue shimmer. The fish is not scaled, but boiling tarragon or wine vinegar is poured over it, and it is left to stand in a cool place for 10–15 minutes. Afterwards it is gently poached in fish stock and served with melted butter. Salmon, trout, carp, pike, eel, and also herrings and mackerel are often cooked in this way. It is the German equivalent of the French au bleu. See also CARP.

blaukraut, a German method of cooking shredded red cabbage with 1 tablespoon caraway seeds, 4 apples, 1 gill (½ cup) wine vinegar, 2 tablespoons sugar, 2 large onions, and 1 pint (2 cups) water. It is cooked for at least 2½ hours, or until tender, and is usually served with game.

blaundesorye, a medieval English dish consisting of curd mixed with minced white meat and almonds. It is probably an early form of *blancmange*.

blawn fish, a traditional fish dish from the Orkney Islands. Blawn means "wind-blown." Either haddock, codling, whiting, or other white fish is used fresh from the sea, cleaned, skinned, and rubbed with salt. To prepare, the eyes are removed and a string passed through the eye sockets. Then it is hung for 1 day in a passage where there is a current of air; the next day it is taken down, rolled in a little flour, and grilled under a slow grill with a little butter. Saithe is also prepared in this way.

blazinde moldoveneşti, Rumanian cheesecakes, made from puff pastry squares filled with a mixture of 1 lb. (2 cups) creamed cottage cheese, 2 egg yolks, 3 tablespoons sugar, and a pinch of salt. The pastry is folded over on top, sealed with water, brushed over with egg yolk, and baked until it is golden.

blé noir, French for buckwheat, also called *gruau de Sarrasin*, Saracen corn. See BUCKWHEAT; SARRASIN.

bleak (*Alburnus lucidus*), a slender, silvery fish of the carp family (*Cyprinidae*), found in many rivers in Europe. It can be cooked in any way as for sprat. The scales are used in France for the manufacture of pearls.

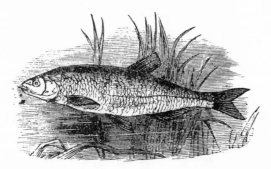

bleak

bleie, SEE BRACHSE.

blennie cagnette, French for a genus of European freshwater fish of the *Blenny* family, most of which are seafishes, a suborder of *Percomorphi*. It has no scales and is about 6 inches long. It is very plentiful in rivers of the Hérault department, where fishermen also call it lièvre and chasseur. The flesh is white and quite good in flavour. It is usually fried, but is also used in a matelote.

blenny, see BLENNIE CAGNETTE.

blette, French name for chard or spinach beet. See POIRÉE.

bleu, au, I. A French culinary term applied to freshwater fish, mainly trout. The fresh fish is plunged into a boiling court-bouillon with vinegar added; sometimes it is soaked in vinegar first. This gives the skin of the fish a blueish colour. It is then simmered until cooked and served with hot melted butter. II. When applied to meat, the term means "blue," that is, very rare. This applies particularly to steak.

bleu d'Auvergne, a French cow's milk cheese from the

Laqueuille and Dores mountains of Auvergne. It has been made only for the last hundred years or so, since the farmers of those districts have begun to imitate the technique used for Roquefort, and to inoculate their cheese with *penicillium glaucum*. The cheese has no crust or rind. Bleu fermier, made in the Cère and Jordanne valleys, is the most important bleu d'Auvergne. The commercial bleus d'Auvergne are made from May to October but are not sold until the following year.

bleu de basillac, a French blue-mould cheese of the Roquefort type. It is made in the Limousin and is in season from November to May.

bleu de Bresse, a fairly recent French cheese made from cow's milk, having a blue-mould vein and containing 50% fat in the dry substance. It comes from the Ain district. It is formed into small rounds about 4 inches across, and is strong, creamy, and good to eat. In common with many French blue cheeses, it does not travel well and spoils easily if kept too long. It is in season all year round. Also called *Bresse bleu*.

bleu de laqueuille, a French *bleu d'Auvergne* cheese from the Puy-de-Dôme department. It is a rather mild cheese of its type, but it does not keep. It is eaten all year round.

bleu de sassenage, a French cow's milk cheese, blue-veined, made chiefly in the Isère department. It is semi-hard, and resembles *gex* cheese in flavour and texture.

bleu du haut-jura, see GEX.

bleu fermier, see BLEU D'AUVERGNE.

bleu naturel de L'aveyron, a French blue-veined cheese made only in small quantities in the Millau and Sainte-Affrique districts. It is one of the best of its type.

blewitt, alternative name for *bluet*.

blinchki s tvorogom, a Russian cheese dish consisting of small, thin pancakes cooked on one side only and rolled up, with a mixture of 1 lb. (2 cups) *tvorog* (curd), 2 egg yolks, 3 tablespoons sugar, 1 grated lemon or orange peel, 2 tablespoons melted butter, 1 tablespoon sultanas, and salt. The filling is put onto the fried side of the pancake. Then it is folded up like an envelope, brushed with egg white, and fried in butter until golden brown all over. These pancakes are very popular in Russia and are sometimes served with meat or eaten instead of cheese.

blind, bake, to bake blind means to bake a pastry shell or flan empty. The bottom is well pricked with a fork and sometimes dried beans or rice are put in to stop the pastry from rising. When cooked, the pastry case is filled with whatever ingredients are desired. This is the way it is done in Britain and the U.S. The method in France is eminently more practical. The pastry is laid over a flan tin that has been placed upside down. In this way no pricking or other means of stopping the bottom of the pastry from rising is necessary. When cooked, the pastry case is merely turned right way up and filled when cool.

blinde vinken, a Dutch dish of stuffed veal fillets. Thin slices of veal, cut from the round, are rolled around a boiled egg or, as alternative stuffings, fried onions mixed with chopped parsley, or ground veal mixed with egg, white bread (softened in milk), seasoning, and nutmeg. The rolls are secured and browned in butter; a little water and lemon slices are added to the pan, which should be covered, and the rolls are simmered until tender for about 45 minutes. Before serving, the rolls are untied.

blintzes or **blinzes**, a Jewish pancake which has its origin in eastern Europe. It is made from flour, egg, salt, and milk, just like an ordinary pancake. Depending on the filling to be used, water sometimes is used instead of milk for religious reasons. It is fried on one side only, then filled with either cream cheese, cottage or pot cheese (or a combination); apple and cinnamon, fruits and preserves; or minced meat. Then it is folded over like an envelope and fried in butter or oil.

blinut, Finnish for bliny, always eaten in Finland at Shrovetide.

bliny, a Russian and Polish yeast pancake, made of half wheat flour and half buckwheat flour, yeast, butter, milk, and eggs. The pancakes are spread with caviar or melted butter and placed one on top of the other until a small pile is made. Blini are always served with sour cream (*smetana*). They used to be eaten a lot in Russia in the carnival time before Lent. The batter uses 1 oz. yeast diluted in 1 pint (2 cups) lukewarm milk, to 1 lb. (4 cups) mixed flours and 4 eggs and 1 oz. (1 tablespoon) melted butter. The batter is left to prove, as in all yeast cookery.

bloater, an English speciality consisting of a herring which is salted and smoked while still closed up, although it is cleaned first. The Yarmouth bloater is thought to be the finest. It is best when fried or grilled, with a knob of butter added at serving time. A popular fish paste called bloater paste is made from filleted, baked, and pounded bloaters mixed with ⅓ of their weight of butter. See also RED HERRING.

bloder, see TOGGENBURGER KASE.

bloemkool, Dutch for cauliflower.

blomkål, Danish, Norwegian, and Swedish for cauliflower. In Denmark and Sweden, cauliflower is often served as a soufflé. See GRÖNSAKER.

blond de veau, French for a concentrated veal broth used for mixing with soups and sauces. It forms a thick jelly when cold, and is invaluable for a chaudfroid or for any sauce which is required to set when cold.

blond de volaille, the same as *fond blond* and as *blond de veau*, but made with chicken. It is often used for braising vegetables such as celery or lettuce. See also FONDS DE CUISINE.

blonde, sauce, a French sauce made from 1 pint (2 cups) sauce velouté beaten with 2 egg yolks, and heated, stirring all the time, until reduced. It is used with white meats and poultry. See also ALLEMANDE.

blondiner, a French word used by the writer Alexandre Dumas to describe frying a sliced onion in butter until it is a pale yellow colour, but not yet brown.

blondir, French culinary term which means to brown very lightly any ingredient fried in butter, oil, or fat.

blondir, faire, the cooking of flour and butter to make a roux.

blood, the red fluid circulating in the veins of higher animals. The blood of the pig and the sheep is used to make black pudding, called boudin in French. The blood of rabbit, hare, goose, and chicken is used to thicken dishes called civets, which must not be heated above 158° F, lest the blood coagulate and the mixture curdle.

blood orange, see ORANGE.

blood pudding, see BLACK PUDDING; DRISHEEN; MORCILLA; PALTEN; VERIPALTTU.

bloodwort (*Rumex sanguineus*), a red-veined variety of dock, used as a potherb and also cooked as spinach or sorrel, or added to those vegetables.

bløtkake, a Norwegian layer-cake made from 4 egg yolks and 4 egg whites, beaten with ½ lb. (1 cup) sugar, then 4 oz. (1 cup) corn flour (cornstarch) and the same of flour. After baking in a slow oven for 45 minutes, it is put on a rack and cooled; when cold it is cut into slices and cream is put between them. It is eaten at the end of the *syttende mai*, the Norwegian Independence Day, May 17, commemorating the signing of the constitution in 1814.

blue Cheshire cheese, begins by being red Cheshire, until spores of *penicillium glaucum* are added which marble the cheese with blue veins. It is a creamy and delicious version of Cheshire cheese, but it is comparatively rare.

blue coco, an alternative name for the *coco bean*.

blue Dorset, an English cheese of the West Country, also known as blue vinny or blue vinid. "Vinny" is a corruption of the old West Country word "vinew," meaning mouldy. It is a white, hard cheese with a bright blue vein running right through like a streak, unlike the all-over marbling of a Stilton. It is made from the skimmed milk of Gloucester-bred cows, and unfortunately is now very difficult to obtain. It was always a farm-made cheese, and the old farms which made it are rapidly disappearing. I have eaten it, locally made, on several occasions and found it extremely good.

blue grouse (*Dendragopus richardsonii*), a large member of the grouse family found in North America. It is native, particularly in the Rocky Mountains, in British Columbia, and from Alberta to Wyoming. On the Mexican border and to the south of it, there is a similar bird called the dusky grouse (*D. obscurus*). It is suitable for use in all recipes for grouse.

blue mold, or blue veined, cheese, the name given in the U.S. to cheeses of the Roquefort type. They are, however, made from cow's milk.

blue vinid, see BLUE DORSET.

blue vinny, see BLUE DORSET.

blue-back, or red, salmon (*Oncorhynchus herka*), a species of salmon similar to quinnat salmon, which inhabits the waters of the Pacific coast. This is not a true salmon, and not so good to eat; it is used largely for canning. It is used extensively on the Atlantic coast of the U.S. in creole cookery. See also DOG SALMON; PACIFIC SALMON; REDFISH.

blueberry (*Vaccinium nitidum*), a small shrub of the *Ericaceae* family which has a genus of over 130 species, some of which are deciduous and others evergreen. The great virtues of the shrub are its small blue-black berries, and the fact that it will grow on the most barren land. It is prolific in Spain, where it is called *arandano*, and also in the U.S. and Canada, where thousands of arid acres are cultivated with this shrub. The fruits are made into pies, tarts, jams, sauces, and are also canned extensively. It is also grown for its ornamental quality, but the fruit is sweet and has a very pleasant flavour. For some unknown reason it is not common in Great Britain, although it was known in Europe by Virgil and Pliny, who mention it. See also MUFFIN.

blueberry grunt, a Nova Scotian speciality made with dough made from ½ lb. (2 cups) flour, 1 heaped tablespoon shortening (butter or margarine), 2 teaspoons baking powder, and approximately ¾ pint (1½ cups) milk (enough to make a soft spongy dough). While the blueberries (1 lb.) are cooking with 6 oz. (⅔ cup) sugar and about ¾ pint (1½ cups) water, spoonfuls of the dough are dropped in, the pan covered, and the whole cooked for 15–20 minutes. It is served hot with cream.

bluefish (*Pomatomus saltatrix*), a medium-sized fish found in the warmer waters of the eastern seaboard of the U.S. and also off Bermuda. It is highly thought of gastronomically and is best baked in the oven with a little white wine and butter, or poached, and served with hot, melted butter and lemon.

bluefort, a fairly recent Dutch blue-veined cow's milk cheese with a distinctive flavour.

bluefort cheese, the trade name of a Canadian "blue" cheese which resembles Roquefort but is made from cow's milk.

bluepoints, see OYSTER.

bluet, blewitt, or bluetail (*Tricholoma personatum*), a kind of mushroom found in the Midlands of England. It has no surface peel and therefore does not dry well. It comes in late September and is best eaten in stews. In taste, it is said to resemble tripe and is therefore excellent cooked with onions. It is called russula or russule in France, where it is very popular.

bluetail, another name for *bluet*.

blumenkohl, German for cauliflower, often made into fritters in Germany.

gebackener blumenkohl, lightly cooked cauliflower baked in cheese and cream sauce.

blunt-snouted Irish char, see CHAR.

blutwürste, see WURST.

boar (*Sus scrofa*), the name given to the male of the domestic pig and, more often, to the male of the wild species of the *Suidae* family. Wild pig is found all over Europe (except in the British Isles, where it is now extinct), Asia, and North Africa. It was introduced into the U.S. from Germany in 1912 and is now plentiful in eastern Tennessee and North Carolina. In culinary terms, boar always means wild boar. Only the young boar is considered good eating and is a delicacy, whether roasted, grilled, braised, or smoked like ham, wherever it is found. In France when under 6 months old it is known as *marcassin;* when between 6 months and a year, *bête de campagne rousse;* when between 1 and 2 years, *bête de campagne.* A boar's head was a festive dish in medieval England, and this still obtains in France, Germany, and Russia. See also CINGHIALE; WILDSCHWEIN.

boar

Mr. Norman Douglas gives the following excellent recipe for wild boar in *Birds and Beasts of the Greek Anthology* (Chapman and Hall, 1928). (Note: 100 grammes is approximately 3¼ oz.)

"Trim saddle of boar and give it a good shape; salt and pepper it, and steep it for 12 to 14 hours in 1 litre of dry white wine, together with the following seasoning: 100 grammes chopped onions, 100 grammes chopped carrots, 2 heads of garlic, 1 head of celery cut in slices, 1 bay leaf, 2 cloves, 10 grammes black pepper, a pinch of parsley and thyme. The saddle should be turned at frequent intervals to absorb the ingredients. Now braise it in a stewpan over a slow fire together with the above vegetables, seasoning, add 100 grammes of butter. Baste the saddle with the liquor in which it was lying and, when this is at an end, with *jus de viande.* The operation should take about two hours, according to the size of the saddle. Then remove from the fire and strain through a sieve the liquor in which it was lying.

"The following hot and thick sauce must meanwhile be held in readiness: Put 30 grammes of sugar into a saucepan and melt brown over the fire; then add a claret-glass of wine-vinegar and bring to the boil. Now add the above strained liquor, together with 25 grammes of roasted pine nuts, 20 grammes each of dried raisins, candied citron peel cut into small squares, and currants (the latter having previously been soaked in water), and 100 grammes of best powdered chocolate. Stir well over the fire. If not sufficiently thick, a little potato flour should be added.

"Serve both as hot as may be. The saddle must be cut in slices immediately, and the sauce poured over the whole. A

single non-assertive vegetable, such as purée of chestnuts or lentils should be served.

"Not a dish for every day some one may remark. Assuredly not. The longer one lives, the more one realises that nothing is a dish for every day. And if anybody will take the trouble to dress a saddle of mutton in the same manner, he will be pleasantly surprised at the result. But I fear we shall go on roasting the beast to the end of time."

bobolink, see REEDBIRD.

bob-white (*Colinus virginianus*), a quail of the genus *Colinus,* found from Canada to Mexico. Its name derives from its call. It is highly thought of as a food and can be prepared as grouse or partridge. It has been introduced into Europe many times, but without success. See also AMERICAN QUAIL.

bocal, a wide-mouthed glass jar used in France for bottling or pickling fruit or vegetables.

bocconcini, an Italian dish which consists of thin slices of veal and ham rolled up with a thin slice of gruyère cheese. These little rolls are fried in butter and served with fresh tomato sauce. It is a variation of *saltimbocca.*

boccone squadrista, an Italian dish of cutlets of fish cooked between two large slices of apple. It is sprinkled with rum and set alight at the moment of serving. It is one of Filippo Marinetti's inventions.

böckling, the Swedish term for a small Baltic herring, which is smoked, and used in many different ways throughout Scandinavia in the preparation of the "cold table." One method is to arrange the herrings in alternate rows with cold scrambled eggs. See also KOLDTBORD; SMÖRGÅSBORD; STRÖMMING.

boczek, Polish for spare ribs.

boczek duszony z kapustą, a traditional dish of beef or pork spare ribs, cabbage, and root vegetables, which are cooked together by braising in stock, and thickening with a roux of butter and flour.

boczek wedzony wypiekany, a traditional dish of boiled, smoked bacon spare ribs and potatoes, parboiled, then sliced and put in layers in an ovenproof dish, covered with sour cream, and baked until cooked.

bodrio, see CALDO.

boerenkool, Dutch for kale.

boerenkool met rookworst, as *boerenkool met worst* but with *rookworst.*

boerenkool met worst, kale with smoked sausage and potatoes, a popular Dutch cold-weather dish. After boiling for about 1 hour the kale is well minced and added, together with fat or lard and salt, to a saucepan containing uncooked potatoes, with water to half cover. It is simmered for about 30 minutes, when the resulting rather dry mixture is mixed well together and served with *rookworst* piled on top.

boeuf, French for beef, which is of excellent quality in France. It is lean and juicy, especially when it comes from charollais cattle, a breed which is now being exported for breeding all over the world. French butchery differs from both English and American. The main methods of cooking are described here.

boeuf à la bordelaise, rump or sirloin is used for this dish. It is marinated overnight in olive oil, with shallots, onion, bay leaf, parsley, and pepper, drained, and roasted with a little butter. Pan juices, after removing excess fat, are mixed with 2 tablespoons butter and 2 tablespoons flour, and well blended; the meat is moistened with strained marinade, 1 tablespoon wine vinegar, and 1 or 2 coarsely chopped gherkins.

boeuf à la bourguignonne, tende de tranche (topside) cut into large squares and marinated for 6–8 hours in ½ pint (1 cup) red wine to barely cover and ⅛ pint (¼ cup) olive oil with a sliced onion, thyme, parsley, salt, and pepper. A slice of salt pork is diced and melted in a heavy pot, and small onions are browned; then both are removed, and the drained, dried beef is sprinkled with flour and sautéed in the fat. When this is blended, the marinade is added, bubbled up, and ½ pint (1 cup) meat stock poured in together with a clove of garlic and a bouquet garni. It is covered tightly and cooked slowly on top of the stove for 2 hours. Then the pork and onion mixture, and some more small onions and mushrooms, are added, and it is cooked for 30 to 45 minutes.

ingredients for boeuf à la bourguignonne

boeuf à la mode, one of the finest beef dishes anywhere in the world. It is superb when served cold. The meat and carrots are set in a soft, natural, wine-and-herb-flavoured jelly, served with a green salad, and perhaps potatoes baked in their skins on a separate plate. It can be served hot, but then it is no different from an *estouffade.* Good beef must be used, preferably *culotte* (rump) or *tende de tranche* (topside) and it should be boned, without gristle, and larded lengthways with seasoned pork fat. For a 5-lb. joint about 4 oz. of pork should be used. Two medium-sized onions are lightly coloured in fat, then the meat. Then 6 tablespoons (¾ cup) warmed brandy is poured over and ignited, followed by ½ pint (1 cup) red or white wine. (Red will give a deeper-coloured and richer jelly.) One split calf's foot, or 2 pig's trotters (feet) are added, parsley, bay leaf, thyme, garlic (1 clove, crushed), salt, pepper, and enough stock or water to barely cover the meat. The lid is *luted,* and all is simmered very slowly for 4 to 5 hours. Carrots are cooked separately and strained. If the dish is to be eaten cold, it is simpler and more efficient to strain off the stock, let it get quite cold, and remove all fat. The beef is thinly sliced and either placed in a deep dish in overlapping slices, or reconstituted, with the carrots arranged around the outside. The jelly is warmed just enough to make it pourable, and spread over the meat and vegetables. The whole dish is left to get cold and jellied. The pig's feet, or calf's foot are the cook's perks, and they are delicious devoured with the fingers, standing up, while admiring the dish of boeuf à la mode. A well-trained dog is useful to dispose of the bones. More conscientious cooks use them for boiling up again, to make more stock. See also BOURGEOISE, À LA.

boeuf bouilli, boiled beef. This is served in many ways in France, the classic dish being pot-au-feu. The cuts used are *gite à la noix, paleron, jarret, plat de côtes,* or *trumeau.* The cold meat, after the first serving, is often reheated or served in the following ways. See also BOUILLI.

BOEUF BOUILLI À LA PROVENÇALE, diced beef browned in butter or oil with lightly fried onions. Five minutes before serving, tomato fondue with chopped garlic is added, boiled up, and all sprinkled with parsley.

BOEUF BOUILLI À LA VINAIGRETTE, thin slices or cubes, sometimes with cold sliced, boiled potatoes added, seasoned with onion, salt, pepper, parsley, olive oil, and vinegar. It is served cold.

BOEUF BOUILLI FROID À LA PARISIENNE, cut in thin slices and served on a long dish surrounded by alternating groups of cooked green beans, peas, carrots, potatoes, tomatoes, hard-boiled eggs, watercress, etc., dressed with sauce vinaigrette, sprinkled with chopped chervil, parsley, and tarragon, and served cold.

BOEUF BOUILLI SAUTÉ À LA LYONNAISE, beef cut into small slices, fried in butter, added to and heated with sliced, fried onions. It is then sprinkled with chopped parsley and a little vinegar which has been shaken round the pan the meat was cooked in.

BOEUF BOUILLI SAUTÉ PARMENTIER, as *lyonnaise* but using potatoes instead of onions.

boeuf en daube, see DAUBE.

boeuf salé et fumé, salt and smoked beef. In Ireland and U.S. salé is called corned beef. In France it is used for pressed beef (boeuf pressé) or as a principal ingredient in a potée.

carbonnade de boeuf, see CARBONNADE.

estouffade de boeuf, a slowly braised dish of tende de tranche (topside) or *tranche grasse* (top rump) browned in butter and the fat from a thick slice of fried, cubed salt pork (in the Languedoc, goose dripping is used), with quartered or small onions, garlic, bouquet garni, salt, and pepper. Red wine and a dash of brandy if possible, and sometimes split pig's trotters (feet) (*pieds de porc*) are added. It is covered and cooked as slowly as possible for about 6–8 hours. It is called *estouffat* in the Languedoc region, and both words come from etuvée, "stoved," i.e., cooked very slowly at the back of the stove.

fricadelles de boeuf, minced raw or cooked (braised or boiled) beef mixed with mashed potatoes, onion, eggs to bind, all seasoned, shaped into flat cakes which are then floured and fried in butter. They are served with sauce piquante or purée of vegetables.

paupiettes de boeuf, see PAUPIETTES.

sautés de boeuf, usually the rump (*culotte*) or centre fillet, which is cut into pieces, seasoned, and sautéed in butter in a *sautoir* (see SAUTER). The outside should be brown, but the inside pink. It is removed, and the pan juices diluted with white or red wine, veal gravy, or demi-glace, and reduced. The meat is reheated, but not boiled, in the sauce. Cream and Madeira (à la crème); red wine and lean bacon (à la bourguignonne); mushrooms sautéed in butter (à la provençale) are alternative sauces.

boeuf strogonoff, see GOVIADINA; BEEF STROGONOFF.

See also AIGUILLETTE; BIFTECK; CONTRE-FILET; HOCHEPOT; MIROTON; POT-AU-FEU; RAGOÛT; TOURNEDOS; and table of beef cuts under BEEF.

bøf, Danish for fillet of beef or beefsteak. See OKSE.

bogavante, Spanish for lobster. See LANGOSTA.

boghvedegrød, a Danish form of porridge made from buckwheat and milk. Butter, beer, sugar, and cinnamon are added to taste.

bogue, a Mediterranean fish, of which two species are known, the common bogue and the bogue saupe. It is a dull yellow on the back, with a silver belly, and is about 14 inches long. It is fried, poached, grilled, and used in bouillabaisse and *matelote.*

bohémienne, I. A French mayonnaise with cream and a little tarragon vinegar added. It is highly seasoned. II. A French garnish composed of pilaf rice, tomatoes, and fried onion rings. III. A French method of serving potatoes. See POMME DE TERRE (POMMES BOHÉMIENNE). IV. A French method of serving chicken. See POULET (POULET SAUTÉ À LA BOHÉMIENNE).

böhmische dalken, an Austrian dough made of 1 lb. (4 cups) flour, five egg yolks, three egg whites, 4 oz. (½ cup) butter, 2 heaped tablespoons sugar, 1 oz.—1 package yeast, 1 gill (½ cup) warm milk, salt, all well mixed, rolled out, and cut into rounds. These are left to rise and the centre is indented with the fingers before baking. When cooked, they are served hot, with either plum jam or red currant jelly in the hollow.

bohnen, German for beans; *grüne bohnen* are french beans.

grüne bohnen mit birnen, french beans cooked with pears. The liquid is thickened with corn flour (cornstarch), and lemon juice is added. It is served with pork.

bohnen (or *linsen*) *mit Backpflauman,* prunes cooked with dried beans. Served with pork, goose, or duck. See also FRANKFURTER BOHNENSUPPE; POMMERSCHE SUPPE; WESTFÄLISCHE BOHNENSUPPE.

boïeldieu, a French chicken consommé garnished with quenelles of foie gras and of chicken, with truffles. See also CONSOMMÉ.

boiled dressing, a type of cooked mayonnaise made from 1 teaspoon salt, 1 teaspoon mustard, 1 tablespoon sugar, cayenne to taste, 2 tablespoons flour, 1 egg, 1½ gills (¾ cup) milk, 2 tablespoons butter, and ⅛ pint (¼ cup) vinegar. The dry ingredients are mixed together, and to these are added the lightly beaten egg, milk, butter, and vinegar (slowly), stirring throughout. The mixture is cooked in a double boiler over boiling water, being constantly beaten, until it thickens. It is then strained and cooled. If bottled, it will keep well in a cold place. See also CHICKEN SALAD DRESSING.

bois de Sainte-Lucie, a French variety of cherry tree, remarkable for the sweet smell of the wood.

boitelle, a French garnish for fish consisting of sliced raw mushrooms cooked with the fish.

bola, a Jewish yeasted cake made from a dough consisting of 1 lb. (4 cups) flour mixed with 2 oz. (¼ cup) butter, and ½ oz. yeast dissolved in ½ pint (1 cup) tepid milk. Then 2 eggs are well mixed in, and it is all covered with a cloth and set in a warm place for an hour to rise. The dough is then rolled and spread with 3 oz. (½ cup scant) butter, folded over, and rolled again. The same quantity of butter is again spread over and rolled. It is cut into two halves, each piece rolled quite thinly and shaped into rounds. One round is spread with a mixture of 4 oz. (1 cup) chopped candied peel mixed with 1 tablespoon brown sugar, and 2 level tablespoons each of ginger, cinnamon, and chopped almonds. This is covered with the other half of dough, and set again in a warm place to rise, for ½ hour. The cake is baked in a hot oven (400° F) for ½ hour, then brushed over with 4 oz. (½ cup) sugar which has been boiled for 10 minutes with 3 tablespoons water. It is cooked again for a further ½ hour. When taken from the oven it is brushed once more with sugar and water, and put back for 5 minutes to dry.

bola, a Portuguese cheese made from cow's milk. It is a semi-hard cheese, not unlike edam in appearance and taste. It is the most popular cow's milk cheese in Portugal and weighs 2–4 lb.

boldro, see PESCATRICE.

bolet, French for boletus. See also CÈPE.

boletus (*Boletus edulis*), a kind of mushroom which is glossy and bun-like in shape. The colour is yellowish to a warm brown, and the gills are honeycombed. It is native to central and northern Europe, and highly thought of gastronomically. See also CÈPE.

bolinhos de bacalhau, a Portuguese fritter delicacy consisting of 1 lb. minced, cooked salt cod mixed with 1 lb. sieved, cooked potatoes, herbs, seasonings, and 3 egg yolks. When well mixed and ready to cook, the egg whites, stiffly beaten, are added, and small spoonfuls of the mixture are dropped into hot oil and fried to a golden brown. They are served with olives, gherkins, or salad and can be eaten hot or cold.

bolitas, Spanish for fritter. See also BUÑUELOS; FRITAS.

boller, Danish for dumplings. In Denmark the housewife specializes in dumplings or "soup balls," which she adds to chicken and meat soups to make them more nourishing. They are made from 6 oz. (⅔ cup) butter, ½ lb. (2 cups) flour, 4 eggs, and 1 egg yolk, with salt and a scant pint (2 cups) boiling water. A roux is made of the butter, flour, and water. Away from the heat, the eggs are stirred in, one at a time, adding salt to taste. The balls are shaped by using 2 teaspoons. They can be cooked in boiling salted water, stock, or soup, and are ready to serve when they rise to the top of the pan. See also KØD; MELBOLLER.

boller, Norwegian for dumplings.

bollito, an Italian national dish, notably of Piedmont, consisting of an elaborate number of meats and poultry, such as calf's head, turkey, beef, veal, pork sausage, and any other various meats all boiled in the same pot. According to the length of time that each requires, these ingredients are put on to cook. They are served with boiled haricot beans and other vegetables, and make a delicious and lavish stew. The resulting stock is also superb.

bollo maimón, a kind of Spanish biscuit (cookie) which is shaped like a bull ring. It is served on feast days in Spain and also at weddings.

bolo, Portuguese for cake. Cakes and pastries in Portugal are extremely good and are often filled with purées of fruit and nuts such as melon, pineapple, or almonds. See also MORGADO DE FIGOS; PASTELERIA ROLO DE OVOS.

bolo podre, cake made from 8 oz. (1 cup) butter creamed with 8 oz. (1 cup) sugar, and 4 eggs, 8 oz. (2 cups) flour, 1 teaspoon cinnamon, and 4 oz. (1 cup) chopped nuts added. A little brandy is poured in, and finally 1 teaspoon baking powder is added. The cake is baked in a hot oven in a greased tin, for about 1 hour.

bolo real do Algarve, a cake made with 4 oz. (½ cup) sugar, 4 oz. (1 cup) ground almonds, and 2 egg yolks, baked in a greased tin in a hot oven for 30 minutes.

bologna sausage, a large sausage of Italian origin, but popular in England, where it is sometimes known as breakfast sausage and the U.S. It is made from minced beef and pork, sage, garlic salt, and pepper. Sometimes it is smoked, but usually it is boiled and served cold in slices.

Bolognese, an Italian method of cooking, from Bologna. It is a rich and delicious cuisine, using white truffles. Bologna is also well-known for *mortadella* sausage. See also RAGÙ.

bomba, a Polish variety of ice cream, made with thick whipped cream like the French *bombe.* The general Polish term for ice cream is *lody.*

bomba di riso, see RISO.

Bombay duck (*Harpodon negereus*), a small gelatinous fish from Indian and south Asiatic waters, which is dried, salted and eaten with curry. The name is a corruption of bombil, a native name for fish. It is impregnated with a plant called asafetida, which is to some Western peoples an offensive-smelling herb.

bombe, French for an ice cream which used to be made in a spherical-shaped mould; nowadays a simple cone is used. Usually the middle is made of a lighter-textured mixture, and the outside of a heavier mixture, such as water–ice. The bombe mixture for the middle is made with 1 lb. (2 cups) sugar boiled to 220°F with ¾ pint (1½ cups) water; this is then put in a double boiler with 12 egg yolks over a high flame. It is whisked constantly until it is like a thick cream, sieved, and whisked again until it is cold, frothy, and pale in colour. An equal quantity of whipped cream is added, and flavouring to taste, and the mixture is now ready for freezing.

ice cream bombe

bomboline di ricotta in brodo, an Italian soup made from broth, with dumplings made from ½ lb. (1 cup) ricotta cheese mixed with 3 heaped tablespoons flour, 2 eggs, a pinch of nutmeg, salt, and pepper. The mixture is shaped into very small rounds, which are left to chill, and are then rolled in flour, fried in oil until golden, and dropped into the hot soup.

bonaparte, a French chicken consommé, garnished with chicken quenelles.

bonaventure potato cake, a Canadian speciality made from 1 lb. (2 cups) mashed potatoes, 8 oz. (1 cup) flour, 4 tablespoons butter, and approximately ¼ pint (½ cup) milk. It is mixed into a flat cake, baked for 30–40 minutes in a moderate oven, then served hot and buttered.

bonbon, French for small confectionery such as caramel, butterscotch, sugared almonds, praliné, or toffees. In the U.S. these are chocolate-covered confectioneries.

bon-chrétien, a French pear of two varieties, one summer and one winter. It is sweet, but has a rough texture and is usually used for cooking.

bondart, a French cow's milk cheese from Normandy. It is a soft cheese in season from October to June.

bondepige med slør, a Danish apple pudding which consists of layers of cooked apple alternated with a mixture of rye breadcrumbs fried in butter, with sugar to taste. It is topped with grated chocolate or jam. The name means "peasant girl with veil."

bondiola, a speciality of the province of Parma, Italy, consisting of a cured shoulder of pork.

bondon, a French cheese from Neufchâtel-en-Bray, made from ewe's milk, or sometimes from a mixture of sour cow's milk and ewe's milk. In some cases the mould *penicillium candidum* is added. It is a small loaf-shaped cheese.

bone(s), any part of a vertebrate skeleton, composed of cartilaginous substance and calcareous salts. Larger bones, such as knuckles, have a soft, fatty substance in the middle, known as marrow. See MARROW. This is often served poached, with toast. Bones are an essential factor in making stock; some varieties contain more gelatine than others, and, when boiled slowly in water for some hours with herbs or vegetables and seasoning, produce jellied stock, or meat jelly (glaze). Carcasses of poultry so treated make excellent soup. Fish bones boiled in water with herbs is the basis of fish court-bouillon. In Edwardian times, in England and France, large beef bones with a certain amount of meat adhering were rubbed with mustard, ketchup, and butter and grilled until brown. They were known as devilled bones. "Boning" means removing the bones from a joint of meat, poultry, fish, or any other food, either cooked or raw. See also MARROW.

bonen, Dutch for beans. See also BRUINE BONEN; WITTE BONEN.

bonito (*Sarda sarda*), a small, delicious member of the tunny (tuna) family, found in the warmer waters of the Atlantic and also in the Mediterranean. It is of a similar texture to tunny (tuna), the flesh being whorled in the same way. It is excellent baked in the oven, or grilled with a sauce of melted butter and lemon juice. It can be prepared in the same way as tunny (tuna), but needs less cooking as it is smaller. In French, it is *bonite,* but it is also called *pélamide* or *pélamyde,* and Normandy fishermen also call it *germon.* See also PALAMIDA.

bonito, a fish found in Spanish waters, a member of the *Scombridae* family. It resembles jureles and is treated in the same way.

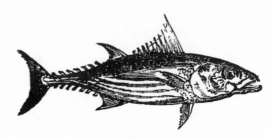

bonito

bonnach grùan, a cod liver bannock made with fresh fish, a traditional recipe from the Isle of Barra, off the Scottish coast. The liver of a fair-sized cod, fresh from the sea, is soaked overnight in salt water. After all stringy parts have been removed, the liver is minced, mixed with a tablespoon of oatmeal, a pinch of baking soda, and seasoned. It is formed into a flat round, put on a plate and placed over a pot of boiling water. The fish from which the liver is taken is placed on top, and it is all cooked slowly until ready. On the Isle of Skye this dish is called *bonnach donn* (brown bannock) and includes a small chopped onion.

bonnag, a traditional Manx soda bread made with plain flour, 1 lb. (4 cups) flour to a teaspoon of baking soda, and the same of cream of tartar and salt. It is mixed to a soft dough with approximately ½ pint (1 cup) buttermilk or sour milk, shaped into rounds and baked for 1 hour in a moderate oven. The same mixture, with less buttermilk added so that the dough shall be stiffer, is rolled into small rounds and baked on a griddle or in a heavy frying pan.

bonnag arran oarn, traditional barley meal bread from the Isle of Man. It is made with barley meal and wheat flour in equal quantities, with a little lard rubbed in and a pinch of baking soda, cream of tartar, and salt added. It is mixed to a stiff dough with buttermilk, as for *bonnag,* then shaped into round loaves and baked for 1 hour in a moderate oven. A similar mixture, made with butter and candied peel, mixed spice, and brown sugar added, constitutes a traditional Manx cake.

bonne femme, I. A French method of cooking meat or poultry, usually in a casserole, and garnished with button onions which have been braised, mushrooms, and bacon. See also POULET À LA BONNE FEMME. II. Poached fillets of sole served with a white wine sauce, with sliced mushrooms, parsley, and shallots added, all lightly browned under the grill. III. A French soup made from finely shredded leeks cooked in butter, to which are added 3 pints (6 cups) white stock and approximately ½ lb. (1½ cups) sliced raw potatoes. At the last moment 2 tablespoons chopped chervil and 4 tablespoons butter are added, and the soup is served with thinly sliced French bread dried in the oven. IV. A French method of serving potatoes. See POMME DE TERRE (POMMES BONNE FEMME).

bonne-dame, the common French name for orach.

bonnefoy, I. A French sauce for meat like a sauce bordelaise, but with white wine instead of red, and chopped tarragon added. It is garnished with chopped, cooked beef marrow and parsley. II. As above without the beef marrow. It is used for fish *à la bonnefoy,* also called *à la bordelaise.*

bonner, Norwegian for beans.

bonner med sennep, a casserole of beans with mustard. It is cooked with 2 chopped onions fried in butter and transferred to a casserole containing ½ lb. baked butter beans; a mixture of 1 tablespoon mustard, 2 tablespoons tomato purée with the liquid from the beans sprinkled over the vegetables. Thin rashers of bacon (the rind already removed) top the dish, which is baked in a hot oven until the bacon becomes crisp.

bønner, Danish for beans.

stuvede bønner, dried, soaked beans (1 lb.) are simmered with sliced onion, chopped bacon, herbs, all barely covered with water, for 3 hours. When the liquid has been absorbed, ½ pint (1 cup) thick tomato sauce mixed with ¼ pint (½ cup) white wine and 4 chopped mushrooms is added, and the dish is cooked for 15 minutes.

bonnet turc, French for a variety of pumpkin known in English as turk's cap.

bönor, Swedish for beans.

bönor och svamp, beans and mushrooms, a vegetable dish served in Sweden with roast veal and some game dishes. It is prepared with 1 lb. string beans, boiled quickly in lightly salted water, and 1 lb. thinly sliced mushrooms, fried in butter until tender. Then ¼ pint (½ cup) cream is added and the contents of the pan allowed to simmer for about 10 minutes, after which they are seasoned. The beans are reheated in butter, with salt and 1 teaspoon sugar. The creamed mushrooms are served round the beans.

bonvalet, a French cake created in the 19th century in Paris, and almost identical with *Beauvilliers.* It consists of about ½ lb. (2 cups) of almonds pounded with the same amount of sugar, to which are added 5 egg whites. In a separate bowl, the 1 lb. (2 cups) sugar is mixed with 4 oz. (½ cup) butter and 4 whole eggs. The two mixtures are combined and (1½ cups) each of rice flour, sifted cake flour, and potato flour are added and well mixed. Finally, 7 more egg whites, stiffly beaten, are folded in. This elaborate cake is cooked in a moderate oven (375°F) in a special tin called a *trois frères.* When cold, the cake is iced with kirsch icing and the centre filled with crème chantilly.

bookmaker's sandwich, see SANDWICH.

boquerones, a Spanish dish of fresh anchovies, floured and joined together by making a small incision above the tail of one fish and slipping the tails of 3 or 4 other fish through this. They are spread out like a hand of cards and fried in the form of a fan in hot oil.

borage (*Borago officinalis*), an annual, short bushy herb with vivid blue flowers that attract bees in quantity. Although an annual, it makes many seedlings each year and is extremely easy to grow. The flowers and stem are now used for flavouring wine cups and other drinks. The young leaves, which contain nitrate of potash, are good in salads. It used to be used for making cordials and has the reputation of making people happy. Gerard, writing in 1597, says of the leaves of borage: "There be also many things made of them, used everywhere for the comfort of the heart, for the driving away of sorrow, and increasing the joy of the mind." The Welsh name for borage is llanwellys, "herb of happiness." It was one of the

four cardinal flowers of the ancients. See also ALKANET; BORAGGINE.

boraggine, Italian for borage. In Genoa it is used in a stuffing for ravioli. Also, the leaves are dipped in batter and made into fritters (*frittelle*).

bord-de-plat, a small dish used in France to protect the border of a dish on which food in sauce is being served. It is round or oval, varies in size, and is usually made of metal.

bordelaise, I. A French sauce for grilled meat made from ½ pint (1 cup) red wine reduced with a little chopped shallot, thyme, bay leaf, peppercorns, and salt. When boiled down to two-thirds the quantity, the same amount of demi-glace (or meat jelly [glaze]) and 1 tablespoon butter are added. It is again reduced, then strained, and garnished with poached, diced beef bone marrow and chopped parsley. Grilled steaks à la bordelaise are often garnished with more marrow. Sometimes this sauce is thickened with a *beurre manié.* II. For fish served à la bordelaise the sauce is made without the marrow and with white wine. It is also called *bonnefoy.* III. The term refers also to cèpes, mirepoix, or globe artichokes and potatoes served as a garnish, especially with *noix de veau.* See also POULET (POULET SAUTÉ À LA BORDELAIS). IV. A French method of serving potatoes. See POMME DE TERRE (POMMES À LA BORDELAISE).

bordure, I. A French culinary term meaning a dish which is served either in or on a substance shaped in the form of a ring or crown. In English it means a border. II. Round or oval-shaped metal utensils put into a dish to keep a garnish in place. III. Ragoût or salpicon served within a border of poached forcemeat (quenelles) prepared in a special ring mould, with *pommes duchesse* round the edge.

borecole, see KALE.

börek, a Turkish national dish of fried or baked phyllo pastry rolls with a filling, generally savoury and commonly of cheese, but sometimes sweet. Traditionally, the filling is made with a mixture of 1 cup feta or other cream curd cheese to 1 raw egg, 1 tablespoon butter, and 2 teaspoons chopped parsley. This is placed between long sheets of the pastry, the top is brushed with more egg or melted butter, and the whole is baked until golden and then cut into small rolls when cooked. *Börek* is popular throughout the Balkans, and in some areas the rolls are made individually, using a filling of gruyère or other hard cheese melted in a thick white sauce, and they are cooked by frying in olive oil instead of being baked. Many other savoury fillings are also used, such as minced meat with or without the cheese, feta cheese and spinach, purée of spinach and onion, chopped ham, fish, chicken livers. Savoury *börek* are generally eaten as an hors d'oeuvre. A popular sweet *börek* is sometimes made with a mixture of 2 egg yolks, 8 oz. (2 cups) flour, 4 oz. (½ cup) sugar, 2 tablespoons brandy, and about 4 tablespoons yogourt. These are combined to form a kind of pastry which is rolled out and cut into strips or made into shapes which are then fried in hot butter until golden brown. They are drained on greaseproof (waxed) paper, and served sprinkled with sugar. *Börek* is sometimes rendered beurrek in English- and French-speaking countries.

borjú, Hungarian for veal. See also BÉCSISZELET; PÖRKÖLT.

borjú vagy disznó paprikásszelet, veal (or pork) chops in paprika sauce. To prepare, 2 bacon rashers for each chop are fried in a little butter and then removed from the pan. The chops are fried in the same fat to which a little hot water is added with salt and paprika. When the chops are tender, approximately ½ pint (1 cup) sour cream is added. This dish is served with boiled rice. The rice is put in the centre of a dish and the bacon laid over it; the chops are placed around the side and the sauce is poured over them.

borjúpaprikás, a dish of chopped veal cooked with onions in hot fat with paprika, salt, water, and, finally, sour cream added.

borjúpörkölt, a national dish of braised veal cooked with onions and paprika. Sour cream is added just before serving. It is traditionally eaten on St. Stephen's Day, August 20, which even today is a national holiday.

töltött borjúhús, shoulder or breast of veal stuffed with goose liver and then baked.

borlotti, the Italian name of a reddish, and a pink and purple-mottled dried bean used in stews and for salads.

boronía, a traditional Spanish vegetable soup, made by sweating diced eggplants, pumpkin, and tomatoes in oil, then adding a little water, heavily flavoured with garlic, salt, allspice, and caraway seeds. When the mixture is cooked, it is sieved, and then thickened with breadcrumbs. A pinch of saffron is added last.

borracho, Portuguese for pigeon, often served roasted with rice or braised with onion, tomato, pimento, and white wine.

borrego, Portuguese for baby lamb often braised with onions, tomatoes, peas, bay leaf, garlic, and potatoes cut into small balls. When roasted on a spit, it is called *cordeiro assado.*

borschkeitto, a Finnish dish consisting of a soup made with beetroot, butter, flour, vinegar, salt, and sugar. Before serving, slices of *frankfurter würstchen* or chopped pieces of meat or ham are added. Sour cream may be served with the soup on a separate dish.

borsch, a traditional beetroot and cabbage soup eaten in Russia, the Ukraine, and also Poland. It is made with pieces of beef, bacon, game, or poultry, with the meat stock, onions, caraway seed, cabbage, and beetroot, and half the beetroot stock. The best results are usually achieved if the meat and vegetables are allowed to simmer in this for some hours, then put through a sieve, after which the rest of the beetroot juice can be added. (If this is allowed to boil, it will turn a pinkish-brown colour.) The soup may be served hot or cold; in either case a liberal quantity of sour cream is poured on top before serving. Borsch is sometimes garnished with *bitkis* (small meatballs) and *vatruschki* (cream cheese tartlets). It is one of the finest soups in the world, and well worth the trouble it takes to prepare. In the Ukraine, dried mushroom stock is sometimes used instead of meat stock, and stewed prunes are added to the vegetables. See also BARSZCŽ.

borsch flotsky, ''navy'' borsch, made as basic recipe, but with the addition of a quantity of diced vegetables.

borsch kholodny, a cold *borsch,* like the Polish chłodnik, made from chopped beetroot and its leaves cooked in stock. It is left to cool, then finely sliced pickled cucumber, spring onions (scallions), sliced hard-boiled eggs, sour cream, seasonings, and kvass are added. It is served very cold, sometimes with crushed ice.

borsch polsky, Polish borsch. A partially roasted duck is finished in rich beef broth, and the broth is then strained and garnished with strips of beetroot and shredded cabbage. Slices of the duck breast, beef, and *pelmeni* are served separately, with beetroot juice and sour cream.

borsch skobelev, same as for basic recipe, with the addition of diced potato, diced salt pork, small fried sausages, and meatballs. This soup is served with a separate dish of small slices of fried bread.

borschok, a national Russian soup whose basic ingredients are shredded cabbage, strips of root vegetables, and red beetroot, cooked with stock from beef, ham bones, chicken, or duck. The soup is always coloured with the juice of raw red beetroots and served with sour cream. *Borschok* is also sometimes served as a plain beetroot soup.

borstplaat, traditional Dutch sweets eaten on St. Nicholas's Eve, December 5. They are boiled sweets made from sugar, water, and fruit or peppermint essence (extract).

bosanski lonac, a Bosnian casserole made from pork, beef, and lamb, with onions, sweet peppers, eggplant, tomatoes, and other vegetables in season, cooked with herbs, spices, and white wine. *Lonac* is the name of the deep earthenware pot it is cooked in. See also GYOVECH.

bossons, a French cow's milk cheese which comes from Provence. It is in season all the year round.

Boston baked beans, one of the most famous American dishes, consisting of baked, soaked dried, navy (kidney), or haricot beans, with salt pork, brown sugar, molasses, salt, and water to cover. Sometimes mustard and/or onions are also added for extra seasoning. They are baked covered in a slow oven for 6 to 8 hours.

Boston baked beans with Boston brown bread

Boston brown bread, an American bread made from 1 cup each of rye flour, corn meal, whole wheat flour, ¾ cup molasses, 1 pint (2 cups) buttermilk or 1¾ cups fresh milk, 2 teaspoons combined baking soda and salt. The dry ingredients are mixed, then molasses and milk added, and the mixture is put in a greased dish (not more than two-thirds full). It is covered and steamed for 1½–2 hours; then with the cover removed, set in a slow oven for 15–20 minutes. Raisins are sometimes added to the mixture.

Boston clam chowder, see NEW ENGLAND CLAM CHOWDER.

Boston fish chowder, a regional soup from Boston, U.S. Chopped onions, diced green peppers, and chopped celery in equal proportions are fried in butter. Fish and fish stock to double the quantity of ingredients in saucepan are added, with cayenne pepper and herbs. Diced potatoes are added at a later stage, and finally milk. The soup is sometimes garnished with flaked cod or other fish. Salted crackers are served separately. See also CHOWDER.

Boston pickling cucumber, see CUCUMBER.

boszorkányhab, an Hungarian pudding made from sieved, baked apples mixed with stiffly beaten egg whites, lemon juice, and sugar. The literal translation is ''witches froth.''

botargo, grey mullet roe which is mentioned in Samuel Pepy's *Diary,* June 6, 1661. He says: ''We stayed talking and singing and drinking great draughts of claret, and eating botargo and bread and butter till twelve at night.'' This seems to imply that it was quite a usual dish to eat. About that time it was also described as a ''sausage made from the eggs and the blood of the mullet.''

Botargo was formerly made into a paste in England by mixing it with the fish blood, salt, and lemon juice. Nowadays this dish is almost exclusively Greek or Turkish. Each year in August when the grey mullet is ready to spawn she is led into false weirs and adroitly speared by Greek fishermen in flat-bottomed boats. The roe is immediately taken from the belly, cleaned, soaked in brine, and dried in the sun. The dried roe can be eaten at once with bread, although it is usually preserved by a coating of beeswax which is removed before eating. In this condition, the roe is sometimes called "red caviar" and is sliced and eaten with bread or toast. The roe is very rich with a unique flavour. In Greece the collecting grounds are called *tzenios*. It can also be used to flavour scrambled eggs or omelettes. See also AVGOTARAHO; CAVIAR; TARAMOSALATA.

boter, Dutch for butter.

boterhamkoek, a national Dutch cake made at Deventer. It consists of ¼ lb. (½ cup) butter, ½ lb. (2 cups) flour, 6 tablespoons corn syrup, ¼ lb. (½ cup) brown sugar, ¼ pint (½ cup) milk, 1 teaspoon each of aniseed, cinnamon, nutmeg, and ginger, and 2 teaspoons baking powder. All dry ingredients are mixed first, then the syrup, melted butter, and milk. The cake is baked in a moderate oven for 30–40 minutes. It resembles a sweet, spiced bread.

botermèlk, Belgian for buttermilk. For every 3 pints (6 cups), 3 oz. pearl barley and a little brown sugar to taste are boiled with the buttermilk. It is cooked for 2 hours, and if the consistency is sloppy a little corn flour (cornstarch), approximately 2 tablespoons, is mixed with cold water and added just before serving. Sometimes treacle or molasses is mixed in to taste.

bottom round, see ROUND.

botvinya, a traditional Russian cold herb soup. Purée of sorrel and young beet tops are mixed with *kvass* (a fermented spirit, only slightly alcoholic, made from wheat, rye, barley, and buckwheat meal) with the addition of sugar and fruit such as cranberries, apples, strawberries, raspberries, etc. This is seasoned with salt, pepper, and sugar. The garnishings are strips of fresh cucumber, chopped tarragon, dill, and fennel. A cube of ice is placed on each plate. Small pieces of cold, cooked salmon or sturgeon and grated horseradish are served separately. Sometimes acid white wine is used instead of *kvass*.

bouche du roi, a term used in France under the ancien régime, to describe the service that dealt with the kitchens of the royal household. These services sometimes employed over 500 people.

bouchées, see VOL-AU-VENTS.

boudin, French for black pudding; also called *boudin noir.*

boudin blanc, a French sausage made from minced chicken, pork, or veal, with breadcrumbs and onions. It is about 1½ inches wide and about 12 inches long.

boudy, a beautiful-looking French apple, but of poor taste. It is mainly used for cooking or decorating fruit baskets.

bouffoir, French word for the bellows used by French butchers to force air under the skin and into the tissues of carcases. This makes a joint considerably more tender since it breaks down gristly particles.

bougon, a soft French goat's milk cheese from Poitou, in season from May to November.

bougras, a soup from the Périgord region of France, prepared from cabbage, leeks, onions, and potatoes, all cooked in the same water in which black puddings have been cooked. It is a speciality at Shrovetide, when pigs are killed and the black puddings are usually made. It is cooked for about 1 hour, sprinkled with flour to thicken, and poured over slices of homemade bread.

bouillabaisse, a French fish soup/stew made in the Mediterranean region, with saffron added. The authentic bouillabaisse can only be made there, because certain of the fishes do not exist elsewhere. Good fish soups are made in all countries, but each makes use of specific fish which have their own characteristic taste and so cannot well be replaced by others if the authentic flavour is required. The fish used are crawfish or lobster, rascasse (hogfish), gurnet, weever, roucaou, john

dory, anglerfish, conger eel, whiting, bass, crab, and chapon. For 6 to 8 people, about 6 lb. assorted fish and shellfish are needed. The heads are cut off all the fish and first boiled in 2 quarts water to make a stock. Three large tomatoes, 2 onions, 4 cloves garlic, 2 sprigs each of thyme, fennel, and parsley, a good pinch saffron, and a twist of dry orange peel are gently sweated, but not coloured in ¼ pint (½ cup) olive oil. Then the fishhead broth is strained and used for cooking the fish. It is all well seasoned with salt and black pepper. The firm fish, such as crawfish, lobster, eel, weever, gurnet, crab, anglerfish, and rascasse, are separated from the other fish, cut into pieces, and cooked first, since they take longer. The soup is boiled very rapidly; in fact the name is thought to come from this feature—"ça bout, ça baisse"—"it boils, it lowers" (i.e., in volume) was the cry of the fisherman's wife who was in charge of the cooking pot, and immediately more liquid and more herbs would be added to the kettle to stop the soup from boiling away. After about 10 minutes, the soft fish are put in and ¼ pint (½ cup) more olive oil is added. It is the fast boiling which makes the oil and broth amalgamate. Cooking time in all is about 15 to 20 minutes. The fish is then lifted out, and the soup poured over slices of stale French bread called *marette*. The fish is arranged on another dish, but both are served together. Sometimes the bread is rubbed with a paste of garlic and olive oil pounded together until thick. Near Perpignan, potatoes are added and sometimes the saffron omitted, but this is nearer a *chaudrée* or a *cotriade*, than a true bouillabaisse. See also BOGUE; BOULLINADA; BRODETTO; BURRIDA; CACCIUCCO LIVORNESE; KACCAVIA.

bouillabaisse à la Parisienne, as above, using leeks as well, and half white wine and half fish stock for the liquid.

bouillabaisse borgne, a Provençal soup, also called *aigosau,* made from potatoes, fish stock, poached eggs (1 per person), and parsley.

bouillabaisse d'épinards, a Provençal dish made from cooked spinach reheated on top of the stove in a saucepan or flameproof casserole with onion, olive oil, sliced potatoes, garlic, and fennel. When the other vegetables are cooked, eggs (1 per person) are broken over them and cooked gently.

bouillade, or *all grenat,* a Cataluña sauce in which snails and also fish are cooked with chopped garlic and red pimentoes, thickened with flour, and moistened with white wine. It is sometimes served poured over cooked diced potatoes.

bouillant, an old French name for a small puff pastry patty filled with a salpicon of chicken and served very hot, hence the name "boiling."

bouillante, an old French name for soup served boiling hot.

bouille, la, I. A French cheese made with cow's milk. It comes from Normandy, and is in season from October to May. II. French for a vessel for carrying milk.

bouilleture or **bouilliture,** a speciality of Poitou and Anjou, France, which is a matelote of various types of fish, especially eels. It is served garnished with slices of toast, sautéed mushrooms, small onions, and sometimes quartered hard-boiled eggs. In Poitou, prunes are added to the garnish.

bouilli, I. A French diminutive of *beef bouilli,* meaning boiled beef. It particularly applies to the meat after cooking in a pot-au-feu. II. A soufflé made from milk, sugar, and flour or starch (boiled until thickened). When cooled, egg yolks, butter, and spices are added and beaten egg whites are folded in.

bouillie, a kind of French porridge made from a variety of grains, maize, millet, buckwheat, or *gruau*. It is mixed into boiling salted water as for porridge, and when thick, a few spoonfuls of pork fat are stirred in. It is poured out to a thickness of about 1 inch, on a coarse linen cloth, and then left to cool. When quite firm and cold, it is cut into uniform slices, dipped in flour, and fried in lard or butter. In the

Périgord it is eaten instead of bread with *civet de lièvre*, or boiled salt pork. If eaten when hot and before frying, it serves as a soup, and if sprinkled with sugar it becomes a sweet course. A universal peasant's dish.

bouillon, French for broth meat stock, with the fat removed, usually used as a basis for a richer soup. The liquid is strained, thus removing any solid particles of meat. It is often given to invalids to encourage appetite. It can also be made from vegetables or herbs, without meat. In culinary French it usually means stock. The name comes from *bouillir*, to boil.

bouillon aveugle, a colloquial French phrase which denotes clear soup without any little "eyes" or fat on top, hence "blind" bouillon.

boula boula, an American soup which came originally from the Seychelles, consisting of turtle soup mixed with an equal quantity of puréed (fresh) green peas. This is heated without being allowed to boil, and a little butter, and seasonings are added. Finally it is flavoured with sherry and put into soup plates with a spoonful of whipped cream on each portion. The plates are put under a grill for a minute or two, then the soup is served at once.

boulangère, à la, a French garnish for meat consisting of sliced raw potatoes and onions, baked with a little stock in the same dish as the joint. The joint is placed on top of the potatoes and onions. Lamb is the most usual meat so cooked.

boulbett, Russian sweet pastry and cheesecakes made from 1 lb. (2 cups) cottage cheese (*tvorog*), whipped, 3 tablespoons sugar, 2 egg yolks, 2 oz. (½ cup) flour, and a pinch of salt, mixed into a dough which is shaped into small balls baked or fried in butter. These are eaten with powdered sugar and sour cream, served separately.

boule de neige, I. A French cake in the shape of a ball, made from sponge mixture and covered with whipped cream. II. An iced pudding made from a bombe ice cream mixture in a round mould and finally covered with whipped cream. III. The name in certain regions of France for edible agaric, a genus of fungi. See also MUSHROOM.

boulette, I. An alternative name for the French cheese *cassette*. II. A French dish made from ½ lb. chopped or minced (usually leftover) meat, poultry, or fish mixed with 1 chopped onion, seasoning, and beaten egg to bind. The mixture is shaped into small balls, dipped in egg and breadcrumbs, and fried in deep oil or fat. They are usually served cold, wrapped in a crisp lettuce leaf.

boulette d'avesne, see DAUPHIN.

boulettes de viande, French for small pastries made with *bouilli* from a pot-au-feu which is minced and enclosed in pastry. They are then baked in a moderate oven until golden brown.

boullinada, a Cataluña version of bouillabaisse. It is not as elaborate as true bouillabaisse, and contains equal proportions of fish and potato. Mussels are sometimes added just before serving.

bouquet garni, a small sprig of thyme, parsley, and a bay leaf, tied together and used in soups, stews, or for the poaching of fish. The bouquet is usually removed before serving the dish. For certain dishes the bouquet is more elaborate and can include basil, chervil, burnet, tarragon, and rosemary.

bouquetière, a French garnish for meat consisting of small *pommes château*, artichoke bottoms filled with diced white turnips and carrots, french beans, peas, and sprigs of cauliflower masked with sauce hollandaise. These assorted vegetables are sometimes arranged in the shape of a bouquet.

bouquetin, French for ibex.

bouquets (*Leander serratus*), French for prawns, also known as crevettes roses.

bourdaines, les, the method in Anjou, France, of cooking peeled and cored apples. The cavities are filled with plum or quince jam; the apples are then wrapped in short pastry, sealed, and baked in a slow oven for about 1 hour.

bourdaloue, a French beef consommé, served plain or garnished with royale garnish of either tomato, asparagus, or carrot. It may also be made from chicken consommé. See also CONSOMMÉ.

tarte à la bourdaloue, a pastry tart filled with almond custard flavoured with kirsch, containing red currant, apricot jelly, and/or macaroons. The pastry is topped with poached pears. The dish was named for Louis Bourdaloue, a 17th-century preacher.

bourekia, Greek for phyllo pastry patties filled with a variety of savoury fillings such as minced meat, cream cheese, and spinach. They are usually fried, come in various shapes, and are served as part of *meze*. They are also called *bourekakia* and are very like the Turkish *böreck*.

bourgain, a French cheese of the Neufchâtel type, made from cow's milk. It is unsalted and the fat content is low. It is very soft and does not travel, so is eaten only locally.

bourgeoise, à la, I. A French garnish for meat consisting of tiny balls of carrot, fried onions, and diced bacon. Sometimes braised fresh celery, chicory, or lettuce is added but carrots are essential. It is also called à la mode. See also BOEUF (BOEUF À LA MODE); POULET (POULET À LA BOURGEOISE). II. A French beef consommé garnished with diced root vegetables and chopped chervil.

bourguignonne, à la, I. A variant, from Burgundy, France, of sauce bordelaise. It is made without the bone-marrow, is more highly seasoned with pepper, and is served with meat, eggs, fish, and poultry. II. A French method of braising beef with red burgundy wine, mushrooms, small onions, and lardoons. This method is also used for poultry, fish, and eggs, but the lardoons are omitted in the case of fish or eggs. III. A French garnish for meat (especially large cuts of beef) of mushrooms sautéed in butter, or diced pickled pork blanched and browned, and small glazed button onions. See also BOEUF(BOEUF À LA BOURGUIGNONNE); POULET (POULET SAUTÉ À LA BOURGUIGNONNE).

bourride, la, a fish soup of the Marseilles district of France, similar to a bouillabaisse, with no saffron, and an *aïoli* added instead. In Provence *sauce rouille* is also used. Usually the fish used are approximately 3 lb. of bass, mullet, sea bream, anglerfish, whiting, john dory, or rock salmon. Almost any white fish will do. It is made as a bouillabaisse, but when the fish is nearly cooked, ½ pint (1 cup) mayonnaise mixed with 3 cloves of crushed garlic is put into a double boiler, and a large ladleful of the hot broth is poured over and beaten with a whisk until it is thick and frothy. This is then poured over slices of toast, and the fish arranged on top.

boursin, a French soft cheese from Normandy, developed only recently. It is made from whole cow's milk. There are several varieties, one being delicately flavoured with garlic and chopped herbs, known as Boursin à l'ail, and one with peppercorns, called Boursin au poivre. It has a rich, creamy consistency.

bourtheto, a speciality of Corfu. It consists of baked fish with sliced onions, tomatoes, and cayenne pepper. It is fiery to the taste.

boutargue, French for the salted roe of the grey mullet and the tunny (tuna) fish. It is soaked in a solution of salt and water, drained, and pressed. Boutargue is eaten as an hors d'oeuvre with oil and vinegar. See BOTARGO.

bowfin (*Amia calva*), a mudfish found in the Great Lakes of America and the Mississippi Valley. It is not very good eating.

box-crab, see CALAPPA.

boxty or *broxty*, a traditional Irish dish, especially popular in County Cavan, made from equal quantities of grated raw potatoes and cooked potatoes stirred into hot milk until they are cooked and firm. The mixture is then put into a warm dish and hot melted butter is poured into a well made in the middle. Boxty is eaten traditionally on the night of Halloween, when a wedding ring is put into the dish and is said to decide the destiny of whoever gets it on his plate. There are several jingles which accompany this ceremony:

> Boxty on the griddle, Boxty in the pan,
> If you don't eat Boxty, you'll never get a man.

Also a counter-Boxty song:

> I'll have none of your Boxty,
> I'll have none of your Blarney,
> But I'll whirl my petticoats over my head,
> And be off with my Royal Charlie.

boxty bread, made with 1 lb. (4 cups) flour, 1 lb. (2 cups) mashed potatoes, and 1 lb. grated raw potatoes mixed with 4 oz. (½ cup) melted butter or bacon fat. The raw potatoes are grated into a clean cloth, which is wrung out tightly over a basin, catching the liquid. The dry grated potatoes are mixed with the cooked ones. When the starch has separated from the liquid at the bottom of the basin, the starch is added, together with salt, pepper, and the melted fat. It is kneaded on a floured board and shaped into 4 round flat loaves, marked with a cross, and baked in a moderate over for 40 minutes; they are then split and buttered while hot.

boxty pancakes, made with equal quantities of grated raw potatoes, cooked mashed potatoes, flour, and 1 teaspoon baking soda to 1 lb. each of the other ingredients, mixed to a thin batter with milk, and cooked like pancakes on the hot plate of a stove or griddle.

boyaux, French for the intestines of slaughtered animals. Pig's intestines are mainly used for making *andouilles* and *andouillettes*.

boysenberry, see HYBRID BERRIES.

bozbash, a Russian country soup made from boiled mutton. The stock is degreased; the meat is boned and cut into largish pieces, then put back in the stock with cooked peas, sliced potatoes, apples, tomatoes, and previously fried onions. It is all cooked for an additional 30 minutes.

Bra, an Italian cheese from Bra in Piedmont. It is a hard, white cheese made from partly skimmed, rennetted cow's milk, with a sharp and slightly salty flavour acquired by immersion in brine or having salt sprinkled on the surface before curing. It weighs up to 12 lb. and was first made by nomads. Nowadays there is also a small soft, creamy, milk cheese of the same name (but spelt Brà), made in the provinces of Cuneo and Turin.

brabançonne, à la, a French garnish for steaks and noisettes of little pastry tarts filled with puréed brussels sprouts or endives, and covered with a sauce mornay. They are served with small potato croquettes.

brachse, German for bream; also called *bleie* or *brasse*. It is often cooked in pale beer with onions, bayleaf, spice, and lemon slices, the stock thickened with beurre manié.

braciola, Italian for escallop used often in Italian cookery, especially with veal which is fried in butter: sometimes Marsala is added to the pan juices.

braciolette or *brasciolette*, an Italian dish consisting of thin slices of veal or beef covered with a slice of ham, and topped with a mixture of grated Parmesan or gruyère cheese, pine nuts, sultanas, and parsley. They are rolled up and secured with a toothpick before being browned in oil, with ¼ pint (½ cup) white wine added to the pan juices and simmered slowly for about 20 minutes. This is a variation of *bocconcini, involtini*, and *saltimbocca* which are all thin slices of meat with various fillings.

bracken or *brake* (*Pteridium*), a genus of fern which occurs almost all over the world. The young unopened leaves (fronds) are edible when they are about 3 inches long, still tightly curled, and young enough to snap off. They are tied in bundles and boiled in salted water for about 30 minutes, then served with butter or melted bacon fat. They have a smoky flavour, rather like raw Indian tea leaves—a distinctive flavour, which is either liked or very much disliked. They are often served with brown bread and butter. They are rich in potash and are highly prized in the Far East. The roots of bracken are also edible. They are boiled until tender, allowed to cool, and served with an oil and vinegar dressing.

In Canada, bracken leaves, known as fiddleheads from their shape, are popular and are tinned for export. In the Canary Islands a kind of coarse bread called goflo is made from powdered bracken roots mixed with barley meal.

braendende kaerlighed, a Danish dish of creamed potatoes covered with cubes of fried green (unsmoked) bacon (smoked bacon can be used equally well). This dish is garnished with fried onions and pieces of pickled beetroot (the latter is optional). The name means "burning love."

bragance, à la, I. A French garnish for steaks and noisettes consisting of tomatoes stuffed with sauce béarnaise and served with potato croquettes. II. A French beef consommé garnished with large sago, minute balls of cucumber, and royale garnish julienne. See also CONSOMMÈ.

braganza cabbage, see COUVE TRONCHUDA.

brains, the convoluted nervous substance in the skull of vertebrates. Gastronomically, sheep's brains are the best, then calves', followed by pigs'. They should be simmered gently in salted water with a dash of vinegar added, then allowed to cool, when all the skin and other matter is removed. They are then excellent if reheated in butter, with capers added, or else dipped in batter, or in egg and breadcrumbs, fried in oil, and garnished with lemon. See also CERVELLES; CROCCHETTA (CROCCHETTE DI CERVELLA); MIALA; SESOS.

braise, to cook in a closed container with very little liquid, usually in the oven.

braisière, French for a braising pan, usually metal, with a tight-fitting lid. It is also called a *daubière*.

bramble, see BLACKBERRY.

bramble curd, see LEMON (LEMON CURD).

bramborovä polévká, see POLÉVKÁ.

bran, the outer coat of the wheat berry. It is sometimes used as a breakfast food, and is also mixed with wheat and made into bread, scones, etc. It has been used as a laxative since the 14th century. See also FLOUR.

brancas, a French beef consommé garnished with chiffonade of lettuce and sorrel, cooked vermicelli, and julienne of fried mushrooms and sprinkled with chopped chervil. See also CONSOMMÉ.

brancino, a perch-like fish found in the Adriatic and eaten especially in Venice. It is usually poached in white wine fish stock and served hot with sauce *genovese* or cold with a mayonnaise.

brandade de morue, a Provençal dish of pounded salt cod, milk, garlic, olive oil, salt, and pepper, served on fast days and also during Lent. It is made with 2 lb. salt cod soaked overnight and then cooked just until all the bones and skin can be removed. It is then pounded with a little garlic and ½ pint (1 cup) milk and ½ pint (1 cup) olive oil are heated separately in 2 saucepans until they are warm but not hot. These are added to the pounded fish, alternately, spoonful by spoonful with a wooden spoon, until all is thick and creamy. The ingredients must never be hotter than just warm, otherwise the oil will crack and spoil the entire dish. This dish is usually eaten tepid, garnished with triangles of fried bread and with thin slices of sautéed truffle if it is *brandade de morue à la nantua* or *aux truffes*.

brandkrapferlsuppe, a traditional Austrian soup composed of beef broth with fried *profiteroles*. These are very small balls of chou pastry cooked in hot fat and used as a garnish.

brandy butter, an English hard sauce eaten especially with Christmas pudding, but also with other steamed puddings and hot mince pies. It is made from 4 oz. (½ cup) butter, 4 oz. (½ cup) sugar well beaten and mixed with 3–4 tablespoons brandy. It is chilled and served cold with the hot pudding. In Cumberland, England, rum is used in place of brandy and the sugar used is the light brown variety. Also a few drops of lemon juice and a pinch of nutmeg is added. This is called rum butter.

brandy sauce, an English sauce made from 2 egg yolks, ½ pint (1 cup) cream, 2 tablespoons brown sugar, and 1 tablespoon brandy. It is well beaten and cooked in a double boiler, stirring all the time to prevent curdling. It is served with steamed sweet puddings, particularly Christmas pudding.

brandy snap, a wafer curl, made from 4 heaped tablespoons each of butter, brown sugar, and flour, and 1 tablespoon brandy, all well beaten. Spoonfuls are put onto a greased baking sheet and baked until golden brown, then curled around a wooden spoon handle while still warm. Wafers are mentioned in the works of Geoffrey Chaucer (1340–1400): ''Wafers piping hot out of the Gleed,'' and were probably known earlier. The wafer irons were usually round, about the size of a small plate, with a long handle to prevent one's fingers burning over the hot coals. These wafer irons went to America with the earliest settlers and came back to us as waffle irons. The wafers were originally called *gaufres*, from *gaufrer*, to flute or crimp, and the old Norman-French word *vaufre*. Brandy snaps are the descendants of the *gaufres*, and were popular with the Flemish weavers who came to England in the 14th century. They are still made and sold at the centuries-old fair held yearly at Hull, Yorkshire.

brandy snaps

brantôme, a French sauce for fish made from ½ pint (1 cup) cream sauce, reduced by half with ¼ pint (1 cup) white wine, 1 tablespoon oyster juice, 1 tablespoon crayfish butter (*beurre écrevisses*) all beaten together. The sauce is seasoned with cayenne pepper and garnished with grated truffles.

branzine, see SPIGOLA.

brasciolette, see BRACIOLETTE.

braten, German for roast. See HASENBRATEN; MILCHBRATEN; ROSTBRATEN; SAUERBRATEN; SCHWEINEBRATEN; WALDMEISTERBRATEN; WURSTELBRATEN.

bratheringe, a German method of sousing herrings. They are first dipped in flour and then fried in oil. When cool, a cold boiled marinade of half vinegar and half water, 2 tablespoons olive oil, a pinch of mustard seed, bay leaves, a sliced onion, and peppercorns is poured over the herrings and left for 24 hours. See also HERINGE; SOUSE.

bratklops, German for *rissole,* usually served with sauerkraut in Germany. In France they are also served plain and in other countries they are sometimes used as an hors d'oeuvre.

bratwurst, a German sausage made from lean pork to ⅙ of the quantity of fat pork, a pinch of saltpetre, salt, and black pepper. This mixture is finely minced; then breadcrumbs (1 lb. to 6 lb. meat), soaked in milk but pressed dry, together with grated nutmeg, and finely minced sage or any other herb are added to the meat mixture before it is packed into skins and the ends are secured. This sausage is often boiled in salted water in Germany, as well as being served fried or grilled. Each district has its own variety, and the name of the town or place prefaces the sausages. See also WURST.

braune suppe mit leberpurée, brown soup made with a purée of ½ lb. cooked liver, 1 onion, and 2 egg yolks.

braunkohl, German for kale or broccoli.

braunkohl Holsteiner art, a recipe from Holstein. The kale is blanched with chopped leeks, sweated in lard, seasoned, and braised in beef stock thickened with a sprinkling of oatmeal. See also PINKEL MIT BRAUNKOHL.

brawn, an English dish of boiled, boned, jellied, and potted pig's head or, at an earlier date, boar's meat. The word is from the Old French *braon*. Brawn is served cold. It differs from galantine in that it is a blend of meat and its own jelly. The head or one-half head is simmered in water with herbs and seasoning until the meat leaves the bone. The boned meat is chopped, fat removed from the stock, and the stock is poured over the meat to cover it completely. When cold, the stock will form a jelly. It is mentioned in Russell's ''Boke of Nurture,'' 1460: ''Set forth mustard and brawne.''

brazil nut (*Bertholletia excelsa*), the edible fruit of a large tree native to South America which is valuable as timber. It will not survive frost and has failed to transplant to colder regions. It fruits from January to June. The large, cream-coloured nut, also known as butternut, paranut, creamnut, and niggertoe, has a dark brown, ridged, three-sided shell, 1–1½ inches long. It is excellent eaten raw and also much used for sweet and cake making.

bread, a food made from a baked dough of flour with salt, milk, or water, and, usually, yeast added. It is a staple food product in many parts of the world, and the making of it dates back to the Stone Age.

The earliest form of bread was probably made from ground acorns and beech nuts, but calcified remains of bread made from coarsely ground grain have been found in Switzerland, in such early settlements as Stone-Age lake-dwellings. The dough was probably cooked in a container covered with hot ashes. Bread is mentioned in Genesis III, where it is said that Lot ''made a feast, and did bake unleavened bread.'' The ancient Egyptians were efficient bakers and kneaded the dough with their feet, as indeed was the practice in Scotland until quite recently. Pliny says that Rome had no public bakers until after the war with Perseus (B.C. 171–168). Wheat was brought to North America by the Spaniards, and the first crop was cut in 1530.

Bread made with wholemeal flour produces a brown loaf, and that made with a refined white wheat flour, a white loaf. Refined white flour is made from wheat, rye, and even bran. White bread is regarded as having almost magical properties by the poorer classes in England. Mrs. Hartley in her book *Food in England* (MacDonald, 1954) thinks this may be due to the whiteness of the pre-Reformation wafer of the Mass, which was made from wheat flour. She points out that the rich or intellectual class will eat and enjoy all types of brown bread, but the poorer the district, the more firmly will the people insist on their right to a white loaf.

In various parts of Europe and North America, bread has flavourings of caraway seeds, currants, saffron, and many other spices. There are many varieties of loaf shape in Great Britain, such as cottage, coburg, cob, tin, Vienna, sandwich, farl, and pan loaf. The best crusty bread is baked in a brick oven. Soda bread, made without yeast but with baking soda, is popular in Ireland; buttermilk or sour milk is used to mix the flour into a dough. Gluten bread is made for diabetics and has gluten added to the dough; it contains 30 to 40 percent starch. Unleavened bread is used in Scandinavian countries, and by Jewish people at Passover. See also BRØD; BRÖD; BROOD; BROT DOUGH; IRISH SODA BREAD; MANCHET BREAD; MATZO; YEAST DOUGH.

Irish soda bread, ready to bake

to bread means to coat something with toasted crumbs of any variety of bread.

bread pudding, an old English pudding, also known as bread and butter pudding, consisting of thin slices of crustless bread, buttered, and scattered with currants, sultanas, and a little sugar and cinnamon. A custard made from 2 eggs, 1 pint (2 cups) milk, and vanilla sugar is poured over, and the whole is baked until firm in a moderate oven. The bread should only half-fill the dish, since it swells considerably.

bread sauce, an English thick sauce used with poultry and game consisting of ¾ pint (1½ cups) milk boiled with a pinch of mace and an onion stuck with cloves. The onion is removed and 1 cup fresh white breadcrumbs, 1 teaspoon butter, 2 tablespoons cream, and seasonings are added and heated until the sauce is thick. It is served hot.

breadcrumbs, stale crustless bread which is rolled into small crumbs. If the bread is not stale, it can be dried in the oven until crisp before rolling. Breadcrumbs are used extensively for coating fish, meat, and some other foods before frying. They are also used to make a crisp top for vegetable and sweet dishes, or for stuffing. Once they are thoroughly dried out, breadcrumbs can be stored in an airtight container; if stored fresh and damp, they will quickly become mouldy.

breadfruit (*Artocarpus communis* or *A. incisa*), a tropical fruit brought to the West Indies from Polynesia by Captain Bligh on the *Bounty*. The fruit has become a staple of the West Indian diet, and is prepared by boiling, baking, or frying.

breakfast biscuit, a crisp rusk-like biscuit made from 1 lb. (4 cups) flour, 4 tablespoons cream, 1 oz. yeast dissolved in ½ pint (1 cup) tepid water, and salt. The mixture is cut into rounds and pricked all over before baking in a moderate oven until golden brown.

bream, a name applied to many varieties of fish. The freshwa-

breadfruit

ter breams (family *Cyprinidae*) and the sea breams (family *Sparidae*) are absolutely distinct. Among species of the former is the common bream (*Abramis brama*), which, like its kindred species (e.g., the white bream and American shiner), is not good eating. One species of sea bream which is very good to eat is the common sea bream, or chad (*Pagellus centrodontus*); it is best either grilled and served with herbs, butter, and lemon worked together, or else cooked in a cream sauce, with mushrooms and a little white wine. Another variety is *Sargus ovis*, known as sargo or *pargo* in Spain and Portugal, and in Britain as sheep's head. There are several varieties of this sea bream, the main two being known as grey bream or red bream. Both are eaten extensively in southern Europe, but red bream (so-called because of its brighter colouring) has the finer flavour and is one of the most valued food-fishes. Porgy (family *Sparidae*) is the variety of bream found in the U.S. See also BESUGO; BRACHSE; DAURADE; GILT-POLL.

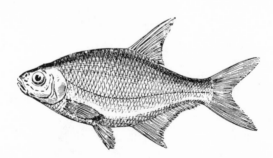

bream (*Pagellus centrodontus*)

brebán, a French garnish for meat, of puréed broad beans on top of artichoke bottoms or cauliflower with sauce hollandaise and potatoes with parsley.

brebis, French for ewe. Many good French cheeses are made from ewe's milk, e.g., Roquefort, *cachat, brebis de Bassillac, banons, brousses, broccio,* and *oloron*. Ewe meat is pickled like pork in the southwestern districts of France and cooked in the same way.

bréjauda, a good traditional soup of Limousin, a region of France, made from stock, sliced cabbage, and diced bacon. Red wine is added to the last few spoonfuls left in the plate, and this is known as *chabrol*. See also GOUDALE.

brema, see SARGO.

brennender pudding, a German pudding, made from 2 oz. (¼ cup) sugar beaten with 4 egg yolks and 2 oz. (½ cup) ground almonds, 2 heaped tablespoons flour, and the same of stale sponge cake crumbs. Finally the beaten egg whites are added. It is steamed in a ring mould for 1 hour. While still hot, the pudding is turned out and lumps of sugar soaked in brandy or other liqueur are put in the middle and set alight at the table.

brent goose, see BARNACLE GOOSE.

bresaola, also called brisavola, a speciality of the province of Lombardy, Italy. It consists of dried salt beef very thinly carved and served with olive oil, lemon juice, and parsley. It is used for antipasti.

bresolles, a French dish probably invented by the chef to the Marquis de Bresolles. It consists of ½ lb. finely chopped lean ham with a chopped medium onion, 3 spring onions (scallions), 4 chopped mushrooms, a clove of garlic, seasoning, a pinch of nutmeg, and 4 tablespoons olive oil. This mixture is layered in a casserole with thin slices of either veal, beef, or mutton, ending with the ham mixture. It is covered and baked in a moderate oven for 30 minutes. When cooked it is turned out and garnished with braised chestnuts and demi-glace flavoured with Madeira wine.

bressanne, a French sauce made from ½ pint (1 cup) sauce espagnole with 2 tablespoons each of Madeira wine and orange juice and 2 cooked puréed chicken livers. It is served with poultry.

Bresse, a district of France famous for the excellence of its poultry.

brestois, a French cake from Brest which is made of 12 eggs to 1 lb. (2½ cups) castor sugar, whisked over a low heat; 5 oz. pounded almonds mixed with 3 eggs and flavoured with a squeeze of lemon and 3 tablespoons curaçao are then added. The whole is whisked to make it frothy, and at the last moment ½ lb. (1 cup) melted butter and ½ lb. (2 cups) sifted flour are blended in. The mixture is put into buttered brioche moulds and baked in a slow oven. If kept in an airtight tin, a brestois keeps well; it used to be known as a *gateau de voyage*—a travelling cake.

breton, a French cake which in spite of its name does not come from Brittany. It was a large cake made by placing different cakes on top of one another and icing each with a different colour, finally decorating the whole with almond paste. It is seldom seen nowadays.

breton far, a commercially made cream flan found in Brittany.

bretonne, I. A French sauce made from ½ pint (1 cup) velouté, ¼ cup white wine, ½ medium onion, ¼ heart celery, and 2 leeks, all sliced julienne, softened in 1 tablespoon butter, and added to the sauce. Sometimes it is flavoured with tomato purée and parsley. It is served with meat. A variant has 3 tablespoons each of cream and butter added, also mushrooms and fish fumet when served with fish. Carême's recipe is without tomatoes. II. A French garnish for joints, of cooked white haricot beans with sauce bretonne. III. A French beef consommé garnished with strips of leek, celeriac, mushrooms, and chervil. See also CONSOMMÉ. IV. A French method of serving potatoes. See POMME DE TERRE.

bretonneau, an Old French name in Normandy for turbot.

brewis, a "tea-kettle" broth made in Wales from oat-husks, soaked in water and then boiled with fat bacon, salt, and pepper. Today it is made with finely cut bread crusts and a lump of butter. See also BROSE.

brézolles, French for slices of veal cut from the inside part of the leg, known as *noix patissìre* or *rouelle.* The latter can also mean slices from the knuckle end, cut across the bone. Brézolles are thicker than escalopes, and are not flattened before cooking.

brézolles lorraines, 1 shallot and 1 tablespoon parsley, both chopped and turned in 2 tablespoons butter with a slice of chopped ham; the veal slices (see above) added, seasoned,

and browned on each side. One-fourth cup white wine is added, then all is transferred to an ovenproof dish, sprinkled with breadcrumbs, dotted with butter, and baked for 20–30 minutes in a moderate oven.

briand, a French chicken consommé garnished with diced chicken, ham, and veal. It is sprinkled with chopped chervil before serving. See also CONSOMMÉ.

brick cheese, one of the few cheeses which originated in the U.S.; it is particularly popular in Wisconsin. It is made from renneted cow's milk and is a sweet-curd, semisoft cheese, with a mild yet pungent flavour. It is like a cross between a mild cheddar and a mild limburger, if such a thing can be imagined. The paste is elastic and slices without crumbling, hence its popularity for sandwiches. It has numerous round and irregularly shaped "eyes." The name is thought to derive either from its brick-like shape or from the bricks used in pressing the cheese.

bricquebec, a French cheese made with cow's milk. It comes from Normandy and is in season all the year round.

brider, French, meaning to truss.

brie, one of the finest French cow's milk cheeses. It comes from the district of La Brie, along the lower valley of the Marne. It is circular in shape and is from ¾ to 1 inch thick, and from 15 to 20 inches in diameter. A smaller brie of 4 to 6 inches in diameter is also made, though it is not as good as the larger cheese. Brie is a soft-paste cheese made from renneted whole cow's milk and is mould-inoculated. It is slightly salted, without rind, but with a golden-brown mouldy crust with white tracings. The inside should be creamy, and slightly runny.

Brie has been praised for its excellence from the 10th century onwards, its crowning distinction being the title *"le roi des fromages,"* given to it during the Congress of Vienna in 1815, which was presided over by Prince Metternich and attended by ambassadors of 30 nations. The chief city of La Brie is Meaux, and the best brie is *brie de Meaux,* which is creamery-made and at its best from November to May; this is known as *gras* (full fat). The spring and summer bries are not as good and are called *migras* (half fat) and *maigre* (low fat).

brie de coulommiers, see COULOMMIERS.

brie de melun, of somewhat thicker texture than other bries, and not inoculated. It is matured over a longer period to produce its own fleur, but it is not always the best of the brie cheeses.

brie de montereau, a near-brie type of cheese, but somewhat thicker than *brie de Meaux.*

briessuppe, an Austrian soup made from stock, blanched chopped calves' sweetbreads, 2 sliced onions, 2 sliced carrots, and a small shredded cabbage. It is garnished with asparagus tips and diced fried bread.

brighton rock, a small English cake made from 4 oz. (1 cup) ground almonds (both sweet and bitter) mixed with 6 tablespoons rose water. Then 2 oz. (½ cup) currants, 8 oz. (2 cups) flour, 4 oz. (½ cup) sugar, and 4 oz. (½ cup) melted butter are added to make a firm mixture, and the whole is well creamed. The mixture is formed into small cakes, which are baked for about 15 minutes in a moderate oven.

brignole, see PRUNE.

brill (*Scophthalmus rhombus*), an extremely good European sea fish which is at its best from April to August. It is a flat fish, white and firm, and can be cooked in the same way as turbot, which it resembles.

Brillat-Savarin, Jean (1755–1826), French gourmet and politician, author of several legal pamphlets, and a gastronomical work entitled *La Physiologie du Goût.* His name is given to various preparations. I. Two French garnishes, one for game, the other for noisettes. The first consists of pastry tarts filled with a soufflé of snipe or woodcock and truffles. The second

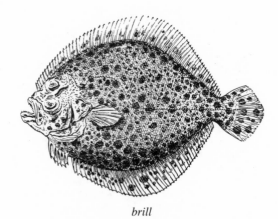

brill

consists of cassolettes of *pommes duchesse* filled with a salpicon of foie gras, truffles, with asparagus tips in butter. II. Two chicken consommés. The first, thickened with tapioca, is garnished with julienne of chicken breast, diamond-shaped pieces of crêpes, chiffonade of lettuce, sorrel, and chervil. The second, thickened with arrowroot, is garnished with sliced mushrooms, truffles, and carrots. See also CONSOMMÉ. III. A French soft triple cream cheese from Normandy made with cow's milk. It is in season all the year round.

brilloli, a Corsican sweet porridge, made from chestnut flour to which milk or cream is added.

brindza, see BRYNDZA.

brine, a solution of salt and water used for preserving or pickling. In the case of meats, saltpetre, sugar, and herbs are sometimes added. See also CURING.

bringukollar, an Icelandic speciality of breast of lamb spiced and soured with pickling brine.

brînză, Rumanian for cheese. See CAŞCAVAL; KASHKAVAL; MONOSTORER; PENETELEU.

brioche, a French yeast dough, very light and crumbly. The finished article varies in shape from a ball with a small head (known as brioche à tête) to a small column (*brioche mousseline*) and brioche en couronne (brioche dough formed into quite a large crown shape before baking). An ordinary brioche dough consists of 1 lb. (4 cups) sifted flour, ½ lb. (1 cup) butter, 4 eggs, ½ oz. yeast, 3 tablespoons sugar, a little salt, and about a gill (½ cup) of warm milk. The yeast is creamed with a little tepid water and mixed into a quarter of the flour, rolled into a ball, covered, and left to double its size. The remainder of the flour is mixed with the eggs and 2 tablespoons warmed (tepid) milk and then kneaded. The sugar (3 tablespoons) and a pinch of salt are dissolved in the rest of the milk, then the softened butter is added. Both doughs are mixed together, and blended thoroughly. They are then put into a warmed bowl, covered, and left in a warm place for 2½ hours, after which the dough is well beaten and kept in a cool place until wanted for use. This dough can be used for cases for sweet or savoury fillings. If it is being used for savoury pies or with grated cheese (4 oz. for 2 lb. dough), omit the sugar.

The word brioche is said to come from two Old French words, *bris*, to break, and *hocher*, to stir, which, put together, have become brioche. "Faire une brioche" means to make a blunder. This arises from earlier days when musicians who played out of tune had to pay a fine; the money was spent on brioches.

brioche goubaud, a form of brioche which resembles a covered tart or flan. A round greased flan tin is lined with brioche dough, and the centre is filled with thinly rolled triangles of the same dough stuffed with chopped preserved fruit previously soaked in a liqueur. These wedge-shaped pieces are arranged so that they fit together, the whole looking like a

segmented tart. It is left in a warm place to rise for ½ hour, then brushed with beaten egg before being baked in a hot oven. When cooked, the top is brushed with strained, diluted, and warmed apricot jam.

brioche mousseline, made with the same quantity of flour as above, but with double the quantity of butter. It is baked in the shape of a small column.

brioli, a Corsican dish made from chestnut meal, prepared as for polenta and served with milk or cream. See also POLENTA.

brionne, alternative name in France for CHAYOTE.

brisket, the breast-meat of animals. In British culinary use it generally refers to salted beef. The upper end is the thickest and leanest, while the lower (navel) end has more fat. In the U.S., brisket is served boiled or braised. Brisket of salted or corned beef is the best cut for boiling, but care should be taken that the butt end is served. In the U.S., first-cut brisket is the best cut and it is boneless. See also RATTLERAN. See meat diagrams, pages xxii–xxiii.

brisling, a Danish and Norwegian term for the young herring, which are very plentiful in Scandinavian waters. See also SILD.

brisling, innbakt i form, Norwegian baked brisling pie. Two medium onions, finely sliced, 6 mushrooms, and 1 sliced green pepper are fried together in butter. Four peeled tomatoes, 1 cup dry white wine, water to barely cover, and seasonings are added to the pan and simmered for 10 minutes. Half of this sauce goes into a pie dish together with the contents of a large can of brislings. They are topped by sliced, cooked potatoes and the remaining sauce with a little parsley. The dish is covered with pastry and baked for ½ hour in a hot oven.

bristol, a French garnish for meat, made from small croquettes of rice, creamed flageolet beans (small kidney beans), and *pommes noisettes*.

brit or *bret*, in England the word for a small turbot. In the U.S. it denotes a small herring.

britannia, a French beef consommé slightly thickened with tapioca and garnished with crayfish royale and julienne of truffles. See also CONSOMMÉ.

British cheeses, see ENGLISH CHEESES.

brněnskýřízek, a Czechoslovak dish of thin veal fillets (scallops) stuffed with a mixture of scrambled eggs, butter, cooked green peas, and chopped ham. These fillets are folded over, secured with a skewer, dipped into egg and breadcrumbs, and fried on both sides in hot fat.

broa, traditional Portuguese yellow corn bread, served with many dishes. It is made from ½ lb. (2 cups) each cornmeal and wheat flour, 2 tablespoons each semolina and corn flour (cornstarch), 1 tablespoon sugar and 2 teaspoons baking powder, all mixed. Beaten egg, milk, melted fat or oil, and salt are added until a slack dough is formed. This is put into a tin and baked in a hot oven for 20–30 minutes. See also BROAS.

broad bean (*Vicia faba*), a bean which should be picked and cooked when young and tender, for the surrounding skin becomes tough and leathery when old. The age can be easily recognised by a black line running along the kidney-shaped side, and all beans with this line should have the skins removed by blanching; otherwise they will be inedible.

Young beans should be shelled and cooked in fast-boiling salted water, with either a good-sized sprig of parsley, or better still savory, for not longer than 15 minutes. They should be drained, and served with more chopped parsley or savory, freshly ground pepper, and butter. They are also excellent cooked as above, drained, and served cold with a sauce vinaigrette, as a salad, or for hors d'oeuvre. For a main course, they can be cooked and some of the bean water reserved and used in equal quantities with milk to make a sauce béchamel.

broad bean

The beans are reheated in this sauce with chopped ham or bacon, chopped parsley or savory, and freshly ground pepper or a pinch of mace. In France this is known as *fèves au jambon,* but it is also an English country dish. In some Mediterranean countries, particularly Italy, broad beans are dried for use in the winter in soups, stews, and casseroles. They are soaked for several hours before cooking. See also BEAN.

broas, small Madeira cakes, particularly popular in the 19th century in Britain, and so called from the Portuguese *broa* meaning millet, as they resembled the yellow corn bread eaten in Portugal which was accompanied with wine. They were eaten with wine, especially Madeira, and originated in the Portuguese island of that name. They are made from ¼ lb. (½ cup) butter mixed into 1 lb. (3½ cups) flour and ¾ lb. (1½ cups) sugar; 1 teaspoon powdered cinnamon, the grated peel of 1 lemon, and 2 beaten eggs are added, with a very little milk if the mixture is too stiff. It is shaped into small round cakes, and baked for 15–20 minutes in a moderate to hot oven.

broccio(u), a Corsican cream cheese made from either goat's or sour ewe's milk. It has a very delicate flavour and resembles a *petit suisse* in appearance. It is at its best from April to November.

broccoli (*Brassica oleracea;* var. *italica*), a cluster-headed vegetable resembling a small cauliflower. (American variety, *Brassica oleracea botrytis.*) The European broccoli first mentioned is a native of Italy; it was introduced into France and Great Britain at the beginning of the 18th century, but did not become popular in the U.S. until after WW I. It is a winter and early spring vegetable, and is highly thought of gastronomically. A new variety, called "calabrese," has been developed in England; it is dark green in colour and can be tinged with purple, for which reason it is sometimes known as purple-sprouting broccoli.

Broccoli "heads" should be trimmed and cooked gently in boiling salted water until the stalks are tender. If hot, they are good served with melted butter, sauce hollandaise, or a béchamel sauce flavoured with cheese. They can also be served cold with a vinaigrette dressing. In Italy, they are sometimes served cold in hors d'oeuvre and salads, or used in soups and as a garnish, besides being served as a vegetable. Broccoli is called by the same name in both Norway and Sweden. See also CALABRESE.

broccoli grateng, a Norwegian broccoli and cheese dish. Broccoli is cooked in the usual way until quite soft, when it is covered with 1 pint (2 cups) white sauce to which 4 tablespoons (¼ cup) cream, a pinch each of salt and allspice, and 1 beaten egg yolk have been added. The dish is then topped with grated cheese and baked in a hot oven until golden brown. See also GRØNSAKER.

broccoli med frankfurterkorv, a Swedish dish of broccoli with frankfurters. Broccoli is cooked in the usual way. Frankfurters split lengthways and halved are laid on top. The dish is topped with slices of cheese and browned under the grill. See also GRÖNSAKER.

broccoli tipper med rørt smør, another Norwegian dish of broccoli tips with lemon butter. The broccoli is cooked in the usual way, and served with a chilled sauce of creamed butter mixed with a dash of worcestershire sauce and a good squeeze of lemon juice. See also GRÖNSAKER.

brochet, French for pike. A small pike is called *brocheton.* Pike is very highly thought of in France, and is prepared in many ways. In Alsace it is baked in white wine and fish stock and served with tartlets filled with sauerkraut and ham. In the area around Nantes in the northwest of France it is poached and served with a (sauce) *beurre blanc;* elsewhere it is braised, grilled, fried, or made into mousse. In Lyons it is made into quenelles known as *quenelles de brochet à la Lyonnaise.* See also QUENELLE.

brochettes, a French method of cooking meat or fish, cut into pieces and threaded on a skewer, then grilled either on the stove or over an open fire.

brócolos, Portuguese for broccoli.

brød, Danish for bread, which is usually made from rye flour.

brød, Norwegian for bread. Bread is so often served in Norway, principally in the form of open sandwiches (*smørbrød*), that it is an important part of the country's food. The main bread eaten is very similar to that eaten in Great Britain, but there are other kinds, notably *flatbrød* and *lefser,* which are popular throughout the country. The Norwegians have a special Christmas bread (called *julekake*), which is something like the pastry made in Denmark. See also BREAD; JULEKAKE.

bröd, Swedish for bread. Open sandwiches are served at informal tea and beer parties in Sweden, where bread also figures very large on the smörgåsbord. It is very often home-baked, and the loaves of *råg* (rye bread), *knäckebröd* (crispbread), *limpa* (fruit bread), and *vetebröd* (coffee bread) are quite excellent. Yeast is used in many Swedish bread recipes. See also BREAD.

brodet, a Yugoslavian fish stew, made from about 3 lb. local red-coloured fish, 2 sliced onions, 2 cups peeled shrimps, 2 tablespoons tomato purée, 4 tablespoons wine vinegar, 4 cloves garlic, 2 tablespoons parsley, grated peel of 1 lemon, seasonings, and red wine and water in equal quantities to cover completely. After sautéeing the onion in oil, it is all cooked together, except for the finely chopped garlic, parsley, and grated lemon peel, which is added finally as a garnish.

brodetto, an Italian fish soup which is more like a stew. It is common to the Marche province and the Adriatic coast. There are different versions for each town, but they do not vary much. The fish used are those caught locally, such as *calamaretti* (squid), eel, red mullet, *spigola* (bass), sole, and a delicate crustacean called *cannocchie* (or *pannocchie* or *cicala di mare*). The heads of all are boiled up with tomatoes, a clove of crushed garlic, parsley, oregano, a dash of vinegar, seasoning, and water to cover. When cooked, this mixture is strained and sieved, and should be fairly thick and a deep reddish colour. The *calamaretti* are first cleaned and chopped; then fried in olive oil with parsley, garlic, and 1 pint (2 cups) fresh tomato sauce thinned with a little water. They are simmered for ½ hour before adding chunks of the other fish, cooking them gently so that they do not break. The sauce should be nearly all absorbed when the dish is ready, and it is served with slices of bread fried in oil or baked in the oven. At the same time the soup, or *brodo,* made from the heads, is served hot, in separate dishes. The two dishes are eaten simultaneously, each person choosing the fish he or she prefers. See also BURRIDA; CACCIUCCO LIVORNESE; CANNOCCHIE; ZUPPA, DI PESCE.

brodo, Italian for broth, which forms the basis for many Italian soups. It is sometimes garnished with small pasta, *anolini,* or *cappelletti.* See also ANOLINI; CAPPELLETTI; PASSATELLI; STRACCIATELLA.

pasta in brodo con fegatini e piselli, a mild, well-flavoured chicken broth containing fine strips of pasta, peas, and chicken liver, all sprinkled with grated Parmesan cheese.

broeselknödel, see KNÖDEL.

broglie, a French sauce for meat, consisting of demi-glace reduced with mushroom stock, butter, and Madeira wine, and then garnished with finely chopped fried ham.

broil, term used in the U.S. meaning "to grill"; it is thought to come from the French *bruler,* to burn. This term was used in England in the form *brule* until about 1500, and the term *broil* up to the end of the 19th century.

broiler, I. The word used in the U.S. for a grill. II. It is also the term used in the U.S. for a young chicken.

brombaer, Danish for blackberry.

brombaersuppe, blackberry soup. Blackberries are barely covered in cold water and simmered gently until the juice is extracted. Then they are strained and the juice is thickened with either corn flour (cornstarch) or potato flour slaked in a little cold water (1 heaped tablespoon for 1 pint juice). The soup, which should be of a creamy consistency, is served chilled, and can be flavoured with grated nutmeg.

brønnkarse, Norwegian for watercress (also called *vannkarse).* It is much used in Norway in the preparation and decoration of *smørbrød.*

brood, Dutch for bread. Many varieties of bread are made in Holland—brown, white, rye (*roggebrood*), and pumpernickel, as well as rolls and currant bread. Dutch for roll is *broodje;* breadcrumbs are *broodkruimels.* Stale bread is the basis of many Dutch pudding recipes.

broodomelet, bread omelette. A small stale crustless loaf is soaked in warmed milk and mashed finely. Then vanilla, lemon peel, 4 tablespoons sugar, and 4 egg yolks are added. Finally, 4 stiffly beaten egg whites are folded in. This mixture is cooked, half at a time, in butter in an omelette pan until each half is brown on both sides. The halves are laid one on top of the other with a layer of orange marmalade spread between. The omelette can be eaten, sprinkled with sugar, either warm or cold.

broodschoteltje, apple charlotte. Apples are stewed or steamed, put through a sieve and sweetened. Alternate layers of this mixture and stale bread (buttered on both sides) are arranged in a casserole, ending with a layer of bread. Cinnamon mixed with sugar is dusted over the top, and the pudding is baked for about 20 minutes in a moderate oven.

broodschoteltje met amandelen, a bread dish with almonds, especially popular with Dutch children. A small crustless loaf is softened in milk and crumbled, before being mixed with 1 cup finely chopped blanched almonds, 2 egg yolks, and ½ lb. (1 cup) sugar. Lastly, 2 stiffly beaten egg whites are folded in and the dish is sprinkled with cinnamon and dotted with butter, and baked in a moderate oven for about 30 minutes.

broodschoteltje met rozijnen, a bread dish made with raisins. A Dutch variation of the English bread and butter pudding. Stale bread is softened in milk and crumbled adding 2 egg yolks, 4 oz. (½ cup) sugar, 3 tablespoons each of raisins and chopped candied orange peel, 1 gill (½ cup) brandy, and 2 teaspoons cinnamon. These are mixed well. Then 2 stiffly beaten egg whites are folded in. The pudding is dotted with butter and cooked for about 30 minutes in a moderate oven.

broodschoteltje met sinaasappels, a bread dish with oranges. One small loaf of white bread without crust is soaked and mashed in warm orange juice. Two egg yolks, ½ lb. (1 cup) sugar, and lemon peel are folded into 4 oz. (½ cup) softened butter. When this mixture is of a creamy consistency, it is mixed with the bread, the stiffly beaten egg whites are folded in, and baked for about 30 minutes in a slow oven. See also TURFJES MET BESSENSAP; WENTELTEEFJES.

brooklime (*Veronica beccabunga*), an edible veronica which grows in bogs, and is known in Scotland as water pimpernel, or purpie. It resembles watercress, and is a good substitute for it.

broom (*Cytisus*), a shrub of the pea family, native to all temperate parts of Europe, Asia, and the U.S. In medieval England the buds were preserved in vinegar and used as capers.

broonie, Orkney Island gingerbread made with oatmeal instead of flour. The word comes from the Orkney and Shetland word which is from the Norse, *brüni,* meaning a thick bannock.

brose, a traditional Scottish dish which consists of boiling water or milk poured over oatmeal. It is a kind of porridge soup. Originally, from the 16th to the 18th century it was eaten mainly by shepherds in the Scottish Highlands. The ground oats were put into a small covered container made of leather or wood called a hoggin and carried on the back. At the nearest brook, water was added to the oats, and by the time the sheep were reached, the movement and body warmth of the shepherd had set up a fermentation which produced a thickish porridge. Today, however, brose more often means a form of soup, such as oatmeal stirred into mutton broth and cooked until it thickens the soup. It is similar to the Welsh *brewis.*

brot, German for bread, of which there are many varieties in Germany, the majority being dark and made from rye flour. Bread is also used extensively in light dumplings (see KLÖSSE), both sweet and savoury. See also PUMPERNICKEL; STOLLEN; ZWIEBACK.

brotkoch, a delicate sweet mould made from ¼ cup breadcrumbs, 3 oz. (3 heaped tablespoons) sugar, 4 egg yolks, and 4 beaten egg whites, steamed, with shredded almonds and fine candied peel lining the mould. It is cooked for 1 hour, and served with a lemon, vanilla, or liqueur sauce.

brotpudding, bread pudding, made with ground almonds and grated lemon peel instead of the dried fruits used in the English recipe.

brotsuppe, an Austrian and German soup made from stale breadcrumbs and veal stock thickened with egg yolk, and flavoured with parsley, salt, and pepper. It is served garnished with cubes of smoked sausage.

brotchán, an Irish word originally meaning porridge but which has now come to mean broth or soup. In ancient times soup was much thicker than it is today, and contained a coarse oatmeal.

brotchán roy, a leek or nettle broth thickened with oatmeal, reputed to be a favourite with St. Columba.

broth, from the Teutonic root *bru,* to boil, is the water in which either meat, poultry, vegetables, or fish have been boiled. Meat broth is the basis of all meat soups, but more usually it is the mixture of meat and vegetables that is used, even if the vegetable is no more than an onion and a sprig of parsley. Nowadays broth means a thin, clear soup. Scotch broth is an exception.

Scotch broth, a mutton-based soup, with chopped onions, carrots, seasonings, and pearl barley. The proportions are 1½ lb. mutton, free of bone, fat, and gristle, 2 large onions, 3 carrots, 3 tablespoons pearl barley, 2 tablespoons chopped parsley, and 2 quarts (8 cups) water.

brótola de fango, a grey fish with reddish fins, about 8–10 inches long found in Spanish waters. It is of the cod family (*Gadidae*) and makes fair eating if cooked whole in the oven in an oiled dish, with sliced lemon, tomatoes, and onion, with grated garlic and parsley on the top. It can also be used in soups and rice dishes.

brousses, a ewe's milk cheese made in Provence, France, which is at its best from March to May, and again in September.

broutes, in the Béarn district of France this name is given to old cabbage shoots or stumps, which are trimmed, washed, and cooked in salted water. They are then drained and seasoned with oil and vinegar. It is a popular Lenten dish. In the Basses-Pyrénées, leeks are sometimes added to the cabbage; the mixture is pressed, and cut into pieces, and called by the same name. See also CABBAGE.

brown betty, an American and also English pudding made from apples, breadcrumbs, butter, brown sugar, lemon juice and peel, cinnamon, and water. They are all put in layers, finishing with the breadcrumbs, and baked in a moderate oven until brown on top. See also APPLE CHARLOTTE; CHARLOTTE DE FRUITS.

brown sauce, see ESPAGNOLE, SAUCE.

brown sugar, see SUGAR.

brown trout, see TROUT.

brownie, an American biscuit (cookie) made from 2 squares (2 oz.) unsweetened chocolate melted and mixed with 2 oz. (¼ cup) butter, 9½ oz. (1¼ cups) sugar, 2 eggs, 2 oz. (½ cup) flour, ¼ cup chopped nuts, with vanilla to taste and a pinch of salt. The mixture is spread in a flat tin lined with greased paper, and baked in a slow oven for 1 hour. When cool, it is cut in squares.

browning, a fluid preparation made from 1 lb. burnt sugar or caramel mixed with ¼ lb. salt, a flavouring such as mushroom ketchup, and water. It is also known as gravy salt and is commercially made and bottled. It is used to colour gravies, soups, stews, etc., although nowadays, with the many good stock cubes and other seasonings that are on the market, it is not used to any great extent.

broye, a dish from the Béarn district of France, consisting of white (uncooked) or roasted maize flour (*troustade*) cooked with vegetable stock until it is thick, and then left to get cold. When chilled it is cut into slices and fried in hot fat until golden. It is the Béarnais version of *polenta*.

bruciate briache, literally "burning drunkards," an Italian dish of baked, peeled chestnuts, sprinkled with sugar, soaked in hot rum, and set aflame.

bruckfleisch, the German term for a collection of beef offal (variety meats), such as sweetbread, liver, heart, and melts (spleen). It is made into a stew with water, root vegetables, bay leaf, seasonings, and herbs, and served with dumplings. Sometimes a cheap beef cut, known as *kronfleisch*, is added.

brugnon, a hybrid fruit grown in France. It is a cross between a plum and a peach, and looks like a red plum. The taste is not unlike that of a nectarine, and for this reason is sometimes now used as an alternative French name for nectarine. Like most hybrids, it does not propagate from seed, but from cuttings. It is in season from the end of July to the end of August. It is a good dessert fruit, but its keeping qualities are poor.

bruine bonen, Dutch for kidney beans (see FRENCH BEANS). These dried brown beans can be cooked whole and served with diced, crisply fried bacon and fried onions. Dill pickles and mustard are served on the side.

   bruine bonensoep, the Dutch way of making a brown bean soup using dried beans. Two cups beans should be washed and soaked overnight in 5 pints (10 cups) water, then sim- mered in the same water for about 4 hours with 4 cloves, salt, 1 bay leaf, and 10 peppercorns. The whole is then sieved and returned to the heat for a further 2 hours, together with the 2 leeks, ½ celery heart (with leaves), 2 carrots, and 2 onions, all of which have been previously browned in fat. Before serving, the soup is given a spicy flavour by the addition of 2 tablespoons each of ketchup and soy sauce.

brukiew, Polish for turnips. One traditional Polish way of serving them is to half-cook them in ham stock, add potatoes, and then finish cooking. They are strained, mashed, and served with cooked, crumbled streaky bacon on top. The liquid is retained for soup stock.

brukselka, Polish for brussels sprouts, often made into a soup in Poland with smoked pork, onion, celery, leek, and parsnip. They are also served as a vegetable topped with breadcrumbs fried in butter.

brun lapskaus, a Norwegian brown beef stew. Slices of stewing beef are dipped into seasoned flour and browned in butter. They are then placed in a covered pan with peppercorns, bay leaf, and brown stock to cover, and cooked for 1–1½ hours. If desired, the sauce may be strained and thickened with potato flour. Potatoes and other vegetables accompany this stew.

brun løksaus, a Norwegian brown onion sauce. It is made with ¼ lb. diced bacon lightly fried in a pan, with ¼ lb. sliced onions or shallots. When lightly browned, 1 heaped tablespoon flour is stirred in, then 1 pint (2 cups) beef stock, and either ½ cup malt or wine vinegar is gradually added. When cooked and thickened, seasoning and a little sugar are included. In Norway this sauce often accompanies the meat balls known as *kjøttboller*. See also KJØTT.

brune kager, Danish spice biscuits, made from 2 heaped tablespoons butter, 4 oz. (½ cup) brown sugar, and 1 cup golden syrup (corn syrup), boiled in a saucepan. It is removed from the heat and mixed with ¾ lb. (3 cups) flour, ½ teaspoon baking soda, ½ cup chopped almonds, ¼ cup candied peel, and a pinch each of cloves, cinnamon, and ginger. It is well kneaded and left for 2–3 days in a cool place, then rolled out and cut into biscuits, which are baked in a moderate oven for 10–15 minutes.

brunede kartofler, see KARTOFFEL.

brunnenkresse, German for watercress.

brunoise, I. A French vegetable garnish for soup made from diced carrots, onion, leek, celery, turnips, peas, and green beans simmered very gently in butter. Consommé is heated separately, then the vegetables are combined and the whole sprinkled with chopped chervil. The peas and beans are added last to avoid overcooking. It is sometimes served with poached eggs, quenelles, or royale garnish as well. See also CONSOMMÉ. II. A method of cutting vegetables into very fine dice, and then cooking them in butter, or other fat until soft, but not brown. III. Various diced vegetables used as a flavouring for crayfish and other foods. A little of the sweated brunoise is often added to other soups or dishes.

brunswick stew, jointed squirrels are put into boiling water, with corn taken off the cob, lima beans, tomatoes, potatoes, onion, a pinch of sugar, salt, and pepper. All are covered and simmered for 2 hours. A few ounces of butter are added 10 minutes before serving.

bruschetta, an Italian, and especially Tuscan and Umbrian, dish of baked slices of white bread rubbed with garlic. Olive oil is poured over them before eating.

brussels lof, Dutch for Belgian endive. A Dutch method of preparing this vegetable is to cook it whole in salted water for about 30 minutes or until tender, then drain and bake it in butter (the dish being dusted with nutmeg) in a hot oven for about 10 minutes. It is sometimes garnished with more melted butter and quartered hard-boiled eggs. See also ENDIVE.

brussels sprouts (*Brassica oleracea;* var. *gemmifera*), a variety of cabbage introduced from the Low Countries into Great Britain in the late 16th century. Its origin is obscure, but a 17th-century English gardener's book says: "The best seed of this plant comes from Denmark and Russia."

The plant does not have a head like the cabbage, but little tight-budded sprouts in the axils of the leaves along the stem. Brussels sprouts are in season from September throughout the winter. The smallest heads are the best eating, and they should be trimmed and a cross cut on the bottom of each stalk. They are usually boiled in salted water, but they should not be allowed to cook for more than 10 minutes as they will lose their bright green colour and crisp texture. They are exceptionally good if turned in butter, after boiling, with the addition of some cooked chopped chestnuts. Another excellent method is to mix them with cooked celery, and serve in a béchamel sauce; also to sprinkle them with celery salt. They are an essential ingredient in the French garnish, *bruxelloise.* See also BRUKSELKA; SPRUITJES.

bruxelloise, à la, I. A French and Belgian sauce for asparagus, consisting of melted butter, salt, pepper, lemon juice, and a sieved hard-boiled egg added finally, and well mixed. II. French garnish for large and small cuts of meat, consisting of brussels sprouts tossed in butter, *pommes fondantes,* and clear veal gravy or thin demi-glace.

brylé pudding, Swedish for crème caramel. One half lb. (1 cup) castor sugar and 3 tablespoons hot water are boiled rapidly in a heavy saucepan to a rich brown syrup. This is poured into the bottom of a soufflé dish and allowed to cool. The sides of the dish are brushed with unsalted melted butter. Into this prepared dish is poured a mixture of 4 eggs, 1½ pints (3 cups) thin cream, 3 tablespoons sugar, and vanilla essence (extract) to taste, all beaten together. The crème caramel is baked (the dish standing in a tin of warm water) in a slow oven until set, when it is turned out and served with whipped cream.

bryndza, a typical Hungarian cheese made from ewe's milk which is rennetted. It has a mildly pungent flavour and smell, and it is very good to eat. It is made in five sizes, which weigh 10, 20, 30, 40, and 60 lb., respectively. This cheese is also made in Czechoslovakia, in the Tatra Mountains.

bryony (*Bryonia dioica*), see BLACK BRYONY.

brysselkäx, Swedish vanilla biscuits. Two oz. (2 heaped tablespoons) vanilla castor sugar (or a few drops of vanilla added to sugar) is beaten into ½ lb. (1 cup) creamed butter; 10 oz. (2½ cups) sifted flour is added and all are lightly kneaded together. The mixture is shaped into a roll about 1½ inches thick, and this is rolled in a mixture of 1 oz. (1 heaped tablespoon) sugar and 1 oz. cocoa. It is then wrapped in waxed paper and chilled. Slices are cut and baked in a moderate oven for 10 minutes.

brzoskwinie, Polish for peaches, often preserved in sugar with white wine.

bubble and squeak, an English dish nearly 200 years old, made of cold salt beef, fried with cooked cabbage. The name obtains from the noise of the frying vegetables. Today the name is more usually given to a mashed mixture of cabbage or greens and potato, fried on each side until brown. See also CABBAGE.

buberts, traditional Latvian pudding, made from 2 tablespoons flour cooked like hasty pudding with ¾ pint (1½ cups) hot milk. When this is cool, 2 egg yolks beaten with vanilla sugar to taste, chopped nuts, and lemon peel are added. Finally, 2 stiffly beaten egg whites are added, and it is left to set. If jam or fruit sauce is served with it, the dish is called *buberts ar auglu mérce.* See also MÉRCE.

bublanina, a Czechoslovak fruit sponge cake. The sponge is put in a baking tin and dotted with stoned cherries or plums. It is baked in a moderate oven until golden brown, and then sprinkled with vanilla sugar.

bublichki or **bubliky,** a Russian sweet bread ring sprinkled with poppy seed. It is made with flour, yeast, butter, eggs, salt, sugar, and water. Sometimes it is made into small ring rolls. They are popular at holiday or festive times.

bucardas, see ALMEJAS.

bucarde, French for cockle.

bucatini, a thin macaroni.

buccin, French for whelk.

buchteln, an Austrian bun, prepared as for yeast dough with ½ oz. yeast, 1 lb. (4 cups) flour, scant ½ pint (1 cup) milk, 2 heaped tablespoons sugar, lemon peel, and 3 egg yolks. The buns have jam inside, and are baked in the oven.

buchty, Czechoslovak yeast buns, made with ½ oz. yeast, 1 lb. (4 cups) flour, 3 tablespoons sugar, ½ lb. (1 cup) soft butter, 2 eggs, and approximately ½ pint (1 cup) tepid milk all mixed together and left for about 1 hour to rise. (See YEAST DOUGH for preparation.) Sometimes lemon peel or vanilla is added to the dough. When it is doubled in size, it is turned onto a floured board and divided into small, round lumps. These are patted out and a little filling of either cottage cheese, poppy seeds, cherries, plums, or other fruit is put in. The dough is folded in to seal it up, and rounded with the hands. The buns are put onto a greased tin, not too close together since they rise a lot. They are left for 30 minutes before baking in a hot oven until golden. While still warm, they are sprinkled with vanilla sugar.

buck, male of the roe and fallow deer, reindeer, chamois, antelope, hare, and rabbit. See also IZARD.

buck rarebit, a very old English dish which consists of welsh rarebit with a poached egg on the top.

bücklinge, an Austrian dish of smoked herring fillets baked with eggs and butter. See also HERRING.

buckwheat (*Fagopyrum esculentum*), the fruit of a herbaceous plant native to central Asia, but also cultivated in Europe and North America. The fruit is similar to beechmast, and it is also known as beech wheat. In the U.S. the seeds are used for a cereal breakfast food; in Russia they are used in making cakes and pancakes. (See also BLINY.) It is also used to prepare *kasha.*

budino, Italian for pudding, usually cooked, and often containing cheese, fruit, or nuts. See also DOLCE.

budino di prugne, a pudding of ¾ lb. soaked prunes barely covered with white wine or water and simmered until soft. When cool, the prunes are finely chopped with 3 tablespoons mixed sultanas, currants, and raisins, and mixed with 2 tablespoons sugar, 4 oz. (1 cup) stale sponge cake crumbs, 1 tablespoon grated lemon peel, 3 tablespoons mixed ground nuts, 2 tablespoons thick cream, and approximately 4 tablespoons of the wine in which the prunes were cooked (if they were cooked in water, Marsala or brandy is added instead). The mixture must not be too dry, but it should not be swamped. It is baked in a pastry case for about ½ hour in a moderate to hot oven and served hot or cold.

budino di ricotta, a pudding made from 1 lb. (2 cups) ricotta cheese, mixed with 4 oz. (½ cup) sugar, 2 oz. (½ cup) ground almonds and 3 crushed bitter almonds, 5 egg whites, and grated peel of 1 lemon. It is poured into a buttered mould, coated with breadcrumbs, cooked for ½ hour, and served cold.

budino toscano, a Tuscan pudding made from 1 lb. (2 cups) ricotta cheese mixed with 2 oz. (½ cup) ground almonds, 2 tablespoons chopped candied orange peel, 4 oz. (½ cup) sugar, 1 tablespoon each of raisins and sultanas, 4 egg yolks and the grated peel of 1 lemon, all beaten together and baked in a buttered mould for about ½ hour. It is equally good eaten uncooked like *crema di mascherpone*.

budyń, the Polish term for a steamed or boiled pudding, whether sweet or savoury. Savoury budyń is often made with pounded fish, shellfish, or poultry; a sweet budyń is made with added sugar and pounded or ground almonds (*budyń migdalowy*).

budyń cielecy, budyń made with calves' brains. Three sets blanched, trimmed, and mashed calves' brains are mixed with ¼ pint (½ cup) cream and 4 separated eggs (the beaten whites added last). This mixture is poured into a greased mould lined with breadcrumbs and steamed for 1 hour. It is served with melted butter and caper or mushroom sauce.

buffalo, see BISON.

buffalo berry (*Shepherdia argentea*), a bushy tree which grows wild in North America, particularly in the Dakotas and Minnesota. It is cultivated in the colder parts of the U.S. for its berries, which are the size of a seedless raisin and either round or oval in shape. The berries are both red and yellow, and acidic, but with a pleasant flavour. They make excellent jam and also the best sauce to eat with buffalo meat, hence their name. The berry is also known as Nebraska currant and rabbit berry.

buffalo currant (*Ribes odoratum*), a cultivated variety of the American currant which grows wild from Missouri to Arkansas. The fruit has a distinctive smell (hence its Latin name) which some people like and others detest. It is used mostly for jam and pies. There is another currant also called buffalo (*R. aureum*) which is also known as golden or Missouri currant. See also GOLDEN CURRANT.

buffalo fish (*Megastomatobus cyprinella*), a good eating freshwater fish which is plentiful in the Mississippi Valley and the Great Lakes of the U.S. It can be prepared and eaten like carp.

buffel-headed duck (*Bucephala albeola*), also known as butterback duck. It is a North American duck, similar to, but smaller than, the canvasback. It is, however, not nearly such good eating. It can be cooked as wild duck.

Bugey, the part of Savoy, France, where Brillat-Savarin, the gastronome, was born at Belley. It is famous for its good food, and especially for the crayfish from the streams around Nantua.

Bugey rissoles, a speciality at Christmastide. They are quite unlike British rissoles and are in fact, puff pastry, filled with chopped roast turkey and tripe which has been poached in aromatic white wine and beef stock, butter, onion, and seasonings, and moistened with good turkey gravy. At the last minute, a few large currants are added. The pastry is cut into pieces 4 inches long and 2½ inches wide and the filling put on. It is folded over, the edges being moistened to secure them, and then brushed over with beaten egg before being baked in a quick oven. The rissoles are eaten hot.

buglosse, see ALKANET.

bugnes, a French fritter made of rolled dough and fried in oil. A speciality of Lyons. The word *beignet* is thought to come from it.

buhara pilâvı, a Turkish speciality of Abdullah's restaurant in Istanbul. One lb. washed rice is cooked gently in 4 oz. (½ cup) butter in a casserole. When translucent, a handful each of skinned pistachio nuts, currants, chopped chicken livers, and grated carrot is added with salt and pepper. This is covered with hot chicken stock to 1 inch higher than the rice. The casserole lid is put on and the contents are cooked slowly until all the liquid is absorbed. It should never be stirred, but sometimes gently lifted with a fork to let out the heat.

buisson, en, a French term employed when describing a dish consisting of various foods, particularly shellfish, arranged to resemble a bush.

bulgare, a French garnish for meat, poultry, or fish, consisting of a mayonnaise mixed with tomato sauce and garnished with cooked, diced celery hearts.

Bulgarian cheeses, Bulgarian has no collective word for cheese, but the country produces very popular native cheeses. See KASHKAVAL; PAPANASH; SIRENE.

bulgur, Turkish for cracked wheat which is used in Turkey and in Mideast in place of rice for a pilaf. In Syria and Lebanon it is used in *kibbeh*. See also PILAVI.

buljong, the Norwegian term for a clear soup, bouillon, or consommé.

buljons ar frikadelém, Latvian for clear soup with quenelles.

bulk cheese, the Canadian slang name for Canadian cheddar.

bullace (*Prunus institia*), a wild plum tree of the Damascus plum variety and the fruit of the tree. The name comes from the Old French word *beloce*. The fruit is rounder and smaller than a plum. It is green in colour and rather sour. However, it makes good wine, bottles well, and can be used like a damson. The same name is given to a sea-fish (*Larimus fasciatus*) with a large head (prized gastronomically in the southern U.S.) and to a small catfish (*Amiurus nebulosus*) found all over the U.S.

bullon de roca, see LABRO.

bully beef, the English name for salted and spiced beef. Bully beef is also pressed and then tinned. I have never heard the name applied to freshly cooked corned or salted beef. The name may be derived from the French *bouilli* meaning boiled; as far as I can find out, it is a British army expression and was current in WW I.

bulrush (family *Cyperaceae*), an aquatic plant known by Pliny as *scirpus*. The leaves and young shoots can be used in salad. The starchy roots are also edible and are used quite frequently in France, where they are known as *massette*.

bulvė, Lithuanian for potato. *Virtos bulvės* are boiled potatoes. See also BULVIŲ DEŠROS.

bulvieriė, a soup made from 2 pints (4 cups) puréed potato soup mixed with ¾ pint (1½ cups) sour cream. The soup is garnished with shredded sorrel, strips of knob celery, strips of smoked goose breast, small fried pork sausages, and 8 halves of hard-boiled egg which have been dipped in egg and breadcrumbs and fried in lard.

bulvių dešros, a potato sausage which is a Lithuanian speciality. It is made from 3 lb. peeled and grated raw potatoes, to which 2 eggs and 1½ teaspoons salt are added with ½ lb. cubed fried bacon and 2 finely chopped onions. This mixture is then put into casings 6–8 inches long or a cloth secured at each end, then baked with butter and basted with ½ pint (1 cup) water, in a slow oven for 2 hours. The sausage is served with sauerkraut.

bun, a small, usually leavened, sweet cake, sometimes also containing fruit and spices. It is of ancient origin, associated with the religious bread offerings of remotest antiquity. Small round cakes were offered by the Egyptians to the goddess of the moon, having had marked upon them a representation of the horns of an ox, which were her symbol. Such sacred bread offerings, being connected generally with the manifestations of the mother-goddess cult associated with fertility and protection, were a widespread practice throughout Europe and Asia—indeed, as far as the cult extended. Among the Greeks, a similar small, sacred cake, containing the finest sifted flour and honey, had the name *bous*, "ox," the accusative of which, *boun*, is thought by many to be the origin of the word bun. The practice of substituting the offering of a sacred bread for what had originally been a blood sacrifice was indicative of the growing adoption of more civilized behaviour. In time, the representation of the horns became a simple cross, though it has also been suggested that this was intended to symbolize the four quarters of the moon. Certainly, in the case of the larger cakes, this marking had also a functional significance in promoting the even rising of the dough and facilitating equitable distribution of fragments among the worshippers. The Romans continued this practice, and such buns were sold at the entrance to their temples. Buns marked with a cross were eaten by the Saxons in honour of the goddess of light, Eoster (the origin of our Easter habit of eating hot cross buns, transposed by the Christian church into a christianized form). The protective association of these little cakes is to be seen in the small, highly spiced buns which are frequently found in Viking-ship burials, and this tradition continues even to the present in English country areas, especially Dorset, where it is thought that the preservation of a hot cross bun, or loaf, marked with a cross and baked on Easter Day, will ensure protection throughout the year.

It has been suggested that the Old French word for a fritter, or swelling, *bugne* (likewise the English word ''bunion'') is probably derived from the classical *boun*.

There are many varieties of English bun, usually made with flour, yeast, sugar, butter, and fruit or spices, such as Bath bun, Chelsea bun, hot cross bun, and the sally lunn. In Scotland, the name is given to a rich spiced cake called Scotch currant bun. In Ulster, Northern Ireland, it is the name for a round plain loaf of bread. It is possible that the crescent or moon shape of the croissant stems from the same source, and in Lyons, France, *bugnes* is a dough fritter fried in hot oil, from which is derived *beignet*. See also CROISSANT.

bundenfleisch, German for salt beef. In culinary use, it means the smoked, salted beef prepared in the Swiss canton of Grisons. It is pickled in brine in November, and smoked and sold in April.

bundeva, Serbo-Croat for pumpkin. This is a very popular vegetable in Yugoslavia. It is often cooked using 2 lb. pumpkin which is peeled, seeded, and cut into thin strips. Then 2 peeled and chopped onions are fried in oil or butter, and 1 tablespoon flour is added, followed by enough hot water (about ½ pint or 1 cup) to make a fairly thick sauce. The strips of pumpkin are then added, together with salt, 1 tablespoon chopped dill, parsley, or fennel, and is simmered for about 1 hour. Finally ¼ pint (½ cup) cream, 2 teaspoons lemon juice, and a pinch of cinnamon are added. Pumpkin is also made into a pie in Yugoslavia, with strudel pastry. A local word for pumpkin is *tikva*.

bündnerfleisch or **bundnerteller,** see BINDENFLEISCH.

bündnerwurst, a Swiss wurst consisting of lean minced pork, diced bacon, powdered cloves, salt, and pepper, all mixed with a little water. The mixture is put into a cleaned calf's bladder and smoked. It is then boiled, and may be served either hot or cold.

bunter hans, a very large light dumpling made with breadcrumbs poached tied in a cloth in water, and served with either stewed vegetables or stewed dried fruits. A speciality of Holstein and north Germany. See also KLÖSSE.

buñuelos, a Spanish fritter batter into which ham, prawns, mussels, chicken, cheese, and potatoes are dipped before being fried in deep oil. The greater the variety of foods used, the better. See also FRITTER.

buñuelos clásicos, a kind of fritter shaped to form a ring. It is made and sold on the spot at all Spanish fairs. The fritter batter consists of 1 lb. (4 cups) flour, ¼ lb. (½ cup) sugar, and 2 oz. yeast, with the addition of 1 pint (2 cups) tepid water. The fritters are tossed into deep boiling oil, and when they swell up, they are drained and sprinkled with sugar. Although not easy to make, they are light and extremely good.

buñuelos de viento, a variation of the above, made without yeast, like choux pastry. One-half pint (1 cup) milk and 4 oz. lard are brought to the boil together in a saucepan. Then ½ lb. (2 cups) sifted flour, 1 tablespoon sugar, 2 teaspoons

cognac, and the grated peel of 1 lemon are added to the liquid in the pan and stirred to a stiff-smooth paste over a gentle heat. The pan is removed from the stove and 6 beaten eggs are well stirred in. Teaspoons of this paste are fried in deep, hot oil. When cool, these fritters are sometimes split and filled with cream. They are traditionally eaten on All Saints' Day in Spain.

buraki, Polish for beetroot which, with cabbage, is almost the national vegetable of Poland and Russia. It is served hot or cold, usually with sour cream, and is also the basis for many traditional soups in both countries. See also BARSZCZ; BEETROOT; BORSCH.

burbot (*Lota lota*), an excellent European river fish. It is the only member of the cod family to inhabit fresh water. A subspecies is also found in the Great Lakes of Canada and the U.S. The flesh does not make particularly good eating, but the liver is very fat and highly prized as food. In France it is used as a pâté, particularly during Lent. It is also known as lote and eelpout. See also BISTOLA DE ROCA.

burdock (*Arctium Lappa*), a perennial plant with burrs, which grows wild in hedgerows. In Scotland, young shoots and peeled roots are cooked and used like salsify. Gerard, writing of these shoots in the 16th century, said ''. . . boiled in meat broth are pleasant to eat, and increase seed and stir up lust.'' The burrs are commonly called bachelor's buttons, or butterbur.

burgonya, Hungarian for potatoes.

burgonya paradicscommal, a Hungarian method of cooking potatoes with an equal quantity of tomatoes, a sprinkling of flour, butter, and sour cream. Traditionally eaten on the great Hungarian holiday, St. Stephen's Day (celebrated in Hungary on August 20, the day the saint's relics were brought to Budapest, and not on September 2, recognised in the ecclesiastical calendar as the feast day).

burgonyaleves, a Hungarian soup made from potatoes and onions, flavoured with paprika, parsley, pimento, and seasonings, and served with sour cream. The suffix *leves* means soup.

rakott burgonya, a potato and egg ragoût. Thick slices of boiled potato are placed on the bottom of a buttered dish with slices of ham over them. They are then covered with alternate layers of sour cream, slices of hard-boiled egg, and boiled cauliflower, finishing with another layer of potato. Finally breadcrumbs are sprinkled on top and the whole is covered with melted butter. The dish is baked in a moderate oven for about 20 minutes.

töltött burgonya, a delicious Hungarian method of stuffing potatoes. Large potatoes of a uniform size are required, and, for the stuffing, cooked minced pork, 3 tablespoons cooked rice, smoked sausages, onions, sour cream, paprika, lard, and salt. The potatoes are peeled and cut lengthwise, and the centres removed. The space is filled with a mixture of the cooked pork and rice, which has been seasoned with plenty of salt and paprika. The onions and the pulp from the potatoes are arranged in layers, with the sausages, in the bottom of an ovenproof dish, and the stuffed potatoes are placed on top. They are covered with a little hot water, baked for 1 hour, and then the sour cream is added when the potatoes are almost cooked. Sweet peppers are also stuffed with meat and potatoes in the same way, and this is called *töltött paprika s burgonya*.

burgonya, Turkish for potatoes.

burgonya köftesi, potato balls. Eight oz. soft-boiled potato, 2 chopped onions, 2 tablespoons parsley, 2 tablespoons grated cheese, and 1 egg are all kneaded together, and the resulting mixture is shaped into balls which are dipped in beaten egg, rolled in breadcrumbs, and fried in boiling oil.

Burgos, a popular soft Spanish cheese made from ewe's milk.

It bears the name of the Spanish province of Burgos, which is the chief area of manufacture.

burma bean, a variety of lima bean. See LIMA BEAN.

burmeister, trade name of a soft, ripened cheese made in Wisconsin, U.S. It is similar to brick cheese.

burnet (*Poterium sanguisorba*), a perennial herb which is a member of the rose family, frequently found growing in chalky, dry soils. The common or salad burnet has an astringent quality, and its name derives from its dark brown flowers. The young leaves have a cucumber flavour, and are used in soups, salads, fish dishes, and also in drinks.

burrida, the name of a Genoese fish soup/stew. Three lb. local fish, such as *gallinella*, *nocciolo*, *pescatrice*, *pesce prete*, *scorfano*, and *sugherello* are used, as well as octopus, mussels, prawns, and clams. One sliced onion, 1 small carrot, ¼ head celery, 1 clove garlic, and 1 tablespoon parsley are first fried in 4 tablespoons olive oil. Then 1 lb. peeled tomatoes, and 1 oz. dried mushrooms (soaked previously) are added, with 3 pints (6 cups) water and 1 sprig basil. If octopus or inkfish (squid) is being used, it should be added to the vegetables at this point and simmered for ½ hour. When these are cooked, the other chopped fish are put in and cooked for 20 minutes. Shellfish or crustacea are added last, and cooking continued just long enough to open the shells. The soup is served with crisp fried bread.

burridà, la, a Sardinian soup made from dogfish cooked in ¼ pint (½ cup) oil, ¼ cup wine vinegar, 3 cloves garlic, ½ cup chopped pine nuts, a pinch of nutmeg, and 1 cup breadcrumbs. These are all covered with water to 2 inches above the ingredients and simmered for ½ hour. The soup is eaten cold.

burrini, an Italian cheese similar to *buttiri*, except that the butter is on the outer layer and not in the middle.

burro, Italian for butter.

burro, al, Italian culinary term meaning served with butter. This applies especially to pasta.

burro, salse di, a butter sauce, made from ½ chopped onion and 1 tablespoon parsley simmered with 1 cup white wine until the wine is reduced by half. Then 2 oz. (2 heaped tablespoons) soft butter is whipped and added gradually. The sauce is seasoned and whipped again. It must not be allowed to brown.

busecca, traditional Italian tripe soup/stew from Turin and Milan. It is made by lightly frying 2 medium chopped onions, 3 leeks, 2 carrots, ½ small cabbage, and 2 sticks celery in 4 tablespoons each olive oil and butter. One-half lb. soaked broad beans, 4 peeled tomatoes, a pinch each of saffron and nutmeg, and 2 pints (4 cups) white stock are added to the other ingredients. Thin strips of blanched tripe (2 lb.) and ¼ lb. chopped bacon are then put in, the stew is seasoned and simmered for 1 hour or until tender. Sliced potatoes are sometimes added at this stage. The soup is served with grated Parmesan cheese and fingers of fried bread which have been rubbed with garlic. See also TRIPE; TRIPPA.

bustard (family *Otididae*), a delicious bird weighing up to 14 lb., and now almost extinct in Great Britain. A smaller species (*Tetrax tetrax*) is still found in the Mediterranean, North Africa, and the Near East, and is highly thought of gastronomically. It is known in France as *bastardau*, and is cooked there by roasting in butter, and served with a red wine sauce.

buster, the name for a crab, especially in New Orleans, U.S., when it is in the stage between hard and soft shell. Such crabs are cleaned, dipped whole into batter, and fried until golden in butter, and are considered a great delicacy. They are often served with sauce béarnaise. See also CRAB.

butifarra, a Spanish sausage made from minced fat pork mixed with white wine, cloves, nutmeg, salt, and pepper. See also CAZUELA A LA CATALANA; CHORIZO.

bustard

butt, an old English and current American cut of pork, part of the shoulder and neck. See meat diagrams, page xxv.

butter, a fatty substance made by churning the cream of the milk of mammals. It is used extensively all over the western world for cooking and also for spreading on bread. It is golden in colour and soft in texture. It dates back to earliest times, and although now it is made only from cow's milk, originally asses', goat's, ewe's, and even she-camel's milk were employed. See also BEURRE; BEURRES COMPOSÉS; BURRO; BOTER.

butter bean, see HARICOT BEAN.

butter cream, an alternative name for butter icing.

butter icing, see ICING.

butterfish, see DOLLARFISH.

butterkäse, an Austrian soft cheese, made in the shape of a loaf and weighing about 4 lb. It is full-cream (*vollfett*) and unsalted, and has a mild but slightly sour taste and smell.

butterknöpfe, a German garnish for soup made from 4 oz. (½ cup) butter creamed and beaten with 3 eggs, 3 heaped tablespoons flour, a pinch of salt, and nutmeg. The batter should be smooth and thick. When the clear soup is boiling, small "buttons" of the batter are put in and cooked gently for 10 minutes.

buttermilk, the liquid left in the churn after the butter has been made. In the U.S. buttermilk is made commercially by adding a culture to sweet (whole or skimmed) milk and often has cream or butter particles added to increase flavour and make a heavier consistency. It is used for soups, cakes, breads, and biscuit making. In Belgium and northern France it is also cooked with vermicelli, rice, semolina, and tapioca. Currants, sultanas, and apples are sometimes added. In Ireland it has been used since earliest times both as a drink (it is reputed to cure a hangover) and for cooking, especially in the making of soda bread. See also BABEURRE; BOTER-MÈLK; HANGOP; KAERNEMAELKSKOLDSKAAL; KARNEMELK PUDDING.

butternockerlsuppe, a traditional Austrian soup consisting of rich beef broth with small dumplings. The dumplings are made with 2 oz. (2 heaped tablespoons) creamed butter combined with 2 egg yolks, 4 oz. (1 cup) flour, 2 tablespoons sour cream, and seasoning, with the stiffly beaten egg whites folded in last. Teaspoonfuls of the mixture are poached gently in water before being added to the broth.

butterscotch, a sweetmeat (confection) made from 4 oz. (½ cup) butter and 1 lb. (2 cups) brown sugar heated to 290° F and flavoured with lemon juice. It is beaten to make it creamy, before leaving it to set. Butterscotch originated in Scotland.

butterscotch sauce, an American sauce made from 1 lb.

(2 cups) brown sugar, 4 oz. (½ cup) butter, ¼ pint heavy cream, and 1 tablespoon lemon juice, cooked in a double boiler for 1 hour. The sauce is served with ice cream; chopped toasted almonds are sometimes added.

buttiri, a Calabrian cheese which can be made from buffalo's or cow's milk, and which has an ''egg'' of butter in the middle. It is cut in such a way that one gets butter and cheese in each slice. It is the Calabrian version of *cacio a cavallo.*

button mushroom, a small mushroom before the gills have opened. It is best eaten raw with cream and lemon juice to preserve the flavour. The large field mushrooms are better for cooking as they have more flavour. See also MUSHROOM.

button onion, the name given to small onions picked at a very early stage, but not before the bulb and brown skin have formed. They are used for garnishes in casserole dishes or as hors d'oeuvre. See also ONION.

byron, a French sauce made from ½ pint (1 cup) red wine thickened with 1 tablespoon each arrowroot and butter, and garnished with finely sliced truffles. Served with meat, fish, or eggs.

C

caballa, see ESCOMBRO.

cabbage (*Brassica oleracea*), indigenous to western Asia and Europe, is one of the oldest and most universally cultivated of edible plants. There are innumerable varieties in cultivation, which may be broadly divided into the smooth-leaved and the curly leaved (or Savoy) classes. There are also derivatives, cultivated for their edible flowers, such as cauliflower and broccoli; for their stems, such as kohlrabi; for their leaves only, such as borecole or kale; and for their miniature cabbage heads, such as brussels sprouts. Some varieties of cabbage are green, others white or red. They can come into season early or late. Cabbage is eaten raw in salads, pickled as sauerkraut, made into soups, and in fact cooked in any number of different ways. Particularly attractive recipes for the cooking of cabbage come from Germany, Russia, and Poland. See also ALIVENCI; BAYRISCHES KRAUT; BROUTES; BUBBLE AND SQUEAK; CALDO VERDE; CHOU; COL; COLE SLAW; COUVE; COUVE TRONCHUDA; FÅR-I-KÅL; FYLT; KAALI; KÅL; KÅLHUDE; KAPUSTA; KOHL; LAHANA; RED CABBAGE; RØDKAAL; ROTKOHL; SARMADES; STAMPPOT.

Savoy cabbage   *York cabbage*

cabbage palm, the name given to the terminal shoots of some species of edible palm. These belong to a large family of trees (*Palmaceae*) which includes the date and coconut. Sago is made from the interior of the stem. The shoots are tied in bunches and cut to about 2 inches long, parboiled in water, then sautéed in good fat or oil. A sauce is made by adding flour, tomato purée, and a little stock. The hearts or young shoots are cooked like asparagus. See also COEUR DE PALMIER.

cabbie-claw, a fish dish from the Shetland Islands, made from very fresh codling, cleaned and skinned, then salted for 12 hours and hung in the open air for 1 to 2 days. It is then put in boiling water with parsley and 1 tablespoon grated horseradish, and simmered gently until cooked. It is drained and filleted, covered with egg sauce made with milk and fish stock, and surrounded by mashed potatoes.

In Shetland dialect a young cod is called *kabbilow,* possibly from the French *cabillaud,* meaning fresh cod.

cabécou, a French cheese made with goat's milk. It comes from Quercy and is in season from April to November.

cabello de ángel, "angel's hair," a delicious Spanish jam, so named because when cooked, the fine strands look like golden hairs. It is made from a gourd called *sidra.*

cabidela, a Portuguese dish of chicken cooked in a rich sauce made from 4 oz. (½ cup) butter, chopped parsley, aniseed, 2 bay leaves, ½ lb. tomatoes, and 1 pint (2 cups) red wine. It is served with boiled rice.

cabillaud, French for fresh cod.

cabinet, pouding de, a French pudding made from alternate layers of sponge (lady) fingers soaked in kirsch or maraschino, chopped crystallized fruits, and cleaned and stoned raisins, also soaked in a liqueur. A mould is filled with vanilla-flavoured custard and baked in a *bain-marie* in a moderate oven for 30 minutes. When cool, it is turned out and served with custard cream (see CRÈME À L'ANGLAISE), *zabaglione,* or various fruit sauces.

cabinet pudding, an English pudding rarely seen today, made from 4 oz. (1 cup) breadcrumbs baked in ¾ pint (1½ cups) of lemon- or vanilla-flavoured custard, with 2 oz. currants added. The dish is cooked in a *bain-marie* in a moderate oven for 30 minutes.

caboc, a Scottish cream cheese which is rolled in fine oatmeal.

cabra, Portuguese for female goat; the male is called *bode.* Young goat or kid is eaten a great deal in Portugal, sometimes cooked in the oven with stock, macaroni, turnip tops, and rosemary; when cooked, a little vinegar is poured over it. See also GOAT.

cabrales, Spanish cheeses made from goat's milk. They are made in the Asturias and Santander highlands by the local peasantry. Some cabrales cheeses have a blue veining similar to Roquefort, and their quality varies according to the skill of the maker.

cabreiro, a Portuguese cheese made in the Castelo Branco district from mixed ewe's and goat's milk. It weighs 1–2 lb. and is shaped like a plate with turned-up and rounded edges. It is creamy and mild when fresh, but if it is to be kept, it is rubbed with salt and matured for about 3 months, which gives it a very sharp flavour.

cabrilla, a collective name for a number of edible fish of the *Serranidae* (sea-perches) family, found in the Mediterranean and also off the coast of California, U.S.

cabrion, a French goat's milk cheese (sometimes made with some cow's milk) made in Burgundy at the time of the vintage. It is soaked in *eau-de-vie de marc de Bourgogne* and is ripened in the husks of the freshly pressed grapes. It is a local cheese only.

cabrito, Portuguese and Spanish for kid. In Spain a kid is sometimes eaten in a stew. See also CABRA; CALDERETA EXTREMEÑA DE CABRITO; CHANFAINA.

cacalaousada, la, a sauce for snails from Montpellier, France, made from minced ham, chopped herbs, and milk, thickened with a little flour and seasoned with a pinch of sugar and salt. See also ESCARGOT.

cacalaus, a dish of cooked snails served with either *aïoli* sauce, or fresh tomato sauce mixed with thyme, savory, and fennel, eaten traditionally in Provence on Christmas Eve, with thorns from the acacia or judas tree as garnish. See also AÏGO BOÜILIDO; CHRISTMAS.

cacao, see COCOA.

cacciatora, alla, an Italian method of cooking, which means literally "hunter's style" and is used generally for game or poultry. When birds or game are used they are browned first in olive oil, then onion, garlic, herbs, tomato, stock, and red or white wine are added. It is all simmered slowly until tender.

abbachio alla cacciatora is 2 lb. young lamb, cubed, browned in oil, seasoned with rosemary, sage, garlic, salt, and pepper. Then a sprinkle of flour is added, ¼ pint (½ cup) red wine vinegar, and ¾ cup stock. It is simmered until tender, then 4 anchovy fillets are mashed into a little of the stock, and added to the lamb and simmered for 5 minutes. It is garnished with parsley before serving.

cacciatori, a small Italian *salame* weighing 6–8 oz. It is made like Milan *salame,* but less salt is used in the curing, and it is matured for a shorter time.

cacciocavallo, see CACIO A CAVALLO.

cacciucco livornese, a Leghorn fish stew, eaten as a main course. It is made of coarse fish, with octopus, inkfish (squid), crabs, and small lobsters added, and cooked in a broth of olive oil, garlic, onion, sage leaves, tomato sauce, and a little white wine, and seasoned with salt, black pepper, red pepper, and bay leaves. It is served with bread fried in oil or baked. It is similar to the Genoese *burrida,* and *brodetto,* for which the method of cooking is the same.

cacen-gri, Welsh griddle or girdle scones made from 1 lb. (4 cups) flour mixed with 1 teaspoon each of bicarbonate of soda and cream of tartar, and 3 oz. (3 heaped tablespoons) butter rubbed in. A pinch of salt, sugar to taste, and 4 oz. (1 cup) currants are added and all are mixed to a light dough with approximately ½ pint (1 cup) buttermilk or sour milk. This is rolled out and cut into rounds, which are cooked on both sides on a hot griddle or in a heavy pan. They are served hot with butter.

cachat, a French cheese made from either ewe's or goat's milk, matured with wine vinegar and then pressed. It is highly flavoured, and is very popular in Provence, where it is made and known as *fromage fort du Ventoux.* Its season is from May to November.

cachelada, a Spanish dish from the province of Léon, consisting of a whole chorizo sausage covered with water and brought to the boil. When the water is boiling, peeled quartered potatoes are added and cooked until tender. They are drained and served together with the sausage, the liquid being kept for use in a vegetable soup.

cachelos, a Spanish vegetable and meat dish, traditional in Galicia. Two lb. cooked potatoes are mixed with 1 small chopped cabbage which has been cooked with 2 oz. ham and 2 oz. chorizo, drained, and then fried in 4 tablespoons olive oil with 3 cloves garlic and ½ teaspoon hot red pepper. The meat and the vegetables are served in separate dishes.

cacio a cavallo, an Italian cheese, known since the 14th century, from the province of Sorrento, but also made in the Abruzzi, Apulia, and Molise. This diversity of manufacture accounts for the fact that it is sometimes spelt *cacciocavallo,* and can be made either from whole or skimmed cow's milk, skimmed milk being the more usual form for it in the area of Naples. The cheese is firm, and moulded into the shape of gourds, tied with raffia at the neck, and left to dry in pairs, straddled on poles, which accounts for the name, *cavallo* being Italian for horse. Its slightly salty flavour is appropriate to a rough red wine, and as a cheese cooked in baked pasta (such as lasagne) it is very good. It travels well, for it will keep some time if unopened. A Calabrian version of cacio a cavallo has an egg of butter inside and is known as *buttiri.*

cacio fiore, see CACIOTTA.

caciotta or *caciotto,* also called *cacio fiore,* a "buttery" semi-hard Italian cheese made in small cylindrical shapes weighing from 1 to 4 lbs. In the Marche it is made from both cow's and sheep's milk; in Tuscany and Umbria from sheep's milk only. In Capri it is made from goat's milk and is used there in the filling for Capri ravioli. In northern Italy, *formagella* is the more common generic name. See also CHIAVARI.

Caerphilly cheese, a white fresh cheese made from cow's milk (originally, when it was still warm) and named after the village of Caerphilly in Wales. It is mild in flavour and popular among the mining communities of south Wales. It is a large, round, flat cheese, and owing to its high moisture content, rapidly deteriorates. Nowadays it is made mostly in Somerset or Wiltshire, and has a much larger sale in the south of England. It is made also in Ireland, but it is not as creamy as the local variety.

caesar salad, an American salad made with 2 heads cos (romaine) lettuce mixed with 1 cup chopped fried croûtons, 6 chopped anchovies, 2 tablespoons grated Parmesan cheese, and 1 raw egg, all tossed very lightly with a dressing made from 1 clove garlic, 4 tablespoons olive oil, 1½ tablespoons lemon juice or wine vinegar, 1 teaspoon Dijon mustard, salt, and pepper.

caïeu d'isigny, see MOULES.

café liègeois, a Belgian sundae from Liège. It consists of vanilla or coffee ice cream, mixed with sweet, strong black coffee until thick and creamy. It is topped with whipped cream.

caille, French for quail. Quails may be served stuffed and baked with *financière* garnish; in pastry shells; grilled; sautéed in butter with brandy; with *riz à la grecque;* or made into a pâté, terrine, or mousse. See also GIBIER.

caille d'Amérique, French for *colin* (the American quail).

cailles à la bonne femme, quails cooked in a casserole with butter, diced bacon, diced, lightly sautéed potatoes, and game stock.

cailles aux cerises, quails cooked in butter in a casserole, with stoned cherries added half-way through cooking time.

cailles aux raisins, as above, but the birds are wrapped in vine leaves before cooking and served with peeled, seeded grapes.

cailles en caisses, boned quails stuffed with forcemeat, the birds' livers, and chopped truffle. The quails are moulded into their original shape and then wrapped individually in waxed paper or foil. They are packed into a pan with a little melted butter, covered with a lid and baked in a hot oven for 15–20 minutes. They are then taken out, the waxed paper removed, and each bird is put in a paper case which has been brushed with oil. The pan juices are reheated with a little game fumet and Madeira wine and poured over the birds in the cases. They are returned to the oven for 5 minutes and then served.

cailles en caisses à la lamballe, as above, but the cases are lined with a julienne of mushrooms and truffles with cream. The pan juices are diluted with port wine and cream.

cailles en caisses à la strasbourgeoise, quails stuffed with foie gras truffé, and cooked en papillote.

cailles en caisses à l'italienne, as above, but a spoonful of sauce italienne is put into the cases first.

Both quails and their garnishes, such as *mirepoix,* truffles, and foie gras, are served together in paper cases and the pan juices are diluted with champagne, brandy, or Madeira. Sometimes the quails are coated with aspic and served cold, or made into a chaud-froid.

caillebotte, the name, in certain regions of France given to curds when eaten fresh.

cailletot, the local name in Normandy, France, for young turbot.

cáis, Irish for cheese. This is a borrowed word, from the Latin *caseus,* and is applied to all types of cheese. Cheese-making was one of the numerous arts which were lost for many years in Ireland in the period of economic and social degradation which followed the English conquests of the 16th and 17th centuries. Nowadays, however, many cheeses of foreign origin are made in the Irish Republic, notably a cheese called carrowgarry, which resembles a port-salut and has been made for some years in a convent in Roscommon. Commercial creameries all over the country produce cheddar, Caerphilly, Edam, gouda, gruyère, samsoe, camembert, and brie, and about one third of the output is exported. Apart from various processed cheeses, the newest and best Irish cheeses are *blarney, clonevan, Irish blue tara,* and *Wexford.* Original Irish cheeses, now, alas, no longer made, are *fáiscre, grotha, gruth, millsén, mulchán, tanag, táth.*

Cheese-making in Ireland

caisse, the French name for a small container of earthenware, china, silver, or paper, in which are served hot or cold hors d'oeuvre.

cake (probably from Old Norse *kaka*), basically an unyeasted bread with other ingredients besides flour, such as currants, fruits, spice, eggs, and sugar, and baked in a tin specially designed for the purpose. However, this is a very plain description for some of the very light, frothy concoctions such as angel cake, baba, chocolate cake, and sponge cake. All over the world, special cakes are made for symbolic reasons, and for festive occasions such as Christmas, Easter, birthdays, christenings, and weddings. These cakes vary from country to country, but generally are rich, fruited, and quite large. Certain cakes are also associated with different counties or provinces, for instance, in Britain, *Eccles cakes, Shrewsbury cakes,* and in Scotland *Dundee cake.* A cake is generally not less than 6 inches across and can attain any size the cook desires; cakes, however, are much smaller and are usually individually cooked for each person. Some buns and small pastries, either fruit- or cream-filled, are also called cakes in common usage. The light pastry cake is of French or Austrian origin, both countries being world-famous for the excellence of their cakes. See also BOLO; GÂTEAU; TORTE.

In Ireland a cake often means a large flat bread, especially the *bastable cake* of County Cork, which is made from brown and white flour and buttermilk. Potato cake is another Irish speciality made from potatoes, flour, and either melted butter or milk. See also BANNOCK; GINGERBREAD; SIMNEL CAKE.

calabacines, Spanish for small marrows (zucchini).

calabacines rellenos, stuffed small marrows (zucchini). After peeling, the small marrows are halved lengthwise and the seeds removed; they are then cooked for 10 minutes in boiling, salted water. Chopped onion and garlic are slowly fried in butter or oil, and peeled, seeded tomatoes, seasoning, and a little sugar are added. Slow cooking of the mixture is continued in a covered pan for 10 minutes before it is used to fill the small marrows (zucchini). Grated cheese is added to a béchamel sauce, and this is poured over the stuffed small marrows (zucchini). Finally the dish is sprinkled with more cheese, dabbed with butter, and baked in the oven until the top is lightly browned.

calabrese (*Brassica oleracea;* var. *ilalica*), also known as green or purple sprouting broccoli. This plant produces, during the late summer and autumn, an abundance of small green flowerets which have a particularly delicate flavour. It is treated in the same way as cauliflower and may be used as a substitute in dishes demanding that vegetable. See also BROCCOLI.

calamai, see FRAGOLINE DI MARE.

calamares, Spanish for a small squid or inkfish. When young, it is good cooked in its own ink, and when larger it is equally good stuffed with chopped ham and onion; the latter dish is called *calamares rellenos.* See also CALAMARY.

calamares en su tinto, inkfish (squid) cut into pieces, fried, and served in a sauce made from the black liquid secreted in the pouch, herbs, and garlic.

calamaretti, Italian for a small version of calamary (squid), eaten with scampi. Both are coated with egg and breadcrumbs and fried in butter, and this is called *calamaretti e scampi alle stecche.* It is also used for hors d'oeuvre or in soup. The word is also a local name for *fragoline di mare.*

calamari, a variety of squid or inkfish popular in Italy. Rings of it are eaten fried in oil, or included in soup. See also CALAMARY.

calamari in umido, stewed inkfish (squid). The calamari, cleaned and seasoned with salt and lemon juice, are cooked in a pan with onions, garlic, tomatoes, tomato purée, red wine, oil, and herbs.

calamaroni, Italian for a variety of inkfish (squid) used generally for making soups. See CALAMARY.

calamary (*Loligo vulgaris*), the English name for a squid found in the Mediterranean and in Spanish waters, and highly thought of as food. It has different names in different parts of Spain: *chocos* in Galicia, *jibiones* in Santander, *chiripúa* in San Sebastián, and *calamares* in Castile; likewise *calamari* in Italy. In England it is also called sleevefish and inkfish or penfish because of the black liquid that it squirts out at enemies, and which is used in the sauce with herbs and garlic. Cuttlefish is related and is served in the same way. The ink is used in painting, as sepia. The calamary is known as *tantonnet* in Provence, where it is fried in oil with garlic. Other French names are *calmar, encornet,* and *seiche.*

calamary

calamint (*Calamintha officinalis*), a small herb with blue thyme-like flowers. (See THYME.) It has a warm, peppery smell, similar to peppermint. It grows easily from seed or cuttings, and is a perennial.

calappa, a crustacean similar to the crab, also called boxcrab.

calas, a traditional rice fritter from New Orleans, U.S. Until quite recently it was sold piping hot in the streets of that city. It is made from ½ cup raw rice simmered until very soft in 2 pints (4 cups) boiling water, then drained and cooled. Half a package (½ oz.) of dry yeast is dissolved in tepid water and mixed well with the rice, covered, and allowed to stand overnight to rise. In the morning 3 well-beaten eggs, sugar, and salt to taste, and a pinch of nutmeg are blended in with just enough flour to make a thick batter. This is covered and allowed to rise for 20 minutes. Then tablespoonfuls are dropped into hot deep oil and fried until golden brown all over. When drained, they are sprinkled with sugar, and served hot. This will make about 20 calas.

calcionetta, an Italian dessert dish, a sort of sweet, fried ravioli. It consists of a ravioli pastry of flour and olive oil mixed with white wine to make a firm dough, with a filling of puréed chestnuts, mixed with honey, grated chocolate, orange peel, ground almonds flavoured with rum, and cinnamon. These ravioli shapes are fried in oil and served hot with castor sugar.

caldeirada, a Portuguese fish stew made from octopus, small squid, prawns, shrimps, and lobster. The shellfish are fried in oil, then onions, bay leaf, and water are added.

caldeirada à fragateira, a traditional Portuguese fish stew, as well known in Portugal as is bouillabaisse in France. Many kinds of fish are used, such as anglerfish, conger eel, hake, and sea bream. The fish are arranged in layers with pimentos, tomatoes, onion, and potatoes (each layer of one ingredient), and the top is dotted with fat and a dressing of olive oil,

cloves, salt, and pepper. Strained stock made of fish heads and bones is added barely to cover; the pot is covered and the stew is simmered for some hours until cooked, A thinner version, more soup-like, is sometimes made, which is served with garlic-rubbed bread slices. If available, lobster, clams, shrimps, and mussels are added, but the former recipe is the more usual.

calderada, a Spanish fish soup from Galicia, similar to bouillabaisse.

caldereta, the general Spanish term for a stew of fish or meat. The name *caldereta* is derived from the word *caldera,* a cauldron, the vessel in which the stew is cooked. See also CORDERO.

caldereta asturiana, a fish stew like the Portuguese *caldeirada,* with shellfish added. It is particularly popular in Asturias.

caldereta de cordero, a stew made from young lamb, with garlic, onions, herbs, saffron, and very little water. It is a traditional dish in Jerez.

caldereta extremeña de cabrito, a kid stew. A disjointed kid is browned in oil and then drained. The liver is fried with red peppers in the same oil. The peppers and liver are then pounded and garlic is added. All ingredients are returned to the oil and 1 glass of wine (*extremeña*) is added, with a bay leaf and boiling water to cover. The whole is slowly stewed for several hours. This is a famous dish in Badajoz. See also GOAT.

caldo, Portuguese for broth. See SOPA.

caldo de grãs, a soup made from chick-peas.

caldo verde, a soup made from finely shredded kale or cabbage boiled in water, thickened with potato.

caldo, Spanish for broth, also called bodrio. See SOPA.

caldo español, a traditional soup made by boiling together diced pork, smoked meat, potatoes, turnips, carrots, cabbage, seasonings, and water. Before serving, slices of smoked sausage are added.

calf, the name given to the young of a bovine animal, especially the cow, for the first year of its life. The meat is culinarily known as veal, but the offal (variety meats) and head are known as calf's head, calf's liver, etc. See also VEAL.

calf's foot jelly, calf's foot simmered for hours in water, then clarified. This makes a firm jelly when cold, and can be flavoured as wished. It is excellent for invalids.

calf's foot pie, an old English dish made from cooked and then sliced calf's foot, veal, suet, currants, mace, nutmeg, grated lemon peel, and orange, quince, or red currant jelly, all baked with a pastry crust. When cooked, wine *caudel* is poured through the hole in the top of the pastry, made from eggs beaten with white wine, a little sugar, and a pinch of cinnamon. The whole is heated, but not allowed to reach boiling point, otherwise curdling will take place.

calf's head, washed and then boiled with onion, lemon juice, salt, and pepper until the meat is ready to leave the bone. It is taken from the bone and chopped (except the tongue, which is left whole and skinned). The meat is put into a mould, the tongue in the centre, and the stock left to get cold and defatted, then just heated and poured around the meat. It is allowed to jell, then turned out, garnished with chopped gherkins, capers, and chopped hard-boiled egg, and served with sauce vinaigrette.

California herring, see HERRING.

California quail (*Lophortyx californica*), a game bird of the American partridge family. It is one of the most handsome of birds, and also one of the most difficult to shoot because it lives in the scrub-covered hills of the western U.S. It is sometimes found at a height of 9000 ft. above sea level. All recipes for partridge are suitable for this bird.

calipash, a corruption of carapace, the shell of the turtle, but in culinary terms it means the gelatinous green fat which is attached to the upper shell. Calipee is the name given to the yellow gelatinous fat of the under-shell.

calipee, see CALIPASH.

callos, Spanish for tripe, which is used a great deal in Spain for stews and soups.

callos a la madrileña, a Spanish dish of tripe cooked with fat, salt pork, and chorizo sausage in white wine, with herbs, bay leaf, and peppercorns. It is served with a sauce of tomatoes, red peppers, and fried onions pounded in a mortar with olive oil and fresh breadcrumbs. See also MENUDOS GITANOS.

călugăresc, a Rumanian word meaning a monk, often given to the large vegetable stews, such as *ghiveci* and *iahnie*.

calville, a Belgian variety of apple with a thin, golden-yellow skin. It is a very good dessert apple, and is also used for apple sauce to serve with chicken or duck. Fried slices of calville apple are served with pike-perch (see PERCH) as a garnish.

calzone, a crescent-shaped turnover made in Naples. It consists of leavened dough with a slice of ham and mozzarella cheese in the centre, fried in smoking oil. It can be baked in an oiled baking dish if preferred.

camarão, Portuguese for shrimp, which is a most popular shellfish in Portugal. It is eaten plain, boiled, or steamed, but is also used in croquettes and in soups. See also LAGOSTINHAS; SOPA.

camarãos ensopados, diced tomatoes, onion, sweet peppers, and parsley are all sautéed in oil before the peeled, steamed shrimps are added. A sauce is made from 1 tablespoon each of butter and flour and the milk from a coconut, and this is poured over the shrimp mixture and the whole heated for a few minutes.

camargue, a fresh cheese made in Provence from ewe's milk. It has a very short season, from April to June.

camarón, Spanish for shrimp, hardly ever used in Spain except as an omelette filling. The large prawn takes its place. See LANGOSTINA.

cambacérès, a French garnish. For fish, a white wine sauce is made with crayfish stock, crayfish tails, mushroom slices, and (sometimes) truffle slices. For entrées, sliced mushrooms, pitted olives, sauce madère, and (sometimes) truffle slices are used.

Cambridge cheese, see YORK CHEESE.

Cambridge sauce, an English substitute for mayonnaise. It is a cold sauce for cold meat or fish dishes, made with ¼ pint (½ cup) oil and 2 tablespoons vinegar dripped into the pounded yolks of hard-boiled eggs, 1 tablespoon capers, 2 filleted anchovies, chopped chervil, tarragon, chives to taste, and a pinch of cayenne pepper.

camembert, a universally known French cheese named after a village in Normandy. It was known in the 12th century and was cited in Thomas Corneille's French Dictionary, published in 1708, as one of the best Normandy cheeses. Camembert is a soft-paste cheese made of whole cow's milk; it is fermented after it has been inoculated with *penicillium candidum*, a white mould introduced by a Monsieur Roger in 1910. It is in season from October to June, and should be soft and slightly runny when perfectly ripe. The place of origin appears on the label, as dictated by French law.

Other similar cheeses are *ervy* and *chaource* from the department of Aube; *olivet* and *saint-benoît* from the departments of Loiret and Thenay, and *vendôme* from the department of Loir-et-Cher.

camerani, I. A French garnish for poultry and sweetbreads. Small tartlets are stuffed with goose liver purée and slices of ox-tongue, with macaroni sautéed in butter after being drained, seasoned with salt, pepper, nutmeg, and grated cheese, and bound with butter. II. A French beef consommé garnished with braised, diced carrots, leeks, celery, and pasta, and served with grated Parmesan cheese. See also CONSOMMÉ.

camosun, an American, semi-soft cheese developed about 1932 by the Extension Service of Washington State College, as a means of using up surplus cow's milk. The drained curd is pressed, and the cheese is salted for 30 hours, then coated with paraffin. It is cured in a humid room for 1–3 months. In taste and texture it is similar to Gouda and monterey.

campos, see CINCHO.

Canadian cheddar (slang name "bulk" or "store"), has been made in Canada since the first cheese factory was opened in Ontario in 1864. It is made from unpasteurized cow's milk, which means that it matures as well as the English variety upon which it is modelled. It is made both white and yellow, and the flavour varies from mild to sharp according to the length of time it has matured. It is the most popular cheese in Canada. Two of the best commercial brands are Black Diamond and Cherry Hill. Black Diamond has a black rind, rather like the American coon cheese. Canadian law requires that no hard or cheddar cheese, when made from unpasteurized milk, be sold for at least 60 days after manufacture. To ensure observance of this regulation, all cheese is dated as it is made.

Canadian cheeses, see BLUEFORT; CANADIAN CHEDDAR; CANADIAN COLBY; EREMITE; OKA; WASHED CURD CHEESE. Imitations of popular European cheeses such as emmenthal, camembert, Gouda, Parmesan, limburger, and danablu are also made, but all bear the label "Made in Canada."

Canadian colby, a Canadian cheese which ripens quickly. It is sometimes called "stirred curd" because the curd is stirred continually while the whey is being drained. It is similar to cheddar, but the texture is looser and the paste softer.

Canadian grouse (*Canuchites canadensis*), also known as spruce partridge, a game bird which inhabits the wooded parts of southeastern Canada and some forests in the eastern U.S., although it is now becoming rare in both places. It is similar to the male grouse, black cock, although not nearly as good, and can be cooked in the same way.

canapés, French appetizers made from rectangular slices of crustless bread either toasted or fried in oil or butter, and then usually spread with meat or fish pâté. Correctly, canapés should be served as an accompaniment to winged game, and spread with forcemeat made from the trail intestines of the birds. Nowadays, however, they usually take the form of small hors d'oeuvre handed round at cocktail parties or with drinks. The name derives from the French canapé meaning "sofa," since these appetizers were eaten before dinner, while sitting in the drawing room.

canard, French for duck. The French domesticated duck is a different bird from the English *aylesbury*, or the American Long Island duck. It is a cross between the wild mallard and the domestic duck, and has a rich and gamey flavour which is quite individual. French ducks are very lean and are prepared differently than the American or English variety. In French classical cookery, Rouen and Nantes ducks are reputed to be the finest. The Rouen duck weighs up to 6 lb.; the Nantes duck is smaller in size but has fine, delicate flesh. The Rouen duck is strangled and smothered when being killed (a method not tolerated in Britain or the U.S.), so that it retains the blood, which makes the flesh stay red and gives it a special flavour; ducks so killed should be cooked the same day, otherwise dangerous toxins can develop. The Nantes duck is bled before cooking. The Duclair duck, which is a variety of Rouen duck, is also popular in France, Barbary duck (*canard d'Inde*), when crossed with the Rouen duck, produces the mulard duck, which is bred specially for its liver and the making of foie gras. Duck pâté is a great delicacy, and the finest comes from Amiens.

In culinary terms, duck is usually described as duckling,

and most French duck dishes are called *caneton* (duckling) *à la* . . . See also CANETON; DUCK.

canard sauvage, French for mallard and wild duck; also called *un sauvage.* It is roasted or cooked on the spit and served with a variety of sauces, such as port, chambertin, orange, or financière. It is also served *à la presse.* See also AYTHYA; CANETON; GIBIER.

canard siffleur, French for widgeon (male); also called *canard garrot.* In culinary French it is often, but inaccurately, called *sarcelle.* See also GIBIER.

canary pudding, see CASTLE PUDDING.

cancalaise, à la, I. A French garnish for fish consisting of poached oysters and shelled shrimps mixed with sauce normande. The name is derived from the small French fishing port of Cancale which is famous for its fat oysters, known as *blonde.* II. A fish consommé thickened with arrowroot, garnished with oysters, whiting, quenelles, and strips of sole, and sprinkled with chervil. See also CONSOMMÉ. III. A French method of serving potatoes. See POMME DE TERRE.

cancoillote, a cheese from the Franche-Comté, made of skimmed cow's milk. Rennet is added and it is cooked in a *bain-marie.* The resulting cheese mixture is very strong, so before serving it is melted and mixed with fresh butter and white wine. At the same time herbs and spices may be blended in to taste. It is used as a cheese spread.

candied peel, the outer coating of, usually, citrus fruit, which is cooked slowly in a syrup of sugar and water until it becomes crystallised. It keeps for some time, and is used, chopped, for cakes, biscuits, and puddings.

candle fish (*Thaleichthys pacificus*), a fish which inhabits the northern Pacific and is extremely good to eat. It resembles an oily smelt, and can be cooked in the same way.

candy, I. Crystallised sugar made by repeated boiling and slow evaporation. Foods preserved by coating them with this substance are known as candied. The word comes from the Arabic-Persian *qand,* which means the crystallised juice of the sugar cane. Certain vegetables, such as carrots or sweet potatoes, are candied by boiling and draining the vegetables, and cutting them into convenient serving pieces. For every lb. (peeled), ¼ lb. (½ cup) butter and ¼ lb. (½ cup) brown sugar are melted in a pan and stirred. The vegetables are added and shaken and turned until glazed all over. Should the mixture become too thick and treacly, about 2 to 3 tablespoons water may be added, while stirring well. II. The word candy is used in the U.S. to denote sweetmeats (confection) or toffees.

cane ribbon syrup or ***cane syrup,*** a syrup made from cane sugar, used in the southern states of the U.S., particularly Mississippi. It is clearer than molasses and of a much lighter consistency. It is used with corn bread and some desserts.

cane sugar, see SUGAR.

canella (*Canella alba*), a large tree from the West Indies. A digestive, aromatic condiment is made from the inner peel.

canelones, the Spanish equivalent of the Italian cannelloni. They are made with a similar paste, and the fillings vary from ham chopped with onion and herbs (*canelones con jamón*) to puréed spinach, or puréed fish and chopped cooked mushrooms. Canelones are not eaten throughout Spain, but they are popular in the environs of Madrid.

canestrato, a Sicilian cheese made from sheep's milk, or a mixture of sheep's and goat's milk. See also PECORINO.

caneton, French for duckling. See also CANARD; DUCK.

caneton à la bigarade, also called *à la orange.* Nantes duckling, braised, grilled, roasted, or fried in butter and then drained. A *sauce bigarade* is prepared using oranges and/or lemons cut in julienne strips and braised in Madeira wine, port, or orange liqueur and poured over the duck.

caneton à la bordelaise, stuffed Nantes duckling fried in butter in a *cocotte,* after which sautéed cèpes are added.

caneton aux navets, Nantes duckling sautéed in butter, then cooked with ½ pint (1 cup) dry white wine, bouquet garni, sauce espagnole, or veal stock. When half cooked, sautéed and sugared small turnips and sautéed button onions are added, and cooking time is resumed. Nantes ducklings are also casseroled, roasted, and served both hot and cold with a variety of garnishes or sauces.

caneton d'albuféra, duckling roasted with Bayonne ham slices, herbs, butter, onion studded with cloves, and a small glass of Madeira wine, in a covered dish in a moderate oven. Before serving, the herbs and onion are removed and 2 tablespoons sauce financière and small mushrooms are added. Carême, the famous French chef, is thought to have invented the name of this dish.

caneton rouennais à la presse, Rouen duckling cooked in butter for 20 minutes. At the table, the legs are removed. The breast is cut into very thin slices and kept hot at table in a chafing dish containing a little reduced hot red wine stock seasoned with freshly ground pepper. The carcase is cut up, sprinkled with a good red wine, and pressed in a special duck press so that all the juices and marrow are squeezed out. Then 4 tablespoons brandy and a little butter are added and the duck is heated up in this magnificent gravy. The legs, which will be too underdone unless grilled, are put at each end of the dish, and the duck is then served. See also WILD DUCK.

caneton rouennais au chambertin, Rouen duckling braised with chambertin wine, with mushrooms and pork or bacon added.

caneton rouennais au porto, Rouen duckling cooked in butter with port wine, and thickened veal gravy added to the pan juices.

caneton rouennais aux cerises, Rouen duckling sautéed in butter then put into a *cocotte* with ½ lb. of stoned morello cherries (called *griottes* in France). The pan juices are diluted with a little veal stock and Madeira wine.

caneton rouennais en chemise, Rouen duckling, with the breastbone taken out. The duckling is stuffed with 1 tablespoon chopped onion, the duck liver and a few other duck or chicken livers, sliced, seasoned, and mixed with 1 tablespoon chopped parsley, all gently sautéed in butter. When cold, the stuffing is pounded or sieved and put into the bird. The bird is reconstituted, and roasted in a very hot oven for 10 minutes. It is then enclosed either in a soaked pig's bladder or a large napkin, tied, and poached in veal stock for 45–50 minutes. It is drained and unwrapped before serving, then garnished with skinned quarters of fresh orange.

caneton rouennais rôti, Rouen duckling stuffed (as for *en chemise*), roasted, and served with sauce rouennaise.

Rouen ducklings are also served cold in chaud-froid, soufflés, suprêmes, and in terrines and timbales.

cangrejo, Spanish for a small sea and estuary crab; also known as *centolla.* These little crabs are eaten extensively in Spain. They are boiled and are eaten either with mayonnaise, or used in soups or in rice dishes such as paella.

canja com arroz, Portuguese chicken soup with rice, root vegetables, onions, tomatoes, herbs, and lightly beaten egg whites. See also FRANGO.

canneler, a French culinary term meaning to flute the edges of pastry or cakes; also to chop vegetables or fruit with an implement which flutes the edges.

cannella, Italian for cinnamon, used in Italy in cakes, puddings, and, sparingly, in some game dishes.

cannellini, the Italian name for an oval, white, dried bean, served either in soups or with an olive oil and vinegar dressing for salad or antipasto.

cannelloni, the Italian name for large squares of pasta which are made from a dough of flour, water, and eggs rolled very thinly (see RAVIOLI for the dough). The squares are poached in boiling salted water, then put into cold water before draining. Each one is stuffed with 1 lb. puréed, cooked spinach, ½ lb. (1 cup) ricotta or other cream cheese, a pinch nutmeg, seasonings, and 2 egg yolks. They are rolled up like a pancake and laid side by side in an ovenproof dish. Butter and a little good stock are added, and it is all generously sprinkled with grated Parmesan cheese before baking in a moderate oven for about 15 to 20 minutes until the top is browned. Unfortunately, in many restaurants cannelloni are used as a receptacle for left-over meat and the whole is covered with a coarse sauce made from diluted tomato purée, which quite destroys the true, delicate flavour of the dish. Cannelloni are served as an entrée.

cannelloni alla toscana, as above, but spread with any type of ravioli stuffing, rolled up and served with a sauce béchamel lightly flavoured with tomato, and grated cheese.

canning, a process of preserving foods. The food is placed in a metal or glass container, hermetically sealed, and then subjected to a definite elevated temperature (which varies for different foods) for the period of time required to destroy putrefactive organisms, after which the cans are subjected to cooling. The permanently sealed container, provided it remains undamaged, prevents reinfection.

Canning was invented in France in 1809 by Nicholas Appert (1797–1847) after the French government had offered a 12,000-franc prize for the discovery of a practical method of food preservation. It was perfected by his brother François Appert, who, in 1810, wrote a book called *Art de conserver les substances animales et végétales* (sic). Napoleon used foods so preserved for his armies in the attack on Russia. In the same year, a patent of the Appert method was taken out in England and later in the U.S., where canning of both lobster and salmon became extensive. In 1823, the Americans William Underwood and Thomas Kensett set up commercial canneries in Boston and New York, respectively, but it was not until 1839 that an Englishman, Peter Durand, conceived and patented a tin-coated steel container, the prototype of the present-day can. Nowadays almost all foods are preserved by this method.

cannocchie (*Squilla mantis*), also called *pannocchie* and *cicala di mare*. A flat-tailed Adriatic and Mediterranean crustacean of the squill fish family, distinguished by lilac marks on its flesh. It has a delicate flavour and is eaten in soups. See also BRODETTO; SQUILL FISH.

cannòli, a Sicilian pastry made from 1 lb. (3½ cups) flour, 8 oz. (2 cups) sugar, 6 oz. (⅔ cup) lard, and 2 eggs, all mixed to a paste with a little red wine. This is rolled out and cut into small ovals about 6 inches long. The ovals are wrapped round small tubes so that the edges meet in a point, and then they are fried in boiling oil. When they are brown and crisp, they are dried on paper and the tubes removed. They are then filled with a mixture of sugar, ricotta cheese, scraped chocolate, candied peel, and chopped pistachio nuts. Other fillings, with a variety of flavours, can be used.

cantal, a French cow's milk cheese from the highlands of the Cantal. The best variety is *cantal haute-montagne*, made of unskimmed milk from one herd only. It is produced during early summer and takes several months to ripen in the cool mountain caves. The cheeses of Cantal were noted and praised by Pliny the Elder.

cantaloup, the name of a melon which originated in Cantalupo, in the province of Ancona, Italy.

cantelo, a Spanish bread baked in a ring shape. It is made especially for weddings, where it is broken into small pieces and given to the guests with a glass of wine.

Canterbury pudding, an old English pudding which consists of a plain baked sponge mixture served with a hot wine sauce.

canvasback duck (*Aythya vallisneria*), perhaps the most highly prized North American wild duck. It is so called because the colour of its back is considerably lighter than its chestnut-coloured head. It is fond of eating wild celery shoots, which give the flesh a delicious and distinctive flavour much admired by gastronomes. It is found in most states of the U.S. It is best braised in ½ lb. (1 cup) butter for about 35 minutes, with 2 tablespoons red currant jelly and a small tumbler (approx. ½ cup) of red wine added to the pan juices to make the sauce. This sauce should be reduced by quick boiling on top of the stove. Cooked wild rice is the perfect accompaniment for this bird, as it is for all game. Despite the high price of wild rice, even in its country of origin, it is a luxury worth indulging in for special occasions. See also DUCK.

capa santa, an alternative Italian name, with *conchiglia dei pellegrini*, for scallops.

capão, Portuguese for capon. See FRANGO.

caparozzolo, the name in Venice for sea truffle.

cape gooseberry (*Physalis peruviana*), a bush-like plant which is a species of *physalis*, a native of Mexico, and North America, and which bears an edible berry. It is grown commercially in warmer parts of Europe, particularly the south of France where it is known by the names *alkékenge*, *coqueret*, or physalis, according to the locality. The fruit is eaten raw, or cooked in syrup, or made into a good jam or jelly. For the jelly, 1 lb. (2 cups) of sugar is used to 1 lb. of juice, and if boiled for ½ hour, it will reach setting point.

The cape gooseberry often found in English gardens is an edible variety (*P. edulis*); the dried orange "lanterns" are used for floral decoration in the winter months. Another variety is known as *strawberry tomato*. See also ALKÉKENGE.

capelin (*Mallotus villosus*), a small fish of the smelt family, which abounds off the coasts of Greenland, Iceland, Alaska, and Newfoundland, where it is very popular. It is also found in the Mediterranean, where it is prepared like whiting.

capendu, the French name for a variety of red apple which has a very short stalk.

caper (*Capparis spinosa*; syn. *C. inermis*), one of a genus of shrubs native to tropical and subtropical regions, which now grows in many temperate countries like France and Britain. It is a straggling, glabrous plant, reaching about 3 feet in height, with ovate leaves. The unexpanded flower buds have a peppery taste, and are pickled in vinegar for use as a garnish, or in sauces for serving with eggs, fish, or meat (particularly boiled mutton). Capers are crushed into butter, which is served cold with fish and called beurre de câpres. A tablespoon of capers can be added to beurre noir, and this is excellent with poached skate. Small young capers, known in France as nonpareilles, are the most prized, after which, increasing in size but lessening in flavour, come superfine, fine, capuchin, and *capot*.

caper sauce, a white sauce for boiled mutton. Equal quantities of milk and of the liquid in which the mutton has been cooked are combined (approx. 1 cup or ½ pint of each). One tablespoon coarsely chopped capers for each cup of sauce is added, and a small amount of the caper vinegar. It is served immediately on adding the capers to avoid curdling. Cream and a little tarragon vinegar can also be added.

capercaillie (*Tetrao urogallus*), also called capercailzie or cock o' the woods, the largest game bird in the British Isles and a member of the grouse family. It has a handsome plumage of green, black, red, and white. It is also found in the pine forests of the Jura, the Alps, the Carpathians, and Siberia. For some time it was extinct in the British Isles, but it has been reintroduced into Scotland and is now plentiful there. Unfortunately it has a habit of feeding on the tops of young pine trees, which gives it a slight flavour of turpentine. To remove this, the bird should be drawn as soon as possible after it is shot and hung for about 5 days. Provided the bird is young, stuffing it with raw potato (subsequently discarded) will ensure that no trace of turpentine remains. It makes good eating. See also GIBIER; TJUR.

capercaillie

capercaillie with sour cream and cheese, a traditional Norwegian dish. The capercaillie is placed in a pan containing 4 oz. (½ cup) butter and browned on all sides. Then 1 pint (2 cups) sour cream and 1 pint (2 cups) stock are added and all is simmered gently for about 2 hours, or until the bird is tender. The bird is removed to a dish and carved into neat pieces. The sour cream sauce is thickened with 4 oz. (1 cup) grated brown Norwegian cheese, seasoned to taste, and poured over the pieces of capercaillie. The top is sprinkled with 4 rashers of bacon which have been cooked till crisp and diced.

roast capercaillie, the bird is prepared for roasting, and stuffed with slices of raw potato. It is placed in a roasting tin, covered completely with fat ham or bacon, and sprinkled with salt and pepper. It is roasted for 15 minutes at 400°F, then the heat is reduced to 375°F and cooked for a further 35 minutes. The potato stuffing is removed, and the bird is served with bread sauce and gravy.

capillaire, a popular 19th-century English flavouring made from the black stems of maidenhair fern boiled with sugar; a little orange flower water is added, and a pinch of saffron to colour. When boiled until thick it turns to a jelly. It used to be eaten as a tonic with stoned and crushed cherries and crushed ice.

capilotade, a French culinary term for a ragoût of several different kinds of reheated poultry. When reheated meats are substituted for poultry, the dish is called *salmigondis.*

capitaine, French for a saltwater fish which is similar to carp and is prepared in the same way.

capocollo, one of the famous pork specialities of cured shoulder of ham which comes from the province of Parma in Italy. Others are *culatello di zibello, coppa,* and *spalla di San Secondo.*

capon (*from Saxon capun*), the culinary term for a castrated cockerel which is specially fed until it is killed between the ages of 6 and 9 months. It is usually very fat and large, and is the best eating chicken there is.

caponata, a Sicilian dish, served as an hors d'oeuvre or as a vegetable course. It is made from fried eggplants, mixed with a sauce made from 2 tablespoons each of capers, olives, celery, and anchovies, all cut into julienne strips and simmered with 1 sliced onion, 2 tablespoons sugar, ¼ pint (½ cup) vinegar, and ½ pint (1 cup) diluted tomato purée. This is piled

into a dome shape, and garnished with slices of tunny-fish (tuna), spiny lobster (crawfish), and *botargo.*

caponata alla marinara, an Italian dish eaten by fishermen and sailors all along the coast. It is made from ship's biscuits or stale bread soaked in water and then moistened with olive oil. Stoned black olives, anchovies, marjoram, and chopped garlic are added, and the dish is made about an hour before it is needed, to give the oil and garlic time to penetrate. It is simple peasant food which goes well with rough red wine.

caponi, Greek for red gurnard.

cappelletti, literally meaning "little hats," are a form of small ravioli eaten in many northern provinces of Italy. They have varying fillings of finely minced veal, ham, and pork, with vegetables, and are always poached in stock or water, and drained. They are served with melted butter and grated parmesan cheese, or in veal or chicken broth.

One variation of stuffing consists of ¼ lb. each of lean pork and veal, and 2 oz. ham and veal brains all chopped and gently cooked in butter with a sliced carrot and 1 stalk celery for 5 minutes. It is moistened with 1 gill (½ cup) Marsala wine and simmered for 15 minutes. Then it is all minced and 1 beaten egg is added with 2 tablespoons grated Parmesan cheese, a pinch of nutmeg, salt, and pepper to taste. See also PASTA; RAVIOLI.

cappelletti in brodo, the name given to the traditional serving of cappelletti in broth in Perugia on Christmas Eve. See BRODO.

cappon magro, a large Genoese fish and vegetable salad, served on a base of ship's biscuits or stale bread first soaked in olive oil and wine vinegar. Despite its being a fast-day dish (*magro-maigre*), it is very filling, and best made for about eight people as a cold buffet. In Genoa, fish such as *spigola* (sea bass), lobster, prawns, crabs, and oysters are mixed with potatoes, carrots, artichoke bottoms, beetroot, cauliflower, french beans, celery, and olives, all (except the last two ingredients) being carefully cooked so that they are still firm and in no way sodden. A sauce is made of 1 cup fresh parsley pounded with 1 large clove garlic and salt. When thick, 1 tablespoon capers, 2 anchovy fillets, ¼ chopped fennel root, and 4 green olives are added and also pounded, then 2 tablespoons breadcrumbs (softened in water and pressed dry). The yolks of 2 hard-boiled eggs and 1 cup olive oil are added, slowly stirring all the time as for a mayonnaise. Finally, 2 tablespoons vinegar are added. The sauce is poured over the salad; the different colours are very attractive.

câpres, French for capers, used extensively in France for sauces and garnishes.

capretto, Italian for kid. See also GOAT.

capretto al forno, roast kid cooked with garlic and rosemary in butter or oil.

capretto al vino bianco, kid cooked with carrots, tomatoes, onion, turnip, celery, garlic, a pinch of coriander seeds, a piece of orange peel, and chopped herbs. The meat and vegetables are first lightly browned in oil. Spice and herbs are added with 1 gill (½ cup) each Marsala and white wine. This is well seasoned, covered, and simmered gently for 2 hours. Before serving juice of ½ orange is added, and the sauce reduced until fairly thick.

capricet des dieux, a post-war French cheese from the Haute Marne district of France. It is a very rich cheese, being 72% cow's milk fat in dry substances, and is a soft-ripened cheese. When in good condition it has a creamy, yet quite delicate flavour, and a soft rind. Also called super capricet des dieux.

capriole, Italian for capers.

capriolo, Italian for roebuck.

capsicum, a genus of plants of the order *Solanaceae,* having some 30 species of which nearly 200 varieties have been described. The fruits of some of these are of considerable culinary importance owing to the extremely distinctive flavouring substances that they contain, chiefly the oleoresin capsaicin, and a volatile oil. They are also useful in a decorative way because of their bright colours of green, yellow, and red. The taste varies greatly with the different varieties. The red and green, small-podded capsicums have a very hot, peppery taste and are known as chillis (*C. frutescens; var. C. longum, fasciculatum*). These small varieties are sometimes commonly called Guinea pepper (*poivron* in French), but they should not be confused with the African tree, Negro pepper (*Xylopia aethiopica*), which is sometimes known by the same name. Chillis, dried, ground, and powdered, are used to make cayenne pepper, a very hot chilli sauce, and, in Portugal, *piri-piri*. The milder varieties of capsicum (*C. frutescens; var. C. grossum; C. tetragonum*) are much larger in size and can be red, green, or yellow. They are known in English as sweet peppers, in French as *piments doux,* and in Spanish as *pimientos*. The taste is not at all hot but characteristically smoky. They can be eaten raw in salads (after the inside seeds have been removed), or cooked, when they may be stuffed with cooked rice, herbs, and small pieces of meat or poultry, as for eggplant, or used in casserole dishes or stews. They are very popular in Italy, Portugal, and Spain.

In spite of their name (*capsicum* comes from *kapto,* to bite), none of these fruits is a true pepper, bearing no botanical relationship to the *Piperaceae,* to which order all the true peppers belong. See also CAYENNE; CHILLI; PAPRIKA; PIMENTOS; PIMIENTOS.

capsuni, Rumanian for strawberries. Rumanian strawberries are remarkable for their size and excellent flavour. They are between 2 and 2½ inches across and have a good, delicate taste, not unlike that of our wood strawberry.

capucijners, Dutch dried brown peas. They are about the size of a chick-pea and are used particularly for soup.

capucijners met spek, soup made from soaked peas cooked with three times their quantity of water or stock, garnished with small potato balls, diced smoked bacon, finely chopped gherkins, raw onion, and sliced hard-boiled eggs.

capucin, I. The name of a variety of caper. II. The name given to the hare by French sportsmen.

capucine, à la, I. A French chicken consommé garnished with shredded spinach and lettuce *chiffonade. Profiteroles* filled with chicken purée are sometimes served as well. See also CONSOMMÉ. II. A French garnish for meats, consisting of cabbage leaves or mushrooms stuffed with forcemeat, made into balls and braised, and all masked with sauce madère.

caracol, Spanish for edible sea- or land-snail.

caramel, four oz. sugar melted on a hot stove, moistened with 4 tablespoons of water then boiled without stirring until it turns brown, but is still liquid and not burnt. Cane sugar is the finest for caramel, since beet sugar takes much longer to brown. It is used for puddings (see CRÈME CARAMEL), for coating nuts or small fruits like the grape, and sometimes for colouring. See also SUGAR BOILING.

caramel sauce, a sauce for sweet puddings made from 6 oz. (⅔ cup) sugar, peel of ½ lemon, and a pinch of cinnamon, all of which are put into ½ cup of cold water, brought gradually to the boil, and simmered for 10 minutes. Into another saucepan are put 4 tablespoons white sugar and 1 tablespoon water. This is melted over heat until the water has evaporated and the sugar begins to brown or caramelize; the first mixture is then passed through a fine sieve and added to the caramel with either a glassful of Madeira or some brandy. Cane sugar, if available, is the best to use, for sugar made from beet retains a lot of moisture and takes really fast boiling for at least double the time to achieve the same result.

caramote, a large Italian prawn. See MAZZANCOLLE.

caranguejo, Portuguese for small crab often used near Oporto for *acepipes.* See also SANTOLA.

caranguejo no carro, is spider crab mixed with fried onion, breadcrumbs, olives, butter, piri-piri sauce, and seasonings. It is baked for 10 minutes and served with parsley and lemon.

carasau, the traditional unleavened bread of Sardinia. The dough is made from 1 lb. (3½ cups) wheat flour, a little salt, and enough water to make a firm paste. It must be kneaded for some hours before it is ready for rolling out to ¼-inch thickness and baking in a moderate oven. It is crisp when first cooked, but soon becomes soft enough to wrap round a slice of meat. The shepherds on the hillsides make a mixture of cream cheese and herbs which is rolled up in a sheet of carasau. See also CHIBARZU.

carassin, the French name for a freshwater fish of the carp family. It can be cooked in the same way as carp, but is mainly used for making soup.

caraway (*Carum carvi*), an easily grown biennial plant which was a great favourite with the Elizabethans, who used it both medicinally and for flavouring. The small, thin brown seeds of the caraway plant have a strong, slightly hot flavour which faintly resembles aniseed. They are often used in the baking of bread, cakes, and other foods, in Balkan and Jewish cooking, and for the making of the liqueur, kümmel, now widely produced in Russia.

caraway seed extract, used in soups, salads, and stews in Latvia. It is made by pouring boiling water over the seeds and leaving it to stand, covered, until cold. It is then strained for use. See BIESŮ SAKNU SALĀTI.

carbohydrate, a general name for one of the important classes of nutrients. All carbohydrates are compounds of carbon, hydrogen, and oxygen, but they differ very widely in their composition, structure, appearance, properties, and nutritional value. The body readily converts carbohydrates into fat and hence it is important that those who wish to reduce limit their intake sufficiently. The two main divisions of carbohydrates met with in the culinary field are starch and sugar.

carbonnade or **carbonade,** I. The French term used to denote the rapid grilling or frying of meat over a hot fire until the outside is crisp and dark brown, the inside remaining red. The word derives from *carbon* (charcoal), and correctly, the fire used for this process should be a charcoal one, although gas and electric stoves can also be used. II. The word can also mean a rich stew.

carbonnade à la Flamande, a Flemish beef stew which is one of the national dishes of Belgium. It is always served with potatoes, which are eaten extensively in that country. The stew is made from 2 lb. cubed lean beef, well-browned quickly in butter with sliced onions, garlic, chopped thyme, parsley, and bay leaf. One tablespoon each brown sugar and vinegar are added, the same of flour is stirred in with ½ pint (1 cup) of a reddish-coloured Belgian beer called Faro, which gives both colour and flavour. A little stock is added to cover, if necessary. The whole is well seasoned, covered, and simmered for several hours. Diced pork fat is sometimes used to fry the meat and onions in. About 15 minutes before serving, the fat is skimmed off and poured onto squares of stale bread. These are spread thickly with French mustard, put on top of the pot and pushed down into the liquid. The pot is then put back in the oven for 15 minutes without the lid in order to let the bread get brown.

carbonnade Nîmoise, a traditional braised lamb or mutton dish from Nîmes, in the Languedoc, France. The meat is larded with very small pieces of bacon and garlic, and left in a single piece about 1 inch thick. It is well-browned quickly in olive oil and fat bacon, seasoned, and sprinkled with thyme or marjoram. About 2 lb. peeled, diced potatoes are added and the dish is put, uncovered, into a very low oven (250°F) for

3–4 hours. The fat should be absorbed into the potatoes by the time the dish is ready. Other vegetables such as chopped fennel root, onions, carrots, or eggplant, according to season, are also sometimes added with the potatoes.

carciofi, Italian for globe artichokes which are so tender in Italy that they are eaten whole, not leaf by leaf as in France and elsewhere.

carciofi alla giudia, a speciality of Rome, of globe artichokes dipped whole into oil and fried until crisp and golden. Only very fresh tender artichokes are used for this dish, which is beloved of Roman Jewish people, whence the name. Easter is the height of the artichoke season in Italy.

carciofi alla maionese, cooked artichokes served with cold mayonnaise.

carciofi alla venezia, these small violet-leaved artichokes are simmered in equal quantities of white wine and olive oil until all the wine is absorbed and only a little oil remains as a sauce.

carciofi alla romana, artichokes stuffed with mint, parsley, and chopped garlic, cooked head downwards in water and white wine with a quarter the amount of olive oil.

carciofi di insalata, artichoke hearts finely sliced and seasoned with lemon juice, oil, and salt.

carciofi ripieni, stuffed artichokes. The artichokes are prepared for stuffing by removing the outside leaves, and cutting off the remainder with a sharp knife, to within about an inch of the top of the leaves. The choke is scooped out so that only the bottom and a ring of the inside leaves are left. The stuffing consists of breadcrumbs, chopped anchovy fillets, and cloves of garlic. The artichokes are simmered in white wine and oil.

cardamine, a common plant of American origin, with violet flower spikes. It has a taste similar to watercress but is not as peppery. It is eaten in salad in France and sometimes in the U.S., where it is known as lady's smock.

cardamom (*Elettaria cardomum*), the fruit or dried seeds of a large perennial herb which belongs to the ginger family (*Zingiberaceae*) and is native to India and Ceylon. It is also known as "grains of paradise," probably from its strong aromatic smell, as well as from its taste, and because it is used in the East for chewing, like betel. Certainly, if chewed excessively in the raw state, it does produce a soporific effect. The fruit has an irregular, angular, three-sided shape and is about the size of a small pistachio nut. The outer shell varies in colour from light brown, through pale green, to a creamy biscuit-colour. The lighter coloured shells with small brown seeds inside have a better flavour than the dark shells with almost black seeds. (In commerce, *Amomum cardamomum* from Siam and Java is sometimes sold as true cardamom.) The shell is peeled off, and the small seeds, used both whole and ground, are an essential ingredient in a curry. In Scandinavia, particularly Denmark, they are used to flavour cakes, breads, pastries, biscuits, or cookies. In the East they are also used in confectionery. From personal experience I recommend their use instead of cinnamon with baked apples; with peeled grapes; or ½ teaspoon of whole seeds sprinkled over a fresh fruit salad, for it imparts a most unusual yet delectable flavour.

cardiga, a mild, hard Portuguese cheese, with a slightly oily texture.

cardinal, the culinary approximation to the colour scarlet. It is usually obtained from the coral of the hen lobster.

cardinal consommé, consommé of lobster, garnished with lobster quenelles. See also CONSOMMÉ.

cardinal garnish, pieces of lobster and slices of truffle in sauce.

cardinal omelette, a French omelette made from plover's eggs, stuffed with salpicon of lobster and truffles in creamed

thick veal gravy, and coated with cheese sauce blended with lobster butter. The whole is sprinkled with grated cheese and browned rapidly under a hot grill. It is one of the haute cuisine French dishes.

sauce cardinal, I. A sauce béchamel made with equal parts of fish fumet and lobster *coulis*. II. A béchamel with fresh cream and some lobster butter added with a little cayenne pepper.

cardinal fish (*Apogon imberbis*), a red fish found off the European coasts, known as "King of the mullets" and cooked like a mullet. Red fish found in eastern U.S. resembles it, and is cooked in the same way. On the west coast of the U.S., red fish is known as spot bass.

cardinaliser, a French culinary term meaning to turn crustacea red by plunging them into a boiling court bouillon.

cardine, see LIMANDELLE.

cardon, French for cardoon, a plant of the same genus as the artichoke. The cardon de Tours is the best, and in France it is first half-cooked in a white vegetable court bouillon, then simmered in the desired sauce. (The most usual sauces are béchamel, crème, fines herbes, lyonnaise, mornay, and parmesan.) Sometimes they are presented with poached bone marrow, and this dish is called cardon à la moelle. They are also cooked and served cold with sauce hollandaise or vinaigrette.

cardons aux anchois, a traditional Provençal Christmas Eve dish of cooked cardoons with an anchovy sauce. See also AÏGO BOUÏLIDO.

cardoon (*Cynara cardunculus*), a close relative of the globe artichoke. It has been long under cultivation in southern Europe and figured prominently in medieval cookery. Its main root, being thick, fleshy, and tender, with an excellent flavour, is lightly boiled and served like celeriac. The ribs and stems of the inner leaves are blanched in boiling salted water to which 1 tablespoon vinegar has been added to keep them white. This part of the plant, known in England and the U.S. as the "chard," should not be confused with chard or spinach beet as it is different botanically, and has a distinct flavour of its own. See also CARDON.

cardoon

Carême, I. A French chicken and veal consommé double garnished with sliced carrots, turnips, lettuce chiffonade, and asparagus tips. II. A garnish for fish of quenelles of fish, truffle slices, cream sauce, and fleurons. III. A garnish for tournedos and noisettes of large pitted olives stuffed with ham forcemeat, madeira sauce, and potato croquettes.

These dishes are the creation of Antonin Carême (1784–1833), a master chef and pastrycook, generally regarded as the founder of haute cuisine. He also wrote four important books on gastronomy. He was one of twenty-five children, abandoned by his poor father, and taken in out of charity by the owner of a simple cook-shop who gave him his first lessons in cooking. Later he went to the famous pâtissier, Bailly, where Talleyrand was a customer. He cooked for all the crowned heads of Europe during his lifetime. See also CANETON (CANETON ALBUFÉRA); CHARLOTTE (CHARLOTTE RUSSE); CHARTREUSE; CHOU; CONSOMMÉ CARÊME.

caribou (*Rangifer tarandus*), a large antlered animal of the reindeer family, found in the most southerly regions of the world, as well as in Canada and Alaska. The caribou is considered excellent game, and is also useful for its hide, which is cured for the making of clothes. The meat is well worth meticulous cooking to retain its flavour, and is treated exactly like beef, except that it is important to trim off all the fat since this does not make good eating. Caribou can also be cooked in the same way as venison.

roast saddle of caribou, the saddle is considered to have the best texture and flavour. A recipe that preserves both, requires a complete saddle of caribou and about ½ lb. fat pork cut into ¼-inch strips. A strip is run through each side fillet (parallel to the backbone) of caribou and 2 garlic cloves are sliced and inserted at intervals into the outer layer of fillet meat. The remainder of the pork is laid over the joint, which is put rib-end down into the roasting tin. It is then cooked for 20 minutes to the lb. in a very hot oven. After 30 minutes the heat is lowered. The joint must be basted every 15 minutes from the time it is put into the oven to prevent its becoming dry. When the meat is cooked it is transferred to a dish and replaced in a very low oven while a gravy is made by adding 1 tablespoon flour to the drippings in the roasting tin and allowing it to cook on top of the stove for a few minutes, stirring and scraping the bottom of the roasting tin all the time. Then ½ pint (1 cup) red wine, salt, and freshly ground black pepper to taste, are added. The gravy is cooked until it thickens, when it is served with the roast saddle. Caribou has a different flavour when marinated; it is an equally excellent dish but needs more time than a straightforward roast. The marinade is made from 1 bottle red wine, tarragon, bay leaves, pepper, and salt; the meat is left in it for 24 hours, and turned so that all the meat gets covered by the wine.

caricolles, a sea snail, and a Belgian speciality. See MOULES (MOULES ET FRITES).

caringue, the French name for a fish similar to saurel, and cooked as such.

Carlsbad plum, a delicious crystallised plum which is a speciality of Carlsbad (Karlovy Vary), Czechoslovakia.

carmélite, à la, I. A French compound sauce which consists of sauce bourguignonne with a julienne of lean ham and glazed button onions. II. A fish consommé slightly thickened with arrowroot, and garnished with rice and fish forcemeat balls. See also CONSOMMÉ.

carmen, a French beef consommé with a fumet of tomatoes and sweet peppers, garnished with a julienne of both rice and sprigs of chervil. See also CONSOMMÉ.

carnatz, a Rumanian speciality, consisting of equal quantities of minced, boiled, or roast beef and minced, lean pork, mixed together and seasoned with marjoram, paprika, salt, and pepper. The mixture is shaped into croquettes, dipped in egg and breadcrumbs, and deep-fried. Fresh tomato sauce is served separately.

carne, Italian for meat: *carne affumicata*, smoked beef; *carne arrosto*, roast meat; *carne brasato*, braised meat; *carne fredda*, cold meat; *carne tritata*, minced meat or hash.

sugo de carne, an Italian meat sauce made from minced beef, onion, carrot, celery, mushrooms, parsley, tomato purée, flour, butter or olive oil, stock, and white wine, all cooked until thick and strong. Served with *pasta asciutta*. See also RAGÙ.

carne, Portuguese for meat. See BIFE; CABRA; CORDEIRO; VITELA.

carne assada, a national stew, made from beef marinated for 8 hours in red wine, lemon juice, and olive oil with garlic, bay leaves, cloves, salt, and pepper. The beef is casseroled slowly with some of the marinade and garnished with fried potatoes, halved hard-boiled eggs, and asparagus or wild asparagus tips.

carne de proco, Portuguese for pork. Pig meat, in all its various forms, is an important element in Portuguese diet. See CHISPE E FEIJÃO BRANCO; FEBRAS DO PORCO; FEIJOADA COMPLETA; LEITÃO ASSADO; PRESUNTO; ROJÕES À MODA DO MINHO.

carne estufada à Portuguesa, a stew, usually of beef, with onions, herbs, and wine.

carne porco com amêijoas, traditional recipe of fried cubes of pork served with a sauce made from small clams.

carne, Spanish for meat. See CABRITO; COCHINILLO; CORDERO; TERNERA.

carne de vaca, Spanish for beef. Beef is not usually good in Spain, since it is very often old and tough, and is best marinated. It is unwise to eat beef when there has been a bullfight in the district, as one is probably eating bull (*toro*). It is better to ask for *ternera* (veal), which is not white as in France, but is in reality baby beef. In Spain, meat is generally fried or made into stews. Roasting is not common except in the central area of the country. Spaniards say their cooking is like their climate—in the north they stew, in the middle they roast, and in the south they fry! See also CAZUELA A LA CATALANA; ESTOFADO; TORO.

carob (*Ceratonia siliqua*), also called locust bean, a leguminous tree which grows in the Mediterranean area and farther east. It has a long pod with many seeds and a sweet pulp. It is used in confectionery, especially for people on diets that exclude chocolate. It is also made into cakes after roasting and mashing.

caroline, a small French pâté à choux (choux pastry) stuffed with a purée of meat or pâté and coated with chaud-froid. It is used for hors d'oeuvre or as a garnish.

carosella, the local name in Naples for a species of fennel closely related to the one we know in England. It is very tender and eaten extensively in the district around Naples. See also FENNEL.

carota, Italian for carrot.

carote al Marsala, an Italian method of simmering finely sliced carrots in Marsala wine.

carotte, French for carrot. The finest French carrots come from the department of Nièvre, and the French garnish, *nivernaise*, always contains carrots.

carottes à la vichy, evenly sliced young carrots cooked in vichy water with salt, sugar, and butter. When soft, the liquid is reduced and the carrots glazed. Before serving the dish is sprinkled with chopped parsley.

carottes en cheveux d'ange, a jam made from 1 lb. carrots to 1 lb. sugar and juice of 2 lemons. This jam was very popular in the southwest of France in the 19th century.

carp (*Cyprinus carpio*), a soft-finned freshwater fish, originally from Asia but now found all over Europe in slow-moving rivers or in ponds. It lives to a great age and can grow to an enormous size. The best season for eating is from November to April. Carp is thought to have been imported into England in the 14th century, or earlier, and is already mentioned as a familiar fish in *The Good Huswife's Jewell* by Thomas Dawson (1596). It also occurs in *Hamlet* and in Ben Jonson's *Forrest* ("Fat, aged carps, that runne into the net," cannot have been a "newfangled" fish). There are many varieties of the carp, two of which are the so-called "leather" and the "mirror" carp; the leather carp has hardly any scales, and the mirror carp only a few very large ones. The carp family embraces other freshwater fish, such as tench, bream, chub, roach, dace, barbel, gudgeon, bleak, and the ornamental goldfish. They are often known as mud-fish, owing to their habit of burrowing into the muddy bottom of rivers and ponds. As they sometimes have a muddy flavour, they should be well washed in running water and, after cleaning, soaked in a weak vinegar and water liquid for a few hours; if prepared in this way they make delicious eating.

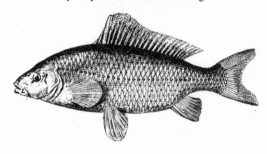

carp

Carp is considered a delicacy in Europe, especially by Jews; in Belgium, Germany, and Hungary, the kollar carp is both abundant and popular. In France, it is often braised in red wine, either with or without stuffing. In Jewish recipes, the fish is prepared with an onion fried in oil to which are added a good sprinkling of flour and a little water; the fish, cut and filleted, is now put in with parsley and garlic, and simmered until cooked, after which it is removed. The stock is boiled down and some oil beaten in before pouring it over the fish. In Russia, carp is cut into pieces, rolled in flour, and baked in white wine; sour cream and a dash of vinegar are added to finish, and it is garnished with sauerkraut, mushrooms, and small pickles. In Germany it is often cooked in beer. In England it is poached, fried, or grilled, but it is not popular. Sometimes it is poached in white wine with herbs, and served cold in its own jelly. Carp roes are thought a delicacy in European countries and, as well as being served as a savoury, are often used as a garnish for a larger braised fish. The most popular variety in the U.S. is golden or winter carp, but the native buffalo fish belongs to the same family and can be eaten in the same way. Carp was imported into the U.S. in 1876 and was distributed to 25 states three years later. It is plentiful today in the Midwest and sold in all cities on the eastern seaboard. See also BLAUFISCH; CARASSIN; CARPE; CARPILLON; CRAP; ICRE; KARP; KARPFEN.

carpe, French for carp. See also CARPILLON.

carpe à l'alsacienne, carp stuffed with breadcrumbs, fish purée, egg, cream, and nutmeg, then poached in white wine and garnished with sauerkraut and boiled potatoes.

carpe à la polonaise, carp stuffed with fish forcemeat and cooked in equal quantities of red wine and fish fumet.

carpe au bleu, a method of cooking popular in France, Germany, and Czechoslovakia. The carp is poached in boiling salted vinegar which turns it blue. It is served hot with a sauce either of melted butter or hollandaise, or cold with *ravigote*.

carpe chambord, carp stuffed and larded with fat bacon and truffles, with herbs.

carpetshell, a clam found off the coasts of Kerry and Cork, Ireland, which is similar to a cockle but has a smooth surface with a slight ridge running vertically over the shell. The local names are *ruacan* and *kirkeen*. Many tons are exported monthly to France, where it is called *palourde*.

carpillon, French for a small carp found in the Rhône, Saône, and other rivers, the flesh of which is tender and delicate.

carpón, see GALLINA DEL MAR.

carrageen (*Chondrus crispus*), also known as Iberian moss, Irish moss, pearl moss, or sea moss, this green or purplish mucilaginous, edible seaweed is common on many coasts of northern Europe and the U.S. In Ireland it is dried, bleached, and used as a vegetable, as a jellifying agent, and for the making of moulds and aspics. It has a very high vitamin content, and is processed and marketed commercially in Ireland, as well as being exported.

carrageen jelly, a jelly made of ½ cup dried carrageen first soaked in water to cover for 10 minutes, then drained. It is then simmered in 1 pint (2 cups) water with 2 heaped tablespoons sugar and 1 tablespoon grated lemon peel or other flavouring (although without flavouring it has a most delicate taste and is not in the least "seaweedy") for about 20 minutes, stirring from time to time. When the mixture is thickened, it is strained; when cooled, it will jell. Cream or a stiffly beaten egg white can be folded in, to taste.

carrageen mould, as above, but using milk instead of water.

The water in which the dried moss has been soaked is often used as the liquid for mixing pastry, breads, or cakes.

carré, French for best end of neck cutlets of lamb, pork, and veal, situated between the neck and the saddle. Left together uncut, but with the backbone chined away, these are known as a rack. In the U.S. this cut is known as centre rib chops, also called a rack when left uncut. In Britain, owing to the different butchery, it is usually known as top of the loin. For carré of pork, see table of cuts of meat, page xxi.

carré à la boulangère, rack of lamb browned in butter, cooked with a lot of sliced onions and sliced potatoes, with butter and a little stock. The rack is placed on the top of the vegetables for cooking.

carré d'agneau beaucaire, as above, then served with Provence artichokes. It is sometimes accompanied by a dish of fresh peeled and chopped tomatoes cooked in butter, with chopped tarragon added.

carré en cocotte à la bonne femme, as above, cooked with small browned onions, diced potatoes, and melted butter.

carré affiné, the name for fermented ancien impérial cheese.

carré de bonneville, a French cow's milk cheese which is in season from September to June and comes from Normandy.

carré de l'est, a French cow's milk cheese with a flavour somewhat resembling a mild maroilles. It is rather soft, slightly salted, and may or may not be mould-inoculated.

carré de l'est fleur, a variety of carré de l'est which is relatively fresh cheese and coated with a white mould.

carré de l'est lavé, a variety of carré de l'est the rind of which is washed. It is at its best from October to June and comes from Lorraine.

carrelet, the French name for a flounder, *plaice,* or sand dab, found off the European Atlantic coast but not in the Mediterranean. It is prepared like plaice, except in Normandy where it is often cooked in the oven in cider barely to cover. Carrelet is very often served *à la dugléré* in France.

carrelet aux oignons, carrelet cooked on a bed of previously cooked onions with 1 teaspoon sugar, salt, pepper, and 4 oz. (¼ cup) butter. A little cider or white wine and lemon juice are added and it is covered with buttered paper and baked for 20 minutes.

carrot (*Daucus carota;* var. *sativa*), a plant native to Europe but cultivated all over the world. It has been known since earliest times and was known as "honey underground" (*Is e mil fe'n talamh . . .*) in early Celtic literature, although it did not become a popular vegetable in England until the reign of Elizabeth I. In Ireland, Scotland, and Wales it was used extensively in soups, stews, and, as late as the 19th century, was also used in Ireland for a pudding. It is grown for its sweet root which can be long and tapering, or short and thick. The valuable minerals contained in carrots are near the thin outer skin, which is the reason they are scraped rather than peeled. Young, tender carrots need only be brushed with a hard brush. They are in season all year, but the finest are the young carrots of early summer, which can be eaten raw in salads or gently cooked with water and a little mint for 10 minutes. When older, they are invaluable in stews, as they do not break up under long slow cooking and also retain both colour and flavour. Carrot juice is good to drink and is also used to dye some cheeses an orange colour. In the U.S. carrots are often served candied. See CANDY. See also CAROTA; CAROTTE; VICHY, À LA.

carrot pudding (from an Irish manuscript book of 1755). "Take the yolks of 6 eggs and 2 whites, beat up with ¼ lb. sugar very well, then add ¼ lb. cooked carrots pounded fine with a glass of brandy. Then have handy 3 ounces butter melted to oil and when cold add to your eggs, and when the oven is hot and ready put in your dish bottomed with puff pastry and bake them as other puddings."

carrowgarry, an Irish cheese made from full cream cow's milk by nuns in a convent at Roscommon, Ireland. It has a good taste, with a creamy, but firm texture not unlike a port-salut.

cartoccio, an Italian method of cooking fish such as salmon, trout, mullet, or *orata*. The fish and a *battuto* are placed in oiled paper (the edges of which must be tightly folded so that the juices do not run out), and then baked in the oven for 30 minutes.

carving, from Old English *ceorfan,* meaning to cut up meat, poultry, or game for service at the table. It can denote either cutting into slices or dejointing, in the case of a bird. Until quite recently this was usually done by the male head of the household, a survival from earlier times when carving was considered an art for noblemen only, its acquisition being much sought after in royal and princely households where the carvers were known as *écuyers tranchants* in France, and where the last tutor provided for young noblemen was a master of carving. The introduction of serving meat and poultry already carved, known in France as *service à la russe,* did away with the *écuyer tranchant;* but in good restaurants the work is done by a carver who ranks as highly as the maître d'hôtel. It is a highly skilled job, involving a good knowledge of anatomy as well as the judging of the grain and texture of the meats. Generally all meat is carved vertically across the grain, except a leg of lamb or mutton, which can be carved either at right angles to the bone (the more usual method), or parallel to the bone, as for a saddle. Ham, whether boned or not, should be carved vertically towards the bone. Chicken and other poultry should have the legs and wings removed first, then the breast sliced. Duck and hare are carved in slices parallel to the breast-bone.

casanova garnish, a French garnish for fish, of oysters, mussels, truffle slices, and white wine sauce.

cascavaddu, a Sicilian cheese similar to *cacio a cavallo*.

cascaval, a ewe's milk, plastic-curd cheese made in Rumania, Serbia, Macedonia, and Bulgaria. The milk is curdled with rennet, and the curd drained, then put in a cloth and matured until it becomes elastic, whereupon it is heated. After this, it is put in metal cans, cooked in water, and then worked like a bread dough. It is formed into spherical shapes weighing about 6 lb. These are put into wood or metal moulds, washed with whey, dried, rubbed frequently with salt, and cured. In taste and texture this cheese resembles the Italian *cacio a cavallo*.

cashew nut (*Anacardium occidentale*), the fruit of the cashew tree, indigenous to South America but now introduced and grown in many tropical countries. The nut is kidney-shaped, and has a sweet taste far superior to that of a peanut. It is sold lightly roasted, sometimes salted. The nut is surrounded by fleshy, juicy pulp, which is slightly tart, but pleasant to taste and is eaten raw without any additions. Cooked with sugar, this flesh makes good jam which is imported into Europe. The juice is used in two ways: first, fermented and made into a wine or alcoholic beverage called cajuáda, and secondly, a vinegar known as anacard. Both are popular in Brazil.

cashew nut butter, a spread consisting of ground, homogenized cashew nuts. It resembles peanut butter in appearance, but is creamier and more delicate in taste.

casigiolu, a Sardinian cheese also known as *panedda* and *pera di vacca*. It is a plastic-curd cheese similar to *cacio a cavallo,* but is made from cow's milk.

casoeula, an Italian speciality from Milan consisting of 2 lb. lean pork cut into thick slices which are browned in butter with 1 large sliced onion, 4 diced carrots, 1 stalk chopped celery, and a 3-inch square of diced fat bacon; then ½ lb. chopped sausage such as *cotechino* is added, a bay leaf, salt, pepper, 1 tablespoon flour, and ½ pint (1 cup) white wine, which should almost cover the meat. A little stock or water may be added if necessary. It is covered and simmered slowly for 1½ hours. Meanwhile a medium-size white cabbage is cooked for 10 minutes in boiling salted water, drained, and cut into quarters. It is added to the casoeula, and the whole is cooked for a further 30 minutes or until tender. Commonly served with slices of plain or fried *polenta*.

cassata, an Italian ice cream from Naples, made in a mould lined with ice cream and containing layers of diced fruit and nuts or macaroons, with more ice cream on top. It is all frozen, and served cut into slices.

cassata alla Siciliana, a Sicilian speciality which consists of a sponge cake cut into three layers, each layer being spread with a mixture of 1 lb. (2 cups) ricotta cheese beaten with 4 oz. (½ cup) fine sugar, 4 oz. grated bitter chocolate, and ½ cup chopped crystallised fruit which has been soaked in maraschino liqueur. The cake is reconstituted, the top being sprinkled with sugar and more chopped fruit. It is well chilled before serving.

cassava, the name given to a number of plants of the genus *Manihot,* native to the West Indies, South America, and Florida in the U.S. The two most important for food are *M. esculenta* and *M. aipi* (sweet cassava). The fleshy tubers, when dried, produce about 40 percent starch, 30 percent glucose, and 10 percent tapioca, leaving a residue of water. Cassava cakes and cassava pie are made from the dried and grated roots, which resemble coarse flour or meal. It is also known as *manioc*.

casse museau landais, a very hard French cake (literally "jaw-breaker"), from the Landes district. It is made from 1 lb. (3½ cups) flour, 4 eggs, ½ lb. local cheeses, a pinch of salt, 1 tablespoon olive oil, and a small glass (1 gill–¼ cup) brandy. The ingredients are well mixed in the order given, and left to rest for 2–3 hours before being divided into portions the size of an egg and baked on a metal sheet in a slow oven for 30 minutes.

casserole, I. A cooking utensil which can be made from a number of materials such as copper, stainless steel, porcelain-covered iron or enamelled cast-iron, flameproof glass, porcelain, or terracotta. It is either round or oval, with handles and a lid. When deep, it is used for oven cooking; when shallow it is called a sauté pan (in French, *sautoir*). II. "To casserole" in the British Isles and France means to use such a utensil to cook meat or poultry with vegetables and liquid, in the oven, with a low heat to ensure slow cooking. III. In France, a cas-

serole also means a dish made with rice, which after cooking is shaped into a casserole shape. It is also known as *timbale*.
IV. In the U.S. a casserole means a dish made of two or more ingredients, usually rice or pasta with meat, vegetables, and gravy. It does not require any other ingredient before serving, straight from the casserole at the table.

Nearly all casserole dishes are better for cooking in advance, leaving to get cold, and then reheating. This applies particularly if wine has been added.

cassette, a Belgian cheese made in the Namur, Dinant, and Huy districts. It is a soft cheese made from cow's milk, which is fermented at a high temperature and seasoned with salt and pepper. It is hand-pressed and shaped into balls which are either wrapped in walnut leaves or pressed into osier baskets. It is also called boulette.

cassia, I. A genus of about four hundred plants of the *Leguminosae* family, found in tropical and subtropical parts of the world. One variety (*Cassia fistula*) has long pods, and the small unexpanded flower buds are known in culinary terms as cassia buds. They look like a small spiky clove and taste like weak cinnamon. They are used mainly for pickling and, when ground, for spicy cakes or breads. Another variety yields the laxative senna pod. II. *Cinnamomun cassia* and *C. zeylanicum* are trees of the *Lauraceae* family, cultivated originally in China. The aromatic bark is a light reddish-brown and is used ground as both a substitute for and an adulterant of cinnamon, for it is cheaper to produce. On account of its origin, it is sometimes known as "China cassia" or cinnamon; in French *cannelle de Chine*.

cassis, French for black currant, used a great deal in France for preserves and also for a liqueur called cassis de Dijon.

cassolette, I. Little French dishes in flameproof porcelain, glass, or metal of varying shapes and sizes, used for holding hot or cold hors d'oeuvre, small entrées, and some desserts. In preparing the latter, the *cassolettes* are filled with fruits poached in syrup, or cream. In the U.S. they are known as individual casseroles. II. A batter case fried in a special mould in deep oil and then filled with a savoury filling such as shrimps in sauce, scrambled eggs and cheese, puréed spinach and cheese, chopped chicken, etc.

cassonade, French for brown sugar (unrefined sugar).

cassoulet, a famous traditional bean dish which originated in Languedoc, France. It is made from soaked dried haricot beans, goose and pork, mutton, and sometimes duck, little sausages, onions, tomatoes, bouquet garni, garlic, good meat gravy, water, and seasonings. The beans should be partially cooked before layering them with the other ingredients, covering with a layer of breadcrumbs, and baking in a slow oven until a thick, fat, golden crust forms. This crust should be broken up about six times in all so that the goodness penetrates the whole dish. The *cassoulet* should be cooked for at least 2–3 hours.

cassoulet toulousain, cassoulet with toulouse sausage as well as the other ingredients. There are several regional versions of this dish. In Carcassonne, Périgord, Gascony, Castannau, and Castelnaudary, the ingredients vary from fresh pork and mutton to calf's foot and pig's cheek. Like those of most good peasant dishes, the name comes from the original clay cooking pot, *cassol d'Issel*, from the small town of Issel near Castelnaudary.

castagnacci, Corsican fritters made with chestnut flour. Also an Italian cake made with 5 oz. (1 cup) chestnut flour, a pinch of salt, and 2 tablespoons almond oil. These ingredients are well blended and mixed with enough boiling water to make a pouring consistency. The mixture is then poured into a square, flat buttered tin, and generously sprinkled with pignoli, sultanas, raisins, and chopped rosemary. The latter is es-

sential to give the authentic flavour. The cake, which has a crumbly texture, is baked in a moderate oven for about 1 hour.

castagne, Italian for chestnuts. See also CHESTNUTS.

castagne al Marsala, chestnuts cooked in equal quantities of Marsala and red wine, with sugar to taste. Served hot or cold, with cream.

castagnole Romagna, small fritters, traditional in Rome, eaten at holiday times. They resemble very light doughnuts and are made with ¼ lb. (1 cup) flour, 2 eggs, grated peel of 1 lemon, 1 tablespoon sugar, a pinch of salt, and sometimes a little brandy. The ingredients are mixed to a dropping consistency with olive oil; then spoonfuls are dropped into boiling-hot oil until golden brown. When drained, they are sprinkled with sugar and lemon juice and served hot.

castañas, Spanish for chestnuts.

castellane, a French garnish for tournedos and noisettes consisting of tomatoes cooked in oil, placed on the meat, and surrounded by small potato croquettes and fried onion rings.

castellane, consommé, a classical French soup made from good meat stock flavoured with snipe fumet. It is garnished with finely cut snipe fillets and a royale made with one-third of snipe purée and two-thirds lentils mashed with the yolks of some hard-boiled eggs. Woodcock may be used instead of snipe. See also CONSOMMÉ.

castello, a Danish cream cheese with a rather sharp taste.

castelmagno, an Italian blue mould cheese, similar to gorgonzola.

castelo branco, a Portuguese cheese, semi-soft and fermented, made from ewe's milk, or from a mixture of ewe's and goat's milk. It is widely distributed all over Portugal.

castelo de vide, a regional, farmhouse-made variety of the Portuguese *serra* cheese.

caster or *castor sugar*, see SUGAR.

castiglione, à la, a French garnish for small pieces of meat. It consists of large mushrooms stuffed with cooked rice and browned in the oven, eggplants sautéed in butter, and slices of poached beef marrow.

castle pudding, a hot steamed or baked English pudding made from a sponge mixture, and cooked in individual *darioles*. It is served with jam sauce. When cooked in one big basin with a little lemon peel added, it is known as canary pudding.

catalane, a French consommé made from beef garnished with a julienne of eggplant, sweet peppers, and tomatoes, with cooked rice. See also CONSOMMÉ.

catalane, à la, I. A French garnish for tournedos and noisettes consisting of artichoke bottoms and grilled tomatoes, demi-glace, and tomato purée and sautéed eggplant and pilaf of rice. II. A demi-glace seasoned with mustard, garlic, and cayenne pepper, flavoured with Madeira wine and garnished with chopped fried onion. III. A style of cooking peculiar to the Catalan province. Poultry, game, or meat is lightly sautéed in oil, and braised in an already-cooked sauce consisting of chopped shallots, tomatoes, garlic, mushrooms, and white wine. The dish is garnished with slices of small fried sausages and braised button onions. See also MOUTON (MOUTON EN PISTACHE).

catchup, see KETCHUP.

catfish, the name generally given to a large class of fish characterized by being scaleless, and having long barbels or feelers about the mouth. Nearly all are freshwater fish, although some tropical varieties also inhabit salt water. The catfishes of North America belong to the *Amiuridae* family, of which there are about 25 species. The most important from a gastronomic point of view is the *Amiurus lacustris* of the Great Lakes, which weighs about 150 lb. Also the *Ictalurus furcatus* and *I. ponderosus*, found in the Mississippi and its tributaries, about 5 feet long with an attainable weight of around 150 lb., are excellent to eat ahd have very few bones. They are a speciality of Memphis, Tennessee. A small or dwarf catfish (*Amiurus nebulosus*), although not closely related to *Larimus fasciatus,* is sometimes called bullhead. It is abundant in New England lakes. It acclimatises well to transplanting, and has been successfully introduced into different localities, as well as being imported into France to stock French rivers. It seldom attains more than 2 feet in length, and has a very delicate flavour. In tropical America the large varieties *Pimelodus* and *Platystoma* are very plentiful. The European catfish (*Silurus glanis*) is about 10 feet long and weighs about 400 lb. It is one of the largest European freshwater fishes, and is found mainly in the Danube, Elbe, Vistula, and Oder. It is very highly thought of as food and considered a delicacy. Another species (*Parasilurus aristotelis*) is found in Greece. It is called *silouros* in Greek mythology and today, no doubt from *ailouros*—cat, an allusion not only to its feelers, but also to its habit of lashing its very long tail as it swims.

The large fish are cooked in thick steaks, usually brushed with oil, and either grilled (broiled) or baked, and served with thick lemon wedges. The small fish (weighing about 3 lb.) are always skinned before cooking either whole or in fillets. Sometimes they are rolled in flour, cornmeal, or batter before frying with herbs and serving with lemon wedges and sauce tartare. See also CHANNEL CAT; DOGFISH; SILURE.

catmint (*Nepeta cataria*), a popular herbaceous plant with strongly aromatic leaves. The delicate young shoots can be used sparingly in green salads.

catsup, see KETCHUP.

cauchoise, a consommé of beef with diced cooked lamb and bacon and julienne of braised vegetables. See also CONSOMMÉ.

escalopes de veau, cauchoise, a speciality of the region of Caux in Normandy consisting of veal escalopes cooked in butter with cubes of sweet apple; flambéed with calvados, and with ¼ pint (½ cup) cream added and reduced.

caudel, or caudle, an extremely old English dish, mentioned as early as the 12th century. It consists of oatmeal stirred into hot water and boiled until thick, with sugar, cinnamon, mace or nutmeg, and lemon rind added. According to taste, either ale, brandy, or sherry was added, and it was eaten hot. It was served before a meal, or in place of one on long cold journeys in a stage-coach. The word can also mean a gravy of cream and wine poured into a pie after baking.

caul, a culinary term denoting a membrane which encloses the paunch of animals used for butcher's meat. The caul, especially that of pig or sheep, is often used to encase mixed minced offals (variety meats) for *faggots.* The French word for it is crépine, and it is used a good deal in France for charcuterie. See also CRÉPINETTES.

cauliflower (*Brassica oleracea*), a member of the cabbage family, cultivated for its flowers which form a large, compact head. It is believed to have come from Cyprus and been introduced into Italy in the 16th century. The famous Scots gardener and horticulturalist John Loudon, writing in 1822, called it "the most delicate and curious of the whole Brassica tribe." Cauliflowers are in season in Europe from June until the autumn, in the U.S. from autumn to spring. They can be used raw, chopped, in salads, cooked in various ways, and in soup. Boiled cauliflower, allowed to get cold and dressed with a vinaigrette to which has been added chopped chives and nasturtium flowers, makes an excellent salad. In 19th century Ireland, the florets were gently cooked in a little milk, a knob of butter, salt, and pepper. See also DUBARRY.

cauliflower fritters, an English dish for which a cauliflower

cauliflower

is washed, trimmed, and parboiled, then drained and torn into strips which are dipped in batter and fried in deep fat. They are served in a folded napkin with sprigs of parsley.

In France, a better method is used. A cauliflower is trimmed, steamed and drained. It is cut up into little sprigs, seasoned with pepper, salt, a little vinegar, and a sprinkling of mixed parsley and chives finely chopped, and allowed to stand for 20 minutes. The sprigs are then dipped in butter and deep fried. They are served with a sauce béchamel or a tomato sauce. See also BLUMENKOHL; CAVOLFIORE; CHOUFLEUR.

cavaillon melon, a melon which comes from Cavaillon in the Vaucluse district of France.

caviar, the slightly salted roe of various members of the sturgeon family (*Acipenseridae*) such as *beluga,* sevruga, sterliad and *sterlet.* The name is common to most European languages and thought to be of Turkish or Tartar origin, but the Turkish word khavyah probably comes from the Italian *caviale.* In Russian the name is *ikrá.* The most common caviar comes from the beluga and is large and pearly-grey in colour. It is made by beating the ovaries and straining through a sieve to clear the eggs of membranes, fibres, and fatty matter. It is then salted with 4–6% of salt. The superb rare albino beluga produces the "imperial" caviar which is unpressed, and does not keep well. For commercial use, however, it is pressed. The de luxe caviar is called malossae—"little salt"—and this keeps well. All cavier will spoil if kept at over 40°F for more than a few hours. For this reason it is often served on ice and is always kept refrigerated. There is a coarse variety in Russia, called *payusnaya,* which is salted more heavily and compressed into more solid form before tinning or putting into jars. This is a staple article of food in Russia and eastern Europe. The name comes from pajus, the adherent skin of the ovaries. Caviar from the sturgeon proper keeps well and is the most easily exportable. Although the sturgeon abounds in Russian rivers and the Caspian and Black seas, nowadays most caviar comes from Iran. Russia is the biggest customer for Iranian caviar, with the United States and the rest of Europe following. It is an expensive and unusual delicacy. Caviar is served with hot toast and butter. Sometimes a squeeze of lemon is added, but nothing else apart from that.

Lumpfish, salmon, tunny (tuna), and mullet are used to make imitation caviar, but it cannot compare with the original. However, the mullet roe is made into an acceptable dish called *botargo.* See also AVGOTARAHO; STERLET; TARAMA.

cavolfiore, Italian for cauliflower, which in Italy is often served with a sauce made from butter, flour, cauliflower stock, lemon juice, and egg yolks. In Naples on Christmas Eve, it is also served, cooked, as a salad, with carp or eel, and called *insalata di rinforz.*

cavoli, Italian for cabbage.

cavoli in agro dolce, an Italian dish consisting of sweetsour shredded cabbage, cooked in a little oil with onion, tomatoes and a little wine vinegar. A spoonful of sugar is stirred in shortly before serving.

cavolo pavonazza, see KALE.

cavour, I. A French garnish for slices of meat consisting of semolina croquettes, timbale of lasagne, and ravioli. II. A garnish for entrées, consisting of round polenta cakes mixed with parmesan cheese, and mushrooms stuffed with chicken liver purée. The gravy is flavoured with tomato purée and marsala wine. III. Chicken consommé with green peas, elbow macaroni, and an unsweet pancake mixture poured through a colander into hot fat, then used as a garnish. See also CONSOMMÉ.

cavourma, a Turkish dish made from spinach, which in Turkey is cooked, drained, and then chopped and mixed with finely-cut onions which have been fried in butter and small pieces of cooked mutton. A poached egg is placed on top of each portion.

cawl, Welsh for soup. See WELSH CAWL.

cayenne, or red pepper, a hot red pepper made chiefly from the dried ripe fruit of *Capsicum frutescens; var. longum.* The fruits are reduced to a powder which is mixed with wheat flour, made into cakes with yeast, and baked into hard biscuits, the flavouring *oleoresin capsaicin* impregnating the whole of the biscuits. These are then ground to a powder, producing a red pepper which, while very hot to most palates, is not as hot as chilli powder. Occasionally, chilli powder is sold as cayenne pepper, and its greater pungency is then very noticeable. See also CAPSICUM; CHILLI.

cayettes, a French flat sausage made from minced pork, herbs, and chopped *blette,* shaped like a large rissole and baked in the oven. It is a speciality of the Ardèche.

cazuela a la catalana, a traditional dish from Lerida, Spain, made in a flat earthenware dish. The bottom is covered with olive oil in which minced beef is fried until brown, and then removed. In the same oil carrots, onions, and tomatoes are fried together, being well stirred to prevent sticking; a small amount of flour is added and cooked a little, then the meat is stirred in, and about 2 cups hot stock or water are added. The mixture is cooked on a slow flame for about 45 minutes, care being taken that it does not get too dry; if this happens, a little more water may be added. When it is cooked, slices of *butifarra* are arranged round the edge of the dish, and the cazuela is given a final heat-through in a hot oven.

cebolha, Portuguese for onion. Onions are of unusual sweetness and mildness in Portugal, and are used both cooked and raw.

cebolla, Spanish for onion.

cebolla Española, a Spanish onion soup made of 2 lb. chopped onions, lightly fried in olive oil and 2 pints (4 cups) white stock and seasonings. Finally, diced bread is added and the soup is simmered slowly until cooked.

cebrero, a Spanish cheese named after the village of Piedrafita de Cebrero, where the best examples of this cheese are made. It is mushroom-shaped, with a pale yellow rind, and a fine texture. The taste is creamy but slightly sharp. Cebrero has a faint blue veining, but not sufficient to call it a "blue" cheese.

cebulka, Polish for shallot.

cebulka glasowana, a Polish shallot dish which has a sweet-sour taste. One lb. shallots or button onions are blanched in boiling water, and when cool the skins are removed and the shallots are lightly turned in butter, then 2 tablespoons sugar is melted in a casserole and allowed to colour slightly; the shallots are then added with stock or bouillon to cover (about 1 cup), and well seasoned. The dish is covered and cooked for 30 minutes, or until the liquid is the consistency of honey.

ceci, Italian for chick-peas, small, hard, yellow dried peas which need lengthy soaking before cooking. In Italy they are mixed with pasta to make a thick *minestra.* After soaking and cooking, and dressed with seasoning and oil, they make an excellent salad with a nutty flavour that goes well with drinks. In Sardinia, Piedmont, and Genoa, thick pancakes called faina are made from chick-pea flour fried in oil, and are sold hot from street barrows in winter. The niçois *socca* is very similar. See also CHICK-PEA; TUONI E LAMPO.

cédrat, see PÂTÉ DE CÉDRAT.

cefalo o muggine, an Italian method of cooking grey mullet. This is very much like the Provençal method for cooking red mullet, that is, carefully cleaned, brushed with oil, and roasted on a bed of wild fennel branches. Flaming brandy is poured over it when cooked. It is sometimes grilled.

céleri, French for celery. This is cooked in numerous ways in France—with sauce béchamel, in cream, puréed, with a sauce of beef marrow (à la *moelle*), and also eaten raw with sauce vinaigrette.

céleri-rave, French for celeriac, usually peeled, quartered, and braised, and served with sauces of various kinds; or blanched in boiling salted water, sliced julienne, and served cold, mixed with mayonnaise. It can also be eaten raw if finely grated.

celeriac (*Apium graveolens;* var. *rapaceum*), also known as turnip-rooted or knob celery, or celery root, this is a variety of celery cultivated for its thick, turnip-like root. It was first introduced into England from Europe during the 18th century. It stores well, and is used, grated, for salads, soups, and purées. Celeriac must be peeled before cooking. It should be boiled slowly in good vegetable stock until tender. It is served with melted butter or a sauce hollandaise or béchamel. It is also excellent, perhaps indeed at its best, boiled, sliced, allowed to cool, and served with a mayonnaise.

celeriac

celery (*Apium graveolens;* var. *dulce*), a plant which is said to have been cultivated by Italian gardeners during the 17th century, from a prototype known in England as smallage. It is now cultivated extensively in Europe for its leaf-stalks, which are blanched in the trenches in which they are grown. In French cuisine, celery is one of the basic aromatics. Celery is in season from autumn, through the winter, until April. It is eaten raw and cooked, and is served both as a vegetable on its own, and in salad, soups, stews, and casseroles.

celery salt, a commercial preparation combining crushed celery seeds and salt, used for flavouring.

celery sauce, an American sauce, composed of a small head of celery, 2 tablespoons each of flour and butter, 1 pint (2 cups) stock or water, 6 tablespoons cream, salt, and pepper. The well-washed celery, including green tops, is chopped, cooked in the stock, and then rubbed through a sieve. The butter is rubbed into the flour, and the celery mixture is added. The whole is brought gently to the boil and simmered, before adding the cream and seasoning. It is sometimes served with boiled mutton, rabbit fricassée and in Ireland with poultry. It is easily made with a liquidiser or blender.

célestine, French chicken consommé, thickened with tapioca, garnished with chopped pancake stuffed with chicken forcemeat and chervil. See also CONSOMMÉ.

cenci, an Italian fried pastry resembling a lover's knot, usually served with a fruit salad, cold mousse, or similar type of sweet. The pastry is made from ½ lb. (2 cups) flour and 1 heaped tablespoon butter, rubbed together, then 2 oz. (¼ cup) sugar to taste, is added and mixed to a stiff but pliable dough with 1 egg, 1 egg yolk, and a little brandy (2 tablespoons). This is rolled very thinly and cut into ribbon-like strips which are tied into lover's knots and fried in boiling oil until golden brown; when drained, they are sprinkled with sugar and served warm.

cendré de la brie, a French cow's milk cheese from the Ile-de-France, at its best between September and May.

center cut, the name given in the U.S. to a thick end of tenderloin.

centolla, see CANGREJO.

cèpe, I. French for boletus. It is found in woods, under oak, chestnut and beech trees, in spring and autumn. It is very much prized gastronomically in France, and is cooked in the same way as mushroom. See also BOLETUS. II. A particular member of the large edible boletus family, *Boletus edulis.* These are the size of a big mushroom, with a thick, fleshy, shiny, brown top, a spongy gill, and a thick white stem. They are found all over Europe but are made particular use of in France, where they are gathered all the summer. They are dried, and can be used in soups, or, after soaking, can be sautéed in oil or butter. They are also bottled and canned commercially. See also MUSHROOM.

cèpes à la gènoese, a French method of cooking cèpes which comes from Genoa in Italy. It can be applied to all members of the mushroom family. Remove the stalks from 1 lb. cèpes, but reserve the heads and sprinkle liberally with coarse sea salt (*gros sel*); leave for 30 minutes, and when water drains out, put them in a hot oven for 2 minutes to dry. Line an earthenware dish with dried vine leaves, and pour over enough olive oil to cover the bottom of ⅓ inch; heat on a gentle flame so that the oil is absorbed but the leaves not frizzled. Add the cèpes in layers, gill-side up, and bake in moderate heat for 30 minutes. Meanwhile cut the stalks evenly and scatter them over the top with 1 chopped garlic clove and seasoning of pepper. Put back for 10 minutes and serve hot from the casserole.

cèpes à la provençale, prepared with 1 lb. cèpes simmered in 4 oz. (½ cup) butter with the juice of 1 lemon, then drained, and sliced if large. Enough olive oil to cover the bottom of a frying pan is heated and the cèpes are sautéed and seasoned. At the last moment before they are ready, 1 tablespoon chopped onion and 2 oz. (½ cup) fresh breadcrumbs, 1 garlic clove, and 1 tablespoon chopped parsley are added. If shallot is substituted for onion and the garlic omitted, it is called *à la bordelaise.*

cerceta, Spanish for teal.

cerdeña, Spanish for sardine.

cerdo, Spanish for pork. See also COCHINILLO ASADO; GACHAS MANCHEGAS; JAMÓN; MANITAS DE CERDO REHOGADAS; SALCHICHA.

lomo de cerdo a la aragonesa, loin of pork, first sliced, seasoned, and floured, then browned on both sides in oil. Garlic and onion are fried in the same oil, and peeled and seeded tomatoes are added. The meat is then casseroled and the sauce, with white wine added, is poured over the meat and sprinkled with cinnamon. Before serving, the casserole is garnished with hard-boiled egg and parsley.

cereal, a word which comes from the name of the Roman goodess of harvest (corn), Ceres, and is used to denote farinaceous foods such as oats, wheat, barley, rye, millet, Indian corn, rice, and buckwheat. All cereals can be made into bread, but wheat and rye are the most usually employed for this purpose. The word can also mean an article of diet made from one or other of the above cereals, and used as a breakfast dish, such as corn flakes, etc. It is also applied loosely to starchy tubers such as arrowroot, cassava, etc.

céréales, French for cereals.

cerejas, Portuguese for cherries.

cereza, Spanish for cherry.

cerf, French for red deer.

cerfeuil, French for sweet cicely and chervil, which are always included in fines herbes mixtures and are used extensively in France as a garnish, especially for potatoes, sauces, and soups. See also CHERVIL SAUCE.

cerfeuil tubéreux, or bulbeux, French for turnip-rooted chervil. It is served plainly boiled, like new potatoes, with butter, or with cream and chopped parsley. When made into a purée, it is known in culinary French as purée *chevreuse.*

cerfoglio, Italian for chervil.

cerignola olives, giant green olives from Puglie, Italy.

cerise, French for cherry. See also CANETON AUX CERISES; CLAFOUTI.

cerneaux au verjus, an unusual hors d'oeuvre from Touraine, France, made from sliced and peeled green walnuts. They are covered with the juice of pressed white grapes and seasoned with pepper and a finely chopped shallot.

černý kuba, a typical Czechoslovak dish of barley porridge simmered very slowly with caraway seeds. When it is thick, cooked, dried, sliced mushrooms and herbs are added with seasonings. In country districts, this makes a filling meal with smoked sausage; in some poorer homes it may constitute the whole meal. It is often served with *halušky.*

certosina, an Italian white, creamy cow's milk cheese from the Veneto, Italy. No doubt it acquired its name from being originally made in Carthusian monasteries.

cervelas, a French sausage made in large and small sizes, so-called because it formerly contained pig's brains. Nowadays it is made from pork meat and pork fat, seasoned with garlic, salt, and pepper. It is also called *saucisse* or *saucisson de Paris.*

cervelas truffé, a large, lightly cured pork sausage containing chopped truffles. It is one of the finest and can be eaten as it is, sliced, as an hors d'oeuvre, or poached for about 1 hour and served with potato salad.

cervelatwurst, a German spreadable wurst made from finely minced and pounded pork and beef fillet, very highly spiced, and smoked. See also STREICHWURST.

cervella, Italian for brains, usually fried in butter or oil after blanching, and served with mushrooms, or served in a fritto misto. See also CROCCHETTA (CROCCHETTE DI CERVELLA); RAVIOLI GENOVESE.

cervelles, French for brains. The most usual method of serving brains in France is called *cervelles au beurre noir.* Poached and skinned brains are cut into slices and seasoned, then fried in butter which, when the brains have been cooked and removed, is allowed to brown. Chopped parsley and capers, with a little of the caper vinegar, are added just before serving. See also BRAINS.

červené zelí, a Czechoslovak method of cooking cabbage. It is finely shredded, and mixed with 1 chopped onion, 1 tablespoon caraway seeds, water, and seasonings, and cooked over a low heat for about 15 minutes. Before serving, ¼ pint (½ cup) sour cream is stirred in and heated up.

cervo, Italian for deer. See also VENISON.

cervo con salsa di ciliegie, a 4-lb. joint of marinated venison is browned in hot oil, with 1 sliced onion and 2 carrots. It is put into an earthenware casserole together with some of the marinade, water barely to cover, 4 dried mushrooms, 1 large garlic clove, 2 stalks celery, 1 tablespoon mixed parsley and thyme, and a bay leaf. On top is put a thick slice of fat bacon. The casserole is then covered, and the contents cooked in the oven for about 3–4 hours. When ready, the venison is served with cherry sauce, made from ½ lb. stoned cherries, ¼ lb. (½ cup) dissolved red currant jelly, a pinch of crushed coriander seeds, black pepper, and 1 teaspoon wine vinegar, all simmered for 15 minutes. The vegetables (cooked with the venison) are sieved, and the sauce added to the resulting purée. Lentils are served with it.

cestinhos de verduras, Portuguese "vegetable baskets," eaten at *Romaria d'Agonia*. They consist of buttered peas, chopped carrots, turnips, and beets cooked in a pastry case.

cetrioli, Italian for cucumber. See also CUCUMBER.

cetrioli alla duse, stuffed cucumbers for ANTIPASTO. Cucumbers are cooked in wine vinegar, after which the seeds are removed and the cucumbers stuffed with mashed, hard-boiled eggs, a pinch of mustard, 1 finely sliced onion, 2 anchovy fillets and 6 radishes, all well mixed with olive oil. It is served cold with raw tomatoes and lemon wedges.

ćevapčići, a traditional Yugoslav dish consisting of 1½ lb. minced beef, ¾ lb. minced pork, 3 cloves garlic, herbs, salt, and pepper, all well mixed with a little water and formed into short fingers. They are grilled over charcoal and served with chopped raw onion. See also PLJESKAVICA.

chabichou, a soft French goat's milk cheese, one of the best from the Poitou district. It is in season from May to November.

chaboisseau, a very ugly fish with a large head, found in the Mediterranean. Its appearance has gained it various names, such as "sea-toad," "sea-devil," and "tadpole." It makes a curious rumbling noise when held, and so is also called "grumbler." The flesh is quite delicate in flavour, but should not be eaten during the spawning season, November to May.

chabot, I. The French name for chub, a freshwater fish of the carp family, also called chevaine. II. A freshwater fish of the *Cottus* family, with a delicate flavour.

chabris, a French goat's milk cheese made in the region of Chabris, a village by the river Cher in the department of Indre. The camembert technique is used in the making and presentation of this cheese.

chabrol, see BRÉJAUDA; GOUDALE.

chacklowrie, a Scottish dish from Aberdeenshire, consisting of cooked cabbage mashed with pearl barley broth.

chad, see BREAM.

chafing dish, a metal dish which stands on a trivet over a gentle heat from either methylated spirits or bottled gas. It is used for heating or cooking at the table. It is quite decorative and extremely useful for such dishes as scrambled eggs, devilled kidneys, or flambéed fruits, chicken or game. Thin steaks are excellent so cooked. It was a popular method of cooking in the 18th and 19th centuries when beautifully designed dishes were made.

chakhokhbili, a Russian dish from the Caucasus made from jointed chicken or lamb. First the meat is fried in oil or butter; then sliced onions, tomatoes, 1 tablespoon vinegar, 1 pint (2 cups) stock, a bay leaf, and seasonings are added, and it is all simmered for 1½ hours. It is served with skinned, sliced raw tomatoes, slices of lemon, and a sprinkling of chopped parsley.

chalber bälleli, a dish from Green County, Wisconsin, U.S. This consists of 2 lb. minced veal and ¼ lb. minced pork mixed with ½ pint (1 cup) light cream and 3 eggs, with a little finely chopped onion, 1½ cups toast crumbs, a pinch of nutmeg, salt and pepper added. The mixture is well beaten and

shaped into egg-sized balls which are first browned all over in butter, then put into a casserole and baked with more butter for 30 minutes. The juices are thickened with flour, and 1 cup milk is added to make a creamy gravy.

challah, a traditional twisted, white, Jewish Sabbath loaf made with 3½ lb. (12 cups) flour, 3 eggs, 1½ oz. yeast, and sometimes a pinch of saffron and 1 tablespoon poppy seeds sprinkled over the top. It is also known as *cholla.* The braided, beehive shape is reminiscent of the shewbread of the Bible, which was made for priestly blessing in the temple.

chamberlain tartelette, a French tart, made in a mould lined with puff pastry and filled with a mixture of chopped apple, breadcrumbs, sugar, cinnamon, grated lemon peel (rind), and rum, then covered with more puff pastry and baked. When cold, it is covered with hard sugar icing.

chambertin sauce, like wine sauce, but using Chambertin as the wine.

chambéry, I. A French salad consisting of 1 large peeled tomato, hollowed out and washed with vinegar and filled with finely diced lobster, salmon, artichoke bottoms, gherkins, and finely shredded lettuce, all bound with mayonnaise. II. A French omelette. The ordinary omelette mixture is mixed with previously cooked, diced leeks, bacon, potatoes, and cheese, and is then folded in the normal way. III. A French method of serving potatoes, see POMMES CHAMBÉRY.

chambord, I. A sauce made from fish stock with mirepoix, herbs and a little red wine. The mixture is reduced; then demiglace is added, and it is cooked and strained. Butter and anchovy essence (extract) are included, and the whole is beaten together. II. A French garnish for fish consisting of large fish quenelles, mushrooms, soft roes, shrimps, large rounds of truffle, and fleurons, with sauce chambord.

chamois, see IZARD.

chamomile (*Anthemis nobilis*), a plant once sacred to the Egyptians and famous throughout the centuries for producing an incomparable herb tea. The dried white flowers, which have the scent of sweet fresh apples, are soaked in boiling water and the resulting brew drunk as a cure for indigestion, headaches, and general weariness. Chamomile grows rather like grass and makes a delightful aromatic lawn. It is found in abundance on mountainsides in Ireland, and at one time the lawns of Buckingham Palace were interspersed with it. It also grows in the U.S. and is spelt camomile. Care should be taken not to confuse the wild chamomile with a noxious plant called stinking mayweed (*A. cotula*), which, however, is easily recognized by its unpleasant smell. The Spaniards call the plant manzanilla which means a little apple, and this is the name of a light sherry flavoured with chamomile.

chamomile

champ, a traditional potato dish from the north of Ireland. It is made from hot mashed potatoes whipped with, most usually, chopped spring onions (scallions) cooked in milk, then seasoned. This mixture is put in a deep dish and a well is made in the middle into which is poured hot melted butter. Champ is also made with young nettle tops, chopped parsley, leeks, or green peas.

champenois, a French cheese made with cow's milk. It comes from the Champagne region, and is in season from September to June.

champignon, the Danish term for the common field mushroom. Other mushrooms and edible fungi are *svamp*. See also MUSHROOM.

champignon sovs, Danish mushroom sauce made with fish stock and cream when served with *fiskebudding* or *fiske klatkage*.

champignon, French for mushroom. See CÈPE; CHANTERELLE; MORILLE; PRATELLE.

champignon de couche, French for cultivated mushroom.

champignon, see PILZE.

champigny, a French pastry made from puff pastry (*pâte feuilletée*) rolled out to a square ⅛ inch thick. The centre is filled with apricot jam flavoured with kirsch and apricot kernels. It is moistened at the edges and covered with another square of pastry ⅓-inch thick, which is pressed down to prevent the jam from trickling through. The surface is brushed with beaten egg, and the pastry is baked for 30 minutes in a moderate oven. When cooked, it is sprinkled with icing sugar.

champinjon, the Swedish term for the common field mushroom. Other mushrooms and edible fungi are *svamp*. *Champinjoner* are often served sautéed in butter, with cream, and are also used for soufflés. See also MUSHROOM.

champinjonsolåda, a Swedish mushroom and egg pie made from ¾ lb. (2 cups) chopped mushrooms lightly fried in butter with 1 chopped shallot or 1 tablespoon onion. Then ½ lb. cooked, diced ham is added and all stirred well; 1 tablespoon crisp breadcrumbs and 2 tablespoons tomato juice are added, with 1 cup (½ pint) white stock. This is well seasoned and poured into a shallow, greased flameproof dish. Then 3 eggs are beaten and mixed with 1 tablespoon chopped parsley or chives, salt, and pepper to taste. This is poured over the mushrooms. The dish is placed in a larger dish half-full of hot water and baked in a moderate oven until set (about 30 minutes).

champoléon, or queyras, a French hard cheese of the *cancoillotte* type. It is made in the Hautes-Alpes from skimmed cow's milk.

chanakhi, a stew from Georgia, Russia. It consists of cubed lamb or mutton put into a casserole with sliced potatoes, onion, green beans, tomatoes, chopped egg plants, pepper and salt. Water or stock is added to cover, and the stew is cooked in a moderate oven for about 2 hours.

chanfaina, a famous stew from the Spanish province of León. It is made from the offal (variety meats) of a young goat or kid, which is cooked with the animal's head and feet, artichokes, chard, lettuce, and peas. It is a rather specialized dish, and not for the unadventurous. It can also be made with lamb's or pig's liver, but this is not strictly traditional.

channel cat (*Ictalurus punctatus*), one of the most highly-prized river fish of the lower Mississippi Valley, U.S. It is served grilled, fried, or baked, and has a delectable taste. See also CATFISH.

chanquetes, a small fish found off the coast of Spain near Malaga. It resembles whitebait and is prepared in the same way.

chantelle, the trade name of a semi-soft, matured cheese made in Illinois, U.S. from fresh whole cow's milk. The technique of making and curing is similar to that used for bel paese, which chantelle is said to resemble in taste and texture.

chanterelle, the French name for a small, yellow, edible mushroom with a delicate flavour. It is formed like a cup, with a frilled edge and thick vein-like gills; there is hardly any stalk. It is also known in France as girolle. See also MUSHROOM.

chanterelle hygrophorus, a variety found in the U.S. It grows in bogs, in clusters, and can be found from June to September.

chantilly, à la, a French method of serving chicken. See POULET À LA CHANTILLY.

chantilly, sauce, I. A classical French sauce, made from ½ pint (1 cup) mayonnaise, to which is added, just before it is served, a few drops of lemon juice and ⅛ pint (¼ cup) (before whipping) cream. II. The hot sauce chantilly is a béchamel mixed with whipped cream in the above proportions. III. When used as a sweet course, chantilly means fresh cream sweetened with vanilla sugar and whipped. Sometimes a stiffly beaten egg white is added, to lighten it and to make the taste less cloying. One egg white is enough for ½ pint (1 cup) cream. IV. Sauce allemande, with whipped cream added as above, just before it is served.

chaource, a French cheese made in the Champagne district from cow's milk. It is in season from October to May.

chap, see BATH CHAP.

chapatti, a flat and unleavened Indian bread made in a round; the food is usually placed on the *chapatti*, as though this were a plate. It is made from a well-kneaded flour (wheat or millet) and water, then baked on a griddle. Chapatti are served with curry in most Indian restaurants.

chapeler, a French verb which means, in culinary parlance, to make breadcrumbs from bread dried in the oven, by crushing with a bottle or rolling pin. *Chapelure blanche* are breadcrumbs made from dried crumbs before they have become golden. *Chapelure blonde* or *brune* are breadcrumbs dried until they are coloured a pale gold. See also PANAGE.

chapon, I. A pinkish red fish (*Scorpaena scrofa*) found in the Mediterranean and used in bouillabaisse. II. In the Mediterranean area it means a slice of bread rubbed with garlic and seasoned with olive oil and vinegar. This bread is often added to a salad of chicory. The Italian dish *cappon magro* comes from chapon. See also POULET.

char (*S. Salvelinus*), a freshwater fish of the salmon family, with a red belly—the name "char" means red—and black spots on its sides. It resembles a trout in flavour, and in the U.S. the name is given to some species of red-fleshed trout. It is widely distributed in deep lakes and rivers in many countries, from Iceland to England and Scotland, Scandinavia, Switzerland, Savoy in Italy, and the U.S. It is probably the "poisson rouge" mentioned by St. Evremond in his epistles, and recommended by him. It is prepared and cooked like trout. A great breakfast delicacy in 19th-century England was potted char made from fillets poached in vegetable stock, then covered with butter and put in earthenware pots in the oven. It was served cold, with toast.

In Lough Dan, Ireland, and a few other Irish lakes only, lives the blunt-snouted Irish char, a most delicate and beautiful fish, black on top with pink spots, and orange underneath. Like the lakes themselves, it had its origins in the Ice Age. It is gradually being replaced by the brown trout, to which family, as well as to that of the salmon, it is related; it is, however, a more slender fish. It is excellent to eat, and can be prepared like trout.

charbonnier, the French name for coalfish, often used in fish soups in France.

charcoal, a black porous residue obtained from partially burnt organic matter, particularly wood; the burning process must be specially conducted according to the nature of the substance. Charcoal gives a steady, even heat when used for cooking and is especially suitable for the grilling of meat or fish. The fumes can be dangerous unless a proper outlet is provided for them. It is an essential for an out-of-door barbecue since, when its burning dies down, it can be fanned into heat again without flaming. It is used extensively in Mediterranean countries.

charcuterie, a French word which means the preparation of cooked meats, particularly pork, in many different ways. Nowadays it has also come to mean the shop where such cooked meats are sold. In 1475 the charcutiers, according to the statutes, could only sell *boudin, cervelas* and other sausage forms of pork. In 1476 the charcutiers got the monopoly for selling pork meat, both raw and cooked; however, they were still not allowed to kill the pigs themselves, and the regular butchers who did so allowed only the fat raw pork to be sold, and reserved the other cuts for themselves. In the 16th century they obtained the right to kill the pigs themselves, but they had to buy them 20 leagues from the city. Today, with abbatoirs in cities, this no longer obtains. The most usual contents of a charcuterie, apart from those already listed, are *jambon* (de Paris), (de Bayonne) and de Campagne, *galantine,* galantine de *marcassin,* foie gras, many different pâtés and terrines, *rillettes,* and *saucisses,* which also includes *crépinettes.* Many foreign sausages are also sold.

There is a ham fair (foire de jambons) which takes place on the Boulevard Richard-Lenoir in Paris, just before Holy Week. All the stalls are laden with charcuterie from all over France and Europe. The fair dates from the 15th century.

charcutière, sauce, a French sauce served with grilled meat, especially pork cutlets. A small onion is finely chopped and cooked until soft, but not brown in lard or butter; demi-glace, consommé, white wine or white stock is added, the sauce is allowed to boil up and is then reduced. Before serving, julienne gherkins are added.

chard, I. (*Beta vulgaris;* var. *cicla*), the true chard, also called Swiss chard, leaf beet, leaf chard, sea kale beet, silver beet, white leaf beet, or spinach beet. It is an annual vegetable, grown not only for its large, spinach-like leaves, but also for its broad, white mid-ribs, which should be stripped from the green parts and steamed separately, then served with melted butter, or in any way suitable for sea kale. Chard is, indeed, two good vegetables in one, for the green part of the leaves is often sold as, and tastes like, an earthy spinach, and can be cooked in any way suitable for spinach. The leaves vary in both colour and form; they can be flat, varying from pale to dark green, or they can be curly and bright green with white veins. The plant withstands dry weather very well, which is no doubt the reason for its popularity in Mediterranean countries. It is called *blette* in France, *acelga* in Spain. In Italy, it is used as part of the filling for *tortelli di erbette.* See also ACELGA; RHUBARB BEET. II. The name given to the blanched summer shoots of the globe artichoke, for use in early winter, or the young flowering shoots of salsify, for use in the spring. III. The name sometimes given, in both Britain and the U.S., to the edible parts of the inner leaves of cardoons. They possibly got this name because they are closely related to the globe artichoke and undergo a similar blanching treatment.

charlotte, originally a French dessert, of which there are several kinds. See also SCHALETH À LA JUIVE.

charlotte de fruits, a dish that is imitated all over the world. A flameproof dish is lined either with slices of bread and butter, breadcrumbs, or sponge (lady) fingers and filled with puréed fruits, generally apple, although apricot, rhubarb,

plum, peach, or any fruit can be used. Butter and lemon peel and sometimes rum are added and the contents covered with more bread, breadcrumbs, or sponge (lady) fingers before being baked for about 30 minutes. If apple is used, the dish is called *charlotte de pommes.* See also APPLE CHARLOTTE; BROWN BETTY.

charlotte glacée à la vanille, like *charlotte russe* but filled with vanilla ice-cream.

charlotte russe, a plain cylindrical mould, known as a "charlotte mould," is lined with sponge (lady) fingers or gateau *gènoise,* and filled with either *bavarois* or *crème chantilly.* This dish is thought to be the invention of the great chef and writer, Antonin Carême (1784–1833).

charlotte mould

charollais, a French breed of cattle which is noted for the quality and leanness of its meat. See also BOEUF.

charollaise, I. A French garnish for slices of meat consisting of cooked cauliflower sprigs *à la villeroi* and *croustades* filled with mashed turnips. II. Clear oxtail consommé garnished with small pieces of braised oxtail, julienne of carrot and onion, also small cabbage leaves stuffed with minced, cooked meat and rolled into tiny balls. See also CONSOMMÉ.

charolles, a French cheese made with goat's milk, from Mâconnais; it is in season from April to December.

charoset, a traditional Jewish food eaten at the religious festival of Passover as a symbol of clay from which the Israelites made bricks during periods of Egyptian slavery, and also forming part of the seder table. The seder begins on the evening preceding the first day of Passover week. Charoset is made from finely chopped, peeled and cored apples, nuts, and raisins, all mixed together with a little cinnamon; a little red wine is added to bind the ingredients. Sometimes honey or sugar and grated lemon peel are added. See also SEDER.

chartreuse, I. The French name for a magnificent dish of cabbage cooked with partridge (formerly it meant a fine Lenten dish of many-layered, sliced vegetables cooked with good stock in a mould). *Chartreuse à la parisienne* is a recipe by the famous French chef Carême consisting of sliced truffles baked in champagne, then finely sliced crayfish tails, chicken breasts with butter, then more crayfish tails. This forms the lining of a mould, and the middle is filled with chicken quenelle mixture and *blanquette* of chicken. The mould is covered and then baked in a *bain-marie;* when cooked it is turned out and garnished with button mushrooms. II. A beef consommé slightly thickened with tapioca; it is garnished with pieces of tomato, small ravioli stuffed with spinach purée, and truffles. See also CONSOMMÉ. III. A famous French liqueur flavoured with angelica and hyssop, made by Carthusian monks in Voiran, France, and Tarragona in Spain.

chasse royale, an old French dish made from various cooked game arranged in a pyramid on a large dish.

chasseur, à la, I. A classical French garnish for small pieces of butcher's meat, poultry, or eggs consisting of sliced sautéed mushrooms, with a little shallot, moistened with white wine. See also POULET, SAUTÉ CHASSEUR. II. A French sauce with a white wine foundation, with mushrooms and shallots. It is used for meat or game. III. Meat or game cooked with shallots, white wine, and mushrooms, strongly flavoured with tomato. IV. A game consommé thickened with tapioca, garnished with julienne of mushrooms cooked in Madeira. It is sprinkled with chopped chervil and served with small *profiteroles* filled with game purée. See also CONSOMMÉ. The literal meaning of the name chasseur is "hunter."

châtaignes, see CHESTNUT.

château, I. A French word which applies to a thick slice of steak taken from the sirloin (uppercut) or a slice from a rib of beef. It is sometimes called an *entrecôte château* in restaurants, and is invariably grilled and served with a sauce such as béarnaise. II. A method of preparing potatoes. See POMME DE TERRE (POMMES CHÂTEAU). III. A name often given in restaurants for sauce châteaubriand.

château salad, a French–Canadian salad composed of cooked frogs' legs, shredded lettuce, and watercress, with an oil and vinegar dressing or mayonnaise. It is garnished with sliced, hard-boiled eggs and lemon wedges.

châteaubriand, the name the French give to a large steak (enough for at least two people) taken from the centre of the fillet or tenderloin. It is grilled and garnished with *pommes château* and served with sauce châteaubriand (frequently called *château sauce*). This way of serving steak fillet was invented by Montmireil, who was Châteaubriand's chef.

châteaubriand, sauce, the classical French sauce which is the true accompaniment for a grilled *châteaubriand aux pommes,* but which is now often superseded by sauce béarnaise. Sauce châteaubriand consists of ½ pint (1 cup) each of white wine and demi-glace, with the addition of 3 chopped shallots, boiled rapidly until greatly reduced. To this liquid are added 3 tablespoons butter (gradually in small pieces) and 1 tablespoon fresh chopped tarragon. Just before serving, the sauce is seasoned with a dash of cayenne pepper and a squeeze of lemon juice.

châtelaine, I. A French garnish for slices of meat consisting of *pommes château,* braised celery, cooked artichoke bottoms, and grilled tomatoes. See also POULET, À LA CHATELAINE. II. Artichoke bottoms stuffed with onion purée, glazed chestnuts, *pommes à la parisienne,* and sauce madère. III. An omelette filling of mashed, cooked chestnuts mixed with meat essence (extract) or gravy. The omelette is surrounded by creamed onion sauce. IV. A salad dressing of mayonnaise mixed with an equal amount of whipped cream. V. A chicken consommé, slightly thickened with tapioca and garnished with royale of artichoke and onion, with chicken and chestnut quenelles. See also CONSOMMÉ.

chatouillard, I. The French name for potatoes which are cut into long ribbons by a special implement, and fried in deep oil. II. The nickname given to an expert fryer or *friturier* in France.

chauchat, a French garnish for fish consisting of slices of boiled potato cut lengthwise and arranged as a border around the fish, with a sauce mornay over them, and gratinéed (see GRATIN) under a grill.

chaud-froid, a classical French sauce for game, chicken, fish, meats, or eggs. It is made from a sauce velouté, aspic jelly, thick cream, and egg yolks. One pint (1 cup) good, smooth velouté is made, to which ¼ pint (½ cup) liquid aspic is added, and reduced, constantly stirring, over a slow fire. When the sauce is thick enough to coat the wooden stirring spoon, the pan is removed from the fire and the ¼ pint (½ cup) cream mixed with 2 beaten egg yolks is added. It is then either whipped or strained through a fine sieve and

cooled until it has almost gelled. It can be coloured with herbs or spinach purée to make it green, tomato purée to make it red, lobster coral to make it pink, or demi-glace to make it brown, according to taste and decorative need. Flavouring such as madeira, red or white wine, game essence (extract), veal or fish velouté can be added. This dish is always served cold, and is sometimes garnished with truffles, mushrooms, shrimps, or crayfish.

The name is thought to come from the Latin of ancient Rome. At Pompeii, fragments of meat in jelly were found in a jar with *calidus-frigidus* (hot-cold) written on the outside.

chaudeau, the Polish term for a sweet sauce.

chaudeau migdałowe, an almond sauce which is rather like a *zabaglione,* made from 1 cup ground almonds, 2 tablespoons sugar, 1½ pints (3 cups) milk, 3 egg yolks, and 1 tablespoon potato flour, all cooked in a double boiler, beating all the time, so that the mixture becomes thick, yet foamy.

chaudeau pończowe, a sauce called "punch," made from white wine, lemon and orange juices, with eggs and sugar, and cooked as above.

chaudeau waniliowe, as above, but with vanilla.

chaudeau z białego wina, as above, with eggs and sugar but without fruit juices.

chaudeau z wina czerwonego, a sauce made from red wine, cinnamon, cloves, raisins, lemon juice, and sugar, simmered together for 10–15 minutes.

chaudée, an apple tart of high quality which is a speciality of the district of Lorraine, France.

chaudrée, a French fish soup made from a court-bouillon of herbs, butter, seasoning, and white wine, in which are cooked conger eel, whiting, sole, plaice, *raiton,* and other fish. The soup and the fish are served separately. It is also called *chaudrée de fouras.* It is possibly the origin of the American word chowder. See also BOUILLABAISSE.

chaudron, French for a small cauldron, usually made from copper, in which preserved goose and pork (*confit d'oie, confit de porc*) are cooked.

chaumont, a French cow's milk cheese from Champagne, in season from November to May.

chausson, French for turnover, usually made from *pâté feuilletée* and often filled with cooked apples or other fruit as well as savouries, before being baked in a hot oven for about 15 minutes. Chaussons are generally eaten warm, but can also be served cold. The term also applies to two rounds of pastry with a filling sandwiched between, baked, and served cold.

chausson à la cussy, turnover filled with a forcemeat of whiting, anchovies, and chopped truffles. It is served hot as an entrée or hors d'oeuvre.

chausson à la lyonnaise, a hot turnover filled with creamed pike and beurre écrevisses (butter mixed with crayfish), crayfish, and truffles moistened with brandy.

chausson à la périgourdine, filled with foie gras and truffles moistened with brandy.

chausson à la reine, filled with purée à la *reine* mixed with finely chopped mushrooms and truffles.

chavignol, a French, soft, goat's milk cheese from Sancerre and the nearby villages in the Berry. It is at its best from May to October.

chayote, French for custard marrow, also called brionne. Before cooking it is blanched and cut into quarters or smaller pieces. It is then served with a cream sauce (à la crème), or au beurre, au gratin, *à la grecque,* à la créole, or braised with stock, and dipped in batter and fried (*fritot*). It may also be served cold, dressed with oil and vinegar, or cut in half crossways, stuffed with various minced meats and baked in the oven. Custard marrows are also popular in California, U.S., where they are often marinated in salt and water before being cooked; they are then drained and dressed with oil and vinegar while warm.

chebureki, a Russian pastry turnover made from 12 oz. (3 cups) flour mixed with 1 egg, about ¾ cup cold water, and salt, then rolled out paper-thin, and cut into saucer-sized circles. These are stuffed with a mixture of 1 lb. chopped cooked lamb or mutton, onion, ½ lb. (1 cup) cooked rice, 1 tablespoon chopped mixed dill and parsley, and seasonings. In the Caucasus, tomatoes and ham are sometimes added to the filling. The edges are moistened and the pastry circles folded over to form semicircles; then the turnovers are fried in deep hot oil until golden.

checky pig, a curious little pasty which was made in Leicestershire, England, until 1940; it resembled a little flat pig. Two thin strips of pastry were laid across a central oval, and one was folded to form the ears, and the other to form a long tail. The pastry was filled with minced meat, chopped onion, and herbs, and was closed in the middle. The name is thought to come from a "cheese peg" which was a cross-handled, awl-shaped tool.

chécy, a French cheese made from cow's milk from Orléanais. It is in season from October to June.

cheddar cheese, a famous English cheese made from cow's milk, and made originally in the Somerset town of Cheddar. Now, however, it is imitated in almost all English-speaking countries. In the late 17th century it was the custom for all the neighbouring and adjoining parishes of Cheddar to pool their milk and make a gigantic cheese, sometimes weighing 100 lb. and maturing for 2–5 years. During Queen Victoria's reign, a cheddar cheese was made weighing 11 hundredweights (112 lb. is 1 hundredweight). This was put on exhibition after having been presented to Her Majesty. It was refused by her and was put in Chancery. Its subsequent fate is unknown to the author.

New Zealand is the country which made the largest cheddar cheese in this century; it weighed 10 hundredweights and was sent to the Wembley Exhibition of 1924. The paste of cheddar should be smooth and fairly hard in consistency; if flaky or rubbery, it means either that it is immature or that it has been badly made. It is golden in colour, but is sometimes dyed with carrot or marigold juice to make it red. Under ideal conditions, it can be a good, tasty, filling cheese, but so many inferior imitations are on the market that it is rapidly losing the good reputation it once had. At its worst, it tastes like an innocuous soap. It is good for cooking and is used almost exclusively in the British Isles and parts of the Commonwealth for such dishes as welsh rarebit, macaroni and cheese, *chou-fleur au gratin,* and cheese biscuits or pastries.

cheese, a food made throughout the world from the pressed curds of milk from many mammals. Fresh cheese comes from unfermented curds and has to be eaten quite soon after manufacture. Fermented curd cheese falls into two categories: the soft cheeses, such as brie and camembert; and the hard cheeses, such as cheshire, edam, stilton, Roquefort, and gorgonzola, which keep indefinitely if uncut and stored in the right conditions. There are also cheeses, for example emmenthal, Gruyère, Parmesan, and port-salut, which are made from scalded curds.

Every country, and every district in that country, has its own variety of cheese. The hard cheeses, and those made from scalded curds, can be cooked; soft and cream cheeses are best eaten with bread or biscuits (crackers), or used as a filling for pancakes, pies, or small savoury tarts known as cheesecakes. Apples and other fruits are considered good to eat with cheese. In England, the cheese is usually served after the sweet course, but in France it is served before.

The name comes from the Latin *caseus,* and the Old English word was *cése.* For varieties see individual entries under country.

cheese blintzes, small pancakes filled with a mixture of 1 lb. cream or cottage cheese, 2 egg yolks (seasoned with salt), and 2 tablespoons sugar, to which is added chopped lemon or orange peel. They are a popular Jewish dish. See also BLINTZES.

cheese sauce, a very good sauce for boiled cauliflower or split baked potatoes. It is made of 1 oz. (1 heaping tablespoon) each of butter and flour, ½ pint (1 cup) milk, salt, and pepper, a little cayenne, and 3 oz. (½ cup) grated cheese. A hard cheese is used, usually Parmesan. The butter is melted and the flour added, stirring until the mixture bubbles gently. The milk is added by degrees, beating constantly until the mixture is smooth and creamy. The pan is removed from the heat and the seasonings and cheese are added. An egg yolk is sometimes included with the cheese to obtain a richer sauce. See also MORNAY.

cheesecake, a traditional dish in 17th- and 18th-century Britain and Ireland, but seldom seen there today in private homes. It is more usually bought from a delicatessen as "Polish curd cake," which, indeed, it resembles. In the 18th century, almost all open tarts made with a mixture of cream and egg yolks, with the addition of lemon, orange juice, and grated peel, or soft, puréed fruit such as apple, were called "cheesecakes"; in fact, the acid fruit juice does have the effect of curdling the cream, making it a flavoured cream cheese. To make a cheesecake, a short pastry case is baked blind and then filled. The filling consists of a mixture of 1 lb. curd and 2 eggs, beaten together, to which are added 2 oz. (¼ cup) butter and 2 tablespoons cream, followed by a pinch of cinnamon and nutmeg, 2 tablespoons castor sugar, a handful of sultanas or the grated peel and juice of 1 lemon, and a little brandy. This is all beaten well, poured into the pastry case and baked for 30 minutes in a moderate oven. Another filling used is a mixture of 4 oz. (1 cup) ground almonds, 4 tablespoons melted butter, 2 egg yolks, sugar to taste, and the juice and grated peel of a lemon or orange. This is well beaten, poured into the pastry case and cooked in a moderate oven until it is golden brown. It is served cold. For either filling the top can be "gilded" with 1 beaten egg mixed with 1 tablespoon each flour and sugar. This process is carried out before cooking, and ensures a thin golden crust on the top. In the U.S. cheesecakes are often homemade. There are many variations. See also CURD (CURD CAKE).

cheesecake

chef's hat, see POLITA.

Chelsea bun, an English yeasted bun which originated in Chelsea, a borough of southwest London, in the 18th century. The original bun factory enjoyed royal patronage until 1839, when it was closed down. A successive factory was in operation until 1888. The buns are still made today by a number of local commercial bakeries. They consist of 2½ oz. (5 tablespoons) butter rubbed into 1¼ lb. (4 cups generous) flour, a pinch of salt, and 2½ tablespoons sugar; 1 oz. (1 package) yeast is added to 1 gill (¼ cup) tepid milk and allowed to work, after which 4 eggs are beaten and poured into the yeast. This is turned into the middle of the flour mixture and kneaded until smooth, then covered, and put in a warm place to rise for 1½ hours. The dough is lightly kneaded again, put onto a floured board and rolled out into a square. Then 5 tablespoons butter is slightly softened and mixed with 2½ tablespoons sugar, and this mixture is evenly spread over the dough, which is then rolled up, folded in half, and rolled out again. It is now sprinkled with 5 tablespoons currants and 1 teaspoon mixed spice, rolled up like a swiss roll, and cut into slices about 1½ inches thick. These are laid on a warm, greased baking sheet and left, covered, for 20 minutes, by which time they will have swollen in size and will touch each other. They are then sprinkled with coarse sugar and baked in a hot oven for 20 minutes. The buns are cooled before being separated, when they will pull apart quite easily. The same mixture, left unrolled, is used for hot cross buns.

Cheltenham pudding, a regional English pudding which consists of a baked suet pudding with dried fruits and preserved ginger added. It is served with brandy sauce.

chemisier, a French culinary term which means to coat either a piece of food, or the lining of a mould, with a thin layer of aspic jelly.

chenelle di semolino, small semolina dumplings used in Italy to garnish broth or soup. They are made with 1 tablespoon butter softened and mixed with 2 eggs; a pinch each of nutmeg, salt, and pepper are added and 2 heaped tablespoons semolina are well blended in. Tiny spoonfuls are dropped into hot broth and cooked for 5 minutes.

cherbourg, a French beef consommé with Madeira wine, garnished with julienne of mushrooms and truffles, poached egg, and ham quenelles. See CONSOMMÉ.

cherry, a fruit-bearing tree of the family *Rosaceae*. There are several hundred varieties of this small fruit, distributed all over the world. Two main species of cherry appear to have been the progenitors of the many cultivated varieties, and both grow wild in Britain. The cherry, although thought to have originated in Persia, was brought to Europe and Britain by the Romans about 100 A.D.; indeed, the many wild cherry trees found along the Roman road, Watling Street (which runs from London, past St. Albans to Wroxeter near Shrewsbury), may be descendants of trees grown from stones thrown away by Roman soldiers, who were fond of eating cherries when on the march.

The two species are the dessert, or sweet, cherry and the "sour" cherry. The sweet cherries come from *Prunus avium* and fall into two groups: the *bigarreaus* or hearts, with firm, sweet flesh and both light and dark skins (well-known varieties are white hearts and black hearts, bing, and Queen Anne); and the *geans* or guignes, sweet, tender, juicy, with dark flesh and both light and dark skins, the most typical being black tartarian, elton heart, and frogmore. The sour cherries (*Prunus cerasus*) are used for all culinary purposes, such as making pies, tarts, jams, or jellies, and for canning or bottling. The main varieties of sour cherry are *morellos,* which have black flesh, and *amarelles,* which have red flesh and (despite their name) can sometimes be sweet enough to eat raw. Both of these are used in the making of cherry brandy. Damasca (also marasca) from Dalmatia is used for the liqueur maraschino. Both are very bitter in taste.

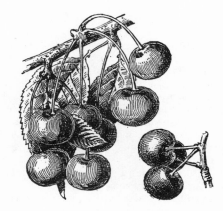
cherry

Duke cherries are a hybrid of sweet and sour cherries; in France, they are known as Royale, in the U.S. as May duke. They originated in Médoc, France. There are some 65 varieties, falling into light-fleshed and dark-fleshed types, of which the prototypes are black duke and red duke or red hortense. They can be used for dessert or for cooking, and are very suitable for bottling in brandy.

Cherry Hill, a commercial brand of Canadian cheddar. See CANADIAN CHEDDAR.

cherry plum, alternative English name for myrobalan, a juicy fruit about the size of a cherry.

chervèni yaytsà, Bulgarian "red eggs." In Bulgaria, as in Greece, Russia, and the U.S. painted hard-boiled eggs are a traditional feature of Easter-Day celebrations. In Bulgaria, a favourite colour for them is red, and the eggs are eaten and also used for a game in which each person tries to crack the challenger's egg, which is held in the palm of the hand. The owner of the egg that survives longest is reputed to be assured of the longest life. See also KOKKINA AVGA; KRASHENIE YAYTSA.

chervil (*Anthriscus cerefolium*), common chervil, a hardy annual pot-herb, Russian and Asian in origin, but now native to Europe. It resembles parsley in appearance, but there is a delicate suggestion of aniseed in its flavour. The leaves are used as a garnish for salads and various cold dishes and as a flavouring for fish and soups, particularly potato soup. Another variety (*Chaerophyllum bulbosum*) is a turnip-rooted chervil, a hardy biennial vegetable, native to southern Europe. It is grown for its roots which are black or greyish outside and golden within; they are eaten boiled or steamed, and have an aromatic, sweet flavour and a floury texture. They may be served either whole, with cream or melted butter, and chopped parsley, or else mashed, to give what in France is known as a *purée chevreuse.*

chervil sauce, a sauce sometimes served instead of bread sauce with poultry or game. It consists of fresh cream seasoned with pepper and salt, to which are added strips of finely cut chervil. It is called sauce *cerfeuil* in France.

chervil vinegar, a vinegar made from chervil leaves removed from their stalks and steeped in double the quantity of white wine vinegar (1 cup chervil to 2 cups vinegar) for 2 weeks. The vinegar is carefully strained off without bruising the leaves, and the same amount of fresh leaves are added and left to macerate for a further 2 weeks, after which it is bottled and corked tightly.

Cheshire cat, alas, not the name of an ever-smiling cat, but an old English cheese measure!

Cheshire cheese, one of the most famous of English cheeses which has been made in Cheshire for at least 300 years. It is a full-cream, hard-pressed, cow's milk cheese with 45 percent

chervil

chestnut

of its total dry matter consisting of butter fat. It has a loose and flaky texture, with a mild, mellow flavour, and can be white, red, or blue in colour. Blue Cheshire, which is perhaps the finest of these three, achieves its colour by a natural process, being red to begin with, until spores of *Penicillium glaucum* appear and vein through it. In Cheshire and Lancashire, the cheese is preferred uncoloured, that is, white, but Londoners and foreigners like it an orangey-red colour, which is obtained by adding carrot juice or *anatto*. Cheshire cheese is cylindrical in shape, with its height about the same as its diameter. It is at its best when 12–18 months old. The cheese made in the late summer or autumn is superior to that made in the spring. Unfortunately, most of the Cheshire today is made in factories, and is sometimes sold too early, which robs it of its mature taste. Cheddar cheese can be imitated in many countries, but Cheshire cheese, to be worthy of the name, must be made in that county, for it is thought that the peculiarly saline quality of the mineralogy of Cheshire grazings is responsible for the singular flavour of the cheese. Cheshire cheese can be used for cooking when stale.

chesnok, Russian for garlic. In Azerbaijan, a pickle consisting of whole garlic bulbs in red wine vinegar is served with pickled cucumbers, fresh tomatoes, and watercress, accompanying a spicy lamb dish. Although it is a regional dish, one finds it in Moscow restaurants which specialize in Azerbaijani cooking. See also GARLIC.

chester français, the French name for Cheshire cheese made at Castres, France.

Chester pudding, an English regional pudding made from a custard mixed with chopped almonds, rind (peel) and juice of 1 lemon, and a little melted butter, baked in a thin pastry case. The top is covered with the egg whites left over from the custard, stiffly beaten, and lightly browned in the oven.

chestnut (*Castanea sativa; also C. dentata, C. mollisima, C. crenata*), the edible nut of several species of trees of the genus *Castanea*. In southern Europe *C. sativa,* the sweet or Spanish chestnut, has been cultivated from Roman times and possibly even before that. Some of the now existing named varieties of *C. sativa* are famous for the flavour and size of their nuts, the large size being obtained by leaving only one nut in the cluster. (In the wild state there may be as many as three, and such nuts are known in French as châtaignes.)

The most famous named varieties of the cultivated *C. sativa* are marron de Lyon and paragon, whose large single nuts are known as marrons, which, after being cooked until soft (by boiling or roasting) and having both outer and inner shells removed, are saturated with a heavy vanilla-flavoured syrup and then dried, to become the famous marrons glacés.

Chestnuts have diverse uses in cookery, being roasted, boiled, steamed, grilled, and mashed. They form the main ingredient of the famous nesselrode pudding, are excellent puréed and served with ham, and provide a valuable component for stuffings for poultry and garnishes.

Chestnuts may be preserved by drying. They can also be ground into a flour, such flour being used in Corsica, for instance, to make a kind of sweet porridge called *brilloli.* See also CASTAGNE; FERINANA.

chestnut sauce, a favourite American sauce for boiled poultry. It is rather thick, made of ½ lb. half-cooked chestnuts, peeled (both outer and inner skins being removed), and boiled in 1 pint (2 cups) white stock. When soft, they are pressed through a fine sieve, or blended. Then 1 heaping tablespoon flour is rubbed into the same of butter and added to the chestnut purée. The mixture is then brought slowly to the boil, stirring constantly. It is removed from the heat, and ¼ pint (½ cup) thick cream and seasonings are added. It is all well beaten before serving.

chevaler, a technical French culinary term used to indicate a symmetrical arrangement of the different combinations of a dish by placing them one upon the other.

chevalet, a French culinary term meaning a slice of bread trimmed and covered with wafer-thin slices of butter or fat pork, before adding raw chicken breasts. The whole is then baked.

cheveux d'ange, I. The French name for a very fine type of vermicelli. II. A kind of French carrot jam. See CAROTTES, EN CHEVEAUX D'ANGE. III. A plain consommé garnished with (I). See also CONSOMMÉ.

chevreau, French for kid. Up to 40 days old, they are called tétards in France, and up to 4 months, broutards. Cabri is an alternative name for kid. See also GOAT.

chèvres longues, see SAINTE-MAURE.

chevret or *chèvreton,* a French, soft, goat's milk cheese called chevret in Bresse and chèvreton in the Maconnais. In season from April to November.

chevreuil, French for roe deer, or roebuck, which is the deer most esteemed gastronomically in France. For cooking purposes, the young animal up to 18 months old does not need a marinade, but does require one after that age. After having been larded, the saddle (*selle*) is roasted for 25 minutes per lb. and served with braised or puréed chestnuts, sauce *poivrade* and gooseberry jelly. The haunch (*cuissot* or *gigue*) is also larded, roasted in the oven or on a spit, and garnished as above. Cutlets (*côtelettes*) are sautéed in butter or oil and served with cream and sauce madère, or with fresh, skinned and pipped grapes soaked in brandy and moistened with *sauce poivrade.* Chestnuts and brown lentils, both puréed, are alternative garnishes. The fillets (filets mignons) are prepared as the cutlets. The shoulders, neck, breast, and the upper part of the loin are used for terrines and pâtés, and also for a civet, which is made as for hare (see CIVET DE LICÈVRE). The neck is sometimes prepared *en daube*. See also GIBIER; VENISON.

chevreuil sauce, the classical French sauce for venison. It consists of ½ pint (1 cup) sauce *poivrade*, with the addition of 1 gill (½ cup) red wine, both reduced, when a *mirepoix* of vegetables and some little pieces of venison are added before serving. See also GRAND VENEUR SAUCE; ROEBUCK SAUCE.

chevreuse, I. A French garnish for tournedos and noisettes. Artichoke bottoms are filled with mushroom purée, and slices of truffle are placed on top. *Pommes noisette* and sauce *bonnefoy* accompany them. II. The French name given to a purée made from turnip-rooted chervil (*cerfeuil tubéreux*).

Chevrier, the French name for a type of haricot bean which stays green, and is cultivated especially in the Arpajon region. It is also called flageolet, but Chevrier is the name of the man who originated it.

chevrotins, small, French, goat's milk cheeses made in Auvergne and Savoie. The best from Auvergne are *chevrotins d'Ambert*. They are eaten from May to November.

chevrotton de Mâcon, a goat's milk cheese from Mâcon, in season from May to September. Also called mâconnais.

Chiavari, an Italian sour milk cheese made from cow's milk. It is a local version of *caciotta*, made in the town of Chiavari.

chibarzu, a traditional bread of Sardinia, made with wheat flour, salt, and yeast (see YEAST DOUGH). It is shaped like a very large English cottage loaf, and is very crusty and good. Also called chivarzu and pane di Sanluri. See also CARASAU.

chícharos, a curious Spanish dish of sweet cakes made with 4 oz. (1 cup) dried peas, 1 lb. (3½ cups) flour, 8 oz. (1 cup) sugar, 6 oz. (⅔ cup) butter, rind (peel) and juice of 1 lemon, and 2 eggs. The peas are soaked overnight, and are then finely chopped before being mixed with the other ingredients. These cakes are a speciality of Zaragoza in Aragon, a region which has a good reputation for cooking.

Chichester pudding, an English regional pudding consisting of 1 pint (2 cups) milk and 2 egg yolks thickened with 1 cup breadcrumbs, sweetened to taste, and made into a stiff custard over hot water. The stiff whites of the eggs are folded in, and the whole is baked until set and brown.

chick-pea (*Cicer arietinum*), originally from western Asia, a plant of the *Leguminosae* family. It was cultivated in Homer's time under the name erebinthos, and is now grown all over the East, Egypt, and southern Europe for its seeds or "peas," which, owing to their resemblance to a ram's head, have gained it the botanical name *arietinum*. These seeds are used both fresh and dried, for soups, stews, and purées. The finest chick-pea is the white species (*garbanzos*) grown in Spain, where it is used extensively for *olla podrida* and allied dishes. It is the basis for the couscous (minute balls of crushed, cooked grain and chick-peas, served with stews) of Arabia. Chick-peas, roasted, are served for *meze* in Greece, and as a substitute for coffee in the Middle East. See also CECI; GRÃO; HUMMUS; POIS CHICHE; REVITHIA; TUONI E LAMPO.

chickasaw plum (*Prunus angustifolia*), an American plum, also called mountain cherry, from the southern states. The fruit is small and not of a very good quality.

chicken, the young bird of a domestic fowl. There are several grades of chicken, designated by their age and, subsequently, their weight. Very young birds (4–6 weeks old), weighing up to 2½ lb., are known by the French name *poussin*, or the American name of broiler. Although tender, the birds have little flavour and also little meat on them. They are best cooked by splitting down the middle and grilling, or by dipping in a batter, or egg and breadcrumbs, and deep frying.

Spring chicken (fryer) is about 2–3½ lb. in weight, and has more flavour than *poussin*. If roasted in a moderate oven for 45 minutes, it will be perfectly cooked; given longer, it will become dry and tasteless. The usual English stuffing consists of 2 cups soaked bread to 1 tablespoon chopped thyme or tarragon, 1 tablespoon minced onion, the chopped liver of the bird, and, if desired, an egg or egg yolk. Spring chickens are also good for jointing, using for pies and sautés, and deep frying or grilling. The bones have a gelatinous quality, owing to the youth of the bird, and are excellent for making jellied soup, or a good stock (which can be done after the chicken has been grilled or roasted). The method for preparing this is to add to the carcase not more than 1½ pints (3 cups) water, together with seasonings, herbs, and a chicken stock cube, and then boil them for 1–2 hours, gently, or for 20 minutes in a pressure cooker.

The best roasting bird in Great Britain is known as roasting chicken. A roaster is under 8 months and weighs 3½–5 lb. If it is a capon, it will have the finest flavour and can weigh from 6–8 lb. It may be stuffed, if desired, although the taste is often better if a small bunch of tarragon and a nut of butter is put inside, rather than a bread stuffing, which naturally absorbs a lot of the flavour. Roasting chicken or the older bird is the best to poach or boil; the others are too small and lack in taste. A 4-lb. chicken should be poached in not more than 2 pints (4 cups) water or stock, with seasonings and herbs, for 1½ hours. If cooked too much, even the best bird will become stringy.

The traditional sauce served generally with boiled chicken in Britain is parsley sauce, made with half milk and half chicken stock, thickened with 1 tablespoon flour or corn flour (cornstarch) to 1 cup stock. Tarragon, however, is the finer herb with chicken and can be used instead of, or with, parsley in the sauce. For cold chicken dishes, such as chicken salad, chaud-froid, or mayonnaise, boiled or poached chicken should always be used, since it is more moist and succulent.

Cockerels can be used as roasting chickens but must be killed at 6 months. They do not compare with the hen, or, more especially, the capon.

Boiling fowl is usually an elderly laying hen of indeterminate age and should be used only for soups or for mincing, unless it is known that its actual age does not exceed 1½ years. See also CHAKHOKHBILI; COCK-A-LEEKY; COUNTY CAPTAIN; CSIRKE; FRANGO; GUMBO; HINDLE WAKES CHICKEN; HOWTOWDIE; KOTOPOULI; KURITSA; KYLLING; POLLO; POULARDE; POULET; SPATCHCOCK; TAVUK.

chicken à la Kiev, see KÚRITSA PO KIEVSKI.

chicken à la king, an original American chicken dish created at the turn of the century in the Brighton Beach Hotel, Long Island, New York, by the chef George Greenwald for his boss E. Clarke King II. It consists of diced, cooked breast of chicken, served in a sauce made from chopped red and green peppers, chopped mushrooms, paprika, chopped onion with lemon juice, cream, and seasonings, all thickened with creamed butter and egg yolks. Sherry is added to taste, and it should be served with cooked noodles, in hot pastry cases, or on hot buttered toast.

chicken and clam broth bellevue, a traditional American soup composed of equal parts of clam broth and chicken broth, served with unsweetened whipped cream.

chicken, southern fried, a southern dish of jointed floured chicken fried on all sides in fat or oil. It is often served with corn bread and fried banana. It is sometimes called chicken Maryland.

chicken corn soup, a very substantial stew-like soup traditional in Philadelphia and all over Pennsylvania, U.S. A whole chicken is jointed and cooked in water to cover, with salt and a pinch of saffron, until tender. The chicken is then removed; the legs and breast and a little stock are set aside. The remaining meat is boned and chopped up and returned to the saucepan; it is brought to the boil, and some noodles and 2 cups fresh corn kernels are added. Both these ingredients are cooked until done; then a little chopped parsley, pepper, and 2 chopped hard-boiled eggs are added. [The breast and legs may be used for a pastry crust pie the next day.] Both the soup and the pie are specialities of the Pennsylvania Dutch country.

chicken cream, a 19th-century English chicken dish using only the breast and thighs of the bird, the remainder being used for casseroles, curry, or soup. It is prepared with 1 tablespoon butter heated and 1 small sliced onion fried in it until golden; then 2 tablespoons flour are stirred in and ½ pint (1 cup) warmed milk. The mixture is well stirred until thick, then left to get quite cold. Meanwhile all skin, bone, etc., is taken from the chicken; and the remaining meat is finely minced and seasoned, added to the sauce, and seasoned again. Then 1 egg yolk is folded in with 3 tablespoons cream. The mixture is put into a buttered basin or small moulds and steamed over boiling water; the time allowed is 1 hour for the large container, 30 minutes for the small, individual ones. The chicken cream can be eaten hot or cold. If cold, it is sometimes covered with aspic jelly to which a little chopped tarragon has been added.

chicken paprika, see CSIRKE PAPRIKÁS.

chicken pie, a popular dish in all English-speaking countries. It is at its best when the bones have been removed before cooking, and fresh herbs (notably tarragon) and a particularly, strong chicken stock are used, the latter so that it can also be eaten cold and jellied. The pastry crust on top can be of either short crust or puff pastry, according to choice. Recipes vary from county to county in Britain, but exceptionally good is the Cornish, made from 1 medium chicken boiled for 30 minutes and left to cool. The meat is removed from the bones, which are put back in the liquid, seasoned well, and simmered for at least 1 hour to make a good stock. A deep pie dish is thickly spread with chopped parsley to a depth of ¼ inch. The chicken meat is mixed with 4 slices chopped lean ham, 1 minced shallot or small onion, a pinch of both sugar and salt; also mace or nutmeg. The dish is filled with strained chicken stock, the edges dampened, and a crust of pastry put over and pressed down at the rim to prevent the juices escaping. A small cross is cut out on top. It is brushed with milk or beaten egg to gild it, and baked in a moderate oven for 35–40 minutes, or until golden on top. It is removed from the oven, and ¼ pint (½ cup) warm cream is poured through a funnel through the slit, and it is served at once. Also good is the Welsh chicken pie prepared as above, but chopped leeks are used to a depth of ½ inch, as well as parsley.

chicken salad dressing, an American mayonnaise dressing made of ½ cup (¼ pint) vinegar, lightly beaten with 4 egg yolks, cayenne, salt, and french mustard. This is added to rich chicken broth, thick cream, and melted butter and cooked in a double boiler, stirring continuously. As soon as the mixture shows signs of thickening, it is strained and ⅓ cup butter and ¼ pint (½ cup) thick cream are added and stirred well. The dressing is served cold. See also BOILED DRESSING.

chicken stock cube, a commercial product which is a compressed cube containing chicken fat and meat, vegetable oil, meat extract, onion powder, yeast extract, spices, herbs, hydrolised protein, monosodium glutamate, and salt. It is extremely useful for enriching stocks, soups, stews, and casserole dishes. There is also a beef stock cube.

chicken turbot, the English name for small-sized, or baby, turbot.

chicorée frisée, French for the annual and biennial plant endive (*Chichorium endivia*), particularly the curly leaved varieties such as Louviers, Anjou, and Meaux, which have green, tending to yellow, leaves, and are invaluable for winter sal-

ads. In France, endive is often braised in good stock and served with cream, butter, or béchamel. The stumps are also utilised. The wild, straight endive known as *barbe-de-capucin* is usually referred to simply as chicorée. There is great confusion over the names endive and chicory. In the U.S., the curly endive is called chicory, and the witloof, with thick, blanched heads, endive. Generally, British usage is the other way round, but there is a tendency in some cities for American usage to be copied. See also ENDIVE.

chicory (*Cichorium intybus*), a vegetable with long, silvery-white, tightly folded leaves. Confusingly, it is known in France and the U.S. as endive. In Belgium, where it is very popular, it is called *chicorée de Bruxelles,* or commonly *barbe-de-bouc* (goat's beard). The witloof (white leaf) is the largest and most popular variety of chicory. A species found in Holland, France, and the U.S., closely related to common chicory, is magdeburg chicory.

Chicory can be eaten raw in salad, when it should be dressed with oil and lemon juice and seasonings; it is particularly good mixed with sliced beetroot and yogourt. Cooked, it is best braised in a little stock, butter, and lemon juice, in a moderate oven for 1 hour. It is delicious with sweet ham or chicken. The lemon juice, which should be used sparingly, prevents it from turning brown. Cream can be added before serving, if desired. Before serving raw or cooked, a little of the stem should be scooped out; this stops the chicory from tasting bitter, which it is inclined to do.

The long, parsnip-like roots are also very delicate to taste. They are roasted and ground to mix with coffee. See also ESCAROLE.

chicory gourilos, stumps of both chicory and endive. When fully grown and tender, they are boiled in salted water, drained, and tossed in either butter or cream. They are served as a vegetable or as an hors d'oeuvre in France.

chien de mer, see SAUMONETTE.

chiffonade. I. A French salad dressing consisting of a sauce vinaigrette mixed with chopped parsley, chopped hard-boiled eggs, and chopped cooked beetroot. II. In France, chiffonade also denotes vegetables (especially sorrel and lettuce) or herbs cut into ribbon-like strips and cooked in butter. It can be moistened with cream sauce. Sorrel chiffonade forms an important part of potage *santé,* or of a sorrel omelette, with or without the cream sauce, according to taste. III. An American chiffonade dressing is made of 2 hard-boiled eggs, 1 cup sauce vinaigrette, 2 tablespoons each of minced parsley and chopped red pepper, and 1 teaspoon minced shallot. The hard-boiled eggs and the red pepper are very finely chopped, and all the ingredients are blended together well and served chilled.

chiftele, Rumanian for meat balls, one of the most common dishes found in Rumania. They are usually made from minced beef, chopped herbs, and grated onion, mixed with a little corn meal and seasonings. Fish or game is also used for this dish, but less frequently.

chikhirtma, a Russian soup from the Caucasus, made from 1½ lb. mutton cut into serving pieces and simmered in water until cooked. These are removed from the stock and the fat is skimmed off. Then 2 onions fried in butter, a pinch saffron, salt, and pepper are all added to the stock which is brought to the boil; 2 tablespoons white vinegar are boiled and added to the soup, together with the mutton, which is heated up. Before serving, 2 egg yolks are stirred into the hot soup, but it is not allowed to reboil.

chilli or *chili* (*Capsicum frutescens;* var. *longum*), the dried fruit of this species of *capsicum,* a strictly tropical and sub-tropical plant. It is sometimes called Guinea pepper. For culinary purposes, the dried fruit is either used whole, being introduced for a greater or lesser time during cooking, or else the soft inside lining of the skin from the fruit is scraped off and added. Alternatively, the whole fruit may be powdered, and small quantities of the powder, which is one of the hottest flavourings known to man, are added to the dish in preparation. The best chillies and chilli powder are said to come from Mexico, and the cuisine of Central and South America is much influenced by the use of this flavouring; but Zanzibar also has a reputation for the production of a good chilli powder with an excellent red colour. The world-famous tabasco sauce is prepared with a small and very hot chilli as an ingredient. Perhaps the hottest chilli sauce in the world is that made by the Chinese; it has a thick consistency and is an essential ingredient for some Indonesian and Chinese dishes. The Portuguese bottled *piri-piri* is also extremely hot. See also CAPSICUM; CAYENNE.

chilli

chilli con carne, a spicy stew of beef, onions, and seasonings, simmered in sauce flavoured with hot chilli, for several hours. It is usually mixed with dried, soaked, cooked red kidney beans. Although originally of Spanish origin, it has now become a mixture of Mexican and American-Indian cooking, such as was practised by the Spanish settlers in California, U.S. It is still a speciality in southwestern U.S.

chilli sauce, I. A sauce that is hot to the taste made from ¼ lb. dry, red chillies cleaned of seeds and cooked in 1 quart (4 cups) boiling water until pulpy. This pulp is sieved to make about 1½ cups of purée. Then 2 tablespoons oil or fat are heated; 1 tablespoon flour is stirred in, and 1 crushed garlic clove and salt are added. The chilli purée is then mixed in and, finally 1 tablespoon vinegar. It is used sparingly—not more than 1 teaspoon to 1 pint (2 cups) stock. II. A milder sauce can be made from 6 chopped green or red peppers, 4 finely chopped onions, 2 lb. peeled tomatoes, 8 tablespoons moist sugar, salt, a pinch of cayenne pepper, and 3 cups wine vinegar, all of which are boiled together gently for about 1 hour, then allowed to cool and, finally, poured into jars for use when required. III. A hot sauce, good for serving with fried fish, consists of 2 small red chillies cleaned of seeds and chopped with ¼ cup capers and a little parsley, to which are added salt, sugar, 3 tablespoons sherry, and the juice of 1 lemon.

chimaja, the root of a wild cherry, used fresh and dried in a large number of Mexican dishes. It forms part of the national *mole* sauce.

China chilo, an old English dish dating from the time of the East India Company in the early 17th century. It was usually served on a clear white and green plate acquired in the East. It is made from raw, finely minced or chopped mutton or lamb,

shredded lettuce, a few chopped spring onions (scallions), butter, and as many green peas as would equal the weight of the meat. With the addition of a little water and seasonings, it is all simmered slowly on top of the stove for about 2 hours. Towards the end of this time, a peeled, diced medium-sized cucumber is added, and cooked until it is soft but not squashy. It is served on a dish of boiled rice.

China orange, see ORANGE.

chinchard, French for an elongated sea fish of the large *Carangidae* family, which includes saurel and caringue and is not unlike a type of mackerel to look at. The inferior horse mackerel is a member of the same family. Chinchard is well thought of as a fish and is generally cooked filleted. In Italy it is called sugherello. See also JURELES.

chine, the bony part adjoining the fillet of a loin, particularly of pork, but also of veal or lamb; or the bony part of a rib or sirloin of beef. It is in fact the backbone containing the spinal cord. Chine of pork is the best known because its gelatinous quality makes it excellent for stock.

Chinese date (*Zizyphus jujuba*), a tropical tree, originally from Asia but now cultivated in California, U.S. The fruit has scratch-like marks on it and contains long pointed seeds; its taste faintly resembles that of a dried date. It can be eaten raw when fresh but is usually sold candied. In appearance it is quite unlike any other fruit. The Chinese name is Hoong joe, and it is also called jujube.

chino, a Spanish conical strainer, or colander, which is used with a small wooden paddle, primarily for sieving the ripe, chopped vegetables for gazpacho.

chinois, I. French for small Chinese oranges, both green and yellow, which are either crystallised or preserved in brandy. II. A French conical strainer with a very fine mesh.

chinois

chiodi di garofano, Italian for clove, used especially in Italy in meat dishes such as *stracotto,* and in the Sienese cake *panforte.*

chiorro, a Basque national dish consisting of 1 lb. onions and 1 small bulb of garlic sliced and chopped and softened in olive oil. Then 1 tablespoon flour, 1 lb. tomatoes, 1 tablespoon tomato purée, and a pinch each of mace, paprika, and cayenne are added; also 1 glass (½ cup) red wine and 1 glass (½ cup) water. These ingredients are brought to the boil and then simmered for ½ hour with the utensil lid removed. Meanwhile, fillets of fish such as turbot, cod, haddock, etc., are cooked with lemon juice and seasonings in a buttered pie-dish. They are served on a large croûton of fried bread, and the sauce is spooned over each serving.

chiozzo, Italian for gudgeon, often used in *fritto misto di mare.*

chipirones, Spanish for small inkfish (squid). For the large ones, *chocos* is an alternative name.

chipirones en su tinta, literally "inkfish in their ink," a dish prepared in El Escorial and other parts of Spain. It is made from 2 large onions, 2 cloves garlic, 3 lb. peeled tomatoes and herbs cooked in ¼ pint (½ cup) olive oil. When the sauce is well cooked, the inkfish (approximately 12) are added, together with their ''ink'' (the fluid they exude), and cooked gently for 20–30 minutes. It is seasoned with salt and cayenne pepper. Rice is served with this dish.

chipolata. I. A French name for small sausages. Originally, the word meant an Italian stew with onions. II. A French garnish for slices of meat consisting of braised button onions, chipolata sausages, mushrooms, whole chestnuts, and small lardoons.

chips, the colloquial word in England for fingers of fried potato. When peeled and sliced, they should be soaked to remove some of the starch, and then dried in a cloth before frying in very hot oil. Ideally, chips should be fried twice, which ensures their remaining much crisper. The first time, they are fried to a very pale golden colour and are then removed and drained on paper; the second time, they are fried to a deeper colour, and remain crisper than if only fried once. See also GAME CHIPS.

chiqueter, a French culinary word which means to mark out with a knife the small round top of a *vol-au-vent* case, or the edge of a tart or flan.

chirinon, see HIRINO.

chispe e feijão branco, a traditional dish from the Algarve, Portugal. It consists of soaked, dried white beans cooked slowly in water with chopped pig's trotter (feet), pieces of pork, sliced garlic, and sliced carrots, all flavoured with chopped parsley and aniseed. It is one of the best dishes of southern Portugal.

chitarra, alla, a form of long, thin pasta made in the Abruzzi. It is cut on a wooden board with wire strings, the chitarra (guitar). It is often served with olive oil, *saetina,* or *paesana* sauce. See also PASTA.

chitterlings, the smaller intestine of the pig. In England, some years ago, they used to be offered for sale already washed and boiled by the pork butcher. They were then dipped in egg and breadcrumbs and fried in bacon fat at home, where they were looked upon as a worthy supper or breakfast. Chitterlings are served a great deal in Russia, and are prepared like tripe, often being served with a sour cream sauce. A lightly smoked sausage with a black skin is made from chitterlings, and is a speciality of Normandy, France. See also ANDOUILLE.

chive (*Allium schoenoprasum*), a member of the onion family and a native of northern Europe. Only the thin spiky green leaves, which have a most delicate flavour, are used, mainly as a garnish, with salads, stews, and soups. The chive is a hardy perennial which increases rapidly in warm soil; it can be kept green all winter in a cool greenhouse or under a cloche. It has a pretty pink bushy flower.

chivry, sauce, a classic French sauce served with poultry, eggs, or fish. In the latter case fish stock is used instead of chicken stock. It is made from ½ pint (1 cup) velouté (*de volaille*) mixed with ½ pint (1 cup) stock, and ½ pint (1 cup) white wine which has been reduced to half by boiling with 1 teaspoon each of shallot, chervil, tarragon, chives, and burnet. It is all well seasoned, and finished with 2 tablespoons *beurre chivry.*

chizze con formaggio, an Italian dish of cheese-filled pastry slices fried in olive oil.

chłodnik, a traditional Polish cold herb soup made from chopped boiled red beetroots, twice the quantity of blanched young beetroot top, sorrel, chopped chives, and dill, juice of pickled cucumbers, sour cream or sour milk, and seasoning. It is garnished with diced fresh cucumber, quarters of hard-boiled egg, crayfish tails, slices of lemon and sometimes flakes of parboiled cold sturgeon. The soup is poured over a cube of ice placed in each plate.

chłodnik gotowany, a chilled soup made from meat stock mixed with sliced hard-boiled eggs, fermented rye, pickled beetroot, and sour cream, garnished with crayfish tails and pickled cucumbers.

chłodnik litewski, a Lithuanian version of the above, with buttermilk added.

chłodnik ogorkowy, a traditional chilled soup, made from juice of pickled cucumbers heated with leaven, then blended with sour milk. It is garnished with diced red beetroot, sliced hard-boiled egg, crayfish tails, chopped chives, and dill, and is served with a cube of ice on each plate.

chocolat, French for chocolate.

chocolate, the substance obtained from the seeds of the chocolate or cocoa tree (*Theobroma cacao*), which is now cultivated in the West Indies, although native to South America and Mexico, where it was discovered by the Spaniards in the early 16th century. It was they who brought it to Europe, and chocolate is still a popular drink in Spain. The name comes from the Aztec word chocolatl (*choco*—cocoa, *latl*—water). The seeds are dried, partially fermented, roasted, and ground. Chocolate reaches the markets in solid blocks or bars, and is a very valuable food which lends itself to a variety of uses in cookery. For culinary purposes, though, only black, or bitter, chocolate should be used. (This chocolate is obtained by cooling the crushed cocoa beans, and removing the fat from the hard block). Unfortunately, most so-called ''cooking'' chocolate has only some of the fat removed and sugar added. This is not to be recommended as it can give it a mawkish flavour; it is preferable to use chocolate in which the fat has been completely removed, and to add sugar to the ingredients when preparing a dish. Other methods include chocolate grated and combined with milk and sugar to form a beverage; eaten as a sweetmeat (confection); or melted and added to cakes and desserts. Chocolate biscuits (cookies) are biscuits dipped in melted chocolate. Chocolate contains small amounts of the alkaloid theobromine, which resembles caffeine in its properties, and is therefore a stimulant. See also CHOKLAD; COCOA; MOLE.

American Indian with chocolate cup and pot

chocolate cake, a cake popular in almost all European countries and in the U.S. It can take many forms, from a sponge mixture flavoured with chocolate, or more usually cocoa powder, to a plain cake thickly iced with melted chocolate. A common recipe uses 4 oz. bitter chocolate dissolved in 1 tablespoon milk. Then ½ lb. (1 cup) butter is creamed with ½ lb. (1 cup) sugar, and 4 eggs are added, one at a time, with 1 tablespoon flour. The chocolate mixture is stirred in, and, finally, 6 more tablespoons flour. When well mixed, this is poured into a greased and lined tin 12 inches by 8 inches and baked in a moderate oven for approximately 40 minutes. See also SACHERTORTE.

chocolate icing, icing made with 4 oz. chocolate melted in 4 tablespoons water. When the melting process is completed,

2 cups icing sugar are worked in until the icing is thin enough to spread.

chocolate mousse, a light dessert made with the whites of 4 eggs, separated and beaten until stiff; ½ lb. plain chocolate is melted in 3 tablespoons water, then removed from the heat, and the beaten egg yolks stirred in gradually, still beating well; finally, either 2 tablespoons fine sugar, or the same of brandy or other sweet liqueur, are stirred in. When the mixture is cool, the egg whites are folded in, and the mousse is chilled. It is the egg whites which make the mixture frothy; if these are omitted, one still has a delicious, dark chocolate dessert, but it is smooth and creamy in texture, not frothy.

chocolate sauce, a sauce made from ¼ lb. chocolate, ½ pint (1 cup) milk, vanilla to taste, and some sugar (if the sauce is to be very sweet) stirred over the fire in a thick saucepan until the chocolate has melted and the milk is about to boil. The pan is removed from the fire and 4 well-beaten egg yolks are stirred in over a very gentle heat. The sauce must not boil again.

chocolate truffles, a delectable sweetmeat (confection) that gets its name from its resemblance to a truffle. It is made from ¼ lb. bitter chocolate melted with 1 tablespoon milk, then beaten with 1½ tablespoons butter and 1 egg yolk. This mixture is left for 4 hours to harden, and is then made into small sausage shapes and rolled in cocoa.

chocos, Portuguese for inkfish or cuttlefish, used a lot in Portugal and prepared like *lula.* See also LULA.

chocos, Spanish for inkfish or cuttlefish, also called *jibia.* See also CALAMARY; CHIPIRONES.

chocos con habas, a traditional Cadiz dish of inkfish cooked in olive oil, with garlic, broad beans, salt, pepper, and a little water.

choesels, see LES CHOESELS.

choisy, I. A French garnish for tournedos and noisettes made of braised lettuce and *pommes château.* II. A omelette filling of braised lettuce with cream sauce.

choklad, Swedish for chocolate.

chokladkola, a Swedish recipe for chocolate toffee fudge. It is made with 1½ lb. (3 cups) sugar, 2 tablespoons butter, 3 tablespoons cocoa, ½ pint (1 cup) golden syrup (corn syrup), and 1 pint (2 cups) thin cream brought slowly to the boil, stirring constantly, and then boiled rapidly until the toffee sets. When a few drops of this boiling mixture, dropped into very cold water, form a ball soft to the touch, the toffee is ready to be poured into a tin and cut into squares.

cholent, the traditional Jewish dish served in Orthodox houses on the Sabbath, a day on which no cooking is permitted. The name is thought to come from two German words, shule ende (end of synagogue service). The contents vary from country to country but in Europe, rib of beef, or brisket, is put into a large casserole with soaked haricot beans, onion, and potatoes. A large dumpling is made from flour, suet, grated onion, parsley, and grated potato, all seasoned, and this is added to the meat and vegetables. The contents are covered with boiling water, and a little sugar is added. A tightly fitting lid is put on, and as late as possible before sundown on Friday evening, the casserole is placed in a slow oven, and the cholent is cooked until midday dinner on Saturday. It is a delicious hot-pot and merits Heine's poem to it, "Princess Sabbath."

cholla, see CHALLAH.

chop, I. To cut up any article of food into various sizes or shapes. II. Meat about 1–2 inches thick taken from the loin of lamb, mutton, pork, or veal. It is called cutlet in the U.S. Chops can be grilled or braised, but grilling is the most usual method. See also CUTLET. III. A chump chop is cut from the end of the loin nearest the tail. It has little bone, and is considerably leaner than a centre cut or loin chop.

chop potato pudding, a traditional Cornish dish made with 4 large potatoes, 2 tablespoons flour, and ¼ lb. suet chopped up together and mixed with a little water. They are then put into a basin and either boiled or steamed for 2 hours. The pudding is served with meat and gravy.

chop suey, a Westernized "Chinese" dish, not known or eaten in China, although popular in American and European Chinese restaurants. Chop suey is spelt "tsa sui" in Mandarin, and means, literally, "mixed fragments," which is indeed the character of the dish, for it is a mixture of small pieces of chicken, ham, or shrimp, chopped mushrooms, celery, water chestnuts, bamboo shoots, stock, and soy sauce. The Chinese dish most resembling it is *chao hui,* which contains pieces of chicken, bamboo shoots, ham, mushroom, and minced pork balls.

There are several stories as to the origin of chop suey in the U.S. One says that it was created by a Chinese cook in the mining district, who, when asked to serve food late at night, used up the remains in his larder. Another says that it was an Irishman working as a waiter in a Chinese restaurant in San Francisco who invented it; a large party came in just as the restaurant was closing, and not wishing to lose his customers, the waiter scooped up the fragments left in all the dishes in the kitchen, mixed them together, and christened the concoction chop suey, i.e., mixed fragments. Whoever was the creator, chop suey has made a great impact on Western palates, and it is even canned for serving in the home.

chopa, see BESUGO.

chopa blanca (*Kyphosus sectatrix*), a fish like the common *rudderfish* from the Gulf of Florida, U.S. It is considered fairly good eating. Also called Bermuda chub.

chorbà, Bulgarian for soup. Many vegetables are used for soup in Bulgaria, also lamb and mutton. Yogourt is incorporated in some cold soups and is also used as a garnish. Lettuce forms the basis for a popular soup which is made in the same way as in Rumania. See also TARATÒR.

àgneshka chorbà, sliced lamb fried in butter, with spinach and chopped spring onions (scallions) then added, paprika to season, and water to cover. When the meat is nearly cooked, a little rice and a few peppercorns are added. Before serving, the soup is thickened with egg yolks mixed with a little yogourt or sour milk, but not reboiled.

sèlska chorbà, village or country soup, made from 1 lb. onions puréed and mixed with 1 grated celeriac root, the onion stock, 2 tablespoons olive oil, and seasoning all brought to the boil. A dash of lemon juice or vinegar is added and the soup is sometimes thickened with an egg yolk.

zèleva chorbà sŭs bekòn, cabbage soup with bacon, a thick, substantial stew–soup which serves as an entire meal. A whole cabbage is shredded or finely sliced and blanched in salted water. Then 1 large onion and ½ lb. bacon are diced and fried in oil, and when brown, 2 tablespoons flour is shaken over. The cabbage and liquid are added, and cooked until all are tender. The whole is seasoned with black pepper and caraway seeds, and sometimes thickened with 1 egg beaten with 4 tablespoons yogourt. It must not be reboiled after the egg has been added.

chorizo, a Spanish garlic sausage. There are two types of sausage in Spain; one is used only in stews and contains beef, pork, garlic, and red peppers: the other is eaten smoked or dried and is made from pork (lean and fat), red and white pepper, and garlic. One of the latter kind is *salchichon,* a delicious pork sausage. See also BUTIFARRA; CACHELADA; CACHELOS; LONGANIZA; MORCILLA BLANCA; PAELLA; SALCHICHA.

chorlito, Spanish for plover, which are plentiful in Spain and cooked like partridge.

choron, a French garnish for tournedos and noisettes consisting of artichoke bottoms, green peas, *pommes noisettes,* and sauce *choron.*

choron, sauce, a classic French sauce, made from a sauce béarnaise blended with tomato purée to taste.

chou, French for a pastry invented by the famous chef Carême, made from 3 oz. (4 tablespoons) butter, a pinch of salt, and 1 tablespoon sugar (only if for a sweet course), all boiled in 1½ gills (⅓ cup) water. When bubbling, the pan is removed from the heat and 3¾ oz. (1 scant cup) plain, sifted flour is beaten in until the mixture is smooth and leaves the sides of the pan. It is left to cool, and 3 well-beaten eggs are added gradually, beating thoroughly until the paste is smooth and shiny looking. When ready, the pastry is pushed through a forcing bag and baked on a metal baking tray. Chou pastry is always used for eclairs, *profiteroles, saint-honoré,* or soufflé fritters. The plain case can be filled with sweet or savoury fillings, or simply whipped cream.

chou, French for cabbage (plural *choux*). *Choux pommés* is French for cabbages with a large heart. In France, cabbage is usually braised with larding bacon, onion, and carrot in a little stock. See also CHOUÉE.

chou farci, stuffed cabbage. The cabbage is blanched for about 10 minutes in boiling salted water, after which the heart is removed, chopped, and mixed with minced meat, vegetables, and herbs. This mixture is put back into the cabbage which is then tied in cloth or muslin and braised slowly in stock for several hours. When cooked, it is drained, and served with a little of the stock.

chou caraïbe, the root of *Arum esculentum,* a plant originally Asian and African but now cultivated in the south of France. It is prepared like swede.

chou rouge, French for red cabbage. After it has been salted, it is served either braised, or shredded and raw.

moelle de chou rouge, the core and stalk of the chou rouge are trimmed and boiled, then chopped and served with butter.

choucroute, French for sauerkraut.

choucroute garnie, the French name for a dish consisting of sauerkraut braised in white wine, or a little wine vinegar and water, a slice of ham, bacon, or pickled goose, frankfurt sausages, and boiled potatoes. This is a traditional dish from Alsace but is served all over France.

chouée, a method employed in the Poitou region of France of serving green cabbage. The cabbage is boiled in salted water, drained and pressed, and a large amount of butter is added. See also CHOU.

chou-fleur, French for cauliflower.

chou-fleur au gratin, a cauliflower is first trimmed, steamed, and drained. It is then separated into flowerlets which are placed in a flameproof dish and covered with a thin white sauce thickened with grated Parmesan or with a sauce mornay. This is then sprinkled generously with breadcrumbs, studded with small dabs of butter, and browned in the oven. An excellent variation is easily accomplished by including small strips of crisply fried bacon in the sauce mornay.

chou-rave, French for kohlrabi, usually served peeled, sliced, then boiled, drained, and accompanied by melted butter, sauce béchamel, or prepared au gratin.

chouriço, a Portuguese pickled pork sausage. Both pork fat and lean leg of pork are cut into small pieces and put in a large basin with salt, white pepper, and chopped garlic, with white wine to cover. This is left for a week, being turned at least every day. It is then drained and paprika is added before it is stuffed into a skin. The sausage is smoked for 4 days, and then kept covered with olive oil. See also SALPICÃO; SALSICHAS.

chouriço de sangue, ''blood sausage,'' a Portuguese blood pudding made from pig's blood. It is usually served with boiled turnip tops tossed in olive oil, and is often accompanied by *farin heiras.*

choux de bruxelles, French for brussels sprouts. In Belgium, they are served not only as a vegetable course, but also as an ingredient for soups, purées, and salads. One method of using them is to sieve them, cooked, with potato, and add them to a chicken stock, with a garnish of cream or top of the milk, and fried bread croûtons.

chowder, a Newfoundland and New England (U.S.) soup, made with fresh fish, clams, shellfish, bacon, and onions simmered in water. The name is thought to derive from the French chaudière (pot) and the Latin *caldaria* (hot). See also BOSTON FISH CHOWDER; CLAM CHOWDER; CONCH CHOWDER; LOBSTER CHOWDER; MANHATTAN CLAM CHOWDER; NEW ENGLAND CLAM CHOWDER; OYSTER CHOWDER; POTATO CHOWDER.

chrane, a Jewish preserve made from cooked beetroots mixed with grated raw horseradish and covered with malt vinegar sweetened with sugar.

chremslach, a traditional Jewish dish similar to grimslich, eaten at the Passover festival. It is made with 3 tablespoons schmaltz or fat, 6 tablespoons hot water, and the rind (peel) and juice of 1 lemon mixed together. Then 4 cups matzo meal are beaten in until a stiff batter is made; 1 tablespoon sugar is added to 4 egg yolks and mixed in, and a little salt is added to the stiffly beaten egg whites, which are put in last. A filling is made of chopped preserved fruit or nuts, such as cherries or almonds, and a little honey, mixed well together. The batter is formed into small balls in which a little filling is inserted and enclosed. Each ball (or chremzle) is flattened into a thick pancake and fried on both sides in hot oil. These pancakes are then drained on paper and sprinkled with almonds and either honey or sugar. Different countries have their own variety of filling.

christe marine, see SAMPHIRE.

Christmas, a festival held in all Christian countries in either December or January, to mark the birth of Christ. The western Church observes the festival on December 25, the date decreed by Pope Julius I in the 4th century; in the eastern Orthodox Church it is celebrated January 6–7. It is the occasion for a family celebration and presents are given to all. Throughout Europe, many traditional dishes are associated with Christmas. It is a true feast, and the principal dish consists of a large cooked bird; in latter years the turkey has been traditional, but goose, duck, and chicken are also served, accompanied by ham and other meats. Spiced beef is traditional in Ireland.

In the British Isles and Ireland, Christmas cake, Christmas pudding, and mincepies are essential dishes. Most European countries have a Christmas cake or other dish, but in Roman Catholic countries it is generally the Feast of the Epiphany (January 6) which is celebrated with a large meal, cakes, and presents. Until very recently, Christmas Eve day was one of fast and abstinence in the Catholic Church, so all dishes served on that day were meatless. See also AIGO BOUÏLLIDO; ANGUILLES, EN CATIGOUT; CACALAUS; CHRISTÓPSOMO; EGGE (EGGEDOSIS); GRØD; INSALATA DI RINFORZ; JOULUKINKKU; JOULUTORTUT; JULGRÖT; JULSKINKA; KOURAB IÉTDES; LEBKUCHEN; LUTFISK; SINT NICHOLAAS AVOND; TOURTIÈRE.

Christmas cake, a cake eaten at Christmas. An original recipe for the English Christmas cake consists of 1 wineglass (½ cup) rum or brandy and 10 eggs mixed slowly together, with the addition of 1 lb. 2 oz. (4 cups) flour, 1 lb. (3 cups) raisins, 1 lb. (3 cups) currants, 4 oz. (1 cup) cherries, 4 oz. (1 cup) almonds, 2 oz. (½ cup) candied peel (rind), 1½ oz. (¼ cup) walnuts (cleaned and chopped), 1 lb. (2 cups) butter and 1 lb. (2 cups) sugar. The mixture is turned into prepared tins and baked in a slow oven for 4–6 hours.

Christmas pudding, a pudding, also known as plum pudding, which is traditionally eaten at Christmas in Britain and Ireland. It is a very rich, fruited, steamed pudding made from 1 lb. raisins, 1 lb. currants, 1 lb. sultanas, 1 lb. grated suet, and 1 lb. breadcrumbs, mixed with ¼ lb. (1 cup) flour, 1 lb. (2 cups) sugar, 2 cups mixed candied peel (rind), 1 cup nuts, a pinch of nutmeg, 1 teaspoon mixed spice, lemon juice and grated peel (rind), 6 eggs, and ¼ pint (½ cup) each of rum, brandy, and stout, or milk. These ingredients are all thoroughly mixed, and custom decrees that various silver trinkets or coins be added, before putting the mixture into 2 greased basins about 6 inches in diameter, or 1 large one, which are covered and tied down and steamed for at least 6–8 hours. Whoever gets a silver token has good fortune throughout the year. The pudding in this form did not appear until about 1675. Before this, it was more of a thick porridge with dried fruits and spices added. It should be made well in advance of Christmas as it improves with keeping. Brandy butter or rum butter is served as a sauce. See also PLUM PUDDING.

christópsomo, a Greek Christmas bread similar to *lambropsomo*, except that the loaf is decorated with a cross of dough and chopped nuts. See also CHRISTMAS.

chrust czyli faworki, Polish for a kind of thin sweet biscuit (cookie) which is fried a crisp brown, and eaten either hot or cold with honey. It consists of 2 cups flour, 4 tablespoons sugar, 1 tablespoon butter, 1 egg, ½ cup sour cream, and a little vinegar (approximately 1 tablespoon).

chrzan z octem, a Polish horseradish sauce made with wine vinegar, sugar, and salt, but without sour cream.

chub (*Leuciscus cephalus*), a freshwater fish of the carp family found in all European and English rivers and streams. It has a long body, sometimes 15 inches, and can weigh up to 10 lb. It is a very bony fish, and not very firm or tasty. It should be eaten immediately after being caught as the flavour deteriorates rapidly. In France it is used in a *matelote*. In the U.S. it is found in the Great Lakes (Lake Superior is the main source), and the fish is known as blackfin or longjaw. It is prepared like carp. See also CHABOT; DOBULE.

chuchel, a Swiss dish sometimes eaten for breakfast or supper. It is made from 3 eggs, whipped with ½ pint (1 cup) milk and a little salt, and enough flour to make it into a thick batter. This is cooked in butter in a frying pan for about 10 minutes, stirring the while, and when ready it is cut with a spoon or knife and served with fruit sauce or syrup. It is also popular in the Swiss-American parts of Wisconsin, U.S.

chuck, one of the cheapest cuts of beef which comes from the neck ribs of the animal. It is usually taken off the bone and used for stews, pies, soups, and stock. It is often known as chuck steak or chuck roast in the U.S.

chudleigh, a small plain yeasted bun traditional in Devonshire, England. It is served split in two and spread with thick or clotted cream and raspberry or strawberry jam. Chudleighs are the Devon equivalent of Cornish splits.

chufa (*Cyperus esculentus*), a European sedge with knotted roots which become swollen and form small, scaly tubers. They are brownish outside but white within, and sweet to the taste. When dried, the flavour improves, and they can be eaten during the winter either raw, or ground and roasted. They are also called rush nut.

chuleta, Spanish for cutlet or chop.

chuletas a la navarra, lamb cutlets browned in oil and then removed. Chopped ham and onion are lightly fried in the same oil, then peeled tomatoes and seasonings are added and cooked until thick to form a sauce. *Chorizo*, cut in fine slices, is served on top of the cutlets, and the sauce poured over the top.

chump chops, lean chops cut from the hind end of the loin before it becomes the top of the leg, in lamb, mutton, pork, and veal.

churros, a traditional Spanish breakfast dish, rather like a doughnut. Churros are usually bought in shops and at fairs; they are cooked in great cauldrons and sold hot. They are not easy to make at home, but consist of 5 oz. (1 cup) flour, a pinch of salt, and ½ teaspoon baking soda, mixed together and then gradually worked to a paste with ¼ pint (½ cup) water. A large pan is half-filled with oil which must be heated until it is smoking; the churros paste is put into a large icing-syringe called a *churrero* which is held strapped to the shoulder, and it is piped into the hot oil in the form of a continuous spiral, starting in the centre and spreading round the pan. This must be done quickly and evenly, so that browning is regular. It is then drained, sprinkled with sugar, and broken into required lengths for serving. Churros are eaten with thick, hot chocolate and a glass of milk.

chutney (from the Hindu word chatni), a condiment or pickle of Indian origin which can be made from a number of differing diced fruits or vegetables mixed together and cooked with sugar, ginger, turmeric, cinnamon, and vinegar until a soft thick mixture is formed. It can be made hot with chillies, if desired. Apples, tomatoes, bananas, onions, celery, mangoes, pimentos, raisins, and many other plants such as vegetable marrow can be used. It is also made commercially, and except for mango chutney, which is eaten with curry, it is usually served as a relish with cold meats.

ciastka, Polish for cakes or pastries.

ciastka francuskie z poziomkami lub jabłkami, Polish pastries after the French style (made from puff pastry), with strawberry or apple filling. The fruit is soaked in rum, sprinkled with sugar, and left to macerate while the dough is being made.

ciasto, Polish for dough and pastry.

ciasto drożdżowe do pierogów, a savoury dish made from yeast dough (*pirozhki*) filled with chopped meat, chopped hard-boiled eggs and cooked chopped cabbage, with seasonings and chopped herbs.

ciasto kruche, Polish pastry made without yeast, the equivalent of short crust, flaky or puff pastry.

ciasto maślane, pastry made with butter and without yeast.

ciasto pólfrancuskie, a kind of French pastry dough made with yeast. See also BRIOCHE.

cibol, see WELSH ONION.

ciboulette, French for chives; also called *civette* and *appétit*, used extensively for garnishes and also in omelettes.

cicala di maro, Italian for squill-fish, used in fish soups. See also BRODETTO; CANNOCCHIE.

cicoria, Italian for chicory. In Piedmont, chopped white truffles with garlic and chopped green olives are added to a salad of chicory.

cider, the fermented juice of fruit, usually apples, used as a beverage, for cooking, or for making other products, as vinegar.

cider sauce, an American sauce made of 1 tablespoon butter, 1 heaping tablespoon flour, ½ cup ham stock, ½ cup cider, salt, and pepper. The butter is melted, the flour is added and then gradually, the ham stock, stirring constantly. It is simmered for a few minutes and the cider and seasonings are added. Served with hot ham.

cielęcina, Polish for veal.

cielęcina nerkowa, loin of veal, a popular joint in Poland, usually either roasted (*pieczona*) or stuffed (*nadziewana*).

cielęcina w majonezie, 3 lb. veal is simmered in water with sliced root vegetables, then drained, cooled, and sliced; the liquid is reduced to about ½ pint (1 cup), then poured over the meat and left to chill and gel. Before serving, the jellied meat is spread with mayonnaise, *macédoine* of vegetables, sliced hard-boiled egg, capers, and sliced pickled cucumber.

cielęcina zakrawana z cytryna, roast veal, garnished with breadcrumbs fried in butter mixed with 2 tablespoons chopped parsley and juice of 1 lemon.

cielęcina ze smietana, veal larded with salt pork and roasted with butter. During the last 30 minutes of cooking, the meat is basted with ½ pint (1 cup) sour cream mixed with juice of ½ lemon; this mixes with the pan juices, which are served with the cooked joint as a sauce.

sznycle cięlece naturalne, veal escalopes rolled in flour and cooked in butter. Anchovies are sometimes used as a garnish.

cietrzew, Polish for blackcock, which is plentiful in Poland and eaten extensively. Grouse (Scotch grouse, *Lagopus scoticus*) is not known outside Britain and Ireland, but related species are found in Poland and are termed "grouse" (głuszec) in Polish. They are prepared in the same way as cietrzew. In Poland almost all game is marinated for 2 days in a marinade made from 1 cup red or white wine boiled with 1 cup wine vinegar, 2 cups water, 1 onion, bay leaf, peppercorns, a bouquet garni, and 6 juniper berries. This is poured over the game when cold. See also BLACKCOCK; DZICZYZNA.

cietrzew lub głuszec duszony w maderze, blackcock or grouse (black) marinated as above, rubbed with crushed juniper berries and salt, casseroled with strips of bacon over the breasts, and simmered for 10 minutes. Then ¼ pint (½ cup) madeira wine is added, a sprinkle of flour, and optionally, 6 shallots and 6 mushrooms. It is covered and cooked in a moderate oven for 1 hour.

cietrzew lub głuszec pieczony, Polish for plain roast blackcock or grouse.

cietrzew lub głuszec ze smietana, roast blackcock or grouse, basted with 2 cups sour cream during the cooking.

cigala, Spanish for Dublin Bay prawn.

cigěr, Turkish for liver.

cigěr kebob, cubed liver, skewered and wrapped in caul and slowly grilled. Then 3 pounded garlic cloves, ½ cup wine vinegar, 2 cups stock, salt, and pepper, are all well stirred, heated, and served over the liver.

cilantro, Spanish for coriander, which is often used whole but slightly crushed, rubbed over the outside of pork or lamb before roasting.

ciliegia, Italian for cherry, used in puddings and as a sauce with venison. See CERVO, CON SALSA DI CILIEGIE.

cima, Italian for stuffed cold veal, a peasant dish and a speciality of Genoa. The breast of veal is filled with a stuffing of veal brains, sweetbreads, chopped leg of veal, eggs, artichoke heart, green peas, butter, Parmesan cheese, and marjoram. It is boiled and then sliced.

cincho, a hard cheese made in the provinces of central Spain from ewe's milk. It is also called *campos*, after the central plain of Tierra de Campos.

cinghiale, Italian for boar. See also BOAR; MARCASSIN.

cinghiale alla cacciatore, literally "hunter's wild boar." It is browned in butter, with onion, carrot, celery, parsley, and seasoning, then simmered in white wine and stock and larded with strips of ham.

cinghiale arrosto, roast wild boar, especially good in Piedmont and Sardinia. It is marinated in olive oil, lemon juice, onion, celery, rosemary, garlic, cloves, bay leaves, salt, and pepper for 24 hours. It is then dried, covered with paper, and roasted, as for pork. Served with boiled mashed chestnuts and red currant jelly.

cinghiale in agrodolce, wild boar with sweet-sour sauce. A saddle of boar is marinated as for venison (*cervo*). After 3 days it is removed, larded with fat ham, and roasted in oil and butter. The marinade is reduced to half by boiling, and sugar, red wine, vinegar, pine nuts, and candied orange peel (rind) are added. This sauce is served separately. See also AGRODOLCE.

cinnamon, the inner bark of *Cinnamomum zeylanicum*, a small evergreen tree belonging to the order·*Lauraceae*. It has been known from remote antiquity, being mentioned in the Bible and by Herodotus. It is now almost exclusively a product of Ceylon. The powder obtained from the bark of *Cassia lignae*, a tree grown largely in China, is somewhat similar, but not so delicate or aromatic.

cioccolata, Italian for chocolate, used not only as a sweet in Italy (see TARTUFI), but also as an ingredient in rich stews to give a sweet-sour (*agrodolce*) taste.

cioppino, a speciality of San Francisco, U.S., made from fresh shellfish and fish cooked over a charcoal brazier in a rich sauce consisting of onion, green pepper, garlic, leek, tinned tomatoes and their juice, tomato purée, bay leaf, seasonings, and white wine. The sauce is usually cooked for some hours before the fish is added—halibut or bass are the best. Any shellfish can also be used, oysters, lobsters, crabs, clams, etc., and they are only cooked for about 15 minutes. Cioppino is served in a large soup plate and garnished with fingers of toast spread with butter which has been worked with minced garlic. It was first made by the Genoese fishermen who live in San Francisco.

ciorbă, Rumanian for meat or fish soup. See also SUPA.

ciorbă de peşte, a substantial fish soup in which one or more varieties of fish can be used. Tomatoes, onions, a leek, a little celery, 3 garlic cloves, a carrot, and a little butter are placed together in a pan and steamed for a few minutes. Then 3 quarts boiling water, salt, and pepper are added. When the vegetables are almost tender, the fish is added (about 2 lb. in all), and when the fish is cooked, the soup is ready. In parts of the Balkans, this soup is sieved, and soured by using a souring agent such as the water in which a cabbage has been boiled, with 1 teaspoon dill or cumin, a carrot, and an onion; or sometimes citric acid is diluted and added.

ciorbă de schimbea, a traditional tripe soup. The tripe is cut into fine strips and cooked in a court bouillon with onions, cloves, pepper, and a little vinegar. It is drained and put into a casserole with shredded pimentos and the strained stock. When the vegetables are just soft, egg yolks and butter are stirred in, but the soup is not reboiled.

ciorbă ţărănească, a soup which can be made either with a small chicken or 2–3 lb. beef or veal. The meat or chicken is put into a pan in small pieces and covered with water; when it comes to the boil, it is skimmed and onions, a carrot, a little chopped celery, 3 tomatoes, a little lovage, and 1 teaspoon paprika are added. The vegetables and meat are boiled for about 2 hours, more water being added as required. When the soup is ready to serve, it is garnished with chopped parsley and thyme.

cipolla, Italian for onion.

cipolla ripiene, stuffed onions, a typical dish of southern Italy. Halves of boiled onions, without their centres, are stuffed with parsley, garlic, anchovies, ham, and black olives, all finely chopped and bound with breadcrumbs. They are then baked in the oven.

passato di cipolla, a thick, puréed onion soup made from 2 lb. onions peeled and cooked in water until very soft, then sieved or electrically blended, and beaten with 1 egg, 1 tablespoon butter, 1 cup grated Parmesan cheese, salt, and pepper. It is reheated and served with triangles of bread fried in butter.

cipollina, Italian for chive, or small shallot or onion.

cipolline in agrodolce, sweet-sour onions, made with 1 lb. small onions cooked in 2 tablespoons each olive oil, wine vinegar, and sugar, 3 cloves, bay leaf, and salt. The sauce turns to syrup after 10–15 minutes. The dish is eaten hot or cold.

cîrnat, Rumanian for sausage, of which there are many varieties. Hot pork sausages are eaten a lot around Christmas time, and with *iahnie*.

ciruela, Spanish for plum.

ciruelas rellenas, a Spanish speciality of stuffed soaked prunes. The stones are removed and the cavities are filled with finely chopped ham; the prunes are then dipped in beaten egg and breadcrumbs and fried in deep hot oil. They are served hot on toothpicks. Plums can also be prepared in this way.

cisco (*Leucichthys artedi*), one of the most prized whitefish found in Lake Superior and the other Great Lakes of the U.S. and Canada. It is also known as lake herring, and in French–Canadian as ciscoette or ciscovet. It can be cooked in any way as salmon.

ciseler, French culinary word which means to make light incisions on the back of fish in order to make the cooking time shorter. It is also applied to the fine slicing of leaf herbs to be incorporated into a chiffonade or a julienne.

ciste, a traditional dish from County Cork, Ireland, seldom seen nowadays. It is made from lamb or pork chops trimmed of fat, lamb or pork kidneys (or liver), sliced onions, carrot, herbs, and seasonings. The chops are placed standing up around the edge of a large saucepan, and all other ingredients are put in the middle with enough stock or water barely to cover the vegetables; the pan is covered and simmered gently for ½ hour. During this time, the ciste paste is made from ½ lb. (1¾ cups) flour, 4 oz. (1 cup) grated suet, a teaspoon of baking powder, salt, and a little milk to mix into a paste. If pork chops are used, a few sultanas are added. The paste is rolled to fit the saucepan exactly. It is then pressed down to meet the stew, and the bones of the chops pressed into it. It is covered with a tight fitting lid, care being taken to see that the dough does not come to within an inch of the top, to allow for rising. It is cooked over a gentle heat for 1–1½ hours. Ciste is served by loosening the crust around the edge with a knife, than cutting it into wedges. These are placed around a deep dish, and the stew is put in the middle. Each portion consists of a chop, kidney, and vegetables. If preferred, it can be cooked in a slow oven for the same length of time.

cîteaux, a French cow's milk cheese made in Burgundy. It is in season all the year round.

citrange, an American citrus fruit resulting from a cross between the sweet orange and the trifoliate orange (*Poncirus trifoliata*). It has a very strong orange flavour, but is more acid than the ordinary orange.

citroen, Dutch for lemon. *Citroen sap* is lemon juice.

citroenvla, a Dutch pudding made from 4 egg yolks and 4 egg whites, ½ cup castor sugar, ½ cup white wine, and juice and grated rind (peel) of 2 lemons. All but the egg whites are heated in a double boiler until thick, then the egg whites are added, beaten very stiffly. The pudding is served cold.

citron (*Citrus medica*), the citron tree and its fruit. In Corsica it is cultivated extensively and the fruit made into a liqueur known as *cédratine*. Generally speaking, however, it is the peel which is most useful to the cook; this is very thick and bumpy and is candied for use in confectionery. It is called cédrat. See also CITRUS; PÂTÉ DE CÉDRAT.

citron, Danish for lemon.

citronsuppe, Danish lemon soup. A syrup of juice from 3 large lemons, 3 heaped tablespoons sugar, and 3 pints (6 cups) water is thickened to a creamy consistency with 3 tablespoons corn flour (cornstarch) (creamed with cold water). The soup is stirred until boiling. It is served chilled and garnished with cherries.

citron, Swedish for lemon.

citronfromage, a Swedish lemon cream dessert made with 2 egg yolks and 6 oz. (⅔ cup) sugar well beaten, to which is added juice and grated rind (peel) of 1 lemon. Powdered gelatine (½ tablespoon) is first soaked for a few moments in 2 tablespoons cold water and later dissolved over hot water; it is then gradually added to the egg mixture, stirring constantly until thickened. The beaten egg whites are folded in, followed by ½ pint (1 cup) whipped cream. The whole is poured into a wet mould and chilled. Served unmoulded and decorated with whipped cream and cherries or grapes.

citronkräm, Swedish lemon cream, used as a filling for some Swedish layer cakes. See KRONANS KAKA. In a saucepan ½ lb. (1 cup) castor sugar, ¼ pint (½ cup) white wine, the same of water, 6 egg yolks, and the grated rind (peel) and juice of 1 large lemon are mixed together. The mixture is stirred constantly while it is cooking. When it has thickened, it is allowed to cool; during this time it is still stirred occasionally.

citronella (*Cymbopogon nardus*), a tropical perennial grass. It has a strong, lemony smell, and the leaves are used sparingly for seasoning and in salads. An oil is extracted from this plant which is disliked by flying insects such as wasps, flies, and mosquitoes, so that it is invaluable as a fly-repellent when rubbed on the skin.

citrouillat, a pumpkin pie made in the Berry district of France.

citrus, the genus of a family of fruit-bearing trees. The *Citrus aurantium* is a tree whose green leaves are called orange leaves and are used for making a *tisane*. The flowers, wrongly called orange blossoms, are used in confectionery. The *C. balontinum* is a kind of orange tree with leaves that have serrated edges. The fruit is not unlike a lemon and is used in the same way. *C. bigarde* is the Seville orange, used for marmalade and for cooking with game. The *C. medica* is a fruit-bearing citron tree cultivated in Provence (Grasse and Nice) and in northern Italy. It is known as *aigre de cèdre* in France.

city chicken, an American recipe for veal and pork cubes which are threaded onto skewers and dipped in flour, egg, and breadcrumbs, and fried. It is then braised for 1 hour in stock barely to cover.

ciuperci, Rumanian for mushrooms.

ciulama de ciuperci, mushrooms in a creamy sauce. Onion is chopped finely and fried in butter; 1 lb. washed, chopped mushrooms are added and are cooked for 5 minutes. Then a little chopped parsley and ½ teaspoon dill are added. Finally, 2 teaspoons flour are mixed with 1 cup sour cream and this is mixed in with the mushrooms. They are allowed to cook for a further 10 minutes, and are then served hot.

ciuperci cu mărar, mushrooms simmered with sliced fennel root, parsley, onion, and nutmeg. It is served with a sauce made from a roux of 1 tablespoon each of butter and flour and ½ pint (1 cup) milk to which chopped fennel leaves, 1 egg yolk, and ¼ pint (½ cup) sour cream are added.

civet, a French word which is particularly applied to a stew of furred game cooked with a little red wine and garnished with small onions, lardoons, and mushrooms. When cooked, the sauce is thickened with the blood of the animal—an essential feature of the dish. The word is thought to come from the French word *cive*, which is a green onion formerly used in the civet. Nowadays, feathered game is also used in a civet, and in the Languedoc there is a civet made with spiny lobster. Generally, however, hare is the more usual ingredient.

civet de lièvre, a method of casseroling hare. The hare is jointed and browned in pork or goose fat, then put into a casserole with shallots, garlic, and bacon or gammon (in the Landes district, jambon de bayonne is used). Red wine, stock, ripe skinned tomatoes, and dried *cèpes* are added. The casserole is then covered and cooked slowly in the oven for 2–3 hours. The sauce is thickened with the blood of the hare which is stirred into the hot stock, warmed, but on no account allowed to boil as this would cause curdling. See also HARE.

clabber cheese, see COTTAGE CHEESE.

clabbered milk, milk which has been soured naturally, so that it is thick and curdy. Natural souring is not possible in the case of pasteurized milk, as it becomes bad before it turns to curd. Nowadays, most U.S. milk is pasteurized. It is drunk a lot in Poland (kwasne) and Finland (*piimä*). The name comes from the Irish *bainne clabair,* "thick milk," and was originally rendered as "bonny clabber" in English. It has been drunk by the Irish since the earliest times.

clafouti(s), a speciality of the Limousin district of France. It is a thick pastry made with 1 cup flour, 2 eggs, and ½ cup sugar, on top of which are put black stoned cherries. It is cooked in a moderate oven for 45 minutes and then sprinkled with castor sugar. It is eaten hot or cold.

claire, the name of the sea enclosures in the Marennes region of France where the oysters are left to go green, thus acquiring a more delicate flavour. See also OYSTER.

clam, the name for a variety of bivalve shellfish which live in wet sand and can be gathered at low tide. They are found on the coasts on both sides of the North Atlantic. Along the French beaches of Croisic and the Bay of Bourgneuf, they are cultivated in special beds. In North America, two varieties are very popular: *Venus mercenaria,* the round or hard clam; and *mya arenaria,* the long or soft clam. They are eaten both raw and cooked, and are prepared as mussels. A delicious American soup called clam chowder is made from them. When eaten raw they are inclined to be tough, compared with oysters. The hard-shelled clams are called "littlenecks" and "cherrystones" in the U.S. In France they are called *palourdes,* but in Provence, *clovisses* or *praires.* Many of the French *palourdes* are imported from Ireland, where they are extensively fished for in County Kerry. See also AMÊIJOAS; CARPETSHELL.

clambake, an American method of cooking fresh clams, lobsters, and other shellfish in the open air. A large pit is dug on the beach, and a fire is started at the bottom of it. When a sufficiently large bed of ashes has formed, the red part of the fire is doused by putting damp seaweed on top. The clams and other fish are placed on top, covered with more seaweed, and then the sand is replaced. Meanwhile the guests swim or lie on the beach for about 1½–2 hours while the food is cooking. Then the sand is shovelled away and in the nest of seaweed is the deliciously fresh, newly baked fish. If available, large stones are placed around the pit to throw out more heat, but providing there is enough hot ash, these are not essential. Fresh corn and potatoes are sometimes added to this magnificent al fresco meal. See also BARBECUE.

clam broth, a traditional soup from the U.S. Scrubbed clams are placed in a saucepan with sufficient water to cover the shells; chopped onions, celery, parsley, and salt are sometimes added, and the mixture is boiled until the clams are cooked. The broth is strained and eaten alone or used as a dip, with butter, for the steamed or boiled clams.

clam chowder, chopped onions and diced green peppers are fried with salt pork. When cooked, fresh chopped clams and clam stock are added, with a little flour, salt, pepper, herbs, and diced cooked potatoes. Before the soup is cooked, sliced cooked tomatoes are added and all is simmered gently for a few minutes. This is Manhattan-style chowder; the famous New England clam chowder has milk and no tomatoes. See also CHOWDER.

Clamart, à la, a French garnish for slices of meat and tournedos, made of tartelettes of artichoke bottoms filled with *pois à la française* or a purée of green peas, and *pommes rissolées* or new potatoes cooked in butter. The pan juices are diluted

with white wine and veal gravy and reduced. Clamart is a region outside Paris where excellent peas are grown. See also POULET, SAUTÉ CLAMART.

omelette Clamart, an omelette stuffed with hot *petits pois.*

clapshot, a traditional vegetable dish from the Orkney Islands, consisting of equal quantities of cooked boiled potatoes and boiled turnips mashed together very thoroughly. Chopped chives, bacon fat, salt, and pepper are added. It goes very well with *haggis.*

clara de huevo, Spanish for egg white.

clarify, a word meaning to clear various food substances by heating and straining or by removing impurities. Butter is clarified by being gently heated and strained so that the whitish deposit is left behind. Bouillon or broth can be made clear by boiling it up with an egg white. It is all beaten with a whip (egg beater) and then strained. Fruit juices can be clarified by straining.

clary, see SAGE.

clavaria, a spindle-shaped fungi which grows capless like a bush fan or coral and has branches of white, pink, and/or purple. It is tough to eat, but is sautéed in oil or butter in France, where it is called *clavaire.*

claviari, see FUNGHI.

clayere, French word for an enclosure of "bed," where oysters are fattened. See also *claire.*

clayon, French word for the small wire trays used by pastry cooks. It can also mean a small straw mat on which cheeses and other foods are put.

clementine (*Citrus nobilis;* var. *deliciosa*), a citrus fruit which is a cross between the wild North African orange and the tangerine. It is very juicy and almost seedless, it is in season during what we know as the winter months.

clermont, I. A French garnish for tournedos and noisettes consisting of fragments of chestnut mixed with a sauce *soubise* poached in a dariole mould, with rings of fried onion added. II. A garnish of stuffed braised cabbage balls cooked with squares of salt pork, boiled potatoes, and demi-glace.

Clifton puffs, a small regional cake from Clifton, near Bristol, England. It is similar to a Banbury cake except that the pastry has a little ground rice and ground almonds (about 1 tablespoon each to ½ lb. flour) added, and also the juice of 1 lemon. The pastry is cut into pieces about 4 inches square, the filling is put in the middle, and then the corners are folded into the centre. They are then baked.

clisse, the French word for a little tray of wicker or rushes used to drain cheeses. The term also applies to the wickerwork around a bottle.

clod, the hanging folds of the neck of an ox. It is used for soups or stews and is called a clod of beef.

clonevan, an Irish cheese made in County Wexford. It is prepared from full cream milk, is round and flat in shape, and tastes creamy but is fairly firm and very pleasant to eat. It is packed like a camembert in a round straw box. It only slightly resembles the camembert however, being a much milder cheese.

cloth of gold plum, see MYROBALAN.

clotted cream, cream which, according to an old Cornish recipe, is best made over a wood fire. New milk is strained immediately into shallow pans and allowed to stand for 24 hours in winter and 12 in summer. The pan is placed in a steamer of water and slowly heated until the cream begins to show a raised ring around the edge. It is then removed to a cool dairy for 12 or 24 hours, depending on the season. The cream is taken off in layers for use. See also CORNISH BURNT CREAM.

cloudberry (*Rubus chamaemorus*), a herbaceous plant which often adopts a trailing character. A member of the huge *Rosaceae* family, it has some 400 varieties. It has an orange-yellow fruit resembling a raspberry. It grows in mountainous and in boggy regions in Great Britain and more northerly countries. In North America it grows in peat bogs, but it is most widely distributed in Scandinavia and Finland where it is gathered in large quantities and used for many dishes such as *mehukeitto* or *puolukkaliemi*. The name derives from the Old English *clud*, a rock or hill, and it was first found in England by the botanist Thomas Penny (*c.* 1530–1588) in the mountain country on the borders of Lancashire and the West Riding of Yorkshire. In Scotland, it is known as avron. In Canada, the berries are called baked-apple berries, and in Quebec, yellow berries.

clouter, a French culinary term meaning to stud a piece of meat, poultry, game, or fish with small pieces of another substance, such as truffle, ham, tongue, anchovy, or gherkin. It is in fact a form of garnishing, and in the U.S., cloves, apricots, peaches, and pineapple are so used to garnish a ham. The noun is *cloutage*.

clove, I. The dried, unexpanded flower bud of a tropical tree (*Eugenia caryophyllata*), a species of myrtle. Coming originally from the Moluccas, it was introduced by the Dutch into Amboyna. The Portuguese, by their discovery of the Cape of Good Hope route to the Far East, had for many years almost a monopoly of the trade in this spice, and a bitter campaign was waged between them and the Dutch, during the course of which unsuccessful efforts were made to extirpate the growth of the tree on the Moluccas. In fact the end result of the struggle was the spread of the clove to many other tropical locations so that today it is grown in Java, Sumatra, Zanzibar, Brazil, Guyana, and most of the West Indian Islands. When freshly dried, cloves contain as much as 18% of a volatile oil with a very powerful and characteristic sweet smell, the chief constituent is eugenic acid. On crushing between the thumbnails, freshly dried cloves readily exude this oil, but old and stale ones fail to show it and are very much less effective as a flavouring agent. Cloves were an essential ingredient in a pomander. They are used particularly with cooked apple and baked ham, as well as in puddings, stews, etc. II. A clove of garlic is a culinary term used to denote one of the half-moon-like sections of a garlic bulb.

clove

clovisse, the Provençal name for *Venus treillissée,* a thick shelled clam. The genus *Venus* has more than 150 species. The Marseilles clovisse has a beautiful mother-of-pearl shell and an exquisite flavour. The clovisse sold in Paris is inferior; it has a soft shell with a wavy edge and is not nearly as good to eat. It is eaten raw, sometimes with a wedge of lemon as the only addition. See also CLAM.

club sandwich, an American double-decker sandwich made usually with fresh toast spread with mayonnaise, lettuce and tomato, chicken or turkey, and a thin slice of cooked bacon. This is covered with a second piece of toast and the filling is repeated and covered with toast again. It is often served with the bacon and tomato in one half and the chicken in the other. Ham, cheese, and other fillings are also used frequently. It may be prepared by toasting the top and bottom slices of bread on one side only. This makes the sandwich less crunchy, and easier to eat.

club steak, the American equivalent of an *entrecôte*.

cluny, omelette, a French omelette. Hot game purée is folded into the omelette. The dish on which it is presented is bordered with fresh tomato sauce.

clupeidae, an important fish family including both saltwater and freshwater fish. Herring, sardine, anchovy, and shad are the best known.

cnicaut, a local French name for an edible wild cardoon that has a cabbagy taste.

coalfish (*Pollachius virens*), a sea fish which is related to the cod and pollack and is extensively fished in the North Sea. It is not as popular as cod, but is much cheaper in price, and it has a delicate flavour when eaten very fresh. It is also called coley. In Scotland it is known as *saithe* and cuddy. In Norway it forms the basis for a speciality called *seibiff*. See also PALE.

coat, to, in culinary terms, to cover food entirely in a batter, or breadcrumbs, before frying it; or a sauce as chaud-froid.

cobnut (*Corylus avellana*), the English name for a type of hazelnut, which differs from the filbert in being rounder, and scarcely covered by a leafy husk. The best known is the thin-shelled, sweet-tasting cosford, which originated in Suffolk in about 1816. The most widely grown today is the Kent cob also known as Lambert's filbert, after its originator Mr. Lambert, who produced it in Goudhurst, Kent, in 1830. This latter name is truer and more descriptive; for it is in fact a filbert, having an oblong nut quite covered by the tapering husk. It has an excellent flavour and is extensively cultivated in Kent. See also FILBERT.

cochifrito, a Spanish lamb and paprika stew, with onions, garlic, lemon juice, and herbs. Hardly any liquid is used, and the meat and vegetables are first fried in oil. This is a popular dish in Navarre, one of the sheep-rearing districts of Spain where the cooking is allied to that of France. Another speciality of the region is *torta de conejo*. See also CORDERO.

cochineal, dried bodies of the cochineal insect which is reared on cactus. It is used for red colouring in cooking, particularly for icing. Carmine is produced in the same way but is deeper in colour.

cochinillo asado del mesón del segoviano, Spanish for roast sucking pig as served in Madrid. The pig, which should be 21 days old, must be well washed and scraped. It is split from mouth to tail and cleaned before being oven-cooked in a large pan, lying belly uppermost. Butter, salt, and bay leaves are placed upon it, and after a few minutes in a hot oven, crushed garlic and marjoram are sprinkled over it. The pig is turned after 45 minutes and the flesh is pricked. Cooking is continued for a further 45 minutes, when the skin will be brown and crisp. See also CERDO.

cochlearia (*Cochlearia officinalis*), a wild plant with a four-petalled flower which grows on the coasts of England, Ireland, and Brittany. It is a kind of wild horseradish, and the mustardy leaves were eaten as salad in France and Ireland. In the late 18th and early 19th centuries it was used as a sandwich filling in England with watercress and sliced oranges, no doubt because of the benefit obtained from the high vitamin C content. It is this last attribute which gives it its unattractive common name of scurvy-grass, although it is also sometimes called spoonwort, on account of the shape of the leaves and from the Latin *coclear,* a spoon.

cochon, French for pig. See PORC.

cochon de lait, sucking pig. Roast sucking pig stuffed with breadcrumbs, garlic, lemon and orange peel, with the juices, nutmeg, and 2 eggs is a speciality of Lorraine in France.

cocido, literally meaning cooked or boiled, a traditional Spanish soup–stew of meats, vegetables, and chick-peas, formerly called *olla podrida,* after the pot, or olla, in which it was cooked. It is also called *puchero* in some parts of the country. The liquid is strained off and served as soup, the cooked meat and vegetables being eaten as a second course. These soup–stews are most common in the north of Spain, but each province has its own method of making cocido. In Seville it is made with rice, sweet potatoes, blood pudding with garlic, assorted pork products, and chick-peas; in the Granada cocido no garlic is used, and it contains white potatoes with rabbit or chicken; in Barcelona, *butifarra* is used; and in Madrid, rice or vermicelli is included. The two essentials are chick-peas and a pork product, and when these two ingredients are present, the dish is always called *cocido* or *puchero.* Other soup–stews are called *calderada, caldereta* (from *caldera*— cauldron), *estofado, guisado,* and *pote* (pot). The Spaniards say their cooking is like their climate—in the north they stew, in the central region they roast, and in the south they fry. See also GARBANZOS.

cocido andaluz, an Andalusian soup–stew made from ½ lb. soaked chick-peas, 1 lb. beef, ½ lb. fat pork, onion, french beans, tomato, garlic, pumpkin, potatoes, saffron, paprika, *morcilla blanca, chorizo* salt, and pepper, with water to cover. It is cooked for 3–4 hours, a glass (¼ pint) red wine being added 5 minutes before serving. The meats and vegetables are lifted out and served with a sauce made from 3 pounded garlic cloves mixed with ½ teaspoon paprika and the mashed pumpkin and tomato, moistened with a little red wine and seasoned to taste.

cocido madrileño, as above, with leek, carrot, green cabbage, potatoes, chick-peas, vermicelli or rice, beef, boiling fowl, *chorizo, morcilla blanca,* pig's trotter (foot), bacon, and ham. The leek, carrot, and cabbage are cooked with the *chorizo* and *morcilla* in water to cover; the liquid is then strained off and the vermicelli added to it (this forms the soup). The other meats are cooked with the chick-peas for 3–4 hours, and sometimes, half-way through cooking time, small meat balls are added, made from 2 oz. each minced beef and breadcrumbs mixed with 1 egg and seasoned with a pinch of cinnamon, salt, and pepper; all the meats are served with the chick-peas (this forms the stew). The drained vegetables are then heated with chopped garlic in olive oil in a frying-pan, and are served with the *chorizo* and *morcilla,* and potatoes, sometimes mixed with a thick purée of tomatoes.

cock, a word which, when used alone, means simply "male bird," of any genus or species whatever. However, it is used particularly to denote the male fowl. When used in combination, as for example in the words blackcock and woodcock, it signifies a particular known species, and does not refer specifically to either cock or hen. See also COCK'S KIDNEYS; COCK'S COMB.

cock-a-leeky, a traditional Scottish soup made with an old cock or hen fowl. This is put whole into a big pot, surrounded with sliced leeks, veal or bacon bones, parsley, thyme, a bay leaf, and seasonings, then covered with water and simmered for 4–5 hours. It is strained and boned; chopped and cooked prunes and the white part of 2 leeks are added as a garnish. Sometimes strips of chicken are added. Talleyrand, the French statesman, when he fled to England during the French Revolution, acquired a liking for cock-a-leeky but thought that the prunes, though stewed with the soup, should be removed before serving. It is also known as cockie leekie.

cockle (*Cardium edule*), a small European marine bivalve mollusc found mainly in estuaries. Cockles are generally cooked by boiling, and are eaten cold with a little vinegar in England and Ireland. However, they make excellent soup, and can in fact be prepared like mussels or clams. They used to be immensely popular in the 19th century in Ireland, whence the song about Mollie Malone, which tells of "Cockles and Mussels alive, alive O!"

cockle

cock's comb, the red, fleshy crest found on the head of poultry. In France it is used for garnishes or for filling savoury tarts. See also CRÊTE DE COQ.

cock's kidneys, the testicles of a male fowl. See ROGNONS DE COQ.

coco, Portuguese for coconut, which is used a great deal in Portuguese cooking.

coco bean (*Phaseolus vulgaris*), a variety of french bean which is becoming increasingly popular because of the flavour of the beans and the decorative appearance of the growing plant, with its purple flowers and climbing habit. The pods are stringless, and the little purple beans change to green in the cooking. When young, coco beans are cooked as french beans, but if they have been allowed to mature fully, they are shelled and cooked in the same way as haricot beans. They are often referred to as blue coco.

cocoa (*Theobroma cacao*), a pulverised form of the seeds of the cacao tree (from which chocolate is also made), which is native to tropical America, but is now cultivated in many other tropical countries. The word cocoa is an English corruption of cacao (Mexican cacauatl), and used solely for manufactured cocoa powder. The seeds are dried, partly fermented, and the husk, germ, and most of the oil or fat removed. This fat is known as cocoa, or correctly, cacao butter, and is used in a pure form in confectionery. The powdered cocoa is used for a beverage, with the addition of milk, water, and sugar, and as a flavouring for biscuits (cookies), cakes, and puddings. According to legend, Columbus was the first European to use cocoa, but it was not until someone thought of adding sugar to it that it became a popular drink. Samuel Pepys (1633–1703) records his first taste of "jucalette" and pronounced it "very good." See also CHOCOLATE.

coconut (*Cocos nucifera*), the fruit of the coconut palm. It consists of an outer fibrous husk enclosing a large nut which contains a white, edible, jelly-like substance (endosperm). When the nut is fresh it contains an opaque liquid called coconut milk. This refreshing fluid can be extracted by puncturing three small holes at the top of the nut, and is used to flavour curries, or, heated with eggs and sugar, to make a custard-like sweet. The coconut is a most valuable product of the tropics,

cocoa branch and vanilla pods

and is used extensively in cake making and confectionery; a dried, grated form called desiccated coconut is sold commercially for this use. It also yields a valuable oil which has been used since ancient times for food; when refined, this is often used in the manufacture of margarines and vegetarian foods, as a substitute for cacao (cocoa) butter in chocolates, and as a cooking or salad oil. The sap of the tree can be fermented and made into palm wine, a strong drink not unlike arrack.

coconut

cocotte, the French name for a round or oval flameproof dish in which meat, poultry, game, and eggs are cooked with butter or sauce, herbs, vegetables or mushrooms. Foods cooked in these dishes are described as en cocotte and are usually served in the dish. See also COQ SOLIDEX; OEUFS EN COCOTTE; POMME COCOTTE.

cocozelle, an Italian vegetable marrow (zucchini) of the bush variety which has oblong fruits reaching about 2 feet in length. The colour is dark green with yellow and darker green stripes. It has an excellent flavour, and is now grown in many parts of Europe and Britain.

cod (*Gadus callarias*), an important soft-finned saltwater fish found in the Atlantic Ocean from Newfoundland to Norway; in Great Britain and Ireland in the North Sea; and in the Baltic. Its back is greyish-brown with yellow and brown spots, and a white belly. The mature fish can weigh up to 80 lb., but the small young codling, weighing 3–4 lb., is also very good to eat.

Fresh, the cod can be fried, grilled, boiled, stuffed, and baked, and served with a large variety of sauces. In many European countries it is also salted; in Spain and Portugal salted cod is used in the *bacalao* and bacalhau dishes, and in France (where its use was introduced by Basque fishermen in the 15th

cod

century) it is the main ingredient in *brandade de morue*. The liver contains a valuable oil full of vitamins. It is also filleted and smoked, in which case it resembles a coarser smoked haddock. See also BAKALIAROS; CABILLAUD; KABELJAU; KABELJAUW; KABELJO; MORUE; SALTFISKUR; STOKVIS; TORSK.

cod liver bannock, see BONNACH GRÙAN.

cod-burbot, a freshwater fish of the cod family, similar to the burbot. In the U.S. it is found in the Great Lakes and also in other lakes and rivers in the northern part of the country, where it is sometimes called freshwater cusk. See also CUSK.

codorniz, Spanish for quail.

codornices asadas, roast quails. The quails are first browned in lard and then pot-roasted in a closed vessel for 1 hour. For each pair of quails, 1 glass stock, 1 glass white wine, parsley, marjoram, thyme, bay leaf, garlic, and seasoning are added. When cooked, the herbs and bay leaf are removed and the sauce is thickened.

coelho, Portuguese for rabbit.

coelho bravo à cacadora, wild rabbit stewed with onion, garlic, pimentos, and white wine.

coeur, French for heart.

coeur à la crème, see FROMAGE BLANC.

coeur de palmier, French for palm hearts, which are usually cooked like asparagus when they are fresh, but can also be stewed in butter or gravy and served with grated cheese or cream. They are usually canned, however, and can then be served in sauce vinaigrette. See also CABBAGE PALM.

coffee (*Caffea arabica, C. liberica, C. robusta*), a shrub which bears an abundance of small round or oval-shaped berries, the seeds of which, when separated from the pulp, are roasted, ground, and used to make the beverage coffee, which was hardly known in Europe before the 17th century. The shrub is a native of Arabia, but is now cultivated in Brazil, the Dutch East Indies, the West Indies, Central America, Kenya, and elsewhere. The best coffee comes from the Blue Mountain (Jamaica), Bogotá (Colombia), and the Yemen. Apart from the place of origin of the beans, good coffee depends on degree of roasting, freshness of grinding, quality of water, and method of making. European coffee is usually highly roasted and coarsely ground, and sometimes has chicory added to it which imparts the well-known bitter taste. Turkish coffee is made from pulverised beans, boiled up with sugar and water. It is very thick and syrupy.

Coffee is also widely used for flavouring. It contains the alkaloid caffeine, which is a stimulant. See also MOCHA.

cogumelos, Portuguese for mushrooms.

cogumelos com arroz, a dish of mushrooms sautéed in olive oil and simmered with rice and stock.

coing, French for quince. A thick quince paste or pâté is made in country districts of France, and a sweetmeat (confection) called *cotignac* is sold commercially in Orléans, where it has been famous for many hundreds of years. See also COTIGNAC; MEMBRILLO.

col, Spanish for cabbage.

sopa de coles, a good cabbage soup, made with onions, garlic, potatoes and chorizo, served over bread, and sprinkled with grated cheese. It is a speciality of the Austurias.

colache, a Mexican vegetable dish, made with onion, garlic, zucchini, tomato, sweet corn, and green beans, all fried lightly in bacon fat with a little sugar, salt, and a dash of vinegar.

colander, a utensil made from metal or plastic, which is usually round, with handles and with small holes punched in the bottom and sides. The colander is used for straining cooked vegetables or any foods which require the liquid separate from the solids. The word is a corruption of the Latin *colatorium* from the verb *colare,* to strain. It is sometimes spelt "cullender."

colbert, à la, I. A classical French sauce made from ½ cup butter, in small pieces, stirred gradually into 2 cups light glace de volaille or some stock and meat glaze. When the boiling point is reached, it is strained and lemon juice and chopped parsley are added. II. A garnish for meat and offal (variety meat) of small chicken croquettes with fried eggs, truffle slices, and sauce colbert. III. The name given particularly to fish which are dipped in egg and breadcrumbs before being fried. IV. Beef or chicken consommé garnished with brunoise of spring vegetables, poached egg, and chopped chervil. See also CONSOMMÉ.

colby, an American cheese made from either fresh or pasteurised cow's milk. It is similar in taste to Cheddar, but has a softer and more open paste. It also contains more moisture, and for that reason does not keep as well as Cheddar cheese.

colcannon, I. A traditional Irish dish served particularly on Halloween. It should be made with equal quantities of cooked chopped kale and cooked mashed potato but, more generally, cabbage is used instead of kale. They are both beaten together with a little hot milk in which either a chopped leek or green onion tops have been boiled; seasoning is added to taste. When it has become a light, fluffy, pale green mixture, it is put into a deep dish, a well is made in the middle, and hot melted butter is poured into it. This is spooned out with the drier potato mixture. The dish can also be fried in bacon fat on both sides until crisp and brown. When served on Halloween a ring is often put in the colcannon, and it is said that whoever gets this will be married within the year. II. Colcannon is also a Scottish Highland dish made from boiled cabbage, carrots, potatoes, and turnips, all mashed together and then put into a saucepan with a large knob of butter, salt, black pepper, and a spoonful of good meat gravy. It is served very hot. See also KAILKENNY.

cold pack cheese, an American commercial processed cheese spread made by mincing different kinds of cheese together, and mixing this, without heating, with another dairy product such as butter, cream, or milk, until a thick paste is formed. To this pounded and blended mixture is added one or more of colouring matter, spices, a sweetening agent, salt, an acidifying agent, and a little cold water. The resulting product is not in the least like a cheese but is very popular throughout the U.S., as a spread or sandwich filling. It is chilled before using.

cole slaw, an American dish of raw, shredded white cabbage, the name "cole" being the general word for all members of the *Brassica oleracea* or true cabbage family. It is made with 3 egg yolks, 1 tablespoon butter, 1 teaspoon prepared mustard, 1 teaspoon fine sugar, ½ cup white wine vinegar, salt, and juice of ½ lemon. The well-beaten yolks are cooked in a double boiler with the vinegar, sugar, butter, salt, and mustard, beating continuously. When they amalgamate, the lemon is added. When thick the mixture is removed from the heat and cooled. Then ½ cup whipped cream is added. The mixture is poured over shredded cabbage and sometimes a small amount of shredded carrot. Sometimes mayonnaise or boiled dressing is used, the former being preferable.

Another method is to soak in iced water for 1 hour the center part of a crisp white cabbage, finely shredded. Then it is drained and ½ cup oil, ¼ cup vinegar, and a pinch each of caraway seeds, paprika, and black pepper are added. Salt is added last so that the crystals do not dissolve.

For hot cole slaw, a well-washed white cabbage is shredded very finely and drained thoroughly. It is put into a pan, and ½ pint (1 cup) boiling water is poured over it with a good sprinkling of salt. It is boiled until nearly tender, when ½ cup milk and a nut of butter are added, and the cabbage further cooked until these are absorbed. A béarnaise or other similar sauce is served with it.

coley, see COALFISH.

colin, colin-loui, the American and Canadian names for the bobwhite. It is a member of the quail family and is known in French as caille d'Amérique.

collar, the word used to describe a neck cut of pork, usually after curing—when it is bacon. It is sold as a joint and also as rashers. It is quite good for boiling, but not so full of flavour for rashers as either streaky bacon or back rashers.

collard (*Brassica oleracea;* var. *acephala*), the collective name given to various cabbages of the kale type, of which the green leaves do not form a compact "head." They are cooked as cabbage and are very popular in the deep south of the U.S. where they are called "collard greens."

collard or *collared pork,* a traditional Irish dish, made from soaked salted pig's head split in two, with onion, turnip, carrot, nutmeg, grated lemon peel (rind), herbs, salt, and pepper all cooked in water until the tenderness of the meat can be tested by pulling it off the bone. The tongue is peeled and sliced and put between the two halves of the head like a sandwich. It is then wrapped in muslin and cooked for a further 2 hours. When cool, it is pressed between two boards with a weight on top. It is served cold in slices with lettuce. It is traditionally eaten on St. Stephen's Day, December 26. See also COLLARED BEEF.

collared or *collard beef,* an English and Irish method of cooking the thin end of the flank which has been first rubbed with salt and saltpetre—as for salting or for corned beef. It is washed and dried, then rubbed with finely minced parsley and allspice, rolled in a cloth, tied, and boiled very gently for about 5 hours, or until tender. It is taken from the liquid, but left in the cloth and pressed under a heavy weight until cold, when it is sometimes glazed with aspic. It is served cold, cut into slices. See also COLLARD PORK; FLANK.

coller, the action of adding dissolved gelatine to a food preparation to make it stiffer.

collier's foot, also called Lancashire foot, a popular northern England pasty which takes the name "foot" from its shape, which resembles the sole of a shoe. Miners in the north used to carry their food in an oval tin and this shape just fitted it. Bacon fat is used to make the pastry, which is rolled out and cut into a pair of "soles." One sole is covered with thin onion rings, thin cheese slices, and, finally, a slice of bacon. Each layer is seasoned and mustard is spread on the bacon. Sometimes a little broth, beer, or even a sliced, peeled apple is added to give moisture. The other sole is pressed on, with water at the edges to make it stick, and the "foot" is then baked in a moderate oven until gently browned and the inside cooked. Collier originally signified a charcoal-burner.

collioure, a French sauce made from 1 cup mayonnaise, to which is added a purée of 6 anchovy fillets, 1 tablespoon chopped parsley, and 1 small grated garlic clove. It is excellent served with cold, poached white fish such as cod.

collop, a very old English and Scottish word meaning a thick or thin slice of meat or offal (variety meat), such as liver or kidney. In Scotland, the collops, or slices, are sometimes minced before cooking and then are known as "mince collops."

colmenillas, Spanish for morels.

colombine, I. A French croquette which has an outer layer of cooked semolina mixed with grated Parmesan cheese. It is served hot as an hors d'oeuvre. II. A chicken consommé garnished with diced carrots and turnips, julienne of pigeon breast, and poached pigeon's eggs. See also CONSOMMÉ.

colonne, a French cooking utensil, used to core fruit such as apples, and to cut root vegetables into the shape of a column.

coloquintes, see GOURDS.

comber, Polish for rack of meat containing a kidney. This cut is taken partly from the loin and partly from the rib of the animal.

comber à la duchesse, a roasted loin or rack of veal larded with pork strips and basted with sour cream. Traditionally this roast is garnished with crayfish and truffles.

comber jeleni ze smietana, a recipe for roasting a loin or saddle of venison. The marinade is made from vinegar and water to which many different root vegetables and herbs are added. It is also used to marinate hare. The Poles often marinate meat and game for several days; it is probably sold freshly killed and is therefore tough. The joint is larded with strips of salt pork and cooked in a moderate to hot oven for 20 minutes to the lb., basting with butter meanwhile. The pan juices are thickened with 1 tablespoon flour and ½ pint (1 cup) sour cream is added and reduced. See also DZICZYZNY.

comber sarni naturalny, a method in which, before roasting, venison is rubbed with olive oil and lemon juice, and then wrapped in a cheesecloth over which a glass of red wine is poured. The whole is refrigerated for 2 days before cooking.

comfrey (*Symphytum officinale*), a member of the *Borinacea* family known in medieval times as "knit-bone" because of its medicinal properties. It has sweetly scented leaves, but its use as a pot herb has been almost forgotten.

commande, sur, a French phrase which, when it appears on a menu, indicates that the food will be cooked to order, therefore it will take time to prepare. It literally means "on order."

commissie, see EDAM.

commodore, I. A French garnish for fish consisting of croquettes of crayfish tails or lobster, fish quenelles, mussels *à la villeroy,* and a crayfish *coulis* or sauce *normande* with crayfish butter. II. A fish consommé thickened with arrowroot and garnished with sliced clams and diced tomatoes. See also CONSOMMÉ.

compote, I. A word used in both French and English to denote a dish of fresh or dried fruit, whole or cut up, which has been cooked in a thick or thin syrup, sometimes with cinnamon, clove, vanilla, and orange or lemon peel added. Dried fruits are soaked before being cooked in the syrup. The compote is usually served cold and can be sprinkled with brandy, kirsch, or other liqueur. II. The name can also mean a dish of game such as partridge or pigeon, which has simmered for a long time in gravy.

compotier, a deep French dish on a raised base used for compotes and other cold sweet dishes.

Comté, a hard, French cow's milk cheese from the Franche-Comté country, where it has been made for generations. It is similar to the Swiss Gruyère and is made in the same way. The "eyes" in this type of cheese are the result of cooling after the cooking process. From the 14th to the 19th century, this cheese was called *vacherin,* but it has come to be known nowadays as Gruyère français. It keeps well and travels well, and it is good for cooking.

concasser, a French term which means either the coarse

chopping of food with a knife, or the pounding up of food in a mortar.

conch, a large edible mollusc found in the warm waters of the Caribbean, off the coast of Florida, U.S., and in the Pacific.

conch chowder, a speciality of Key West, Florida, made from conches boiled for 10 minutes and then taken from their shells. The meat is beaten until it falls apart and then is covered with fresh lime juice and left for 2 hours. Diced green pepper, onion, and garlic are sautéed in oil until soft; tomato purée and water are added and the seasoning adjusted. Peeled, sliced potatoes are put in, and when these are half cooked, the conch meat is added and cooked until the potatoes are done. See also CHOWDER.

conchiglia, Italian for shell, but particularly it can refer to small shellfish such as clams or cockles. See also ARSELLE; COZZE; VONGOLE.

conchiglia dei pellegrini is the term for scallop, and it is also called *capa santa.*

concombre, French for cucumber. In France, as well as being eaten in salad, cucumbers are poached in water with butter, drained, and served with cream sauce with grated Parmesan cheese or sauce mornay; or they are braised in stock and/or water and served with the braising liquid. See also CUCUMBER.

concombre farci, stuffed cucumber. It is peeled and blanched and with its seeds removed is stuffed with a mixture of various minced meats or poultry and chopped herbs and seasonings, bound with an egg or a little thick béchamel. It is then baked with a little stock for about 30–40 minutes in a moderate oven.

condé, I. A French rectangular cake, made from flaky pastry covered with almond icing, powdered with icing sugar, and baked on a tray in a moderate oven. II. A French method of preparing apricots, pears, peaches, or pineapples. The fruit is peeled, cored, and lightly poached in syrup, then arranged on hot cooked rice flavoured with vanilla, coated with hot apricot sauce, and garnished with chopped angelica or cherries. III. A purée of red haricot beans flavoured with red wine and garnished with fried croûtons. It is eaten as a thick soup. IV. A French garnish for meat made from puréed red haricot beans cooked with bacon cut into triangles and mixed with a red wine sauce whipped with butter.

condiments, the name applied to a number of seasonings added to prepared food.

conejo, Spanish for rabbit.

pastel de conejo, a dish from Navarre. A rabbit is stewed and the bones are removed. The meat is sprinkled with thyme and rosemary and placed on a sheet of pastry made with 1 lb. baked potatoes to 5 oz. flour, a little oil, salt, and 1 egg. It is covered with a second sheet of the potato pastry, and the edges are sealed. If large, the pastry is baked in the oven; if small, it is fried in hot oil.

torta de conejo, a similar dish from Alicante which consists of rabbit stewed with onions, tomatoes, red peppers, seasoning, and water, and all put into a pastry case which has been baked blind. See also COCHIFRITO.

confectionery, the branch of cookery which is concerned with the making of sweetmeats (candies).

conference pear, see PEAR.

confettura, Italian for jam.

confettura di fichi, fig jam made of green figs, sugar, and grated rind (peel) and juice of 1 lemon, all cooked for 1½ hours.

confit, I. French for fruits or vegetables preserved in sugar, vinegar, or brandy. II. Meat of goose, pork, duck, turkey, or chicken cooked in its own fat and preserved by immersing and covering it in that fat so that air is excluded.

confit de porc, a Gascon dish of preserved pork which is marinated with salt and spices and cooked in melted pork fat. When cooked, it is put into a stone pot and covered with the fat.

confit d'oie, French for preserved goose. See OIE, CONFIT D'.

conger eel (*Conger conger* and *Muraena conger*), a large saltwater fish, sometimes reaching 8 feet in length, and scaleless. It is a sea eel, and coarse in flavour compared with the common eel. The small ones are the best to eat. Conger eel (*congre* in France) is used a great deal for fish soups, mainly bouillabaisse, but it can also be baked, boiled, or fried. See also CONGRIO; SAFIO.

conger eel

congrio, Spanish for conger eel. In Spain, conger eel is often stuffed with milk-soaked bread, chopped garlic, parsley, and grated cheese all mixed and bound with an egg, then baked in butter. It is also used for soups. See also CONGER EEL.

congro, see SAFIO.

coniglio, Italian for rabbit. In Italy young rabbit is often stuffed, roasted, and basted with warm wine and water mixed.

coniglio agrodolce, a Sicilian recipe for rabbit cooked in a casserole with sugar, sultanas, onion, herbs, stock, pine nuts (pignoli), and a little wine vinegar.

coniglio alla cacciatore, rabbit cooked as *coniglio in padella* but with red wine and rosemary.

coniglio al marsala, jointed rabbit sautéed in butter with ham or bacon and celery stalk; when it is browned, crushed skinned tomatoes, garlic, marjoram, salt, and pepper are added, then a glass of Marsala wine and enough stock just to cover all the contents of the pan. They are simmered gently for an hour. Then a small unpeeled aubergine (eggplant) is added, diced, and a diced red or green pepper; cooking is continued, but terminated before the pepper or aubergine (eggplant) show any signs of becoming too soft.

coniglio in padella, the Roman way of cooking jointed rabbit. The rabbit is soaked for some hours in cold water; it is then dried and rubbed with salt, pepper, and herbs. The joints are browned in oil, with garlic, diced bacon, and chopped parsley; a glass (½ cup) of white wine is poured over, and when this has almost evaporated, peeled tomatoes and a pint of stock are added. It is covered and simmered for at least an hour.

consolante, a word used in French restaurant kitchens for an alcoholic drink given to the cooks while they are working.

consommé, a French word used to describe a rich, concentrated, and clear soup. There are 2 basic types of consomme: *consommé simple,* made from fish, game, meat, poultry, or turtle, with root vegetables, herbs, and seasonings, simmered slowly with water for 5–6 hours, and then strained; *consommé double,* obtained by the fortification of one good stock by another rich stock, or by the addition of more meat, fish, game, etc. It is afterward strained and is sometimes clarified,

with egg whites whipped to a froth, heated, and then strained. The shells can also be added. Allow 1 egg white for 2 pints stock. It is served hot or cold, the latter being known as *consommé froid.* If the cold consommé forms a jelly, it is called *consommé en gelée.*

In many classical French recipes, the clear consommé is thickened with rice, sago, tapioca, or pearl barley, but these are used as a garnish. Basically, consommé is a clear soup. There are many varieties of consommé and garnishes for them. Many are of 19th-century origin; some are of great importance, but others are culinary curiosities that are seldom encountered today. See also ADÈLE; ADELINA PATTI; ALBION; ALSACIENNE; AMBASSADEUR; AMBASSADRICE; AMÉRICAINE; AMIRAL; ANDALOUSE; ANJOU; ANVERSOISE; AREMBERG, D'; ARTAGNAN, D'; AULAGNIER, D'; AURORE, À L'; BASQUAISE, À L'; BEAUHARNAIS. À LA; BÉHAGUE; BERCHOUX; BERNY; BIS-MARCK-SUPPE; BIZET; BOÏELDIEU; BONAPARTE; BOURGEOISE, À LA; BRAGANCE, À LA; BRANCAS; BRETONNE; BRIAND; BRILLAT-SAVARIN; BRITANNIA; BRUNOISE; CAMERANI; CANCALAISE; CAPUCINE, À LA; CARDINAL CONSOMMÉ; CARÊME; CARMÉLITE, À LA; CARMEN; CASTELLANE CONSOMMÉ; CATALANE, À LA; CAUCHOISE; CAVOUR; CÉLESTINE; CHAROLLAISE; CHASSEUR, À LA; CHÂTELAINE; CHERBOURG; CHEVEUX D'ANGE; COLBERT, À LA; COLOMBINE; COMMODORE; CRÉCY; CROÛTE-AU-POT; CUSSY, À LA; CYRANO; CZAREVITCH; CZARINA; DALAYRAC; DANOISE; DAUDET; DAUMONT, À LA; DIANE; DORIA; DOUGLAS; DUBARRY; DUCHESSE; DUFFERIN; DUMESNIL; ÉCOSSAISE, À LA; FAVORITE; FERMIÈRE, À LA; FLAMANDE, À LA; FLEURY, À LA; GAULOISE, À LA; GEORGE SAND; GERMAINE; GERMINAL; GRIMALDI; HOLLANDAISE, À LA; IMPÉRIALE, À LA; JENNY LIND; JUDIC, À LA; JULIENNE; KLÉBER; LAFFITE; LAGUIPIÈRE; LILLEOISE, À LA; LONGCHAMP; LORETTE; LUCULLUS, À LA; MACDONALD; MADRILÈNE; MANCELLE; MARIE-LOUISE, À LA; MARQUISE, À LA; MÉDICIS; MERCÉDÈS, À LA; MESSINE; METTERNICH; MIRETTE; NESSELRODE; NIMROD; NIVERNAISE, À LA; OEUFS DE PLUVIER, CONSOMMÉ AUX; ORLÉANS; ORSAY, D'; PARISIENNE, À LA; PLUVIER, À LA; PRINCESSE, À LA; PRINTANIÈRE, À LA; RACHEL; RAMPOLLA; REINE; RÉJANE; ROYALE; SAINT HUBERT; SARAH BERNHARDT; SAVARIN; TALLEYRAND; VALENCIENNES, À LA; VÉRON; VERT PRÉ, AU; XAVIER; YVETTE; ZOLA; ZORILLA.

consommé all'uovo, an Italian beef broth heated to just under boiling point and poured over a beaten egg mixed with the juice of ½ lemon. It is beaten until smooth and served with grated cheese. See also STRACCIATELLA.

conti, I. A French garnish for slices of meat. Rectangles of lean bacon are cooked with lentils which are then sieved before serving. II. A French puréed soup made from cooked lentils mixed with butter and garnished with chervil and fried croûtons.

contiser, a French culinary term which means to stud fillets either of poultry, game, or sole with truffles soaked in egg white (to make them stick), inserting these into regular incisions made in the fillet before cooking.

contre-filet or **faux filet,** a French term for a steak cut from the top of the sirloin. It can also be cut as a joint when it is trimmed of any gristle or sinew and tied for roasting. The North American equivalent for the former is sirloin steak, and for the latter, eye of sirloin.

conversation, a French pastry tart made from puff pastry half filled with a mixture of ½ lb. (1 cup) sugar, ¼ lb. (½ cup) blanched almonds, 2 eggs, ¼ lb. (½ cup) butter, and a tablespoon rum, all well mixed and then covered with pastry. On top of this is put a layer of royal icing, with crosswise strips of pastry placed across. The tarts are cooked in a moderate oven for about ½ hour.

cookie, a small flat biscuit in the U.S., and a plain bun in

Scotland. In 19th-century England, cookie was a common word and is mentioned several times in the novels of Anthony Trollope, but it is not in use in England today. It is thought to derive from the Dutch *koekje*, which is the diminutive of *koek* (cake).

coon, an American cheddar cheese cured by a special patented method which is used only for a cheese of high quality, since both the temperature and humidity present while curing are higher than is required for the making of the usual cheddar cheese. The outside of coon cheese is a dark brown colour, and the flavour is very sharp and pungent. The paste is crumbly. It is popular in the U.S. with people who like a matured, but sharp cheddar.

coot (*Fulica atra*), a rather small bird which is not much valued as food today in Great Britain, as it weighs only 2 lb. In some parts of central Europe, however, smoked coot is an essential winter food. The bird must be skinned as soon as it is shot, and it is at its best from September to December.

coot, grilled, a method according to which the marinated birds are taken from the liquid, and the breast and legs are cut off with a sharp knife and then sliced into thin cutlets. They are sautéed in hot bacon fat, a little marinade is added, and it is all simmered for about 20 minutes or until tender. The meat is removed from the pan and browned under a hot grill, basting with the pan juices. It is served with sauce *Italienne*.

copate, small, wafer-like cakes, a speciality of Siena, Italy.

copeaux, small French cakes known also as petits fours. The mixture is composed of 8 oz. (1 cup) sugar, ½ pint (1 cup) cream, 9 oz. (2 cups) sieved flour, a vanilla pod, and 5 stiffly beaten egg whites. The mixture is beaten well and put through a forcing (pastry) bag onto a greased baking tray in little strips about 1 inch apart. Baking takes about 15 minutes. While the strips are still warm, they are rolled on a small stick into twists. See also PETITS FOURS.

coppa, I. Italian for a cured shoulder of pork, a speciality of the province of Parma. II. In Rome, coppa is a brawn made from pig's head. III. In the Veneto, it is a meat loaf comprised of slices of cooked ham, tongue, and *mortadella* sausage. IV. In Corsica, it is a kind of highly flavoured sausage made from pork and spices.

coprin chevelu, French for the shaggy cap mushroom. See MUSHROOM.

coq, I. The French word for a male chicken, i.e., cock, but in dishes prefaced with "coq," a chicken of either sex, or often a hen, is used. II. The term is also the French name for the chef on a ship.

coq au vin, the bird is cut into 6 portions and browned in an ovenproof dish with diced breast of pork, onions, and butter. Then chopped garlic, morels, and a bouquet garni are added. Excess fat is skimmed off, a little brandy added and set alight, and a pint of red wine poured over. This is covered and cooked in a slow to moderate oven until tender. The sauce is sometimes thickened with the cooked, pounded liver of the bird, and a beurre manié.

coq en pâté, the bird is cleaned, and then the breastbone is removed. A stuffing of foie gras, truffles, and minced veal, moistened with brandy and seasoned, is inserted in the cavity. The bird is trussed, with the legs inserted into its sides, and is then browned all over in butter. It is covered with sliced carrot, sliced celery, and a medium-sized onion, seasoned with thyme and powdered bay leaf, salt, pepper, butter, and a little sliced ham. It is then wrapped in either a pig's caul or thin salt pork. Finally it is encased in pastry (a *pâté brisée* made from flour, butter, and an egg), and is all brushed over with beaten egg. A small hole is made in the top for the steam to escape, and the bird is cooked in a moderate oven for about 1 hour. Another method of preparation is to put the garnished

bird into an oval terrine dish and cover with the same pastry. Sauce *Périgueux* is served separately.

coq solidex, a French transparent egg poacher with a clip-on lid. The advantage of this is that the cooking can be observed through the glass, therefore overcooking is less likely. Butter or cream, herbs, mushrooms, etc., according to taste, are put into the container with the egg. The utensil is put in a pan of boiling water for 7 minutes, if a "set" egg with a runny yolk is required. See also COCOTTE.

coque du Lot, an Easter cake which is a speciality of the Lot region of France. It is made from 2 lb. (7 cups) flour, 4 oz. (½ cup) butter, 3 oz. chopped candied lemon peel, 1 oz. yeast, and 6 eggs all blended into a dough and flavoured with 1 teaspoon each of lemon essence (extract), orange flower water, and rum. It is shaped into an oval, left to rise, and baked in a hot oven for 1–1½ hours.

coquelicot, French for poppy. See also HUILE D'OEILLETTE.

coques à petits fours, a small French cake of the petit fours type made with 1 lb. pounded blanched almonds, 1 lb. (2 cups) sugar, and 1 stiffly beaten egg white. This mixture is put through a forcing (pastry) bag to form small balls, and these are sprinkled with icing sugar before being cooked in a slow oven until golden brown. These small cakes are then sandwiched in pairs, flat sides together, with a filling of either jam or thick chocolate spread, and then glazed on top with icing.

coquilles, I. French for shells, especially fish shells. In France, these are used as utensils in which to cook fish, meat, or vegetables. II. A kitchen utensil filled with charcoal and used in France for cooking joints on the spit.

coquilles Saint Jacques, French for scallops. This term is also used in England for a scallop dish with a sauce mornay. See also PECTEN.

coquinas, small brightly patterned clams found an inch or so beneath the wet sand on nearly all beaches in the Gulf of Florida, U.S. They make an excellent broth, which is eaten both hot and cold, sometimes with the addition of a little worcestershire sauce and Tabasco.

coquines, see ALMEJAS.

coral, the ovaries of hen lobsters which are used as the basis for most lobster sauces. Raw, they are soft and greenish in colour, but they turn red when cooked.

çorba, Turkish for soup.

balık çorbası, a fish soup, generally made with grey mullet. The fish is filleted and browned in oil and cooked with 3 onions, parsley, mint, saffron, and water. Then 3 egg yolks are beaten with juice of 1 large lemon, or an equivalent quantity of wine vinegar, and this is put into a warmed soup tureen; then the boiling soup is poured onto it, stirring rapidly to prevent curdling.

düğün çorbası, a beef soup made from beef broth thickened with blended flour and water, to which are added melted butter, diced beef, and, before serving, paprika. See also DÜĞÜN ETI.

pirinç çorbası, a soup in which 4 oz. rice is boiled in 4 pints (8 cups) chicken or meat broth. The finished soup is poured into the tureen over a beaten mixture of egg yolks and lemon juice, as described for *balık çorbası*. It is sprinkled with cinnamon before serving.

čorba, the Serbo-Croat word for a thick soup. Soup is very popular in Yugoslavia, and there are many varieties.

čorba od ikre, one of the best-known Yugoslavian soups, made from fish roe, root vegetables, onion, and bay leaves, all simmered together. An egg yolk beaten with sour milk and lemon juice is added at the last moment.

jagnéca čorba, a soup made with lamb and root vegetables.

piléca čorba, chicken soup made by boiling a fowl and giblets with onions in water for 2 hours. To the strained soup is added 1 onion which has been fried in butter and mixed with 3 tablespoons paprika, a little water, and seasoning. The whole is then boiled up with carrots, parsnip, and green peas until these are tender. The soup is thickened with 2 egg yolks mixed with ¼ cup sour cream and flavoured with lemon juice.

piléca čorba sa rezancima, a chicken soup with noodles.

srpska kisela čorba, a Serbian sour soup made with the stock strained from chicken that has been boiled with root vegetables, sweet pepper, and bay leaves. A roux is made with oil, flour, and paprika, and the stock is added to it. Finally an egg yolk is beaten with equal quantities of cream and lemon juice, and this mixture is poured slowly into the hot soup.

cordée, a French culinary term employed when describing pastry which is soggy because too much water has been used in the mixing. The verb is *corder.*

cordero, Spanish for lamb. Lamb is extremely good in the north of Spain, particularly sucking lamb, but in the south the quality is poor. See also CALDERETA; COCHIFRITO.

cordero asado, Spanish for roast lamb which is usually roasted with lard and basted with red wine.

cordero lechal en chilindrón, a dish of sucking lamb cooked in the same way as *pollo chilindrón.*

cordero lechazo asado, roast, sucking lamb seasoned with bay leaf, garlic, and white wine.

cordula, a traditional Sardinian dish which consists of sheep's gut rubbed with herbs and oil and roasted on a spit.

coriander (*Coriandrum sativum*), an attractive plant of Eastern origin introduced into Britain by the Romans. It is the aromatic fruits of this plant which constitute the famous valuable spices, not the seeds, as is generally supposed. In India, the fruits are ground and used in curry powder. The leaves are used for flavouring soups, but the fruits enhance stews, cheeses, pickles, puddings, and pastries. When covered with icing or a silver substance, they decorate cakes and sweetmeats (confections). The small silver balls on wedding or christening cakes have a coriander inside. It is called cilantro in Mexico, South America, and the Caribbean, where it is much used. It is also sometimes called Chinese parsley.

It is an annual plant, but seeds itself well, even in cold climates. The fruits should never be eaten when green, as they have a very unpleasant flavour when unripe.

coriandro, Italian for coriander, the fruits of which are used in Italy with pork, lamb, and fish.

cormorant (*Phalacrocorax carbo*), a sea bird which feeds entirely on fish. Only the young cormorant, or squab, is suitable for cooking and eating, because the older birds have dark and strong-smelling flesh. Young roast cormorant is rather like hare, and when served with red currant jelly is highly esteemed by the northern islanders in the Hebrides, Orkneys, and Shetland Islands. The best months for eating the cormorant are August–December. To prepare the bird for cooking, the skin is slit down the back, the wings and feet are chopped off, and the skin is then peeled off completely. In the last century, a cormorant soup used to be made in County Kerry, Ireland. It was said to resemble hare soup. See also SQUAB.

corn (*Zea mays*), alternatively Indian corn, sweet corn, or maize. Strictly speaking, the word corn covers any kind of grain, such as oats or wheat, but in culinary terms it always means specifically maize or Indian corn. It is grown all over the world, more particularly in America and Africa, and there are two main species: *indentata,* which is maize or Indian corn proper; and the variety *saccharata* or sweet corn, which is used as a fresh vegetable. The grain of *indentata,* being starchy, is used in the preparation of corn flour (cornstarch), hominy, etc. *Saccharata,* with its sweet and starchy grain, is

eaten while soft and not fully ripe. If not eaten at that stage, it must be canned. Freshly picked young cobs are either roasted in front of a brisk fire (only until the grain is lightly browned) and then eaten on the cob with salt and melted butter or olive oil, or boiled in salted water. The grain is also pounded, when it is known as corn meal, and used to make bread, cakes, and pastries. In the southern states of America, the coarsely ground grain, after the removal of chaff, is called hominy, and, if more finely ground, hominy grits. The early ripening varieties suit the English climate and flourish there. They include Early Fordhook, Golden Early Market, and Golden Bantam. Corn was introduced into France in the 16th century and grows especially well in the vine-growing districts. See also CORN FLOUR; POLENTA FLOUR.

corn

corn and onions, cream of, a traditional soup from the U.S. Chopped onions and sweet corn are simmered in butter. Flour is sprinkled over them and white stock added. When cooked, milk is added and the whole strained. It is then strongly seasoned, and butter and cream are added.

corn bread, a bread made from ground Indian corn or maize and sometimes flour as well. It is a speciality of the southern states of the U.S. Although the basic mixture is more or less the same in several states, the method of cooking varies. In Mississippi, the ingredients consist of 4 oz. (½ cup) stone-ground cornmeal, 1½ teaspoons baking powder, and a pinch of sugar and salt, all mixed together and moistened with 1 egg and 1½ cups milk beaten up. A baking tin, or individual small cake tins, are greased, and the mixture is poured in to half-way level, baked in a moderate to hot oven for 30 minutes, and served hot with fried chicken or ham, or as a hot dessert with cane ribbon syrup.

In Texas, the cornmeal is mixed with the same amount of flour, and the mixture is sometimes moistened with buttermilk. It is poured into a heated skillet greased with bacon dripping, and cooked over a low heat on top of the stove. When brown round the edges, it is turned over and browned on the other side. The pan must not be covered, or the bread will sweat. It is served with the cooked green leaves of turnip and baked ham hocks, or with pork cheeks (jowls) and cooked cow-peas.

In the Far West and some northern states, corn bread is made from ½ lb. (2 cups) cornmeal, 2 cups boiling water, 2 tablespoons butter, and a pinch of salt, all well mixed. Then 2 eggs are added, together with 1 pint (2 generous cups) milk, and finally 2 teaspoons baking powder are stirred in. The mixture is baked in a heavy, greased iron skillet in a hot to medium oven for about 1 hour. The mixture is batter-thin, but when cooked it resembles a flattish loaf or cake. It is often eaten hot for breakfast with grilled sausages or ham. Stale corn bread is used for stuffing fowl. See also CORN, PONE; COUNTRY SPOON BREAD; CRACKLING CORN BREAD; CREOLE COUSH-COUSH.

corn chowder, a soup made in southern U.S. from ¼ lb. salt pork, browned and crisp, with 1 lb. minced potatoes, an onion (also minced), 1 lb. tinned creamed corn, seasonings, and water to cover. It is covered and baked in the oven for about 1 hour until thick; then 1 pint (2 cups) warm cream is added. Sometimes it is served with grated cheese (browned on top under a broiler) or with a sprinkling of chopped chives or onion tops and diced fried ham. Fish can be used instead of pork, and milk used instead of cream.

corn and fish chowder

corn oil, the oil extracted from Indian corn or maize. It is a nonhydrogenated and polyunsaturated oil, which makes it extremely suitable for people suffering from heart conditions or hypercholesterolemia. It is excellent for frying or pastry-making, but does not have the fine and particular flavour of a good olive oil for dressing salads.

corn on the cob, a dish of freshly picked sweet corn. The outer husks are removed, and the tender inner husks are opened sufficiently to remove the ''silk'' which covers the corn and then closed again. (Some claim that it is better to remove the ''silk'' after boiling.) The corn is put into a pan full of boiling water, to which sugar and salt in equal proportions have been added. After allowing the water to boil again, the corn is simmered for about 20 minutes, depending on the size of the cobs. It is then removed from the water and the husks are detached. Butter is provided to smear over the corn. It is held in the hands and eaten off the cob.

corn pone, the name for small corn cakes which are a speciality of Alabama, U.S. They are made from 1 lb. (3 cups) white cornmeal mixed with salt and 3 tablespoons melted bacon fat. Then about 5 cups boiling water are poured in and mixed until the consistency is that of a thick batter. Spoonfuls of the mixture are dropped to form stick shapes on a greased baking sheet and are baked in a hot oven for about 40 minutes. The cakes are usually eaten with the main course.

corn pudding, a speciality of the Mississippi delta and the South generally. It is made from a 1 lb. can of creamed sweet corn, 1 tablespoon sugar, 3 tablespoons melted butter, 5 eggs, 1½ pints (3 cups) milk, and a little salt, all well mixed and thickened with 1 tablespoon corn flour (cornstarch) dissolved in water. This is poured into a greased shallow baking dish and baked for about 1 hour until it is firm like a custard. Sometimes the eggs are separated, and the stiffly beaten egg whites are added just before baking.

corn sugar, a product of corn flour (cornstarch), a dextro-rotatory form of glucose, known chemically as dextrose.

corn syrup, a product of the partial hydrolysis of corn flour (cornstarch). It is a yellowish-coloured liquid which does not easily crystallise and is used in the manufacture of jams, preserves, biscuits (cookies), and sweetmeats (confection).

corn Washington, cream of, a U.S. regional soup. Equal quantities of chopped onions, leeks, and celery are simmered in butter and sprinkled with 1 tablespoon flour to 2 lb. chopped vegetables. Chicken, or white stock, to 4 times the quantity of chopped vegetables, and ½ cup stewed corn are added; the mixture is simmered for 1 hour, then strained. Fresh whole corn kernels, finely chopped red pimentos (enough to garnish), 2 egg yolks, and 4 tablespoons whipped cream per quart of soup are added before serving.

corn flour (cornstarch), the starch of maize very finely ground and pulverised. (In some eastern countries rice is treated in the same way.) It possesses the property of thickening liquids when it is activated by first mixing with a little cold liquid, then added to the larger amount, and the whole brought to the boil. It is used in this capacity for soups, stews, and puddings, especially hasty pudding. Another use is as an ingredient in various cakes and pastries, where its other property, that of producing a light texture, is of value; the ratio of corn flour (cornstarch) to flour in these instances is 1 tablespoon corn flour (cornstarch) to 4 tablespoons flour. The Chinese use it in many of their dishes, which gives the finished dish a slightly glazed aspect and thickens the sauces as well.

corn salad (*Valerianella olitoria*), alternatively lamb's lettuce, a wild European herb which has yielded to long and intensive cultivation and become a very popular winter salad vegetable in France and Italy. The French varieties are round-leaved and the Italian longer-leaved and lighter in colour, with serrated edges called rughetta. When it is accompanied by thin slices of cooked red beetroot and thin sticks of raw celery, it becomes salade *lorette*.

corn salad

corncrake or **landrail** (*Crex crex*), a small migratory bird, once a common sight in English meadows, but nowadays becoming more and more rare; consequently, in England it is protected from extinction by law. It is particularly popular in France (roi des cailles as it is known there) for eating purposes, and is at its best from October to November. Corncrake is cooked in the same way as snipe, quail, or grouse.

corned beef, the Irish and American name for salt beef. See also BULLY BEEF.

corned beef hash, see HASH.

cornelian cherry (*Cornus Mas*), a deciduous shrub or small tree of the *Cornaceae* family. It has early, showy yellow flowers, and a bright-red, oval, edible fruit nearly 1 inch long. It is very hardy and will grow from a seed or cuttings. It is used in Russia, where it is known as *kizil*, for many sauces, and also for making *kisel*. In France, the fruit (*cornouille*) is preserved in honey or sugar, and also in pickle, like olives. It is also called a cornel.

cornet, I. A pastry or ice cream in the form of a horn. II. A thin slice of ham, tongue, or other meat rolled up to resemble a horn. III. In France, the larynx of a large mammal, such as the ox, is also called a cornet. IV. Originally, before the days of the forcing (pastry) bag, paper would be twisted into a horn shape and used to form certain cakes, or icing motifs. This also was called a cornet.

cornhusker, an American cow's milk cheese, first introduced in 1940 by the Nebraska Agricultural Experiment Station. It is similar to cheddar and colby, but it has a softer paste and contains more moisture, which means that it does not keep as well.

Cornish burnt cream, a traditional dish made by alternating layers of baked custard and clotted cream in a pie dish, covering the top with thinly sliced citron sprinkled with castor sugar, and lightly browning. See also CLOTTED CREAM; CUSTARD.

Cornish fairings, traditional Cornish biscuits (cookies) made of 3 lb. (10½ cups) flour, 1½ lb. (3 cups) sugar, 1 lb. (2 cups) butter, lard, ½ lb. (1 cup) candied lemon peel, 1 lb. (2 cups) syrup, 1½ tablespoons baking powder, 1 tablespoon ground ginger, and 1 tablespoon mixed spice. The fat is rubbed into the flour, and spices, a pinch of ammonium bicarbonate powder, and the ginger and sugar are added. The baking powder is boiled in a little water (½ gill or ⅛ cup), whisked into the syrup, and added to the other ingredients, together with the lemon peel. A soft paste is made, which is cut into 1-inch cubes. These are baked on a greased tin in a warm oven for about 15 minutes.

Cornish pasty, a traditional Cornish pastry turnover with a variety of possible fillings. The pastry should not be too flaky or too rich; the most usual pastry is made from 1 lb. flour to ½ lb. combined lard and suet, and salt, mixed with water to a dryish paste. A circle is then cut out, and usually raw, thin steak, cooked onion, and cooked potato (all cut small and seasoned) are put on half the pastry; the edges are moistened with water and the other half of pastry is folded over and well pressed down. A slit is cut on top before the pasty is baked in a quick oven. Each member of the family has his or her initial marked at one corner, and in this way individual tastes regarding fillings can be catered to. The true way to eat a Cornish pasty is to hold it in the hand and begin to bite from the opposite end to the initial, so that should any remain uneaten, there is no danger of its being consumed later by anyone but its rightful owner!

Cornish pasties

It is said in Cornwall that the Devil never crossed the River Tamar into that county for fear of the Cornish woman's habit of putting anything and everything into a pasty. The following Cornish rhyme is well known.

Pastry rolled out like a plate,
Piled with turmut,[1] tates,[2] and mate.[3]
Doubled up, and baked like fate,
That's a Cornish Pasty.

(*Anon.*)

[1] turnip.   [2] potatoes.   [3] meat.

Alternative fillings include: apple; blackberries; broccoli; chicken; dates; eggs and bacon; herbs, spinach, and onion; jam; mackerel; parsley and lamb; pork, potatoes, onion, and herbs; rabbit; rice, sugar, and egg; sorrel; star-gazy (herring); and turnip and potato.

Cornish splits, traditional Cornish rolls made from 1 lb. (3½ cups) flour, 2 tablespoons butter, 1 oz. yeast, 1 tablespoon sugar, ½ pint (1 cup) milk, and salt shaped into small round cakes, put in a warm place for 1 hour to rise, then baked in a moderate oven for 20 minutes. When cooked, they are split and buttered while hot, then served with cream, jam, or treacle. Splits eaten with Devonshire cream and treacle are known as "thunder and lightning." Another variety is sometimes made without yeast, but with 2 teaspoons baking powder, and the appropriate amount of buttermilk, instead of milk.

Cornish squab cake, a traditional Cornish recipe from Penzance. Mashed potatoes, seasoned with salt and pepper, are spread over the top of a rich pastry crust and covered with strips of pickled pork. The cake is then browned in the oven. Cream is sometimes mixed into the potato.

cornstarch, see CORN FLOUR.

cos lettuce, a variety of lettuce with long, crisp leaves, and no heart; it is also called romaine. See also LETTUCE.

cosford, a variety of hazelnut which is of good quality and size.

costolette, Italian for cutlets.

costolette Bolognese, veal cutlets as cooked in Bologna. This dish has two forms. Veal cutlets dipped in egg and breadcrumbs, then fried, and topped by a slice of ham and a covering of grated Parmesan cheese and dabs of butter; or escalopes of veal cooked in butter, stock, and a little Marsala wine, topped by grated Parmesan. In Bologna, they are often served with a dish of white truffles.

costolette d'agnello alla Marinetti, Marinetti's lamb cutlets. The cutlets are braised with bay leaves, rosemary, garlic, pepper, white wine, and lemon and are served with dates stuffed with salted pistachio nuts. See also MARINETTI.

costolette Milanese, veal cutlets as cooked in Milan. The cutlets are coated with egg and breadcrumbs, fried in butter, and garnished with lemon wedges and chopped parsley. Spaghetti is sometimes served with them. They make an excellent dish when well cooked.

cotechino, an Italian pork sausage, a speciality of Emilia, Romagna, and Modena. A pork salame (salami), salted for only a few days and weighing 1–2 lb., is pricked, wrapped in muslin or linen, and simmered for 2–3 hours according to weight. It is served with cooked, soaked, white haricot beans, lentils, or mashed potato.

côtelettes, French for cutlets. Traditionally, each person is served 2 lamb cutlets, as is also the custom with noisettes. Côtelettes découvertes are a French cut of veal, identical with the *côtes découvertes* of lamb butchery.

côtelettes de poisson, thick cutlets cut across a large fish such as cod or salmon. See also DARNE.

côtelettes de volaille, chicken cutlets (similar to a suprêmes, i.e., the name given to a breast of fowl or chicken, divided into two along the sternum, with the humerus bone of the wing adhering to the carcase). They are usually rolled in flour, cooked in butter, and seasoned; a few drops of lemon juice are added. They must be served as soon as they are cooked, otherwise they become dry and insipid.

côtelettes parisiennes, see TENDRONS.

cotenna, Italian for pork rind, used for larding lean beef, particularly in a stew.

côtes de boeuf, a rib of beef also consisting of the muscles which cover the ribs and backbone. The fourth to the seventh vertebra is sometimes called *train de côtes découvert,* and the eighth vertebra to the end, *train de côtes couvert.* When the joint has been boned and the meat cut into slices, such a slice is known as an *entrecôte.* The joint is often roasted or braised. See also ENTRECÔTE.

   côtes de boeuf à la bouquetière, beef which is first sautéed in butter and then covered and cooked gently in more butter. The pan juices are diluted with demi-glace and Madeira, and the dish is garnished with small heaps of young, fresh vegetables, boiled, drained, and turned in butter. Other garnishes used are *bourgeoise, bourgignonne, dauphine;* if the joint is roasted, *duchesse, à la jardinière, à la lyonnaise, à la nivernaise, à la parisienne,* etc.

côtes de filet, French for a chop cut from the centre of the loin of lamb or mutton.

côtes découvertes, French for middle neck cutlets of lamb, known in the U.S. as rib chops nearer to the neck.

cotherstone, an English double cream cheese made in Yorkshire but now very difficult to obtain. It is farmhouse made and resembles a stilton in shape and size.

cotignac, an old French sweetmeat (confection), for which Orléans was famous. It was said to have been presented to Joan of Arc when she made her first triumphal entry into that city. It was based on medlars; now quince is used, and it is made and sold commercially. The quinces are put whole into a low oven until soft, then carefully sliced, the peel being left on. An equal quantity of sugar is added, and it is boiled gently in a preserving pan until it begins to candy at the sides and bottom. Constant stirring is necessary. It is poured into shallow dishes and left to get cold, and then is dried out for several hours in an oven at the lowest possible temperature. When quite firm, it is cut into squares, wrapped in foil, and kept in a tin. See also COING; MEMBRILLO.

cotogna, Italian for quince.

   cotognata, an Italian preserve made of a very sweet quince paste.

côtoyer, a French culinary word which means to turn a joint of meat when it is cooking in the oven so that all sides get the maximum heat.

cotriade, a Breton fish soup similar to bouillabaisse, but using john dory, mackerel, sardine, hake, conger eel, and other Atlantic fish. It also contains onions fried in lard, potatoes, and herbs. The liquid is served in a tureen on large slices of bread; the fish and potatoes are served separately on a large dish.

cotronese, an Italian cheese of the *pecorino* type made from a mixture of ewe's and goat's milk, from Crotone in Calabria. It is a peppery drawn-curd cheese, also known as crotonese. See also FOGGIANO.

cottage cheese, probably the oldest form of soft cheese. It is made from skimmed milk which is heated and then soured. The whey is drained from it, but it is never hard-pressed, so a certain amount of moisture remains in it. It is usually eaten within two or three days of being made, but if it is kept for a little while, it becomes what is known as clabber cheese. Because of its low fat content, it is eaten a great deal by people on a fat-free diet. It exists in many countries, where it is used in a number of ways in cooking, or is eaten fresh with bread and salads. When it is made with cream or full cream milk, it is known as cream cheese. It is white in colour and has a clotted appearance. See also SERNIK; TVOROG.

cottage pie, see SHEPHERD'S PIE.

Cottenham, a rare double cream, semi-hard, blue-veined cheese which comes from Cottenham in Cambridgeshire. It is like a rich creamy stilton in taste, but flatter and broader in shape. It is also called double Cottenham.

Cottslowe cheese, see CREAM CHEESE.

coucher, a French culinary word which means to make pâté, stuffing, purée, or other preparation into a round or oval shape on a baking sheet, by the use of a forcing (pastry) bag having either a round or a fluted nozzle. The verb coucher means to sleep, thus to form a bed on the baking sheet.

coucouzelle, French for the fruit of a variety of *courgettes* which is picked when quite small. It is called zuchetti or zucchini in Italy, and the latter name obtains in the U.S. and in Britain.

couennes de porc, French for fresh pork rinds used often in country stews to add richness and a gelatinous quality to the gravy.

coulibiac, see KULEBYAKA.

coulis, I. French for Old English cullis, which is a rich meat gravy. Precisely, it means meat juices obtained naturally, that is, the fresh juices which run out of the meat. II. Liquid purées of poultry, game, fish, and vegetables are sometimes referred to as coulis. III. Nowadays, the word is often used to denote a thick soup made from the purée of a crustacean.

coulommiers, Brie façon coulommiers, a cheaper cheese than Brie de Meaux. It is available from November to June, and is sold before it has had time to acquire the reddish-brown crust that is typical of Brie. Though a good ordinary cheese, it is quite inferior in flavour to the splendid Brie. See also BRIE.

country spoon bread, a bread from the southern states of the U.S. made from 1 cup cornmeal and 2 cups milk, cooked for about 10 minutes in a large saucepan until the mixture resembles porridge. It is then removed from the heat, and salt, 1 teaspoon baking powder, 2 tablespoons butter, another cup milk, and 2 egg yolks are added. They are all blended well, and then 2 stiffly beaten egg whites are folded in. The bread is baked in a greased dish in a slow to medium oven for 1 hour. It is spooned into warm dishes and topped with butter. See also CORN, BREAD.

county captain, an Anglo-Indian dish of curried chicken, with raisins and apples added. The chicken is jointed and sprinkled with lemon juice before being rolled in flour and cooked with curry powder and the other ingredients. It is served with boiled Patna rice and mango chutney. It is sometimes called "country captain." The word captain is thought to be a corruption of capon.

coup de feu, I. A French culinary term which means that an article of food has been subjected to too strong a heat and has become blackened. II. The expression is used among chefs to describe the hours spent in serving up a meal.

coupe Jacques, a French dessert which, when correctly served, should consist of various fruits soaked in liqueur and arranged between lemon and strawberry ice cream. The top is decorated with chopped almonds and glacé cherries. Alas, nowadays, it too often means canned fruit with a dollop of inferior vanilla ice cream. See also COUPES GLACÉES.

coupes glacées, a collective name for French ice cream puddings (sundaes) made with fruit soaked in a liqueur, covered with one or more kinds of ice cream, and decorated on top with fresh or crystallised fruit, or with *crème chantilly.* They should be served in a stemmed round cup of glass or silver, known as a coupe (in the U.S. it is called a sundae glass). *Coupe Jacques* is perhaps the most usual variety.

courges, French for vegetable marrow (zucchini), squash, or pumpkin. Local names include *bonnet de prêtre* and *pâtisson.* When cutting any variety of courges it should be started from the flower end to avoid bitterness. See also COUCOUZELLE; GOURDS.

courgettes, a small variety of edible gourd, which has a short succulent fruit. It is used in ratatouille and called zucchini in the U.S. and Italy. See also COUCOUZELLE.

couronne, French for crown of meat.

court bouillon, an aromatic liquid which originated in France, used for poaching meat, fish, and various vegetables. In each case, the court bouillon is boiled before adding the substance to be cooked.

For meat, the most usual recipe is 2 tablespoons diced carrot and the same of onion, a clove of garlic, peppercorns, a bouquet garni, and salted water to cover. It is boiled for at least 15 minutes before the meat is added. For fish, it is made from salted water, sliced onion, sliced carrot, parsley, thyme, bay leaf, peppercorns, the fish trimmings, if any, and a little of either wine vinegar or white wine. Leeks and celery can also be added, if available. For vegetables, it is made from chopped onion sweated in olive oil, white wine, and water with lemon juice added; then garlic and fresh herbs are also included.

couscous, is of Berber origin and the national dish of the Maghreb, the north African countries of Algeria, Morocco, and Tunisia, which has been adopted by other countries. It is not easy to make unless you have been doing it for some time and have the correct grain. It consists of 1 lb. fine semolina sprinkled with a little fine flour so that each grain is coated to keep them separate when steamed over water, broth, or a stew. The flour-coated semolina is mixed with a little cold water, worked with the fingers to prevent lumps forming. When the stew or broth is nearly cooked, the couscous is mixed with a little cold water until it becomes about the size of rice, but no larger. It is put into a *couscousier,* a pot with holes in it, not unlike a steamer, which fits over the stew saucepan. The grains are stirred to let air to them and help them to swell. They are simmered, uncovered for about 30 minutes; then turned into a bowl, sprinkled again with cold water, and stirred to separate them. They are salted and sometimes a tablespoon of olive oil is added, before returning to the *couscousier* for another ½ hour. They are served piled onto a wooden or earthenware dish and mixed with butter before serving either separately, or with the stew poured over the top. Couscous can be served cold mixed with yogourt, in which case it is cooked over water. In Algeria, sugar and dried fruits are added for a sweet dish drunk with milk and served as an entrée. See also CUSCUSU TRAPANESE.

cousinette, a soup from the Béarn region of France, made with finely chopped spinach, sorrel, lettuce, and various green herbs.

couve, Portuguese for cabbage, a vegetable much eaten in Portugal, where several varieties including kale are grown. See also CALDO, VERDE; COUVE TRONCHUDA.

couve à mineira, a dish of strips of scalded cabbage (or kale) fried with diced bacon. These are well stirred over the heat and salt and pepper are added to taste.

salada de couves, a salad using cabbage as its main ingredient. Minced onion is mixed with finely chopped raw cabbage, green sweet pepper, and parsley, and the salad is well chilled before a dressing of olive oil, vinegar, sugar, salt, and pepper is poured over.

couve tronchuda (*Brassica oleracea;* var. *tronchuda*), a variety of cabbage with white midribs which are cooked like seakale, but with a head which is cooked like an ordinary cabbage. There is also a curly leaved type with small midribs which is like kale. This form of cabbage withstands frost better than almost any other. It was introduced into England from Portugal in 1821, and is still most commonly known by its Portuguese name, couve tronchuda, although it is also called variously Portugal cabbage, Braganza cabbage, and sea-kale cabbage.

Coventry godcakes, traditional English cakes, triangular in shape, from Coventry, where they are sold on New Year's Day and at Easter. Godparents used to give them as presents to their godchildren. They are made of puff pastry filled with mincemeat and can vary in size from 6 to 18 inches across.

cow, a female ox, of which either virgin cows (heifers) or sterile cows are used for eating. Old cows are extremely tough to eat and have little flavour.

cow heel (foot), used in soups, stews, and with tripe and onions and highly prized for its gelatinous properties. It is split in half and scalded. Jellied cow heel (foot) cooked with bacon makes a good brawn, much enjoyed in the north of England.

cow parsnip (*Heracleum sphondylium*), a weed which grows in many English hedges. The leaves can be cooked in the same way as spinach and have a faint flavour of asparagus; it makes quite a pleasant green vegetable. In Siberia, the young shoots are eaten like asparagus; in Poland, a strong beer is made from the stems and seeds.

cow pea (*Vigna sinensis*), a herb more closely related to the bean than to the pea. It grows wild in many tropical countries, but is cultivated in the southern states of the U.S. where it is known as white-eyed pea or black-eyed pea. The dried "peas" can be both black and white.

cowslip (*Primula veris*), a sweetly scented spring flower, sometimes eaten with fresh cream or crystallised in sugar as a sweetmeat (confection). It is chiefly used, however, to make wine, vinegar, mead (with honey), or syrup.

cozido, a Portuguese culinary term for any boiled dish. It may consist of meat, beans, vegetables, smoked sausages, and/or smoked ham—in fact, as with most country stews, of any vegetable or meat that is at hand. When used in connection with fish or vegetables, it means simply "boiled."

cozido à Portuguesa, a stew of beef, ham, salt pork, sausages, rice, shredded cabbage, tomato sauce, and chick-peas. It is served in three courses: first the liquid with the rice, as a soup; then the cabbage and peas with tomato sauce, and finally the boiled meat with boiled potatoes.

cozonac, an elaborate raisin bread traditional in Rumania. It is made with flour, yeast, butter, sugar, milk, and about 1½ dozen eggs. Sometimes it has walnuts, almonds, or poppy seeds as flavourings.

cozze, Italian name for mussels in Naples and along the Tyrrhenian coast. In Venice they are known as *peoci* and in some parts of Tuscany as *militi* and *muscoli. Arselle,* strictly speaking, are clams, but this name is also used for mussels in Genoa and Sardinia. See also ZUPPA, DI COZZE.

cozze al vino bianco, mussels cooked in oil and served in a sauce made of their stock together with white wine, garlic, and parsley. They should be served opened, on the half-shell, and eaten cold. Sometimes they are served on croûtons and in this case are called *crostini di mare.*

cozze pelose, Italian mussels with a shell covered with hair. They are found mainly on the coast around Genoa. They are cooked in the usual way, and have an excellent flavour.

crab, the name for any crustacean of the order *Decapoda.* Crabs are found off the coasts of Europe (*Cancer pagurus*), off the Atlantic and Pacific coasts of America (*C. magister*), and in Alaskan, Russian, and Japanese waters, the large, so-called king crab (*Paralithodes camtschatica*). In Europe, the best edible varieties are the common crab, the giant crab, and the spider crab. In the U.S., soft-shelled crabs (taken at the time they discard their shells) are a delicacy, as are also the tiny baby crabs found inside some oysters off the New England coast. Both these varieties are often stewed in wine and cream and are eaten whole, shell and all, or they are fried in butter and eaten plain or sprinkled with grilled almonds.

A medium-sized, heavy crab makes the best eating. The best and kindest way to kill a crab is to put it in cold, salted

crab

water, bring it gradually to the boil, and simmer for about 15 minutes. When cold, the crab is dressed, that is, all the meat from body and claws is mixed with cream, seasonings, and sometimes breadcrumbs, put back in the shell and served cold (the stomach sac and ''dead men's fingers,'' long, soft claw-like appendages adhering to the round under shell, having been removed). This method is the most usual in England, and is known as ''dressed crab.'' Crab is excellent in soups or bisques; cooked, after the preliminary boiling, with garlic, tomatoes, and saffron, and served with rice; with a cheese sauce (Mornay) or with mushrooms; devilled or newburg. There are any number of variations.

Commercially, crabs, especially the king crabs, are canned, and are also made into a crab paste and sold in jars. See also BUSTER; MOLECCHE; SPIDER CRAB.

crab apple (*Pyrus baccata*), a tree which came originally from Siberia and northern China, but is now cultivated all over the world for the beauty of its blossom and fruit. Most of those in the British Isles and America are hybrids of *Pyrus malus* (the apple) and *Pyrus baccata* (the Siberian crab apple). The fruit is used for jams, jellies, and preserves.

crab apple jelly, the jelly made from crab apples, particularly good with cold meats or poultry. After the apples have been covered with water and cooked, they are drained in muslin. Then 1 lb. sugar for every pint of juice is boiled up with the juice for about 1 hour (or until a small amount, put on a saucer, jellies when cold).

crackers, American usage for unsweetened biscuits. See also CREAM CRACKERS.

crackling, in the British Isles the roasted skin or rind of pork which has been scored into thin strips to make it easier to eat. To make brittle and crisp crackling, the joint should be raised on a small grid in the pan. If the skin fries in the boiling fat, it becomes as tough as leather; in fact, the Normans used to manufacture it especially to make armour plate to withstand battle-axes and arrows. It was called cuir bouillie.

crackling corn bread, a creole speciality, made in the same way as corn bread, but with pork crackling chopped and added to the batter. It is poured into a hot greased iron pot and baked in a hot oven for about ½ hour. See also CORN BREAD.

crakeberry, see CROWBERRY.

cramique, a Belgian brioche with raisins added.

cranberry (*Vaccinium oxycoccus;* var. *palustris*), a small European shrub with acid, crimson berries that ripen in the autumn. They are mentioned in Lyte's translation of Rembert Dodoens' *Niewe Herball* in 1578, where they are also called ''fenberries.'' In Ireland, they are known as ''bogberries.'' The name in England was originally ''craneberry,'' either because the unopened flower and corolla resemble a crane's head and neck, or because the marshy bogs where they grow were haunted by cranes.

They are very popular in the U.S., and there are many varieties of this genus now cultivated commercially there. Cranberry sauce is traditional in the U.S. served with roasted turkey, and with some game; in addition, the berries are made into pies, tarts, bread, jams, and jellies, and are also used for garnishes. They must be cooked with sugar; this gives them a pleasant, smoky, yet slightly bitter taste.

cranberry sauce, an American sauce for turkey, chicken, and game, made of ripe cranberries, sugar, and water. To prepare it, 1 lb. (about 3 cups) washed berries are placed in an enamel saucepan with ½ pint (1 cup) water, and covered closely. They are glanced at occasionally during the cooking, and when all the cranberries have burst open, the sugar, to taste, is added, and the sauce is uncovered and simmered gently for 20 minutes without being stirred. Sometimes very fine strips of orange or lemon peel are added with the sugar.

crandall, see GOLDEN CURRANT.

crap, Rumanian for carp, which is eaten extensively in Rumania. The roe is treated like caviar (see *icre*) and is very good.

crap umplut, a whole 4-lb. carp is stuffed with 1 cup chopped olives mixed with 1 crushed garlic clove, 1 tablespoon each fennel, parsley, and olive oil, with 2 tablespoons lemon juice. It is baked with sliced root vegetables, tomatoes, and 1 lemon (sliced), all seasoned and covered with ¼ pint (½ cup) olive oil.

crapaudine, I. A classic French sauce. This is a sauce piquante with the addition of chopped mushrooms and a little mustard diluted in tarragon vinegar. II. A French method of preparing and cooking certain birds, particularly pigeon. The birds are split horizontally from the tip of the breast to the wings. They are opened, flattened slightly, and spread with melted butter, salt, and pepper, and grilled on both sides until cooked. Sauce diable is sometimes served separately, and the dish is garnished with chopped gherkins. It is possible that the name comes from the toad-like shape the bird presents when so cooked (*crapaud* means toad).

crappie (*Pomoxis annularis*), a good freshwater fish found in the waters of the Mississippi Valley. It is related to the calico bass. See also BASS.

crappit heids, a traditional Scottish dish of stuffed heads of haddock. It used to be a favourite supper dish and is mentioned in Sir Walter Scott's novel, *Guy Mannering*. The name comes from the Teutonic kroppen or krappen meaning to fill or stuff.

Originally, the stuffing was simply oatmeal, suet, or butter, onions, salt, and pepper, but nowadays it often contains crab, lobster, anchovy, egg yolk, and breadcrumbs. The head is cut off well into the shoulder, stuffed, and gently simmered in fish stock for ½ hour. On the Isle of Lewis, the fish livers are added to the stuffing. See also HADDOCK.

craquelin, a French dry biscuit made from ½ lb. (approximately 2 scant cups) flour, ½ lb. (1 cup) butter, 2 egg yolks, 2 tablespoons sugar, a pinch of salt, and about 1 gill (½ cup) milk. The dough is rolled out to ⅛-inch thickness, cut into squares, brushed with beaten egg, and baked quickly in a hot oven. When cool, the biscuits are sprinkled with vanilla sugar. Roubaix, in northern France, is noted for them.

craquelots, French name for a herring which is only half-smoked. It is good to eat, but does not keep very long, unlike the fully smoked bloater. They are also called harengs bouffis.

craquelots de Dunquerque, a speciality of Dunkirk, France, these herrings are smoked with the leaves of the hazelnut tree.

crawfish (*Palinurus vulgaris*), a large crustacean, also known as the spiny lobster. It is found off all the Mediterranean coasts, the coasts of England and Ireland, of Chile, and also in the warm waters of Bermuda and the West Indies. The meat is very like lobster and can be served in the same way, but crawfish is in fact very much less popular than lobster, since it has thin, whip-like antennae instead of the large claws typical of the lobster, which are reputed to contain the best-flavoured meat. The crawfish can attain a weight of 20 lb., but this is exceptional. It is extensively canned.

crawfish

crayfish, a freshwater lobster found in European and American rivers and lakes. There are three different kinds. *Astacus fluviatilis* is the larger kind found in Europe, distinguished by the red underside of the large claws; *Astacus pallipes* is small, 3–4 inches long and found in British and Irish rivers; and *Cambarus affinis* is a slightly different species, found in American rivers. See also RÁK; RAK; RAKI; RAVUT.

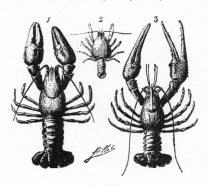

crayfish

The crayfish has firm and delicately flavoured flesh and should be served as simply as possible in order to preserve that delicacy. Boiled and pounded, it is used as the basis of sauce *nantua* and of *bisque d'écrevisses,* but it can be prepared and served like lobster. A crayfish found in estuaries in Spain is called *langosta.* See also ÉCREVISSES; LANGOSTA.

cream, the fatter part of milk. It was originally separated from the whole milk by allowing it to stand in shallow bowls in a cool room, when the fatty fractions rose to the surface and were skimmed off, the thinner remainder being known as skimmed or skim milk. Nowadays, it is usually made by placing the whole milk in a special machine centrefuge called a separator. Many of the larger commercial dairies today use separators which divide the cream into two varieties, one of a very much higher fat content than the other, which are marketed at different prices as "single" (light) and "double" (heavy) cream. The fat content of the former is often too low to enable the cream to be satisfactorily whipped, while that of the latter is so high that some of the water-soluble flavouring substances are left behind, thus producing an extremely rich, fatty cream, with a rather insipid flavour. For general culinary purposes, the best cream is either that made in the original manner, which has the finest flavour, or that derived from a single-fraction separator, which has all the milk fat together

with enough of the water-soluble substances to give the cream a good flavour. Except in the case of Devonshire cream, milk set for cream should not be pasteurized, i.e., heated. See also CREMA; CRÈME; DEVONSHIRE CREAM.

Cream, both fresh and sour, is used a great deal in the cooking and garnishing of sauces, soups, and stews; fresh, it is whipped for soufflés and other sweet dishes. It is also used plain with fruit, pies, and tarts. It is the main ingredient of butter. See also CRÈME FRAÎCHE; SOUR CREAM.

cream dressing, an American dressing of German origin, made of ¼ pint (½ cup) thin (light) cream, 1 tablespoon mixed mustard, 1 tablespoon vinegar or lemon juice, salt, and pepper. Onion juice is optional. The cream is beaten until stiff; the salt, pepper, and mustard are added, and then the vinegar very slowly, beating continuously. The onion juice is added if desired. This dressing is sometimes used for potato salad, when chopped parsley, onion, or chives are added.

cream horns, a pastry made in the shape of a horn or cornet and filled with fresh whipped cream, or, in France, *crème pâtissière.*

cream sauce, see CRÈME, SAUCE.

cream sauce for oysters, an American sauce usually served with baked oysters. It is made with 3 tablespoons butter, 3 shallots, 3 medium mushrooms, 2 teaspoons flour, ¼ pint (½ cup) cream, 1 egg yolk, salt, cayenne, ½ teaspoon parsley, and 1 tablespoon grated cheese. The chopped shallots and finely chopped mushrooms are simmered in a pan in half the melted butter for 15 minutes. Meanwhile, the flour is added to the remainder of the melted butter over the heat, and when the mixture bubbles, the cream is gradually added and stirred until the mixture is smooth and thick. It is then slowly mixed into the beaten egg yolk, and the shallots and mushrooms, in their butter, are added. The sauce is rather highly seasoned with cayenne pepper and salt, and chopped parsley is added. The grated cheese, with paprika, is sprinkled on top of the oysters, according to taste.

cream cheese, a cheese made from full cream milk, or from single or double cream. It is prepared as cottage cheese, but with the full fat milk content. There are several English commercial varieties such as St. Ivel, made at Yeovil; Victoria, made at Guildford; Horner's, made in Worcestershire; Cottslowe, made in the Cotswolds; Farm Vale, made in Somerset. Cream cheese needs to be eaten when fresh. The best cream cheeses in Britain today come from Cornwall and Devonshire. The commercial varieties contain a certain amount of preservative.

In Shakespeare's time, and for many years after, the best-known cream cheese was called *slipcote* or slipcoat. It was made with full cream milk which was soured with rennet, drained, and set to dry on green rushes for 8 days. In the 18th century, dock leaves were also used in place of rushes.

cream crackers, plain, flat biscuits, usually eaten with cheese, invented and first marketed by W. and R. Jacob and Co. Ltd., Dublin, Ireland, in 1885. Jacobs were also the first people to pack them in an airtight carton, and this led to their being exported all over the world at an early date. They are immensely popular in the U.S., where they are commonly called "crackers." They are made from flour, mixed with salt, and a very little fat, and moistened with milk or milk and water; this mixture is then rolled very thin, pricked on top, cut into squares, and baked until very pale brown.

cream of tartar, a purified form of acid potassium tartarate with the appearance of a fine white powder. In the past it was made from tartar, a by-product of wine production. Its mildly acidic properties are used to liberate carbon dioxide gas from sodium bicarbonate (bread soda) and thus to act as a raising agent in bread and cake made without yeast, and in the composition of baking powder. It is also used to perform the same function in order to cause effervescence when water is added to some forms of lemonade powder. See also BAKING POWDER.

cream soups, thickened soups made from either vegetables, poultry, or fish, not necessarily with cream added, but of a creamy consistency.

crécy, I. A French soup made from puréed carrots. II. A French garnish made from carrots sliced julienne. All preparations prefaced à la Crécy must contain carrots in some form or other. III. Chicken consommé garnished with *brunoise* of carrots and chopped chervil. See also CONSOMMÉ. IV. A French method of serving potatoes. See POMME DE TERRE (POMMES À LA CRÉCY).

creier de vițel pane, a Rumanian dish of pancakes filled with mashed calves' brains, onion, parsley, and eggs. When filled and rolled up, they are dipped in egg and breadcrumbs and fried in deep fat.

crema, a Greek corn flour (cornstarch) pudding, a popular dish in Greece. It is seldom served at the end of a meal but, like *rizogalo*, eaten between meals as a snack. It is made from 2 oz. corn flour (cornstarch) mixed with 1½ pints (3 cups) hot milk and 4 oz. (½ cup) sugar, boiled gently until thick and sometimes flavoured with orange or tangerine peel and vanilla essence (extract). It is served chilled, garnished with cinnamon or chopped nuts, in small glass bowls.

crema, Italian for cream in the north of Italy; it is known in the south as *panna*.

crema di mascherpone, an Italian sweet made from 1 lb. mascarpone cheese, 4 oz. (½ cup) sugar, 4 egg yolks, and 2 or 3 tablespoons of a liqueur such as kirsch, all beaten together until they are of a thick consistency and then iced for 2 or 3 hours.

crème, French for cream. However, the French word applies not only to fresh cream, but also to custard cream sauces and custard cream used to garnish cakes or flans, as well as to certain soups and sauces which can contain cream (à la crème).

à la crème, the title given to meat dishes which have their pan juices mixed with cream. It is also applied to vegetables that are tossed in cream after boiling and lightly sautéeing in butter.

crème à l'anglaise, a French sauce or garnish used for cold sweet dishes, cakes, or pastries. It is made from 8 egg yolks worked with ½ lb. (1 cup) castor sugar until they are entirely amalgamated. The mixture is moistened gradually with 1½ pints (2½ cups) boiled (scalded) milk, which has been flavoured to taste with vanilla, lemon, or orange, and mixed well again. It is stirred continuously over a low flame until it almost reaches boiling point and has thickened like a custard. It is then sieved and kept for use. It can be made with 6 eggs—instead of 8—and with about 1 teaspoon arrowroot added, which prevents clotting due to overheating. These amounts make about 2 pints of sauce. Gelatine is added for certain cold sweets such as *bavarois.*

crème à l'anglaise collée, crème à l'anglaise whipped with 1½ teaspoons dissolved gelatine (or 8–10 leaves), and with 1 tablespoon of liqueur added. It is whipped until cool, and used in cold desserts.

crème au beurre, made like a *crème à l'anglaise,* but butter and cream are used instead of milk. It can be flavoured in many ways, with pounded almonds, or with chocolate, coffee, praline, or any liqueur, or ½ lb. (1 cup) butter can be beaten gradually into tepid *crème à l'anglaise.*

crème au miroir, a custard cream browned on top, originally with a salamander, but nowadays usually under a grill.

crème chantilly, a dessert made from cool fresh whipped cream, with a little sugar, and flavouring added when it has reached double its original volume. It is served as it is, cold,

or sometimes with puréed fruit, when it is called crème chantilly aux fruits. It is also used as a filling for *bonvalet* or *beauvilliers.*

crème pâtissière, or confectioner's custard, used for filling small and large cakes. It is made from half the quantity of flour, i.e., 4 oz. (½ cup) to ½ lb. (1 cup) sugar, and 6 eggs, all worked well together, then 1 pint boiling milk is gradually added and stirred constantly. Flavouring is added according to taste.

crème plombières, as *crème pâtissière* with 1 tablespoon rice flour instead of flour, and 3 tablespoons whipped cream added when the mixture is ready. It is served either in small pots, in a special biscuit case, or a dish lined with almond paste.

crème Saint-Honoré, as *crème pâtissière* with stiffly beaten egg whites added when the cream is hot.

crème brûlée, an extremely old English dish which is a speciality of Trinity College, Cambridge, and is therefore sometimes known as Cambridge cream. It is also a popular dish in the U.S. Crème brûlée is made from 4 egg yolks mixed with a little sugar, then added to 1 pint good cream brought to scalding point (180°), but not boiled, and in which a vanilla pod has been infused. It is all well stirred, returned to a double boiler and allowed to thicken. This operation must be performed carefully, stirring all the time, or else the cream will curdle. The vanilla pod is taken out and the cream is poured into a dish and left to get cold. Originally, it was sprinkled with castor sugar and browned on top with a salamander, but this implement is quite forgotten now. Instead, the crème brûlée is sugared with white or brown sugar and put under a hot grill until brown, but it is served cold.

crème caramel, also known as *crème moulée au caramel,* a French pudding made from custard prepared as for *crème royale,* but first the mould is lined with a mixture of sugar and water (five heaped tablespoons sugar to 3 tablespoons water) which have been allowed to boil without stirring, and become caramelised. The pudding is then baked in the caramelised mould in a *bain-marie* in the oven, when cooked if it is turned out upside down, it is called *crème caramel renversée.* It is served cold. See also BRYLÉ PUDDING.

crème des vosges, small fresh cream cheese from Alsace, available only during the summer months.

crème fraîche or **crème double,** is French cream, in which the lactic acids have been allowed to work so that it thickens and has a distinctive flavour. It also has the advantage in that it can be boiled without curdling. Crème fraîche can be made by adding 1 tablespoon of sour cream, yogurt or buttermilk to ½ pint fresh double (heavy) cream, then heating it to under 85°F and leaving it to stand in a warm room (72°F) for about 6 hours. It should be stirred well and will keep refrigerated for about a week.

crème frite, a French dessert which consists of *crème pâtissière* cooled in an even layer about ¼ inch thick, which is then cut into regular-sized squares or circles, dipped in egg, and rolled in breadcrumbs before being fried in deep, hot oil. After draining, they are sprinkled with sugar and served with apricot sauce.

crème renversée, a French custard like *crème caramel,* but turned out upside down when cold.

crème royale, a French pudding made from 3 whole eggs and 2 egg yolks stirred with sugar, then mixed with 1 pint hot milk which has been flavoured with vanilla. This is baked in a buttered mould in a *bain-marie,* turned out, and eaten when cold.

crème sauce, a classical French sauce. For fish, egg dishes, poultry, and vegetables, it is made with a mixture of two parts of reduced béchamel to one of fresh cream. The pan is removed from the heat, a little butter and some more cream are added, and the whole is passed through a fine sieve. For roast veal, it consists of a roux blanc, with cream added.

cremeboller, Danish for chocolate pastry buns made with *wienerbrød* pastry (recipe I). The dough is spread with either almond paste or with a paste of beaten butter and sugar (in equal quantities). It is then cut into pieces 4 inches square, the centres are filled with vanilla cream, and the corners are folded into the centres. The buns are baked upside down in a hot oven until golden brown and afterward are coated with chocolate icing.

crémets, French cow's milk cheeses made in Anjou. They are in season almost all the year round.

crémets d'Angers, French cream cheeses to which fresh whipped cream and stiffly beaten egg whites are added. They are put into a perforated mould and left to drain in a cool place. Before serving, they are turned out onto a deep dish and covered with fresh cream.

crémets nantais, small, fresh cream cheeses from the country of the lower Loire in France. They are available only during the summer months.

cremini, an Italian generic term for various small, soft, factory-made cheeses, sold under brand names and wrapped in tin foil.

crempog, a Welsh pancake made from 4 oz. (¾ cup) flour, 1 tablespoon melted butter, ½ pint (1 cup) buttermilk, an egg, and a pinch of baking soda, and cooked in the usual way.

créole, à la, I. A French culinary term used to denote a variety of dishes which contain rice, either as a garnish, or as a pilaf with its own garnish of sweet peppers and tomatoes simmered in a little olive oil. II. It can apply to sweet dishes made from rice and usually flavoured with orange. III. It is also used to describe eggs, poultry, and entrées served with a garnish of risotto, stuffed sweet peppers, and sauce créole.

creole cheese, a cream cheese made in Louisiana, U.S., for the New Orleans market. It is a rich, unripened cheese, made by mixing equal quantities of a cheese of the cottage type and full cream.

creole coush-coush, a creole bread popular in Louisiana, U.S., made from 1 lb. (2½ cups) cornmeal, 1 teaspoon salt, 1 teaspoon baking powder, and ¾ pint (1½ cups) milk, well mixed. The mixture is poured into a well-greased and well-heated iron pot and left on top of a hot stove until a crust forms. It is then stirred, and the heat is lowered to simmering point; it is covered and cooked for 15 minutes. It is served with milk and sugar, or with cane ribbon syrup and crisply fried bacon.

creole sauce, a traditional American sauce, popular in parts of the U.S. as an accompaniment for grilled steak. It is made of 2 tablespoons each of chopped onions, mushrooms, and chopped green peppers; 1 tablespoon each chopped red peppers and chopped parsley; 2 tablespoons butter; salt and pepper to taste; and 1 pint (2 cups) *sauce espagnole.* All the vegetables are simmered gently in the butter for about 10 minutes. The *sauce espagnole* is added, with rather strong seasonings, and the whole allowed to simmer for 1 hour before serving.

crêpe, a French pancake made from a batter of eggs and flour. A little sugar is added if the dish is to be a sweet one; it is replaced by a good pinch of salt if savoury-filled pancakes are required. The most usual crêpe batter consists of ½ lb. (2 cups) flour to 4 eggs. Then are added 2 tablespoons each of cream, melted butter, and cognac, then ¾ pint (1½ cups) milk, and all are very well beaten. The mixture is fried in spoonfuls. Savoury crêpes can be filled with minced meat, poultry, shellfish, caviar, or various cheeses mixed with a little cream or sauce béchamel. See also PANCAKE.

crêpe making in Brittany

crêpe suzette, a very thin pancake made with crêpe batter, flavoured with curaçao and a little orange juice (approximately 2 tablespoons in all). When cooked, the pancake is spread with butter mixed with sugar, beaten with orange zest and a little curaçao. It is folded in four, a little spirit such as brandy is poured over and lit, and it is served very hot.

crêpes de pommes de terre, potato pancakes made with 1 lb. grated raw potatoes, seasoned with salt, pepper, and nutmeg and mixed with 2 eggs beaten with ¼ pint (½ cup) milk and 3 oz. (½ cup) *beurre noisette.* This batter is well beaten and fried in spoonfuls in hot oil.

crépinettes, small flat French sausages encased in caul (*crépine,* also *toilette*) found in all French charcuterie shops. They are usually made from minced pork, lamb, veal, or chicken, and are buttered before grilling or heating in the oven. They are generally accompanied by a purée of potatoes, and sometimes by sauce *périgueux* if they have truffles in them.

crescenza, an Italian cheese of the *stracchino* family. It is soft, creamy, slightly sweet, uncooked, and pale yellow in colour. It is made in Lombardy from cow's milk.

crescione, I. Italian for watercress. II. A small crescent-shaped pasta used for garnishing soups.

crescioni, an Italian dish consisting of 1 lb. cooked drained spinach with 2 chopped shallots, 1 tablespoon chopped parsley, 1 tablespoon raisins and currants. It is all simmered in ¼ pint (½ cup) olive oil, salt, pepper, and a little sugar to taste, mixed together, then enclosed in small squares of pastry (*pasta frolla*) and fried in deep, hot oil.

crespolini, very special Italian pancakes filled with a mixture of ½ lb. (1 cup) cooked spinach, 4 oz. (1 cup) cream cheese, 1 egg, 1 oz. grated Parmesan cheese, and 2 or 3 chicken livers (sautéed in butter). The pancakes are filled with this mixture, rolled up, and layered in a casserole, with sauce béchamel, finishing with a layer of spinach-filled pancakes. It is surmounted by slices of thin bel paese, sprinkled with grated Parmesan cheese, and dotted with butter, and then baked in a hot oven for 20–30 minutes.

cress or *garden cress* (*Lepidium sativum*), a plant native to Persia; it must not be confused with watercress. Cress can be grown quickly under almost any conditions. It is used for garnishes and sandwich fillings. In England, it is grown with mustard, which is sown a week later because its growth is faster; they are used together as a salad or for sandwiches. Cress is also a frequent ingredient in hors d'oeuvre.

cresson alénois, French for cress or garden cress, often added, chopped and blanched, to hot consommé.

crête de coq, French for cock's comb, which is used for entrées and garnishes. The combs are lightly pricked and put under a cold running tap to wash out the blood. Then they are put in a saucepan with cold water to cover, and heated to just under 114°F, when the skins will begin to curl off. The combs are drained, rubbed with a clean cloth, and sprinkled with salt. Then the outer skins are removed completely and the combs left to soak until they become white. After this they are cooked for ½ hour in a boiling court bouillon.

attelets de crêtes, a French dish of cock's combs threaded on skewers, sometimes coated with aspic or chaud-froid. They can also be coated with egg and breadcrumbs, and fried. They are diced and mixed with sauce allemande or velouté for a *salpicon,* and sometimes this mixture is used to fill small tartlets for hors d'oeuvre. See also ATTELET.

crever, a French culinary term which means to overcook rice to the bursting point.

crevettes, see SHRIMP.

crevettes grises, French for shrimps.

crevettes roses, French for prawns, or larger shrimps which turn pink when boiled.

crevettes, sauce, a classical French sauce consisting of a fish velouté with shrimp *coulis.*

cricket teal, see GARGANEY.

crimping, I. The making of fluted patterns on the edge of a pie or flan. II. A cruel way of cutting fish when alive, which used to be an English practice, but is no longer used. Large gashes were made on both sides, from head to tail, at a space of 1½–2 inches apart. It was thought that this barbarous method stiffened and contracted the flesh, making it particularly delicious. Whole or sliced, crimped fish was always boiled in salted water, and all sauces that were appropriate for boiled fish were used. A little of the stock in which the fish had been cooked was usually served, as well as a sauce. The fish mainly used for crimping were cod, haddock, salmon, and skate, the two latter fish cut into slices or larger pieces.

crinkleroot (*Dentaria diphylla*), an American toothwort. Its knotted roots are very succulent to eat, after cooking in boiling, salted water, and draining.

crispelle, an Italian speciality made from small rounds of either pizza dough or salted bread, fried on both sides in very hot olive oil.

crisps, see GAME CHIPS.

croaker, a small but excellent fish of the *Sciaenidae* family, supposed to make a grunting noise. The *Micropogon undulatus* is one variety of many and the best gastronomically. It is found all along the eastern seaboard of the U.S. The large (50 lb. or more) freshwater drumfish of the Great Lakes and the Mississippi Valley is related to the croaker.

crocchetta, Italian for croquette.

crocchette di cervella, brain croquettes. Calves' brains are boiled in water with 1 tablespoon of vinegar for 15 to 20 minutes, drained, pounded into a paste, seasoned, then dipped in beaten egg and flour, and fried in butter. See also BRAINS.

crocchette di patate, potato cakes made from mashed, cooked potato, butter, grated Parmesan or Gruyère cheese, raw egg, seasoning, and nutmeg. These are mixed, and formed into croquette rounds, which are rolled in egg and breadcrumbs and fried.

crocchette di spinaci, as above, but using spinach, Parmesan cheese, nutmeg, seasoning and egg.

croissant, a French crescent-shaped roll made with an especially leavened dough or, more generally, with *pâté feuilletée.* It is said that it was first created in Budapest during the siege of that city by the Turks in 1686. The all-night bakers gave the alarm that the Turks had tunnelled underground passages into the city, whereupon swift action was taken and the attack repulsed. In recognition of their resourcefulness on this occasion, the bakers were granted the privilege of employing in some way in their confections the crescent emblem, which was part of the Ottoman flag. It is also possible, however, that the crescent shape stems from much earlier, pre-Christian sources.

The croissant is very light and is best served with butter. Jam is sometimes added, but it can detract from the simple yet excellent flavour. In France, they are served, warm, for breakfast. When made with butter they are called *croissant au beurre,* and these are the best. Others are made with lard. See also BUN.

croissant au beurre, a dough consisting of 1 tablespoon butter, 1 teaspoon salt, and 1½ tablespoons sugar put into a mixing bowl with ½ pint (1 cup) of warm, boiled milk, mixed lightly and left until it is tepid. One oz. yeast is mixed with 4 tablespoons of tepid water and left to work, then added to the butter and sugar. One lb. (4 cups) flour is added and kneaded well until the dough is light and elastic, then covered and left in a warm place for about 1 hour or until doubled in size. It is kneaded again for 1 minute then chilled for 2 hours. The chilled dough is rolled into a strip three times as long as it is wide. Then spread with ½ lb. (1 cup) butter over the dough and the ends of the strip folded in towards the centre, envelope fashion. The dough is turned half round and rolled across it. It is chilled for ½ hour, then this operation is repeated twice more, the last time leaving the dough in the refrigerator for 1 hour. It is then ready for use. Roll out the dough to a ¼-inch thickness and cut into 4-inch squares. Divide each square into 2 triangles and starting with the longest side, roll each triangle towards the point, so that the pointed end will be in the middle. Bend slightly into crescents, brush with 1 egg yolk mixed with 2 tablespoons milk, and put onto an unbuttered baking tray, and leave for ½ hour. Bake in a moderate oven for 15–20 minutes, until golden. This amount makes about 20 croissants.

cromesqui or *kromesky,* French-Polish croquettes which are popular in Russia and Poland. They can be made from finely diced meats, fish, shellfish, poultry, eggs, game, or liver, sometimes with mushroom or truffle added, and bound with a thick sauce, either demi-glace or a cream sauce to which an egg yolk is sometimes added. The mixture is then formed into cone or ball shapes. In Poland these are then wrapped in a very thin pancake and deep-fried; in Russia they may be wrapped in a pig's caul, covered in batter and then fried. In France, where the dish originated, cromesqui are not wrapped, but dipped straight into batter, and deep-fried in oil. They are served in France as a hot hors d'oeuvre or a small entrée; in Poland and Russia as an entrée or first course.

crooner (*Trigla lyra*), a fish of the gurnard family, sometimes also called piper. It is rather bony, and not as good as the gurnard to eat.

crop, the gullet of birds. In grain-eating birds, this forms a pouch, and before poultry and winged game are cooked, the contents of the crop are removed and a stuffing inserted.

cropadeu, a traditional Scottish dish that consists of oatmeal and water made into a dumpling, in the middle of which is put a well-seasoned haddock's liver. The dumpling is boiled in a floured cloth for at least 1 hour. The liver dissolves into the oatmeal and the whole makes a tasty peasant dish.

croquant, a small French pastry which crunches when bitten. It consists of 6 oz. (1½ cups) pounded, blanched almonds mixed with 4 egg whites, and 1 lb. (2 cups) castor sugar flavoured with vanilla. The paste is made into boat shapes which are rolled in brown sugar, put on a buttered baking sheet, and cooked in a slow to moderate oven. They resemble a meringue with an almond flavour.

croquante, I. An elaborate centrepiece, hardly ever seen today, for a buffet supper in France. It consisted of a large mould with trellised bands of marzipan set on a pastry base, and the marzipan top filled with small rounds of *pâte feuilletée* with a preserved cherry in the middle. II. A sweet shaped like a basket, made of marzipan, and filled with ice cream.

croque au sel, à la, a French culinary term which means food usually eaten raw with no other seasoning but salt. Foods frequently eaten in this way are celery, young nuts, small globe artichokes, etc.

croquembouche, a French word for all kinds of pastries or fruits which crunch or crumble in the mouth when eaten. The most usual is a small choux pastry profiterole, glazed with sugar, which is cooked to the crack stage 289°F, until it is almost toffee-like, called in French *au cassé,* from the verb *casser,* to crack. Small puff pastries and meringues are also so treated, and some croquembouches are fashioned into elaborate pyramid shapes. Orange segments, free of pith, and grapes are also dipped in the syrup made from sugar, allowed to harden, and sometimes set in a pastry base. The toffee-apple of childhood would come under the heading of croquembouche in France.

croque-monsieur, a French hot sandwich which is served as a small entrée or as a snack. It is a large, thick, crustless slice of bread, buttered on one side only, and on top a thin slice of Gruyère cheese and a slice of lean ham is placed. Another slice of bread is put on top of that, and the whole is fried in butter until it is golden on all sides. It can also be made with a slice of *pain perdu* at the bottom and the cheese and ham on top, then all covered with a thick cheese sauce. It is slightly grilled until the top is golden.

croquets, almond biscuits which are a speciality of Bordeaux, France. They are made from ½ lb. peeled and ½ lb. unpeeled almonds, 1 lb. (2 cups) sugar, ¼ lb. (½ cup) butter, 2 eggs, grated zest of 1 lemon or 1 orange, 1 oz. packet powdered yeast, and a pinch of salt. The ingredients are all pounded into a dough, which is shaped like a large sausage, and baked on a metal sheet. When cooked, slices are served.

croquettes, small oval or cylindrical shapes made from a variety of mixtures, both sweet and savoury, and, when formed, dipped into egg and breadcrumbs before frying in hot oil. Finely minced or chopped fish, meat, poultry, or game is usually bound with a stiff sauce béchamel or velouté before shaping. Mashed potatoes can be mixed with egg and then made into croquettes. Rice, macaroni, and semolina are also made into croquettes, sometimes mixed with either grated cheese or cooked fruit. See also CROCCHETTA; CROMESQUI.

croquettes la varenne, a different type of croquette. They are made from thin pancakes filled with chopped mushrooms cooked in butter and bound with thick tomato sauce. When rolled, they are dipped in egg and breadcrumbs before frying, and are served at once.

croquignolles-parisiennes, I. A Parisian pastry made from 1 lb. (4 cups) flour, 1¼ lb. (4½ cups) icing sugar, 10 egg whites, and a liqueur. When well mixed, it is put through a forcing (pastry) bag onto a buttered sheet, and left to dry for a few hours before cooking in a moderate oven. These pastries are made in many regions of France besides Paris, and only differ slightly in content and flavouring. II. A speciality of New Orleans, U.S., are small crunchy, sweet, fried cakes made from ½ lb. (1 cup) sugar beaten with about 2 tablespoons water, to which are added 2 beaten eggs, then 12 oz. (2¾ cups) flour, 1 teaspoon baking powder, and a pinch of nutmeg. This dough is rolled on a floured surface to ¼-inch thickness and cut into rounds which are fried in deep hot oil like doughnuts.

crôsnes, see JAPANESE ARTICHOKE; STACHYS.

crosse, French for the knuckle or butt-end of a shin of beef or veal. See diagrams, pages xxiii and xxiv.

crostini, Italian croûtons, made from slices of bread covered with various kinds of cheese and baked for about 10 minutes in the oven. The most usual cheeses are bel paese, provatura, provolone, Gruyère, or Parmesan, and the crostini take their name from whichever cheese is used, i.e., *crostini di parmigiano* (Parmesan). They are served as hors d'oeuvre or with soups. If served with a clear broth (*brodo*), they are sometimes garnished with anchovy fillets, chopped, and heated in butter. See also CROÛTONS.

crostini di fegatini, popular in Tuscany and Umbria, these croûtons are traditionally served with broth (*brodo*) on New Year's Eve in Siena and in other places in the north of Italy. They consist of chicken livers and a little ham chopped, cooked in butter, and slightly floured, a little chicken stock, lemon juice, and seasoning added. When cooked, the mixture is all well mashed and spread on bread croûtons which have been fried in butter.

crostini di mare, see COZZE, AL VINO BIANCO.

crotonese, see COTRONESE.

croustade, a French dish made usually with a pastry case filled with the same mixture as a *vol-au-vent,* of meat, poultry, fish, shellfish, or vegetables bound with cream or a thick sauce béchamel or sauce velouté. The container can also be made of mashed potatoes, cooked cold noodles, cooked rice, semolina, or, perhaps the best of all, half of a hollowed-out stale loaf with the crust left intact. Small round rolls can be so treated and filled with grated cheese and beaten egg, then cooked in a hot oven for 10 minutes until the filling has melted and risen.

croûte-au-pot, a French culinary term which applies to *pot-au-feu* after it has been left to get cold, and the fat removed. Squares of toasted or oven-dried bread are put in the bottom of a casserole, and the liquid and small pieces of meat and vegetables are reheated and poured over. Croûte-au-pot is served with one piece of bread per person, and grated cheese is handed round separately. Also known as consommé croûte-au-pot. See also CONSOMMÉ; DIABLOTINS.

croûte-au-pot à l'ancienne, croûte-au-pot with hollowed-out crusts of bread filled with mashed stock pot vegetables, and browned under the grill.

croûtes, I. French for crusts and for delicious slices of brioche. The bread is fried until crisp and dried in the oven, and served with soups or as an hors d'oeuvre. II. A kind of small *croustade* made from stale bread, cut as for a *vol-au-vent,* fried, drained, and filled with various fillings. Croûtes for mixed entrées are usually made from either short or puff pastry, baked blind in a flan dish, and filled afterwards. For these entrées, the pastry should be cooked but not allowed to colour if reheating is required.

croûtes à la nantua, as *croûtes au fromage gratinées,* but with crayfish tails or shrimps substituted for the cheese.

croûtes à la normande, as *croûtes montmorency,* but with apple purée flavored with calvados, then thick cream and apple sauce with calvados.

croûtes à la reine, as *croûtes au fromage gratinées,* but with purée of chicken instead of cheese.

croûtes au fromage gratinées, thick oval slices of bread fried until golden, then covered with sauce béchamel with thick cream and grated cheese added, then a thick slice of Gruyère sprinkled with breadcrumbs and melted butter. It is browned either in the oven or under a grill, and served at once.

croûtes aux fruits, a *savarin,* or conical shapes cut from a white loaf and fried in butter, then garnished with cooked pear or apple, decorated with angelica or glacé cherries, and covered with hot fruit sauce flavoured with kirsch. The hot fruit sauce can be apricots, peaches, nectarines, and plums, etc., all cooked in syrup.

croûtes aux truffes, as *croûtes aux fromage gratinées,* with truffles and sprinkled with grated Parmesan cheese before grilling.

croûtes dorées, stale brioche cut into slices which are soaked in sweetened cold milk and beaten egg, then brushed with melted butter. In another version, these slices are fried on both sides in butter until golden and, finally, sprinkled with castor sugar.

croûtes montmorency, stale brioche cut into half-moon slices sprinkled with sugar and glazed in the oven. Each slice is then covered with *frangipane* pastry cream flavoured with cherry brandy. The slices are arranged in a crown shape, and the centre is filled with cooked, stoned cherries, and decorated with chopped almonds, angelica, and cherries. It is covered with red currant jelly mixed with cherry brandy.

croûtes Saint-Hubert, as *croûtes au fromage gratinées,* but with game instead of cheese.

III. Croûtes can also be used for sweet dishes.

croûtons, I. Slices of crustless bread fried to a golden brown in good game or poultry dripping or butter and used as an accompaniment for soup and game. The slices are cut diagonally in some cases, but for soups they are diced into ½-inch cubes. Croûtons for soup can also be made from crustless bread dried in the oven until it just starts to colour, then broken into small pieces. Diced fried croûtons are added to scrambled eggs when they are ready to serve, and are also used as a garnish for vegetable purées, particularly spinach, and for blanquette de veau, *civet,* chicken fricassee, and salmi. The shape in which they are cut is a matter of individual choice. II. Another form of croûton is a thick slice of crustless bread fried on both sides in a good game or poultry dripping, or butter, then split open. The unfried side is spread with pâté de foie gras or a good liver pâté. These croûtons often serve as a mount for game or tournedos. See also CROSTINI; PARKER HOUSE CROÛTONS.

crow (family *Corvidae*), a large blue-black bird which is edible when very young. It is best skinned, filleted, and made into a pie, although it can be used to flavour a soup which has other good ingredients.

crowberry (*Empetrum nigrum*), the fruit of a hardy shrub which is found growing wild in the mountainous districts of Russia, Scandinavia, and Scotland. The berries are used like cranberries. They are also called crakeberries.

crowdie, I. The Scottish Highland name for a soft cheese made from soured milk curd or buttermilk. See also ABERDEEN CROWDIE. II. A dish made of buttermilk poured onto finely ground oatmeal until it is as thin as pancake batter, then stirred. This was at one time a universal breakfast dish in Scotland. The name was applied to all foods of the porridge type, and ''crowdie-time'' meant breakfast time, witness *The Holy Fair* by Robert Burns: "Then I gaed hame at crowdie-time. . . .''

crown, I. A word used to denote a method of dressing a dish in the form of a crown, or a cake baked in that shape. II. A term in English and American butchery. All the rib chops of lamb are preserved as a single joint, and the skin on the less meaty side is cut through, but the thick top end remains joined. The joint is folded inside out and fastened together (by skewers or sewing) so that a ''crown'' effect is achieved. On top of each standing bone, cubes of bread and salt pork are impaled alternately, and the joint is roasted in a hot oven. When cooked, the inside of the crown is filled with mashed potatoes or cooked green peas. In the old days, the bread and pork were removed before serving, and a cutlet frill was put on each spike. This is a pretty dish, and very succulent if not cooked for too long. It is known in the U.S. as ''crown roast.''

cruchade, a kind of porridge, similar to polenta, made from maize (cornmeal) and milk or water. It is a dish which originated in the Bordeaux and Lot regions of France. See also MILLAS.

crudités, a French dish of raw vegetables, such as radishes, carrots, spring onions (scallions), etc., eaten as a first course. If large, the vegetables are sometimes grated and served with an oil and vinegar dressing.

cruibeen, Irish for pig's trotter (foot), a traditional Saturday night dish in the old days, in Irish pubs, and still eaten in country districts. It is served cold, after boiling. See also PIG'S TROTTERS.

cruller, an American small fried cake with ingredients similar to those of a doughnut, but with nutmeg and ginger in the dough, and mixed with buttermilk or sour milk. Another version has yeast added to the dough, but all crullers are fried in deep hot oil until golden brown. No doubt their origin lies in the *Aberdeen crulla.*

crumpet, a British tea-time delicacy made from 2 lb. (7 cups) flour, 1 oz. yeast, salt, 1½ pints (3 cups) milk, and ½ pint (1 cup) water, mixed into a batter. This is poured into special crumpet rings on a heated baking sheet or griddle, and cooked on one side only over a brisk heat. The top, which is uncooked, should be full of small holes. Crumpets are eaten toasted, bottom-side done first, and liberally spread with butter, with a pinch of salt on top. They are delicious on a winter's day. For breakfast, they are good toasted and buttered with a poached egg or bacon on top; and a crumpet with honey or syrup makes an excellent change from toast and marmalade. They resemble the Welsh *pikelet,* but are not sweetened, and are first cooked only on the one side.

crustacea, see SHELLFISH.

crystallised fruits, small fruits, or segments of larger ones, immersed in a thick syrup usually brought to 220°–224°F (32°–36°C). They are soaked for some time, then drained. Crystallisation takes place during the draining and drying period. See also SUGAR BOILING.

csipetke, small flour dumplings which are an important feature of all Hungarian soups and stews. They are made from a dough consisting of 2 eggs to 1 lb. (3½ cups) flour, kneaded together with a little salt. The dough is rolled into strips about ½-inch thick from which small pieces are broken off and shaped into tiny balls about the size of a marble.

csirke paprikás, the famous and traditional Hungarian dish, known throughout the English-speaking world as chicken paprika. A 4-lb. bird is cut into serving pieces and rolled in seasoned flour, 4 tablespoons butter or oil are melted, and 2 large onions, peeled and sliced, are lightly sautéed until soft and golden. Then 1 tablespoon paprika, a pinch of salt, and black pepper are stirred in and the chicken joints added and lightly browned on all sides. Chicken stock is poured over to barely cover (about ¾ pint or 1½ cups); it is covered and cooked in a slow to moderate oven for 1–1½ hours. Finally, ½ pint (1 cup) sour cream is mixed into the stock, and it is reheated. The dish is usually served with boiled rice, potatoes, noodles, or little dumplings. See also CHICKEN; GALUSHKA.

csurgatott tészta, a Hungarian egg dumpling made from ½ lb. (2 cups) flour, 2 eggs, 1 tablespoon lard or butter, and a little sour milk or buttermilk. These ingredients are mixed quickly and lightly together, and the mixture is made into tiny little balls which are poached for a few minutes in boiling hot water or soup. They are served with *csirke paprikás.* See also DUMPLINGS; GALUSHKA.

cuajada, I. Spanish for junket. Sweet desserts or puddings are not common in Spain, where meals are almost invariably finished with fresh fruit. II. The term is also Spanish for cottage cheese.

cuauhtemoc, a Mexican dish, also popular in the U.S., consisting of cooked dried black beans, puréed, lightly fried in oil with tomato, onion, and garlic. Eggs with the yolks unbroken are set on top and all is baked in a hot oven for about 20 minutes until the eggs are cooked.

cucumber (*Cucumis sativus*), a creeping plant reintroduced into England in 1573 from India. It had been first brought by the Romans, but by the time of Edward III it was only eaten by the poor. Today it is cultivated in greenhouses, cold frames, and in the open where weather permits. Its fruit is generally eaten raw for its subtle and cooling flavour, but it is also cooked as a vegetable, and pickled. When cutting cucumber it should always be started from the pointed flower-end as this prevents any bitter taste. The same applies to zucchini or *courgettes*. There are many varieties of the cucumber family (*Cucurbitaceae*), some with white skins, some with yellow, but most have dark green shiny skins. There is a small variety called gherkin used for pickling in vinegar, and the green Paris *cornichon* and the Boston pickling cucumber of the U.S. The ridge cucumber, used in all the ways already described, is short and thick, several times larger than a gherkin, but much shorter than the ordinary cucumber, with raised strips along the skin; it grows better on ridges of soil than on level ground.

Cucumber is rich in vitamin C. It is thought by some to be indigestible, but any adverse effects can be obviated by not removing the peel, slicing the cucumber thinly, sprinkling it with salt, and leaving it covered with a plate for at least 1 hour before dressing or serving. This draws out the moisture, and the liquid is poured off before the dressing is added. In the U.S. cucumber may be rendered more digestible by removing the skin which is usually coated with wax and by removing the seeds, which are the sources of indigestion. See also AGURK; AGURKE; ANGOURIA; CETRIOLI; CONCOMBRE; KURKKU; GURKA; GURKE.

baked cucumber, a whole cucumber, with a slice cut off at one end and the seeds removed, stuffed with a mixture of minced meat, onion, and herbs. A carrot is used as a stopper, and the cucumber is baked in the oven for an hour with about 1 pint (2 cups) stock.

buttered cucumbers with Marsala, an 18th-century dish. The cucumbers are peeled and cut in half lengthways, then into slices. They are fried very gently in hot butter until soft but not brown, seasoned, then moistened with a glass (½ cup) of Marsala wine, which is allowed to boil and reduce slightly. It is served hot or cold.

cucumber sauce, a traditional American sauce, particularly good with salmon. It is made of 1 small cucumber, ¼ pint (½ cup) thick (heavy) cream, 2 tablespoons vinegar, salt, and pepper. The cream and vinegar must be thoroughly prechilled. The cream is beaten until thick, but not stiff. The vinegar is added gradually, beating continuously, then the seasonings. Just before serving, the grated or finely diced cucumber is folded in.

cucumber soup, I. An 18th-century recipe. Diced, peeled medium cucumber, a medium-sized onion, a handful of sorrel or spinach, and 1 stick of celery are cooked gently in 2 tablespoons melted butter until they are soft, but not brown. Then 1 tablespoon flour is shaken over, and 2 pints (4 cups) chicken stock are added. All are boiled, then simmered for ½ hour. The soup is then sieved or electrically blended, seasoned, and a small pinch of mace is added; then it is reheated, and ¼ pint (½ cup) cream is stirred in just before serving. On festive occasions, the soup was garnished with small chunks of cooked lobster. II. A traditional English soup. Peeled, sliced cucumbers are stewed in butter. White stock and seasoning are added. When cooked, the mixture is thickened with arrowroot, strained, and egg yolks and milk are added. It is made hot but is not boiled and is garnished with shredded sorrel.

cuddy, see SAITHE.

cuillère à bouche and *cuillère à soupe,* French for 1 flat tablespoon of dry ingredients, approximately ½ oz. *Cuillère à café* is the French for 1 small flat teaspoon of dry ingredients; *cuillère à pot* denotes a small soup ladle of liquid, approximately 4 tablespoons, or 2 fluid oz.

cuire à blanc, I. French for baking blind. II. The term also applies to the cooking of white offal (variety meats), such as brains, in a court bouillon.

cuire bleu or *cuire blanc,* a French culinary term denoting the cooking of steaks and chops so that they are very rare.

cuisse, French for the thigh of certain animals and birds, usually chicken or frog. *Cuisses de grenouilles* is the French for frog's legs.

cuisson, I. The French equivalent of our noun ''cooking,'' used to denote various culinary processes and details, especially the cooking time. II. The liquid used in the cooking, i.e., the stock or clear soup used with mushrooms, brains, or calf's head, etc. This is referred to as a ''cuisson de tête de veau,'' and so on.

cuiths, see SAITHE.

cul, see QUASI.

culatello di zibello, a rump of pork cured like ham, a speciality of the province of Parma, Italy. It is the best and most expensive Italian pork. In winter, it is steeped in white wine for 2 or 3 days before cutting. See also PROSCIUTTO.

cullen skink, an old Scottish stew–soup made from finnan haddock (haddie), onion, mashed potato, butter, milk, pepper, and salt. See also SKINK.

culotte de boeuf, a French joint of beef, the end of the loin towards the hipbone, used for braising or poaching. In England, it is part of the rump and is treated as such, and a steak cut from this part is rump steak. In North America, it is the end of the sirloin towards the hipbone, and a steak cut from that part is a sirloin steak. See diagrams, pages xxii–xxiii.

Cumberland sauce, a traditional English sauce served with cold meats or game. The ingredients are 1 lemon, 1 orange, ½ pint (1 cup) port wine, 1 lb. (2 cups) red currant jelly, 1 tablespoon vinegar, cayenne, salt, and approximately 12 chopped glacé cherries. The orange and lemon are thinly peeled without removing the pith. The peel is finely shredded and blanched in water for 5 minutes. The liquor is strained off, and to the shredded peel are added the port, red currant jelly, cayenne, salt, the juice of the orange and lemon, and the vinegar. The mixture is boiled for a few minutes. When cold, the cherries are added.

cumin (*Cuminum cyminum*), the ancient aromatic fruit of a herbaceous plant of the *Umbelliferaceae* family, which flavours much of Oriental and Balkan cooking. The fruit is so small that it is usually referred to as a seed. It is highly prized as a stimulant to the appetite, and is an invariable constituent of a good curry. Wild cumin is used in münster cheese. It has been known from very early times and is mentioned in the New Testament, when Jesus Christ says to the Pharisees: ''Ye pay tithe of Mint, and Anise and Cumin, and have omitted the weightier matter of law; judgement, mercy and faith.''

cunner (*Crenilabrus melops*), a small but good eating fish found in the Atlantic. In the U.S. *Tautogolabros adspersus* is also known as cunner.

cupate, Tuscan honey cakes from Italy. They consist of equal quantities of chopped dried nuts and honey boiled together. A little grated orange peel and ground aniseed are added and all are cooked until golden. A pastry (*pasta frolla*) is made with flour and eggs and rolled out thinly. The hot nut mixture is spread on half and covered tightly with the other half. It is baked for 5–10 minutes, and served cold, cut into small squares.

curd, the coagulum formed in milk which has been subjected to the action of rennet, or acted on by lactic ferments or acid.

When milk is subjected to this process, it solidifies and becomes surrounded by liquid. This liquid is known as whey, and the solid that remains when it has been drained off (in a mould, or a bag made from cheese muslin) is the curd. Curd can be eaten as it is, with a little salt or sugar, or with cream, or it can be used with other foods such as eggs, to make curd cake, or, again, as a stuffing for pancakes. Curdling is the first operation in the making of cheese.

curd cake, a traditional speciality of Russia and Poland, where it takes many forms and is very delicious. These cakes are very popular in the U.S., as they were taken there by Russian, Polish, and Jewish immigrants. In England they are known as cheesecakes, and were highly thought of in 17th- and 18th-century Britain. See also BLAZINDE MOLDOVENESTI; CHEESECAKE; PLACEK SEROWY NA KRUCHYM SPODZIE; SER (SERNIK); TVOROG.

curé, a French cheese made in Brittany from cow's milk. It is in season all the year round. It is also called *nantais.*

curing, the preserving of all kinds of food from decomposition. One of the earliest methods of curing, known to man even in prehistoric times, was drying, that is, exposing food to the sun, or even simply to the air alone. This practice is still continued in many parts of the world, notable examples being the *blawn* fish of the Scottish Islands, the *bindenfleisch* of Switzerland, and the elvas plums of Portugal. In South Africa, *biltong* is air-dried meat, as is pemmican, first made by the North American Indians. The Bombay duck, which is often served with curry, is a small Indian fish cured in the same way.

As soon as man found out how to make fire, smoking became the second most important means of preserving fish and meat. Even today, many smoked meats such as ham (*prosciutto crudo, jambon de Parme,* etc.) or sausage are eaten raw, as are smoked eel, mackerel, salmon, and trout. Fish such as bloaters, haddock, and kippers are salted beforehand. The opposite process, freezing, was another method of preservation used in cold countries by primitive man, but it cannot really be called curing. However, foods buried in the bogs of Ireland (bog butter) were actually cured through the action of the humic acid that was present.

The third, and perhaps most generally used means of curing, came with the discovery of the curing properties of salt. This no doubt was made by the Mesolithic people who inhabited the seacoasts all over the world. Nowadays, we use the same principle of rubbing the article with one tenth of its weight of salt, so that all sides are completely covered. This will preserve foods from decomposition and also alter their taste, so that they become specialities quite unlike the fresh variety. In the case of meats, various other ingredients are added. These do not help the preservation, but add flavour— except in the case of saltpetre, which has a powerful preservative action and makes the meat turn a curious pink-red colour instead of the brown that the salt alone would produce. Sugar, on the other hand, keeps the meat soft by counteracting the hardening effect of the saltpetre. The latter must be used very sparingly; $1/40$ of the weight of salt used is recommended. Saltpetre is used principally in curing beef, mutton, or pork. Ham and bacon have sugar, treacle, or beer with the salt, and are afterwards smoked.

Other curing ingredients include vinegar and pepper, also alcohol, mainly wines, spirits, and beer. Vegetables cured in vinegar can be called pickles. Many fruits are cured in alcohol, that is, they are totally immersed, uncooked, in spirit. They do not decompose, yet have a flavour which is quite different from that of the fresh fruit. This is the essence of cured foods, that, unlike refrigerated foods, they remain in edible form, yet have a taste quite different from the original article.

See also BRINE; DEEP FREEZING; DEHYDRATION; SALT; SMOKE, TO; TROUT, CURED.

curled dock, see DOCK.

curlew (*Numenius arquata*), a migratory bird of the snipe, sandpiper, and plover family. In Scotland, it is also called a *whaup.* Although not relished as good game today, the bird can make an excellent dish if eaten when young. When the curlew feeds on berries, grups, and insects inland, rather than on fish, the flavour is considered by some to have great gastronomic merit. They used to be eaten in salmi in Ireland and were highly prized.

curnieura, the local name in Liguria, Italy, for marjoram.

currant, I. The berries of several different kinds of currant bushes extensively cultivated all over Europe, belonging to the *Saxifragaceae* family. The three most important are the black, the red, and the white currants. All can be cooked and made into pies or tarts, but are used mostly for making jellies and jams. Bar-le-Duc, in France, is famous for its currant preserves. Black currants are used to make *cassis de Dijon,* a liqueur which has become world famous. Red currant jelly is served with roast venison and mutton. II. Small, seedless raisins which came originally from Corinth and are now grown commercially in the Levant. The French name is *raisin de Corinth.*

currant jelly sauce, a sauce made from sauce espagnole passed through a strainer, and a somewhat lesser amount of red currant jelly added, stirring gently over a mild heat until the jelly is well mixed and the sauce quite hot.

currany 'obbin, a traditional Cornish cake. A stiffish paste is made of flour, lard, salt, and milk or water. It is rolled out thin and strewn lavishly with currants or raisins. It is then rolled up, the ends pressed together, and brushed with egg white, and baked in a moderate oven.

curry, an Indian and Far Eastern method of cooking with a combination of many different dried and ground spices and herbs. Curry has been popular in the British Isles since the East India Company was formed in the 18th century, but it must be stated that, except for what is served in a few good Indian restaurants, curry in the British Isles never bears much resemblance to a good genuine Indian or Burmese curry. This, mainly, is because of the use of commercially canned curry powder which, because it is used infrequently, lingers on the kitchen shelf for some months and, like ground pepper and ground coffee, quickly loses its fragrance and becomes stale through prolonged exposure to air. Excellent curry pastes submerged in oils are on the market, and these keep their fragrance and freshness. It is better to grind the spices freshly, and according to taste, as is the practice in the country of origin. Although curry has the reputation of being a "hot" (in the sense of peppery) dish, there is no need for this to be the case. In India and particularly in Burma and Malaya, mild curries are just as popular as hot curries. The "heat" of a curry depends on the amount of chilli put into the mixture. The principal ingredients of curry powder, known in India as *garam masala,* are allspice, anise, bay leaves, capsicum, cardamom, cinnamon, chilli, coriander, cumin, fenugreek, ginger, mace, mustard seed, black and white peppercorns, saffron, and turmeric. These are all sun-dried, or slow-oven-roasted, and freshly ground in a mill. If the spices are fresh and are stored in a really airtight container, they will keep well for about a month. If these fruits and seeds are bought already dried, then they must be ground straightaway.

Many foods can be curried. In the case of meat or poultry, these are cut up and fried in clarified butter with onions, then the curry powder is added, followed by stock, coconut milk (or yogourt in northern India), garlic, and water. It is all simmered slowly until cooked. Eggs are hard-boiled before being added to the prepared sauce. Vegetables are lightly fried first, and the same principle is applied. A curried dish is served with boiled and/or fried rice, mango chutney, lime pickle, and, if a true Indian flavour is required, *chapatti* and poppodums. See also GARAM MASALA.

cuscusu trapanese, a Sicilian dish, similar to the Arabian couscous, introduced into Sicily by the Arab population of Trapani on the west coast of Sicily. It consists of a fish soup served with couscous, which is prepared in Trapani in a special round-bottomed saucepan called a pignata di cuscusu, and another one with sloping sides called a mafaradda. Both together are something like our double boiler.

Cuscusu is prepared from a few handfuls of coarsely ground semolina which are put into a large basin and sprinkled with water with one hand, while mixing continuously with the fingers of the other until it becomes a mass of grains the size of rice. It should not become a paste. It is tipped into a coarse sieve and shaken so that any loose semolina falls through. The couscous is then put on a cloth to dry. For the final cooking, water or stock is put in the lower saucepan to boil and the couscous, seasoned with olive oil, chopped garlic, onion, salt, and pepper, is put into the upper saucepan, covered, and set to cook over the boiling water. Meanwhile, eel, lobster, and any firm white fish which will not break easily during cooking, have been turned in hot oil and then cooked with the onion and herbs in water. The couscous is moistened with some of the fish stock and covered with a thick cloth for 30 minutes, or until it has swollen and absorbed the liquid. The grains are separated with a fork, seasoned with a little ground cinnamon, clove, nutmeg, and a little more black pepper, and put onto a warmed dish with the fish piled on top. The taste is excellent but, in my opinion, the dish is completely spoilt by the mass of small fish bones. See also COUSCOUS.

cusk (*Brosme brosme*), a large sea fish related to the cod and found off the northern coasts of Europe and America. In the U.S. it is often served steamed with a cream sauce. It is also called tusk or torsk. See also COD-BURBOT.

cussy, à la, I. A French garnish for tournedos, noisettes, and chicken consisting of large grilled mushrooms stuffed with chestnut purée, *rognons de coq,* and small whole truffles cooked in Madeira wine. II. A classic French sauce made with demi-glace mixed with poultry jelly and flavoured with Madeira. III. A game consommé garnished with cubes of chestnut and partridge royale, partridge quenelles and julienne of truffles. Before serving, brandy and sherry are added. See also CONSOMMÉ.

custard, I. An old English sauce used with stewed fruit or various steamed puddings made from a mixture of 4 egg yolks to 1 pint (2 cups) milk, sweetened to taste, and usually flavoured with either vanilla sugar or a vanilla pod. It is brought to scalding point, or until the mixture will coat the back of a spoon, in a double boiler. This mixture is incorporated into many puddings, such as bread and butter pudding, diplomatic pudding, and trifle. With the egg whites stiffly beaten and added last, the mixture can be frozen and made into a delectable custard ice cream. Or, when poured into a pastry case, sprinkled with grated nutmeg, and baked in the oven until set, it becomes custard pie. It also forms the basis of cold soufflés. True custard sauce is hardly seen today, and the word custard has steadily been debased since a custard "powder" was produced commercially, in the middle of the 19th century, which is now used in countless homes where a true custard has rarely, if ever, been tasted. The word is believed to come from the obsolete French crustade. II. When used as a pudding on its own (baked custard), the yolks and whites of eggs are used and it is baked in an ovenproof dish in a *bain-marie* in the oven until set. The top is usually sprinkled with grated nutmeg. This method is used for crème caramel, called caramel custard in English. See also CORNISH BURNT CREAM.

custard apple, see ANNONA.

custard marrow (*Cucurbita pepo;* var. *ovifera*), one of the more decorative varieties of the squash family. It is called custard squash or chayote in the U.S. The fruit is broad and flattish, with regularly scalloped edges, and the flesh firm and rather floury, not very sweet. Custard marrows are identified according to their skins, whether yellow, green, orange, striped, or warted. They are also called "elector's caps," and are cooked in the same way as squash. See also CHAYOTE.

custard saus, a Dutch custard sauce served in Holland either as a dessert or as a filling for pancakes (*pannekoeken*). It is made with 2 oz. (¼ cup) sugar and a pinch of salt added to 3 lightly beaten egg yolks, after which ½ pint (1 cup) each scalded milk and cream are slowly stirred in. The mixture is cooked over a low fire, stirring constantly, or in a double boiler, and served cool. It is sometimes flavoured with vanilla or other flavouring.

cutlet, I. A very good cut of meat taken from the top rib-bone of lamb or mutton, also known as best end of neck. It should be grilled rather than fried. See also CHOP. II. A veal cutlet can come from the same part of the animal as does a lamb cutlet, but it can also come from the leg. Cutlets can be grilled, or dipped in egg and breadcrumbs and fried. They are sometimes served with a devil sauce. III. A cutlet can also mean a cut from the ribs or leg of any meat or fowl, or a piece of fish. The cutlet can be fried in butter alone. See diagrams on pages xxiv–xxvii. See also COSTOLETTE.

cutlet bat, a heavy flat metal bat with a handle used for flattening cutlets, escalopes, or steak. It also tenderizes the meat by breaking up any gristly tissues.

cuttlefish (*Sepia officinalis*), a mollusc belonging to the same class as squid and octopus, closely related to the calamary (squid), found in the Mediterranean and Adriatic Seas. When frightened, it squirts out an ink which is used in sepia paint. It can be cooked in the same way as calamary, and is beaten hard before cooking. It is popular in Spain and Italy.

cwikła, a Polish beetroot and horseradish sauce used with boiled beef and other meats. It consists of 2 medium-sized cooked beetroots cut into thin strips, combined with 2 oz. (1 cup) grated horseradish, salt, and pepper to taste. It is covered with ¼ pint (½ cup) wine vinegar and water.

cynaderki, Polish for kidneys.

cynaderki cielęce smażone, Polish for veal kidneys dipped in batter and fried in butter, and served with either a sharp sauce or lemon slices.

cynaderki duszone, lightly fried veal kidneys simmered in a sauce made of bouillon, sour cream, paprika, and marjoram.

cyrano, a French duck consommé, with small duck quenelles which have been covered with sauce suprême and grated cheese and browned in the oven. See also CONSOMMÉ.

czarevitch, a French game consommé garnished with strips of truffle and hazel grouse quenelles and flavoured with sherry. See also CONSOMMÉ.

czarina, a French beef consommé flavoured with fennel and garnished with diced cooked *vesiga.* See also CONSOMMÉ.

Czechoslovakian cheeses, see OST.

czyściec bulwiasty, Polish for Jerusalem artichokes. In Poland they are usually peeled, boiled in salted water until tender, then drained and served with a garnish made from breadcrumbs tossed in melted butter. They are also baked in their skins and served with butter, like jacket potatoes. See also KARCZOCHY.

D

dab (*Limanda limanda*), a small saltwater fish, between 8 and 12 inches long, and the most highly valued member of the plaice and flounder family. It is found in the Atlantic and Pacific Oceans. The flesh is white and soft and can be prepared and cooked like plaice or flounder. The American dab is slightly different, and is called sandy or rusty dab (*L. ferruginea*).

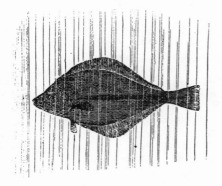

dab

dace (*Leuciscus leuciscus*), a freshwater fish (also known in the north of England as dar or dart) of little gastronomic value. It is found in rivers all over England and Europe, and in France, where it is called dard or vandoise and is used

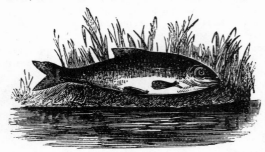

dace

mainly for soups or *matelotes*. A fish of the same name but of a different species (*Rhinichthys atronasus*) is found in the U.S., also horned dace (*Semotilus atromaculatus*) which is related to carp.

daddel, Norwegian for date.

dadel, Dutch for date.

dağ kebab, see KÈBAB.

daguet, French for a young stag. The word comes from *dague* (dagger) and refers to the shape of the horns.

dahorp, traditional Yugoslavian mutton stew. Raw mutton is diced and boiled in water with salt, onions, and herbs. The meat is removed, then the stock is strained and used to boil rice with diced green peppers. When cooked, the rice and peppers are combined with the mutton and lightly sprinkled with vinegar before serving.

dahorp kisela, another stew dish consisting of 2 pounds of cubed mutton boiled for 1 hour in water with 2 pounds of mixed sliced carrots, celery, turnip, and chopped parsley. When cooked, the mutton is removed and mixed with ½ pound half-cooked rice, 2 chopped, lightly fried onions, and a little of the strained stock. One tablespoon each of paprika and vinegar are added to this mixture and cooking is completed in a casserole in the oven for half an hour.

daim, French for fallow deer, which are quite rare in France. The young deer has a very delicate taste. See also VENISON.

daisies, types of American cheddar cheese.

dalayrac, a French chicken consommé thickened with tapioca and garnished with julienne of chicken, mushrooms, and truffles. See also CONSOMMÉ.

dalle, see DARNE.

damascenes, also known as Shropshire damsons or black jack damsons, an inferior variety of the common damson, with smaller and rounder fruit.

dame-blanche, a French cold dessert which is a kind of *plombières* ice cream.

dampfnudeln, a German yeast pastry shaped into small balls before being baked and served hot with stewed fruit, jam, or vanilla sauce. The dough is made from ½ lb. (1¾ cups) flour, 1 tablespoon sugar, 2 egg yolks, 2 oz. (¼ cup) melted butter, ¼ pint (½ cup) milk, ½ oz. yeast, grated lemon peel, and a pinch of salt.

damson (*Prunus domestica*), said to be derived from the Damascus plum tree (*Prunus institia*). The fruit resembles a small rounded bitter plum with a deep blue skin and greenish flesh. The damson is closely related to the hedgerow sloe. The fruit is used for jams, pickles, preserves, puddings, and pies. Damson jam was formerly known in England as "damson cheese." See also PLUM.

danablu, a Danish blue-veined cheese known as blue cheese or "Danish blue," which is exported all over Europe. It is made of homogenized milk, ripens quickly, and has a sharper flavour than most Danish cheeses. It weighs between 5½ and 6½ lb.

danbo, a type of Danish cheese of the samsoe variety. It is a hard, oblong, yellow cheese with shiny-rimmed holes and a mild flavour. It weighs about 13 lb.

dandelion (*Taraxacum officinale*), a plant which grows wild all over Europe and will flourish in any soil, however poor. It is valued in parts of Europe, Asia, and the U.S. for its bitter-tasting, pinnated leaves, which, after the larger outer ones have been discarded, may be blanched by obscuring them from light and used as a salad, or, when young, as a vegetable, cooked in the same way as spinach. In England, a cordial is made from dandelion flowers. The long tapering roots of this plant, when dried, roasted, and ground are used in parts of Europe as an admixture in coffee. A variety is cultivated in France called *plein coeur amélioré*.

dangleberry, the original name for tangleberry, from the very long pedicels which characterize the fruit.

Danish cheeses, see OST.

danoise, a French wild duck consommé garnished with quenelles of game and diced mushrooms and all flavoured with Marsala. See also CONSOMMÉ.

dansk armbaand, literally, Danish bracelets, a Danish dish of bacon and tomato patties. Pork and part of a lean collar of bacon are minced together with seasoning and crushed herbs. This mixture is shaped into patties about 1 inch in thickness, and each is wrapped securely in a rasher of bacon from which the rind has been removed. The patties are baked in a moderate oven, first for 10 minutes, then, after being turned, for a further 5 minutes, after which they are brushed with melted butter, a slice of peeled tomato is placed on each one, and they are returned to the oven for 5 minutes more. They are served with potato chips, round a bed of green peas, and garnished with minced parsley and chives.

dar or **dart,** see DACE.

darazsfeszek, biscuits from Hungary, rather fancifully known as "wasp's nests." They are delicious either hot or cold, and are the favourite coffee cakes of the country. A dough is made from 1 oz. yeast, 9 oz. (2 generous cups) flour, ¼ pint (½ cup) milk, 2 teaspoons sugar, and 3 egg yolks. The dough is beaten well to let air into it and left to rise. It is then rolled out to a thickness of ½ inch and covered with a mixture of creamed butter and sugar, to which have been added ground almonds and sultanas. This dough is made into a roll and cut into slices, which are placed on a baking tray and left to rise again. They are baked for about ½ hour and sprinkled with sugar while still warm.

darblay, a French potato soup with finely chopped (julienne) vegetables added; it is thickened with egg yolks and cream.

dard, see DACE.

dariole, I. A small cylindrical mould for cooking pastries or vegetables, either hot, when they are to be used as a garnish, or set in aspic. II. A small French cake cooked in a dariole mould. The mould is lined with pastry and filled with *frangipane* cream mixed with chopped almonds and flavoured with a liqueur. This is baked in the oven and, when cooked, the cakes are turned out and sprinkled with sugar.

darne, the French name for a thick slice of raw fish, either on the bone or filleted, used for poaching, grilling, sautéeing, frying, or braising. It used to be called a *dalle* (slab). Salmon is the most usual fish to be served as a darne. See also CÔTELETTES DE POISSON.

dartois, I. A French garnish for sliced meat consisting of small pieces of boiled carrot and turnip, braised celery, and *pommes rissolées*. II. A small hors d'oeuvre similar to allumettes except that a garnish of anchovy, spinach, foie gras, sweetbreads, or poultry, etc., is enclosed in two bands of puff pastry, which are cut into rectangles when they are cooked. III. A French sweet pastry made from puff pastry layered with almond-flavoured French pastry cream (*crème pâtissière*). When baked, the top is sprinkled with icing sugar and the pastry put back in the oven until it becomes brown and glazed.

Darwen salmon, the local name in Darwen, near Blackburn, in Lancashire, England, for a dogfish (*Acanthias vulgaris*). It is sold very cheaply without its head. See also DOGFISH.

date (*Phoenix dactylifera*), the oblong-shaped fruit, with grooved seed, of a palm tree which is indigenous over a huge area stretching from Persia through Arabia and North Africa to the Canaries and is now cultivated also in Arizona and California, U.S. The food value of the date is very important to the native population of the former regions. There are three varieties of date: large, soft, and juicy, rich in saccharine; dry and hard, the mainstay of the Arabs' diet; and fibrous, with a low sugar content, not good for keeping. Of these, only the first category reaches distant markets. The date is mostly eaten raw, but is also added to cakes and boiled or steamed puddings. In Elizabethan cookery, dates were included in ragoûts of pork, with grapes, oranges, and lemons. They were also cooked with artichokes in a cream sauce. They impart a delicious flavour if used sparingly. See also DATTE.

date

dátil, Spanish for date.

datte, French for date. See also DATE.

   dattes fourrées, stoned dates stuffed with marzipan flavoured with a liqueur and topped with a nut.

dattel, German for date.

datteri di mare, literally, sea dates, small shellfish found off the Genoese coast. They are similar to mussels and have a very hard shell. They have a delicate flavour and are used in sea date soup, a speciality of Porto Venere.

dattero, Italian for date.

daube, a French method of braising meat, poultry, and game in stock to which wine as well as herbs have been added. However, if the word daube appears on a menu without qualification, it generally means larded sliced or cubed beef, casseroled in stock and red wine, with a little diced salt pork, gammon, onions, carrots, bouquet garni, and seasonings, all braised very slowly for 4 or 5 hours in a large pot (commonly called a *daubière* but given the special name *toupin* in the Béarn). When cooked, the sauce can be strained off, left to get cold, and the fat removed. The beef and sliced carrots are put into a deep dish and the slightly warmed stock is poured over. This is left to get cold and jellied, when it is eaten with a hot baked jacket potato and salad.

Jean-Jacques Rousseau, the Swiss writer, added a calf's or pig's foot to the beef, thus ensuring that the stock jellied, and he used white instead of red wine. I have favoured his recipe for many years. In Provence, a tomato is added, but it can destroy the pure beef flavour. In the Béarn, dried red pepper is put in, but in both these places the daube is eaten hot. It is a far superior dish when served cold and jellied, as it always used to be.

Pheasant, rabbit, and turkey *en daube* are usually served cold and are cooked with stock and white wine. Sometimes the animals are stuffed with forcemeat and foie gras as well as being barded.

Daubes of all kinds including goose are specialities of the Dauphiné district.

daube à l'avignonnaise, a daube made with mutton and served hot.

daubière, a French cooking pot used for the cooking of *daubes.* It may be made from a variety of materials, including earthenware and copper lined with tin. In early times, the daubière stood on three legs and had a very deep lid so that the top could be covered with hot embers. See also TOUPIN.

daudet, a French chicken consommé garnished with julienne of celeriac, lobster quenelles, and cubes of chicken and ham royale. See also CONSOMMÉ.

daumont, à la, I. A French garnish for fish consisting of large cooked mushroom heads, sauce *nantua,* fish quenelles, and soft roes dipped in breadcrumbs and fried. II. A sauce hollandaise flavoured with oyster liquid and lemon juice and garnished with chopped mushrooms, truffles, and oysters. III. A French beef consommé thickened with tapioca and garnished with strips of mushroom, cooked ox palate, and rice. See also CONSOMMÉ.

dauphin, a French cow's milk cheese from Flanders. It is in season from September to June.

dauphine, à la, I. A French garnish for sliced meat consisting of *pommes dauphine* in straw potato nests, demi-glace, and Madeira wine. II. A mixture of *pommes duchesse* and chou paste shaped into small balls and deep fried. III. Fillets of sole poached in Madeira which has had mushroom or truffle infused in it. They are cooled, drained, and masked with *sauce villeroi* and *beurre écrevisses.* Then they are coated with breadcrumbs and fried in butter just before serving. The dish is presented with a border of fish forcemeat garnished with cooked mushrooms, small fish quenelles, crayfish, and truffles, and covered with sauce velouté. Sauce *nantua* is served separately.

dauphinoise, à la, a French method of cooking potatoes in the oven. The potatoes are sliced thinly and placed in a dish with milk or cream barely covering them, layered with grated Gruyère cheese with a pinch of nutmeg, and baked for 1–1½ hours. Sometimes a beaten egg is added to the warm milk, but it is not essential. The dish is also called *gratin de pommes à la dauphinoise.*

daurade (*Chrysophrys aurata*), French for gilt-poll, a saltwater fish of the sea bream family. It is a delicate-tasting fish, found in the Mediterranean and off the British Isles, and is best served à la meunière, or poached and accompanied by melted butter. It is sometimes spelt dorade in France, but this name is often used by fishmongers to pass off other inferior golden-glinted fish as sea bream or gilt-poll. See also BREAM; DORADA; ORATA.

daventry, an English cheese similar to a ripe stilton, but very rich in taste and a darker green in colour.

decize, a French cow's milk cheese from Nivernais which is not unlike a brie. It is in season all the year round.

découpage, French for carving.

deep freezing, a method of preserving foods so that the flavour is unimpaired for some months by storing them in mechanically refrigerated chests at a temperature between −40°C to −18°C. See also BIRDSEYE.

deep frying, the immersion of foods in a large deep pan of hot or boiling fat or oil. Different foods require differing temperatures; for instance, vegetables and fish are cooked in moderately hot oil, as they would not be cooked through if subjected to too much heat initially, whereas precooked food, small foods, such as shrimps in batter, and foods coated with egg and breadcrumbs, need very hot oil to seal them immediately. Raw foods in batter are better if fried twice, once in moderate oil so that they cook and become just golden, and the second time in boiling oil to colour the batter and to heat it through. This also applies particularly to potato chips.

deep frying basket, a wire basket with a handle which fits just inside a deep-fat pan and allows the food to be lifted out and drained.

deer, the name of many different members of the *Cervidae* family, which are antlered, ruminant quadrupeds. The best for eating purposes is the roe deer, followed by the fallow deer, the red deer, and moose deer, and the reindeer, in that order. In culinary terms, deer is always referred to as venison. Young deer is rather tasteless although tender; deer liver is a delicacy, but it must be eaten fresh. After the middle of September, an old stag's liver tastes too strong, so a hind's liver is always preferable from that time on. See also CERVO; CHEVREUIL; DOE; ELK; VENISON.

braised deer liver, the liver is sliced and soaked in cold milk or water for 1 hour. It is then fried lightly on both sides, in butter, removed from the pan, and kept warm. It must not be allowed to become curled with too much heat. Then ½ pint (1 cup) good stock or 1 glass (½ cup) red wine is added to the butter and liver juices in the pan. This is boiled up rapidly for a few minutes, reduced, and then served over the liver slices. A little lemon juice is also recommended.

déglacer, a French culinary term meaning to use liquid, usually stock or wine, to dilute the pan juices left after roasting or sautéeing meat, game, or poultry. Cream or vinegar can also be used.

dégorger, a French culinary term meaning to soak food in water before cooking to release some of their juices and make them less bitter. It can also mean covering certain vegetables, such as eggplant or cucumber, in salt to soften them before cooking or further preparation.

dégraisser, a French culinary word meaning ''to take the fat from'' either soup, stew, sauce, or pan juices; or even to cut away excess fat from a joint.

dégraissis, the fat skimmed off soups or sauces, known in France as ''economy fat.'' It must be clarified before further use.

dehydration, the process of keeping dried foods for long periods of time because the moisture has been extracted from them, either naturally, or artificially, by air or heat and, in some cases, both, for bacteria cannot grow on dry materials. It is also nature's method of preservation, i.e., berries, seeds, or nuts. The water content must be reduced to below 8 percent or 10 percent to be immune from attack. The flavour, colour, and taste of dried foods is changed, but not necessarily impaired; it is different, as will be noted in dried apples, apricots, figs, prunes (plums), peaches, pears, grapes (currants, raisins, sultanas), etc. These fruits are dried by exposure on wooden or iron trays in a warm temperature, but there have been continual immense improvements, notably accelerated freeze drying (A.F.D.) in which Ireland is very far advanced. A.F.D. is a modern improvement using quick freezing and vacuum techniques to produce sublimation of ice and controlled heat changes, all of which result in the least possible loss or change of flavour, but as the finished product must not be allowed to accumulate moisture from the air, it is sealed in packs with an inert gas such as nitrogen. In this form, the food will keep for years without refrigeration as long as the pack is intact. Coconut is grated before drying and known as desiccated coconut. Vegetables are either dried in factories where climatic drying conditions are reproduced by radiant heat, or by A.F.D. Vegetables such as peas are prepared whole as above, but french beans, carrots, onions, or sweet peppers, etc., are sliced before drying to facilitate the operation by presenting a greater surface area. Eggs are dried, whole, or yolks and whites separately and widely used in commercial bakeries. Condensed or evaporated milk is milk which has had its water content (approximately 87 percent) partially reduced. Dried or powdered milk was first made by Grimwade in England in 1855 by a spray method, which, under high pressure, passes the milk through fine apertures at 270°. Today to spray-dry a liquid such as milk, it is forced through a very tiny orifice against a crystal or agate, which atomizes the liquid; there is a temperature variation in the vat into which the atomized liquid falls, and in the process of falling, it becomes dehydrated. The water having evaporated, the resulting powder from the bottom of the vat is dried milk. This milk mixed with wheat and barley malt is known as malted milk powder, and was first made in England in 1887.

Meat is rarely dehydrated whole, with the exception of dried beef (*bindenfleisch*). The process used for the production of dried milk is also used for the production of meat extracts which have been broken by centrifugal spinners, similar in action to a domestic spin dryer, an operation pioneered in 1847 by the German chemist Baron Justin von Liebig with Max von Pettenkofer. Yeast when treated in like manner yields an extract very similar in taste.

Fish particularly shellfish such as prawns or scallops lend themselves to the method of preserving by air drying which has been used for many centuries for foods in Far Eastern countries. A.F.D. is a modern development of those methods, and is equally successful. Many dried vegetables, sometimes mixed with small quantities of meat or fish, are used in the manufacture of package soups. It is a satisfactory method of preserving, not only for its keeping qualities, but because large quantities of food weighing very little are thus easily transported. This has many important applications in the economics of food storage and transportation, particularly for that of extraterrestrial alimentation. With the exception of some fruits such as figs and plums which can be eaten raw, all foods so preserved need the addition of water or another liquid in cooking. See also CURING; EXTRACT.

délice, originally a type of French pastry. Nowadays, it is a word used in menu terminology to imply that a dish is delectable. It may apply to any dish and should be regarded with caution.

delmonico steak, an American steak cut from the rib of beef. Its European equivalent is an entrecôte.

demerara sugar, see SUGAR.

demi-deuil, à la, a French culinary term, meaning literally "half mourning," applied to poultry which is larded under the breast skin with thin slices of truffle, and then poached in a cream sauce. It is garnished with small pastry cases filled with chopped sweetbreads and mushrooms.

Demidoff, the name of a princely Russian family. Prince Anatole was a renowned gourmet of the Second Empire, who gave his name to several dishes. In culinary terms the name signifies several preparations. I. A chicken, sautéed or roasted in butter, served with a purée of root vegetables, artichoke hearts, sauce madère, and fried onion rings, with a slice of truffle on top. II. A braised chicken with puréed vegetables, and, at the last moment, the addition of crescent-shaped truffle pieces, and rich veal stock mixed with a little port. III. A sterlet poached in white wine with fennel, celeriac, and pickled cucumber, then garnished with poached crayfish tails and sliced truffles.

demi-espagnole, formerly the word for demi-glace.

demi-glace, a sauce made from ½ pint (1 cup) *glace de viande* or *fonds brun* added to 1 pint (2 cups) sauce espagnole, which is then reduced to half by simmering on a slow fire. The consistency should be such that it will half glaze, or "coat," the food with which it is being used. It can be flavoured with a little Madeira or sherry.

   demi-glace tomatée, a demi-glace with the addition of tomatoes.

demi-sel, a French wrapped cream cheese, small and fresh, of which the best is made in Normandy. The deluxe version of the *demi-sel* is known as *double-crème* and has a higher butter fat content.

demoiselles de Caen or *demoiselles de Cherbourg*, French culinary names for quite small lobsters.

dénerver, a French culinary term meaning to remove tendons from poultry or game; this includes gristle and membranes, etc., from meat.

denier, en, a French term sometimes applied to potato crisps if cut in the shape of a coin. The word is thought to come from the Latin *denarius*.

dent-de-loup, the name in France for triangles of bread or other foods used as a garnish. It means literally, "wolf's fang," and the garnish is meant to resemble this.

dente, al, an Italian culinary term meaning, literally, to the teeth. It denotes pasta cooked so that it is not too soft, that is, able to be chewed.

denté, French for dentex.

dentelle, the name in Brittany for a very thin crêpe, so called because of its lacy texture.

dentex (*Scomber colias; S. maculatus*), a saltwater fish found in the Atlantic and Mediterranean. It has pinkish-white flesh and is characterised by its dentition. It is sometimes called Spanish mackerel since it resembles a mackerel and is prepared and cooked as such. See ESTORINO. In the U.S. *Cybium maculatum* is also known as Spanish mackerel and is found in warm waters. See also ESCOMBRO.

dentice, Italian for dentex. It is usually grilled or baked in Italy.

dépouiller, a French culinary term meaning to add drops of cold water to a sauce while it is being cooked, so that any fat or scum will rise to the surface. This fat or scum is removed, and the operation repeated until the liquid becomes clear. It is used particularly in the making of demi-glace. The fat or scum may also be removed by skimming the surface with a ladle that has small holes in it called in French an *écumaire*.

derby, a French method of preparing and cooking chicken. It is stuffed with rice, goose liver, and truffles, cooked in port and rich veal stock, and garnished with slices of foie gras and truffles.

Derby or *Derbyshire*, a hard-pressed cow's milk cheese made in Derbyshire, England. It is more flaky than cheddar but firmer than Cheshire, and should be kept for 6 months before being used. It is a good, plain cheese when matured, but too much is sold after only 6 weeks of keeping because it tends to shrink during the ripening period. At Christmas and at harvest time, smaller cheeses weighing about 15 lb. each used to be made, flavoured with sage leaves; these leaves were pulped, and the juice was added to the curd. However, the sage juice gave the cheese an unattractive brownish colour, so spinach juice was often used instead, giving it a pleasant green tinge. This cheese is known as sage Derby.

dérober, a French culinary term meaning particularly to skin shelled broad beans, but generally to peel vegetables.

desiccation, the process of drying or dehydrating foods. The word is applied particularly to coconut. See also DEHYDRATION.

desosser, French for to bone.

dessécher, a French culinary term meaning to dry out certain boiled vegetables for a few minutes on a high heat, before sautéeing or preparing them in some other way. It is also used in connection with chou pastry or a *panade* when these are made on top of the stove.

dessert, the last course of a meal. In France, it can mean cheese, sweets, and fruit. In England, it used to mean nuts and fruit and a dessert wine such as port. Nowadays, and particularly in the U.S., it means the sweet course. All condiments should be removed from the table before the dessert course is served.

dessert cheese, see FRÜHSTÜCKSKÄSE.

desserter, Danish and Norwegian for dessert.

détrempe, a French culinary term meaning to make a mixture of flour and water. It is used in making pastries.

devil, I. "Devilling" was very popular in 18th- and 19th-century Britain. Boswell, Dr. Johnson's biographer, frequently refers to partaking of a dish of "devilled bones" for supper. It is an excellent way of serving cold poultry, game, or rib of beef bones. In Britain, there are three distinct kinds of devilling, all with different devil sauces, i.e., brown devil, wet devil, and white devil. They all contain spicy ingredients and can be served with hot cutlets, chops, steak, or hard-boiled eggs. II. Fish can be cooked in the same way, but this is not usual. See also DIABLE. III. Devilling, in France, means to split poultry open along the back, flatten, season, and grill. When cooked, it is served with sauce à la diable.

brown devil, a sauce made with 4 oz. (½ cup) butter mashed with ¼ the amount of flour, and 1 teaspoon mustard powder. French mustard, chutney, and worcestershire sauce are added to taste. The cold cooked remains of rib of beef are covered with this paste, and all are heated either in the oven or under a slow grill. The bones should be crisp and brown when served.

wet devil, a sauce made with grilled poultry or game joints first dipped in melted butter; then ½ pint (1 cup) cream is mixed with 1 tablespoon curry powder, and 1 teaspoon mustard powder. The grilled joints are put into this and heated up.

white devil, a sauce made with cold cooked poultry, game, or rib bones heated in a little good stock or gravy and kept hot. Slightly whipped cream is mixed with French mustard, mushroom ketchup, worcestershire sauce, salt, and pepper to taste. This mixture is poured over the joints and grilled until brown on top.

devil fish, see ANGLERFISH.

devil's food, a rich chocolate cake popular in the U.S. made with ½ lb. cooking chocolate melted with 6 oz. (⅔ cup) brown sugar, ½ pint (1 cup) milk, and 1 lightly beaten egg yolk over hot water until it becomes a smooth paste, then cooled. Meanwhile, 2½ oz. (⅓ cup) butter is creamed with 4 oz. (½ cup) sugar, and 2 egg yolks; 9½ oz. (2 cups) flour, a pinch of salt, and 1 teaspoon baking soda are added to the butter mixture alternately with ½ pint (1 cup) milk. Then the chocolate mixture is stirred in, and finally, 3 stiffly beaten egg whites combined with 4 oz. (½ cup) sugar. The whole is poured into a greased dish and baked for 35–40 minutes in a moderate oven. The cooled cake can be divided into 2 and sandwiched together with cream or icing.

devils on horseback, a British savoury, like angels on horseback, but made by stuffing prunes with chutney and rolling them up in rashers of bacon. They are then placed on buttered bread, sprinkled with grated cheese, and cooked in a hot oven or under the grill.

Devonshire cream, a very deep yellow, clotted cream from Devonshire, England. It is prepared with fresh cow's milk put into a wide, shallow pan, and left to stand for 12 hours in summer and double the time in winter. It is then placed on a hotplate and scalded as slowly as possible. A circle will rise on the crust of cream when it is properly scalded. The time for scalding varies, but it is essential to wait for the circle to rise. The cream is taken from the fire, but is skimmed into open dishes only when absolutely cold. The top will be a yellow crust and underneath the consistency will be very creamy. It is a very delicious cream and is always used in Cornish splits and in buns, in Devonshire. Cornish cream is made in the same way, but is sometimes rougher in texture.

dewberry, a plant with a trailing bramble which bears a fruit similar to blackberry.

dextrose, see CORN, SUGAR.

dhania, the Indian name for finely ground coriander which is used a lot in curries.

diable, I. A French cooking pot made of two porous, earthenware dishes (each with a handle), one of which forms the lid. Chicken or vegetables, such as potatoes and chestnuts, or fruit can be cooked in it without liquid. This form of cooking imparts an excellent flavour, but cooking time is considerably longer, i.e., small potatoes require at least 1 hour. It is ideal for slow solid fuel cookers. II. A French draught-sheet of metal used for cookers.

diable, à la, a classical French sauce made with 2 shallots, ½ pint (1 cup) white wine, and 1 tablespoon wine vinegar simmered until greatly reduced. Then ½ pint (1 cup) demi-glace is added and the mixture is boiled for 5 minutes, after which it is finely sieved. Fines herbes are added before serving. See also DEVIL.

diable à l'anglaise, as above, but with the addition of a little tomato purée, Harvey's sauce, cayenne pepper, and worcestershire sauce to taste.

diable de mer, French for devil fish.

diablotins, I. A French garnish for clear soup or consommé consisting of round slices of French bread, about ¼-inch thick, covered with a very thick sauce béchamel flavoured with grated Parmesan cheese and cayenne pepper. II. *Consommé aux diablotins* is a chicken consommé, slightly thickened with tapioca, served with diablotins garnish, as above, sprinkled with more Parmesan cheese, and browned under the grill. See also CROÛTE AU POT. III. A hot hors d'oeuvre consisting of puff pastry mixed with Parmesan cheese and seasoned with cayenne pepper. It is shaped into small dumplings, poached in boiling water, drained, sprinkled with grated Parmesan cheese, and browned under the grill. IV. Commercially made French chocolates accompanied by a motto, and wrapped in tinfoil. V. A kind of fritter made by French pastry cooks in the 19th century.

diablotki, Polish cheese croûtons made from 2 tablespoons butter, 3 egg yolks, 3 tablespoons grated Parmesan cheese and a good pinch paprika, all mixed together, spread on thin slices of bread and baked until golden brown.

diamondback, see TERRAPIN.

diane, I. French partridge consommé garnished with truffle semi-circles and game quenelles, with a glass of Madeira added at serving. See also CONSOMMÉ. II. A classical French sauce consisting of sauce *poivrade* flavoured with game essence (extract) and thickened with cream and butter. III. A method of preparing steak by sautéeing or broiling it and adding A-1 sauce, worcestershire sauce, cream, and butter. Some variations include sherry, shallots, brandy, and a garnish of pâté.

dicoccum, see WHEAT.

dieppoise, à la, I. French garnish for fish consisting of shredded shrimps, bearded mussels, and mushroom heads, all simmered gently in stock or butter. II. A fish velouté blended with shrimp butter. III. A fish, especially brill, cooked in white wine, garnished with (I) and masked with the thickened stock of the fish and cooked mussels.

digester, the forerunner of the pressure cooker, invented by Denis Papin (1647–1712), a Frenchman from Blois, who came to England about 1675 and became a member of the Royal Society in 1680. He worked closely with the Irishman, Sir Robert Boyle, on the steam engine and died in London in total obscurity in 1712.

The digester had a tightly fitting lid so that under pressure the contents could be raised to a high temperature. It was mainly used for softening bones to make jelly for invalids.

Dijon mustard, a product of Dijon, famous for its mustard-making since the 18th century, and said to be the region from which come the finest mustard seeds grown in France. The well-known mustard *blanc de Dijon* is a variety which is stronger than most French mustards, but not as aromatic, since it is without the rich combination of herbs which gives the others the special flavour judged in Britain and the U.S. to be that of "French" mustard. *Blanc de Dijon* is rather like a superbly blended English mustard; it is very pale in colour and is mixed with verjuice, not vinegar. See also FRENCH MUSTARD; MUSTARD.

dill (*Peucedanum graveolens*), a lacy, delicate, umbelliferous plant, an annual of quick growth, reaching about 3 feet in height. The seeds have a faint caraway flavour and are greatly prized in northern and Scandinavian countries. Dill pickles were, until recently, very popular in Britain, and a soothing water made from dill was given to babies because of its mildly soporific effect. Dill is used in a great many German and Russian recipes. The name is a derivative of an old Norse word *dilla,* which means "to lull." The plant is much used as a garnish for fish, meats, soups, sauces, and pickles in the Scandinavian countries. It resembles fennel in appearance, but not in taste. Dill once had a sinister reputation as a potent magic herb; it was enough to condemn an old man or woman as a witch if it was found growing in the garden. See also DILL, SÅS; SOS, KOPERKOWY.

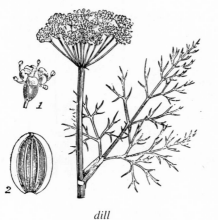

dill

dill pickles, 1 gallon water is boiled with 1 lb. coarse salt and allowed to cool. Sliced cucumbers are layered in a jar, with dill and grape or black currant leaves, then covered with the brine, sealed, and left for 2 to 3 weeks before use.

dill, Norwegian for dill.

dill, Swedish for dill.

dill sas, dill sauce, which usually accompanies roast meats in Sweden. A roux of sifted flour and butter is made, to which hot stock is added. When the mixture is boiling, a little vinegar, chopped dill, sugar, and seasoning are put in. An egg yolk and a little of the sauce are beaten together, and this mixture is used to thicken the sauce, which is never reboiled after the egg yolk is added, as it would curdle.

dille, Dutch for dill.

dillesk, see DULSE.

dillisk, see DULSE.

dinde, French for turkey, usually referred to on menus as *dindonneau* (young turkey). It was originally spelt d'Inde, i.e., from India, as in the early days America, where it came from, was called the West Indies.

dindonneau, French for young turkey. French cooks usually stuff a turkey with shelled, cooked, mashed chestnuts mixed with a little minced pork, or sausage meat, shallot, and parsley. In northern France, apples are sometimes added. The bird is roasted in butter or oil, and the pan juices are mixed with a little Madeira or other sweet wine.

diosmos, Greek for mint, used in salads, sauces, and stews.

diostekercs, a Hungarian yeast cake eaten at Christmas. It is made from 10 oz. (2½ cups) flour mixed with 3 heaped tablespoons butter, 1 heaped tablespoon sugar, and a pinch of salt; ½ oz. fresh yeast is creamed with 8 tablespoons tepid milk and when it has proved 1 egg yolk is stirred in. This is mixed into the flour mixture, kneaded well, covered with a cloth and left to rise in a warm place for 1 hour, or until double in size. Meanwhile, 2 heaped tablespoons sugar are dissolved in 5 tablespoons tepid milk; 1 cup each chopped walnuts, sultanas, and 2 heaped tablespoons butter are added and all warmed up together and left to cool while the dough is well-kneaded for 5 minutes before rolling out on a floured board to a flat, rectangular shape which is spread with the nut and fruit mixture. This is rolled up like a Swiss roll, left to rise on a greased baking sheet for 15 minutes, brushed with beaten egg, and baked in a hot oven for 35–40 minutes.

dip, a savoury mixture, originating in the U.S., into which are dipped small biscuits, crackers, raw vegetables, or pieces of food, such as shrimps. It is usually served at parties or large buffets. It consists mainly of a cream or cream cheese base, sometimes mixed with mayonnaise, and heavily spiced with bottled sauces such as tabasco or worcestershire, tomato ketchup, lemon juice, onion juice, and so on. It can have puréed avocado pear, crab, prawns, or cheese, etc., mixed with it. The contents depend more on the hostess's imagination than on specific recipes.

diples, sweet Greek pastries. This word is also sometimes rendered *thiples* in English and other names for these pastries are *avgokalamara* and *xerotiyana.* They are made from phyllo pastry cut in small pieces, and sometimes formed as bowknots and other shapes, fried in hot oil, and served with syrup, cinnamon, and finely chopped nuts. A stiff dough is made from 2 lb. (8 cups) flour, 1 teaspoon baking powder, salt, 4 eggs, and water flavoured with ouzo or orange juice. It is rolled very thinly, then cut into thin strips which are tied into bows or other shapes, then fried in deep boiling oil until golden. These are laid in layers; each layer is sprinkled with cinnamon, coarse sugar, chopped walnuts, and a syrup made from 1 cup honey to 1 cup water, the juice of ½ lemon, and a small piece of cinnamon.

diplomate pudding, a pudding served in France and Britain (where it is known as diplomat pudding), made with crystallised fruit placed at the bottom of a greased mould which is then filled with alternate layers of sponge (lady) fingers soaked in liqueur and *bavarois*. On each layer of sponge (lady) fingers, currants and sultanas, previously soaked in warmed syrup, are scattered. The top layer is of *bavarois*. The pudding is served cold. Fruits other than the dried currants and sultanas can be substituted, peeled, sliced, and soaked in a sweet liqueur.

diplomate, sauce, I. A classic French sauce made from sauce *normande* mixed with lobster *coulis* and mushroom essence (extract). It is garnished with diced truffles and lobster meat. II. A French garnish of sliced calf's sweetbreads, cock's combs, cock's kidneys, and small mushrooms, all bound with sauce madère.

dippie, a traditional dish from Penzance, Cornwall, consisting of potatoes and pilchards boiled in thin cream or dippie. Since cream has become a valuable commercial commodity, this dish has almost disappeared from use.

divinity fudge, an American sweetmeat (confection) made from 1 lb. (2 cups) sugar, ¼ pint (½ cup) corn syrup, 1 teaspoon vanilla, 2 egg whites, and 1 cup pecan nuts. The first three ingredients are boiled with ¼ pint (½ cup) water to 248°F (firm ball stage) then poured over the stiffly beaten egg whites, beating constantly with a wire whisk until the mixture holds its shape when dropped from the spoon. The chopped nuts are added at the end.

dobosh torta, a Hungarian sponge cake which is thinly layered and filled with a chocolate, butter, and egg filling. The cake is cut into sections before topping with burnt sugar icing, which becomes hard, like a caramel when cold. It is perhaps the best known of Hungarian cakes, and it is light, as well as rich and creamy. In Austria, it is called *dobos torte*.

dobrada, Portuguese for tripe, which is extremely popular throughout Portugal. *Tripas a moda do porto* also contains tripe mixed with other intestines and offal (variety meat).

dobrada à Portuguesa, a stew of tripe, sausage, ham, dried white beans, onion, and chicken. It is the traditional Sunday dinner dish throughout Portugal. In poorer districts, it consists only of tripe and beans. The beans are soaked overnight and, with pieces of tripe, cooked slowly for about 2 hours, then the other meats are added. Diced onions are browned in oil then added to the pan, together with peeled, chopped tomatoes and seasonings. All are gently simmered for a further ½ hour.

dobule, common French name for the chub. It tastes not unlike *féra*, and is cooked in the same way.

doce d'oves, a Portuguese pudding made from egg yolks and sugar. It is very sweet and rich, with a somewhat cloying flavour.

dock (*Rumex alpinus, R. patientia, R. crispus*), sorrel and rhubarb are both members of the large dock family, which also includes mountain rhubarb or patience dock and curled dock, which are used as pot herbs for flavouring, or, when cooked as vegetables, are added to spinach, sorrel, or lettuce. All docks contain a valuable alkaloid called rumicin, as well as chrysophanic acid, useful for intestinal complaints and for the liver. The red-veined variety, *R. sanguineus* is also known as bloodwort.

dodine de canard, I. A rich French stew made from duck, onions, herbs, and red wine. II. A galantine of duck which is a speciality of Tours, France.

doe, female of the deer. It is good when marinated, but must not be eaten during the mating season, as the flesh is coarse and tasteless. See also DEER; VENISON.

dog salmon (*Oncorhynchus keta*), a fish allied to blue-back, or red salmon, and quinnat salmon, found in the rivers of the Pacific coast of America, and of Asia. Like those mentioned, it is not a true salmon; in fact it is very inferior, and is used mostly for canning. See also BLUE-BACK SALMON; PACIFIC SALMON; REDFISH.

dogfish, a name covering a large number of different species

of fish including catfish (*Galeichthys marinus*); *Acanthias vulgaris* (formerly called *Squalus acanthias*), a coarse-eating shark-like fish common in American and European waters; and *Cynias canis* or smooth dogfish, so called because it has no dorsal fins. At the turn of the century, the dogfish was salted by the fishermen of the west coast of England. The name also applies to a variety of blackfish in the U.S. The flesh is good for soup, and some species, such as catfish, are good to eat. See also BURRIDÀ, LA; CATFISH; DARWEN SALMON; ROUSSETTE.

dolce, Italian for a sweet dish which applies in culinary usage to cakes, pastries, and puddings. There are many traditional cakes to be found in all provinces of Italy. See also AMARETTI; BUDINO; COPATE; CREMA, DI MASCHERPONE; PANFORTE; PRESNITZ; ZUPPA INGLESE.

dolce mafarka, an Italian sweet invented by Marinetti. It is made of coffee, rice, eggs, lemon peel, milk, sugar, and orange flower water. It is cooked, and then cooled in a mould on ice, and served with biscuits (cookies). See also MARINETTI.

dollar fish (*Poronotus triacanthus*), a small sea fish of the *Stromateoidea* genus, common during the summer months on the Atlantic coast of North America. A variety of the dollar fish is the butterfish. It is usually fried or grilled and is quite good to eat.

dollma me vaj, an Albanian speciality of green peppers stuffed with cooked rice mixed with tomato, parsley, lemon juice, and salt. They are simmered in water or stock until cooked, but are served cold with meat or fowl.

dòlmà(s), Turkish for "stuffed," but now the name for stuffed vine leaves, although it is a shortening of *yàlàndji-dòlmàs*, the full name for them. The leaves are stuffed with a mixture of fried onions, cooked rice, and seasonings. Then they are rolled up, put into a dish with lemon, and sometimes tomato juice. A plate is put on top and they are simmered for ½ hour. The juice of sour grapes and plums, when they are in season, is used instead of lemon. The stuffed vine leaves are eaten cold as a first course. See also DOLMADAKIA; DOLMADES.

dolmadakia or *dolmathakia*, Greek for very small stuffed vine leaves (about 1 inch long), like *dolmades* but smaller. They are eaten hot or cold, but if they are served hot and meat stuffing is used, they are accompanied by *avgolémono* sauce.

dolmades or *dolmathes*, Greek for stuffed vine leaves. Vine leaves are found throughout Greece, either fresh or preserved in brine, according to the season. (In England, a tinned variety is now available, which can be stuffed equally well.) Stuffed vine leaves are usually eaten as an appetizer, either hot or cold, this last factor determining the type of stuffing used. To prepare these, the leaves are first dropped in hot water and are then spread out, so that a choice can be made. Only the best are selected for stuffing, of which a spoonful is placed on each leaf; the leaves are then rolled up, the edges being turned in in the process, like a parcel. The leaves measure about 2 inches across and, when stuffed, resemble a small fat sausage. The discarded leaves are used to line the cooking pan and to pack in between the dolmades to prevent movement while cooking. Water or stock mixed with tomato purée and lemon juice is poured over the rolls, and they are cooked slowly for about 2 hours. If served hot, a sauce is made by straining the liquid from the pan and stirring in a little yogourt. If served cold, they should be left in the pan until quite cold before serving, when they are eaten without a sauce. See also YEMISSIS ME KREAS KE RIZI; YEMISSIS ME RIZI.

domaci beli sir, a Yugoslavian salted cheese lightly pickled in brine. It is very white in colour and is usually eaten with raw hot peppers and sliced raw onions.

domates, Greek for tomatoes.

domates, saltsa, Greek for tomato sauce, the most popular sauce after avgolémono. It is made with pulped fresh tomatoes, onions, garlic, and seasoning. Sometimes nutmeg and ground ginger are added.

domates yemistes, tomatoes stuffed with onions, rice, currants, pine nuts, parsley, mint, garlic, and seasoning. They are either baked or cooked covered on a low flame on top of the stove.

domates yemistes me kima, tomatoes stuffed with minced meat mixed with tomato pulp, herbs, and seasoning, and baked.

domates yemistes me melitzanes, tomatoes stuffed with eggplant. Onions are first simmered in oil, then the pulp from the tomatoes is added and simmering continued. Chopped eggplant (which should not be peeled) is added and cooked until soft. The mixture is then allowed to cool slightly, when grated cheese is well blended in, and lastly, beaten eggs (2 eggs for enough mixture to fill 9 large tomatoes) are briskly stirred in. A little sugar and salt is sprinkled inside the tomatoes which are filled with the mixture. The open tops are sprinkled with a small amount of breadcrumbs and oil, and the tomatoes are stood in about 1 inch of water and baked in a moderate oven for about ½ hour.

domates yemistes me yarithes, raw tomatoes stuffed with cooked shrimps and mayonnaise.

dòmātiz, Turkish for tomato which is used a lot in Turkish cooking.

donkey, see ASS.

donkey pepper, see POIVRE D'ÂNE.

donzelle, a small eel-like fish found in the Mediterranean, and also known as girelle. It is used in bouillabaisse.

dopp i gryten, Swedish for "dip in the pot." During the day of Christmas Eve, when the Swedish housewife is too busy with Christmas preparations to provide normal meals, she will leave the skimmed stock in which the Christmas ham has been boiled on the stove, and adding beef stock to it with seasoning. The family will satisfy their hunger by dipping pieces of rye bread into the pot. See also JULSKINKA.

doppskov, a Swedish dish made from leftover boiled or roasted veal, beef, and ham, diced small, and sautéed in butter with sliced onions. It is then simmered in a cream sauce mixed with diced boiled potatoes. A fried egg per person is served on top.

dorada, a fish like gilt-poll and sargo, found in Spanish waters, with black marks and gold stripes on the head. It is very good to eat and is at its best stuffed and baked. See also DAURADE.

dorado, Spanish for john dory.

doree, see JOHN DORY.

dorée, French for john dory. Also called Saint Pierre.

St. Pierre à la deauvillaise, dory fillets, poached then covered with onion sauce made with fish stock, cider, and cream.

dorer, a French culinary term meaning to brush pastry, or a dish like *pommes duchesse,* with egg or egg yolk mixed with a little water, before cooking, thus ensuring a "gilded" appearance when cooked.

doreye au riz, Belgian rice tarts. The crust is made from ½ lb. (2 scant cups) flour, 2 oz. (¼ cup) sugar, 6 tablespoons butter, 2 teaspoons olive oil, 2 egg yolks, and ½ teaspoon lemon peel mixed with 1 tablespoon cold water. It is filled with a mixture of 6 oz. (¾ cup) rice cooked with 2 pints (4 cups) milk and 10 oz. (1½ cups) sugar. When cool, 6 egg yolks, 4 oz. (½ cup) soft butter, and a flavouring are added. Then 1 cup whipped cream and the stiffly beaten egg whites are folded in before the tart is baked in a moderate oven until golden brown. These quantities make either 1 large 10-inch tart or 18 small ones.

doria, I. A French garnish for eggs, entrées, and fish, consist-

ing of cucumber cut into pieces the size and shape of olives and cooked slowly in butter. The cucumber is covered with a lid so that the steam prevents it from browning. It is accompanied by *pommes noisette.* II. A French salad, see SALADE, DORIA. III. A chicken consommé garnished with chicken quenelles, olive-shaped cucumber pieces, small balls of fried cheese croûtons (made from puff pastry), and chopped chervil. See also CONSOMMÉ.

Dorset knobs, small, round, knob-like biscuits common to Dorset, England. They are made from flour, eggs, and water, and are very crisp to eat, not unlike a thick rusk. They are usually eaten with butter and cheese.

dory, alternative name for john dory.

dotterel (Eudromias morinellus), a fat and delicious bird which is a visitor to England during the summer and a member of the plover family. It is, however, now protected by law in England, but is eaten in France *(guignard)* where it is cooked in the same way as plover.

double cottenham, see COTTENHAM.

double-crème, see DEMI-SEL.

double d'agneau, a cut of lamb, peculiar to France, comprising the two hind legs of the animal roasted in one piece.

double Gloucester, see GLOUCESTER CHEESE.

doubler, I. A French culinary term meaning to fold in two. It applies to a cut of meat, fillet of fish, or layer of pastry. II. It also means to cover, with foil or paper, pastries which are being cooked, in order to protect them from too much heat and the danger of burning.

doucette, alternative French name for corn salad; also called *dragonet.*

dough, a mixture of flour and a liquid used for making bread, pastries, buns, or scones. Water or milk is the most common liquid, but sometimes eggs are added. Yeast is essential to dough if it is meant to rise. All bread, excepting soda bread and unleavened breads, is made with yeast, and it must be kneaded before cooking. The word comes from the Old English word *dāh.* See also BREAD; SODA BREAD; YEAST, DOUGH.

dough bird or *Eskimo curlew (Numenius borealis),* an American species of curlew. It used to be one of the best birds to eat, but, no doubt due to that very fact, it is now almost extinct. It eats berries and seeds in the summer and cockles and rock snails in the winter.

doughnuts, a small round fried cake, sometimes having a hole in the centre, forms of which exist all over Europe and the U.S. They are eaten hot or cold. In the U.S., the ones with a hole in the middle are often used by children and adults to "dunk" in milk or coffee. In Great Britain the round, whole ones are popular and have a spoonful of jam pressed into the dough before frying. In the U.S. these are called simply jelly doughnuts. The lightest and best are made with yeast, and these are known as raised doughnuts in the U.S. They consist of ½ pint less 2 tablespoons (¾ cup) milk, scalded and cooled to tepid, with ½ oz. (packet) yeast dissolved in it. Then 4 oz. (½ cup) sugar, a pinch of salt, and 4 oz. (1 cup) flour are worked in; the mixture is covered and left to double its size. Then 3 oz. (⅓ cup) butter is melted and cooled, before being added to the dough, followed by 1 beaten egg, a pinch of nutmeg, and another 4 oz. (½ cup) sugar, all mixed in well. Up to 2 more cups (½ lb.) flour are added, but care should be taken not to make the mixture too floury. It is covered and left to rise again, whereupon it is kneaded well and rolled out to ½-inch thickness, cut into small rounds, and left to rise again. The doughnuts are then fried in deep oil (350°F), being turned frequently until brown all over, and, when cold and drained, they are rolled in sugar. They are also eaten plain, or with glazes of sugar, cinnamon, icing sugar, or chocolate. These ingredients make about 24 doughnuts. They can also be made without yeast, using 2 teaspoons baking powder and 1 egg instead of the yeast. The dry ingredients are mixed together, and the butter is melted and added with the eggs and milk. See KRAPFEN; MILOSTI; OLADYI; PONCHIKI.

douglas, French beef consommé garnished with slices of cooked sweetbreads, artichoke bottoms, and asparagus tips. See also CONSOMMÉ.

douillon, see RABOTTE.

dove (family *Columbidae*), a small member of the pigeon family. In England it is a common pet, but the wild bird makes an excellent dish. Doves are at their best when young, at which time they are known as squabs. The older bird must be casseroled or subjected to some other form of long, slow cooking to make the flesh palatable. Allow 1 bird per person. Any recipe for pigeon can also be used for dove. See also TAUBE.

dowitcher or **redbreasted snipe** (*Limnodromus griseus*), also known as the long-billed snipe. There are two birds in the U.S. which bear this name. Both may be prepared for table in the same way as snipe.

doyenné, a French dessert pear. There are several varieties, all of which are very sweet and juicy and can be said to melt in the mouth. *Doyenné blanc* possesses a skin with a cinnamon tinge, is very juicy and delicious, and is ripe in October. *Doyenné d'hiver* is shaped like a large egg, has a rough greenish-yellow skin; its flavour is the least good, and it is ripe in November. *Doyenné de comice* is the largest, has a pale green skin with a russet blush, is the most delicious doyenné of all, and is ripe in October. *Doyenné de juillet* is the smallest variety, has a good flavour, and is ripe in July.

drachena, a large Russian pancake which consists of 2 eggs beaten with ½ pint (1 cup) milk, with 4 oz. (1 cup) flour, 2 tablespoons cream, salt, and pepper added. The pancake is cooked on both sides in butter and arranged flat on a round dish, or it can be baked in a greased dish in the oven for ½ hour. It is served covered with brown butter. It can also be made as a sweet pudding by adding 1 oz. sugar instead of salt and pepper. This version is sprinkled with more sugar and butter before serving.

dragée, a French sweetmeat (confection) consisting usually of whole nuts with a hard sugar or sugared chocolate coating.

dragon marine, Spanish for weever.

dragonättika, Swedish for tarragon vinegar.

dragoncelle, Italian name for tarragon, also called *serpentaria*. In Siena, it is used to flavour stuffed globe artichokes, but is not generally used in other parts of Italy.

dragonet, alternative French name, with *doucette,* for corn salad.

dragonfish (*Trachinus draco*), a saltwater fish, also called weever, found off the European and Mediterranean coasts. It is prepared and cooked in the same way as whiting and is also used in soups and bouillabaisse. There is a smaller variety, sometimes known as dwarf dragonfish, chiefly used for bouillabaisse. However, in Italy and Sicily, it is fried, poached, grilled, and sometimes marinated in oil and lemon juice before cooking and serving with Italian salad. See also DRAKENA; VIVE; WEEVER.

dragoni, Italian for dragonfish.

drakena, Greek for weever or dragonfish, served baked (*plaki*), also in *bourtheto, kaccavia, psari picti,* etc.

dravle, a Norwegian pudding consisting of curds and cream.

drawn butter sauce, a sauce prepared by putting 6 oz. (6 heaped tablespoons) butter in a double saucepan and stirring in 2 tablespoons flour, moistening it with 1 pint (2 cups) water, and seasoning with pepper and salt to taste. The mixture is left to simmer until it thickens, stirring so that it is smooth. Then, little by little, ½ oz. (1 level tablespoon) butter is added, being beaten continuously, until the sauce becomes quite white. The juice of 1 lemon is squeezed in, and the sauce is stirred once more and strained through a fine sieve before serving.

dredging, an operation which used to be carried out between bastings of a spit-roasted bird or meat. The food was sprinkled with seasonings, spices, herbs, juices, or wine, which the hot fat sealed into the crevices and skin. Before serving, it was dredged with flour, oatmeal, or breadcrumbs, and this dredging, with a last basting, crisped and browned the outside. Nowadays, dredging usually refers to the shaking of flour over roasting meat or other food before sautéeing. See also BASTE; FROTHING.

dresdner stollen, see STOLLEN.

dressing, I. See STUFFING. II. The plucking, drawing, singeing, trimming, and trussing of poultry or game. III. The scaling, gutting, and trimming of fish. IV. The name used in the U.S. for various sauces served with salads or cooked vegetables. See also SALAD DRESSING.

drie in de pan, see PANNEKOEKEN.

dried beef, beef air-dried and finely sliced, known as chipped beef, used in the U.S. as a garnish, or served on toast in a cream sauce. It is the same as the Swiss *bindenfleisch.*

dripping, the fat and sediment from roasting meat or from fried bacon. Beef dripping is considered the best, but good pork dripping is used in many country cakes and pastries. Dripping should be poured into a bowl when hot, and left to harden. It should then be turned out, and the brown jellied juice and gravy at the bottom scraped off and used for gravies, soups, and stews; this is what the French call *jus* and it is the essence (extract) of the meat. What is left can be used for roasting, frying, or pastry making.

   dripping toast, an old English nursery treat, not to be despised. Hot toast is spread with the dripping and some of the essence (extract), sprinkled with salt, and eaten before the toast gets cold.

drisheen, an Irish blood pudding which resembles a long, thick sausage, larger in diameter than the more usual black pudding. It is eaten mostly in the counties Kerry, Limerick, and Cork, where it originates, but it is possible to buy it nowadays in Dublin. In Kerry and Cork pig's blood is used, but sheep's blood is used in the classical Limerick drisheen. The blood is stirred to cool it and prevent coagulation, then salt is added before straining. In the finest drisheen, cream, white breadcrumbs, pepper, mace, and herbs are added. (Two pints of blood to 1 pint cream and 1 pint breadcrumbs are used.) The ingredients are then put into a casing of membrane and boiled for about 20 minutes. For re-use, it is either fried, grilled, or simmered in a little stock. Nowadays a "cereal" is added to commercial drisheen, and it is doubtful if any cream is used at all, as small diced lumps of suet seem to have taken its place. The drisheen should be eaten very fresh, when it is as good as, if not better than, the best French *boudin.*

   It is still a traditional Sunday morning breakfast, or Saturday night supper, in Ireland, served with either tripe or fried rashers of bacon and sausage. It is called "packet" in some districts. At my home in county Clare, drisheen was also made with goose blood, and it was very delicious. The mixture was poured into small and large casseroles, and baked in a *bain-marie* in a slow-to-moderate oven for about 1 hour. Tansy is the traditional drisheen herb, but parsley, a little thyme, and a small pinch of mace are very good. Turkey and hare blood can also be used. See also BLACK PUDDING; MORCILLA; WHITE PUDDING.

drob de miel, a Rumanian national dish of calf's stomach filled with lamb's liver, lungs and heart, onion, eggs, and herbs, all minced and tied up before being simmered in water or stock. It resembles *haggis*.

drop scones, British, but particularly Scottish, pancakes which are cooked on a griddle or in a heavy pan. They are made from 1 lb. (3½ cups) flour, 1 tablespoon sugar, and 2 teaspoons each of baking soda and cream of tartar, an egg, and ¾ pint (1½ cups) milk all beaten together until a fairly soft batter is formed. Spoonfuls, not larger than 3 inches across when spread, are dropped onto the warm griddle, and when brown on one side, are turned so that the other side can be browned. They are best eaten hot with butter, honey, or syrup and are an excellent teatime dish.

drumfish, the name given to a number of fish of the family *Sciaenidae* of which the red drumfish (*Sciaenops ocellata*), found in the South Atlantic, is the best to eat. See also CROAKER.

drupe, an English and French word for a fruit with a single stone.

druva, Swedish for grape.

druvgelé, grape jelly. A cinnamon stick and whole cloves are tied in a bag and added to 5 lb. grapes and 8 tablespoons vinegar during cooking. When the grapes are soft, the juice is strained through a jelly bag. The juice is then boiled for about 30 minutes, after which preserving sugar (1 lb. to 1 pint juice) is added and boiling continued until the jelly sets, which varies between 45 and 60 minutes.

dry goose, see FITLESS COCK.

drying, of foods, see CURING; DEHYDRATION.

duBarry, I. A French garnish for slices of meat, consisting of cooked cauliflowers with sauce mornay, sprinkled with grated cheese and breadcrumbs, and then browned. II. A garnish of cauliflowerets and a demi-glace mixed with diluted meat juices of the main dish. This is served with joints. III. There is also a duBarry soup made from cauliflowers and stock with cream added. IV. Beef consommé slightly thickened with tapioca, garnished with cubes of royale, cauliflowerets, and chervil. See also CONSOMMÉ.

Dublin Bay prawns (*Nephrops norvegicus*), delicious small shellfish which are not prawns at all, but Norway lobster. They are not scampi, which are a variety of *Nephrops norvegicus* found only in the Adriatic, and are larger.

Dublin Bay prawns and smoked salmon platter

The Dublin Bay prawn gets its name in a curious way. About 150 years ago, when all the fishing boats were sailing ships and had no refrigeration to speak of, all shellfish caught in the nets were cooked immediately and eaten, as they would soon have gone bad if kept. They became the "perks" or gratuity of the crew and their womenfolk on board. Sailing ships of all nations used to anchor in Lambay Deep, a sheltered spot off the coast of north Dublin, before setting sail to fish their way home. All the freshly caught shellfish would be cooked by the women, who would sell them in the streets of Dublin as "Dublin Bay prawns." The money they got for them was theirs to spend on what they wanted.

Dublin Bay prawns are found in most of the colder waters of the European continental shelf and, as they breed all the year round, they are always in season. Freshly caught ones should not be used for a prawn cocktail; they are too delicate in flavour. They are best steamed, then shelled, and turned in butter with salt and a little lemon juice. Many of the Irish catch are frozen and exported to France and Germany as well as England, where they are usually sold as scampi, and served fried, curried, and in a cream sauce. The frozen ones are not to be compared in flavour to the freshly cooked ones.

Dublin coddle, a traditional Irish dish which used to be eaten on Saturday night in Dublin after the pubs closed. It consists of sliced onions, sliced potatoes, thick rashers of bacon, and sausages put in a saucepan in layers. It is well seasoned and water to the depth of ¼ of the saucepan is added; it is covered and cooked slowly for 1½–2 hours.

Dublin lawyer, a traditional Irish dish consisting of a live lobster split in two. The flesh, cut into chunks, is cooked in butter; it is flambéed with 2 tablespoons warm Irish whiskey, then 1 cup cream is added. The whole is heated, put back in the shells, and served.

Dublin rock, a 19th-century Irish cold sweet, made from butter or very thick cream beaten with double the quantity of ground almonds, sugar, and a little brandy, until the mixture is light, white, and stiff. It is left until the next day in a cold place, then broken up into rough lumps, piled on a dish, and decorated with sliced angelica and shredded split almonds.

duchesse, I. A French garnish for meat consisting of *pommes duchesse* made into varying shapes and sizes, with sauce madère. See POMME DE TERRE (POMMES DUCHESSE). II. A cream sauce beaten with butter and cream and garnished with chopped cooked tongue and mushrooms. III. A chicken consommé with sago, shredded lettuce, and plain royale. See also CONSOMMÉ.

duchesse d'angoulême, an excellent French pear which ripens and keeps throughout the winter. It is large and of a rather ugly, knobbly shape, with a mottled skin.

duchesses, small French petit fours made from 2 oz. pounded sweet almonds and the same quantity of pounded filberts (hazelnuts), blended with an egg white. Then 1¼ lb. (2½ cups) sugar and 2 oz. grated bitter chocolate are added, with 3 more egg whites. The mixture is put into a pastry bag, piped into little balls, and then baked in a moderate oven.

duck, a web-footed water bird of which there are many varieties. Many of these are bred domestically; some for food, others for their eggs, and some for their decorative quality. In Great Britain, the white Aylesbury duck is the largest and the best to eat; whereas the Indian runner, and khaki Campbell, are the best layers. The Aylesbury, dressed, weighs about 4/5 lb., and is usually stuffed with a mixture of breadcrumbs, chopped onion, and a little fresh sage. After roasting, it is served with applesauce. The meat is dark and succulent. The traditional British vegetable to serve with the domestic duck is green peas. Young birds, under 6 months of age, are called duckling.

There are several British varieties of wild duck, the largest and the best being undoubtedly mallard. (This duck, incidentally, does not taste fishy as, contrary to sources which indicate otherwise, it feeds on seeds and marsh plants.) It is in season from autumn to spring, but is at its best from November to January. It is usually roasted lightly, and served with a sauce of port or red wine mixed with the pan juices, lemon or orange juice, mushroom ketchup, cayenne pepper, black pepper, and salt. A little brandy is added and is poured over the bird and set aflame. Wild duck can also have an orange sauce or salad served with it. Widgeon and teal are varieties of wild duck and are prepared in the same way but, as they are smaller, the cooking time is less. See also ANITRA; BUFFEL-HEADED DUCK; CANARD; CANETON; CANVASBACK DUCK; EEND; ENTE; KACZKA; LONG ISLAND DUCK; OSTROPEL; PATO; PILES CEPETIS; RATE; SCOTER; UTKA; WILD DUCK.

salt duck, is a speciality of Wales. The duck is cleaned, then immersed in a cooled brine made from 2 lb. salt, 1½ lb. brown sugar, 1 oz. saltpetre, 8 pints (16 cups) water, 1 bay-leaf, thyme, and peppercorns, for 2 days. It is then washed and cooked with half water and half cider to cover, for 2 hours. It is served with hot onion sauce.

dufferin, A French fish consommé slightly curried and garnished with rice, small pieces of sole, and curried fish quenelles. See also CONSOMMÉ.

dugléré, à la, a French method of cooking and serving white fish, such as halibut, turbot, sole, etc. It was devised by the French chef Dugléré at the ''Aux Trois Frères Provençaux'' restaurant in 1786. It is poached in white wine and butter with chopped shallots, parsley, and seasonings. The stock is reduced, and cream, peeled and chopped tomatoes, more butter, and a squeeze of lemon juice are added, allowed to cook, and then poured over the fish. It is often used for *carrelet.*

düğün is a Turkish word for a feast held on the occasion of a wedding or circumcision. See also ÇORBA.

düğün eti, a Turkish mutton stew for which the mutton is cut into large cubes and fried with quartered onions in mutton fat. The mutton and onions are then covered with water and a squeeze of tomato purée and a flavouring of lemon juice is added and all is stewed.

dulce de leche, a Spanish pudding made from 10 egg yolks whipped with ½ lb. (1 cup) white sugar, 4 tablespoons flour, and 1 teaspoon grated lemon peel. Then 1 pint (2 cups) milk is heated, combined with the egg mixture, and stirred over heat until it thickens, as for custard. It is poured into a greased shallow dish and is left until cold. Then it is cut into fingers, dipped in stiffly beaten egg white, rolled in breadcrumbs, and fried in butter.

dulceatza, a Rumanian sweet made from various fruits and rose petals from the world-famous Valley of Roses near Kazanluik, which provides three quarters of the world's attar of roses.

dulse (Rhodymenia palmata; Dilsea carnosa), the common name for 2 edible seaweeds which are entirely unrelated but very similar. Also both are a purplish-brown, edible seaweed, and both are rich in mineral salts. Dulse is also called dillisk or dellesk, and it is collected on parts of the Scottish coast, the west coast of Ireland, and on the northern shores of the Mediterranean. It requires lengthy boiling. The celebrated cook, Soyer, whose name was execrated in Ireland because of the poverty of the soups recommended by him to feed the famine victims of 1847, included dulse as an ingredient of his St. Patrick's soup. Dulse can be bought dried in Dublin and other Irish towns. If dried, it should be soaked in water for a few hours before being cooked, then put in a saucepan with milk to cover it, 2 tablespoons butter, salt, and pepper and simmered for about 3 hours. It is then chopped finely, and added to mashed potato, soups, or broth. It is also used in making jellies. Very small quantities, raw and dried, are pleasant to chew with drinks, but should be taken sparingly as the salt induces thirst.

dumesnil, a French consommé of beef garnished with slices of poached beef marrow, vegetable julienne, and chopped chervil. See also CONSOMMÉ.

dumplings, I. Small round balls made of various farinaceous ingredients, such as flour, breadcrumbs, or even mashed potato, mixed with fat, water, or egg or egg white, and salt. In England, they are usually made with double the quantity of flour to grated suet, salt, and water, and are poached with a stew or soup. They are a traditional accompaniment of boiled salt beef and are an important constituent of some beef stews. They are light and filling, and should not be larger than a big walnut before being cooked, as they swell. II. Sweet dumplings are also traditional in Britain, especially apple dumplings. A peeled, cored, and sugared apple is encased in the dough (made as described above) and wrapped in a cloth before being boiled in water for at least 1 hour. They are drained and served with cream or custard. III. Dumplings are eaten a great deal in Germany, in many forms; sometimes yeast is added to them. They are also popular in Austria, Scandinavia, Poland, Hungary, and Russia, but many of these dumplings bear little relation to the British one. The quenelle and gnocchi are a very superior form of dumpling. See also BOLLER; CSURGATOTT TÉSZTA; ERDAPFEL, KNÖDL; KLETSKI; KLUSKI; KNAIDLACH; KNAIDLE; KNEDLE; KNEDLÍKY; KNÖDEL; GALUSKA; GALUSHKI; MELBOLLER.

dumplings for garnishing soups, are made from ½ pint (1 cup) cold water with 4 oz. (½ cup) butter in it brought to the boil, and 4 oz. (1 cup) flour is added, and the mixture is stirred over a low heat until it comes away from the sides of the pan. When cool, 4 egg yolks are beaten in, one by one, and a pinch of ground cardamom and of salt are added. Lastly, the egg whites are folded in, and balls the size of a marble are formed. These are simmered for about 2 minutes in boiling, salted water until they rise to the surface, and are then skimmed off and added to hot clear soup.

Dundee cake, a famous Scottish fruit cake made like a Christmas cake, but with blanched and split almonds generously sprinkled on top. These are added after the cake has been baking for 1 hour, so that they become browned by the end of cooking time.

Dunlop, the only Scottish hard cheese, named after the town of Dunlop in Ayrshire, where it was first made by Barbara Gilmour in 1688. It is similar to cheddar in flavour but is whiter and has a thinner rind. It has a high moisture content, so does not keep or travel well. It is good for cooking, especially for toasted cheese dishes.

durian (Durio zibethinus), the fruit of a Malayan tree which varies in size from 5 to 8 lb. and is covered in prickles. It has a soft, cream-coloured pulp, which, when properly mature, has an almond-custard taste. However, if over-ripe, it smells and some think it tastes like rotting vegetable refuse. It is used for cakes, ice cream, jam, and canning.

duroc, a French method of cooking chicken by sautéeing it in butter with mushrooms and herbs. It is garnished with tomatoes and new potatoes. See also POULET, SAUTÉ DUROC.

Dutch cheeses, see KAAS.

Dutch sauce, see HOLLANDAISE.

duveč, a traditional Yugoslavian meat casserole. It is made from any meat, but more usually pork or lamb, cut into fillets or chops, and first browned in oil. Onions, potatoes, rice, tomatoes, green peppers, and often other available vegetables are added. All are well seasoned with salt, pepper, paprika, and herbs, barely covered with water, and cooked gently until the meat is done and almost all the liquid is absorbed. Duveč simply means casserole and the dish could also be made with fish.

duxelles, a culinary preparation of 4 shallots, 2 tablespoons parsley, 1 onion, and 1 lb. mushrooms; all are chopped finely, squeezed in a towel to remove the moisture, and stewed slowly together with 1 heaped tablespoon butter until every trace of moisture has evaporated, leaving a dry residue with a predominating aroma of mushroom and shallots. Dry duxelles is kept in a screw-top jar and used for flavouring as the need arises.

duxelles sauce, a classical French sauce made of ½ pint (1 cup) white wine and 2 small chopped onions and shallots boiled until reduced by half. Then ½ pint (1 cup) sauce velouté is added together with 1 tablespoon duxelles. It is reboiled before serving with fish, rabbit, veal, or vegetable dishes. Mushroom sauce is sometimes called duxelles sauce, but correctly it should be made as above.

dynia, Polish for pumpkin or edible gourd. Pumpkins, when young, may be served fried like an eggplant; they are also sometimes boiled in salted water, drained, and eaten with bread sauce.

dynia duszona, a favourite way of preparing pumpkin by parboiling, then simmering in milk, butter, and herbs. This sauce is thickened by the addition of 2 egg yolks to 1 pint (2 cups) of liquid, and is reheated, but not reboiled, or it will curdle.

dyrejøtt, Norwegian for deer. See HJORTEKJØTT.

dyrekølle, Danish for venison.

dyrekølle stegt, roast leg of venison, which is prepared by first skinning the meat and removing any sinews. Strips of fat salt pork are seasoned and inserted at intervals along the leg, which is then rubbed in oil and baked in a moderate oven on a rack for about 3 hours, basting frequently with melted butter.

When the meat is tender, a wine sauce is made, consisting of the strained gravy from the pan, blended with a paste of creamed butter and flour (*beurre manié*), together with ½ pint (1 cup) fresh stock, 2 tablespoons apple vinegar, 1 tablespoon red currant jelly, 1 tablespoon grated orange peel, and 1 gill (¼ cup) Madeira or sherry. This mixture is cooked until thickened, then ¼ pint (½ cup) sour cream is added and the sauce used for further basting of the meat. Finally, the sauce is strained and served separately.

In parts of Denmark, this dish is served with a simple sour cream and gravy sauce.

dziczyzna, Polish for game, of which all kinds, both feathered and ground, abound in the vast forests of Poland. Hunting is a tradition among both the rich and the poor, and game often finds its way into the peasant's stew pot. The famous hunter's dish, *bigos,* has been immortalized in Polish poetry. Sour cream and red cabbage are usual accompaniments. See also BAŻANT; BEKASY; CIETRZEW; GAME; JELENIA; KUROPATWA; PRZEPIORKA.

dzikie geşi, Polish for wild goose. The same method of preparation can be used for wild duck which is called *dzikie kaczki.*

dzikie geşi duszone, is one recipe for braised wild goose; first, the birds are marinated for two days in a cold solution of boiled vinegar and water (double quantity of water), onion, carrot, herbs, and spices. After being rubbed with ground juniper and salt, they are browned in butter and then casserole-cooked, covered in an equal mixture of the marinade and stock with 1 tablespoon capers and 6 mushrooms; then ½ pint (1 cup) sour cream blended with 1 teaspoon flour is added 1–1½ hours later. Macaroni, rice, or wild rice can accompany this dish.

Another method is to omit the sour cream but to add olives, Madeira (or sherry), a bay leaf, a sprig of thyme, and a pinch of nutmeg.

dzikie geşi pieczone, a Polish recipe for roast wild goose or wild duck. To preserve tenderness, the birds are cleaned immediately upon killing, although plucking may be deferred. After hanging for one week, boiling marinade is poured over them. The game are then wrapped in moistened cheesecloth and refrigerated a further 2 days. At the time of cooking, they are salted further, rubbed with marjoram, stuffed with onion and apple, and roasted in a moderate oven for 15–20 minutes to the lb., being basted frequently with melted butter. Toward the end of cooking time, they are sprinkled with cold water to brown the skin. They are served with a sharp jelly (see GŁÓG).

ear-shell, see ORMER.

earth nut, I. *Buniun flexuosum; Conopodium denudatum,* a small form of truffle about the size of a hazelnut, which grows all over Britain and Ireland in woody places. At one time in Ireland, where it is also called fairy potato or pig nut, a serious study was made of their potential as a food-source, but their small size and the labour and expense involved in digging them out made the proposition uneconomic. They are eaten widely in Europe, particularly in Holland.

When the "nut" is ripe, the leaf is light green, feathery, and hairy; the long white stem goes deep into the soil, with the little nut at the bottom. After washing, the nut is eaten raw. II. It is also another name for peanut (*Arachis hypogaea*).

East India mayonnaise, an Anglo-Indian sauce served with fish cakes or boiled salmon. To prepare it a finely sieved clove of garlic and 1 teaspoon good curry powder are added to ½ pint (1 cup) of thick mayonnaise.

Easter, a festival celebrated by the Christian Church to mark the Resurrection of Christ. The word comes from the name of the Anglo-Saxon goddess of Light and Spring, Eostre. Special dishes were cooked in her honour, so that the year would be endowed with fertility. A small spiced bun was baked, and it is possible that the hot cross bun derives from this. Simnel cake is an Easter cake in Britain. Chocolate Easter eggs are given as presents. All over the world, celebrations are held and special dishes are made for Easter. See also ARNAKI STI SOUVLA; BUN; KOULOURAKIA; KULICH; LAMBROPSOMO; MAYIERITSA; PASKHA; PRESNITZ.

ebleskiver, a North American fried cake, popular in Wisconsin among people of Danish origin. They are made from a thin batter of ½ lb. (2 cups) flour, 1 teaspoon baking soda, 2 eggs, 1 pint (2 cups) thick sour milk or cream or buttermilk, and a pinch of salt. They are cooked in a *skiver pan* which is specially made for such cakes and is set with hollows. A little fat is put in each hollow, and the batter is spooned in just to half fill each one. The cakes are allowed to brown and are then turned; all the cooking is done on a low heat, so that the insides of the cakes are properly cooked. It is served hot with brown or white sugar, jam, or jelly. See also AEBLESKIVER.

ébouillanter, French for to scald, a process used to facilitate the peeling of certain food, such as almonds; it is called blanching in English.

écailler, French for to scale, that is, to remove the scales of a fish with a knife before cooking.

écalottes, see ANODONTA.

écalure, a French word meaning the outer skin, peel, or shell of fruit, nuts, and vegetables both soft and hard. It is also the shells of eggs and shellfish.

écarlate, à l', French for a process whereby pork or beef is pickled in brine and then boiled. The saltpetre added to the brine gives the meat a reddish tinge, hence it is known in France as à l'écarlate (scarlet).

Eccles cakes, small English cakes similar to Banbury cakes, except that there is no candied peel in them, and they can be round as well as oval in shape. Originally, Eccles cakes were filled with black currants and chopped mint leaves.

échalote, French for shallot, which is used a great deal in France to flavour stews or braised dishes, and as a garnish.

beurre d'échalote, made with 6 peeled shallots cooked in water to cover for 10 minutes, then pounded in a mortar. When cool, the equivalent amount of butter is blended in, then all is sieved. It is served cold, in cubes, with grilled meats, in cold hors d'oeuvre mixtures, or as a sauce ingredient.

essence d'échalote, made from ½ pint (1 cup) white wine or white wine vinegar boiled for 5 minutes with 4 tablespoons chopped peeled shallots, then strained and bottled for subsequent use in sauces.

semoule d'échalote, a commercially made product consisting of dried and finely ground shallots, sold in small tins; it is known in English as shallot powder. It is excellent for adding to any dish calling for fresh shallots.

échaude, a French pastry which is poached in water before being cooked in the oven. This is an extremely old method of pastry making and it is mentioned in a Charter of 1202, where there is a reference to "buns called eschaudati." Hot water used to be poured onto pastry dough to make it rise.

échine de porc, French for chine or spareribs of pork, usually cooked as a loin; also called épinée (dialect) and *palette.* It comprises the shoulder or bladebone, with 4 ribs from the neck attached. It is not the same cut as the American spareribs. See diagram page xxvi.

éclair, a French pastry made with chou paste, and usually filled after cooking with *crème pâtissière* and iced on top. It can also have savoury fillings, as for hors d'oeuvre. The most usual shape is a long thick finger, but the savoury ones are often round. See also RELIGIEUSE.

écorce, French for the outer skin or rind of fruits, such as lemon or orange, and for bark, such as cinnamon. When the rind is grated it is called zeste.

écossaise, à l', a French consommé made from mutton broth, with pearl barley and a *brunoise* of carrot, celery, and leek. See also CONSOMMÉ.

écosser, French verb meaning to pod peas and beans.

écraser, French for to flatten, pound, or crush aromatic fruits or seeds; or to make oven-dried bread into breadcrumbs by the same method.

écremer, French for to skim cream from milk. *Écremeuse* is the word for a separator, a mechanical device used in dairies for the skimming process. It also applies to a French china gravy boat marked G (*grasse*) at one end and M (*maigre*) at the other. The M end has an inner enclosed spout which prevents fat from being poured with the gravy onto the plate. Known in 19th-century England as a creamer.

écrevisses, French for freshwater crayfish. *Écrevisses à pattes blanches* are the smaller kind of crayfish, *écrevisses à pattes rouges* are the larger kind, also called *écrevisses de la Meuse.*

écuelle, French for a deep dish used for serving vegetables.

écume, French for scum on stock or jams; *écumer* is the verb form signifying the removal of this scum; *écumoire* is a perforated spoon used for skimming scum from stock.

écureuil, French for squirrel; the French cook it in the same way as rabbit. See also GIBIER.

Edam, a Dutch cheese made from cow's milk, which gets its name from the town of Edam near Amsterdam. The fat content must not be less than 40%. The rind is a bright red and the cheese an orange-yellow colour; it is mild in flavour, and not very distinguished. It weighs from 1 to 5 lb. and is spherical in shape, with a flattened top and bottom; there are larger versions of Edam called *commissie* (6–9 lb.) and *middelbare* (10–14 lb.). Edam is widely exported, and in France it is known as tête de maure.

edamer, an Austrian cheese, made in the Steiermark and Salzburg; it is a copy of the Dutch Edam.

eddik, Norwegian for vinegar.

eddike, Danish for vinegar.

edelpilzkäse, one of the most popular Austrian soft cheeses, which comes from the Steiermark. It is a full-cream (vollfett) cheese and weighs nearly 12 lb. The paste is white or ivory, with slight blue veining; it becomes crumbly if kept for long. It has a sharp and distinctive, slightly mouldy flavour, quite unlike any other cheese.

edge-bone, see AITCH-BONE.

Edinburgh fog, a Scottish pudding made from stiffly whipped cream, with vanilla sugar to taste, and with crushed ratafia biscuits and some blanched and chopped almonds mixed with it. It is served cold.

Edinburgh gingerbread, as gingerbread, but with nuts added.

Edinburgh rock, a Scottish sweetmeat (confection) made from crushed lump sugar, cream of tartar, water, colouring matter, and flavouring. The sugar and water are dissolved (1 lb. sugar to ½ pint water) and, when nearly boiling, ½ teaspoon cream of tartar is added, and it is boiled without stirring until it reaches 250° F. It is removed from the heat, and the colouring and flavouring are added. It is then poured onto a cold buttered slab. When cool, it is pulled until it becomes dull and opaque, cut into pieces with scissors, and left in a warm room for at least 24 hours. It should be powdery and soft.

Edirne, a Turkish soft white cheese made from ewe's milk. It is one of the most popular Turkish cheeses and gets its name from the important city Edirne in northwest Turkey, near the Graeco–Bulgarian frontier. It is also made in the Vilayets region and in the provinces of Ankara, Konya, and Bursa.

eel (*Anguilla anguilla*), a snake-like, migratory fish which inhabits rivers and streams but goes to the sea to breed. There are four kinds of eel: the grig, the snig, the sharp-nosed, and the broad-nosed. The two latter kinds are the best to eat.

eel

Eels must be kept alive until they are required for a meal, for it is better to skin them just before cooking as it makes them more digestible; their flesh is nourishing and gelatinous, and they are considered a delicacy throughout Europe. Holland is a great eel-eating country, but English and Irish eels are sweeter to the taste. In England they are mostly smoked, but in the East End of London, jellied eels have been sold on barrows for several hundred years. Eel pie used to be very popular, but it is not seen very often nowadays. In France, eel is used in soups and matelotes; it is fried, grilled, and braised in white or red wine; stuffed with breadcrumbs, herbs, and pounded fish and baked; and made into a hot or cold *ballottine* (an old name for galatine).

Every country has its own method of cooking eels, and uses in its recipes whatever ingredients are its particular specialities. For instance, in Hungary, cream and paprika are used; in Spain, ground almonds, oil, and garlic. In Russia eels are sometimes used in a *kulebyaka*. See also AAL; AALSOEP; ÅL; ANGUILA; ANGUILLA; ANGUILLE; AOL; EIROS; ELVERS; PALING; WĘGORZ.

eelpout or **barbot** (*Lota lota*), I. A European and North American freshwater fish, and a relative of the marine cod. The liver is very fat and highly esteemed as a food, but the flesh is not very good eating. II. *Zoarces viviparus* is also called eelpout, but is of a different suborder. It resembles a large, fat eel, and is coarse to eat. See also BURBOT.

eend, Dutch for duck, popular and plentiful in Holland. See also DUCK.

gevulde eend, stuffed duck. Chestnut stuffing is prepared by first making two slits across the flat side of the chestnuts, which are then boiled in water for about 25 minutes, whereupon they are peeled and cooked in water or stock for a further 20 minutes. Meanwhile, the duck has had boiling water poured over it, and its inside rinsed with the boiling water and rubbed with seasoning. The bird is stuffed with the chestnuts and roasted in butter in a moderate oven for about 1½ hours; the pan should be very close-fitting and the basting frequent.

effeuiller, a French verb meaning, in culinary terms, to strip the leaves or petals from a plant, such as a globe artichoke or an herb.

efterrätter, Swedish for the dessert, sweet, or pudding course. This course is an important part of Swedish eating, and fruit soups (*fruktsoppe*) and fruit creams are as popular in Sweden as in other Scandinavian countries. Cream is an ingredient in many dessert recipes and usually accompanies all dessert and pudding dishes. Jam is also much used in puddings, as well as in fillings for open tarts. The *fromage* desserts (see *citronfromage*), which are a form of mousse, are traditional. Pancakes and layer cakes are also popular. See also BÄRKRÄM; FRUKT; GRÄDDE.

egg, the spheroidal body produced by the females of birds and some reptiles, containing the germ of a new bird or reptile, surrounded by a rough membrane or shell. Fish also produce eggs, but these are known as roe. All eggs can be used as food, but the one most generally eaten is the egg of the domestic hen.

Eggs are very nutritious, and are composed of the white or albumen, a thick transparent liquid in which is enclosed the yolk or vitellus. The yolk is composed of fats and minerals. It is high in cholestrines, which makes it unsuitable for people on fat-free diets, for whom not more than 2–3 per week are recommended.

Eggs can be eaten raw, either beaten up in milk, or with the addition of spicy sauces. Boiled eggs, fried eggs, poached eggs, scrambled eggs or eggs beaten with, or without, a little milk or cream and cooked in butter, are the most usual methods of serving. Cooked in a small cocotte pot with butter or oil, they are called *en cocotte*. See also OMELETTE. Eggs are also much used, either whole, or the white and yolk separately, in the making of cakes, puddings, soufflés, and sauces. It is essential that they are fresh when used. The simplest way to find this out is to put them in a bowl of water; if they are fresh, they will sink to the bottom; if bad, the gas in them will cause them to rise to the top. Eggs can be preserved by rubbing them all over with fat, or immersing them in isinglass solution.

Eggs which are boiled for 7–10 minutes are known as hard-boiled eggs. These can be served in a number of sauces, such as cheese, onion, and curry, or used as a garnish. They can also be served as stuffed eggs; they are sliced in half and the hard-cooked yolks taken out, mashed, and mixed with grated cheese, melted butter, and herbs, and then put back in the white halves.

See also AEG; ÄGG; AVGA; EGGE; EI; EIEREN; HUEVOS; JAJA; OEUFS; OMELETTE; OVOS; UOVO; YAITSÁ.

stuffed eggs

egg and parsley sauce, see EGG SAUCE.

egg butter, a Finnish garnish made from hard-boiled eggs mashed into butter.

egg sauce, a Scottish sauce consisting of a light béchamel with the addition of sieved yolks of hard-boiled eggs and the whites cut into thin strips. Chopped parsley is sometimes added, and the sauce then is known as egg and parsley sauce. This is often served with boiled fish.

In the U.S. there are many ways of serving eggs which are not practised in Europe. The most usual are described here:

creole egg-bake, eggs baked in individual casseroles, on a bed of puréed onion, celery, and green pepper, mixed with a little flour and tomato sauce. The top is sprinkled with crushed cheese crackers, and the dish is cooked for about 20 minutes in a slow oven.

eggs Benedict, poached eggs placed on top of split toasted English muffins, with a slice of cold boiled ham. Sauce hollandaise, diluted with cream, is poured round.

eggs Huntingdon, hard-boiled eggs put into a white sauce made with milk and chicken stock. The mixture is put into a buttered dish, sprinkled with grated cheese, cayenne pepper, and buttered cracker crumbs, and then baked until the top is brown.

eggs New Orleans, as *creole egg-bake*, but covered with grated cheese before baking.

scalloped eggs, hard-boiled eggs put in a buttered baking dish on top of buttered cracker crumbs and covered with white sauce and chopped cooked ham, chicken, veal, or shellfish. More sauce is put on top, then cracker crumbs. It is baked until the top is browned.

scrambled eggs, country style, butter is heated in an omelette pan, and when it is melted, eggs are broken in, whole. The yolks only are pricked with a fork, and the eggs are cooked until the whites are partially set, then stirred until all is creamy.

shirred eggs, see OEUFS EN COCOTTE.

egge, Norwegian for egg.

eggedosis, a national dessert consisting of 10 yolks and 1 white of egg beaten together with 2 teaspoons cold water and 8 tablespoons castor sugar. This is usually done over hot water in a double boiler, although some versions are made simply by beating. A little brandy or Madeira wine is poured into individual glasses, which are then filled with the egg mixture. If the alcohol is omitted, a glass of Madeira is served with the dessert, together with macaroons and meringues. This dessert is served by tradition after church on Christmas Day, and on other feasts. See also CHRISTMAS.

eggplant (*Solanum melongena*), a plant native to Asia, the fruits of which are eaten as a vegetable and are of many different kinds. Some are egg-shaped, others long like cucumbers, and yet others round like tomatoes. They are usually deep purple in colour. They may be peeled or not, and are baked, fried, frittered, stuffed, and used as an ingredient in various dishes, particularly in those of the Balkans, Turkey, Yugoslavia, and Albania (see IMAM BAYILDI). Before cooking, they are usually cut in half, salted, and left for about an hour. The moisture is poured off before further preparation. It is known sometimes as aubergine in England, and always by that name in France. An alternative French name is melangène. See also BAKLAZHANY; BERENJENA; MELANZANE; MELISA; MELITZANES; MOUSAKÁ; PATLIDJAN; VINETE.

églefin, French for fresh haddock; also called *aiglefin*, *aigrefin*, *egrefin*, *morue noire*, *morue St. Pierre*.

eglefin fumé, French for smoked haddock.

égouttoir, French for a wide-mouthed earthenware jug which has a drainer for cheese curds on top. The top is called a *faiselle*. It is a convenient utensil for making small quantities of cottage cheese at home. The jug catches the whey and dispenses with hanging up the muslin to drip.

égrapper, a French culinary term meaning to take grapes or, berries from their stalk.

egrefin, an alternative name for *eglefin*, French for fresh haddock.

égrener, a French culinary term meaning to detach corn or other grain from the stalk.

égruger, a French culinary term meaning to pulverise in a mortar or mill, to grind. *Égrugeoir* is the French word for a wooden salt mill.

Egyptian onion, an alternative name for tree onion. See
ONION.

ei(er), German for egg(s); also *eigelb* (egg yolk) and *eiweiss*
(egg white). *Ruehrei* is scrambled egg. See also EGG.

eierkäse, egg cheese, a German sweet-savoury pudding
made from 6 eggs beaten with 1½ pints (3 cups) milk and 3
tablespoons sugar, with a few drops of lemon juice. It is
strained and cooked over a low heat until it starts to curdle,
when it is immediately removed, stirred well, and put in a
wetted mould in a cool place. A pint (2 cups) of cream is
boiled (scalded) with 2 oz. (2 heaped tablespoons) sugar, a
little cinnamon stick, and lemon peel. Then 2 egg yolks are
beaten with 1 tablespoon milk and a pinch of corn flour (cornstarch) or potato flour. This is stirred into the boiling cream
(the cinnamon stick having been removed) until a smooth
sauce is made. It is poured over the cold, turned-out mould.

eiernockerln, a variation of the German nockerln made
from 2 or 3 eggs whipped up and poured over nockerln in a
frying pan. The contents are stirred with a fork until a consistency resembling that of scrambled eggs is achieved. It is
served at once, with a green salad.

eierstich, a baked custard made from 3 eggs, ½ pint (1 cup)
milk or stock, and 1 teaspoon potato flour all baked in a *bain-
marie* and cut into strips when cold. In Germany it is used as
a garnish for clear soups.

eider duck (*Somateria mollissima*), a bird chiefly prized for
the down on its breast, used for eiderdowns. The flesh is not
worth eating, but the eggs are a great delicacy and particularly relished in Iceland, the Farne Islands, and Spitsbergen,
Norway.

eierapfel, German for eggplant; known also as *eierfrucht* and
eierpflanze.

eieren, Dutch for eggs. See also EGG; SPIEGELEIER.

gebakken eieren met uien en kaas, a dish of baked eggs and
onions with cheese. A medium-sized onion is grated and
lightly browned with 3 tablespoons butter in a baking dish,
and sprinkled with 4 tablespoons hard grated cheese over
which 6 eggs are broken, keeping the yolks intact. Then ¼
pint (½ cup) cream is then poured over, and the dish topped
by more cheese and baked in a moderate oven.

eierkuckas, an Alsatian pancake, made with a batter mixed
with cream and red currant jelly.

einbren, the Yiddish word for a flour or matzo used to thicken
gravy. The word itself means thickening.

einkorn (*Triticum monococcum*), a coarse grain wheat, cultivated in poor soils in Spain, Italy, Switzerland, south Germany, and formerly in Provence. It is usually known by this
German name which means "one grain," but it is also called
German wheat. Macaroni is said to have been made from this
grain originally. See also ÉPAUTRE.

einlauf, a Jewish and German garnish for soup made from
about ¼ lb. (1 cup) flour mixed with salt and 1 egg mixed with
a little water. This is poured very slowly over the back of a
spoon into boiling soup, which is then covered and allowed to
cook for 3 minutes.

eiros, Portuguese for eels, which are often used in *caldeirada
à fragateira.* See also EEL.

eisbein, a German dish consisting of boiled, pickled shank of
pork, served with pease pudding, boiled potatoes, and sauerkraut.

ekshili tchorba, a Turkish mutton soup made from 3 pints (6
cups) mutton broth to which is added a thickening of 1 tablespoon flour, 2 eggs, 2 tablespoons lemon juice, and 2 tablespoons water. Diced cooked fat mutton is added as a garnish.

elbo, a Danish cheese of the samsoe variety which has the
same properties as danbo. It differs from samsoe both in
shape and in the colour of the rind, which is brownish red.
The curd is golden, but has fewer eyes in it than samsoe.

elder (*Sambucus nigra*), a very common European tree, bearing clusters of strongly aromatic white flowers which are followed by purplish black berries in equal profusion. Both the
berries and flowers are used in the making of country wines
and cordials, and a red wine is made from the berries. Elderberries are also often added to wines made from other wild
fruits because of their deep, rich colour and their muscatel
flavour. They are used, too, in the making of jam, jellies,
chutney, and ketchup. The flowers alone make a pleasant
white wine and are also used for flavouring—for instance, if a
bunch is added to gooseberries while they are cooking, it imparts a grape-like flavour to the fruit. When dried, the flowers
make a tea with a soothing quality.

elder

elder flower fritters, the heads of elder flowers are washed
in salt and water, dried carefully, then dipped in a batter and
fried until golden in deep hot oil. They are sprinkled with
sugar before serving.

elecampane (*Inula helenium*), a wild perennial plant, with
round, yellow blossoms rather like small sunflowers; it grows
freely and looks attractive in the garden. The Latin name
derives from a starchy property called inulin from which is
extracted a sugar called laevulose, giving the plant a commercial value today; the English name is born of a traditional association with Helen of Troy. The roots of elecampane were
once eaten, candied, as a sweetmeat (confection), and also
boiled as a vegetable.

elector's caps, SEE CUSTARD MARROW.

elgbiff, Norwegian for elk. Young elk is popular game in
Norway; it can be eaten roasted, stewed, or fried, or in some
parts of the country, it may be larded and pot-roasted like
venison. See also ELK.

elgbiff stekt på grill, grilled elk steak. The steak should be
at least 1-inch thick. It is brushed with butter and grilled for
about 10 minutes on each side. During the last 5 minutes,
large mushrooms brushed with butter are grilled with the
steak, which is garnished with more butter and seasoning.

elk (*Alces alces*), the largest existing member of the deer family, whose flesh, hide, and antlers are used to great advantage
by the Eskimos in Alaska. The American variety is called
moose. The flesh may be cooked as venison (all recipes can
be used), but there is a Russian recipe which is widely used in
North America. Smoked elk tongue is considered a delicacy.
See also DEER; ELGBIFF; OLÉN; REINDEER; VENISON.

ellies, Greek for olives. Greek olives are thought to be among
the best in the world and much of Greece's economy depends
on a successful olive harvest. The end of the harvest is a time
for celebration in feasting and merry-making. The fruit is considered most valuable and nourishing, and a Greek can always
make a satisfying meal from a dish of olives and brown bread.
Olive oil is an essential ingredient in Greek cooking; olives

are also pickled in brine, and great barrels of them can be seen in the town markets.

The history of the olive is as old as the mythological history of Greece. When the goddess Athene battled for supremacy against Poseidon, the gods decided in her favour because she owned an olive tree, which was deemed a more important gift to mankind than the salt spring that Poseidon, with his trident, had caused to flow from the rock on which stands the Acropolis. From the wood of the olive were made the sceptres of kings and so also, in contrast to the image of peace that the olive branch provides, were the arrows of Heracles. The wood served a domestic purpose too, being used in the making of many household goods and shepherds' crooks were also made of it.

Elvas plums, see AMEIXA.

elvers, the young of the European eel. They are about 2 inches long, transparent, and pale amber in colour. In the Severn River, England, they are caught by the million at the end of March and, after washing, are delicious cooked as whitebait. Sometimes they are also boiled in a cloth for several hours, then turned out and, when cold and jellied, cut into slices. At Epney, Glos, England, they are cooked in bacon fat until milky, then beaten eggs are added. They are eaten with the cooked bacon rashers, garnished with lemon.

elzekaria, a Basque peasant soup made with a large onion sliced and sautéed in pork or goose fat, a small white cabbage, shredded, ½ lb. soaked, dried haricot beans, 3 crushed garlic cloves, salt, pepper, and 2 quarts (8 cups) water, all simmered for at least 3 hours. A few drops of wine vinegar are poured into each plate before serving.

emballer, a French culinary term meaning to wrap a joint of meat, game, or poultry, or a pudding, in a cloth; or, in the case of meat, to wrap it in a slice of pork fat or a pig's caul before cooking.

émincé, French for a dish made from leftover roasted or braised meat. Contrary to what one might expect, it does not mean minced meat, which is *hachis,* but thin slices heated in a sauce. Poultry can also be served in this way. The verb is *émincer,* meaning to cut into thin slices (meat, poultry, vegetables, or fruit).

Emmenthal, a cheese from the Emmental valley in the Swiss canton of Berne. (It is known as Gruyère almost everywhere except in Switzerland.) The name Emmenthal has been current since the 16th century, but the character of the cheese has changed; it used to be made only in Alpine dairies but is now prepared in modern valley dairies with up-to-date machinery. It is made from cow's milk and is pale yellow in colour, with holes in the curd which vary from the size of a pea to that of a large round nut. These holes or "eyes" are formed by the influence of propionic acid bacteria. The rind is a dark yellow in colour, and dry. Emmenthal takes about 4 months to mature and keeps in good condition for years if well made. It is slightly milder in taste and softer in texture than a true Gruyère, and is without the faint smell of ammonia one associates with the latter. The principal difference is, however, the size; for export, it must weigh at least 143 lb., but it often attains 170 lb. It is a good cheese and is exported all over the world, when it must bear the word Switzerland stamped in red, as it is copied in many countries especially Germany where it is called emmenthaler.

emmer wheat (*Triticum dicoccum*), one of the earliest types of wheat grown in southern Europe, especially Switzerland and southern Germany.

empadinhas, small Portuguese pastries filled with chopped fish, olives, game, or mushrooms, and served hot or cold.

empanadas de batallon, small Spanish pasties filled with chopped ham, *chorizo,* or shellfish, and red peppers, slightly flavoured with onion. They are deep fried in hot olive oil and served hot.

empereur, an alternative French name, with *espadon,* for swordfish.

empotage, a French culinary term listing all the ingredients for a braise. *Empoter* is the verb meaning to put all the ingredients in the braising pot.

enchaud de porc à la périgourdine, a French method of cooking loin of pork, from Périgord. The 5- to 6-lb. loin is boned, the rind taken off, and the flat meat studded with small thick pieces of truffle and a few slivers of garlic; salt and pepper are added. It is rolled up and tied with string, like a thick sausage, and is then roasted with the bones and trimmings of meat. When golden, a pint (2 cups) of good stock is added, and it is covered and cooked slowly for about 2½ hours. When ready, the stock is poured off, allowed to get cold, and the fat removed. The jelly underneath is chopped and served round the cold, aromatic joint.

enchiladas, a spicy, rolled pancake of Mexican origin, popular in the U.S., especially near the Mexican border. A large flat griddle-cooked pancake is dipped in hot oil to soften, then in chilli sauce. It is sprinkled with grated cheese and rolled up. More chilli sauce and grated cheese are poured over before serving. (Chilli sauce in the U.S. varies in piquancy. It can be quite peppery, though nothing like the Chinese kind; generally, it is more like a tomato chutney.)

encornet, French for sleeve-fish, a variety of calamary.

endaubage, I. The French culinary term for the supplementary ingredients used in a *daube*. II. The French slang term for "bully" or corned beef.

endive (*Cichorium endivia*), a plant which was brought to Europe at a very early date from the East. In France and the U.S. what we know as endive is called chicory, and what we known as chicory is endive. To make things even more confusing, there is some tendency (though not general) to follow the U.S. usage in England!

There are many varieties of endive, but unless otherwise stated, the word endive denotes one of the curly leaved varieties such as the Anjou, the Meaux, the stag's horn, etc. The broad-leaved varieties are called Batavian endive. The bleaching or "hearting" of endive is produced by placing a piece of slate or shard in the centre of the plant when it is practically full-grown.

endive

Endive is an excellent salad but may also be braised and served as a vegetable. See also ANDITHIA; BRUSSELS LOF; CHICORÉE FRISÉE; ESCAROLE.

endive de Bruxelles, French for the witloof variety of chicory. In the U.S. it is known as Belgian endive.

endive gourilos, stumps of the curly endive blanched in salted water containing lemon juice or wine vinegar. After blanching they are drained and either sautéed in butter, fried in batter, or served *à la grecque.* A certain amount of the trimmed curly leaves, looking rather like a rosette, are left on the stump before cooking.

endivia, Italian for endive (curled-leaf, green).

endivie, German for endive (curled-leaf, green).

engelswurz, German for angelica.

English cheeses, see BATH CHEESE; BLUE CHESHIRE CHEESE; BLUE DORSET; CAERPHILLY CHEESE; CHEDDAR CHEESE; CHESHIRE CHEESE; COTHERSTONE; COTTAGE CHEESE; COTTENHAM; CREAM CHEESE; DAVENTRY; DERBY (DERBYSHIRE); DUNLOP; ESSEX; GLOUCESTER CHEESE; HORNERS; ILCHESTER; LANCASHIRE CHEESE; LEICESTERSHIRE CHEESE; LINCOLN CHEESE; ORKNEY; POT CHEESE; SAGE (SAGE CHEESE, SAGE LANCASHIRE); ST. IVEL CHEESE; SLIPCOTE; STILTON; SUFFOLK CHEESE; TRUCKLES; VICTORIA CHEESE; WENSLEYDALE CHEESE; WILTSHIRE CHEESE; YORK CHEESE.

English wheat, a variety of wheat called *forment renflé* in France. It is not cultivated in the British Isles in spite of its name, but is grown mostly in the Mediterranean region of France.

enkephalos, Greek for brains.

enoyauteur, a French implement for cracking nuts or fruit stones without crushing them.

enrober, French meaning for to coat one food with another.

ensalada, Spanish for salad. Usually in Spain, salad means lettuce with a dressing of oil and vinegar, but there are also salads of red or green peppers, tomatoes, cooked artichokes, and other vegetables.

ensalada de pimientos, sweet peppers are grilled, peeled, cut lengthways in half, and finely sliced (the stalks and seeds having been removed). Tomatoes, likewise skinned and seeded, and chopped onions are added. These ingredients are mixed together with a vinaigrette dressing and sprinkled with parsley.

ensalada de Sevilla, a salad of raw chicory chopped with stoned olives, sprinkled with tarragon, and dressed with vinaigrette dressing.

ensopado, Portuguese for thick soup, almost the consistency of a stew. It is made from a variety of vegetables and stock.

ente, German for duck. See also DUCK; GEFLÜGEL.

ente gedampfte, duck steamed with root vegetables, bay leaf, and sage.

entrada, a Greek dish rather like a pot roast, made with meat, usually beef, and vegetables such as onions, carrots, celery, tomatoes, and potatoes. The meat is left whole and cooked slowly, with only a little liquid, for several hours until it is quite tender.

entrecôte, a French cut of steak which means "between the ribs," and is usually taken from the top of the sirloin and ribs of beef. The word is sometimes used for the *contre-* or *faux-filet,* but a true entrecôte is cut between the ribs, the "côtes." It is usually grilled or fried. In the U.S. it is known as rib steak. See also CÔTES DE BOEUF, and diagram pages xxii–xxiii.

entrecuisse, a French culinary term for the second joint, or thick thigh, of poultry or winged game.

entrée, a French word meaning the dish following the fish course and coming before the meat. Nowadays, when it is not so common to eat a great number of courses, it can even consist of fish and be the third course. Or again, a dish that is termed an entrée, such as vol-au-vent, sweetbreads, or brains, a meat or fish course, can be the main course of a light meal. In the U.S. this is the most common usage. It can also be a cold dish.

entrelarder, I. A French culinary term for cooking meat with alternate layers, interlarded, of pork fat. II. It can also mean "streaky," i.e., meat with natural streaks of fat.

entremeses, Spanish for hors d'oeuvre, usually consisting of sardines, sausage, olives, onions, sweet peppers, etc. See also ESCABÈCHES; HORS D'OEUVRE.

entremets, a French culinary term which means literally "between dishes," but nowadays refers to the sweet or dessert course, served in France after the cheese.

enyrer, Norwegian for kidney.

enzyme, a complex organic chemical compound, usually a complex protein, which promotes a chemical reaction, acting as a catalyst—often, however, within a narrow operating temperature range. Enzymes have a very important part to play in digestive processes, in the tenderising of meat, in the production of milk curds, and in fermentation.

épaule, French for a shoulder cut of meat, for example,

épaule d'agneau, shoulder of lamb, etc. See table of cuts, page xxi.

épautre, a coarse grain wheat which used to be grown in Provence. It is supposed to be the wheat originally used for macaroni. It is also known as German wheat. See also EINKORN.

epergne, a centrepiece for a dining table, with little bowls attached to an ornamental stem. Epergnes were popular in Britain in Victorian times and held sweetmeats (confections), fruits, or nuts. In France today they are used for raw hors d'oeuvre. Although epergne appears to be a French word, the article itself is known in France as a *ménagère.*

éperlans, French for smelts.

éperons Bachiques, a French term meaning literally "spurs of Bacchus." It is used for highly spiced cold hors d'oeuvre, implying that they cause thirst, which they undoubtedly do.

épices, French for spices.

épigramme, a French cut of lamb which consists of the "eye" or best part of the end of neck or breast of lamb cutlet. Sometimes it is blanched first, and when cold, dipped in egg and breadcrumbs and grilled or fried. It is sometimes used as a garnish for a *blanquette* of lamb.

épinard, French for spinach, is used in many dishes in France; it is the essential ingredient in the French garnish, *Florentine.* New Zealand spinach is called *tétragone* in French. It is grown extensively in the south of France. See also SPINACH.

épine d'Espagne, French for azarole.

épine d'hiver, a French winter pear of excellent quality and very fragrant.

épinée, see ÉCHINE DE PORC.

épine-vinette, French for barberry. In France the green berries are often pickled in vinegar, like capers. The ripe ones are used for syrups, jam, and jelly, and are also candied and then dried. See also BARBERRY.

Epiphany, or Twelfth Night, January 6th, is the occasion in Europe for the giving of presents and feasting. In all Catholic countries, cakes are eaten. In France, *galette des rois* is made of flaky pastry or yeast dough shaped like a crown. In Italy *panettone* is served. Twelfth Night is known as "the little," or "women's Christmas" in Ireland, and goose or poultry is often served there.

épluchage, a French culinary term for the removal of the skin of fruit or vegetables.

époisses, an important French cow's milk cheese from the Côte d'Or (Burgundy). It is a soft cheese made from whole milk and is mould-inoculated. It is usually eaten fresh during the summer months. Époisses is sometimes flavoured with black pepper, cloves, or fennel seeds and soaked in white wine or *eau-de-vie de marc.* It is then called *époisses confits au vin blanc* or *au marc de Bourgogne.*

éponger, I. A French culinary term meaning to dry parboiled vegetables by putting them on paper or a cloth to absorb surplus moisture. II. It also means to drain fried foods in the same way.

équille, French for sand eel which is like a small smelt and is cooked in the same way.

érable, tarte à l', a tart, from the province of Quebec, Canada, which consists of a pastry shell with a cream filling to which has been added maple syrup.

erbsen, German for peas, usually dried, although green peas are sometimes called grünen erbsen. The more usual name is *schoten*.

erce, a French cheese made from cow's milk, from the Ariège district. It is in season from November to May.

erdapfel, south German for potato. In other parts of Germany it is *kartoffel*.

erdapfelknödl, an Austrian potato dumpling made from 1 lb. (2½ cups) mashed, baked jacket potato mixed with 3 tablespoons butter, 2 egg yolks, 2 tablespoons each of flour and semolina, and 1 tablespoon chopped chives. These are all mixed together, shaped into small dumplings, with minute croutons pressed into the middle of each one, and poached in salted water. See also DUMPLINGS.

erdbeer, German for strawberry.

erdbeer kaltschale, a German soup made from wild strawberries, puréed and mixed with sugar and white wine. It is served chilled and garnished with sugared whole wild strawberries.

erdélyi tokany, a traditional Hungarian stew from Transylvania; it is both simple and economical to make, and consequently very popular. Beef is cut into squares and placed in a saucepan with fat bacon, salt, pepper, and a little water and simmered until the meat is tender. Sliced onion is then added, and when this is tender, the tokany is ready to serve.

eremite, the trade-name of a blue cheese made in Canada. It is of the Roquefort type, but made from the milk of cows, not ewes.

Ermite, French for an old boar, which is used for making pâtés.

erte, Norwegian for pea.

ertesuppe, pea soup, served often as a main course followed by a dessert.

erve doce, Portuguese for an herb which is used a great deal in the south of Portugal. It is generally used dried and tastes like a mild, sweet marjoram. The name means literally "sweet grass."

ervilhas, Portuguese for green peas used often in stews or *cozido*.

ervy, a French soft, cow's milk cheese, not unlike a camembert in taste and texture. It is in season from November to May, and is made in the Champagne district.

erwt, Dutch for pea.

erwtensoep, pea soup. This soup should be left to stand overnight and served reheated and seasoned. It is made with 1 lb. (3 cups) split peas soaked overnight and cooked in water. When they are just tender, 2 pig's feet are added and simmered for 2 hours; then a piece of fresh bacon, about 1 lb. in weight, is included in the pot, together with 2 tablespoons parsley, 1 medium celeriac, 3 celery stalks with foliage, and 3 leeks and 2 onions which have been lightly browned in butter. Simmering is continued for a further hour, after which diced frankfurters are added. Before serving, the bacon is removed and served separately, by cutting it into slices and spreading it on pumpernickel bread.

eryngo (*Eryngium maritum*), sea-holly, an English seaside weed with thistle-blue flowers, greenish-blue leaves, and fleshy cylindrical roots. There is a similar *Eryngium* which grows wild on some of the northern coasts of the U.S., but its roots are fetid and unfit to eat. In the 17th and 18th centuries, jam used to be made from eryngo roots. The proportions were 1 lb. roots to ¾ lb. (1½ cups) sugar and 2 pints (4 cups) water.

eryngo candy. The roots are scraped and sliced, then after boiling they can be candied like angelica. It makes excellent toffee if the sliced root is cooked in water to cover and then this water added to the sugar and butter solution just as it is ready to set.

érythrin, the generic name for several varieties of thick freshwater fish with large heads and round jaws. They make excellent eating, and can be prepared and cooked as bass.

escabèches, a Spanish and Provençal hors d'oeuvre made from small fish such as anchovy, sardine, whiting, smelt, or mullet, all fresh. The fish is dipped in hot olive oil, then put in a deep earthenware pot. A marinade is made, mostly of olive oil but also of water and a little vinegar, with a carrot and onion, garlic, thyme, bay leaf, parsley, and pimento. This is poured over the fish and all is left in a cool place for 24 hours. The fish is served with the marinade.

Partridges are also prepared in a similar way, with the addition of white wine (see PERDIZ). See also ENTREMESES.

escalope, a French term used to describe a thin piece of meat (scallop) usually veal or fish flattened and fried in butter or oil.

escalope de veau, veal escallop. It is cut from the leg or fillet.

escargot, French for snail. The most popular variety, used in restaurants and for canning, are *helix pomatia*, often known in France as *hélices vigneronnes* or vineyard snails, from their fondness for vine or apple leaves as food. However, the small garden snail, *helix aspersa,* is most generally eaten by country people and is renowned for its succulence. This snail is known by many names in different parts of France: aspergille, colimaçon and jardinière in the north; caraguolo in Montpellier; cagouille, limaou, and limat in the Bordelais; caragaou, contar, and escargot escourgol in Provence; banarut in Arles; and bajaina at Grasse. All snails are first starved for about 10 days. They are then soaked in salted water with vinegar, and then rinsed and blanched in boiling, salted water until they emerge from their shells. Only the snails that emerge are edible; the others should be discarded. Then they are simmered in a court bouillon with white wine or stock. After this they are removed from their shells and the hard black part at the end of the tail, the cloaca and intestine, is removed. The snails are then ready to serve, and there is a variety of sauces which may accompany them.

Snails can also be fried in batter or cooked on skewers. Many millions are exported every year from France to all parts of the world. See also SNAILS.

escargot à l'arlésienne, 4 dozen prepared snails are put into a sauce made from 4 oz. diced salt pork browned in a saucepan. Then 2 tablespoons flour are stirred in, together with ½ bottle white wine, 3 garlic cloves, and 2 tablespoons chopped parsley. This is all boiled and slowly simmered until it has thickened, when 4 tablespoons Madeira wine and a pinch of cayenne pepper are added. The snails are removed, put back in their shells, and then replaced in the sauce. The mixture is stirred and boiled for 5 minutes, before serving with a squeeze of lemon and more parsley sprinkled on top.

escargots à la bourguignonne, 4 dozen prepared snails are put back in their shells with a sauce of ½ lb. (1 cup) softened butter thoroughly worked into a purée with 1 cup freshly chopped parsley, 1 finely grated shallot, and 2 large pounded cloves of garlic, all seasoned with a pinch of nutmeg, salt, and pepper. When the shells have been filled they are put onto a flat metal plate, or a snail dish which has indentations to hold the snails and is known in French as an escargotière, and are then heated, either in a hot oven or under a hot grill, for 5 minutes. This is the method used in Burgundy. In Gascony, olive oil is used instead of butter, chopped chives and leeks are added, and the sauce is called *l'aillada*. In Bordeaux, the *aillada* is made with 1 cup breadcrumbs soaked in milk, 1 tablespoon flour is added, and 1 egg yolk. This mixture is heated in a double boiler before pounding it up with herbs, garlic, shallot, etc., as above. It is sometimes flavoured with cloves and a pinch of allspice. In Montpellier, chopped ham and garlic are sautéed in butter, thickened with 2 tablespoons flour and a pinch of sugar, before adding ½ pint (1 cup) white wine. This is called *la cacalousada*. In the Languedoc, aïoli is used.

escargots à la poulette, ½ pint (1 cup) sauce *poulette* is mixed with 1 large browned, sliced, and chopped onion which has been moistened with a little white wine. The snails are heated in this for about 5 minutes.

escarola, Spanish for endive or escarole used a lot in salads and cooked as a vegetable. See ESCAROLE.

escarole (Chicoree scarole), a variety of curly leaved endive, also called Batavian endive. The leaves are broad and not as curly as those of *chicorée frisée.*

escarole

The central leaves are often blanched by covering them with a slate, or cultivating the plant in a cellar. All methods for preparing endive or chicory can be applied to escarole. It is very popular in France and other countries, but is not seen very often in Britain. It is also eaten a great deal in the U.S. and is regarded and treated there as a variety of chicory, both in its use as a salad, and as the base for an excellent soup. This latter is made by pouring boiling beef stock onto the chopped escarole leaves, already mixed with 2 beaten eggs, and 2 tablespoons grated Parmesan cheese. See also CHICORY; ENDIVE; SCAROLA.

eschalot, the English form of the French *échalote,* formerly used as an alternative word for shallot.

escolar (Ruvettus pretiosus), a large, rough-scaled, mackerel-like, deep-sea fish of gastronomic merit. It lives at depths of from 100 to 400 fathoms in the Mediterranean, mid-Atlantic, and southern seas. It can be prepared and cooked as mackerel.

escombro, Spanish for mackerel. Small mackerel are either fried or grilled; if large they are seasoned and then baked having first been dabbed with butter and covered with buttered paper. They are served with either sauce tartare or *salsa verde.* Estornino and caballa are also Spanish names for mackerel. Jureles is the Spanish name for horse-mackerel.

Eskimo curlew, see DOUGH BIRD.

espada, Portuguese for swordfish, which is extremely good to

eat. It is served in cutlets, either fried, grilled or boiled. If boiled, it is first rubbed with coarse salt and left for several hours, then gently poached in water or fish stock with a few cloves, a little parsley, and a clove of garlic.

espadon, French for swordfish, also called *empereur,* which is cooked like fresh tunny-fish (tuna). Or 1 lb. of steaks of swordfish are marinated in olive oil, lemon juice, salt, and pepper for 1 hour, then sautéed in oil with 1 medium onion, 2 crushed and peeled tomatoes, garlic, and herbs with ¾ cup of white wine. Cooking is completed in a moderate oven for ½ hour. Sometimes sauce espagnole is added to the juices.

espagnole, sauce, also called brown sauce; together with velouté and béchamel, this is one of the three *grandes* or basic sauces of French cooking, from which many other sauces are made—for example, with Madeira wine it becomes sauce *madère;* with orange peel, *bigarade;* with gherkins, sauce *piquante,* etc. The ingredients of the classic sauce espagnole are: trimmings of raw lean veal and ham, or rabbit, pork, or game (about ¼ lb.), 1 onion, 1 clove, 1 carrot, 1 tablespoon flour, 1 pint (2 cups) hot stock or bouillon, a small bouquet garni, salt, and pepper. The pieces of meat, chopped onion, clove, and sliced carrot are put into a heavy iron pot with a tight cover and slowly cooked until a rich brown gravy is obtained. The flour is worked in, and the hot stock or bouillon is added gradually, with salt, pepper, and bouquet garni. It is cooked for about 4 hours over a very low heat, until it reaches a creamy consistency, when it is skimmed and strained through a fine sieve. These quantities make about 1 cup of sauce. The sauce may be kept bottled in a cool place for 3–4 days. Nowadays a tablespoon of tomato purée is often added. In my opinion, tomato should be used very sparingly, otherwise it dominates the flavour.

espargo, see ASPARAGO.

esparguetes, Portuguese for spaghetti used in both savoury and sweet dishes in Portugal.

espárrago, Spanish for asparagus.

espárragos amagueros, a Spanish recipe for asparagus from Málaga. The asparagus is boiled in salted water and drained. Red peppers, parsley, garlic, and breadcrumbs are fried in oil before being pounded in a mortar, 1 dessertspoon vinegar being added at the last moment. This mixture is poured over the asparagus. Finally, 4 eggs are broken over all, and the dish is heated in the oven until these have set.

especie, Spanish for spices.

esperlán, see ESCABÈCHES.

espinaca, Spanish for spinach. In the south of Spain, there is no spinach grown. See also ACELGA.

espinafres, Portuguese for spinach.

espinafres com sardinhas, a gratin of spinach and sardines.

esquinado, French Provençal name for the spider crab.

esquinado à l'huile, a purée of 1 large esquinado, with 2 hard-boiled egg yolks, 1 teaspoon dry mustard, 2 tablespoons lemon juice, ¼ pint (½ cup) olive oil, 1 tablespoon parsley, salt, and pepper. It must be well pounded, and put back in the shell to be served with any plainly cooked white fish, or with rice, or on toast as an hors d'oeuvre.

esrom, a fragrant Danish cheese, yellow in colour, and, although rich, having an extremely mild flavour. It weighs 1–3 lb.

essence (extract), I. In the French kitchen, the word essence describes the natural juices of foods such as meat, poultry, fish, herbs, vegetables, mushrooms, or tomatoes, which result from cooking them, either without liquid, or with a minimum (to prevent burning); the resulting juices are boiled down or reduced to half the volume, acquiring in the process the maximum of flavour with the minimum of bulk. This essence, which in the case of meat, poultry, or fish is often a jelly, is used to flavour sauces or soups, for even a small amount gives a strong taste. II. A liquid, sometimes oily and volatile, extracted by distillation and used sparingly for flavouring, i.e., essence (extract) of almond, anise, cinnamon, cloves, lemon, orange, etc. These products are made and sold commercially. See also EXTRACT.

essex, a cheese which is not made any longer; and from the quatrain here quoted by Dorothy Hartley in her book *Food in England* (Macdonald), it is not difficult to see many reasons for its disappearance.

> Those that made me were uncivil,
> They made me harder than the devil;
> Knives can't cut me, fire won't light me,
> Dogs bark at me but can't bite me.

essig, German for vinegar. Fruits such as pears and plums are pickled with a cold, boiled mixture of sugar, vinegar, cloves, and cinnamon in Germany. The juices are also used separately as vinegar.

esterházy-rostélyos, a Hungarian dish, known in English as esterházy steaks. To prepare this, 4 small sirloin steaks are required as well as 2 onions, 2 carrots, 2 parsnips, 1 tablespoon paprika, 2 tablespoons lard, salt, and ½ pint (1 cup) sour cream. The sliced vegetables are browned in the lard and the steaks are then added, having first been lightly grilled. The paprika and cream follow and are brought to just below the boiling point. The steaks should be served slightly underdone, in the sauce.

estofado, Spanish for braised or casseroled meat.

estofado de vaca, beef and bacon stew, made with garlic, onions, mixed herbs, pimento, tomatoes, white wine, stock, a little vinegar, and salt. Towards the end of cooking time, small, new, peeled potatoes are added and cooked in the stew. See also CARNE DE VACA.

estouffade, I. An alternative name for *fonds brun.* II. French for a dish of which the ingredients are slowly stewed. The main ingredient is usually beef. It is also called *étuvée.* The Languedoc dialect word for this is estouffat, and there the dish is usually composed of cooked dried haricot beans and pork. In Gascony, a *daube* is called l'estouffat. See also BOEUF, ESTOUFFADE DE.

estragon, French, Danish, German, Spanish, Swedish, and Norwegian for tarragon, one of the most fragrant of the garden pot-herbs. See POULET, À L'ESTRAGON; TARRAGON.

ésturgeon, French for sturgeon.

esturion, Spanish for sturgeon.

étain, papier d', French for oven foil used for cooking.

étouffée, a French method of cooking, with little or no liquid, in a tightly closed pot; the dish is called *étuvée.*

étourdeau, French name in some country districts for a young capon.

étourneau, French for starling, often used in pâté in France.

étuve and *demi-étuve,* full- and half-size, semi-hard Dutch cheeses made from cow's milk. They are made all year round.

étuvée, a l', French for a dish of meat, poultry, or vegetables that has been stewed slowly with little or no liquid, but butter or oil. Also called *étouffée.* See also BOEUF, ESTOUFFADE DE; ESTOUFFADE.

evaporated milk, milk either sweetened or unsweetened from which about 40% of the water has been extracted by evaporation under a vacuum. The unsweetened form is usually made from full-cream milk and can be used for infant feeding. The sweetened variety is generally made from skim milk, the sugar being added after evaporation. Both are sold in tins. Generally, in Britain, and in the U.S. the sweetened variety is called condensed milk. It can be used for making puddings.

evarglice, a popular Yugoslavian cheese, usually eaten with peppery raw vegetables such as peppers or radishes.

evora, queijo de, a local name for a farmhouse variety of serra cheese. See SERRA.

ewe, an old female sheep, whose milk is used for many European, particularly French and Italian, cheeses. Pickled ewe meat is made in southwestern France. See also ALENTEJO; BREBIS; BROCCIO; BROUSSES; BURGOS; CINCHO; EDIRNE; FÉTA; KAČKAVALJ; LIPTÓI TÚRÓ; PECORINO; RABAÇAL, QUEIJO DE; ROQUEFORT; SERRA; SZÉKELY SAJT.

excelsior, I. One of the finest French soft cheeses, from the Vallée de Bray in Normandy. It is made from cow's milk and has 72% fat content. It resembles a *fromage de monsieur* but is far creamier and more delicate. It is not a common cheese, even in France, but is well worth hunting out. It is available all the year round. II. A French garnish for tournedos and noisettes, consisting of braised lettuce and pommes fondantes.

Exeter pudding, an excellent, almost forgotten English pudding, made from 6 eggs beaten with 2 tablespoons rum and 6 oz. (⅔ cup) sugar. The same amount of breadcrumbs and butter, or grated suet, with the grated zest of lemon, is added and well beaten. An ovenproof dish is lined with sponge cakes studded with raisins; some of the mixture is poured in and layered with black currant jam, the final layer being the mixture. The pudding is baked in a moderate oven until it has risen and is firm, and it is served with melted black currant jelly with the addition of a little sherry. Blackberry may be used instead of black currant.

exocoetus, a sea fish, also known as flying-fish, which is quite good to eat and is prepared as mackerel.

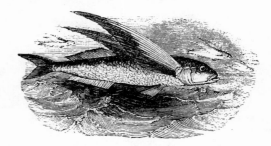

exocoetus

extract, a concentrated product obtained by evaporation, or a preparation containing the active principle of a substance in concentrated form. In culinary terms, it means the residue left after cooking meat, game, or poultry, usually by roasting. Extracts of fish are called fumets or essences. Soya sauce is a vegetable extract, and extracts can also be obtained from yeast, mushrooms, and truffles. Meat extract is commercially made and used for enriching meat dishes. See also DEHYDRATION; ESSENCE; FUMET.

eye of sirloin, American phrase for a joint of sirloin.

eyebright (*Euphrasia officinalis*), a European herb which is dried and used to make a kind of medicinal "tea."

eye-of-the-round, American phrase for the eye of silverside, a cut of beef.

F

faarekød, Danish for mutton, which is usually braised with root vegetables, the sauce thickened with cream and egg yolk, and the whole garnished with a large amount of fresh chopped dill. Lamb is often served the same way.

fabada asturiana, a famous Spanish dish of dried white haricot beans. It is made from 2 lb. beans which have been soaked overnight and then simmered; to them are added ½ lb. salted pork or bacon, 1 pig's ear (a piece of ham can be substituted), ½ lb. *morcilla asturiana,* 1 oz. longaniza or salted beef, water to cover, and seasoning. The pan is covered and the contents are cooked, either in the oven or over a low fire, until the beans are tender. When the stew is half-cooked, after about 2 hours, 2 oz. (2 tablespoons) melted lard mixed with 1 teaspoon saffron, which has been diluted with a little of the cooking stock, is poured in.

fadennudeln, German for vermicelli usually made into a sweet dish. See NUDELN.

fadge, a local name in counties Derry and Donegal, Ireland, for griddle or pan-fried potato cakes. The word is derived from the old French word *fouace* or *fougasse* from the Latin *focus* (hearth), i.e., the flat cakes were laid on the hot stones to cook, which became fadge: a flat bannock in Scotland.

fågelbo, a Swedish dish consisting of heaps of anchovy fillets, chopped raw onion, cooked beetroot, cooked sliced potatoes, with a raw egg yolk in the middle, all garnished with chopped chives and parsley. It means literally "bird's nest." Without the potatoes it is known as *sologa* (sun-eye) and both are eaten for smörgåsbord.

faggots, a traditional north of England and Welsh dish. Faggots are rich forcemeat squares made with pork offal (variety meats), such as minced liver and lights (lungs), mixed with an equal quantity of breadcrumbs or oatmeal soaked in milk, with chopped marjoram, sage, minced onion, salt, pepper, and mace to taste. (In some districts a sprig of bog myrtle is also mixed in.) The mixture is pressed into a large tin and covered with pig's caul, a fine membrane larded with fat, then baked slowly in the oven. When it has cooked for 1 hour, it is removed from the oven and marked with a knife into squares, then cooking is continued until the top is crisp. It is left to cool in the pan and, when cold, the squares are broken apart. Faggots are served cold with salad or reheated and served with gravy and apple sauce. They are also known as savoury ducks, and are not unlike a coarse *crépinette.*

fagiano, Italian for pheasant. In Italy, pheasant is often braised in white wine, and in Leghorn, it is garnished with mushrooms and sliced fried yellow boletus.

fagioli, Italian for dried beans. See also FASOEIL AL FURN; HARICOT BEAN.

fagioli all' uccelletto, a Tuscan recipe for cooking soaked, dried beans with garlic, sage, peeled and chopped tomatoes, olive oil, and enough water to cover. They are cooked slowly until the beans are tender and the sauce is thick. The title literally means "beans like birds," so named because the ingredients are supposed to make the beans taste like a game dish.

fagioli Toscani col tonno, a Tuscan recipe for beans with tunny (tuna) fish, one of the best known Florentine dishes. The beans, white fat Tuscan haricots or butter beans, are cooked with onion, water, and plenty of oil, and are served with a generous helping of tunny (tuna) fish, preferably *ventresca.*

fagiolini, Italian for french or string beans. See also FRENCH BEAN.

fagiolini col tonno, french beans cooked and drained, then treated in the Italian manner, mixed with hot olive oil in place of butter, lemon juice, and seasoning. The beans are covered in the dressing and served at room temperature with flaked tunny (tuna) fish.

sformato di fagiolini, french beans cooked in a sauce béchamel, and served with fonduta.

fagoue, the French butchery term for calf's sweetbreads or the pancreas. See RIS.

faina, see CECI.

fair maids, a Cornish term for pilchards, probably a corruption of the Spanish fumade, meaning smoked. The Spanish fishing fleets used to assemble off the Cornish coast, and pilchards were salted and smoked in large pits. See also PILCHARD.

faisan, French for pheasant. Pheasant is also served cold as a ballottine, as a chaud-froid, or as a *daube.* It is made into pâtés, terrines, and soup. See also GAME; GIBIER.

faisan à l'alsacienne, the pheasant is half-cooked in butter, then put in a braising pan with cooked sauerkraut flavoured with game fumet, goose fat, and a little fat bacon and saveloy sausage. It is covered and cooked in the oven for 25 minutes.

faisan à la bohémienne, pheasant with the breastbone removed, stuffed with foie gras, truffles, and paprika, then cooked for 15 minutes in Madeira. After this, the legs are trussed against the breast, and the bird is finished by cooking in butter. Before serving, a little brandy and a few spoonfuls of game fumet are added, and it is flamed.

faisan à la languedocienne, jointed pheasant cooked with a *mirepoix* of vegetables, lean ham, thyme, and bay leaf, moistened with red wine and a little stock. When half-cooked, it is drained and put into an ovenproof dish with small mushrooms, a truffle, and 2 tablespoons brandy, which is ignited. The strained sauce is poured over and a little butter added. The dish is covered and the contents baked for 25 minutes.

faisan à la Normande, pheasant browned in butter and casseroled with lightly browned sweet potatoes and butter, then cooked in a slow oven. Just before serving, cream and a little calvados are added.

faisan à la Périgueux, pheasant pot-roasted with truffles and wine, then served with game forcemeat balls mixed with truffles.

faisan aux choux, see PERDRIX, AUX CHOUX.

faisan en cocotte, casseroled pheasant, cooked with mushrooms and butter, and garnished with cooked potato cut into little pear shapes.

faisan en cocotte à la crème, as above, with ½ pint (1 cup) cream added half-way through cooking.

suprêmes de faisan, pheasant breasts sautéed in butter and served with various sauces or garnishes.

faisán, Spanish for pheasant.

faisán al modo Alcántara, a dish which originated in the old monastery at Alcántara, in the Extremadura, where some of the finest Spanish cooking is found. The cleaned pheasant, from which the breastbone has been removed, is stuffed with 4 duck livers mixed with an equal amount of butter, seasoned, and sieved; to this mixture are added large pieces of truffle cooked in port wine. The stuffed bird is marinated for 3 days in port, after which it is salted and cooked in butter. When nearly cooked, the marinade is reduced and small truffles are added. The marinade is then poured over the bird, and all is cooked for 10 minutes. The sauce is poured round the pheasant. Partridge can be cooked in the same way.

faisandage, the French culinary term for red meat which is "high" and has developed a marked, but not unpleasant smell. It naturally derives from *faisan* (pheasant), which has to be hung before cooking to reach perfection. It can be quite tough and tasteless if not hung, unless eaten the same day it is shot.

faisão, Portuguese for pheasant, which is usually cooked like partridge in Portugal. See PERDIZ.

fáiscre grotha, an early Irish cheese no longer made. The name means literally "a compression of curds." It was eaten fresh and is thought to have been a small cheese, as one source says that a woman could carry several in the fold of her cloak.

faisselle, a French osier or pottery utensil with holes in it used for draining the moisture from fresh cheeses. See also ÉGOUTTOIR.

fait-tout, see RONDIN.

faki, Greek for brown lentils; the word is also used for the brown lentil soup which is traditionally eaten on Good Friday, sprinkled with vinegar.

faki me pasta, see ALVEROF.

falla de San Chusep, St. Joseph's Day celebrations in Valencia, Spain, which begin on March 13 and end on the 19th, the official St. Joseph's Day. In Valencia dialect, *falla* means a pyre, and the name originated with the annual burning of shavings cleared out of carpenters' shops at this time. Now, by local tradition, wooden effigies of animals or people are made here, which are burnt after a tremendous feast at mid-

night on March 19. Many traditional dishes are eaten during this week-long feast, including *turrón jijona.*

fallfish, the name given in the eastern states of the U.S. to the chub.

fallow dear, see DEER.

falscher hase, a German dish whose title means "false hare." It is made from 1 lb. each chopped beef, veal, and pork, mixed with 2 eggs, 2 sliced sautéed onions, 1 tablespoon each of capers, lemon juice, butter, and seasonings. It is shaped like a beef fillet, rolled in breadcrumbs, and baked in butter. The pan juices are boiled up with cream and poured over the meat loaf.

falszywy losoś, a Polish veal dish, the name meaning "mock salmon made with veal." Veal is simmered in stock made from vegetables, veal bones, and wine vinegar to taste. When cooked, the meat is left overnight in this liquid. Served with a cold sauce of mashed hard-boiled eggs, into which olive oil and lemon juice have been well beaten.

famiglioli, an edible Italian fungus. See FUNGHI.

fanchette or *fanchonette,* an early French cake, hardly ever seen today. It has a *pâté feuilletée* casing, filled with *crème patissière* mixed with cream and flour, with vanilla to taste. It is baked in a slow oven and topped with meringue.

fancy brisket, the American term for the best cut of salt (corned) beef, easily identified as it is boneless. See BRISKET and diagram page xxii.

fangri, Greek for sea-bream, used a lot in Greece.

fänkålsås, Swedish for fennel sauce, made from 1 pint (2 cups) stock added to a roux made of 1 tablespoon each of butter and sifted flour, and when this has thickened, 1 tablespoon vinegar, 2 tablespoons chopped fennel, 2 teaspoons castor sugar, and salt are added; all are stirred until boiling. A little of the sauce is gradually added to a beaten egg yolk, and this mixture is poured into the main body of the sauce, which is cooked over a low heat until almost boiling. (If the egg yolk is allowed to boil, the sauce will curdle.) It should be served at once.

fanshell, a shellfish resembling the scallop found off the European and American Atlantic coasts and also in the Mediterranean, where it is called *pèlerine.* It is prepared and cooked like scallop.

far, I. A French porridge made from hard wheat flour. II. A name for a Breton flan made from *crème pâtissière* and sold commercially.

får, Norwegian for mutton. In Norway, mutton is often smoked, like ham, and served either boiled, with new vegetables, or sliced and fried, with eggs. See also FENALÅR; SPEKEPØLSE.

fårepølse, a sausage made from minced mutton, goat, and beef, preserved with alcohol, salt, and sugar.

fårerull, a speciality of cured mutton made into a roll.

får-i-kål, a dish of braised mutton, white cabbage, and black peppercorns cooked with a little stock for 2 to 3 hours in a casserole.

far poitevin, a dish of many shredded raw vegetables (approximately 1 lb.) such as cabbage, lettuce, sorrel, and spinach, combined with a little diced pork fat and ¼ pint (½ cup) cream, mixed with 1 raw egg, and flavoured with chives, parsley, salt, and pepper. It is all wrapped in large cabbage and lettuce leaves, put in muslin, and boiled with fresh and salt pork and root vegetables. It is a speciality of Poitou, France, and is also called farci.

faraona, Italian for guinea fowl, often cooked with stock, butter, and wine, and flavoured with juniper berries. It is sometimes called *gallina faraona.* See also GUINEA FOWL.

farce, I. French for forcemeat. II. An Old English word meaning to stuff meat, poultry, etc.

farci, I. A dish from the south of France. Usually it is a cabbage stuffed with sausage meat, wrapped in muslin and cooked in stock. II. French for stuffed. See FAR POITEVIN; FARCIDURES; POMME DE TERRE (POMMES FARCIES); SOUFASSUM.

farcidures, a speciality of Limousin, France, consisting of small balls made from buckwheat flour mixed with sorrel and beetroot, then wrapped in cabbage leaves and simmered in cabbage soup, as a garnish.

farfalle, a form of Italian pasta, literally meaning "butterfly" so called because of its shape like a butterfly.

farfallini, a much smaller version of farfalle, used to garnish soups. See PASTA.

farfel, a Jewish speciality, made commercially nowadays, which consists of a very stiff noodle-like dough made from barley with eggs added. The dough is allowed to harden and then is grated or chopped finely; it is not unlike Hungarian *tarhonya.* It is used to garnish soups or stews (*tzimmes*), and is also cooked with lentils and other vegetables, sprinkled with grated cheese, and served as a course on its own. It is very popular with Russian and Balkan Jews.

farigoule, a Provençal name for wild thyme; also called frigolet and used a lot in cooking.

farin heiras, a Portuguese dish of smoked fat pork rolled in flour and cooked in red wine. It is often eaten with turnip tops that have been boiled and then tossed in olive oil, or with *chouriço de sangue,* a kind of blood pudding.

farina, I. A fine flour made from a kind of grain, root, or nut. II. The purified middlings of hard wheat other than durum. III. A commercially packed, fine wheat flour used in the same way as arrowroot or semolina. IV. A fine powder made from potatoes and used for thickening. See FECULA.

farina dolce, an Italian *fecula* made from dried and ground chestnuts.

farinaceous, an adjective which means containing flour, meal or corn, nuts, or starchy roots such as potato.

farine, French for flour. *Farine de froment* is the French for fine wheat flour, or alternatively *farine de gruau. Farine de maïs* is the French for maize flour or polenta, used for country cakes; also for corn flour. *Farine de sarrasin* is the French for buckwheat flour, used in Brittany for pancakes, and *farine de seigle* is French for rye flour, used for bread and *pain d'épice.*

fårkött, Swedish for mutton, served boiled with vegetables, or smoked. See also FÅR.

farl, a term used in both Scotland and Wales to mean a quarter of a round oatcake, or bannock. Bakers sometimes use the word to mean a thin quarter, using bannock for a thick quarter.

farofias, a Portuguese pudding, made from whipped egg whites poached in milk, and served with custard. The word means "sweet clouds"; it is the Portuguese version of floating island.

färserade, Swedish for stuffed. See LÖK, FARSERADE LÖKAR.

farseret, Danish for stuffed. See HVIDKAAL, FARSERET.

farsz, Polish for stuffing. The Polish have many different stuffings for their various dishes. A few are included here:

farsz pasztetowy, a stuffing of liver pâté made from ½ lb. minced veal and ½ lb. minced pork liver and lights (lungs); added to many root vegetables such as sliced onion, celeriac, carrot, parsnip, etc.; 2 eggs and ½ cup breadcrumbs. It is used to stuff roast pork or whole sucking pig.

farsz z kasztanów, a feathered game or poultry stuffing of 1 lb. sieved cooked chestnuts, 4 tablespoons cream, 2 tablespoons butter, 2 eggs, 1 teaspoon sugar, and 3 tablespoons breadcrumbs. Sometimes the eggs are separated, and the stiffly beaten whites added last. This will make enough for 2 pheasants, or equivalent birds.

farsz z kaszy, a stuffing of 1 cup cooked buckwheat groats and parts of the pig's offal (variety meat), mixed with 2 me-

dium grated onions, 1 teaspoon marjoram, and 1 egg moistened with a little stock. It is used for stuffing a whole sucking pig.

fasan, German for pheasant, which in Germany is often stuffed with sieved, cooked chestnuts and cooked in butter. Compotes of apples or pears, or grape or red currant jellies are served with it, and braised red cabbage often accompanies it. In Austria, the bird is sometimes roasted in butter, basted with sour cream, and served with braised red cabbage or sauerkraut.

fasan nach bohmischer art, a method of cooking pheasant in which the bird is stuffed with chopped, cold roast snipe, which is mixed with herbs and truffles. When cooked, it is flambéed with brandy.

fasaner, Danish for pheasant. A popular method of cooking it is to brown it in butter and then to pot-roast it in a little stock. It is accompanied by green peas and *kartofler brunede.*

faschierter braten, an Austrian and German meat loaf made from ½ lb. minced beef, and ½ lb. minced pork, 2 thick slices soaked bread, 2 eggs, chopped herbs, and seasoning to taste. It is shaped into a loaf and baked in a little fat for 1 hour. Thirty minutes before it is cooked, ¼ pint (½ cup) sour cream is added to the pan juices. It is served with rice or macaroni.

faschingskrapfen, see under KRAPFEN.

faséole, a variety of haricot bean grown in Mediterranean areas.

fasoeil al furn, a Piedmontese bean dish which, by tradition, is cooked on Saturday night and eaten for Sunday lunch after Mass. The red kidney beans are soaked for 12 hours and then baked slowly in the oven for 4–6 hours with parsley, garlic, pepper, cinnamon, ground cloves, mace, and strips of pork rind or bacon rashers, with stock or water to cover. See also FAGIOLI.

fasola, Polish for beans. Fresh cooked beans are often served with a dressing of lemon juice and butter. Fasola sucha is Polish for dried beans. See also BEANS; FRENCH BEAN; HARICOT BEAN.

fasola lub soczewica na kwaśno, dried cooked beans or lentils served with a sauce made from a small sautéed onion, 1 tablespoon flour, ¾ pint (1½ cups) of the liquid the beans were cooked in, and flavoured with 3 tablespoons wine vinegar, salt, and pepper. The sauce should be as thick as a béchamel and mixed thoroughly with the beans.

fasola na kwaśno ze śmietana, a dish made from 2 lb. french (string) beans simmered in bouillon, strained, and then added to ½ pint (1 cup) sour cream, 1 tablespoon butter, 1 teaspoon flour, and lemon juice to taste.

fasola po francusku, a way of cooking french (string) beans. When tender and drained, the beans are added to a grated onion (already browned in butter), herbs, and lemon juice, and the whole is simmered for a further period until it has amalgamated.

fassolada, also spelt *fassolatha,* a traditional Greek soup made from 1 lb. soaked dried beans, cooked with 3 stalks celery, 2 large carrots, 2 large onions, 2 tablespoons tomato purée, ¼ pint (½ cup) olive oil, 1 tablespoon parsley, 3 quarts (12 cups) water, and seasonings. All ingredients are cooked gently for 2–3 hours or until the beans are soft. It is really the national dish of Greece. Beans are cheap, so it makes a solid meal for large, poor families, although it is not despised by richer ones. See also FASSOLAKIA FRESKA; FASSOLIA.

fassolakia freska, Greek for green (string) beans. Like many Greek vegetable recipes, the following is meant to be eaten as a course on its own. Onions are fried in a little oil or butter until they begin to change colour. Tomato purée is added, followed by the beans (which have been snapped into pieces) and sufficient boiling water to cover. It is all well seasoned and cooked slowly. See also FRENCH BEAN.

fassolakia freska me domates, cooked green (string) beans snapped into pieces and lightly fried with onion, tomatoes, parsley, and seasonings.

fassolakia freska salata, a salad made of 1 lb. fresh green (string) beans boiled and then served cold with a dressing of 4 tablespoons olive oil, the juice of ½ lemon, and 2 tablespoons wine vinegar.

fassolatha, see FASSOLADA.

fassolia, Greek for haricot beans, which the Greeks claim were discovered by Alexander the Great in India and brought back by him to Greece, thus giving Europe one of its major vegetables. See also HARICOT BEAN.

fassolia me hirino, made from 1 lb. soaked dried beans cooked slowly for 2–3 hours with 1 large onion, 3 large tomatoes, 1 lb. cubed pork. The ingredients are first lightly fried in olive oil and then covered with water or stock.

fassolia salata, soaked dried beans cooked and served as a salad with olive oil.

fassolia yahni, a dish of dried beans boiled with vegetables. One lb. dried beans should be soaked overnight, after which they are boiled in water for 35 minutes (half-way through the cooking a pinch of baking soda is put in). After draining, they are combined with ½ pint (1 cup) olive oil, 1 tablespoon diluted tomato purée, root vegetables such as carrots, celery, onions, etc., and seasoning. The mixture is covered with hot water, brought to the boil, and allowed to cook gently until it is tender.

fassolia yiachni, is the name of a dish made with soaked dried beans, garlic, thyme, and tomato purée, all fried in a good quantity of olive oil for about 10 minutes, before being covered with boiling water and simmered for about 3 hours, or until tender. Lemon juice, raw onion rings, and black pepper are added when the fassolia is cooked. It is usually served as a first course, or cold as a salad called fassolia salata.

fassolia yiandes plaki, soaked dried beans cooked with chopped tomatoes, onions, garlic, mint, sugar, salt, pepper, and olive oil, as *fassolini yahni.*

fasùl yahniya, a Bulgarian traditional dish of stewed dried white beans with onion, red and green peppers, and tomatoes. It is often served with pickles or a salad.

fat, a substance found in the connective and nervous tissue of all animals, as well as in parts of some plants, particularly in the fruit, seeds, and nuts. All fats are chemically classified as esters, that is, combinations of alcohols and acids. Those fats having the most general culinary importance are combinations of the tri-hydroxy alcohol glycerol, more commonly known as glycerine, with three of the so-called fatty acids: stearic acid, palmitic acid, and oleic acid. These fatty acids consist of relatively long linear chains of carbon atoms having, other than their bonds to neighbouring carbon atoms, only attachments to hydrogen atoms. The last atom of carbon is attached to the acid radicle—COOH which contains, as well as the hydrogen atom, two of oxygen.

An exceedingly important difference exists between oleic acid and the other two fatty acids, stearic and palmitic; oleic acid has, half-way along its molecule, a double bond (where one of the hydrogen atoms is absent from each of two adjacent carbon atoms). This peculiarity makes fats which contain a high proportion of oleic acid liquid at room temperature, that is to say, at room temperature they are not solid fats, but oils. The greater the proportion of oleic acid in the make-up of a fat, the more easily digestible it is, particularly by those who have a deficient pancreas or liver. More important still, these high oleic acid fats, or fats having a high proportion of double bonds (known as polyunsaturated fats or oils), are particularly recommended in the diet of those who are subject to atherosclerotic degeneration of the arteries,

whether or not high blood pressure is present; or indeed for anyone having a blood cholesterol level which is above normal. The more unsaturated the fat (oil), the more satisfactory it is as an article of diet for such conditions.

In order of increasing saturation, the culinary oils may be arranged as follows: safflower seed oil, sunflower seed oil, corn oil, sesame seed oil, peanut oil, olive oil, while in order of increasing saturation, the animal fats may be arranged as follows: salmon fat, herring fat, pork fat, mutton fat, beef fat.

In cooking terms, fat usually means a thick grease made from animal tissue which melts at a low temperature. It can also mean the white layers interleaving and encompassing a carcase, which are melted and rendered down to an oily substance which hardens when cold. This is known as dripping (drippings), as well as fat. Fats are also derived from certain vegetables. Butter and most margarines come under the heading of fat, although they are not made from carcase fat. Fat is used mostly for frying, roasting, or pastry making. See also LARD; OIL.

fat hen, see ORACH.

fat rascals, a Yorkshire tea cake which is made from ½ lb. (2 cups) flour, 3 oz. (3 heaped tablespoons) butter, the same amount of sugar and sultanas, ½ teaspoon mixed spices, and 1 teaspoon baking powder, all mixed with 1 egg and about ⅛ pint (¼ cup) milk, to make a firm dough. The mixture is put into small patty pans before baking for 10 to 15 minutes in a moderate oven. They are served hot, split, and spread with butter.

fattigmann, a Norwegian biscuit. Literally translated, the name means "poor man," although the ingredients used are hardly consistent with poverty. It is made with 5 egg yolks, 3 tablespoons cream, 2 teaspoons brandy, and 3 tablespoons fine sugar, all beaten together very well, and flavoured with cardamom seeds. A soft dough is produced by the addition of about ¼ lb. (1 cup) flour to give a thick, but dropping dough, and this is chilled for 12 hours. It is then rolled out on a floured board and made into biscuit shapes which are fried in hot oil or lard until they rise to the top and are golden in colour.

faubonne, I. A thick French soup (*potage*) consisting of *saint-germain* soup, with a julienne of sautéed vegetables and chopped chervil added. (Dried peas and beans can also be used.) II. A pheasant purée garnished with pheasant strips and a julienne of truffles.

faux éperlan, see ATHÉRINE.

faux-filet, see CONTRE-FILET.

fava, Italian for broad bean often dried in Italy and used for soups.

fave al guanciale, a favourite Roman dish consisting of fresh broad beans cooked with butter, chopped onion, and chopped bacon. They are first sautéed for 5 minutes, then barely covered with water and served undrained after about 20 minutes of cooking. It is seasoned to taste.

fava, Portuguese for broad bean.

favas à algarvia, are broad beans cooked with onion and sausage in ham and chicken stock. It is often served for *acepipes.*

faverolles, a name given in the south of France to many kinds of haricot bean.

favorite, I. A French garnish. For tournedos and noisettes, it consists of sliced foie gras, truffles, and cooked asparagus tips; for slices of meat, it consists of artichoke bottoms cut in quarters, braised celery, and small *pommes anna* or *pommes château.* II. A consommé thickened with tapioca garnished with julienne of artichoke bottoms and mushrooms, and small potato balls, sprinkled with chervil. See also CONSOMMÉ.

fawn, a young roe deer or fallow deer.

fazant, Dutch for pheasant. Pheasants are popular and plentiful in Holland.

gebraden fazant, roast pheasant. Boiling water is poured over the outside and inside of the bird before salt is sprinkled inside and a good knob of butter inserted. Butter is melted in a skillet just large enough to take the bird, which is browned and then cooked, covered, in a moderate oven for about ½ hour, being basted frequently. It is served with a sauce consisting of 1 tablespoon flour (browned in a little of the pan drippings), ½ pint (1 cup) thick cream, and salt. When smooth, brandy and a dash of spicy bottled sauce are added.

feather fowlie, a Scottish soup, possibly a French inheritance. It is made from jointed fowl cooked with 2 slices of ham, 1 chopped heart of celery, 1 sliced onion, a pinch each of thyme, parsley, and mace, and a quart (4 cups) of water. It is simmered for 1½ hours, then the stock is degreased and put into another saucepan; 1 large spoonful chopped parsley and the chopped breast meat of the bird are added, and all cooked for 15 minutes. Then 3 egg yolks are beaten with 1 tablespoon cream and added to the hot soup. It is not reboiled or it will curdle. The name could be a corruption of oeufs filés, or "fowlie," alone a corruption of *volaille*.

febras do porco, a Portuguese dish consisting of pork cooked with pimento, garlic, and cumin seeds in a red wine sauce.

fecula, the name given to the starch-like powder obtained from potatoes, chestnuts, arrowroot, cassava, and other vegetables. It is known as "flour," is very finely ground, and used for thickening soups and sauces. See also FLOUR.

fécule, French for fecula. *Fécule de maïs* is the French for corn flour, and *fécule de pommes de terre*, potato flour.

fedelini, a very narrow, ribbon-shaped Italian pasta used mainly in soups. The name means "the faithful."

fegatelli, Italian for slices of pig's liver. Sometimes used in *spuma di fegato* which is a liver mousse.

fegatini, Italian for chicken and poultry livers.

salsa di fegatini, a sauce made of ½ lb. floured chicken livers cooked in 2 tablespoons butter with 4 oz. mushrooms, ½ gill (4 tablespoons) Marsala or white wine, seasoning, and ½ pint (1 cup) chicken or meat stock. It is served with potato gnocchi.

fegato, Italian for liver.

fegato alla Veneziana, a speciality of Venice, made from gently stewed onions served with calf's liver cut wafer-thin and cooked in butter for 1 minute on each side.

fegato di vitello al Marsala, calf's liver fried and then simmered in Marsala wine.

fegato di vitello alla Milanese, calf's liver cut in slightly thicker slices than for *alla Veneziana*, seasoned with pepper, salt, and lemon juice, dipped in beaten egg and breadcrumbs, and fried in butter. Served garnished with parsley and halves of lemon.

feige, German for fig.

feijão, Portuguese for dried bean. Dried beans of all kinds and colours are almost the staple diet of many Portuguese people, and they are cooked and served in many ways, even to being eaten together with rice, as the accompaniment for curry. There are red, yellow, white, and green beans, and they are used for soups, stews, and salads, and as a vegetable. The colours make the dish very attractive and the protein value is high.

The big white haricot bean is often stewed in milk thickened with barley or rice and flavoured with chopped herbs. It is also cooked with whole red peppers.

feijão vermelho com molho, a traditional Portuguese kidney bean stew which consists of 1 lb. soaked dried kidney beans simmered for 2–3 hours in ¼ pint (½ cup) olive oil and water to cover. When cooked, fried onions, tomatoes, cumin seeds,

and sometimes sausages are added. See also FEIJOADA COMPLETA.

feijão verde, Portuguese for green bean. These beans grow prolifically in Portugal and have a good flavour. They are invariably served with *cozido* of meat or fish, particularly in the Algarve. See also FRENCH BEAN.

feijoada completa, an elaborate dish of pork and beans which is very popular in both Portugal and Brazil. A good feijoada can include as many as 15 different kinds of meat, such as sausages, salted and dried bacon, salted pig's, lamb's, or calf's tongue, fresh pork (including ears and tails), and fresh beef. Dried black beans are soaked overnight in water, and, in a separate pan, the dried meats are treated in the same way. The meat is drained, added to the beans and bean water, and then simmered over a slow heat or in the oven. Fresh pork and beef are put in after 1 hour and more water is added from time to time if necessary. It is all cooked slowly for 4–5 hours, or until everything is tender. A sauce is made by sautéeing in oil chopped onions, tomatoes, mashed garlic, bay leaves, and parsley. Then 1 spoonful of beans from the stewpot is added before all the sauce is put into the meat and bean dish. The feijoada is served by putting the fresh meats on one side of the platter and the dried ones, including the tongue, on the other. The beans and sauce are served separately, and sometimes shredded cabbage, sliced oranges, and a hot pepper sauce (piri piri) are also served as side dishes. It is an elaborate but satisfying repast. See also CARNE DE PORCO; FEIJÃO, VERMELHO COM MOLHO.

felchen, German for whitefish and féra. It is one of the important freshwater fishes found in Germany and it is prepared in any way as for trout.

fenalår, a Norwegian speciality which is leg of mutton, slightly salted, wind-dried, and usually smoked. It is used on the *koldtbord*. See also FÅR.

fenchel, German for fennel, used extensively with fish dishes.

fennel (*Foeniculum vulgare* syn. *officinale*), a free-growing umbelliferous European herb. It grows to a height of 5 or 6 feet; its leaves are delicate and feathery, and its blossoms yellow. The Romans, who gave the plant its name, used the leaves and seeds both for flavouring foods and for making perfumes. Today, the pungently scented seeds, which taste slightly like aniseed, are still used for flavouring; the feathery leaves, and their stalks, are excellent cooked with grilled or fried fish. The seeds of the cultivated or garden-fennel are used in confectionery, for flavouring figs and sausages in Italy (*finocchiona*), and both leaves and seeds are used in the making of a Swedish fennel sauce (*fänkålsås*).

Florence fennel   fennel

A very important variety from the culinary point of view is Florence fennel (*F. vulgare;* var. *dulce*). This is a thick, low-growing plant yielding 2 crops per year, a native of Italy, where it is called *finocchio* or *cartucci*. It is a perennial and grows well by the sea. The enlarged leafstalks at the base of the stem are used as a salad and a vegetable in both France and Italy; indeed, they are a staple food in southern Italy, where they are prepared in any way that is suitable for celery. The leaves are used as a garnish and are excellent in fish sauces, particularly with salmon. At one time the herb was thought to have slimming properties, and was called marathron by the Greeks from the verb *maraino*, to grow thin. It has a pleasant taste, slightly resembling aniseed. See also FENOUIL.

fennel flower (*Nigella sativa*), another name for black cumin, and, in spite of its name, bears no relation to fennel proper. It is a pretty, pale blue garden flower known as "Love in the Mist." Its aromatic seeds are use in confectionery and in German are called Schwarzkummel.

fennel pear, a variety of French pear which has a slight taste of aniseed, like fennel. There are three varieties grown in France: fenouillet gris, fenouillet gros, and fenouillet rouge. It is also known as "fenowlet" in England.

fennikel, Norwegian for fennel where it is used a lot in pickling.

fenouil, French for fennel. The dried stalks are used in Provençal cookery for grilling mullet and sea-bass, and for flavouring court bouillon in which fish will be cooked. The leaves are used for sauces and salads as well as for garnishes. See also FENNEL.

fenouil tubereux, French for Florence fennel, which is served cooked or raw in any way that is suitable for celery.

fenouillet, see FENNEL PEAR

fenugrec, French for fenugreek.

fenugreek (*Trigonella foenum-graecum*), also known as "Greek hay," a herb indigenous to the Mediterranean region. The seeds from its pods yield a somewhat fatty, bitter oil, formerly esteemed in veterinary practice. The seed is used as an ingredient in curry powders.

fer á glacer, an alternative name, with pelle rouge and salamandre, for salamander.

féra (*Coregonus ferus*), a kind of salmon trout found especially in Lake Geneva, but also in some other lakes in Switzerland, Bavaria, Austria, and France. It is related to whitefish. The flesh is very delicate and delicious to eat. The colour of the fish changes with its habitat—in deep waters it is white; in medium waters, black—and the young, or blue, féra has a blueish shimmer on its back. The finest féra are caught on the sandbank (*travers*) of Lake Geneva round about May, and these are called *féra de travers*. Féra is best cooked simply, to preserve the flavour; either *à la meunière*, grilled, *au bleu,* or in any way that is suitable for trout.

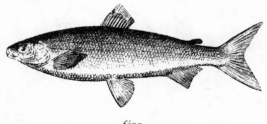

féra

ferchuse, a speciality from Burgundy made from pig's offal (variety meat). Traditionally, it was served when the home farm pig was killed. It consists of pluck (heart, liver, and lungs) fried in diced pork fat, cut into squares, seasoned with salt, pepper, and spices, and browned. Flour is then sprinkled on top, and when the pluck has been cooked slightly, it is moistened with red wine and covered with water or stock. When boiling, shallots, garlic, and bouquet garni are added, and it is all cooked slowly for about 1 hour. The name comes from fressure, which is French for pluck.

ferinana, a Corsican chestnut porridge with olive oil added. See also CHESTNUT.

fermière, à la, I. A French garnish for poultry and braised or pot-roasted meat consisting of carrots, turnips, onions, potatoes, and celery or celeriac, all braised gently in butter, together with the natural juice of the meat or poultry. See also POULET, SAUTÉ FERMIÈRE. II. Small half-moon slices of carrot, celeriac, turnip, and shredded leek, simmered in butter and mixed with either veal velouté or white wine sauce, according to what it will be served with. This is sometimes called a fondue de legumes. III. A beef cosommé double garnished with julienne of cabbage, diced french beans, and squares of pasta. See also CONSOMMÉ.

fern, see BRACKEN.

fersken, Norwegian for peach.

fesa col prosciutto, a leg of veal larded with ham, a speciality of Parma, Italy. The slices of ham, together with slices of carrot, are inserted into incisions made in the veal. The meat is cooked in butter, olive oil, and white wine.

festa di San Giuseppe, St. Joseph's Day, March 19, is celebrated as a holiday all over Italy. Every village prepares its own tavola di San Giuseppe (table of St. Joseph), consisting of elaborate cakes, pasta, and pastries, and all the orphans, beggars, and other poor people are invited to partake. Presents are given to all. The custom is that cheese is not eaten on that day.

In Sicily, the feast is celebrated with the visit, from house to house, of an elderly carpenter, a poor girl, and an orphan child, who, dressed in robes and crowns, accept gifts of alms and food to be shared among all the poor of the community, and the Church. See also BIGNÉ; FRITTELLE, DI SAN GIUSEPPE; SFECIN, DI SAN GIUSEPPE; SPAGHETTI, SPAGHETTI E FINOCCHI ALLA SICILIANA; ZEPPOLE ALLA NAPOLETANA.

festy cock, see FITLESS COCK.

féta, an extremely popular soft, white, Greek cheese made from ewe's milk, which comes from the mountain regions north of Athens. It is made like cottage cheese but is heavily salted and is kept for about a month. It is the basis of many other Greek cheeses. Because of its high water content it does not travel, and so is only eaten locally. There is, however, a variety for export which is made from pasteurised milk.

fetta, a salty white cheese made in Sardinia. It closely resembles the Greek féta.

fettuccine, the Roman name for homemade egg noodles or tagliatelle. See PASTA.

feuillantine, French cakes made from puff pastry rolled out, folded into thirds, turned, and rolled 6 times. It is then rolled out and cut in strips about 2 inches long. They are brushed with egg white and sprinkled with coarse sugar before being baked in a moderate oven. Feuillantines are served with tea, coffee, or ice cream.

feuille de dreux, a French cheese made in the Île-de-France from cow's milk. It is in season from October to June.

feuilleton, a delicious French meat dish made from thin slices of flattened veal spread with various stuffings or salpicons and then placed one on top of the other until they are about 6 inches high. This is then wrapped in pork caul and braised. When cooked, it is drained, glazed in the oven, served with *bourgeoise* garnish, or braised vegetables such as celery or chicory, and eaten hot. It can also be served cold in jelly. In the Périgord, it is stuffed with a mixture of foie gras and truffles and braised in Madeira wine.

feuilleton berrichon, a speciality from the Berri district of France consisting of a mixture of chopped pork, veal, herbs, and seasoning encased in flaky pastry, like an exceptionally good sausage roll.

fiambre, Portuguese for cold cooked ham. See PRESUNTO.

fiatole, French for a Mediterranean fish with golden bars and spots on a dark grey skin. It is flat and almost square, but has a good taste and is prepared in the same way as turbot.

ficelle, à la, a French method of cooking fillet of beef. It is often bound tightly with string, browned in a hot oven for 10 minutes, then put, while hot, into boiling consommé for 15 minutes or longer if liked well done. See also FILET.

fico, Italian for fig. Figs grow extensively all over Italy, the Sicilian ones being notable. They are eaten raw and dried, and are also made into jam. The dried figs of Bari are flavoured with fennel seeds, and are particularly delicious. Fresh figs are often served with thin slices of prosciutto crudo; it is a delectable combination. See also FIG.

fideos, Spanish for fine spaghetti.

fideos a la malagueña, a spaghetti recipe from Málaga, one of several that may be found in Spain. The spaghetti is first boiled, then tossed in oil. Squares of potato and red pepper are fried separately and are then mixed with cooked, shelled peas and the spaghetti. *Boquerones* decorate this dish.

fides, a Greek variety of pasta which is eaten extensively in Greece, especially in soups. See also SPAGHETO.

fidget pie, also spelt figet pie, is a Welsh border speciality consisting of 1 lb. each peeled, sliced potatoes and apples layered in a pie dish with ½ lb. sliced onions and 1 lb. un-smoked, diced bacon. It is seasoned to taste, barely covered with stock or water, then covered with short crust pastry before baking in a moderate oven for 40–60 minutes. The name is a corruption of flitch, the country English word for a side of bacon.

fiélas, the name in Provence, France, for the conger eel, which is used in bouillabaisse and in matelote.

fieldfare (*Turdus pilaris*), a bird, about the size of a large thrush, which is a winter visitor to the British Isles and southern Europe. It is highly thought of as food in the south of France. In Italy it is often cooked in the same way as thrush, pigeon, or snipe. See also TÀCCULA; UCCELLETTI.

fig (*Ficus carica*), the fruit of a wide variety of fig trees. Figs are of many different shapes and colours; some have purple skins, some green, others green and brown. The pulp also differs in colour from red to a yellowish brown, according to type. The fig is native to the Middle East and the Mediterranean Coast. Sicilian figs are celebrated for their flavour in Italy. Smyrna figs are the most prized in the Middle East; they are grown extensively in Europe and are eaten fresh as dessert fruits, but are also used commercially in the dried form for puddings, cakes, and preserves. In central Europe, roasted figs are ground and used in the same way as the French use chicory to flavour coffee. The wild fig has been successfully introduced into California, together with the insect which fertilises it, and it now grows extensively in the warmer states of the U.S. See also FICO; FIGOS; FIGUE; HIGOS.

figado, Portuguese for liver.

figado à transmontana, a speciality of thin liver slices stuffed with a mixture of hard-boiled eggs, parsley, chopped ham, and garlic. The slices are rolled up, secured with thread, and put into a baking dish. Lightly fried onions and a little stock are poured over, and the liver is baked in a hot oven for about 30 minutes. On being removed from the oven, it is covered with scrambled eggs made from egg yolks and the juice of ½ lemon. See also ROLINHOS DE FIGADO.

figado de cebolada, liver fried with onions and pimentos.

figado estufado, liver braised with vegetables. See also ISCAS.

figatelli, a Corsican sausage made from pig's liver.

figeater or *figpecker* (*Sylvia curruca; S. borin*), a member of

fig

the warbler family of birds, found in all Mediterranean countries. It is rarely seen in the British Isles, but may occasionally be found nesting there in the spring. Quite erroneously, it is said to feed on figs and grapes; it eats neither, but only the insects which cluster round these fruits when they are ripe. It has always been considered a great table delicacy, and the only bird which epicures of ancient times considered should be eaten bones and all (Aulus Gellius quoting Favorinus). It is always eaten freshly killed, without being drawn; it is sometimes wrapped in vine leaves before cooking. All methods for serving ortolan or plover can be applied. See also AMBELOPOÙLIA; BECCAFICO; TÀCCULA; UCCELLETTI.

figgie hobbin, a traditional Cornish pastry, sometimes called figgy duff, which is said to have been displayed in a shop window bearing the legend: "Figgy Duff 4d. lb., more Figgier 5d" (a "fig" being a raisin). Figgie hobbins are still eaten by descendants of Cornish miners who settled in Colorado, U.S., about 1862.

A little suet and a little lard are rubbed into flour with baking powder. Raisins are added to taste, and a stiff paste made of milk or water. The dough is rolled, cut into thin squares, and baked. In Colorado, a light short pastry is rolled out thinly, scattered with raisins and grated lemon peel, and rolled up with a light pattern scored on top before being baked in a moderate oven. It is also called figgy 'oben.

figgy duff, see FIGGIE HOBBIN.

figos, Portuguese for figs, which are very good in Portugal, both fresh and dried. In the south, the dried figs are often combined with blanched almonds to make elaborate animal or fish shapes. See also FIG; MORGADO DE FIGOS.

figue, French for fig. The most highly thought of figs in France are the Marseillaise, which have a yellowish-white skin and white sweet pulp; the *bellona,* purple skin and red pulp; the banisotte, large with purple skin and red, sweet pulp; the blanquette of Argenteuil, green skin and white, sweet pulp; the dauphine of Argenteuil, purple skin and pale red pulp; and the barbillone, purple skin and white pulp. See also FIG.

filbert (*Corylus avellana;* var. *maxima*), an English oblong variety of hazelnut entirely covered by the tapering, leafy husk. There are 3 separate varieties, characterised by the colour of their skin: the white filbert (white aveline); the red filbert (red aveline); and a frizzle filbert which is much less common and has a frizzled husk. Curiously, one of the most popular filberts is called a cob nut or Kent cob. This nut has a more vigorous growth than the aforementioned varieties and is cultivated extensively in Kent. The name is thought to derive from St. Philibert whose feast day, August 22, falls in the ripening period of the nut. See also COB NUT.

filé powder, an essential ingredient in the famous creole soup–stew called gumbo. It comes from the dried, tender young leaves of the sassafras tree and was made originally by the Choctaw Indians, whose squaws spread out the leaves to dry, then pounded them and passed them through a fine sieve. Both the bark and the leaves have a very aromatic flavour. When using the filé powder in gumbo, it must be added after the pot has been taken from the fire, and the stew must never be reheated, as the powder would render it stringy and unfit for use. For this reason, filé powder is usually stirred into the soup in each individual soup plate. See also GUMBO.

filet, French for fillet. I. In beef (filet de boeuf) it is a cut of meat taken from the fillet or undercut of sirloin. See diagram page xxiii. There are many French methods of cooking this staple and excellent cut. It is usually grilled or fried in butter, sometimes flambéed with brandy and served with a sauce béarnaise or hollandaise. The centre protion of a fillet is often baked in the oven after larding with small strips of fat bacon, and served with a variety of garnishes, such as *andalouse; anversoise; béatrix; bouquetière; châtalaine; clamart; dauphine; dubarry; duchesse; favorite; financière; forestière; frascati; godard; hussarde; jardinière; Italienne; Languedocienne; massenet; mentonnaise; moderne; niçoise; nivernaise; Parisienne; piédmontaise; Portugaise; printanière; provençale; renaissance; riche; Richelieu; romaine; romanoff; Saint-Germain; sarde; Talleyrand.* See also FICELLE; FILLET; TOURNEDOS.

II. In veal (filet de *veau*) it is a cut from the middle and back loin. III. In pork, lamb, or mutton, it is the cut of meat from the loin nearest to the hind leg. It is known as loin in England. IV. In fish (filet de *poisson*) it denotes fish taken off the bone before cooking. It is also the word for a thick slice of fish, called alternatively a *darne* or tranche, which has part of the bone left in, and is the same as the English fish steak. V. In poultry or game (filet de *volaille* or filet de *gibier* de plume), it means the breast and wing. It is also called suprême.

filet de boeuf à la gelée, roast fillet of beef served cold in aspic, with a cold sauce such as mayonnaise, rémoulade, tartare, etc., and sometimes with individual timbales or darioles of macédoine of vegetables set in aspic.

filet garni, fillet served with a variety of cooked vegetables, also mushrooms and tomatoes.

filet mignon, I. A small cut of meat taken from the small end of the fillet (of beef). Originally, it was a small muscle from inside the rib weighing about ¼ lb. II. When referring to lamb or mutton, it denotes the undercut of a saddle.

fillet, I. In beef, it is the undercut of sirloin. It is called tenderloin in the U.S. II. In veal and pork, it is a thick slice from the top of a hind leg. In Ireland and the U.S., it is the undercut which constitutes the pork or veal fillet, as is the case with beef. III. In lamb or mutton, it is a joint from the top of the hind leg. IV. In fish, it is fish taken from the bone; or, in the case of thick fishes, such as cod or salmon, a thick slice is often called a fillet, although it is more properly a steak, since it retains a portion of the backbone. See also FILET and Table of Cuts of Meats, page xxi.

filleted, a term meaning ''boned,'' usually applied to fish.

filo, see PHYLLO.

fin, the wing-like membranes used by the fish for balancing and guiding its body. Certain fins, such as those of the turtle, are a great delicacy. Shark fin is used for a soup; and, in skate, the fin or wing is the best part of the fish to eat.

fin de siècle, a French cheese from Normandy, made of cow's milk; it is in season all the year round.

financière, à la, a French garnish for poultry and sweetbreads, consisting of chicken quenelles, cock's combs, *rognons de coq,* truffles, mushroom caps, and stoned olives, with sauce *financière.* This garnish is also used to fill bouchées and *vol-au-vents.*

financière, sauce, a classical French sauce. Brown sauce is heated, and to it are added half the amount of chicken broth, truffle trimmings, and chopped mushrooms. This is cooked until the liquid is greatly reduced, then, after lowering the heat, sauterne or Madeira, ¼ pint (½ cup) to ¾ pint (1¼ cups) sauce, is gradually added. It is strained and served hot.

findik keuftessi, Turkish mutton dumplings. A mixture is made of 2 lb. finely chopped mutton, 2 medium chopped onions (previously fried in butter), 2 eggs, 2 tablespoons creamed butter, a pinch of cinnamon, seasonings, and 4 tablespoons flour. It is shaped into walnut-sized dumplings which are lightly rolled in flour and then fried in butter. They are then simmered with chopped fresh mint leaves in very little water or mutton stock for 30 minutes.

fines herbes, a mixture of many herbs, such as tarragon, burnet, chervil, thyme, marjoram, chives, and parsley, all chopped. Sometimes it is used to mean only chopped parsley, used for flavouring an omelette, salad, meat, or fish. See also HERBES.

finikia, also spelt fenikia, the Greek popular name given to the small honey-dipped cakes called melomakarona, which are said to be taken from a recipe dating back to the Venetians, who invaded Greece towards the end of the 17th century. These small round cakes are made from 1½ lb. (6 cups) flour worked into 3 tablespoons brandy, 3 oz. (⅓ cup) sugar, 2 tablespoons orange juice, and ½ pint (1 cup) olive oil (the oil is well beaten and then well mixed with the other ingredients before the flour is added). Then 1 tablespoon honey, 1 teaspoon baking powder, ½ teaspoon cinnamon, 2 teaspoons lemon juice, and 1 tablespoon grated orange peel are added to the mixture. They are baked in a fairly hot oven (375° F) for 20–25 minutes. After cooling, the cakes are dipped into a syrup of 1 lb. (¼ pint or ½ cup) melted honey, and 1 teaspoon lemon juice which have boiled together for 15 minutes and then been left to cool. Finally they are garnished with sesame seeds.

finker, a Danish recipe for using up cold roast beef with an apple sauce, which is made from 6 sliced apples simmered in a sauce consisting of 2 tablespoons butter, 1 heaped tablespoon flour, 1 pint (2 cups) rich brown stock, and 2 teaspoons vinegar. When the apples are tender, the sauce is thickened by the addition of creamed flour and butter. Small squares of the beef, together with a pinch of sugar and seasoning to taste, are added to the apple sauce. It is served with mashed potatoes and boiled carrots, the latter being coated with butter mixed with chopped parsley.

finnan haddie, a smoked haddock from Findon (pronounced Finnan) in Kincardineshire, Scotland, which is a pale yellow colour and justly world famous for its delicate taste.

The haddock is cleaned thoroughly and split; after removal of the head, it is well salted and left overnight—that is, if it is required to be kept for more than a week. It is then hung for 2 or 3 hours in the open to dry, then smoked in a chimney or a smoking machine over peat or hardwood sawdust. The heat must be kept as even as possible, or it can spoil the fish. It should acquire the desired golden yellow colour in 12 hours. See also ARBROATH SMOKIE; HADDOCK.

Finnish cheeses, see JUUSTO.

finnlendskaia, a traditional Finnish garnish for soup. Slices of pancake, made with sour cream added to the batter instead of milk, and with 2 tablespoons grated Hamburg parsley root stirred into it, are placed on small pieces of toast; they are thickly spread with grated cheese, sprinkled with breadcrumbs, and dotted with butter, before being browned under the grill. They are served as a side dish with strong beef broth, and the two together constitute a complete dish on their own.

finocchio, see FENNEL.

finocchiona, an Italian sausage flavoured with fennel seeds. It is one of the best in Italy.

finte (*Alosa finta*), a fish which comes to European rivers to spawn and is considered a gastronomic delicacy in France. It is related to the shad; it is more elongated in shape, but tastes like shad and is prepared in the same way.

fior di latte, literally "flower of milk," an Italian cheese similar to mozzarella, but it is made from cow's milk, has less flavour, and is more rubbery in texture. It should be eaten very fresh. In Italy fior di latte is often used in place of mozzarella, as the buffalo, with whose milk the latter should be made, is getting rare.

fiore sardo, a hard Italian cheese made from ewe's milk. When it is unripe it is used as a table cheese, but when fully cured it can be grated and used with pasta or soups.

fiorentina, an Italian garnish and sauce from Florence. The garnish always has spinach as one of the main ingredients; the sauce is usually a cheese sauce with leaf spinach added.

fiouse, a local name in Lorraine for quiche lorraine.

firespecier, a Danish biscuit (cookie) which is a kind of shortbread and is extremely good to eat. It is made with 1 lb. (2 cups) butter rubbed into 1 lb. (4 cups) flour, then 1 lb. (2 cups) castor sugar—which has previously been mixed with 2 oz. (½ cup) ground almonds—is gradually kneaded in. After chilling, this dough is rolled out thinly, and rounds, about 1¾ inches across, are cut out. These are baked in a fairly hot oven for 10 minutes. The name, translated, means "four species."

first cut brisket, see FANCY BRISKET.

fisch, German for fish. See also AAL; FELCHEN; FORELLE; HERINGE; KABELJAU; KARPFEN; ZANDER.

gespickter fisch, an Austrian and German speciality of a whole fish larded with bacon and baked with small onions, sliced root vegetables, and butter. Rice is often served with this dish.

fischmilcher, German for soft roe often used poached, then mashed with a little mustard and white wine, then served as a sauce with herrings baked in white wine.

fish, an animal living in water either fresh or salt. It is a vertebrate, cold-blooded creature with gills and limbs modified into fins. Almost all varieties are edible. See also FISCH; FISK; PESCADO; PESCE.

fishballs, balls consisting of boiled, flaked fish mixed with an equal quantity of mashed potatoes, herbs, salt, and pepper to taste, bound with 1 raw egg per lb. of mixture. The mixture is shaped into balls, rolled in either flour or egg and breadcrumbs, and then fried in deep hot oil. In Norway, they are poached. See also FISKEBOLLER.

fishcake, as above, but shaped into flat round cakes and fried in shallow oil. In Norway, a more elaborate form called *fiskkaggen* is made.

fish kettle (poacher), see KETTLE.

fisk, Danish for fish. There is a wide variety of fish on sale in Denmark, where, in the large towns, the fishmongers sell it live from the tank, rather than from the slab, as in Britain. The most general ways of cooking and serving fish in Denmark are given here. See also AAL; HELLEFLYNDER; HORNFISK; LAKS; PIGHVARRE; RØDSPAETTE; SILD; SØTUNGE; STØR; TORSK.

fiske klatkage, fish fritters. Small pieces of filleted plaice are dipped in batter and fried in butter or cooking oil. A sauce is made of 2 oz. (2 heaped tablespoons) each butter and flour, and 1 pint (2 cups) boiling fish stock, to which 2 oz. olives, 6 chopped chestnuts or mushrooms, and, lastly, 3 tablespoons white wine and seasoning. The sauce is poured over the fish and the dish garnished with slices of pastry.

fiskebudding, Danish for fish pudding, for which cod, hali-

but, trout, or turbot are equally good. The skin and bones of about 2 lb. of fish are first removed, and can be saved for stock. Then 2 tablespoons flour, ½ pint (1 cup) cream, and 1 teaspoon salt are mixed with the minced fish, after which 3 stiffly beaten egg whites are folded in. A greased mould lined with breadcrumbs is filled ¾ full with the mixture and is placed in a pan containing a little hot water. It is covered, and the contents are left to cook in a slow oven for about 1 hour. This is a deliciously light, mousse-like dish. The fish may be garnished with dill, fennel, or parsley and served with a mushroom sauce made with the fish stock and milk in equal quantities, the chopped mushrooms added last. See also KLIPFISKE (KLIPFISKEBUDDING).

fiskefrikadeller, fried fishcakes, which in Denmark are usually made with 2 lb. of cod, pike, haddock, or salmon, which should be skinned and filleted, well mashed, and seasoned. Then 1 pint (2 cups) very thick white sauce is prepared, 2 beaten eggs are stirred in, and the fish are blended with the mixture to produce a batter consistency. Cream or milk is added as necessary. The mixture is formed into rounds and fried in butter on both sides until brown. These cakes are garnished with parsley and lemon slices and served in a tomato sauce.

fiskegratin, a Danish fish soufflé consisting of 3 oz. (3 heaped tablespoons) butter, the same of flour, ½ pint (1 cup) milk (or fish stock), 3 eggs, ½ lb. filleted, flaked, boiled fish, and seasoning. The eggs are separated, and the whites are stiffly beaten and folded into the mixture last of all. The dish is baked in a greased mould, standing in a tin of hot water, in a moderate oven for 1 hour.

fisk, Norwegian for fish. Norway is renowned for the excellence of her fish which are caught in her own waters all the year round. Salted fish, which is much used in Norway for smørgåsbord, is generally bought from the shops already salted. As in some Mediterranean countries, fish is sold alive, to be killed just before cooking. As well as grilling, frying, etc., the Norwegians make much use of fish pies which can also be mixed with potatoes or vegetables. Fish soup (*fiskesuppe*) is popular throughout the country. See also LAKS; ØRRET; PALE; SILD; TORSK.

fiskeboller, fishballs, which are also sometimes served (very small ones) as a garnish for soups. A 3-lb. haddock is cleaned, skinned, and boned, before being minced several times. It is then mixed with 2 tablespoons corn flour (cornstarch), salt, and ½ pint (1 cup) milk (the latter being added very gradually at first), and 2 separated eggs, and the stiffly beaten whites are folded in last. The resulting dough is rolled out and made into small balls. These are simmered in salted water until they rise to the surface. Instead of boiling them, the Norwegians sometimes fry these balls in butter if they are to be used as a main course and not as a garnish. See also FISHBALL.

fiskepudding, a delicious fish mousse. A 2-lb. boiled haddock is skinned, and the flesh, when flaked, is removed from the bone and minced. Salt, 1 tablespoon flour, and 2 eggs are blended with the fish, then ½ pint (1 cup) milk, nutmeg, and 3 more beaten eggs are gradually included. Finally, ½ pint (1 cup) beaten cream is added and the dish is steamed for 2 hours and served with a *hummer* sauce. See also PLUKKFISK.

fiskesuppe, a fish soup which can be made with almost any kind of fish. Usually cod or coalfish is used, with carrot, onion, and celery or leek. They are all simmered in water or fish stock to cover until tender, and then strained; then the soup is thickened with 2 egg yolks beaten with ¼ pint (½ cup) sour cream or yogourt to 1 quart soup. It is garnished with tiny fishballs, called *fiskeboller*.

fiskkaggen, a dish made of 1 lb. boiled, flaked white fish mixed with 4 oz. (½ cup) butter, 2 egg yolks, ¼ lb. (1 cup) fresh breadcrumbs, and 2 stiffly beaten egg whites. It is seasoned with salt, pepper, and nutmeg. It is put into a greased soufflé dish, baked in a hot oven, and eaten cold.

fisk, Swedish for fish. Throughout Sweden, fish is eaten a great deal, and the many dried, pickled, canned, and smoked varieties are almost as popular as fresh fish. Fish recipes are very varied. Fish is often served cold, when it may be boiled and set in aspic, or served in mayonnaise. When boiling fish, Swedish cooks use a court bouillon. Fish mousse, fish pudding, and fish soups are also very popular. See also FLUNDRA; GÄDDA; HEL FISK I KAPPROCK; LAX; SILL; STRÖMMING; TORSK.

fiskfars, a fish mousse. A 3-lb. fresh haddock is filleted and the flesh ground in a mortar and made into a paste by the addition of 12 oz. (1⅔ cups) butter. Then ¼ pint (½ cup) cream is gradually beaten into 4 egg yolks, followed by 2 heaped tablespoons flour, 1 teaspoon castor sugar, and seasoning. The fish paste is stirred into this mixture, alternately with 1 tablespoon more cream. One teaspoon anchovy essence (extract), or 1 tablespoon white wine may be added as flavouring. Lastly, 4 stiff egg whites are folded in, and all is poured into a soufflé dish that has been buttered and lined with breadcrumbs. The dish should be only ¾ full. It is covered with paper and the contents steamed for 1½ hours. It is served unmoulded, with parsley and a fish sauce—*fisksas, hummer saus,* or shrimp sauce.

fiskgratin, fish au gratin. Fillets of flounder or sole are seasoned before being simmered in a fish stock. They are then put into a sauce made from milk and fish stock thickened with corn flour (cornstarch)—1 tablespoon to ½ pint (1 cup) liquid. The dish is topped with grated breadcrumbs and grated cheese, and baked in a fairly hot oven for about 10 minutes.

fiskpudding, a fish pudding. I. One lb. filleted sole is pounded down to a paste with the gradual addition of 4 tablespoons fish stock. This is rubbed through a sieve and gradually stirred into ¾ pint (1½ cups) whipped cream. Seasoning and nutmeg are put in, and the mixture poured into small buttered moulds, which are then covered with greaseproof paper and the contents steamed or cooked standing in boiling water for about 20 minutes, when they are unmoulded and served. It is garnished with either chopped dill or parsley, with a lobster sauce. II. Another Swedish fish pudding made from 2 lb. pounded fish, chopped herbs, and 1 cup cooked rice bound with 2 tablespoons cream mixed with 2 eggs, and cooked as I. It is served with a cream and cheese sauce. See also RÖKT-FISKPUDDING.

fisksås, fish sauce. A roux is made of 2 oz. (2 heaped tablespoons) each butter and flour, to which 1 pint (2 cups) strained fish stock is added. Two egg yolks are beaten into ¼ pint (½ cup) cream, and this mixture is added to the fish stock, which is then heated until thick (but never allowed to boil) in a double boiler. Finally, seasoning and a pinch of sugar are included. See also HUMMERSÅS; KROGVÄRDENS SÅS; SKARPSÅS.

fisksoppa, fish soup. A fresh haddock, about 2 lb. in weight, is divided into equal portions and simmered in 4 pints (8 cups) salted water in which a sliced carrot, celery foliage, bay leaf, cloves, and peppercorns are included. After 45 minutes, the soup is strained and the best pieces of the fish are reserved as a garnish. A roux of butter and flour is made, to which milk and then the fish stock are added. This is enriched and thickened by the addition of ¼ pint (½ cup) cream mixed with an egg yolk, but is not reboiled.

kokt fisk, boiled fish. The fish is boiled in a court bouillon of cold water, bay leaf, salt, parsley, and thyme, with lemon juice, sliced root vegetables, an onion, and a fish head with trimmings. All simmered for about ¾ hour and then allowed to cool. It is served with melted butter sauce as for *stekta fiskfiller.*

stekta fiskfiller, fried fish fillets. The fillets are seasoned, dipped in egg and breadcrumbs, and left to stand for several minutes before being fried in butter. They are served in a sauce of 4 oz. (½ cup) melted butter and 1 tablespoon lemon juice with either chopped dill or parsley to taste.

fissurelle, a gasteropod mollusc with a conical shell like a limpet. There are many varieties, and they inhabit warm, tropical waters. They are common in the Mediterranean, and in Greece there is a variety called "St. Peter's ear." Fissurelle can be cooked in the same way as calamary (squid).

fistulane, a French name, for a headless mollusc with a tubular shell. It is prepared like a cockle. It is also called gastrochère.

fistuline hépatique, French for beefsteak fungus; also known in France as *langue-de-boeuf* and *foie-de-boeuf.* Known as liver fungus in the U.S. See MUSHROOM.

fitless cock or **festy cock,** a corruption of Fastern meaning "fast eve." It is a Scottish Highland dish, seldom seen now, which used to be eaten on Fastern's Even, the evening which precedes the first day of Lent, Shrove Tuesday. Cockfights used to be held in parish schools on that day in the eighteenth century. It consists of oatmeal, suet, onion, salt, and pepper, bound with an egg, shaped into the form of a fowl and boiled in a cloth like a dumpling. In the south of Scotland it was roasted in the kiln ashes and was known as "dry goose." It is a form of white pudding found in all Gaelic-speaking countries.

fjaderfa, Swedish for poultry; also fågel. Chicken, turkey, and goose are all found in Sweden, but on the whole are apt to be reserved for the more festive occasions. This is particularly true of goose. However, dishes made from boiling fowl are often a feature of Swedish menus. See also GÅS; HÖNS; KALKON; KYCKLING.

fjaerkré, Norwegian for poultry (also called fugl). Duck, goose, and chicken are most popular as table birds in Norway. Turkey is also eaten, usually for a celebration dinner. See also AND; GÅS; HØNE; KYLLING.

fjerkrae, Danish for poultry. Ducks, chickens, and geese are all popular in Denmark. At Christmas, goose has the same importance there that turkey has in England. Roast chicken and horseradish sauce, and boiled chicken served with the soup, are popular Danish country dishes but, generally speaking, chicken will most often be stuffed with parsley and butter and served with a *rabarberkompot,* as the Danes like soursweet flavours. Likewise, a goose may be stuffed with apples and prunes, like the Norwegian *sviske-fylling.* Cream and stock are incorporated in most Danish poultry recipes.

fladene, a Corsican tart made with *broccio* and flavoured with vanilla.

flaeske, Danish for pork. In Denmark, pigs are very carefully bred for the table, being reared under the most hygienic conditions. They are fed mainly on skim milk and mashed barley, and their flavour is delicious. Pork rashers are cut very thinly and cooked slowly until the rind is crisp (the latter is seldom removed). Danish bacon is an important export. See also SVINEKØD.

flæske æggekage, a pork pancake. Thin fillets of pork are browned in butter, seasoned, and set aside. A batter is made and cooked in a little butter until nearly set, when the fillets are laid on top and cooking continued. The dish is garnished with chives and parsley.

paneret flæske med ærter og gulerødder, fried pork served with green peas and carrots. For this dish, pork chops are dipped in seasoned flour and in egg and breadcrumbs, and then fried in butter. A sauce béchamel is made with butter, flour, and vegetable stock, to which the cooked vegetables are added, together with parsley and seasoning. This sauce is poured round the chops.

flæskesteg, rodkaal, kartofler og sauce, roast pork and gravy, served with red cabbage and brunede *kartofler*. Boiling water is first poured over the rind, which is then scored. The 4-lb. loin joint is sprinkled with salt and roasted in a moderate oven until tender (after cooking for 15 minutes, 2 cups boiling water are added). The gravy is strained and thickened with creamed flour and flavoured with beef extract.

flageolet, see CHEVRIER; HARICOT BEAN; LIMA BEAN.

flaish un kais, Dutch-American individual turnovers. The pastry is made with 4 oz. flour, ¼ lb. (½ cup) butter, 3 oz. cream cheese, and 1 teaspoon curry powder; the turnover is filled with a mixture of 4 oz. mashed boiled chicken livers, 2 hard-boiled eggs, 1 teaspoon grated onion, 4 tablespoons thick cream, and 1 teaspoon curry powder. They are well pressed at the edges and baked in a moderate oven for ½ hour. They are particularly popular in Pennsylvania.

flake, the name in some parts of England for dogfish. This ugly fish has many names, mostly in order to disguise its unprepossessing appearance and to make it saleable, although in fact it has a good flavour. It is popular in France where it is known as *bar*.

flaki, Polish for tripe. See also TRIPE.

flaki po Francusku, tripe cooked in the French way, with white wine, tomato purée, celery, root vegetables, herbs, ginger, and onions thickened with a little flour. This is not in any way a traditional French method, but an adaptation of tripe à la mode de caen. (This sort of thing frequently happens when regional dishes cross frontiers.)

flaki po Warszawsku, the Warsaw way of cooking tripe. It is simmered with root vegetables, leeks, celery, and hamburg parsley for several hours. The stock is thickened with *beurre manié*; salt is added, but not until the end, because it is thought to discolour the tripe. This dish is served with *pulpety z łoju lub szpiku*.

flaky pastry, see PASTRY.

flamande, a la, I. A garnish, originally Flemish, for pieces of meat. It consists of braised cabbage and carrots, turnips, and bacon cooked with the cabbage. It is also made with *saucisson* and plain boiled potatoes. II. A method of poaching fish in fish stock with light beer, usually the Belgian light red variety called faro. The stock is thickened with a *beurre manié*, and chopped herbs are added. III. A butter sauce seasoned with a little French mustard, lemon juice, and chopped parsley. IV. Melted butter seasoned with French mustard, lemon juice, and parsley. V. A method of serving asparagus hot with melted butter and halves of hot hard-boiled eggs which are mashed into the butter by the diner. VI. A beef consommé with royale of puréed brussels sprouts, peas, and sprigs of chopped chervil. See also CONSOMMÉ.

flamber, to pour warmed spirit, such as brandy, whisky, rum, etc., over food and set fire to it. It gives a good distinctive liquor flavour to certain cooked foods such as meat or game, puddings, pancakes, and fruit.

flamiche, I. A French pastry tart filled with 2 lb. sliced leeks cooked in butter until tender and mixed with 3 egg yolks beaten with ¼ pint (½ cup) cream, salt, and pepper. It is covered with more pastry and baked until golden brown. This is a speciality of Burgundy and Picardy. II. In other parts of France, it can be pastry mixed with egg yolk, yeast, sugar, and rum or brandy. This is a sweet rather than a savoury dish. In parts of northern France, a variety is called flamique.

flamingo (*Phoenicopterus*), a long-legged, rosy-coloured water bird which is sometimes eaten in Sardinia but not considered to be very good, although the Romans thought highly

flambéing in a Belgian restaurant kitchen

flamingo

of it. Flamingoes are called *gente rubia*, or red folk in Sardinia.

flamique, see FLAMICHE.

flamri, a French pudding made from ½ lb. semolina boiled with 1 pint (2 cups) white wine and the same of water. When it has thickened, 10 oz. (1¼ cups) sugar, 2 eggs, and a pinch of salt are added and, at the last moment, 6 stiffly beaten egg whites (three times the number of eggs already used). It is baked in a *bain-marie*. When cool, it is turned out and covered with a purée of any sweetened raw, red fruit.

flamusse, a French Burgundian tart. A 10-inch tin is lined with pastry and filled with cheese-flavoured cream—4 oz. (1 cup) Gruyère cheese to 1 pint (2 cups) cream—mixed with 3 raw beaten egg yolks, and the tart is baked in a moderate oven until golden brown on top.

flan, an open pastry case usually filled with fruit, although savoury flans are also made. The name comes from the metallurgical flan, which is simply a metal disc, and flan tins are made of flat metal and sometimes have a fluted or crimped edge. The flan is extremely old and is mentioned by the Latin poet Fortunatus (530–609 A.D.). The word flan is common to most European languages.

The pastry used to line the flan tin is usually short crust, often with an egg and a little sugar added if the filling is to be sweet. It differs from a tart in that it is never covered with pastry (although in the U.S. a flan is called a tart or pie). Sometimes the pastry is lightly cooked before putting in the filling, or the inside is painted over with beaten egg. This is the most satisfactory method, as it ensures that the pastry will not be heavy. See also PISSALADIÈRE; QUICHE LORRAINE. Some European recipes are included here.

flan à la Portuguesa, a Portuguese flan filled with ½ lb. rice cooked in 1 pint (2 cups) red wine and mixed with 3 tablespoons butter, 6 oz. (⅔ cup) sugar, 2 egg yolks, 1 cup stoned sour cherries, and 2 stiffly beaten egg whites. It is baked in a moderate oven and served cold.

flan de Pascuas, Spanish for an Easter dish from Ibiza. In a 9-inch pastry case are placed, in the order given, 6 thin slices of cheese (made from a mixture of goat's and sheep's milk), about 1 tablespoon sugar, 6 eggs (broken in one by one and left whole), again a little sugar, another egg which has previously had chopped mint beaten into it, and lastly, sprigs of mint. The flan is oven-baked for about 40 minutes.

flan de poireaux, a French savoury flan or quiche filled with 2 lb. sautéed chopped leeks, 2 oz. diced ham, 3 egg yolks mixed with ½ pint (1 cup) cream, salt, and pepper; all baked until golden brown on top. It is eaten hot or cold.

flan, the name for crème caramel in the south of Spain and Andorra.

flanchet, French for flank of beef. See diagram page xxiii.

flangnarde, a pudding made in the Auvergne and Limousin, from 3 tablespoons flour mixed with 3 eggs and a little salt. When smooth, 1½ pints (3 cups) cooled boiled milk, flavoured with vanilla, are added. The mixture is poured into an ovenproof dish, dotted with butter, and baked in a very hot oven. It is served either hot or cold.

flank, a cut of beef taken from the flap below the loin and following on from the ribs. It is flat and lean and good for stuffing and braising. It must have long slow cooking to make it tender. The alternative English name is skirt. See also COLLARED BEEF. See diagram page xxii.

flannel cakes, American griddle cakes (pancakes) made from ½ lb. (2 cups) flour, 1 teaspoon baking powder, 2 tablespoons butter, salt, 2 eggs separated (whites stiffly beaten and added last), all mixed to a soft dough with 1½ pints (2½ cups) buttermilk. They are baked on a hot greased griddle and topped with chicken or turkey heated up in a thick cream and vegetable sauce; this is known as chicken or turkey hash. However flannel cakes are often eaten simply with butter and maple syrup. Other grains such as whole wheat, oatmeal, corn meal, etc., can also be used and often a small amount of sugar is included in the batter.

flapjack, I. A biscuit made from 12 tablespoons rolled oats, 2 tablespoons brown sugar, 4 tablespoons melted butter, and 2 tablespoons golden syrup, all mixed and baked in a flat tin. The mixture is cut into squares or fingers while still warm. II. In parts of England and the U.S., flapjack is also a griddle cake, like a drop scone.

flask, Swedish for pork. Of the various meats eaten in Sweden, pork is one of the most popular, particularly at Christmas time, and recipes are very varied. See also JULSKINKA; PLOMMONSPÄCKAD FLÄSKKARRÉ.

flaskpannkaka, a Swedish baked pork pudding made with ¼ lb. pickled pork diced and fried until it is well browned and the fat is clear. Then 2 pints (4 cups) milk is gradually added to 2 beaten eggs, into which is stirred 10 oz. (2½ cups) sifted seasoned flour. The resulting batter is poured into a greased dish, with the meat sprinkled on top, and the whole is baked in a fairly hot oven for about 45 minutes. The pudding is served cut into squares, with cranberry sauce.

flatbrød, a Norwegian bread made of rye flour and potatoes; it is often eaten in conjunction with a slimming diet. Three lb. mashed potatoes and 1 lb. rye flour are mashed to a paste and left to stand, covered, for 12 hours. The mixture is then rolled out into very thin rounds, the size of the pan in which each is baked. Sometimes, in Norway, the shape will be a thin oblong one instead of round. Baking is done over a moderate heat, with frequent turning, until cooked through. When cool, this bread is crisp. See also LEFSER.

flats, a type of American cheddar.

flead, the inner membrane of a pig's stomach, a fine thin skin, full of pieces of pure lard. It is beaten into flour to make lard cake. Flead pastry is made by clearing the flead from the membrane, and folding and rolling it into the flour. Flead cakes have spices, sugar, and egg added. See also GROVEY CAKE.

fleckerln, a variety of very small, square, German and Austrian noodles. They are used as a garnish in soups and also as an accompaniment to meat. Schinkenfleckerln are fleckerln with the addition of sour cream and minced ham.

fleckerlsuppe, a traditional Austrian soup made of strong beef broth garnished with fleckerln.

fleisch, German for meat.

fleischklösse, minced meat and herb dumplings.

fleischknoedel, see KNOEDEL.

fleischkuchen, a German meat loaf made with 1 lb. minced cooked pork, 2 medium-sized grated raw potatoes, and 1 onion bound together with 2 raw eggs and seasoned, and the mixture is then baked or fried, with the top browned under the grill. The loaf is served with onion sauce, potatoes, and sauerkraut.

flensjes, Dutch for the thin pancakes popular in Holland. There are several ways of preparing flensjes, but the basic method uses 3 beaten eggs and a pinch of salt well mixed with 3 oz. (¾ cup) flour, to which ½ pint (1 cup) milk is gradually added. A little butter is melted in a skillet and a small quantity of batter is browned on one side only, rolled up, and sugared (sometimes ginger, jams, or marmalade are substituted for sugar). Another method is to make the flensjes the day before they are required, but this time leaving them unrolled, and serving them flat, in layers, with a filling of custard sauce in between each layer, and well chilled. See also PANNEKOEKE.

flet, French for flounder. See also CARELET.

flétan, French for halibut often served baked in foil, with lemon juice and rosemary. The fish is wrapped in bacon rashers before securing the foil by folding at the top.

fleuriste, a French garnish for tournedos and noisettes consisting of tomatoes, scooped out and filled with a *jardinière* of vegetables and *pommes château.*

fleurons, a common form of French garnish consisting of very thinly rolled scraps of puff pastry, usually crescent shaped, baked or fried, and served hot as a garnish for soup or entrées. See also GARNISH.

fleury, à la, a consommé of chicken, garnished with small chicken quenelles and green peas. See also CONSOMMÉ.

flitch, a side of bacon, that is, half a pig slit down the back with the legs and shoulders taken off. In Dunmow, Essex, England, a "Dunmow Flitch" used to be awarded to a married couple who could prove they had not quarrelled for about twenty years.

floating island, a pudding of which there are two varieties, the more usual variety being large spoonfuls of stiffly whipped egg whites, sweetened, poached on both sides in boiling vanilla-flavoured milk. They are drained and the milk is made into a custard with the egg yolks and more sugar. The custard is poured into a dish with the cooked balls of egg white heaped on top and often served with caramel dribbled over it. It is usually served cold. In the less common variety the French fill a cake tin with sponge cake layers soaked in kirsch and spread with apricot jam, chopped blanched almonds, and currants. This is repeated until the tin is almost full, then it is topped with crème *chantilly* and decorated with chopped nuts and currants. Just before serving, a chilled vanilla-flavoured custard is poured round it.

flocon, a form of French cornflake used in France as a garnish for soups, or for making a kind of porridge.

fløde, Danish for cream which is used extensively in Danish cooking, especially in pastries and desserts.

flohkrebs, German for prawns.

Florence fennel, see FENNEL.

florendine, an 18th-century English meat pie, always made from veal or some part of the calf. It usually consisted of loin of veal with the kidneys and their fat all minced and mixed with the yolks of hard-boiled eggs, rice, currants, a pinch of sugar, salt, nutmeg, thyme, and cream; it was covered with puff pastry and baked. By the 19th century it had become too lavish, with oysters or anchovies, pork, lemon, shallots, mace, butter, consommé, and white wine added. It is, however, an excellent dish and should be revived.

florentine, à la, I. A French garnish for fish and sweetbreads consisting of a sauce *italienne* and garnish *fiorentina* (cooked spinach). II. Fish served with leaf spinach and sauce mornay. III. Meat served with tiny spinach pancakes and Parmesan-flavoured semolina croquettes with demi-glace.

florentines, very thin sweet biscuits (cookies) containing minced nuts, candied peel, and dried fruits mixed into melted butter, sugar, and cream and baked in a moderate oven on a greased baking sheet. They are then coated with melted chocolate which is "brushed" to give them wavy lines.

florian, a French garnish for slices of meat composed of braised lettuce, browned button onions, carrots cut into ovals like olives, and *pommes fondantes.*

Florida dusky duck (*Anas fulvigula*), an American duck common in Florida and the southern states of the U.S. where it has a variety of names such as Florida black duck, summer mallard, Texas dusky duck, and Mexican mallard. The flavour is said to be comparable to that of a mallard, and this duck may be cooked in the same way.

fløteost, a type of Norwegian mysost cheese.

flounder (*Platichthys flesus*), a common saltwater flatfish of the same family as dab, brill, sole, and turbot, found off the sandy coasts of both sides of the Atlantic. Although generally found only in the sea, it has been discovered in fresh water, especially in the river Seine, France. It can be prepared and cooked like plaice.

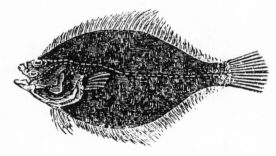

flounder

In Scandinavian countries, especially Norway, flounders are also dried and smoked for winter use. In the U.S., they are used in place of sole and turbot, which do not inhabit American waters. They have quite a delicate flavour, but are not as milky as brill or turbot.

In the U.S. the name is also given to two kinds of freshwater fish, the sunfish (*Eupomotis gibbosus*) and the red-breasted bream. See also CARRELET; FLOUNDER; FLUNDRA; PLAICE.

flour, the ground and sifted meal of wheat, rye, buckwheat, oats, barley, and maize, which are the grains most commonly used, although other corn of inferior quality is also made into flour. Usually, when flour is mentioned, wheat flour is meant, as it has the highest content of gluten and is used for the daily bread in most European countries, as well as in North America. There are many kinds of wheat flour from the finely sifted to the unsifted (or unbolted) flour ground from the

whole kernel. In white flour, bran, the outer husk, is discarded, but this is left on in the more nutritious whole ground flour. More varied amounts of bran are left in the differing kinds of stone-ground flour than remains in the flour which undergoes the more modern method of steel-rolling. This flour is usually brown. White flour is in fact pale yellow when fresh, but becomes white with age. Chemicals can hasten the whitening, but the vitamin content is depleted.

Graham flour is named after an American dietitian, Sylvester Graham, who in 1840 pioneered a flour which was made from unsifted whole meal, ground from the whole kernel and not refined. In England, it is called Grant flour. This flour is used a great deal in Finland, for rusks known as *grahamkorputs.*

Rye bread, which is made from rye meal, is dark in colour and very popular in Germany, Russia, central Europe, Scandinavia, and the Baltic States. It is a hard, but tasty bread, and very good with salty dishes such as cheeses or cured fish, such as herrings.

The grinding or milling of flour dates back to prehistoric times, and the earliest method was the crushing of the grain between large stones. The Romans invented conical millstones called querns, turned by hand, and many querns still exist in Europe. About the time of Christ, water-propelled mills were invented, and flat, rather than conical, millstones were found to be more satisfactory.

Flour is used as an ingredient in many dishes, and particularly in bread, buns, cakes, pastries, and puddings; it also serves as a thickening agent in sauces, soups, and stews.

Certain farinaceous products called "flours" are made from cassava, chestnuts, potato, soya bean, and rice. See also BRAN; BREAD; CORN; FÉCULA; GLUTEN; SEMOLINA; WHEAT; WHEAT GERM; YEAST.

floutes, an Alsatian quenelle, made from a mixture of 1¼ lb. (4 cups) finely mashed potatoes, 2 eggs, 2 oz. (½ cup) flour, and a pinch each of nutmeg, salt, and pepper. It is formed into small cork-like shapes, poached in salted boiling water, drained, and served with hot *beurre noisette* which has a spoonful of freshly fried breadcrumbs in it. See also QUENELLES, DE POMMES DE TERRE À L'ALSACIENNE.

floyeres, Greek for almond-stuffed pastry rolls, which are very popular in Greece. Sheets of phyllo pastry are each cut into 4 strips and brushed with slightly melted butter. On each are placed 4 oz. (½ cup) crushed almonds mixed with 2 oz. (¼ cup) sugar and 1 egg. The strips are then rolled up in the manner of an English swiss roll and baked in a moderate oven until golden brown. After that they are dipped in a simmering syrup of sugar, water, lemon juice, and cinnamon. They are eaten cold.

fluke, see WITCH FLOUNDER.

flummery, I. An extremely old British and Irish sweet pudding, seldom seen nowadays. It is made from oatmeal soaked in water overnight, the liquid then strained off and boiled until it becomes thick and gelatinous. In Ireland, sugar, raisins, and sometimes almonds are added; in England, cream and stewed fruit; and in Wales, sugar, cream, and a flavouring such as orange flower water, or sherry. It is eaten cold. See also FRUMENTY. II. In Scotland, flummery is a custard, with sugar, nutmeg, and currants soaked in sherry, added to it while it is cooking. It is served hot.

flunder, German for smoked plaice and flounder; see SCHOLLES.

flundra, Swedish for flounder, which is held in high esteem gastronomically in Scandinavian and Baltic countries. As well as being used in many ways when fresh (*fiskgratin*), it is also preserved by drying and smoking, for winter use. See also FISK; FLOUNDER.

fluss-krebs, German for crayfish which are quite common in many German rivers and lakes.

flute, to cut vegetables or fruit with an implement which serrates the edges; to do likewise with pastry or cakes.

flûte, a long French loaf sold in Paris.

flûte à potage, a long French roll used for making *croûtes,* which are served with soups and stews.

flyndre, Norwegian for flounder which is of exceptional quality in Norway.

focaccia, the Genoese name for a bread made with flour mixed with olive oil and salt. See PIZZA, ALLA GENOVESE.

focaccia di pomidoro, an Italian savoury flan made from short crust pastry baked blind, then filled with a mixture of cooked fried onions, tomatoes, zucchini, parsley, sage, garlic, and seasonings. The top is covered with 1 or 2 beaten eggs, sprinkled with grated Parmesan cheese, then baked in a fairly hot oven until the eggs are set and gently browned.

fofos de bacalhau, Portuguese for small fried balls made from puréed salted cod. See also BACALHAU.

fogas (*Lucioperca sandra*), a giant pike-perch which can weigh up to 20 lb., found in the river Tisza and Lake Balaton, Hungary, and eaten a great deal there. It is a most delicious white-fleshed freshwater fish. It is also found in the Danube, but as it must swim against a powerful river current there, it is not as tender as that found in the Hungarian locations. Very small fogas, weighing 2 lb. or less, are called fogasullo. Genuine fogas from Lake Balaton is marked with a lead seal to authenticate it.

In Hungary, it is often simmered whole in sour cream, or poached and served with a cream and paprika sauce. It is also fried, grilled, and baked. See also FOGOSCH.

foggiano, an Italian cheese which is made in Apulia from ewe's milk. It is similar to *cotronese.*

fogosch, a very delicately flavoured fish found only in Lake Platen, Austria. It grows to a large size and can attain 20 lb. in weight. The raw flesh is almost transparent, but when cooked it is very white, like the *fogas* of Lake Balaton, Hungary, to which it is related. It can be fried, grilled, baked, or braised in cream or wine, but its flavour is so good that it should not be disguised by too elaborate a sauce. See also FOGAS.

foie, French for liver. All kinds of liver are used in France for pâtés and terrines, as well as being cooked alone. Goose liver pâtés is renowned. See FOIE DE CERF; FOIE GRAS.

foie-de-boeuf, an alternative name for fistuline hépatique.

foie de cerf, French for deer liver. It is usually cut in large dice, and browned in butter with chopped onions, then seasoned, sprinkled with flour, moistened with stock and baked or simmered for 40 minutes. The sauce is finished with a few drops of vinegar and a little french mustard.

foie gras, the liver of a goose or duck, specially fattened by forcible feeding and made into a paste or pâté. The main region for this somewhat brutal way of making a gastronomic delicacy is Strasbourg, France, although excellent fois gras pâtés are made in Toulouse, Nancy, and Perigueux, where the goose livers can attain the abnormal weight of 4 lb. Other European countries, especially Hungary, Luxemburg, Czechoslovakia, and Austria, also produce good foie gras. The colour of a good goose pâté de foie gras is a guide to its quality; it should be a light creamy-brown tinged with pink and firm to cut. Duck pâté de foie gras, although very delicate, is less firm to cut. In the Périgord, chopped black truffles are added to the paste, which is then known as foie gras truffé.

Foie gras is served in various ways: as it comes from the jar, with bread or toast; in jelly (*foie gras à la gelée*); with garnishes, pancakes, mousse, terrines, and quenelles; and in pastry cases.

foil, also known as aluminium foil or ovenfoil. It is a thin silver sheet of paper used for refrigeration, or for sealing food from air or direct heat in cooking. It is of comparatively recent origin.

foin, I. French for the choke, or feathery part, of the globe artichoke. II. To cook au foin is a farmhouse method of boiling a ham on a bed of sweet hay, with water to cover. This method is also practised in the country in Ireland. Foin is French for hay.

fold, to fold foodstuffs in means to incorporate one with the other gently, without breaking. It can also mean to blend a light mixture into a heavier one. It is applied particularly to egg whites which are required to remain frothy after whipping—if beaten, rather than folded in, the froth would be absorbed. Also applied to delicate foods such as artichoke hearts, brains, or soft fish roes.

fondant, a kind of French icing for cakes, made from 2½ lb. (5 cups) sugar and 1½ pints (3 cups) water, with 2½ teaspoons glucose or 1 teaspoon cream of tartar, boiled to 238–240°F (soft-ball stage) and then beaten until white and solid. Various flavours are added as desired. It is also used for making candy and for glazing fruits.

fondants, French for very small croquettes made from vegetable purées or *crème pâtissière* mixed with grated cheese to taste, then fried. Served as hot hors d'oeuvre.

fonds brun, also known as *estouffade,* one of the principal French *fonds de cuisine,* consisting of highly seasoned beef broth. It is used for preparing sauces, soups, gravies, or casseroles. See also FONDS DE CUISINE.

fonds d'artichauts, French for artichoke bottoms, used extensively for garnish and in hors d'oeuvre. They are also filled with *salpicons.* See also ARMÉNONVILLE; BEAUGENCY; CLAMART; MARIE LOUISE.

fonds de cuisine, basic culinary preparations considered indispensable in large establishments as foundations for the preparation of soups, sauces, etc. The chief fonds de cuisine are fonds blanc (veal broth), fonds blanc de volaille (veal broth in which fowl has been cooked, sometimes called fonds blond), *fonds brun* or *estouffade* (beef broth), and fonds de gibier (game broth to which white wine has been added during cooking). All of these broths are highly seasoned. See also BLONDE DE VEAU; FONDS BRUN.

fonds de poisson, fish stock, highly seasoned, with the addition of white wine. This is often known as fumet.

fondue, I. A Swiss national dish made from grated or chopped cheese heated, but not boiled, in a special fireproof dish called a *caquelon,* from which it is served. Heating takes place over a spirit stove (chafing dish), which continues to keep the fondue warm throughout. The fondue is eaten communally, by guests taking small chunks of bread singly on a fork and dipping them in the mixture; custom decrees that anyone who loses a piece of bread in the dish supplies the company with a bottle of wine. When the "crust" at the bottom, which is considered a delicacy, is reached, it is lifted out and eaten with a fork.

The dish is prepared with 1½ lb. diced cheese (usually Gruyère) first rubbed in flour or corn flour (cornstarch), in dish rubbed with garlic. One bottle of white wine is heated in the caquelon and the cheese is added, being gently stirred until it is all melted. A few spoonfuls of kirsch, or other liqueur, are blended in, and seasonings. Almost every Swiss canton has its own variant. See also FONDUE AU FROMAGE; FONDUE BOURGUIGNONNE; FONDUTA; RACLETTE.

II. The name for vegetables such as carrots, celery, tomatoes, or leeks, finely sliced, and cooked gently in butter or oil in a covered pan until they become a purée.

fondue de tomates, a name used for all dishes à la provençale, à la *Portugaise*, or à la madrilene. It is also served with eggs, and is cooked as II.

fondue Fribourg, a cheese fondue made from the soft vacherin cheese. No flour is employed.

fondue Neuchâtel, cheese fondue made from both fresh and stale Gruyère.

fondue Valais, cheese fondue made solely from *valais raclette* cheese.

fondue au fromage, the name which Brillat-Savarin, the famous French gourmet and politician, gave to a dish he made of scrambled eggs and grated Gruyère cheese.

fondue bourguignonne, a Swiss national dish made with the same utensils as fondue and also eaten communally, but consisting of different ingredients. The caquelon is filled with hot olive oil, and strips of raw fillet steak on long forks are dipped in it and cooked to taste. Various sauce accompaniments, such as mustard, horseradish, béarnaise, and others, are made available separately, and the hot meat is dipped into one of them before being eaten. See also FONDUE.

fonduta, an Italian cheese fondue. A very famous Piedmontese dish made with fontina cheese, a buttery cheese of the region. Three oz. diced cheese is soaked in milk to cover, then melted into a thick cream with 1 beaten egg, 1 tablespoon butter, and seasoning. On top are placed fine slices of raw white truffles; it is a delicious combination. This quantity is enough for one person. When eaten with rice, this dish is called *riso ricco* or *riso con la fonduta*.

fonduta alla parmigiana, a comparatively new dish which was introduced to show that Parmesan cheese could be used equally as well as fontina for a fonduta. It consists of slices of Parmesan cheese alternating with sliced white truffles, and grated Parmesan cheese on top; it is heated gently in the oven.

fontainebleau, I. A French garnish for tournedos and noisettes consisting of bouchées made of pommes duchesse and filled with a mixture of diced spring vegetables in a cream sauce. II. A rich cream cheese made in the country districts round Fontainebleau from cow's milk, and eaten as a sweet or dessert course, mainly in the summer. It is also made commercially, when it is very light and fluffy. III. A soft and rather insipid version of *fromage blanc*, made chiefly during the summer months. *Triple-crème*, a superior grade of this cheese, can be obtained all the year round.

fontina, a famous Italian cheese made in Piedmont. It is like a buttery, creamy kind of Gruyère, but with much smaller holes. It can be rich if eaten alone, but it is perfect for the Piedmontese *fonduta*, for which it is always used.

fontine, a French cheese from Franche-Comté, made from cow's milk, and in season all year round.

fool, an English dish of puréed fruit. The fruit is left raw if a soft fruit such as raspberry is used, but is cooked if the dish is to be made with a hard fruit such as apple. It is sweetened and, just before serving, half its quantity of either whipped cream or whipped egg white is added. It is served in individual glasses, with a sweet biscuit (cookie). The name comes from the French verb "fouler" to crush.

fool quail, see MASSENA QUAIL.

forcemeat, from the French *farce* (stuffing), usually a very rich and highly flavoured mixture which is used either by itself or as part of the stuffing for various meats, fish, or fowl. It is also used for patties or vegetables. There are innumerable recipes for forcemeat, one of which uses ham and chicken or veal minced together, then pounded in a mortar with onion, salt, pepper, lemon peel, breadcrumbs, and chopped parsley. The mixture is bound with an egg to which milk is added, if necessary. See also GODIVEAU; GRATIN FORCEMEAT; PANADE; STUFFING.

forcing (pastry) bag, a funnel-shaped bag, fitted with nozzles

of different sizes. Creamy mixtures, and certain soft pastry mixtures, such as chou, are put into the bag and piped through the nozzle into decorative shapes. The forcing bag is also called a pastry bag in both Britain and the U.S.

forel, Russian for trout.

forel s vinom, trout poached in white wine or kvass (a Russian alcoholic drink made from rye, like a beer) with onion and herbs and served hot or cold with a little of the juice over it.

forelle, German for trout, usually cooked au bleu, or poached in fish stock and served with melted butter and lemon wedges. See also FISCH.

for-eller mellomrett, Norwegian for hors d'oeuvre. See also SMØRGÅSBORD.

forestière, à la, I. A French garnish for meat consisting of either sautéed *cèpes* or sautéed morels (depending on the season), cooked, diced, lean bacon, and *pommes noisette*. See also POULET SAUTÉ FORESTIÈRE. II. A French sauce made from demi-glace flavoured with sherry, with sliced sautéed mushrooms added.

Forfar bridies, a kind of Scots Cornish pastry made with strips of rump steak, with a hole cut on top to let out the steam. Sometimes chopped kidney and onions are included in the filling; if onion was included the baker indicated its presence to the customer by putting 2 holes in the bridie. Forfar bridies used to be served hot from the baker in Forfar, Scotland, in the 19th and early 20th centuries.

forlorne kyllinger, a Danish dish of veal rolls. Literally translated, the name means "mock chicken." Slices of beaten leg of veal are spread with a mixture of butter, minced parsley, and seasoning, before being rolled up and secured. The rolls are dipped in flour and fried until brown, when near-boiling cream is added to the pan and the whole simmered for about 45 minutes. Afterwards, the sauce is seasoned and poured back over the rolls, which are accompanied by creamed potatoes and buttered green peas.

formagella, see CACIOTTA.

formaggini, an Italian generic term for small soft cream cheeses made in factories. They are cylindrical and flat in shape but have distinctive flavours. They are sometimes eaten with olive oil and also used in cooking.

formaggini di Lecco, an Italian cheese from Lecco, Lombardy, made from cow's milk to which some goat's milk may be added. It can be eaten fresh or at any stage of its maturity. It is sweet when immature, but very piquant when fully ripe. The shape is small and cylindrical.

formaggini di Montpellier, a soft Italian cheese made from curdled cow's milk and white wine, with thistle blossoms added.

formaggio, Italian for cheese. See ASIAGO; BAGOZZO; BATTELMATT; BEL PAESE; BITTO; BRA; BURRINI; BUTTIRI; CACIO A CAVALLO; CACIOTTA; CANESTRATO; CASIGIOLU; CASTELMAGNO; CERTOSINA; CHIAVARI; COTRONESE; CREMINI; CRESCENZA; FIOR DI LATTE; FIORE SARDO; FONTINA; FORMAGGINI; FORMAGGINI DI LECCO; FORMAGGINI DI MONTPELLIER; FRESA; GORGONZOLA; GRANA; GROVIERA; LODIGIANO; MASCARPONE; MOLITERNO; MONCENISIO; MONTASIO; MOZZARELLA; NOSTRALE; OVOLI; PAGLIERINO; PANEDDA; PARMESAN; PECORINO; PECORINO SARDO; PEPATO; PERA DI VACCA; PRESSATO; PROVATURA; PROVOLA; PROVOLA DI PECORA; PROVOLONE; QUARTIROLO; RAGUSANO; RAVIGGIOLO; RICOTTA; ROBIOLA; ROBIOLINA; SCAMORZA; SCANNO; STRACCHINO; TALEGGINO; TALEGGIO; TOMINI DEL TALUCCO; TRECCIA; UOVA DI BUFALO; VENETO; VEZZENA.

forshmak, a Russian dish made from 1 lb. minced cold meat or poultry mixed with half a minced salt herring, 3 medium potatoes mashed, 1 medium onion fried, 1 tablespoon but-

ter, 3 tablespoons thick sour cream, 2 tablespoons breadcrumbs, and seasonings. This mixture is put through the
mincer, and then 3 raw egg yolks are added, followed by 3
beaten egg whites. It is all put into a greased oven dish,
sprinkled with either grated cheese or breadcrumbs and a
little melted butter, and baked for about 30 minutes. It will
come away from the sides of the dish when it is ready.
Forshmak is usually served with a sour cream and tomato
sauce, and is eaten hot for *zakouski*.

fouace, an old form of French pastry not unlike a *galette*,
made from fine wheat flour. It was originally cooked on the
hearth on hot stones and was covered with a round lid on
which hot ashes were placed. It is made in country districts in
all French provinces, but in the Auvergne a grand yeasted one
is made, with cognac, eggs, and butter, which is shaped like a
crown and baked in the oven. The word derives from the
Latin *focus* (hearth) as does also the Scottish and Irish *fadge*,
meaning a flat bannock or potato cake baked on a griddle.

fouée, a speciality of the Poitou region of France. It is a circle
of bread dough, uncooked, covered with either cream, butter
or olive oil, baked in a very hot oven. The word means
"faggot."

fougasse, a traditional round trellis of bread made from fine
flour and olive oil, and flavoured with aniseed. It is eaten at
Christmas in Provence. See also AïGO BOUïLLIDO.

fourme d'ambert or *fourme de montbrison*, a French cow's
milk cheese from the highlands of the Monts Forez. It is a
blue cheese, fermented, and mould-inoculated. It has a rich
blue marbling inside and is red or yellow outside. It is in
season from May to March.

fourmes de cantal, see CANTAL.

fournitures, French for salad greens and fresh herbs.

fowl, the generic term for chicken, but it is used particularly
for the older birds, which should be cooked by slow boiling,
braising, or steaming. Fowl is used for broth and as a basis
for soups, in forcemeat stuffing, in fillings for *vol-au-vent*,
and for quenelles and croquettes; it can also be boiled and
served cold with a salad or with mayonnaise. See also COCK-
A-LEEKY.

foyot, sauce, a classical French sauce composed of 1 cup
sauce béarnaise blended with 1 tablespoon meat glaze.

fragole, Italian for strawberries. They are used to great advantage in ice cream in Italy (*gelato di fragole*). *Fragole dei
boschi* is the Italian for wood strawberries, which are available all through the summer and are eaten with sugar and
sometimes orange or lemon juice, not with cream, which does
not go very well with them. They have an excellent flavour.

fragole or *fragoline di mare*, Italian for "sea strawberries."
These are tiny fish, very succulent and tender, members of the
squid and inkfish family. They are used mainly for *insalata di
frutti di mare*, a salad of small shellfish. They are also known
as totani, calamari, calamaretti, seppie, moscardini, and sepolini, according to local dialect. See also POLIPETTO.

fraise, French for strawberry. Fraise de bois is the French for
wood strawberry often served with coeur à la crème.

fraise de veau, French for calf's mesentery. This is eaten in
France, and the usual method of preparation is first to boil it
in a court bouillon and then cut it into pieces which are
dipped in egg and breadcrumbs before being fried in deep hot
oil. A sauce *piquante* is served with it.

framboeza, Portuguese for raspberry.

framboise, French for raspberry. Also for the French liqueur
made from distilled raspberries. The best raspberries come
from outside Paris and on the Côte d'Or.

framboos, Dutch for raspberry.

frambuesa, Spanish for raspberry.

francolin (*Francolinus*), a bird not unlike a partridge found in
all warm European countries, especially Greece and Sicily. It
varies in size and taste according to its diet, but when this has
been satisfactory, it is good to eat. It can be served in any
way that is suitable for partridge.

frangipane, a cream used in various desserts, cakes, and pastries, believed to have been created in France during the reign
of Louis XIII by an Italian called Frangipani. The mixture
consists of ½ lb. (1 cup) sugar, 6 oz. (1¾ cups) flour, and a
pinch of salt, mixed with 4 eggs and 4 egg yolks, and 3 pints
(6 cups) milk that has been boiled (scalded) with vanilla.
These ingredients are gently heated and cooked for 2–3 minutes, stirring all the time, after which ½ lb. (1 cup) butter and
2 cups crushed macaroons or pulverized almonds are well
mixed in.

panade à la frangipane, a French name for a cream prepared like frangipane but without the macaroons and sugar. It
is sometimes added to poultry and fish forcemeat, like a *panade*.

frango, Portuguese for pullet. See also CANJA COM ARROZ;
GALINHA.

frango a modo da Beira-Alta, alternate layers of cooked
chicken and pasta in a cheese or tomato sauce.

frango com ervilhas, chicken cooked by braising with
smoked ham (*presunto*), onions, bay leaf, and peas in port
wine barely to cover, seasoned to taste.

frango guisado, see GUISADO.

frango no fomo, chicken roasted in butter.

frankfurter bohnensuppe, a German regional soup from
Frankfurt, made from 1 lb. soaked kidney beans boiled in 4
pints (8 cups) water with 2 diced turnips, 2 carrots, 2 onions,
and seasonings. Before serving a generous amount of butter
and sliced frankfurters are added to the unstrained soup.

frankfurter würstchen, German for frankfurter sausage,
which originated in Germany but is now well known all over
Europe, and, particularly in the U.S., where it is also known
as the hot dog. It is made from minced pork and beef with salt
and spices. Frankfurters are sold ready cooked, lightly
smoked, either loose or canned, but may also be heated by
gentle boiling for a few minutes only, or grilling. Frying
makes them leathery, and is not advised. In Germany and
Austria, the most popular methods of serving them are hot
with sauerkraut or cold with potato salad. See also WÜRSTE.

frankfurters, see FRANKFURTER WÜRSTCHEN.

frappé, French for iced, used especially in the description of
creams, fruit, sweets and liquids.

frascati, à la, a French garnish for meat, consisting of thin
slices of foie gras, asparagus tips, mushrooms, and truffles.

frasye, see FROISE.

frattaglie, Italian for giblets used in Italy as a stuffing for
some ravioli.

frémissement, French for simmering, literally "shuddering,"
which describes the action perfectly.

french beans or *string beans* (*Phaseolus vulgaris*), a class of
beans which includes also kidney beans, snap beans, wax
beans, and wax-pod beans, and is grown almost exclusively
for the pods which are gathered before the seeds reach maturity. Their flavour is best when they are small and stringless,
and of course they command a higher price in this condition
than when grown to a commercial standard. Most French or
string beans are green, but some are white, yellow, or purple,
and there are dwarf as well as climbing varieties; the latter
must not be confused with runner beans. They have a very
high vitamin content.

French bean is the English name; string bean, the American. The former is due to the fact that the plant was introduced into England by Huguenots during the reign of
Queen Elizabeth I, having been brought to Europe from South

America; the American name is due to the fact that the pods become tough and stringy when allowed to mature. However, American string beans are often packaged under the name of French beans when they are cut on a diagonal in thin strips.

There are many varieties of this class of bean. The English wax-pod bean (American wax bean) has tender yellow pods which, when the beans inside are practically mature, are stewed slowly, whole. In France they are called mange-tout. The purple variety, which turns green in cooking, has an excellent flavour and is known as blue coco. Both the pods and the dried seeds of the kidney bean can be eaten. Haricot beans are the ripe seeds which are taken from the mature pods. See also BEAN; BOHNEN; BRUINE BONEN; FAGIOLINI; FASOLA; FASSOLAKIA FRESKA; FEIJÃO VERDE; JUDIAS VERDES.

French cheeses, see FROMAGE.

french dressing, an American term, although nowadays it is sometimes used in Britain, for a salad dressing consisting of 4 parts olive or salad oil to 1 part wine vinegar or lemon juice, seasoned with salt, freshly ground pepper, and sometimes prepared mustard; all are shaken well together before use. Purists insist, rightly, that only oil, vinegar, and seasonings be used for a true French dressing; however, in the U.S., sugar, paprika, cayenne pepper, curry powder, herbs, and even tomato purée, or ketchup can find their way into this dressing. Any of these strong flavourings completely changes the character, and is not advised.

french fried onions, the name given in the U.S. to large onion rings, dipped in batter, and fried in deep, hot oil. The term is also used in British restaurants.

french fried potatoes, the name given in the U.S. to fingers of deep-fried potato. They are called *pommes frites* in France, and chips in Britain.

French mustard, mustard from France, usually regarded as particularly fine. In France mustard flour is sold and is mixed with verjuice, wine vinegar, and many combinations of aromatic herbs. The finest French mustard comes from Dijon. In Bordeaux, a special mustard flavoured with allspice of the Pays Basque is made, which is extremely good. See also DIJON MUSTARD; MUSTARD.

french spinach, see ORACH.

fresa, another variety of the Italian cheese, *caciotta,* but made in Sardinia from either plain cow's milk or a mixture of cow's and goat's milk. The best fresa is made in the autumn and is eaten fresh. It is called fresa di Atunza.

fresa, Spanish for strawberry.

fresa di Atunza, see FRESA.

fressure, French for pluck; also called issues. See FERCHUSE; VENDÉE FRESSURE.

frétins, French for small fry, like whitebait, found in the Mediterranean.

friand, French for a hot hors d'oeuvre often including a sausage roll, that is, sausage meat enclosed in puff pastry. Literally friand means "dainty" or "nice."

friar's fish-in-sauce, a 19th-century Scottish recipe, perfected by Meg Dods, the owner of a memorable inn in Scotland, circa 1826. This excellent dish was made with either trout, carp, or perch, cleaned and, if large, split and divided, then rubbed with salt and mixed spices. The fish were put in a stewpan and covered with good fish stock, a few onions stuck with cloves, black peppercorns, and mace being included. After 5 minutes, a couple of glasses of claret or Rhenish wine, a boned anchovy, juice of a lemon, and cayenne were added. It was all simmered gently until the fish was cooked, then lifted out and kept hot. The sauce was thickened with flour rubbed into butter, and a dash of mushroom ketchup and a few oysters were put in. It was all strained and served hot over the fish.

friar's omelette, an old English sweet omelette made with cooked and sweetened apple, with butter and lemon juice added. It is made with 1 lb. apples puréed and left to cool. This is beaten with 2 raw eggs and put into a buttered baking dish strewn with breadcrumbs. It is covered thickly with more breadcrumbs, baked for 30 minutes, then sprinkled with sugar and served hot or cold.

fribourg, see BABA.

fribourg vacherin, a type of Gruyère cheese with a considerably high fat content and a white curd. It is produced only in Fribourg, Switzerland, and is not exported. It is eaten alone, or mixed with Gruyère for a Fribourg fondue.

fricadelles, French for small flat cakes of 1 lb. minced meat mixed with herbs, milk, 2 slices soaked bread or cooked potatoes, and 2 raw eggs, all rolled in flour or egg and breadcrumbs and fried.

fricandeau, I. A long thick piece from the top rump of veal. It is also used to describe a dish made from *noix de veau,* larded and braised or roasted. II. A dish made with the above joint, larded and braised. The best-known version is *fricandeau à l'oseille:* veal braised with sorrel and stock. Other garnishes served are: bouquetière; à la bourgeoise; à la clamart; à la florentine; à la jardinière; macédoine; à la milanaise; à la piémontaise; or with various vegetables such as braised celery, chicory, lettuce, or mushrooms. III. Slices or fillets of sturgeon or fresh tunny (tuna) fish, braised in fish stock.

fricandelles or *fricadelles,* Belgian pork balls made from 2 lb. minced pork with 1 minced onion, 2 slices bread soaked in milk, 1 gill (½ cup) white wine, 2 egg yolks, and 2 stiffly beaten egg whites. They are rolled in flour and fried till brown, then poached in 1 pint (2 cups) stock with a bouquet garni and 4 quartered potatoes. They are also put into *les choesels.*

fricandelles

fricassée, I. A French white ragoût, like a *blanquette.* It also usually applies to poultry, either cooked or reheated in a white sauce, or thickened white stock and/or white wine with various vegetables. II. Certain vegetables cooked in oil or butter with ham and garlic. III. In the Périgord, it means to remove the vegetables from a pot-au-feu before they are quite cooked; then to drain, slice, and brown them in butter or oil, sprinkle them with flour, and put them back to finish cooking. This is called fricassée Périgourdine.

fridatten, an Austrian garnish for soups consisting of a pancake cut into match-like strips and added to the soup just before serving.

fridatten suppe, a rich beef broth garnished with strips of fridatten and sprinkled with chopped chives.

friesian, a Dutch cheese similar to *leyden,* but with a mixture of cloves and cumin added to the curd. It weighs between 16 and 20 lb. and is seldom exported.

frigolet, alternative Provençal name, with *farigoule,* for wild thyme used a lot in Provençal cooking, especially with rabbit.

frijole, the Mexican name for bean, including pink, black, kidney, or pinto beans, which are cooked as Boston baked beans.

frijoles con queso, a Spanish-American dish of soaked, dried tepary beans cooked in water to cover until they can be mashed; then crisply fried bacon and diced or grated cheese are added, and all are heated until the cheese is melted. In Mexico, where this is eaten a great deal, green and root vegetables are added to the beans while they are cooking, and the dish is made hot with chilli. It is served with tortillas.

frikadeller, Danish meatballs made with pork and beef. One lb. of each meat is well minced (ground) and then mixed with 2 tablespoons chopped onion (optional), seasoning, and 4 tablespoons flour. In some parts of Denmark, breadcrumbs are substituted for flour. Then 2 lightly beaten egg whites are blended into the dry ingredients with a little milk, enough to make a mixture that holds its shape. (Sometimes whole eggs are used.) The mixture is formed into balls or cakes about ¾ inch thick and 2½ inches across. These are fried in butter until cooked through. See also KØDBOLLER.

frikadeller med rodkaal, fried meatballs served with cooked red cabbage. To make this dish more filling, some boiled, mashed potatoes may be mixed with the meat and flour.

frikadeller, I. Swedish meatballs made from minced veal, breadcrumbs, herbs, and egg white, like the Danish dish of the same name, and fried. They are then simmered in sour cream or yogourt. See also KOTT (KOTTBULLAR). II. Very small Swedish meatballs made from ½ lb. finely minced beef mixed with 1 tablespoon breadcrumbs, 1 tablespoon butter, 1 teaspoon potato flour, ¼ pint (½ cup) milk, and seasonings. They are then rolled with floured hands into tiny balls before poaching in boiling salted water. They are used as a garnish for soups.

frinault cendré, a French cow's milk cheese coated with wood-ash from Orléanais. It is in season from September to June.

frischkase, German for fresh, soft, cream cheese made from cow's milk, to be eaten within a few days of its production. Some cheeses under this heading are speisequark, schichtkäse, rahmfrischkäse, käsenach, liptauer art, and a type of gervais.

frischling, German for young wild boar, used to make an excellent pâté in Germany. See also WILDSCHWEIN.

fritas, Spanish for fritters. A Spanish fritter dish, good for an informal supper, is made from ¼ lb. minced chicken and ¼ lb. minced ham slowly cooked in 1 cup white sauce. When a fairly solid paste is formed, it is pressed between two pieces of stale bread. These sandwiches are coated with beaten egg and breadcrumbs and are fried in very hot oil.

fritot, French for any type of fritter made with small pieces of meat, fish, poultry, brains, sweetbreads, fruit, vegetables, etc. The pieces are dipped in batter, deep fried in oil, drained, and served with lemon; or for savour fritters, with a sauce such as tomato or tartare.

frittata, a flat Italian omelette that is not folded over like a French one. See also OMELETTE.

frittata aromatica, also called frittata al formaggio, is an omelette made with eggs beaten with grated Parmesan cheese to taste, chopped basil, marjoram, parsley, and seasonings, poured into a little hot olive oil or butter. The eggs are shaken round the pan and, when set underneath, a little more Parmesan cheese is sprinkled over the top, and all is gently browned under a grill. In country districts where there are no grills, a plate is put over the top and the omelette turned out onto it, then slipped back into the pan to allow the other side to brown gently.

frittata genoese, a Genoese omelette, made with basil, grated cheese, and sometimes cooked spinach added to the beaten eggs. The whole is cooked as *frittata aromatica.*

frittatine imbolitte, Italian stuffed pancakes, which consist of ordinary pancakes rolled up with a stuffing as for ravioli, garnished with butter and grated cheese, and cooked in a little meat or chicken broth.

frittelle, Italian fritters, often made of squares of fresh uncooked ravioli pasta, filled with pieces of bel paese or another cheese and ham, fried in oil, and served hot.

frittelle di arigusta, lobster fritters. The claw or tail meat of lobster or crawfish is seasoned and dipped in batter, fried, and served hot with mayonnaise.

frittelle di mele, apple fritters; for the batter, see PASTELLA.

frittelle di San Giuseppe, fritters made from ¼ lb. sweetened soft rice which has been cooked in 1 pint (2 cups) milk flavoured with vanilla and grated orange and lemon peel. The rice is cooled, then mixed with 2 beaten eggs, a glass (¼ cup) Marsala wine, and 2 tablespoons potato flour or plain flour. The mixture is left overnight, then shaped into croquettes and sometimes rolled in breadcrumbs and fried in deep, hot oil. It is always eaten, especially in Sicily, on St. Joseph's Day, March 19th. See also FESTA DI SAN GIUSEPPE.

fritter, in Britain and the U.S., any piece of food, sweet or savoury, dipped into batter and fried in deep hot oil. The most usual sweet fritters are made from apple, banana, or pineapple; the savoury ones are made from minced meat, poultry, or fish and are bound with a thick sauce béchamel so that they are firm before dipping in the batter. Generally speaking, however, a fritter in England means something sweet. See also BEIGNET; BUÑUELOS; CROMESQUIS; FRITAS; FRITTELLE; FRITTO MISTO; KUNGULL ME KOS; LOUKOUMADES; RIS (RISKLATTER); TIGANITES.

fritto misto, I. An Italian dish made with varying ingredients, all fried. It usually contains a few thin veal scallops, brains, artichoke hearts, slices of aubergine (eggplant), mushrooms, and cauliflower. Each ingredient is coated with batter (*pastella*) and fried in deep olive oil. It is served with halves of lemon.

fritto misto alla fiorentina, chicken breasts, brains, sweetbreads, artichoke hearts, and mozzarella cheese, prepared as above.

fritto misto di mare, a dish popular all along the coast. It consists of inkfish or squid cut into rings, unshelled prawns, and red mullet, all dusted with flour and fried in olive oil. It is served with halves of lemon.

fritto misto di verdure, a fried mixture of vegetables including aubergines (eggplants), small marrows (zucchini), and mozzarella cheese, all cut up and dipped in batter (*pastella*) before frying.

fritto misto Milanese, thinly sliced veal, calf's liver, calf's brains, croquettes, cock's combs previously cooked, sliced artichoke hearts, cauliflower flowerets, and chips of zucchini. All is coated with egg and breadcrumbs and fried in clarified butter. II. In France, fritto misto means calf's head fritters with tomato sauce.

friture, I. A French word for fried food of any kind, including fish, meat, and poultry. It can also mean the oil or fat used for the frying process. Une friture, although incorrect, is often used to describe a dish of small fried fish such as whitebait or smelts. II. In French, it is the term for deep frying. Friture à l'italienne is French for *fritto misto.*

friturier, see CHATOUILLARD; RÔTI.

frog, one of the many varieties of batrachian leaping amphibians. There are over 20 species, and in France, the European country where they are most popular as food, the green frog (*R. esculenta*) and the mute frog are those most generally eaten. In the U.S., the bull or bellowing frog (*R. catesbeiana*) and the leopard frog (*R. pipiens*) are the ones used for food.

They are at least twice the size of the European frog. Only the hind legs of the frog are used, and they are very delicious, tasting not unlike a very tender and delicate chicken. See also GRENOUILLE; RANA; ŻABKI.

frogfish, see ANGLERFISH.

froise, a term which occurs in old English cookery books. Its meaning is uncertain but seems to have denoted food which is fried, sometimes in batter. It is thought to be onomatopoeic, and to represent the sound food makes when dropped into deep fat. Palgrave, writing in 1530, mentions "Froyses of egges," which were eggs fried. In 1575, it is quoted as being a pancake with bacon on it. It is also found spelt as "frasye." By 1650, Cotgrave refers to a "Frasye," which appears to be a braise of chicken giblets, head, feet, liver, and wings, with parsley, butter, saffron, and hardly any liquid. It is like a fondue de légumes.

fromage, French for cheese. Many new cheeses are to be found from year to year in France, where there are over 300 varieties. The best known are those listed below, and individual entries are listed in this book. See AISY CENDRÉ; AMOU; ANISÉ; AUTUN; AYDES, LES; BANON; BARBEREY; BEAUFORT; BEAUMONT; BEAUPRÉ DE ROYBON; BLEU D'AUVERGNE; BLEU DE BASILLAC; BLEU DE BRESSE; BLEU DE LAQUEVILLE; BLEU DE SASSENAGE; BLEU DU HAUT-JURA; BLEU FERMIER; BLEU NATUREL DE L'AVEYRON; BONDART; BOSSONS; BOUILLE, LA; BOURSIN; BRICQUEBEC; BRIE; BRIE DE COULOMMIERS; BRIE DE MEAUX; BRIE DE MELUN; BRIE DE MONTEREAU; BRILLAT-SAVARIN; BROCCIO; BROUSSES; CABÉCOU; CACHAT; CAMARGUE; CAMEMBERT; CANCOILLOTTE; CANTAL; CARRÉ DE BONNEVILLE; CARRÉ DE L'EST; CHABICHOU; CHAMPENOIS; CHAOURCE; CHAROLLES; CHAUMONT; CHÉCY; CHESTER FRANÇAIS; CHEVRET; CHEVROTINS; CHEVROTTON DE MÂCON; CITEAUX; COMTE; COULOMMIERS; CRÈME DES VOSGES; CRÉMETS; CRÉMETS D'ANGERS; CRÉMETS NANTAIS; CURÉ; DAUPHIN; DE-CIZE; DEMI-SEL; EMMENTHAL; EPOISSES; EXCELSIOR; FEUILLE DE DREUX; FIN DE SIÈCLE; FONTAINEBLEAU; FONTINE; FOURME D'AMBERT; FRINAULT CENDRÉ; FROMAGE À LA CRÈME; FROMAGE BLANC; FROMAGE DE MONSIEUR; FROMAGE FORT; FROMAGE SEC; FROMGEY; GAPERON; GÉROMÉ; GERVAIS; GEX; GLUX; GOURNAY; GRIS DE LILLE; GRUYÈRE; HAUTELUCE; HUPPEMEAU; LAGUIOLE; LANGRÉS; LARRON, LE; LEVROUX; LIGUEUIL; LIVAROT; LUCHON; MANICAMP; MAROILLES; MAROILLES GRIS, LE; METTON; MIGNON, LE; MONSIEUR BLANC; MONT-CENIS; MONT-DES-CATS; MONT D'OR; MORBIER; MOTHE-ST-HÉRAYE, LA; MUNSTER; MUROL; NANTAIS; NEUFCHÂTEL; NIOLO; OLIVET BLEU and OLIVET CENDRÉ; OLORON; PALADRU; PAVÉ DE MOYEAUX; PELARDOU; PETIT SUISSE; PICODON; PITH-IVIERS AU FOIN; POIVRE D'ÂNE; POMMEL; PONTGIBAUD; PONT-L'ÉVÊQUE; PORT-DU-SALUT; POULIGNY-ST-PIERRE; PROVI-DENCE; PUANT MACÉRÉ; QUART, LE; REBLOCHON; RÉCOLLET; RICEYS CENDRÉ, LES; RIGOTTES; ROCAMADOUR; ROI, LE; ROL-LOT; ROMANS; ROQUEFORT; ROUENNAIS; SAINT-AGATHON; SAINT-BENÔIT; SAINT-CLAUDE; SAINT-FLORENTIN; SAINT-MARCELLIN; SAINT-NECTAIRE; SAINT-PAULIN; SAINT-RÉMI; SAINTE-ANNE-D'AURRAY; SAINTE-MAURE; SASSENAGE; SELLES-SUR-CHER; SEPTMONCEL; SORBAIS, LE; SOUMAINTRAIN; TAMIE; THENAY; TIGNARD; TOMME; TOMME AU FENOUIL; TOMME AU MARC; TOMME DE BELLAY; TOMME DE CANTAL; TOMME DE PRASLIN; TOMME DE SAVOIE; TOMME GRISE; TRÔO; VACHERIN; VACHERIN D'ABONDANCE; VACHERIN DE JOUX; VACHERIN DES BEAUGES; VALENCAY; VENDÔME; VENDÔME BLEU; VENDÔME CENDRÉ; VÉZELAY; VIC-EN-BIGORRE; VILLEDIEU.

fromage à la crème, a French fresh cream cheese made from cow's milk and cream which must be eaten within a few days of making. It is sometimes put in a heart-shaped mould, and is then called coeur à la crème. See also FROMAGE BLANC.

fromage au raisin, see TOMME AU MARC.

fromage blanc, also called fromage à la pie, the simplest

A selection of French cheeses, clockwise from upper right: cantal, pont l'évêque, coulommiers, reblochon, monsieur blanc, Valençay, roquefort.

form of cheese produced in France. It is made from un-skimmed cow's milk which is left to sour, then placed in a butter-muslin bag and, like cottage cheese, allowed to drain over a basin in a cool place. It is eaten sprinkled with salt and pepper. It can also be mixed with cream and eaten with sifted sugar, and is then known as *fromage à la crème.* When drained from a small, heart-shaped wicker basket, from which it acquires its shape and its name, it is called coeur à la crème and is often served with wild strawberries. All these varieties are made with fresh curds and must be eaten within a few days of making.

fromage de Bruxelles, a local Belgian cheese from the Hal district and Louvain. It is soft and fermented, and made from skimmed cow's milk.

fromage de curé, see CURÉ.

fromage de monsieur, a white, creamy, slightly fermented cheese from Normandy, made from cow's milk, with a fairly high butterfat content. It is usually sold in small round wooden boxes. When in peak condition, it is good. See also MONSIEUR BLANC.

fromage de porc, French for brawn made from pig's head and tongue.

fromage d'Italie, a French type of brawn made from pig's liver.

fromage d'ors, see LARRON, LE.

fromage fort, a French cheese paste popular in the district around Lyons. Layers of grated or thinly sliced cheese, with salt, chopped mixed herbs or leek juice, and cream are put into stone pots. The pots are filled up with white wine mixed with a little brandy, and hermetically sealed, and are left in a warm place for 2 or 3 weeks to ferment.

fromage mou, see MAQUÉE.

fromage sec, a dry French cheese made from cow's milk. It is a speciality of the Nivernais and Morvan district of France. It is made by drying white cheese in straw baskets, draining well, and dusting with pepper.

fromager, a French culinary term meaning to add grated cheese to a sauce or to dough stuffing, or to sprinkle it over a dish to be browned under the grill or in the oven.

froment renflé, a variety of wheat grown in the Mediterranean countries, though not in the British Isles despite its common name, English wheat. It is of low gluten content and makes poor quality bread.

fromenteau, a variety of French dessert grape.

fromgey, a white cow's milk cheese from Lorraine, France, which, when eaten locally, is spread on bread and sprinkled with chopped shallots or onions.

froschkeulen, German for frog's legs. See GRENOUILLE.

frosting, an American word for the icing on cakes.

frothing, an old English method of finishing many spit-roasted joints, which involved the meat being taken from the fire, dredged with flour, and having boiling water trickled over it for a few moments before being replaced in front of the fire for a final crisping. Today, a similar process takes place, whereby the meat is sprinkled with salt and basted with wine, cider, beer, or a good stock. This action is known as "to froth." See also BASTE; DREDGING.

fructose, a hexose sugar, that is to say, one having six carbon atoms in its molecule—the chief sugar found in fruit juices. It has a most delicious flavour but has recently (1967) been found to be associated with atherosclerotic conditions, though as yet no indication has been found that, when eaten by the normally healthy, it produces any undesirable results.

frugtsuppe, a Danish recipe for raspberry and red currant soup. The fruit is slowly simmered until all the juice is extracted. The juice is then strained and served chilled with a little whipped cream as a first course. The fruit can be sieved, and the resulting purée mixed with equal quantities of whipped cream and served as a dessert.

frühstückskäse, a rather soft German cheese of the limburger type made from whole or partly skimmed cow's milk. It is sometimes eaten after slight curing. During curing, yeasts and moulds grow on the surface of the cheese first, followed by the so-called red cheese bacteria and the formation of the surface smear. The names breakfast cheese, dessert cheese, or appetite cheese usually refer to cheeses of the frühstückskäse type. See also KASE.

fruit, the edible product of a plant or a tree, with seed or seeds enclosed in its flesh. Many fruits such as cucumber, eggplant, marrow (zucchini), and tomato are eaten as vegetables. All fresh raw fruits are rich in vitamins, and the citrus fruits are particularly rich in Vitamin C. Certain fruits, such as figs, plums, apricots, raisins, currants, and apples, are dried. They are soaked before cooking. See also FRUKT.

fruit salad, a dish prepared with innumerable different combinations of fresh fruits, the choice depending on individual taste and on availability. The general principle is the contrasting of flavours: the sharpness and piquancy of oranges, grapefruit, etc., opposed to the sweet blandness of peaches, pears, bananas, and so on. Colour also plays an important part in the composition of a fruit salad. The dressing is provided by the natural juice of the fruit, with some sweet liqueur and a few drops of lemon juice.

fruit kernel, the soft part inside the hard shell of a stone fruit. It is usually edible and, although inclined to be bitter, adds a good flavour to jams; this applies particularly to the apricot kernel. Nuts are fruit kernels.

fruits de mer, French for a dish of assorted crustacea and shellfish, all served together, either raw or cooked. It is used in particular for a plate of oysters or sea urchins. If the shellfish is cooked, it is served in certain cases with rice, as for a risotto.

frukt, Norwegian and Swedish for fruit.

fruktsoppa, Swedish for a dried fruit soup made from ¼ lb. each of prunes, dried apricots, and raisins soaked overnight in water and then stewed until tender, when they are put through a sieve. A cream is made of 3 heaped tablespoons sugar, 2 tablespoons corn flour (cornstarch) and 1 pint (2 cups) cold water, and this is added to the purée, which is reboiled for a few minutes. Swedish soups are served hot or cold, with rusks, or sometimes with Swedish cold dumplings.

frumenty, I. An old English dish which used to be prepared at harvest time in medieval England. New wheat was steeped in water and left on a low fire for 36 hours, so that the kernel was very soft. The liquid was strained, and the drained wheat boiled with milk, sugar, and spices such as cinnamon, mace,

or nutmeg. It was no doubt the forerunner of *flummery.* It is also spelt furmenty. II. A custard pudding made in the west of England. III. Children's food in the U.S. made with sugar and raisins, the yolk of an egg being added before serving. This is also known as furmenty.

frushie, a Victorian fruit flan popular in the west of Scotland. It has a trellis work of pastry over the fruit and is served with whipped cream. Frushie is an old Scots word meaning literally "brittle" or "crumbly," and it signifies the type of pastry with which the flan is made.

fry, I. A fish when it is still very young and not more than a few inches long. II. The intestines of pig and lamb are sometimes known as pig's fry and lamb's fry. See also HASLET.

frying, cooking in hot oil, butter, lard, or other fat. It is one of the most important ways of cooking and includes sautéing and deep frying.

deep frying is used for foods, sometimes covered by a batter and fried in a deep kettle or frying pan. The fat or oil (better for this kind of frying), which must be clean and which requires straining after use, has to come half-way up the pan, but not higher, for the water content of the foods causes it to rise, which can result in boiling over; also the fat or oil must be hot, but not smoking. A small cube of bread dropped in the oil should brown in 1 minute if the temperature is correct. The food is immersed completely in the hot oil and cooked to the desired degree, after which it should be drained on paper. Potato chips should be fried twice to obtain the best results. The first time they should only be a pale gold, then drained. Just before they are needed they should be refried in the hot oil to the desired colour. In this method they become very crisp. See also CHIPS.

dry frying, or pan frying, is used for steaks, chops, pancakes, griddle cakes, or other foods, sometimes breaded, and cooked in a heavy pan. Very little fat is put into the pan, just enough to lightly grease the entire base. For meats, the fat from the meat itself is often sufficient. The pan must be hot before the food is added. The food is browned on one side and turned at least once.

shallow frying, or sautéing, is used for all fish, eggs, croquettes, and meats which are sometimes coated with egg and breadcrumbs. A little clarified butter or fat, enough to cover the bottom of the pan is heated before adding the food. The food is seared in the hot fat to seal in the juices.

frying pan, a metal utensil made in varying sizes and used for frying.

fuaróg, see ABERDEEN CROWDIE.

fucetola, the name in the south of Italy for the figeater, a member of the warbler family, known elsewhere in the country as beccaficio. It is usually grilled on a skewer. See also UCCELLETTI.

fudge, a sweetmeat (confection) made from 1 lb. (2 cups) sugar, 1½ gills (¾ cup) milk, and 2 oz. (¼ cup) butter, with flavourings such as 3 tablespoons cocoa, chocolate, coffee, or 1 teaspoon vanilla. It is heated to about 240°F and then beaten to a thick cream before being poured into a shallow pan to set. It is cut into squares when cold. For nut or fruit fudge, chopped nuts, dried fruits, and ginger are also added.

fuggan, a traditional Cornish oval-shaped cake, marked on top with a criss-cross design made with knife strokes. It is made from 1 lb. (4 cups) flour, a pinch of salt, 8 oz. (½ cup) grated suet or lard, and 1 cup currants or raisins, mixed with ½ pint (1 cup) sour milk or buttermilk, or sometimes water, and then baked in a moderate oven. See also MEATY FUGGAN.

fugl, see FJAERKRÉ.

fulmar (*Fulmarus glacialis*), an Arctic petrel, an oceanic bird similar to a herring gull in size and colour. On St. Kilda, an island off the Scottish coast, numbers used to be snared annually for food, which made them nearly extinct. However, the fulmar now breeds much more extensively, as far south as southern Ireland. The eggs are highly prized as food on some Scottish islands, and the birds themselves are still salted and smoked for winter use.

fumet, this is a highly concentrated essence (extract) of fish or vegetables, obtained by stewing them in wine or stock until the liquid is greatly reduced. See also EXTRACT.

funcho, Portuguese for fennel, which grows wild in Portugal and is particularly in evidence in the south. It is used chiefly in soups, but seldom with fish—which in other Mediterranean countries is one of the major uses for fennel.

funghetti, an Italian culinary term applied to certain vegetables, such as eggplant, which, retaining their skins, have been cut into small pieces and fried. It does not mean that there are mushrooms in the dish, as might be imagined from the name.

funghi, Italian for mushrooms. There are many varieties in Italy, the most common being funghi porcini, the boletus (*Polyporaceae*). It is gathered in large quantities in early autumn and dried for winter use. Funghi ovoli (*Amanita caesarea*) are vivid scarlet and orange mushrooms which are also very popular in Italy; they are usually served either grilled or roasted. Funghi gallinaccii (*Cantharellus cioarius*), the French *chanterelle,* are rubbery yellow mushrooms found in the north. Funghi trun (*Armillarea mellea*) are delicious apricot-coloured mushrooms found in Piedmont. There are many others which are not mushroom-shaped but are edible and common in Italy: claviari (*Clavariaceae*), which is branch-shaped and coral in colour; famiglioli, which has a red flat top with yellow underneath; grifole (*Clavariaceae*), which is a very hard, fan-shaped grey fungus and grows from the bark of oak or chestnut trees, having to be boiled before it is edible; lingua di castagno (chestnut tongues), a vivid carmine colour, which looks spectacular growing on the bark of chestnut or oak trees; and poliporo, which has the same habit of growth but is brilliant yellow in colour. The last two fungi are related to *Fistulina hepatica,* the beefsteak fungus. *Grifole, lingua di castagno,* and *poliporo* all belong to the type of fungi known as "fleshy." *Ferlengo* is a large, fleshy, light brown mushroom found north of Rome. It is excellent fried in oil with garlic and parsley. See also MUSHROOM.

funghi alla graticola, large mushrooms grilled with garlic, olive oil, marjoram, and seasonings.

funghi fritti, perhaps the most typical Italian way of cooking mushrooms. They are dipped in batter (*pastella*) and then fried in olive oil.

funghi in umido, mushrooms cut in thin slices and stewed in olive oil with garlic, chopped mint, salt, and black pepper.

funghi ripieni, large mushrooms stuffed with chopped ham or bacon, garlic, parsley, grated Parmesan cheese, breadcrumbs, and seasonings. They are brushed with olive oil, covered, and baked in the oven.

salsa di funghi, a mushroom sauce served in Verona, and usually made from ½ lb. dried mushrooms, which are soaked and added to a small sliced onion, parsley, and 1 clove garlic, then fried in a mixture of butter and olive oil. It is sprinkled with flour, seasoned, and simmered. (The water from the soaked mushrooms should be enough liquid.) It is served with pasta, risotto, veal, or poultry.

fungi, see MUSHROOMS.

furmenty, see FLUMMERY; FRUMENTY.

fusilli, helix, a thin spiral-shaped spaghetti formed into a twist like a corkscrew. The name means literally "twists." See also PASTA ASCIUTTA.

fylt kålhode, a Norwegian dish of cabbage stuffed with minced meat and braised.

fynbo, a Danish cheese of the samsoe variety, but smaller. It is made on the island of Funen and is a hard, rich, yellow cheese with shiny holes. There are little cheeses from ½ lb. to 2 lb. in weight, and larger ones up to 15 lb. See also OST.

fyrstekake, Norwegian for almond flan. There are two different recipes. In one a sandwich tin is lined with a pastry made from 1 oz. sugar, 4 oz. (½ cup) butter, 8 oz. (2 cups) self-raising flour, and 1 egg. Then 8 oz. (1 cup) sugar is mixed with 4 oz. (1 cup) minced Jordan almonds, and together they are once more put through the mincer, after which the mixture is combined with 3 egg yolks, followed by 3 beaten egg whites. This forms a filling for the flan case, and the whole is baked in a reasonably hot oven, the heat being reduced after the first 15 minutes, and baking continued for a further 30 minutes. In another recipe 6 oz. (⅔ cup) butter, 5 oz. (½ cup plus 1 tablespoon) sugar, and 10 oz. (2½ cups) flour are sifted together and an egg yolk, beaten with 1 tablespoon cream, is added to the dry mixture. The resulting dough is rolled out and used to line a 9-inch flan tin which is filled with a mixture composed of 3 beaten egg whites into which are beaten in small amounts 8 oz. (1 cup) sugar and 4 oz. (1 cup) ground almonds. The whole is baked in a fairly hot oven and served cold.

G

gachas, a curious sweet dish from Cádiz, Spain. It is made from 2 tablespoons flour added to 3 tablespoons olive oil in which 1 teaspoon aniseed has been fried; it is stirred until it bubbles, but not brown. Then ½ pint (1 cup) boiling water is added, and the mixture is simmered and whipped until it is like a fine porridge or baked custard. It is served hot with sugar, honey, and milk.

gachas manchegas, a traditional dish from La Mancha, Spain. It is made of 1 lb. pig's cheek or chap, cut into small pieces, and fried gently in oil. The meat is removed, and to the oil are added 2 oz. *almorta* flour, a pinch of paprika, caraway seeds, pepper, 1 clove, and ½ pint (1 cup) boiling water. This is simmered until thickened, and is served with the pieces of pig's chap in it, as an entrée. See also CERDO.

gädda, Swedish for pike. In Sweden pike is often simmered in salted onion stock and served garnished with dill or parsley and horseradish sauce or melted butter. See also FISK.

ugnstekt gädda, baked pike. The gills are removed from a young fish about 2 lb. in weight, but the head is left on. The fish is then rubbed with salt, brushed with egg, sprinkled with breadcrumbs, seasoned, and baked with butter in a moderate oven, being basted frequently with ½ pint (1 cup) of hot fish stock or milk. It is garnished with parsley and lemon.

gade, the French name in Normandy for red currant, from which a delicious jam is made. It is called *gadelle* in western France. See also BAR-LE-DUC.

gadwall (*Anas strepera*), a wild duck which is highly thought of for the table and is not unlike the mallard. It breeds in Europe, North America, and North Asia, and migrates south in summer. It is sometimes known as the gray or sand widgeon in the U.S. It can be prepared for table in any way as for wild duck.

gaffelbidder, the Danish name for cured herrings of exceptionally fine quality. Each coastal town or village has its own secret curing process. Some of the finest of these herrings are almost purple in colour. They are served on their own, with onions, or sometimes with boiled potatoes and beetroot. See also HERRING.

gaffelbitter, "fork bits," the Norwegian equivalent of the Danish *gaffelbidder,* applied to slices of raw pickled herrings which are canned commercially with dill and often in a wine sauce. See also HERRING.

galaktopolia, a Greek shop where one can order and eat a small bowl of yogourt, ice cold *rizogalo,* or *crema.* These small eating places can be very welcome on a hot day after sampling the *vin du pays* too generously, or climbing the steep slopes to the Acropolis, and visiting other places of interest to the traveller in Greece.

galangal (*Alpinia officinarum*), an Arabian plant from the root of which a mild form of ginger is produced. It should not be confused with galingale.

galantine, a dish made from boned, cooked, stuffed white meat, poultry, game, or fish, which is put into its own jellied stock and served cold. The stuffed food is usually restored as far as possible to its original shape and wrapped in muslin before cooking. The galantine is pressed when cold, and the outside is often glazed. This was a popular dish in Edwardian England. It is not known whether the name comes from the Gothic root *gal* (jelly) or from the Old French *galine* (chicken). A name for a similar dish is *ballotine,* but this can be served hot or cold. *Galantyna* is Polish for galantine which is a popular dish in that country.

A cold buffet with galantine of duck and galantine of chicken

galareta, Polish for jelly.

galareta z ryby, fish jelly. A whole pike, perch, or carp is poached in court bouillon. The stock is reduced, then whipped with egg whites (2 egg whites to 1 pint stock) and poured over the fish. When cold it is garnished with prawn, sliced hard-boiled eggs, and truffle.

galathée, the French name for a species of crustacean rather like the freshwater crayfish, which inhabits the European coasts of the Atlantic and the Mediterranean. It is prepared and cooked as lobster.

galatoboureko, an elaborate vanilla cream or custard pie made in Greece, from 20 sheets of phyllo pastry layered with a custard sauce. The sauce is made in a double boiler, with 6 oz. semolina, 4 pints (8 cups) milk, 1 lb. (2 cups) sugar, 6 eggs, 2 teaspoons grated lemon peel, and vanilla to taste. Before cooking it is all brushed with melted butter, and sprinkled with cold water to prevent the pastry leaves curling up. When the pie is cooked, after about 1½ hours in a moderate oven, a syrup made from 1 lb. (2 cups) sugar, 1 teaspoon lemon juice and grated peel, and 2 pints (4 cups) water is poured gradually over it. It is served cold. These amounts make approximately 12 to 15 portions.

galerts, a traditional Latvian dish of jellied, potted veal. It is made from calf's head and feet, 3 onions, 3 turnips, 2 bay leaves, and seasonings, all cooked in water to cover until tender. The bones are then removed and all is strained and minced. Hard-boiled eggs, sliced cooked carrots, parsley, and butter are now added and the stock is poured over. It is left to jelly and then served in slices with grated horseradish or mustard.

galette, I. A thin round French cake made from different kinds of grain: wheat, barley, oats, buckwheat, or maize. II. A puff pastry cake, or a dough with yeast. The best known are described here. III. A round, savoury cake, often made from potato, and sometimes using *pommes duchesse.*

galette bretonnaise is made from 4 oz. (1 cup) flour, 2 oz. (¼ cup) butter, 4 oz. (½ cup) castor sugar, and 2 small eggs with the grated peel of ½ lemon. This is well mixed as for pastry, with the addition of 5 oz. (1 scant cup) of currants. The mixture is divided into pieces the size of a small egg, put onto a greased baking sheet, and flattened slightly. They are brushed with beaten egg, marked with a knife, and baked in a fairly hot oven for about 15 minutes.

galette de plomb, made from ½ lb. (2 cups) sieved flour mixed with 2 eggs, 4 tablespoons thick cream, 2 tablespoons sugar, and a pinch of salt, all well kneaded, then left in a cold place for 2 hours. The dough is rolled out and cut into circles about 4 inches across, brushed with egg, scored on top with a knife, and baked in a hot oven for 10 minutes.

galette de pommes de terre, peeled and finely sliced potatoes fried in overlapping slices in a mixture of olive oil and butter, seasoned with salt, black pepper, and nutmeg. As soon as this ''cake'' starts to cook, it is covered and the heat lowered. It is then left for 15 minutes. By this time the potato will have formed a pancake, which is turned over and gently browned on the other side.

galette des rois (cake of kings), a cake traditionally eaten in France on Twelfth Night, January 6, the Feast of the Epiphany. It is a light, flaky pastry cake made from *pâté sucrée.* The pastry is baked blind and then filled with jam and whipped cream. In the south of France, yeast is incorporated into the dough. It is thought to have originated in pre-Christian times, when it was usual to bake a dried bean in the cake; whoever found the bean was made king for the day, and all the family had to fulfill his wishes. This custom prevails to the present day.

galettes de maïs, little cakes made from maize flour, fried in butter and served with many meat dishes in the Savoie and Bordelais regions of France. They are also called *millas, millias,* or *milliassou.* See also MILLAS.

galettes suisses, Swiss almond biscuits made from 4 oz. (1 cup) flour, 2 egg yolks, 4 oz. (½ cup) sugar, ½ cup ground almonds, 1 teaspoon vanilla, and 2 tablespoons soft butter, all worked to a dough. This is chilled, then rolled out thinly and cut into small rounds which are brushed with beaten egg, sprinkled with sugar and shredded almonds, and baked in a hot oven for 10 minutes.

galichons or **calissons,** small almond cakes with icing. A speciality of Aix-en-Provence, France.

galicien, a French cake-like dessert, extremely light, made with 1 lb. (2 cups) sugar, 12 oz. (3 cups) flour, and 16 eggs. The eggs and sugar are whipped together over a very gentle heat, and when the mixture is three times its original bulk, it is taken off the heat and the flour is stirred in very gradually. It is then poured into a baking tin and baked in a fairly hot oven. When cool, the cake is sliced across and filled with *crème au beurre* flavoured with pistachio nuts. It is covered with icing blended with more nuts, and decorated.

galingale (*Cyperus longus*), a plant whose tubers are edible and not unlike a faintly gingery hamburg parsley root. It is used in France and called souchet or, colloquially, amandes de terre. The roots are a pinkish colour when cooked and smell of roses. It was used a great deal in medieval England as a spice. In Geoffrey Chaucer's *The Canterbury Tales,* the cook was to ''boil the chicknes and the marybones and poudre marchant tart and Galingale.'' ''Poudre marchant'' was a tart kind of flavouring powder. See also POUDERS.

galinha, Portuguese for hen. See also FRANGO.

galinha corada, a Portuguese method of cooking chicken with 1 tablespoon paprika, ½ pint (1 cup) Madeira wine, 4 oz. chopped bacon, 4 tablespoons butter, and 2 tablespoons parsley. It is roasted for about 1½ hours in a moderate oven.

galletas, popular small Spanish cakes or biscuits made from 8 oz. (2 cups) sifted flour, 4 eggs, 1 lb. (2 cups) sugar, 6 oz. (¾ cup) butter, grated peel of 1 lemon, and ½ teaspoon salt all well mixed, then rolled into long strips. These are twisted into different shapes, such as plaits (in Madrid) or small round cakes with a hole in the centre, and they are often variously flavoured with cinnamon or brandy or other liqueurs. They are brushed with egg yolk and baked on a greased baking-sheet in a moderate oven for about 20 minutes.

gallimaufry, a medieval chicken stew, with bacon, verjuice, ginger, mustard, and wine. It was originally French, but was introduced into Britain by the Normans.

gallina, Spanish for hazel grouse which is quite plentiful in Spain and cooked as for partridge.

gallina del mar, Spanish and Maltese for gurnard, a red fish with an ugly large head. It is excellent to eat, and in Spain is either baked with 2 tablespoons butter, ½ pint (1 cup) white wine, and 1 tablespoon chopped parsley, or poached with herbs. Other Spanish names for gurnard are *carpón* and *trigla.*

gallina faraona, see FARAONA.

gallinaccio (*Cantharellus cibarius*), a rubbery yellow mushroom found in Italy. See also FUNGHI.

gallinella or **capone** (*Trigla lyra*), a spiny fish found in Italy and used in fish stews and soups. It is often known as sea-hen in English.

gallinule, an alternative name for moorhen, but also the name given to another genus of the same family (*Rallidae*), of which there are two particularly well-known species. The European purple gallinule (*Porphyrio porphyrio*), which is twice as big as the moorhen, ranges in colour from purple to sky blue, and breeds in Europe, mainly in southern Spain, Sardinia, and Sicily. It is also found as far away as New Zealand. The American purple gallinule (*Porphyrula martinica*), which is similar to the moorhen in size, has plumage predominantly of a rich purple, and is found in areas ranging from the southern U.S. and the West Indies to southern Central America. Gallinule can be cooked in the same way as moorhen.

gallo de San Pedro, Spanish for john dory. Baked whole, covered with slices of lemon, a little garlic and onion, and sprinkled with white wine and olive oil, these fish make a delicious dish. The name means "St. Peter's cock," and the fish is supposed to bear the mark of St. Peter's thumb upon it; another Spanish name for it is *dorado.*

gallopoulo, Greek for turkey.

gallopoulo yemistos, roast stuffed turkey. It is usually stuffed with 1 lb. boiled, chopped chestnuts or walnuts, 4 oz. chopped almonds, 1 tablespoon pignoli, the chopped turkey liver, 2 cups fresh breadcrumbs, 2 sticks chopped celery, 3 tablespoons sultanas, and 1 small chopped onion. The fowl is rubbed with lemon, salt, pepper, and butter, before roasting. Plenty of stuffing is made, and any that cannot be fitted inside the bird is made into little cakes which are fried and served as a garnish. Minced lamb, lamb's liver, rice, tomato, herbs, and spices are also used for stuffing.

galo das urzes, Portuguese for grouse, which is usually braised in red wine with herbs and garlic.

galuptzi, see HOLISHKES.

galuska, a small Hungarian egg dumpling, used as a garnish. The dumplings are made from 8 oz. (2 cups) sifted flour, 1 egg, salt, and enough water to make a stiff dough. They are usually served with *csirke paprikás* and with other stews and soups. See also CSURGATOTT TÈSZTA.

galushki, Ukrainian dumplings, usually made from 10 oz. (2½ cups) flour, ½ cup melted butter, 2 eggs, and salt, mixed to a soft dough with ½ cup sour cream. This is rolled out to a thickness of ½ inch and cut into small pieces which are poached in boiling salted water and served with either melted butter or sour cream. After poaching they are sometimes fried in butter.

galushki s syrom, as above, but with the addition of 8 oz. (1 cup) dry *tvorog* to the dough. Galushki s syrom are sometimes put into an ovenproof dish, covered with butter and sour cream and baked until golden brown.

gamba, Spanish for prawn; langostina and *cigala* are other varieties. These abound in Spain, and are cooked in many ways. They form part of paella, and are also cooked in the oven in their shells with garlic, parsley, and olive oil for *tapas,* as well as being served plain with drinks.

gambas al jerez, shelled raw prawns (shrimp) marinated for 2 to 3 hours in olive oil, with garlic, salt, parsley, and sherry to barely cover. They are then either grilled (broiled) or sautéed until cooked, and served hot with cocktail sticks.

gamberetti, Italian for prawn (shrimp). Often served poached in court bouillon, then marinated in olive oil and lemon juice.

gambero do mare, Italian for lobster. True lobster, however, is seldom found in Italian waters, and what is sold and eaten as lobster is very often crawfish (*aragosta*).

gambero imperiale, see MAZZANCOLLE.

game, wild animals, birds, or fish that are hunted for sport or food; also the flesh of these creatures. The most common all over the world are deer, rabbit, hare, bear, boar, duck, goose, pheasant, partridge, grouse, quail, snipe, woodcock, and pigeon. In some countries game laws restrict the seasons, and in some cases prohibit the killing of certain birds or animals that are scarce or in danger of extinction. Entries for these birds (known as feathered game) and animals (known as furred game) will be found in their alphabetical place in the book. Cold cooked game and their carcases make a variety of dishes, such as game salad, game cutlets, game quenelles, pies, pâtés, terrines, and soups. A famous game soup made from old game birds is called potage *St. Hubert,* St. Hubert being the patron saint of hunters. Game fish are usually large,

like barracuda for example, and are sometimes coarse to eat. See also AMBELOPOÙLIA; CODORNIZ; DZICZYZNY; DZIKIE GESI; FAISÁN; GIBIER; HAAS; HASE; JÄNIS; KOUNELI; LAYOS; OLEN; PERDIZES; PERDREAU; PERNICE; PERTHIKES; PINGIÀDA; POROL; RIEKKO; TÀCCULA; TETERKA; UCCELLETTI; VILDT; VILT; WILD; ZAJĄC; ZAYATS.

game cutlets, minced cold game mixed with its weight in either breadcrumbs or cold mashed potato, chopped parsley, basil, salt, pepper, and 1 or 2 eggs (depending on the amount of game mixture; 1½ lb. of mixture requires 2 eggs). It is rolled into small flat cakes which are dipped in flour and fried in hot oil on both sides. They are sometimes served with a fresh tomato or mushroom sauce.

game quenelles, see QUENELLES, OF GROUSE.

game salad, another method of using leftover game. The scraps are mixed with an equal quantity of cold boiled rice, a finely sliced onion, a green or red pepper, and a little diced cucumber or large gherkin is added. They are mixed well together, and some olive oil, a very little wine vinegar, and a tablespoon of yogourt are poured over. It is served cold as an hors d'oeuvre.

game soup with lentils, made with black lentils which have been soaked overnight, and with either game or venison stock to cover. The soup is simmered gently with 1 sliced onion and chopped herbs for 2½ hours. Diane and Royale garnish are used for game soups.

game chips, wafer-thin slices of potato cut across the tuber and fried until golden brown in deep oil at 395°F. They are served with game and poultry, but when served with drinks or cocktails they are called crisps. The packaged variety are not at all bad if salted and warmed up in the oven. I have found them much improved if a little crisply fried onion is added to them, but this should be done just before serving, so as not to make them soggy. See also CHIPS.

game crumbs, dry breadcrumbs fried in melted butter until golden, drained, and served separately with feathered game which has been roasted.

gammelost, the most popular Norwegian skimmed cow's milk hard cheese, made from curd which is naturally soured, not rennetted. Gammel means "old"; however, the name "old cheese" does not mean that the cheese is eaten when old, but refers to the method of using naturally soured milk as opposed to rennetted milk. It is a round, flat cheese weighing between 6 and 9 lb. although sometimes larger cheeses weighing up to 25 lb. are made. It has a green-blue-brownish veining throughout, which in factories is induced by piercing the cheese with needles impregnated with *Mucor ramosus* and *Penicillium roqueforti,* but on farms this process occurs naturally, as the rooms are full of the fungus spores which settle in the cheeses. The curing period is about a month. Sometimes, when the gammelost is partly cured, it is put in chests lined with straw which has been treated with juniper extract, and this gives the cheese a flavour that cheese gourmets strongly object to. Gammelost is made mainly in the west of Norway, and the finest comes from the Hardanger and Sogn districts. See also OST.

gammon, an English term originally meaning the cured foreleg of a pig. The hind leg is usually reserved for hams, but nowadays a slice of gammon is often taken from the top of the ham. It is generally a whole slice, cut thickly, and is grilled or fried. It can be smoked or green (unsmoked). A thick slice of gammon is often called a ham steak, particularly in Ireland and the U.S.

ganga, a type of hazel grouse common in the Pyrenees.

gannet or ***solan goose*** (*Sula bassana*), a large white seabird with black-tipped wings, found breeding on the Faroe Isles and also in the Gulf of the St. Lawrence. Up to the late 19th century, the gannet was considered very good eating in the British Isles, but now it seems to have gone out of fashion. However, the fishermen in the Outer Hebrides still enjoy it, and the young birds are salted for winter use. The eggs were relished by English royalty in the 19th century. Gannet can also be prepared for the table and cooked in the same way as wild goose. See also GOOSE.

gans, Dutch for goose, traditional Christmas fare in Holland.

gebraden gans, roast goose. Boiling water is first poured over the bird both inside and out; it is then stuffed with 10 medium peeled and sliced cooking apples and roasted in butter in a moderate oven, being basted fairly frequently. Allow 25 minutes per lb. When half cooked, the bird should be seasoned and then returned to the oven.

gans, German for goose. The finest German birds come from Nordling in the south. Goose is more popular in Germany than in the British Isles, and is always served at Christmas, having been especially fattened for this occasion. It is frequently roasted and stuffed with boiled chestnuts and chopped apples, and sometimes served with cooked, chopped *nudeln* and hot, cooked red cabbage, or sauerkraut. This is called gänsebraten. In Thüringen, dumplings made from grated raw potatoes are the usual accompaniment. Prunes, apples, and raisins or sultanas, mixed with breadcrumbs and a pinch of cinnamon, constitute another stuffing which is particularly popular in Mecklenburg. Every part of the bird is utilised, the liver being a particular delicacy. See also GEFLÜGEL; GOOSE.

gänseklein, a dish of cleaned and chopped goose giblets cooked with an onion stuck with cloves, parsley, and water to cover, then simmered until very tender. Meanwhile, 3 or 4 pears or apples are peeled, cored, and sliced, simmered in butter, and when cooked, mashed to a smooth purée. The onion and parsley are removed from the giblet gravy, which is thickened with breadcrumbs and then has the fruit purée stirred into it. See also GIBLETS.

gänseleber, goose liver, which is usually cooked separately. As a result of the special fattening of the bird, the liver can be enlarged from 4 to 6 inches across. A simple but delicious way of cooking it is to encase it in gänseschmaltz and then to roast it for approximately 20 minutes in a hot oven. It should be pink in the middle and soft in texture. It can also be cut into thick slices, dipped in egg and breadcrumbs, and fried in butter, or goose fat. Perhaps it is best of all poached in port- or Madeira-flavoured veal stock, and when cold, covered with aspic jelly. It can also be sautéed in butter, mashed, and served as a pâté or pie. See also GIBLETS; LEBER; LIVER.

gänseleber mit äpfeln und zwiebeln, goose liver soaked in milk for 1 hour, then dried and rolled in salt, paprika, and breadcrumbs before lightly frying in butter on both sides. Then 2 peeled, sliced apples and 1 large sliced onion are added, and fried until golden. Some German cooks omit the breadcrumbs and fry each ingredient separately, serving them in small piles on the same dish, covered with a sauce made from the pan juices reduced with ¼ pint (½ cup) Madeira, and 1 large sliced mushroom or truffle.

gänseschmaltz or *gänsefett,* preserved goose fat, used for many dishes which require rich, clarified fat. When the goose is drawn, all fat and the giblets are removed from the inside, and when the bird is half-roasted, half the fat is drained off. The fresh fat and the drippings are put into a saucepan with a few slices of apple and a little salt. It is simmered until clear, then strained and put into small jars covered with paper or foil, and stored in a cool place. It is often served plain on rye bread, or on boiled or jacket potatoes.

gänseschwarzsauer, German goose soup made from goose stewed in water with vegetables, prunes, bay leaf, cinnamon, clove, lemon, salt, and pepper; the stock is thickened with goose blood.

ganslsuppe, Austrian and German goose soup. The legs, wings, feet, and gizzard of a goose are boiled in white stock which is then strained, seasoned, and thickened with a roux of flour and butter. It is garnished with cauliflower sprigs, marrow dumplings, and the chopped giblets. See also GEFLÜGEL (GEFLÜGELKLEINSUPPE).

ganso, Spanish for goose. It is also called *oca.* Goose is sometimes eaten on festive occasions in Spain, but generally duck, or the cheaper pheasant, is preferred. See also GOOSE.

gantois, Flemish pastries made from ½ lb. (2 cups) flour, ½ lb. (1 cup) brown sugar, 10 tablespoons butter, 2 eggs, 1 teaspoon cinnamon, ½ teaspoon ground cloves, and a pinch of baking soda. The dough is rolled and cut into 5 rounds which are cooked in a moderate oven for 15 minutes, then spread with greengage jam and put one on top of the other. The whole is coated with a concentrated apricot jam, and then covered with ¼ cup icing (confectioners') sugar mixed and flavoured with 3 tablespoons ground almonds, 1 tablespoon candied orange peel, and 1 egg white. It is then gently browned in a slow oven, and served cold.

gaper (*Mya truncata*), a bivalve which lives buried in the sand or mud flats at the mouths of rivers and estuaries. It is found all round British and French coasts. Large quantities are collected at low tide, boiled, and eaten like cockles. Around Belfast, Northern Ireland, they are called cockle brillion. Kunyu is the name for them in the Orkney Islands, spoon-shell in Devonshire, brélin in Brittany.

gaperon, a French cow's milk cheese from Limagne. It is in season from September to July.

gar (*Lepisosteus osseus*) or **garpike,** a freshwater pike-like fish found in the U.S. It is poor to eat and can only be used for pounding up and making into quenelles.

garam masala, the Indian name for the mixture of ground spices such as cardamom, cloves, cinnamon, cumin, coriander, mace, ginger, turmeric, and black pepper, known as curry powder in Europe and the U.S. In India it is always freshly ground and is seldom available ready made.

garbanzos, Spanish for chick-peas. In Spain they are used extensively in stews, casseroles, and salads, as well as being made into a thick puréed soup. Ingredients for the soup are 2 onions, 1 leek, 1 bay leaf, 2 cloves garlic, a pinch of saffron, 1 tablespoon herbs, 2 tablespoons butter, and 3 eggs, with 1 lb. soaked chick-peas and 3 pints (6 cups) water. The eggs and butter are added last, being stirred into the hot soup before serving. See also CHICK-PEA; COCIDO; POTAJE.

garbanzos a la madrileña, chick-pea soup (as above, but without the egg mixture) diluted with beef stock and garnished with croûtons. Sometimes diced *chorizo* is added, and on fast-days ½ lb. soaked *bacalao,* cut into small pieces, is cooked with the peas.

garbure, a thick soup (from the word garbe, a sheaf or bunch). It is Béarnaise in origin and is traditionally made in an earthenware pot.

garbure à la Bayonne, a soup–stew from Bayonne in the Basses-Pyrénées. It is made from 1 young, green, shredded cabbage, ¼ lb. bacon, 2 tablespoons goose fat, some slices of the rye bread popular in that district, a joint of *confit d'oie,* and ¼ lb. *confit de porc* (known locally as *méthode*). All are immersed in 4 pints (8 cups) water, are well seasoned, and simmered for about 3 hours.

garbure à la béarnaise, a traditional soup–stew from the Béarn, which varies widely in preparation. It is generally made from ½ lb. salt pork (known there as *trébuc*), slivers of preserved goose, carrots, garlic, potatoes, cabbage, fresh green beans, and seasonings all cooked slowly with water to cover for 2–3 hours. It is strained, and the salt pork and goose are sliced and arranged in layers on a dish, moistened with the stock, then sprinkled with a mixture of grated cheese, breadcrumbs, and butter; it is browned and served from the dish after the soup. See also GOUDALE.

garbure à la paysanne, another traditional soup–stew. Sliced carrots, turnips, leeks, onions, and potatoes (approximately 2 of each), and cabbage are simmered until cooked in a white ham stock to cover. The mixture is seasoned, mashed, and spread on triangles of bread, with a little fat stock added, then covered with grated cheese, breadcrumbs, and butter, and browned. These croûtons are served hot on a plate, separate, with rich beef broth, like the Italian *crostini.*

garden relish, a relish from the U.S. often served with cooked turnip greens or cooked meats, especially hamburgers. It consists of 2 tomatoes, 2 stalks celery, 1 cucumber, 1 green pepper, and 2 tablespoons onion all chopped finely, mixed together, then dressed with 2 parts olive oil to 4 parts vinegar, salt, and pepper.

garfish (*Belone belone*), known also as the sea needle or sea eel, this fish is sometimes described as a cross between an eel and a mackerel. It is a thin fish, 2 to 3 feet in length, its head projecting forwards into a very long, thin snout. The sides and belly are a black and silver colour, the back green, marked with a dark purple line; the bones are bright green. It makes its appearance in northern waters in the summer. It is considered good to eat, although the bones can be annoying. The most usual method of cooking is to grill or fry it in butter. It is popular in Mediterranean countries as well as in Scandinavia. In Italy quite small ones, about a foot long, are eaten. It is sometimes known as garpike, and is no relation to the freshwater gar.

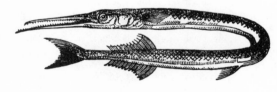

garfish

garganey or **summer teal** (*Anas querquedula*), one of the smallest members of the duck family, commonly found breeding on the Norfolk Broads, where it is also known as cricket teal. It is not esteemed very highly by the gastronome because its flesh has a certain marshy flavour in the spring, but it is thought a good bird in the autumn. It is best when marinated before cooking. See also TEAL.

garibaldi, a biscuit (cookie) of Italian origin, and named after the general Garibaldi, but very popular in Britain, where it is known by children as ''squashed-fly'' biscuit (cookie). It is a flat sweet biscuit made from 1 lb. flour, 6 oz. (⅔ cup) sugar, 3 tablespoons syrup, 1 heaped teaspoon baking powder, ½ teaspoon mixed spice and salt, with currants sandwiched between 2 thin layers of the dough. It is pricked on top, brushed with egg, and baked in a quick oven.

garides or **garithes,** Greek for shrimps. Shrimps caught in Greek waters are as large as Dublin Bay prawns. They are popular in Greece and are used in *pilafi,* brushed with oil and grilled or fried, and also braised.

garides me saltsa, a dish for which shrimps or prawns may be used. The shellfish are braised with onions, tomatoes, tomato purée, parsley, olive oil, and seasoning, then removed, shelled, and returned to the sauce to be served.

garides yahni, 2 lb. boiled shelled shrimps are sautéed in oil with 1 lb. peeled chopped tomatoes, 2 sliced onions, 3 tablespoons parsley, and seasoning, then simmered for 20–30 minutes in 1 cup stock from that available after the shrimps are cooked.

garlic (*Allium sativum*), a plant of the onion family, most useful if treated with discretion. Although it was decreed in Ancient Greece that people who ate garlic should not be allowed inside the temple of Cybele, it has been esteemed from earliest times as an intestinal antiseptic. Pliny gives a long list of the complaints it is said to cure, and it is still much used in medicine today. In the Middle Ages in Europe it was thought to be a cure for leprosy and lepers were sometimes referred to as ''pilgarlics.'' It is also thought to counteract evil supernatural forces. A 9th-century Irish poem runs as follows:

> *Is leighas air gach tinn*
> *Cheamb 'us im a Mhàigh*
> *Ol 'an flochair sid*
> *Bainne-ghobhar bán.*

> (Garlic with May butter
> Cureth all disease
> Drink of goat's white milk
> Take along with these.)

The sections of the garlic bulb are known as cloves of garlic. It is excellent with lamb or mutton, tiny slivers being inserted in the meat before cooking; it is very good in most stews, and an important ingredient in some sauces, soups, and salads. The wild ''crow garlic'' (*A. vineale*) and field garlic (*A. oleraceum*) grow prolifically. The leaves can be used for flavouring, in the manner of chives, and if eaten by cows, they can flavour the milk. To flavour a green salad, especially chicory, the interior of the bowl is rubbed with a cut clove of garlic. If a strong flavouring is required, a *chapon* is made and placed in the dressing to soak for a while before adding the salad. See AÏLLADE; AÏOLI; AJO; BEURRE AÏL; CHESNÓK; USTUROI.

garlic vinegar, 2 oz. peeled and bruised garlic is added to a quart of white wine vinegar which is then kept in a cool place for about a month. At the end of this period it is filtered and bottled.

garnaal, Dutch for shrimp. The shrimps found in Dutch waters are small but of excellent quality, and they are a popular seafood throughout Holland. When fresh they are usually eaten steamed or boiled, on slices of bread with a little lemon juice or vinegar and pepper, or in salads with mayonnaise.

garnalen croquetten, shrimp croquettes made with 1 lb. (2 cups) peeled minced fresh shrimps, ½ teaspoon grated nutmeg, and 1 tablespoon chopped parsley, all heated gently with 3 tablespoons butter, 2 heaped tablespoons flour, and ½ pint (1 cup) milk until it is a thick paste. The resulting mixture is allowed to cool before being made into individual shapes. Each croquette is rolled in breadcrumbs, then in a mixture of beaten egg and water, and then once again in breadcrumbs. They are left to stand for about 30 minutes before being fried on both sides in oil until golden.

garnalen saus, shrimp sauce, a useful accompaniment to cooked sole. It is prepared with ½ lb. (1 cup) peeled shrimps, 1 tablespoon chopped parsley, and a little mace all mixed into 2 cups white sauce made from 3 tablespoons butter, 3 tablespoons flour, and 1 pint (2 cups) fish stock or milk. When blended, pepper and beaten egg are added, but the sauce is not allowed to reboil.

garnish, tasty and decorative accompaniment to whatever is the main item of a dish. Garnishes are designed not only to appeal to the eye, but also to stimulate the palate by complementing or underlining the flavour of fish, meat, or fowl, whichever it may be. It may consist of a single ingredient, such as butter, wedges of lemon, or a chopped herb. The most common are described here. See also GARNITUR; GARNITURE.

breadcrumbs. butter is heated until lightly smoking; then coarse, stale white breadcrumbs are added, and lightly tossed until crisp and golden. They are sprinkled with salt and served hot with vegetables such as cauliflower, or with game birds and turkey.

croûtes, larger versions of croûtons, on which small birds or entrées are served.

croûtons, rather stale, close grained, and crustless pieces of bread are cut into plain dices, or else stamped with special cutters into small decorative shapes. They are sometimes rubbed with garlic. Butter is heated until almost smoking, and in this the croûtons are tossed to fry on all sides. They are served as a garnish for soups, vegetables, eggs, or entrées.

fleurons, a common French garnish made of very thinly rolled scraps of puff pastry, shaped into an oval or crescent, baked or fried, and served hot to garnish soup or entrées.

freshly cooked vegetables, both root and green, are also used as a garnish. Also raw tomato, lettuce, or watercress.

fried parsley, washed and dried parsley, with the large stalks removed, is fried in boiling fat until crisp. It needs careful handling and is mainly used as a garnish for fish dishes or *oeufs au beurre noir.*

quenelles, are also used as a garnish in both Britain and France.

suet dumplings, salt and pepper are added to sieved flour with finely chopped suet and mixed to a stiff dough with cold water. This is shaped into small balls which are poached in boiling water or stock.

garnitur, German for garnish. See BACKERBSEN; BUTTER-KNÖPFE; EINLAUF; FLECKERLN; FRIDATTEN; GRIESWURFEL; REIBGERSTL; SCHÖBERL.

garniture, French for garnish of which there are several hundreds in French cuisine. They comprise various ingredients which blend with the foods and flavours of the main dish. Simple garnishes consist of a single element such as cream or butter worked with herbs or another component (see BEURRES COMPOSÉS). Lemon slices, or a sprinkling of herbs or grated cheese can also constitute a garnish. The numerous French classical garnishes are in the main what are known as composite garnishes, that is garnishes made up of a number of ingredients, sometimes including a sauce of the same name, with vegetables, shellfish, foie gras, truffles, mushrooms, or quenelles added, as well as croûtons, fleurons, tartelettes filled with *salpicon* or a purée, rice, pasta, etc. French classical garnishes are rigidly bound by their main ingredient, and the names are a guide to the uninitiated. For instance, *dubarry* must contain cauliflower; *florentine,* spinach; *parmentier,* potatoes; and *vichy,* carrots. Classical French garnishes can be found in their alphabetical order throughout the book, and largely take their names from the creator or the place of origin. The main French soup garnishes consist of small croûtons, fleurons, quenelles, royale, or simply grated cheese.

garoupa, Portuguese for a large variety of *besugo,* usually served *cozido.*

garpike, see GARFISH.

garum, also called liquamen, was a basic condiment or sauce used by the Romans. It was made from the entrails of small fish, such as anchovy, atherine, sprats, small mackerel, or scomber, put into a vessel and salted. It was left to dry in the sun for about 2 months, when it was strained and potted. Later it could be flavoured individually with either vinegar, oil, or pepper, the latter being the most popular and called *garum nigrum.* Several towns were famous for their factory-

made garum, and in the ruins of Pompeii a small jar was found bearing the inscription "Best strained liquamen. From the factory of Umbricus Agathopus."

gås, Danish for goose. Geese are eaten in Denmark nearly all the year round, but particularly around Christmas time, when the goose is traditionally served for the Christmas Eve dinner. As is the case with most Danish meats, it comes to the table carved, garnished with its own stuffing and parsley, and served with boiled potatoes and red cabbage.

gåsestegt med æbler og svesker, roast goose with an apple and prune stuffing. The fat from the inside of a 12-lb. bird is removed and covered with cold water, before being drained and melted (it is used later for basting requirements). The inside of the bird is rubbed with seasoning and stuffed with a mixture of ½ lb. each peeled, cored, and sliced apples, and chopped, stoned prunes, 1 cup breadcrumbs, and seasoning. It is then rubbed with salt and roasted in a hot oven, with some goose fat, first on one side and then on its back, stock from the neck and giblets being used for basting. To make the skin crisp, 2 or 3 tablespoons cold water are poured over the bird 15 minutes before serving. The gravy is strained of excess fat and thickened with potato flour or corn flour (cornstarch) (1 tablespoon to 1½ cups stock), boiled up, and reduced before serving in a heated gravy boat. See also GOOSE; KRÅSE.

gås, Norwegian for goose. Geese cooked in the Norwegian manner have a prune stuffing (*sviske fylling*). See also FJAERKRÉ.

gås, Swedish for goose, a bird which is highly thought of throughout Sweden. On November 11, the annual feast day of St. Martin, it is the custom to serve a dinner of roast goose, preceded by giblet soup garnished with slices of goose liver sausage, and followed by a layer cream cake. See also FJADERFA.

stekt gås, roast goose. The goose should be young and weigh about 10 to 12 lb. It is first rubbed with seasoning inside and out, then roasted with 1 pint (2 cups) veal or chicken stock in a fairly hot oven for about 2½ hours with frequent basting. For a goose, the Swedish housewife invariably chooses an apple and prune stuffing. Quartered and peeled cooking apples are placed inside the goose alternately with stoned prunes. Roast goose is served already carved in Sweden, but the bird's shape is ingeniously maintained. It is accompanied by hot braised red cabbage, browned potatoes (*potatis*), and a gravy which is made by creaming corn flour (cornstarch) with potato flour and cold stock, and is added to the liquid in the pan and seasoned.

A Swedish way of using up the leftovers from a goose is to mince pieces from the bird's carcase with lean cooked ham (½ lb. goose to 1½ oz. ham); the mixture is pounded down to a paste, and ½ the quantity of butter is added, by degrees. The paste is seasoned with curry powder, nutmeg, or mace. This potted goose is sealed in jars with clarified butter and served with dry bread or toast. Goose leftovers can also be devilled like chicken (*kycklinglår med ris*). See also GOOSE.

gastrochère, see FISTULANE.

gastronome, I. A French garnish for fish, poultry, and sweetbreads consisting of glazed chestnuts, truffles, *rognons de coq,* and morels. II. A sauce consisting of ½ pint (1 cup) demi-glace mixed with 3 tablespoons champagne, Madeira, and a pinch of cayenne pepper, all reduced before serving.

gâteau, French for a large cake usually iced and layered with various creams. It can be served as a sweet course. See also CAKE.

gaudes, a French porridge not unlike *polenta* and made from maize flour; it is peculiar to the Franche-Comté, Burgundy, and other districts. After being cooked and left to get cold, it may be eaten sliced and fried in butter, or served hot or cold with cream and sugar.

gaufre, the Belgian and French waffle made from a batter mixture, sometimes with yeast or baking soda. To prepare them 1 lb. (3½ cups) flour is mixed with ½ lb. (1 cup) butter, 2 oz. (¼ cup) sugar, 3 eggs, 1½ teaspoons baking soda, and 1 teaspoon vanilla. All is well mixed and allowed to stand before being cooked on the heated irons. For yeast waffles, 1 oz. fresh yeast or ½ oz. dried yeast is substituted for the baking soda. Sometimes two waffles are sandwiched with a filling of cream. See also BRANDY SNAP; WAFERS; WAFFLES.

gauloise, à la, I. A French garnish served with consommé, consisting of cock's combs and cock's kidneys, both poached, julienne of pancake, and chervil. See also CONSOMMÉ. II. A garnish for *vol-au-vent* having cock's kidneys as the chief ingredient, with chopped tongue and truffle, all in a Madeira-flavoured sauce suprême. III. A chicken consommé garnished with cock's combs, cock's kidneys, and cubed ham royale. IV. Small cakes made of *pain de gênes* mixture, cooked in special tins, and topped with apricot jam and grilled chopped almonds.

gautrias, a French cow's milk cheese from Mayenne. It resembles port-du-salut.

gaves, a delicious river trout from the streams and rivers of the Béarn district of France.

gayettes, flat sausages made from 3½ lb. pork liver and 3½ lb. fresh bacon, both finely chopped with 2 garlic cloves and seasonings, wrapped in pork caul, and baked in the oven for 30–40 minutes. They are served cold as an hors d'oeuvre in Provence.

gazpacho, a Spanish soup. See SOPA. *Gazpacho colorado,* literally red gazpacho, is gazpacho served hot with crusty bread.

gean, Scottish dialect name for a wild cherry. The word comes from guigne, old French for Anjou, and it was from here that this cherry was brought to Scotland. These cherries, which have now been cultivated, may be red, black, or white; they are firm and fairly sweet. In France they are used to make a liqueur called guignolet which is a speciality of Angers. See also CHERRY.

gebie, a small crustacean not unlike a shrimp, but whitish in colour. It is found off the French coast and cooked as shrimp, but mainly used for bait.

gefillte fish (*stuffed fish*), gefüllt is German for stuffed. This traditional Jewish method of cooking fish was specifically designed to give the utmost flavour to the freshwater fish eaten by Jews in those countries far from the sea. Nowadays, however, with deep freezing, sea fish are also used. Large bream or carp are used but whitefish or pike are still the most popular. Large gashes are made across the back which are then stuffed with a mixture of herbs, breadcrumbs, matzo meal or cracker crumbs, and vegetables. Nowadays the fish is usually cut right through, and each section is skinned and filleted before being stuffed; but the most common modern method of all is for about 3 lb. cooked fish to be minced with 2 onions, 1 tablespoon chopped parsley, 2 stalks celery, and 1 carrot, and then thoroughly mixed with 1 cup breadcrumbs, cracker crumbs or matzo meal, 2 eggs, and seasoning, before being made into balls and poached in fish stock. A little stock is poured over each drained ball which jellies when cold. They are delicious and usually eaten cold.

gefillte helzel, a Jewish dish of chicken or other poultry neck stuffed with various ingredients, such as a mixture of cooked chestnuts, breadcrumbs or flour, onion, herbs, and schmaltz, roasted or boiled with the bird. Sometimes it is cooked with *kasha, tzimmes,* or *nahit.* See also GIBLETS; HELZEL.

geflügel, German for fowl or poultry. See also ENTE; GANS; HUHN.

geflügel ragoût, an Austrian and German stew made from giblets, liver, and leftover poultry, with onions, caraway seeds or cumin, tomatoes, and stock. It is cooked as below.

geflügelkleinsuppe, a soup made from the giblets and wings of a large bird such as goose or turkey, which are cleaned and cooked with 1 onion, 2 leeks, and 2 carrots, in 3 pints (6 cups) water with seasonings for 2 hours. Then 1 lb. peeled, raw potatoes are added to the strained stock, and cooked until tender. It is thickened with a *beurre manié,* the giblets are chopped and put back in the soup tureen, and finally 1 tablespoon chopped parsley and 2 tablespoons sour cream are added to the soup. See also GANS (GANSLSUPPE).

gehirnwürst, a German würst made from blanched pig's brains and pork (lean and fat in equal parts), seasoned with mace, salt, and pepper. It is served cooked in butter.

geitost, "goat cheese," the Norwegian term for cheese made from the whey of goat's milk and often served in Norway at breakfast time. This type of cheese is also eaten in Sweden, where it is called *getost.* There are several varieties of geitost: *ekte geitost,* "genuine goat cheese," is made exclusively from goat's milk whey; *blandet geitost,* "blended goat cheese," is made from a mixture of cow's and goat's milk whey. There is also a special type of geitost made in the Gudbrandsdal valley, *Gudbrandsdalsost;* this must contain as much as 35% butterfat, and is sweeter than the other types. The paste of this cheese is a medium brown colour, and the texture is hard. It is a coarse cheese. See also MYSOST; OST.

gekruid ijs, a Dutch spiced ice cream made with 2 slices stale black rye bread, ground and mixed with 2 tablespoons maraschino and ½ teaspoon each of ground cloves and cinnamon. This is mixed with 1½ pints (3 cups) soft vanilla ice cream and frozen hard.

gelatine, a brittle, transparent, slightly yellow substance, tasteless and colourless, made from prolonged boiling of bones, tissues, skin, tendons, and ligaments of fish or mammals. It is sold in sheets or powdered, and when mixed with hot water forms a viscous substance which is used to set liquids when they are left to get cold. It is used for making aspics, sweet jelly, and certain mousses both sweet and savoury. It is sold commercially, and instructions for use are sold with the packet.

gelato, Italian for ice cream. See also ICES; TORTONI.

gelderse rookworst, a Dutch smoked sausage with a spicy flavour. See also ROOKWORST.

gélinotte des bois, French for hazel grouse, which is cooked in ways similar to those used for partridge in France. See also PERDREAU; PERDRIX.

gendarme, I. A popular slang term in France for a pickled herring. II. A dry, very hard sausage made in Switzerland.

génévoise, sauce, a classical French sauce made from 1 pint (2 cups) white roux moistened with the liquid obtained by cooking certain kinds of fish and, when blended, 1 tablespoon butter, 1 teaspoon finely chopped parsley, 2 thinly sliced mushrooms which may or may not have been simmered in butter, a few drops lemon juice, a chopped shallot, and a small wineglass (½ cup) dry white wine, if wine has not been already used in the fish dish, are all added. The whole is reduced by slow cooking and is strained and served hot. A little anchovy essence (extract) is sometimes added. The liquid used to make the roux may be further flavoured by cooking in it the bones, head, and debris of the fish and reducing greatly, when it becomes a fish *coulis.* It is served particularly with salmon or salmon trout. This was originally called *génoise.*

genièvre, French for juniper. French for juniper berries is *baies de genièvre,* and they are used a lot in game cooking. They also form an essential part of Liégeoise cooking.

genoa cake, a cake like the French *genoese,* but in England it is made with half the number of eggs, and the butter and sugar are creamed together before adding the flour and eggs. It is more like a Victoria sponge.

génoise, see GENÉVOISE.

genoese, a cake made from 1 lb. (4 cups) flour, 1 lb. each (2 cups) sugar and butter, a trace of vanilla, and 16 eggs. The sugar, vanilla, and eggs are whisked in a double boiler over hot water until very frothy; then the flour and the softened butter are beaten in. This amount makes three large cakes; they are baked in a moderate oven for about 45 minutes. The cake may either be iced or cut into layers and filled with chocolate or creams. It is a spongy, light, rich cake. See also PAIN DE GÊNES; SAINT-MICHEL.

genovese, salsa, a Genoese sauce for serving with pasta made from 1 large onion sliced and fried in butter with a carrot, 3 tomatoes, 1 tablespoon soaked dried mushrooms, 1 stalk celery, and ¼ lb. chopped veal. Then 1 tablespoon flour is added with ½ pint (1 cup) white wine. When bubbling, ½ pint (1 cup) stock is added. The sauce is seasoned and then simmered for 30 minutes. It can be served as it is, or put through a sieve.

gentleman's relish, the popular name for *patum peperium.*

Georges Sand, a French fish consommé with fish quenelles, cooked sliced morels, *beurre écrevisses,* and croûtons with carp soft roe. See also CONSOMMÉ.

georgette, a French name for certain foods, particularly potatoes, when they have been stuffed with braised crayfish tails.

geräucherte bratwürste, German smoked würste, made from 6 lb. lean pork and 1 lb. fat bacon, mixed with 2 oz. salt, 2 oz. saltpetre, and black pepper. The pork is finely minced and the bacon coarsely minced, before the mixture is put into casings and smoked for about a week.

germaine, a French chicken or meat consommé, garnished with chicken quenelles and cubes of green pea royale, sprinkled with chopped chervil. See also CONSOMMÉ.

German cheeses, see KÄSE.

German sago, a potato flour coloured with oxide of iron, or sugar burnt to a yellowish white.

German wheat, see EINKORN; ÉPAUTRE.

germbutterteig or *germteig,* an Austrian and German puff pastry made with 1 oz. yeast dissolved in ¼ pint (½ cup) tepid milk, 2 oz. (¼ cup) butter, 2 oz. (¼ cup) sugar, and 5 egg yolks, with 1 lb. (4 cups) flour. When all the ingredients are well mixed, 3 whole eggs are well beaten and mixed in and the dough is then left to rise in a warm place. Germbutterteig is used for many Austrian pastries.

germinal, a French meat consommé with tarragon garnished with green peas, beans, and chopped chervil. See also CONSOMMÉ.

germon, I. The local name in Normandy, France, for bonito caught off the Atlantic Coast. II. The name for the small long-finned tunny (tuna) fish (*Thunnus germo*), also called albacore, found in the Mediterranean. It has a white flesh which is very good to eat. It can be used for all recipes for tunny (tuna) (*Thunnus thynnus*). See also ALBACORE; ATUN; BONITO; TUNNY.

géromé, a French cow's milk cheese from the valleys of the Vosges, first made in the valley of Gérardmer. It is made with whole milk and is fermented. It has a rather soft consistency and a strong flavour; the paste is yellow and the rind brick red. It is eaten from November to April. Sometimes the géromés are flavoured with fennel, aniseed, or cumin seeds, and are then known as *géromé anisé.*

gerste, German for barley.

gerstensuppe, a beef or mutton broth cooked with barley, popular in Germany and the German-speaking parts of Switzerland, particularly Engadine. See also ULMER GERSTLSUPPE.

gerty meat puddings, a traditional Cornish dish, and the West

Country haggis. The insides of a pig are thoroughly cleansed with salt and steeped overnight in brine. The lights (lungs), melt (spleen), heart, and kidneys are covered with cold water and brought to the boil. When they are cooked, the liquid is set aside. The fat and lard surrounding the offal (variety meat) are melted and mixed with the minced cooked entrails. Then 1 part of groats to 3 of the liquid are boiled until cooked, and added to the minced ingredients with salt and pepper. The skins are filled with this mixture and boiled gently for 45 minutes. Gerty meat puddings become known as "black pots" with the addition of pig's blood to the mixture before it is put into the skins.

gerty milk, a traditional Cornish breakfast dish, often used, even in comparatively recent times, instead of porridge or bread and milk. It is prepared with 4 oz. (1 cup) flour and 2 pints (4 cups) milk (the flour being first made into a smooth paste with cold milk) boiled together, but kept runny, and seasoned with salt and pepper. It is eaten hot. There are two old Cornish sayings about gerty milk: If a man was hacking old stumps he would say, "Gerty grey, if you won't come up there you may stay," or "Gerty milk, if you won't come up I'll break the hilt." Gerty grey is made with water instead of milk.

gervais, a cheese made in Normandy from cow's milk and sold in packets. It is like a *demi-sel.*

geś, Polish for goose. See also GOOSE.

geś pieczona nadziewana kasztanami, roast goose stuffed with chestnuts, minced fresh pork, buttered shallots, nutmeg, and marjoram.

geś pieczona nadziewana pasztetem, roast goose stuffed with minced goose liver, veal, breadcrumbs, thyme, truffles, and egg.

gęsia szyja nadziewana na zimno, goose neck stuffed with the minced goose liver, ½ lb. minced veal, and 3 oz. chopped salt pork, 3 tablespoons breadcrumbs, 4 small cooked sliced mushrooms, 1 tablespoon butter, and 2 egg yolks. The neck is secured with a fine skewer, and pricked here and there with a needle to allow for swelling. It is then simmered in stock for 1 hour. When cool it is pressed between boards with a weight on top. It is served cold, carved into slices, with a sharp sauce such as tartare.

geschnitzeltes mit rösti, a Swiss dish of finely chopped veal simmered in white wine and broth, served with *rösti.*

geselchtes, the word in southern Germany and Austria for cured and smoked pork. See KASSELER RIPPENSPEER; SCHWEINE-FLEISCH.

gęsinka, a traditional Polish soup. Strips of celeriac, carrots, onions, and mushrooms are cooked in butter, with a little water; then they are rubbed through a sieve, mixed with a little beef broth, sour cream, and egg yolks. The soup is seasoned with salt and lemon juice, and garnished with cooked pearl barley.

gespickter fisch, see FISCH.

gesztenye, Hungarian for chestnut.

gesztenyekrém, a Hungarian pudding made from ½ lb. (1 cup) sieved cooked chestnuts mixed with 1 pint (2 cups) rich custard, 2 tablespoons rum, and ¾ pint (½ cup) whipped cream. It is served cold.

getost, the Swedish "goat cheese." It is made from the whey of goat's milk in both Sweden and Norway. See also GEITOST; MYSOST.

gevetch-de-peshte, a Jewish fish and vegetable dish, basically Rumanian, but eaten by Jewish people in many other parts of the world as well. It consists of 4 lbs. pickerel or trout, 3 tablespoons oil, 4 tablespoons flour, ½ lb. (1 cup) green beans, 1 cup chopped celery, 1 cup chopped cabbage, 2 chopped carrots, 1 small eggplant, 1 cup peas, 1 green pepper, 4 sliced potatoes, 4 skinned tomatoes, 2 diced turnips, 3 sliced onions,

½ pint (1 cup) water, salt, and pepper. First the fish is rubbed inside and out with oil and dusted with flour. The vegetables are sliced and mixed; some are used to fill the fish, the rest laid evenly on the bottom of an oval dish large enough to contain all those listed above. The stuffed fish is then placed on the bed of vegetables and sprinkled with diced onion. Water is added, and the dish is baked at about 350°F for 45–50 minutes, or until the potatoes and beans are tender. During cooking the sauce should be level with the fish, but should not cover it. Salt and pepper are added to taste in a cupful of sauce taken from the dish and then returned to be reheated. The dish is ready when the fish is lightly browned and all vegetables are tender. The fish is lifted out carefully onto a large serving platter and surrounded with the vegetables; sometimes the vegetables and gravy are served separately. This dish is closely related to *ghiveci*, to the Greek *yiouvetsi*, and the Bulgarian *gyuvèch*. It varies according to available foods and national cooking habits.

gex, a French blue-veined cow's milk cheese from the uplands of the Jura mountains and the Pays de Gex on the Franco-Swiss border. The paste is floury-white with blue veinings, and the rind is yellow or red. It is also called bleu du haut-jura.

ghagin fin, a very small star- or coin-shaped pasta served in meat broth or vegetable soups in Malta.

gherkin (*Cucumis anguria*), the small, ridged fruit of a plant of the cucumber family. Gherkins are pickled either in vinegar or brine or both. A variety of herbs are used to flavour the pickle, the commonest being dill. Gherkins are used mostly as a garnish, as cocktail savouries, and for sauces.

gherkin

gherkin sauce, a sauce of ½ pint (1 cup) wine vinegar, 2 teaspoons thyme, a bay leaf, a clove of garlic, 2 finely chopped shallots, pepper, salt, and a sprinkling of cayenne pepper boiled gently together in a heavy saucepan over a low heat. After 30 minutes, ½ pint (1 cup) stock, thickened with flour, if desired, is added. When the mixture boils again, 2 tablespoons finely chopped parsley and 12 minced pickled gherkins are added.

ghiozzo, Italian for gudgeon, often used in fritto misto di mare, and in soups.

ghiveci, a Rumanian national dish of casseroled chopped or sliced vegetables such as onions, eggplants, potatoes, peas, beans, green peppers, leeks, celery, tomatoes, cabbage, and many other vegetables sautéed in oil and then simmered with herbs and more oil in a large casserole. Sliced fried onions and garlic are put on top before serving, and sometimes chopped meat or fish is added during cooking. The name means "flower-pot," and it is so called from the shape of the original cooking pot. It is the Rumanian equivalent of the Yugoslavian *duveč*, the Bulgarian *gyuvèch* and the Greek *yiouvetsi*.

gianchetti, an Italian fish which is very small, boneless, and white. It forms the basis for *insalata di frutti di mare*.

gianduiotto, Italian chocolates or nougat from Alba or Cremona.

giant crab, a large variety of the common crab. See also CRAB.

giant perch, a very large variety of perch found in some of the rivers of France and Germany. See also PERCH.

gibanica, a famous Yugoslavian pastry like the Bulgarian *bànitsa*, filled with unsweetened cream cheese and served hot. It is very rich and made with a great deal of butter. It is a prominent item on holidays and festivals.

gibassier, a traditional Christmas Eve cake eaten in Provence, France. The name is connected with the word "gibbous," referring to its lumpy surface. See also POMPE.

gibelotte, a rich French stew made from rabbit, bacon, onions, herbs, and seasonings all cooked in either red or white wine. It is similar to *civet de lièvre* except that gibelotte uses either white or red wine and potatoes can also be added.

gibier, French for all wild animals and birds which are hunted for food. The word gibier comes from *gibecer*, Old French for hunting. *Gibecer* comes from the Latin *gibbosus* (hunchback), the explanation being that the large bag or sack used to transport the dead game gave the hunters the appearance of hunchbacks as they carried it home in the evening over their shoulders. Gibier de plume is winged or feathered game. See also ALOUETTE; BÉCASSE; BÉCASSEAU; BÉCASSINE; BÉCASSINE LA SOURDE; CAILLE; CANARD SAUVAGE; CANARD SIFFLEUR; CAPERCALLIE; FAISAN; GÉLINOTTE DE BOIS; ORTOLAN; PERDREAU; PERDRIX; PIGEON; PINTADE; PLUVIER; SARCELLE. Gibier de poil is furred game. See also CHEVREUIL; CIVET; ÉCUREUIL; IZARD; LAPEREAU; LEVRAUT; LIÈVRE; MARCASSIN; VENAISON.

giblets, the head, legs, neck, heart, gizzard, and liver of poultry, and in France the cock's comb and cock's kidneys (testes). The gizzard must be opened by slitting it down the centre and the grit or food taken out, also the scales of the legs should be scaled off. All giblets should be boiled up with double their volume of water and/or wine and with herbs; this makes excellent stock or sauce. The liver should either be used in the stuffing or cooked separately, as it can become bitter if boiled. Turkey and chicken necks are often stuffed. Stuffed goose neck is popular in Germany, Poland, and Russia. See also GANS (GÄNSEKLEIN, GÄNSELEBER); GEFILLTE HELZEL; GEFLÜGEL, RAGOÛT; RASSOLNIK.

giblet sauce, fowl's giblets, an onion, a clove, mace, and sometimes peppercorns are simmered together in stock or water for a few hours. When tender, the giblets are removed and the liquid strained into another saucepan. It is thickened if desired, and the giblets, very finely chopped, are added to it.

gigot, French for a leg of lamb or mutton. The word is also used in Scotland and in some parts of the U.S. In Ireland, gigot chops are neck chops, used for Irish stew. They are lean, but not tender enough to fry or grill. A *manche de gigot* is a culinary metal appliance used in France; it is attached to the bone of the leg of lamb to keep it steady for carving.

gild, to brush pastry or other foods with egg yolk to make them turn golden on top when cooked.

gilderne soup, a special Jewish soup served on 25th and 50th wedding anniversaries. It is made from chicken, and the golden globules of chicken fat must be left floating on the top as an omen of further happiness for the couple who are celebrating their anniversary.

gilthead, a saltwater fish of the sea bream family found in the Mediterranean and warmer Atlantic waters. It is prepared and cooked like *gilt-poll*.

gilt-poll (*Pagellus centrodontus*), a saltwater fish which makes good eating and has a delicate flavour. It is closely related to sea bream. It has a brilliant golden crescent between the eyes, and because of this was known by the ancients as "golden eyebrow." See also BREAM; DAURADE.

ginepro, Italian for juniper. Juniper berries are used in Italy in

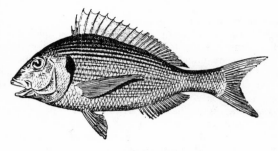

gilt-poll

game stuffing, giving an aromatic, bitter flavour. They are also excellent with pork and mutton.

ginger (*Zingiber officinale*), a perennial reedlike plant, a native of the warmer parts of Asia. It has been known from very early times, the Greek and Latin botanical names being derived from the Sanskrit. The spice, which has a peppery, piquant flavour, is derived from the rhizome or underground stem, and the root stock. The rhizomes are washed, scraped, and dried in the sun. The portions nearest the stem, known as stem ginger, are of a more delicate flavour and are preserved in a heavy syrup or crystallised in sugar which acquires the characteristic flavour of the ginger itself. The lower portions are sun-dried and sold in pieces, and the product is known as root ginger. Root ginger is the source of powdered ginger. Green ginger comes from the lower portions, but is not dried; it should be peeled before adding to stews or sauces. It has a delicate, aromatic smell and is much used with beef and chicken in Chinese cookery. All gingers, except the kind in syrup, are used for chutneys, curries, and pickles.

ginger

ginger snap, a round crunchy biscuit (cookie) with a ginger taste.

ginger snap sauce, an American sauce made by mixing together 4 ginger snaps, ½ pint (1 cup) stock, juice of 1 lemon, 4 oz. (½ cup) brown sugar, ¼ pint (½ cup) vinegar, 2 tablespoons raisins, and ½ teaspoon onion juice, and cooking gently until a smooth sauce is obtained. It is usually served with tongue, occasionally with fish, when, of course, fish stock is used. This sauce is of German origin, for ginger biscuits (cookies) or bread are incorporated in a beer sauce with cod in Germany. See also KABELJAU, IN BIERSAUCE.

gingerbread, an English and Irish ginger cake. The earliest form of gingerbread was not so much a cake as a solid block of honey baked with flour, ginger, and spices, which was then decorated to resemble a piece of tooled leather. In medieval

times it was a popular present, not unlike a box of chocolates today. When cooked, the slab was in fact gilded; cloves with a touch of gold paint on their heads were driven in like nails and arranged to form a fleur-de-lys pattern. Sometimes small box-tree leaves were also gilded and alternated with the green ones to form heraldic devices. The gilding of gingerbreads went on in England until the late 19th century. Until quite recently, it was applied while the cake was still hot. It was painted first with egg white, and then gold leaf was pressed on in whatever pattern was desired. A true gingerbread should always contain some honey. An old recipe still used today comprises 2 oz. (¼ cup) butter melted with 1 tablespoon honey, 2 of molasses, and 1 of brown sugar. Then 6 tablespoons flour, 1 flat teaspoon ground ginger, the same of baking soda, and a pinch of salt are mixed in. A tablespoon of milk and an egg are beaten into the mixture, then chopped candied peel, sultanas, and preserved or crystallised ginger are added, about a tablespoon of each. This is well beaten and poured into a greased tin, baked for 1½–2 hours in a moderate oven, and cut into squares when cool. See also GRASMERE GINGERBREAD; PARKIN.

gioddù, a particularly good Sardinian yogourt, which is very thick and is made either from cow's milk or the milk of ewes and goats.

giouvarlakia, Greek meatballs, usually of lamb or mutton, cooked in simmering stock. The stock is thickened with *avgolémono sauce* just before serving.

giouvetsi, see YIOUVETSI.

girdle, see GRIDDLE.

girella (*Labrus vulgaris*), a delicate-tasting saltwater fish with beautiful colouring, found in the Mediterranean. The common girella is violet with an orange stripe, the red girella is bright scarlet, and the Turkish girella is green with turquoise-blue stripes. It is a member of the wrasse family, and is often called rainbow wrasse. It is used a lot in bouillabaisse, and can also be fried.

girolle, see CHANTERELLE.

gîte à la noix, French for the silverside cut of beef. *Gîte à la noix cote ronde* is the French for eye of silverside. See diagram page xxiii.

gizzard, the second stomach in birds and poultry, used by the bird for grinding up its food after this has been mixed with the gastric juices in the first stomach. The saclike membrane on one side is slit open and the half-digested grain removed, before the remaining meaty pouch is washed and trimmed. The gizzard is always added to the giblets when making stock, and it is frequently eaten by country people all over Europe.

gjouveč, see DUVEČ.

glaçage, a French word used in cooking, which has no true English equivalent. It means glazing or browning in a hot oven or under the grill, but it can also be used in relation to freezing or icing a food. See also GLAZE.

glace, French for ice cream. See also BOMBE; COUPE JACQUES; GLACÉ; PARFAIT GLACÉ; PLOMBIÈRES.

glacé, I. French for glazed, applied particularly to fruits dipped in a syrup which hardens when cold. The most common is the glacé cherry which is used for cakes and puddings. II. The term also means "iced" with reference to the shiny icing on a cake. A *glacière* is the French term for a sugar-dredger, used to sprinkle icing (confectioners') sugar on cakes. In English, it is also called a muffineer, from being formerly used to sprinkle sugar on muffins. See also GLAZE.

glace de viande, glace de volaille, glace de gibier, and *glace de poisson,* a concentrated stock obtained by reducing a *fonds brun,* a *fonds blanc de volaille,* a *fonds de gibier,* and a *fonds de poisson,* respectively. See also FONDS DE CUISINE.

Glamorgan sausage, a traditional Welsh sausage mentioned by George Borrow in *Wild Wales*, ''breakfast was delicious buttered toast and Glamorgan sausage.'' It differs from the usual sausage in that it is meatless, but is nevertheless very good. It consists of 4 oz. grated Caerphilly cheese mixed with a good pinch of black pepper, 1 teaspoon dry mustard, 6 oz. (2 cups) dry breadcrumbs, 2 slices minced onion, 1 tablespoon chopped parsley, salt to taste, and 1 beaten egg. The mixture is rolled into sausage shapes on a floured board, and fried in hot lard until brown on both sides. The sausages are served hot.

glanis, see SILŪRE.

glarus cheese, see SCHABZIEGER.

glaserade ägg, a Swedish dish of eggs in aspic. One tablespoon gelatine is soaked in ¼ cup cold water for 5 minutes, before being dissolved in ¾ pint (1½ cups) boiling white stock. The yolks are removed from 9 hard-boiled eggs and mixed with 3 oz. liver pâté, and this in turn is flavoured with 1 tablespoon Madeira wine and bound with 2 tablespoons of cream. (Swedish caviar can also be used instead of the pâté, but then the wine and cream are omitted.) This mixture forms the stuffing for the egg whites, with the aspic liquid spooned over the eggs (when it has cooled to the consistency of raw egg white) so that they are well glazed when cold.

Glasgow bailies or *Glasgow magistrates*, a Scots method of cooking herrings. It is made by stuffing 6 filleted herrings with 1½ cups fresh breadcrumbs mixed with 2 tablespoons chopped parsley, 1 tablespoon grated lemon peel, 2 tablespoons melted bacon fat, and an egg yolk. The herrings are then rolled up tightly, secured, and placed one against the other, with their tails uppermost, in a pie dish. They are barely covered with a mixture of half vinegar and half water, 1 bay leaf, salt, and peppercorns to taste, then baked with the lid on for 30 minutes in a moderate oven. They are eaten hot or cold with bannocks.

glassmestersild, a Norwegian dish of glazed herring.

glasswort (*Salicornia herbacea*), a variety of samphire which grows extensively on salt marshes. It has bright green cylindrical branches, with no leaves. After steeping in malt vinegar, the shoots are pickled and sold under the name of marsh samphire. Glasswort is inferior to samphire.

glattes mehl, a fine white flour milled in a special way from Italian or Hungarian wheat and used in Austria for all pastry making and for certain breads. It is known as Vienna flour in England. See also MEHL.

glaze, I. Meat glaze is dark, strong meat stock reduced by boiling until it is syrupy. When cold it sets like a jelly. It is added to sauces and gravy to improve the taste, and when melted, is used to brush over galantines or cold tongue. It is firm when cold, dark brown, and shiny. Nowadays gelatine is often added to strong meat stock to make it set. Fish stock boiled down in the same way is also a glaze, but its technical culinary name is fumet. II. Glaze for flans and cakes usually consists of warm apricot, blackberry, or red currant jelly, which is brushed on the top and sets, and is shiny when cold. See also GLACÉ. III. To glaze can also mean to make shiny by grilling, in the case of a white or cheese sauce, for example, or to brush with egg, sugar, or milk and water before grilling or baking so that the finished article is shiny on top. See also GLAÇAGE.

glessie, an old-fashioned Scots sweetmeat (confection) made from 8 oz. (1 cup) brown sugar, 1 tablespoon butter, 1½ lb. (4 cups) golden syrup (corn syrup), 1 teaspoon cream of tartar, and 2 tablespoons water all boiled without stirring until a little sets in cold water.

gliny, the local name in the West of England for guinea fowl, which is very popular there and often braised in cider with root vegetables.

globe artichoke, see ARTICHOKE.

głóg, Polish for hawthorn berry. The berries are picked in the autumn before the frost. They should be red in colour and still firm. They are often used in Poland for jams, jellies, and sauces, and a special preserve is made from them which is served with game and cold meats. See also ACAROLE; HAWTHORN.

konfitura z głogu, hawthorn berry jam. The berries are slit and the seeds removed, also any fibres. They are covered with boiling water and left until cool and the fruit softened, and then drained. A syrup is made using the same amount of sugar as berries, with an equal amount of water, and the berries are put into this and left to steep overnight. The syrup is reheated adding half again as much sugar, also lemon juice to taste, and this is simmered for 10 minutes before putting back the berries. It is then simmered for about 20 minutes or until of setting consistency.

powidła z głogu, hawthorn berry preserve for serving with game and cold meats. The berries are prepared as for *konfitura* and they are put into a bowl without water, covered with a dish and weight on top. They are left to stand until soft enough to mash, then they are pressed through a sieve and mixed with an equal amount of sugar and simmered without water, stirring frequently, until it begins to thicken and the berries are still a red colour. It is then bottled and sealed down.

glorias, a Spanish pastry turnover filled with a mixture of 1 teaspoon cinnamon, 4 oz. (1½ cups) icing (confectioners') sugar, 4 oz. (1 cup) flour, 1 lb. sweet potatoes, 4 oz. (1 cup) ground almonds, 3 tablespoons each of rum and aniseed added to make a firm paste. The top of the turnover is painted with egg white before being baked for 15 minutes in a hot oven.

glossa, a Greek fish resembling a sole or flounder and used extensively in Greek cooking.

Gloucester cheese, a cheese first made in the 18th century in the Vale of Gloucester and the Vale of Berkeley, from the milk of a breed of Gloucester cows. It is made in two colours, pale yellow and red, and in two sizes, single and double. The single Gloucester is an undistinguished mild cheese, but the double Gloucester, which is coloured with annatto, is quite delicious. It has a mild creamy flavour and is probably the best red cheese in England. It keeps well and should mature for about 6 months. It is good for cooking when stale.

Gloucester sauce, an English sauce mainly used for dressing meat salads. It consists of a mayonnaise flavoured with cayenne pepper, chopped chives, lemon juice, and worcestershire sauce, with a little sour cream added.

glukhar, Russian for capercaillie, a bird which is more popular in Russia than in the British Isles.

glukhar s smetanym sousom, the most traditional Russian way of cooking capercaillie. The bird is roasted and served with a sour cream sauce.

główka, the Polish culinary term for an animal's head.

główka cielęca, a Polish dish of boiled calf's head, which is made like brawn and served hot or cold.

główka cielęca smażona z sosem tatarskim, calf's head cooked, boned, then sliced, fried in egg and breadcrumbs, and served with sauce tartare.

glucose, a sugar found in many fruits, particularly grapes. Powdered glucose is used for infants and invalids as it is easy to assimilate and gives energy. In liquid form, it is a thick clear syrup known as corn syrup in the U.S. and made from maize. It is useful in making jam and confectionery, as it does not crystallise.

głuszec, see CIETRZEW.

gluten, an albuminous, sticky substance found in wheat, which gives strength to flour. The gluten content in flour can be altered by chemical processes, but the more gluten in the flour, the better the bread. Diabetic bread has gluten added. See also FLOUR.

glux, a French cow's milk cheese from the Nivernais. It is in season all the year round.

glycerine, a sweet, syrupy, colourless liquid extracted from fats. It is added to commercially made cakes and icing to keep them moist, and makes icing easier to work. It is sometimes used in place of sugar in diabetic foods.

glyko, Greek for jam or fruit preserve. In Greece it is the custom for a guest to be offered a tray bearing one or more such preserves (*glyka koutaliou* or "spoon sweets") in small bowls, with a glass of water, a spoon, and either a liqueur or a cup of Turkish coffee. Etiquette demands that the guest shall eat a spoonful of the preserve, then, still holding the spoon, drink the water, and finally return the empty glass to the tray with the spoon in it. Afterwards the liqueur or coffee is drunk, and the hostess and family are wished health and good fortune in a toast. See also NERANDZI GIRISTO.

glyko nerandzaki, a preserve of bitter oranges or lemons. This is a classical *glyka koutaliou* recipe, and it is made by most Greek housewives. The fruit used must be small, about the size of a tennis ball and very unripe, being dark green and extremely bitter. First the pits are removed and the fruit is soaked in cold water for 24 hours. Next the fruit is covered and brought to the boil in water containing a good pinch of baking soda. When the fruit is soft enough to slip off a testing needle, it is drained, and again soaked in cold water for a number of hours. After drying, the fruit is cooked gently for several minutes in a syrup of sugar and water. This is covered and left to stand overnight. The fruit is then removed and the syrup reboiled until thick. The lemons or oranges are once more returned to the pan to be simmered until the moisture in them has been absorbed, when they are cooled and sealed in jars.

Greek housewives have a small gadget for removing pits from oranges or lemons which is very useful. It looks like an exceptionally slim marrow spoon, and has the effect of coring the fruit, in just the same way as apples are cored.

glyko triantafillo, a rose-petal jam, a speciality of the island of Chios and now exported. It is often served for breakfast in Greece with coarse brown bread. The roses used should be fresh, large, dark red, and fragrant. The white base should be cut off, and the washed petals layered in a saucepan with sugar and left overnight. In the morning, a syrup of 2 lb. sugar to 1 cup water and the juice of 2 lemons is added to it. When the mixture begins to thicken, it is bottled in heated jars and sealed.

karpouzi glyko, a preserve made from 1 lb. watermelon rind, cubed and then boiled with 12 oz. (1½ cups) sugar, ¼ pint (½ cup) honey, 2-inch cinnamon sticks, and ¼ pint (½ cup) water for 1–1½ hours. When cooking is finished, toasted chopped almonds and a little lemon juice are added.

lemoniou glyko, Greek for orange and lemon blossom preserve or jam, which is a speciality of the island of Chios. It is made in the same way as *glyko triantafillo,* using the orange and lemon instead of rose petals. Tangerine blossoms are also used.

vissino glyko, morello cherry preserve, a type of syrup-preserve which is very popular throughout Greece as *glyka koutaliou.* Layers of stoned, sour black cherries are placed in a pan and each layer is sprinkled with sugar; water to cover is added, and the whole rapidly cooked until the resulting syrup is as thick as honey. Then ½ cup lemon juice is added. Any scum which may rise to the surface is removed.

gnocchetti sardi, a traditional Sardinian pasta made from white flour and shaped like tiny shells. They take longer to cook than spaghetti. They are served with tomato sauce,

chunks of lamb, and cheese. In the local dialect they are called *malloredus.*

gnocchi, Italian for small savoury corklike shapes made from various basic farinaceous or vegetable foods. They were originally called ravioli and are still given this name in parts of Tuscany, although all ingredients are mixed together, not enclosed in an envelope of pasta as is the case with modern ravioli. The most common gnocchi are made with 3 oz. (⅔ cup) flour combined with 4 oz. grated Parmesan cheese, 2 oz. (2 heaped tablespoons) butter, 2 eggs, a pinch of nutmeg, salt, and pepper. It is all well mixed and shaped into small cork-sized shapes, rolled in flour, and poached gently for about 5 minutes, or until they rise to the top. They are drained and served with melted butter or garnishes which vary from district to district.

In France and Austria, gnocchi are made from chou pastry, using milk instead of water. When ready, grated Parmesan cheese is added and the mixture piped out of a forcing (pastry) bag with a large nozzle, into boiling water. When drained, the gnocchi are covered with sauce mornay and browned in the oven.

gnocchi alla romana, gnocchi made with semolina or maize flour stirred into boiling milk (approximately ½ lb. semolina to 1 quart milk). When thick, 2 egg yolks are added and the mixture is seasoned with salt, pepper, and nutmeg. When cool, it is cut into small corklike shapes, put into a baking dish, covered with melted butter and grated Parmesan cheese, and baked in a slow oven.

gnocchi di patate, an Italian savoury dish made from 2 lb. floury potatoes baked in their skins until tender, then split and the pulp removed. This is mixed with a slice of chopped boiled ham, 1 tablespoon grated Parmesan cheese, and 2 tablespoons butter. Then 2 beaten eggs are well blended into the mixture, and finally enough sifted flour to make a workable consistency. With floured hands, long sausage shapes are moulded and cut into thick slices which in turn are shaped into small balls and poached in boiling salted water until they rise to the surface. They are drained, served on a gratin dish, and covered with thick, fresh tomato or béchamel sauce sprinkled with grated Parmesan cheese, *pesto,* sugo, or chicken liver sauce.

gnocchi di ricotta, as *gnocchi verdi,* but without spinach. It is served in Genoa with *pesto,* or with melted butter and grated Parmesan cheese.

gnocchi verdi, as plain gnocchi, but with chopped cooked spinach and ricotta cheese added; it is served with melted butter and grated Parmesan cheese.

goat (Capra), a horned ruminant. Goats are too tough to eat, but the milk of the female makes excellent cheese and is very nutritious. The hide is also used, and the hair of the Cashmere breed is most valuable for spinning. Goats are found almost all over the world and will eat almost anything. The young goat, or kid, is excellent eating, but it should be killed while it is still milking the mother. See also CABRA; CALDERETA, EXTREMEÑA DE CABRITO; CAPRETTO; CHEVREAU; KATSIKAKI; MICISHJA, LA.

goat's beard (Tragopogon pratensis), a wild relative of salsify which grows freely in meadows. The roots are coarser than salsify but may be prepared in the same way. The shoots, when blanched by the exclusion of light, are prepared as chard.

goby (Gobiidae), the family name of a large number of saltwater and freshwater fish with broad heads and large mouths. The black variety is the best to eat; it is quite small, but much prized gastronomically in France on account of its very delicate flesh, rather like a gudgeon. It is usually eaten fried.

gocce d'oro, literally "drops of gold," a delicious golden plum grown particularly in the region of Venice, Italy.

godard, a classical French garnish for poultry and sweetbreads consisting of large and small chicken or veal and mushroom quenelles, large mushroom caps, diced ox tongue, cock's combs, kidneys, lamb's sweetbreads, and truffles, with sauce godard. It is sometimes used as a garnish for meat, if it is served as a second course. It is named in honour of Eugène Godard, the organiser of the aerial post during the siege of Paris 1870–71.

godard, sauce, a French sauce made from ½ lb. raw, finely chopped ham, a sliced carrot, and onion, all simmered in ¼ lb. (½ cup) butter for about 5 minutes. A half bottle of dry champagne is added and the mixture cooked gently for 30 minutes. The liquid is then strained into a stewpan, and a quart of sauce espagnole, with a quantity of chopped, previously cooked, mushrooms, is added. The sauce is cooked gently until a thick creamy consistency is achieved. It is strained and kept hot until required.

godiveau, a veal forcemeat used in certain French garnishes. To prepare, 1 lb. fillet or knuckle of veal, 2 veal kidneys, and 1½ lb. beef suet, with salt, pepper, and finely chopped herbs are pounded together in a mortar. Then 4 eggs are added, and the pounding is continued until the suet cannot be distinguished from the rest. It is kept on ice for use as required. It is often formed into small corklike shapes and used for quenelles. See also FORCEMEAT; GRATIN FORCEMEAT.

godiveau lyonnais, equal quantities of boned pike and chopped veal kidneys, eggs (2 to each lb. of fish and meat), and 2 cups breadcrumbs are pounded together in a mortar until a smooth paste is obtained. It is used for quenelles and other French garnishes. See also MOUSSELINE, FORCEMEAT.

godwit (*Limosa*), a bird which resembles the curlew, but is much finer eating. It is found in Europe, North America, Siberia, and New Zealand. There are several varieties, but the two most common are the black-tailed godwit and the bartailed godwit. The Maoris cook the birds undrawn, the trail being delicious. They also pot them for use in winter. The godwit can be cooked like a curlew or woodcock. In the U.S there is a large marbled godwit and a small one called the Hudsonian godwit.

goémon, the colloquial French name for a type of seaweed from which swallows extract a glutinous substance to make their nests, and from which we make *bird's nest soup.*

gogol-mogol, a Ukrainian custard made from 3 egg yolks beaten with 4 oz. (½ cup) brown sugar. This mixture is put into a double boiler with 1½ pints (3 cups) milk and vanilla to taste and heated until it thickens, being beaten continuously. It is served cold, garnished with chopped walnuts.

gogoşari, Rumanian for the large capsicum or sweet pepper. This is eaten extensively in Rumania, raw in salads, cooked in stews, and stuffed with rice, meat, and herbs before baking. The Rumanian term for the small hot capsicum or chilli is ardei iute.

gogues, a French bacon and vegetable dish from Anjou. Equal quantities of onions, spinach beet, and lettuce are chopped, salted, and left overnight. The next day they are drained and fried in lard until soft. Some finely diced bacon is added and all is cooked, together with enough pig's blood to make a rather thin mixture. It is well seasoned. Thin slices of beef are filled with this mixture, rolled up like a pancake, and secured. They are simmered in salted water for 2½ hours, then drained. When cold, they are sliced, tossed in butter until brown on both sides, and served hot.

goguette, a flat French sausage, highly spiced, made from pork sausage meat.

gołąbki ze słodkiej kapusty, a Polish dish of stuffed cabbage. Individual cabbage leaves are stuffed with rice and seasoning, rolled up, and casserole-cooked in bouillon or fermented rye liquor. In Russia, a traditional recipe is cabbage stuffed with sauerkraut or minced pork.

golden buck, an English savoury made from ¼ lb. grated cheddar cheese mixed with 1 tablespoon butter, 2 beaten eggs, 1 tablespoon cream, 3 tablespoons of a dark beer such as brown ale, a pinch of cayenne pepper, and a dash of worcestershire sauce, all heated gently until they are melted but not boiling, as the eggs will curdle. The mixture is poured onto hot toast and eaten at once.

golden currant (*Ribes aureum*), the fruit of a wild North American currant which grows mostly on the banks of streams around Minnesota and westwards. This currant can be round or oval, usually yellow but sometimes so dark as to be black. It has now been cultivated by American horticulturists and the best known strain is called crandall. It is also known as Missouri currant and is used for pies, tarts, jams, and jellies. See also BUFFALO CURRANT.

golden drop, the Irish name for soda bread made with ½ lb. (2 cups) each corn meal and flour mixed with 1 teaspoon baking soda and 1 teaspoon salt. These are formed into a dough with ½ pint (1 cup) buttermilk. (If fresh milk is used, 1 teaspoon cream of tartar should be added.) The dough is laid on a floured baking sheet in a round about 1½ inches thick, marked with a knife in the form of a cross, and baked in a moderate to hot oven for 35–40 minutes.

golden plover, a small bird found mainly in Ireland and the U.S. There are 3 varieties found in Ireland. *Pluvialis apricaria altifrons* is a visitor from the north, very like the native *Pluvialis apricaria,* except that it has a black head; both are excellent eating. The latter is known in Irish as feadóg. *Pluvialis dominica* is the American golden plover which, although it breeds in North America, is found in Mayo, Kerry, and Meath, southern Ireland. It is a smaller bird than the other two, and it has been noticed that after its long flight across the Atlantic the weight loss is only about 2 oz. See also PLOVER.

golden sauce, an English sweet sauce. For one of the many versions of it, 4 oz. (½ cup) butter is warmed in a basin before the fire and beaten by hand until creamy; then, with the basin standing in hot water, 2 oz. (2 heaped tablespoons) brown sugar are stirred in until melted, followed by beaten yolk of egg, stirring all the time until the sauce thickens, when a generous amount (approximately 1 wineglass) of brandy is added. The stirring is continued over a gentle heat until the sauce is hot. It is dusted with grated nutmeg.

golden syrup, an English golden treacle (which resembles corn syrup in texture and colour) made from refined sugars. It is used for sauces, cakes, and puddings. See also TREACLE.

golden thistle (*Scolymus hispanicus*), a native thistle of southern Europe with a white fleshy root, not unlike salsify. It is also called the Spanish oyster plant.

golden-eye (*Bucephala clangula*), a duck which breeds in northern Europe and Asia, and migrates south in the winter. (There are two species of golden-eye in the U.S., but they are not often used for food.) It is generally known as the "whistler" because of the whistle produced by its wing beats. As a table duck, it is not of the best, being fatty and oily, and it is never eaten if redhead, canvasback, ringneck, or scaup are available. However, the eggs are greatly prized in Ireland and Scandinavia.

gołębie, Polish for pigeon.

gołębie na sposób dzikich ptaków, 4 pigeons are rubbed with crushed juniper berries and salt, then casseroled with bacon, onion, root vegetables, celery, bay leaf, pepper, thyme, marjoram, and red wine. The ingredients are covered and simmered for about 30 minutes, then 1 tablespoon breadcrumbs is added and a little more wine, and the dish is returned to the oven for 30 minutes. The sauce and vegetables are strained off, sieved, and then poured over the birds. A cup of sour cream is added, and the whole is heated up before serving.

gołębie pieczone, roast stuffed young pigeon, covered with bacon strips and cooked in butter.

golonka, a Polish speciality from Poznań, which consists of leg of pork rubbed with salt, browned in oil, and pot-roasted with root vegetables, caraway seeds, allspice, and marjoram, seasoned to taste, with very little liquid, for 4–5 hours. It is eaten with *groszek puree i kapusta.*

gomost, a curdled milk which is eaten with salt or sugar in the country districts of Norway.

good King Henry (*Chenopodium bonus henricus*), a common European herb of the spinach family, found all over the English countryside. The origin of the name is obscure but thought to come from the German household sprite Heinz or Heinrich, a figure similar to our Robin Goodfellow. Other legends concerning the name link it with Henry VIII's notorious sore legs, which it was thought to have cured, and indeed some of the names given to this plant by English farmers lend credence to this idea: "blites," "fat hen," and "loblolly" are among them. The entire plant is edible, but the fresh tops bear some resemblance in flavour to asparagus. It is a valuable source of iron, and can be eaten as spinach or in salads.

goose, the generic name for a considerable number of birds of the genus *Anser,* which are larger than ducks and smaller than swans. Goose is one of the most important of the domestic fowls. All the species of goose which are used as food all over the world are bred from the wild goose (*Anser ferus; A. segetum*). The male bird is called a gander, but in culinary terms, both sexes are known as goose. Up to 6 months old it is known as gosling or "green goose" in English, and this bird is not stuffed. Although the goose lives to a great age, it is no use for eating after the age of 2 years. A young goose will still have down on its yellow legs, and the underbill will be soft. The large white goose is preferred in England to the smaller grey goose, which is favoured in France. Roast goose can be very fatty, so, to counteract this, in both Poland and Ireland the custom is to stuff the bird with potatoes flavoured with a little onion and herbs. The potato absorbs a lot of the fat and makes the bird more palatable. The traditional English stuffing is made from 1 large chopped onion mixed with 2 fresh chopped sage leaves, 2 cups fresh breadcrumbs, 1 egg, and seasoning. Chestnuts and apples are used in France. Braised goose with young vegetables is a very acceptable dish, likewise any goose casseroled with dried beans or lentils. Goose is very popular in Germany, especially at Christmas time, and is stuffed there with either apples, chestnuts, raisins, or prunes with apple, and served with either shredded white cabbage or sauerkraut. Goose liver is often baked whole with butter and a little Madeira wine. Potted goose is an old English way with goose. In Great Britain, Ireland, and the U.S. either apple sauce or cranberry sauce is served with roast goose, although formerly in Ireland onion sauce was served, and the goose is stuffed with sage and onion. In Russia it is cut into pieces and simmered with stock, herbs, and mushrooms, then thickened with sour cream mixed with chopped boletus. See also BARNACLE GOOSE; GANNET; GANS; GANSO; GÅS; GĘŚ; GUS; GUSKA; HINA; HUSA; LIBA; OIE.

potted goose, for this, only the breast meat of the birds is used. All skin and fat are removed from cold, cooked birds, and the breast meat is cut off, then minced, and after that, pounded until it becomes a smooth paste. Then ½ lb. butter is added for each 1 lb. of meat, and they are further pounded together with a pinch of mace, salt, and pepper. The mixture is all passed through a wire sieve, put in a pot, and pressed

roast goose with apples

down very firmly with a spoon. It is then set in a very low oven to heat through, once again pressed down with a spoon, and finally, while still warm, covered with melted butter.

preserved goose, see OIE, CONFIT D'.

gooseberry (*Ribes grossularia*), a shrub indigenous to Europe and North Africa, introduced into England in the Middle Ages. There are many varieties, the oval berries differing in size, colour, and texture of skin; they can be red, yellow, green, or white, smooth-skinned or covered with small hairs. The choicer varieties are eaten as dessert fruits, but they are also much used in cooking in England, and gooseberry pie used to be eaten traditionally at Whitsuntide. Gooseberries have been used in puddings and preserves since their first introduction; a typical medieval dish was a pie of gooseberries and chicken, with butter and egg yolks mixed with verjuice. One of the best ways to cook gooseberries is in a little water with plenty of sugar. When they are just soft, plunge in a bunch of elderflowers, which are in bloom at the same time. Leave them to boil for about 5 minutes. This gives the gooseberries a Muscat grape flavour. Gooseberry fool is a well-known English pudding. Classical French cuisine hardly mentions the gooseberry, but gooseberry sauce with mackerel is well known in Normandy and Brittany.

gooseberry

gooseberry sauce, an English and French sauce for boiled or baked mackerel. Finely chopped, well-boiled sorrel leaves, butter, sugar, salt, pepper, and a sprinkling of nutmeg are blended into a purée of gooseberries. The purée is then reheated and served. In 18th- and 19th-century Ireland, this sauce was popular with the addition of chopped fennel leaves, to taste. See also GROSEILLE À MAQUEREAU.

gorenflot, see BABA.

gorenjski želodec, a Yugoslavian sausage, a speciality of Gorenska, which consists of pig's stomach stuffed with meat from the head, then cooked with salt, pepper, and garlic. After cooking, it is pressed to get rid of all excess liquid, then air-dried. The name means literally "stomach from Gorenska."

gorge, I. French for the elongated "throat" sweetbread which is, in fact, the thymus gland. See RIS. II. French for the neck flap adjoining the front leg (*pied*) of pig.

gorgonzola, an Italian cheese made from cow's milk. The curd is allowed to mature till a natural mould forms; alternatively, copper wire may be used to induce mould. It is a creamy, strong cheese produced in Lombardy. There is a white variety called pannerone, but it is comparatively unknown.

gosling, see GOOSE.

göteborgs sallad, a Swedish salad from Gothenburg, and a popular party dish in Sweden. It is made with 3 calves' sweetbreads and 8 sets of brains soaked for 1 hour in cold water. Then they are removed to fresh cold water, to cover, and brought to the boil, together with juice of 3 lemons, 1 bay leaf, 3 sprigs parsley, 3 shallots, and black peppercorns. The stock is skimmed, and simmering continues for about 20 minutes, after which, when cool, the skins and membranes are removed and the meats are once again left to stand in cold water for about 30 minutes, then cut into pieces. Then 1 tablespoon powdered gelatine is dissolved in cold water, then added to ½ pint (1 cup) hot white wine. When this liquid is cool, 1 pint (2 cups) mayonnaise is gradually beaten in and 1 tablespoon each of parsley and of dill is added. Each piece of meat is dipped into this sauce then laid on a bed of shredded lettuce. The salad is served chilled.

Gotham pudding, a speciality of the small town of Gotham, outside Nottingham, made from ½ pint (1 cup) milk, 3 eggs, and 2 heaped tablespoons flour beaten well; when smooth, a pinch of salt and 4 oz. (1 cup) chopped candied peel are stirred in, and the mixture is again well beaten. Finally 1 teaspoon baking powder is included, and the mixture is poured into a greased mould and steamed for 1½ hours. When cooked, the pudding is turned out and served with sugar.

götterspeise, a German dessert consisting of 1 pint (2 cups) *chantilly* cream mixed with ½ cup grated pumpernickel and 3 tablespoons grated chocolate.

Gouda, a Dutch cheese made from whole cow's milk, and called after the town of that name near Rotterdam. It is perhaps the best known of the Dutch cheeses abroad, is widely exported, and is produced in other countries as well today. It is cured in brine, and ripened for almost 12 months. When freshly made it is a creamy cheese with a rich yellow colour, but as it ages it becomes firmer and also darker. It is cylindrical in shape with a yellow rind and can attain nearly 50 lb. in weight; it only weighs less than 6 lb. when made in a "midget" size of about 1 lb., but this is not thought to have the quality of the larger ones. There is also another type of Gouda cheese which is coloured, salted, and pressed like the large Gouda, but it is smaller in size, contains more moisture, and is therefore softer in texture. See also LUNCHEON CHEESE.

goudale, a *garbure*, to which red or white wine is added. When the bread and vegetables have been eaten from this very substantial soup, a generous glass of wine is mixed with the liquid at the bottom of the plate and drunk with relish. The goudale is thought to be the pièce de résistance of this Béarn dish, and a safeguard against illness. Goudale is called chabrol in Limousin. See also BRÉJAUDA; GARBURE, À LA PAYSANNE.

gouère aux pommes, an apple dish from the Berry region of France. It is made from peeled, sliced, and cored apples soaked with a little brandy and sugar. The apples are soaked for about 1 hour and put into a greased baking dish; batter is poured over them and the whole is cooked for about 45 minutes in a moderate oven. It is eaten hot preferably, but also cold, sprinkled with coarse sugar.

gougère, a French cheese cake from Burgundy. It looks like a large éclair and is made in much the same way. Four oz. butter, ½ pint (1 cup) water, and salt are brought to the boil; then 4 oz. flour are well stirred in. When this mixture is cool, 4 eggs are beaten in, one at a time. Finally, 4 oz. finely diced gruyère cheese are worked into the mixture. This is cooked on a greased baking sheet, or in a buttered pie dish, in small spoonsful placed on top of each other, then painted with egg yolk and sprinkled with more cheese, before baking for 40 minutes in a moderate oven. This is the traditional gougère, but sometimes the paste is used to line a soufflé dish, and it is then filled with either fish, tomatoes and cheese, chicken, or game. It is baked until brown and eaten hot or cold.

gougnette, a type of doughnut from the Lot region of France. The doughnuts are made from 1 lb. (4 cups) flour, 5 eggs, 3 oz. (⅓ cup) sugar, and ½ oz. yeast; they are left to rise, then cut into small pieces, and fried in deep oil. When golden they are drained, sprinkled with sugar, and arranged in a pyramid.

goujon, en, the French culinary term for small fried strips of plaice or sole. It is thought to derive from the gudgeon, which is small, fried like whitebait in France, and is also called goujon.

goulash, see GULYÁS; GULYÁSLEVES.

goumi (*Elaeagnus multiflora*), a Chinese berried shrub which grows wild in both China and Japan. It has been introduced into the U.S. with great success and thrives in the eastern states. The berries, which ripen in midsummer, are very pretty, being a reddish-orange colour with tiny silver flecks. They are not eaten raw but make excellent pies and preserves.

gourd, a name given to various plants of the *Cucurbitaceae* family, represented in two genera, *Cucurbita* and *Lagenaria*. The former includes pumpkins, squashes, and vegetable marrows (zucchini). The majority of gourds are cultivated for their decorative, rather than their culinary value, being fantastically shaped and richly coloured (known in France as coloquintes).

Of the edible varieties, the turk's cap and the turban are the most important, with orange flesh which is thick, floury, and sweet. Small Chinese turban gourds from the Far East have been found to proliferate in England; their flesh is yellow. Gourds are used for soups and as vegetable courses. There are many delicious edible gourds cultivated in China, India, and Africa.

gourilos, see CHICORY.

gournay, a French cow's milk cheese from Normandy, in season from November to June.

gouronopoulo, Greek for sucking-pig. See also KREAS.

gourounaki yemisto me feta, a speciality of roast sucking-pig, stuffed with feta cheese, rubbed with marjoram and olive oil, and roasted in the oven. Lamb and game are sometimes cooked in the same way. See also HIRINO PSITO.

govyadina, Russian for beef. See also BASTURMA; BEEF STROGANOFF; FORSHMAK; PIROZHKI.

govyadina soldatskaya, sirloin steak lightly fried in butter, then braised in beef stock with shredded cabbage, shredded Hamburg parsley root, balls of carrot and turnip, and herbs.

govyadina varennaya, beef boiled or pot-roasted, sliced, then covered with a sauce made from ½ pint (1 cup) reduced stock, ¼ pint (½ cup) sour cream, 2 tablespoons grated horseradish, with 2 teaspoons vinegar. Breadcrumbs are sprinkled over, and the dish is dotted with butter and browned in the oven.

grädde, Swedish for cream. See also EFTERRÄTTER.

gräddtårta, cream layer cake, made from ½ lb. (1 cup) creamed butter with a little salt and ½ teaspoon almond essence (extract). Then 1 lb. 5 oz. (2¼ cups) castor sugar are gradually added, and the mixture is beaten until fluffy; 6 egg yolks are added one at a time, and also beaten, and 1 lb. 5 oz. (4½ cups) flour mixed with 5 teaspoons baking powder are added alternately with ¾ pint (1½ cups) milk. Finally, the 6 stiffly beaten egg whites are folded in carefully. This mixture is put into 6 buttered 9-inch sandwich tins and baked in a moderate oven for approximately 12 to 15 minutes. When cool, the cake is layered with red currant jelly and almond-flavoured whipped cream. See also MANDEL (MANDELSKORPOR).

gräddvåfflor, sour cream waffles made from 1 pint (2 cups) stiffly whipped sour cream mixed with ¾ lb. (3 cups) flour and ¼ pint (½ cup) cold water. When quite smooth, 2 oz. (¼ cup) melted butter is added. The batter is poured in spoonfuls onto a heated waffle iron and cooked until golden.

graham flour, see FLOUR.

grahamkorput, Finnish for rusks made with 1 lb. (3½ cups) graham flour and 8 oz. (2 cups) wheat flour mixed with 4 oz. (½ cup) melted butter, 2 tablespoons corn syrup, and 2 oz. yeast dissolved in 1 pint (2 cups) tepid milk or water, all well kneaded, shaped, and left to rise before baking for 20 minutes in a moderate oven. They are very popular in Finland.

graining, I. An alternative name for dace. II. A term used in boiling sugar. When heated beyond 250°F, it will form crystals, or "grain." To prevent this, a pinch of cream of tartar or liquid glucose is added. This is known as "cutting the grain."

grains of paradise, see CARDAMOM.

graisse, French for fat. Graisses alimentaires or graisses végétales are vegetable fats, margarines, etc.; graisse de rognons de boeuf is rendered down beef kidney fat, thought by many French cooks to be good for deep frying.

graisse Normande, a special cooking fat made in Normandy by melting together, and then clarifying, equal parts of pork fat and suet flavoured with root vegetables, herbs, salt, and pepper. The distinctive flavour permeates the foods that are cooked in the fat.

gramolatas or **gramolates,** a kind of French sherbet made from iced fruit syrup.

grana, a local Italian name for Parmesan cheese, so called from the graining which a good Parmesan should have. In Parma it is called *grana parmigiana,* but at Lodi, Lombardy, it is called *grana lodigiana,* and likewise grana reggiana in the district of Reggio Emilia. It is also made in Modena, Bologna, Ferrara, and Piacenza. See also PARMESAN.

granadilla (*Passiflora edulis*), passion-fruit, of which there are several different kinds cultivated in tropical and subtropical areas. The fruit, encased in a hard skin which has to be cut open, is sweet and aromatic, and is generally eaten raw as a dessert. An occasional taste is very pleasant, while too much of the fruit is inclined to be cloying. The giant granadilla of tropical America (*Passiflora quadrangularis*) has yellow-skinned fruit, 15–20 cm. long.

grancevole or **granceole,** the common crabs of the Adriatic. They are large, bright scarlet, and spiky, but of unspectacular flavour. The edible parts are eaten in Italy in the shell, with oil, lemon, and mayonnaise. They are common in Venice. The giant crab is called *granchio.*

grand sallett (grand salad), a 16th-century English salad made from cold chicken or pike, mixed with minced onion, tarragon, capers, olives, samphire, broom buds, mushrooms, oysters, lemon, orange, raisins, almonds, blue figs, sweet potatoes (known then as Virginia potatoes), peas, and red and white currants. All the ingredients are dressed with olive oil and vinegar and garnished with sliced oranges and lemons. This dish is also called salamagundi and is mentioned in *The Good Huswives Treasure* (1588). This salad is ideal for adaptation to modern tastes, using cold poultry, fish, or meats, and sliced potatoes or cooked rice with a variety of cooked vegetables and also fruits, particularly crisp, sweet apples.

grand veneur, sauce, a classical French sauce made from 1 pint (2 cups) sauce poivrade with the addition of 3 tablespoons venison essence (extract), 3 tablespoons red currant jelly, and ¼ pint (½ cup) cream. It is served only with venison and furred game.

grand-duc, French garnish for fish and fowl, composed of truffles and asparagus tips. Crayfish is also used for fish dishes, with sauce mornay.

granita, Italian water ice, formerly called sherbet (later sorbet). It used to be served in the middle of large banquets to revive tired appetites and is very refreshing in hot weather.

granita al caffé, coffee granita made with ¼ lb. (½ cup) sugar, 2 pints (4 cups) water, and 6 oz. coffee infused together, strained, and then frozen till set. It is sometimes served with cream.

granita di fragole, strawberry granita made with 2 lb. wood strawberries sieved with lemon and orange juice, added to a syrup made from ½ lb. (1 cup) sugar boiled for 5 minutes with ¼ pint (½ cup) water, and then frozen.

granita di limone, lemon granita made with ½ pint (1 cup) fresh lemon juice and syrup, as above.

grant loaf, a coarse English wholemeal bread, perfected some years ago by Doris Grant; it is the counterpart to graham bread, made from graham flour in the U.S. Flour, yeast, and liquid are mixed together, turned straight into bread tins, and left to rise there. This cuts out the proving which is part of most breadmaking. It is also called a granary loaf.

granulated sugar, see SUGAR.

grão, Portuguese for chick-pea, used extensively in Portugal, especially for a thick soup, caldo de grão. See also CHICK-PEA.

grape, the fresh fruit of a vast number of different varieties of *Vitis vinifera,* the European grape vine. Apart from wine-making with its ancillary products, grapes are eaten fresh as dessert and used for jams and preserves. They are also dried for use in cookery and are then known as currants or raisins. White grapes (in fact pale green in colour), peeled and seeded, are used for garnishing and in sauces such as *à la véronique,* and usually known as muscat grapes. The most delicate in flavour is white frontignan (muscatel) although there is a very good black muscat called muscatele. The larger purple grape is considered a good dessert grape, perhaps the Black Hamburg or Black Alicante being the best. However, the skin of the dark grape is tougher and should be removed before eating. See also DRUVA; PITTE CON NIEPITA; RAISIN; UVA.

grapefruit (*Citrus paradisi*), a citrus fruit derived from the coarser shaddock. It was first called pompelmous, a cognate of the French name for grapefruit, *pamplemousse.* There are two classes of grapefruit, one with a yellow pulp and the other with pink or red, and many varieties of each class. The fruits are large and may be round or oval. They are used in salads, fruit cups, preserves, and in fact in most of the ways that oranges are used. When eaten alone, they are generally served cut in half, the sections loosened, sprinkled with castor sugar, and eaten with a spoon, as a first course. Prepared in this way, sprinkled with gin or rum, and then grilled under a hot grill until gently browned, they make a pleasant first course to a meal. The grapefruit is also called pomelo. See also SHADDOCK.

grapiaux, a speciality of the Nivernais and Morvan region of France, large pancakes cooked in heated pork fat.

gras-double, French for tripe. The two most famous methods of cooking and serving tripe in France are described here.

gras-double à la lyonnaise, tripe cut into thin strips and fried in hot butter or lard, added to fried onions and cooked together until the tripe is browned and tender. A little vinegar and chopped parsley are added before serving.

gras-double or *tripes à la mode de Caen,* tripe simmered slowly with calf's foot, carrots, leeks, garlic, thyme, parsley, and bay leaf, allspice, salt, pepper, and either cider or water with a little Calvados added. The lid should be luted.

grasløk, Norwegian for chives, a popular herb in Norway and often used on the various types of *smørbrød.*

gräslök, Swedish for chives. See also GRÖNSAKER.

gräslökpotatis, a Swedish recipe for potatoes with cream, flavoured with chives. Two lb. sliced boiled potatoes are fried in butter until a golden colour, when they are generously flavoured with chives. Then ½ pint (1 cup) cream is gradually stirred into the potatoes, which are simmered gently for a further 10 minutes and served. In Sweden they generally accompany scallops of veal, game, or fried chicken dishes.

grasmere gingerbread, originally made of fine oatmeal, but nowadays wheat flour is used. It consists of ½ lb. (2 cups) oatmeal or flour to ½ lb. (1 cup) sugar and ¼ lb. (½ cup) fat, 1 tablespoon syrup, ½ teaspoon cream of tartar, ½ teaspoon baking soda, and 1 teaspoon ginger, all well mixed. The mixture should be dry and is baked in a greased tin and left until cold before turning out. It resembles that other North Country gingerbread or ginger cake called *parkin.* See also GINGERBREAD.

grass snake, a nonpoisonous snake sometimes eaten in France, and prepared like eel. In French it is known as *anguille de haie,* hedge eel.

grater, a utensil with a rough pierced surface used to grate into coarse fragments such foods as cheese, nuts, nutmeg, fruits, and vegetables.

grateron, the common French name for rennet which is used extensively in cheese making.

gratin, I. The French culinary term for the thin crust formed on top of certain dishes when browned under a grill or in the oven. This can be achieved with butter, breadcrumbs, or cheese. When the latter is used the dish is sometimes called *au gratin,* and the verb meaning to prepare food in this way is *gratiner.* II. A fireproof dish with handles used for the above dishes.

gratin forcemeat, a French forcemeat which is spread on croûtons and canapés, and sometimes used as stuffing. Chicken livers are browned in hot pork fat with a shallot, mushroom stalks, a sprig of thyme, and half a bay leaf and well seasoned with salt, pepper, and a pinch of mace. It is pounded in a mortar or electrically blended to a purée. It will keep in a cold place for some days. For stuffings it is sometimes mixed with white bread soaked in milk, or breadcrumbs. See also FORCEMEAT; GODIVEAU.

grattons or **gratterons,** names given in the southwest of France to the remains of the melted fat or rind of pork, goose, or turkey. It is salted while hot and eaten cold for hors d'oeuvre.

gravenche, a fish of the salmon family peculiar to the lakes of Switzerland, mainly Lake Geneva, and Bavaria. It is similar to the fera and is often taken for that fish. However, it has a lighter colouring on the scales and a more curved back. It is also smaller and not as delicious. It can be prepared as trout.

gravieri, Greek for a cheese made in Crete, similar to Gruyère. It can be extremely good.

gravlaks, a Norwegian national dish of cured salmon. The preservative is a mixture of sugar and salt, beer, and dill. It is served raw with either a mild mustard sauce made with sour cream, or a dill sauce. See also GRAVLAX; RØYKTLAKS.

gravlax, Swedish for raw pickled salmon. The backbone from the middle cut of a fresh salmon is removed and the fish divided into two fillets. These are rubbed with a mixture of ½ lb. salt, ½ teaspoon saltpetre, 1 tablespoon sugar, and 10 crushed peppercorns. One of the fillets is then placed skin side downwards, sprinkled with dill and spices, and covered by the other fillet with skin side uppermost. The fish is weighted down and left for at least one day and night (or up to 36 hours, according to taste) in a cold place. When served, it is accompanied by a French dressing with mustard and garnished with dill. See also GRAVLAKS; LAX; RØYKTLAKS.

gravy, the English term for the juices and sediment that come out of meat during and after cooking by roasting, frying, or grilling. To form a dressing for the meat, this sediment can be mixed with a little thickening agent as flour or corn flour (cornstarch), although this tends to spoil the flavour, followed by wine, stock, or water, and seasoning. It must be well boiled up before serving. If well reduced by boiling it will jelly when cold. Unfortunately, this essence is frequently ruined by the addition of commercially made gravy powders.

gravyer, a Turkish hard cheese made from ewe's milk. It tastes similar to Gruyère and is a high quality cheese made in the modern, well-appointed creameries known as *mandira.*

gray widgeon, see GADWALL.

grayling (*Thymallus thymallus*), one of the finest European freshwater fishes found in Great Britain, Europe, and Scandinavia. In the U.S. there are 3 slightly different kinds: the Arctic grayling (*Thymallus signifer*), Montana grayling (*Thymallus montanus*), and Michigan grayling (*Thymallus tricolor*). The European type is a member of the salmon family and is a most delicate feeder. It has a smell, when first caught, of thyme (hence its Latin name), cucumber, and river mint, all of which faintly pervade the flesh when cooked. It rarely weighs more than 4 lb., its usual weight being about 2 lb. It should be cooked simply with butter and an herb such as lemon thyme or parsley in order that the full flavour of the flesh may be tasted, but recipes for trout are also suitable.

Great Lake herring (*Coregonus clupeiformis*), a whitefish found in the Great Lakes of North America. It is one of the largest and, gastronomically speaking, best, of the North American whitefish.

great snipe (*Capella media*), the largest snipe found in the British Isles, mostly in the eastern counties. It is smaller than a woodcock, but considered very good to eat. It breeds in northern Europe and is very popular in Sweden. It can be cooked in the same way as woodcock; but braising in stock with sour cream, as for *aarfugl,* is a common way of cooking it in Scandinavian countries.

gregen or **grebenes,** a Jewish dish which consists of the fat and skin from the neck, thigh, and rear of poultry, particularly chicken, which is fried over a low heat with an equal quantity of onion until crisp. Sometimes water to cover is added and it is cooked until the water evaporates. When the cracklings are crisp and brown they are drained on kitchen paper, and the fat (*schmaltz*) is stored for future use in cooking. Grebenes are eaten plain on toast, or used for stuffing poultry, and also in potato croquettes. See also SCHMALTZ.

grecque, à la, not usually a dish of Greek origin, but a method used in France for serving vegetables, particularly mushrooms and globe artichokes. They are cooked in equal parts of white wine and water, or a court bouillon, with the juice of 4 lemons, or 6 tablespoons wine vinegar, ½ pint (1 cup) olive oil, fennel, 2 small onions, 1 stalk celery, 1 bay leaf, a sprig of thyme, and 2 teaspoons coriander. They are served cold in the liquor. Eggplants are often served in the same way.

Greek cheese, see TYRI.

Greek hay, see FENUGREEK.

green bacon and **green ham,** a term used for cured, but unsmoked, bacon or ham. It has a milder flavour than the smoked variety, and if cured with sugar, it can be very sweet.

green cheese, see SAGE CHEESE.

green fish, see LING.

green goose, see GOOSE.

green pea, see PEA.

green plover, see PLOVER.

green sauce, see VERTE, SAUCE.

green turtle, see TURTLE.

greengage (*Prunus institia*), the popular name for all "gages," a distinct group of the plum family and the sweetest and most fragrant of all dessert plums. They are round in shape, with small stones, and most of them are green in colour, ripening to amber. The Cambridge gage is considered the best English variety. The French Reine-Claude, a somewhat larger fruit, is named after the queen of Francis I of France. Apart from their use as dessert fruit, greengages are used for jams, preserves, tarts, and puddings.

greengage

greenshank (*Tringa nebularia*), a bird allied to the snipe but a little larger, with greenish legs and a 2-inch beak. It is seen in England and Ireland, in small flocks during spring and autumn when it migrates to and from Europe. It may be hung, prepared, and cooked in the same way as woodcock, but when young, it is best roasted and served with an orange sauce or salad.

grelos, Portuguese for dandelion leaves, which are often cooked as a vegetable in Portugal. Grelos has also come to mean "greens," so that grelos de nabos means turnip tops—also frequently eaten as a vegetable in Portugal.

gremolata, the Milanese name for a prepared mixture of ½ cup chopped parsley, 1 garlic clove, chopped, and grated peel of ½ lemon. It is always sprinkled on top of a traditional *ossi buchi alla milanese* before serving.

grenade, French for pomegranate, very popular in France, especially the juice, which is the basis of grenadine syrup.

grenadier, a river fish of France, so called because the shape of its head resembles a French grenadier's cap. It has a delicate flavour, and seldom exceeds more than 15 inches in length. It is usually poached with soft *beurre maître d'hôtel* as a garnish.

grenadins, the French term for small slices cut from the fillet or leg of veal. They are triangular or rectangular and are larded with bacon and braised with white wine, onion, carrot, and stock barely to cover. Turkey is cooked in the same way. The meat is garnished with braised and glazed carrots, endive, chicory, spinach, or celery. Each grenadin is in fact a small *fricandeau*.

grenouille, French for frog. The green frog and the mute frog are those generally eaten in France, the European country where the frog is most popular as food. Since frogs are not regarded as meat, they can be eaten on meatless days in Catholic countries. They are often "farmed" in France, then frozen for export to America and other countries. Only the hind legs of the frog are used, and they are delicious, tasting not unlike a very tender and delicate chicken. The legs are cut off and skinned, and the feet removed. They are soaked in cold water for several hours to swell the flesh and then dried. Usually, 3 pairs are allowed per person. Sometimes the legs are marinated in white wine, with a bay leaf, thyme, parsley, chives, and a bruised clove. The most common method is to dip them in batter and fry them in deep oil, when they are known as grenouilles frites. They can also be casseroled with butter, wine, and cream (à la crème), or fried in butter and served with sauce béchamel mixed with cream. À la meunière and à la *poulette* are other classic methods. In the south of France, particularly in Provence, frogs' legs are cooked with olive oil and garlic. See also FROG.

grenouilles à la poulette, frogs' legs poached in white wine with butter, a squeeze of lemon juice, 1 small onion, and a bouquet garni. When the stock is boiling, sliced mushrooms are added, and when the frogs' legs are cooked, the stock is boiled down and thickened with egg yolk and cream.

grenouilles à la provençale, a method of preparing frogs' legs, with olive oil, parsley, chives, milk, garlic cloves, flour, juice of 1 lemon, butter, salt, and pepper. Medium-sized frogs' legs are steeped in milk and then rolled in seasoned flour. The butter is heated with about half the olive oil and allowed to get hot but not smoky. The legs are added and are then cooked through on both sides (about 10 minutes), when they should be nicely browned. They are sprinkled with the lemon juice and chopped chives and parsley and seasoned to taste. They are then put on a serving dish and kept warm. After the remaining butter and olive oil have been slightly browned in a clean pan, the crushed or chopped garlic cloves are added, and the sauce is poured over the frogs' legs. They are served with slices of lemon.

grenouilles, chartreuse de, an elaborate old French method of serving frogs' legs, seldom seen nowadays. It consists of a risotto cooked with the meat from the legs (after they have been poached in white wine), chunks of boned pike, and chopped prawn or crayfish tails. When cooked, it is sprinkled with grated Parmesan cheese and quickly browned under a hot grill before serving.

grenu, French for lumpy, used to describe dough or other mixtures which are not thoroughly kneaded.

gresiller, a French culinary term, meaning to shrink by heating.

grey mullet, see MULLET.

grey snapper, see RED SNAPPER.

gribiche, sauce, a classical French sauce, which is made as follows. Three yolks of hard-boiled eggs are pounded to a paste, into which ½ pint (1 cup) olive oil is worked (as in the making of mayonnaise). Three tablespoons wine vinegar are added, also chopped gherkins, capers, parsley, chervil, and tarragon, and lastly a julienne of the whites of hard-boiled eggs. The sauce is served cold with cold fish or shellfish.

griby, Russian for mushrooms. Generally this refers to varieties found in woods. The common European mushroom (*Psalliota campestris*) was for many years thought to be a toadstool in Russia, but in later years it has been known there by the French name champignon. Mushrooms are much used in Russia, for they have a good flavour. They are often dried, and are excellent for soups and stews.

griby marinovannye, pickled mushrooms, which are prepared by first boiling the mushrooms in salted water, then draining them. When cold, they are packed in a jar with salt and peppercorns and covered with previously boiled vinegar. Finally some oil is added to seal the flavour in, and a tight-fitting lid is put on.

griby solenye, salted mushrooms. Mushrooms are layered with salt in a large jar (sometimes with the addition of sliced onion and peppercorns), then the jar is covered tightly. The mushrooms are for use during the winter.

griby v smetannom souse, mushrooms simmered in butter and sour cream.

griddle or **gridiron**, one of the earliest implements, with the spit, used for cooking. The word is probably derived from the Old French *grédil* (gridiron), although the hot stones used for baking by the Gaels were called *greadeal*. A griddle (also spelt girdle) is a thick round sheet of iron, with a handle. It is used to cook bannocks, drop scones, flapjacks, soda bread, and many other dishes. These flat cakes are sometimes known as griddle cakes. A griddle was originally placed over hot coals, but nowadays electrically controlled griddles are available and are much in use in the U.S.

griess, German for semolina.

griessschmarrn, an Austrian semolina milk pudding with raisins. See SCHMARRN.

griessknödel, semolina dumplings. See also BAYRISCHE GRIESKLÖSSE; KNÖDEL; PFLÜTTEN.

griesswürfel, a German garnish made from the boiled stock of chicken or veal to which enough semolina is added (about 2 heaped tablespoons to ¾ pint stock) to make a stiff paste. Butter, pepper, and salt are added, and the mixture is poured on a large cold dish to a thickness of ½ inch. When quite cold, it is cut into small cubes and added as garnish to hot strong soup.

griesčiai, Lithuanian for parsnips, used a great deal for soups and stews, and as a vegetable with roast meats.

griesspudding, a Swiss pudding mainly given to children, made with ⅔ cup farina, 2 egg yolks, 4 oz. (½ cup) sugar, 2 pints (4 cups) milk, 1 teaspoon vanilla, and 3 tablespoons raisins, all cooked gently together, preferably in a double-boiler. The 2 stiffly beaten egg whites are added when the above mixture is cool. It is served cold with raspberry or fruit syrup.

grifole, an edible Italian fungus. See FUNGHI.

grig, a small freshwater eel.

grignon, French for a piece of dry bread, baked very hard; it is also the end crust of a loaf.

grill, to, to cook by means of radiant heat; an important method of cooking as it extracts the fat from the food but does not impair the flavour. Grilling can be done with gas or electricity, or on an open woodfire or charcoal. The latter gives the finest results because there is a high proportion of radiant heat and little flame.

grillade, French for grilled food.

grillade au fenouil, a famous Provençal method of grilling fish such as sea bass, red mullet, and loup de mer over a bed of dried fennel stalks. The fish are painted with olive oil and flambéed with a little warmed brandy.

grillardin, the chef in charge of all the grilling in a large French restaurant. See also POISSONNIER; RÔTIR.

grille, French for deep frying basket.

grillettes, a French word used in former times for thin slices of pork fried in butter or fat.

grilse, the name for a young salmon when it first leaves the sea to go upstream. When cooked, it is usually stuffed and left whole. See also PARR; SMOLT.

grimaldi, a French chicken consommé with tomato fumet garnished with julienne of celeriac and tomato royale. See also CONSOMMÉ.

grimslich, a traditional Jewish Passover dish in Europe, of matzo fritters. Two matzos are soaked in cold water until soft, then squeezed dry and beaten with a fork. The yolks of 2 eggs are added, also 4 oz. dried chopped fruits, 2 oz. ground almonds, a pinch of cinnamon, and 2 oz. fine matzo meal. Lastly, the stiffly beaten egg whites are folded in. Spoonfuls of the mixture are dropped into hot, shallow oil, fried on both sides, and served hot sprinkled with sugar. An elaborate version is called *chremslach*, and these are eaten in the U.S.

griottes, the French name for the bright red bitter morello cherries, used for *caneton rouennais aux cerises*.

gris de lille, a cow's milk cheese from northeast France, in season from November to July.

griskin, an unusual English word for the spine, chine, or backbone of the pig, which is cut away when preparing a side for bacon. It can also apply to an inferior, thin loin of pork.

grissini, long sticks of hard-baked, rusklike bread from 10 to 30 inches long. They are Italian in origin and made from bread dough brushed with milk or egg and salted well with coarse sea salt before cooking.

grits, a corruption of the word groats. See HOMINY.

groats, I. An oatmeal. See also OATMEAL. II. The seeds of oats taken from their husks by a machine, sometimes left whole, sometimes crushed. They are used for thickening soups, or for making gruel. When this word is used for the seeds of other grains, it is prefaced by the qualifying adjective, i.e. buckwheat groats, etc.

grød (also called *risengrød*), a rice pudding covered with cinnamon and pieces of butter, eaten on Christmas Eve in Denmark. Inside the pudding is one almond, and whoever finds it gets a present and good fortune. If it is found by an unmarried person, it indicates early marriage. Grød is usually followed by roast goose. In some parts of the country a little of the grød is set aside for the julenisse, a little gnome thought to live in the barn or attic, who looks after the family.

groente, Dutch for vegetables. Vegetables are good and plentiful in Holland and much use is made of them. Sometimes, particularly in winter, they are mixed with potatoes, meat, or bacon to make filling dishes such as *stamppot witte kool* or *hutspot met witte bonen en spek*. When in season, hot lettuce dishes are popular. Many vegetables are found in Holland, including spinach, cauliflower, chicory, cabbage, onions, leeks, asparagus, brussels sprouts, and sorrel. See also ASPERGES; BIETEN; BRUINE BONEN; BRUSSELS LOF; SPINAZIE; SPRUITJES; STOOFSLA; ZURING.

groentesoep, Dutch for vegetable soup, often garnished with meatballs (*soepballetjes*).

grondin, French for gurnard or gurnet, a fish so called because of the grunting sound it makes when it is caught. It is also called gurneau.

grønnsaker, Norwegian for vegetables. During the long Norwegian winter, fresh vegetables are scarce and much use is made of frozen vegetables and potatoes. The latter are sometimes made into potato cakes and eaten in place of bread. During the summer, most of the vegetables grown in Britain are also available in Norway. Beans, peas, carrots, cabbage, leek, beetroot, spinach, and parsnip are all popular in season. Usually Norwegian vegetables are boiled, drained, and coated with parsley butter, but sometimes they are cooked up with a cream sauce. See also BONNER; BROCCOLI; GULEROT; KÅL; MAISKOLBE; PURRE; SURKÅL.

grønsager, Danish for vegetables. The Danes make very good use of vegetables, leftovers often being mashed up and shaped into rounds which are then dipped in breadcrumbs and fried. Frequently two different kinds of vegetables are cooked together and served in a white sauce made from the cooking stock. Vegetable soufflés (*grønsagsgratin*) are also popular, and are made as *grönsaksufflé*. Butter is an essential ingredient in the cooking and serving of all vegetable dishes. Sugar is also discreetly used as flavouring and, as always in Denmark, much care goes into their garnishing. See also BØNNER; GULEROD; HVIDKÅL; LØG; RØDKÅL.

grönsaker, Swedish for vegetables (also vaxt). Vegetables, usually boiled and served with melted butter and a little sugar, are eaten with the main course in Sweden; but, probably owing to the long winters, the Swedish housewife relies very much upon frozen vegetables, and at the time of publication Sweden has one of the highest consumptions of frozen food in the world. However, in season, most of the fresh vegetables known in Great Britain are also found in Sweden, where there are delicious hot vegetable dishes such as soufflés, which are served on the smorgåsbord. See also ÄRT; BÖNOR; BLOMKÅL BROCCOLI; GRÄSLÖK; GURKA; LÖK; POTATIS; ROTMOS.

grönsaksufflé, a vegetable soufflé. A base is made, consisting of 1 oz. butter, 3 tablespoons flour, ½ pint (1 cup) cream or milk, and 4 tablespoons cauliflower stock. When the sauce has been removed from the heat, 3 egg yolks are beaten in one at a time, after which the sauce is well beaten for several minutes and then seasoned. Boiled cauliflowerlets are stirred in, followed by 3 beaten egg whites. The whole is poured into a buttered dish which has been previously dredged with breadcrumbs, and it is baked in a moderate oven for about 35 minutes (the dish should stand in a tin containing a little hot water). The soufflé is accompanied by a sauce of melted butter, and sometimes by bacon or sausages. Spinach, mushrooms, etc., can also be used for this soufflé.

grönsallad, see SALLAD.

gros-blanquet, a French pear with a greeny yellow skin. It is sweet, but a little gritty in texture.

gros sel, French for a crystalline unrefined sea-salt. It is greyish in colour, but has a good flavour. It is sometimes used in salt mills by people who find the taste superior to iodized salt. It is also used for pickling in brine and is known then as "freezing salt."

groseille, French for currant. *Groseille blanche* is white currant; *groseille rouge,* red currant. *Groseilles rouges de bar* is the famous French red currant preserve, originally made at the town of Bar-le-Duc in eastern France.

groseille à Maquereau, French for gooseberry.

groseilles, sauce de, a classical French sauce in which stewed green gooseberries are blended with an equal amount of sauce bâtarde. It is served with mackerel in Brittany. See also GOOSEBERRY, SAUCE.

g'röstl, an Austrian hash dish, often known as *tiroler g'röstl.* It is made from fried onion rings, fried cooked potatoes, and sliced, cooked beef, seasoned with caraway seeds, salt, and pepper.

groszek, Polish for peas.

groszek purée i kapusta, pease pudding and cabbage.

groszek zielony duszony, green peas, melted butter, and salt, half covered with water and simmered. The stock is thickened with flour, and a pinch of sugar and chopped dill are added.

groszek zielony zaprawiany żółtkami, peas cooked in bouillon and served in a sweet sauce of beaten egg yolks with sweetened cream.

ground rice, rice ground to a fine powder; it is used for cakes and puddings, and to thicken soups, stews, and sauces.

groundhog, see WOODCHUCK.

groundnut, see PEANUT.

grouper (*Epinephelus morio*), a large sea fish found in warm American waters. It has a firm flesh which is good to eat, and it can be prepared and cooked in the same way as bass.

grous or **groux,** a Breton name for a thick gruel made from buckwheat flour and milk or water.

grouse (*Lagopus scoticus*), generally considered to be one of the best game birds in the world to eat. It is a very clean feeder, living on berries and young, tender shoots of heather, which abound where it is bred in Scotland, Yorkshire, and Ireland. From mid-September to mid-October is the best time to eat grouse born in the same year. The older bird of the year before cannot be compared in flavour and is most suitable in a braise, a terrine, or a pie. The young bird is easily recognisable by its clean claws with no noticeable moulting ridge and its soft breastbone tips. The grouse is usually hung for a week in warm weather, longer in cold weather. Many birds all over the world are called grouse, but in the British Isles it means red or Scotch grouse. Grouse to be roasted is not stuffed like poultry, but in the Highlands of Scotland the small wild mountain raspberries or rowanberries are mixed with butter and put inside the little birds. The fruit almost melts away, but the spicy buttery juice is excellent with the bird. The flavour of grouse is unique and so good that young birds should be cooked very simply. When they are older, the old Scottish method of grouse pie and potted grouse are really the best, or they may be braised with stock and mushrooms, or made into a salmi.

grouse

The true grouse does not exist in the U.S. The bird nearest to it is the bob white, called a quail in the North and a partridge in the South. The nearest relative to grouse is the blue-grouse, found in the Rocky Mountains as far north as Wyoming. Further south, it is replaced by the dusky grouse, which appears as far south as New Mexico. There is also a ruffed grouse, known more generally as beech partridge, and in Pennsylvania the local name is mountain pheasant. All the birds are larger than the Scotch grouse. Two other well-known but almost extinct species are the sharp-tailed grouse and the spruce grouse of Canada. See also GAME; QUENELLES; SALMI.

grouse pie (also a good recipe for partridges, pigeons, or pheasants), all tough skin and fibre are removed from breasts and the meat is cut into fairly small pieces and beaten flat. A mixture of lean pork with just a little fat, minced with 1 medium onion, pepper, and salt is spread to a thickness of about ⅛ inch on the little fillets. An ovenproof dish is lined with thin slices of streaky bacon and the fillets are laid inside, one on top of the other, until the dish is full. They are covered with more slices of bacon, and the dish is half-filled with a good stock made from the other parts and bones of the birds. The dish is covered and stood in a tin, with water half-way up, and cooked slowly for 2 hours in the oven. Care should be taken that the liquid does not cook away. The rest of the stock is reduced, and when the pie is cooked, this reduced stock is added to the fillets. The dish is cooled, then covered with greaseproof paper with a light weight on top, until cold. If there is any grease on the top it is removed, and the pie is served cold and cut into slices. It can be covered with pastry before cooking, if desired, but in Scotland a pie does not always have a pastry crust.

potted grouse (also for partridge and pigeon), four birds are plucked and prepared as for roasting. The necks, livers, and gizzards are retained. The birds are cut down the backs and the bones broken by beating them with a rolling pin. Plenty of cayenne, black pepper, and salt to taste are worked into about 1 lb. butter. The birds are rubbed all over with this, and the rest of the seasoned butter is placed inside the birds, which are closed up after that. All the giblets are placed in an earthenware dish and the birds put on top. The lid is put on, sealed round with a flour and water paste, and baked for 2 hours in a moderate oven. The birds should be so well done that the bones are easy to extract. After the bones have been extracted, each bird should be pressed down inside a potting dish, and some of the gravy and butter in which it has been cooked is poured over it. The birds are left to get cold and then covered with melted butter. It is a mistake to be sparing with either butter or pepper in this recipe.

roast grouse with white grapes, two birds are wrapped in fat bacon, and a knob of butter is put into each bird, as the flesh tends to dry when cooked. They are put into a hot oven with 4 oz. (½ cup) butter and cooked for 25 minutes. After 20 minutes, a glass of port is poured into the roasting tin and the birds are basted frequently until cooked. They are removed from the oven and kept warm. The liquor in the roasting tin is reduced by half, and the grouse is served with hot game chips and a bowl of peeled and pipped white grapes in their own juice.

grovey cake, a heavy cake made, according to a traditional Cornish recipe, with the dried "groves" (flakes of fat) remaining after pig-killing, when the fat has been rendered down to lard, and barley, flour, and salt. The cake is cut into squares when hot and eaten immediately. See also FLEAD; LARD, CAKES.

groviera, an Italian cheese, similar to Gruyère.

gruau, I. French for husk. II. A French name given to a very small pasta made from potato flour. It looks like sago and is used for a sort of porridge (*bouillie*), in soups, and also in sweet dishes.

gruau d'avoine, oatmeal, frequently used in France for soups, with milk, egg yolks, and butter.

grue, French for crane, which is sometimes eaten in France, where it is prepared in the same way as bustard.

gruel, oatmeal boiled in milk or water so that the consistency is liquid, unlike the thicker porridge.

grus, an old Irish hard-pressed cheese made from cow's milk, and similar to *tanag*. It has not been made for many years.

gruszki, Polish for pears.

gruszki smazone w miodzie, pears candied in honey and rolled in sugar. It is a favourite party dish. Sometimes, in Poland, pears are preserved in alcohol.

gruth, the modern Irish word for curd; it was also, in former times, an unpressed cheese made from either buttermilk or skimmed milk. Gruth, together with oatmeal and vegetables such as leeks or onions, nettles and carrots, was the main diet in many monasteries all over Ireland.

grützwurst, see PINKELWURST.

Gruyère, I. A cheese called after the Gruyère valley in the Canton of Fribourg, Switzerland. However, the cheese is also made in Vaud, Neuchâtel, the Bernese Jura, in the French Jura, and in Savoy. Unlike *emmenthal,* which it closely resembles, it is made from cow's milk, in both upland and valley dairies; it is more liberally salted than *emmenthal,* the

holes in the curd are smaller, and the curing period is about twice as long. Gruyère is also slightly harder in texture, and the rind is not dry. It has been known since the 12th century and has changed less than *emmenthal.* It is an excellent cheese to eat and very good for cooking, especially in a fondue. It is exported in large quantities all over the world. An entire cheese weighs about 80 lb. See also SAANEN. II. Greek for a ewe's milk cheese made in the same way as the famous Swiss Gruyère. It can be very good, but is not comparable with the Swiss variety.

Gruyère de Beaufort, see BEAUFORT.

Gruyère français, see COMTÉ.

grybai, Lithuanian for mushroom. Dried mushrooms are used extensively in Lithuania, especially in a delicious soup, see ŠALTI BARŠČIAI.

gryczanki, Polish buckwheat cakes. They are made in much the same way as griddle cakes, using buckwheat flour and sour cream for the dough. Sometimes they are made sandwich-style, and given a cheese and egg yolk filling.

grzanki, Polish for croûtons, sometimes made from pumpernickel.

grzanki faszerowane zajączem, a pâté of hare, used for garnishes or hors d'oeuvre and served on croûtons. See also ZAJĄC.

grzybek śmietankowy, a Polish sweet dish which is a rich pancake mixture made from 6 eggs, 1 tablespoon butter, 4 tablespoons icing (confectioners') sugar, ½ lb. (2 cups) flour, and ¾ pint (1½ cups) sour cream, which are all well beaten, the 6 stiffly beaten egg whites being added last. The mixture is fried in 2 thick rounds, in butter, and sandwiched together with jam. It is no doubt called a "mushroom" cake because of its appearance when cooked. It can be baked instead of fried, but then it has raisins added.

grzyby, Polish for wild mushrooms. Cultivated mushrooms (*pieczarki*), are seldom used for there is a wide variety of wild mushrooms in Poland, and many traditional mushroom recipes, of which those described here are the best known. *Grzyby suche* are Polish dried mushrooms; they are particularly well flavoured and are widely exported. See also PIECZARKI, FASZEROWANE.

grzyby marynowane, 1 lb. small button mushrooms simmered for 15 minutes with 1 sliced onion and salt in ¼ pint (½ cup) water, tightly covered; then 3 tablespoons wine vinegar, 2 bay leaves, peppercorns, and allspice are added. The ingredients are boiled up twice more and, when cool, are bottled and sealed.

grzyby panierowane, 1 lb. mushrooms lightly sautéed in butter with ½ minced onion, then dipped in egg and breadcrumbs before frying in butter or oil.

grzyby ze śmietaną, 1 lb. mushrooms stewed in butter, seasoned, and mixed with ½ pint (1 cup) sour cream blended with 1 teaspoon flour.

guacamole, a Mexican dish, or sauce, used as an hors d'oeuvre, a dip for chips, or a filling for tacos and tortillas. It is popular in the U.S. It is made from very ripe avocado pears, mashed and whipped with very little crushed garlic, lemon juice, onion, chillis or chilli pepper, sometimes tomatoes, and salt to taste. It may be served with poultry.

guards' pudding, an English pudding made from 6 tablespoons breadcrumbs mixed with the same amount of grated suet, 4 tablespoons brown sugar, 3 tablespoons strawberry or raspberry jam, 1 egg, and a pinch of baking soda all well mixed and steamed in a pudding basin for ⅔ hours. The pudding is served hot with melted jam or cream. It is also sometimes called Burbridge pudding.

guarracino, an ugly black fish found in Italian waters, and used principally for Italian fish soup. See ZUPPA, DI PESCE.

guastiedda siciliana, a Sicilian savoury made from fresh hot bread rolls sprinkled with sesame seeds. The rolls are split open and filled with a mixture of ricotta cheese and matchstick-thin strips of *cascavaddu* cheese, the latter having been first tossed in hot lard.

gudbrandsdalsost, see GEITOST.

gudgeon (*Gobio gobio*), one of the best freshwater fishes, found on the sandy bottom of almost all the rivers and lakes of Europe. It is a small fish belonging to the carp family. It is either used in a garnish (*batelière*); or dipped in flour or batter, fried in deep oil, like smelts or whitebait, and served as a separate course.

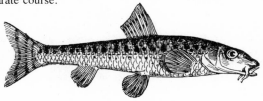

gudgeon

guglhupf or **gougelhopf,** a traditional Austrian yeast cake baked in a fluted dish made from copper, aluminum, or preferably fireproof pottery. There are eldness recipes for guglhupf, but generally it consists of 1 lb. (4 cups) flour, 1 oz. yeast, 3 egg yolks, 6 oz. (⅔ cup) butter, 4 oz. (½ cup) sugar, ½ pint (1 cup) tepid milk, grated peel of 1 lemon, ½ cup raisins, and ½ cup blanched almonds, all well kneaded, covered, and set to rise in a warm place as for yeast dough. It is baked in a hot oven (400°F) for about 40 minutes. See also KUGELHUPF.

marmorguglhupf, "marbled guglhupf," in which half the mixture is made with the addition of grated chocolate.

rahmguglhupf, as above, with cream added.

guigne, French for gean, one of the 2 main types of sweet cherry. A great many varieties of gean are cultivated in France.

guignette, I. Also called maubèche. French for sandpiper, a small wading bird not unlike a plover or snipe, which is cooked in France in the same way as snipe. II. The name in the south of France for a mollusc called littorine.

guillemot (*Uria aalge*), a sea bird common on European and American coasts. The birds are not eaten, but their eggs are collected and eaten like plover or gull eggs. They are about twice the size of the latter, but not so good to eat, as they contain too much egg white in proportion to yolk.

guindilla, I. Spanish for chilli. Chillies are used fresh and dried in Spain to flavour stews, rice dishes, etc. II. Spanish for morello cherry.

guinea fowl (*Numida mealeagris*), a West African bird, crested, and originally called turkey in 16th-century England. There are several wild varieties through Africa. When not domesticated, the guinea fowl can be tough and rather dry, and for this reason it is best when it is simmered gently, or braised in the oven. It is now domesticated in Europe and the U.S. and is quite common today. In the west of England, it is known locally as gliny, (where it is often cooked in cider) and in the U.S. as guinea hen. It is reasonably priced and can be served in numerous ways. Having a very good flavour, not unlike a bronze turkey, it is excellent roasted and basted with red wine, and can be cooked in the same way as pheasant, which is a similar size. See also FARAONA; PERLICZKI PIECZONE; PINTADE.

guinea pepper, see CAPSICUM.

guinea pig (*Cavia porcellus*), once a popular dish in England, but now these endearing little animals are used almost exclu-

sively for laboratory work or are kept as pets. They were native to Peru, Ecuador, and Colombia, and were domesticated by the Indians long before the arrival of the Spaniards. They were prized for their meat, which was considered a delicacy, and they were imported into Europe for this reason, after the discovery of America. They are still a staple feature of diet in Brazil and other South American countries. They are prepared for cooking by scalding and should not be skinned; then they are roasted, braised, or stewed in the same way as rabbit.

guisado, a Portuguese stew, made usually with chicken, goose, game, or turkey, with tomatoes, onions, port wine, garlic, and herbs. Sometimes raw beaten eggs are stirred into the hot sauce, which must not be reboiled or it will curdle.

guisado, a Spanish game stew for hare, partridge, rabbit, goose, or pheasant. The meat is cut up and, if possible, the blood, liver, and giblets are saved; the pieces should not be washed but wiped with a cloth. First the joints are fried in ½ pint (1 cup) olive oil, with 1 large sliced onion, until brown. The meat and oil are then transferred to a fireproof dish (*olla*), and equal portions of wine (Valdepeñas is best) and of stock or water are added to cover, together with a piece of bacon, some button onions, pimentos, garlic, thyme, parsley, salt, and pepper. The dish is covered and the stew is allowed to simmer gently for 1½–2 hours; it should be constantly stirred with a wooden spoon, and any fat should be carefully skimmed off. About 30 minutes before serving, the giblets are added. Finally the blood is added to thicken the stew, which must not reboil or it will curdle.

guisado de trigo, a Spanish stew made from about 6 wheat ears and ½ lb. soaked chick-peas, with 1 pig's trotter (foot), 2 large tomatoes, 2 sweet peppers, 2 garlic cloves, and 2 onions, all finely sliced, and herbs. The wheat, pig's trotter (foot), and chick-peas are first covered in water and simmered; then the other ingredients, having been sautéed in oil, are added to them, and cooking is continued until all are tender. This is a common dish in Albacete, La Mancha, the home of Don Quixote. Wheat, the outstanding feature of this dish, is cultivated in La Mancha—which also explains the presence of the windmills encountered there by Don Quixote and Sancho Panza. Most parts of Spain are too mountainous or infertile to encourage wheat growing.

guisantes, Spanish for peas. In Bilbao, they are first sautéed with a small onion in oil, then small new potatoes to the same weight as peas, 1 garlic clove, and ½ pint (1 cup) stock are added. The whole is seasoned to taste, and sometimes a little more fried garlic is added before serving. Peas are also used for soups, stews, and cakes.

guisias, a variety of wild pea, almost white in colour, which is found in Spain and Ibiza. A vegetable stew is made with them. See also QUINAD.

gül receli, jam made from fresh rose petals (usually red), a Turkish speciality. The petals from 2 dozen roses are cooked in a syrup made from 1 lb. sugar, 2 tablespoons lemon juice, and ½ pint (1 cup) rose water. The petals are soaked overnight in this, then simmered for about 1 hour until the syrup starts to thicken.

gulasch, an Austrian national dish, not to be confused with the Hungarian *gulyás,* although it is similar. Gulasch is called pörkölt in Hungary, and can be made from any meat or poultry. The meat or poultry is cubed or jointed and fried with an equal weight of onions in fat until brown. Then 1 tablespoon paprika, ¼ cup water, 1 tablespoon tomato purée, salt, marjoram, caraway seeds, and 1 tablespoon vinegar are added. The dish is covered, simmered gently until tender and served with *nockerln.* If veal is used, sour cream is added 5 minutes before the gulasch is ready.

gulasz wieprzowy, Polish for *gulyás* made from pork. Parboiled potatoes are added during the last 30 minutes of cooking time.

gulerod, Danish for carrot. In Denmark young carrots are often boiled and then cooked like brunede kartofler (see KARTOFFEL). They are also used for stews and soups. See also GRØNSAGER.

gulerot, Norwegian for carrot. See also GRØNNSAKER.

gulerotsuppe med ris, a soup made from 1 lb. minced carrots and ½ lb. minced turnips, first fried in butter, then seasoned, covered with stock, and simmered until cooked. Then 1 cup mashed potato is added with 4 pints (8 cups) stock. All are cooked for 30 minutes, then poured over 3 beaten egg yolks and 1 cup hot boiled rice in a tureen.

gull, the name given to sea birds of the family *Laridae.* Today, gull's eggs are valued more than the flesh of the bird, which has a very fishy flavour. To make a gull palatable, it must be caught alive and fed on milk or buttermilk for 2 or 3 weeks; this eliminates the unpleasant taste.

gull's eggs, very delicious hard-boiled and eaten with a little celery salt. In Ireland, the gulls are larger, and consequently the eggs are larger than those sold in England. They can be made into a good omelette or used as hen's eggs, for they have no taste of fish.

gulyás, the national dish of Hungary, and called goulash in English. Gulyás means "cowherd," so called because the true goulash was an invention of the wandering cowherd. All the ingredients, meat (often mutton), potatoes, tomatoes, sweet peppers, onions, herbs, and paprika were put into one pot and cooked over a wood fire. Now the recognized form of the dish is a beef stew, but in fact a whole range of stews goes by the name, and, also, different localities have their own version, for almost any meat may be cooked by the same method. Sour cream is often added before serving, and caraway seeds are nearly always used. For preparation, 2 lb. meat are cubed and browned with ½ lb. onions, then 1 tablespoon paprika is stirred in, and potatoes, tomatoes, sweet peppers, and herbs are added. All are covered with stock or water and simmered slowly for 2 hours, or until tender. Then ½ cup (¼ pint) sour cream is stirred in before serving. See also GULYÁSLEVES; PAPRIKÁS; PÖRKÖLT.

marha gulyás, a stew made with lightly fried onions, garlic, beef, ox heart, liver, and udder; seasoned with paprika, caraway seeds, marjoram, and salt; moistened with stock, water, or diluted tomato purée; and then cooked for several hours. Diced potatoes are added half-way through cooking, and 10 minutes before serving, *csipetke* are put in and cooked.

szegedigulyás, as gulyás, with sauerkraut added 30 minutes before serving.

székelygulyás, is prepared as gulyás, and a few caraway seeds are added. About 1 lb. sauerkraut is washed and cooked in a pan with a little chopped bacon and ¼ pint (½ cup) water. When cooked, any water is strained off and the goulash mixed in well. Shortly before serving, a mixture of 1 teaspoon flour and 1 gill (½ cup) sour cream, buttermilk, or yogourt is beaten into the gulyás and it is cooked for a few minutes more. This dish is popular in Transylvania.

gulyásleves, a dish which is related to the famous Hungarian *gulyás,* but is a thick type of soup. It can be made with several different kinds of meat used either in combination or separately. The main ingredients are beef or other meats, onions, fresh tomatoes, red or green peppers, potatoes, paprika, salt, lard, and water. The onions are cooked in the lard, and the diced meat is added. The rest of the ingredients, except potatoes, are then added and all simmered for 45 minutes. At this point, about 3 pints (6 cups) hot water are added slowly and the soup is simmered for another 2 hours. Thirty minutes before serving, the peeled and quartered potatoes are put in with some slices of smoked sausage. While basically a soup, served with fresh bread or a salad, this dish often makes the main meal of the day for the Hungarian peasant. See also GULYÁS.

gumbo, from the French gombo, meaning okra, is a distinctive and original creole dish inherited from Africa and the West Indies, and perfected by the Acadians (a people from the district of Acadia or Acadie), in what is now Nova Scotia and eastern New Brunswick, which was land disputed between the French and English, although colonized by France in 1604. It became English under the Treaty of Utrecht, 1713, and in 1755, when war with France was imminent, England forcibly deported the Acadians and destroyed their settlements, as celebrated in Longfellow's poem "Evangeline." One party made its way to Bayou Teche, Louisiana, and their descendants still inhabit that area and are known as Cajuns. The Acadians adapted the dish to foods grown in Louisiana, and it is a unique speciality of that American state. Gumbo is a soup–stew which usually has okra, onions, celery, and green peppers in it, as well as the most important and essential item, filé powder. Fluffy rice is served with gumbo, and the most famous gumbos are made with chicken, turkey, rabbit, squirrel, crab, shrimp, oyster, or simply green vegetables. See also FILÉ POWDER.

chicken gumbo, a creole dish from Louisiana, U.S., made from jointed, floured chicken browned in chicken fat, and then covered with hot water. Then 1 green pepper, 2 garlic cloves, 2 onions, ½ cup celery, and 1 lb. okra, all sliced, are added, and the ingredients are covered tightly and simmered for about 1 hour, having been seasoned to taste. A pinch of filé powder is put into each bowl and the hot soup poured over and stirred, or 1 teaspoon of filé powder is put in a warmed tureen, and the soup–stew poured over. (Okra has a gelatinous quality not unlike that of filé powder, and it is sometimes used in place of it, but they can be used together.) Cooked rice is served with it as well. Once the filé powder has been added, the gumbo must not be reheated, as it makes the meat stringy and unfit for further use. Gumbo is usually kept hot in a *bain-marie.* Chicken gumbo is also made with a mixture of chicken and 2 lb. large chopped prawns (called shrimps in the U.S.), and is known as chicken–shrimp gumbo.

crab gumbo creole, a soup from New Orleans. Onions and green peppers are diced and simmered in butter with chopped celery and leeks, until cooked. Strong fish or white stock is added with seasoning. The soup is garnished with shredded crab (or shrimp), boiled rice, and diced tomatoes, and filé powder is added to each bowl, as above. See also CRAB.

lobster gumbo, a traditional American soup. Chopped onions, diced peppers, and strips of ham are simmered in lobster butter; white wine, and fish stock or white stock are added and, at a later stage, okra and diced tomatoes with seasoning. The soup is garnished with diced lobster. Filé powder is added to each bowl, as above.

z'herbes gumbo, green gumbo made from turnip tops, spinach, cabbage, beetroot tops, mustard, green vegetables, garlic, green onions, pickled pork, and 1 green sweet pepper, all heated in water until a thick purée is formed. Filé powder is added, as above.

gundy, a Scots sweetmeat (confection) similar to *glessie,* but flavoured with a little aniseed or cinnamon.

gurka, Swedish for cucumber. See also GRÖNSAKER.

inlagd gurka, pickled cucumber. Thinly sliced cucumbers are covered with salt and left weighted down for 1 hour, after which they are drained and sprinkled with a dressing consisting of sugar, pepper, water, vinegar, and also parsley or dill. It is served slightly chilled.

pressgurka, cucumber salad. A French dressing is sprinkled over thin, unpeeled slices of cucumber and the salad is served chilled, garnished with parsley or dill.

stekt gurka, fried cucumber. Peeled slices of cucumber are dipped in egg and stale breadcrumbs (which have previously been seasoned with salt, pepper, and ginger) and fried in butter until golden brown. They are served with fried or grilled meat and fish.

gurke, German for cucumber, which in Germany and Austria is often served stewed in stock. It may also be served stuffed or as a salad which is dressed with cream, chopped dill, and chives, with a sprinkling of vinegar. *Salzgurke* is German for pickling cucumber or gherkin.

gefüllte gurke, cucumber blanched and stuffed with equal quantities of minced, cooked meat and soaked white bread, flavoured with dill, salt, and pepper. Rashers of fat bacon are wrapped round, and the whole is covered with stock and casseroled for 1 hour.

gurnard or **gurnet** (*family Triglidae*), a saltwater fish found in the warmer waters off the Atlantic coasts and in the Mediterranean. There are two main species: *T. cuculus,* the red gurnard, sometimes called sea cockoo; and *T. hirundo,* the yellow gurnard, a rather inferior fish. Both have large heads, and the former is sometimes wrongly sold as red mullet as it has a reddish tinge; however its taste is coarse in comparison with the mullet, although recipes for mullet can be used. *Crooner* is one of the gurnards.

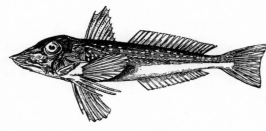

gurnard

gurneau, an alternative French name, with *grondin,* for a species of furnard, found in the Mediterranean, the Baltic, and British coastal waters.

gurnet, see GURNARD.

gury, a traditional Russian dish which comprises a whole raw white cabbage soaked in brine with beetroots and red peppers. It is extremely decorative as it becomes a soft shade of red. It is a speciality of Georgia, U.S.S.R.

gus, Russian for goose. See also GOOSE.

gus farshirovanny kashey, goose stuffed with kasha. Usually the goose is first boned (and the bones simmered with root vegetables and dried mushrooms), then filled with a mixture of the chopped mushrooms and kasha, sewn up, and roasted. It is basted with a little stock from time to time.

guska, Serbo-Croat for goose, which in Croatia is often roasted and served with cooked noodles, when it is called pečena guska s mlincima. See also GOOSE.

guska na podvarku, goose on sauerkraut. A young 10-lb. goose is rubbed with salt and goose fat, both inside and out, then roasted for 2 hours. Then 2 large onions are sliced, fried in oil, and, when golden, 2 lb. sauerkraut, 1 teaspoon paprika, salt, and pepper are added. When hot and well coloured, these ingredients are put in a large dish, with goose gravy and the goose on top, and roasted for a further 20–30 minutes.

gutui, Rumanian for quince.

gutui ca carne, quinces with meat. Prepared with 1 lb. either veal or beef cut into pieces and fried in fat until cooked, when 1 teaspoon flour is added. When this has browned, the pan is filled with stock. About 6 or 7 quinces are prepared, quartered, and fried in a separate pan. They are then added, with a little caramelised sugar, to the meat, with which they are cooked until tender. A small chicken may be substituted for the meat. See also VĂCUŢĂ, CU GUTUI.

gwyniad, the Welsh name for *Coregonus lavaretus,* found in Wales in Lake Bala. It is a herringlike fish, one of the freshwater whitefish. The same fish is caught in Loch Lomond and Loch Eck, Scotland, where it is known as powan, and in Ullswater, Hawes Water, and the Red Tarn in the Lake District, where it is known as schelly or skelly. It is of the same family as the *pollan,* and the *lavaret* and *fera* of France, Austria, and Switzerland. It is good to eat and can be fried, grilled, or baked.

gymnètre faux, a saltwater fish about 20 inches long, found in the Mediterranean. It is flat, silver in colour, and has red fins. It tastes like cod and can be prepared and served with recipes that are suitable for cod.

Gyulai kolbàsz, a Hungarian sausage from Gyulai, often served as a first course, like salame.

gyuvèch, a dish which is eaten, with slight variations throughout the Balkans, but is also one of the national recipes of Bulgaria. It is made with beef, veal, lamb, or pork, or a mixture of meats (about 2 lb.) cubed, trimmed of fat or gristle, and placed in a saucepan with a little butter and seasoning, then barely covered with water and simmered for 15 minutes. Any scum which rises is taken off. Then chopped vegetables, such as tomatoes, potatoes, eggplant, french beans, bahmyas, green peppers, and green tomatoes, with the juice of ½ lemon are added and just blanched for 5 minutes. A flameproof dish is buttered and the drained meat and vegetables are layered in it, with the tomatoes on top, and 1 pint (2 cups) of the stock is poured over before baking for about 1½ hours, or until the meat is tender, in a moderate oven. Ten minutes before serving, 2 eggs, 1 tablespoon flour, and the juice of ½ lemon are mixed together and poured over the top. The dish is returned to the oven and baked for a further 10 minutes or until the top is cooked and golden brown. See also BOSANSKI LONAC; DJUVEČ; GEVETCH-DE-PESHTE; GHIVECI; TURLU GYUVÈCH.

haantjes, Dutch for cocks. See KIP.

haas, Dutch for hare. Hare is featured very often on Dutch menus, and there are various methods of preparing it. The methods described here are also suitable for rabbit. See also GAME; HARE; HAZEPEPER; KONIJN.

gebraden haas, roast hare which has been marinated in vinegar for 2 hours, then scalded with boiling water. It is rubbed with salt and dry mustard, larded with bacon, then roasted in butter for about 2 hours. The pan juices are mixed with ¼ pint (½ cup) each of red wine and sour cream, and reduced. Finally, ¼ pint of hare's blood is added, heated but not reboiled, and seasoned to taste.

gestoofde haas, stewed hare. The legs are divided into 2 pieces and the saddle into 6; all are sautéed in butter for about 20 minutes and then sprinkled with seasoning. They are put into a pot which is lined with slices of fat smoked bacon, together with the pan drippings. Then 1 pint (2 cups) sour cream is added, the pot is covered, and the hare is cooked for up to 3 hours in a slow oven. A fairly thick cream sauce is made by mixing 3 tablespoons flour with 2 tablespoons butter and adding these to the pot after the removal of the game; after blending, ½ pint (1 cup) bouillon is added, the sauce is sieved, and pepper and some grated lemon peel are included.

habas, Spanish for broad beans, used extensively in Spain for casserole dishes with bacon or ham and other vegetables. Every province has its own version.

habas a la montañesa, broad beans mountain-style. Enough olive oil is poured into a casserole to cover the bottom, and ½ lb. finely chopped bacon is browned in it with 1 large sliced onion. Then 2 sliced sweet peppers are added, together with seasoning, 1 tablespoon flour, and ¼ pint (½ cup) stock, white wine, or water; 2 lb. shelled beans, parsley, thyme, and mint are included, the casserole is tightly covered, and the contents are cooked on a very low flame until tender. Variations of this dish include potatoes and carrots, or tomatoes, or garlic, 1 bay leaf, and paprika.

haberdine, also spelt haburden, an old English name for salt cod. The two spellings are both a corruption of the place name Aberdeen, Scotland, where large quantities of this dried, salted fish were exported in former times. See also LABERDAN.

habillage, the French term for the dressing of poultry, game, or fish.

haburden, see HABERDINE.

hachage, French for either chopped food, or the action of chopping, although the term generally used to describe food when it is served chopped is *hachis.*

hâché, a Dutch meat stew or hash made with 4 onions fried in fat or oil and then removed from the pan and replaced by 2 lb. cubed round steak. The steak is browned, after which the onions are returned and both ingredients are sprinkled with flour. Then 1 pint (2 cups) water, 2 bay leaves, 2 tablespoons vinegar, 6 cloves, salt, and 1 tablespoon worcestershire sauce are all added, the pan is covered, and the whole is simmered for about 2 hours. The stew is served with cooked red cabbage and boiled potatoes.

hachis, I. French for chopped food, thus hachoir, French for a crescent-shaped chopping-knife. See also HACHAGE. II. French for hash, served in France with a border of *pommes duchesse.*

hachis à la parmentier, chopped cold meat, usually cold roast beef, mixed with demi-glace sauce and served in large, partly scooped-out, (jacket)-baked potatoes.

hachis à l'indienne, hash with curry added.

haddock (*Gadus aeglefinus*), one of the smaller fish of the cod family. It is found in the North Atlantic from Iceland to France, and in the American Atlantic waters. In Newfoundland it is known as âné or *ánon.* Around Scotland, England, and Ireland it is at its best during the autumn and winter months. It is a good-eating white fish, quite delicate in flavour when served fresh, and can be cooked like cod or hake. In Ireland fresh haddock can be stuffed with equal parts of breadcrumbs and grated suet, with 1 tablespoon grated lemon peel and a pinch of mace, and baked with butter and ¼ pint (½ cup) Madeira wine. This is an 18th-century Irish recipe that should be used more today. In England haddock is usually grilled, fried in batter, or poached in milk or cream. If poached, the liquid when cooked is thickened with flour and the fish served with melted butter, or, alternatively, with egg sauce. Cheese sauce (or sauce mornay), too, is a popular accompaniment with poached haddock. The Norway haddock is bright red in colour and much prized gastronomically in Scandinavian countries.

Haddock is also smoked, particularly at Findon (pronounced "Finnan") in Scotland, and finnan haddie is extremely popular both in the British Isles and in the U.S. It is served either poached or grilled, with a pat of butter and pepper, and sometimes a poached egg accompanies it. In Scotland haddock is often smoked over turf, oak, or silver-birch sawdust to which a few juniper twigs or pine-cones are added. *Arbroath smokies,* from Auchmithie, Scotland, are haddock smoked to a copper colour; the fish is smoked, gutted, but closed up, unlike the Findon haddock which is split open. Another curing method is *moray firth.* Smoked haddock can also be used for fishcakes, soufflés, or composite dishes such as *kedgeree.*

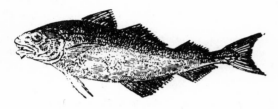

haddock

Sir Walter Scott mentions haddock in the Waverley novels, and says that the fish used to be dried over smouldering seaweed and sprinkled with seawater, which gave it a unique flavour. If haddock is dried in the sun, it is known as rizzared haddock; if dried in the wind, it is known as blawn. Haddock can also be rock-dried or earth-dried (a process applied particularly to skate), i.e., left on the grass for a day or two with a grassy sod over it. There are many Scottish recipes for this fish. See also FINNAN HADDIE; NORWAY HADDOCK; RÖKT-FISKPUDDING.

ham and haddie, a delicious dish from Glasgow. Smoked haddock is cooked with a slice of smoked ham or bacon in a very little water, in a pan with a close-fitting lid. See also CRAPPIT HEIDS.

hagebutten, German for rose hips used in Germany for soups, sauces, and preserves.

hagebuttenmarmelade, 2 lb. rose hips are marinated in ⅓ pint white wine vinegar for 3 days, being stirred frequently. On the 4th day, the resulting purée is sieved, and to every 1 lb. of purée ¾ lb. lump sugar, first soaked and brought to just below the boiling point, is added. The preserve is heated but must not boil.

hagebuttensuppe, a rose hip soup made from ½ lb. soaked rose hips boiled until soft in 1½ pints (3 cups) water with the peel of 1 lemon, a 2-inch cinnamon stick, and 3 cloves. It is then sieved and 1 oz. flour is browned in 1 oz. butter, and this mixture is added gradually to the soup, which is sweetened to taste, flavoured with 2 tablespoons white wine, and served hot.

hagejordbaer, Norwegian for cultivated strawberries. See JORDBÆR.

haggamuggie, a Shetland Island fish haggis. The stomach (muggie) of a large fish is well washed and tied at one end with string. It is two-thirds filled with toasted oatmeal, the chopped fish liver, salt, and pepper. The top is tied down and the whole boiled in salted water for 30 minutes. It is eaten in its entirety, hot, with potatoes. No doubt the word "huggermugger" (secret) comes from this.

haggis, a Scots national dish made from the minced heart, liver, and lights (lungs) of a sheep, mixed with suet, oatmeal, and a little chopped parsley and onion, and seasoned with nutmeg, pepper, cayenne pepper, and salt. This is all put into a cleaned sheep's stomach or paunch; it is pricked to allow for expansion, tied securely, boiled for 3–4 hours in salted water, and then left to get cold in the water. To serve, it is reheated, then set on a large dish with a napkin underneath, and, tradi-

tionally, surrounded with mashed turnips and boiled potatoes. Whiskey is the accepted drink to serve with it. Haggis made from deer pluck is a superior variation, since deer liver is a gastronomic delicacy.

haggis

Haggis is often served to the accompaniment of pipe music from Highland pipers at *Hogmanay* and on Burns's Night (January 25), the anniversary of the birth of the great Scots poet Robert Burns, who even wrote a poem called "To a Haggis." Haggis was probably brought to Britain by the Romans. A dish almost exactly like it (apart from the addition of more herbs and eggs) occurs in Caelius Apicius' cookery book *De Re Coquinaria:* it appears in Chapter VII under the general heading of "Ventiiculi." Caelius Apicius was a famous epicure who lived during the reigns of both the Emperors Augustus and Tiberius. He finally hung himself after having spent his fortune on eating and entertaining.

The name is thought to come from the Scottish word hag, to hack or to chop, although some think it derives from the French *hachis.* See also AFRONCHEMOYLE.

hákarl, an Icelandic speciality consisting of smoked shark. It is an acquired taste.

hake (Merluccius), a sea fish of the cod family, but not quite as large as the cod, and a little firmer in texture; it also has fewer bones. Hake is found almost all over the world, even in Pacific waters; the silver hake, found off the eastern seaboard of the U.S., is a finer fish than the European variety. Fresh hake can be cooked and served like cod or haddock; large hake cut into steaks is delicious poached in fish stock and served with lemon-flavoured melted butter. In Europe, though, hake is often dried; this is called merluche in France. See also MERLUZA.

hakkebøf, Danish for hamburgers. They are made with 2 lb. finely minced steak shaped into shallow rounds which are rolled in seasoned flour and fried on both sides in butter until cooked through. A sauce consisting of 2 pints (4 cups) beef stock and 3 tablespoons cream thickened with 2 tablespoons corn flour (cornstarch) is poured over the hamburgers, which are served with brunede kartofler (see KARTOFFEL) and sliced onions which have been fried until crisp and brown. Sometimes in Denmark the hamburgers are shaped into balls, dipped in seasoned flour, and then fried in lard with onions. The accompanying sauce for these balls consists of boiling beef stock thickened with corn flour (cornstarch) creamed with a little cold water.

hal, Hungarian for fish.

halaszlé, a traditional fish stew which consists of 4 onions fried in butter and seasoned with salt and paprika, and 4 lb. assorted fish such as eel, pike, *fogas,* shad, and carp, all cut into pieces and covered with a mixture of 2 tablespoons tomato purée, water, sour cream, fish stock, and 1 tablespoon lemon juice. This is cooked until the fish is tender; then the sauce is thickened with egg yolks and reheated, but not reboiled for fear of curdling.

halkocsonya, fish in aspic, usually poached carp, trout, or *fogas.* It is served as an hors d'oeuvre.

tejfeles hal, fish, such as pike or carp, baked in ½ pint (1 cup) water with parsley, onion, and green peppers underneath, and sliced tomatoes and butter on top. The sauce is made by serving the vegetables with the stock and adding ½ pint (1 cup) sweet or sour cream and a pinch of paprika.

halibut (*Hippoglossus hippoglossus*), the largest flat fish found in northern waters. It can attain a length of 10 feet and a weight of 300 lb. It is a delicious fish, firm yet milky, and it is cooked and served in the same way as turbot, which it resembles. It bakes very well as it does not go dry. Young halibut under 3 lb. in weight are called chicken halibut and they are excellent; in Ireland these small halibut are often lightly smoked and served in the same way as smoked haddock.

halicot, a former French culinary term from the verb halicoter, for food chopped very finely; it has since been corrupted to haricot. See also HARICOT DE MOUTON.

halloumi, a very good Greek goat's milk cheese made in Cyprus.

Halloween or **All Halloween,** held on October 31, is the eve or vigil of Hallowmass or All Saint's Day, November 1. It is thought to have been originally a Druidic festival, and in the distant past it was chiefly marked by the lighting of bonfires (or bone fires, since the bones of near relatives were burned at this time) to honour the Sun God in thanksgiving for the harvest, and by the belief that it was the one night in the year during which the unquiet spirits, or ghosts, and witches were most likely to walk abroad. It was also a Druidic belief that Samhain (pronounced Sow-án), the Lord of Death, summoned together the evil souls that had been condemned to inhabit the bodies of animals. November 1, or Samhain, was also the Celtic New Year, and the oatmeal porridge called *sowan* or sowans was eaten at this time, as in fact it still is. Indeed, in parts of Ireland Halloween is still known in Irish as Oidhche Shamhna, the watching, or vigil, of Samhain. Ireland, Scotland, parts of the north of England, and the U.S. still observe Halloween. In the south of England, Guy Fawkes night, on November 5, is the more popular celebration, although not confined to that region. Certain features of the celebrations of the early festival of Pomona, the Roman goddess of fruit trees, have become part of the Halloween festivities; for instance ''apple bobbing''—the game of catching a floating apple with the teeth—and the burning or roasting of nuts.

There are, perhaps, more traditional Irish dishes for Halloween than for any other day, and different counties have their own specialities. County Armagh has a sweet cake made from potato and apple with flour, sugar, butter, and eggs. There are boxty bread and pancakes, colcannon, and, most general throughout Ireland, barm brack. At Halloween all these dishes have a ring mixed into the ingredients, and the belief is that whoever gets it will be married within the year. It is the night for fortune telling and practical jokes, and even as recently as 25 years ago, men and women changed clothes, as in earlier saturnalia. It is still a common practice to hang cabbages or turnips on the doors of neighbours, the survival of a custom known in Munster and Connaught as ''battering away hunger.'' In County Clare, a half loaf of bread is used for the same purpose. In Scotland, the bonnach samhthain (Sow-án bannock) is baked, and also an elaborate fruit cake which is iced in the Halloween colours of orange and black. These too have rings and charms concealed in them. In the U.S., it is often descendants of people from Ireland and Scotland who carry on the traditions of their homeland.

halorini, Greek for a cheese of Greek-Cypriot origin, usually made from ewe's milk; it is folded over like dough and filled with pounded coriander seeds.

halušky, a typical Czechoslovak luncheon dish, made from 1 lb. boiled noodles mixed with 1 large chopped fried onion and ½ lb. stewed, dried mushrooms. The ingredients are put into an ovenproof dish, and 2 eggs and 1 pint (2 cups) milk are beaten together and poured over. The dish is baked for about 30 minutes or until golden brown, and is sprinkled with parsley before serving. It is often served with *černý kuba.*

halva or **halvah,** a Greek and Turkish sweetmeat (confection) made from 1 lb. (2 cups) semolina added to a syrup made from 1½ lb. (3 cups) sugar boiled with 2 pints (4 cups) water and cooked until pale gold. Then 1 cup fried chopped almonds is put in, before baking in a moderate oven for 15 minutes. The mixture is pressed when cool, then sprinkled with cinnamon and more almonds. Commercially made halvas is usually made with sesame seeds instead of the more expensive almonds.

halvas, a Greek Easter cake, made by combining 1 lb. (2 cups) semolina with 6 oz. (⅔ cup) butter, 6 oz. (⅔ cup) sugar, 4 oz. (1 cup) chopped almonds, 4 eggs, and 1 teaspoon cinnamon and baking for about 40 minutes in a moderate oven. A thick syrup of 1 lb. (2 cups) sugar, 1 teaspoon lemon juice, a 1-inch cinnamon stick, and 2 pints (4 cups) water, all boiled until syrupy, is poured over the cake after baking. It is served cooled and cut into squares. See also LAMBROPSOMO; TSOUREKIA.

halvas toufournou, also *halvas tis rinas,* as above, but with 3 tablespoons brandy and 2 teaspoons baking powder added. The eggs are separated, the whites being added at the end after being beaten until stiff. It is always baked in a hot oven, as opposed to a moderate one for plain halvas.

ham, the hind leg of a pig which has been cured and smoked. Nowadays some hams sold are shoulder of pig and, although good, are fatter and have less flavour than a true ham. The most prized English variety is York ham, originally lightly smoked over the smouldering sawdust embers left during the building of York Minster. Bradenham hams are exceptionally good; they have a coal-black skin and also come from Yorkshire. Suffolk hams are very sweet, but are seldom seen these days. Limerick ham, from Ireland, is world-famous. It is said that the best ones come from the left leg; the right leg is used by the pig to scratch his ear and this is thought to toughen the meat! In the U.S., the most famous hams are the peach-fed, sweet, smoked Virginia ham and the drier Smithfield and Kentucky hams, although many of the foreign hams are now being imitated there.

In Britain, Ireland, and the U.S. hams are usually soaked overnight in cold water, before the skin is scrubbed and the ham simmered with herbs in water or cider for 25 minutes to the pound. Hams should never be rapidly boiled; it makes them dry. They are cooled in the water, then the skin is peeled off, and they can be reheated in the stock and served with a variety of sauces, such as parsley, lemon, or raisin and celery, all based on the ham stock. Or they can be covered with pineapple rings, apricots, or peaches, and brown sugar, studded with cloves, and baked in the oven with a little juice for about an hour. Ham is good to eat hot or cold, and is usually served at a cold buffet and at Christmas time. There are many varieties of delicious foreign-cured ham, some so delicately smoked that they are eaten raw, finely sliced. See also JAMBON; JAMÓN; JOULUKINKKU; JULSKINKA; PAIO; PRAŽSKÁ ŠUNKA; PRESUNTO; PROSCIUTTO; PRŠUT; SCHINKEN; SKINKA; SKINKE; ȘUNCĂ; SZYNCA.

ham steaks, slices cut from the whole ham, usually grilled or fried, sometimes with pineapple juice.

ham, Dutch for ham, often served chopped, mixed with bread or potatoes, raw eggs, and either fried or steamed; this is called hamballetjes.

hamantaschen, a three-cornered Jewish pastry filled with poppy seeds and chopped nuts and raisins mixed with honey or, in some countries, thick prune butter (*lacqua*). It symbolizes the purse or the three-cornered hat of Hamam, and is eaten at the Purim festival, or the Feast of Esther, which commemorates the downfall of the wicked councillor Hamam. See also NAHIT; PURIM, FRITTERS.

Hamburg parsley, see PARSLEY.

hamburger, a minced beefsteak with seasonings and sometimes a little chopped onion, all mixed lightly together before being shaped into cakes and dry (pan) fried. Nowadays they are thought of as purely American; in fact, they originated on the German Hamburg-Amerika line boats, which brought emigrants to America in the 1850s. There was at that time a famous Hamburg beef which was salted and sometimes slightly smoked, and therefore ideal for keeping on a long sea voyage. As it was hard, it was minced and sometimes stretched with soaked breadcrumbs and chopped onion. It was popular with the Jewish emigrants, who continued to make Hamburg steaks, as the patties were then called, with fresh meat when they settled in the U.S. Today, hamburgers are served in various ways in the U.S.: with fried onions, a sour cream and dill mixture, olives and tomato sauce, kidney beans, cheese, ketchup, or bacon. They may also be simmered in stock or a rich tomato sauce after frying. They are most often made into a hefty sandwich, served on a roll or muffin. As meat balls, they are served with spaghetti and tomato sauce, gnocchi, and other pasta. See also HAKKEBØF.

Hamburger aalsuppe, a German regional soup from Hamburg. It consists of 2 lb. eel cut up and boiled in 3 pints (6 cups) strongly seasoned stock. Then 1 lb. pears is peeled, quartered, covered in red or white wine with lemon peel and sugar to taste, and simmered. The stocks from the eel and the pears are strained and combined. Then 2 finely diced, cooked carrots, 2 leeks, 1 Hamburg parsley root, and 1 cup green peas are added to 1 cup rich beef broth and simmered until tender. The broth is then slightly thickened with a brown roux, combined with the eel and pear stock, and reheated (or the roux is dispensed with and the combined broth and eel and pear stock are thickened by pouring them, when hot, over 2 beaten egg yolks in a warmed tureen). Small flour dumplings, together with the eel meat and pears remaining after the stock has been strained, are placed in a tureen and the soup is poured over them. See also AAL (AALSUPPE).

Hamburger rauchfleisch, German for smoked brisket of beef, boiled, then sliced very thinly when cold and served with grated horseradish; this is a speciality of Hamburg.

hamburgerrygg, a Danish smoked loin of pork in a large sausage shape, bought whole, boiled, and served hot with horseradish cream sauce and carmellised potatoes *kartoffel*.

hamlet, I. (*Epinephelus striatus*), a large sea fish of the grouper family which is considered very good eating. It abounds in American subtropical and tropical waters. II. In the West Indies, a large black and yellow eel, which is highly thought of gastronomically, has the same name.

hammel, German for mutton. Hammelrippe is the German for mutton cutlet, hammelschulter for shoulder of mutton, often braised with cucumbers and onion. Hammelzungen is German for sheep's tongue. See also MUTTON; SCHÖPS.

hammelkeule als wildbret, German for leg of mutton cooked like venison. It is boned and soaked for several days in sour milk; then dried, larded with strips of fat bacon, rolled, and roasted with butter and a very little water. When

cooked, 1 pint (2 cups) sour cream, and 1 teaspoon meat extract mixed with 2 tablespoons flour are added to the pan juices; this mixture is thickened by boiling up, and is served with red currant jelly, with the meat.

hammelwürste, a German dish consisting of fat pork, garlic, marjoram, a pinch of ginger, and mutton sausages. See also WÜRST.

hand, an English cut of pork or ham consisting of the foreleg and part of the shoulder. It is known in the U.S. as picnic shoulder.

hand cheese, an American sour cow's milk cheese. It is made from a mixture of skimmed milk and buttermilk. The curd is ground in a curd mill, and caraway seeds are sometimes added. The cheese is made by farmers of German descent in Pennsylvania, as well as by a few factories in Wisconsin and Illinois. It is so called because originally it was moulded into its final shape by hand.

hangikjöt, Icelandic smoked leg of lamb, which is a traditional speciality in Iceland. It is always boiled or braised, and served with a nutmeg sauce (white sauce flavoured with nutmeg), green peas, and potatoes. See also LAMBASTEIK.

hanging, of meat and game, a method which adds more flavour and also tenderises. The meat or game should be hung on a hook in a dry, cool, but well-aired place.

hangop, Dutch for "hang up," an expression referring to the making of a dessert dish of that name consisting of creamed buttermilk. To prepare it 2 quarts (8 cups) buttermilk are brought to a cream-like consistency by being placed in a bag which is hung up to drain for about 6 hours; the buttermilk is then mixed with ¼ pint (½ cup) whipped cream. It is eaten well chilled, with cinnamon to taste and brown sugar, together with some broken zwieback rusks. (Sometimes sugar is mixed with the creamed buttermilk and pineapple is added.)

hanoi, a small pink fish found in Greek waters, used with celery, carrots, onions, and parsley to make soup in Greece. *Avgolémono sauce* is generally added to the soup before serving.

hapukapsa salat, an Estonian national dish which consists of 1½ lb. (3 cups) sauerkraut made into a salad with 2 large raw chopped apples, 1 large sliced onion, and ¼ pint (½ cup) sour cream. A little sugar and salt are added, and the dish is usually served with meat.

hapupiim, Estonian for sour milk, which is often served as a drink with meals in the Estonian S.S.R.

harcsa, a kind of white shad found in the Danube and Tisza Rivers; it is very popular in fish stews and soups.

hard sauce, in the U.S. a hard sauce is made by working two parts of castor (powdered) sugar into one part of butter. The mixture is beaten until it reaches the consistency of clotted cream, when a few drops of lemon juice or brandy or rum are worked in. It is kept refrigerated until required, when pieces are cut off and shaped for serving. The English version of this sauce is known as brandy butter or rum butter.

hardfiskur, a traditional Icelandic fish dish. The fish is cleaned and then cut in half. It is dried out-of-doors and is eaten with butter as an hors d'oeuvre.

hare, a wild rodent with dark, well-flavoured flesh. There are two kinds of European hare (*Lepus europaeus*): the mountain hare, also known as Scotch blue in Scotland, and the common hare, which varies in colour from greyish brown in England to tan and golden in Normandy, Touraine, Champagne, Beauce, and Brie, the districts of France which have the finest hares. The mountain hare is smaller, but more delicate in flavour. Young hares are called leverets in English, and are still young at 1 year old; they are easily recognised by a little rounded prominence on a bone under the leg joint, which disappears as they grow older, and the skin of the ears splits more easily on a young hare. Females remain tender for 2 years. Hare can be eaten freshly shot, but if left to get cold, like all other game it must be hung head downwards for at least 3 days—perhaps longer in extremely cold weather—and not drawn until ready for use. It must be skinned, and the blood, which collects under a piece of membrane in the ribs and is used to thicken and enrich the gravy when the hare is jugged or casseroled, is kept carefully in a container. Young hare is usually roasted; the older hare is made into pâtés and pies, and is potted, jugged, or casseroled.

hare

In all European countries, the saddle, which is the body with the legs removed, is often roasted separately, sometimes larded and at other times stuffed. The legs are made into pies, etc., or casseroled. The American hare (*L. californicus, L. americanus, L. articus*) are often called rabbit in the U.S. *L. californicus* is known as the jack rabbit; *L. americanus* is the snowshoe rabbit; *L. articus* is the Arctic hare, which closely resembles the blue or Scotch hare, and likewise changes its coat to white in the winter. They are all good to eat and can be prepared like the European hare. See also AÏLLADE, DE LEVRAUT; CIVET, DE LIÈVRE; HAAS; HASE; HAZEPEPER; HUBERTUSLEVES; IEPURE; JÄNIS (JÄNISPAISTI); LAYOS; LEPRE; LIEBRE; PAPRIKÁS (PAPRIKÁSNYÚL); ZAJĄC; ZAYATS.

jugged hare, the English equivalent of *civet de lièvre*. The hare is usually marinated overnight in wine, a little vinegar, onion, bay leaf, and peppercorns. The joints are dried and browned in oil or bacon fat, then put into a casserole (or, as was originally used, a deep earthenware pot) with celery, onion, carrot, allspice, and the peel and juice of a lemon, all sliced finely. Stock is poured over barely to cover, the lid is tightly sealed, and the contents are cooked in a slow oven for about 3 hours. When cooked, the gravy is strained off into a pan; it is thickened with a *beurre manié* and boiled. Then ¼ pint (½ cup) strained marinade (see hare) is added, and 1 tablespoon red currant jelly. This is boiled and allowed to reduce slightly before the blood of the hare is added. The sauce is reheated, stirring all the time, but it must not reboil or it will curdle. It is poured over the warm hare and served. See also JUGGED.

potted hare, the old English way of making a hare terrine. The slightly cooked hare is minced and mixed with a pinch each of nutmeg, mace, salt, and pepper. It is put in layers in an ovenproof dish with sliced ham or pork, and a little stock and melted butter is poured over; it is covered and cooked in a slow oven for several hours. When cool, fresh melted butter is poured over and it is left to get cold. The dish is served cold, sliced, with toast. The hare liver is very good and can be incorporated in the terrine. Excellent soup can be made from hare, with root vegetables, and herbs. Red currant jelly is the usual accompaniment to roasted hare.

hareng, French for herring. *Harengs bouffis* are half-smoked herrings; see CRAQUELOTS. *Harengs frais* are fresh herrings, *harengs fumés* are smoked herrings, and *harengs salés* are salt herrings, a speciality of the Boulogne fisheries. All these varieties are used extensively in France.

haricot, French for bean. *Haricots blancs frais* are fresh haricot beans; *haricots blancs secs,* dried haricot beans. *Haricot de Java* is the soya bean; *haricot de Lima,* lima bean; *haricot d'Espagne,* runner bean; *haricot verts,* french beans. All these beans are used a lot in French cooking. See NORMANDE, À LA.

haricot de mouton, French for haricot of mutton, a stew made with chopped mutton, turnips, and potatoes. See also HALICOT.

haricot bean (*Phaseolus vulgaris*), also called kidney bean and navy bean. In Europe the term haricots is applied to the fully ripened seeds of the french (string) bean and its many varieties. Some are large and white, such as white rice and comtesse de chambord; others, such as the flageolet, are smaller and are green, purple, or brown according to variety. (See *chevrier.*) There is a red variety used in Italy and called *borlotti*. America produces many other varieties of bean besides these, the more important being the lima bean or butter bean and the tepary (pinto) bean. Beans are used in Europe and in the U.S. as a vegetable, in soups, and in salads. See also BOHNEN; BØNNER; BÖNOR; CASSOULET; FABADA ASTURIANA; FAGIOLI; FASOEIL AL FURN; FASOLA; FASSOLADA; FASSOLIA; FASÙL YAHNIYA; FEIJÃO.

haring, Dutch for herring, which, as well as being an important commercial commodity, for both the home and export markets, is a national dish in Holland, and known as "the poor man's oyster." The season starts in May, and the first day of the catch is something of a festival, as crowds gather to watch the herring fleets, each boat being decorated with bunting and flags. The skipper of the first craft to return with a full catch within 24 hours gains nationwide fame, and it is from his hands that the Queen of the Netherlands receives the first herrings of the season, packed in a traditional barrel. While the season lasts, these fresh young herrings ("green" herrings, as the Dutch call them) are eaten raw, but lightly salted, everywhere, even in the streets, where small carts bearing the words "Hollandse Nieuwe" (Holland New Ones) and decorated with the national emblem do a good trade among all classes. In restaurants herrings are usually served on ice, with toast and butter. When not in season they are served either pickled in herbs and vinegar, or salted. See also MAATJES.

haringsla, herring salad. This is a popular Dutch horsd'oeuvre. Chopped and mixed together with seasoning, oil and vinegar, are 2 apples, 2 pickled herrings, 2 boiled beets, 2 hard-boiled eggs, 3 dill pickles, and cold mashed potatoes. This mixture is spread on the inner leaves of a lettuce and covered with mayonnaise. The salad is garnished with more hard-boiled egg, dill pickle, and parsley.

harnois de gueule, slang French expression for food, similar to the English word "grub."

hartkäse, a generic German term for cheese which is firm and hard enough to be cut into slices.

hartshorn, I. A European weed (*Plantago coronopus*), which grows freely in sandy places near the sea and is cultivated for its green leaves, which make a good salad when young. It is also known as star of the earth and buckthorn plantain. II. The name for the antlers of deer, the chief source of ammonia, and of gelatine in former days.

harvey sauce, one of the oldest English bottled sauces. It is rather more of a relish than a sauce, but it is not hot to the taste. It is an essential ingredient in devil sauces and certain cheese, fish, or meat dishes. A very early recipe from *The Compleat Servant Maid* (1677) makes a sauce which keeps for a good year if kept tightly covered. It is made from 12 pounded anchovies, cayenne pepper, mushroom ketchup, and the juice from pickled walnuts, all to taste—not more than 1 tablespoon of the two latter ingredients. A chopped shallot, 2 oz. chopped garlic, and 4 pints (8 cups) vinegar are added, and the sauce is left to stand for 2 weeks, stirring twice or three times a day. It is then strained and bottled.

harze, a Belgian cow's milk cheese which tastes not unlike port-du-salut.

harzer käse, the German version of *harze.*

hase, German for hare, which is extremely popular in Germany. See also GAME; HARE.

hasenbraten, a famous German and Austrian dish of larded young hare covered in red wine and simmered with herbs and root vegetables. The gravy is strained, and ¼ pint (½ cup) sour cream and the hare's blood are added gradually. The gravy is reheated but is not allowed to boil. It is served with either stewed currants or red currant jelly.

hasenbraten in bier, jointed hare rolled in seasoned oatmeal, browned in butter, then simmered in light beer.

hasenpfeffer, a method of cooking hare which is traditional in Germany and Austria. The hare is simmered in red wine, with 1 chopped, thick gammon rasher, 3 onions, 1 oz. grated chocolate, 2 tablespoons chopped herbs, and seasonings. It is served with fine cooked macaroni and red currant jelly.

hasenrücken mit meerrettich, larded saddle of hare braised for 1 hour, or until tender, with ½ pint (1 cup) red wine containing a pinch of grated nutmeg and cinnamon. Just before serving 3 tablespoons red currant jelly and 1 tablespoon grated horseradish are added.

haselhuhn, German for hazel grouse, which abounds in German pine forests and is cooked in the same way as pheasant. See *faisan.*

hash, I. This usually signifies a meal made from leftovers of meat, fish, or poultry, and can be prepared in various ways. Sometimes the meat is diced and served in a white or brown sauce, or gravy, with freshly cooked root vegetables. II. In Britain and the U.S., it can also mean pan-fried vegetables, particularly potatoes, which are mashed and fried until a brown crust has formed.

corned beef hash, diced or mashed corned beef mixed with mashed potatoes and fried onions, then fried in very little oil until brown. Holes are made in this cake, and eggs are dropped in and allowed to half-cook; then the cake is put under the grill or boiler to cook the top of the eggs. See also PYTT-I-PANNA. A hash of cold fish can be prepared in the same way.

haslet or *harslet,* an old English country dish, formerly made from pig's fry. It consisted of the heart, lights (lungs), liver, and sweetbread, broiled gently for ½ hour. It was then drained, cut into small slices, seasoned, rolled in flour, then fried in hot dripping or lard with about ½ pound of sliced pork or streaky bacon. Cassell's *Dictionary of Cookery* (1877) suggests serving a sauce with it, made from 3 tablespoons of claret mixed with a cup of gravy seasoned with prepared mustard, salt, and pepper. A little sliced onion was also sometimes added to the sauce. Nowadays when it is found in country districts, particularly the Midlands and the North, the fry is chopped very small with a little fat pork or bacon and onion, then put into a tin and covered with the fatty membrane known as flead before baking in a moderate oven for about 1½–2 hours. The finished dish resembles a meat loaf and is served either hot or cold, cut into slices. The name comes from the Old French, hastelet, haste, spit, from the Latin *hasta,* spear. This implied that originally it was cooked over a spit. See also FRY.

hasty pudding, one of the oldest English puddings, which

stems from the days when, with milk, flour, butter, and spices always in the house, the pudding could be made reasonably quickly to put before unexpected callers. Before 1800 an egg was an essential ingredient, but since then the pudding has been made without and many consider this an improvement. Almost any sweet spice can be used, or even a bay leaf, as a substitute. To prepare it, 2 oz. butter is melted and 2 oz. flour is stirred in; ¾ pint (1½ cups) warm milk is then added gradually, stirring to remove any lumps. When smooth, the spices (a pinch of mace or nutmeg) are included. The mixture is poured into a buttered dish and covered thickly with sugar and powdered cinnamon, with a few pats of butter added. The pudding is grilled until the top is melted and browned; it can be eaten hot or cold, but it is better hot. In the U.S. it is still popular, but made with corn flour (maize flour) instead of wheat flour. See also MALVERN PUDDING.

hâtereau, I. An old French word for little balls of pork liver, not unlike gayettes except that they are round. II. A hot hors d'oeuvre or entrée of small pieces of food coated in egg and breadcrumbs, fried, then put onto skewers and covered with an appropriate sauce. See also ATTEREAU.

hattelle and *hâttelette,* Old French words used to describe small birds, livers, giblets, etc., roasted on skewers. The word comes from *attelet* (skewer).

hauki, Finnish for pike.

uunissa paistettu hauki, pike stuffed with a mixture of rice, spinach, eggs, and salt, then sewn up, placed in a casserole with butter, and sprinkled with breadcrumbs. Boiling water is added to half-way up the fish and it is cooked for about 40 minutes.

haunch, the word for the hind quarters of certain wild mammals. In culinary parlance, it applies to deer or venison.

haussulz, an Austrian dish of brawn. It is made from either pig's or calf's head, cooked with pig's trotter (foot) or half a calf's foot, root vegetables, bay leaf, 1 gill (½ cup) wine vinegar, and water to cover them, all simmered for 3–4 hours. When cool, the meat is taken from the bones and finely chopped. The stock is defatted, and well seasoned, then poured over just to cover the meat. When cold and jellied, the brawn is turned out, and garnished with chopped gherkins, capers, and slices of hard-boiled eggs.

hauteluce, a French goat's milk cheese from Savoy, which is in season from May to September.

havarti, a Danish cheese known as the "ladies" cheese. The name originated from Havarti, a farm in New Zealand where, about 100 years ago, a farmer's wife made a study of cheese-making in Europe and as a result produced a cheese with an unusual flavour which was adopted by the Danes. When fresh it is rather acid, but when mature the acid taste changes to a sharp, aromatic tang. It is round in shape, has large and small holes, and weighs between 8 and 11 lb. See also OST.

haver, from the Norse *havre* (oats), the name in the north of England, particularly the West Riding of Yorkshire, for a thin oatcake or loaf. It was introduced into Yorkshire by the armies of John of Hainault in the 12th century. Later on, the Lancashire Regiment were known as the "Havercake Lads." The haver consists of fine oatmeal, yeast, and warm water, and originally it was baked on the flat, hot hearthstone from which the ashes were brushed back. The bread keeps very well and used to be stored in "haver racks," shaped like a large square harp, which were suspended from the ceilings of cottages. In the South a similar smaller oatcake is called a clapper, from the practise of making it very thin by clapping it between the two hands.

havre, Swedish for oats.

havregryns bollar, coffee balls consisting of ½ lb. porridge oats, 2 heaped tablespoons castor sugar, 1 heaped tablespoon cocoa, 4 oz. (½ cup) butter, and ¼ pint (½ cup) strong cold coffee. The oats, sugar, and cocoa are mixed together and added, alternately with the coffee, to creamed butter. Small balls are shaped and rolled in castor sugar.

havregrynskakor, biscuits made with porridge oats. First, 2 oz. (¼ cup) sugar is well beaten into 6 oz. (⅔ cup) creamed butter, after which 8 oz. oats and 2 heaped tablespoons self-raising flour are stirred in, and the mixture is shaped into equal-sized balls which are baked in a moderate oven until golden brown.

hawfinch, a European seed-eating bird, highly thought of as food in France where it is usually known as gros-bec. It is generally roasted.

hawksbill turtle, the aquatic tortoise which is the chief source of tortoise shell. It is not eaten, but the eggs are considered a delicacy.

hawthorn, a shrub or small tree of which the fruit, when ripe and red, makes a good jelly, especially if a few apples are added. The berries and apples are both boiled together and the resulting mixture dripped through a muslin. Then 1 lb. sugar is added for every pint of juice. In the country districts of England this jelly used to be served with cream cheese. In Poland, cooked hawthorn berries are made into a sauce with flour, butter, white wine, or cream, and served with game or veal cutlets. See also GŁOG (KONFITURA Z GŁOGU).

hazel grouse (*Terrastes bonasia*), a game bird which lives mostly in the pine forests of Europe, from France to Russia. It feeds on berries and young shoots and has tender succulent white flesh. It is thought a great delicacy in France where it is known as *gélinotte des bois.* It is also called hazel hen and wood grouse. It used to be plentiful in France in the Ardennes, but nowadays it mostly comes frozen, from Russia, especially Vologda, Archangel, and Kazan. Like the *capercaillie,* it feeds on fir cones, and it is advisable to clean the bird when it is first shot, and to soak it in milk for a few hours before cooking. As with all birds, the young are best roasted and the older birds braised or made into terrines, pâtés, or pies. It can be cooked like partridge, but the best methods are those used in Russia, where it is roasted in butter and basted frequently with sour cream. See also TETERKA.

bitki of hazel or grouse, made from two filleted hazel grouse, the bones being barely covered in water and boiled with salt and peppercorns until the liquid is reduced by half, then strained. In another saucepan, 1 tablespoon grated cheese is added to ¼ pint (½ cup) sour cream or yogourt, and the reduced stock is thoroughly mixed in. The fillets of game are rolled in flour and fried on both sides in hot butter until they are just cooked through. The heated sauce is poured over before serving.

hazelnut (*Corylus avellana;* var. *maxima; barcelonensis; pontica*), the fruit of a shrub cultivated since earliest times in Europe, Central and Russian Asia, and North Africa. Theophrastus mentions two kinds: one round like the English cobnut and one oblong (filbert). They were called Heracleatic nuts, possibly introduced from Herakleia, now Ponderachi, on the Black Sea. Others were called Pontic nuts (from Pontus in Asia), and avellana (from Abellana) was the name used by Pliny. Nowadays the majority sold in Europe and Great Britain are the large broad Spanish variety (*barcelonensis*), which is thick-shelled and reddish brown in colour with a very sweet taste. Hazelnuts can be eaten on their own, but are also used a great deal in confectionery. They are also pounded and mixed with butter, this being known in France as *beurre noisette. C. rostrata* and *C. americana* are related American varieties. Hazel wood is legendary for its use in divining-rods and in magical investigation.

hazepeper, a Dutch dish of spiced hare. A large hare is divided into 10 or 12 pieces which are left overnight in a marinade of 3 parts red wine to 1 part vinegar. The next day, they are sautéed in butter and a sauce made of 2 sliced onions sautéed in more butter, to which 5 tablespoons flour is added followed by the marinade. The hare and its butter are put into this sauce, together with 2 teaspoons sugar, seasoning, 3 cloves, 1 bay leaf, and 2 tablespoons soy sauce, and all are simmered for at least 3 hours. See also HAAS; HARE.

heart, the hearts of all mammals or birds are used in cooking. The best are calf's or lamb's hearts which are usually stuffed with breadcrumbs and herbs, then braised with vegetables and stock, which makes a rich brown gravy. See also LOVE-IN-DISGUISE; MOCK GOOSE.

heathcock and *gorcock,* see BLACKCOCK.

hecht, German for pike. This fish is much more popular in Germany and Austria than in the British Isles, where it is seldom eaten. See also SCHWARZFISCH.

hedgehog (*Erinaceus europaeus*), an insect-eating quadruped covered in spiny quills and having a pig-like snout. It is said to taste like a cross between chicken and sucking-pig and is much enjoyed by the gypsies, who sometimes bake it in clay or grill it over an open fire. It is at its best in the autumn.

hel fisk i kapprock, a Swedish dish of stuffed mackerel or trout baked whole in paper. To prepare it, 4 mackerel or trout are slit down the back and their backbones removed. A stuffing is made with a mixture of 1 heaped tablespoon beaten butter, ½ cup chopped parsley, 1 small chopped onion, 2 tablespoons chopped chives, pepper, and 2 tablespoons lemon juice or white wine. The fish are carefully washed before being stuffed, and each is then wrapped individually in buttered wax paper and baked in a moderate oven for about 12 minutes. The fish are brought to the table still wrapped in the paper. Lemon juice and parsley are served as accompaniments. See also FISK.

helder, à la, I. A French garnish for tournedos. Tournedos are sautéed in butter and put onto fried croûtons, with a ring of sauce béarnaise on top, in the middle of which is thick fondue de tomates. It is served with *pommes parisienne,* and with the pan juices reduced with white wine and veal gravy. II. A French garnish for noisettes. Artichoke bottoms are filled alternately with asparagus tips, chopped tomatoes, and small fried potato balls, and covered with sauce béarnaise.

hélianthe, a tuberous vegetable, not unlike a Jerusalem artichoke in appearance, but tasting somewhat like a potato. It must not be cooked too soft and can be prepared like the Jerusalem artichoke. It is eaten in France and Germany.

hélices vigneronnes, see ESCARGOT.

helleflynder, Danish for halibut, which is among the finest fish caught in Danish waters. It is equally good cut into steaks and served like *laks,* or filleted, dipped in egg and breadcrumbs and fried in melted butter. It is used particularly for *fiskegratin.* See also FISK.

helleflyndre, Norwegian for halibut, also called kveite. It is of exceptional quality in Norway and is served poached, grilled, fried, baked, or used for *fiskepudding.*

helston pudding, a traditional Cornish dish made with 2 oz. each of raisins, currants, suet, sugar, breadcrumbs, and ground rice, 1 tablespoon chopped candied peel, ½ teaspoon baking soda, ½ teaspoon mixed spice, 2 oz. flour, salt, and ½ pint (1 cup) milk. The soda is dissolved in the milk, which is then added to the cleaned fruit, finely cut peel, and all the other dry ingredients. The mixture is poured into a well-greased basin and covered with greased paper and a well-floured pudding cloth. It is then boiled for 2 hours in water.

helvella, a genus of European fungus, also known as false morels, which grow in wet grass and at the base of fir trees. There are several edible varieties, namely *Cyathipodia macro-*

pus, Helvella crispa, and *H. lacunosa,* distinctive by their crinkly appearance. They are eaten with impunity by some people but can cause indigestion in others. *H. crispa,* which is the commonest variety in Britain, tastes like a morel. It should be prepared for cooking by first simmering or blanching for 5 minutes in water; the water may be poisonous and should be thrown away, but the fungus will be harmless and ready for cooking in any way that is suitable for morel. On no account should it be eaten raw. See also MOREL.

helzel, German for neck of poultry, which is often stuffed in its skin casing and cooked with the goose, duck, or chicken. It is a traditional Jewish dish, known throughout Europe. See also GEFILLTE HELZEL.

hen de la wake, see HINDLE WAKES CHICKEN.

hénon, the local name in Picardy, France, for a delicious cockle which is abundant in the mouth of the river Somme.

Henri IV, I. A French garnish for tournedos and noisettes of watercress and *pommes pont-neuf.* II. A French garnish for tournedos and noisettes of artichoke bottoms, *pommes noisette,* and sauce béarnaise. III. A sauce béarnaise mixed with liquid meat glaze. IV. A clear strong beef broth with strips of chicken breast, sliced carrots, and herbs.

herbes, French for herbs, which play an important part in classical French cooking. See also BEURRES COMPOSÉS; BOUQUET GARNI; FINES HERBES.

herbes à tortue, a mixture of basil, marjoram, savory, and thyme used for flavouring turtle soup and turtle sauce.

herbs, plants used in cookery for their flavouring and medicinal properties and their capacity to scent a dish. The most generally used culinary herbs are angelica, basil, bay, borage, burnet, celery, chervil, chives, dill, fennel, garlic, lemon thyme, lovage, marjoram, mint, parsley, rosemary, sage, savory, shallot, thyme, and tarragon. Sage, basil, dill, fennel, lovage, marjoram, chervil, parsley, and thyme may be dried for winter use by tying in bunches in paper bags and hanging in a dark dry place. The leaves are then powdered and bottled. The other herbs will dry, but will quickly lose their flavour if kept. The best way to preserve them is to chop a mixture finely, cover them with lemon juice, and put them into a screw-topped bottle. Both the juice and the herbs are aromatic and delicious. Herbs can with profit be added to almost any dish. A few herbs freshly chopped and added to soups or stews lend a flavour which nothing else can give; they can bring the taste of summer into the wintertime. Mint is excellent added to cooked and raw fruits. Many herbs, and their fruits and seeds, are used in all forms of cooking and in the best confectionery. See individual entries for herbs. See also SPICES.

heringe, German for herring, eaten a great deal in Germany, fresh, cured, and salted. When fresh, they are served baked, fried, or grilled; when lightly salted they are eaten raw on ice, with lemon. See also BISMARCKHERINGE; BRATHERINGE; FISCH; HERRING; MATJESHERINGE.

heringe in weinsauce, fresh herrings baked in equal quantities of white wine and water, with salt and peppercorns, for 30 minutes. They are served cold, with dry mustard mixed to a thin cream consistency with the liquid used for baking the fish.

gebratene heringe, heavily salted herrings first soaked for several hours in milk or wine, then coated with egg and breadcrumbs and fried.

pikante heringe, fresh herrings with roes poached in white wine mixed with stock or water, with 1 small onion, garlic, parsley, and 2 cloves. The sauce is thickened with butter and flour and served over the fish.

Herkimer cheese, a cow's milk cheese which used to be made in Herkimer County, N.Y., U.S., and resembles cheddar, al-though the paste is whiter and the texture crumbly. The flavour is rather sharp. Nowadays it is a rather rare cheese.

hermit crab (*Paguridae*), a crustacean which has no shell, only a shell-like band round its middle. It swims about until it finds a mollusc of a suitable size, whereupon it eats the owner and creeps into its shell. It can be cooked like shrimp, or simply baked or grilled with butter.

hernekeitto, Finnish pea soup, made with dried soaked peas, water, chopped pork, and seasoning. It is served very hot as the main dinner dish, and is eaten at the beginning of Lent in Finland.

heron (*Ardea cinetea*), a long-legged river bird which is common in Europe but is now becoming rarer in the British Isles. The heron is not eaten very much these days, but the classic English dish is heron pie or pudding, which is recommended by the gastronome. It can only be cooked if the heron has no broken bones, since they contain an unpleasant fishy fluid which contaminates the whole bird.

herrgårdsost, the most popular Swedish cheese, made from whole cow's milk. It is produced in two qualities: full cream (herrgård-elite), which is matured for 4 to 6 months, and half cream (herrgård) which is matured for 3 to 4 months. The first is not unlike a Swiss *emmenthal* in taste and texture, although the paste is not so hard, nor are there so many holes in it. The lower grade cheese is more like a Gouda in taste and texture. The name means "manor cheese," and it was originally farm- or homemade in western Sweden; however, nowadays there are factories making it all over the country. It weighs from 25 to 40 lb. See also OST.

herring (*Clupea harengus*), one of the most abundant sea fishes, also one of the cheapest and most nutritious. The flavour is very good, and because of the oil they contain, herrings are best grilled, soused, or stuffed and baked. They have been eaten since earliest times and traces of them have been found ossified in prehistoric cave dwellings. Allied species of the European herring are found all over the world; the most important gastronomically is *Pomolobus pseudoharengus,* called wall-eyed herring in the U.S. and alewife in Britain. This is found in Atlantic waters, as is the silver sild of the family *Clupeidae,* and the thread herring (*Opisthonema oglinum*). In the north Pacific Ocean the finest is the California or Pacific herring (*Clupea pallasii*). They are all prepared and cooked like herring.

Herring can be salted, smoked, dried, or pickled, and each European country has its speciality. Holland uses young female herrings for a particular process after which they are called *maatjes.* Germany is renowned for the *bismarckheringe.* In Russia and Poland herrings are coated with flour and baked on sliced boiled potatoes, with sour cream, shallot, and *kabul* sauce poured over them. In France and Belgium they are often poached in white wine, also grilled and served with sauce *ravigote.* In England they are usually grilled or fried in breadcrumbs, and served with mustard sauce. However, in Yorkshire they are made into a layered pie with potatoes and sour apples. This is called Yorkshire herring pie.

Scotland is the home of cured herrings. The Loch Fyne kipper, as a smoked herring is called, is a delight. Fresh herrings in Scotland are usually rolled in oatmeal before frying. They are also slightly salted and baked in vinegar, a little sugar, onions, and a little water, and are known as soused or pickled herring. Oatcakes are served with most herring dishes in Scotland, and also potato, either hot or cold, depending on the dish. Excellent wood-smoked kippers are also found in the Isle of Man. An old Irish recipe for herrings which have been smoked is mentioned in *Larousse Gastronomique.* They are soaked in milk for 2 hours, drained, and dried, then layered in a pie dish with onions, thyme, and bay leaves; on top are

herring stuffed with gooseberries

placed the hard and soft roes, a little whiskey is poured over and set alight, and when the flame has died down the dish is ready to eat. Both the hard and soft roes are delectable and are served in many ways. See also BLOATER; BÖCKLING; BUCK-LINGE; GAFFELBIDDER; GAFFELBITTER; HARING; HEERINGAD PIIMÄ SAUSTIGA; HERINGE; PILCHARDS; RED HERRING; ROLL-MOPS; SILD; SILL; SILLI; SLEDZIE; VÄIKSED.

Herve, a soft, fermented Belgian cheese made from whole cow's milk. It is pressed according to a technique peculiar to the Herve country, whence its name. It is a small cheese, shaped like a cube and weighing about 6 oz. It comes in three qualities: full cream, cream, and partly skimmed milk.

hete bliksem, a Dutch winter dish which means literally "hot as lightning." It consists of equal amounts of puréed apples and potatoes mixed well with butter or lard, with fried bacon on top. It is served very hot.

hickory, the name for several species of American hardwood tree of the genus *Carya*. The fruit of the tree, the hickory nut, is used in confectionery. The wood is used in the U.S. for smoking hams, also for flavouring salt used for cooking steaks, pies, cutlets, soups, stews, etc. See also SPICED SALT.

hickory

hideg gyumolcsleves, a cold fruit soup often served in Hungary.

hideg tlöételek, Hungarian for cold hors d'oeuvre or appetizers. This course usually consists of sausage which has been smoked (*kolbasz*), goose liver pâté (*liba*), or a fish (*hal*) in aspic. See also HORS D'OEUVRE.

hidrellez, a traditional spring festival held in Turkey on May 1. Special foods, notably baklava and *lookoumi*, are eaten on this day.

higado, Spanish for liver. Hígado de pollo is chicken liver; hígado de ternera, calf's liver, etc. See also LIVER.

hígado á la asturiana, a recipe for either calf's or sheep's liver. Fat bacon is fried in butter, and 1 lb. sliced liver and 1 large sliced onion are added. After cooking for a few minutes, 4 peeled tomatoes and ½ pint (1 cup) white wine are put in. The dish is seasoned and cooked, covered, for 1 hour. A paste is made of 2 oz. (½ cup) pounded almonds and 1 large garlic clove, to which is added approximately ¼ pint (½ cup) water; this is poured over the liver after it has cooked for 30 minutes. The dish is served with a border of triangles of toasted bread.

high moisture jack, a cheese similar to Monterey, but made from whole cow's milk and by a slightly different process. It is semi-soft in texture.

high tea, see TEA.

higo, Spanish for fig. Figs grow extensively all over Spain, having been imported by the Moors many centuries ago. One variety grown there produces two kinds of figs on the same tree—first a white one, then a black, both equally good to eat. Fresh figs are eaten raw, served with a heavy syrup or with wine. They are also dried, as in Portugal; and, recently, pickled in syrup with vinegar, mustard, peppers, and spices, then canned. These are called *higos pikles*. See also FIG.

higos con vino malagueño, 12 fresh figs are sliced and layered in a bowl with a dusting of icing sugar and a pinch of cinnamon, then moistened with brandy and left for 1–2 hours. Before serving, 3 tablespoons Málaga wine or sweet sherry are mixed in. It is served with cream.

hilopites me kima, a Greek dish of 1 lb. minced lamb fried in oil or butter, with 1 large chopped onion, 2 garlic cloves, 4 tomatoes, and seasoning simmered in the oil until it is like a thick sauce. It is served with cooked noodles heated in the sauce and well mixed together.

himmel und erde, literally "heaven and earth," a German dish consisting of equal quantities of sliced apples and sliced potatoes cooked in broth with a bay leaf and seasoning. It is strained, made into a purée, and served with black pudding or pork. See also KARTOFFEL (WESTFÄLISCHE KARTOFFELN).

hina, Greek for goose.

hina yemisti, Greek for stuffed goose. The bird is roasted in the usual manner, but the Greeks stuff their goose with apples and chestnuts, sometimes adding pignoli and chopped onion.

hindle wakes chicken, a very old English method of cooking fowl which has come down through the ages unchanged. The name is a corruption of hen de la wake and is thought to have been brought to the north of England by the Flemish spinners who settled at Bolton-le-Moor in the 14th century. The "wake" was the feast held on the eve of the dedication of the early churches; it subsequently degenerated into a fair, with much eating and drinking. The 1797 edition of the *Encyclopaedia Britannica* ends its long article as follows: "Indeed several of our ancient fairs appear to have been usually held, and have been continued to our time, on the original Church holidays of the places: besides, it is observable that fairs were generally kept in churchyards, and also on Sundays, till the indecency and scandal were so great as to need reformation." Nowadays, the "wake" has come to mean an ordinary fair, and these are still held in parts of the north of England, particularly at Wakefield, Yorkshire, on All Saint's night.

For the dish of hindle wakes chicken, a large boiling fowl is cooked before the wake and brought out on the night. The white meat, with its black filling and yellow and green garnish, looks just as garish as did its counterpart on the medieval table. Recipes vary slightly, but the essential filling of dark fruit and spice remains as it has been for centuries. The bird is stuffed with a mixture of 2 cups fresh breadcrumbs, 2 tablespoons grated suet, ½ lb. soaked and stoned prunes with their pits, mixed chopped herbs, a pinch each of mace and cinnamon, and the juice of 1 lemon, all seasoned to taste. The bird is firmly secured and put in a saucepan with water to cover, together with an onion, brown sugar, and ¼ pint (½ cup) vinegar. The pan is covered and the bird cooked slowly for about 4 hours or until tender, and left to cool in the stock. When required, it is taken out, skinned, and placed on a serving-dish. A sauce is made by thickening the stock with a roux, then adding the juice of a lemon. When slightly cooled, this sauce is poured over the bird, which is garnished with grated lemon peel. Just before serving it is decorated with halved prunes and wedges of lemon and sprinkled thickly with chopped parsley. It takes pride of place on the table and is eaten after a long day at the fair. See also CHICKEN.

hirino, Greek for pork or pig. This word is sometimes pronounced chirinon in English. See also KREAS; PIHTI HIRINO.

hirines brizoles krassates, pork chops in red wine. Thirty minutes before preparing this dish, the chops should be rubbed with seasoning and lemon juice. They are simmered in boiling water until partially cooked, when they are drained, browned in butter, then further simmered in the wine.

hirino me selinorizes, an Athenian speciality of 3 lb. lean pork cut into serving portions and browned in butter, then cooked with 1 large head chopped celery or celeriac, 2 onions, herbs, and red wine to cover. *Avgolémono sauce* is added 5 minutes before serving.

hirino psito, the traditional dish of young sucking-pig, stuffed with herbs, then roasted while on a spit in the open air, being basted with olive oil and lemon juice. It is served with *skorthalia* sauce. See also GOUROUNOPOULO.

hirn, German for brains. See also GEHIRNWÜRST.

hirnpofesen, an Austrian speciality consisting of calf's brain fried in butter with a small onion, parsley, and seasoning. An egg is stirred in and then some of this mixture is put between two slices of milk-soaked bread. The sandwich is dipped in egg and breadcrumbs and then fried on both sides. It is served with spinach.

hirnschoberlsuppe, a traditional Austrian brain soup. A cold, boiled set of calf's brains is strained and mixed with 2 tablespoons butter, 2 egg yolks, 1 cup breadcrumbs, and the stiffly beaten egg whites; nutmeg, salt, and pepper are added. The mixture is baked in a well-greased tin and cut into lozenge shapes as garnish for rich beef broth.

hıyar taratorv, a Turkish sauce or green salad. Almonds or pistachio nuts are skinned and pounded with a little salt and a few garlic cloves. They are then mixed with half their quantity of soaked, crustless bread until a paste-like consistency is achieved. The mixture is then beaten with enough vinegar or lemon juice to give it the consistency of cream, and it is poured over the salad. Finally, the whole is sprinkled with 1–2 tablespoons olive oil.

hjortekjøtt, Norwegian for red deer meat, which is very popular in Norway.

stekte hjortekoteletter, a Norwegian method of frying venison cutlets. Tender cuts from the loin are marinated for up to 2 hours in lemon juice and oil. After drying, the cutlets are seasoned and coated in flour, egg, and breadcrumbs. They should be fried in butter, turning frequently. A currant jelly is added to the pan to make a gravy, and this is poured over the joint, which is garnished with watercress.

hladna zakuska, the Serbo-Croat term for an assortment of *charcuterie,* served as an hors d'oeuvre. See also HORS D'OEUVRE.

hobelkäse, see SAANENKÄSE.

hocco, a turkey-like gallinaceous bird from Central America. Importation of them, live, into France took place quite recently. The flesh is white and succulent and highly prized.

hochepot, a Belgian speciality which is a magnificent hot pot made from brisket of beef, pig's trotters (feet) and ears, veal, mutton, herbs, cabbage, carrots, onions, leeks, celery, turnip,

chipolata sausages, and seasonings. They are all cooked slowly for about 3 hours, except the *chipolata* sausages which are added for the last hour only. Then the meat is removed and served with a little of the strained stock. The remainder is served as a soup. See also HOT POT.

hock, an alternative name for knuckle of pork in Britain. In the U.S. it is also used for the foreleg pork shank.

hodgils, a Scottish border name for oatmeal dumplings. They are made from oatmeal mixed with herbs, salt, and a little fat. They are cooked in boiling broth and served with boiled meat, usually beef.

hogfish, I. *Scorpaena scrofa,* a sea fish with a large and spiny head, and spikes which can be poisonous. This is the French *rascasse,* which is used only for bouillabaisse or other fish soups; French fishermen call it *diable de mer* (sea devil) and *crapaud* (toad). See also SCORFANO. II. *Lachnolaimus maximus,* a large fish found off the Florida coast in the U.S., very good to eat when cut into large steaks. It can be baked, fried, or grilled.

hogget, the English name for a yearling lamb.

Hogmanay, the Scots' New Year's Eve. It is characterized by the playing of the bagpipes, the drinking of whiskey, punch, and hot-pint (hot ale spiced and laced with whiskey), and the eating of certain traditional foods, such as bannock, haggis, Scotch currant bun. Parties are held which go on into the early hours of the morning, the next day being a national holiday in Scotland. On the morning of Hogmanay small bands of children go from door to door, singing:

> Hogmanay,
> Trollolay,
> Gie's o' your white bread and nane o' your grey

and ask for small gifts, usually a cake. Descendants of Scottish families that have settled in the North of Ireland also celebrate Hogmanay. In the Clogher Valley, mummers with blackened faces and straw or rabbit skins tied round their legs are known as ''Hogmanay men.'' Cakes are given to the performers. The origin of the word Hogmanay is dubious, but is thought to come from Old French *aguil'anneuf* through Norman French *hoguignané,* ''to the new year.''

hoisin, see SOY SAUCE.

holishkes, stuffed cabbage which is a traditional Jewish fare for Succoth and other festive holidays. It is also known as *praekes, galuptzi,* or *sarmale* in the Balkans, and consists of meat-filled cabbage leaves which are prepared in the following way. One pound of minced beef and 4 oz. (⅔ cup) raw rice are mixed with 1 egg, 1 grated onion, 1 grated carrot, and salt. Ten large cabbage leaves are blanched by covering them with boiling water for 2–3 minutes, after which they are drained. A ball of meat mixture is placed in the centre of each cabbage leaf and rolled up, tucking in the ends. The stuffed cabbage leaves are placed close together in a heavy frying-pan, and 3 tablespoons lemon juice or vinegar, 4 oz. (½ cup) brown sugar, and ½ pint (1 cup) tomato juice are added, with water to cover. The lid is put on tightly and the ingredients simmered for 1 hour, followed by baking in the oven, to brown slightly, for 20 minutes. If necessary, small quantities of hot water may be added during baking.

hollandaise sauce, a classical French sauce of Dutch origin. It is also known as Holland or Dutch sauce. Four oz. (½ cup) best butter is cut into halves. One piece is placed in the top of a double boiler over hot water (the water must not be allowed to boil). When melted, 2 or 3 well-beaten egg yolks are added, stirring gently until the mixture thickens. The remainder of the butter is slowly added in very small pieces, stirring gently each time, followed, if desired, by cream, with a little lemon juice or tarragon vinegar, salt, and pepper.

mock hollandaise, an American version of the sauce made

from 2 egg yolks, 1 tablespoon water, salt, and 1 tablespoon lemon juice, thoroughly mixed together and put in a double boiler. Then 2 tablespoons butter are melted in a small pan and 1 tablespoon flour added; when smooth, 1 cup (½ pint) hot water is included. After beating well, this mixture is added to the contents of the double boiler, and the whole mixed well and seasoned with pepper, sometimes also with paprika.

oyster hollandaise, an American recipe with oysters. A mock hollandaise is made, using some of the strained liquor of the oysters instead of water. The oysters are gently cooked in the remainder of their own liquor and a little salted water until the edges curl. They are drained, and added to the sauce when serving, with lemon juice and a sprinkling of cayenne.

hollandaise, à la, I. A method of serving fish poached in court bouillon, with hot melted butter and potatoes served separately. Hollandaise sauce sometimes accompanies it, but not always. II. A consommé seasoned with paprika, and garnished with tiny quenelles of calf's liver, bone marrow, and chervil. It is also called à la hongroise. See also CONSOMMÉ.

hollandse erwtensoep, a traditional Dutch peasant soup made from dried split peas, puréed and chopped leeks, onions, celeriac, pork, and bacon. It is garnished with slices of *gelderse rookworst.*

hollandse koffietafel, the traditional Dutch dish served at the midday meal, which takes place at about 12:30 P.M. The name often figures on the Dutch menu and is a dish comprising a variety of sliced sausages, cold meats, breads, jams, and sweet spreads, with fresh fruit, and coffee. All are placed on the table together; sometimes one hot dish is included, which will usually be made from leftovers. In Holland the main meal of the day is the evening meal, eaten at about 6 P.M.

hollandse palingsoep, traditional Dutch eel soup, often eaten during Lent. It is made from 2 lb. eels skinned, cut up into small pieces, parboiled, and then simmered in butter with 2 chopped onions, 2 leeks, and the heads and trimmings of sea fish. Then 3 pints (6 cups) water, ½ pint (1 cup) white wine, salt, peppercorns, and cloves are added, and the mixture is boiled until the fish is cooked. The pieces of eel are removed and the stock is strained, seasoned with cayenne pepper, and thickened with 2 egg yolks and 2 tablespoons butter. The soup is then poured into a tureen over croûtons, strips of cooked leek, celery, and parsley root. See also PALING.

holstein, a French garnish for veal escalope (scallop), which has been dipped in egg and breadcrumbs and fried. The garnish consists of a poached or fried egg, chopped gherkins, cooked beetroot, olives, capers, anchovies, and lemon wedges.

holsteiner schnitzel, see SCHNITZEL.

holundersuppe, a German soup made with elderberries, apples, lemon, sugar, and salt; it is usually served with small semolina dumplings. It is sometimes made without the apples. In the north of Germany almost all soft fruits are made into soups. See also OBST (OBSTSUPPE).

homard, French for lobster. An egg-carrying hen lobster is known as a paquette in France. See also LOBSTER.

homard à l'Américaine (also Armoricaine), raw lobster is first sautéed in oil, then removed from the pan. Next 2 tablespoons finely chopped onion are added and cooked until soft, then 2 shallots are added, and 2 peeled tomatoes, with a touch of garlic, parsley, and tarragon. The lobster is put on top of this and moistened with a glass of white wine, a little fish stock, and 4 tablespoons brandy, and seasoned with a pinch of cayenne pepper. The mixture is brought to the boil, covered, and simmered gently for about 20 minutes. Coral, if any, is added at the end to thicken the sauce.

homard à la newburg, cooked or raw lobster sautéed in but-

ter with cream, sherry, and fish stock, all thickened with egg yolks. It is served with rice and is also called homard à la crème.

homard à la Provençale, virtually the same as *à l'Américaine.* They are both served with rice.

homard au gratin à la normande, cooked lobster served in a rich sauce béchamel to which have been added a little grated Gruyère cheese and cream.

homard cardinal, lobster cooked in court bouillon, the flesh of the tail sliced, and the claw flesh diced. The half shells are filled with a purée of mushrooms and truffles bound with lobster sauce, and the slices of lobster, arranged alternately with truffle slices, are placed on top and covered with sauce *cardinale,* a little grated cheese and butter.

homard thermidor, boiled or raw lobster which has been baked in the shell, then split lengthwise, and the flesh diced coarsely. It is covered with sauce *bercy* mixed with a little English mustard, sprinkled with grated Parmesan cheese and melted butter, and browned quickly in the oven.

hominy, coarsely ground, hulled, and split maize. After sifting, the resulting coarse meal is known as hominy grits, sometimes abbreviated to grits. The origin of the word is open to question; some think it comes from the North American Indian word *auhuminea,* meaning "parched corn," or from rockahoming, a word from Algonquin dialect, with the same meaning. It is much used in the U.S., especially in the South and West, for the making of cakes, croquettes, and puddings. An excellent porridge-like breakfast dish is made by adding 1 cup grits and a pinch of salt to 3 cups boiling water and gently cooking, covered, for about an hour. The grits are removed from the heat and when lukewarm, 4 lightly beaten eggs, 4 oz. (½ cup) butter, and ½ pint (1 cup) milk are blended in. The mixture is poured into a greased casserole and baked in a moderate over for 35 minutes, then grated Parmesan or cheddar cheese is sprinkled over and it is baked again until the cheese is melted and brown. This is served surrounded with crisp fried bacon or *chipolata* sausages. Milk is sometimes used instead of water, and egg yolks rather than whole eggs. The dish is not unlike polenta, and is very good served cut into squares, with roast meat and salad.

homogenize, to render uniform, generally applied to the production of a smooth mixture of uniformly sized solid or liquid particles or globules in a liquid continuous phase. The making of mayonnaise is one example; the production of purées is an example of a similar operation, but one in which the proportion of solid to liquid components is balanced more in favour of the former. In the case of milk, the most commonly homogenised product, it is the process of breaking up the fat globules into uniform, fine particles. It is usually done by forcing the mixture through minute holes. This makes the particles uniformly small and evenly distributed in the liquid.

høne, Danish for fowl. See also KYLLING.

kogt høne med peberrod, a recipe using boiled fowl with horseradish. A sauce is made from 2 heaped tablespoons each chicken fat and flour and 1 generous pint (2½ cups) stock. When smooth, 3 tablespoons grated horseradish, 1 tablespoon sugar, salt, and 2 tablespoons tarragon vinegar are all blended in, and pieces of the boiled fowl are added. It is garnished with boiled potatoes and parsley. It can also be served cold with mayonnaise mixed with horseradish.

høne, Norwegian for fowl, used for soups or casseroles and sometimes served with rice. See also FJAERKRÉ; KYLLING.

honey, a sweet, sticky, yellowish fluid, the nectar of flowers collected by bees, and put by these insects into wax cells inside the hive. Honey was the chief sweet food of early times, when cane sugar was unknown or a rarity. In commercial apiaries, section or comb honey is often sold, and the wax is eaten as well as the liquid. Superfine honey is extracted under sun or gentle heat, but the varieties which use greater heat in order to give it a preservative quality should be avoided, since overheating destroys many of its health-giving properties. To make thick honey liquid, stand the jar in warm water on a strip of wood. All pure honey granulates; that it does so is proof of its purity, and the speed of the process depends on the floral source. Granulated honey is better for the human physiology than liquid honey, for it is high in sugar dextrose which goes direct to the bloodstream.

Honey is antiseptic, for no germs will live in it. The sugars of honey are fruit sugars, dextrose and laevulose. The taste of honey varies according to the type of flowers from which the bees have collected it: heather, rosemary, lime, and thyme honey are distinctive and delicious. The honey from Mount Hymethus in Greece is world famous; it has a lovely resinous flavour. Honey and vinegar mixed are good for a sore throat, and if walnut juice vinegar is substituted for the vinegar, it is the finest cure for a "tickly" cough. Honey is eaten with bread and toast, and used in the cooking of fruit and cakes. Even some meat, such as pork, ham, chicken, and duck, is excellent spread with honey. Honey is very good for children, but is forbidden to diabetics. See also HONIG.

honey fungus or *honey agaric* (*Armillaria mellea*), a fleshy edible fungus not unlike a *cèpe* in appearance, except that it is a glorious apricot-yellow colour. It is just as good to eat as the *cèpe*, and is highly esteemed in Italy, where it is called funghi trun by the Piedmontese (see FUNGHI).

honeydew melon, see MELON.

honeyware, see BADDERLOCKS.

hongroise, à la, I. A French garnish for meat composed of sprigs of cauliflower, with a sauce mornay and paprika, boiled potatoes or pommes fondantes. II. It is also fish poached in white wine and fish stock, with chopped onions previously turned in butter, paprika, and diced tomatoes, all reduced, with thick cream added. III. A white wine sauce mixed with either veal glaze or diced salt pork sautéed in demi-glace seasoned with paprika, and sour cream added. IV. A consommé (see HOLLANDAISE, À LA). V. A French method of serving potatoes, see POMME DE TERRE (POMMES À LA HONGROISE). VI. A French method of serving chicken; see POULET, À LA HONGROISE.

hongroise, sauce, a classical French sauce consisting of a sauce suprême to which are added chopped onions already cooked in white wine, and paprika. It is served with eggs, fish, poultry, and meat (except pork).

honig, German for honey, which in Germany is used a great deal in cakes.

honigskuchen, Swiss spiced honey cakes which are a speciality of the province of Appenzell. They are made by mixing 2 tablespoons milk, 1 egg, and 4 oz. (½ cup) sugar together, then adding 1 cup melted honey. Ground cinnamon, cloves, and finely grated nutmeg are added to taste, and finally 4 cups of flour. The mixture is all worked into a dough, then left for 4 hours. It is rolled out to ½-inch thickness and cut into round shapes, then baked in a moderate oven for 30 minutes.

höns, Swedish for fowl. Boiling fowl are popular in Sweden, and there are various recipes for boiled chicken. See also FJADERFA; KYCKLING.

höns i pepparrotsmajonnäs, a salad of chicken in mayonnaise. Grated horseradish and dry mustard, to taste, are stirred into 1 pint (2 cups) slightly beaten mayonnaise, then 3 tablespoons whipped cream are folded in. Shredded, boiled chicken is mixed with chopped, cooked celeriac and shredded celery, together with diced apples, and these are stirred into the sauce. The dish is decorated with asparagus tips.

hönsfrikasse, fowl fricassé. Portions of a boiled fowl are dipped in seasoned flour and are then gently fried in a little butter. A sauce is made from 2 tablespoons each butter and flour, and 1 generous pint (2½ cups) chicken stock; to this, when off the heat, 2 tablespoons cream are gradually added. The sauce is seasoned and the chicken reheated in it. (Sometimes chopped mushrooms or grated horseradish, to taste, are added to the sauce.) The dish is garnished with parsley and served with rice or mashed potatoes, and green peas.

hop (*Humulus lupulus*), an herbaceous twining plant, the sole representative of its genus. It grows wild in the hedges and thickets of England and Ireland and is fairly common in all the nontropical parts of the world. The cultivation of hops for use in the manufacture of beer dates from an early period. In the 8th and 9th centuries, hop gardens, called humularia, existed in France and Germany. In 18th-century England, a hop sauce was made by first boiling the buds, then adding them to melted butter; it was served with fish, chicken, or boiled mutton. Soup was also made by adding the buds to dried peas and onion and cooked until soft, in water.

In France, hop shoots are boiled and served tossed in butter and cream or veal stock. In Belgium, where the hop shoots are much prized, they are served as a vegetable, garnished with poached eggs and croûtons fried in butter. The young, tender tops of the hop are also cut off in spring to be used in the same way as asparagus tips. See also HOPFENSALAT.

hopfensalat, German for a salad of young hop buds which are tied in bundles and cooked like asparagus and then served cold with mayonnaise and lemon juice. If eaten hot, they are served with melted butter. See also HOP.

horehound (*Marrubium vulgare*), also called white horehound to distinguish it from the evil-smelling black horehound, a species of perennial herb and a member of the mint family. It was included by Hippocrates in his list of "simples," and it has not since fallen from favour, for it is still used in certain cough-sweets (cough drops) and in a brown, brittle candy made for sore throats. The scent of the leaves and flowers is very pleasant, and it is a very useful flavouring herb for cakes, stews, and sauces in place of a bay leaf. Horehound ale was once a popular drink, and specialists in honey greatly prize the honey that is made by bees who have absorbed their nectar from the tiny tubular white flowers of the horehound.

hornazo, a savoury Spanish tart or pasty, traditional fare in Salamanca, particularly in the town of Castilla la Vieja, and served on the Monday following Easter Monday. The pastry is made with 8 oz. (2 cups) flour, 4 oz. (½ cup) butter, 1 egg, and water to mix. The filling consists of 2 oz. sliced *chorizo*, 2 oz. chopped ham, 1 cup cooked pieces of poultry, and 2 sliced hard-boiled eggs, all seasoned and moistened with stock. Hornazo is made in the form of a Cornish pasty and is suitable for taking on picnics as it can be eaten cold.

horned dace, see DACE.

horner's cheese, a cream cheese made in Worcestershire.

hornfisk, Danish for garfish. See also FISK.

stegt hornfisk, fried garfish. The fish is filleted and the fillets split in two, then sprinkled with salt. After standing for 10 minutes, they are rinsed, rolled in flour, dipped in egg and breadcrumbs, then fried in butter until brown. They are served with more butter and boiled potatoes, and garnished with lemon slices.

hors d'oeuvre, the French name for a series of small savoury dishes which are served usually as a first course, but even as a whole light meal. They can be hot or cold, but when they take the form of several small pastry tarts filled with chopped fish, meat, poultry, or eggs in a sauce, they are generally served hot. Fresh vegetables served as a small salad, with hard-boiled eggs, anchovies, and mayonnaise are a usual hors d'oeuvre in France. Canapés garnished with smoked fish or roe, meats, salame, etc., can also constitute an hors d'oeuvre. Generally speaking, however, hors d'oeuvre in France is a mixture of piquant and tasty mouthfuls of any savoury food. The name literally means "outside the main work," that is, an addition to the main body of the meal.

The hors d'oeuvre resembles the Greek *meze* and the Russian *zakouski,* except that these are served with drinks some time before a meal, whereas in France the hors d'oeuvre is definitely part of the meal. A whole vegetable (such as a globe artichoke with dressing), or pickled herrings, are sometimes served as hors d'oeuvre, but usually it takes the aforementioned forms.

In Great Britain and the U.S. the name usually refers to small dishes of various cooked and raw vegetables dressed with mayonnaise or oil and vinegar, also of hard-boiled eggs, fish, sausages, salame, olives, mushrooms, shellfish, etc., served cold and all set out on a large trolley from which the individual diner makes his choice. The canapé can be hot or cold but is strictly for serving with drinks both in Europe and the U.S. See also ACEPIPES; ANTIPASTI; ENTREMESES; HIDEG TLŐÉTELEK; HLADNA; MEZES; PIKKULÄMPIMÄT; SMÖRGÅSBORD; VOILEIPÄPYÖTA; ZAKUSKI.

horse mackerel, I. *Trachurus trachurus,* a sea fish which, despite its name, is not a mackerel. It is found off the European coasts of the North Atlantic, and, when young, is sometimes tinned in Portugal and sold as inferior sardines. It is coarse to eat. II. *Trachurus symmetricus,* a species of saurel found only in northern Pacific waters. III. *Thunnus secundodorsalis,* a species of tunny fish (tuna) found off the northern Atlantic coast of the U.S.

horsemeat, meat from *Equus caballus,* the horse, domesticated since prehistoric times. It is taboo for Jews, and also for the Irish, since it was the subject of a curse placed on Neman by St. Colmiclle; it also figures in poems of the 12th century as a penance or degradation. However, horsemeat is eaten in many parts of the world, particularly in France and Belgium. The taste is inclined to sweetness, and needs garlic or some other strong herb to disguise this, when it can pass as beef. All methods of serving beef can be applied to horsemeat.

horseradish (*Cochlearia armorica*), a plant originally from the East, with a root that has a strong, peppery flavour. This is occasionally just grated and used as a condiment, especially in Poland, Russia, and other northern countries, but more generally it is used to make a savoury sauce. It is served in the latter form with roast beef in Britain, or with smoked fish such as trout or mackerel. See also KHREN; MEERRETTICH; PEBERROD; PIPARJUURI; RAIFORT.

horseradish

horseradish and mustard sauce, an American sauce used for hamburger steaks. It is made with 2 tablespoons flour well mixed with 4 tablespoons melted butter and moistened with ½ pint (1 cup) stock. The mixture is beaten until smooth, after which salt, pepper, 1 tablespoon finely chopped onion, 1 heaped teaspoon mixed mustard (French and English), and 1 tablespoon grated horseradish are added. They are all cooked gently together for 20 minutes and strained. Then 2 tablespoons cream and 2 tablespoons lemon juice are added gradually.

horseradish frozen sauce, an American sauce for which ½ cup finely grated horseradish, 1 tablespoon finely chopped and salted pistachio nuts, 1 heaped teaspoon French mustard, 2 tablespoons chilli sauce (not the hot variety), and 1 tablespoon lemon juice, with seasonings as desired are folded into ½ pint (1 cup) thick whipped cream. The sauce is then poured into an oiled mould, which is allowed to stand in the freezer of a refrigerator until set. The sauce is a popular accompaniment to cold fish in hot weather.

horseradish mayonnaise, an American dressing for cold boiled fish or salt beef consisting of 2 cupsful mayonnaise, to which are added, just before serving, 3 tablespoons very finely grated horseradish.

horseradish sauce, an English sauce for which there are 2 methods of preparation. In one, 1 small teacup grated horseradish and half that amount of thick cream are added to 1 cup sauce béchamel with seasoning to taste. The sauce is well blended and simmered for only a few minutes after the horseradish and cream have been added. It is served with roasted or boiled beef, hot or cold, and also with smoked trout. However, the more generally used horseradish sauce is made with 3 tablespoons grated horseradish, 2 teaspoons sugar, salt, pepper, ½ teaspoon made English mustard, and 1 tablespoon white wine vinegar blended together. Then ¼ pint (½ cup) cream is whipped and stirred slowly into the mixture, which is then chilled. It is sometimes frozen and served cut in small cubes, with grilled salmon.

horta, Greek for green vegetables such as spinach, cabbage, etc., and salad greens such as lettuce and dandelion. *Horta soupa* is Greek for green vegetable soup. See also LAHANIKA.

hoşaflar, Turkish for sherbets, often made with morello cherries in Turkey.

hoshaf, an Albanian fruit compote, usually made from many delicious fruits such as cherries, melon, the native dark blue plum, apricots, and peaches, sometimes mixed and cooked in a syrup. In wintertime it is made with dried fruits.

hot cross bun, an English yeast bun containing a little spice and currants. Traditionally it is eaten on Good Friday and has a cross marked on the top. See also BUN; CHELSEA BUN.

hot dog, in the U.S., a frankfurter served hot, often accompanied with pickles, ketchup, mustard, or relish in a soft bread roll. See also FRANKFURTER WÜRSTCHEN.

hot pot, a stew traditional in the Midlands and north of England, the most famous being the Lancashire hot pot. The name comes originally from "hodge-podge" (mixture) and from the old earthenware dish in which it used to be cooked, and which had the words "hot pot" painted on the side. The stew is made from boned neck cutlets of mutton or lamb, layered with onions, sliced potatoes, seasonings, and, in the old days, a few oysters. Good fatless broth is added, with a thick layer of sliced potatoes on top. The hot pot is baked, covered, in a slow oven until all the ingredients are tender; the lid is removed for the last 30 minutes so that the potatoes are crisp and brown on top. Sometimes lamb's kidneys are sliced and added, but this is not strictly traditional. In the North, a side-dish of pickled red cabbage is always served with this excellent stew. In country districts, the cutlets sometimes retained the bones and were arranged round the interior of the pot, with the bones vertical. The vegetables were put in the middle, but potatoes still formed the top layer. This resembles the early Irish stew. It is common in varying forms to many European countries. See also HOCHEPOT; HUTSPOT.

hot pot

hot water crust, see PASTRY.

houblon, French for hop. *Jets de houblon* are the top shoots or edible flowers, which are cooked like asparagus, served with melted butter, or used as a garnish. See also ANVERSOISE, À LA.

hough, a Scots dish of boiled shin of beef (together with the bones), peppercorns, mace, and salt to taste. When the beef is really tender, it is chopped and put back in the stock which is then reduced by rapid boiling. The hough is put into pots and covered with the stock, which is a thick jelly when cold. This is known as potted hough.

hovĕzí maso, a succulent Czechoslovak beef stew made like a pot-au-feu, with shin beef and many root vegetables and garnished with sliced pickled cucumbers. Dumplings *knedlíky* are often added or served instead of potatoes.

howtowdie, a Scottish dish which is plainly French in origin, probably introduced by Mary of Lorraine, Duchess of Guise and wife of James V of Scotland, who had considerable influence on Scottish cuisine. The name is thought to come from the Old French for a pullet, hutaudeau. The dish consists of a roasting chicken stuffed with breadcrumbs soaked in milk, shallot, tarragon, parsley, salt, and pepper. It is roasted in butter with onions or shallots, a pinch of mace, 2 cloves, and seasonings; after 30 minutes ½ pint (1 cup) hot stock is added. The dish is covered and cooked for a further 30 minutes or until tender. The stock is strained into a saucepan; the chopped chicken liver is added to it, and when cooked, it is mashed into the stock and ¼ pint (½ cup) thick cream is stirred in. Two lb. spinach has meanwhile been cooked and drained and is arranged round the bird and the sauce is poured over the chicken, but not over the spinach. In the 19th century, poached eggs were arranged on top of the spinach round the bird, and then the dish was called in Scotland "howtowdie with drappit" (dropped, that is, poached) eggs. See also CHICKEN.

hrachová polévka, see POLÉVKA.

htapodi, Greek for octopus, a popular mollusc in Greek cuisine although it is tough and needs beating before cooking. See also OCTOPUS.

htapodi krassato, the octopus is cleaned and the inkbag discarded. The octopus is then cooked in a pan without liquid until it turns red, when the tentacles are removed first and cut up; later the body is sometimes peeled (this is optional) and then cut into equal pieces. Then ½ cup olive oil is heated and 1 lb. sliced onions are cooked until soft but not brown. Garlic and the octopus flesh are now added and cooked for 5 minutes, before adding ½ cup wine vinegar, 1 pint (2 cups) red wine, pepper, salt, 2 stalks celery, and 1 bay leaf. The pot is covered and it is all simmered for about 3 hours or until the octopus is tender. The dish is served with cooked rice. It is particularly popular in Cyprus.

htapodi stifado me kremidia, baby octopus simmered as above, with onions, 2 tablespoons diluted tomato purée, garlic, wine vinegar, and white wine.

hubertusleves, Hungarian hare soup, made with legs of hare, onions, peppers, red wine stock, paprika, and seasonings, garnished with sour cream.

huchen, German for huck.

hucho, an alternative English name for huck.

huck, a freshwater fish of the salmon family found in the Danube and many rivers north of the Alps. It is also called hucho. It is prepared and cooked like salmon.

huckleberry (*Gaylussacia*), a wild North American berry of which there are several edible species, the principal being *Gaylussacia baccata*. It was given its botanical name in honour of the celebrated French chemist Gay-Lussac (1778–1850). The berry is used for making tarts, pies, preserves, and syrups. It resembles a blueberry, but the huckleberry seeds are larger. The fruit can be white or pink (*G. leucocarpa*), and these berries have the better flavour; but it can also be a blue-black or purple (*G. baccata; G. brachyrea; G. dumosa*—dwarf), and these berries are the firmest for sending to market. *G. ursina* is an inferior variety called bear huckleberry or buckberry.

huesos de santo, "saint's bones," a Spanish sweet from Granada, eaten on All Saints Day. It is made from 1 lb. (2 cups) sugar, ½ pint (1 cup) water and grated peel of 1 lemon boiled together until thick, when 1 lb. ground almonds is mixed in, and lastly a purée of ½ lb. potatoes. After cooling, this mixture is rolled out, cut into strips about 3 inches by 2 inches, rolled around a skewer or sugar cane, and oven cooked. Once the pastries are cooked the skewers are removed, and when the pastries are cool, they are filled with a creamy sauce made from a warm mixture of 4 oz. (½ cup) dissolved sugar and 6 egg yolks, gently heated and stirred well with 1 tablespoon water. The pastries are then iced with icing flavoured with lemon juice.

huevos, Spanish for eggs. Yema de huevo is egg yolk (see YEMAS). Huevos cocidos and huevos duros are both Spanish for hard-boiled eggs; huevos escalfados, poached eggs; huevos fritos or huevos estrellados, fried eggs; huevos pasados par aqua, soft-boiled eggs; huevos revueltos, scrambled eggs. There are, of course, many other egg dishes eaten in Spain, including the popular tortilla. See also EGG.

huevos a la casera, a traditional household soup. Salt and a little olive oil are added to boiling water, then fresh white breadcrumbs to thicken. Eggs are poached in the soup as a garnish.

huevos al plato, a regional egg dish from Álava. Fried tomatoes, garlic, and parsley are placed in the bottom of a dish with slices of fried *morcilla blanca* placed on top. Eggs are broken over this mixture, and grated cheese is sprinkled over all before baking in a hot oven for 10–15 minutes, or until the eggs are set.

huevos a la tórtola, "turtle-dove eggs." Whole eggs are broken into a flat dish and covered with spinach, artichoke hearts, chicken liver, salt, and lemon juice, all cooked together. Butter and grated cheese are put on top and the whole baked in the oven for about 20 minutes.

huevos arriba, the eggs are separated, the yolks put on

toast, the whites stiffly beaten with grated cheese, and put over and around the yolks. All are then baked for 15 minutes.

huevos con berenjenas, as *huevos al plato,* using fried eggplant, onion, tomato and garlic, but without *morcilla blanca.*

huevos con mariscos, eggs with shellfish; scallops are generally used. The scallops are baked in their shells, then removed, chopped, and covered with lemon juice. Then 2 eggs are beaten with 1 spoonful milk and seasoned; the mixture is poured over the scallops and cooked over a low heat until set. It is served garnished with shelled prawns and sprinkled with parsley.

huevos empanados, poached eggs, sometimes drained and then dipped in flour, egg, and breadcrumbs before frying in oil.

huevos rancheros, peeled and chopped tomatoes simmered with onion, garlic, a sweet pepper, and a chilli until puréed. Then eggs are broken whole on top, seasoning is added, and the dish is covered and baked in a hot oven until the eggs are set, but not hard. A popular dish in the southern states of America as well as in Spain.

huevos rellenos, hard-boiled eggs stuffed with anchovy, mayonnaise, cheese, herbs, etc.

huevos de mújol, Spanish for grey mullet roe. See BOTARGO.

huff paste, the name in Scotland and the north of England for a pastry made with flour, suet, and water, which was used to enclose food such as a marrow bone, ham, salmon, chicken, goose, etc., during the baking process. The idea was to keep in the juices and smell while cooking, and this it did admirably. Sometimes the crust was broken open and not eaten; but if the rich drippings of a ham or goose were concerned, bits were cracked off and served to those who liked them. This type of pastry was also used to enclose food during the boiling process, but this pastry was always eaten afterwards. It is sometimes used today, especially for ham or salmon, in private homes. The Scotch black bun (Scotch currant bun) is often made with huff paste outside, instead of short crust pastry.

huhn, German for chicken. Spring chicken is *junghuhn;* roasting chicken, *brathuhn;* capon, *kapaun;* castrated hen, *masthuhn;* and boiling fowl, *suppenhuhn.* See also GEFLÜGEL.

boiled chicken, served cold in aspic and with mayonnaise.

huhn mit reis or *hühnchen in weisser sauce,* boiling fowl cooked with 1 tablespoon mixed herbs, in salted water to cover, for 2 hours or until tender; the bird is skinned and jointed, but kept hot in the stock. Then ½ pint (1 cup) water and 1 pint (2 cups) of chicken stock are boiled up, and ¼ lb. rice is added and cooked for 15–20 minutes, or until it is done and the liquid absorbed. A roux is then made from 2 tablespoons butter, 1 heaped tablespoon flour, and 1 pint (2 cups) stock; it is flavoured with lemon juice, seasoned to taste, and just before serving 1 egg yolk is stirred in. This sauce is served over the drained chicken joints, which are placed on the dish in a ring of rice.

huhn nach bauernart, chicken cooked peasant style. The bird is jointed, dipped in egg, rolled in breadcrumbs mixed with grated hard cheese, and then fried in butter. Mushrooms are also fried in the same butter, seasoned, and then ½ pint (1 cup) white sauce, ¼ pint (½ cup) white wine, and a squeeze of lemon juice are added. Sometimes 2 beaten egg yolks are stirred in, but then the sauce must not be reboiled. The sauce is served over the fried chicken.

huhn nach jägerart, chicken hunter's style. Jointed chicken is fried in oil until cooked, then kept hot; 4 oz. mushrooms and 6 oz. shallots are fried in the same pan. Then 1 tablespoon diluted tomato purée, 1 tablespoon mixed herbs, and 4 tablespoons brandy are added. It is all boiled and served over the chicken.

hühnerbraten, roast chicken, often stuffed with breadcrumbs, onion, and mushrooms all bound with an egg.

hühnerleberpastete, chicken liver pâté.

paprikahuhn, chicken larded, then cooked with paprika, giblet stock, onion, and sour cream. This is a popular dish in Austria and Hungary.

Sacher huhn, a dish created by the late Madame Sacher of the famous Viennese restaurant, the Hotel Sacher. It consists of a young chicken stuffed with 2 cups sausage-meat, 1 minced goose liver, and 2 lamb's sweetbreads. It is cooked in 1 cup melted butter and 4 tablespoons Madeira wine, then garnished with cooked asparagus, cooked peas, cooked new carrots, and cooked new potatoes tossed in butter.

saures huhn, sour chicken. The bird is jointed and then simmered in water to barely cover, with one-third the quantity of wine vinegar, 1 bay leaf, 1 sliced onion, 4 cloves, salt, and pepper until it is tender and the liquid almost absorbed. The bay leaf and cloves are removed. Then ¼ pint (½ cup) sour cream or cottage cheese is thinned down with 1 tablespoon each olive oil and vinegar and is added to the chicken mixture and simmered gently for a further 10 minutes. It is served with boiled potatoes and green beans or peas.

huile, French for oil which is used a great deal for cooking purposes in France. There are many varieties.

huile d'amandes douces, almond oil, good for frying fish, or cake making.

huile d'arachides, ground nut or peanut oil, good for frying and for sauces for persons whose systems cannot tolerate olive oil.

huile de carthame, safflower seed oil, used for all purposes, especially dietetically. It has a good flavour.

huile de coton, cottonseed oil, used in margarine.

huile de mais, corn oil, used for frying and salads.

huile de noix, walnut oil, strongly flavoured and thus not liked by everyone. It is used particularly in southwestern France.

huile d'oeillette, oil extracted from the seeds of the opium poppy. It is also known as olivette in France and can be used like olive oil.

huile d'olive, see OLIVE OIL.

huile de sesame, sesame seed oil, which has a rich nutty flavour.

huile de tournesol, sunflower seed oil, used for salads.

huitres, French for oysters. In France oysters are served both hot and cold, for hors d'oeuvre, in *barquettes,* or brochettes (*en broche*), as *beignets,* in soups, garnishes, and soufflés. Other very common ways of cooking them are à la crème, *colbert, diable, florentine,* au gratin, mornay, *normande,* and *villeroi.* In the Archacon region, oysters are called gravettes. See also CLAIRE; MARENNES; OYSTER.

huitres fourrées, a Breton speciality consisting of hot oysters stuffed with a cream sauce which is thickened with egg yolks and breadcrumbs and mixed with finely chopped mushrooms.

huitrier, French for the wading oyster-catcher, a bird which, when young, is relished as food in France. It is prepared like plover. See also OYSTER CATCHER.

hummer, Danish for lobster, which is of excellent quality in Denmark. Lobster sauce is often served with sole or *fiskbudding.* It is made by blending puréed lobster mixed with cream into sauce hollandaise.

hummer, German for lobster.

hummer in weissbier, a dish of lobster served with a sauce made from light beer, shallots, caraway seeds, pepper, and flour.

hummer, Norwegian for lobster. Norwegian lobster is of good quality. See also LOBSTER.

hummer saus, lobster sauce. The tail flesh is removed from the lobster and cut up; the rest of the flesh is pounded with butter in a mortar, and sieved. More butter, together with cream, seasoning, cayenne pepper, and mace is heated with the chopped lobster almost to boiling point, when the pounded lobster and more cream are included. It is served with sole or *fiskepudding.*

hummer, Swedish for lobster.

hummer sas, lobster sauce, often served with *fiskepudding.* It is made from 1 cup chopped lobster mixed into ½ pint (1 cup) white wine sauce, flavoured with mace and lemon juice.

hummus, a purée of 1 lb. soaked boiled chick-peas, well mixed with a sauce made from ½ pint (1 cup) sesame seed paste (*tahina* or taratoor), 4 tablespoons cold water, 2 cloves pressed garlic, 3 tablespoons chopped parsley, juice of 3 lemons, pepper, and salt. Two tablespoons of olive oil is mixed with a little paprika and dribbled over the top. Hummus is also used as a dressing for fish, meat, and vegetables such as cooked cauliflower, eggplant, etc. Hummus bi tahina is known throughout the Arab world; it is also to be found in Turkey and in the Jewish cuisine of several European countries. It makes a delicious and unusual hors d'oeuvre or a dip, when it is served with crusty bread.

humpback, see PACIFIC SALMON.

hundreds and thousands, see NONPAREILLE.

Hungarian cheeses, see SAJT.

hünkâr beğendi, literally ''the King liked it,'' a Greek and Turkish speciality which consists of a lamb stew served with a purée of eggplants. It is made with 2 lb. cubed lamb sautéed in butter with 2 large sliced onions; then 2 teaspoons tomato purée diluted in ½ pint (1 cup) water is added, with seasonings, and the whole is covered and simmered for 2 hours. The eggplants are first grilled, then skinned and mashed, before mixing with ½ pint (1 cup) each of cream and milk, 2 tablespoons butter, the same of grated *kefalotyri* cheese, and ½ cup breadcrumbs. This is seasoned to taste and heated up, stirring well; the lamb is served on top, garnished with rings of green pepper.

Hunyadi töltött, a traditional Hungarian dish of 2 lb. thin sirloin steak beaten flat and covered with a mixture of 2 tablespoons creamed butter, 1 egg yolk, 3 oz. chopped ham, 1 cup chopped cooked macaroni, 1 stiffly beaten egg white, salt, and pepper, all rolled up, secured with twine and browned in fat. Then stock is added, barely to cover, with 1 large fried onion in slices, 3 tomatoes, 2 chopped green peppers, and 1 tablespoon paprika. All are covered and cooked for 1 hour, when ½ pint (1 cup) sour cream is added and cooking resumed for a further hour. This and the following dish are named after the famous Hungarian statesman and warrior Janos Hunyadi (1387–1456), who liberated Hungary from the Turks.

Hunyadi torta, a Hungarian cake made from ¼ lb. (½ cup) sieved chestnuts mixed with 6 oz. melted chocolate, 5 beaten egg yolks, and 2 tablespoons breadcrumbs until creamy. Finally, 5 stiffly beaten egg whites are folded in, and it is baked in 2 round flan tins in a moderate oven for 20 minutes. When cold, the cake layers are sandwiched together with jam or whipped cream.

huppe, French for a kind of lark which has a tufted head. It is cooked like lark, but sometimes has a rather strong flavour.

huppemeau, a French cow's milk cheese not unlike a brie. It is in season from October to June and comes from the Orléanais.

hure de porc, a French dish consisting of potted pig's head. The head, ears, and tongue, which have been salted for 3 days, are braised gently in water to cover for 4–5 hours, and then all bones are removed. The meat is well seasoned with

quatre épices; the liquid is reduced and defatted and then poured over the sliced meat. It is pressed down when cold, and served cold in slices, like brawn.

hurt, a local English name in Surrey for bilberry, as is hurtleberry.

husa, Czech for goose.

pečená husa se zelím, a festive dish of stuffed roast goose. The stuffing consists of fried onion mixed with sauerkraut, caraway seeds, and pepper, heated up until boiling, and then having a large raw potato grated into it. This dish is served with *knedlíky.*

husarenfilet, an Austrian speciality which consists of a fillet steak larded with ham and strips of pickled cucumber, all browned lightly and then stewed for 1½ hours in a thin cream sauce. It is served with boiled potatoes.

husarenfilet-fleisch, small, thin beaten slices of fillet steak, pork, and veal, dredged with flour, browned, and simmered with a very little stock to barely cover and 1 teaspoon of vinegar for 30 minutes; then ½ pint (1 cup) sour cream is added and it is cooked for another 30 minutes. It is served with boiled potatoes.

hush puppies, a kind of drop scone popular in the southern states of the U.S., made with a mixture of 1½ cups white corn meal to ½ cup flour, 2 teaspoons baking powder, an egg, salt, ½ pint (1 cup) buttermilk, and sometimes approximately 2 tablespoons finely grated onion. When the mixture has become a firmish batter, spoonfuls are dropped into deep hot fat or oil and are fried until golden brown. They are an accompaniment to fried fish of many sorts in the U.S. The ingredients can vary slightly, for example cream can be used in place of buttermilk, and parsley is sometimes added.

husk, the outer casing of a grain of wheat, oats, or barley. That of the wheat is the richest in gluten. The smooth, husked grain of the barley is known as pearl barley.

húsleves májgombóccal, a clear chicken soup, eaten traditionally on St. Stephen's Day, August 20. It is garnished with small dumplings (*májgomboc*) of chicken liver, flour, and egg.

hussarde, à la, I. A French garnish for meat consisting of tomatoes hollowed and stuffed with sauce *soubise,* grated horseradish, grilled mushrooms, and *pommes duchesse.* II. A sauce made from chopped shallots and onions sautéed in butter. White wine is added and reduced, then demi-glace, tomato purée, raw ham, garlic, and herbs to taste are included, and all are simmered together, strained, and garnished with grated horseradish, chopped ham, and parsley.

huszárrostélyos, Hungarian fried bread, which is usually fried in goose fat, sprinkled with salt, and rubbed with garlic.

hutspot, a Dutch word meaning hodge-podge or hot pot. These ''hodge-podge'' dishes, consisting of meat with vegetables, worst, or bacon, etc., are much eaten during the winter in Holland. Here are two typical examples. See also HOT POT.

hutspot met klapstuk, a hot pot made from 2 lb. flank end of boiling beef put into 2 pints boiling water and salt, and then simmered for 1½ hours when 3 lb. diced carrots are added to the pot. After simmering for a further 30 minutes, 3 lb. diced potatoes and 2 lb. onions are added, with water as necessary. Before serving, the meat is removed to be served separately, and the vegetables are flavoured with pepper.

hutspot met witte bonen en spek, hot pot with white haricot beans and bacon. First, 2 lb. salt pork is boiled in water for 1 hour after which 2 lb. diced carrots, 2 lb. quartered potatoes, and 2 lb. sliced onions are included and cooked until the pork is tender. It is then removed, and the simmering of the vegetables is continued until they are cooked. Before serving, the pork is sliced, then returned to the stew, together with a 1-lb.

tin of haricot beans (if the water in which the pork has been boiled is too salty, fresh water is used) and is heated up.

hvidkål, Danish for white cabbage. See also GRØNSAGER.

farseret hvidkål, stuffed cabbage. Large blanched cabbage leaves are stuffed with a mixture of 4 oz. boiled rice, 1 tablespoon herbs, ½ lb. minced meat, 1 egg, and seasonings. The leaves are rolled up, then casseroled for 1 hour in stock with 1 large sliced onion. The dish is garnished with cream before serving.

hvidkål salat, a cabbage salad made like cole slaw.

hvidkålsuppe, a recipe for cabbage soup and pork. A 3-lb. chine of pork is brought to the boil in water to cover and the scum removed. Salt, parsley, thyme, bay leaf, and root vegetables such as carrots, leeks, and onions are added to the pot, and the whole is simmered for 30 minutes. Then a quartered cabbage is added, and simmering continues for about 3 hours, or until the pork is tender (the vegetables are removed as they become cooked). The pork is served sliced in the soup.

hvit sagosuppe, a Norwegian pudding consisting of 4 oz. sago cooked in 4 pints (8 cups) milk and water mixed, ¼ lb. (½ cup) sugar, and 5 egg yolks, which are stirred in just before serving, hot, with cream.

hvitkål, Norwegian for white cabbage. See KÅL.

hyben, Danish for rose hip.

hybensuppe, rose hip soup. It is made with 1 lb. dried rose hips, soaked for 12 hours in 2 quarts (8 cups) water, before being brought to the boil in the same water. They are gently simmered into a pulp and the juice is then strained off. Sugar is added to the juice, which is brought to boiling point and thickened with 2 tablespoons corn flour (cornstarch), which have previously been creamed with cold water. The mixture is then simmered for a short time. This soup is lightly garnished with whipped cream, sprinkled with shredded almonds, and served chilled or tepid, according to season.

hybrid berries, berries which are the result of crosses between established or wild berried fruit canes or bushes. One of the earliest of these hybrids is the loganberry (American dewberry crossed with the raspberry) which is now used for further crosses. The wineberry, or Japanese wineberry as it is sometimes called, is the fruit of a bramble native to China and Japan, introduced into the U.S. in about 1889 and now cultivated, but not so far used for crossing. Newer hybrids and their qualities are given here.

boysenberry, parenthood unlisted, but certainly includes the eastern black raspberry (*Rubus occidentalis*) and loganberry. The fruits are large, wine-coloured, and contain fewer seeds than do either of the two parents. They have a good flavour and are treated as loganberry. They are popular in the U.S. and are available canned as well as fresh. Opinions differ, but, personally, I consider the finest to be the wineberry and the worcester berry, for both quality and decorativeness.

Japanese wineberry, see WINEBERRY.

king's acre berry, blackberry crossed with raspberry. The fruit is very dark and known as "black"; it is sweet, but not a profuse grower. It is treated as loganberry.

loganberry, see LOGANBERRY.

lowberry, a blackberry hybrid, parents unlisted. It is a "black" berry, very sweet, not unlike loganberry but less acidic. It is treated as loganberry.

nectarberry, arrived in Europe as a sport of the lowberry. The fruit is a deep wine colour, has a small core, and few seeds. The flavour is sweet, and the fruit ripens later than boysenberry or youngberry, but is treated as loganberry.

phenomenal berry, larger and brighter, and certainly sweeter, than the loganberry, which is definitely one of its parents. It ripens later than the loganberry but is treated similarly.

veitchberry, blackberry crossed with November Abundance raspberry. The fruit is mulberry-colour, about twice the size of a blackberry. It ripens between the end of the raspberry season and the start of the blackberry season. It is treated as loganberry.

wineberry, see WINEBERRY.

worcester berry, thought to be gooseberry crossed with black currant, although there is some doubt about it. The size of the fruit is between that of each parent, and the worcester berry grows freely in clusters of a deep reddish-purple colour. The flavour is between that of its parents, gooseberry and black currant. It fruits in May–June and sometimes again in September. The strong stems are covered in vicious spikes, which could account for the fact that the fruit is seldom seen in shops. It is, however, truly delicious and easily grown. It is treated like gooseberry.

youngberry, a dewberry crossed with a phenomenal berry, raised by Mr. Young of California, U.S. It has large, very juicy fruit, deep red changing to black when ripe. It is treated like loganberry.

hyldebaer, Danish for elderberry.

hyldebærsuppe, elberberry soup. The stems of 1 lb. elderberries are removed and the berries cooked in 4 pints (8 cups) water with lemon peel, and a 1-inch cinnamon stick. The juice is then strained off, sweetened to taste and thickened with 1 heaped tablespoon corn flour (cornstarch) to 1 pint (2 cups) juice. The corn flour (cornstarch) is creamed with cold water. The soup is stirred until boiling and clear. It is served hot, with *melboller* and quartered apples, or white bread croûtons which have been fried in butter and sprinkled with sugar.

hyssop (*Hyssopus officinalis*), an aromatic mint-flavoured herb, native to southern Europe and Asia, which takes its name from the Hebrew word *zrob* (honey). It grows to about 4 feet in the British Isles. A hyssop tisane, which has a bitter flavour, is said to be good for the complexion. The herb is used in France in the famous liqueurs Benedictine and Chartreuse, and also as a flavouring for fat sausages, as it is thought to aid the digestion. It is also said to be good for bruises. It is good for stews or salads. When in bloom, the hyssop has flowers of dark blue, pink (*H. rubra*), or white (*H. alba*); they are strong and slightly bitter in taste, but have a delightful sweet scent. Hyssop attracts bees, and in the Middle Ages it was used as a strewing herb. It is quite easy to grow, either from seed or with cuttings taken from an established plant. The hyssop mentioned in the Bible is in fact the caper plant (*Capparis spinosa*).

I

iahnie, Rumanian for ragoût or stew, often, like ratatouille, made entirely from vegetables, and sometimes served with meat dishes or fried eggs. Vegetables are of exceptionally good quality in Rumania, large in size yet of good flavour. *Ghiveci* is another vegetable stew which, however, sometimes has meat in it. It is also called *călugăresc,* which means "monk," and it was eaten a lot in early monasteries.

iahnie de cartofi, potato ragoût. It is made with 2 lb. potatoes peeled and sliced, and 2 large onions. The onions are fried until golden in oil, then the potatoes are added, followed by 1 lb. peeled, sliced tomatoes, 2 bay leaves, salt, pepper, and ¾ pint (1½ cups) water. They are covered and simmered gently until the potatoes are cooked and then garnished with chopped parsley.

iahnie de ciuperci, a ragoût of mushrooms with lightly fried onions mixed with tomato purée, seasoned with dill, salt, and pepper.

iahnie de fasole, boiled and drained haricot beans mixed, while still hot, with oil and sliced, fried onions; it is seasoned with lemon juice, chopped dill, salt, and pepper.

iahnie de rosii cu praji, peeled tomatoes and leeks simmered in oil with seasoning, until tender but still firm. The leeks are chopped into 2-inch pieces.

Iberian moss, see CARRAGEEN.

ibex (*Capra ibex*), a type of wild goat that inhabits mountain districts all over Europe. It is quite rare and difficult to shoot because of its habitat. The flesh is said to be very good, tasting like a gamy mutton, and it can be prepared like kid.

ice and *ice cream,* general terms used for a type of confection which takes two main forms. It was Italy that introduced ices of both kinds to the rest of Europe. Buontalenti, one of the cooks taken to France by Catherine de Medici in 1533, delighted the French court with his iced confections, which were previously unknown in France. Two Italians, de Mirra and de Marco, brought ices to the court of Charles I and, much later in the 19th century, another Italian, Giovanni Bosio, first sold ices in the U.S. About 1670, a Sicilian, Francisco Procopio, opened a café in Paris for the sale of ices to the French public. This was the Café Procope in the rue des Fossés-Saint-Germain-des-Prés (now rue de l'Ancienne Comédie).

"Cream ices" were popularised by Tortoni, owner of a Paris café in the late 18th century, when it became the fashion to serve a *bombe glacée* at the end of a formal meal in France. Water ices, or *sorbets,* used to be served between courses during a meal, to refresh and clear the palate for the next course, in the way that a bowl of clear soup is served in China. Nothing is quite as refreshing as a water ice, and it is a pity that they are not more generally eaten.

The French and Italians have many excellent ices (see BOMBE; CASSATA; COUPES GLACÉES; GRANITA; MELBA; PARFAIT).

A light sponge cake may be covered with ice-cream and the whole frozen so that it becomes an iced pudding. Fruit, both fresh and crystallised, and nuts, especially hazelnuts and pistachios, may be combined with the ice cream mixture to make a delectable sweet. See also ALASKA, BAKED; BOMBE; CASSATA; COUPES GLACÉES; GRANITA; MELBA; PARFAIT; PARFAIT GLACÉ.

ice creams, strictly speaking, should be made only from cream, eggs, and whatever flavouring is required. Originally, cream and eggs were added to the fruit syrup used for water ices. Proportions are 3 egg yolks and 1 pint (2 cups) cream, sweetened with 3 tablespoons sugar dissolved in ¾ gill (½ cup) water. This is known as a mousse base; if whole eggs are used, the mixture is known as a custard base. To make a light, smooth-textured ice cream, the mixture should be churned until thick while in the freezer. Most modern, commercially produced ice cream is made with synthetic ingredients and can never have the true "cream ice" flavour.

water ices, made of frozen fruit-flavoured syrups which

ibex

consist of 6 oz. (⅔ cup) sugar to 1 pint (2 cups) water. They are also known by their French name sorbet or the Italian word for them, *granita*. These have been made since very early times, both by the Arabs, who called them sherbets, and by the Chinese. It is thought that the Chinese passed on the method of making these water ices to the Indians and the Persians, and that the great Venetian traveller Marco Polo (1254–1324) brought the idea back to Italy. On the other hand, it is also possible that the method was introduced through Arab influence in Sicily.

iceberg lettuce, see LETTUCE.

icing, a coating made from sugar, and used to fill and decorate cakes, biscuits (cookies), and pastries. There are several different kinds of icing.

butter icing, a creamed mixture of 2 tablespoons butter and ½ lb. (1 cup) icing sugar, with a flavouring such as chocolate or coffee. It is used in Britain and the U.S. to sandwich together layers of cake or pastry. Margarine is sometimes used instead of butter.

fondant icing, an icing made from a thick syrup (boiled to 240°F) containing 2½ lb. (5 cups) sugar to 1½ pints (3 cups) water and 1 teaspoon cream of tartar, worked with a spatula until white and smooth. When cool, this is diluted with a little syrup and flavoured as desired. It is slightly warmed before use. It is suitable for light cakes, such as a sponge or *genoa*, and is sometimes coloured with vegetable dye. It is a hard icing.

frosting, an alternative American name for icing. The most common American icing is made from 2 beaten egg whites added to 12 oz. (1½ cups) sugar heated with ¼ pint (½ cup) water, then all whisked together over heat. The mixture is flavoured to taste and beaten until stiff enough to be spread over the cake.

glacé icing, icing (confectioners') sugar worked into a syrup until it resembles a thick cream.

royal icing, a much harder icing than the others, made from 3 egg whites whipped with approximately 3 lb. (1½ cups) icing sugar and ¼ teaspoon cream of tartar or 1 tablespoon lemon juice until quite stiff. It is often used for wedding or birthday cakes and, if it is required to be very firm, the iced cake is put into a cool oven to harden a little.

icing sugar, see SUGAR.

icre, Rumanian for roe.

icre de crap, carp roe, which is highly esteemed in Rumania and is eaten a great deal. The fresh roe is salted and left overnight, then rinsed in water and the outer membrane removed. It is pounded in mortar, then beaten with olive oil and lemon juice until it attains a thick consistency. It is served cold with black radishes, black olives, and sliced onion dressed with oil, and toast. It is not unlike *taramosalata*.

idrijski žlikrofi, "idrian balls" a ravioli stuffed with puréed vegetables and kajmak, popular in Slovenia, Yugoslavia.

iepure, Rumanian for wild rabbit or hare. *Iepure de casă* is a tame rabbit.

iepure cu masline, jointed wild rabbit or hare simmered with 4 pints (8 cups) water, root vegetables, and herbs such as lovage, bay leaf, thyme, and a pinch of ginger, for 1 hour. The meat is taken out and the stock reduced. Then 1 large onion is sliced and fried in oil, 4 tablespoons flour are stirred in, and then the hot stock. This is flavoured with 3 tablespoons tomato purée, 1 tablespoon vinegar, 2 cloves, peppercorns, 1 stalk chopped celery, 1 tablespoon parsley, 1 tablespoon grated lemon peel, and 1 teaspoon sugar. Finally the rabbit is included. It is covered and simmered gently for 30 minutes or until tender. Before serving, 6 tablespoons sherry or red wine and 24 ripe black olives are added, and it is

cooked for a further 10 minutes. The dish is eaten hot or cold, with boiled rice or *mămăligă*.

igname, French for yam, which is imported into France from the West Indies, and is very occasionally served there in the same way as sweet potatoes.

ikrá, Russian for caviar, which is eaten extensively in Russia. See also BELUGA.

Ilchester, a recent, commercially blended cheese made in Ilchester, Somerset, from cheddar cheese, pale beer, spices, and chives. It is made in ¼-lb. and ½-lb. sizes and is rather sharp in taste.

ilha, queijo da, a Portuguese cow's milk cheese which is hard, like a matured cheddar.

imam bayıldı, a Turkish and Greek speciality which means "fainting imam," *imam* being Turkish for priest. There are many reasons given for the priest's fainting, ranging from the richness of the dish to his parsimonious horror at the cost of the amount of olive oil used in its preparation. The stalks are removed from 4 eggplants and incisions are made along the sides, deep, but not so deep that they cut the bottom skin; then they are salted and left for a few hours while the stuffing is made. Three chopped onions, 2 peeled and chopped tomatoes, 2 cloves garlic, 1 tablespoon parsley, 1 chopped bay leaf, and seasonings are sautéed gently in ½ pint (1 cup) olive oil. When it has cooled, this mixture is spooned into the cuts in the drained eggplants, getting in as much as possible. The eggplants are put into a casserole and olive oil and the juice of 1 lemon are poured over them until the liquid reaches halfway up their sides. The casserole is then covered and the contents cooked very slowly for about 1 hour in the oven, until they are quite soft. It is served cold.

impératrice, à l', a French name for various sweet dishes and cakes with a rice base.

riz à l'impératrice, one of the principal sweet dishes bearing this name. It is made from ¼ lb. rice cooked with 2 pints (4 cups) milk and vanilla flavouring and left to get cool. Then 1 cup chopped crystallised fruit, previously soaked in kirsch, is added, together with ½ pint (1 cup) thick custard mixed with 1 cup whipped cream. The mixture is poured into a mould lined with gooseberry jelly, and chilled. Other fruits such as peaches or pears may be used in place of the jam. Many fruits are served in conjunction with riz à l'impératrice, particularly dessert pears, which are peeled and cored and placed around the edge.

impériale, à l', I. A French garnish for fowl, consisting of slices of foie gras, truffles, mushrooms, and quenelles or braised sliced sweetbreads. Cock's combs and cock's kidneys are sometimes added, and it is all covered with sauce madère. See also POULET, À LA IMPÉRIALE. II. A chicken consommé slightly thickened with tapioca, garnished with small rounds of poached chicken forcemeat, and peas and chopped chervil. Cock's combs and cock's kidneys are added when available. See also CONSOMMÉ. III. A French method of serving potatoes, see POMME DE TERRE (POMMES DE TERRE À LA IMPÉRIALE).

imperial frischkäse, an Austrian, skimmed milk, soft cream cheese. It is slightly salted, and is made and eaten only in country districts.

indeyka, Russian for turkey.

indeyka s vishnevim sousom, turkey slices rolled in flour then sautéed in butter; wine is added, and they are served with a sauce made from boiled cherries, sugar, mixed spices, and water. See also PASHTET.

Indian corn, see CORN.

Indian lettuce, the name given to two quite distinct plants, *Montia perfoliata* and *Pyrola americana,* both of which have round leaves and are eaten as a winter vegetable in the U.S., rather like spinach.

Indian pudding, a speciality of New England, U.S. It is a sweet pudding made from cornmeal boiled in a great deal of milk (1 quart to 5 tablespoons cornmeal) for 20 minutes, stirring well. Then 2 tablespoons butter, ½ cup molasses, ½ cup brown sugar, ½ teaspoon each of ginger, nutmeg, and cinnamon, and 2 eggs are beaten in. The mixture is poured into a greased 2-quart casserole, and 1 cup cold milk is poured over, but not stirred—it is absorbed as the pudding cooks. It is baked for about 1 hour in a moderate oven until set and served warm with ice cream or hard sauce.

Indian rice, a term which designates rice grown in India, chiefly Basmati or Patna.

indianky, rich little cakes popular in Czechoslovakia. A very light sponge mixture is made by whisking 3 egg whites with 1 oz. (1 heaped tablespoon) sugar, and mixing this with 3 egg yolks, 2 oz. (¼ cup) sugar, and 3 heaped tablespoons flour. It is shaped into small rounds which are baked in a hot oven. While still warm, the rounds are split open and filled with 1 pint (2 cups) whipped cream and 2 tablespoons icing sugar, and the tops are also decorated with icing which is sometimes flavoured with chocolate.

indienne, à la, I. A French garnish for poultry or meats, of rice with curry sauce. II. A white wine sauce with mushroom and lemon juice, flavoured with curry powder. III. A cold mayonnaise seasoned with curry powder.

indienne, sauce, a classical French curry sauce which can be made in two ways. One, 1 slice of raw, chopped ham and a slice of onion are fried until brown, and 2 tablespoons butter, a sprig of thyme, and 12 small whole peppers are then included. Then 1 teaspoon curry powder mixed into ½ pint (1 cup) velouté is added to this mixture, and the whole is gently boiled for about 10 minutes. The mixture is then strained into another saucepan and 2 tablespoons fresh cream, the yolks of 2 eggs, and lemon juice are blended in. Two, 1 large onion is sautéed in 2 tablespoons butter, then 1 stalk chopped celery, parsley, thyme, 1 bay leaf, a blade of mace, 2 tablespoons flour, and 1 teaspoon curry powder are all added and stirred well in. Then 1 pint (2 cups) consommé or stock is poured in, and the sauce is simmered for 30 minutes. It is strained, and finally ½ cup cream and a squeeze of lemon juice are added.

indvolde, Danish for tripe.

indvolde stegte, a recipe for roast tripe. The tripe is cut into a round, and a stuffing consisting of minced onion, breadcrumbs, grated lemon peel, crushed mixed herbs, and seasoning, all moistened with milk, stock, or water, is spread over one half of the tripe; the other half is rolled over and stitched down. Rashers of Danish bacon are placed on the roll, which is put in a buttered tin and baked in a slow oven for about 2 hours, basting frequently. It is served cut into slices, though the roll shape is retained. Beef gravy is poured over it, and it is accompanied by mashed potatoes.

indyk, Polish for turkey.

indyk pieczony, stuffed roast turkey. In Poland, turkey is often filled with a stuffing of 1 lb. mashed cooked chestnuts, 4 tablespoons heavy cream, ½ lb. each pork and veal forcemeat, 2 grated sautéed onions, ½ cup breadcrumbs soaked in milk, 1 egg, and seasoning. Sometimes the meat and onions are omitted, in which case 2 tablespoons butter and 3 eggs are used instead.

indyk w sosie maderowym, turkey with sauce madère. The bird is first larded with truffles soaked in white wine (half the quantity is kept back for adding to the stuffing, which is the same as for *indyk pieczony* except that the chestnuts are omitted). The turkey is rubbed with butter and, half-way

through cooking, is basted with a mixture of ¾ pint (1½ cups) Madeira wine and ½ pint (1 cup) bouillon or giblet stock. The pan juices are thickened to make the sauce.

kotlety z indyka, cutlet-shaped turkey cakes, made from 1 lb. minced meat from the breast of the bird, creamed with 2 egg yolks, 1 tablespoon butter, 2 truffles or 4 small mushrooms, and the juice of a ½ lemon. The patties are shaped, dipped in melted butter, and fried. They are served with a purée of chestnuts or mushrooms, or sometimes a sauce madère.

in-far cake or **dreaming-bread,** a very old Scottish cake, like a rich oatcake with flour and butter added. The Roman rite of conferratio, in which a consecrated cake was eaten to effect the ceremony of marriage, is the basis of a similar practice involving in-far cake in Scotland. When the bride arrived on the threshold of her new home, an in-far cake was broken over her head and the pieces were given to the unmarried guests to put under their pillows and "dream" on. In the 19th century in the Orkney Islands, the minister placed the cake on the palm of one hand and held it over the bride's head; with the other hand he smashed the cake, and the crumbs were scattered to be scrambled for by the guests, who thought it a sign of great good luck if they were able to catch one before it reached the floor.

ingberlach, a small Jewish honey cake eaten at Passover. It is made from ¾ cup honey, boiled with ½ lb. (1 cup) sugar for 10 minutes, then taken from the stove. A mixture of 2 beaten eggs, 1 cup matzo meal, ½ cup ground almonds or walnuts, and 1 tablespoon ground ginger is stirred into the honey, and it is cooked very gently for 10 minutes, stirring constantly. Then the mixture is turned out onto a wet board, shaped into a flat round, and sprinkled with sugar and ginger. When cool, it is cut into squares or diamond shapes.

ingefära, Swedish for ginger.

päron i ingefära, ginger pears. A clear syrup is made from 2 lb. sugar and ½ pint (1 cup) water, and 3 lb. peeled whole pears are simmered in it for about 2 hours, together with 3 small pieces stem ginger (which have been crushed and tied in a piece of muslin). The ginger-bag is removed before the pears and syrup are stored in covered jars.

ingladsild, Norwegian for pickled herring, of which there are many excellent varieties, each small Norwegian port having its own secret, closely guarded recipe.

ingwer, German for ginger, used a great deal for cakes in Germany, especially for *lebkuchen*.

inkfish, see CALAMARY; CUTTLEFISH.

inky caps (Coprinaceae), a well-defined genus of fungi, characterised by black spores on the gills, the gills themselves being distinctive by running parallel to each other, not driving in, wedge-shaped, toward the centre of the cap like those of most other mushrooms. When the fungus first appears above ground, it seems to have scarcely any cap, but during growth this gradually expands. There are several varieties of inky caps, all of which are edible. The common ink cap (*Coprinus atramentarius*) is bell-shaped, pale grey in colour, and about 2 inches long before it starts expanding. When young it should not be eaten with alcoholic drink. The shaggy ink cap (*C. comatus*) is torpedo-shaped before expanding, and 2 to 4 inches in height. It must be eaten the day it is picked, as rapid deterioration soon sets in. The magpie ink cap (*C. picaceus*) is so called because of its mottled, magpie appearance.

inky pinky, a Scottish hash, made from thin slices of cold roast beef simmered in good beef stock or gravy, with 1 large whole onion, carrots, and seasoning. Just before serving, 1 tablespoon vinegar is added, the onion is removed, and the gravy is thickened with corn flour. It is served with triangles of toast.

insalata, Italian for salad, of which there are many varieties in Italy. Generally they are made from cooked vegetables of various kinds, mixed together with an oil and vinegar dressing. Cooked dried beans are also used.

insalata di frutta, a fruit salad, usually made with figs, plums, apricots, and peaches.

insalata di frutti di mare, a salad of mussels, prawns, and *fragoline di mare,* a very small and tender kind of inkfish (squid), which are mixed with twice their quantity of *gianchetti.* Sometimes a few slices raw mushrooms are added. All are mixed well together and served with lemon.

insalata di raperonzoli, Italian for corn salad which is eaten a lot in winter.

insalata di rinforz, a special salad which is eaten on Christmas Eve in Naples. It usually accompanies eel (see ANGUILLA) or carp. It is made from a cooked cauliflower broken into sprigs, with garlic, black olives, and capers, the whole covered with a sauce made from ¼ cup olive oil, lemon juice to taste, 1 teaspoon sugar, 1 teaspoon mustard, 1 clove garlic, salt, and pepper, all well mixed and shaken. See also CAVOLFIORE.

insalata verde, Italian green salad, made from raw green stuffs, such as lettuce, chicory, and the weeds common to Italy, known as rughetta and puntarella which have a distinctive flavour.

salsa per insalata, the typical sauce for an *insalata.* It is usually made as vinaigrette, though lemon juice is more generally used than vinegar. In Milan, pounded anchovy fillet and a clove of garlic are sometimes added.

interlarding, a process whereby lardoons are sewn through the outer surface only of meats in order both to flavour and to decorate. See also BARDING; LARDING; PIQUAGE.

involtini, see SALTIMBOCCA.

iridée, an edible, irridescent French seaweed which has a variegated colouring. It is eaten raw in salads, or boiled in water like a green vegetable.

Irish bread, see SODA BREAD.

Irish cheeses, see CÁIS.

Irish moss, see CARRAGEEN.

Irish pease pudding, the classical accompaniment to hot pickled pork. It is made from 1 lb. dried peas, either green or yellow, soaked overnight and then boiled in a cloth in 2 quarts water for about 2 hours, or until tender. They are drained and rubbed through a sieve; then a beaten egg, 2 tablespoons butter, and salt and pepper are added. The country method is simply to soak the peas overnight, and then to put them, together with a chopped onion, into a muslin bag. The bag is tied and the pudding cooked in the saucepan with the pickled pork for several hours; when ready, it is seasoned and whipped with a fork. It is sometimes flavoured with worcestershire sauce to taste.

Irish potato cakes, see POTATO, CAKES.

Irish stew, one of the classical Irish dishes, now known all over the English-speaking world and also in France. Well made, it is a delicate hot pot, but too often it is served swimming in liquid, and with additions to the original recipe which are not traditional and change the character of the dish. In earlier days, Irish stew was undoubtedly made, not with lamb or mutton, but with young male kid which was both lean and tender. It is essential to have good meat to make a real Irish stew, as the meat should only take as long to cook as do the sliced potatoes. If older meat is used, it should be partly cooked beforehand. First 2 lb. lamb or mutton should be trimmed of fat and bone, and 1 lb. each potatoes and onions are peeled and sliced fairly thickly. The ingredients are layered in the saucepan or casserole: first a layer of potatoes, then the onions. The meat, which is well seasoned and sprinkled with a little chopped thyme is put on top, then more onions; and finally more potatoes, but cut much more thickly, to cover the top. Only about 2 cups water are added, and the saucepan is covered with a tightly fitting lid and cooked either in a slow oven or on top of the stove for about 2 hours. The potatoes at the bottom should dissolve and absorb the meat juices, and the whole should be creamy and just moist. This is the real Irish stew; the addition of carrots or any other vegetable renders it a "stew" only.

isabelita, Spanish for angel fish. This name is used particularly in the West Indies, and is also common usage in some southern parts of the U.S.

isard, see IZARD.

iscas, a Portuguese dish of thin slices of liver, highly seasoned and fried in oil. See also FIGADO.

ischl, a Hungarian biscuit (cookie) made with 5 oz. (1 cup plus 1 tablespoon) flour, 4 oz. (½ cup) butter, 2 heaped tablespoons sugar, a pinch of baking soda, 1 egg yolk, and 2 oz. roasted hazelnuts, all well mixed. The mixture is cut into small rounds, baked for 15 minutes in a moderate oven, and when cooked, the rounds are stuck together in twos with jam, before being topped with chocolate icing.

isinglass, a gelatine made from the dried bladders of fish, especially sturgeon. Not only is it used as gelatine, but it is also dissolved in water and used to preserve eggs.

issues, French for pluck. The word is used only of animals, never of birds.

istiridyè, Turkish for oysters. See also OYSTER.

istiridyè külbastisi, oysters removed from the shell, sprinkled with salt, pepper, and a few drops of olive oil, and grilled, preferably over charcoal.

istiridyè pilâkisi, shelled oysters (about 3 dozen) cooked in hot olive oil on a bed of chopped parsley. Two cups water are added and they are simmered for 10 minutes. Then 2 egg yolks are beaten up in a saucepan with 4 tablespoons oyster liquor and juice of 1 lemon, and beating is continued over a low heat until the mixture thickens (it must not boil). The sauce is served poured over the oysters.

Italian cheeses, see FORMAGGIO.

italienne, à la, I. A French garnish for meat, consisting of artichoke bottoms, mushrooms, and macaroni croquettes, with sauce *Italienne.* II. A French method of serving chicken, see POULET, À L'ITALIENNE.

italienne, sauce, a classical French sauce. I. One heaped tablespoon fresh butter is put into a saucepan over a slow heat. Then 2 tablespoons chopped parsley, 1 tablespoon chopped mushrooms, 1 tablespoon chopped shallots, and finally, 1 pint (2 cups) dry white wine are added. The mixture is boiled until it has reduced by half, then ¼ pint (½ cup) stock and ½ pint (1 cup) velouté are added, and the sauce is gently boiled until thick. It is skimmed and served hot with meat, fish, poultry, or eggs. II. There is also a cold sauce Italienne, which consists of a mayonnaise garnished with a purée of cooked calf's brains and chopped fines herbes.

ivoire, sauce, a classical French white sauce made from 1 pint (2 cups) of the liquor in which poultry or fish has been cooked, boiled until reduced by half. Then 1 tablespoon flour or corn flour (cornstarch) mixed with 2 tablespoons water is stirred in, and stirring is continued until the flour is cooked and the sauce smooth. The saucepan is removed from the heat, and 2 eggs beaten in a little water are well mixed in. It is seasoned to taste, and stirring continued over a very low heat until the sauce is thick. If serving with sweetbreads or poultry, 3 tablespoons of veal gravy for every ½ pint (1 cup) of sauce is added.

ivrogne de mer, a small fish found in Mediterranean, Adriatic, and Atlantic waters. It has red scales, and is tough to eat, but is used for soups or stews. The name means, literally, ''drunkard of the sea.''

izard or *isard* (*Rupicapra rubicapra*), a reddish-coloured goat-like antelope, also called chamois; it is found in the mountainous districts of central and southern Europe, particularly the Pyrenees (where the species is called *R. pyrenaica*), and in western Asia. Because of its swiftness of movement, it is hard to shoot. It is very popular as food in Andorra and is prepared there by first being steeped in a marinade of dry white wine to cover, with allspice, bay leaf, orange peel, parsley, thyme, marjoram, cinnamon, onions, and tomatoes. Then a greased casserole is lined with slices of *petit salé* or fat bacon, and thick chunks of izard are laid on top. The marinade is poured over, garlic and seasonings added, the lid firmly put on, and the ingredients cooked in a slow oven for about 3 hours, or until the meat is tender. The liver of the izard is a speciality, and is often baked in wine with onion. See also GIBIER.

izmir köftesi, a Turkish dish of chopped mutton. First 1 lb. raw mutton is chopped into small pieces and mixed with 3

izard

slices crustless, soaked white bread, 2 eggs, 1 tablespoon onion juice, salt, pepper, and a pinch of nutmeg. The mixture is then formed into sausage-shaped rolls and fried. They are covered with a sauce made by boiling together tomato purée and a little water. See also KÖFTE.

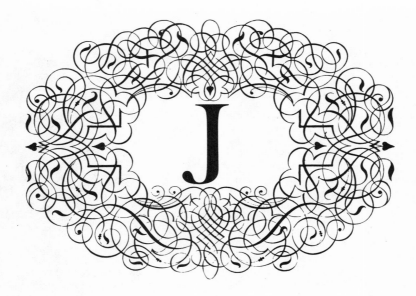

jabalí, I. Spanish for wild boar. A young boar is a jabato, and is cooked in any way that is suitable for pork. See also CO-CHINILLO ASADO DEL MESÓN DEL SEGOVIANO. II. Spanish for a fish of the bass family. It is not unlike halibut and is good to eat. It is also called *rayon*.

jabłka, Polish for apple.

jabłka nadziewane na winie, peeled, cored apples sprinkled with sugar. The centres are filled with a mixture of orange peel simmered in butter, raisins, chopped almonds, and sugar, and the apples are then baked in white wine until tender.

jachtschotel, a Dutch dish, known as "hunter's dish," using left-overs of game (meat may be substituted). Onions are fried in butter and mixed with cooked, chopped game or meat; to these are added stock to barely cover, made from meat juice and water, seasoning, worcestershire sauce, and nutmeg to taste. A dish is filled with alternate layers of this meat mixture, mashed potato, and thinly sliced apple. The last layer, potato, is dotted with butter and sprinkled with cheese. The contents of the dish are baked for about 30 minutes in a moderate oven.

jack cheese, an alternative name for Monterey jack cheese.

jack rabbit, see HARE.

jack snipe (*Lymnocryptes minima*), a smaller bird than the common snipe, but similar to it in every other way. Seen in England in September, the jack snipe is easy to shoot because it is slow to rise when disturbed. It is prepared for the table in any way that is suitable for common snipe, and is thought to be equally as good, if not better. Jack snipe is called *bécassine la sourde* in France.

jägersuppe, "hunter's soup," a German dish which is more of a stew than a soup. It is made from roasted partridge, diced ham, carrot, onion, celery, stock, and red wine, all seasoned and simmered for about 1 hour.

jägerwurst, "hunter's sausage," a very hard, flat wurst made from minced pork spiced with paprika, and smoked. It is hard and dry, but quite tasty, and is eaten raw. See also WURST.

jagnje, Serbo-Croat for lamb.

jagnje kuvano u mleku, a Yugoslav speciality which consists of a whole baby lamb simmered in milk with onions and herbs.

jagodowa, Polish for bilberry, one of the most popular wild fruits in Poland. Bilberries are not only used for the many dishes usually associated with this fruit, but also for a soup which is served either hot or cold and with or without sour cream.

jaja, Polish for eggs. Polish egg dishes are many and varied and very often have sauces added to them. The most usual of these consists of sour cream slightly thickened with flour, and in this the eggs are poached. Sorrel sauce made with cream is another favourite used to garnish all kinds of egg dishes. See also EGG; SOS, SZCZAWIOWY.

jaja nadziewane, stuffed eggs. Cooked egg whites are stuffed with the sieved cooked yolks, anchovy fillets, raw egg, breadcrumbs, sour cream, and parsley. The whole is then covered with sour cream and baked. (Crayfish and shrimps are also used as egg stuffing.)

jaja sadzone z sosem maderowym lub truflowym, fried eggs served covered in a truffle sauce or sauce madère.

jajecznica, scrambled eggs, a favourite breakfast dish in Poland. It is usually served sprinkled with chopped chives.

tebaliki z Jaja, the Polish version of *oeufs en cocotte,* served with anchovies.

jalousies, small French cakes made from flaky pastry covered with almond paste. When cooked, the top is spread with apricot jam.

jam, a mixture of fresh or dried fruit and sugar, boiled together until the confection becomes quite firm. The length of time this takes depends a great deal on the amount of pectin in the fruit being used: some fruit, apples for example, have a high pectin content and set easily; some, such as strawberries, which are low in pectin, can have lemon juice added to hasten and improve the setting. The amount of sugar used is about 1½ lb. to 2 lb. fruit. Preserving sugar (chippings of cane sugar) is the best to use, as it does not crystallise as readily as granulated sugar or sugar made from sugar beet. When ready, the jam is put into warmed and sterilized jars or bottles and must be covered to exclude air to prevent fermentation or mold or botulism.

jam sauce, jam heated and boiled up with a little white wine. It is served hot, usually with steamed puddings. It is sometimes sieved before serving. See also VICTORIA SPONGE.

jamaican pepper, see ALLSPICE.

jambalaya, a rice dish from the southern U.S. It is not unlike a risotto, and can be made with pork, chicken, or shellfish, or a mixture of 2 or 3 of them. Onion and garlic are gently sautéed in oil or fat; then a variety of vegetables are added such as green or red peppers, tomatoes, and celery (2 cups in all), followed by 2 cups in all of diced ham, poultry, prawns, or oysters, 3–4 cups water or stock, 1 cup raw rice, seasoning, and chopped herbs. The ingredients are covered with a lid and simmered gently without stirring for 30–40 minutes, or until the rice is cooked and all the liquid absorbed. Shrimp or prawn jambalaya is the most usual variety.

jambe, French for leg, usually of meat.

jambe de bois, a country name for a clear soup, the main ingredient being part of a leg of beef.

jambon, I. French for ham. The quality of French ham is excellent, and there are many varieties, the best known being jambon de Bayonne which is cured at Orthez in the Basses Pyrénées. This can be eaten raw (sliced thinly) or cooked. It forms a part of various sauces and stews, but it must not be boiled. Jambon de Toulouse is salted and dried, can be eaten raw, or can be cooked in the same way as Bayonne ham.

jambon and sausages

All over France, there are a large number of different provincial salted and smoked hams (*jambons de campagne*), for example the hams of Brittany, Burgundy, Morvan, Touraine, Limousin, Lorraine, Savoy, Alsace, the Ardennes, and the Auvergne. Nearly all these can be eaten raw or cooked. Jambons Blanc, demi-sel, and de Paris are more like the English or American hams; they are only very lightly smoked, and can be boiled. They are called jambons glacés by French pork butchers. Fully salted and smoked hams are known as jambons de porc salés et fumés. Many varieties of cold ham are found in *charcuteries* all over France: hams in aspic, shoulders of ham boned and rolled, jambon de Dijon cooked with parsley, and the boned, cooked jambon de Paris mentioned earlier. Ham is also cooked in a red wine, such as Chambertin: the dish takes the name of the wine. Foreign hams, such as the English York ham, German Westphalian or Mainz ham (*schinken*), Prague ham, Parma ham, and Hungarian ham, are also popular in France, especially the Prague ham (*Pražska šunka*).

The preliminary cooking of French ham is very like the English method. Afterwards, it is served in many ways: with cream or spinach, in pastry, or as a mousse. See also HAM; JAMBONETTES.

jambon à l'alsacienne, an Alsatian dish of boiled, hot ham served with sauerkraut, Strasbourg sausages, and boiled potatoes.

jambon au foin, a French farmhouse method of boiling a ham in water on a bed of sweet hay.

jambon persillé de bourgogne, an Easter day dish in Burgundy. The 5 lb. of ham is cooked with white wine, veal knuckle, calf's foot, chervil, tarragon, and a bouquet garni. It is very well cooked, and then drained and flaked with a fork into a deep bowl. The stock is clarified and poured over it, with 1 spoonful tarragon vinegar added. When it begins to set, 2 tablespoons or more finely chopped parsley are added. It is served cold. II. French for a leg of fresh pork.

jambon de poulet, French for chicken leg, generally boned and stuffed, then braised in stock with Madeira wine.

jambonneau, French for a foreleg of pork, or a knuckle from the fore or hind leg, which is cut and cured separately from the ham, usually pickled or salted for only about 1 week. (This cut is called picnic ham in the U.S.) It is then simmered in water with carrots, onions, bouquet garni, and a bay leaf. When cooked, it is skinned and the flesh is removed from the bone and pressed down, so that it looks like a small ham. It can be bought in most *charcuteries*.

jambonneau de volaille, French for a large chicken leg, boned and stuffed, then braised in stock. It can be served hot, or jellied and cold, and it is prepared in the same way as *ballottine*.

jambonnettes, a speciality of the Ardèche, France. This is a delicious dish consisting of a boned knuckle-end of ham stuffed with fresh pork and sewn up into a cushion shape. It is sold at fêtes and on feast days.

jamón, Spanish for ham. The finest Spanish ham comes from the Estremadura; it is home-cured, not smoked, and is eaten raw in thick slices. The Asturias ham is the mildest Spanish variety with a delicate flavour not unlike a York ham. In Granada a delicious dried and smoked ham is produced, called *jamón serrano*. When ham is served cooked, it is usually accompanied by dried or fresh beans, as is illustrated by the recipe given here from Granada. See also HAM.

jamón

jamón con habas a la granadina, shelled broad beans (which must be young and fresh) tossed in hot oil or lard; when nearly cooked, slices of ham are added and the whole is mixed well together.

jänis, Finnish for hare.

jänispaisti, casserole of hare, a very popular game dish in Finland. The hare, which is at its best in winter, should be hung for several days and then soaked in a weak vinegar solution for a few hours. After that, the fore and hind legs should be severed and tied together, with rashers of bacon between them. The back is divided in the same way, and the three bundles are browned in a casserole. The stock made from the offal and ribs is then poured over. When cooked, the strings are removed and the hare cut up. Sour cream is added to the stock, and the hare and the sauce are served separately. See also GAME; HARE.

Jansson's frestelse, literally, "Jansson's temptation," a Swedish dish which is also eaten in Norway. I have not been able to discover who Jansson was, or what became of him as a result of eating this delicious appetiser. I suspect he met a sudden death but, on the other hand, he may have lived to be a patriarch of 90, so it's worth taking the risk! Sliced potatoes, anchovies, minced onions, butter, cream, and anchovy juice are layered alternately, finishing with a potato layer, then baked in the oven and eaten hot.

jānu siers, a Latvian cheese, literally "St. John's cheese," eaten especially on the Latvian national holiday, St. John's Day, June 24th. It is served with bacon, and beer is drunk with it.

Japanese artichoke (Stachys sieboldi), also called Chinese artichoke and knotroot, and known in Oriental markets as choroqi, is an Eastern perennial plant cultivated in Europe and the U.S. for its tubers or underground rhizomes. These taste not unlike the tubers of a delicate-flavoured Jerusalem artichoke, and are used in the same way, but require less cooking. See also JAPONAISE, À LA.

Japanese bunching onion (Allium fistulosum), a species of onion very like the Welsh onion, which it is often mistaken for. The Welsh onion, however, is smaller.

Japanese quince (Chaenomeles lagenaria), an ornamental shrub which came originally from Japan but is now grown all over Europe. It bears hard, yellowish-green, round or oval berries. They are exceedingly bitter when fresh, but they are aromatic, and make excellent preserves and jellies.

Japanese wineberry, see HYBRID BERRIES; WINEBERRY.

Japonaise, à la, a French garnish comprising tartlets filled with Japanese artichokes parboiled and tossed in butter, with croquette potatoes.

japuta (Brama brama, Brama rayi), Spanish for a sea bream, known as Ray's bream in English, which is found off the north coast of Spain and fished for with nets. It is considered fair eating and is usually poached in wine with onion and parsley, grilled, or fried in fillets. It is also eaten in Italy where it is called *pesce castagna.*

jardinière, à la, I. A French garnish, consisting of all manner of fresh vegetables, plainly boiled and arranged round a joint or portion of meat. They are separated according to kind, with an eye to colour juxtaposition. II. Sometimes the term used to describe meat braised with many vegetables.

jardinière, sauce, a classical French sauce made with 1 tablespoon butter and 1 teaspoon of sugar placed in a saucepan over a moderate heat, with the addition of medium-sized, finely cut carrots, turnips, and peeled button onions (3 of each). They are fried gently for 20 minutes, when 1 pint (2 cups) broth is added and the mixture simmered gently until the vegetables are cooked. The mixture is then boiled quickly for a while, to reduce the liquor, and the fat is skimmed off. Some cauliflower sprigs, asparagus heads, green peas, and french (string) beans are now added to 1 pint (2 cups) freshly made sauce espagnole, together with the pre-cooked vegetables, and all are boiled gently together for some 15 minutes. The sauce is seasoned with salt and pepper, and is served hot.

jarmuż, a Polish dish of quartered stewed white cabbage which has been cooked in stock, bound with a brown roux, and then mixed with sour cream. It is garnished with braised chestnuts.

jaroba, see LABRO.

jarosse or jarousse, the French name for a cultivated vetch which is known in Britain as everlasting pea. It is used for food in France, particularly in the Auvergne, where it is known as the Auvergne lentil.

jarret, French for shin or knuckle, for instance, knuckle of veal is jarret de veau.

jarrett steak, a popular dish from Cornwall and the west country of England, made from 2 lb. cubed shin of beef rolled in flour, then casseroled with chopped celery heart and ½ lb. rolled bacon rashers, seasoned, and barely covered with ½ pint (1 cup) water mixed with 1 tablespoon worcestershire sauce and 2 tablespoons tomato sauce. It is covered and cooked slowly in the oven for about 2 hours.

jaseur, French for waxwing, a member of the finch family. It is cooked in the same way as lark in France.

jay (Garrulus glandarius), a bird which is beautiful in appearance but has a screeching cry; it is common in most European countries, but has become rare in England. It can be eaten, but is not specially recommended, except when young; its flavour is insipid and, if the bird is old, it must be put in a simple marinade before cooking. However, in France, the young birds are considered a delicacy. The jay is skinned, not plucked, and does not require hanging.

jelenia, Polish for venison, which is eaten a great deal in Poland since the numerous forests in that country are inhabited by many varieties of deer. Venison is always marinated after hanging, and the marinade consists of root vegetables, herbs, allspice, peppercorns, and generally wine vinegar, diluted with twice the quantity of water. The shoulder is usually braised. Steaks and cutlets are fried or grilled with butter, and sometimes red wine is added to the dripping, boiled up, and served as a gravy; or they are casseroled in red or white wine with onion and herbs. Grills and roasts are served with sauce. See also DZICZYZNA.

jelenia ze śmietaną, marinated loin or saddle of venison, larded with salt pork and either roasted or cooked on a spit, basted with butter and sour cream. The drippings are thickened with a little flour, well mixed to avoid lumps. The dish is served with a sour compote of fruit or a jelly.

potrawka z jelenia, marinated shoulder of venison rubbed with pepper, crushed juniper berries, and thyme, and sautéed with onion and bacon. It is then casseroled with red wine, prunes, apples, walnuts, and 1 cup rye breadcrumbs. When cooked, it is served with noodles and puréed beetroot.

jelly, I. Soft, firm, semi-transparent food, consisting chiefly of gelatine made from bones, carrageen, etc. It can be savoury or sweet. Fruit jellies, with predominately synthetic flavouring, are sold commercially. These only need boiling water added to them, and then they are put in a cold place to set. II. A kind of jam made by cooking fresh fruit in water to barely cover, then letting it drip through muslin until all the juice is extracted. This juice is boiled up with sugar—1 lb. sugar to 1 pint (2 cups) juice—for about ½ hour or until it sets, when it is cooled. It is put into sterilised jars or pots and covered to exclude air. As with jam, preserving sugar (chippings of cane sugar) is the best to use.

jelly bag, an old-fashioned bag made from coarse woollen cloth used for the purpose of clarifying jelly, which, when hot, is dripped through it. Also called a tammy cloth in Scotland.

Jenny Lind, named after the Swedish opera singer, is a French consommé made from game, garnished with strips of quail and sliced mushrooms. See also CONSOMMÉ.

Jersey wonder, a small doughnut-like cake which is a speciality of Jersey in the Channel Islands. It consists of a dough made from 8 oz. (2 cups) flour, 4 oz. (½ cup) butter, 2 heaped tablespoons sugar, and 2 eggs, formed into bow-knots which are deep-fried in oil. When hot, the cakes are served with a fruit sauce.

Jerusalem artichoke (*Helianthus tuberosus*), knobby tubers, with a sweetish taste and a flavour faintly resembling that of the globe artichoke, which was first introduced into France from Canada in 1607. In France, Jerusalem artichokes were first called poires de terre and artichauts de Canada; later they were known as *topinambours* after a tribe of savages of the same name, from Brazil, who had been brought to France for exhibition at about the time that these artichokes became popular. The tubers reached England via Holland, under the name *artischo-kappeln van ter neusen,* which some authorities claim became anglicised to Jerusalem artichoke. Others, although this theory is now discounted, claim that the name is a corruption of the Italian name for them, *girasole.* In 19th-century England, Jerusalem artichoke soup was invariably known as ''Palestine soup,'' under the assumption that Jerusalem artichokes came from Jerusalem.

Jerusalem artichokes are rich in carbohydrates, particularly in inulin. They are steamed or boiled, with or without their skins, until tender; they are baked and fried, are made into soup, or are used cold for salads. Their distinctive flavour is acclaimed by many gournets. See also ARTICHOKE; CZYŚCIEC BULWIASTY; PARMENTIER.

jesiotr, Polish for sturgeon.

jesiotr pieczony, a Polish way of baking sturgeon in a sour cream sauce. The fish is first cut into portions, dipped in flour, egg, and breadcrumbs, and fried in butter. It is then sprinkled with dill and parsley before sour cream, to cover, is added. Traditionally it is eaten at *Wigilia.*

jesse, a carp-like fish found in almost all European rivers. Although the taste is good, the fish is extremely bony, so is not used as often as carp. The flesh becomes yellowish when cooked.

jésuite, I. A small French pastry made from flaky pastry, of which half is spread with almond paste, then covered with the other half and sprinkled with praline. It is cut into triangles and baked in a moderate oven. II. The popular name in many country districts in France for a turkey, from the belief that this bird was first imported into France by the Jesuits, who bred it on their farms, particularly near Bourges.

jésus, a Swiss sausage made from pig's liver.

jewfish, a name for any of the large groupers found off the west coast of Mexico, the West Indies, and Florida. It applies particularly to *Promicrops itaira,* which is a game fish not highly thought of gastronomically.

Jew's ears (*Auricularia auricula-judae*), a fungus resembling a human ear, found almost exclusively on dead elder branches. It dries successfully, and when soaked in hot water is excellent for adding to soups. It grows freely all over Europe, or where elder trees abound, and is simple to dry. It is used in many Chinese dishes and is also known as Chinese fungus. It is soaked in boiling water before use and gives a most interesting texture and taste to many braised dishes.

jibia, see CHOCOS.

jibiones, the name given to calamary in Santander.

Job's tears (*Coix lacryma-jobi*), a coarse grass cultivated in the arid parts of Spain and Portugal. The hard seeds are used to make a coarse bread.

jogurt, Serbo-Croat for yogourt, which is used a lot in cooking in Yugoslavia as well as being eaten on its own.

jogurt ''tava,'' roast lamb served with a sauce made from 2 egg yolks whipped with 1 pint (2 cups) yogourt and 1 heaped teaspoon paprika. The egg whites are beaten stiff and added to the mixture, before it is poured over the meat and all baked in the oven until set, about 15–20 minutes.

john dory (*Zeus faber*), an ugly but delicate-tasting sea fish with a very thick skin and small scales. It exists in all European waters and there is a similar species in Australia. In the U.S., the porgy bears the closest resemblance to it. It can be cooked whole, baked, grilled, or poached. When filleted, it can be cooked in the same way as brill, turbot, or sole. In France it is used in bouillabaisse and is called Saint Pierre. In the British Isles its appearance does not recommend it to the buyer, but it is nevertheless an excellent fish, and as the demand is small, sells very cheaply. It is sometimes called doree in English.

john dory

johnnycake, a speciality of Rhode Island, U.S. It is a griddle-fried cake made from white cornmeal and eaten for breakfast with sausages, eggs, or syrup. To prepare them 3 cups white cornmeal (known as johnny cake meal) and a little salt are scalded with 1 quart boiling water. It is thinned down with about ½ cup milk until it is the consistency of a thin batter. Spoonfuls are dropped onto a hot, well-greased griddle, and they are cooked on both sides.

johnnycake toast, left-over johnnycakes can be used for milk toast (cubed toast soaked in warm milk). They are split, laid in a baking dish, dotted with butter, covered with milk or cream, then heated but not allowed to boil. They are served slightly salted.

joinville, I. A French garnish for fish consisting of a salpicon of cooked mushrooms, shrimps, and truffles, with sauce joinville. II. Fillets of sole poached in fumet, drained, and arranged in a circle on a round dish, with a peeled shrimp on each fillet. In the middle is put joinville garnish, and the fillets are coated with some of the sauce joinville. On top is placed a truffle glazed with fish jelly. III. A cake made from flour, butter (half the quantity of butter to flour), and milk. These ingredients are made into a firm dough, which is rolled out to form two equal squares; one square is spread with raspberry jam and is then covered with the other square, and the edges are pressed down. The top is pricked and then baked for about 30 minutes. When cooked, the cake is sprinkled with sugar.

joinville, sauce, a classical French sauce. It is a combination of ½ pint (1 cup) sauce normande and 2 tablespoons coulis of crayfish and shrimps. Sometimes a julienne of truffles is added. It is served with fish, particularly sole.

jorbkäse, a German cheese made from sour milk. See also MAINZER KÄSE.

jordbaer, Danish and Norwegian for strawberry.

jordbærkake, Norwegian strawberry layer cake, made from 3 heaped tablespoons castor sugar beaten with 3 egg yolks and 1 tablespoon water; 3 heaped tablespoons flour are then sifted in gradually. The beaten egg whites are folded in, and the cake mixture is baked for 15–20 minutes in 3 sandwich tins in a moderate oven. Frozen strawberries are mashed and used as a filling, and syrup and whipped cream are poured over the top of the cake.

joue de porc fumée, French smoked pig's cheek, not unlike a bath chap.

joulukinkku, a traditional Finnish method of cooking ham at Christmas. It is eaten either hot, as a joint, or cold with the smörgåsbord. The fresh ham is rubbed with salt, sugar, and saltpetre and left for a day. It is then placed in brine for 2 weeks, when it is removed and boiled for 4 hours. It is then skinned, smeared with mustard, sprinkled with breadcrumbs and sugar, and baked until it has browned. See also HAM.

joulutortut, Finnish for small round or square pastry cases stuffed with pulped prunes. Their edges are folded to the centre and pressed together. These are traditional fare at Christmas. The pastry is made from 12 oz. (3 cups) flour, 1 teaspoon baking powder, and 9 oz. (1 cup and 1 tablespoon) butter, mixed with ¾ pint (1½ cups) stiffly beaten cream. See also VIIPURIN RINKELI.

jowl, an alternative name for the American butt cut of pork.

judas tree (*Cercis siliquastrum*), a very beautiful tree which grows in southern Europe, the U.S., and Asia. In early summer, it has a profusion of bright purplish-red, strongly scented flowers which, when in bud form, can be pickled in vinegar, like capers.

judías, Spanish for beans. Judías encarnadas are (dried) red beans; judías verdes are french (string) beans.

judías encarnadas a la madrileña, red beans as served in Madrid. First they are soaked, then boiled with thinly sliced bacon and *chorizo,* in water to cover until they are tender. Chopped garlic and onion are fried in olive oil, and when golden, a little flour is stirred in; some of the hot bean stock is poured over, and stirring is continued to avoid lumps. This mixture is added to the beans and simmered with them for 5 minutes before serving. See also MADRILEÑO.

judías verdes a la española, french (string) beans Spanish-style. The beans are boiled in salted water. Chopped garlic, parsley, and red sweet peppers which have already been baked, skinned, and cut into strips, are all fried in oil, and this mixture is then combined with the french string beans.

judic, à la, I. A French garnish for entrées, consisting of stuffed braised lettuces, cock's combs, truffles, and *pommes château.* II. A consommé double garnished with rounds of truffle, quenelles of chicken, and chopped braised lettuce. See also CONSOMMÉ.

judru, a French sausage of cured pork, not unlike salame. It is a speciality of Chagny in the Côte d'Or.

jugged, food, especially hare, cooked in an earthenware pot of jug. See also HARE.

juhannus, "Day of Light," which is Midsummer Day. The midnight sun heralds the beginning of the 24-hour day. Many traditional dishes, such as *kesäkeitto* and *mansikkatorttu,* are eaten.

juice, I. The liquid squeezed from raw food, whether animal or vegetable, and in particular from fruit. II. The blood that runs out of meat or poultry when roasting. III. The liquid surrounding certain shellfish when first opened, for example, oyster juice.

jujube, see CHINESE DATE.

julekake, a Norwegian Christmas bread, filled with spiced apples or dried fruit, candied peel, and almond paste. It is baked in a variety of shapes such as a half moon, figure eight, or a tricorne. To prepare it, ½ oz. yeast is creamed with 1 teaspoon sugar, and ½ cup tepid water mixed with 1 egg. Then 1 lb. (4 cups) flour and ¼ teaspoon salt are mixed with 3 tablespoons sugar, and 3 heaped tablespoons butter are rubbed in. Into a well in the centre of this mixture is poured the yeast liquid, and a little of the flour is sprinkled over. It is covered and set in a warm place to rise for 20–30 minutes, until the yeast has bubbled through. The flour is "pulled" in from the sides, and kneaded lightly. Then 1 cup mixed dried fruit, 1 teaspoon cardamom or caraway seeds, and ½ cup mixed candied peel are added. The mixture is again covered and put in a warm place until it doubles in size; it is then kneaded again, and put into a large, well-greased and floured bread tin. It is cooked in a moderate to hot oven for 45–60 minutes.

Jules Verne, à la, a French garnish for meat consisting of potatoes and turnips filled with whatever stuffing is desired, and then braised, with mushrooms simmered in butter.

julgröt, a Swedish Christmas dish consisting of a rice pudding cooked in milk with a single almond in it. Whoever gets the almond will be the next person to marry during the following year.

julienne, I. A French garnish of finely shredded vegetables. II. Any foodstuff, whether vegetable or animal, cut into match-like shapes. III. A consommé to which is added a mixture of finely chopped or shredded vegetables. It can also be garnished with quenelles, *profiteroles,* or royale. See also CONSOMMÉ.

julskinka, the Swedish Christmas ham. (In Sweden, a baked or boiled ham always appears as part of the smörgåsbord for Christmas Eve dinner.) A cured ham is brought to the boil in cold water, skin side uppermost. After the stock has been skimmed, herbs such as bay leaf, cloves, and allspice are added, and the ham is gently simmered until tender (about 3½ hours for a 10–12-lb. ham). The skin is then removed, and the ham allowed to cool in the stock. The ham is glazed after that, by spreading over the fat side a mixture of 1 beaten egg, 1 tablespoon prepared mustard, 3 tablespoons brown sugar, and 3 heaped tablespoons breadcrumbs. A little fat is brushed over this, and the ham browned in the oven or under the oven-grill. It is beautifully garnished, sometimes with little bunches of black and green grapes and sections of orange, and the knuckle is dressed with a festive paper frill. The liquid in which the ham has been cooked is reserved for the traditional "dip in the pot," which is also eaten on Christmas Eve. See also DOPP I GRYTAN; HAM.

jumbles, an American biscuit or cookie made from 10 oz. (1¼ cups) butter and 10 oz. (1¼ cups) sugar creamed together, followed by 2 eggs, a flavouring such as lemon, 1 lb. 4 oz. (5 cups) flour, and a pinch of nutmeg. These ingredients are all well mixed, and the mixture is then refrigerated for several hours before being rolled out very thinly and cut into 2½-inch rounds. These are baked for about 8 minutes. Jumbles used to be made in 19th-century England, and ground almonds were added to the dough.

juneberry, an American berried shrub of the genus *Amelanchier.* The fruit is sweet and juicy and varies greatly in size and also in colour, ranging from red to black. The North American Indians eat a great deal of it both fresh and dried, and horticulturists have cultivated several varieties of the shrub.

jungfernbraten, an Austrian dish made from fillet of pork, larded and browned, then cooked on top of a bed of sautéed onions and carrots, a little stock and sour cream. It is braised until tender, and a few drops of vinegar are added before serving.

jungschweinskaree, an Austrian way of cooking loin of pork, which is scored and rubbed with salt and crushed caraway seeds. It is roasted, and served with the pan juices.

juniper (*Juniper communis*), a shrub-like tree whose berries are very aromatic and yield a valuable alkaloid called juni-perin. The tree grows wild in Europe, and is to be found in England in the Lake District. The berries are used to flavour gin. In cooking, they are included in the preparation of marinades, boiled mutton, roast game (particularly venison and partridge), and, in parts of Ireland, with wild duck. The world-famous Limerick ham acquired its reputation from being smoked over juniper branches and berries.

juniper

juniper sauce, 1 slice chopped ham and 2 medium onions are sautéed in butter, then 1 tablespoon crushed juniper leaves and berries and ½ pint (1 cup) red wine are added. All is reduced, mixed with 2 tablespoons demi-glace, boiled again, then strained. If the sauce is to be served with game, strong stock made from game bones and trimmings is used instead of red wine.

junket, an old English milk pudding composed of milk set to a solid curd by the addition of rennet, in the proportion of 1 teaspoon to 1 pint milk. The milk must not be hotter than blood temperature, or it will not set. Flavourings can be added, also sugar, and the top is usually sprinkled with ground nutmeg. In Cornwall, clotted cream is also put on top. The name probably comes from the Norman French *jonquette,* the word for a rush basket used for draining soured milk or cream curd.

jurel (*Trachurus trachurus*), Spanish for horse mackerel, also known as scad. It is good when baked with butter, with either young green peas, or served with *salsa verde.* Another variety (*T. picturatus*) is found in the eastern Atlantic and sometimes in the Mediterranean, and can be cooked in the same way. See also CHINCHARD; HORSE MACKEREL; SAUREL.

jus, I. French for the liquid that is exuded from meat during roasting or grilling and remains after the fat has been skimmed off. It may be hot or cold, but in the classical French cuisine the phrase *jus de viande* refers invariably to the hot *jus;* when cold, it becomes jellied and is known as *jus en gelée.* II. French for fruit or vegetable juice. III. The juices extracted from meat, poultry, or game by compressing them in a special press after they have been lightly cooked. (The best example of this is *caneton Rouennais à la presse.*) This is also called *jus de viande.*

jus lié, a French term for a fatless veal gravy thickened with arrowroot.

juusto, Finnish for cheese. See PIIMÄJUUSTO; POHJALAINEN LEIPÄJUUSTO; UUNIJUUSTO PIHKAMAIDOSTA.

jydske terninger, a Danish sandwich made from short crust pastry filled with a thick mixture of ½ lb. chopped tinned pork, 1 sliced onion, 1 sliced potato, 1 heaped tablespoon butter, grated lemon peel, and parsley, all moistened with ½ cup gravy or a white sauce. The top pastry crust is brushed with milk, and all is baked in a moderate oven for 30 minutes. It is served cold, divided in four squares, which are once more cut crosswise into serving portions.

jydske terninger

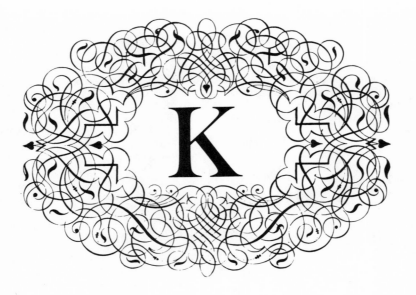

kaali, Finnish for cabbage.

kaalikääryleet, cabbage rolls. A large cabbage is cooked until tender, and then the larger leaves are stuffed with a mixture of ½ cup cooked rice or pearl barley, ½ cup breadcrumbs, 1 tablespoon butter, 1 lb. minced meat, ¼ pint (½ cup) cream, and pepper. This mixture is placed on the leaves, which are wrapped around it as though it were a small parcel. The top of the rolls are smeared with a thin syrup not unlike corn syrup, and cooked in a hot oven; then, when brown, they are covered with boiling water and stewed. They are served hot with the thickened stock and cranberry jam.

kaalikeitto, a type of cabbage soup. This soup is made with 1 lb. chopped breast of mutton, to which are added 1 onion, 4 pints (8 cups) hot water, salt, and 6 allspice berries. After cooking for 30 minutes, a shredded cabbage and 1 teaspoon marjoram are added. The soup is served as a main dish for dinner.

kaalipiirakka, a cabbage pasty. This pasty is made with a *pulla* dough, as used for coffee bread, which is divided into two pieces. The filling is made with cabbage which has been boiled and then fried in butter. The larger piece of dough is pressed out and the filling placed on top. Slices of hard-boiled egg are arranged on top of the filling, and then the other piece of dough is placed over the top and the edges sealed down. The pasty is cooked in a hot oven, and is served hot as a smörgåsbord dish.

maitokaali, a type of cabbage soup made with cabbage, butter, flour, sugar, milk, salt, and water.

kääresyltty, a Finnish form of salted brawn, made from 5 lb. fat, salt bacon flavoured with pepper, ginger, and allspice, cooked in salted water for 4 hours, then drained, cooled, and pressed.

kaas, Dutch for cheese. All Dutch cheeses must bear the mark of the Government Cheese Control, which is a casein disk; this is in blue ink for full cream cheeses, in black ink for the others. See BLUEFORT; EDAM; ÉTUVE; FRIESIAN; GOUDA; KANTER; KERNHEM; LEYDEN; LUNCHEON CHEESE; SPICED CHEESE.

kaas en broodschoteltje, a bread and cheese dish made with 2 beaten eggs and ½ pint (1 cup) milk poured over 5 sandwiches of crustless stale bread and slices of cheese. The dish is left to stand for 30 minutes, before being dotted with butter and baked for about 30 minutes in a moderately hot oven. It can be served hot or cold and is very good with a green salad.

kabak, Turkish for courgettes (zucchini), often served stuffed with rice and herbs, for *meze.*

kabeljau, German for young cod or codling. See also COD; FISCH.

kabeljau in biersauce, a codling (about 3 lb. in weight) baked on a bed composed of a 2-inch square of chopped gingerbread, 1 sliced onion, 2 sliced carrots, and a bay leaf. It is seasoned, barely covered with brown ale, and baked with the lid on for 30 minutes in a hot oven. Then the fish is removed and the remaining mixture is sieved, thickened with butter and flour, and served over the fish. Squares of toast surround the dish, sometimes with an oyster on each piece. See also GINGERSNAP SAUCE.

kabeljauw, Dutch for young cod, eaten both fresh and dried. See also COD.

gestoofde kabeljauw, 6 fillets of cod are layered with sliced potatoes and onions, ending with a layer of potatoes. Then a mixture of 3 eggs beaten with ½ pint (1 cup) sour cream, sometimes flavoured with nutmeg, is poured over the dish, the top is sprinkled with breadcrumbs, and it is baked in a moderate oven for about 30 minutes.

gestoofde kabeljauw of schelvis, a dish of baked fillets of haddock or cod. Salt and nutmeg are added to 1 pint (2 cups) white sauce. When off the heat, 2 egg yolks are beaten in, then 2 egg whites are folded into the mixture, and 2 lb. fish is covered with the sauce, then topped with breadcrumbs and baked in a moderate oven for about 30 minutes. For variety, other ingredients may be included in the sauce, such as parsley, mushrooms, shrimps.

kabeljo, Swedish for dried or cured cod. See also COD; TORSK.

kabeljopudding, dried cod pudding. To prepare it, 1 lb. fish is soaked in water (which is changed every 4 hours) for 12 hours, before being placed in a pan of boiling water and boiled until the flakes fall apart. Then it is boned and shredded, 2 lb. potatoes are mashed with black pepper, 1 egg yolk, ¼ pint (½ cup) hot milk, and 1 tablespoon butter, and, lastly, the fish is mixed in. The whole is topped with breadcrumbs and a little more butter, and baked until golden brown.

kabul sauce, a commercially bottled Russian sauce with a very poignant flavour. It is used for flavouring other sauces, and salads. See also SMITANE, SAUCE.

kabuni, a traditional Albanian dish, consisting of 1 lb. (2 cups) rice sautéed in 6 oz. (⅔ cup) butter, to which 2 pints (4 cups) stock are added and the whole cooked for 10 minutes. Then 2 cups raisins are included, and cooking continues until all the liquid is absorbed and the rice is cooked. Before serving, 1 cup sugar mixed with 1 teaspoon cinnamon is added. This dish is eaten with the meat course, or, particularly, with boiled chicken.

kaccavia or *kakavia,* Greek fish soup or bouillabaisse. The Greeks claim to be the inventors of this type of dish, citing an ancient soup brought by them to the Marseilla Phocaem colonies. In those days the fishermen cooked their fish in a special earthenware pot called a *kakave,* which was placed in the middle of the boat. This name was translated by the French as *bouillote* (pot), whence bouillabaisse. A traditional recipe for kaccavia, as prepared by fishermen from the Greek Islands, consists of about 3 lb. mixed small fish put into the pot, with water to cover. To these are added ¼ pint (½ cup) olive oil, 2 sliced onions, 4 tomatoes, and seasonings, and all the ingredients are cooked until soft. This mixture is sieved, and the thick stock put back into the pot as a base for 2 lb. of the larger fish, and shellfish, lobsters, etc., which are then included. Water to cover is added, together with herbs such as garlic, bay leaf, celery tops, and parsley, and all is cooked briskly for 20–30 minutes. It is a very simple dish, but good. It is always eaten on *Tou Sotiros.* In restaurants it is served with fried croûtons. See also BOUILLABAISSE.

kačkavalj, a cheese made in Yugoslavia from ewe's milk, and very popular there.

kaczka, Polish for duck. *Kaczka faszerowana* is roast, stuffed duck. Sometimes duck is simmered with capers in giblet stock, which is thickened to make a gravy and called *kaczka duszona z sosie kaparowym.* See also DUCK.

kaczka duszona z kapustą gerwoną, duck braised in a casserole with red cabbage, onions, caraway seeds, bay leaves, shallots, and stock or red wine. See also POTRAWKA (POTRAWKA Z KACZKI Z RYZEM).

kadayif, a traditional sweetmeat (confection) in Turkey and the Middle East. It consists of fine noodles, butter, almonds, honey, and salt. The noodles are cooked in boiling water, then drained well. They are put into a shallow oblong pan, and when solid are turned out and cut into squares. These are placed on a greased baking sheet and covered with finely sliced almonds or hazelnuts. Honey is poured over and the whole is baked in a moderate oven for 30 minutes. To serve, more chopped nuts and a trace of honey are added. Kadayif is eaten hot or cold.

kadın budu, traditional Turkish beef and rice patties, made by mixing equal quantities of raw chopped beef and boiled rice, chopped parsley, 1 egg (to 1 lb. of meat and rice), and salt to taste. The mixture is shaped into flat oval dumplings which are then boiled. When cold, they are dipped into beaten egg and fried.

kaerlighedskranser, Danish biscuit rings made from 4 oz. castor sugar beaten into ½ lb. (1 cup) creamed butter; 4 oz. (1 cup) flour is then blended in, followed by 4 hard-boiled egg yolks which are well beaten into the flour mixture, vanilla to taste, and sufficient extra flour to form a dough. After chilling for 1 hour, the dough is rolled out, and rounds about 2½ inches in diameter are cut. The centre of each circle is removed and all the pieces baked in a moderate oven until golden brown. Sometimes the centre pieces are put back, either with jam, or when they are dipped in icing and desiccated coconut, or with butter cream, when they are dipped in hot jam and chopped nuts. The name means "love rings."

kaernemaelk, Danish for buttermilk.

kærnemælkskoldskal, buttermilk soup, a popular farmhouse dish in Denmark. It is made with 2 eggs, juice of 1 lemon, 4 tablespoons sugar, and ½ teaspoon vanilla essence (extract) beaten together. This mixture is gradually folded into 2 pints (4 cups) buttermilk. The soup is topped with whipped cream. If this dish is used as a dessert, as it sometimes is in Denmark, it is served with small meringues and sweetened fruit.

kærnemælkssuppe med solbær, a buttermilk soup with black currant jam. It is prepared from 4 oz. (1 cup) flour stirred into 2 pints (4 cups) buttermilk; then a further 4 pints (8 cups) buttermilk are brought to boiling point and stirred into the first mixture. The whole is again brought to the boil, stirring constantly. Then 2 egg yolks are beaten with 4 oz. (1 cup) sugar, and the buttermilk mixture is gradually stirred in. Lastly, ½ lb. jam is added. This soup is served chilled.

kager, Danish for pastry, of which there are many different kinds, always of high quality. Perhaps wienerbrød is the most popular and the most varied, although the Danes usually buy this ready-made from the shops. See also WIENERBRØD.

kail, an alternative spelling for kale, often synonymous with cabbage in country districts of the British Isles.

kail and knockit corn, a Shetland Island method of serving cabbage which has been boiled with pork or smoked mutton, then drained, seasoned, and mixed with knocked corn. (Knocked corn is a barley which is dried, then put into a knocking stone with a little warm water, and bruised with a mallet to break the husks, which float off; it is not unlike pearl barley.)

kailkenny, a Scottish dish from Aberdeenshire and the northeast, resembling *colcannon.* The word is possibly a corruption of colcannon, and the dish was no doubt originally made with kale, and not cabbage. It consists of equal quantities of cabbage and potato, mashed together, with a cup of cream added.

kaïmaki, a Greek cream which is so thick that it can be cut into slices. Perhaps Devonshire cream is the nearest equivalent, but it does not really approximate. It is more like a fresh, hard, cream cheese, and is used in cooking particularly with *kouneli* as well as being eaten fresh.

kaiserfleisch, an Austrian speciality which is a rack of smoked pickled pork, boiled, and served with sauerkraut and dumplings made with white bread, or a purée of green split peas. In his book *Together* (Chapman and Hall, 1923), Norman Douglas describes it as "a dish which alone would repay the trouble of a journey to this country from the other end of the world, were travelling fifty times more vexatious than it is."

kaiserschmarrn, see SCHMARRN.

kajgana, a Yugoslavian omelette-like dish. It is not unlike the Portuguese *omeleta. Kajgana od jaja* is plain scrambled eggs.

kajmak, a thick Yugoslavian cream made from boiled, cooled, and skimmed ewe's milk, which is then salted in a jar. It is often served as an hors d'oeuvre, like a cheese, with homemade bread.

kakaviá, see KACCAVIA.

kaker, Norwegian for cakes. Sometimes in Norway, the rich sponge or layer cakes (*lurifakser*) are served as a dessert. They are also served with coffee instead of biscuits (cookies).

kakor, Swedish for cakes. Cakes and biscuits (cookies) are served with coffee throughout Sweden. The standard of cake-making is high; the cakes are usually rich and always extremely good. Butter is invariably used and cream is often an ingredient. In Sweden, cakes frequently take the place of puddings for dessert.

kål, Danish for cabbage; see HVIDKÅL.

kål, Norwegian for cabbage. In Norway, one way of preparing it is to cook it shredded, with sour cream, caraway seeds, and seasoning for about 15 minutes. See also GRØNNSAKER.

kålruletter, cabbage rissoles. The cabbage leaves are boiled until soft in salted water, and the hard parts of the stalks are then removed. Sausage meat is placed on each leaf, which is rolled up and secured. The rissoles are simmered in water for about 30 minutes, when the ties are removed and the rissoles served, coated with parsley sauce. See also SURKÅL.

kål, Swedish for cabbage. See also GRÖNSAKER.

kåldolmar, cabbage rolls. First 2 oz. rice is cooked in ½ pint (1 cup) water until the latter is absorbed, then simmered in ½ pint (1 cup) milk for about 30 minutes. When cool, ¼ lb. each of minced pork and minced beef or veal are mixed in, also chopped parsley, 1 egg, 2 tablespoons cream or milk, and seasoning. Spoonfuls of this mixture are placed on boiled cabbage leaves, which are rolled up and secured; the rolls are browned in butter and then baked in a mixture of water and meat stock, with a little brown sugar sprinkled over all, in a slow oven until tender (1–1½ hours). After that, the stock is thickened with a mixture of flour and cream and is poured back over the rolls before serving.

kålsoppa, a cabbage soup. Shredded cabbage is lightly browned in butter. Then 1 tablespoon golden syrup is well stirred in over the heat, beef stock and seasoning are added, and the soup is simmered for about 3 hours. It is served with *frikadeller*.

kala, Estonian for fish. The people of Estonia are very fond of fish and eat it salted, smoked, baked, and in soup. A shop sign with 3 fish on a dark brown background means that fresh fish is for sale. Prazdnik is the festival which opens the fishing season, and the fishermen drink mead and cider on that day. See also VÄIKSED HEERINGAD PIIMÄ SAUSTIGA.

kalasupp, a fish soup, often made with both saltwater and freshwater fish. About 2 lb. filleted fish are cooked with 2 onions, a bay leaf, and seasoning in 5 pints (10 cups) water. The fish is removed when cooked, and 1 lb. sliced potatoes is cooked in the stock. Then 2 pints (4 cups) milk, 2 tablespoons parsley and dill, and the fillets of fish are added and simmered for 10 minutes. The soup is served with lemon slices.

kala, Finnish for fish. See also AHVENMUHENNOS; LIPEÄKALA; LOHI; MADE; MATEENMÄTI; MUIKKU; PAPERISSA SAVUSTETTU KALA; SILAKAT; SILLI.

kalakeitto, a fish soup, made with 3 lb. fresh fish, 2 tablespoons butter, 2 pints (4 cups) milk, 2 tablespoons flour, 1 onion, 1 lb. potatoes, seasoning, and allspice, garnished with chopped chives and parsley. The fish is boiled with the sliced potatoes in water, which is then thickened with a roux made from the butter, flour, and milk.

kalakukko, a fish pasty. Pastry made with rye meal is shaped on a baking board into an oval ¾ inch thick, 20 inches long, and 12 inches wide. On it are arranged pieces of dried fish, often a tiny white fish called *muikku*, and slices of pork, with salt between the layers. The pastry is folded over the filling, and the edges are sealed. It is baked until the pastry becomes golden brown, then the heat is reduced and cooking continued in a cool oven for a further 3 hours. The pasty is then wrapped in damp greaseproof paper and several layers of ordinary paper, and returned to the oven for 6 hours. It is left in the oven overnight and served cold with butter or sour milk (*viilipiimä*), either as a snack or as a meal. In some parts of the country it is called *patakukko*.

keitetty kala, plain boiled fish, served with a sauce made from its thickened stock, to which hard-boiled eggs and chives are usually added. With pike, grated horseradish is added to the sauce.

paistettu kala, fried fish. The fish are cleaned, rolled in flour, and fried in butter.

kalafjory, Polish for cauliflower, often used in soup in Poland, and also served boiled with fried, buttered breadcrumbs as a garnish.

kalafjory po wlosku, parboiled cauliflower covered with chopped ham, sautéed mushrooms, and tomato sauce, all sprinkled with Parmesan cheese and cooked in the oven.

kalamara, Yugoslav for squid, often served in risotto in Yugoslavia.

kalamaria, Greek for squids. The very small and tender squids, called kalamarakia, are particularly delicious and are eaten as appetizers. They are either fried au naturel in deep oil, or first dipped in egg and breadcrumbs and then fried. Larger squids are apt to be tougher and are best when braised. Squids are also eaten a good deal in Cyprus.

kalamaria yemista, larger squids stuffed with a mixture of cooked rice, parsley, dill, onions, pignoli, and olive oil. They are put into an oiled baking dish with ½ cup red wine, ½ cup olive oil, ½ cup tomato juice, and enough water to cover, before baking for 1 hour, or until tender. Usually served cold.

kalarepka, Polish for kohlrabi. See also KOHLRABI.

kalarepka faszerowana, kohlrabi with the centre scooped out, and the cavity then stuffed with minced beef, lamb, or pork, raw egg, and grated onion before braising in stock which is thickened before serving.

kalb, German for veal, often cooked in Germany, Austria, and Hungary with paprika and sour cream. See also SCHNITZEL; VEAL. *Kalbsbrust* is breast of veal; *kalbsfuss*, calf's foot; *kalbshirn*, calf's brain; *kalbskopf*, calf's head; *kalbsleber*, calf's liver; *kalbsmilch*, calf's sweetbreads; *kalbsnierenbraten*, roast loin of veal; *kalbskeule*, leg of veal; *kalbshesse*, shin and knuckle of veal; *kalbsveegerl*, stuffed, boned knuckle of veal; *kalbszunge*, calf's tongue.

gefüllter kalbsbraten, a delicious dish of boned leg of veal, stuffed with onions, breadcrumbs, kidney, and anchovies, all chopped. The stuffed leg is rolled up and roasted, then served with hot sour cream.

kalb Holstein, veal cutlets or escalopes (scallops), coated with egg and breadcrumbs or flour, fried on both sides in pork fat or butter. It is garnished with a poached egg on top of each piece of meat, surrounded by sliced gherkins, beetroot, olives, capers, anchovies, and lemon slices, sprinkled with chopped parsley.

kalbsrippe, veal cutlets, often served fried in butter, with a sauce made from sour cream, paprika, and caraway seeds mixed with the pan juices. This is called *kümmelsauce*.

kalb, the word for veal in the German-speaking parts of Switzerland, where it is very popular and is eaten in a variety of ways. See also GESCHNITZELTES MIT RÖSTI; SCHNITZEL; WIENER SCHNITZEL.

garniertes kalbsfilet, fillets of veal which are floured, then fried in butter, and garnished with asparagus tips, green peas, and little balls of mashed potato fried in butter.

geschmorte kalbshaxe, braised shin of veal. A 3-lb. shin is first browned in fat, then 1 pint (2 cups) stock, ¼ pint (½ cup) white wine, 1 onion, 2 Hamburg parsley roots, 1 bay leaf, 2 cloves, thyme, and seasonings are added. All are simmered slowly until tender. It is served with root vegetables and potatoes which have been sautéed in butter and then simmered in stock in another pan.

kalbsrouladen, thin veal slices stuffed with chopped, sautéed mushrooms and onion, with nutmeg, parsley, and seasonings. They are rolled up and simmered in tomato and veal stock to cover, for about 1 hour.

kale (*Brassica oleracea*; var. *acephala*), also *kail*, borecole, cole, and colewort; any cabbage with sprouting, curled, finely dented leaves not forming a close-knit heart or head. There are several forms of kale, tall and dwarf, green and variegated. The variety called Labrador is among the best. The curly leaves are used in winter and the little sprouting shoots in early spring. All kale is cooked like cabbage, or served as a green salad. Kale is used particularly in Scotland, and to be asked to "kale" means to be asked to a meal, though not necessarily of kale. Kale withstands frost better than any other green vegetable, indeed the frost gives it a more mellow flavour. It was probably originally used in place of cabbage in Colcannon in Ireland, hence the name. There is a type of kale called cavolo pavonazza or Neapolitan curled borecole, grown in Italy; its stem swells a few inches from the ground and it is good when cooked and eaten like kohlrabi. See also BOERENKOOL; BRAUNKOHL; KAIL.

kale

kale brose, a traditional Scots soup. Beef jowl (cheek) and kale are cooked in beef broth. The soup is thickened with oatmeal and garnished with triangles of toast.

kalfsvlees, Dutch for veal. Kalfskoteletten are veal cutlets; kalfslever, calf's liver.

gebakken kalfsnieren, sautéed veal kidneys. Two kidneys are soaked for 2 hours in water, which is changed twice during this time, and are then simmered, together with a bay leaf, ½ onion, and seasoning, in bouillon for about 30 minutes. After this they are sliced; each slice is again seasoned, then dipped in an egg and water mixture, rolled in breadcrumbs, and sautéed in butter. See also NIER.

gestoofde kalfsborst, stewed breast of veal. (Other parts of veal, cut in 2-inch cubes may be substituted for breast.) The breast of veal is beaten until tender, when boiling water is poured over it. It is drained and then baked in butter for about 15 minutes in a moderate oven, when 3 pints (6 cups) bouillon, root vegetables, parsley, mace, salt, and ½ sliced lemon are added, and the stew is covered and simmered for a further 1¼ hours. A brown sauce is made with butter, flour, and gravy from the stew; this is strained, and lemon juice and mushrooms are added. Rice accompanies this dish.

gevulde kalfsborst, stuffed breast of veal. An incision is made in the breast, which is then stuffed with a mixture of 1 lb. ground veal, 3 crustless slices white bread softened in milk, 2 eggs, salt, and nutmeg to taste. (Mushrooms are sometimes added to the stuffing.) The meat is then baked (about 30 minutes to the lb.) in a slow oven, during which time it is basted frequently; a little cold water is added periodically. A gravy is served with the meat, consisting of a roux of butter and flour added to the pan dripping, to which seasoning, powdered herbs (marjoram, tarragon, etc.) and either Madeira or sherry is added.

kalfsoester, veal escalopes (scallops), usually prepared by dipping in egg and breadcrumbs, frying in butter, and garnishing with lemon and anchovies. See also BLINDE VINKEN.

kalfsvlees in gelei, jellied calf's tongue and foot. A calf's foot is split and simmered for about 3 hours in water containing a bay leaf and salt. The meat is taken off and put through a mincer, and then mixed with ½ lb. minced smoked tongue, canned sliced truffles, and 4 dill pickles. Then 3 tablespoons vinegar are added, together with the meat mixture, and all are poured into a mould and chilled. The jelly is garnished with lettuce, tomatoes, and mayonnaise.

kalia, a traditional Polish soup. Rich chicken broth is flavoured with the juice of pickled cucumbers and garnished with diced chicken, celery root, parsley root, and carrots.

kalkoen, Dutch for turkey. The Dutch prefer goose to turkey at Christmas. However, the custom, prevalent in Britain and elsewhere, of eating turkey on Christmas Day, is gaining favour in Holland. It is usually stuffed and roasted.

kalkon, Swedish for turkey, a bird seldom eaten in Sweden, goose, chicken, or game birds being preferred. However, it is gaining popularity in the cities, where it is usually roasted, as in Britain or the U.S. but with a stuffing of apples and prunes (*sviske fylling*). Swedish housewives are adept at utilising leftovers, and turkey or chicken remains are often served in the following way. See also FJADERFA.

beignet på kalkon eller kyckling med skinka, rolled bacon fritters stuffed with turkey or chicken. First ¼ lb. (1 cup) turkey or chicken is minced with 1 slice ham or bacon, then mixed with a pinch of ground mace and a chopped bouquet garni. Thin rashers of bacon with the rind removed are stuffed with this mixture, rolled up (using 2 cloves to secure each roll), and dipped into a thick batter before frying until golden in deep, hot oil. The rolls are drained before serving hot, garnished with chopped parsley and lemon wedges.

kallun, Danish for tripe.

stegt kallun, roast tripe. The tripe is cut into a round, and a stuffing, consisting of minced onion, breadcrumbs, grated lemon peel, crushed mixed herbs, and seasoning, all moistened with milk, stock, or water, is spread over one half of the tripe; the other half is rolled over the stuffing and stitched down. Rashers of Danish bacon are placed on the top of the tripe roll, which is then put in a buttered tin and baked in a slow oven for about 2 hours, basting frequently. It is served cut into slices, although the roll shape is retained. Beef gravy is poured over it, and it is accompanied by mashed potatoes.

kalteszal, a Polish beer soup made from 4 beaten egg yolks, 6 oz. (⅔ cup) sugar, juice of 2 lemons, a 2-inch stick of cinnamon, and 3 pints (6 cups) beer, all cooked in a double boiler, stirring constantly. It is served chilled, with rum and raisins added to taste. This soup has a sweet-sour taste.

kaltschale, literally "cold bowl," a German cold soup, made from fruits and their juices, which is also eaten as a dessert. Fruits such as orange, strawberry, or raspberry are puréed and mixed with sugar and white or red wine. Micheál Mac Liammóir, in his book *Each Actor on his Ass* (1961), describes it perfectly: "A cold soup made of fruits and their juices, much eaten here (Hamburg) and called *kaltschale*, should be introduced into Ireland: it tastes agreeably of Summertime and subtly invokes fine weather even when there isn't any." Kaltschale is very popular in Russia, where it is served with tiny fruit *pel'meni*, a ravioli-like accompaniment. See also ERDBEER; OBST.

kalvekjøtt, Norwegian for veal. Kalvebrissel are calf's sweetbreads. See also KJØTT.

kalvekyllinger, veal rolls with a cream sauce. Escalopes (scallops) should be cut from either the shoulder or the leg and well beaten. Butter, parsley, and lemon juice are laid on each one, and seasoned. The escalopes (scallops) are then rolled up and secured, before being browned in butter; boiling milk is added gradually, followed by cream. The whole is covered and simmered for about 20 minutes until tender.

kalvekød, Danish for veal. Kalvekoteletter are veal cutlets. See also KØDO.

kalvehjerter, casserole of calves' hearts. The tubes and sinewy parts are removed from the hearts, which are then stuffed with parsley and raw onions. Before being transferred to a casserole, together with root vegetables, a bay leaf, seasoning, and boiling water, they are browned in butter. The dish is slowly baked for about 2 hours until tender, when ¼ pint (½ cup) cream is added. Mashed potatoes and a green salad are served with this dish.

kalve fricandeau, braised breast of veal. Veal is cut into small squares, seasoned, and covered with warm water, when it is brought to boiling point and drained, then sprinkled with cold water and drained once again. It is half covered with beef or veal stock and brought to the boil, after which it is skimmed. Onions, turnips, and a bouquet garni are now included, and all are simmered until tender, when the remaining stock is strained off. A gravy is made with a roux of butter and flour added to the stock, along with seasoning and a pinch of ground mace. The meat is reheated in the gravy. Two egg yolks may be added during preparation, to thicken the gravy, but it must not be reboiled or the yolks will curdle.

kalvkött, Swedish for veal. Veal is a most popular meat in Sweden. There are a number of different ways of cooking it, and cream or sour cream is usually included in the gravy. See also KÖTT.

kalvbräss, calf's sweetbreads. In Sweden these are very popular on the smörgåsbord, where they are presented in a variety of ways, sometimes creamed in a sauce béchamel flavoured with Madeira, or they are sometimes served as the main course of a Swedish meal. Whatever the method of preparation, they are always soaked beforehand in cold water and then simmered in a mixture of water, vinegar, and salt for about 15 minutes, after which they are put straight into cold water. One method of cooking them is to remove the tubes and membrane as soon as the sweetbreads are cool, and then they are diced when quite cold. A roux of butter and flour is prepared, to which are added some stock and cream. This sauce is further flavoured with lemon juice or sherry and seasoning, and the sweetbreads are then gently cooked in it. See also MEDALJONGER (KALVBRÄSS MEDALJONGER).

kalvkycklingar, veal rolls with a cream sauce. A 3-lb. fillet of veal is cut into as many portions as are required; each one is beaten and then seasoned. A knob of parsley butter is placed on each and it is rolled up and secured. The rolls are browned in butter and then simmered in veal stock until tender; they are served untied, garnished with asparagus tips and with a sauce made from the strained stock, to which cream is gradually added.

kalvstek, pot-roasted veal. A small leg of veal is seasoned and then browned in butter, when veal stock and sliced carrots and onions are added. All is simmered for about 1½ hours until tender. (Additional stock may be added if required.) A sauce is made from the strained stock, with flour, heated cream, and seasoning.

kamper steur, a Dutch dish of hard-boiled eggs covered with mustard sauce. The sauce is made with 4 tablespoons each of butter and flour, with 1 pint (2 cups) bouillon to which 1½ tablespoons prepared mustard and 1 tablespoon capers are added. The dish takes its name from the town of Kampen, where it originated.

kanin, Norwegian for rabbit which is popular in Norway and often cooked with butter, sour cream, and a little mustard. It is also roasted and served with red cabbage.

kaninchen, German for wild rabbit. A tame or hutch rabbit is zahmes kaninchen. A popular method of cooking rabbit in Germany is to joint it and brown it in butter; then to casserole the joints (which have been rolled in flour) with onion, prunes, and beer. Young rabbits are also stuffed and roasted and served with hot braised red cabbage.

kanter, a Dutch cheese resembling *friesian,* but no spices are added to the curd. The inside is dark yellow. See also LEYDEN.

kapakoti, literally "with the cover on," a Greek term for pot-roasting.

kapamà, a Balkan dish which consists of large slices of lamb simmered in stock with a shredded lettuce, a bunch of spring onions, and a little chopped dill. It takes about 2 hours to cook.

kapaun, German for capon. See HUHN.

kapers, Danish for capers.

kapersovs, a sauce to accompany mutton, fish, and boiled fowl, consisting of 1 tablespoon butter, 2 tablespoons flour, and 1 pint (2 cups) hot stock, to which 2 tablespoons capers and 1 tablespoon of the vinegar from the pickled capers are added. Cream or an egg yolk is put in just before serving and well mixed but not reboiled.

kapłon, Polish for capon. See also KURCZĘ; PULARDA.

kapłon z kremem z pieca, capon simmered in stock and served with sour cream sauce mixed with egg yolks and some of the stock.

kāpostu, Latvian for cabbage, which is a popular vegetable in Latvia. See also PĪRĀGS; SKABU KĀPOSTU SUPA.

káposzta, Hungarian for cabbage, which is cooked in many ways in Hungary. In Transylvania and Bácskai it is cooked with pig's trotters (feet), caraway seeds, paprika, onion, and sour cream. See also BÁCSKAI KÁPOSZTA; KOLOZSVÁRI KÁPOSZTA.

káposztaleves, cabbage soup. The ingredients comprise either pork or mutton, 1 onion, tomatoes, ½ pint (1 cup) sour cream, flour, lard, paprika, and salt. The cabbage (about 2 lb.) is shredded with the onion and cooked in a little fat. The meat is then cubed and added, with the tomatoes, salt, and paprika. The ingredients are simmered for about 30 minutes, then hot water is added gradually, and the soup is covered and simmered for a further 1½ hours. About 30 minutes before it is cooked, 1 cup sour cream mixed with 1 tablespoon flour is stirred in. This is quite a substantial dish, and in Hungary a soup of this nature, served with a salad and bread, constitutes the main meal of the day.

káposztáspalacsinta, pancakes made with finely shredded, boiled cabbage which is sautéed and added to the normal pancake batter. A popular addition to the filling is a little chopped ham.

rakott káposzta, a sauerkraut ragoût. First 1 lb. sauerkraut is braised with ¼ lb. smoked bacon, then layered with ½ lb. lean diced pork, 2 chopped onions, 1 garlic clove, ¼ lb. sliced sausage, and 1 tablespoon paprika, all first browned in lard. The final layer of sauerkraut is covered with ½ pint (1 cup) sour cream, and the ragoût is baked in a moderate oven for 30 minutes.

töltött káposzta, stuffed cabbage prepared in the same way as *töltött burgonya.* See BURGONYA.

vörös káposzta és alma, a dish of cooked red cabbage, apples, sugar, white wine, and salt. The shredded cabbage is fried in hot lard for a few minutes, then the other ingredients are added and it is simmered slowly for about 2 hours.

kapr, Czechoslovak for carp, one of the most popular Bohemian fishes. A festive dish is made with poached carp served with a raisin sauce.

kapr v aapiku, carp poached and served cold, set in aspic made from pig's trotters (feet).

kapusta, Russian for cabbage which, with beetroot, is the most popular vegetable in Russia. It is served for soups and stews and stuffings; is pickled, stuffed, and salted; and is often served with sour cream. In fact there is a Russian adage which says "Shchi da kasha pishcha nasha" (Cabbage soup and kasha is all we eat). Red cabbage is also served with game and pork dishes, after being shredded and cooked with stock, celeriac, Hamburg parsley roots, sugar, allspice, and cloves, for 2–3 hours. See also PIROZHKI; SHCHI; SOLYANKA.

kapusta, Polish for cabbage, which is cooked in several ways in Poland.

kapusta czerwona duszona, red cabbage cooked with bacon fat, stock, and lemon juice for several hours. When half cooked, red wine and dill or caraway are often added to taste.

kapusta na kwaśno, white cabbage cooked with tart apples, tomatoes, and onion in water flavoured with lemon juice.

kapusta na słodke z kminkiem, salt pork or bacon minced with 1 onion and caraway seeds are added to white cabbage. The whole is then simmered in bouillon for about 1 hour.

kapusta czerwona, Polish for red cabbage.

kapusta czerwona duszona, red cabbage cooked with bacon fat, stock, and lemon juice. When half-cooked, red wine and dill or caraway are often added.

satatka z kapusty czerwonej, a salad of blanched, shredded red cabbage sprinkled with lemon juice, salt, pepper, and olive oil to taste.

kapusta kiszona or *kapusta kwaśna,* Polish for sauerkraut.

kapuśniak, a traditional sauerkraut soup. Sauerkraut, marrow bones, slices of pork, bacon, carrots, celery root, parsley root, onions, and pork sausages are boiled in water until cooked. The soup is then thickened with flour and butter, after which the vegetables are removed. It is garnished with the meat, bacon, and sausages. This soup is also made with fresh cabbage.

kapuziner, German for nasturtium leaves, used a great deal in salads in Germany.

karakot, a sweetmeat (confection) from Uzbekistan. To prepare it 2 lb. sieved, stewed fruit is mixed with 1½ lb. (3 cups) sugar, 2 oz. ground almonds and ½ teaspoon vanilla, and cooked in 1 pint (2 cups) water. It is thickened with 2 egg yolks, then finally 2 stiffly whipped egg whites are whisked in and the mixture is beaten well. The mixture is put into a flat tin and left to dry off in a cool oven. When set, it is cut into slices and left to get cold. Karakot is served with lemon tea.

karaoloi, Greek for snails. They are particularly eaten, boiled, at Boghaz on the Karpas peninsula in Cyprus.

karczochy, Polish for globe artichokes which, after boiling, are usually served cold with an olive oil and vinegar dressing; if served hot, melted butter accompanies them. See also ARTICHOKE; CZYŚCIEC BULWIASTY.

karczochy na winie. After cooking with herbs and water for 10 minutes, the globe artichokes are cut into quarters and the hairy chokes are removed. The artichoke quarters are then arranged in a casserole, with butter and a glass of dry white wine, and simmered for 20 minutes. A dash of olive oil and wine vinegar is sprinkled over before serving.

kardy, Polish for chard, a popular vegetable in Poland. It is stripped from the stalk (which is cooked and served separately with melted butter and lemon), then simmered in water with salt and lemon juice or wine vinegar, about 1 tablespoon. When cooked it is well drained and served with various garnishes, such as breadcrumbs turned and lightly browned in butter, sour cream, and grated cheese, or thickened bouillon or meat gravy.

karides, Turkish for shrimps; larger prawns are *büyük karides.* Both kinds are eaten extensively, either plainly steamed or in a *pilâvi.*

karithopita, a Greek walnut cake, a speciality of Athens. First 4 oz. (½ cup) butter and 10 oz. (1¾ cups) sugar are creamed together. Then 8 egg yolks are beaten in and added one by one. Four of the 8 beaten egg whites are folded in, followed by 2 teaspoons cinnamon, 1½ lb. (6 cups) flour, and 2 teaspoons baking powder. Next 1½ lb. less 2 tablespoons of ground fresh walnuts are included. The mixture is beaten continuously, after which the remaining egg whites are folded in. Before placing the prepared tin in the oven, to be baked for about 40–60 minutes, the top is sprinkled with the 2 tablespoons of ground walnuts. After baking, a syrup made from 1 pint (2 cups) water, 12 oz. (1½ cups) sugar, and ½ cup brandy is poured over. The cake is eaten cold.

karjalanpaisti, Finnish Karelian hot pot. It is the prefix *kar* which indicates that the dish comes from the province of Karelia, famous for the excellence and variety of its food and cooking. Small pieces of beef, mutton, veal, and pork are placed in an earthenware pot with a generous sprinkling of whole black peppercorns, barely covered with salted water, and cooked slowly for 6 hours. The hot pot is served direct from the pot, and is accompanied by potatoes boiled in their skins.

karjalanpiiraat, Finnish Karelian pasties, which, like *karjalanpaisti,* have their origin in the province of Karelia. Pastry, made from 1 lb. (4 cups) rye flour, salt, and about ¾ pint (1½ cups) water, is shaped into balls which are then flattened and rolled until they are paper-thin. The pieces of pastry are placed on a baking-board, and 1 tablespoon cooked rice is spread evenly over the centre of each piece. The sides are folded in, leaving a narrow gap down the centre, and the edges are crimped with the fingers (the pasties resemble large, curled leaves when made). They are baked rapidly and, when cooked, are brushed with melted butter and cream. They are served with Finnish egg butter, which is made from the yolks of hard-boiled eggs (sometimes the finely mashed whites are added too) mixed with an equal amount of butter and seasoned with salt and pepper. The pasties are eaten hot as part of the smörgåsbord, or indeed of any meal. They can also be filled with meat, fish, or vegetables, like the Russian *pirogi domaschany,* for a main dish. See also KEITINPIIRAAT.

karl xv tårta, a Swedish recipe for an almond and apricot tart. A batter is made, consisting of 8 oz. (1 cup) butter, 12 oz. (1½ cups) sugar, 4 eggs, 4 oz. (1 cup) flour, and 8 oz. (2 cups) ground almonds, each ingredient being included in the order given and well beaten in as it is added. Half of this mixture is poured into a cake tin, followed by a layer of tinned, drained apricots, and then the remainder of the batter. The whole is baked for about 3 hours in a slow oven. The tart is served cold, decorated with sweetened whipped cream and glacé cherries.

karmonadle, Polish pork schnitzels, which are pork chops dipped in egg and breadcrumbs and fried.

karnemelk, Dutch for buttermilk.

karnemelk pudding, buttermilk pudding made from ½ pint (1 cup) hot lemon juice to which 1 lb. (2 cups) sugar has been added, and 2 tablespoons gelatine which has been soaked in water and then dissolved in a little hot water; both are added to 1½ pints (3 cups) buttermilk. The whole mixture is then poured into a mould and chilled. It is served with whipped cream. See also HANGOP.

karnı yarık, a Turkish vegetable dish. An incision is made in the side of an eggplant, and the flesh removed and chopped. The flesh is then mixed with cooked mutton and onions fried in butter, and reinserted in the eggplant, which is placed in a greased baking-dish with a little water, covered with melted butter and cooked in the oven. See also MELISA; PATLICAN.

kärntner nudeln, a German speciality of noodle paste rolled into thin oval shapes and filled with a mixture of chopped, soaked, dried fruit, sugar, and cinnamon, all thickened with fine breadcrumbs soaked in cream. The filling is put on half the area of the paste ovals, which are then folded over, with the edges dampened and pressed down. They are then placed in a shallow dish, covered with milk, and baked for about 45 minutes. When cooked, they are drained, brushed with melted butter, and sprinkled with sugar.

karotte, German for carrot. See also MÖHRE. A popular way of serving carrots in Germany is to boil 1 lb. carrots until tender; they are drained, then mixed with fat bacon rashers which have been fried until crisp. Then a little butter, 1 tablespoon wine vinegar and 1 teaspoon caraway seeds are all heated until very hot, in the fat remaining in the frying-pan and poured over the bacon and carrot mixture.

karottensauce, a sauce made from 2 large sautéed, grated carrots, 2 oz. butter, seasoning, nutmeg, parsley, and ½ pint (1 cup) stock, all cooked until smooth and thick. It is served with boiled salt beef, or cheese and tomato pie.

karp, Polish for carp. There are several ways of serving this fish in Poland. If boiled or steamed, it is garnished with parsley or mushrooms; it can also be served fried in egg and breadcrumbs, or it can be casseroled with vegetables. Sometimes it is eaten chilled in aspic. See also CARP.

karp nadziewany. Before baking, the fish is stuffed with the fish liver, truffles, and mushrooms. It is served with either a lemon or a caper sauce.

karp po polsku w szarym sosie. A large carp is simmered for about 1½ hours with onions, carrots, leek, parsnips, bay leaf, parsley, and peppercorns, and served with a sweet-sour sauce made from butter, sugar, flour, and fish stock, to which raisins, prunes, almonds, red wine, and wine vinegar or lemon are added. It is thickened with honey cake crumbs. Traditionally, this dish is eaten in Poland at *Wigilia.*

karpfen, German for carp. This is a very popular fish in Germany and Austria, especially in the parts of the country that are furthest from the sea. It is served baked, with cream, sometimes flavoured with paprika, or poached and then served cold in aspic, as well as being fried, grilled, or boiled. Traditionally, carp is eaten on Christmas Eve in northern Germany. Whichever method of cooking is used, the scales are not removed, so that everyone eating it can save one scale which he keeps throughout the year as a lucky charm. See also BLAUFISCH; CARP; FISCH; SCHWARZFISCH.

gebackener karpfen,. a traditional Austrian Christmas Eve dish, consisting of fillets of carp fried in egg and breadcrumbs. The head, skin, and bones are used to make a stock for carp soup which, with vegetables and the roe added, comprises another traditional Christmas dish.

karpouzi, Greek for watermelon, a favourite fruit in Greece. See PASSA TEMPO MAN. See also GLYKO.

kartofel, Russian for potatoes, which are eaten a great deal. They are often fried or boiled and served with sour cream. See also ZAPEKANKA.

kartoffel, Danish for potato.

brunede kartofler, a national dish of 2 lb. boiled potatoes drained, then sliced and fried in a mixture of 2 oz. (¼ cup) butter and 2 oz. (¼ cup) sugar heated in a frying-pan with 1 tablespoon water. It is often eaten at *Juleaften* (Christmas Eve).

stuvede kartofler, Danish creamed potatoes. A pinch of sugar is added to a white sauce, and the sliced, boiled potatoes are heated up in the sauce. The dish is garnished with parsley and butter.

kartoffel, German for potato. In south Germany a potato is called *erdapfel.*

kartoffelklösse, very light dumplings, or *klösse,* made from

karpouzi

4 oz. (1 cup) breadcrumbs, ¾ lb. (2 cups) mashed potato, 3 tablespoons butter, a pinch of nutmeg, 2 oz. grated cheese, a pinch of salt, 2 egg yolks, and 2 whole eggs, all well mixed, shaped into small egg-sized pieces and poached in boiling salted water. It is served with tomato sauce. These dumplings are also made without cheese; sometimes sugar is used instead, and the *klösse* are not boiled but rolled in beaten egg and breadcrumbs and fried. These are called gebratene kartoffelklösse, and are served with cinnamon, fruit sauce, or jam. See also ERDAPFEL; KLÖSSE; KNÖDEL; PFLÜTTEN.

kartoffelsalat, potato salad, which is eaten extensively in Germany. The best way to make it is to slice the cooked potatoes while they are still hot, and to cover them with olive oil and a little vinegar; this will be absorbed by the potatoes, and will give them a delicious flavour when cold.

Westfälische kartoffeln, a Westphalian potato dish, consisting of mashed potatoes mixed with a purée of half the quantity of cooking apples and butter. The top is sprinkled with breadcrumbs and heavily dotted with more butter, before being browned in the oven or under a grill. See also HIMMEL UND ERDE.

kartul, Estonian for potato. *Keedetud kartulid* are boiled potatoes, served with almost every meal in Estonia.

karve, Norwegian for caraway.

karvekjeks, caraway biscuits (cookies) made with 4 oz. (½ cup) beaten butter mixed with 8 oz. (2 cups) sifted flour, salt, and 1 teaspoon baking powder. Eight oz. (1 cup) sugar is added gradually; then 1 beaten egg, 2 teaspoons caraway seeds, and 2 tablespoons brandy are also included. The resulting dough is rolled out to an ⅛-inch thickness and cut into various shapes, before being dredged with icing sugar and baked for 15 minutes in a moderate oven.

karveli, a coarse brown Greek bread which is very delicious, soft and crumbly, and has the real flavour of wheat.

kascha, see KASHA.

käse, German for cheese. See ALLGÄUER BERGKÄSE (ALLGÄUER LIMBURGER, ALLGÄUER RAHMKÄSE); BACKSTEINKÄSE; FRISCHKÄSE FRÜHTÜCKSKÄSE; HARZER KÄSE; JORBKÄSE; LIPTAUER; MAINAUER KÄSE; MAINZER KÄSE; MÜNSTERKÄSE; NIEHEIMER HOPFENKÄSE; QUARK; ROMADUR KÄSE; SCHNITTKÄSE; TILSITER KÄSE; WEICHKÄSE; WEISSLACKERKÄSE; WILSTERMARSCHKÄSE. See also AUSTRIAN CHEESES; SWISS CHEESES.

käsekuchen, cheese cake. A sweet pastry case is filled with a mixture of ½ lb. (2 cups) cottage cheese or curds, 3 tablespoons sugar, 4 tablespoons chopped raisins or sultanas, 1 tablespoon nuts, 1 tablespoon flour, and a pinch of cinnamon, all well mixed together, before baking in a moderate oven for 30 minutes. Raw egg is sometimes added to the filling.

käsestrudel, see STRUDEL.

kasen, German for curds, used a lot for cooking.

kaser, a very popular Turkish semi-hard, pressed cheese made from ewe's milk. It has a pleasant taste.

käsestangen, Swiss cheese twists made from 1 lb. (4 cups) flour, 6 oz. (⅔ cup) grated cheese, 4 oz. (½ cup) butter, 4 oz. (½ cup) lard, 1 egg, and ½ pint (1 cup) milk all mixed well. The mixture is rolled out and cut into strips which are twisted together, brushed with egg, sprinkled with more cheese, caraway seeds, and salt, and then baked on a baking sheet in a hot oven (400°F) until brown.

kasha or **kascha**, Russian for boiled or cooked cereal, often buckwheat (*grechnevaya kasha*), although rice (*risovaya kasha*) or semolina (*mannya kasha*) are also used. It is a staple food-all over Russia, particularly in country districts where an old saying runs "Shchi da kasha pishcha nasha," which, roughly translated, means "We get nothing but cabbage soup and kasha." It is like the oatmeal of Scotland and Ireland, the *mămăligă* of Rumania, and the pasta and polenta of Italy. Kasha is used for both savoury and sweet dishes, as a stuffing for fish, meat, and poultry, as a garnish for soups, or served with mushrooms and onions or other vegetables, and butter or sour cream. It can also accompany cooked meats, game, or poultry.

It was always a favourite of Russian Jews and is still eaten by them, not only in Russia but all over the world. To make a kasha of something derives from a Yiddish phrase which means to make a mess or "hash" of things. In Jewish cookery kasha is sometimes made from a combination of dried beans, barley, or lentils. Kasha made from the more traditional buckwheat is used as a filling for kreplach, *knishes, pirogi*, and pirozhki, and also as a substitute for potatoes.

Kasha is eaten also in Poland with the addition of grated Parmesan cheese, eggs, and sour cream; or with the buckwheat replaced by semolina, in which case the dish is a sweet one, not unlike hasty pudding. See also KASZA.

grechnevaya kasha, made with 1 cup buckwheat flour spread out in a large frying-pan and fried until coloured slightly. It is then put in an earthenware pot with salt, a lump of butter, and water to cover. The lid is put on and it is cooked in a slow oven for 2–3 hours. It is carefully watched to see that it does not dry out, and when it is soft and the liquid has evaporated, it is ready to serve with sour cream or melted butter, or as a garnish for soup, meat, or vegetables. It can also be made into puddings with sugar, cream, or fruit.

gurievskaya kasha, a rich, sweet form of kasha eaten in Russia on festive occasions. It is made from 1 cup buckwheat flour or semolina, boiled in 1 pint (2 cups) sweetened rich milk for 10 minutes, when 2 eggs and 2 tablespoons butter are stirred in. It is put into a deep dish lined with pastry and layered with apricot jam, chopped crystallised fruits, chopped walnuts, and so on until the dish is full. It is sprinkled with breadcrumbs and baked in the oven. When cold, it is coated with icing sugar and browned with a salamander or a hot iron held close.

nachinkoy kasha, a kasha stuffing. It is prepared as grechnevaya kasha, with veal and cooked game added before serving. Sometimes mushrooms are also added. It is also used for stuffing poultry, game, or meat.

varnitchkes kasha, a popular dish with Russian and Polish Jews. It is made from 1 cup buckwheat groats browned in a heavy pan, then coated with the yolks of 2 eggs. Some recipes coat the buckwheat with the eggs first. Then 2 pints hot water are added very slowly, and the buckwheat mixture is constantly stirred until soft and cooked. Finally 2–3 oz. butter and 1 cup cooked noodle shapes are added, and the mixture is browned under a grill. It is served plain, or with meat gravy.

kashkavàl, one of the best of the Bulgarian national cheeses.

It is made from ewe's milk. There are three sizes: *balkàn*, about 4 inches thick; *semi-balkàn*, 2–3 inches thick; *field kashkavàl*, 2–2¼ inches thick and about 12 inches in diameter. It is a cylindrical cheese slightly bulging at the waist, with a smooth firm crust. The paste, amber in colour, is fairly soft and creamy. It has a distinctive and attractive milk smell and flavour, a little salty, but delicate. It takes at least sixty days, at a temperature of 58°F (15°C) to mature. It is also made in Rumania from partly skimmed ewe's milk, when it is heavily salted and weighs between 4 and 6 lb.

kasseler rippenspeer, a German way of serving smoked spareribs and loin of pork, usually roasted (though sometimes boiled) and served with the pan juices, sauerkraut, braised red cabbage or spinach, and potatoes.

kasseri, a Greek cheese made from either goat's or ewe's milk (sometimes a mixture of both), a softer version of *kefalotyri*. It is white, firm, and mild in flavour and used for grating but also eaten fresh.

kastana, Greek for chestnuts. In many Greek homes, chestnuts and potatoes are interchangeable as vegetables. The chestnut man, selling chestnuts, nuts, and roasted seeds on the street corner, is a feature of Greek life. He is called the "passo tempo" man. Chestnuts are also used in cakes and puddings.

kastana purée, a favourite dish. First 2 lb. chestnuts are cooked, skinned, puréed, and mixed with sugar to taste, then simmered in 1½ pints (3 cups) milk and vanilla, until all liquid is absorbed. The purée is then sieved, mixed with 1 glass brandy and ignited. It is topped with whipped cream and grated chocolate.

kastanie, German for chestnut.

kastanien-bisque, a creamed chestnut soup which is popular in Switzerland. Puréed, cooked chestnuts are added to thickened chicken stock, and the soup is garnished with a lump of butter.

kasza, Polish for buckwheat.

kasza gryczana sypka, a dish cooked in the same way as kasha and served with sour cream or cooked mushrooms, or anchovies and capers. See also KASHA.

kasztany, Polish for chestnuts. Chestnuts are used in Poland to stuff goose, turkey, ham, and chicken. Kasztany w cukrze is Polish for glazed chestnuts. See also ORZECHY (ORZECHY WŁOSKIE Z CUKRZE).

kataifi, a Greek pastry made by professional pastry-makers. Although kataifi pastry should not be difficult to make oneself, it often goes wrong, even in the hands of experienced cooks, so it is best left to the expert. Elaborate Greek pastries can in fact be bought, uncooked, at special pastry shops, then stuffed with various fillings and cooked at home. The bought rolls of kataifi look, but do not taste, like stuffed shredded wheat, for the pastry is made in long thin strands resembling spaghetti. Delicious sweet rolls can be made from kataifi pastry filled with walnuts, butter, sugar, and cinnamon, and covered, while still hot, with a lemon syrup. See also PHYLLO.

katalu, a Turkish vegetable dish which consists of eggplants and green peppers, both cut into cubes, quartered tomatoes, sliced green beans and okra, all simmered in oil with garlic and chopped parsley.

katsikaki, Greek for kid.

katsikaki psito, Greek roasted kid. The Greeks arrange their goat breeding so that the kids are born in spring, and when these are ready for cooking, a feast of roasted kid is held. Their method of preparing it is to rub a whole kid with lemon juice and seasoning, and to insert garlic in the skin. It is baked in olive oil, with herbs added, in a moderate oven. When the meat is almost tender, water is added to the baking pan and the kid is basted frequently. Cooking is continued until the flesh is almost dropping off the bones.

For the Greeks, the goat has been a mythological symbol since the time when its agility inspired the mountain shepherds to create Pan, embodiment of the joy of living. The goat has also been the subject of songs by ancient classical writers such as Sophocles, Euripides, and Aeschylus. In the theatre of Dionysus, dramas in honour of the god of spring, of corn, and of wine, had actors clothed in goatskins in the chorus. One day, an actor broke line and started an argument with the leader; his name was Thespis (hence ''Thespian''), and he was the first actor to speak dialogue in the Greek theatre. To this day, the spoken performance is called ''trayodia,'' meaning goatsong. The goat was also thought to be a suitable sacrifice to the gods.

Today, goat is popular in Greece not only for its flesh but also for its milk and its butter. The milk has more vitamin B and albumen content than cow's milk, and makes good cheeses. The milkman selling goat's milk is a familiar sight in Athens. The butter, too, is said to have a higher content of vitamin B. The Greeks prefer kid to mutton, which they seldom eat. See also KID; KREAS.

katzenjammer, German for a hangover, and also for a dish often eaten in Germany and Austria as a cure for hangover. It is essential to make it the night before it will be needed, because with a really bad hangover the preparation of it might prove too difficult. It is made by slicing cold beef very thinly and covering it with two parts olive oil to one part wine vinegar, a little french mustard, salt, and pepper. It is left for 2 hours. The meat is then lifted out and folded into a mayonnaise made from egg, egg yolk, vinegar, mustard, sugar, water, salt, and pepper and whisked over hot water until thick. When cool, 1 tablespoon olive oil is whisked in. Sliced gherkins and potatoes are added.

kaura, Finnish for rolled oats, which are an important part of Finnish diet. *Kaurapuuro* is Finnish for rolled oat porridge; *kaurasuurimovelli,* for rolled oat gruel.

kavalli, a Maltese dish consisting of whole mackerel baked between layers of sliced potatoes, moistened with olive oil and lemon juice.

kavkazky plov, see PLOV.

kaymak, Turkish for thick cream, like the Greek *kaïmaki.*

kèbāb, a Turkish speciality, but well known all over the Balkans and particularly in Bulgaria, Greece, and southern Russia. It consists of small pieces of meat threaded on long skewers, or sometimes on a spit, then rubbed with cinnamon, or olive oil, herbs, lemon juice, salt, and pepper, before grilling over charcoal or under a grill. It can also mean cubes of meat cooked in very little liquid. In the Balkans lamb or mutton is the meat most frequently used, but kèbābs are also made with game, liver, fish, and poultry. Pieces of liver or bacon are sometimes threaded between the pieces of meat, also bay leaves, slices of mushroom, tomato, or onion. Kèbābs are usually served with rice and wedges of lemon. See also KEBÀP; SHASHLYK.

dağ kèbābı, pieces of veal skewered with slices of onion and tomatoes, sprinkled with chopped thyme, and grilled. Garnished with sliced okra and served with *pilâv.*

döner kèbābı, a Turkish, Greek, and Balkan method of cooking long strips of lamb, cut from the rump, wound round the crossbar of a continuously turning spit (hence *döner,* ''turning''). The meat is highly seasoned with garlic, herbs, and spices. As it cooks, very thin slices are carved off vertically into a special tin pan with a handle, so that the underlayer of meat is exposed to the charcoal. Each slice is served on a mixture of finely chopped onion and parsley, and sprinkled with paprika. *Döner kèbābı* is served with rice. It is an excellent way of dealing with tough meat.

Turkish kebabı

kèbābı cacık-kebassı. The meat from a leg of mutton is cut into cubes which are marinated with onion in lemon juice, then seasoned with salt and pepper, and grilled on skewers. These kebabs are served sprinkled with sliced roasted almonds and covered with sour cream.

kirmà tàvuk kèbābı, made with chickens rubbed with cinnamon, salt, pepper, and onion juice, and cooked on a spit. They are basted with hot butter.

kuş kèbābı, as kirmà tàvuk kèbābı, using mutton.

osmaniye kèbābı, fat mutton is cut into cubes which are marinated in vinegar with chopped onions, salt, and pepper, then grilled on skewers. Sometimes the skewered cubes are stewed in very little water. This dish is served with *pilâv.*

şiş kèbābı, as osmaniye kèbābı, the mutton being rubbed with cinnamon and basted with fresh tomato sauce.

tavşan kèbābı, skewered, grilled pieces of hare, basted with a mixture of butter, garlic, and vinegar.

tencere kèbābı, cubes of fat mutton fried with chopped onions in oil until brown, then stewed in very little water with chopped parsley. For Greek kebab specialities, see also ARNI (ARNI SOUVLAKIA); DÖNER KEBAB; TAS KEBAB.

kebàp, Bulgarian for kebab.

kebàpcheta (little kebabs) are made from minced (ground) meats, mixed with onion, garlic, mint, and parsley, moist bread, eggs, and seasonings. It is formed into small balls, threaded on skewers and grilled like kebabs. See also KYUFTÈ.

kedgeree, an English dish of Indian origin, which made its appearance in England in the 18th century, during the time of the East India Company. The Indian word from which it comes is *khicharhi,* and originally the dish consisted of rice, onion, red lentils, Indian spices, fresh limes or lemons, butterfat, and fish. In the 19th century it was often seen on the sideboard at breakfast time, together with the grilled kidneys, bacon, eggs, cold ham, and other dishes for that meal. Nowadays it is not specifically a breakfast dish. It is usually made as follows: 1 lb. cooked, boiled rice; 1 large flaked, smoked haddock; 1 chopped, hard-boiled egg; 3 tablespoons butter; 2 tablespoons cream; salt; and pepper are all mixed together and heated in the oven. Sometimes a squeeze of lemon juice is added before serving.

kefalotir, the Yugoslavian version of the Greek cheese, kefalotyri.

kefalotyri, a Greek hard, very salty yellow cheese made in various parts of the country and known under several names. This particular name comes from the shape of the cheese, which is like a hat, or head (*kefalo*). It is used for grating, like Parmesan. It can be made from either ewe's or goat's milk.

keftedakia or **keftethakia,** Greek for little keftedes, very small meat balls that are served for *mezes.*

keftedes, keftethes, or **kephtethakia,** the Greek for the meat balls or rissoles that are popular throughout the Balkans, the Middle and Far East. The balls, which are about the size of a walnut, are lightly floured and fried in butter or oil. They are made from a paste of 2 lb. very well minced (ground) raw meat, 6 oz. (1½ cups) moistened breadcrumbs, 3 small minced onions (which have previously had boiling water poured over them), 2 beaten eggs, 1 tablespoon chopped parsley and mint, 1 tablespoon grated cheese, seasoning, and either *ouzo* or lemon juice to moisten. This dish is usually eaten hot. Keftedes are served throughout Greece on festive occasions and picnics. When made for home consumption, they are a little larger and are served with pilaf rice, vegetables, or salad.

keitinpiiraat, Finnish for small pasties made with rye flour pastry. The pastry is divided into pieces which are thinly rolled out and are half spread with cooked rice; then the other half is folded over the filling, and the edges are sealed down. The pasties are deep fried in fat and served hot. See also KARJALANPIIRAAT.

Kentish chicken pudding, see PUDDING.

kephalos, Greek for grey mullet, a favourite fish in Greece, often served *plaki.* See also TARAMOSALATA.

kepta veršiena, a Lithuanian method of cooking veal, a traditional dish for *Pabaigtuves* the national Harvest Festival. First 2 carrots, 1 onion, and 2 Hamburg parsley roots are grated and mixed with dry mustard until they form a paste. This is rubbed into the meat until it is absorbed; then the meat is put in a bowl, covered, and pressed down under a heavy weight for 4 to 5 days. It is then well salted and covered with bacon rashers and fat, before roasting with a little hot water. It is cooked until tender, and served with a sauce made with the pan juices, flour, and sour cream.

kermakakku, Finnish for a sour cream cake, made with 1 pint (2 cups) sour cream, ¾ lb. (1½ cups) sugar, 4 oz. (1 cup) potato flour, 6 oz. (1½ cups) wheat flour, 2 teaspoons vanilla sugar, and 1 teaspoon baking soda. The cream is whipped, and the other ingredients are added to it. The mixture is poured into a greased cake tin, sprinkled with breadcrumbs, and baked in a moderate oven for 30–40 minutes.

kermesse, aux boudins, the name given to a gathering sometimes arranged by small Belgian restaurateurs for their patrons, during which a whole meat carcase, usually lamb, pork or veal, and the various internal organs, such as liver, heart, sweetbreads, brains, are cooked and eaten. The ingenuity of the chef who decides how this feast is to be cooked, and the appreciation of the guests, both combine to make the party a success.

kernhem, a Dutch cream cheese, very strongly flavoured and of recent manufacture.

kerry or **kerrie,** Dutch for curry and curry powder, which figure quite frequently in Dutch cooking as a result of strong connections with the East Indies. See also RIJSTTAFEL.

kerryschoteltje, a Dutch curry dish for using up leftover cooked meat. First 4 onions are browned in butter, then 1 tablespoon curry powder and salt are stirred in. One lb. diced meat, 3 cups boiled rice, and 1 pint (2 cups) stock are added, and all are well mixed together and put in an ovenproof dish. The top is dotted with butter and sprinkled with breadcrumbs, and the curry is then baked in a moderate oven for about 30 minutes.

kervel, Dutch for chervil, used to make a soup with veal stock thickened with 3 egg yolks just before serving.

kesäkeitto, meaning "summer soup," a Finnish mixed vegetable soup, always prepared when the vegetables are at their peak and usually eaten on *juhannus.* It is made with milk and is served hot with a garnish of butter and chopped parsley.

ketchup, catchup, or **catsup,** a spicy sauce or condiment, which correctly, should be made from the juice of cooked fruits or vegetables such as walnut, tomato, or mushroom, with vinegar. Tomato ketchup has onions, green or red peppers, sugar, and sometimes soya added. Ketchup is used as a relish and, if homemade and used sparingly, can add piquancy to cold meat, sausages, cheese dishes, and fried fish. It is not unlike a chutney, except that it is puréed, and, in the case of mushroom ketchup, strained so that it is entirely liquid. Most ketchup today is commercially made and bottled, and the taste is synthetic. The name is thought to come from the Chinese kôe-chiap or kê-tsiap which means the brine of pickled fish, an early relish similar to the Roman *garum.*

kettle, I. A metal receptacle used for boiling water. II. A fish kettle (poacher), an oval metal receptacle with a drainer or slotted tray, on which fish is cooked in water or court bouillon. When the fish is cooked the drainer can be lifted out, leaving the fish unbroken and strained. (The expression "a pretty kettle of fish" comes from "kiddle" of fish; this was a large illegal trap set in the river to ensnare the fat trout or salmon from the lord of the manor's protected waters.) III. A word often employed in the U.S. to describe any metal pan used on top of the stove for cooking a variety of foods.

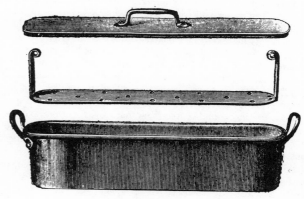

fish kettle

kettle broth, see KIDDLEY BROTH.

keule, German for leg of meat. This word is always put after the designation (for example, lammekeule, leg of lamb).

kharcho, a Russian soup from the Caucasus, made from cooked boiled brisket of beef. The fat is strained from the stock and the meat cut into pieces. Then finely chopped onion, garlic, rice, stoned cooking plums, salt, and pepper are added and cooked for 30 minutes. Finally, tomatoes are fried lightly in butter and added 5 minutes before serving. The soup is garnished with chopped parsley or dill.

khlodnik or **kholodets,** a Russian dialect word for any cold soup. See BORSCH.

khren, Russian for horseradish, often mixed with sour cream in Russia, and served with boiled meats or baked fish. See also HORSERADISH.

khvorost, literally means "twigs," "kindling," the Russian name for sweet biscuits (cookies) which are cut into strips like twigs and twisted, 2 or 3 together, before being cooked in hot oil or butter. First 1 gill (½ cup) milk is mixed well with 1 tablespoon sour cream, 3 egg yolks, 1 tablespoon sugar, a good pinch of salt, and 2 tablespoons brandy or vodka. Then 10 oz. (2½ cups) flour is gradually added to make a thick smooth dough which is rolled very thin, then cut into narrow strips about 4 inches long and 2 or 3 strips are twisted together, the ends secured by painting with egg white. After being fried until golden they are drained on paper and sprinkled with sugar and cinnamon.

kichlach, a basic traditional Jewish pastry, made from 6 oz.

(1¼ cups) flour, 2 tablespoons sugar, 3 eggs, and salt. Various spices or poppy seeds are sometimes added to the mixture, before it is dropped onto a greased sheet in spoonfuls, as drop scones, and baked.

kid, a young goat. It makes excellent eating when 3 or 4 weeks old, before it leaves the mother, but should not be eaten when more than 3 months old. In Italy it is an Easter speciality. To prepare for eating, the whole kid is stuffed with apples and garlic and the outside rubbed with olive oil and ginger; then it is roasted for 15 minutes to the lb. See also CABRA; CABRITO; CAPRETTO; KATSIKAKI; MICISHJA, LA.

kiddley broth or **kettle broth,** a traditional Cornish soup, made from bread cut into squares, a few marigold heads, a few stalks of *scifers* chopped fine, butter, pepper, and salt. The ingredients are put into a basin and boiling water is poured over them. The broth is eaten straight away.

kidney beans, see FRENCH BEANS.

kidneys, a pair of glandular organs in the abdominal cavity of mammals and reptiles. Almost all are edible and all are classed as offal (variety meats). Cock's kidneys, as they are called in culinary terms, are in fact the testicles of the cock. Calf's and lamb's kidneys are the most delicate, and are usually grilled or sautéed, although calf's kidney is delicious simmered in butter and white wine (see *rognons de veau à la liégeoise*). This kidney has a cluster shape and is very good left whole in its fat and gently baked so that the fat is brown and crisp and the inside delicately pink. This method is also excellent for lamb's kidneys, which are usually overcooked if fried or sautéed in butter. They are improved if Marsala, Madeira, sherry, or a little brandy is added to the pan juices. Lamb's kidneys should be included in a mixed grill. Pig's kidneys are larger and coarser, but make excellent pâtés and a very good braise, for the flavour of the gravy is strong and good. Ox kidney is inclined to be tough and strong-tasting, but is essential to a steak and kidney pie or pudding, for it makes delicious gravy. It is also acceptable cut up, browned in fat with onions, herbs, and stock, then braised in a slow oven. See also NIER; NIERE; NJURE; NYRE; POCHKI; ROGNON; ROGNONE.

sautéed kidneys with brandy

kiełbasa, the general Polish word for sausage. However, in the U.S. the word has come to mean a particular type of garlic sausage, mild in flavour, and sold in rings. It is also known as Polish sausage. There are many varieties of Polish sausage, some resembling frankfurters and known as knockwurst. The most esteemed are those smoked over juniper wood. Some sausages take the name of the place in which they originated, such as kiełbasa krakowska (Cracow) and kiełbasa tuchówska

(Tuchów). Kiełbasa szynkowa is made from ham. Kiełbasa wiankowa, or ring sausage, is called after its shape. All can be eaten cold or simmered in stock or beer and served with red cabbage. See also RZEPA; SOSISKI.

kılıç şiş, Turkish for fish cooked on a spit.

kilki, the Russian name for a Norwegian variety of anchovy, which is eaten mostly as an hors d'oeuvre and is much appreciated in Russia. Tallin, Estonia, is the chief processing centre.

kilki krutiya yaytsa, a dish of small smoked kilki, served on a thin slice of hard-boiled egg and rye bread. It is often served for *zakuski*.

kima, Greek for minced meat used for making a sauce, generally for pasta.

kingdom of Fife pie, a traditional Scottish dish consisting of a rabbit and pickled pork, with grated nutmeg, forcemeat balls made from the liver, breadcrumbs, egg, herbs, and white wine; all covered with puff pastry.

kingfish (*Scomberomorus*), a large sea fish of which there are many different species found all over the world. In the U.S., the name refers to the fish of the *Menticirrhus* family. Kingfish is good to eat, the flesh being firm and white, and it is prepared like tunny (tuna) fish.

king's acre berry, see HYBRID BERRIES.

kip, Dutch for fowl or hen. See also KUIKEN.

gebraden kip, Dutch for roast chicken. Boiling water is poured over and inside the bird, after which the inside is salted and butter is inserted. The bird is then lightly browned all over in butter, over a strong heat. The heat is reduced, the pan half covered, and cooking continued until the bird is tender (about 20 minutes for a young chicken). The liver is added during the last 5 minutes, and the bird is served with potatoes, young peas, and a compote of fruit. A good bouillon is made from the neck, giblets, and underpart of the legs, with a pinch of mace, salt, and water.

kipfelschmarrn, see SCHMARRN.

kipfler, a Dutch potato, yellow and waxy, which is the best variety for frying or making into chips. It is also good for *pommes de terre Anna*.

kipper, a name which usually refers to a split herring, mildly salted and smoked. The best kippers are a pale copper colour; the very dark ones are sometimes dyed, and have not been gently smoked over oak chips, as they are on Lochfyneside, Scotland, and also in Peel, the Isle of Man. In Scotland they are grilled and served with baps or oatcakes. They are now served also in France, Germany, and the U.S., usually grilled, with pepper and a pat of butter added before serving. They can also be soaked in lemon juice overnight, then sliced and eaten raw, like a coarse smoked salmon.

In Scotland, salmon is also kippered. It is filleted, salted for 24 hours, then drained and left to drip for 6 hours. When dry, it is rubbed with olive oil and left for a further 5 or 6 hours; then it is drained and rubbed with a cloth soaked in rum or whisky, before being covered with demerara (brown) sugar and left for 24 hours. The sugar is then wiped off and the olive oil process repeated. After this, the olive oil is wiped off completely with the spirit-soaked cloth and the fish is ready for smoking. The fire is made from peat, oak chips, and oak sawdust, and is lit at about 6 P.M. on two successive evenings. During the day, when the fire has gone out, the fish should be left hanging in the kiln. After two firings the fish is ready to eat. Trout may be treated in the same way.

kirchweih or **kirtag,** "church day," a Bavarian festival which is held on the third Sunday and Monday in October. It is to celebrate the weih, the inauguration of churches in town and country. The great feast begins after mass, when large numbers of doughnuts (kirchweihkrapfen), fritters, and noo-

grilled kipper on toast

dles (kirchweihnudeln) are eaten, and roast goose and red cabbage is served. Schnaps and beer are plentiful, and the day ends with the *kirtagtanz,* a ball consisting of traditional dances accompanied by musicians playing zithers, guitars, and accordions. It is usually held in a hall or barn decorated with lanterns and garlands.

kirkeen, see CARPETSHELL.

kirxa bil-haxix, a Maltese hot pot made with tripe and vegetables.

kisel, a Russian and Baltic dessert made from 1 pint (2 cups) red fruit juice and 4 oz. (½ cup) sugar. It is thickened with 2 tablespoons corn flour (cornstarch) or arrowroot. It can also be flavoured with wine, and is served cold. The word derives from the common Slavonic word *kisly,* "sharp, sour."

kisela dahorp, see DAHORP.

kisela riblja čorba, a traditional Yugoslavian fish soup. Huck, a local fish, is cut up into small pieces, salted, and allowed to stand. Sliced onions and green peppers are simmered in oil or lard; water and seasoning are added to double the volume of vegetables and boiled for 20 minutes. The fish is poached in this stock and, when cooked, is carefully removed. After straining, 2 egg yolks and 2 tablespoons cream are added for 2 pints stock. The soup is garnished with boiled rice and the pieces of huck. See also RIBA.

kiseló mlyàko, see PODKVÀSA.

kishmish, Armenian for dried fruits (although nowadays, in colloquial Russian, it means a "hash" or a mix-up). It also describes a particular preparation of dried fruits. A variety of them, such as apricots, prunes, figs, sultanas, and apples, are soaked overnight in water. Next day the water is strained off and boiled with sugar, lemon peel, cinnamon, nutmeg, and allspice, until it is slightly syrupy. The soaked fruit is then put in and cooked until soft.

kisiel, a traditional Polish cold dessert, a "fruit cream" made from tart berries cooked with sugar and water, thickened with potato flour. A vanilla pod or unsweetened chocolate, heated in milk or thin cream, is sometimes substituted for the fruit. The vanilla is removed before the mixture is turned into a mould.

kisielius, a Lithuanian porridge-like gruel made from oatmeal which has fermented. It is often served with stewed fruit at Christmas time.

kitchen, the room or area containing the cooking facilities, also denoting the general area where food is prepared.

kıymalı börek, a Turkish pancake filled with chopped meat or mushrooms, rolled like a cigar and fried in shallow fat or oil. It is also popular in Russia.

kızartma, a kind of Turkish meat stew, made with 2 lb. meat which is parboiled, then rubbed with fresh curds and browned in butter, with onions and seasoning. It is usually served at

A 16th-century Italian kitchen and its 20th-century counterpart in Belgium.

weddings or festivals. Mutton is the most usual meat, and sometimes tomatoes are added.

kizil, Russian for cornelian cherry, a fruit used a great deal in Russia for making sauces which are served with chicken dishes and shashlyk. See also KISEL.

varenye iz kizila, jam made from cornelian cherries, eaten for tea as well as with desserts.

kjeks, Norwegian for biscuit (cookies), also known as *småkaker.* The Norwegian housewife makes a variety of biscuits at Christmas, which are stored and offered, together with a cup of coffee or a glass of wine, to guests who call between meals. See also BERLINER KRANSER; FATTIGMANN; KARVE (KARVEKJEKS); SJOKOLADE, KNASK.

kjot, Icelandic for meat.

kjotsupa, a traditional Icelandic meat stew with rice and turnips. Lamb, often the saddle, is usually used.

kjøtt, Norwegian for meat: beef, lamb, mutton, and veal are all eaten in Norway; pork is especially popular at Christmas time. Smoked meats are as popular in Norway as is smoked fish. Every autumn mutton is smoked for consumption during the succeeding summer, when it is sliced and fried with egg or boiled with young vegetables. Meat salads and meat in aspic are also popular in the summer, while meat cakes are eaten throughout the country all the year round. See also BIFF; FÅR; FENALÅR; KALVEKJØTT; LAMMEKJOTT; OKSE; SVINEKJØTT.

kjøttboller, meat balls. Norwegian housewives often can these balls for future use as fried meat cakes or stuffing for cabbage, etc. Minced steak is lightly floured and shaped into balls which are simmered for about 5 minutes in salted water or beef stock before being canned.

kjøttfarse, Norwegian meat stuffing. Minced steak is much used in Norway as a stuffing for vegetables, etc.

kjøttgelé, Norwegian for meat jelly, an ingredient often used in Norwegian cookery, particularly in the preparation of some kinds of smørbrød.

kjøttkaker, meat cakes made from 4 oz. shredded suet and 1½ lb. round steak are minced (ground) together; 2 teaspoons flour and seasoning are added. Then about 3 tablespoons cold water are worked gradually into the mixture, and it is shaped into flat cakes and fried in butter. Onions are also fried in butter and piled on the cakes before they are served. Sometimes spices are incorporated in the seasoning. Kjøttkaker are often served with cranberries, apples, and pears cooked with sugar and water. See also MEDISTERKAKER.

kjøttpudding, meat pudding. First 1 lb. chuck steak is minced (ground) several times before being mixed with salt and 2 tablespoons of either corn flour (cornstarch) or potato flour, and is then minced (ground) once again. Then 1 pint (2 cups) cold milk which has been boiled is gradually stirred in, and the whole is well beaten, after which 2 oz. shredded suet are stirred in. The pudding is steamed in a pudding basin for 1 hour, and served with white sauce, with chopped celery added.

kjøttsalat, meat salad. Small squares of lean, cooked beef or veal are mixed with a few gherkins and a stiff mayonnaise. This salad is garnished with tomatoes and lettuce.

kjøttsaus, meat gravy; see SAUS.

kléber, I. A French beef consommé garnished with green peas, diced celeriac, tiny goose liver quenelles, and chopped chervil. See also CONSOMMÉ. II. A French garnish consisting of artichoke hearts stuffed with goose liver purée and truffle sauce. It is served with tournedos and noisettes.

kleik, Polish for gruel, made with barley and bouillon.

klejner, Danish for pastry crullers. First 3 eggs, 6 oz. (⅔ cup) castor sugar, grated peel of 1 lemon, and 6 oz. (⅔ cup) butter are well beaten together. Then 1 lb. (4 cups) flour and 3 tablespoons cream are stirred in. The resulting dough is chilled before being rolled out thinly and cut slantwise into long narrow strips. A slit is cut in the centre of each, through which the thinner end is drawn to form a knot at the centre. The crullers are deep-fried (care being taken that they do not touch one another) in fat or oil until golden and, when drained, are sprinkled with castor sugar.

klephtes, a traditional method of cooking in Greece. It came into being during the 200-year occupation of that country by the Turks, when a Greek guerrilla named Klepht (literally "thief") managed, with a few followers, to maintain independence in the mountains. The outlawed bands were confronted with the possibility that while cooking their food, the aroma of it might be the means of revealing their position to the enemy. To lessen this danger, the food was cooked in a paper wrapping. It was in fact an earlier version of the French method en papillote. Herbs and oil are rubbed over the meat before enclosing it in parchment. Another version of klephtes cooking was to place meat, game, vegetables, and herbs in a covered earthenware pot called a *stamna*. This was laid on its side in a little pit dug at the edge of a bank of earth, and covered. Another small pit was dug underneath the *stamna*, and a fire was made of wood or charcoal. The slow, even heat

produced excellent results. The method is similar to that used in the American beach barbecue or clambake. However, today in towns and cities all over Greece, klephtes cooking means baking with oil, lemon juice, and herbs in greased paper or parchment in a moderate oven.

kletski, the general Russian term for dumplings or quenelles. A typical recipe is for 8 oz. (2 cups) flour mixed with 3 oz. (½ cup) creamed butter and 4 egg yolks, 2 small lightly fried onions, 2 slices chopped ham, and 3 tablespoons breadcrumbs with the stiffly beaten egg whites added last. The mixture is shaped into small balls which are poached in salted water. Sour cream is served separately. Kletski are also made with semolina, like the Italian gnocchi. One cup semolina or oatmeal flour is mixed with salt, 1½ pints (3 cups) water, and 4 tablespoons butter and are boiled and stirred together for 10 minutes. When cool, 5 eggs are beaten in one by one. Small spoonfuls of the mixture are then poached in boiling salted water, drained, and served with melted butter or sour cream. See also DUMPLINGS.

klevera, a Czechoslovakian sweet sauce made from minced plums. They are cooked rapidly in very little water. Sugar is added, and then the plums are boiled up again. The fruit is removed from the heat, rum is stirred in, and the klevera are potted and covered. The sauce is poured over fruit dumplings (*knedlíky*) and spread on pancakes and doughnuts, as well as used as an accompaniment for puddings.

klimp, Swedish for dumplings, served in Sweden in clear soups. A chopped cabbage leaf is mixed with chopped root vegetables, diced peas, beans, and seasonings. All are cooked in butter until tender, when thick, grated Parmesan cheese is stirred in. Small French roll crusts, with the inside bread removed, are stuffed with this mixture. Some more cheese (Parmesan or Gruyère) is sprinkled on top, and the dumplings heated for a few moments in the oven before the hot soup is poured over them.

klip or *klipfish*, cod which has undergone a special salting and smoking process which is peculiar to Norway. It is first cut up, then salted and smoked in the open air. It is prepared and cooked like salt cod, and served with melted butter or parsley butter.

klipfisk, Danish salted and smoked cod, like the Norwegian *klip*.

klipfiskebudding, Danish salt fish pudding usually made with cod. For this dish 1 lb. salt fish is soaked, skin side uppermost, for 12 hours in milk, after which it is skinned, filleted, and flaked. Then 1 pint (2 cups) white sauce is made and the fish blended in. After the mixture has cooled slightly, 5 beaten egg yolks, seasoning, and a pinch of mace are mixed in. Lastly, the 5 stiffly beaten egg whites are folded in. The whole is steamed gently for about 2½ hours, when it should be firm. It is served with sauce hollandaise or mushroom sauce. See also FISK (FISKEBUDDING).

klobase, the Slovene word for sausage.

kranjske klobase, a pork sausage made in the Kranj district of Slovenia. It is often served with sauerkraut.

klops czyli zając falszywy, a Polish meat loaf called "false hare." It is made with 2 lb. minced steak, ½ lb. fat pork, 4 crustless slices of bread soaked in milk, ½ onion, 4 bacon rashers, and 2 raw eggs all mixed together, rolled in flour, and browned quickly in butter. The loaf is then baked with a cup of stock or bouillon for 1 hour. Ten minutes before it is ready, 1 cup sour cream mixed with a small spoonful of flour is added to the gravy. Sometimes sliced hard-boiled eggs are put inside the meat loaf before it is cooked.

klösse, the German word for very light dumplings. Klösse is really the generic term for them, but in some parts of Germany they are called *knödel*, and the two words are interchangeable. See also BAUERNKLÖSSE; BAYRISCHE GRIES-KLÖSSE; BUNTER HANS; KARTOFFEL (KARTOFFELKLÖSSE); KNÖDEL; KÖNIGSBERGER KLOPSE; MARK; NOCKERLN; REIS (REISKLÖSSE).

kluseczki z wątróbki, a Polish dish made from a whole minced calf's liver mixed with 2 tablespoons breadcrumbs, onion (fried until golden) a pinch of nutmeg, and 2 eggs. The mixture is shaped into small patties or croquettes, rolled in flour, and poached in boiling salted water. When these rise to the top, they are allowed to cook in the steam for a few minutes. They are drained and served with drawn-butter sauce and minced fried onion.

kluski, Polish for very light dumplings or noodle strips, generally used for garnishing soups. About 1 tablespoon butter is mixed with 2 egg yolks, and then about 1 heaped tablespoon flour is sprinkled in and lightly stirred. Teaspoonsful of the mixture are dropped into boiling soup a few minutes before serving. See also DUMPLINGS.

kluski francuski, kluski made like small quenelles, from eggs, butter, and flour, and used as a garnish in soup.

kluski krajane ze serowym, noodles cooked and served with cheese.

kluski z makiem, a Polish traditional noodle dish eaten on Christmas Eve (*Wigilia*). Boiled noodles are baked with scalded and pounded poppy seeds and butter.

klyukva v sakhare, Russian for cranberries coated with beaten egg white and icing sugar, and put in a very slow oven until the sugar has set.

knäckebröd, Swedish for crispbread, made from ¼ lb. each of rye flour and rye meal. The rye flour is sifted together with the coarse rye meal, 1 tablespoon sugar, and 1 teaspoon salt; about ¼ pint (½ cup) milk is then added to make a dough. The dough is rolled out thinly and shaped into small rounds. The centre of each round is removed, pricked, and then baked for about 10 minutes in a slow oven. The outer circles are baked on a baking tin (cookie sheet) for about 20 minutes; they are often stored by being slung on a pole near the ceiling of the kitchen.

knackwürste or *knockwürste,* German sausages made from 5 parts lean pork, 3 parts lean beef, and 2 parts fresh pork fat, seasoned with garlic, cumin seeds, salt, and saltpetre. They are tied in pairs, dried for 4 days, then smoked. They are served after being poached for 10 minutes in water. See also WÜRST.

knaidlach, a traditional small Jewish dumpling, made from a mixture of 2 egg yolks, ½ cup matzo meal, and salt, to which the 2 stiffly beaten egg whites are added. The mixture is made into small balls which are poached in boiling clear soup. Many fillings are put into these dumplings, from minced liver and herbs, to nuts with ginger or cinnamon. Sometimes cold mashed potatoes are used instead of matzo meal, and often a mixture of both. The stuffed knaidlach are called knaidlach mit neshomes, "dumplings with souls." See also DUMPLINGS; KNAIDLE; PRUNE JAM KNAIDLACH.

knaidle, a large Jewish dumpling made from 4 oz. (1 cup) flour, 2 oz. (½ cup) suet or vegetable shortening, ½ teaspoon baking powder, salt, herbs, and 3 tablespoons cold water. It is often added to *cholent* in the centre of the pot, for overnight cooking. See also DUMPLINGS; KNAIDLACH.

knaidle mit neshomes, literally "dumplings with souls," a traditional Passover recipe. The dumplings are stuffed with either chopped liver, *greben,* or sometimes simply with matzo meal mixed with egg and hot fat.

knaost, see PULTOST.

kneading, an important part of bread making. When the flour, yeast, and liquid have been mixed to a dough, the dough must then be kneaded on a flat surface. This is done by bringing the edge of the dough to the centre, and then pushing it outwards with the knuckles of the folded hand. This must be done at least a dozen times, for it develops the gluten which makes the bread good. Many electric mixers have a bread hook attachment which enables the kneading to be performed mechanically.

knedle, Polish for dumpling. Sweet dumplings are often made in Poland, with a prune or apricot or other fruit wrapped in the dough before cooking in boiling water. These dumplings are served with sugar and melted butter. See also DUMPLINGS.

knedlíky, the name in Czechoslovakia for dumplings, which are also popular in adjoining countries. They are used not only in soups, but also as an accompaniment for roasts, stews, and fish dishes. Fruit knedlíky can be eaten as a sweet and are also served with game. They are generally made with 4 oz. breadcrumbs (though potato or semolina may also be used), 8 oz. (2 cups) flour, 2 tablespoons melted butter, and 2 separated eggs (the stiff whites being added last), formed into small balls which are poached in boiling water or stock. Sometimes a small quantity of crumbled crisp-fried bread is added to the knedlíky dough. See also DUMPLINGS.

játrové knedlíky, as knedlíky, but with the addition of a little minced liver to the dough.

ovocné knedliky vařené are fruit dumplings made with 2 oz. each butter and sugar creamed together and mixed with 2 eggs, 1 lb. (2 cups) cottage cheese, and ¾ lb. (3 cups) flour, all beaten well and moistened with about 6 tablespoons milk. The dough is rolled out and cut into squares. A stoned plum or apricot, or some chopped apple, is placed in the centre of each, then the sides of the square are folded over, the corners pinched together, and the dumplings are rolled into balls which are then poached in a large quantity of boiling salted water for about 10 minutes, or until they float to the top and stay there for several minutes. These dumplings can be served as a sweet course with melted butter, sugar, and cinnamon or poppy seeds.

švestkové knedliky, the knedlíky dough is made, rolled out, and cut into squares. On each square is placed a stoned plum (the national fruit), sugar, and cinnamon; the edges are moistened to make them stick, and the squares folded over and sealed up before poaching. Afterwards they are sprinkled with sugar. Apricots or apples can also be used.

knelki, Polish for quenelles.

knelki z cielęciny lub drobiu, tiny quenelles made with minced veal or chicken, used as a garnish for soups on festive occasions or for a meat ragoût.

knelki z ryb, fish quenelles.

knishes, a traditional Jewish dish rather like an Irish potato cake, made from 1 cup mashed potato mixed with an egg, 1 tablespoon schmaltz, salt, and enough flour to make a stiff dough, which is cut into rounds which are baked until browned. This is the basic recipe, but various fillings are popular, such as chopped, leftover meat, chicken, liver, cheese, or hard-boiled eggs, each mixed with a raw egg; a hollow is made in the middle of the round to hold the filling. *Greben* and *kasha* are also used as fillings. A sweet version of knishes is made with chopped nuts, raisins, cinnamon, or nutmeg, grated lemon peel, and grated cheese to which an egg is added, all well mixed. The top is brushed with melted butter and sprinkled with more cinnamon, sugar, and chopped nuts before being baked.

knoblauch, German for garlic.

knoblauchwurst, a German wurst made from a mixture of minced beef and pork, with large pieces of fat and garlic in it.

knobs or *knobbards,* small marine molluscs similar to whelks. They are mentioned in Shakespeare's *Henry V.*

knockwurst, see KNACKWÜRSTE.

knödel, very light German dumplings, also called *klösse*. These are immensely popular in Germany and Austria, and there are many varieties. They are made with flour, sometimes with breadcrumbs, potato, semolina addes, and eggs and butter. They can be sweet or savoury, and are often filled with minced meat or liver. See also DUMPLINGS; KLÖSSE; TOPFEN (TOPFENKNÖDEL).

knödel stuffed with apricots

broeselknödel, dumplings made from 4 oz. breadcrumbs, 2 tablespoons butter, a pinch of nutmeg, 1 egg, salt, and 2 teaspoons flour. The dough is shaped into tiny rounds which are poached in boiling salted water or stock.

fleischknödel, dumplings made in the same way as *broeselknödel*, but filled with meat.

griessknödel, dumplings made with 3 oz. semolina, 1 pint (2 cups) milk and water mixed, 1 tablespoon butter, and a pinch of salt, all heated together. Finally, 2 eggs are stirred in.

semmelknödel, dumplings made with stale rolls. To prepare them 8 oz. stale crumbs, soaked in water and squeezed out, is mixed with 3 egg yolks, salt, 1 oz. melted butter, 1 oz. flour, and, finally, 3 egg whites.

serviettenknödel, one large dumpling made from 2 oz. (2 tablespoons) semolina, ½ lb. cream cheese, 1½ oz. (2 tablespoons) butter, 2 eggs, a pinch of salt and of sugar. The eggs are separated and the yolks creamed with the butter, salt, sugar, and semolina. The stiffly beaten whites are mixed, with the cream cheese, into the above mixture. The whole is put into a damp table napkin and boiled for 30 minutes. It is served with either meat or, when sprinkled with sugar and melted butter, stewed fruit.

speckknödel, dumplings made with stale rolls (*semmelknödel*) but with the addition of bacon.

zwetschkenknödel, small dumplings made with 1 lb. boiled, mashed potatoes, 1 tablespoon melted butter, 2 eggs, and 2 tablespoons flour. This mixture is wrapped round small, blue plums which have a lump of sugar in place of the stone. The dumplings are poached in boiling water, then tossed in butter, and sprinkled with sugar.

knöderl, a smaller version of the German *knödel*, used mainly in soups.

knot or **knott** (*Calidris canutus*), a European sandpiper, which breeds in the Arctic in the spring and migrates to the British Isles later in the year. Knot is larger than snipe but has shorter legs. It can be prepared and cooked in the same way as snipe.

knuckle, the projection of carsal or tarsal joints on quadruped mammals; those of sheep and calves are particularly known for their succulence and gelatinous quality. The knuckle contains a small fleshy muscle much appreciated by connoisseurs. The French cut, *jarret de veau*, usually includes the knuckle as does the famous Italian dish of *ossi buchi*. Knuckle of veal is also highly thought of for soups and stews.

knysz, a Polish and Russian kasha cake or strudel consisting of very thin strudel dough on which is placed a mixture of 2 cups cooked buckwheat groats, 2 tablespoons chopped bacon, and 1 small onion. The whole is then baked and served with a mushroom sauce.

köche, a German culinary term, usually denoting light, steamed or baked puddings. It comes from the verb kochen, to cook. These puddings can be sweet or savoury; in the latter case they are often made with parsnips or potato, but are nevertheless served with a fruit sauce. They are always cooked in a basin or mould. See also WIENER KOCH.

kød, Danish for meat. The quality of meat in Denmark is high, and a lot of care goes into its preparation for cooking. Fat or dripping is seldom used for basting: the meat is first browned in butter, and a little boiling water or wine is used as a baste. Joints are generally brought to the table already carved, and always garnished. The gravy is often made with cream. See also FLÆSKE; KALVEKØD; SKINKE; SORT GRYDE; SVINEKØD.

kødboller, Danish for small meat balls. Equal quantities of lean pork and beef are well minced and mixed with flour (2 tablespoons to 1 lb. meat) and seasoning. A combination of 1 egg yolk and ¼ pint (½ cup) milk is then stirred in, and the mixture shaped into small balls which are cooked in boiling salted water until they float to the surface. They are used to garnish clear soup.

Another Danish recipe for meat balls uses minced beef and shredded beef fat. These are well mixed with flour and egg before adding, gradually, a combination of milk and water. Before shaping, salt and grated onion are included. These balls are put into water which is just off the boil, and simmered gently. When cooked, they are placed in cold water to prevent them sticking together. See also FRIKADELLER.

koekjes, Dutch for the sweet cakes or biscuits usually served at the traditional mid-morning coffee break. The word cookie is thought to come from koekjes.

köfte, Turkish meat balls. A mixture is made of 2 lb. raw chopped mutton, 4 slices crustless bread which have been soaked in milk or water, 2 eggs, and 2 crushed garlic cloves, with cinnamon and salt added. It is moulded into small sausage shapes which are fried in mutton suet. These meat balls are also eaten in India, where curry spices are added to the ingredients, and various types of meat ball are a staple item of diet in most Balkan countries. See also BURGONYA, KÖFTESI; IZMIR KÖFTESI; KEFTEDES; KYUFTÈ.

ekşili köfte, chopped raw beef mixed with bread which has been soaked in water, beaten eggs, chopped parsley, and seasoning of salt and pepper, as described for köfte. The mixture is formed into balls which are cooked in a sauce made with chopped onions simmered in butter, tomato purée, and water. Before serving, crushed garlic, cinnamon, and a little vinegar are added to the sauce.

terbiyeli köfte. Ground beef is mixed with soaked bread, salt, and pepper, and the mixture is shaped into flat cakes which are first fried in butter and then simmered in stock. A sauce is made of 2 tablespoons flour mixed with a little cold water, to which are added 2 egg yolks, 2 tablespoons lemon juice, salt, and paprika. The sauce is served poured over the köfte.

kohl, German for cabbage, the vegetable used more than any other in Germany. White cabbage is served in many ways, usually chopped and cooked lightly in salted water, then put into a sauce of sour cream. The sauce can be flavoured with caraway seeds, nutmeg, onion, or a variety of chopped herbs. In Bavaria, chopped lean bacon is added to the cabbage during cooking, and in Swabia cabbage is baked with chopped onions, beaten eggs, diced, fried bacon, and seasoning. Pickled white cabbage is known as sauerkraut, and in certain parts of Germany is served with almost all meats and game. Red cabbage is popular as an accompaniment to game. See also BAYRISCHES KRAUT; ROTKOHL.

gefüllte kohlwürstchen, an Austrian dish comprising cabbage leaves stuffed with minced (ground) cold meat, herbs, onion, and egg. The leaves, with the stuffing included, are rolled up, covered with white wine, and simmered in a saucepan lined with bacon rashers.

kohlrabi (*Brassica oleracea;* var. *caulocarpa*), a hybrid of the cabbage family, mostly grown for its swollen base stem, which has a delicate nutty flavour. It is essential that it be grown quickly in good ground, to prevent its becoming woody and flavourless. As the distinctive flavour is in and around the skin, the vegetable is best steamed or boiled before being peeled or pared. It can be prepared in any of the ways that are suitable for turnip, or, when cooked and cold, it can be cut in thin slices and served with an oil and vinegar dressing or mayonnaise, like celeriac. The young, sprouting green leaves can be cooked in the same way as spinach. It is very popular in Germany and Austria where it has the same name, and in Bavaria it is boiled, sieved, then mixed with sauce béchamel flavoured with nutmeg. In Vienna it is diced, parboiled, simmered in butter with a pinch of sugar, sprinkled with flour, and finished in stock. In Hungary it is cooked in paprika sauce, and in Russia in sour cream, then served with slices of smoked sausage. See also KALAREPKA.

kohlrabi

kokilki z ryb, a Polish dish called ''leftover fish shells,'' made from leftover cooked fish mixed with sautéed mushrooms. Scallop shells are filled with this mixture, which is topped with sauce béchamel and grated parmesan cheese, and baked.

kokkelipiimä, a clotted, thicker variety of *viilipiimä*, which is put in a very cool oven until it coagulates and the curds separate from the whey. When it has cooled, the whey is poured off and the clotted *piimä* is mixed with buttermilk and served as a drink or with porridge. See also VIILIPIIMÄ.

kokkina avga, Greek for scarlet Easter eggs. The eggs are either painted or dyed with harmless vegetable dye. There are several traditional Greek Easter recipes, one of which is *lambropsomo*, a special bread. See also CHERVÈNI YAYTSÀ; MAYIERITSA.

kokorétsi, a spiced Greek sausage, tasting rather like salami. It is made from the offal (variety meat) of lamb coarsely chopped and skewered, with the lamb intestines wound round

the outside. It is highly seasoned, and flavoured with marjoram. This sausage, which is long and fairly thick, is grilled slowly on a spit for several hours, while being basted with olive oil and lemon juice. It is sometimes cut into slices and served for *mezes*.

kokòshka, Bulgarian for chicken.

kokòshka sǔs domàti, chicken sautéed in oil, seasoned, then roasted with 2 lb. fresh, skinned tomatoes. It is served with boiled potatoes or rice.

kokoška, a Serbo-Croat word for hen or poularde. Chicken in Yugoslavia is often jointed, parboiled in water which is thickened with 4 eggs mixed with 2 tablespoons flour, blended with 2 pints (4 cups) sour milk, 1 tablespoon oil, and ½ pint (1 cup) chicken stock, and flavoured with garlic and paprika.

kokospudding, Swedish coconut pudding. To prepare, 2 tablespoons corn flour (cornstarch) are creamed with a little salt and milk, then stirred into 1 pint (2 cups) boiling milk to which 2 tablespoons sugar and 2 oz. desiccated coconut are added. Two beaten egg yolks are stirred into this mixture, and the whole is cooked for a few minutes until it has thickened (it should not boil). Jam is spread in a buttered baking dish, and the mixture poured over and baked in a slow oven until set. A meringue is then made, consisting of 2 beaten egg whites, 1 tablespoon castor sugar, and vanilla essence, all well mixed, and the pudding is topped with this mixture before being returned to the oven for about 15 minutes. It is served either hot or cold.

koláč, a Czechoslovak cake which can take many forms. It can be made with yeast, and can have dried fruits, cottage cheese, or lemon incorporated in the sweet yeast dough.

domažlický koláč, a cake made from a dough consisting of 1 oz. yeast mixed with a pinch of sugar, 2 tablespoons flour, and 4 tablespoons of milk to sponge; then 3 tablespoons sugar, grated peel of 1 lemon, ½ cup melted butter, 14 oz. (3¼ cups) flour, 2 egg yolks, and salt are beaten in. The mixture is left to prove for 1½ hours, then shaped into rounds which are filled with a fruit or a cheese mixture, according to taste, and baked for 40 minutes.

makový koláč, a poppy seed cake made like a sandwich, from ½ lb. (1 cup) sugar creamed with 2 oz. (¼ cup) butter, then 6 egg yolks added, together with ¾ cup powdered poppy seeds, grated peel of 1 lemon, a pinch of clove and cinnamon, ½ cup sultanas, 4 oz. (1 cup) flour, and finally the stiffly beaten egg whites. The two layers are filled with jam and sandwiched together.

kolbasa, Russian for sausage, of which there are many varieties in Russia. Kolbasa Ukrainskaya is Ukrainian sausage, which is thick and about 4 feet long.

kolbász, Hungarian for sausage, of which there are many varieties in Hungary, both smoked and fresh. They are often served as *hideg tlöételek*.

kolbászos rántotta, a Hungarian dish of scrambled eggs with sausages. Smoked sausages, a little green bacon, and a green pimento are cut into small pieces, seasoned with salt and pepper, and fried in butter. Then 6 eggs are beaten in a bowl and the fried ingredients are added to these. The mixture is poured into a buttered pan and stirred constantly until set. It is a dish which must be eaten at once.

koldtbord, the Danish and Norwegian ''cold table,'' which includes the hors d'oeuvre and open sandwiches popular in all Scandinavian countries. An entire meal could easily be made from the koldtbord, which can include hams, turkey, fish, etc. See also SMØRGÅSBORD.

koldūnai, Lithuanian dumplings with a meat filling; they are boiled in meat stock. A traditional dish at *Pabaigtuves*. See also DUMPLINGS.

lietuviški koldūnai, a Lithuanian form of ravioli, also popular in Poland. The squares of dough are filled with a minced mixture of good beef, lamb, bone marrow, onion, and herbs. Another square is put on top and the edges damped and pressed down, before the ravioli is poached in boiling salted water. Cooked dried mushrooms and beef is an alternative filling.

kolja, Swedish for haddock. As well as fresh haddock, smoked and dried haddock is popular in Sweden. See also FISK; RØKTFISKPUDDING.

kolokassi, Greek for sweet potatoes, boiled or baked in their skins and served with butter. They are a popular dish in Cyprus.

kolokithakia, Greek for vegetable marrow (summer squash). See also LAHANIKA.

kolokithakia yahni, cubed vegetable marrow (squash), onions, tomatoes, and parsley, lightly fried in olive oil. A little water is added and the ingredients simmered gently until soft but not too mushy. It is sprinkled with grated cheese before serving.

kolokithokeftedes, Greek marrow (squash) fritters. About 2 medium halved marrows and a chopped onion are cooked in boiling salted water. They are then drained well and mashed with salt, grated cheese, breadcrumbs, melted butter, and 2 eggs. This mixture is left standing for 1 hour, then small flat cakes are formed and fried in equal parts of butter and oil until brown.

kolokithopita, a Greco-American recipe comprising vegetable marrow (summer squash), tomatoes, and onions, all sliced, to which are added breadcrumbs, parsley, dill, and seasoning. The sliced vegetables and a sprinkling of breadcrumbs are all placed separately in layers in a dish, ending with tomatoes, and a little olive oil is poured over them before they are baked for about 1 hour.

kolozsvári káposzta, a Hungarian method of preparing pork and sauerkraut. An onion is fried in a little butter until golden brown, when a quartered tomato, paprika, and about 1 lb. diced lean pork are included, a little water added, and the ingredients simmered until tender. The sauerkraut, which has been washed and drained, and chopped pieces of bacon are placed in a little hot butter in a separate pan for a few minutes. Water is then added and the contents simmered until the bacon is cooked. The meat is removed from the first pan and laid, with the sauerkraut and some previously cooked rice, in alternate layers in a baking dish. The sauce from the meat is thickened with flour and sour milk and poured over. The dish is then cooked in the oven for about 30 minutes.

kolyva, a traditional dish from Ancient Greece. Nowadays, it is eaten by families belonging to the Eastern Orthodox Church 40 days after a death and on the first and fourth anniversaries of a death. The ingredients, 2 lb. wheat boiled with 1 cup dried fruit and garnished with pomegranate seeds, have a symbolic meaning: wheat represents everlasting life, fruit represents joy and sweetness, and pomegranate seeds represent plenty. See also PANSPERIMA.

komkommer, Dutch for cucumber.

gevulde komkommer, cucumber stuffed with beef or veal. A large cucumber is peeled, and sliced lengthwise into halves and then crosswise into three pieces. The pulp is removed and the pieces parboiled in water for about 8 minutes, then they are drained and stuffed with a mixture of white bread (previously soaked in milk), ground meat, grated onion, nutmeg, and seasoning. Liquid made from stock or a bouillon cube is poured over them, and the dish sprinkled with breadcrumbs and grated cheese. It is baked in a moderate oven for 30 minutes.

konfektbröd, Swedish for macaroons. To prepare them, 2 lightly beaten egg whites are added gradually to a mixture of 1½ cups sifted icing (confectioners') sugar and 1½ cups

ground almonds. When a paste of a firm consistency is achieved, teaspoonfuls of the mixture are dropped onto a baking sheet, brushed with melted butter, and sprinkled with flour, before being baked in a slow oven for 30 minutes. See also MANDEL (MANDELSKORPER).

kongesuppe (royal soup), a traditional Norwegian soup made from stock, peas, carrots, parsley, butter, and flavoured with sherry, to which little meat balls are added before serving. It is popular at *Syttende Mai* celebrations.

königsberger klopse, German meat dumplings, made from 1 lb. each raw mixed beef and pork, combined with 4 crustless slices of bread soaked in water, 2 chopped onions, 3 anchovies, 2 eggs, and seasoning, then shaped into balls and poached in boiling salted water with sliced onion, bay leaf, and allspice. They are served with a sauce made from thickened stock mixed with chopped anchovy fillets and capers. The balls are heated in the sauce before serving. See also MEAT BALLS.

königswurst, a large German "royal" sausage made from equal parts of pounded chicken and partridge. Chopped truffle and mushroom are added, and the mixture is bound with raw eggs, seasoned with mace, salt, and pepper, and flavoured with a little Rhenish wine. These large sausages are braised, sliced when cold and served as hors d'oeuvre. See also WÜRSTE.

konijn, Dutch for rabbit. Rabbit is eaten very often in Holland, and the Dutch housewife has many recipes for it. See also HAAS.

kool, Dutch for cabbage, an important winter vegetable in Holland. See also STAMPPOT.

kopanisti, a Greek cheese, which is féta cheese with blue veining. It is more mature than féta and has a finer texture, but the flavour is sharp and peppery.

koper, Polish for dill, extensively used in Poland for flavouring garnishes, sauces, and soups.

zupa koprowa, Polish dill soup, made from 2 cups chopped raw dill sautéed in butter for 3–4 minutes, then added to 2 pints (4 cups) chicken stock. One tablespoon flour is well mixed with ¼ pint (½ cup) sour cream, which is then added to the stock, well stirred, and simmered for 5–10 minutes. The soup is garnished with fried croûtons and slices of hard-boiled egg. See also SOS (SOS KOPERKOWY).

koppen, a Czechoslovakian sour milk cheese made by herders in the Sudetic Mountains between Bohemia and Silesia. It is made from goat's milk and has a pungent flavour and smell. The cheeses are salted and cured and are made in two shapes, one conical and the other cylindrical, each weighing about 2 lb. The cheese is also called *bauden.*

kopūstai su grybais, a traditional Lithuanian dish consisting of soaked dried mushrooms, chopped bacon, onion, apple, and sauerkraut. It is baked in the oven for about 3 hours.

korint, Swedish for dried currant.

korintsås, currant sauce made with 1 cup dried currants well rinsed in warm water and then simmered in water until tender. A roux is made of 1 tablespoon each of butter and flour, to which are added the currants, currant stock, 1 tablespoon vinegar, 2 teaspoons castor sugar, and 1 teaspoon of either golden syrup or honey. All are simmered for about 12 minutes. This sauce accompanies croquettes of minced meat.

körözött, see LIPTAUER.

korv, Swedish for sausage.

korv ragu, sausage casserole. First 1 heaped tablespoon flour is sprinkled onto 2 tablespoons melted butter, and ½ pint (1 cup) vegetable stock, 1 lb. boiled potatoes, 3 carrots, 2 onions, 1 lb. pricked pork sausages, seasoning, and herbs are added. All are simmered for about 30 minutes.

korvasienet, a species of Finnish morel which appears between April and May, and grows on pine-covered heathland.

It is very popular in Finland and has a delicious flavour. See also SIENET.

kørvel, Danish for chervil.

kørvelsuppe, Danish for chervil soup made with 2 carrots cooked in 2 pints (4 cups) white stock and then removed and cut into thin slices. A roux is made from 2 oz. each butter and flour, and half the hot stock; the sliced carrots are then returned to the saucepan, together with the rest of the stock and 4 tablespoons stemmed and minced chervil and seasoning. It is simmered for about 3 minutes.

koryushki, Russian for smelts, which are very popular in Russia. They are often served pickled or smoked, for *zakuski.*

koryushki marinovannye, literally, "marinated smelts." The fish are cleaned, sprinkled with salt, rolled in flour, and fried on both sides in oil. They are then drained and put in a deep earthenware dish. Vinegar, containing carrot, onion, celery, bay leaf, cloves, nutmeg, parsley, and seasoning, all of which have previously been boiled in it, is poured over while still warm. The dish is left to stand overnight, or longer.

koryushki zharenye, boned smelts coated with a thick mushroom and prawn sauce, rolled in flour, and dipped in beaten egg. They are then fried in hot fat until golden brown. They are usually served with green peas.

korzhiki, Russian biscuits (cookies), made from 2 cups flour, 2 tablespoons butter, ⅔ cup sour cream, 3 tablespoons sugar, 1 egg, and ½ teaspoon baking soda. The mixture is formed into rounds which are pricked on top with a fork, brushed with beaten egg, and baked in the oven.

kos, Albanian for sour milk, which is used a great deal in cooking, and is drunk with all meals in Albania. It forms the basis of a cold soup called *tarator* and also a sauce served with fritters, *kungull me kos.* See also REVANI ME KOS.

košeliena, a Lithuanian national dish of pig's trotters (feet) and goose giblets and wings, cooked with bay leaves, allspice, onions, salt, and peppercorns, all simmered until the meat leaves the bones. The pork and goose meat are separated from the bones and all is poured into a deep dish and left to jelly. When set, it is garnished with parsley, dill pickles, and hard-boiled eggs.

kotlet, Polish for cutlet. Sometimes the word kotlet is also used to describe patties of fish, poultry, or meat, ground or minced and shaped like cutlets. See also INDYK (KOTLETY Z INDYKA).

kotlety or **kotletki,** the Russian term for patties or rissoles of minced foods shaped into ovals to resemble cutlets. They are usually made from salmon or chicken, and are served with sour cream.

kotlety po kievski, chicken in the Kiev style, a delicious method which is world-famous. The raw chicken is skinned and the breast removed and cut in flat slices. Each slice is seasoned and sprinkled with finely chopped mushrooms. About 4 ox. (½ cup) hard ice-cold butter, sometimes worked with herbs and garlic, is cut into fingers which are placed on each slice of chicken, before each is folded up and secured. If they are not to be cooked immediately, these fillets must be kept in a very cold place. Before cooking they are dipped in batter or rolled in egg and breadcrumbs; then they are fried in deep hot fat or oil. They should be golden brown all over before being served; when cut for the first time, a stream of golden melted butter should pour out. It is said that in some restaurants the cooked chicken fillet rolls are injected with melted butter by means of a hypodermic syringe: in a hot kitchen it could indeed be difficult to keep butter cold enough for use in the older method. However, there is little doubt that the chicken is more succulent if the butter is inserted before cooking.

kotlety pozharskie, is made from 1 lb. minced chicken mixed with 1 cup soaked white breadcrumbs, 4 tablespoons melted butter, and seasoning. The mixture is made into small cutlet-shapes which are rolled in breadcrumbs and fried in butter.

kotopoulo, Greek for chicken. See also CHICKEN.

kotopita, a Greek chicken pie made with a phyllo pastry crust. To the boned chicken are added an onion purée, *kasseri* cheese, nutmeg, beaten eggs, butter, and seasoning. It is also eaten in Cyprus.

kotopoulo bahmies, a Balkan method of preparing chicken. A chicken is roasted in butter until half cooked, when it is cut into small pieces. The pieces are placed in a casserole with ½ cup butter to 1 cup diluted tomato purée, and about ½ lb. bahmies (okra) is arranged around the chicken pieces. The ingredients are simmered for about 30 minutes.

kotopoulo hilopites, a Peloponnese dish of young chickens simmered in white wine, onions, garlic, celery, parsley, tomatoes, and seasoning. It is served with noodles and grated *kasseri* cheese. A pinch of cinnamon is added to the chicken 10 minutes before it is served.

kotopoulo kapama, jointed chicken rubbed with a mixture of lemon juice, cinnamon, cloves, salt, and pepper, fried in oil and then simmered in thick tomato sauce until the meat leaves the bone.

kotopoulo riyanato, roast chicken with marjoram.

kotopoulo sti stamna, an Athenian speciality of young chicken cooked in an earthenware pot (*stamna*) with wine, butter, and herbs, one of the most delicious ways of cooking a chicken. Other meats and game are cooked in the same way.

kotopoulo tis hydras, a chicken dish from the island of Hydra, made with jointed chicken, ½ cup brandy, butter, thick cream, and seasoning.

kotopoulo tis sharas, chicken grilled on a spit, one of the best of Athenian dishes. The chickens, which must be young and tender, are rubbed with garlic, lemon juice, and seasoning, and left to stand for 1 hour. They are grilled over a low heat and served with *skorthalia* sauce.

kotopoulo tis sharas me saltsa, as above, but served with a sauce of olive oil, lemon juice, thyme, dry mustard, and seasoning, all heated.

kotopoulosoupa, chicken soup, usually enriched with beaten egg and lemon juice. Sometimes cooked rice is added.

kött, Swedish for meat. Roasts and pot roasts are popular in Sweden, where meat is eaten extensively. Roast lamb, mutton, and beef are often accompanied by dill sauce. Finely minced meat is used for meat balls and soup balls, as well as for other dishes—the Swedish cook minces her own meat at home. Pork is perhaps the favourite meat, and joints of pork and ham are served at the Christmas dinner. Veal is also much in demand. See also FLASK; JULSKINKA; KALVKÖTT; LAMM; SKINKA.

köttbullar, meat balls or rissoles made from 1 lb. each minced pork and beef mixed together well. Then 1 cup breadcrumbs are soaked in water and ½ cup cream for some minutes and added to the meat, together with 1 small minced onion, salt, pepper, egg yolk, and sugar (optional). The mixture is shaped into small balls, and these are fried slowly in butter. A thick sauce is made, consisting of a little juice from the pan, flour and milk or cream, and seasoning. This is poured over the balls, which are served with caramellised potatoes (see *potatis*), creamed, mixed vegetables, and pickled gherkins, with cranberry sauce. See also FRIKADELLER.

köttfärssvepta ägg, a variation of Scotch eggs. An egg white is slightly beaten and brushed over hard-boiled eggs, which are then coated with a mixture of pork sausage meat and chopped anchovy fillets, dipped in egg and breadcrumbs, and fried in fat. These eggs may be served hot, with a tomato sauce, or cold with mayonnaise.

pepparrotskött, boiled meat and horseradish. Brisket of

beef is cooked in boiling water and the liquid is then skimmed; root vegetables are added, together with seasoning, and when the water is again boiling, it is skimmed once more. The ingredients are then simmered until all are tender (about 2½ hours). The dish is garnished with shredded horseradish and served with a horseradish sauce. Sometimes the Swedish housewife adds potato dumplings 15 minutes before cooking is finished; these are served round the meat with the vegetables.

koukia, Greek for dried broad beans, used for soups or salad. Koukia freska are fresh broad beans. Both are used extensively in Greece.

koulourakia, small Greek Easter cakes made from 1½ lb. (6 cups) flour, 1 lb. (2 cups) sugar, ¾ lb. (1½ cups) butter, 2 eggs, sesame seeds, cinnamon to taste, and ½ pint (1 cup) cream. The tops of the cakes are sprinkled with sesame seeds before cooking.

koulouria, a sweet Greek bread shaped like a large ring. This is popular in Greece where it is delivered to the householder still warm and smelling of sesame seeds. It may also be bought at any street corner in a Greek town, and can be eaten on the spot, or taken to a coffee shop to be enjoyed with coffee. It is made with 1½ lb. (6 cups) flour, 4 oz. (½ cup) sugar, 6 oz. (⅔ cup) butter, 2 eggs, 1 teaspoon baking powder, vanilla, sesame seeds, and milk.

koulouria

kouneli, Greek for rabbit.

kouneli me kaïmaki, a speciality from Salonika, consisting of jointed rabbit marinated in vinegar, fried in butter, then simmered in a little of the marinade and stock. Then 1 pint (2 cups) thick cream (*kaïmaki*), 1 bay leaf, 3 cloves, and seasoning are added 30 minutes before serving.

kouneli riyanato, rabbit braised with garlic, lemon juice, and marjoram.

kouneli stifado, a rabbit stew. Pieces of rabbit are first browned, and then removed from the pan and kept hot. Small whole onions are browned with crushed garlic, after which the rabbit is returned to the pan. A thick tomato sauce is made with tomatoes, white wine (or wine vinegar), cinnamon, parsley, bay leaves, and seasoning, and is added to the pan. Water to cover is included, and all is well stirred and then allowed to simmer for at least 3 hours. The only accompaniment served with this dish is brown bread.

kounoupidi or *kounoupithi,* Greek for cauliflower.

kounoupidi yahni, cauliflower cooked in tomato juice. Chopped onions and pounded garlic are fried in oil until brown, then a tin of tomato juice is added, followed by salt, pepper, and parsley, and all is brought to the boil. Cauliflower (in separate flowerets) is added and cooked. The sauce, which may be thickened with flour, should be served separately.

koupepia, a Greek dish of vegetable marrow (summer squash) stuffed and baked with minced (ground) meat.

kourabiédes or *kourabiethes,* Greek for a kind of shortbread which is made by tradition for Christmas and New Year celebrations. It is of ancient origin and there are several interesting allusions to it. A cake of it is said to have been mentioned by St. John Chrysostom in one of his sermons. Today, when it is made in the form of individual biscuits (cookies), each of these is stuck with a clove representing the gift of spices which the Three Wise Men brought to the infant Christ. Recipes vary with different families, as do those for the English Christmas pudding. The real secret, according to the Greeks, rests in the time spent creaming the butter and sugar, which should be beaten by hand for at least 30 minutes. One lb. (2 cups) butter is creamed with 6 oz. (⅔ cup) sugar as described; then 4 tablespoons *ouzo* and vanilla to taste are added, followed by 2 egg yolks and 1¼ lb. (5 cups) flour, already well sifted with 1 teaspoon baking powder, to make a dough. Pieces of the dough are formed into biscuit shapes, stuck with a clove, and baked in a moderate oven for 20 minutes. While still hot, they are twice sprinkled with icing (confectioners') sugar and rose water. They keep fresh for several weeks.

kourabiédes me amygdalo, as above, but with the addition of 4 oz. (1 cup) chopped almonds, both blanched and roasted, added before the *ouzo.* Walnuts can also be used.

köyhät ritarit, literally "poor knights," a very popular Finnish dessert made with slices of stale rye or wheat bread dipped in a mixture of egg and milk, fried quickly in butter and served hot with cream and jam.

kozunàk, a traditional Easter cake eaten at the Bulgarian *Vŭzkresènie.* It is conical in shape and is made from 2 lb. (8 cups) flour, 4 tablespoons sugar, ¼ lb. (1 cup) butter, 1 oz. yeast, and 5 eggs, to which are added 2 oz. crushed almonds, 8 oz. raisins, and vanilla to taste. It is prepared in the same way as yeast dough, and when cooked is sprinkled with chopped candied peel.

kraftbruehe, an Austrian soup made from 2 lb. freshly minced (ground) lean beef, shredded carrot, onion, Hamburg parsley roots, and the white part of a large leek, together with a pint of cold water, salt, and 2 egg whites. It is brought gently to the boil on a low flame, and 3 pints of consommé are added, after which all the ingredients are simmered very slowly for 1 hour. The soup is then strained and served.

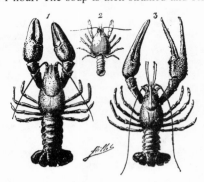

kräfttiden, the Swedish celebration of the opening of the freshwater crayfish season. This begins at midnight on August 7 and continues throughout September; it is a season of party-giving and festivity. The initial feast is often held in the open air, and there is a ritual method of eating the boiled or steamed crayfish. The remains and shell of the fish have to be tastefully arranged round the empty dish, which is a special plate engraved or painted with crayfish. Another tradition is that a glass of schnaps or aquavit should accompany the eating of each claw, and needless to say, this custom gives rise to great revelry. Enormous numbers of these fish are eaten daily in Sweden. Not only are they regarded as a delicacy but at kräfttiden they are actually feted, for large effigies of them decorate restaurants, houses, gardens, and balconies at this time.

krapfen, I. A small German and Austrian pastry which may be made in one of several forms, the most usual being that of a doughnut; in fact it can be made in the same way, with yeast or with baking powder. It is known as *nusskrapfen* if chopped nuts are an ingredient, and *pfannkrapfen* if jam is an ingredient, but these two kinds are usually reserved for New Year's Eve, for they are traditional fare on that occasion. See also DOUGHNUT.

II. Short crust pastry, cut into squares which are filled with minced (ground) meats. The squares of pastry, with the meat inside, are folded over and the edges dampened and pressed down. Then they are either poached in boiling salted water or fried in hot oil or fat. They are made in various sizes. Very small ones, not more than an inch across, are used as a garnish for soups; the larger varieties are eaten as an entrée or main course and known as *zillertalerkrapfen*.

backpulverkrapfen, krapfen made with baking powder. First 4 eggs are beaten with ½ pint (1 cup) milk, then 2 teaspoons baking powder and 1 lb. (4 cups) flour are mixed in to form a dough. Spoonsful are fried in hot oil, drained, and rolled in sugar. They are served with jam heated with water and thickened with arrowroot.

faschingskrapfen consist of ½ oz. yeast creamed with 1 teaspoon sugar, to which 2 tablespoons tepid cream and a pinch of flour are added. This is left to rise and bubble. Meanwhile 3 egg yolks, 1 tablespoon sugar, 2 tablespoons cream, 1 teaspoon each of orange and lemon juice, finely grated lemon peel, and 2 teaspoons rum are all whisked together. Then ½ lb. (2 cups) flour, the yeast, and 4 tablespoons melted butter are folded in. This is beaten well with a wooden spoon, until the dough leaves the sides of the bowl cleanly. It is sprinkled with a little flour and left in a warm place, covered with a cloth to rise. It should double in size, and this usually takes about an hour. It is kneaded afterward, rolled out to ⅛-inch thickness and cut into rounds about 2½ inches across. A little apricot jam is put in the middle of half the number of rounds, the edges are dampened, and the remaining rounds are pressed down on top of the others. When all the dough has been used up, the cakes are left on the tray to rise again, covered with a cloth. Then they are fried on both sides in shallow hot oil or fat (a special fat called *krapfenschmalz* is used), until golden brown, a characteristic white band being left round the middle. They are drained and then dusted with icing (confectioners') sugar. They resemble a doughnut but are far superior in flavour and texture. The Viennese *wiener krapfen* are very similar.

krapiva, traditional Russian nettle soup. Chopped onions and young nettle shoots are simmered in butter; beef broth and a piece of brisket are added to them, and all are cooked for some hours. The soup is garnished with the diced brisket and pearl barley.

kråse, Danish for giblets.

kråseragout, a ragoût of giblets, popular in Denmark during the Christmas season, at which time it is usually made from goose giblets. The giblets are first scalded and then dipped in seasoned flour, after which they are fried in melted butter (to which grated onions have been added), and a pinch each of curry powder and paprika. All the ingredients are then put into the pan together, with boiling water to cover, and simmered for about 2 hours. When they are tender, a little Madeira or sherry is added to taste. The ragoût is reboiled and served with potatoes.

kråsesuppe, giblet soup. For this soup, prunes should be soaked in water overnight. A set of goose giblets, together with the bird's feet, wings (divided), gizzard, and neck (cut into three pieces and the gullet and windpipe removed) are all brought to the boil in cold, salted water which is then skimmed. Root vegetables, including celery and its foliage, are added with peppercorns and mace (optional). The whole is covered and simmered for several hours until the giblets are tender, when the stock is strained and put aside. Sliced, peeled apples and prunes are cooked with sugar in the prune water. A roux is made of butter, flour, and prune stock, to which the giblet stock is added, with more sugar and vinegar to taste. The vegetables, meat, and fruit are diced and added to the soup, which is served with *boller*.

krashenyie jajtza, elaborate and beautifully coloured eggs which, at Easter in Russia, are served from a dish containing fresh green leaves. See also CHERVÈNI YAYTSÀ; KULICH; YAYTSA.

kräuter, German for herbs.

kräuterbutter, a butter which is mixed with chopped herbs such as chives or parsley, and sometimes a third of the quantity of a grated hard cheese of the Parmesan variety. It is often served on slices of pumpernickel or with *nudeln*. It is quite popular in Europe, and the manufacture of the ground herbs has begun both in Europe and the U.S. They are called Kräuter-butter seasoning.

kreas, Greek for meat. When meat is mentioned, the modern Greek thinks first of lamb, then of goat, then of pork. Homer told of the delights of the roast beef on which his friends feasted, but today, although beef is still eaten in Greece, it is not considered to be the best of meats. Butchers' shops are full of carcases, for Greek housewives like to see the pieces of their choice being hacked off: carefully displayed joints are unknown. The best meat cooking is done on the ancestral spit. In days gone by, small dogs and men rotated the huge spits. Today they are still operated by manpower, although in some of the smarter *taverna* the electric rotary spit has been introduced. See also ARNAKI; ARNI; GOURONOPOULO; HIRINO; KATSIKAKI; MOSCHARI; SOFRITO; VODINO.

kreas ke lahanika stin catsarola, a Macedonian dish of casseroled sliced beef, white cabbage, potatoes, tomatoes, green peppers, dried white beans, red cabbage, onions, white wine, and seasoning. The ingredients are chopped or sliced and arranged in layers; then a lid is put on and they are cooked slowly for several hours. An aromatic and delicious dish.

kreas me ellies, slices of beef or veal cooked with tomato sauce and green olives.

kreas me kastana, veal or beef cut into chunks and simmered in stock with onions and chestnuts.

kreas me kydonia, a Greek method of cooking cubed meat of any kind, with onions, quinces, butter, sugar, water, and seasoning.

kreatopita or *kreatopites*, a meat pie, a popular carnival and Ascension Day dish on the island of Cephos. It is very rich, the chief feature being that three different kinds of meat are used, usually lamb, female goat or kid, and the dark meat of a chicken. The other ingredients are onions, tomatoes, rice, bay leaves, grated *kasseri* or Parmesan cheese, sugar, raisins, eggs, white wine, garlic, and seasoning. Short crust pastry is laid at the bottom and sides of the pie-dish as well as being used to cover the top.

kreatines, a Greek word referring to the two-week period of meat fasting. See also APOKREO.

krebs, Danish for crayfish, which often grace the cold tables of Denmark.

krebs, German for crayfish; also flusskrebs.

krebssuppe, a traditional German soup from Hamburg. To

prepare it 2 lb. crayfish, unshelled, 2 carrots, 2 onions, ¼ lb. lean bacon, a little celery, thyme, and bay leaf are fried in butter. Then 2 tablespoons brandy are poured over and ignited. The ingredients are then cooked in a mixture of 1 pint each of stock and white wine. The crayfish are removed and shelled; then, with the pounded shells, they are sweated in butter, with a sprinkling of flour and seasoning. The stock is added and the soup is boiled up for 10 minutes, then strained and garnished with cooked green peas, small dumplings, and the crayfish tails, which can easily be picked out of the strainer.

krem, Polish for cream.

krem z herbaty, tea-flavoured cream, made from 1 pint light cream, 1 vanilla pod, and 1 tablespoon dry tea-leaves boiled together, then cooled, and the vanilla pod removed. Next 2 cups heavy whipped cream, 8 egg yolks, and ½ lb. (1 cup) sugar are whipped together. The two mixtures are then combined, 4 tablespoons rum are stirred in, and 1 tablespoon dissolved gelatine is added to make it set.

kremidia, Greek for onions. *Kremidakia* are small onions, and *kremidakia freska* is the term for spring onions.

kren, see MEERRETTICH.

krendel, a Russian cake made for birthdays or ''name days'' (days of the saints after whom particular members of the family are named). To prepare it 1 oz. yeast is dissolved in ½ pint (1 cup) warm milk and left to work. Meanwhile 10 egg yolks, 10 oz. (1¼ cups) butter, and 1 lb. (2 cups) sugar are creamed together, then 2 lb. (8 cups) flour and the yeast are worked in. Finally, 8 ox. (1 cup) sultanas are put in and the mixture is covered with a cloth and left to rise. To make the krendel, the mixture is turned out onto a floured board and shaped into the letter B. It is brushed with beaten egg, sprinkled with 4 oz. chopped almonds, and baked in a hot oven for 40–50 minutes. It is put on a wire rack to cool, and is sprinkled with sugar. Small individual cakes may also be made instead of one large cake; they are called *krendelki.*

kreplach, a traditional Jewish dish resembling ravioli, for it is made from noodle dough cut into squares and stuffed with a filling of cheese, chicken, meat, or kasha. They are poached in boiling salted water and served with clear soup or a meat sauce. They are usually eaten at Succoth in October, a week-long celebration which marks the first stop made by the Israelites on their flight from Egypt. Kreplach are also eaten at Shevuoth in May, when they are made with cheese. See also HOLISHKES.

kritharaki, Greek for a fine barley kernel used a great deal in casseroles and soups. *Kritharosoupa* is barley soup.

krofne, small fried Yugoslavian yeast cakes, made from a dough consisting of 12 oz. (3 cups) flour, 2 oz. (¼ cup) butter, ¼ pint (½ cup) warm milk, 3 eggs (yolks and whites separated), and ½ oz. yeast. They puff up when fried in deep oil, and resemble doughnuts in size and taste.

krogvärdens sås, literally ''innkeeper's sauce,'' a Swedish cold sauce for boiled or steamed fish. For this sauce, a double boiler is used. One tablespoon butter is melted, and to this are added 2 egg yolks, ½ teaspoon dry mustard, 1 teaspoon sugar, and 1 teaspoon minced onion, together with 1 tablespoon chopped tarragon and pepper to taste. When thick, the sauce is removed from the heat and chilled. See also FISKSÅS.

krolik, Russian for rabbit, which is made into stews and pies, and is often roasted with sour cream and garnished with hot cooked beetroots and pickled cucumbers.

kromesky, see CROMESQUI.

kronans kaka, Swedish for crown cake. It is made with 12 oz. (1½ cups) sugar beaten into 4 oz. (½ cup) creamed butter; then 3 egg yolks and 4 oz. grated raw potato are gradually added, and the whole well beaten for about 30 minutes. Then 6 oz. (1½ cups) ground almonds are included and, lastly, 3

stiffly beaten egg whites are folded in. The cake is baked in a slow oven 300°F for about 45 minutes. It is left to stand in the tin for 15 minutes before being turned out and, when cool, is layered with lemon cream.

kronfleisch, German for a cheap beef cut such as flank, brisket, or shin.

kruid, Dutch for herb. *Kruiderijen* is Dutch for spices, *kruidnagel* for clove, and *kruidnoot* for nutmeg, all of which are used extensively in Dutch cooking.

krupnik, a Polish barley soup made with bone stock with the addition of meat scraps or giblets, and mushrooms.

krupovka, a Czechoslovakian country dish made from barley cooked to a purée like a porridge and served with sausage or smoked meat. See also ČERNÝ KUBA.

krydderfedt, a spiced lard very popular with Danish cooks. It is made from bacon or pork fat, a small minced onion, and a sprig of rosemary or thyme, all heated together, and, when a pale brown colour is achieved it is strained before using.

kuchen, I. The basic term in German for a cake, or small cakes; usually the flavouring is designated first, for example *honigkuchen,* honey cakes. Popularly, it means anything that is baked. II. The general term used in both Germany and Austria to describe a fruit tart or flan, named according to the particular fruit used to fill it. The pastry used to line the tin is usually puff, or rich short crust pastry, although some varieties employed contain yeast. Cream cheese is also used as a filling. Small tarts are called *törtchen.* See also LEBKUCHEN; NÜRNBERGER LEBKUCHEN; PFEFFER (PFEFFERKUCHEN); STRUDEL.

kugel, a Jewish pudding which is a holiday dish. There are several theories about the origin of the name, all related to the shape of the pudding: Kugel, German for cannonball or ball, and *ke-igul,* Hebrew for ''like a circle'' or a heap of manna. Whatever the origin of the name, kugel is particularly associated with Channukah which in the Hebrew calendar is an 8-day celebration of the anniversary of the Battle of the Maccabees, which took place in 105 B.C. Kugel can be made from vegetables and noodles and served as a side dish with meat.

apple kugel, a mixture of thinly sliced apples spiced with cinnamon and nutmeg, then coated with breadcrumbs, honey, and vegetable fat, and layered with thin pastry, until a final layer of the spiced apple mixture is reached. Apple kugel is baked in a moderate oven for about an hour.

kugelhupf or **guglhupf,** a yeast cake which is an Alsatian speciality. It is of Austrian origin, and was popularised in France by Marie Antoinette. It is made from 12 oz. (3 cups) flour, 6 oz. (⅔ cup) butter, 2 oz. (¼ cup) sugar, 3 eggs, ½ oz. fresh yeast, ½ cup currants, 12 sweet chopped almonds, and salt. The dough is baked in a special kugelhupf mould, which is round and has a ray-like pattern on the bottom and sides. On April 1, kugelhupf is baked in a mould shaped like a fish, a practice related to the custom which prevails in France, whereby anonymous gifts in the shape of fish are made to friends on April Fool's Day. There are several theories about the origin of the custom, one of them associating it with the sign of the zodiac, for it is in April that the sun leaves Poissons (Pisces). See also GUGLHUPF.

kuiken, Dutch for chicken. Chicken is popular in Holland, and is often eaten there on Sundays instead of a weekend joint. Prices for chicken compare favourably with those for meat. In most Dutch chicken dishes, butter is used liberally, and the bird is often fried on top of the fire in a pan, instead of being roasted in the more usual way employed in Britain and elsewhere. This is perhaps because ovens are by no means universal in Holland. See also KIP.

kulajda, a Czechoslovakian soup, made with ½ lb. mushrooms simmered in 1 pint water with a few caraway seeds, to which is added a sprinkling of flour. Then 1 pint (2 cups) sour cream is mixed in, and 4 large sliced, raw potatoes. The ingredients are cooked for 15 minutes. Before serving, 2 raw eggs, salt, and a dash of vinegar and chopped dill are stirred in, but it is not reboiled lest it will curdle.

kulebiak z kapustą i grzybami, a Polish rich short crust pastry which is filled with cooked cabbage, mushrooms, and eggs, folded over, secured at the edges, and baked in a moderate oven until gently browned. It is similar to the Russian *kulebyaka.*

kulebyaka, a traditional Russian fish pie. In Russia it is usually made with pike-perch or sterlet, but when these are not available, salmon and turbot are used. A thin sheet of yeast dough, also made with eggs and butter, is placed on a baking-sheet; it is covered with the fish fillets, chopped onion, herbs, sliced hard-boiled eggs, and layers of cooked semolina, kasha, or rice. The filling is topped with butter and chopped *vesiga,* and the dough is then wrapped over, the edges being moistened to ensure that they adhere, and the pie is painted on top with beaten egg before being baked in a slow oven for 1½ hours. Melted butter is served with the hot pie. It is generally known as *coulibiac* in English-speaking countries.

kulich, a cylindrical yeast dough cake, sometimes nearly 2 feet high, which is a traditional Easter cake in Russia and some Baltic states. A rose or a lamb made from butter is sometimes used to decorate the top. It is made with 2 lb. (8 cups) flour, 1 oz. yeast, 4 oz. (½ cup) sugar, ½ lb. (1 cup) butter, 5 eggs, 1 cup raisins, 2 oz. chopped candied peel, ½ teaspoon vanilla, 1 tablespoon lemon juice, and ¾ pint (1½ cups) milk, all mixed and prepared as yeast dough. It is very light, and resembles the Italian *panettone.* When cool, it is sometimes iced and decorated with more peel. The table on which it is served is decorated with brightly coloured eggs (*krashenyie jajtza*), *paskha,* and other delicious Russian foods. The older members of the family stay at home on Easter Day to welcome the many callers, but the young ones visit from house to house. See also EASTER; KRASHENYIE JAJTZA; PASKHA.

kümmel, German for caraway seed. This is used a great deal in Germany, in the cooking of cabbage, cakes, and stews. It is also the basis of the liqueur kummel.

kümmelsauce, a delicious sauce made with ½ pint (1 cup) sour cream, 1 teaspoon each of paprika and of caraway seeds, mixed with the pan juices of veal cutlets that have been fried in butter.

kümmelstangen, small sticks made out of a short crust pastry to which grated cheese and an egg have been added. They are sprinkled with caraway seeds before being baked.

kumquat (*Fortunella japonica*), a shrub native to Japan, but now grown extensively in Florida and California. The fruit is small and bitter–sweet, like a tiny orange, but is excellent for preserves, candying, and confectionery. It is also excellent halved and cooked in syrup, and served with ice cream. Preserved in syrup, it is exported to Europe. It can also be pickled in wine vinegar, like melon. In France, the fresh fruit is sometimes cooked and used, like orange, as a garnish for braised duck.

kundzar, an Alaskan dish eaten by the Ten'a Indians. It consists of a white fish roe pounded with slightly unripe cranberries. A little snow is added, and it is all frozen before eating. Other Alaskan foods are bear, reindeer, and salmon, as well as native berries such as blueberries and salmon berries. Tea has been the most popular drink there since it was introduced by the Russians at the beginning of the 19th century, when they established their first trading posts. See also KUN-TU; NA-TLÖDA.

kungull me kos, an Albanian dish of fritters made with vegetable marrow (summer squash). The batter is made by mixing 4 oz. (1 cup) flour with 1 teaspoon baking soda, a pinch of salt, and 1 beaten egg; about ¼ pint (½ cup) water is beaten in until the mixture is smooth. The marrow (squash) is peeled

and cut into small pieces which are dipped in this batter, then fried in hot oil until golden. A sauce of thick sour milk (*kos*) flavoured with salt and pounded garlic is served cold on top of the hot fritters. See also FRITTER.

kun-tu, an Alaskan speciality made from fermented salmon roe and eaten by the Ten'a Indians instead of Russian caviar. The roe is removed from the salmon during the early run up the Yukon River and, before the frost sets in, is stored underground in birchbark baskets until it ripens. The roe is often boiled, but is also eaten raw. It is also known as *kun-tsidla.* See also KUNDZAR; NA-TLÖDA.

kürbis, German for pumpkin and squash.

kürbiskraut, an Austrian method of cooking vegetable marrow (summer squash). The marrow is peeled, sprinkled with salt, and left for about 1 hour. It is then sautéed in butter, with a small onion, until golden brown. Then 1 tablespoon flour, 1 tablespoon chopped parsley, dill, and paprika to taste are added, followed by about ½ pint water or stock to make a thick sauce. Finally, 1 cup sour cream and lemon juice are added. The whole is covered and simmered for about 30 minutes.

kürbisse, an Austrian method of cooking vegetable marrow (summer squash) in a roux of 2 tablespoons each of butter and flour and 2 pints (4 cups) hot stock, to which are added a little vinegar, caraway seed, and seasoning.

kürbisse mit paprika, as above, but with sour cream instead of stock, and paprika instead of caraway seed.

kurczę, Polish for young chicken or *poussin.*

kurczeta pieczone po polsku, a young roast chicken stuffed with breadcrumbs, butter, liver, dill, and parsley.

kuře, Czech for chicken.

kuře plzeňské, chicken braised with sultanas and Pilsen beer.

kúritsa, Russian for chicken. See also CHAKHOKHBILI; CHICKEN

kúritsa nevskaya, chicken in the Neva style. The chicken is opened from the back and the breast-bone removed. It is stuffed with fine chicken forcemeat which has foie gras and truffles added. The breast fillets are put back, and the chicken is trussed and then poached in chicken stock for 1½ hours. It is allowed to cool, and when cold is covered with chaud-froid sauce made with some of the stock. It is set on a bed of cooked rice and garnished with small domes of vegetable salad mixed with mayonnaise (Russian salad), and decorated with truffle pieces and little shapes of chicken jelly.

kúritsa po kievska, chicken in the Kiev style. See KOTLETY, PO KIEVSKI.

kúritsa s orekhovym sousom, chicken boiled or roasted, and served with a sauce made from crushed walnuts, garlic, and finely chopped onions, all seasoned and mixed well with vinegar and parsley. Rice is eaten with this dish.

kúritsa s vishnevym sousom, boiled chicken served with a sauce made from cooked stoned cherries, raisins, sugar, and chicken stock. (If cornelian cherries are used, the dish is called *kúritsa s kizilnym soúsom.*)

kúritsa so smetannym sousom, chicken fried or roasted, and served with a sauce made from ½ pint (1 cup) sour cream added to the chicken juices left in the cooking pan, which have been boiled up and reduced a little.

kúritsa tabaka, chicken grilled whole on a skewer or spit. It is basted with butter during cooking and served with *sous tkemali* (see SOUS), and garnished with salted cucumbers and tomatoes.

kurka wodna, Polish for coot, often spit-roasted in Poland; see PRZEPIÓRKA.

kurkku, Finnish for cucumber.

kurkkusalaatti, salad made with thinly sliced cucumber and served with a dressing of sour cream, vinegar, oil, sugar, dill, pepper, and salt. If not to be served immediately, it is covered over to prevent a hard skin forming.

suolakurkkut, pickled cucumbers. Small cucumbers are pickled in a salt and vinegar solution, and are then placed in large jars with layers of black currant and oak leaves, dill, grated horseradish, and garlic. The dill gives a characteristic flavour. See also DILL, PICKLES.

kurnik, a Polish chicken pie which is a most elaborate and delicious dish. A pie dish is lined with puff pastry and filled first with a very thin pancake, then with boiled rice mixed with chopped hard-boiled eggs, chopped onions, and sauce béchamel, then with another pancake, then a sliced yellow boletus mixed with sour cream and diced chicken with cream sauce, then with a further pancake, and finally with more pastry to close the pie. It is served hot with sauce suprême.

kuropatwa, Polish for partridge. See also DZICZYZNA.

kuropatwy w śmietanie, a Polish dish of partridges rubbed with salt and larded with salt pork, then browned in butter, halved, dredged with flour, and, finally, covered with sour cream. The pot is covered tightly and the contents cooked for 3–4 hours. Sometimes hot red cabbage is served with this dish.

kutja, a sweet wheat pudding eaten in Byelorussia and in the country regions of eastern and southeastern Poland at Christmas. It is served in a large bowl and placed in the centre of the table. It is blessed by the head of the family before eating. The buckwheat is soaked overnight, then boiled in water and strained. It is covered with water again and simmered for about 5 hours. Boiled poppy seeds, sugar, butter, honey, and sultanas are added. Then a thin cream is mixed in. The pudding is served cold, with chopped almonds sprinkled over it.

kuzu, Turkish for lamb.

kuzu dòlmasi, stuffed with a mixture of fried onions, cooked rice, and seasonings, then roasted.

kvargli, a Hungarian soft cheese made by small farmers and peasants for their own consumption. It can be made from cow's, ewe's, or goat's milk, and is usually very highly flavoured with spices.

květáková polévka, see POLÉVKA.

kyckling, Swedish for chicken. In Sweden, chicken is usually reserved for festive family occasions. See also FJADERFA; HÖNS.

kyckling mousse, chicken mousse. A boiled chicken is well minced and mixed with ½ pint (1 cup) thick cream. The resulting paste is rubbed through a sieve, and ½ pint (1 cup) whipped cream is added and the mixture seasoned. Sherry or Madeira to taste is then included. Then, 1 rounded tablespoon powdered gelatine is soaked for 5 minutes in ¼ pint cold water; half of this mixture is added to 4 tablespoons heated stock taken from ½ pint. When dissolved, the gelatine liquid is stirred into the chicken mixture. The rest of the gelatine liquid is added to the remaining stock, and some of this latter mixture is used to line a rinsed mould (the lining is decorated with beetroot, hard-boiled egg white, and stuffed olives). When the lining is about to set, the remaining gelatine is put into the mould, which is then filled with the chicken mixture. The contents are chilled and turned out before serving.

kycklinglår med ris, devilled chicken drumsticks with rice. Chicken drumsticks are brushed with melted butter and are grilled slowly and evenly until tender. The chicken is served round a dish of boiled *patna rice*, and a boiling sauce is poured over it. The sauce is made with a roux of butter and flour, to which are added chicken stock, meat extract, worcestershire sauce, mustard, and cayenne.

kydonia, Greek for quinces. Ripe quinces are frequently made into compotes in Greece, for serving with meat. The same word is used for sea-quinces, delicious small shellfish which are often peddled by street vendors in Greece. They are eaten as *mezes*.

kydoni peltes, quince jam. After the fruit has been peeled, cleaned, and stoned, the peel and stones are tied in a bag of muslin and the fruit is cut into thick slices and cooked, with the bag, in water for 1½ hours. The bag is then removed and the fruit strained through muslin. For every 2 cups of the resulting juice, 1 cup sugar is added. The mixture is returned to the pan, together with a few young leaves from the ivyleaf geranium, or vanilla. The jam is simmered until set. The pulp may be retained for the making of a traditional quince paste, *pastokydona*.

kydoni xysto, Greek quince cheese. The fruit is peeled and coarsely grated, then gently cooked in water until soft and beginning to set. Over an increased heat, sugar is added gradually until the syrup thickens, at which point lemon juice is poured in. Shortly before the mixture jellies, 1 or 2 geranium leaves, or vanilla, are included.

kylling, Danish for chicken. See also CHICKEN; FJERKRÆ; HØNE.

stegt kylling med smør og persille, roast and stuffed chicken. A 3-lb. bird is stuffed with dry sprigs of parsley and seasoned butter. Butter is also spread on the outside of the bird, which is baked for about 6 minutes in a hot oven; then boiling water is added and the dish covered. Cooking is continued in a moderate oven for a further 65 minutes or until the bird is tender. The gravy is thickened with either corn flour (cornstarch) or arrowroot.

kylling, Norwegian for chicken. Chicken is very often served in Norway as the main course at dinner. Usually it is stuffed with parsley butter, pot-roasted, and served with a cream gravy. See also CHICKEN; FJAERKRÉ; HØNE

kylling med ris, chicken with rice. A boiling fowl is jointed and simmered in salt and water until half cooked. A sauce is made, consisting of the chicken stock thickened with flour and flavoured with salt, cayenne, grated nutmeg, and chopped tomatoes. This sauce is poured over the fowl, which has been placed in a fireproof dish, and both are covered and set aside while the rice is cooked. Then ½ lb. rinsed patna rice or other long-grained rice is brought to the boil in a mixture of ¾ pint milk and the same of water, with salt added, and slowly simmered for 30 minutes, when a mixture of ground mace, 1 teaspoon castor sugar, 2 oz. chopped almonds, and 2 tablespoons butter are stirred into it. The rice mixture is left to cool, and when cold, 2 beaten eggs are stirred in and the whole is spread over the fowl joints. The centre of the "pie" is cut to allow steam to escape, and the dish baked until the fowl is tender. The rice is glazed with egg; breadcrumbs moistened with melted butter are laid on top, and the pie is sprinkled with paprika and served with gravy made from chicken stock and butter.

stekt kylling, young chickens split and fried in butter. They are then covered in milk and cooked for 30 minutes, after which sour cream, parsley, and a little sherry are added to the dish, and it is heated up and served.

kythonia, see KYDONIA.

kyufté, the Bulgarian version of the ubiquitous Balkan meat ball or rissole, the equivalent of the Greek *keptethes* and the Turkish *köfte*, and similar to the Russian *kotlety*. Onions, a garlic clove, a little each of chopped parsley and mint, with seasoning, are fried together in a little butter; this is added to a mixture of 1–2 lb. minced meat, 1–2 cups moist bread, and 2 eggs. The two mixtures are blended together and shaped into small balls which are dipped in flour and fried in deep fat. Sometimes the mixture is cooked in a single piece like a large sausage; sometimes the meat balls are grilled on skewers, when they are known as *kebàpcheta*.

L

la frita, the general Spanish term for fried food, and also a Spanish tortilla, consisting of eggs mixed with chopped, stewed onions and grated cheese.

la reine soup, see LORRAINE SOUP.

laberdan, the name for cod which is salted and packed in barrels immediately on being landed at port, not subsequently at a factory as is the case with most salt cod. It has a finer flavour than the usual salt cod. Like *haberdine,* the name is a corruption of Aberdeen, where cod was first treated in this way.

labro, Spanish for wrasse, a good fish to eat in Spain, and usually baked with butter and lemon juice, or poached and served cold with mayonnaise or sauce vinaigrette. Alternative regional names are *bullon de roca, jaroba margota,* and *tordo de mar.*

labrus (*Labridae*), a European sea fish known for its brilliant colouring. It is also called wrasse and is used for bouillabaisse and other fish soups or stews.

labskaus, a popular fisherman's dish from Oldenburg on the northern coast of Germany. It is really a coarse kind of fishcake, made with chunks of fish, coarsely mashed potato, onions, bay leaf, and seasoning. This is fried in hot bacon fat. Each ingredient should remain distinct, not mixed into an unidentifiable paste. If fish is scarce, the dish is made with chunks of salt pork, corned beef, or other meat.

lache, a small sea fish which is cooked in France like a smelt. It is very good to eat, with a delicate flavour.

lacón con grelos, a Spanish dish, from León, of boiled shoulder of salt pork and white cabbage cooked together in water until tender.

lacqua, thick prune butter, made from puréed cooked prunes and grated peel and juice of lemons, used in Jewish cookery. See also HAMANTASCHEN.

lactic acid, an acid produced through the souring of milk, and known chemically as ochydroxypropionic acid. The preservative action of this acid means that sour milk can be used in the preserving of meat. It also has a tenderizing effect and is used in Bulgaria and Lithuania as a marinade.

laderes, Greek for foods braised in olive oil until cooked. They are usually served cold or lukewarm.

ladies' delight, a home-made English pickle for which there are various recipes. One of them uses equal quantities of peeled and chopped onions and apples, with a quarter the amount of chopped chillis. All are put into a pickle jar; then white wine vinegar, which has been boiled with salt, is poured over them. The pickle is ready for use after a few days. There is obviously more than a hint of irony in the name of this pickle.

ladies' fingers, see OKRA.

ladoxido, Greek for salad dressing or sauce vinaigrette. To prepare it 3 tablespoons each of olive oil and lemon juice or wine vinegar, a pinch of mustard, 2 teaspoons cold water, and seasoning, are all shaken together and chilled. Sometimes a pinch of wild marjoram or a tablespoon of capers is added when the sauce is to be served over grilled or baked brains.

lady's smock, see CARDAMINE.

laffitte, a French chicken consommé flavoured with Madeira and garnished with chopped *rognons de coq* and cock's combs, truffle, mushrooms, cucumber, and stoned olives, all sliced. See also CONSOMMÉ.

lagopède (*Lagopus*), the Pyrennean partridge, which is, however, misnamed, as it is an important member of the grouse family. It has tawny plumage with thin, black streaks in summer, and in winter turns white except for touches of black on the tail. Because of the winter plumage it is sometimes called snow partridge. It feeds on myrtle berries, rowan berries, and birch shoots, which give it a slightly bitter flavour much prized by gastronomes. It can be prepared for the table in the same way as grouse.

lagosta, Portuguese for lobster, although in Portugal crawfish (*lagostim*) is very often served under the guise of lobster. It is not as fine a flavour, and has no claw meat. See also LOBSTER.

lagosta à Portuguesa. A sauce is made from fried chopped onions, skinned tomatoes, garlic, salt, pepper, and a sprinkling of flour. These ingredients are all simmered, and when cooked, sieved. A little brandy is added, and the sauce is poured over the shelled and chopped lobster meat. Meat and sauce are simmered together for 5 minutes, then left to get cold in order to draw out flavour. Finally the dish is reheated and served with hot boiled rice. Lagosta is also sometimes painted with olive oil flavoured with chilli (*piri-piri*), and baked in the oven.

lagostim, Portuguese for crawfish, which is very often presented as lobster (*lagosta*) in Portugal.

lagostinhas, Portuguese for Dublin Bay prawns, which are excellent in Portugal, and best served steamed and cold, in a bowl of ice, and eaten with mayonnaise. *Camarão* is the word for shrimp or prawn, but the two words *lagostinhas* and *camaráos* are used loosely; however, it is essential to insist on lagostinhas if the larger variety is required.

laguiole, a French cow's milk cheese from the Auvergne, which is in season all the year round.

laguipière, a French consommé of game, garnished with poached pigeon's eggs and game royale. See also CONSOMMÉ.

laguipière, sauce, a classical French sauce consisting of ½ pint (1 cup) fish fumet, butter, and glaze, seasoned with lemon juice. Nowadays, it is often made with sauce *normande* flavoured with truffles infused in Madeira wine. It is named after the great 18th-century French chef of the same name. He was Carême's tutor, and died during the retreat from Moscow in 1812, after he had accompanied Prince Murat to Russia.

lahana, Greek for cabbage, a vegetable with a long and proud history in Greece; even in the earliest times, it was never simply cooked in water, but in stock and olive oil with a number of fresh spices, including cumin and coriander. See also LAHANIKA.

lahana dolmades me hirino, cabbage leaves stuffed with minced pork, tomato, rice, onion, and seasoning. They are simmered in water or stock and served with *avgolémono* sauce.

lahana yahni, a dish of braised cabbage, for which only the tender leaves are used. Onions are lightly cooked in oil, followed by root vegetables, tomatoes, and seasoning. Lastly, the cabbage leaves are added to the mixture, with enough water to prevent burning, and cooked until tender. When the cabbage is half cooked, a few capers are added.

soupa lahana, a soup made from shredded white cabbage, onion, tomatoes, olive oil, parsley, freshly chopped aniseed, and stock.

lahanika, Greek for vegetables, which are greatly esteemed in Greece and are generally served there as a separate course, as in France. Alexander the Great was responsible for introducing into Greece many vegetables which are today quite common all over Europe; he brought the onion from Egypt and the haricot bean from India. The onion was thought to be an aphrodisiac, or at least to inspire ardour; perhaps Alexander hoped to inspire martial ardour in his army with it. The cabbage was thought to be a sound precaution against drunkenness, as was parsley; it was always cooked with spices such as cumin, coriander, or caraway. Erasistratus, the physician and anatomist, born in 300 B.C. on the island of Chios, thought cabbage was a cure for paralysis. Leeks, too, were sometimes cooked with cabbage as a cure for various diseases. Even today, in the country regions of Greece, certain herbs such as wild spinach and wild artichokes are still used for health reasons, as they were in England many years ago. Dandelions are still thought to cure stomach disorders. See also ANGINARES; FASSOLAKIA FRESKA; FASSOLIA; HORTA; IMAM BAYILDI; KOLOKITHAKIA; LAHANA; SPANAKI.

lahna, Finnish for bream, which is of excellent quality in Finland and eaten there extensively.

lahnahyytelö, a Finnish method of serving bream. The fish are scaled, gutted, and cut into small pieces, then placed in cold water to cover, with vinegar, allspice, onion, and salt. They are cooked gently for about 1 hour, then removed, and the strained liquid poured over them, before both fish and liquid are set in a cool place. When the fish is served the following day, the liquor has set as a soft jelly.

laitue, French for cabbage (head) lettuce, so called because of the milky juice it exudes when cut. In France, lettuce is often served cooked, as well as raw in salads. *Laitue romaine* is cos (romaine) lettuce. Lettuce is also deep fried in batter; braised, served with sauce mornay or white sauce; and used for soups and for chiffonades. Lettuce stumps are cooked as chicory. See also LETTUCE; ROMAINE.

laitues braisées au gras, lettuce braised with bacon rinds, sliced onion, carrot, and stock.

laitues braisées au maigre, as above, but without the bacon rinds and with water instead of stock. If served with browned butter, it is called laitues au beurre noisette.

lake herring, see CISCO.

lake trout, I. A large variety of trout found mostly in the Swiss lakes. It is prepared like salmon trout and salmon. II. A large trout found in American lakes.

lakerda or **lakertha,** a Greek speciality of pickled fish, usually tunny (tuna), swordfish, or *palamida*. It tastes a little like smoked salmon and is served in Greece for hors d'oeuvre (*meze*).

lakror, a black bird of the thrush family, found in Albania, where it is eaten in pies.

laks, Danish for salmon, one of the finest fish caught in Danish waters. It is baked, grilled, or fried, or poached and served with sauce hollandaise.

laks, Norwegian for salmon. See also RØYKTLAKS. A Norwegian way of baking the middle cut of a salmon is to first roll it in waxed paper, then in two sheets of newspaper, and finally tie it securely. It is baked on the rack of a very moderate oven for about 2 hours, when the parcel is unwrapped. The skin is removed and the fish is served with either a sauce hollandaise or a mayonnaise.

Salmon is often caught when young and served fried, with butter creamed with mustard and lemon juice as a sauce.

laksørred, Danish for salmon trout.

lamb, the young of a sheep when it is less than a year old. After a year it is a *hogget* and for culinary purposes becomes mutton. Baby lamb is the animal before it has been weaned; the meat is tender, but insipid in taste compared with that of an older animal. It is very popular in Italy where it is called *abbacchio*. In France the unweaned lamb is called *agneau de lait* and the best type is *Pauillac*. All lamb should be cooked as simply as possible, with a few herbs and seasoning. The flavour is so delicate that it is easy to destroy it by overwhelming with elaborate sauces. Fresh mint sauce is the traditional accompaniment for roast lamb in the British Isles.

There is a tendency nowadays, especially in Britain and the U.S., to refer to all meat of the sheep, no matter what the age, as lamb. The famous English dish of boiled mutton and caper sauce invariably appears as "lamb," doubtless to indicate that it will be tender. It is unjust to imply that meat from sheep is not of good quality, for although old ewe mutton can be hard and stringy, the meat of young or middle-aged sheep has far more flavour than meat that is technically lamb. See also AGNEAU; AGNELLO; AGNESHKA CHURBA; ARNAKI; ARNI; AVIES KOJA; BARANINA; CORDERO; LAMBASTEIK; LAMM; LAMMAS; LAMSVLEES; MUTTON.

lamballe, a French name given to several dishes, particularly to a soup made from meat broth cooked with tapioca and then added to *potage Saint-Germain.*

lambasteik, an Icelandic lamb dish. Icelandic lamb is much smaller than British lamb, and this gives it a finer texture and flavour. It is the most popular meat dish in Iceland. Lambasteik is prepared both grilled and pot-roasted. See also HANGIKJÖT; LAMB.

lambropsomo, a Greek Easter bread made from 2 lb. (8 cups) flour, 2 oz. yeast, chopped peel of 1 orange, and sesame seeds. The yeast is first dissolved in ¼ pint (½ cup) warm milk, with a little of the flour gradually added; this is left standing in a warm place overnight. The next day a dough is made by adding 1 pint (2 cups) warm water and salt to this mixture, and kneading well. Enough is then used to shape into a long loaf which is well rolled in the sesame seeds. The remaining dough is shaped into two sausage-like pieces which are likewise rolled in the seeds and pressed onto either side of the loaf. Five depressions are then made for five *kokkina avga* (scarlet eggs) which are placed, one at the centre of the loaf, and one at each of the four points of the compass; to the Orthodox Greek these are symbolic of the five wounds of Christ. The loaf is baked in a hot oven for about 45 minutes, having first been lightly brushed with a mixture of beaten egg yolk and cold water. The same recipe is used for *christopsomo* or Christmas bread, which has a cross instead of the scarlet eggs, and is sprinkled with chopped nuts. See also HALVA; TSOUREKIA.

lamb's lettuce, see CORN SALAD.

lamm, German for lamb. *Lammkeule* is leg of lamb and *lammrippchen* is a lamb cutlet.

gebackenes lammernes, an Austrian method of serving a shoulder of lamb. The meat is boned and cut into squares which are dipped in egg and breadcrumbs and fried in lard. This dish is accompanied by a lettuce salad.

lamm, Swedish for lamb. See also KÖTT; LAMB.

kokt lamm, boiled lamb. Breast or shoulder of lamb is placed in boiling water, seasoning and herbs are added, and simmering is continued until the meat is tender (up to 1½ hours). It is served with a dill sauce made with the stock and garnished with parsley.

lammstek, roast lamb. A small leg of lamb is rubbed with seasoning and roasted until evenly browned, when onions and carrots are added to the pan and the oven temperature is lowered. Then ½ pint (1 cup) meat stock is poured over the joint and the cooking continued for about 1½ hours, with occasional basting. After this time ¾ cup sweetened coffee, mixed with ¼ cup cream, is added, and cooking continued until tender (about another hour). The joint is served with caramellised potatoes (*potatis*) and a gravy consisting of the juices in the pan mixed with flour and stock.

lammas, an old English festival of the wheat harvest, held on August 1. The word comes from the Old English *hlaf* (loaf) and *maesse* (mass). Some rents are still payable in England at Lammastide, but the festival is no longer celebrated. It is observed in Scotland on August 12, and bannocks are eaten. In the north of Ireland, it is celebrated with a famous fair at Ballycastle, County Antrim, on the last Tuesday of August. It is a mixed fair, with sheep sales in the morning and dancing and drinking in the afternoon and evening. It is thought to have been established by the Scottish MacDonnells in the 14th century. A delicious honeycomb toffee called yellowman is traditionally sold, and it has been made by the Devlin family for generations.

lammas, Finnish for mutton or lamb. See also LAMB; LIHA; MUTTON; TILLILIHA.

lammaskaali, Finnish mutton or lamb stew with cabbage. The pieces of meat, carrots, and cabbage are arranged in layers in a dish, covered with water, and simmered. The stew is garnished with parsley.

lammekjøtt, Norwegian for lamb. It is sometimes dried and salted in Norway and Denmark.

lam eller får i form, a charlotte of lamb or mutton. Breadcrumbs, slices of cold roast meat, sliced tomatoes, seasoning, and minced onions are arranged in layers, in that order, until the dish is full, ending with a layer of breadcrumbs. The dish is dabbed with butter, covered, and then baked in a moderate oven for 30 minutes, after which it is uncovered and baked for a further 15 minutes. Potatoes accompany this dish.

lammefilet, boned fillet of lamb, salted and dried, and sold as a cured meat, either whole or sliced. It is often used for *smørbrød.*

lettsprengt lammebryst, boiled, salted breast of lamb. Every day for 5 days, a breast of lamb is rubbed with a mixture of

salt, brown sugar, and saltpetre, being kept meanwhile in a cool place. It is then brought to the boil in cold water, skimmed, and kept simmering until tender (allowing 30 minutes per lb.). It is served with carrots, turnips, and potatoes.

lampreia, Portuguese for lamprey, which is considered a great delicacy in Portugal. It is in season only in the spring. Lampreys are also cooked in light flaky pastry in Portugal, and served hot. See also LAMPREY.

cozido de lampreia, a popular method of serving lampreys, in a stew with herbs, onion, vegetables, and red wine. Served with boiled rice.

lampreias do minho, lampreys braised with onion in red wine and served with rice.

lamprey, a fish of which there are two important types: the sea lamprey (*Petromyzon marinus*) and the lampern or river lamprey (*Lampetra fluviatilis*). Both are externally eel-like creatures with no vertebral column or jaws, which live by attaching themselves with their powerful suckers to fish and drawing nourishment from them. Both types may be prepared in any way that is suitable for cooking eels, and both have two filaments on the back which should be removed before cooking, as they are poisonous. The sea lamprey is highly prized gastronomically (especially in Portugal, see LAMPREIA), and is found in the Atlantic and the Mediterranean. It is also common in the Severn Estuary, England, and was a delicacy of the 19th century: it is still eaten but not as generally. Its flesh is delicate to eat, but as it can be rather fatty, small or medium-sized lampreys are preferred (about 20 inches long). The lampern is also considered a great delicacy and is in season from October until early spring. The most usual way of cooking it is in wine, flavoured with the lampern's blood, and mushrooms. In France it is sometimes called *sept-oeil* (seven-eye), and the eggs are also given this name. See also LAMPREIA; LAMPROIE.

lamprey

lamproie, French for lamprey. See also LAMPREY.

lamproie à la bordelaise, chopped lamprey is put into a buttered pan with sliced onions, carrots, garlic, bouquet garni, salt, pepper, and red wine to moisten. It is boiled for 15 minutes, then the lamprey is removed. The white part of leeks is cooked in butter with raw chopped bacon, and the fish is put into a pot with alternating layers of leeks, covered with a roux mixed with the stock, and simmered until cooked. The sauce is thickened with the blood, and it is all garnished with croûtons.

lamsvlees, Dutch for lamb, which is not eaten very often in Holland, perhaps because it is expensive and the supply is small. Whatever the reason, there appear to be many Dutch people who have never tasted it. See also LAMB.

gevulde lamsborst, a Dutch way of roasting stuffed shoulder of lamb. The boned shoulder is rubbed all over with garlic, and one side should be open, so that it can be filled with boiled rice mixed with a curry sauce made with 2 onions lightly fried in 3 tablespoons butter, to which are added 2 tablespoons flour, ½ pint (1 cup) milk, and the same of water. One tablespoon raisins, 1 apple, salt, and 2 teaspoons curry powder are then simmered in the sauce, and finally 1 tablespoon chopped parsley is included. The stuffing is well secured and the joint roasted (for about 40 minutes per lb.) in butter in a slow oven, basting frequently. It is served with fried bananas, more boiled rice, and a green salad.

lamscoteletten, lamb chops or cutlets. First 4 onions are partly fried in butter and removed from the pan; the cutlets are treated likewise and placed, with the onions, in a casserole with 1 tablespoon vinegar, 4 sliced and peeled tomatoes, 1 teaspoon celery salt, 1 tablespoon parsley, 1 bay leaf, salt, 1 teaspoon paprika, and the pan drippings, which have been boiled up with ½ pint (1 cup) bouillon to make a sauce. The contents of the casserole are cooked for about 3 hours in a slow oven, and about 1 tablespoon red currant jelly is added just before serving.

lamstongetjes in madeira saus, lambs' tongues served in a sauce madère. Usually one tongue is allowed for each person. The tongues are brought to the boil and simmered for 30 minutes in water, with mace, bay leaf, salt, and either celery or parsley. After draining, the tongues are skinned, trimmed, and thickly sliced. The slices are lightly browned with garlic in butter, and the sauce is made by adding flour and stock to the pan drippings. The Madeira is put in last, the sauce is sieved, and the dish is accompanied by boiled rice.

Lancashire cheese, an English cow's milk cheese from the Fylde district of Lancashire, and perhaps the finest English cheese for cooking. It has a mild flavour, and when about 3 months old it is as soft and easy to spread as butter. It becomes harder as it matures, but it does not keep well. At the turn of the century it was a farm-made cheese, but nowadays there are many factories in Lancashire which produce it. It is made in three sizes: a small one, loaf-shaped and weighing about 10 lb.; a medium one weighing about 30 lb.; and a large one weighing about 50 lb. Before World War II a small amount of sage Lancashire was made by mixing chopped sage leaves with the curds.

Lancashire foot, a curious foot-shaped turnover traditional in the north of England. The pastry is cut like the double sole of a shoe, and a filling of chopped meat, onion, and potato is placed on half of it; the other half is folded over, the edges dampened and pressed down, and the turnover baked in a slow to moderate oven for about 30 minutes. It is made in this shape in order to fit into the food tin or inner pocket of the worker.

Lancashire hot pot, see HOT POT.

lancen pie, see LAUNCESTON PIE.

lances, another name for sand eels, and a traditional Cornish delicacy. The sand eels are cured by soaking for 12 hours in strong brine, then strung on twine in lots of 20 to 30, and hung to dry in the sun. They are taken down as required, and soaked overnight in water before being boiled. Fresh sand eels are also eaten fried, the heads having first been pinched off and the eels washed and dried.

land cress, see AMERICAN CRESS.

landrail, another name for the corncrake, a small bird very much appreciated as food in Europe, but protected by law in England. It is prepared in the same way as quail.

lane ciasto, Polish for a soup garnish of batter noodles made from flour and eggs (2 eggs to 4 oz. flour). The mixture is poured in a thin stream into boiling soup, and cooked for 2–3 minutes.

langosta, the most common Spanish word for lobster, although *bogavante* is also used. *Langosta* is also the word for crawfish, which is plentiful in Spain and is prepared in any way that is suitable for lobster. In fact the inferior crawfish is often sold as lobster in Spanish restaurants, therefore it is wise to insist on *bogavante.* See also CRAWFISH; LOBSTER.

langostina, Spanish for large deep-sea prawns that have dark red shells covered with large black spots. They must be well scrubbed, and are delicious grilled in their shells on a hotplate over charcoal, and eaten hot. They are also cooked with white wine and herbs, sometimes with a little brandy added. They are used in paella and *calderada. Langostina* is a misleading name, since these prawns are not like the French langoustines, (Dublin Bay prawns) which are known in Spanish as *cigala.* See also CAMARÓN.

langrès, a soft French cow's milk cheese, the making of which is said to date from the time of the Merovingian kings. It is from the Haute-Marne and somewhat resembles *livarot.* It is at its best from November to June.

langue de boeuf, French for ox tongue. Tongue is cooked like braised beef in France, and can be served with any number of garnishes: *Alsacienne* (with sauerkraut and lean bacon), bourgeoise, bourguignonne, florentine, milanaise, and nivernaise. The following sauces are also suitable accompaniments: diable, lyonnaise, madère, poivrade, and tomato.

langue de boeuf à la diable, slices of cold, poached, salted tongue are spread with mustard and dipped in melted butter. Then more melted butter is poured over them, and they are grilled or fried, and served with sauce diable.

langue de chat (*cat's tongue*), a thin, flat French biscuit (cookie), not unlike a cat's tongue in shape. They should be crisp and dry. To make them ½ lb. (1 cup) castor sugar and ½ pint (1 cup) cream are well mixed; then ½ lb. (2 cups) flour, 1 teaspoon vanilla, and 5 stiffly whisked egg whites are beaten in until the whole is quite smooth. The mixture is piped out of a forcing bag onto a greased tin. Sometimes the bottom and edges are dipped in chocolate, but this is an addition to the traditional langue de chat. Chocolate manufacturers also make a langue de chat in plain chocolate.

languedocienne, à la, I. A French garnish for meat, consisting of stuffed eggplants, minced cèpes cooked in oil, tomatoes, and parsley, with *pommes de terre château.* II. Dishes from the Languedoc region of France. Sauces served with these dishes are always flavoured with garlic. See also POULET (POULET À LA LANGUEDOCIENNE).

lantern flounder, a flat fish of the flounder family, also called megrim.

lanttu, Finnish for swede or Swedish turnip. See also SWEDE.

lanttukukko, pasties made with 2 lb. (8 cups) rye flour, 1½ cups water, 2 tablespoons fat and salt, filled with finely sliced, salted swede. The edges are secured, and the pasties are baked. It is the same as *kalakukko,* but using a swede instead of fish.

lanttulaatikko, swede pudding made from 2 lb. peeled, diced swedes cooked until soft in salted water, then drained. They are mashed, then mixed with 3 tablespoons breadcrumbs which have been soaked in 4 tablespoons cream, 2 eggs, and a pinch of nutmeg. The top is sprinkled with breadcrumbs and dotted with butter, and the pudding is baked in the oven. It is served with meat dishes, or for *pikku lämpimät.*

lapereau, French for young rabbit. Rabbit is cooked in many different ways in France. It is grilled, fried, and also made into a terrine or pâté with pork. In Normandy it is often cooked in cider with onions; it is also made into a rich stew called *gibelotte* which is prepared as *civet de lièvre,* except that white wine can be used instead of red. See also GIBIER; LAPIN.

lapereau en blanquette, a jointed rabbit is fried quickly in butter, sprinkled with flour, barely covered with white stock, and simmered for 1 hour. Then button onions and mushrooms are added, and the sauce is thickened with egg yolks and cream, or a *beurre manié* and cream.

tourte de lapereau à la paysanne, made in a tart tin lined with pastry, filled with pork sausage meat mixed with soaked bread, chopped onions, parsley, and thick cold slices of rabbit fillet, finishing with a layer of sliced mushrooms and butter. A pastry lid is put on, and the tart is baked in the oven. Sometimes a little gravy is poured through a hole in the centre after the tart has been cooked.

lapin, French for fully grown rabbit. *Lapin de chou* or *lapin de clapier* is a tame or hutch rabbit.

lapin aux pruneaux, a famous Belgian method of cooking rabbit. The rabbit is marinated in red wine and a little vinegar, then sautéed in butter and rubbed in flour. It is casseroled with prunes, water, and a little of the marinade for several hours. Red currant or gooseberry jelly is stirred in before serving. See also LAPEREAU.

lapskaus, Norwegian for a dish of boiled salt meat. The meat used for this dish varies; green bacon, salted silverside of beef, and salted mutton are all equally good. The meat is simmered in water for 1 hour, when it is removed, cut up, and returned to the stock, together with diced root vegetables. The pan is covered and simmered for another hour. Minced parsley is used for garnishing.

lăptucă, Rumanian for lettuce, used in a traditional soup, as well as for salad.

ciorbă de lăptucă, lettuce soup made from 3 heads lettuce, torn into pieces and simmered in 3 pints (6 cups) water with 6 chopped spring onions (scallions), 1 head (not a clove) of minced garlic, salt, and pepper. When it has cooked for about 10 minutes, ¼ cup mild vinegar is added and simmered for 5 minutes. Then 2 egg yolks are beaten into ¼ pint (½ cup) cream, and when the vegetables are tender this mixture is poured slowly into the very hot soup and stirred. The soup must not boil again after the egg yolks have been added. It is seasoned to taste and garnished with chopped parsley.

lapwing or **green plover,** see PLOVER.

lard, the fat obtained from the melting down of pork fat. It is clarified, and should be a pure white with scarcely any smell. Lard is obtained by chopping up the fat and putting it into a deep pot with 1 gill (5 oz.) water for each lb. of fat. It is stirred frequently over a gentle heat so that it is all fully melted. As soon as steam stops rising from the fat, it is strained through either a very fine strainer or a cloth. It is good for making cakes or pastry and, after oil, is the best fat for frying. See also FAT; OIL.

lard cakes or *lardy cakes,* old English cakes, made with 8 oz. lard or flead of the pig, 4 oz. (½ cup) sugar, 1 lb. (4 cups) self-raising flour, and a little nutmeg, cinnamon, or allspice. The mixture is put into a greased tin and scored across and down with a knife before baking. When cooked the cake is broken, never cut. These cakes were always made about the time of pig-killing at the home farm. See also FLEAD; GROVEY CAKE.

lard, French for bacon. *Lard gras* is the term for the fat of pork between the skin and the flesh of the *chine*. *Lard maigre* is the fat from the pig's belly which is interspersed with lean pork, eaten fresh in France and also used for larding. See also BACON.

larding, the threading of pieces of fat pork, either salted or fresh, into very lean meats such as game or fillets of beef or veal in order to provide interior fat. The implement used for this is called a larding needle. In France the pieces of fat are known as *lardons* or *lard à piquer*, and the larding needle is a *lardoire*. See also BARDING; INTERLARDING; PIQUAGE.

lardoons, strips of fat cut into varying shapes and thicknesses, threaded through a needle made for the purpose, and inserted into meat, game, or poultry to give additional flavour. This process is known as larding. In France the word is *lardons,* and is used to mean coarse or finely chopped salt pork or bacon.

lark (*Alauda arvensis*), a small, brown song bird, once a very popular food in England, especially for lark pie, although this is now never seen. However, the lark has a most delicate-tasting flesh and is still sought after in France and Italy, especially in France for the pâté de *pithiviers*. Otherwise larks are grilled on skewers, or boned and cooked in butter and served on bread. They can be roasted or casseroled as well. See also TÀCCULA; UCCELLETTI.

larron, le, a French cow's milk cheese. It is an inferior *maroilles*, made of skimmed milk and ready to eat within six or seven weeks. A variety of this cheese is made called *fromage d'ors*.

lasagne, an Italian speciality which consists of large strips (2 inches by 4 inches) of pasta, either green and flavoured with spinach (*lasagne verdi*), or plain. It can be bought commercially, for home cooking. The strips are poached in boiling salted water, and when soft are plunged into a saucepan of cold water, before continuing with further preparations. See also LAZANKI; PASTA.

lasagne

lasagne al forno, the most usual method of serving lasagne. The cooked strips are layered in a fireproof dish with a coating of *ragù*, and sauce béchamel flavoured with nutmeg. Grated Parmesan cheese or sliced mozzarella is thickly sprinkled on top of the final layer of lasagne, and it is baked in the oven for about 30 minutes.

lašagne alla piemontese, as above, with finely sliced white truffles.

lasinietis, a Lithuanian white yeast bread, baked with whole peppercorns and crisp bacon rinds. It is served spread with butter and eaten at dinner or tea.

läskisoosi, see SIANLIHA.

latholémono, a Greek sauce made from equal quantities of olive oil and lemon juice beaten until frothy and creamy. It is sometimes flavoured with herbs.

lathoxitho, see LADOXIDO.

latkes, a traditional Jewish dish eaten in December at Channukah, the Feast of Lights, which celebrates the battle of Maccabees. It is a home festival in which the children take part, and candles are lit each evening. Latkes are made from 1 lb. grated raw potatoes mixed with 2 raw eggs and 3 tablespoons flour to bind, salt, and pepper. These ingredients are made with 2 spoons into little cakes which are fried in hot oil. Sometimes grated cheese or onion is added to taste.

latte, Italian for milk, often used for braising or stewing poultry and meat in central and northern Italy. See MAIALE, AL LATTE.

Łatwy i tani piernik, in Polish, "cheap and easy honey cake." It is a sponge mixture made from ½ lb. (2 cups) flour, 4 oz. (½ cup) sugar, and 3 egg yolks, well beaten, to which 1 tablespoon baking powder, 1 lb. honey, 1 cup chopped walnuts, and spices to taste are added. Finally 3

stiffly beaten egg whites are folded in, before baking in a
greased tin for 1 hour in a moderate oven.

laubfrösche, "tree frogs," a Swiss method of serving large
spinach leaves. They are blanched in boiling water, then
stuffed with a mixture of 6 crustless slices bread soaked in
water and squeezed, 2 chopped fried onions, 2 scrambled
eggs, chopped parsley, nutmeg, salt, and pepper to taste. The
leaves are rolled up, put side by side in a dish, and simmered
in bouillon for 20 minutes. When cooked, they are served
with a sauce crème.

Launceston pie or **lancen pie,** a traditional Cornish dish,
consisting of sliced raw meat seasoned with salt and pepper
and placed in the bottom of a pie dish. Over it are placed
layers of sliced potato until the dish is almost full. More
seasoning is added, and the top is finished with a few small
whole potatoes and a border of pastry round the edge of the
dish. The pie is cooked in a slow oven, which approximates
as closely as possible the traditional method of baking in a
"kettle." This was a round disc of iron with two handles at
the sides, known as a "hearth," which was heated over glowing embers; any ash on its upper surface was cleared off and
the food to be baked was placed on the disc, and a kettle or
cylindrical iron pot previously heated in the same way as the
disc and having the same diameter, was inverted over the
food. A layer of ash was placed round the rim to keep smoke
from getting in, and a fire of small wood or furze was made
over the whole. As the fire burned away to ashes, these surrounded the kettle and finished the baking.

lavallière, à la, I. A French garnish for fowl and sweetbreads,
consisting of sautéed truffles served whole, lamb's sweetbreads larded with truffles, and small steamed crayfish. II. A
French garnish for tournedos and noisettes, consisting of artichoke bottoms, filled with asparagus tips, *pommes château,*
and sauce bordelaise.

lavallière, sauce, a classical French sauce. A sauce madère or
demi-glace is flavoured with game essence (extract). A julienne of tarragon and truffle is added, and the sauce is thickened with cream.

lavaret, the French name for the whitefish (*Coregonus ferus*),
a salmonlike fish found in the deep waters of the Savoy lakes.
There are 4 separate breeds to be found in French lakes and
rivers, and also a saltwater lavaret which sometimes runs to
the rivers. The most highly prized lavaret is found in Lake
Bourget. It has a very delicate flavour and is prepared like
trout or salmon trout. It is also called *féra* when found in
Swiss and Bavarian lakes.

lavender (*Lavandula spica*), a fragrant, spiky-leaved, evergreen plant which grows in the Far East as well as in Europe.
There are several varieties, with flowers ranging from a
mauve-blue to purple and even white (*L. nana alba*). The
leaves are used both fresh and dried, in drinks and in pot-
pourri. Sparingly, they are included in marinades (especially
for venison), in jellies (particularly apple jellies), and in stews.
Lavender honey has a delicate, scented taste, that made at
Chamonix in France being particularly notable. Oil is extracted from lavender and used for toilet preparations.

laver (*Porphyra laciniata*), an edible seaweed found on many
shores of Britain and Ireland. Red laver, called slouk in Scotland and sloke in Ireland, is a filmy, reddish-purple seaweed,
rich in iodine. It makes a good pickle and is at its best from
June to March. Green laver (*Ulva latissima*), whose fronds
are bright green and crinkly, is also known as lettuce laver.
Laver is prepared by washing well in several changes of fresh
water, then steeping for several hours, after which it is boiled
gently until tender. The surplus water is poured off and a little
salt beaten into the pulp, which may then be stored for about a
week and after that period, prepared by adding 1 lb. of the

pulp to 3 oz. butter or meat extract, lemon juice, and pepper,
which are all heated in an aluminium saucepan and stirred
with a wooden spoon or silver fork. It is served very hot with
roast meat. Laver served in a silver chafing dish with a sprinkling of Seville orange juice is a traditional accompaniment to
Welsh mutton.

Laver is also mixed with vinegar or lemon juice, a sprinkling of olive oil, pepper, and salt and served cold on toast.
The taste is said to be reminiscent of a mixture of olives and
oysters. In Wales and Scotland, laver is also mixed with oatmeal and fried in flat cakes. Laver bread is a traditional Welsh
speciality, but is not to everyone's taste.

lavraki, a Greek way of baking fish with butter, a little water,
cream, and lemon juice.

lax, Icelandic for salmon, which is served freshly cooked in
Iceland, either hot or cold, and is also pickled, smoked, and
salted.

lax, Swedish for salmon. *Rökt lax* is smoked salmon. See also
FISK; GRAVLAX.

laxpudding, salmon pudding. A 1-lb. fish is rubbed with salt
and then left to stand for 24 hours in a cool place. A pie
dish is well buttered and filled with alternate layers of boiled,
sliced potatoes and salmon, finishing with potatoes. A mixture
of 2 beaten eggs, 1 pint (2 cups) milk, pepper, and 2 teaspoons melted butter is poured over, and the pudding is sprinkled with breadcrumbs, baked in a moderate oven for about
30 minutes, and then served with melted butter.

röktlaxlåda, a custard made with 4 oz. smoked salmon, cut
finely into pieces, mixed with 3 beaten eggs and 1 pint (2
cups) warm milk seasoned to taste. It is baked in a *bain-
marie,* for about 1 hour in a moderate oven.

layos, Greek for hare.

layos me saltsa, a recipe for hare in a white wine sauce,
with a small glass of brandy stirred in before serving. A
jointed hare is cleaned and marinated overnight, the marinade
consisting of equal parts vinegar and water, with parsley and
root vegetables. The next day the joints are dried, rolled in
seasoned flour, and fried in deep, hot oil. The pieces are then
removed to a casserole. A little flour is browned in a small
amount of the remaining oil, and wine is stirred in gradually.
After it has come to the boil, the sauce is strained and poured
over the hare. Slices of bacon (which are cut up when
cooked), garlic (optional), tomato purée, bay leaf, and seasoning are added, and the casserole is baked. The bay leaf is
discarded before serving.

layos me saltsa karidia, a hare, marinated as above, is simmered in stock with a pinch of cinnamon, 1 bay leaf, lemon to
taste, and a little brandy. Just before serving, about 20
crushed walnuts are rolled in flour and added to the stock.

layos stifado, a hare stew, with onions, garlic, tomato
juice, cloves, sugar, currants, bay leaf, and seasoning.

lazanki, Polish for lasagne, usually served in Poland, after the
preliminary boiling, with a mixture of sour cream, egg yolks,
and grated cheese. Lazanki is also served as an accompaniment to cooked cabbage, sauerkraut, or simmered dried
mushrooms. See also LASAGNE.

le roi, see ROI.

leaf beet or **leaf chard,** see CHARD.

leaven, a mixture of 1 oz. yeast, 2 tablespoons flour, and ½
cup tepid water, sometimes also containing 1 teaspoon sugar,
which has been kept in a warm atmosphere until the yeast has
begun to "work," that is, to ferment the sugar and starch
with the production of carbon dioxide gas. The leaven is then
added to the dough, with which it is thoroughly mixed or
kneaded, and allowed to rise further before being made into
bread, cakes, etc., and baked.

leber, German for liver, which is eaten a good deal in Germany and Austria. Goose liver is a speciality. See also GANS (GÄNSELEBER); LIVER; TIROLER LEBER.

leberknödelsuppe, a strong consommé with calf's or pig's liver dumplings, traditional in Upper Bavaria.

lebernockerln, see NOCKERLN.

leberreis, see NOCKERLN.

leberspiessli, skewered calf's liver wrapped in bacon with sage leaves interspersed, grilled over charcoal or vine-wood stumps. It is a speciality of Zurich, Switzerland.

lebersuppe, an Austrian soup made with liver, salt pork, stock, herbs, onions, and carrots, all sieved, and served with croûtons.

leberwurst, a liver wurst made from pork, pig's liver, allspice, and seasoning. See WÜRST.

lebkuchen, small cakes made from 4 oz. honey, 4 oz. treacle (molasses), 3 teaspoons mixed spices, 6 oz. (⅔ cup) brown sugar, 1 lb. (4 cups) flour, 2 oz. candied peel, 2 oz. nuts, peel and juice of 1 lemon, and 2 eggs. They resemble gingerbread and are eaten at Christmas time in Germany and the German-speaking part of Switzerland. They are often baked in elaborate and beautifully carved moulds.

lebkuchen

leche, Spanish for milk.

leche crème, a custard made from 6 egg yolks, 3 tablespoons sugar, and ¾ pint (1½ cups) milk, flavoured with vanilla or lemon, thickened with 3 tablespoons corn flour (cornstarch), and cooked in a double boiler until it thickens. When cold it is dusted with powdered cinnamon.

leche frita, a custard made with 3 eggs, 1 pint (2 cups) milk, and 3 tablespoons flour, cooked until quite thick, then poured into a tin to cool. The custard is then cut into small pieces, which are dipped either in whole beaten egg or egg white, fried in deep oil, and drained. They are sprinkled with sugar before serving. This is a speciality of Valencia. See also ARROZ, CON LECHE.

lechefrite, the French name for the tin placed underneath spit-roasted foods to catch the fat and juices.

leckerli, a rectangular biscuit (cookie) which is a Swiss speciality. It is made with 1 lb. honey, ¼ lb. (½ cup) sugar, 1 lb. (4 cups) flour, 2 tablespoons chopped almonds, 3 tablespoons chopped candied peel, 2 tablespoons cloves, mixed nutmeg, and ginger, and 1 teaspoon baking soda. They are all well combined, and then the mixture is baked on a well-buttered square tray and brushed with milk just before being taken

from the oven, then cut into pieces while warm. In Basel it is sometimes flavoured with kirsch.

lecrelet, a speciality of Basel, Switzerland. It is a light, delicious pastry, flavoured with orange or lemon and sweetened with honey.

lecsó, a Hungarian dish of simmered green peppers, onions, and tomatoes. When they have become a purée, a little paprika is added and several eggs are beaten in. They are cooked like scrambled eggs, and then the whole dish is served with potatoes or rice.

ledvinková polévka, see POLÉVKA.

leek (*Allium porrum*), considered by some to be the most delicately flavoured of all the members of the onion family. Native to Europe, it is one of the most useful of winter vegetables and is a very important ingredient of vegetable soups and stews. Leeks can be baked, boiled, steamed, and braised. They are, of course, the main feature of the famous Scotch *cock-a-leekie,* the Irish brotchàn roy, and the Welsh cawl (the leek being the national vegetable of Wales). The trimmed green part should be eaten as well as the white. To clean, cut across on the green end and stand that end down in a deep jug of cold water. This releases the grit which is lodged in the closely coiled leaves. They are excellent boiled until just tender, then served with hot melted butter and a squeeze of lemon, or boiled and served cold with sauce vinaigrette. They are also the main ingredient in the savoury flan de poireaux and *flamiche.* See also POIREAU.

leek

leek pie, a traditional Welsh dish, consisting of chopped leeks, bacon, and cream, baked with a pastry crust.

lefser, a Norwegian flat potato and rye bread, made from the same ingredients as flatbrød, but when being cooked it is turned only twice, as it should remain soft, hence its name "soft cakes." When cooked, the bread round is slipped from the pan into a clean cloth. Half the bread is spread with a mixture of equal parts of sour cream and creamed butter, well blended and sprinkled with sugar, and the other half is folded over this. It is cut into triangles and kept in the cloth until needed.

legumbres, Spanish for vegetables. See MENESTRA DE LEGUMBRES FRESCAS.

legumina, the Polish word for a sweet pudding.

legumina kasztanowa, a chestnut pudding, made from 1 lb. cooked, shelled chestnuts mixed with 1 cup soaked and drained dried fruit, 3 tablespoons vanilla sugar, and 2 egg whites stiffly beaten and spread over the top. This mixture can be baked, or served chilled; if the latter, sweet whipped cream is poured over before serving.

Leicestershire cheese, a hard, flaky-textured cheese made in Leicestershire, as is the world-famous Stilton. It is not unlike a single Gloucester in taste, but has more flavour when it is fully ripe at 6 months. It is usually coloured a pale orange by the addition of annatto. A very delicious Leicestershire cheese used to be sold in Loughborough market place: it was a milk cheese with a cream cheese set in the centre.

leipä, Finnish for breads and for loaf.

hapanleipä, rye bread (literally "sour" bread).

hiivaleipä, yeast bread, which is sometimes spiced with aniseed, fennel, or caraway seed in Finland. See also PULLA-TAIKINA.

leipziger allerlei, a speciality of Leipzig, Germany, consisting of diced, cooked root vegetables, peas, green beans, asparagus, and morels, all mixed together, tossed in butter, and bound with a white sauce mixed with crayfish tails. It is garnished with more tails, and very small *krödeln* made from semolina.

leipziger schnitzel, see SCHNITZEL.

leitão assado, a Portuguese national speciality of roast suckling-pig cooked with herbs and spices. It is the traditional dish of Barrada. It is usually served hot, but is also excellent cold, for a picnic. See also CARNE, DE PORCO.

lekach, a traditional Jewish honey cake eaten at Rosh Hashanah, the Jewish New Year, in late September or early October. It consists of ½ lb. honey to 12 oz. (3 cups) flour, ¼ lb. (½ cup) sugar, 2 eggs, a little nut oil, ginger, ground mixed spices, walnuts or almonds, and a pinch of baking powder. The eggs and sugar are beaten together, then a few tablespoons of oil and warmed honey are added. All dry ingredients are mixed in alternately with about ¼ pint warm water, although some variations give warm coffee instead. The mixture is beaten to a smooth batter, turned into a shallow greased tin, sprinkled with the chopped nuts and baked in a moderate oven for about 1 hour.

lemon (*Citrus limonium*), the fruit of the lemon tree, originally native to India, but now grown in the Mediterranean area, California, and other subtropical regions. The juice, rich in citric acid, has been used in cookery and as a flavouring agent for many centuries. It has rapidly gained favour as a replacement for vinegar in salad dressings, and is served as a garnish for fish all over the world. It is also used for the national sauce of Greece, *avgolémono*. The peel yields a valuable oil, and is also used in cakes, biscuits, water-ices, and puddings. Grated peel, known as zest of lemon, can also be obtained for sweet dishes by rubbing a lump of sugar against the outside of the lemon. See also CITROEN; CITRON; LEMONI.

lemon butter, an English sauce which is served over steamed puddings. To prepare, 1 heaped tablespoon corn flour (cornstarch), 2 tablespoons castor sugar, and the grated peel of 1 lemon are mixed thoroughly in a saucepan over heat. The juice of a lemon is added to ½ pint (1 cup) boiling water, and this, with a small piece of butter, is added to the sauce. Then the beaten yolks of 2 eggs are gradually stirred in. The sauce must not be allowed to come to the boil.

lemon curd, a delicious English thick lemon custard which is bottled in jars and eaten like jam. It is made by rubbing 1 lb. lump sugar over the rind of 4 lemons, then squeezing the fruit and adding the juice to the sugar. Then ½ lb. (1 cup) butter is put into a double saucepan, the sugar mixture is added, and when melted but not boiling, the beaten eggs are mixed in and constantly stirred until the mixture becomes thick. It must not boil, or the eggs will be scrambled. It makes a good filling for tarts as well as sandwiches. Bramble

jelly is made in the same way, but blackberry juice is used instead of lemon.

lemon sauce, an American sauce chiefly served with boiled fish. First 2 eggs are well beaten, then 1 teaspoon corn flour (cornstarch) is added to 1 cup fish stock, and, with the eggs, juice of 2 lemons, 1 tablespoon butter, salt, and pepper, it is cooked in a double boiler and stirred until thick and creamy. Sometimes thinly sliced almonds are added to the sauce just before serving. It can also be served with boiled chicken, when it is of course made with chicken stock instead of fish stock.

lemon balm, see BALM.

lemon sole (*Limanda limanda*), a European saltwater flat fish which is thought to get its name from the French limande-sole. It is not a sole, being rather more like a dab; the flesh is inclined to be tasteless unless very fresh, when it is milky and delicate, but it can be prepared as sole or dab. It is advisable to serve a good sauce with this fish. Or grill the whole fillet sandwich fashion with butter and herbs in between. This brings out the delicate flavour.

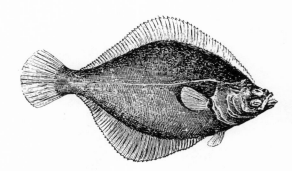

lemon sole

lemon thyme, see THYME.

lemoni, Greek for lemon, used perhaps more in Greece than anywhere else in the world. It is used in juice form for *avgolémono* sauce, which can be served with meat, fish, or vegetables. The small island of Poros, not far from Piraeus, specialises in green, bitter-sweet pickled lemons. See also GLYKO (LEMONIOU GLYKO).

lengua, Spanish for tongue.

lengua a la aragonesa, a speciality of Aragon, consisting of washed and trimmed tongue cooked in boiling water just long enough to allow the skin to be peeled off. Then it is turned in hot oil and more oil is added, followed by garlic, tomatoes, green peppers, root vegetables, parsley, thyme, cloves, and 1 tablespoon grated chocolate. The pan is covered, and it is simmered gently for about 3 hours. When ready, the tongue is drained and sliced, and served with the strained stock and young boiled carrots.

lenticchia, Italian for lentil. The variety used in Italy are the brown or green lentils, which are traditionally eaten on New Year's Day, often with *zampone di Modena*, to ensure a fortunate year. They are made into an excellent thick soup, almost like a porridge, which is eaten hot or cold with a little olive oil added. See also LENTIL.

lenticchie in umido, lentils stewed in olive oil with a sliced onion. When the oil is absorbed, water to cover, garlic, and fresh mint are added. The lentils are covered and simmered slowly until almost all the water has cooked away, and then seasoned with salt and pepper. The lentils are also eaten cold, with a little fresh olive oil and sliced hard-boiled eggs.

lentil (*Lens escuelenta*), the seed of a small branching annual plant of the vetch family. These seeds are dried and keep for a very long time. There are two main varieties of lentil: the Egyptian, which is orange in colour, small, and usually sold split in two; and the French, which is twice as big, greenish-grey outside and yellow within, and is sold whole. The Egyptian lentils have far less flavour than the French, and cook quite quickly. They make soup and salads and are the basis of the Indian dahl. They grow all over India, Africa, and Egypt, and are thought to be the lentil for which Esau sold his birthright (Genesis XXV: 34). The French variety, sometimes called brown or green lentils, have much more taste and make a good, rich brown soup. In Italy they are cooked with rice and eaten hot or cold. They are extremely nourishing and contain a lot of protein. A Hindu proverb says, "Rice is good, but lentils are my life." The lentil's country of origin is not known, but it was probably one of the first plants to be brought under cultivation by mankind. Lentils have been found in the Bronze Age dwellings of St. Peter's Island in Lake Bienne, Switzerland. See also LENTICCHIA; LINSEN.

lentils

léopold, a French meat consommé, thickened with semolina, with julienne of sautéed sorrel and chopped chervil. See also CONSOMMÉ.

lepiote, French for parasol mushroom. The cultivated variety best known in France is called *columelle.*

lepre, Italian for hare. See also HARE.

lepre alla montanura, hare simmered with sugar, pinenuts, cinnamon, ½ lemon, and sultanas, in red wine to cover. In the Trento and the Veneto it is served with polenta and green salad.

lepre in agrodolce, marinated hare simmered in stock with ham and marjoram until tender. It is served with *agrodolce sauce.*

les choesels, a Belgian speciality, consisting of oxtail, mutton, veal, sheep's trotters (feet), ox kidney, and sweetbreads all simmered with herbs, cloves, nutmeg, and onions, the main meat ingredients being added in turn, according to the length of cooking-time each requires to become tender. Finally, *fricandelles* are added, with mushrooms and a flavouring of Madeira wine. It is a most delicious stew.

leshch, Russian for bream.

leshch s kaschey, bream stuffed with kasha mixed with chopped hard-boiled eggs, onions, and herbs. It is then baked with melted butter and a little water, and sprinkled with breadcrumbs. Before serving, sour cream is stirred into the fish stock.

leshch s khrenom i yablokami, a dish of poached bream. A 3-lb. fish is poached in ½ pint (1 cup) vinegar for 10 minutes, then added to sliced onion, celery, leek, and herbs, with salted water to cover, and simmered until all is tender. Then the fish is drained, and served sprinkled with horseradish which has been well mixed with grated raw apple and sugar and diluted with a little vinegar.

leshta yahnìya, a Bulgarian dish made in the same way as *fašùl yahnìya,* but made with lentils instead of beans.

lesso rifato, Italian for reheated meat, usually beef. It is sliced thinly and heated with lightly fried onions, a clove of garlic, a little stock, salt, and pepper. Before serving, a squeeze of lemon is added and a small handful of chopped parsley.

lettuce (*Lactuca sativa*), the name given to a wide variety of annual salad plants. The chief varieties are cabbage (head) lettuce, which has a firm heart in a round and spreading head; cos (romaine) lettuce, which is erect and oblong with a small heart; and cutting (leaf) lettuce. This last is a very valuable type, as it does not run to seed but produces a succession of leaves for cutting during the summer months. Perennial lettuce is an uncultivated variety which grows freely on light and chalky soils in parts of France, and produces leaves rather like those of the dandelion, which are used for salads in early spring. Wild lettuce is found in many places, especially the Caucasus and India. The well-known Webb's wonder, also known as iceberg lettuce, is cabbage-shaped, very crisp and juicy, but without the fine flavour of the cabbage or cos lettuce. Lettuce is mainly used in salads, but it is also braised like chicory. It has a crisp texture and fresh taste. It figures in the Passover ritual, and in early times it was thought a sacred plant.

Lettuce is thought to have originated in Asia Minor, and was eaten by Persian kings as early as 550 B.C. Its easy growth led to its being cultivated all over Europe from an early date, and by the 14th century it was being eaten in Britain, largely by the poor people. In the 16th century John Gerard, the famous herbalist, wrote that it "cooleth the heat of the stomach called heartburn, quencheth thirst, and causeth sleep." In the 18th and 19th centuries in England, lettuce was thought to have faintly narcotic properties; in fact the milky juice of the lettuce contains a small trace of an alkaloid similar to that found in the opium poppy. It is possible that a variety called the "strong-scented lettuce" (*Lactuca virosa*) contains an alkaloid resembling hyoscyamine, which has the power of dilating the pupils. See also LAITUE; LĂPTUCĂ; STOOFSLA.

lever, Danish for liver. See also LIVER.

leverpostej, a liver pâté, which consists of ½ lb. minced liver, ¼ lb. minced bacon, and a small minced onion, mixed together and added to ½ pint (1 cup) sauce béchamel, with a beaten egg and 1 teaspoon anchovy essence. It is then put into a round mould lined with bacon rashers and baked for an hour in a *bain-marie* in a moderate oven. When cold, it is turned out and eaten with toast or salad. In texture it resembles a mousse.

lever, Norwegian and Swedish for liver. *Leverpølse* is Norwegian for liver sausage, which is of good quality and eaten a lot in Scandinavia, especially in open sandwiches or on the cold table.

leveret, see HARE.

levraut, French for leveret. Up to the age of three months a leveret is called a *financier;* up to six months, a *trois quarts;* at a year, a *capucin* or *lièvre pit.* See also AÏLLADE DE LEVRAUT; GIBIER; LIÈVRE.

levroux or **livroux,** a French goat's milk cheese from the Berry district. It is pyramidal in shape and at its best from April to November.

Leyden, a Dutch spiced cheese made from either whole or skimmed cow's milk. The curd is ground and mixed with cumin seeds. It is a cylindrical cheese, lightly coloured outside, with a hard crust, the inside light yellow veined with green. The spices are all in the centre of the cheese. The cheese is marked with two crossed keys in black, taken from the coat of arms of the University at Leyden. It can weigh from 7 to 20 lb. and is not exported to any great extent. See also FRIESIAN; KANTER; SPICED CHEESE.

liaison, a French and an English word for the preparation used to thicken liquid foods such as soups, sauces, or stews. The most common is a roux of various flours and butter, called a *beurre manié,* and the most delicate is a mixture of egg yolks and cream. The latter must not be reboiled after adding to the soup, sauce, or stew, or it will curdle. The blood of certain animals is also used as a liaison, as for example, hare's blood in jugged hare. Soups can also be thickened by the addition of arrowroot, sago, semolina, or tapioca, or starchy vegetables such as potato or potato flour.

liarder, a French culinary term meaning to cut foods into thin round slices. It applies especially to potato crisps. A liard was originally an old coin.

liba, Hungarian for goose. Geese are of high quality in Hungary, some being especially fattened to produce large livers which are made into a pâté called *libamájkrém,* rather like pâté de foie gras. A large goose is often cut into joints which are cooked separately; the legs are often used for a casserole dish with mushrooms, onions, and sour cream or milk, or used in a risotto; the breast is frequently served either fried in batter or minced. See also GOOSE.

vagdalt libamelle, the raw goose breast is finely minced with the goose liver, and 1 tablespoon minced fried onion is added; this is further mixed with 3 crustless slices of bread which have previously been soaked in milk, and enough flour to hold the mixture together. It is well seasoned, then put into a greased loaf tin and baked for 45–60 minutes, being basted with goose fat. It is served hot with gravy, or cold, in which case it is often baked with a pastry crust.

liche (*Lichiamia*), a tunny (tuna)-like fish found in the deep Mediterranean where it attains about 3 feet in length. It is prepared and cooked in the same way as tunny (tuna).

lički kupus ribanac, a Yugoslavian dish of alternate layers of sauerkraut and pork chops, cooked in a casserole and served with boiled potatoes.

licorice, see LIQUORICE.

liebre, Spanish for hare. See also HARE.

liebre estofada con judías, hare casseroled with olive oil, garlic, bay leaf, thyme, a little vinegar, and white wine to cover, in a slow oven for several hours. Half-cooked chopped french beans are added and cooked for 20 minutes. Just before serving, small pieces of hot chilli are put in.

Liederkranz cheese, the trade name of a soft cheese made from whole cow's milk in Ohio, U.S. In smell, taste, and texture it resembles Limburger.

liégeoise, à la, a classical French and Belgian method of cooking, using juniper berries. It applies particularly to veal kidneys, which are braised in butter with juniper berries and flambéed with a little gin. Thrushes are also prepared in the same way.

lièvre, see CIVET (CIVET DE LIÈRE); LEVRAUT.

râble de lièvre, saddle of hare. (Correctly, râble is used exclusively for hare; the term for saddle of venison, mutton, etc., is sells.) The legs of the hare are generally used for a civet or a terrine; when the hind legs are left attached to the saddle, it becomes *train de lièvre.*

râble de lièvre à la crème, saddle of hare baked with shallots, ¼ cup red wine vinegar, 1 pint (2 cups) good cream to cover, and pepper. It is cooked in a covered dish in a low oven for 1½ hours. Salt is added to taste when it is cooked. In Alsace this excellent dish is served with cooked noodles and *pflütten.*

lights or **lites,** the lungs of a mammal, especially the ox. They are used in haggis, and in stews in various parts of Europe. See also BEUSCHEL; VENDÉE FRESSURE.

ligueuil, a French cow's milk cheese from Touraine. It is in season from October until June.

liha, Finnish for meat. See LAMMAS; PATAPAISTI; PIPARJUURI-LIHA; PORON.

lihakeitto, a meat broth. The soup is made with 1½ lb. shin beef, 4 carrots, ½ lb. swedes (turnips), ½ lb. potatoes, salt, 5 allspice berries, 1 onion, and 5 pints (10 cups) water, all boiled gently for 1½ hours. It is garnished with chopped parsley. The potatoes are left whole, and the meat removed, cut into pieces, and then returned to the soup.

liha-makaroonilaatikko, a meat and macaroni pudding made with ½ lb. macaroni cooked in boiling salted water and 1 lb. minced meat browned with 1 onion, then mixed with ¼ pint (½ cup) cream or stock, salt, and pepper. The meat mixture is placed in layers with the macaroni in a dish, covered with a mixture of 2 eggs and 1 pint (2 cups) milk beaten up together, then sprinkled with breadcrumbs, dabbed with butter, and baked for 1 hour. It is served for dinner, with a salad.

lihapullat, small meat balls made from minced (ground) pork and beef, with onions, breadcrumbs, and cream, served in gravy. They are intended as a hot and quite substantial *pikkulämpimät.*

lihapyörykät, meat balls made from 1 lb. minced (ground) meat mixed with 1 chopped onion, ½ cup breadcrumbs which have been soaked in ½ cup cream and ½ cup water, 1 beaten egg, salt, and pepper. The mixture is shaped into small balls and served hot for dinner, with gravy made from water poured into the pan juices and cream, or cold as a smörgåsbord dish. See also MEAT BALLS.

likky pie, a traditional Cornish pie made of leeks and green (unsmoked) bacon, with cream, eggs, and some milk as a sauce. Leeks cut in small pieces are scalded for 10 minutes in boiling water. Very thin slices of bacon are placed in the bottom of a pie dish, then a layer of leeks is placed on top, then another layer of bacon, and so on, with the layers repeated until the dish is full. Seasonings are added, and the dish is covered with suet crust and baked in a slow oven for 30 minutes. Then the crust is taken off and the liquid is drained from the dish. A mixture of ¼ pint (½ cup) cream and 2 eggs (the whites and yolks beaten separately) are added, with ¼ pint milk, to the bacon and leeks, the crust is replaced, the top covered with foil, and the pie is put into the oven for a further 40 minutes.

lilleoise, à la, a consommé double of beef, with chopped tarragon and chervil; garnished with chopped roasted almonds and julienne of truffles and mushrooms. See also CONSOMMÉ.

lima bean (*Phaseolus lunatus*), a native of South America. It is a fast climbing bean cultivated for its short, flat, kidney-shaped seeds, which are usually pale green or white. The Sieva bean, which is closely related, is often called by the same name. Both types of bean are very nutritious and in fact form part of the staple diet of Brazilians. They are floury in texture and are eaten both fresh and dried. In the U.S., where they are rightly popular, they form the basis of succotash. Dried lima beans resemble flageolets and are often used in the same way. Three varieties of this bean are imported into England: Burma beans, Rangoon beans, and the larger, white Madagascar butter beans.

limandelle, a saltwater flat fish, about 12 inches long, which is good to eat and popular in France. It is prepared as brill or plaice. It is also called *cardine* and *mère de sole*.

limaou or **limat,** see ESCARGOT.

limassade, the Provençal name for a sauce vinaigrette served with snails.

limat, see LIMAOU.

Limburger, a Belgian cheese which was first made in the province of Liège and sold at Limbourg. It is made from cow's milk—whole milk, skimmed milk, or partly skimmed milk. It is a square cheese, weighing about 2 lb., and has a very strong smell and a fairly soft texture. This popular cheese has been copied in many parts of the world; in fact there is more Limburger made today in the U.S., Germany, Austria, and Alsace, than in Belgium.

limburger käse, I. An Austrian *Limburger,* which is a soft cheese made in the north and south of Austria, and extremely popular. It is shaped like a brick and attains anything up to 1 lb. in weight. It has either a full cream (*vollfett*) or three-quarter cream (*dreiviertelfett*) content. The cheese is covered in a red wax coating and has a rather sharp taste. II. A German Limburger käse which is a soft cheese with a distinctive bouquet, regarded by cheese makers as one of the most difficult and delicate cheeses to make. Fresh milk is set at a temperature of 91–96°F (33°–36°C), with enough rennet to coagulate it in about 40 minutes. The curd is broken and stirred for a while, and then poured into rectangular cheese-moulds, placed on a draining-board to drain off the whey. The moulds are turned frequently. When the curd has set firm, the curd shapes are removed from the moulds and their surfaces are rubbed with salt. When the surfaces show signs of slipperiness, the cheeses are ripened at a constant temperature of 60°F for 1–2 months, their surfaces being rubbed frequently with salt to foster the distinctive flavour.

lime (*Citrus aurantifolia; medica acida*), the sweet lime and the West Indian lime, perhaps the finest of the citrus fruits. The lime is cultivated in most sub-tropical countries, especially the West Indies, but there are several varieties in Europe. The flavour of the juice is more aromatic and delicate than the juice of the lemon, which it resembles. It is exceptionally thirst-quenching, makes delicious chutney, pickle, and marmalade, and is also used to flavour ice creams and desserts.

lime, see LINDEN.

limousine, à la, a French method of cooking red cabbage in bouillon, with bacon fat. When cooked, it is garnished with braised chestnuts. Meat or poultry, garnished with cabbage so cooked, are titled *à la limousine*.

limpa, a Swedish bread made from 1 lb. coarse rye flour, 2 oz. fresh yeast, 3 lb. white flour, 1 lb. (2 cups) treacle (molasses), 1 tablespoon chopped fennel, 2 oz. chopped candied peel, 4 tablespoons butter, 2 pints (4 cups) tepid milk, and 1 pint (2 cups) warm ale. It is made with the same method as yeast dough and is delicious, more like a cake than a bread.

limpet (*Patella vulgata*), a gasteropod mollusc with a tent-shaped shell, which clings tightly to rocks. Although not much valued as food in the British Isles, limpets have real merit and can be used in place of oysters.

limpet stovies, a traditional dish from the Isle of Colonsay, Scotland. The limpets are well washed, and boiled with water to cover. They are taken from the shells, the sandy trail is removed, and they are layered in a dish with sliced, raw potatoes, pepper, and salt, and a cupful of limpet stock. Butter is put on top, then all is covered with a cloth and simmered slowly for at least an hour. In the 18th century the broth was drunk by nursing mothers in the belief that it would increase their milk.

lin, Polish for tench, frequently eaten in Poland and served in any way that is suitable for carp.

lin duszony, tench cooked in red wine with grated red cabbage.

Lincoln cheese, a soft English cream cheese about 2 inches thick, which does not keep longer than two or three weeks.

linden or **lime** (*Tilia americana; Tilia cordata*), an American and European tree whose scented flowers are infused to make a kind of tea and also produce an excellent honey. Linden is also the German word for the linden tree.

ling (*Molva molva*), the largest member of the cod family, also called long cod or sea burbot. It is quite good to eat, and is often salted and smoked. In medieval times in England it was called greenfish. It is particularly popular in Ireland and Scotland. There is a Gaelic saying that ling would be the beef of the sea if it had always salt enough, butter enough, and boiling enough. In Morayshire it is served boiled, with a sauce of melted butter which has had dry mustard added to it to taste. In the U.S. the same name can apply to the freshwater burbot.

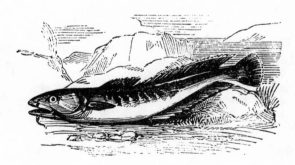

ling

lingonberry (*Empetrum nigrum*), a small wild cranberry found in Scandinavia, Russia, and Scotland, where it is used extensively in purées, compotes, and fruit soups, particularly in the first two areas. Probably it is related to the English lingberry, so-called because it always grows in heather-covered bogs (ling is an old name for certain kinds of heather). It is also called crowberry, no doubt because it is eaten a lot by crows. See also MEHU (MEHUKEITTO).

lingua de vaca, Portuguese for calf's tongue.

lime

lingua de vaca à Portuguesa, calf's tongue cooked in butter with tomatoes and a little Madeira wine.

lingua di bue, Italian for ox tongue. In Italy it is usually boiled, and then served cold in thick slices, with a sauce composed of 1 cup olive oil, 2 tablespoons lemon juice, 2 tablespoons capers, 2 chopped anchovy fillets, and 6 tablespoons chopped parsley. This is called *lingua con salsa verde*. It is also served warm with sautéed eggplant, garlic, and red sweet peppers, seasoned with salt, pepper, and lemon juice.

lingua salmistrata, cold, spiced tongue, a speciality of Verona.

lingua di castagno, an edible Italian fungus. See FUNGHI.

linguado, Portuguese for sole, one of the finest fish caught in Portuguese waters. *Linguado grelhado* is grilled sole. Sole is also served poached in stock after first being rubbed with salt; this is called *linguado cozido*.

lingue, I. French for ling. II. The French name for an eel-like sea fish which is about 3 feet in length. It is prepared as conger eel.

linguisa, a Portuguese smoked sausage. See also PAIO.

linsen, German for lentils. The lentils used in Germany are the so-called French lentils, greenish-brown in colour and about twice the size of the orange Egyptian lentil. They have considerably more flavour than the latter. They are used for soups and salads, and also make an excellent vegetable, particularly with game and duck. They require soaking overnight before being cooked.

linser, small Swedish custard tarts. These tarts are cooked in heartshaped baking tins half-filled with vanilla custard and covered with a pastry lid. To make the pastry dough, 3 tablespoons sugar are well beaten into 6 oz. (⅔ cup) creamed butter; 2 egg yolks are beaten into this mixture one by one, followed by ½ lb. (2 cups) sifted flour. This dough is kneaded and then chilled. The tarts are filled with the vanilla custard, then covered with more pastry and baked in a slow oven until golden brown, when the tops are sprinkled with icing (confectioners) sugar.

linzer torte, an Austrian pastry made from rich short crust, with 6 oz. (⅔ cup) butter creamed with 6 oz. (⅔ cup) sugar and 2 egg yolks or 1 egg, mixed with 6 oz. ground almonds, 6 oz. (1½ cups) flour, grated peel of ½ lemon, and a pinch of cinnamon. The dough is left to rest, preferably for several hours or overnight. Then it is rolled out rather thickly to fit a buttered flan tin, coated generously with raspberry jam or red currant jelly, and latticed with strips of the dough. It is brushed with beaten egg, baked in a slow oven, glazed with warm jam, and decorated with blanched, split almonds.

lipeäkala, a very old Finnish fish dish known as lye fish. (See LYE.) It is an important part of the Christmas fare in Finland and its preparation is usually started early in December. Dried cod or pike is cut into pieces about 8 inches long, skinned and pounded. It is then soaked, in frequently changed cold water, for a week. Meanwhile the lye solution is prepared from 6–7 pints of sifted birch ash and a cup of slaked lime to 5–7 lb. of fish. The ash is placed in a tightly bound cloth bag and put in a tub containing 20–30 pints of water. This is boiled for 30 minutes, cooled, and poured over the fish, which is left to soak in it for 3–5 days. The fish is now transferred to fresh cold water for a further week, the water being changed every day. When the fish is to be cooked, it is tied in a clean cheese-cloth and boiled slowly in salted water for 15 minutes. It is served with a thick white sauce.

lipski sir, a Yugoslavian soft cheese, not unlike *liptauer* which is also eaten in Yugoslavia.

liptai, see LIPTAUER.

liptauer or **liptai**, a German cheese made from sour milk, equally popular in Austria, Hungary (where it is called *Körözött*), and Holland. It does not keep long. About 2½ pints sour milk are strained in a muslin bag for about 12 hours until the curd is drained. About the same quantity of creamed butter is then beaten into the curd. Chopped capers, salt, chopped anchovies, chopped onion, french mustard, caraway seeds, a little pepper and paprika, all to individual taste, are then added, and mixed thoroughly before the cheese is put in a mould. It is decorated with capers and paprika.

liptói túró, a Hungarian soft, white cheese made from ewe's milk. It has a mild, creamy flavour and is sold in jars.

liquorice or **licorice** (*Glycyrrhiza glabra*), an herb which is believed to have its origins in southern Europe or Asia, although it grows well in most climates. It is a slow-growing, long-lived plant with a deep taproot. It grows from cuttings. It has smooth, bright-green leaves, and violet, hanging flowers which are very attractive. Extract of liquorice is used in the flavouring of stout and porter. Traditional Yorkshire gingerbread is also flavoured with this herb. To make sweetmeats, roots of the plant, about 3 years old, are boiled and mashed until the paste sets solid. In the reign of Elizabeth I liquorice was found to grow exceedingly well at Pontefract in Yorkshire, hence *Pontefract cakes*, which are lozenges of liquorice stamped with the impression of Pontefract castle.

lisa, Spanish for grey mullet, excellent baked, grilled, or fried in oil. There is another grey mullet with black horizontal bands known as mujol, mugil, or albur. The roe is the best part of the latter fish.

lithrini, Greek for sea bass, usually served *plaki*. See also PSARI.

litorne, French for fieldfare, which is cooked like thrush in France.

litovski sup, a Lithuanian soup made from 2 pints (4 cups) puréed potato soup mixed with ¾ pint (1½ cups) sour cream. The soup is garnished with shredded sorrel, strips of knob celery, strips of smoked goose breast, small fried pork sausages, and 8 halves of hard-boiled egg which have first been dipped in egg and bread crumbs and fried in lard.

lívance, Czech cakes or pancakes made from a dough consisting of 1 lb. (4 cups) wheat flour, ½ pint (1 cup) milk, 6 oz. (⅔ cup) butter, 6 oz. (⅔ cup) sugar, and 2 egg yolks; the stiffly beaten egg whites are folded in last. The mixture is either made into pancakes which are somewhat similar to crêpes suzette, or it is formed into small balls which are placed in a well-greased dish and baked until golden brown on one side, then turned so as to brown the other side. They are served hot, smothered in thick prune jam with sugar and cinnamon sprinkled on top.

livarot, a traditional soft cow's milk cheese from Normandy. It is made from skimmed milk of the evening milking, with whole milk of the following morning's milking, salted and mould-inoculated. It takes 2 or 3 months to ripen in the cellars, when it is fairly strong in flavour. It is eaten from October to July.

liver, a large glandular organ, which is an important and nutritious food. It is edible, whether from animals, birds, or fish, although some types are more delicate than others. It is classed as offal (variety meat).

Calf's, lamb's, ox, and pig's liver are those most generally offered for sale. The first two are almost always sliced and fried quickly in butter or fat, sometimes with bacon. Liver should not be overcooked as this makes it leathery. Pig's liver can also be fried, but has a harder yet more spongy texture, and is best casseroled with herbs and onion, or made into a pâté. Ox liver is only suitable for pâtés or terrines, as it is strong-tasting and inclined to be tough.

Poultry liver, particularly goose liver, is excellent baked whole, and, when the bird is artificially fattened, it is used for foie gras. Chicken, turkey, and duck livers can be braised, fried, or made into pâtés and terrines. The texture when cooked is soft and crumbly with a delicate flavour. The livers of game, both furred and feathered, are also excellent, particularly deer liver, which is a delicacy.

The liver of the lote, turbot, and skate are sought after by gastronomes, and valuable oils are extracted from cod and shark liver. See also CIGĔR; FEGATO; FIGADO; GANS (GÄNSE-LEBER); HIGADO; ISCAS; LEBER; LEVER; MÁJ; MAKSA; SIKO-TAKIA; WATRÓBKA.

liver fungus, a large, rather tasteless edible fungus which grows on the trunks of oak trees in the U.S.

loach (*Nemachilus barbatulus*), the name of several types of European freshwater fish. The common loach is quite delicate in flavour and is found in mountain streams. It is cooked like smelt, or used for a soup or stew.

loaf, I. A shape of moulded bread when baked. There are many kinds of loaf: cottage, cob, tin, pan, Vienna, etc. See also BREAD. II. Any minced food baked in a rectangular loaf tin, for example meat loaf.

loaf cheese, the term for cheeses which resemble a cottage loaf. Almost any cheese can be made in this shape, and in times past cheese from Cheddar, Wiltshire, and Gloucestershire were so made. Such shapes of cheese, however, are seldom seen today.

loaf,sugar, sugar crystallised en masse in a mould, the shape of which it retains when turned out.

lobina, see SERRANO.

lobio, a Russian bean salad, made from soaked, dried, cooked, and puréed beans. It is a speciality of Georgia, Russia.

lobscouse, an English adaptation of labskaus, a dish from Schleswig-Holstein, Germany. It was a popular fisherman's dish there, made from chunks of fish. It changed on its journey to England, being made in England with neck portions of mutton, with a variety of root vegetables and leeks, all layered, and with a sprinkling of thyme on top, and whole potatoes which should steam above the stew. It is cooked for some hours in a covered dish in a slow oven. It is also good with salted or corned beef. It is somehow a very masculine dish, but excellent on a cold day, or for cooking where conditions are primitive.

lobster, a large saltwater crustacean found only in the Northern Hemisphere. *Homarus gammarus,* the common European lobster, is found from Norway to the Mediterranean, and *H. americanus,* the common North American lobster, is found from Labrador to Cape Hatteras. (In the Southern Hemisphere the spiny lobster and crawfish take over, but these do not have the delicate taste or the large claws of the true lobster.) The lobster grows slowly, being only about 5 inches long at 5 years, but later it grows more quickly. It is in the characteristic large claws that the most delicious flesh is to be found. The male lobster is called the cock, and the female, the hen. The hen carries the eggs in her tail, and an egg-carrying lobster is known as *paquette* in France. These eggs make a delicious sauce. The eggs are known as coral.

There are many ways of cooking lobster, but if it is really freshly caught it should be served simply, to preserve the delicate flavour. According to tests made in the Jersey Marine Biological Laboratory, it is much kinder to put all shellfish into cold saltwater (preferably sea water) and bring them to boiling point, as against plunging the creatures into boiling water. The tests showed that no discomfort was shown in the cold water method until temperature reached 70°F when the lobster fainted and died almost immediately. However, plunged into boiling water, many attempts were made to get out and life continued for nearly 1 minute. It is thought that when put into cold water in which the heat is raised slowly, it penetrates gradually and destroys the nervous system painlessly. The cold water method, apart from being more humane, also seems to make the lobster more tender. When the lobster is so cooked, it should be served by separating the tail from the body and removing the claws. Usually the tail is split in two, but some prefer to use electrical side-cutters which cut easily through the shell of both tail and large claws, so that the flesh from both comes out in one piece. A mayonnaise is prepared, and the juice and cream from the inside of the shell is added. If a hen lobster is used and she is carrying eggs, these should be pounded up and added to the sauce, or used as decoration.

Another simple method is to grill the lobster. The most humane way of killing the lobster for this method is to run a skewer into the spinal cord at the joint between the tail shell and the body. This kills the creature instantaneously, and it can then be split down the middle. The shell and flesh are brushed with oil, and it is then grilled under a very hot grill and seasoned with salt, cayenne, and butter. In both France and Ireland, a grilled lobster is sometimes "finished" with either brandy or whiskey which is warmed and poured over the lobster, then lit before serving. This latter dish is known as Dublin lawyer in Ireland and simply *homard flambé* in France. See also ASTAKO; DUBLIN BAY PRAWNS; HOMARD; HUMMER; LAGOSTA; LANGOSTA; SCAMPI.

lobster butter, made in the same way as beurre d'écrevisses. See BEURRES COMPOSÉS.

lobster chowder, an American soup. Chopped onions, celery, salt pork, leeks, and green peppers are simmered gently in butter, then sprinkled liberally with flour. Fish or meat stock or stock made from boiling the shells, is added, also seasoning, bay leaves or sage, and thyme. Diced potatoes and tomatoes are added at a later stage in the cooking. The soup is garnished with diced lobster. See also BISQUE; CHOWDER.

lobster sauce, for this English sauce the meat from a freshly boiled hen lobster is cut up finely, mixed with the coral, and placed in a saucepan with fresh butter and a generous amount of thick cream. It is stirred over the fire until steaming hot.

locust bean, see CAROB.

lodigiano, an Italian cheese of the *grana* type, made in Lodi, south of Milan. It is a yellow cheese, sharp and fragrant, sometimes bitter, with smaller eyes than Parmesan or Reggiano.

lody, Polish for ice cream, usually made in Poland from a custard mixture of 1½ pints (3 cups) milk or thin cream, thickened in a double boiler with 5 egg yolks, sugar, and desired flavouring to taste. It is well beaten, cooled, and frozen for 3 to 4 hours. When the egg yolks and sugar are beaten together without heating, over ice, and whipped double cream is added before freezing, the ice cream is called *bomba.*

loempias, a Dutch-Indonesian dish which has become a national speciality of Holland. It consists of pancakes filled with shredded fried chicken, bean sprouts, chopped celery, chives, and roasted pork moistened with soya sauce and oil. It is all mixed well together before putting on the pancakes, which are then folded and the edges brushed with egg white. They are then fried in deep oil until crisp and golden. It forms part of the *rijsstafel.*

løg, Danish for onion. See also GRØNSAGER.

løgsauce, onion sauce. A white sauce is made using hot milk, to which minced, boiled onions are added together with seasoning and sugar. It is good with fried herrings.

loganberry (*Rubus loganobaccus*), an edible berry which is a hybrid of the American dewberry and the true raspberry (probably the Red Antwerp variety). It was first produced in

1881 by Judge J. H. Logan in California. It is used for jams, preserves, tarts, pies, and as a dessert fruit with cream; it has quite a distinct flavour of its own, slightly reminiscent of pomegranate, and with larger pips than either of its parents.

lohi, Finnish for salmon, which is of excellent quality in Finland.

lohilaatikko, a Finnish method of preparing salmon au gratin, using salted salmon. A 4-or 5-lb. salmon is cut into thin slices and placed in layers in a dish with 2 small, fried, chopped onions and 2 lb. thinly sliced potatoes. It is covered with a sauce made from 2 eggs and 1 pint (2 cups) milk, sprinkled with breadcrumbs and dabs of butter, and baked for about 1 hour. This dish is usually served for dinner.

riimisuolainen lohi, a Finnish method of salting salmon. The whole fish is split open and filleted, then laid flat, skin-side down, and rubbed with a mixture of 5 tablespoons sugar to 2 tablespoons salt, then put in a flat dish and sprinkled with coarse salt and dill. At least 4 oz. salt are needed for 2 lb. fish, and it should be placed both on the top of the fish and underneath it. Then a light weight is put on top and the dish is kept for at least two days in a cool, dark place. The fish is eaten raw in thin slices, and is extremely good.

loin, the part of an animal from the ribs to the tail, with the flank removed. It is usually split down the backbone. If not, it is a double loin, which in the case of beef is known as a baron, and in lamb as a saddle. According to national custom, and to the meat concerned, loin of mutton, pork, and veal are either cut into chops, or left in a single large portion suitable for roasting.

lök, Swedish for onion. See also GRÖNSAKER; ONION.

farserade lökar, baked stuffed onions. The centres of the onions are removed and mixed with chopped fried bacon, chopped fried mushrooms, chopped tomatoes, sieved breadcrumbs, and either chives or parsley, together with seasoning. The onions are stuffed with this mixture. Grated cheese and some more parsley are sprinkled over them, together with a little beef stock, and the whole is baked for about 1 hour in a moderate oven.

glaserade lökar, glazed onions. The peeled onions are dredged with salt and sugar, and then simmered gently in butter and a small amount of water until the latter has evaporated. Cooking is continued until the onions are glazed. They are served with some poultry dishes.

loksinu su aguonais, a Lithuanian national dish of egg noodles with poppy seeds. First ½ lb. poppy seeds are soaked in water for 2–3 hours, drained, and pounded, then mixed with 7 tablespoons honey and 2 tablespoons brown sugar, both melted. Then ¼ pint (½ cup) cream is added, and when the mixture is thick, 2 tablespoons chopped blanched almonds are stirred in. Next 1 lb. noodles is cooked in boiling water and drained, and ¼ lb. (½ cup) melted butter is poured over them. Finally the poppy seed sauce is folded into the hot noodles. This dish is eaten after the main course.

lokum, see RAHAT LOKUM.

l'ollada, the Catalan national soup, called after the earthenware pot or *oulle* in which it is made. First 1 lb. soaked dried haricot beans are cooked in water in a pot. In another pot are cooked 1 medium-sized shredded white cabbage, 5 medium-sized potatoes, 2 onions, 4 oz. bacon, 1 carrot, 1 turnip, 2 garlic cloves, 1 tablespoon pork fat, herbs, and seasoning. When ready, this is combined with the beans. Small pieces of garlic, onion, and parsley, fried in bacon fat, are used as a garnish.

lonac, a traditional Yugoslavian dish of meat, whole spices, dried peppers, and many kinds of whole vegetables including onions in their skins. It is simmered for 3 hours, often with the lid sealed with a paste of flour and water to keep in the steam. Lonac is also the term for the deep earthenware pot in which such stews are traditionally cooked. See also BOSANSKI LONAC.

London broil, American terminology for a beefsteak, usually flank steak, broiled quickly on both sides and sliced thinly against the grain. It is often served with sauce béarnaise or sauce bordelaise.

long cod, see LING.

Long Island buck, an American savoury, made from ½ lb. grated cheddar cheese well mixed with 3 tablespoons beer, 1 teaspoon paprika, worcestershire sauce to taste, and 2 egg yolks. It is put on toast and baked in the oven until browned on top. Served hot.

Long Island duck, the finest American domestic duck. They are descended from the Peking duck, and were imported into North America about 1873, when an American poultry breeder named James E. Palmer brought some fifteen ducks over from China, six of which died at sea. They have rounded bodies, and reach a considerable weight in the space of about three months. See also DUCK.

longaniza, a Spanish sausage made with lean pork, garlic, wild marjoram, and seasoning. See also CHORIZO.

longchamp, a Parisian soup, which consists of shredded sorrel and vermicelli cooked in 1 pint (2 cups) consommé. When ready, a purée of 1 cup fresh green peas is stirred in. See also CONSOMMÉ.

longe, French for the top end of a loin of veal. It is frequently used, however, to describe the same part of pork, mutton, and beef.

longhorn, see AMERICAN CHEDDAR.

longjaw, see CHUB.

lonza, an Italian speciality of fillet of pork cured like ham, but flavoured with spices, wine, and garlic. It is very good if not oversalted; it is served raw in very thin slices.

lonzo, a Corsican speciality consisting of a boned fillet of pork which is steeped in brine with herbs, and then air dried. It is eaten raw, carved in very thin slices, as an hors d'oeuvre; or in a light meal consisting of soup, lonzo, and cheese. It is extremely good.

loquat (*Eriobotrya japonica*), the small orange-coloured plum-like fruit of an Eastern tree, now introduced into California and Florida as well as the Mediterranean countries. It has not much flavour eaten raw, but makes excellent jams and preserves.

lorette, I. A French garnish for entrées consisting of chicken croquettes, asparagus tips, and slices of truffle. II. Chicken consommé with paprika, garnished with asparagus tips, truffle strips, and chervil, with tiny balls of *pommes lorette* served separately. III. Corn salad (mâche), accompanied by thin slices of cooked red beetroot and thin sticks of raw celery. IV. A French method of serving potatoes, see POMME DE TERRE.

Lorraine, I. A region of France with many gastronomic specialities. See POTÉE, LORRAINE; QUICHE LORRAINE; TOURTE, À LA LORRAINE. II. A cheese made in Lorraine, France. See ANISÉ. III. A French garnish for meat consisting of braised red cabbage and *pommes fondantes*.

Lorraine soup, also called *la reine*, a Scottish soup named after Mary of Lorraine, wife of James V of Scotland, whose influence on Scottish cuisine was considerable. The soup consists of ½ lb. each of cooked chicken and veal, pounded in a mortar with 2 oz. blanched almonds and 2 hard-boiled egg yolks. Then 2 tablespoons breadcrumbs are soaked in 2 tablespoons boiling milk, and when cold, beaten into the meat mixture; 2 quarts (8 cups) good white stock, salt, pepper, a pinch of mace, and a squeeze of lemon are added, and it is all heated until piping hot. Just before serving, cream is added to taste.

łosoś, Polish for salmon.

łosoś pieczony z maderą, salmon baked with butter, herbs, and Madeira wine.

losos, Russian for salmon. See KULEBYAKA. Smoked salmon is *kopchennaya losos*. Both are used extensively in Russia.

lote (*Lota lota*), another name for the freshwater burbot, found mostly in the lakes of Savoy and sometimes in English lakes. The flesh is not very good eating, but the liver is large and has gastronomic merit. In Geneva it is used for making an omelette.

lote

lotier, French for a plant called bird's-foot trefoil in Britain, and lotus in the U.S. The plant grows profusely in meadows and has a most pleasant smell. In France it is used to flavour marinades and for stuffing wild rabbit before cooking. See also BIRD'S-FOOT TREFOIL.

lotte, French for lote. The most usual method of serving lotte is *à la dugléré;* baked fillets of the fish, with tomatoes, onion, parsley, and white wine to cover.

lotte de mer, French for anglerfish used mainly for soups or stews. It is also called *baudroie.*

lotus, see BIRD'S-FOOT TREFOIL.

lou trebuc, preserved goose or pork, a speciality of the Bearn district of France. They are preserved by being cooked in their own fat and then covered with salt. See also OIE, CONFIT D'.

Louisberg chicken pie, an American regional pie, made with 1 lb. chicken fillets, ½ lb. mushrooms, ½ lb. sausage meat shaped into tiny balls, and scooped raw potato balls of the same size, all covered with stock and puff pastry.

louise-bonne, a French variety of pear. It is large, coloured yellow with a red flush and red spots; the flesh is white, sweet, juicy, and delicious. It ripens at the end of September, and keeps for about 2 months.

Louisiana hot sauce, a commercially made American sauce consisting of chillies, salt, and vinegar, all pounded and mixed together. It resembles Tabasco, but the consistency is thicker. It is very hot to the taste, and should be used sparingly. It is used in the preparation of *tacos.*

Louisiana rice pudding, made in Louisiana, and other southern states of the U.S., from 1 pint (2 cups) milk boiled in a double boiler with ½ cup raisins, then 1½ cups cooked rice are added and cooked for 5 minutes. Next 2 egg yolks, 4 oz. (½ cup) sugar, ¼ teaspoon cinnamon or nutmeg, and a pinch of salt, are beaten together, mixed into the rice mixture and cooked for 3 minutes. The 2 stiffly beaten egg whites and 1 tablespoon sugar are placed on top, and the whole is gently browned in a slow oven.

Louisiana soup, a regional soup from the U.S., consisting of 2 pints (4 cups) clear chicken broth garnished with ½ cup cooked chopped okra, 1 cup crab meat, ½ cup boiled rice, ½ cup diced shrimps or lobster, and ½ cup sliced sweet peppers. The soup is coloured with a pinch of saffron.

Louisiana yam nuggets, yams or sweet potatoes cooked, peeled, and mashed, then rolled into balls, covered with stiffly beaten egg whites and baked until pale golden. They are served warm with meats.

louisiane, à la, a French garnish for fowl or meat, consisting of sweet corn fritters and rice darioles on sautéed sweet potatoes and rounds of fried banana. They are served with poultry or veal gravy.

loukanika, Greek sausages. They are served hot with slices of lemon for meze, or fried with eggs and tomatoes. They are made from chopped pork, beef, garlic, cinnamon, allspice, orange peel, cracked whole peppercorns, wine, and lemon juice.

lou-kenkas, small spicy sausages from the Basque and Bordelais coasts. They are often grilled and served hot with ice cold, raw oysters.

loukoumades or **loukoumathes,** Greek yeasted honey fritters, traditionally eaten in front of a fire in the winter time, although they can be ordered at any *kafenion* (coffee shop), usually with a bottle of mineral water called Negrita which takes away from the cloying taste of the very sweet pastries eaten throughout Greece. There are several varieties of these fritters, and they can be made with baking powder instead of yeast. For one type 2 oz. yeast (2 packages) are dissolved in tepid water, just enough to cover the yeast, and 1 cup (4 oz.) flour is scattered over it. It is left to rise until it doubles in size (this takes about 2 hours), then 12 oz. (3 cups) flour are added and enough warm milk or water to make a soft batter. This is covered and left in a warm place until the mixture bubbles (4–5 hours, or overnight). The batter is stirred down and mixed well, then dropped from a tablespoon into deep hot cooking oil (360°F), 2 or 3 spoonfuls at a time, and fried until golden all over. Then the fritters are drained on absorbent paper, and dipped into hot syrup made from 1 cup honey, 1 cup water, 2 cups sugar, a squeeze of lemon juice, and a piece of cinnamon, all boiled for 15 minutes. The cinnamon is removed before using. For another variety 1 pint (2 cups) yogourt with the grated peel of 1 orange or lemon, ½ teaspoon salt, and ½ cup brandy are beaten well, and 8 oz. (2 cups) flour are added gradually to make a batter. It will be the right consistency if it pulls away from the bowl without breaking; if it breaks it is too dry. The batter is left for 2 hours, then the fritters are fried as in the first variety. They can be garnished with icing (confectioners') sugar, chopped nuts, and more cinnamon. See also FRITTER; TIGANITES.

loukoumi, the Greek version of Turkish delight, a sweetmeat (confection) very popular in Greece. It is made from 1 lb. (2 cups) sugar, ¼ pint (½ cup) water, and 3 tablespoons gelatine, flavoured with orange or lemon, and with roasted almonds or pistachio nuts added, all simmered for about 20–30 minutes, then poured into a flat tin to get cold. It is called Turkish delight in English. For the authentic Turkish "Turkish Delight," which should not be made with gelatine, see RAHAT LOKUM.

loup de mer, a Provençal name for sea bass, a literal translation of our alternative English name for the same fish, "seawolf." The name is made good use of, as the formal French word for sea bass, *bar,* can also mean quite another fish (*Galeichthys marinus*), which might be confusing. Loup de mer is usually served *grillade au fenouil.*

loup marin, French for wolf fish. In France it is usually fried, poached, grilled, or served à la *bercy,* à la doria, à la génevoise.

lovage (*Levisticum officinale*), a perennial plant, a member of the parsley family, *Petroselinum,* and sometimes called "love parsley." In appearance it closely resembles the angelica, and its flavour is like a cross between a strong celery and parsley. It is one of the most valuable culinary herbs and always featured strongly in the monastic gardens of medieval Europe. It enhances salads, soups, stews, and sauces, but as the taste is very strong, it should be used sparingly. Lovage seeds can be used in the same way as celery seeds, and in the U.S. they are used to advantage in cookies and cakes. There is also a Scotch variety called *shunis* which is eaten raw as a salad, or cooked like celery. Lovage is used extensively in Rumanian and Balkan cooking.

love-in-disguise, an old English dish made from cleaned and soaked calf's heart, wrapped in fat pork or bacon and simmered in water until tender. It is then dried, coated with veal forcemeat, rolled in breadcrumbs, and roasted in fat in a moderate oven for about 30 minutes. It is basted frequently. A gravy is made from the stock thickened with corn flour (cornstarch). This dish can also be made with the much smaller lamb's hearts, and sausage meat is sometimes substituted for veal forcemeat. See also HEART.

lowberry, see HYBRID BERRIES.

luccio marino, Italian for hake; also called *nasello,* a word which can also be used for whiting. Neither fish is prolific in the Mediterranean, for both prefer colder waters.

luchon, a French cow's milk cheese from the Pyrenees. It is at its best from April to November.

lucullus, à la, I. A French garnish for fowl and sweetbreads, consisting of truffles cooked whole in Madeira, then hollowed out and filled with quenelles of chicken forcemeat and the chopped truffle centres. II. A French velouté soup of chicken blended with purée of calf's brains, flavoured with sherry, and garnished with diced cucumber. III. A consommé of beef, garnished with diced carrots and turnips, cauliflowerets, and quenelles. See also CONSOMMÉ.

luganeghe, northern Italian sausages from Romagna, made from pure pork. They are usually fried slowly in oil, with a little sage. When browned they are covered with a fresh tomato sauce or raw, peeled, and sliced tomatoes and simmered for 15 minutes. It is called *salsicce alla romagnola.*

lukànka, Bulgarian pork sausages, which are spiced and slightly salted. They are served a good deal in the winter, either raw or cooked, in slices.

lula, Portuguese for small squid, eaten in many ways in Portugal, usually fried or made into a risotto (*arroz de lulas*).

lulas recheadas, squids stuffed with the chopped tentacles, herbs, and *piri-piri,* and baked in oil. The taste is very good when the lulas are small, no larger than 4 or 5 inches across. It is one of the best Portuguese dishes.

lumache, Italian for snails, which have been esteemed in Italy since earliest times. Pliny says that the best were imported from Sicily, Capri, and the Balearic Isles. Parks for fattening snails, like the special beds in which oysters are cultivated, were said to have been devised by the Roman Fulvius Lupinus, and the snails were fed with special plants mixed with soup and sometimes wine. In the last century, snail soup was sold in the streets of Naples, and modern Romans have an annual feast of snails on St. John's Day, June 24. Generally in Italy, snails are not served in their shells but, after starving and preparing, are presented in a special sauce. See also ESCARGOTS; SNAILS.

lumache in zimino, 4 dozen prepared snails are heated in 1 pint (2 cups) olive oil, cooked with ½ lb. mushrooms, 3 cloves garlic, 1 small sliced onion, 1 tablespoon each chopped parsley and rosemary, with salt and pepper to taste.

lumber pie, see UMBLES.

lump sugar, see SUGAR.

lumpfish or *lumpsucker* (*Cyclopterus lumpus*), a large sea fish which gets its name from its lump-like first dorsal fin. It is found on both sides of the North Atlantic, but it is more prolific further north in Scandinavian waters. In spring it hollows out large holes on the stony sea-bottom off these coasts, where it deposits immense quantities of pink eggs; many of these are taken by fishermen and, after a long process of salting, pressing, and colouring, they are sold as Danish or German caviar. It is not as fine as true caviar, but it makes a reasonable and inexpensive substitute.

luncheon cheese, a variety of Gouda cheese which is brick-shaped and does not exceed 2 lb. in weight. See also GOUDA.

lurifakser, Norwegian pastry-layer slices made from 6 oz. (⅔ cup) sugar beaten into ½ lb. (1 cup) butter; 12 oz. (3 cups)

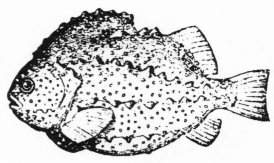

lumpfish

flour and an egg are blended into this, and 1 teaspoon baking powder is added. The mixture is kneaded into a soft dough which is divided into two parts, 2 tablespoons cocoa and a little more flour being kneaded into one part. Both are rolled out into strips ⅛ inch thick, the plain part is brushed with milk, the coloured one laid over this, and the whole rolled up. The roll is well chilled before slices ⅛ inch thick are cut; these are baked for up to 7 minutes in a moderate oven.

lute, a paste of flour and water which is used to seal the lids of casseroles or terrines. This process is known as "luting," and is done to keep steam inside the cooking receptacle. It is particularly important for coq au vin and the cooking of terrines. It is called *lut* in France.

lutefisk, a Norwegian speciality of dried cod, which has been preserved in a lye of potash. The taste does not appeal to foreigners. It is often served at Christmas. See also LIPEÄKALA.

lutfisk, a Swedish traditional Christmas speciality. A fish is soaked in a mixture of wood ash, lime, soda, and water until it is four times its original size. After the fish has been pickled in this mixture for some time, it is dried. It is very much an acquired taste, and foreigners take some time to get used to it. Usually it is followed by *julskinka* and *julgröt.*

lychee (*Nephelium litchi*), the fruit of a Chinese tree called soapberry, cultivated also in India and elsewhere. The outer skin is hard and yet brittle, reddish brown, and with warty marks on the outside. However, the inside is a translucent white, very sweet and succulent. Lychees are stoned, and canned and exported all over the world. When canned, they have what might be described as an almost scented taste, not unlike a very sweet muscat grape.

lye, a solution of water alkalised by lixivation of vegetable or wood ashes. It is a strong alkaline, and used to preserve fish in Scandinavia and Finland. See LIPEÄKALA; LUTEFISK; LUTFISK.

lyonnaise, à la, I. A French garnish of 6 medium-sized braised onions fried in butter, with 1 pint (2 cups) of half white wine and half wine vinegar boiled down to half and added, together with 3 tablespoons demi-glace. II. A method of cooking potatoes by slicing them, tossing them in butter until golden, and then mixing them with fried onions and sprinkling with chopped parsley. III. Any dish which is a speciality of the Lyonnais region of France, especially omelettes, tripe, *quenelles de brochet à la Lyonnaise,* and *saucisson en brioche.* The region is famous for the excellence of its onions and potatoes. See also POMME DE TERRE (POMMES À LA LYONNAISE).

lyonnaise, sauce, a classical French sauce consisting of chopped onions fried in butter, with a mixture of ½ pint (1 cup) white wine and ½ pint (1 cup) wine vinegar, boiled down and added, together with 3 tablespoons demi-glace.

lyutenìtsa, a Bulgarian salad made from green vegetables, garlic, and hot peppers boiled, drained, chopped, and seasoned with vinegar. It is eaten cold.

M

maatjes, a Dutch cured herring which is very popular in Holland. Maatjes means "virgin," and they are so called because only the very young female herrings are used for the process. See also HARING.

macadamia (*Macadamia ternifolia*), the commercial synonym for the Queensland nut, indigenous to Australia but now exported to the U.S., where it is very popular. It is round in shape, with a smooth brown shell and a white kernel. It resembles a large hazelnut, and for this reason is sometimes known as Australian hazel.

macaroni, the English name for maccheroni, a pasta made in the form of a tube. See also MACARONISCHOTELTJE; MACARRÃO; MACCHERONI; MAKARON; PASTA.

macaroni cheese, boiled macaroni put into a cheese sauce and baked in the oven. An egg is sometimes added. If well made it is quite acceptable, but the whole success of the dish depends on the quality of the sauce. In the U.S. this dish is referred to as macaroni and cheese and is very popular.

macaroni pudding, an English milk pudding made with 3 oz. raw macaroni, 2 oz. (¼ cup) sugar, 1 pint (2 cups) milk, and a bay leaf. Sometimes an egg is added. It is baked for several hours in a slow oven until the liquid becomes curdy. It was popular in Victorian times but is now prepared mainly for children.

macaroni, the same word in French as in English. It is used in many French garnishes such as *bayonnaise, milanaise,* and *Talleyrand.*

macaroni à l'italienne, 1 lb. boiled, drained macaroni combined with 6 oz. grated mixed Gruyère and Parmesan cheese and 3 tablespoons butter, seasoned with a pinch of nutmeg and salt. When browned in the oven or under a grill, it is called macaroni au gratin.

macaroni à la milanaise, as above, with tomato-flavoured demi-glace mixed with several tablespoons of *milanaise* garnish.

macaroni à la napolitaine, as *macaroni à l'italienne,* with tomato sauce and grated cheese.

macaronischoteltje, a Dutch dish of macaroni with ham and cheese. First ½ lb. (1½ cups) macaroni is boiled in 3 pints (6 cups) water for 15 minutes, then left to stand in the liquid for another 15 minutes. After draining, it is well mixed with 4 oz. (1 cup) chopped, boiled ham, 1 cup grated Parmesan cheese;

and 3 tablespoons butter. The dish is topped with breadcrumbs and dotted with butter, before being baked in a moderate oven for about 30 minutes. There are several variations of this dish in Holland, made by adding sautéed onions, celery salt, worcestershire sauce, or tomato paste to the macaroni.

macaroon, a small, round, crunchy almond biscuit (cookie), originally from Italy but brought to France in the 16th century. It rapidly gained favour, and by the 18th century it had become customary for French nuns to make macaroons, which they offered to visitors with a glass of wine. The most famous French macaroons are made at Nancy.

Macaroons are very good, and simple to make, consisting of ½ lb. pounded blanched almonds, ½ lb. sugar, and 2 egg whites. The mixture is usually piped from a forcing (pastry) bag onto rice paper, and baked in a moderate oven until a pale gold. In Italy macaroons are found in many forms. See also AMARETTI; MANDORLA; PINOCCATE.

macarrão, Portuguese for macaroni. It is eaten boiled, drained, and sprinkled with cinnamon and is also often used in stews, as is vermicelli.

maccheroni, the Italian spelling of macaroni, a pasta made either in long tubes, which are sometimes cut into pieces and known as "elbow" macaroni, or in shorter, quill-like tubes called *penne,* usually about ¼–½ inch across. Legend has it that a Neapolitan cardinal, being served with the dish for the first time, exclaimed: "Ma caroni!" (my dears), hence the name.

maccheroni al forno, a baked macaroni dish, made with the large-sized macaroni. It is cooked like *maccheroni alla carbonara* and then covered with a sauce of 1 lb. tomatoes, 3 oz. mushrooms, 2 tablespoons parsley, 3 oz. grated cheese, seasoning, and 1 pint (2 cups) thin béchamel. It is then baked in a moderate oven for 30 minutes.

maccheroni alla carbonara, a Roman dish. To prepare it 1 lb. macaroni is cooked in 8 pints (16 cups) boiling salted water and drained in the usual way. Matchstick lengths of ham or coppa are gently fried in butter and, at the last moment before serving, a little red pepper and 2 beaten eggs are added and stirred until lightly set. The ham and egg mixture is then stirred into the hot pasta. Then 4 oz. grated Parmesan or pecorino are also added, and more of this cheese is served separately. The creamy sauce fills the holes in the pasta and is very good. Many kinds of pasta, such as *bucatini* (thin macaroni), *penne,* and *rigatoni* can be used for this dish.

maccheroni alla matriciana, cooked macaroni served with a sauce made from lightly fried sliced onion, 4 oz. chopped pickled pork, bacon, or coppa, 1 lb. skinned tomatoes, and 1 chopped clove of garlic, cooked over a fast heat for 7–10 minutes. It is all well seasoned and poured over the macaroni, which is served in Rome with grated *pecorino Romano* cheese, a speciality of that city. This method is also used with *bucatini* (thin macaroni), *penne,* and spaghetti.

maccheroni alla napoletana, cooked macaroni served with the appropriate sauce (*napoletana*), made from tomatoes, bacon, onion, garlic, celery leaf, carrot, butter or oil, a little sugar, and seasoning of salt, pepper, and basil. Grated Parmesan cheese is served separately.

maccheroni alla siciliana, a Sicilian dish of macaroni with either broccoli or aubergines (eggplants). *Penne* is the best type of macaroni to use for this dish. First 1 lb. pasta is cooked and drained, and the same amount of vegetables are cut up and lightly tossed in hot lard seasoned with black pepper. The pasta and the vegetables are placed in alternate layers in a baking dish, with ricotta cheese between each layer, beginning and ending with pasta. Then 2 eggs, beaten up with 2 tablespoons grated cheese are poured over the top, and the dish is baked in the oven until a golden crust forms, usually after about 30 minutes.

maccheroni ripieni alla toscana, a Tuscan dish of short wide macaroni tubes filled with a meat stuffing and served with tomato sauce and grated cheese. Although not specifically a Tuscan pasta, tufoli is the best macaroni for this method. See also RAVIOLI; TORTELLINI.

timballo (sformato) di maccheroni, a dish baked in a round *timbale* mould lined with cooked macaroni. The hollow centre is filled with a sauce made of cooked chopped sweetbread, chicken livers, mushrooms, onion, stock, butter, and a sprinkling of flour, all flavoured with cognac.

macdonald, a French meat consommé; garnished with royale of lamb's brains, diced cucumber, and small ravioli. See also CONSOMMÉ.

mace (*Myristica fragrans*), the husk of nutmeg, ground finely and used for flavouring mashed potatoes and cauliflower, cheese dishes, fish, meat, and custards and puddings. It is also used in the form known as "blade" mace, fragments ½–1 inch in length, which may be left to cook in the dish in preparation for a greater or lesser time, depending upon how much of the flavour it is desired to impart. It was used extensively in English cookery from the 16th to the 19th century. The flavour is more delicate than that of nutmeg, and the colour should be a rich orangey-brown.

macédoine, French for a mixture of raw or cooked fruit or vegetables, served either hot or cold. The name is thought to come from Macedonia, and is also used in English.

macédoine de fruits, fruits served in a heavy syrup.

macédoine de légumes, mixed vegetables served with butter, mayonnaise, cream, or an olive oil and vinegar dressing. It may also be set in aspic.

macérer, a French culinary term, meaning to soften by soaking or infusing in liquid. It usually refers to fruit soaked in spirits. The English word is macerate, and in English this also covers the process of soaking foods in brine.

maceron, French for the herb alexander, which is used in casseroles, especially of rabbit.

mâche, French for corn salad; also called *doucette.* It is used a lot in winter salads, especially *salade lorette.*

mackerel (*Scomber scombrus*), a smooth-scaled sea fish,

about 14 inches long and with irridescent colouring when fresh. It is found in the Atlantic, the North Sea, the Baltic, and the Mediterranean, as well as in the Pacific Ocean. It is a very fatty, strong-tasting gamey fish, not liked by everyone, but eaten fresh and cooked without fat, it is excellent. It is best poached with a little fennel in court bouillon or white wine, and served with a gooseberry purée. Another excellent method is to stuff it with breadcrumbs, chopped fennel, and parsley, with a little grated onion and lemon peel, cover with foil, and bake for 30 minutes in the oven. It is also good painted with mustard and grilled, then served with *beurre maître d'hôtel* and lemon. A popular English and Scottish method is to bake it with sliced onion and peppercorns in a solution of half water and half vinegar barely to cover. This is eaten cold, and called soused mackerel. In Cornwall, England, half milkless tea and vinegar is used, and is extremely good. See also ESCOMBRO; MAKRELE; MAKRELL; MAQUEREAU; SPANISH MACKEREL.

mâconnais, see CHEVROTTON DE MÂCON.

mâconnaise, à la, the French title given to a meat dish flavoured with red wine.

macreuse, I. French for widgeon (female). II. A French cut of beef, comprising parts of the neck and shoulder.

made, Finnish for burbot, a popular fish in Finland.

mademuhennos, stewed burbot. A 3-lb. fish is cut into pieces and cooked in a pan with pepper and salt, 1 pint water, dabs of butter, and 6 allspice berries. The liver and milt are also added. The fish is served with a sauce made from the stock, 3 tablespoons whipped cream, 1 egg yolk, and 1 tablespoon lemon juice.

Madeira cake, an English cake which used to be served with a glass of Madeira wine. It is a plain cake, with a higher proportion than is usual of eggs and butter to flour. The yolks and whites of 5 eggs are whipped separately, then blended together. Then 6 oz. (⅔ cup) sugar, 6 oz. (1½ cups) self-raising flour, and 6 oz. (⅔ cup) softened butter are beaten in and flavoured with finely grated lemon or orange peel and juice. All are thoroughly mixed, and then baked in a tin lined with greaseproof paper, in a slow-to-moderate oven, for 1½ hours. Halfway through cooking, the top is decorated with 1 tablespoon of thinly sliced candied citron peel. Lemon can be used instead of orange, or 1 tablespoon caraway seeds instead of fruit peel and juice (the cake is then called seed cake).

Madeira sauce, see MADÈRE, SAUCE.

madeleine, à la, I. A French garnish for meat, consisting of artichoke bottoms, *sauce soubise,* and puréed white haricot beans in tartlets. II. A garnish for fish, of cream sauce whipped up with crayfish butter, diced celeriac, and chopped crayfish tails. III. A small French cake thought to have been invented by the pastrycook Avice when he was in the service of the French statesman Talleyrand. It figures in the books of Marcel Proust. It is baked in a special oval mould with a shell-like bottom. A mixture sufficient for about 20 cakes consists of 6 eggs, ½ lb. (1 cup) sugar, ½ lb. (2 cups) flour, 5 oz. (⅔ cup) melted butter, 1 teaspoon baking soda, grated peel of a lemon, and a little salt, all well mixed, put into the buttered moulds and baked in a slow oven until golden brown. The most famous French madeleines come from Commercy, and are sold in oval boxes. IV. A small English cake, made of a sponge mixture baked in a small round mould 3 inches high. When cooked, the cakes are brushed with warmed red jam, rolled in grated coconut, and topped with a glacé cherry.

madère, au, I. A mixture of ½ pint (1 cup) demi-glace reduced with ¼ pint (½ cup) Madeira wine. Served with certain beef dishes, and with braised ham. See also MADÈRE, SAUCE.
II. A French fruit pie served with Madeira-flavoured apricot

sauce, and called croûte au madère. III. *Sorbets,* with Madeira poured over just before serving, are known as sorbets au madère.

madère, sauce, a classical French sauce and one of the most useful wine sauces. First ½ pint (1 cup) sauce piquante is made, with white wine instead of water, and with the pickles and vinegar omitted. To the strained sauce are added 4 medium-sized, thinly sliced, fresh mushrooms and ¼ pint (½ cup) of the gravy from the roast or ham that the sauce is to accompany (after the fat has been skimmed from the top). Then 4 tablespoons good Madeira are added about 5 minutes before serving, and the sauce is simmered gently. Occasionally, sliced fresh truffles are added. See also MADÈRE, AU.

madrileña, salsa a la, a Spanish sauce for roast chicken from Madrid. Stock is made by boiling the legs, neck, heart, lungs, and liver of a chicken in 4 pints (8 cups) water; then it is seasoned and, after several hours of cooking, well reduced to about 1 pint (2 cups). Meanwhile the chicken is roasted and then carved (the skin being added to the stock). Then 1 finely chopped onion is fried in oil, with 1 tablespoon chopped parsley, 1 teaspoon wild marjoram, and 1 bay leaf. The boiling stock is added to this, and the sauce simmered for 30 minutes before being poured over the chicken.

madrilène, a French and American consommé flavoured with tomato juice or tomato fumet, usually served jellied, with a slice of lemon on top. Diced cooked sweet peppers can be added. See also CONSOMMÉ. It can refer to various other dishes flavoured with tomato juice.

madrileño, in Spanish culinary usage the term for a dish traditional in Madrid, where some of the best Spanish cooking is done. See also CALLOS, A LA MADRILEÑA; COCIDO, MADRILEÑO; JUDÍAS, ENCARNADAS A LA MADRILEÑA; POTAJE, MADRILEÑO.

consommé madrileño, a meat or chicken consommé served with a garnish of 3 medium-sized finely chopped onions fried with 1 cup fresh breadcrumbs in 3 tablespoons olive oil, with seasoning for 3 pints (6 cups) consommé. These are well mixed, 3 beaten eggs are stirred in, and the whole is then left to cool until firm. The mixture is then formed into small balls which are fried in oil; these are placed in the soup tureen, and the hot soup is poured over them just before serving.

mądrzyki, a Polish fried cheese pastry, made by mixing 1 lb. finely grated dry cheese with 4 egg yolks, 2 tablespoons sugar, and ¼ pint (½ cup) sour cream, until thoroughly blended. Then the stiffly beaten egg whites are added, and just enough flour (about 3 tablespoons) to make a rollable dough. It is rolled out, and cut into fingers which are fried in very hot oil. The fingers should be crisp, and are served at once with sour cream and sugar. The name means "wise men."

magdeburg chicory, see CHICORY.

mageritsa, see MAYIERITSA.

maggiorana, Italian for sweet marjoram. It has a more delicate flavour than wild marjoram, and is used in Italy for flavouring stews, soups, and fish.

magistères, the French name for certain soups which are extremely nourishing and are often given to invalids. They are generally made from root vegetables, fowl, and beef, with the water content reduced so much in cooking that what remains is essence (extract); the soup is strained before serving. Veal, pigeons, and crayfish, with butter and vegetables, are used to make another magistère.

magyar gulyásleves, traditional Hungarian *gulyás* soup, made by frying 4 chopped onions in lard until golden, then adding 1 lb. small cubes of beef and 1 tablespoon each paprika, marjoram, and crushed caraway seeds, with salt to taste. Then 6 pints (12 cups) water are added and, as the cooking pro-

gresses, 1 sliced red pepper and, later, ½ lb. each tomatoes and potatoes. Strips of pasta are added 10 minutes before the soup is ready for serving.

magyar halleves, traditional Hungarian fish soup. First 2 onions are chopped and fried in lard, and sprinkled with flour which has been well flavoured with paprika. Then 3 pints (6 cups) good fish stock are added and, when cooked, ½ pint (1 cup) sour cream is blended in. The soup is garnished with small flakes of different kinds of fish, and carp roe. Just before serving, irregularly shaped pieces of noodle dough are added and allowed to cook for about 5 minutes.

mahallebi, a Turkish rose cream made with 1½ pints (3 cups) milk and 4 oz. (½ cup) sugar boiled together and mixed with 1 oz. rice flour or ground rice blended with ¼ pint (½ cup) cold water. This is cooked to a thick creamy consistency, flavoured with rose water, then poured into a mould and chilled. Before serving, it is turned out and sprinkled with cinnamon or chopped nuts. This dish is also eaten in Greece and Bulgaria.

mahleb, a spice which comes from Syria and is used a great deal in Greek breads and cakes (*tsourekia*). It is made from black cherry kernels and is finely ground before using.

maia, Balkan soured milk, soured by a tablespoon of sour milk from a previous fermentation. It is used in yogourt.

maiaiul, a Rumanian cake, made with ½ lb. maize flour which is scalded in 2 pints (4 cups) milk and left to cool. Then 1 oz. yeast is mixed with 1 teaspoon sugar, ¾ pint (1½ cups) tepid milk, and 6 oz. (1½ cups) flour into a light dough, and set aside. The maize flour, when cool, is mixed with the yeast dough and this is put aside to ferment. After 1 hour, 2 tablespoons warmed butter, 1 teaspoon dill, and about ¼ pint (½ cup) *maia* are thoroughly mixed with the dough, which should then have the consistency of bread. A little more *maia* can be added if it is too stiff. This mixture is placed in a buttered tin, brushed with a mixture of flour and water, and baked in a moderate oven. It can be eaten hot or cold with sour cream.

maiale, Italian for pork, also called porco.

costa di maiale alla griglia, grilled pork chops. The Italians have an excellent way of preparing pork chops, marinating them for a few hours before grilling in olive oil to cover, with chopped fennel, garlic, and juniper berries. This gives them an original flavour.

lombata di maiale con castagne, a loin of pork cooked with garlic, rosemary, and cloves stuck into the fat. It is roasted with 2 inches of hot water in the pan and garnished with cooked and peeled chestnuts.

maiale al latte, a boned loin, or ½ leg of pork without rind, rolled with a garlic clove, 1 teaspoon crushed coriander seeds, and 2 teaspoons marjoram or basil. It is rubbed outside with salt and pepper, and browned in oil with 1 sliced onion and 2 oz. ham. When brown, milk (1 pint for 1 lb. of meat) is poured over to reach halfway up the meat, and it is gently simmered, uncovered, for several hours. The liquid will be absorbed, and care must be taken to avoid burning, but the meat will be encrusted, and tender inside. It can be eaten hot or cold. See also ARISTA FIORENTINA.

maiale con salsa di prugne, roast pork basted with white wine and served with ½ lb. soaked prunes, 1 large onion, 2 oz. bacon, 1 sprig thyme, and ½ pint (1 cup) white wine, all cooked to a purée.

maiale ubriaco, literally "drunken pork," consisting of pork chops rubbed with lemon, salt, and pepper, then fried. When brown on both sides, ½ pint (1 cup) red wine is added, and the chops are simmered until almost all the liquid has been absorbed.

maids of honour, small English cakes, reputed to have been first made at the court of Henry VIII, and still sold in many cake shops in Richmond, Surrey. About 1 lb. of puff pastry is made into 20 cases which are filled with a mixture of 4 oz. (1 cup) almonds, 3 eggs, 1 cup breadcrumbs soaked in ½ pint (1 cup) hot milk, 2 tablespoons sugar, grated peel of 1 lemon, and 3 tablespoons butter. The cakes are baked in a moderate-to-hot oven until golden brown. They are very light and delicious.

maigre, I. (*Sciaena aquila*), a large sea fish found in European waters. It makes good eating. II. French for "without meat." A *jour maigre* is a fast day.

maillot, à la, I. A French garnish for meat, especially ham, consisting of carrot and turnip, cut into coarse shreds or oval-shaped pieces which are cooked in broth, with glazed button onions, braised lettuce, green peas, and french beans tossed in butter, with a thick veal gravy or demi-glace. It is also called *porte maillot*. II. As above, but consisting only of coarsely shredded carrots, turnips, and french beans tossed in butter.

mainauer käse, a cream cheese made from cow's milk, similar to Radolfzeller käse, another local cream cheese. It is named after an island in Lake Constance, which is bordered by Germany, Switzerland, and Austria.

maintenon, à la, I. A French garnish for veal cutlets or steaks. These are stuffed with sliced mushrooms bound with thick onion purée and cream, then sautéed, and garnished with truffle slices and truffle sauce (a sauce béchamel with added cream and sliced truffle). II. A French sauce, made from a mixture of ½ pint (1 cup) each purée *soubise* and thick sauce béchamel, bound with 2 egg yolks, and 4 oz. sliced mushrooms cooked in butter. It can also be made with sliced truffles and 2 oz. finely chopped tongue. It is served with veal or lamb cutlets.

Mainz ham, see SCHINKEN.

Mainzer handkäse, an Austrian sour milk cheese from the western province. It weighs only about 2 oz., and is covered by a reddish-brown or yellow wax. The paste is yellow on the edges and white in the middle. It has a sharp, acid taste and a pungent smell.

Mainzer käse, a soft German cheese made from sour milk. The curd from partly skimmed and naturally soured milk is kneaded by hand, and pressed into small rounds which are dried and cured in a cool cellar. Some other cheeses made from sour milk are Bauernhandkäse, jorbkäse, kochkäse, harzer käse, Mainzer handkäse, stangenkäse, spitzkäse, quargelkäse, halbschimmelkäse, schimmelkäse, krauterkäse, nieheimer hopfenkäse.

maionese, Italian for mayonnaise. See also MAYONNAISE.

maionese tonnata, ½ pint (1 cup) mayonnaise mixed with 2 oz. puréed tunny (tuna) fish (tinned or freshly cooked). It is served with cold chicken, veal, or hard-boiled eggs, or is used as a filling for raw tomatoes, as a spread for open sandwiches, or is served for *antipasti*.

maionese verde, mayonnaise with pounded parsley or basil, with pignoli and pistachio nuts added.

maioneza, Greek for mayonnaise, made with egg yolks, with a little mustard, olive oil, and lemon juice added. See also MAYONNAISE.

maischolle, see SCHOLLE.

maiskolbe, Norwegian for corn on the cob. This is cooked in the usual manner and sprinkled with salt and paprika. It is then tossed in hot butter or served with tomato sauce.

maito, Finnish for milk.

maitokiisseli, milk *kiisseli*, a popular dessert dish in Finland. It is made with 2 pints (4 cups) milk, ½ cup fine wheat flour, and 3 tablespoons sugar mixed together in a pan and cooked, stirring all the time, for 10 minutes. When the mixture thickens, it is removed from the flame and poured into a dish, and decorated with jam when cold.

maître d'hotel, sauce, see BEURRES COMPOSÉS (BEURRE MAÎTRE D'HÔTEL).

maize, see CORN.

máj, Hungarian for liver, which is served in many ways in Hungary. Goose liver is very highly thought of, and is used for pâtés and also cooked whole. See also LIBA; LIVER.

májgombóc, Hungarian liver dumplings. These dumplings are made with 8 oz. of any kind of liver, 2 egg yolks, 1 tablespoon butter, 2 tablespoons each of breadcrumbs and flour, salt, pepper, and chopped parsley to taste. The ingredients are mixed into a dough and then formed into about 12 small balls which are usually boiled and served in soup. If the quantities are doubled, they can also be served as a separate dish with a butter sauce. When they are served in chicken consommé, they constitute the first course of the traditional St. Stephen's Day dinner. St. Stephen is the national saint and hero of Hungary and his day is celebrated there on August 28.

majonez zwykły, Polish for mayonnaise. See also MAYONNAISE.

majonez z jaj na twardo, mayonnaise made from 4 hard-boiled egg yolks sieved and beaten with the same aount of raw yolks. It is then beaten with ½ pint (1 cup) olive oil, trickled in, until it becomes thick and light in colour, and is seasoned with lemon juice, salt, and pepper to taste.

majoran, German for marjoram.

majoranfleisch, an Austrian dish, made from rump of beef cut in thick slices and browned in lard with sliced onions and then stock to cover. Marjoram and seasoning are added, and all is braised for some hours until the meat is tender.

makagigi, Polish almond and honey biscuits (cookies). These excellent little biscuits are made by boiling 1 lb. (4 cups) chopped blanched almonds, 4 oz. (½ cup) sugar, ¼ lb. (½ cup) honey, and ¼ cup water until the mixture sets (it usually takes about 30 minutes). It is poured onto a cold moistened surface, and rolled out with a china rolling pin, then cooled and cut into strips.

makaron, Polish for macaroni. In Poland it is combined with various meats or with cheese; it is sometimes cooked and then mixed with flavourings, such as chopped ham or shrimps and sauce béchamel, before being heated with grated cheese in a pastry case. See also MACARONI.

makaron z szynką i pomidorami, a casserole of ½ lb. cooked macaroni, ½ lb. shredded ham, 3 oz. grated cheese, and ½ pint (1 cup) tomato sauce, all layered. The top is sprinkled with ½ cup melted butter, and the whole baked for 35 minutes.

makaronada, a Greek dish of macaroni and meat sauce. See also SPAGHETO.

makkara, Finnish for sausage. Sausages are made in various shapes in Finland and are usually large enough for 2–3 servings.

paistettu makkara, roast sausage. The sausage most often used for this dish in Finland is a large thick one, curved into the shape of a horseshoe. It is skinned, an incision is made lengthwise (not right through to the bottom), and then it is liberally brushed with mustard. The cut is then stuffed with 2 medium-sized onions, sliced and browned in fat, and the sausage placed in the oven. When it has browned, 1 pint (2 cups) boiling water mixed with 2 tablespoons tomato purée and salt are added, and the sausage is cooked for 20 minutes, being basted at least twice.

mákos, Hungarian for poppy seeds, traditionally used in Balkan cooking, especially at Christmas, for they are thought to bring the eater good fortune.

mákos és diós kalács, a traditional Hungarian pastry roll

eaten at Christmas. It is made from ½ oz. dry yeast dissolved in ¼ cup lukewarm milk, added to 10 oz. (2½ cups) flour, 6 oz. (¾ cup) butter, 4 oz. (½ cup) sugar, ½ teaspoon salt, and a further ¼ pint (½ cup) milk, all kneaded, then left to rise for 1 hour. The dough is divided in half, each half rolled to ¼-inch thickness and then spread with a mixture of 6 oz. (¾ cup) sugar, 1½ cups ground poppy seed, 5 tablespoons raisins, ¼ pint (½ cup) milk, and the grated peel of 1 lemon, all boiled together until thick (about 20 minutes). Each part is rolled up, brushed with egg, left to rise for 30 minutes, and baked in a moderate oven for 30 minutes. Chopped nuts can also be added. The cake will keep for some weeks.

mákostészta, a cake garnished with poppy seeds. A dough is made with 1 lb. (4 cups) flour, 2 egg yolks, ¼ pint (½ cup) milk, and 3 tablespoons sugar. It is left to stand for about 1 hour, then rolled out to ½-inch thickness and covered with ground poppy seeds mixed with a little thick cream, sugar, and grated lemon peel. It is baked in the oven, and is delicious either hot or cold.

makovy kolach, see KOLÁČ.

makowiec, a traditional Polish Christmas roll, made from 12 oz. (3 cups) flour, 8 oz. (1 cup) butter, ¼ lb. honey, ½ pint (1 cup) cream, 1 oz. yeast, 2 eggs, 3 oz. chopped candied peel, 3 oz. chopped almonds, and ½ teaspoon cinnamon. The dough is prepared in the same way as yeast dough with butter and eggs, the honey, fruit, nuts, and spice being rolled in it. It is baked in large enough quantities to last throughout the holiday. The top is heavily sprinkled with poppy seeds before baking.

makrele, German for mackerel. In Austria, mackerel is often served grilled or steamed with horseradish added to a sauce béchamel. See also MACKEREL.

paprika-makrellen, a German and Austrian dish of 4 filleted mackerel baked with sliced onions, 1 tablespoon paprika, and 1 pint (2 cups) sour cream.

makrell, Norwegian for mackerel. See also MACKEREL.

makrellmarinade, boiled or steamed mackerel steeped in a marinade before serving. The boiled or steamed fish is skinned, and a marinade is made consisting of the stock from the mackerel, wine vinegar, butter, bay leaves, cloves, mace, pickling spice, and peppercorns, the four spices being tied in a bag. After seasoning, it is brought to the boil and simmered for 1 hour, then strained. When cold, the marinade is poured over the fish, which is left to stand in it for 12 hours, and then served with lettuce and mayonnaise.

maksa, Finnish for liver. See also LIVER.

maksalaatikko, liver pudding. This is made with 1 cup boiled rice, to which are added 2 small browned onions, 1 pint (2 cups) cold milk, 12 oz. minced liver, 2 tablespoons raisins, 1 teaspoon ginger, 4 tablespoons corn syrup, 1 teaspoon marjoram, and 1 beaten egg. The mixture is placed in an ovenproof dish, sprinkled with breadcrumbs, dotted with butter, and baked in a moderate oven for 1–1½ hours. It is served with cranberry jam and melted butter.

malác, Hungarian for pork.

malác kocsonya, Hungarian brawn, made from pig's head cooked with garlic, carrot, onions, Hamburg parsley, salt, and spices. It is boned and sliced when cooked, and then the reduced stock is poured over it. When jellied, and before serving, it is sprinkled with paprika.

ropogós malácpecsenye köritéssel, a suckling pig roasted with vegetables.

Málaga raisins, large raisins made from the muscat grape. They are very sweet and used mostly as a dessert fruit. See also RAISINS.

mălai, a Rumanian bread, popular with Rumanian Jews. It is made from 4 oz. (1 cup) flour, 2 cups cornmeal, 2 table-

spoons fat, 3 teaspoons baking powder, 2 separated eggs, 1 quart (8 cups) buttermilk, and ½ cup hot water. The cornmeal is stirred into hot salted water until smooth; the egg yolks and buttermilk are beaten together, and are mixed into the cornmeal. The flour is added gradually, and finally the stiffly beaten egg whites are folded in. A pan is coated all over with melted fat, and the mixture turned into it and baked in a moderate oven for 45 minutes. It is eaten hot.

malaxer, a French culinary term meaning to knead a substance in order to soften it.

malfatti, see RAVIOLI.

mallard (Anas platyrhyncha), the most common species of wild duck to be found in the Northern Hemisphere. The mallard makes extremely good eating, particularly in the autumn when it has a much finer flavour. The inland birds which live on lakes have a superior flavour, for some coastal birds may taste fishy on account of their diet. Mallard is also known as moss duck or muir duck, and in the Orkney Islands as stock duck. See also WILD DUCK.

mallard

malloredus, see GNOCCHETTI SARDI.

mallorquina, I. A traditional Spanish fish soup from Mallorca. First 3 chopped onions are fried in olive oil. Then 3 sliced tomatoes, 2 garlic cloves, and 1 tablespoon chopped parsley are added, followed by 2 quarts (8 cups) rich fish stock and 1 cup white wine, with seasoning. When cooked, the soup is garnished with slivers of bread fried in oil. II. A vegetable soup traditional in Mallorca. It is made from 4 onions, 3 red peppers, 1 small cabbage, 3 garlic cloves, 4 tomatoes, and parsley all fried in oil, then covered with water and simmered until cooked. The base of a casserole dish is covered with thin slices of bread, and the strained vegetables are put on top of them, then more bread is added and the stock poured over all. The contents are baked until almost all the liquid has been absorbed and the remainder is a thick purée.

mallow (Malva sylvestris), a pretty flowering plant which grows wild in Europe. The pale mauve flowers can be dried to make an herb tea, and the young leaves can be cooked like spinach.

malt, barley in which the starch content has been converted into sugar by fermentation. It is used in extract form for breads, and in vegetable extracts used to enrich soups or stews, as well as being used for drinks.

maltaise, à la, the title given to various garnishes and culinary preparations which have the juice of blood oranges added to them.

maltaise, sauce, a classical French sauce made from ½ pint (1 cup) sauce hollandaise or mayonnaise, with the addition of the juice of 2 blood oranges and 1 teaspoon very thinly shredded pieces of the peel. It is served with steamed or boiled vegetables, particularly asparagus. When mayonnaise is used, it is served with cold vegetables.

Maltese orange, see ORANGE.

Malvern pudding, a hasty pudding mixture layered with sweetened apple purée, with grated lemon peel and sugar. The top is strewn with more sugar and cinnamon or nutmeg, then baked in a moderate oven for 20 minutes. It is served either hot or cold. See also HASTY PUDDING.

mămăligă, a type of very thick porridge, rather like a cake, made with maize flour. It is eaten with many dishes in Rumania in place of bread, like *mălai*, with thick soups or stews, bacon, mushrooms, or fish. It is also a traditional Jewish dish. To prepare it, first 1 cup maize flour is shaken into 1¼ pints (2½ cups) boiling water and stirred. When it begins to thicken, it is left to simmer for about 20 minutes. It is particularly served, very hot, with eggs, either scrambled or poached, or sometimes fried. In certain parts of the country, it is eaten with cheese or sour cream, as is *mămăligă cu brînză*. When cold it is sometimes cut into squares which are dipped in beaten egg, sprinkled with grated cheese, fried until golden, and then served with yogourt or sour cream. It is eaten by rich and poor, and is sometimes called *mămăligă de aur* (bread of gold).

mămăligă cu brînză, alternate layers of mămăligă and grated Gruyère cheese are placed in a buttered ovenproof casserole, beginning and ending with mămăligă. A few nuts of butter and a beaten egg are placed on top and the contents baked until brown. It is usually eaten with butter and soft-boiled eggs. It is a national dish.

mămăligă cu ochiuri Românești, mămăligă cooked as above, served with poached eggs, then covered with melted butter. Sour cream is served separately.

mammella, Italian for udder. Calf's udder is one of the ingredients of *ravioli Genovese.*

mämmiä, a traditional Easter Sunday dessert made in Finland. It is served with sugar and cream. To prepare it 4 tablespoons dried orange peel are soaked overnight, then cooked in the same water until soft, then strained and the peel returned. Next 1 lb. (4 cups) rye malt and 3 lb. (12 cups) rye flour are sifted together, and 4 pints (8 cups) water are heated and kept at lukewarm temperature. About 1 cup of the mixed flours is sprinkled into the lukewarm water, stirring all the time until it is like gruel. Then a thick layer (about 3 cups) of the flour is sprinkled on top of the gruel without stirring. It is covered with a cloth and a lid and kept at an even temperature below boiling point. Every hour 2 pints (4 cups) more water are added at a time, together with a good sprinkling of the flour mixture, until 12 pints (24 cups) in all have been used, as well as all the flour. The mixture is returned to the stove after each addition but not allowed to boil, and it must be stirred continuously. When all the flour and malt have been well-mixed, the mixture is cooked for 30 minutes then taken from the heat and the chopped orange peel, 3 tablespoons treacle (molasses), and 3 teaspoons salt are added. (In country districts the orange peel is omitted.) The mämmiä is then placed in an ovenproof dish and baked slowly for a further 3 hours. When cooked, it is covered lightly and stored in a cool place. Originally mämmiä was baked in baskets made from birch bark, but this is now prohibited owing to the enormous damage done to the trees.

manatee (*Trichechus*), a herb-eating mammal, living in tropical coastal waters and estuaries, related to the dugong or sea cow. The American species of manatee (*T. manatus*) is highly thought of for its meat and also for bones and hide. It is a native of the Caribbean and the warm waters off Florida. There is also a South American species (*T. inunguis*), found in the estuaries of the Amazon, which is hunted for both skin and flesh; the latter is cut into steaks and grilled or stewed, when it makes a very delicious gravy. The fat is said to be very

good and sweet, and is used for making pastry when rendered down. It tastes very like pork, and in the West Indies a kind of bacon is made from it.

mancelle, a French game consommé garnished with cubes of game royale and poached chestnuts. See also CONSOMMÉ.

manche, French for a cutlet bone. *Manchette* is the paper frill used for decorating this.

Manchester pudding, a regional English pudding made from 1 lb. (4 cups) breadcrumbs boiled in 2 pints (4 cups) milk with peel of 1 lemon and 6 oz. (⅔ cup) sugar. These are then beaten with 4 oz. (½ cup) butter and 2 egg yolks and poured over a layer of apricot jam. Then more jam is placed on top, and the stiffly beaten egg whites, and a little sugar put on last of all. It is baked in a slow oven until just set and can be eaten hot or cold.

manchet bread, the 14th-century English name for a hand-made and hand-shaped loaf (usually round, with a "waist") made from the finest wheat flour. It was generally baked for noblemen and the aristocracy, so that it came to be symbolic of riches and nobility; it was also, in those pre-Reformation times, associated with the white Mass wafer which was made from the finest wheat flour, and so was credited with almost magical properties. Its reputation was further enhanced by its being quite inaccessible to the poor. Halliwell, in *A Dictionary of Archaic and Provincial Words, Obsolete Phrases, Proverbs and Ancient Customs* (1852), says that the poor usually contented themselves with bread made from rye, barley, oats, or even peas. Today in England, however, it is the poorer people who eat most white bread. The brown wholemeal loaves are not only not seen in their homes, but are actively disliked.

The word comes from the French manche (sleeve). The name survives in Cornwall today, spelt "manchant," referring to bread shaped by hand. See also BREAD.

manchon, I. A French petit four, shaped like a little muff. It is filled with praline cream and each end is dipped in chopped green almonds. II. A small French cake made of flaky pastry, shaped like a muff.

mandarin (*Citrus nobilis*), see ORANGE.

mandel, Danish for almond. See also ALMOND.

mandel kager, almond *wienerbrød,* a special Danish pastry. When the dough (see WIENERBRØD III) is rolled out, it is spread with an equal mixture of castor sugar and ground almonds, moistened with beaten egg, and rolled up. It is cut into slices before baking in a hot oven. When cooked, the slices are coated with a boiled mixture of 2 tablespoons sugar and 2 tablespoons water, then dried out for a few minutes in the oven.

mandel, German for almond. See also ALMOND.

mandelkren, I. An Austrian cold sauce made from 4 pounded hard-boiled egg yolks and 1 cup ground almonds, seasoned with salt and sugar, then beaten with ½ pint (1 cup) olive oil and vinegar to taste, as for a mayonnaise, and mixed with 3 tablespoons grated horseradish. II. A hot sauce is also made from horseradish sauce with cream, mixed with grated almonds.

mandel, Norwegian for almond. See also ALMOND.

mandelkaker, small traditional Norwegian cakes or biscuits (cookies), eaten particularly on *Syttende Mai.* They are made from equal amounts of flour, butter, and sugar, with one quarter the amount of ground almonds. These are all well kneaded so that they are like a paste. Finally, 2 stiffly beaten egg whites per pound of flour are folded in. The mixture is chilled, then rolled out very thinly before cutting into shapes and baking for about 10 minutes in a moderately hot oven. See also FYRSTEKAKE; MOR MONSEN.

mandel, Swedish for almond. See also ALMOND.

mandelskorpor, almond rusks made from ½ lb. (1¼ cups)

castor sugar well beaten into ½ lb. (1 cup) creamed butter. Then 3 eggs and 4 tablespoons cream are stirred in. To this mixture 2 oz. (½ cup) finely chopped almonds are added, and ¾ lb. (3 cups) flour sifted with 2 teaspoons baking powder is gradually stirred in. This dough is divided into 3 portions which are shaped into rolls of equal size. The rolls are baked until evenly browned in a fairly hot oven, when they are cut into slices ½ inch thick. When required, these pastry rusks are split and toasted. See also GRÄDDE; KONFEKTBRÖD; POLYNÉER; SPRITSAR.

mandolin, a French utensil for slicing fruit or vegetables, consisting of a rectangular piece of wood or metal with sharp blades fitted in it, which are adjustable to the required width.

mandorla, Italian for almond, used extensively in Italian cooking, especially for puddings and cakes. See also MACAROON; TORTIGLIONE.

manestra, a Greek pasta not unlike barley.

mangel or **mangel wurzel** (*Beta vulgaris*), a coarse variety of the beet grown both for winter cattle feed and for human consumption. It should be eaten when small, and may be prepared in the same way as beet. Also called mangold. See also BEETROOT.

mange-tout, see FRENCH BEAN.

mange-tout pea, see SUGAR PEA.

mango (*Mangifera indica*), a fruit indigenous to Malaya and the West Indies, but innumerable varieties are now grown in most tropical countries. The choicest mango has no fibre in the pulp and is said to have a flavour unrivalled by any other fruit. Mangoes are picked when ripe and allowed to mature for some days. After stoning, the fruit is cut up and used for curries, pickles, preserves, jellies, and salads. It is used, both green and when ripe, in a variety of ways, but is usually found in the European market in the form of mango chutney, which is served with curry.

mangold, see MANGEL.

Manhattan clam chowder, a traditional American soup made in the same way as New England clam chowder, but with the worcestershire sauce omitted and diced tomatoes added. Crushed salted crackers are served separately. See also CHOWDER.

manicamp, a French cow's milk cheese from Picardy. It is at its best from October to July.

manicotti, the Italian word for homemade cappelletti. See CAPPELLETTI.

manier, a French culinary term meaning to work a mixture by hand, covering, for example, the process of kneading or of mixing fat with flour.

manitas de cerdo rehogadas, Spanish for fried pig's trotters (feet). After cleaning and boiling, the bones are removed, care being taken not to destroy the shape of the feet. They are then floured, dipped in egg and breadcrumbs, and fried in oil. See also CERDO.

mannavelli, Finnish for semolina gruel. It is made in the same way as *ohrajauhovelli*.

manos de ternera, Spanish for calves' feet used a lot in soups and stews in Spain. See also TERNERA.

manouri, Greek for a sweet, soft cheese which hardens as it matures. When fresh, it is eaten with honey.

manqué, literally "failed," a French sponge cake, made from ½ lb. (2 cups) flour, 12 oz. (1½ cups) sugar, 9 separated eggs, 4 oz. (½ cup) butter, and 3 tablespoons rum, the stiffly beaten egg whites being added last. It is baked in a special tin called a *moule à manqué*. The cake is said to have acquired its name because the pastry-cook had intended to make a Savoy cake, but when it turned out badly, he renamed it.

mansikka, Finnish for strawberries.

mansikkalumi, a dessert made with crushed Arctic wild

strawberries mixed with sugar, beaten egg whites, and whipped cream.

mansikkatorttu, a Finnish national sponge cake, which is filled with Arctic wild strawberries.

mantecados, small dry Spanish biscuits (cookies) made in the cities of Antequara and Ronda. To prepare them ½ cup white wine or rum is mixed with 2 tablespoons sugar and 8 oz. (1 cup) lard; flour being gradually added until the mixture becomes firm. It is then cut into rounds about ½ inch thick which are baked in a hot oven. They are a good accompaniment for sherry. In Astorga, León, mantecados are biscuits (cookies) served with coffee, and are made by creaming 8 oz. (1 cup) butter with 8 oz. icing (confectioners') sugar, then adding 6 eggs one at a time, 8 oz. (2 cups) flour, and ½ teaspoon cinnamon. Tablespoonfuls of the mixture are cooked in paper cases. Another variety, called *almendrados,* are made by whipping 2 egg whites, then gradually mixing in 1 tablespoon ground almonds, 1 tablespoon sugar, 1 teaspoon cinnamon, and the grated peel of 1 lemon. Teaspoons of the mixture are baked on a greased baking-sheet for 10 minutes in a moderate oven.

manteche, an Italian cheese like a provolone, but flask-shaped. In the middle of the cheese a small quantity of butter is sealed, which stays fresh for a long time. The method of making the cheese is a closely guarded secret.

manti, a Greek pasty made from 1 lb. minced (ground) meat, 2 minced onions, 1 cup cooked *trahana,* and seasoning, all wrapped up in pastry then baked in a slow oven for 1 hour. When cooked, 1 pint (2 cups) hot chicken broth is poured over, and the pasty is left to stand until this has been absorbed.

Manx broth, a traditional soup from the Isle of Man, made from 2 lb. brisket or shin of beef, a knuckle-bone of ham, 2 cups pearl barley, 1 cabbage, 1 turnip, 3 carrots, and 4 leeks, all chopped with 2 sprigs thyme, plenty of chopped parsley, pepper, and salt. All are boiled for at least 3 hours in 2 quarts (8 cups) water, and the liquid is skimmed as it boils. The soup should be very thick, more like a stew.

manzana, Spanish for apple. See also APPLE.

manzanas fritas, apple fritters with beer and brandy made from 2 lb. peeled, cored, and sliced raw apples sprinkled with sugar and soaked overnight in brandy. A mixture of 3 tablespoons flour, 4 tablespoons sugar, and 1 teaspoon cinnamon is made, and ¼ pint (½ cup) beer is added gradually. The apples are coated with this mixture and then fried in butter.

manzo, Italian for beef. *Manzo ripieno* is stuffed beef; *manzo stufato* is braised meat of any kind, not just beef. See also BEEF; BISTECCA; STRACOTTO; STUFATINO; VITELLONE.

manzo arrosto, roast beef, usually cooked with rosemary and chopped onion.

manzo bollito, boiled beef, usually served cold with mayonnaise.

costa di manzo al vino rosso, a 4-lb. rib of beef marinated for 24 hours in strong red wine containing onion, carrot, celery, bay leaves, garlic, and black pepper (this marinade is excellent for making the toughest beef tender and tasty without being stringy). The meat is removed and browned in butter, then simmered for 3 hours in the marinade, which is then strained and reduced by half. It is especially good when served with potato gnocchi and grated Parmesan cheese.

rondello di manzo, a lean 4-lb. joint is rubbed with garlic, salt, and pepper and soaked for 24 hours in a marinade of 1 pint red wine which has been boiled with sliced onion, carrot, celery, 3 cloves, and 6 peppercorns and then cooled. The meat is turned several times during this period. It is then dried, browned in butter, and simmered gently in a saucepan in the marinade.

maple (*Acer saccharinum*), a large tree native to Canada and the U.S., from which natural syrup is obtained by tapping the trunk. The resulting product, maple syrup, is delicious served with waffles or pancakes, or used for flavouring cold sweets and soufflés.

maple

maple sugar, see SUGAR.

maquée, a soft Belgian cheese made from cow's milk. It comes in two qualities: one made from rennetted, skimmed milk drained in small osier baskets or cheesecloth bags; the second is made by heating the whey. It is also called *fromage mou.*

maquereau, French for mackerel. Young mackerel are called *sansonnets. Maquereau mariné* is soused mackerel. See also MACKEREL.

   maquereau à la boulonnaise, mackerel cut into thick slices, poached in court bouillon with vinegar, drained, and skinned. It is served with shelled, cooked mussels and sauce beurre made with the fish stock.

   maquereau à la dieppoise, poached mackerel fillets in white wine, surrounded by *dieppoise* garnish and with white wine sauce made with the fish stock.

   maquereau à la flamande, a Flemish method of cooking mackerel. It is poached in a court-bouillon, then covered with a sauce made from 2 tablespoons flour, 2 tablespoons butter, 2 teaspoons french mustard, and 1 pint (2 cups) fish stock.

   maquereau à la lyonnaise, mackerel fillets, laid on a bed of onions which have been cooked in butter and moistened with vinegar, covered with more of the onions, moistened with white wine, then dotted with breadcrumbs and butter before baking.

   maquereau à la normande, thickly sliced potatoes, onions, garlic, and bay leaf, simmered in 1 inch of water or cider; when the potatoes are half-cooked, chunks of mackerel and a knob of butter are added. The pan is covered, and cooking is continued until the fish and potatoes are ready.

maraîchère, à la, I. A French garnish for roasted or braised meats, composed of small braised onions, stuffed braised cucumber, braised salsify, and artichokes, with *pommes château.* II. A French dish of veal cutlets sautéed in butter and served with salsify and tiny brussels sprouts.

marasca, Italian for the morello cherry, from which maraschino liqueur is made.

marcassin, French for young wild boar, which is the best for eating. In France almost the whole of the animal is eaten in various forms, but it is usually marinated first. It can be cooked in the same way as ham or pork, and is often served with chestnut purée. It is also made into an excellent terrine, with minced veal, herbs, and red wine. See also CINGHIALE.

marchand de vin, sauce, not a classical French sauce for beef, but a popular American one, probably from the New Orleans region, which is similar to sauce bordelaise, but it is not essential to use Bordeaux wine. It consists of 4 finely sliced small onions or shallots fried in butter, 2 oz. mushrooms, 2 tablespoons beef marrow are optional, and ½ pint (1 cup) red wine, all well seasoned and cooked for about 10 minutes. It is served with steaks. See also BEURRE, MARCHAND DE VINS.

marchew, Polish for carrots. This vegetable is eaten in several different ways in Poland. When very young, carrots are often simmered in butter and bouillon, or combined with peas or asparagus.

Mardi Gras, see SHROVE TUESDAY.

maréchale, à la, I. A French garnish for entrées, consisting of truffles and asparagus tips. II. A French garnish for sweetbreads, meat, and poultry, of chicken quenelles with chopped truffles bound with *sauce italienne,* cock's combs, and a demi-glace flavoured with Madeira. III. A French method of cooking escalopes (meat scallops), poultry, and small cuts of meat, by dipping them in egg and breadcrumbs before frying in butter. They are garnished as in I.

marée, the collective name in France for all seafood sold in a fish market.

marena, a freshwater fish of the salmon family, related to the lavaret. It is found mainly in northern German lakes and is prepared like trout.

marengo, a chicken dish named after the Battle of Marengo in 1800. It is said that Napoleon never ate until a battle was over, and if the campaign had been a long one, foods were scarce. This dish was made from the only food the cook could find in the farmhouses close at hand and derived from the natural resources of the immediate vicinity. It consists of jointed chicken, fried in olive oil with garlic and tomatoes. A little water and brandy are added, barely to cover, and crayfish are steamed on top and used later as a garnish. The dish is also garnished with fried eggs.

   veal sauté marengo, veal prepared in a similar way, but garnished with onions and mushrooms.

marennes, the name given to oysters of a white and green colour which come from Marennes, a small port in the Charente-Maritime district of France. They are of exceptionally good quality and are bred on a large scale.

marette, a special bread made in Marseilles, France, and used in *bouillabaisse.*

margarine, a fat used mostly in cooking, made from a large variety of fatty animal and vegetable substances, of which homogenised animal fat is the most usual but the least good. The invention of margarine was the culmination of experiments by the French chemist Mège-Mouriez in about 1869. Some margarines are a mixture of animal fat and vegetable oil. The finest is that made entirely from nut, seed, or vegetable oils, such as sunflower, safflower, sesame, peanut, or corn oil; this makes excellent pastry, cakes, and sauces, and in addition, is quite acceptable for all cooking in which animal fat should be avoided. Margarine resembles butter in appearance, but must have the word "margarine" printed clearly on the wrapping. The taste is not as delicate or complex as that of a good butter, but margarine should be regarded as a substance in its own right, and not as a butter-substitute.

margota, see LABRO.

marguéry, à la, a French garnish for tournedos, consisting of artichoke hearts filled with salpicon of truffles à la crème, sautéed morels, cock's combs, and cock's kidneys. The pan juices are boiled up and reduced with port wine and cream.

marguéry, sauce, a classical French sauce consisting of sauce hollandaise flavoured with fish essence (extract) and purée of oysters.

marha gulyás, see GULYÁS.

maribo, a Danish cheese which is large, round, and full of irregular holes. It weighs from 26 to 30 lb. Unlike most cheeses, it is well whipped to let the air in and to encourage the acidity to develop. It has a delicious aftertaste. See also OST.

marides or ***marithes,*** Greek for whitebait or small smelts native to Greek waters and eaten a great deal in Greece. They are rolled in flour, fried in deep hot oil and served whole with lemon wedges. They are delicious and are served as *mezes* with the aperitif *ouzo.*

Marie Stuart, a French garnish for entrées consisting of tartlets filled with purée of turnips or onions, with rounds of marrow bone fat on top, covered in demi-glace.

Marie-Jeanne, à la, a French garnish for noisettes and tournedos consisting of tartlets filled with purée of mushrooms topped with a slice of truffle.

Marie-Louise, à la, I. A French garnish for entrées consisting of artichoke bottoms filled with mushroom purée, lightly sprinkled with grated cheese, and gratinéed. Green asparagus tips are also used for this garnish. II. A French consommé of chicken garnished with royale and peas. See also CONSOMMÉ.

marignan, a Parisian cake which consists of a *savarin* baked in the same mould as is used for a *manqué,* served soaked in liqueur-flavoured syrup, and covered with meringue.

marigny, à la, I. A French garnish for entrées consisting of tartlets filled with green peas and french beans cut into lozenge shapes, with *pommes fondantes.* II. A French sauce of 4 tablespoons demi-glace boiled up with 1 tablespoon tomato purée, ¼ pint (½ cup) mushroom stock, and ¼ pint (½ cup) white wine, garnished with sliced mushrooms and stoned olives. III. A French chicken consommé, with chicken quenelles, chopped cucumber, and chervil.

marigold (*Calendula officinalis*), a plant which Nicholas Culpeper, the famous 17th-century astrologer and medical writer, called "a herb of the sun." It was cultivated in medieval monastery gardens and was used by 16th-century herbalists "in possets, broths and drinks as a comforter to the heart," and is sometimes called "pot marigold" on account of its culinary use. Care should be taken to use this herb sparingly, as it is very strong. It can be used in place of saffron in rice dishes, and the fresh petals are sometimes sprinkled on salads, giving a piquant flavour. Both fresh and dried petals are used extensively in Holland, where a fresh petal is sometimes put in a custard, imparting a subtle flavour, and dried, pulverised petals are used to give a delicious piquancy to soups.

marillenstrudel, see STRUDEL.

marinade, a highly seasoned liquor in which game, meat, or fish is left to soak, to be given flavour and to release flavour, as well as to be tenderized. However, it is important to remember that marinating should not be applied to game that is to be eaten before rigor mortis has set in. A French marinade usually includes wine, sometimes vinegar, also olive oil, lemon peel and juice, pepper and salt, bay leaves, onions, shallots, thyme, parsley, cloves, garlic, and other herbs. This is called *marinade crue* in French. If it is brought to the boil, and also sometimes seasoned with coriander or juniper, it is known as *marinade cuite.* Fish marinade usually consists of salt, pepper, onions or shallots, herbs, oil, and lemon juice. See also VENISON, MARINADE FOR.

The appropriate verb, actually adopted from the French

marigold

before the noun, is to marinate, meaning to soak for hours or days in the marinade.

mariné, French for marinated, sometimes also used to mean pickled.

marinebraten, an Austrian beef dish, made from fillet steak placed on top of sliced onions, carrots, and celeriac, with butter added and all just moistened with a mixture of stock and white wine, then browned in a hot oven. The dish is basted frequently, and when it is cooked as required, the stock is strained off, boiled up with fresh cream mixed with more of the same sliced vegetables, and then poured over the steak. *Spätzle* or rice are served with the dish.

Marinetti, Filippo Tomaso (1876–1944), a well-known Italian futurist poet who, in 1930, launched a much-publicised campaign against the traditional Italian forms of cooking, and particularly against the consumption of *pasta asciutta.* Futurist cooking was to be liberated from "the ancient obsession with weight and volume." He claimed the nutritive values of pasta to be deceptive and said that it induced sloth and pessimism, and did not encourage either martial ardour, or physical ardour towards women. Marinetti was not by any means the first to question the nutritional value of pasta. There had been a campaign against it in the 16th century, and another in the 19th century led by the scientist Michele Scropetta. But in a country as poor as Italy, the people considered pasta their sole security against starvation, for it was a food available at low cost. Whether or not it was "a barbarous legacy from the Ostrogoths" mattered little to hungry peasants. In 1932 Marinetti published his book on futurist cooking, *La Cucina Futurista,* with Mussolini's blessing. It contained, for the most part, recipes mixing unusual and exotic flavours. He and his friends shocked the conservative element of the public with their suggestions of nougat, pineapple, sardines, and salame, all served in black coffee flavoured with eau de Cologne, and an aphrodisiac drink of pineapple juice, eggs, cocoa, caviar, almond paste, cayenne pepper, nutmeg, cloves, and Strega. However, not all Marinetti's recipes were as exaggerated as this.

Another of Marinetti's ideas was that the food should be eaten with a fork held in the right hand, while the left stroked suitable materials, such as velvet or silk. Of course all diners were also to be sprayed with scent, but as Marinetti was against almost all foreign goods, presumably sweet Italian scent would be the only perfume allowed. His strong nationalistic tendencies also led him to oppose cocktail parties, jazz, and French cooking. See also BOCCONE SQUADRISTA; COSTO-

LETTE, D'AGNELLO ALLA MARINETTI; DOLCE, MAFARKA; RISO, VERDI; UOVA, DIVORZIATE.

marinière, à la, I. A French method of cooking fish or shellfish in white wine. It is particularly applied to mussels, one of the most famous French dishes being *moules à la marinière.* It can also apply to other fish, such as brill, cooked in white wine and garnished with mussels. II. A French garnish for fish, consisting of bearded mussels cooked in white wine, with shredded shrimps and sauce marinière. III. A French sauce made from sauce bercy and mussel stock, whipped with a little butter, and served with the bearded mussels.

marinovannye, Russian for marinated or pickled. See BAKLAZHANY for Russian pickled aubergines (eggplants); SLIVA for Russian pickled ripe plums.

marisco liso, see VIERAS.

mariscos, Spanish for mussels, although the word can also be used collectively to mean shellfish in general. Mussels are also called *mejillones.* They are used a lot in Spain, especially in *paella.*

marithes, see MARIDES.

marjoram (*Labiaceae*), an aromatic herb with many varieties, the most common in the British Isles being the wild marjoram (*Origanum vulgare*) which grows on chalky soil and has clusters of purple flowers and a sweet smell. In the 15th and 16th centuries in England, it was used especially for flavouring milk and curd dishes, as well as soups and stews. It is a perennial and grows freely. The second variety grown in the British Isles is sweet knotted marjoram (*O. majorana*) which is an annual and has a stronger flavour than the former.

A third variety, pot marjoram or French marjoram (*O. onites*), is a Mediterranean herb, and although perennial in warm climates, must be treated as a half-hardy annual in cold ones. It is known as *origan* in France and *oregano* in Italy, where it is used extensively for soups, stews, sauces, and forcemeats, and especially with veal and beef. There are also Egyptian and Cretan varieties. The oil of all varieties of marjoram was used for perfumery, and marjoram tea was drunk to alleviate chest infections, both in England and by New Englanders in the U.S. See also MAJORAN; RIGANI.

mark, German for bone marrow. See also MARROW.

markklösschen, Swiss dumplings, made with 6 oz. beef or veal marrow mixed with 4 oz. soaked breadcrumbs, 1 tablespoon parsley, 1 teaspoon lemon peel, a pinch of nutmeg, and seasoning. The ingredients are bound with a beaten egg, made into 1-inch balls and poached in stock. They are served in clear soups.

markknödlsuppe, a traditional Austrian beef marrow dumpling soup. To prepare it 4 oz. beef marrow, known as *zerschleichen* in Austria, is slightly warmed, chopped, and rubbed through a sieve. Then 1 egg, 2 tablespoons flour, seasoning, and 2 slices crustless bread which have been soaked in ¼ pint (½ cup) milk, are added. Small dumplings are then shaped from the mixture and boiled in salted water. They are used as a garnish for rich beef broth.

Marlborough pie, a speciality of Massachusetts, U.S., which is often eaten at Thanksgiving Day dinner. First 1 cup apple sauce is combined with 3 tablespoons lemon juice, ½ lb. (1 cup) sugar, 4 eggs, 2 tablespoons butter, ½ teaspoon nutmeg, and a little salt, to make the pie-filling. This is poured into a 9-inch pastry shell and baked for 1 hour in a slow-to-moderate oven, until the top is golden and the filling set. (In Britain, of course, this would not be a pie but a flan or tart, since it has no top crust.)

marling, an old English name for whiting.

marly, a French chicken consommé, garnished with a julienne of leek, celery, chicken, shredded lettuce, chopped chervil, and croûtons, and sprinkled with grated Parmesan cheese. See also CONSOMMÉ.

marmalade, a word which derives from *marmelo,* the Portuguese word for quince, for quince jelly was the original marmalade. It is now, unless otherwise specified, a preserve of bitter or Seville oranges and sugar. In the British Isles it is eaten with toast and butter for breakfast. It is also used to flavour steamed puddings. More recently, other citrus fruits, in particular limes, lemons, and grapefruits, have been used in the making of differently flavoured marmalades. Scottish marmalade, originally made at Dundee, is considered very good, and in Scotland there is a legend which associates the preserve with Mary Queen of Scots. It is said that, when ill, she frequently asked for an orange preserve she had been fond of in France. It became known at her court as "Marie-malade," and marmalade is thought by many Scottish people to be a corruption of those words. Dundee marmalade is world famous and has been made by the Keiller family since the 18th century.

marmalade sauce, a popular English sweet sauce made from 1 cup orange marmalade and ¼ pint (½ cup) white wine stirred together in a saucepan over a gentle heat until very hot, then strained. It is served with steamed puddings.

marmelade, I. The name in almost all European countries for a thick jam made from apples or apricots, figs, melon, peaches, plums, quince, etc. Oranges are seldom used. II. In France, it is also the name for fruit stewed with very little water until it becomes a thick purée. The same purée is made in Spain, but only with apple; it is so thick that, as well as being used for flans, it is sold cut into cubes as a sweetmeat (confection).

marmelo, see MARMALADE.

marmite, I. A French metal or earthenware covered pot, used for long slow cooking either on top of the stove or in the oven. It varies in size and shape, and there is a special type made for cooking on board ships, which can be hung up. II. *Petite marmite,* a clear, strong, savoury broth served in an earthenware vessel. It is a Parisian speciality and should contain lean meat, oxtail, poultry, root vegetables, and beef marrow. It is garnished with dried bread or rusks sprinkled with grated cheese. In Paris it is often called *petite marmite Henri IV.* III. A yeast and vegetable extract, used as a drink or for flavouring soups or stews.

marmotte, French for marmot, a rodent about the size of a large cat which lives in the Alps and the Pyrenees, where it is eaten. In the autumn, before it hibernates, it has a good deal of flesh on it. Although this has a musky flavour, it can be eliminated by marinating for a long time.

maroilles or *marolles,* a French semi-hard cheese with an illustrious history. In 1174, the Abbot of Maroilles in the Thiérache hills ordered the inhabitants of four villages adjacent to the Abbey to make cheese of the milk they would have on the eve of Saint Jean, June 24, and to give it to their parish priest on the day of Saint Rémi, October 1, for delivery in due course to the Abbey. To this day, Saint Rémi's day is Maroilles Day in the vineyards of Champagne. Maroilles is made of unskimmed cow's milk. It is slightly salted, and is fermented not inoculated. It is eaten from October to July.

maroilles gris, le, a French cow's milk cheese of the *maroilles* type, but rindless. It comes from Picardy and is at its best from October to July.

marolles, see MAROILLES.

maronen, German for chestnuts. They are often served cooked and puréed, also after preliminary boiling and shelling, simmered in red wine. When soft, they are also puréed and used as a garnish for veal or poultry. They are used in savoury stuffings, as well as in sweet dishes.

marquer, a French culinary term meaning to prepare foods before cooking. It can also mean to put food into a buttered dish.

marquise, à la, I. A French garnish for noisettes and tournedos, consisting of poached calf's marrow cut in pieces, with asparagus tips, julienne of truffles, and sauce suprême. II. A sauce hollandaise, with caviar to taste added at the last minute and stirred well in. III. A French variety of pear which is sweet, pyramid-shaped, and ripens at the end of November. IV. A French consommé of beef, flavoured with celery and garnished with chicken quenelles, beef marrow, and chopped hazelnuts. See also CONSOMMÉ.

marron, see CHESTNUT. One of the best varieties of French cultivated chestnut is the *marron de Lyon.*

marrow, I. The gelatinous fatty substance found in the middle of bones, from which it is extracted by means of a long, thin silver or silver-plated spoon, known as a marrow spoon. The shank bone of ox is particularly rich in marrow, and an old English dish is made of it, steamed or boiled, wrapped in a napkin, and served with dry toast. It forms an important ingredient in many French sauces, particularly bordelaise, and in masséna garnish. See also BONE; MARK; MOELLE; OSSI BUCHI. II. A gourd-like vegetable, known in the U.S. as summer squash. See VEGETABLE MARROW.

marseillaise, I. A French garnish for tournedos and noisettes, consisting of stuffed olives with anchovy fillets in hollowed tomatoes previously sautéed in olive oil, large fried potato chips, and sauce *provençale.* II. A mayonnaise mixed with a purée of sea-urchins.

marshmallow, a sweetmeat (confection) originally made from the roots of the marsh mallow plant (*Althea officinalis*), but nowadays made from sugar, water, cream of tartar, flavouring and colouring, and stiffly beaten egg whites. It is spongy, gelatinous, and made in 1-inch squares. In the U.S. it is used commonly for icing and desserts, and it is toasted on an open fire as a sweet.

marsh rabbit, see MUSKRAT.

marsh samphire, see GLASSWORT.

marsouin, French for porpoise, useful mainly for its oil.

maruzze, shell-shaped pasta, used for garnishing soups, and also served *asciutta* in sauce. See also PASTA.

marzipan, originally a solid cake and called first St. Mark's pain from the French *pain* (bread), later marchpane, finally marzipan. It is a firm paste made from ½ lb. ground almonds, ½ lb. (1 cup) sugar, and 2–3 egg whites. The dry ingredients should be gently warmed until they can be kneaded before adding the egg whites. It is used to make little sweets and cakes, and also to decorate both large and small cakes. It has a very early origin, and is thought to have been first made by an order of nuns. It is also called almond paste. See also MASSEPAIN.

mascarpone or *mascherpone,* fresh little Italian cream cheeses, sold in white muslin parcels. They are eaten with sugar or fruit, and are very similar to the French *coeur à la crème.*

mascotte, I. A French garnish for fowl or meat, consisting of quartered artichoke bottoms sautéed in butter, *pommes cocotte,* and truffles. II. A sauce consisting of 3 tablespoons meat juice mixed with 4 tablespoons white wine and boiled up with ½ pint (1 cup) veal gravy. All preparations for *sauce mascotte* are cooked *en cocotte.* III. A French cake made by filling a *génoise* with mocha butter cream (see CRÈME, AU BEURRE) mixed with pounded roast hazelnuts.

mash, to, to crush or pound. In culinary terminology it is generally used in connection with vegetables, such as potatoes, turnips, etc. Mashed potatoes are common in the U.S., and their nearest equivalent in France is a purée. The word is also applied to boiled grain, such as bran, when it has been made into a soft pulp by crushing and mixing with water. The Old English word was *masc,* cognate with the German *meisch,* used to describe crushed grapes, malt, etc.

mashlum bannock, a bannock made from mixed flours. See BANNOCK.

masking, the covering of food by a sauce.

maslo, Polish for butter. *Maslo sardelowe* is the Polish for anchovy butter, and *maslo szczypiórkowe* for chive butter. Both are used a lot as garnish for fish, meat, and vegetables.

masséna, a French garnish for tournedos and noisettes, consisting of artichoke bottoms covered with a sauce *périgueux* or sauce béarnaise, and slices of poached marrow bone fat or truffle placed on the tournedos or noisettes.

massena quail (*Cyrtonyx montezumae*), sometimes called massena partridge, the most handsome of the American partridges, found in the mountainous parts of the southwest of the U.S., and also in Mexico and in Central America. It is very tame, and is sometimes called the fool quail because of this. It is well thought of as food, and can be prepared and cooked in any way that is suitable for partridge or quail.

massenet, à la, a French garnish for tournedos and noisettes, consisting of artichoke bottoms filled with poached marrow bone fat, french beans, *pommes anna,* and sauce madère.

massepain, French for marzipan. Small biscuits (cookies) made from almond paste are also called massepains. See also MASSILLONS.

massillons, a French petit four in the shape of a tartlet, made from marzipan. See also MASSEPAIN.

masthuhn, German for pullet. See HUHN.

mastic (*Pistacia lentiscus*), an evergreen resinous shrub native to southern Europe, the sap of which is used as a culinary flavouring. See also MASTIHA.

mastiha, Greek for mastic and for the crystals obtained from the sap, which are used as flavouring. It is an important Greek export to the Middle and Far East. It is said that in the days of the Turkish occupation, the ladies of the Sultan's harem were allowed the proceeds from the sale of mastic gum as pin-money. On the island of Chios there are still some 4 million shrubs. The gum, which tastes faintly of liquorice, is obtained by making incisions in the bark of the tree, from which the small clear crystals fall like tears onto the sand that has been sprinkled round to catch them. The sorting of crystals for quality is still done by hand. They are used a great deal in Balkan cooking for cakes and biscuits (cookies), and a liqueur is also made from mastic.

mateenmäti, a Finnish dish prepared from skinned, mashed burbot roe seasoned with salt, pepper, and a small grated onion, finally mixed with 2 or 3 tablespoons cream. It is served as a component of a smörgåsbord, and also used as a filling for *blinis.* Traditionally, it is eaten at Shrovetide in Finland.

matefaim, a coarse pancake cooked in certain parts of France, especially the Jura and the Loire valley.

matelote, I. The name used in French cooking for a rich fish stew made with either red or white wine. To be correct, it should be made from freshwater fish, but *matelote à la Normande* uses sea fish, such as conger eel, sole, and gurnet, and cider instead of wine. The matelote most often made consists of 2 onions and 3 garlic cloves fried in butter, with about 3 lb. of fish, such as carp, eel, bream, or barbel, chopped into equal pieces and added. Bay leaf, parsley, and thyme are put in, with 1 litre (3½ cups) dry wine. After boiling the mixture, 1 glass (½ cup) brandy is added and set aflame. The cooked fish is taken out and drained, and for subsequent pleasure in eating, the fish bones should be removed, although this is not often done. The stock is then reduced, when cooked button mushrooms and small cooked button onions are added, and the fish put back. It is all thickened with a *beurre manié,* and simmered gently. The matelote is served in a deep bowl and garnished with pieces of fried gudgeon or other freshwater fish and freshwater crayfish. It is also known as a *meurette* when prepared *à la bourguignonne*, or a *pochouse*, but the latter often has a garnish of fried diced belly of pork as well as one of heart-shaped pieces of fried bread. The Belgian *waterzoi* is a matelote. II. A French garnish for fish, consisting of onions, mushrooms, croûtons, and crayfish. III. A French method of serving chicken. See POULET.

matelote à la bourguignonne, as above, but cooked with burgundy and marc.

matelote, sauce, a classical French sauce, consisting of a wine court bouillon in which fish has been cooked, reduced by simmering to ½ pint. Then 4 tablespoons fish demi-glace are added, the sauce is sieved, and 2 tablespoons butter, in small pieces, and a dusting of cayenne, are added before serving.

matignon, a French garnish consisting of a fondue of root vegetables, celery, bay leaf, thyme, salt, and a pinch of sugar. When very soft, a cup of Madeira is added, and the whole is reduced to an essence (extract). Sometimes a little lean raw ham, cut into very thin slices, is added. The garnish is used particularly with artichoke hearts.

matjesheringe, German for young, salted herrings, like *maatjes*, which are eaten a great deal in Germany, particularly in the Bremerhaven district where the big catches are made. See also HERINGE.

matzo, matzot, or *matzos*, Jewish unleavened bread, which is made from fine wheat flour and water only. It is formed into flat cakes or biscuits, either round or square, which are white with brownish baking marks, not unlike a water biscuit. It is thought to have originated in the "shewbread" of the Bible. Matzo flour is also milled in varying degrees of coarseness. The spelling is variable, sometimes appearing as *matzoth*. It forms a part of the ritual service of Passover. See also BREAD.

maubeche, French for sandpiper, which is prepared and cooked in the same way as snipe in France. See GUIGNE.

maultaschen, a dish of the ravioli type, traditionally eaten in Wurtemburg, Germany, on Good Friday. The dough is made from 4 oz. (1 cup) flour, 1 egg, and approximately 4 tablespoons water. It is rolled very thinly, half-covered with cooked spinach; the other half of the dough is folded over, and the whole cut into squares. These are poached in boiling salted water for 15 minutes, drained, and served with hot brown butter, with breadcrumbs sprinkled on top. Puréed brains are added if it is not eaten on a fast-day.

mauviette, French for lark. See ALOUETTE.

may duke, see CHERRY.

mayieritsa or *mageritsa*, a traditional Greek Easter soup eaten in the early hours of Easter Sunday after the *Proti Anastasis* (Resurrection) celebrations. It is made from odd bits and pieces—offal (variety meats), feet, tail, head, etc.—from the lamb which will be roasted later in the day. A good stock is first made from the lamb bones, heart, and intestines (the latter tied in a bundle). The meat is then stripped from the bones and returned to the stock, together with the heart, which is now sliced. Then spring onions (scallions), celery, parsley, dill, and seasoning, all chopped, are added. Lastly, rice is put in and cooked rapidly. After removing from the heat, *avgolémono sauce* is stirred in. The soup is then left to stand, covered, for 5 minutes before serving. See also ARNI; EASTER; KOKKINA AVGA.

mayonnaise, a classical French cold sauce used all over the western world. There is great controversy over the origin of the name. In Ireland, it is firmly believed to be the invention of the chef of the Irish General MacMahon, and that the name is a corruption of "mahonnaise." This theory has a certain amount of support in France. It is also possible that it was given this name by the Duc de Richelieu after he won the battle of Mahon in Minorca in 1757. Carême, the famous

French chef of the early 19th century, thought it was derived from *magnonaise* from the French verb *manier*, to stir. The compilers of *Larousse Gastronomique* consider it a corruption of *moyeunaise*, from the Old French word *moyeu*, the yolk of an egg. In Bayonne, a town in the Basses-Pyrénées department of France, it is believed that the sauce was originally called *bayonnaise*, and was invented there. Each theory has its own supporters; none can be proved right or wrong.

It is essential to have all ingredients at room temperature before starting to make mayonnaise, which is prepared with 2 egg yolks, without a trace of the egg white, put in a medium-sized bowl with a little salt and pepper and a few drops of tarragon vinegar. Then, drop by drop, a large cup of olive oil is added, beating all the time. If too much oil is added initially, the mixture will separate. Once it becomes thick, the oil can be added a little more freely, but care must still be taken. When it is very thick, the sauce can be thinned down with more vinegar or lemon juice. If it is to be kept for as long as a week in a screw-top jar, it is advisable to incorporate 2 or 3 teaspoons boiling water, beating all the time, when the sauce is made. This prevents it from curdling. If the sauce separates or curdles while it is being made, it should be dripped, drop by drop, into another egg yolk, being beaten all the time until it thickens again. An excellent mayonnaise can be made by starting the sauce with olive oil until it is thick, then transferring to a good corn oil, sunflower seed oil, or safflower seed oil. This makes a more digestible sauce, and one that is not as strongly flavoured as the ordinary mayonnaise and, therefore, very good for eating with delicate-tasting foods such as fresh prawns or lobster. It forms the basis for many other cold sauces, particularly *aïoli, andalouse, collioure, indienne, maltaise, mousquetaire, niçoise, orientale, rémoulade, russe, tartare à la, varenne, verte*, and *vincent*. If melted meat jelly or aspic is whisked into the mayonnaise, it can be used to coat eggs, fish, chicken, or vegetables.

The term mayonnaise is also used to denote cold dishes made from fish, poultry, eggs, or vegetables covered with the sauce. See also MAIONESE; MAIONEZA; MAJONEZ ZWYKŁY.

mazagran, I. A French tartlet made from *pommes duchesse* and filled with a *salpicon*, then baked in the oven. II. French for cold coffee served in a glass.

mazanotz, a traditional Czechoslovakian Easter cake, made from 1 oz. yeast, 1 lb. (4 cups) flour, 4 oz. (½ cup) sugar, 6 oz. (⅔ cup) butter, 4 egg yolks, 2 oz. (¼ cup) sultanas, 2 oz. (½ cup) almonds, and grated peel of 1 lemon. The dough is left for a couple of hours to rise, as for yeast dough, then formed into a round loaf. A cross is cut into the top, which is then brushed with beaten egg white, and the loaf is baked in a hot oven for 40 minutes. When cool, it is liberally sprinkled with vanilla sugar. See also EASTER.

mazarin, an elaborate round French cake made from a *génoise* mixture. When the cake has been baked, the middle is scooped out whole, leaving a thin layer of cake at the bottom. The conical shape removed is iced with pink *fondant* icing, and the well left is filled with chopped crystallised fruit, syrup, and apricot jam flavoured with kirsch. It is all covered with more jam, and the iced cone placed on top and decorated with more chopped fruits.

mazarine, à la, I. A French garnish for entrées, consisting of artichoke bottoms filled with a jardinière, croquettes of rice, quenelles, and mushrooms. II. A French garnish for fish of tartlets filled alternately with diced truffles, and shrimps in shrimp sauce.

mazurek pomarańczowy, a Polish orange dessert made from 2 cups ground almonds, ½ lb. (1 cup) sugar, and enough lemon juice to make the paste spread. It is baked on wafer paper in a greased tin in a very slow oven for 15–20 minutes, and is not allowed to get brown. When cool, it is spread with finely grated orange peel and the mashed pulp of 2 oranges and 1 lemon, which has been boiled until thick with 1 lb. (2 cups) sugar and ¼ pint (½ cup) water. Dates, raisins, and chocolate are also used for this dessert, and beaten egg whites are added when this is the case.

mazurki, a Russian sweetmeat (confection), made from 4 oz. each of chopped raisins, almonds, walnuts, figs, prunes, and candied fruit, sprinkled with about 2 oz. (½ cup) flour, and mixed well with 2 separated eggs, the whites added last. The mixture is spread on a buttered baking sheet and baked for 30 minutes. While still hot, it is cut into bars or other shapes and left to cool on a wire rack. See also KISHMISH.

mazzacuogno, see MAZZANCOLLE.

mazzancolle (Penaeus caramote), an Italian variety of very large prawn with the English name caramote. *Mazzancolle* are excellent to eat, not unlike scampi, and can be cooked and served in the same way. They are also called *gambero imperiale* and *mazzacuogno.*

meadow cress (Cardamine pratensis), also known as "lady's smock," a free-growing European wild plant with leaves that have a biting, peppery flavour. When young, they make a pleasant salad, and they are also used in soups, in much the same way as sorrel.

meadow-sweet (Spirea ulmaria), a pretty, feathery, sweet-smelling wild plant with a cream-coloured flower. The leaves can be chopped and a few used in soup, while the flowers are dried in country districts to make a tea said to be good for curing colds.

meal, I. The edible part of some grain (often excluding flour) or pulse, ground to a powder, either finely or coarsely. The word is particularly used in the case of maize, or corn as it is usually called. II. The customary time of eating; the food taken at this time. III. The quantity of milk given by a cow at a milking.

mearns quail, a near relative of the *massena quail,* but much lighter in colour. It is cooked in the same way as quail and partridge.

meat, the flesh of edible mammals and birds. The word is also used for the flesh of certain shellfish, as in lobster meat, crab meat, etc., and also for the flesh of some nuts, such as walnut. Until the 17th century in England, the word meat was used to denote foodstuff generally, in expressions such as funeral meats, sweetmeats, etc. See also CARNE; KØD; KÖTT; KREAS; LIHA; MANZO.

meat balls, small round balls, shaped from a mixture of approximately 1 lb. minced (ground) meats, 1 tablespoon herbs, and sometimes a small grated onion, bound with 2 tablespoons flour, or about 2 oz. soaked bread or an egg. They can be fried or poached in water or a sauce. Originally a German and also a Turkish invention, they are now almost universal, though called meatballs only in the U.S. There is no traditional British recipe. They are served with a variety of sauces, usually with a tomato base. See also BITKI; BITTER BALLEN; CHIFTELE; KEFTEDES; KØD (KØDBOLLER); KÖFTE; KÖNIGSBERGER KLOPS; KÖTT (KÖTTBULLAR); LIHA (LIHAPYÖRYKÄT).

meat loaf, a universal favourite in the U.S. It is made from 2 lb. minced (ground) beef, pork, or veal (or a mixture of all three) mixed with 1 finely chopped onion, 1 green pepper or celery, 1 cup breadcrumbs, a pinch of allspice, ¼ cup tomato juice, a pinch of sage, 2 teaspoons parsley, salt, and pepper to taste, and 2 eggs. All are well blended, then put into an oblong loaf tin and baked in a slow-to-moderate oven for 1–1½ hours. Other meat loaves include varied ingredients according to individual taste; some are made entirely from beef. Worcestershire sauce, mustard, etc., can be added to the mixture which should be spicy and tasty as desired. A meat loaf can be eaten hot or cold, and is sometimes served with bottled tomato ketchup, chilli sauce, chilled sour cream, or a brown sauce or tomato sauce.

meaty fuggan, a pastry case in which dough is made with water, flour, salt, lard or suet. It is rolled into an oval shape, and a long cut is made down the middle to about half the depth. The edges are pulled apart so that the cut can be filled with chopped, seasoned, fresh beef or pork, then pinched together again, and the pie baked in a hot oven. See also FUGGAN.

mecklenburger bratwürst, a German würst from Mecklenburg, made from equal quantities of lean and fat pork, seasoned with allspice, salt, and pepper. If homemade, a little brandy is often mixed with the ingredients. See also WÜRSTE.

médaillon, a French term which designates food, particularly beef or veal, cut into small rounds or ovals. Tournedos is a good example, and foie gras cut into that shape, served either hot or cold, is called by this name.

médaillon sucré, a sweet pastry (*pâté sucrée*) used for flans or cakes, iced and marbled with chocolate or icing of a contrasting colour. See also PÂTE, SUCRÉE.

medaljonger, Swedish fritters or médaillons.

medaljonger kalvbräss, calf's sweetbread fritters. To prepare, 1 lb. sweetbreads are soaked, partly-cooked, and cleaned in the usual way (see KALVKÖTT) and while they are still warm, they are mashed and mixed with 1 heaped tablespoon seasoned flour and a pinch of ground mace, and the mixture spread out on a wet plate. When cold, rounds are cut out, and these are dipped in egg and breadcrumbs, then fried in butter. See also KALVKÖTT (KALVBRÄSS).

räkmedaljonger, shrimp fritters. To prepare 1 lb. large split shrimps are mashed with 4 sardines and ½ cup cream cheese, then formed into small cakes which are dipped in seasoned flour, egg, and breadcrumbs, and fried in hot oil or fat. These fritters are garnished with chopped chervil or parsley.

medg or *meadhg,* Irish for whey, which used to be drunk a lot in Ireland, and is considered very health giving.

médicis, à la, I. A French garnish for tournedos and noisettes, consisting of artichoke bottoms filled with cooked green peas, carrots, and turnips, or with carrots *vichy* and green peas, *pommes noisette,* and sauce *choron.* II. A sauce béarnaise lightly flavoured with tomato purée and 2 tablespoons reduced red wine. III. A French consommé of beef, slightly thickened with tapioca, and garnished with a purée of carrots royale, shredded sorrel, and purée of peas.

medisterkaker, Norwegian fried meat cakes. First 1 lb. each belly of pork and chuck steak are minced several times and seasoned; then ½ pint (1 cup) cold boiled milk is whisked in gradually, and it is seasoned with ginger, salt, and pepper. With floured hands, the mixture is shaped into cakes about 2½ inches in diameter which are fried in butter. *Surkål* accompanies this dish. See also BIFF; KJØTT (KJØTTKAKER).

medisterpølse, Danish sausages, lightly cooked, and sometimes smoked. They have an excellent flavour.

medlar (Mespilus germanica), the fruit of the medlar or mespil tree, which is indigenous to Europe. It has a curious flavour all its own. A famous French sweetmeat (confection) called *cotignac* was made chiefly from medlars in Orléans. It was offered to the Sovereign on entering the town, and is said to have been the first gift offered to Joan of Arc by the townspeople after the siege. In England, medlars are picked when ripe and are then allowed to get soft before being eaten. They are also used in making jelly. In Italy they are eaten fresh and raw, and are called *nespola.* They were introduced into the U.S. by the Jesuits and now grow freely in many states.

medved, Russian for bear. Bear steaks are marinated and then braised with root vegetables and some of the marinade. The gravy is often thickened with sour cream. Bear's paws are a delicacy. See also BEAR.

mee kook, an Estonian honey cake, made from a mixture of 12 oz. (3 cups) flour, 1 teaspoon each of cinnamon and nutmeg, ½ teaspoon ground cardamom seeds, and 1 scant teaspoon each of cream of tartar and baking soda, to which 6 oz. (⅔ cup) melted butter, 2 tablespoons lard, 1 tablespoon white sugar, and 3 tablespoons brown sugar are added; then 3 beaten eggs, ¾ lb. (1½ cups) honey, and ¼ pint (½ cup) sour cream are mixed in. The mixture is poured into a flat tin, garnished with blanched, split almonds, and baked in a moderate oven for 30 minutes. This cake keeps for weeks in a tin.

meerrettich, German for horseradish; in southeast Germany it is known as *kren.* See also HORSERADISH.

meerrettichsauce, horseradish sauce, made from béchamel with fresh grated horseradish added. It is served warm.

megrim, a flat-fish of the flounder family, called lantern flounder in the U.S.

mehl, German for flour. See also GLATTES MEHL.

mehlnockerln, tiny German and Austrian flour dumplings made with 4 oz. (1 cup) flour mixed with 2 egg yolks and 2 stiffly beaten egg whites, 1 tablespoon melted butter, and salt. They are poached in soup or stews for 10 minutes, and rise to the surface when they are done.

mehlsuppe, also called sweet and sour soup, made from 4 onions and 4 leeks, sliced and sautéed in butter. Then 2 tablespoons flour are sprinkled over, and 1½ quarts (6 cups) stock or water are added. The soup is stirred well, and simmered for 30 minutes. At the last moment, a cup of fresh cream and a large lump of butter are added.

mehu, Finnish for juice.

mehukeitto, a Finnish fruit juice soup, made with the juice of lingonberries, cloudberries, raspberries, blackberries, or bilberries. It is thickened with 4 tablespoons potato flour to 2 quarts liquid, and sugar is added to taste. It is also served cold as a sweet, with small biscuits or rusks and whipped cream.

mehukiisseli, fruit juice thickened with potato flour (4 tablespoons to 2 quarts liquid), and served as a cold dessert, with cream. It looks like a transparent blancmange when set, and is the Finnish version of the Russian *kissel.*

mejillones, see MARISCOS.

mejorana, Spanish for sweet marjoram. Wild marjoram is called *orégano,* and both are used a lot in soups and stews.

mel, Norwegian for flour. *Hvetmel* is wheat flour; *rugmel,* rye flour. All are used extensively in the various cakes and breads eaten in Norway.

melachrino, a traditional Greek spiced cake eaten at Easter and on many festive occasions. It is made from 8 oz. (2 cups) flour, 6 oz. (¾ cup) butter, 12 oz. (1½ cups) sugar, ¼ pint (½ cup) milk, 1 teaspoon cinnamon, a pinch of cloves and mace, 1 tablespoon lemon juice, and 3 eggs.

melachrino xantho, literally "brunette and blonde," a layer cake of yellow sponge mixture, with a layer of meringue mixed with finely chopped nuts.

melanzane, Italian for eggplant, cultivated in Italy since the 15th century. Eggplants are usually served fried in oil, or stuffed and baked, after sprinkling with salt and leaving for an hour or two, to extract excess water. Garlic, fresh tomato sauce, and cheese are often added to the baked eggplants. See also CAPONATA.

melba, I. A French garnish for small cuts of meat, composed of small tomatoes filled with a salpicon of chicken, truffles, and mushrooms mixed with sauce velouté, sprinkled with breadcrumbs and browned. It is served with braised lettuce. II. A French method of preparing a sweet known as peach melba, created by Escoffier for Dame Nellie Melba, the opera singer. Peach melba consists of a purée of fresh raspberries poured over a ripe peach poached in vanilla syrup, set on vanilla ice cream. Unfortunately it is seldom served correctly, and usually a tinned peach on inferior ice cream, with raspberry jam on top, is substituted. See also ICE. III. A form of toast. Very thin slices of bread are dried in a low oven until golden brown.

melboller, Danish for chou pastry balls, used to garnish soups. A roux is made, consisting of 4 oz. (½ cup) butter, 4 oz. (1 cup) flour, and ½ pint (1 cup) water. After cooling, 4 beaten eggs are gradually blended in, and the whole is well beaten and seasoned to taste. The mixture is dropped from a teaspoon into boiling soup, and cooking is continued until the balls float to the top. In another version, the roux and egg are treated in the same manner, but a little sugar is added. Teaspoonfuls of this dough are formed into balls and dropped into water or soup stock which is just off the boil. When cooked, they are placed in cold water to prevent them from sticking together. See also BOLLER.

meli, Greek for honey, an essential ingredient in national sweet dishes and cakes, as almost all Greek pastries are soaked in honey. The best honey is said to come from Hymettus, where the bees swarm on the mountain slopes, sucking the nectar from wild thyme. In the region of Delphi the honey is said to be especially good also. See also BAKLAVA; LOUKOUMADES; PASTELLI; DIPLES.

melogarida, a type of wafer biscuit (cookie) made with honey and walnuts pressed together. It is very good to eat.

melomakarona, honey-dipped cakes. See FINIKIA.

melopita, a cheese honey pie, a dish which has survived from the days of ancient Greece. A flan tin is lined with pastry made from 12 oz. (3 cups) flour, 1 teaspoon baking powder, 6 oz. (⅔ cup) butter, and salt, with a little water added as necessary. The filling consists of 1½ lb. (3 cups) beaten unsalted *mizithra* cheese, 4 oz. (½ cup) sugar, 2 teaspoons cinnamon, and ½ lb. honey. Then 5 eggs are added singly, each one being well stirred in. The mixture is then sieved, before being put in the flan case. It is baked in a slow-to-moderate oven for about 1 hour, or until set. When cold, it is sprinkled with cinnamon.

melilot (Melilotus officinalis), a perennial leguminous plant which is common in the eastern counties of England. The leaves and flowers, when dried, are aromatic and are used as flavouring in marinades and stews. Melilot is used in France in the stuffing for tame rabbits, and in Switzerland, where it is known as *ziegerkraut* (literally "curd herb"), in the green cheese, *schabzieger,* and in Gruyère. The farinaceous root can be eaten like a carrot and is used in this way in Iceland.

melisa, Turkish for aubergine (eggplant); see also PATLICAN.

melisa dolması, eggplants scooped out from the top and stuffed with a mixture of cooked rice, minced lamb, tomatoes, onions, pignoli or walnuts, lemon juice, and seasoning. They are then simmered in hot water, olive oil, and lemon juice barely to cover. Although essentially a Turkish dish, this is also eaten in Armenia.

melitzanes, Greek for aubergine or eggplant, technically a fruit, but served as a vegetable throughout Greece and the Balkan countries. There are several varieties, ranging in colour from black to almost ivory white; in shape, from tiny balls to long sausage-shapes. Eggplant purée is almost always served as a *mezes* in Greece.

melitzanes glyko, a preserve of eggplants, rather like a jam, made with sugar, water, cloves, cinnamon, and lemon juice. A speciality of the island of Crete.

melitzanes salata, eggplants puréed, mixed with olive oil, parsley, and lemon juice, and served cold as a salad.

melitzanes tiyanites, eggplant fritters. The eggplant should first be sliced to a ¼-inch thickness, sprinkled with salt, and left for 2 hours between two plates. After being well wiped, the slices are lightly floured and fried until brown in deep boiling olive oil. They should be served very hot.

melitzanes yahni, eggplants fried in hot oil with onion, tomatoes, garlic, parsley, and bay leaf. This dish is similar to ratatouille.

melitzanes yemistes, eggplants stuffed with tomatoes, onion, garlic, parsley, and then baked. See also PAPOUTSAKIA.

melogarida, see MELI.

melomakarona, see FINIKIA.

melon (*Cucurbitaceae*), the fruit of a number of plants which have flexible stems and tendrils with which they attach themselves to any available support. Melons are true fruits, although often mistakenly classed as vegetables. They rank as a dessert fruit, but are sometimes served at the beginning of a meal, chilled, with sifted sugar and sometimes grated nutmeg or ginger. As melon served in this way is not easily digested, it should be followed by a small glass of vodka, brandy, or old Madeira. Small cubes of melon are sometimes used too in fruit cocktails, in salads, or with rice. Melons may also be made into jam, pickled in wine vinegar, or used in the same way as gherkins or chutney. Some popular varieties of dessert melon are described here.

cantaloupe melon (*Cucumis melo cantalupensis*), said to have been first grown in Cantalupo in the province of Ancona, Italy, from seed brought from Armenia. The rind is veined and warty, and the flesh, either dark orange or pale green, is juicy and sweet. Charentais melons, a small type of French cantaloupe, are sweet and aromatic and are becoming increasingly popular in Europe. The serpent melon (var. *flexuosus*) and the chito melon (var. *chito*) are used almost solely for making preserves, chutney, etc.

cantaloupe melon

musk or *nutmeg melon* (*Cucumis melo*, var. *reticulatus*), often called cantaloupe in the U.S. These are of varying shapes and sizes, with white, green, or red flesh, all with a "netted" or lace-patterned rind. When ripe, they are juicy and sweet. The cassaba melon, grown in California, and the winter melon, which travels well but is practically flavourless, also belong to the musk variety. Honeydew melons are another small variety with ribbed, dark green skins and very sweet white flesh, although some varieties have a yellow skin and pale green or greenish yellow flesh.

watermelon (*Citrullus vulgaris*), belonging to a different genus from the other melons and originally a native of Africa. Their red flesh is juicy and refreshing when ripe. Before these melons are ripe, they are often stuffed and cooked as a vegetable. The citron melon (*Citrullus vulgaris*, var. *citroides*) is a variety of watermelon; its rind is used in preserves. It is used extensively in Greece where it is called *karpouzi*.

melon, French for melon. Melon served chilled as an hors d'oeuvre is known as *melon au naturel*. See also MELON.

melon au porto, melon, usually of the cantaloupe variety, with the top cut off and the seeds removed. The centre is filled with port and the whole is chilled. For serving, it is not sliced, but the flesh is scooped out with a large spoon and the juice poured over it. Other wines, such as Madeira, Marsala, muscatel, and Frontignan are all used.

melon de malabar, French for the good quality Siamese pumpkin, which may be cooked as an ordinary pumpkin.

melongène, see EGGPLANT.

melts, the spleen of an animal. It is brown in colour, spongy in texture, and included, minced, in some dishes where mixed offal (variety meats) is used. It is not the same as milt, which is the roe of a male fish. See also BRUCK-FLEISCH; VENDÉE FRESSURE.

melwel, the old English name for hake.

membrillo, Spanish for quince. A traditional Spanish speciality is a quince jam, so thick that it is like a paste. It is good served on its own, or with a semi-hard mild cheese. Nowadays, quince paste is canned commercially for export. It should be pink in colour; if it is golden, it is made of apple or mixed with apple, and not true quince. It will be quite inferior in flavour. See also COTIGNAC.

ménagère, see EPERGNE.

mendiants, see QUATRE MENDIANTS.

menestra de legumbres frescas, a Spanish vegetable and egg dish. It is made with 4 oz. chopped ham simmered in oil, together with 2 chopped onions, 1 carrot, 1 celery stalk, 1 turnip, and 3 potatoes, all sliced, a quartered globe artichoke, ½ cup shelled peas, ½ cauliflower, and 1 cup cooked haricot beans. After 15 minutes, 3 seeded and skinned tomatoes are added and the mixture is cooked further; 1 heaped tablespoon flour is then mixed in, and lastly ½ pint (1 cup) stock and seasoning are added. The pan is covered and all cooked slowly for a further 10 minutes. The vegetables are placed on a dish and decorated with cooked asparagus and 4 poached eggs.

menta, Italian for mint, used extensively in Italian cooking with vegetables, particularly mushrooms, and with fish, soups, and some salads. *Nepitella* is a particular Florentine variety of mint.

menthe, French for mint. *Menthe de Notre-Dame* is French for the pennyroyal variety.

menthe, sauce, see MINT, SAUCE.

mentonnaise, à la, I. The French term for a particular method of cooking certain foods, notably rock-pool fish. The prominent ingredients are garlic, tomatoes, and black olives. The name comes from Menton on the French Riviera. This is very close to Italy and cooking has a strong Italian influence. II. A French garnish for meat consisting of chard stuffed with dux-elles, artichoke bottoms filled with tiny potato balls first sautéed in butter, and meat gravy. III. A French garnish for meat, consisting of sliced zucchini stuffed with rice and tomato purée, small cooked artichokes, and potatoes cut to the size of olives and cooked in butter. It is served with demi-glace.

menudos gitanos, literally "gypsy tripe," a well-known dish of tripe which is a speciality of Andaluz in Spain. It is cooked with 2 onions, 2 tomatoes, 2 sweet peppers, and 2 carrots, all chopped, 1 lb. soaked chick-peas, ½ lb. *chorizo*, ¼ lb. *morcilla*, 8 garlic cloves, 2 teaspoons paprika, herbs, and 2 calf's feet. The tripe and calf's feet are first soaked in wine vinegar, lemon juice, salt, and water to cover, then brought to the boil about 4 times in water which is thrown off each time it has boiled. It is then all simmered with herbs, peas, and root vegetables for 2–3 hours, when the *chorizo* and *morcilla* are added and cooked for 1 hour. The tomatoes, peppers, and onion are fried in oil and poured over the tripe and sausage stew. It is finally sprinkled with saffron and nutmeg. See also CALLOS.

mérce, Latvian for sauce.

augly mérce, fruit sauce, made from cranberries cooked with water and sugar, and thickened with potato flour. It is served with *buberts.*

mercedes, à la, I. A French garnish for meat, consisting of grilled tomatoes, grilled mushrooms, braised lettuce, and potato croquettes, with sauce madère. II. A French chicken or beef consommé with sherry added; it is garnished with cock's combs and cock's kidneys cut into star shapes. See also CONSOMMÉ.

mère de sole, see LIMANDELLE.

meringue, a small confection made from stiffly beaten egg whites and sugar. The creation is attributed to a Swiss pastrycook called Gasparini, who first made it in about 1720. There are 3 varieties.

meringues

meringue chantilly or *meringue suisse,* is made with 4 stiffly whipped egg whites, with ½ lb. (1 cup) castor sugar folded in. The batter is dropped onto a baking tin in spoonfuls or from a forcing-bag and cooked in a very slow oven until set but not browned. Sometimes a little lemon juice is added. When cool, two meringues are sandwiched together with *crème chantilly.* It is also used to top puddings. In bakeries, a little baking powder is added to the egg white and sugar mixture to ensure that the meringue will be crisp.

meringue cuite, as above, but with the egg whites and sugar whisked together over a gentle heat until very thick. This is used for petits fours, and to make "baskets" or other shapes, for it keeps stiff for some time. It can be flavoured with a liqueur.

meringue italienne, is made with 8 stiffly whisked egg whites well beaten with a syrup consisting of 1½ lb. (2 cups) sugar and ½ pint (1 cup) water, boiled to 290°F. It is beaten until very thick and used in pastries, or to cover ice cream in such desserts as baked alaska or *bombe glacée.*

merlan, I. The regional name in Provence, France, for hake. Dried hake is called *merluche.* II. French for whiting.

merlan en colère, whiting cooked with its tail in its mouth.

merlango, Spanish for whiting, which is more tasty than English whiting, and served either fried, or baked with tomato,

with lemon slices. They are never served with their tails in their mouths, as they are in England.

merlano, Italian for whiting, also called *nasello.* As whiting are fish which prefer cold water, they are very rare in the Mediterranean and are often classed with cod, hake, or haddock as *merluzzo.* Local fish, such as *branzino* or *spigola, orata, pesce san pietro* (john dory), *ombrina* (umbra), etc., are all plentiful, of good quality, and widely eaten. See also MERLUZZO.

merle, see BLACKBIRD.

merlin, the local name in Corfu for a Washington navel orange, which was introduced into the island by a British consul called Merlin at the turn of the century. See also ORANGE.

merluza, Spanish for hake, although haddock and fresh cod are also sometimes called by the same name. Small hake is often called *pescadilla.*

Hake is also stuffed and baked in Spain, poached in white wine, and served cold with mayonnaise, or fried with potatoes and served with a sauce made from a roux with stock, chopped parsley, onion, and garlic added, and all garnished with asparagus tips and sliced hard-boiled eggs. See also HAKE.

cazuela de merluza verde, a speciality of Santander. Hake is cut into thick steaks and casseroled with leeks and garlic which have been fried in oil. Flour is sprinkled over, 1 pint (2 cups) water is added, and 1 cup shelled peas and parsley.

merluzzo, Italian for cod, haddock, or whiting. None of these fish is eaten much in Italy, as they are scarce and expensive; however, when they are cooked, they are either fried and served with lemon, or cooked in a casserole with mushrooms, tomatoes, onion, parsley, and white wine. Pignoli or almonds are sometimes added to the casserole. When cod is served, it is usually salted cod, and is known as *baccala.* See also MERLANO.

mérou, a sea fish about 3 feet long, allied to the *Serranidae* family and sometimes called rock cod in English. It is found off the Mediterranean coast of France. It is not unlike a tunny (tuna), with firm white flesh which can be cut into steaks and grilled or fried, or used in soups and stews. It is very good to eat.

merrythought, the forked bone between the neck and breast of chicken and turkey, known generally as the wishbone. It is covered with succulent meat which is considered a delicacy. Other birds have a similar bone but as it is not called a wishbone it has no tradition of magical properties.

merveille, a French pastry, made from 1 lb. (4 cups) flour, ½ lb. (1 cup) butter, 1½ tablespoons sugar, 4 eggs, and a pinch of salt. It is rolled out very thinly, cut into various shapes, and deep-fried in boiling oil. When drained, the pastries are sprinkled with vanilla sugar and eaten hot.

mesentery, a fold of the peritoneum which attaches part of the intestinal canal to the back wall of the abdomen in mammals. Calf's mesentery is eaten in France. See also FRAISE DE VEAU.

mesost, the Swedish term for any cheese that is made from cow's milk whey. See also MYSOST.

messine, petite marmite consommé, garnished with small, poached and skinned chipolata sausages and tiny cabbage rolls. See also CONSOMMÉ.

methi, Greek for intoxication. The ancient Greeks had many herbal recipes for preventing this, parsley being particularly used as it absorbed the fumes of wine. Convivial friends used to wear garlands of parsley on their heads during a drinking bout. Cabbage was eaten in various forms for the same reason, and today yogourt is thought to be good.

méthode, a local Bayonne name for *confit de porc,* a speciality of that region of France. See also GARBURE, À LA BAYONNE.

mets, a French word for any food that has been prepared for eating.

metternich, a French consommé made from pheasant, and garnished with artichoke royale and julienne of pheasant. See also CONSOMMÉ.

metton, a French cow's milk cheese from the Franche-Comté. It is at its best from October to June.

mettwürst, a German smoked würst made from pork and spices, its name meaning ''spreading'' sausage. It is served just as it is bought, and is spread on rye bread. See also STREICHWÜRST; WÜRST.

meunier, see MILLER'S THUMB.

meunière, à la, I. A French method of cooking fish. It is lightly floured, seasoned, and fried in hot foaming butter. When cooked, the fish is removed and the pan cleaned, and fresh butter is heated until golden brown, when lemon juice and herbs such as parsley are quickly stirred in. The liquid is then poured over the fish, and it is served at once. II. A French method of serving chicken. See also POULET, SAUTÉ À LA MEUNIÈRE.

meurette, see MATELOTE.

mexicaine, à la, I. A French garnish for meat consisting of grilled mushrooms, grilled sweet peppers, tomatoes, and eggplants cut lengthways, with highly seasoned meat gravy and tomato juice. II. A mayonnaise flavoured with anchovy essence (extract) and garnished with chopped red and green peppers.

Mexican saffron (*Carthamus tinctoria*), a plant of the *Compositae* family with large orange flower-heads; from the stigmas an inferior substitute for saffron is made, and this gives the plant its other name of safflower. It is widely distributed through southern Europe. The plant has increased in importance since the recent discovery that from its seeds can be extracted an oil that is richer in polyunsaturated fats than any other. This is of the first importance to all who require a diet which will promote the reduction of blood lipides.

mezes, Greek for hors d'oeuvre. The word is also used in Cyprus and Turkey. Foods served for mezes have also to be suitable accompaniments to wines and spirits, since no Greek would think of drinking without eating. The eating of mezes is a social occasion which may last an hour or two before the main meal is served, so the foods presented are many and varied, some seasonal, many the original creations of the cook concerned. However, olives, nuts and féta cheese, fish and shellfish, are among the standard appetizers. Among the tavernas that abound on the sea shore, every conceivable kind of small fish is sold, being served with *karveli. Dolmades, lakerda, taramosalata,* and *bourekia* are also served for mezes. *Mezedakia* or *mezethakia* is a popular Greek diminutive of mezes.

mezzaluna, a crescent-shaped, two-handled vegetable cutter used in Italy.

miala, Greek for brains. See also BRAINS.

miala salata, a salad of lamb's brains. The brains are first whitened by being soaked in cold water for at least 1 hour. They are then simmered until tender in fresh water, with seasoning, parsley, lemon juice, and chopped onion added. When cool, the membrane and skin are removed and the brains left in cold water for 30 minutes. They are then dried, cut into pieces and dressed with olive oil, lemon juice, and chopped parsley. In Greece this salad is sometimes served for mezes.

micishja, la, a Corsican method of preparing young goat. The strips of goat fillet are slightly salted and dried. A favourite method of cooking them is to thread the strips on skewers of green and aromatic wood, and to grill them over a wood fire. A pan is put beneath the meat, with slices of garlic-rubbed

bread in it; the juicy drippings fall on the bread, which is eaten with the meat. See also GOAT.

middelbare, see EDAM.

midia or *mithia,* Greek for mussels. See also MUSSELS.

midia pilafi, cooked mussels served with boiled rice, onions sautéed in olive oil, and diluted tomato purée. The cooking method is the same as that for *pilafi.*

midia tighanita, cleaned raw mussels rolled in flour, then sautéed in olive oil and served with *skorthalia* sauce.

midia yemista, steamed mussels left in the shell and stuffed with rice cooked with a pinch of allspice, pignoli, currants, onions, pepper, chopped parsley, and a little salt.

midye, Turkish for mussels, often served in *pilâv.* See also MUSSELS.

midye dolması, stuffed mussels. First 4 dozen scrubbed mussels are cooked with ½ pint olive oil and 2 finely sliced onions. The mussels are removed from the pan when open, and bearded. Then 1 lb. rice, ½ cup pistachio nuts, 1 tablespoon currants, a pinch of cinnamon, salt, and pepper, and ½ pint (1 cup) water are put in the pan, with the oil, and simmered until the water is absorbed. The mussels in their shells are stuffed with this mixture, and the shells are closed. They are then arranged in a stew pan, barely covered with water, and boiled with the lid on the pan until almost all the liquid is absorbed. They are served hot or cold, and are very delicious.

mie-de-pain, French for fresh breadcrumbs rubbed through a coarse sieve. They are used with beaten egg for coating fish or meat.

miel, French for honey. The most distinctive French honey comes from the Narbonne district, from bees which take the nectar from rosemary flowers. Another excellent variety of honey, *Gâtinais,* comes from the Orléanais. Several spiced breads in France, such as *pain d'épice,* a speciality of Dijon, are made with honey and rye flour.

mien or *mi,* Chinese for noodles, which originated in China and are made from a mixture of wheat and dried ground beans. They are produced in many different lengths and types. There is a transparent variety, called *fun-szu* (powdered silk) in Chinese, which resembles strips of cellophane and is very gelatinous. It is called cellophane noodle in the U.S. There is also a very thin ochre-coloured noodle called ieh fooh mien, which is rather like vermicelli.

Mien are particularly good for making crispy noodles. They are first boiled in water, without salt, for only 3 minutes, then drained and washed in cold water. When well drained, small helpings are fried in a very little hot oil until they are crisp and golden. They must never be submerged in oil, for this only makes them greasy and sodden. See also NOODLES.

miežu putra, a traditional stew from Latvia, made from pearl barley, 1 large onion, and ½ lb. diced smoked meats such as bacon or sausage. To prepare, ½ lb. (1 cup) barley is first lightly toasted, before being put in a covered pot with 3 pints (6 cups) water and the other ingredients. When ready to eat, it is a thick porridge-like dish with very little liquid left. For a poor family this makes a nourishing and substantial meal. At Christmas time it is served with a pig's head and additional slices of sausage.

miga, literally ''crumb,'' an enormous Andalusian pancake, about 18 inches across, made only with flour, water, and olive oil. It forms the usual Sunday luncheon in this part of Spain, and is eaten with small white grapes.

migas, I. A medieval Spanish dish for which small squares of bread are soaked, usually in milk, and then fried in oil. In some parts of Spain, migas served in just this way is a common breakfast dish; however, it can also be accompanied by small pieces of meat fried in oil and flavoured with garlic, when it may be eaten at any meal. In Aragon the migas are moistened with water, sprinkled with salt, and left in a cloth overnight. They are then fried in oil with garlic and served with tomato sauce or ham. Curiously, they are also sometimes served as a sweet, with grapes or chocolate. Their origin is thought to be Celtic. II. An Andalusian soup made with 6 garlic cloves and 2 cups breadcrumbs fried in ¼ pint (½ cup) olive oil; then 3 pints (6 cups) boiling water are added. On very special occasions an egg is broken whole into it and lightly poached, or a very thin sliver of cheese is served to be eaten with the soup. It is the staple soup for a large proportion of the population.

migliaccini, small versions of *migliaccio.*

migliaccio, an Italian bread-like cake, made from chestnut flour and sprinkled thickly with pignoli. It is often served with grilled small birds.

migliassis, a Corsican cake usually made from chestnut flour, oil and water, baked in the oven on chestnut leaves. It may be made as one large cake or small individual ones.

mignon, à la, a French garnish for fowl and sweetbreads, consisting of artichoke bottoms filled with buttered green peas and round quenelles with truffles, with the gravy reduced with white wine, and melted butter stirred in.

mignon, le, a French cow's milk cheese of the *maroilles* type.

mignonette, French for coarsely ground white pepper or a mixture of white and black pepper. Formerly it was used to denote a muslin bag filled with spices, which was dipped into a stew to impart a piquant flavour. See also NOUET.

mignot, I. A soft French cow's milk cheese, which has been made in the department of Calvados for more than 100 years. It resembles *livarot. Mignot blanc* is eaten, fresh, from April to September; *mignot passé* is ripened, and is available throughout the year. II. A dry biscuit popularised in Paris in the 17th century by a pastry cook called Mignot.

Mihaliç, a Turkish soft cheese called after a town of the same name. It is made from ewe's milk.

mijo, Spanish for millet, which is used a great deal in Spain as it grows well on poor land.

mijoter, a French culinary term meaning to cook gently over a low heat, or to simmer.

mikado, à la, I. A French garnish for tournedos and noisettes, of fried tomato halves, Chinese artichoke sautéed in butter, and sauce *provençale.* II. Small mounds of curried rice, or tartlets filled with bean shoots with cream. They are served as canapés, or with escalopes (scallops) of veal, or with chicken.

milanais, a French cake made like *génoise* and flavoured with anisette liqueur. When cold, it is spread with apricot jam and iced with fondant icing flavoured with anis (an aniseed drink liqueur).

milanaise, a la, I. A French garnish for escalopes (scallops), and poultry, consisting of julienne of tongue, mushrooms, and truffles, and sometimes ham, added to spaghetti or macaroni with a little fresh tomato sauce, grated cheese, and a pat of butter. II. A sauce *allemande* mixed with tomato purée, diced tomatoes, and pignoli added. III. A demi-glace mixed with tomato purée and meat glaze, flavoured with garlic and garnished with a julienne of sautéed mushrooms. IV. A method of preparing risotto. See RISOTTO. V. Foods cooked *à la milanaise* are usually dipped in egg and breadcrumbs mixed with grated Parmesan cheese before being fried in clarified butter.

milch, German for milk.

milchbraten, a German pot roast consisting of 2 lb. rump beef simmered with 1 lb. smoked bacon and milk to cover. The meat is larded with some bacon strips, and it is cooked without the lid, until the meat is tender and the sauce reduced.

milchrahmstrudel, see STRUDEL.

milchig, a term used in Jewish cookery for a dish in which some dairy product—milk, cream, butter, or cheese—is one of the ingredients. According to orthodox Jewish laws, meat cannot be combined with these ingredients. In common usage, it denotes that the food is meatless to conform with Jewish dietary laws.

milfoil, see YARROW.

miliasse, see MILLAS.

milieu de tendron, a French cut of beef comprising part of the brisket. See diagram page xxiii.

milk, a cloudy white liquid secreted by the mammary glands of mammals. It has great nutritive value, as it contains proteins and sugars, as well as calcium and other minerals. In Europe and the U.S., cow's milk is the most commonly employed for everyday purposes. It is used in many branches of cooking and, with or without the cream, in the manufacture of many cheeses. Butter is made from cream. The richest cow's milk is given by Jersey cows, and the milk and cream are a deeper yellow than that of other cows. The bulk of milk sold is pasteurised, that is, heat-treated to improve its keeping properties and to prevent the spread of any infection from the cow. From a culinary point of view, pasteurisation is in many ways to be regretted, as it destroys the lactic acid bacteria which are naturally present in milk once it has left the cow, and which promote normal souring. In fact pasteurised milk will go bad rather than turn sour, and this makes it almost impossible for it to provide good curds for cheese making. Goat's milk also has a high food value; it is strong, but good to drink and to cook with, and makes excellent and strong-tasting cheeses, such as *chevret.* Ewe's milk is used extensively throughout Europe, and is the basis for the world-famous roquefort cheese and *pecorino.*

Nowadays milk is also prepared in tins, sometimes with sugar added; the former is called evaporated milk, and the latter condensed milk. Dried milk, partly or entirely skimmed, is extremely useful, as it keeps indefinitely in an airtight tin, and can be used for puddings or sauces. See also BUTTERMILK; LECHE; MAITO; MILCH; MLEKO; PASTEURISATION; WHEY.

milk puddings, see PUDDINGS.

milk sauce, an English sauce for fish, veal, or poultry. First 2 tablespoons butter are melted over a low heat; 2 level tablespoons flour are stirred in, and after a few minutes' cooking, 1 pint (2 cups) of mixed milk and fish stock are also stirred in gradually, until the mixture boils. The heat is then reduced and seasoning added. After a few minutes' simmering, chopped parsley is mixed in. The saucepan is then removed from the heat and 1 tablespoon lemon juice and 1 beaten egg yolk are gradually added, and sometimes also a little thick cream. If the sauce is intended to accompany boiled fowl or veal, the liquor in which the meat was cooked is used as stock.

milkweed (*Asclepias incarnata,* var. *pulchra*), the name applied in the U.S. to a group of plants whose stems contain a sweetish, milky juice, and which are used in salads.

millas or *miliasse,* a kind of polenta or porridge made in the Languedoc region of France from corn meal. Perhaps it was originally made with millet, which used to be widely grown in that region. It is made in the same way as porridge and eaten in various ways. It can be left to get cold, then cut into chunks, fried, and eaten with rich stews such as *daube* or *civet;* or with sugar, or with cooked fruits such as cherries, apples, peaches, etc. In the Lot-et-Garonne region it is known as *cruchade* or *rimote.* See also GALETTE, DE MAIS.

millefanti, traditional Italian bread soup, made from 3 tablespoons grated Parmesan cheese, 2 eggs, and a pinch each of salt, pepper, and nutmeg, mixed with 3 tablespoons fresh white breadcrumbs, and then poured into 2 pints (4 cups) boiling beef broth. The mixture is stirred thoroughly with an egg whisk and allowed to boil very slowly for about 10 minutes. It is whisked up again before serving.

mille-feuille, a French pastry, composed of layers of flaky (puff) pastry filled with whipped cream and raspberry or strawberry jam. The top is sometimes covered with icing or simply scattered with icing (confectioner's) sugar. It is baked in a large tin and cut into rectangular pieces, or alternatively it can be made into a single large round cake. The name means literally "thousand leaves."

miller's thumb (Cottus gobio), the local name in the north of England for a freshwater fish which is also called bullhead. It is usually eaten fried in England, but used in a *matelote* in France, where it is known as *meunier.*

millet (Panicum miliaceum), one of many species of grain-bearing grass. It has been grown since prehistoric times and is still cultivated for food, particularly in Egypt, India, and parts of Russia and Europe. It has been introduced into the U.S. under its Russian name, *proso.* The best edible variety is common millet. It is yellow in colour and sometimes called "golden millet." It makes a coarse bread and a porridge, and it is used in the preparation of the North African dish *couscous.*

millsén, an early Irish sweet curd cheese, which was made from fresh milk with rennet added to it. It is no longer produced.

milosti, a Bohemian speciality which was probably the forerunner of the doughnut. It is a thin, light fried pastry made from 3 oz. each of creamed butter and sugar, to which 1 egg and 2 egg yolks are added. Then 1 tablespoon each of milk, grape juice, and grated lemon peel are mixed in. Finally, ½ lb. (2 cups) flour is gradually worked in until a soft dough is obtained. It is rolled out very thin and cut into small squares, which are fried in deep hot fat or oil until golden brown. When drained, they are sprinkled with sugar.

milt, the soft roe, that is, the male gonad in fish. It makes a delicious savoury, poached, strained, and served with butter, pepper, and lemon. See also ROE.

mimosa salad, a salad made from almost any variety of vegetables, raw or cooked. When arranged in the salad bowl, they are sprinkled with coarsely chopped, hard-boiled egg yolks which resemble mimosa flowers and give the salad its name.

mincemeat, meat preserved by an early method which did not entail either smoking or salting. It was chopped, mixed with dried chopped fruits such as raisins, currants, etc., spices, and alcoholic spirit, then sealed with wax to keep it airtight. After about 1650, the practice of adding the juice or grated peel of citrus fruits developed.

Nowadays, the only ingredient which remains to remind us of the meat is grated beef suet. Traditionally, mincemeat is eaten in pies at Christmas time, and should contain 1 lb. each of raisins and currants, 4 oz. chopped candied peel, 1 lb. peeled, cored, chopped apples, zest of lemon and orange, ½ lb. (1 cup) brown sugar, nutmeg, clove, cinnamon to taste, 4 oz. chopped beef suet, and brandy or rum to taste. It should be made a good month before it is wanted, and kept in an airtight jar. In the U.S., cooked beef or venison is often included in mincemeat, as in the early days.

mince pies, small individual flaky (puff) pastry pies filled with mincemeat. They have pastry top and bottom. Short crust pastry is also used if it is preferred. The pies should be served hot, with a little extra brandy or rum, or brandy butter or rum butter. See also COVENTRY GODCAKES.

minciunele, a Rumanian biscuit (cookie), made from 3 egg yolks, 8½ oz. (2 cups plus 2 tablespoons) flour, 4 tablespoons thick cream, and 2 tablespoons rum or whiskey. The dough is rolled thinly, then cut into strips which are formed into twists and fried in hot fat or oil. The name, literally translated, means "little lies."

minestra, Italian for a thick soup usually made from root vegetables and mushrooms or lentils cooked with water or stock, although in Venice a little chopped salt pork, calf's foot, liver, or ham is sometimes added. *Minestra fredde* is any minestra served cold, a popular method in summertime. See also ZUPPA.

minestra al pomidoro, a traditional Italian tomato soup made with 2 chopped onions and 1 clove garlic fried in oil to which 2 lb. sliced peeled tomatoes, a chopped sprig each of sweet basil and marjoram, salt, and pepper are added. Then 4 pints (8 cups) water are included, and the soup is simmered for 20–30 minutes. It is strained, and then sometimes garnished with cooked rice. Grated parmesan cheese is served separately.

minestra torinese, a regional soup from Turin, made from diced celery root, leeks, chopped green cabbage, ham, and chopped tomatoes, all fried in oil. White stock is added to double the quantity of vegetables, and they are cooked for 1 hour. The soup is flavoured with garlic and saffron. It is garnished with cooked rice, and grated Parmesan cheese is served separately.

minestra veneziana, a regional soup from Venice, made by boiling chopped salt pork, onions, chopped cabbage, blanched calf's foot, calf's ears, liver, and tomatoes in water, and seasoning with salt, pepper, bay leaves, marjoram, and allspice. It is strained, and garnished with cooked rice.

minestra, a word used in Malta to describe a vegetable soup usually made from a mixture of pumpkin, kohlrabi, and turnips.

minestrone, an Italian national soup. Sliced carrots, turnips, leeks, shredded cabbage, diced salt pork, and tomatoes are fried in oil. Crushed garlic, cooked dried beans, green peas, and green beans are added, with stock or water to double the quantity of vegetables, and seasoning. The mixture is then boiled for 1–2 hours. Shortly before the vegetables are cooked, small pasta is added. Grated Parmesan cheese is served separately with the soup. See also ZUPPA.

minho, see PAIO.

minnow (Phoxinus phoxinus), a small freshwater fish found in almost all streams. It is not eaten in the British Isles, but in France it is sometimes used instead of gudgeon in *fritures,* although it is not nearly as good to eat.

mint, a perennial plant with more than a dozen varieties. Mint is one of the most cooling and refreshing herbs, and in the Middle East is made into a mint "tea." The ancient Greeks considered it a cooler of the blood and a refreshment for the brain. The most commonly used culinary mints are: spearmint *(Mentha spicata),* used for flavouring and also for making sauces and jellies. Apple mint, or roundleaved mint *(M. rotundifolia),* which has a white variegated leaf and is thought by epicures to have a more subtle flavour than spearmint; and horsemint *(M. longifolia).* Lesser-known varieties, but admired by specialists, include: black peppermint *(M. piperita vulgaris),* a very pungent variety with purple-bronze leaves and stem; *M. piperita crispa,* a decorative, crisp-leaved peppermint with crimson-purple stems and mauve flowers; bergamot, lemon mint, or eau-de-Cologne mint *(M. citrata);* pineapple mint *(M. citrata);* red mint *(M. rubra),* a handsome mint, but with a coarse flavour; and pennyroyal *(M. pulegium),* an herb that is rarely used nowadays, except for medicinal purposes. See also MENTA; PEPPERMINT.

mint jelly, more popular than mint sauce in the U.S. and Canada, is prepared in several ways. One is to stir 1 tablespoon granulated gelatine into hot water until entirely dissolved. Then 1 cup vinegar, sugar to taste, and finely chopped mint are added, and if desired, a few drops of green vegetable colouring. The mixture is cooled in small pots, and is stirred occasionally during the jellying process to prevent the mint from sinking. Allow to cool slightly before bottling. The jelly is served in a small glass dish. A little cooked apple was used with the mint in early English recipes. It is a useful standby in the winter, when fresh mint is not available.

Another method uses 6 tart, rather underripe, quartered apples not peeled or cored. They are covered with water and gently cooked to mush, then put into a jellybag and left to drip overnight. The juice is then boiled up, and warmed sugar added, in the proportions of 1 lb. (2 cups) sugar to 1 pint (2 cups) juice. When the sugar has melted the heat is increased, but before reaching boiling point, chopped mint and vinegar or lemon juice are added. Fast boiling is continued until the mixture jellies.

mint sauce, most usually eaten with lamb or mutton. Horsemint is supposed to have been the mint of Scripture, as it is extensively cultivated in the East; it was one of the bitter herbs with which the Paschal lamb was eaten, and no doubt our present-day practice of eating mint sauce with lamb derives ultimately from this custom. To make it, young, freshly picked mint leaves are washed, dried in a cloth, and very finely chopped. They are then mixed with wine vinegar and sugar, in the proportions of 2 tablespoons chopped mint to 2 tablespoons sugar and ¼ pint vinegar. The sauce is allowed to stand for a few hours before being served. An alternative version, for use with hot roast lamb, consists of mint, very finely chopped, heaped on thin slices of lemon and sprinkled with sugar and more lemon juice. This is an early English form and is extremely good with lamb chops. A good method for use through the winter is to wash, dry, and finely chop mint leaves which are put into a large bottle and then filled up with good white wine vinegar and tightly corked. The bottles are sealed to retain the aroma. Sugar is added, dissolved in a little hot water before serving. Fresh vinegar and sugar are added to replenish the supply as it is used.

Mint is also used in salads, for cooking with green peas, and with certain fruits. It also makes an excellent tea.

miolos, Portuguese for brains. See also BRAINS.

miolos com ovos, brains with eggs. The brains are blanched in salted water, and then fried in oil. Then 2 beaten eggs are added to ½ lb. cooked brains and the whole is stirred together so that the result is like scrambled eggs. It is usually served with fried potatoes and lemon wedges.

miques de mais, a speciality of the Périgord region of France. It consists of a stiff dough made from 1 cup each corn meal and wheat flour, 3 oz. pork lard, salt, and enough tepid water to make a firm paste. The mixture is shaped with floured hands into small balls and poached, like dumplings, in boiling salted water for nearly 30 minutes. Miques are eaten in place of bread in the Périgord, and usually accompany such dishes as *civet de lièvre* or *salé aux choux.* They can also be fried in butter after poaching, and sprinkled with sugar before being served as a sweet course.

mirabeau, à la, I. A French garnish for grilled meat, consisting of anchovy fillets arranged crosswise, stoned olives, and chopped tarragon, with *beurre d'anchois* served separately. II. A sauce *allemande* flavoured with garlic and beaten with *beurre maître d'hôtel.*

mirabelles, see MYROBALAN.

mirepoix, very small cubes of uncooked carrot, onion, and ham or belly of pork, lightly sautéed in butter, with the addition of bay leaves and thyme. The mirepoix is used as a garnish and can be added to certain sauces, particularly *espa-*gnole,* and to braised meat or poultry to enhance the flavour. When the ham or pork is omitted, the vegetable mirepoix (*mirepoix au maigre*) is sometimes added to crayfish and to some white sauces. See also BORDELAISE.

mirette, I. A French beef consommé, garnished with chicken quenelles and a julienne of lettuce and chervil. II. A French method of serving potatoes, see POMME DE TERRE (POMMES MIRETTE).

mirlitons de Rouen, small tarts, which are a speciality of Rouen in France. To prepare them, ½ lb. flaky (puff) pastry is used to form linings for tartlet tins, and these are filled with a mixture of 4 egg yolks, 3 tablespoons sugar, ½ teaspoon vanilla, 4 oz. (½ cup) butter, which has been heated until it is gently browned, and a small teaspoon of orange flower water. The tarts are sprinkled with castor sugar and baked in a hot oven.

miroir, au, a French culinary term which properly applies to eggs which are baked in the oven or finished under a grill so that the white forms a shiny surface over the yolk. It is also loosely applied to other dishes which have a polished, mirror-like finish.

miroton, a kind of French stew of cooked meat, usually beef, flavoured with onions. The cooked meat is arranged in thin over-lapping slices on a thick foundation of sauce *miroton* or sauce *lyonnaise,* and sliced, lightly fried onions. More sauce is poured over and topped with a little melted butter or dripping. Then the dish is gently heated in the oven. See also BEEF.

miroton de boeuf parmentier, as above, with a thick border of mashed potato.

sauce miroton, a classical French sauce made from 2 finely chopped onions lightly browned in 2 tablespoons butter. Then 1 tablespoon flour is added, and the mixture is moistened with 1 cup good stock or bouillon. It is simmered gently for 20 minutes, when pepper, nutmeg, salt to taste, 1 teaspoon mustard, and a little wine vinegar are added. After further simmering for about 20 minutes, the sauce is ready for use; it is not strained. It is garnished with fried onion rings, and it is used as a basis for *miroton de boeuf.*

mirto, Italian for myrtle, often used with *tàccula* in Sardinia, and also to flavour roast suckling pig. A cooking oil, made illicitly, is also extracted from the myrtle berry in Sardinia, and used for frying fish.

mischlingkäse, a hard cheese made in the western highlands of Austria. The name means "blended" cheese. It is loaf-like in shape, and varies in size from 16 to 40 lb. The paste is a greenish-yellow, semi-hard, and with no "eyes." It has rather a pungent smell and a sharp flavour.

mish me bamje, a traditional Albanian dish, consisting of lamb or mutton stewed with onions, tomatoes, and okra. It is served with boiled rice.

Missouri currant, see BUFFALO CURRANT; GOLDEN CURRANT.

mitan, an old French culinary term meaning "middle." It is now used for the middle or centre cut of salmon.

mithia, see MIDIA.

mititei, Rumanian for pork sausages, usually served grilled.

mitili, a local name for mussels in Tuscany, where they are also called *muscoli.* Each region has its own local name for them. See also COZZE.

mitonner, a French culinary term meaning to simmer bread for a long time in soup or stock.

mixed grill, an English dish consisting of a combination of broiled meats: lamb chop, kidneys, bacon, sausage, a small piece of steak, and sometimes a slice of liver are included. All should be grilled according to the length of time each meat requires, and the dish can be very good. However, the ingredients are more often fried and comprise only a chop, bacon, and sausage, with perhaps a fried tomato or mushroom.

mixtamal, see TORTILLA.

mizerja, Polish for large cucumber used for salad; it is often served *ze śmietana,* that is with a sour cream dressing. See also OGÓRKI.

mizithra or *myzithra,* a mild, soft, moist Greek cheese, excellent as a table cheese or for cooking with baked pasta dishes. It is not unlike a cottage cheese, and is used in many Greek dishes. It is made from the whey drained from *féta,* mixed with ewe's milk. Shepherds in the neighbourhood of Athens make this cheese under primitive conditions and sell it for export to the Greek islands.

mleczko, Polish for sweetbreads. See also SWEETBREADS.

mleczko cielęce smażone, calf's sweetbreads par-boiled and skinned, rolled in flour, dipped in egg and breadcrumbs, then fried. It is garnished with lemon, green peas, spinach, or cauliflower.

mleczko cielęce w potrawie, calf's sweetbreads prepared as above, then finished in a white sauce with lemon, and garnished with croquettes of minced veal and grilled mushrooms.

mleko, Polish for milk.

mleko kwaśne, soured or clabbered milk, often served as a drink in Poland, like buttermilk. A large dish of boiled potatoes served with *mleko kwaśne* constitutes a typical peasant meal, although it is enjoyed by all classes.

mlyàko, Bulgarian for milk. See PODKVÀSA.

mocha, a variety of coffee bean originally grown in Mocha, Arabia. In culinary usage, the word is applied to any dish or preparation that is flavoured with coffee. See also COFFEE.

mocha cake, a French cake made from *génoise* mixture flavoured with coffee, and layered with coffee-flavoured icing or *crème au beurre. Mochatines* is the name given to small versions of this cake.

mock goose, an English north country dish made from a well-washed and cleaned bullock or ox heart. It is simmered in water to cover, with onion, bay leaf, salt, pepper, and a meat cube for 4–5 hours or until tender. It is drained, and the fat skimmed from the stock. It is then stuffed with a mixture of breadcrumbs, the chopped boiled onion from the stock, sage, and seasoning, all bound with an egg. The heart is then dusted with flour, rashers of bacon are put across the top, and it is roasted in a little stock in a quick oven for 30 minutes. The mock goose is garnished with a ring of sausages, and is served with roast potatoes and apple sauce. In texture and flavour it bears a resemblance to goose. See also HEART.

mock turtle, a very substantial English soup, so called because it has a very gelatinous quality, not unlike turtle. It is made from ½ calf's head, 1 thick slice of ham or bacon, 1 lb. shin of beef, and a knuckle of veal with a little meat on it. The meats are chopped and fried in fat until they are lightly browned; root vegetables cut into quarters, salt, pepper, and a bouquet garni are added, covered with water and slowly boiled, skimmed, and left covered with a lid for 3–4 hours. The soup is then strained, left to jelly, and defatted. It is boiled up with stiffly whipped egg whites and the crushed shells, to clarify, then strained again. Marsala, Madeira, or sherry is added to taste, and it is seasoned again if necessary, and garnished with cubes of the gelatinous meat.

mode, à la, I. A French term which means "in the style of." See BOEUF, À LA MODE. II. In the U.S. it also means with ice cream, such as pie à la mode, which is fruit pie served with ice cream.

moderne, à la, a French garnish, consisting of individual dariole moulds of layered carrot, turnip, green beans, and peas, sealed with forcemeat and cooked in a *bain-marie.* They are turned out before being served with small cuts of meat.

modolla di pane or *mollica di pane,* see PANE.

moelle, French for bone marrow, used in sauces such as *bordelaise,* and for garnishes (*marquise*), and also for a sweet pudding. See also MARROW; MOELLE, SAUCE.

pouding à la moelle, ½ lb. marrow is melted in a double sauce pan, and 2 tablespoons beef suet are added. When cool, this is beaten in a basin with 1½ cups sugar, ⅔ cup crustless bread soaked in milk, 3 whole eggs and 8 yolks, 2 cups chopped crystallised fruit and 1 tablespoon each stoned raisins and sultanas. It is poured into a buttered and lightly floured mould and cooked in a *bain-marie* in a slow-to-moderate oven for about an hour, or until set. It is served with a rum-flavoured *zabaglione.*

moelle, sauce, a classical French sauce consisting of sauce *bordelaise* based on white wine instead of red, with the addition of some pieces of poached beef marrow-bone fat.

mohnstrudel, see STRUDEL.

möhre, German for carrot. See also KAROTTE. A Rhineland method of preparing them is as follows. They are scraped and sliced lengthwise, then cooked in boiling water with a little sugar until almost tender. They are then mixed with fried onions, the cooking liquid, and an identical quantity of peeled, cored, and sliced apples. All are simmered until tender, when the mixture is seasoned and sprinkled with lemon juice.

moist sugar, see SUGAR.

molasses, a thick brownish liquid, the residue from the refining of cane sugar. It does not crystallise, and is used in many puddings and cakes, particularly in the southern states of the U.S. It is known in the British Isles as "black treacle."

molbo, a Danish cheese of the samsoe variety. A large, red, and almost round cheese, it is rich and aromatic. The paste is a little darker than the standard samsoe, and there are fewer holes in it. It is very good eaten with radishes. See also OST.

mole, the name of a traditional Mexican sauce used with Mexican dishes of turkey, chicken, and meats, and particularly with *tacos.* Unlike many Mexican sauces, it need not be so fiery that it is unacceptable to more moderate palates. It is made from several kinds of sweet pepper, avocado, tomato, sesame, and aniseed, garlic, coriander, a little cinnamon, cloves, chilli powder, *chimaja,* and grated chocolate, all pounded together. The degree of hotness depends on the the amount of chilli used. The sauce is chocolate coloured and extremely popular in the U.S.

mole de guajolote, a dish of turkey cooked with the above ingredients in a casserole with a little stock or water. The bird is often stuffed with a purée of raw avocado pears before roasting.

mole powder, a Mexican seasoning available in the U.S., made from powdered herbs and spices with chillis and dried sweet peppers.

molecche, Italian for soft-shelled crabs. At the end of April, in Venice, the crabs are changing their shells and are easy to catch. They are a dull green colour and about 2 inches across. While still alive, they are dipped in batter and fried in oil. The whole of the crab is edible, and although the cooking procedure is barbarous, the dish is delicious. In 17th-century Italy they were sometimes served with fritters of dried fig. See also CRAB; GRANCEVOLE.

molho, Portuguese for sauce. There are not many Portuguese national sauces, but those that exist are often highly individual. Molho francês is French dressing.

molho à portuguesa, is made with ½ pint (1 cup) port reduced by half, then 1 cup meat juice, a squeeze of lemon juice, and 1 tablespoon finely grated lemon and bitter orange peel are added. This is boiled up, thickened slightly with 2 tablespoons creamed corn flour (cornstarch), and reduced a little. Finally 2 teaspoons each of dried raisins, chopped blanched almonds, chopped sweet pepper, and lemon juice are added. This sauce is served with meats. See also PIRI-PIRI.

molho de aves (sauce for birds), a speciality of Oporto, Douro, and Trás-os-Montes. To prepare it 1 tablespoon corn flour (cornstarch) is added to the pan juices of poultry; then ½ pint (1 cup) giblet stock and ¼ pint (½ cup) port wine are poured over and the sauce is reduced rapidly on top of the stove, stirring well.

molho escabeche, is composed of 2 sliced onions that have been fried in olive oil, 2 garlic cloves, 2 tablespoons white wine vinegar, and 1 bay leaf. This sauce is used as a marinade for fried fish; it is poured over the fried fish, which is allowed to remain in the marinade for 2 days before it is eaten.

moliterno, an Italian cheese, also known as *pecorino moliterno.* It is very similar to *cotronese.*

mollusc, a large group of invertebrate animals belonging to the *Mollusca* subkingdom of soft-bodied and sometimes hard-shelled animals. Almost the only edible land mollusc is the snail. The marine molluscs include the limpet, cuttlefish, oyster, mussel, octopus, scallop, and squid. Some of these, such as oysters, are eaten raw, but the majority are cooked. See SHELLFISH; SNAIL.

moncenisio, an Italian factory-made blue-mould cheese of the *formaggini* type.

mondseer schachtelkäse, see MONDSEER SCHLOSSKÄSE.

mondseer schlosskäse, an Austrian cheese made and eaten only in the Mondsee district. It is shaped like a small loaf and does not exceed 2 lb. in weight. Mondseer schlosskäse is the full-cream variety and mondseer schachtelkäse (chalet mondseer cheese), three-quarters or half-cream. The smell and taste are similar to that of a *limburger käse.*

monégasque, à la, I. A French chicken consommé thickened with arrowroot. It is garnished with *profiteroles,* with grated cheese in the mixture. II. A French garnish for entrées, composed of slices of fried calf's brains, fried ham, mushrooms, and a demi-glace with julienne of mushrooms and truffles. III. A dish of fried or poached eggs (*oeufs à la monégasque*) served on a bed of tomatoes that have been fried in oil mixed with chopped tarragon and garnished with anchovy fillets and surrounded by tomato sauce.

moniatos, a variety of sweet potato, orange in colour, which is native to Málaga, Spain. See also BATATAS.

monkfish, the American name for the fish known in England as angelfish (*Squatina squatina*).

Monmouth pudding, a regional Welsh pudding from Monmouth, made from 2 cups fresh breadcrumbs soaked in 1 pint (2 cups) boiling milk, then beaten with 2 oz. (¼ cup) sugar, 2 tablespoons butter, and 3 stiffly whisked egg whites. It is placed in a pie dish in alternate layers with a red jam, ending with the breadcrumb mixture, and is baked in a slow oven until just set.

monosodium glutamate, MSG, a neutral salt of glutamic acid, a constituent amino acid of protein, which, because of its stimulating effect upon the taste buds, is introduced into many packaged foods to render them more appetizing. For this reason it is also to be found in various commercial seasonings. Monosodium glutamate is sold unadulterated, in the form of a white powder, under a number of trade names such as Accent, Ajinimoto, Mei Jing, etc. These can be obtained in most regular and Oriental food shops. American scientists have recently discovered that taken in excess of one tenth of an ounce, it can cause chest pains and burning sensations in the body and face in susceptible persons.

monostorer, a Rumanian cheese from Transylvania, made from ewe's milk which is very popular in Rumania.

monselet, à la, a French name applied to dishes cooked or garnished with artichoke hearts, truffles, and *pommes de terre parisienne* or *pommes de terre monselet.* Sauce *foyot* accompanies it, if the garnish is for tournedos or noisettes.

monsieur blanc, a white, unfermented Normandy cheese, of high fat content (usually about 50–55%) made from cow's milk. Being free from added herbs, it has a very delicate, clear flavour. See also FROMAGE DE MONSIEUR.

monstera, a decorative plant with deeply incised leaves, a member of the *Arum* family. It is indigenous to the West Indies and tropical America, but nowadays is grown all over Europe in greenhouses. *Monstera deliciosa* has a succulent edible fruit with a flavour reminiscent of pineapple. The common name is Swiss cheese plant.

mont blanc, a French dessert made from sieved, cooked chestnuts served in a border, for *crème chantilly* which is piled in a dome shape in the centre. In Italy it is also popular and called *monte bianco.*

mont-bry, à la, a French garnish for small cuts of meat, consisting of little cakes of cooked spinach with cooked Parmesan cheese, *cèpes* in cream, and the pan juices blended with white wine and thickened veal stock.

Mont-Cenis, a blue-mould, hard cheese from the district of Mont Cenis in the southeast of France. It is usually made from a mixture of cow's, ewe's, and goat's milk.

mont-des-cats, a French cow's milk cheese from Picardy, which is in season all the year round.

mont d'or, I. A French cheese from that part of the Doubs department nearest to Switzerland. It is a cow's milk cheese, rather similar to *münster.* It is in season from October to May. II. The best-known cheese of the Lyonnais, made from the milk of stable-fed goats near Lyons. It is nowadays very rare, being made more usually from cow's milk.

montasio, an Italian hard cheese from the Veneto, made from whole cow's milk. It is eaten as a table cheese when fresh, but is mainly used in cooking. It is like a coarse *asiago.*

Monte Cristo, see MONTPENSIER, Á LA (II).

Monterey (Jack), a cheese from Monterey, California, first made there in 1892 and also known as Jack cheese. It may be made from pasteurised whole, partly skimmed, or skimmed cow's milk. The whole milk Monterey is semi-soft, the variety made from partly skimmed and skimmed milk, called dry Monterey or dry Jack, is hard and is used for grating.

Monterey Spanish mackerel (*Scomberomorus concolor*), a fish related to the Spanish mackerel, found off the Californian coast.

montglas, see SALPICON, À LA MONTGLAS.

monthéry, a French cow's milk cheese from Seine-et-Oise. It is a soft, surface-ripened cheese, similar to brie.

montmorency, à la, I. A French garnish for tournedos or noisettes, consisting of artichoke bottoms filled with either marble-sized pieces of carrot and *pommes noisette,* or asparagus tips and macedoine of vegetables. II. Montmorency is the name of a variety of cherry grown in the Paris region; consequently a variety of dishes both sweet and savoury, which have cherries added, are described as montmorency or à la montmorency, for example, *savarin* montmorency, *caneton* à la montmorency.

montone, Italian for mutton, hardly ever mentioned on a menu and usually referred to as *agnello.* Nevertheless, it is used in Italian cooking, and is often served, especially minced, in dishes such as *polpette* or *polpettone.* See also MUTTON.

montpellier, see BEURRE, DE MONTPELLIER.

montpensier, à la, I. A French garnish for tournedos, noisettes, and sweetbreads, consisting of artichoke bottoms filled with asparagus tips, julienne of truffles, and *pommes noisette.* The pan juices are diluted and boiled up with white wine or

Madeira, and whipped with butter. II. A French flan also called Monte Cristo. A 9-inch flan tin is lined with *pâte sucrée* and filled with a mixture of 4 oz. (1 cup) ground almonds, 8 oz. (1 cup) sugar, 3 heaped tablespoons melted butter, 1 teaspoon vanilla, ½ pint (1 cup) water, and 5 stiffly beaten egg whites. It is baked in a slow oven for 45 minutes.

moonfish, see OPAH.

moorcock, moorgame, or *muir fowl*, Scottish regional names for grouse, sometimes used for blackcock in England.

moorhen (*Gallinula chloropus*), a small water bird, coloured dark brown, grey, and white, very common all over the British Isles. It is rarely eaten, as the flesh is inclined to be stringy; however, if properly treated it can make quite a good meal, particularly if it is braised and served with a good mushroom and tomato sauce. It should be skinned, not plucked. It is also called water hen and *gallinule*.

moorhen

moose deer, see DEER.

mor monsen (*Mother Monsen*), a Norwegian cake. First 5 eggs are added, one at a time, to a creamed mixture of ½ lb. each of butter and sugar, beating constantly; ½ lb. (2 cups) flour is gradually whipped in, and all poured into a greased cake tin. Then 2 oz. (½ cup) chopped almonds and 2 oz. seedless chopped raisins are sprinkled on top, and the cake is baked in a slow oven for about 40 minutes. It is cut into diamond shapes when cool. See also MANDEL (MANDELKAKER).

moray eel (*Muraena helena*), a very voracious and dangerous large eel. It is said that they were especially bred by rich gourmets in ancient Rome, and the legend grew that slaves who displeased their masters were thrown to them as food. Be that as it may, there is at least one verified modern account of an incident in which the decapitated head of a moray eel bit the foot of a Portuguese fisherman in Bermuda so severely that he had to remain in hospital for 5 months. There are several varieties: spotted black and white; a virulent mottled shade of green; and a mottled cream and dark brown. However, moray is reputedly excellent to eat, especially in the Mediterranean and anyone brave enough to kill one should cook it in any way that is suitable for eel. See also MURENA.

Moray Firth, one of the three mid-19th-century Scottish methods of curing fish which originated in Moray Firth. The Moray Firth curing of smoked haddock makes the fish a very pale colour; Finnan haddie is golden yellow; and *Arbroath* is copper-coloured. See also HADDOCK.

morbier, a French cow's milk cheese from the Franche-Comté. It is at its best from March to October.

morcilla, Spanish black pudding. The mixture varies according to the province in which it is made, but the traditional Spanish black pudding is the morcilla of Asturias, a province renowned for its good cooking. It is from the cuisine of this province that most South American dishes are derived. See also BLACK PUDDING; DRISHEEN.

morcilla asturiana, a black pudding made with pig's blood mixed with pork fat, onions, cayenne, black pepper, marjoram, and salt, put into a pig's bladder and boiled in water.

morcillas negras, Andalusian black puddings made with onions, rice, breadcrumbs, lard, parsley, peppercorns, nutmeg, cinnamon, pimentos, garlic, and minced almonds, all mixed with pig's blood and put into pig's bladders before being boiled in water.

morcilla blanca, I. A Spanish sausage made from minced chicken, hard-boiled egg, fat bacon, black pepper, parsley, and seasonings. See also CHORIZO. II. A Spanish white pudding made from minced pig's lights (lungs) and tripe, with fat and cereal.

morcillón, see VIERAS.

morel (*Morchella esculenta*), an edible fungus or mushroom found in wood clearings in the spring. Morels have a yellowish-brown crinkly cap 1–2 inches tall and make extremely good eating. They also dry well for winter use. Some smaller species have conical or pointed caps and are black. See also HELVELLA; MORILLE; MUSHROOM.

morello, a very dark red, almost black, sour cherry, used for jams and a liqueur. See also CHERRY.

morgado de figos, a Portuguese cake made from chopped dried figs, marzipan, sugar, and chocolate, all flavoured with cinnamon. See also FIGOS.

morille, French for morel, one of the finest mushrooms in France. It is usually found in spring-time in wooded country. The most highly prized variety is small and pointed, with a black, crinkly skin on top, but often *helvella* or false morel is used instead. They should be well trimmed and washed, then simmered in butter in the same way as *cèpes*. See also MOREL.

mornay, sauce, a classical French sauce made from 1 pint (2 cups) sauce béchamel heated in a double boiler. When ready to serve, 2 oz. each of grated Gruyère and Parmesan, together with a few grains of cayenne, are added, well stirred, and heated until all are amalgamated. Fish fumet is added to the béchamel if the sauce is to accompany fish. De Mornay was a friend of Henry IV of France who took a great interest in cookery, and it is to his experiments that we owe this sauce. All dishes coated with sauce mornay, mainly fish, eggs, or vegetables are described as mornay or à la mornay. The coated top is usually glazed under a hot grill.

morpølse, a Norwegian sausage made with beef, mutton, and reindeer meat.

morros de ternera, a Basque dish consisting of calves' cheeks cooked with onions, red peppers, garlic, herbs, and seasoning.

mortadela, a Spanish sausage made from lean minced (ground) pork, brown sugar, saltpetre, spices, seasoning, and brandy or any hard liquor.

mortadella, a famous Bolognese sausage. The best variety is made of pure pork flavoured with coriander and white wine, but the cheaper kind can be a mixture of pork, veal, tripe, pig's head, donkey, and potato or soya flour, with colouring essence. Mortadella is not cured with salt but cooked by a steam process. It is a large sausage, measuring some 4–6 inches across. It is rather insipid, nothing like as good as a raw salted and cured salami.

mortar, a bowl made from stone, or stone with wood at the top, in which food-stuffs are pounded or mixed with a pestle.

mortifier, a French term meaning to hang meat or game.

morue, French for salt cod. *Morue noire* and *morue St. Pierre* are names for fresh haddock. *Morue séchée* is the French for klipfish and stockfish, which are often eaten in the south of France, particularly in Nice, and in Corsica. See also BRANDADE DE MORUE.

morue séchée à la niçoise, salt cod soaked for at least 3 days, then scraped, boned, and cut into pieces. For every 2 lb. of fish, 3 onions are sautéed lightly in olive oil, and when soft, 4 large tomatoes, 4 crushed garlic cloves, basil, and a bouquet garni are added, and all is cooked for 20 minutes. The fish is then put in the pan, with enough water to cover, and simmered for 1 hour. Large, thick slices of potato and black olives are put in to cook, and when these are done the dish is ready.

moscardini, see FRAGOLE.

moschari or **moskari,** Greek for veal. See also KREAS.

moschari kapama, braised veal, an extremely popular dish in Greece. To prepare, 2 lb. chopped veal are browned in butter or oil, with 1 chopped onion and crushed garlic. Then a little flour is added, also seasoning and cinnamon. The whole is covered in red wine and gently simmered until the meat is tender. Herbs, tomatoes, and parsley may be added, to taste.

moschari ragoût, a stew of veal, onions, garlic, bay leaf, red wine, and seasoning, with *avgolémono sauce* added 5 minutes before serving.

moschari stifado, a Dodecanese method of preparing the *maschari ragoût.* It is made with a really large quantity of onions and without the *avgolémono sauce.*

moscovite, à la, a cold sweet dish similar to a *bavarois* or a jelly. It is made with fruit or liqueurs to which whipped cream is sometimes added just before the jelly sets, and it is placed in a hexagonal mould with a hinged lid, which is embedded in crushed ice. Jellies treated in this way are covered with a thin layer of rime.

moscovite, sauce, a classical French sauce, consisting of ½ pint (1 cup) sauce *poivrade,* with 4 juniper berries, 1 tablespoon each sliced almonds and raisins, and 3 tablespoons of Málaga or Marsala added at the time of serving.

moss duck, see MALLARD.

mostek, Polish for breast of meat.

mostek barani faszerowany, breast of lamb stuffed with veal or lean pork, mushrooms, onions, bread, parsley, and egg, then rolled, secured, and simmered in stock. If white wine is used, it becomes *mostek barani faszerowany na winie.*

mostek nadziewany wątróbką, stuffed breast of veal. The meat is stuffed with 1 cup breadcrumbs that have been moistened with milk, mixed with ¼ lb. raw, minced calf's liver, chopped dill and parsley, seasoning, and 1 egg. The meat is secured with skewers, rubbed with butter and roasted in a moderate oven for about 1½ hours, being basted alternately with the pan juices and cold water.

mostelle or **mostèle** (*Gaidropsarus mediterraneus*), names given in the south of France to a fish of the whiting family, found in the Rhone estuary and the Mediterranean. It has a delicate flavour, but must be eaten fresh, as it goes bad quickly. It is used in bouillabaisse, and its liver is highly thought of by gastronomes. It is also called *motelle, moutelo, mustèle,* and *mutelle.*

motelle, see MOSTELLE.

Mothering Sunday, original name for Mother's Day. See SIMNEL CAKE.

Mothe-St. Héraye, la, a French goat's milk cheese made in Poitou. It is at its best from May to November.

mouette, French for gull. Gull's eggs are a delicacy.

moufflon (*Ovis musimon*), the name given to various types of wild sheep. The European moufflon, found mainly in Sardinia and Corsica, is the ancestor of the domestic sheep. There is also an American moufflon or mountain ram, a slender animal with spiral horns and very long legs. The meat is like that of an *izard,* and should be marinated before cooking; it can be prepared in any way that is suitable for venison or mutton. In Corsica, where it is eaten a great deal, it is called *mufione* or *mufoli.*

mould, I. A container for foodstuffs, made in various materials to a specific shape, which it gives to the food it holds. The best known are of French origin. In England, special jelly moulds are made in glass or aluminium, with varying fluted patterns on the bottom. Generally they are oval in shape, and not unlike a child's sandcastle with rounded turrets. Clip moulds are moulds used for raised pies, usually made with hot water crust. They have either hinged sides, which are clipped into place, or a removable bottom, and these features ensure that the lightly cooked pastry case can be filled without fear of its collapsing, and that the pie can easily be removed when it is cooked. Hinged sides also have the advantage that they can be opened during cooking to allow the pastry to brown. See also MOULE. II. A cold dish, either sweet or savoury, usually set with aspic or gelatine, and turned out of a shaped mould. Cakes may be baked in moulds, but are not themselves described as moulds because they take the name of the particular mould used, as in the case of *cornet, savarin,* etc. See also MOUSSELINE.

moule, French for mould. The most important French moulds include *bombe,* a mould for shaping ice cream, usually made of copper with a tight-fitting lid; *bordure,* a plain mould, ring-shaped, with a flat top so that fish or meat can be arranged on top of a vegetable cream or jelly that has first been cooked and set in the mould; *charlotte,* a deep tin or copper mould with sloping sides which are lined with slices of sponge or bread. A fruit or cream filling is placed in the centre. It can sometimes have a lid. *Cornet,* conical in shape, used especially for cream horns; *dariole,* a plain cylindrical mould used for steaming or baking, also called castle moulds when used for castle pudding. *Moule à doville* is a ring mould. *Savarin* is a plain ring mould with a rounded top: *timbale,* a straight-sided mould like a high cake tin; *trois frères,* a round mould with diagonally fluted sides and base with a well in the centre. It is used for cooking the gâteau *bonvalet. Moule à pâte,* a hinged, round, or oval mould used in France for pâtés cooked in a crust of pastry.

moules, French for mussels. The French mussel beds of Isigny have a great reputation, and a variety of mussel known as *caïeu d'Isigny* can attain a length of up to 4½ inches. There is also the Provençal mussel, bred in sheltered pools at Toulon and Marseilles. See also MUSSEL.

moules à la marinière, the best-known method of cooking mussels. Four dozen mussels are well washed and brushed to remove sand and other particles; any already open before cooking should be discarded. They are put in a saucepan with a chopped shallot, parsley, thyme, and bay leaf, a little butter and ½ pint (1 cup) dry white wine, covered, and cooked on a high heat until the shells open. The mussels are then removed from the heat, and the small weed-like beards and empty hinged half-shells are thrown away. The stock is thickened with a *beurre manié,* more chopped parsley is added, and then it is poured over the mussels. If more liquid is added, a soup can be made from this stock, with just a few mussels floated on top. The mussels should not be re-boiled, as this makes them rubbery.

moules et frites, a Belgian speciality consisting of mussels and fried potatoes, sold from little push-carts in Belgium and often eaten on the spot. Also sold on the carts are *caracoles* (little sea-snails), crabs, and *scholles* (sun-dried plaice). See also CARICOLLES.

mouli, a French utensil for making purées of fruit or vegetables for soups, sauces, etc. It is made in metal with a stand, coarse and fine cutters which are interchangeable, and a rotating handle for operating the press, which pushes the food through the cutters. For cooks without an electric mixer (blender) it is invaluable and produces a purée in a matter of seconds. The *moulinette* is a smaller mouli which is good for grating cheese or nuts. It is also called a mouli-grater, and in the U.S. is known as a food mill.

mountain cherry, see CHICKASAW PLUM.

mountain hare, see SCOTCH BLUE HARE.

mountain plum, see TALLOW WOOD.

mountain rhubarb, see DOCK.

mousaká or *moussaká,* a dish of minced (ground) meat, usually lamb, with eggs, minced onions, and eggplants, eaten all over the Balkans, Turkey, and the Middle East. It is particularly a Greek speciality. To prepare it 2 lb. minced (ground) meat is fried with 3 onions. Then 8 medium eggplants are sliced crosswise, sprinkled with salt, drained, then mixed with parsley, marjoram, and seasoning. The eggplant and meat is put alternately in an oblong tin in layers until the dish is full, when ½ pint (1 cup) meat stock, or 2 cups fresh tomato sauce, or 1 pint (2 cups) sauce béchamel is added, and the dish is cooked for 30 minutes. A custard made with 2 egg yolks and ½ pint (1 cup) milk is poured over all. Sometimes grated cheese is sprinkled over the top. It is further cooked in the oven for 30 minutes, or until the crust is golden brown. It is delicious when hot, but is also very good cold. In Turkey it is sometimes cooked in the eggplant-skins, the pulp included with the meat. See also MUSAKA OD PLAVIH PATLIDŽANA.

mousquetaire, sauce, I. A classical French sauce, served with boiled meats. To 1 pint (2 cups) mayonnaise are added 2 finely chopped shallots which have been softened in white wine, and a garnish of chives. It is seasoned with cayenne, and with 2 tablespoons veal jelly (glaze) stirred in as flavouring. II. A sauce *provençale,* with chopped tarragon and other herbs.

mousse, a light, smooth dish, usually cold or iced, which may be sweet or savoury. The chief ingredients are pounded or puréed foods, eggs, and cream. Savoury mousse is usually made with fish (also smoked fish such as salmon, trout, or mackerel) or shellfish, poultry, cheese, hard-boiled eggs, or foie gras, all minced or pounded, mixed with cream and stiffly beaten egg whites, and either cooked in a *bain-marie* or stiffened with aspic or gelatine. A sweet mousse can be made from 8 oz. melted plain chocolate mixed with 4 egg yolks, the stiffly beaten whites being added when the mixture is cool. Cream is served with this sweet mousse, but it is not necessary to include it among the actual ingredients. Any puréed fruit can be used in the same way. The term also covers jellies whipped with or without cream so that they are spongy in texture when chilled. The jelly must be the consistency of raw egg white before whipping.

The mousse was brought to Britain by the Normans, and early manuscripts spell it *moyse* or *mouse.* Although not quite as frothy in texture as the present-day mousse, the *moyse* always had beaten eggs as part of the ingredients. Apple *moyse* was the most common in the 14th and 15th centuries. See also MUS.

mousseau, a French loaf made from whole wheat flour.

mousseline, a name given to many preparations which have whipped cream added to them. It refers particularly to small or large moulds, either sweet or savoury, served either hot or cold. See also MOULD.

mousseline cake, made from 8 oz. (1 cup) castor sugar worked with 7 egg yolks and a little powdered *banille* or ½ teaspoon vanilla. When frothy, 7 oz. (2 cups) corn flour (corn-starch) and flour, mixed in equal quantities, are very gradually added, followed by the stiffly beaten egg whites. The cake is baked in a moderate oven, in a *génoise* cake tin which has been buttered and dusted with sugar. It can be sliced when cold, and layered with various creams.

mousseline forcemeat, a recipe which makes the most superb quenelles of all. First 2 lb. skinned and boned fish are well pounded with salt, nutmeg, and pepper; 4 egg whites are added a little at a time, and the mixture is put in a liquidizer or through a sieve to make it really smooth. After this it must be left on ice to get very cold. Then 1 pint (2 cups) fresh cream is added gradually, and gently stirred in. This mixture is also good for stuffing a large fish before baking or braising it. Chicken, game, or liver can also be used as the basis of this forcemeat. See also GODIVEAU, LYONNAIS.

mousseline pudding, an Edwardian English dish consisting of 6 separated eggs, the yolks beaten with 5 oz. (⅔ cup) sugar, 5 oz. (⅔ cup) butter, and the juice and peel of 1 lemon. The mixture is then thickened in a double boiler over heat, but must not be allowed to boil. It is stirred until cold, when the stiffly beaten egg whites are lightly mixed in. It is put into a greased basin and steamed for 55 minutes, then turned out and served hot. It is quite delicious. See also POMME DE TERRE (POMMES MOUSSELINE).

mousseline, sauce, a classical French sauce. Sauce hollandaise is mixed with an equal amount of stiffly whipped cream. This is heated with extreme care in a double boiler until warmed through (it must *never* be allowed to boil), whipping gently all the time. It is seasoned to taste. It is also called *sauce mousseuse.*

moustartha, saltsa, a Greek lemon and mustard sauce, made with 4 crushed garlic cloves, 8 tablespoons olive oil, and 1 teaspoon dry mustard gradually added to the strained juice of 2 lemons. It is well stirred until blended. This sauce is served separately, with egg or fish dishes, and is sprinkled with chopped parsley.

moutarde, see FRENCH MUSTARD; MUSTARD.

moutelo, see MOSTELLE.

mouton, French for mutton, which is used extensively in France. Especially popular is *pré-salé,* the meat of sheep pastured on the sea coast, where the salt marshes and many sea plants are included in the animal's diet, thus giving the meat a special flavour. Mutton in France is usually cooked slowly, with aromatic herbs and stock or wine, to ensure tenderness. *Civet* is one well-known method; others include haricot, daube, braised leg of mutton with sauce *soubise, navarin,* ragoût, and boned stuffed shoulder of mutton braised and served cold in its own jelly. See also MUTTON.

mouton à la boulangère, see VEAU (EPAULE DE VEAU À LA BOULANGÈRE).

mouton à la bretonne, boned and braised shoulder or leg of mutton, always served with cooked haricot beans either whole or puréed.

mouton à la flamande, as above, but cooked with shredded red cabbage.

mouton à la poitevine, thick slices (each weighing about 1 lb.) cut from a leg of mutton, first browned in butter then cooked with ¼ pint (½ cup) brandy, the same amount of water, and 12 garlic cloves until the liquid boils, then covered and simmered as slowly as possible for 2–3 hours.

mouton en ballon or *mouton en musette,* boned shoulder of mutton, well seasoned, then rolled into a flattish ball. It is firmly tied with string and braised with garlic, root vegetables (turnips are very often used), herbs, white wine, stock, and seasoning. It is untied when cooked, served with some of the stock and one of a variety of possible garnishes, such as *bretonne, boulangère, flamande,* or *soubise.* It is sometimes stuffed with sausage meat or other forcemeat before cooking.

mouton en pistache or *mouton à la catalane,* a method of preparing leg of mutton which comes from the southwest of France, particularly the Catalan. The leg is first boned, rolled lengthwise and tied, then put into a saucepan lined with unsmoked ham, sliced onion, and carrot. It is seasoned, and several spoonfuls of goose or pork fat are poured over; then it is covered, and cooked gently for 30 minutes. It is removed, and the pan juices are thickened with flour, and 2 cups each of white wine and stock are added. When well stirred and thickened, it is strained, and the meat is put back in the pan with the stock, 50 blanched garlic cloves, a bouquet garni, and a piece of dried orange peel. It is covered and cooked in a moderate oven for 1–2 hours. Partridge and pigeon can also be cooked by this method.

mouvette, French for a wooden spoon for stirring sauces.

moya, the Spanish name for a coarse and not very appetising fish of the cod family. It is cooked in the same way as *bacalão.*

moyeu, an Old French word for the yolk of an egg. See MAYONNAISE.

mozart, à la, a French garnish for entrées, consisting of artichoke bottoms filled with a purée of celery or celeriac, *pommes copeaux,* and sauce *poivrade.*

móżdżek, Polish for brains. See also BRAINS. They can be parboiled, skinned, mashed with butter, seasoned, bound with egg, and shaped into cutlets before being fried.

móżdżek cielęcy, calves' brains parboiled in salted water, drained and skinned, then simmered with stock to cover, an onion, celery, carrot, bay leaf, ½ lemon, and seasoning for 30 minutes. The stock is thickened with 2 egg yolks and ¼ cup cream, flavoured with juice and peel of ½ lemon.

móżdżek smażony z jajkami, parboiled as above, then skinned and chopped coarsely, mixed with a lightly browned fried onion, and fried for about 10 minutes on all sides. It is served with a raw egg in the centre of each portion which is forked over the dish while eating.

móżdżek w białym sosie, brains prepared as for *móżdżek cielęcy,* then served in a white sauce.

mozzarella, an Italian cow's milk cheese, which is very popular in Naples and elsewhere in Italy. It should be eaten very fresh, when it is dripping with buttermilk. When it is dry, it is used for cooking with such dishes as pizza napoletana and *crostini,* lasagne. It was formerly made from buffalo milk. *Mozzarella affumicata* is a smoked mozzarella with a golden skin; *mozzarella treccia* is a plaited mozzarella; *uova di buffalo* are egg-shaped mozzarellas. All these cheeses are made in the province of Campania, and also in Apulia, the Abruzzi, and Calabria.

mozzarella alla milanese, slices of mozzarella dusted with flour, dipped in beaten egg and breadcrumbs, then fried in hot fat or oil.

mozzarella in carrozza, crustless sandwiches of mozzarella, soaked in beaten egg and fried in olive oil. The literal translation of the name is "mozzarella in a carriage."

muckalica, an excellent Yugoslavian stew, made from chopped pork, onions, sweet peppers, eggplant, and chillis, together with stock or water, all gently simmered for several hours. It is served throughout Yugoslavia, but the town of Leskovac is considered to make the best.

mudjemeri, traditional Turkish mutton rissoles. They are made with 1 lb. cold boiled rice passed through a mincer and mixed with 1½ lb. chopped raw mutton, 3 chopped onions, and 2 eggs. Salt and chopped herbs are added. Flattish oval cakes are formed, and these are fried in mutton fat. They are sometimes served with fresh tomato sauce.

muesli or **müsli,** a Swiss national breakfast dish or pudding, made by soaking raw rolled oats in water overnight so that they swell and absorb all the water. In the morning, grated apple or other fruit is added, also condensed milk or cream with lemon juice. It is sometimes decorated with chopped nuts. It is now made commercially and sold in packets. Commercially made muesli does not need to be soaked and is served with fresh milk or fruit juice.

muffin, an old English tea-cake, seen seldom today in England, but still found in Ireland and the U.S. Until just before World War II, the "muffin man," with a large tray of muffins and crumpets balanced on his head and ringing a large handbell to advertise his wares, was a common sight in the streets of London. He was very welcome on a cold winter's afternoon. The muffins would be toasted in front of the fire and eaten hot, smothered in butter. Muffins are made from a yeast dough with a little sugar, similar to crumpet mixture, but muffins are thicker than crumpets and are browned on both sides. The dough is cooked in a metal "muffin ring." When muffins are served, they should not be cut, but pulled apart. In the U.S., blueberry muffins are made by adding blueberries sprinkled with flour to the dough. Corn muffins are made with a dough made of half corn meal, and half wheat flour. The American dish of eggs benedict is served on a toasted English muffin.

muffin pudding, an English north country dish, made by splitting muffins and packing them tightly into a greased basin with spoonfuls of honey and a scattering of a spice such as nutmeg, and filling the hollows with a light batter made from 4 oz. (1 cup) flour, ½ pint (1 cup) milk, and 2 stiffly beaten egg whites. It is covered, and boiled or steamed for an hour. It is very light and good.

mufione or **mufoli,** see MOUFFLON.

muge, see MULET.

muggety pie, an old Cornish recipe. A sheep's pluck is soaked in water and thoroughly cleaned. It is boiled for several hours and is then finely minced. Lavish seasoning, some currants, and parsley or spices are added and well mixed in. It is put in a pie dish, covered with a good short crust pastry, and baked.

mugwort (*Artemisia vulgaris*), a European perennial plant with aromatic, faintly bitter leaves. They are used as a flavouring in stews, stuffings, and sweets.

muikku, Finnish for the fry of whitefish, often served like whitebait and eaten with chopped raw onion. They are also often cooked with pork in pies and pasties. See also KALA (KALA KUKKO).

muir duck, see MALLARD.

muir fowl, a local Scottish name for grouse or blackcock.

mujdei de usturoi, a Rumanian garlic sauce served with meats, particularly pork cutlets, and with fish or with vegetables. It is made from 4 large garlic cloves pounded into ¼ pint (½ cup) olive oil and well mixed. This sauce is commonly known for short as *mujdei.*

mújol, see LISA.

mulberry, a fruitberry of which there are several varieties. They may be used in any way that is suitable for blackberries or loganberries although they have a distinctive flavour of their own, and should be very ripe before eating.

black mulberry, the fruit of several varieties of *Morus nigra.* It is thought to have come originally from Persia, but has been grown in Europe for a very long time.

red mulberry (*M. rubra*), a native of the U.S. Its long red berries are delicious in pies and tarts, or they can be eaten as a dessert fruit when very ripe. This applies to the black mulberry also. They also make an excellent jelly, a liqueur, and mulberry gin, which is far better than sloe gin.

white mulberry (*M. alba*), a native of China. The berries

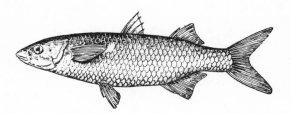

grey mullet

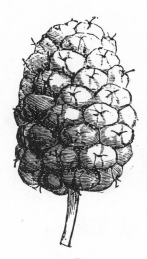

mulberry

are almost white, and sweet, though not very flavoursome. The leaves of the white mulberry are the sole food of silkworms. The Latin poet Ovid relates the story of Pyramus and Thisbe, which tells how white mulberries were turned to red by the blood of the ill-fated lovers.

mulchán, an unpressed Irish cheese, made in country districts from buttermilk. Nowadays it is only made privately.

mule, the hybrid offspring of a male donkey and a mare, or a stallion and a she donkey. When young, it is highly prized as food in parts of Europe where horsemeat is popular. All methods of cooking used for horsemeat are suitable for mule.

mulet or **muge,** French for grey mullet. *Mulet cabot* is the French for surmullet, and *mulet rouge* or *rouget* for red mullet. Red mullet is often called rouget in France, but as several other very inferior red fish such as gurnet are also given this name, it is as well to insist on mulet rouge. The following dishes are prepared with red mullet wherever possible, as it is much the finer fish, but grey mullet can also be used. See also MULLET.

mulet rouge à la bercy, mullet brushed with oil, seasoned, grilled, and served with sauce *bercy.*

mulet rouge à la bordelaise, prepared as above but served with sauce *bordelaise.*

mulet rouge à la niçoise, a popular method of serving mullet in the south of France. The fish are baked with tomatoes, butter, lemon, and tarragon and garnished with anchovies.

mulet rouge aïoli, poached mullet served with sauce *aïoli.*

mulet rouge au fenouil, seasoned, oiled mullet, grilled on a bed of dried fennel stalks, flambéed with brandy or another spirit, and garnished with chopped fresh fennel.

mulet rouge en papillote, mullet brushed with oil, seasoned, cooked in oiled paper or foil, with chopped mushrooms, herbs, and garlic.

mullet, a common European fish with two distinct varieties. See also MULET.

grey mullet (Mugil auratus), a much coarser fish than the red mullet, but nevertheless very good and not unlike a bass. It is found in both European and American waters where it is known as striped mullet and in Florida as black mullet. *Botargo* is made from the roe of this fish. Other varieties are *M. cephalus; M. capito; M. saliens; M. chelo.* See also AVGOTARAHO; LISA.

red mullet (Mullus surmuletus and *M. barbatus),* an exceptionally fine eating fish. Some epicures call it the "woodcock of the sea," implying that it should not be drawn before cooking. The flesh is firm and white, and the mullet is best baked, or grilled with a little olive oil and fennel, or grilled and served with *beurre maître d'hôtel.* The liver is considered a delicacy. The best red mullet are found in the Mediterranean, but it is also a speciality of Weymouth, Dorset, England. See also BARBOUNIA; SALMONETE; TRIGLIE.

red mullet

mulligatawny soup, an Anglo-Indian soup, made from 4 chopped onions fried in butter or oil and sprinkled with rice flour or flour, seasoning, and curry powder to taste (1 tablespoon to 2 pints liquid). To this 2 pints (4 cups) strong beef broth are added (ox tail broth is excellent), and the mixture simmered slowly. When the soup has been cooking for 20 minutes, 2 tablespoons lentils (the orange Egyptian variety) per quart of stock are added, with ½ teaspoon ground coriander. It is garnished with crisp onion rings fried to a deep brown, and dried. The name comes from two Tamil words: *molegoo* (pepper) and *tunee* (water). In India it is served with a side plate of cold bananas and tomatoes, peeled and sliced.

multer, Norwegian for cloudberries, which are plentiful in all Scandinavian countries.

muna, Finnish for egg. See also MUNAKAS.

munavoi, egg butter, made with 2 chopped hard-boiled eggs beaten into 4 oz. (½ cup) butter. This is served in Finland with hot scones.

munakas, Finnish for omelette. See also OMELETTE.

uunissa kypsennetty munakas, an omelette made with smoked ham, eggs, and milk, baked in the oven. Baked omelettes are widely served in Finland for breakfast or lunch.

mung bean *(Phaseolus mungo,* var. *radiatus),* an Indian bean commonly known in that country as the golden or green gram. The beans are round, greenish in colour, and only half the size of a pea. They can be boiled like peas, and are also dried and ground into a floury meal which is rich in protein. If kept in a warm damp place, the bean will germinate, and the resulting bean sprouts are used for many Chinese and Indian dishes.

münsterkäse, a whole milk, semi-hard cheese made from

cow's milk and flavoured with wild cumin. It is the national cheese of Alsace and is made in the valleys and uplands of the Vosges. In season from November to May.

mürbeteig, a sweet German pastry case made with 12 oz. (3 cups) flour, 4 oz. (½ cup) butter, 1 egg, 2 tablespoons sugar, and 2 tablespoons water or rum, but it is often used for savoury pasties also. It is the equivalent of rich short crust pastry.

murena, a moray eel used in Italy in a Roman fish soup. See ZUPPA (ZUPPA DI PESCE ALLA ROMANA). In Calabria *murene* are sometimes roasted with oil. The milky-white flesh is tender and delicious. See also MORAY EEL.

murol, a French cow's milk cheese made in the Auvergne region, and in season almost the whole year round.

mus, Polish for mousse.

mus z wina, a wine mousse dessert made from 1 pint (2 cups) sweet white wine, and 2 tablespoons gelatine dissolved in water, beaten into a syrup made from 8 oz. (1 cup) sugar boiled with ¼ cup water and 1 teaspoon lemon peel. When this is cool, the juice of 2 lemons and 5 stiffly beaten egg whites are added, and all is beaten until stiff.

mus z zająca, hare mousse. For this dish the hare is not marinated. Before being put through the mincer, the hare is simmered with many root vegetables and spices for about 1 hour. Then the bones are removed from the animal, and all the rest of the hare minced twice. When the minced hare is cool, ¼ cup brandy, 1 cup cream, and 1 tablespoon chopped pistachio nuts are beaten in. Finally 2 tablespoons aspic or gelatine are dissolved in water and added to make the mousse set. It is all beaten until light and fluffy, then put in a damp mould. It is eaten cold.

musaka od plavih patlidzana, a Yugoslav mousaka made with 1 lb. each minced pork and mutton laid on a bed of 2 medium-sized eggplant slices fried in batter, and 3 sautéed onions. The meat is covered with another layer of 2 eggplants, sliced and fried, and the whole has a mixture of beaten egg mixed with 2 tablespoons flour, ¾ pint (1½ cups) milk, and seasoning poured over and allowed to trickle through it. Nutmeg is sprinkled on top before the musaka is baked for 40 minutes in a moderate oven. See also MOUSAKÁ.

muscadelle, a French variety of winter pear with a musky flavour.

muscat, very sweet white or black grapes, usually without pips. The best, and the easiest to grow are white frontignan (muscatel), muscat of Alexandra, Cannon Hall muscat (white), muscat Hamburg, and moscatelo (black).

muscoli, an alternative Italian name in Tuscany for mussels; also known as *mitili*. Each region of Italy has its own local name for mussels: in Naples they are *cozze*, in Venice *peoci*, in Florence *telline*, and in Genoa and Sardinia, *arselle*. They are used extensively in Italy in *pizza*, in spaghetti dishes, in soups, and in salads. See also COZZE; ZUPPA (ZUPPA DI COZZE).

muscovy duck or **musk duck** (*Cairina moschata*), a duck native to Central America, though now domesticated over most of the world. It is thought to have been imported into Europe in the middle of the 16th century. It can be cooked as wild duck. The young birds make good eating, but the old ones have a strong smell and are rather tough.

museau, French for muzzle or snout; for example, *museau de boeuf* (ox muzzle or cheek) and *museau de porc* (pig's snout). These are often sold cooked, having been well seasoned with chopped shallot, parsley, and a sauce vinaigrette. They are not unlike brawn, and constitute one of the cheapest hors d'oeuvre in France.

mush, an American dish, a sort of porridge which is made by boiling ½ cup ground rice in 1½ pints (3 cups) milk or water

white muscat grapes

until it is mushy. It is served chilled, cut into slices, dipped in flour, and sautéed in butter or bacon fat. The slices are served with maple syrup or molasses. Mush is also a common American word for any gruel-like concoction.

mushroom, the name applied generally to edible fungi. There are nearly 2000 known species which grow in a wild state in fields and woodlands, all over the world. They have little food value, although they are rich in minerals and vitamins. They are prized chiefly for their peculiar and delicate flavour.

When edible mushrooms are picked at the "button" stage, they may be eaten uncooked, dressed with lemon juice, olive oil, cream, or yogourt and a few grains of salt. Mushrooms give a unique flavour to soups and stews, but they are also delicious simmered in butter, olive oil, or cream as a dish in their own right, when the secret of success is not to overcook and to keep the dish covered during cooking. Serve the mushrooms, with hot toast or bread, in the dish in which they have been cooked. Mushrooms are also grilled and served with meat or bacon, or in an omelette. An essence (extract) is made from them by extracting the juice by long slow cooking, and a mushroom ketchup is produced commercially and marketed for use as a condiment. A mushroom seasoning used as a stuffing and in gravies and sauces is known in culinary French as *duxelles*. When used as stuffing for small game birds, the chopped bird's liver may also be added. Mushrooms also form a part of many important French garnishes. See also BARIGOULE; BEEF STEAK FUNGUS; BOLETUS; BLUET; CÈPE; CHAMPIGNON; CHAMPINJON; CHANTERELLE; CIUPERCI; DUXELLES; FUNGHI; GRIBY; GRZYBY; HELVELLA; INKY CAPS; MOREL; RAGOULE; SVAMP.

mushroom sauce, 4 oz. fresh, thinly sliced mushrooms added to 1 pint (2 cups) sauce béchamel and cooked gently in a double-boiler for about 30 minutes. Alternatively, the sliced mushrooms are lightly sautéed before adding to the sauce, with the strained butter in which they have been cooked.

The best known mushrooms are described here.

fairy-ring mushroom (*Marasmius oreades*), very popular, especially in France, Italy, and the U.S. It has the advantage of being more flavoursome when it is dried.

field mushroom (*Agaricus campestris*), the best known and the most prized. As well as growing wild, this mushroom is cultivated commercially all the year round in hotbeds, sheds, and cellars, but the flavour of the cultivated mushroom is never as good as that of the wild mushroom. This mushroom is also known as edible agaric, and as *champignon de Paris,* for it is grown extensively in the Paris region.

horse mushroom (*Agaricus arvensis*), larger than the field mushroom, the caps sometimes reaching a diameter of 8 inches. It is also coarser, with a stronger flavour. It has a faint smell of aniseed which distinguishes it from the inedible variety, *A. xanthoderma.* It grows in damp meadows and shady places.

parasol mushroom (*Lepiota procera*) and the *shaggy parasol* (*L. rachodes*), both delicately flavoured mushrooms, and much prized.

red-staining mushroom (*Agaricus silvaticus*), similar to the field mushroom, is found in coniferous woods. If young, there is a characteristic pinkish-red staining of the cap when the mushroom is cut across the stalk. It is excellent to eat.

Other edible mushrooms include the following.

Acetabula vulgaris, which changes from bright red in spring to orange-yellow in autumn, and *Acetabula sulcata,* a dark brown variety which has merit.

elm mushroom (*Pleurotus ulmarius*), grows only on elm stumps, and is fawn and white in colour, with caps 3–4 inches across. It has a very pleasant smell and taste.

Galerina mutabilis, a common fungus which resembles the honey fungus (*Armillaria melea*) in having the same deep golden brown colouring. It is edible, but without much flavour and is best when dried.

Laccaria laccata, and var. *amethystina,* small but edible. The former is reddish in colour, the latter a deep violet.

oyster mushroom (*Pleurotus ostreatus*), very good to eat when young. It is thick and fleshy, with shell-shaped caps often 6 inches across, and a bluish-oyster colour, with white flesh. It grows on the stumps of hardwood trees, especially beech, in late autumn and winter. It can also be artificially grown.

polyporus, a large genus of mushrooms, several of which are edible. They are usually found at the foot of old oak trees.

saffron milk cap (*Lactarius deliciosus*) has a sweet, pleasant taste.

It must always be remembered that a good many fungi are extremely poisonous, in particular some members of the genus *Amanita,* which are rendered even more dangerous by their very close resemblance to several of the commonest edible mushrooms. In fact, when gathering wild mushrooms, reference should always be made to a good book on the subject which contains clear colour photographs; however, the following examples are those to be particularly watched for.

death cap (*Amanita phalloides*), the deadliest of poisonous toadstools. It does resemble a field mushroom in shape, but has a ring or frill about an inch down the stalk. It grows particularly in broad-leaved woods.

destroying angel (*Amanita virosa*), a deadly killer, looking very like a field mushroom, except that it has white gills and a ring or frill about an inch down the stalk. It can also be distinguished from the field mushroom by cutting the stalk with a knife. The stalk of *Amanita virosa* will turn yellow. However, it should be noted that after about 15 minutes the yellow staining disappears, and the stalk is the same colour as an ordinary mushroom again. The destroying angel is found mainly in open spaces, and is uncommon in woods.

fly agaric (*Amanita muscaria*), a red fungus with white spots, resembling the fairy-ring mushroom. It is highly poisonous and used to be used to kill flies. It grows mostly under birch trees.

panther (*Amanita pantherina*), similar to *A. muscaria,* but smaller, and often tinged with olive. It is very poisonous.

muskellunge (*Esox masquinongy*), a large freshwater game fish found in North American and Canadian lakes, related to the pike. It is also known as "freshwater tiger." It makes excellent eating and is usually baked, broiled, fried, or served in any way that is suitable for pike.

muskrat (*Ondatra zibethica*), also known as marsh rabbit, an aquatic rodent which is very prolific in many parts of Canada and the U.S. It is canned and sold for food in parts of Canada, and although very full of bones, it makes a good stew. The flesh is dark red and has a gamey taste.

mussel (*Mytilus edulis*), an edible mollusc found in all oceans of the world. Those from the colder regions have the finer flavour. There are 2 main species: the common mussel, which has a long shell with a slight roughness along the back, and the Provençal mussel which is larger, and the shell is sharper along the edges. The latter is found in the Biarritz area of the Atlantic as well as in the Mediterranean; it is bred in salt water pools at Toulon and Marseilles, and although tougher, is highly thought of as food. Care should be taken in gathering mussels that they are picked from clean coastal waters, and the addition of a pinch of baking soda for every 2 pints of water used is a useful precaution to take when cooking all home-gathered mussels. Mussels can cause poisoning if they have been taken from a contaminated harbour, and if they have indeed taken in unwholesome matter, no amount of cooking will reduce the risk. Mussels can be steamed like clams, and fried in batter after opening, or used as a garnish or in a sauce.

mussel

One species of mussels (*Unio pictorum*) lives in fresh water. In the Avonmore and other Irish rivers, pearl-carrying mussels have been found; in Muscatine, Iowa, in 1891, a Mr. Boepple founded a pearl-button industry, using the shells of the freshwater mussels found in the vicinity. See also COZZE; MIDIA; MIDYE; MOULES.

mussel and onion stew, a dish traditional in Dirleton, East Lothian, Scotland. Mussels have always been a very popular food here, and a nearby town is called Musselburgh. To make, 60 mussels are scrubbed, then heated in 1 pint (2 cups) white wine, and when cooked and open, the small weed-like beards and the shells are removed. Then ¼ lb. (½ cup) butter is melted in a saucepan, 3 tablespoons flour are stirred in, and 1 pint (2 cups) milk and the mussel stock are also added. A large onion is peeled and finely sliced, and cooked in this stock. Finally, 3 tablespoons chopped parsley, ¼ pint (½ cup) cream, and the mussels are added, and the stew is gently heated without boiling.

mustard, the seed of the mustard plant (*Sinapis*), known in England in former times as "senvy," and very hot to the taste. It is ground to a fine powder which is mixed to a paste with water or wine to accompany meat, particularly ham or beef. It is also used for sauces.

English mustard, as we know it today, was first made in Lancashire in about 1730 by an old woman named Clements, who kept the secret of its preparation for many years and made a small fortune by going from town to town on a pack-horse, selling it. George I was one of her patrons. In Shakespeare's day, mustard seeds had been pounded and put into a thick creamy white sauce which was poured over slices of meat, particularly brawn; but Mrs. Clements was the first to popularise a mustard powder or flour which only needed the addition of water. Mustard was known to the Romans and imported into Gaul by them. The seeds were pounded and added to their sauces.

There are many varieties of mustard found wild throughout the world, but at least 3 are cultivated commercially: black mustard (*Brassica nigra*), with dark reddish-brown seeds; brown mustard (*Brassica juncea*), whose cooked leaves can also make a useful winter vegetable; and white mustard (*Sinapis alba*), with yellowish seeds.

The leaves can be used as well as the seeds. When young and green they can be included sparingly in salads, garnishes, and sandwiches, usually with cress, or cooked with other green vegetables.

There are many other types of mustard beside the English. *Blanc de Dijon*, made from the ground seeds of the *Sinapis alba* grown in the Dijon district, mixed with white wine, is considered to be one of the finest mustards in the world. It is stronger than the other French mustards, but not as hot as the English, and some of the German, mustards. The Italian Cremona mustard contains crystallised fruit chopped very finely. Florida mustard, made at Magenta-Epernay, France, from mustard seed, spices, salt, and wine from the Champagne district, is very good. It is pale in colour, hot, yet subtle; it is excellent with beef and ham, and blends well into sauces. *Moutarde de meaux* is made from whole grains mixed with spices and herbs, with an excellent taste. Many mustards are mixed with wine vinegar as well as wine. See also DIJON MUSTARD; FRENCH MUSTARD.

mustard pickle, see PICCALILLI.

mustard sauce, ½ pint (1 cup) white sauce thoroughly heated, with 1 teaspoon French mustard and ½ teaspoon English mustard blended into it. It is served with grilled herrings or mackerel.

mustèle, see MOSTELLE.

mustikka, Finnish for bilberry.

mustikkakeitto, a soup made with bilberries cooked in water, thickened with potato flour, and with sugar added to taste. It is served cold as a dessert, with cream or rusks.

mustikkapiirakka, a bilberry tart. The tart is made with *pulla* dough filled with bilberries and sugar. The dough is spread on a large baking dish and covered evenly with bilberries. The edges of the dough are turned over, and any dough left can be cut into strips and placed on top to form a lattice work. It is served with coffee, or as a dessert.

mutelle, see MOSTELLE.

mutton, the meat of a sheep over 1 year old. There are several good breeds of sheep in Britain and Ireland, and they vary in shape, size, and taste, according to whether they are reared in mountainous districts or on flat pasture lands. The small Welsh sheep is undoubtedly the best of the mountain breeds, for the flocks feed on wild thyme which gives the meat a unique flavour. A leg of this breed may not exceed 4 lb. in weight, but is lean, sweet, and good. The black-faced horned sheep of County Kerry and other western districts in Ireland are equally good. The heather-feeding sheep of the Wicklow Hills, although their flavour is stronger than that of the Kerry sheep, is also of excellent quality. Many of the

sheep in the west of Ireland have a *pré-salé* flavour as a result of being pastured on land reclaimed from the sea. In the Orkney Islands, particularly North Ronaldsay, there is a very small breed of sheep which feeds entirely on seaweed, and dies if forced to feed only on grass. When shorn, they are little bigger than a large hare, but the mutton is of exceptional quality, and the wool of extraordinarily fine texture. A similar small breed exists in Iceland. The fattest and most succulent English mutton comes from the Southdown sheep, especially those that feed on grass growing on the chalk downs. Romney Marsh sheep are very large, and the legs weigh between 10 and 12 lb. The meat is good, although coarser-grained than Welsh or Irish mutton, but the marsh grass gives it a *pré-salé* taste. In the 19th and early 20th centuries, both Romney Marsh mutton and Welsh coast-pastured animals were served in England with a sauce made from laver or samphire. In Ireland, dulse or sloke was used. Other good lowland breeds in England are Leicestershire and Shropshire. Mountain mutton should be cooked differently from the fatter, lowland variety; they require much more fat, and a slower cooking time, whereas the problem with lowland mutton is keeping it from being too greasy. As mutton can be tough if old, it is usually used for slowly cooked, braised dishes, such as hot pot or Irish stew; in Scotland, where the black-faced mountain sheep is often used, it is sometimes poached in milk with onions, carrots, thyme, parsley, and rosemary, for 3–4 hours. A sauce with capers is made from the stock.

A lot of mutton is sold as lamb; in fact the word mutton has almost disappeared from restaurant menus. However, if the animal is young enough (under 4 years of age), mutton roasts very well. The classical English sauces served with young roast mutton are red currant jelly, rowanberry jelly, onion sauce, and mint jelly or sauce. Thyme is used in stuffings, and rosemary is good roasted with the meat. Wild garlic is also used in country districts, but seldom the cultivated kind.

Mutton is also used with pork in Scotland, for sausages. Sheep and lamb provide the best kidneys for grilling or frying. See also BARANINA; FÅR; HAMMEL; KÈBAB (KÈBABI CACIK KEBASSI); LAMB; LAMMAS; MONTONE; MOUTON.

boiled leg of mutton with caper sauce, the classic English mutton dish. The leg is simmered in water with mint, thyme, onions, pepper, and salt for several hours, and the sauce is made from the stock.

smoked mutton hams, a speciality of the Scottish border. The leg is rubbed with a mixture of salt, saltpetre, brown sugar, allspice, coriander seeds, and black pepper. It is basted with brine every other day, and kept covered for a fortnight. Then it is taken out and pressed under a heavy weight for one day before being smoked over sawdust and juniper branches. It is soaked before cooking, like a ham.

mycella, a Danish cheese of the *Danablu* variety. Coloured a cream-yellow with green veining, this is a particularly delicious cheese. It gets its name from the mould *mycelium* which produces the veining. It is a larger cheese than *Danablu*, weighing 11–20 lb., and in taste it is closer to gorgonzola. It is sometimes eaten with wild strawberries. See also OST.

myrobalan (*Rosaceae*), the name given to varieties of plum indigenous to the East Indies but now grown widely in Alsace and Lorraine, and to a lesser extent in other parts of France where they are known as *mirabelles*. Perhaps the most prominent variety is *Prunus cerasifera*, known in England as cherry plum and sometimes cloth of gold. The fruit is like a small golden plum with red dots. It is a juicy fruit, about the size of a cherry, with a very thin skin and a sweet taste. It is mostly used in France to make the liqueur *mirabelle*, but it is also good for pies, tarts, jams, and jellies. See also PLUM.

*roast mutton with herb and breadcrumb crust
and mint sauce*

myrtille, French for bilberry, used, when cooked, as a com-pote, jam, syrup, or for a liqueur.

myrtle (*Myrtus communis*), an evergreen shrub with aromatic leaves and seeds, both of which were used in Roman cookery, and are still in use today as an alternative to bay leaves in marinades and stews. They are used particularly in Sardinia. Another member of the myrtle family is pepper myrtle or Jamaican pepper, more commonly known as allspice. In spite of its name, bog or Dutch myrtle is not a true myrtle. See also SWEET GALE.

mysost, the Norwegian term for any cheese that is made from cow's milk whey (*myse* meaning whey). The Swedish term for a cheese of this type is mesost. The whey is first cooked very slowly in huge, copper pans over a wood fire to get rid of the excess moisture. As the water evaporates, the residue becomes a brown, caramellised paste called *prim,* and it is because of this that whey cheese is sometimes called primost in Norway. The mysost is packed into wooden moulds hold-ing anything from 4 to 8 lb. of paste. As soon as it is set, it is ready to eat. The colour varies from light to dark brown, and the paste is hardish. It is sweet to the taste, but rather strong. Sometimes cream is added to the paste, and the resulting cheese is called *fløteost* (*fløte* meaning cream). By govern-ment ruling, mysost must not contain less than 80% dry mat-ter, and according to whether it is made from full cream or skim milk whey, it is termed *helfet* (not less than 33% butter fat), *halvfet* (not less than 20%), and *mager* (under 20%). To produce *helfet* and *halvfet,* cream is usually added. Plain my-sost, or magerost, is given trade names, for example Taffel-ost. All mysost cheese gets dry very quickly, so it is sealed with paraffin wax before being stored. It is served in very thin slices, and is definitely not a cheese for epicures. See also GEITOST; OST.

myzithra, see MIZITHRA.

nabos, Portuguese for turnip. Turnips are eaten extensively in Portugal; both the root and the green tops are used, the latter being called *grelos de nabos.*

nadzienie, Polish for stuffing.

nadzienie z całych kasztanów, a Polish stuffing for turkey or goose consisting of 1½ lb. whole cooked chestnuts mixed with 4 tablespoons butter.

nage, à la, a French method of preparing shellfish, mainly crayfish, crawfish, and lobsters. They are cooked in a court bouillon with herbs, and are eaten hot or cold, and served with the court bouillon.

nageoires de tortue, French for turtle flippers. (When applied to fish, *nageoire* means fin.) Turtle flippers are usually braised for 2–3 hours in strong stock, with Madeira or white wine added to taste.

nageoires de tortue à la financière, turtle flippers braised in Madeira and served with *financière* garnish, the stock being reduced.

nageoires de tortue grillées sauce madère, turtle flippers simmered in water for 2 hours, then brushed with melted butter and grilled on both sides. They are seasoned, basted with 1 cup white wine, and cooked on top of the stove until tender. They are served with sauce madère.

nahit, a traditional Jewish dish eaten at Purim or the Feast of Esther. It is prepared by soaking 1 lb. dried chick-peas overnight, covering them well with water and cooking until soft. Sometimes rice, onion, or brisket of beef are added. See also HAMANTASCHEN; PURIM, FRITTERS.

nalésniki, Polish for crêpes or pancakes made from 4 oz. (1 cup) flour mixed with 1 pint (2 cups) milk, 1 tablespoon melted butter, salt, and 3 eggs.

nalésniki z mięsem albo mózgiem, pancakes with a filling of cooked puréed calves' brains mixed with 2 tablespoons sour cream. Other fillings are sometimes substituted, such as whipped cream with jam or chopped almonds, cottage cheese, or minced meats.

nalisniki, Russian for pancakes filled with a mixture of tvorog and butter. After they have been rolled up, the pancakes are dipped in melted butter and deep fried in oil. Sometimes they are served for *zakuski.* See also PANCAKE.

nalisniki s tvorog, cheese pancakes, made in exactly the same way as *blinchki s tvorogom* and with an identical filling, but rolled up instead of being folded over, brushed with bea-

ten egg, rolled in breadcrumbs, and fried in butter. They are served with sour cream or jam.

namaycush (*Salvelinus namaycush*), a large char sometimes referred to as lake trout, found in the Great Lakes of North America. It usually weighs about 40 lb. but can attain as much as 80 or 100 lb. It makes indifferent eating, and is fished more for sport than for use as food.

nantais, I. Small French almond biscuits (cookies). A mixture of 1 lb. (4 cups) flour, 1 cup ground almonds, 1 lb. (2 cups) castor sugar, ½ lb. (1 cup) butter, 3 eggs, and ¼ pint (½ cup) kirsch is cut into small rounds which are brushed with egg yolk and then baked. II. A French tartlet made from 8 tablespoons each of butter and sugar, a pinch of salt, ½ teaspoon baking powder, and the peel of 1 lemon or orange creamed together. Then 2 eggs and 4 oz. (1 cup) flour are added, and the mixture is put into buttered tartlet tins, sprinkled with finely chopped almonds, and baked in a moderate oven. When cool, the tartlets are brushed with warm apricot jam before being iced with maraschino-flavoured *fondant.* III. A French cow's milk cheese made in Brittany. See CURÉ. IV. A French Nantes duckling. See CANARD.

nantaise, à la. I. A French garnish for meat, consisting of glazed turnips, green peas, and mashed potatoes, with a thick meat gravy. II. A French method of serving chicken. See POULET, À LA NANTAISE.

nantua, à la, a French garnish also for fish and chicken, consisting of poached crayfish tails, sauce *nantua,* and truffles. See also POULET, À LA NANTUA.

nantua, sauce, a classical French sauce, composed of ½ cup sauce béchamel mixed with ½ cup cream and 1 cup fish fumet, 1 tablespoon *mirepoix* of vegetables, 4 tablespoons crayfish butter, and sometimes 2 fresh peeled tomatoes, or tomato purée to taste. It is garnished with crayfish tails and seasoned with pepper, salt, and a dash of cayenne. It is often served with eggs, fish, and shellfish.

napoletana, alla, a phrase which indicates that the preparation concerned is cooked according to the method common in Naples, Italy. The range of such dishes is not as varied as that of Bologna or Milan, and the most common Neapolitan preparation is a sauce that is served with various types of pasta. This is made with 1 lb. fresh, peeled, sliced tomatoes sautéed in oil with celery leaf, 1 onion, and basil, then covered with water, seasoned, and simmered until a thickish purée is formed. It can be strained or not, as desired. Garlic is sometimes added.

Tomatoes and olive oil are popular ingredients in much Neapolitan cookery. Even bread is fried, covered with cheese, and then topped with fried tomatoes mixed with herbs and seasoning. Chicken is commonly boiled, then served in a thick sauce of tomato, garlic, mushroom, and rosemary—a sauce which is also served with fish or meat. The pizza is of Neapolitan origin, as is salsa *pizzaiola,* which is used for fish, meat, and pasta dishes.

napolitaine, à la, I. A French garnish for escalopes (scallops) and cutlets, consisting of cooked spaghetti, fresh tomato sauce, and grated Parmesan cheese. II. A French garnish for fish, consisting of cooked spaghetti, grated Parmesan cheese, and butter, all covered with sauce mornay. Tomato sauce is poured round. III. A French sauce, consisting of 2 tablespoons of fine mirepoix reduced in Marsala wine, with 2 cubed peeled tomatoes, boiled up with 2 tablespoons demi-glace, and 1 tablespoon butter. IV. A salad dressing of 1 tablespoon lemon juice and 3 tablespoons olive oil, mixed with pounded garlic, chopped parsley, salt, and pepper.

napolitains, large ornamental French cakes, formerly used to decorate buffet dinners.

napper, French for to mask, that is, to cover food with a sauce.

narceja, Portuguese for snipe. *Narceja estufada* is braised snipe; *narceja grelhada,* grilled snipe.

narceja à Lisboeta, snipe served Lisbon style, which is sautéed in olive oil, with pimento, garlic, and tomatoes.

naseberry (*Achras zapota*), the fruit of the American sapodilla tree. It is lemon-shaped, grey-brown in colour, and similar to a medlar. The pulp is reddish-yellow and very sweet when the fruit is fully ripe. In France it is called *nèfle d'Amérique.*

nasello, Italian for whiting, or fresh haddock. See also MERLANO; MERLUZZO.

nässelkål, a Swedish soup made from 2 lb. young nettle tops, which are rinsed in several lots of fresh water before being simmered in boiling salted water until tender (about 10 minutes), then put through a sieve. A roux is made from 2 tablespoons each of butter and flour, and 2 pints (4 cups) hot nettle stock is added to this, followed by the nettle purée and seasoning. The soup is garnished with sliced hard-boiled eggs. See also NETTLES.

nassi goreng or ***nasi goreng,*** a Dutch-Indonesian dish of fried rice. Although in Holland the rice is generally cooked by the usual method and then fried up after it has become cold, traditional Indonesian way of doing it is to wash the rice well, bring it to the boil in water (1 cup rice to 2 cups water), and simmer it gently with the lid on for about 20 minutes. The pan is then wrapped in newspapers, and laid between pillows for at least 30 minutes. Rice treated in this way will, if needed, keep hot for hours, and the grains will become crisp and dry. The next step is to fry 2 finely chopped onions in oil, together with 2 crushed garlic cloves, 1 finely chopped red chilli, and salt. The cooked rice is then added to the pan and fried until golden brown, when ½ lb. diced cooked pork and ham are included; then all ingredients are fried for a further 5 minutes. (Cooked chicken, prawns, or shrimps may be substituted for the pork or ham.) Lastly, a plain 4-egg omelette is made and cut into thin strips which are laid lattice-style on top of the rice mixture (a lightly fried egg may be substituted for the omelette). This dish is eaten with spoons and forks from soup plates, and beer is drunk with it. Roasted peanuts, slices of cucumber cut lengthwise, baked bananas (*pisang goreng*), and chutney are served as side dishes.

Indonesian foods and cooking methods have been introduced into Holland over the years by Dutch colonials. Although some of these dishes are complicated to prepare, they are extremely popular in Holland, where there are Indonesian and Chinese restaurants in most of the towns. Indeed, some oriental dishes have been so far adopted as to become almost a traditional part of Dutch eating, and some, including nassi goreng, may be ordered at any snack bar counter. See also RIJSTTAFEL.

nassi goreng

nasturtium or ***Indian cress*** (*Tropaeolum majus*), cultivated mainly for its brilliantly coloured yellow, orange, and red flowers. The flowers are edible, and were among those (the others being primroses, violets, hollyhocks, and chrysanthemums) used by the Marquis d'Albignac, the French émigré who, according to Brillat-Savarin, started a fashion for them after the French Revolution and made a considerable fortune by visiting large English houses purely to dress salads. The leaves are a useful addition to sandwich fillings, and the green seeds are pickled in white vinegar and used as a substitute for capers. The name "Indian cress" has reference to the Peruvian Indians, for it was from the land of the Incas that Indian cress was brought back by the Spaniards. It was first grown in England in 1596. There is a tuber rooted variety (*T. tuberosus*) grown in Bolivia; its flowers have vivid red stripes on a yellow ground, and the tuber can be cooked like a parsnip, although the taste is very different.

nasturtium

natives, the popular English name for oysters bred in Kentish or Essex oyster beds, such as those at Whitstable and Colne.

na-tlöda, an Alaskan delicacy eaten by the native Ten'a Indians. It is made from bear fat, moose tallow, and sometimes seal oil heated and melted together. It is constantly stirred while it cools, and fresh snow is then added. If snow is not used, a dry substance such as minced, dried fish or berries is added. The whole mixture is frozen before eating. See also KUNDZAR; KUN-TU.

natron, naturally occurring sodium sesquicarbonate, an alkaline salt which is similar in some of its properties to bread soda and is used in place of it in the parts of Norway, Sweden, and the U.S. where it is found.

navarin, I. The French name for a ragoût or stew made from mutton, onions, and potatoes. If it contains other root vegetables, it should be called *ragoût à la printanière*. II. A French soup made from a purée of green peas, garnished with crayfish tails, green peas, and chopped parsley.

navy bean, see HARICOT BEAN.

Neapolitan ice, ice cream made in several different coloured layers, although there is little, if any, difference in taste between layer and layer when it is commercially made. It is sold in the shape of a brick, and served cut into slices.

Neapolitan medlar, see AZAROLE.

neat, an Old English name, sometimes still used in country districts, for an ox; for instance ox tongue can be called neat's tongue.

Nebraska currant, see BUFFALO BERRY.

nebuka, see ONION.

neck, a word which, in the language of butchery, covers not only the neck of the animal, but also the shoulder and ribs. There are three grades of neck cut: *scrag* or *scrag end*, which covers the neck itself and is used for soups and stews; *middle neck*, the portion immediately adjoining, which comprises part of the shoulder and the beginning of the ribs, and is used whole as a roast, or cut into cutlets (gigot chops in Ireland); and lastly, *best end of neck*, which covers the ribs as far as the saddle or loin, and can be used for roasts if left whole, especially crown roast in lamb, or can be divided into chops. These three cuts apply to lamb, mutton, and veal. See Table of Cuts of Meats, page xxi.

nécoras, Spanish for spider crabs which are eaten a lot in Spain, usually boiled or steamed and served with garlic and olive oil.

nectarberry, see HYBRID BERRIES.

nectarine (*Prunus persica*), one of the choicest varieties of peach. The fruit is smooth-skinned and has firm flesh ranging in colour from white to yellow and, somewhat rarely, red. The flavour is delicious. Nectarines are excellent as dessert fruits, but are sometimes also used in cookery and confectionery and for jams and jellies.

neep or **nep,** a Scottish and Old English word for a root vegetable, for example pars-nip (nep) or tur-nip. See also PUNCH-NEP.

   neep brose, a thick Scottish soup from Aberdeenshire, consisting of 2 lb. diced swedes or turnips, 4 oz. bone marrow, 4 tablespoons oatmeal, 2 pints (4 cups) milk, 1 pint (2 cups) water, salt, and pepper. The ingredients are all simmered gently until cooked, and the finished soup should be very thick. The turnips may be puréed if preferred.

   neep purry, Scottish for turnip purée mixed with butter and a good pinch of powdered ginger.

nèfle, French for medlar. *Nèfle d'Amérique* is the French for naseberry, and *nèfle du Japon* French for loquat. All of which are used for tarts and conserves.

neige, French for grated ice, used in the presentation of certain dishes. It is grated with a special grater and the food is placed on top.

nectarine

neige de Florence (Florentine snow), a very fine, light, flake-like white pasta, made in France. Guests put it into their own consommé. It is melted by the hot soup and needs no further cooking.

nelusko, I. A French petit four made from stoned cherries in brandy, filled with *groseilles rouges de bar,* then dipped in *fondant* icing. When cold, they are put into little paper cases, and must be kept at a very low temperature. II. A French soup, made from 2 pints (4 cups) chicken-based velouté mixed with 2 tablespoons *beurre noix* made with filberts (hazelnuts), and garnished with chicken quenelles which have ground filberts mixed with the quenelle forcemeat.

nemes édes, Hungarian for a variety of paprika. It means literally "noble and sweet." A Hungarian dish cooked with paprika has the word *paprikás* added to its title, for example *csirke paprikás* (chicken paprika).

Nemours, à la, I. A French garnish for entrées, consisting of green peas, carrots, and *pommes duchesse.* II. A French garnish for entrées or meat, of sautéed mushrooms, and potatoes cut into olive shapes, also sautéed. III. A French soup of puréed potatoes and mushrooms mixed with milk and garnished with tapioca and mushroom strips. IV. Small French tartlets, made with flaky pastry and filled with a little *mirabelle* (myrobalan) jam, with chou pastry piped on top. They are sprinkled with icing (confectioners') sugar and baked quickly in a hot oven.

nepitella, see MENTA.

nerandzi giristo, Greek for preserved orange rolls, a classical *glyka koutaliou* recipe in which thick-skinned, ripe, golden-yellow oranges are used. The oranges are lightly grated before being washed and scored into quarters. Each quarter of skin is neatly peeled off and rolled up. A threaded needle is passed through these rolls and, when 15 or 20 are on the one thread, this is tied at the ends to make a necklace of orange-skin rolls. The process is repeated until all the quarters are threaded. They are cooked in water until soft, after which they are left standing in cold water for 24 hours (the water being changed several times). They are then drained and the threads removed. Finally, they are boiled up in a syrup of sugar and water, before being sealed in jars. A jam is also made in Greece from oranges. See also GLYKO.

nerkówka, see CIELĘCINA.

neroli, the oil distilled from orange blossoms and used in flavouring confectionery.

néroli, I. French for neroli. II. A small French cake made with 6 oz. (¾ cup) pounded almonds first beaten with 3 eggs, then 12 oz. (1½ cups) sugar, 6 oz. chopped candied peel, and

4 tablespoons orange flower water are added and well mixed. Finally 5 tablespoons melted butter and some corn flour (cornstarch) (about 1 tablespoon for each egg used) are added to absorb the liquid. The mixture is poured into small buttered tins, sprinkled with chopped almonds, and baked in a moderate oven.

nespola, see MEDLAR.

nesselrode, à la, I. A French method of cooking fish, with a particular stuffing and garnish. It was created by Mouy, chef to the Russian Comte de Nesselrode who lived in Paris. Fillets of fish are stuffed with pike and lobster forcemeat, wrapped in puff pastry, and baked in the oven. Lobster sauce with oysters is served separately. II. A French garnish for meat, consisting of glazed chestnuts, mushrooms, and truffles in sauce madère. III. A French soup consisting of puréed woodcock and chestnuts, garnished with woodcock, quenelles, and croûtons. IV. A French game consommé with a predominating flavour of hazel hen, garnished with royale garnish with chestnuts, strips of hazel hen, and chopped mushrooms. See also CONSOMMÉ. V. A French iced pudding, also made famous by the chef of the Comte de Nesselrode. It is made from ice cream or custard flavoured with maraschino and then mixed with half its own quantity of chestnut purée and chopped candied orange peel, with crystallised cherries, currants, and sultanas which have been soaked in Màlaga wine, to taste. The mixture is put into a charlotte mould, sealed, and frozen. When required for serving, it is turned out and the base surrounded with marrons glacés. VI. An American pudding made by soaking 2 tablespoons gelatine in 1 cup (½ pint) milk, then scalding 2 cups (1 pint) milk in a double boiler and adding ⅔ cup (6 oz.) sugar and 5 beaten egg yolks. When cooked to thicken slightly, and cooled, the soaked gelatine is added and stirred until dissolved. Then ⅔ cup chopped raisins, 4 tablespoons chopped crystallised fruits, and ¼ lb. crushed macaroons are added and 2 tablespoons brandy or rum. Finally the 5 egg whites are stiffly beaten and folded in. It is put into a damp mould, chilled, and served with whipped cream.

nettles (*Urtica dioica*), chiefly known as very common and troublesome weeds; however, young nettles (which should be picked, of course, with gloves on) are palatable and very nutritious. The young tips are washed, boiled, and treated in any way that is suitable for spinach. The liquor remaining after the nettles have been cooked (mostly in their own steam, like spinach, for little water is required) was used by generations of country people as a general purifier of the system. Cooked nettles have a dry, bread-like texture. In the 19th century, nettle stalks were used in Scotland to make excellent cloth, thought to be more durable than linen. Nettle shirts are mentioned in the Scandinavian fairytale "The Twelve White Swans." See also NÄSSELKÅL.

nettle brotchán, a broth made from 2 lb. nettle tops, 4 tablespoons flake oatmeal, 2 quarts milk or stock, parsley, and seasoning. In R. W. Joyce's *Lives of the Saints* (1875), it is stated that this soup was a great favourite of St. Columba's. *Brotchán* is the Gaelic word for broth, which at one time was almost as thick as porridge.

nettle kail, a Scottish soup traditionally eaten in Scotland on the evening of Shrove Tuesday. In *Rob Roy,* Sir Walter Scott writes that it was once customary for nettles to be forced under glass for this soup. It is made by stuffing a young cockerel with oatmeal and chopped onion, and simmering it with 2 quarts water, seasoning, several good handfuls of young nettle tops, a handful of oat or barley meal, 2 oz. butter, and a little wild garlic, onion, or mint. The ingredients are cooked until tender.

neufchâtel, a French cow's milk cheese from the Pays-de-Bray district of the department of Seine-Inférieure, Normandy. Neufchâtel is a whole milk cheese which is rennetted while fresh, so that the setting of the curd is delayed a little. After draining, the curd is broken in a mill known as a *lisse-cuille.* It is then lightly salted and packed in tin moulds of various shapes, one of which is loaf-shaped and called a *bonde.* After a few days in the cellars, the cheese develops a white, velvety down of mould. At this stage it may be eaten as *neufchâtel fleur;* if allowed to ferment and ripen, it becomes firmer and pungently flavoured, and is known as *neufchâtel affiné.* It is in season from October to May.

neva, à la, the French title given to a dish of cold stuffed chicken served with Russian salad and mayonnaise. See also POULET, À LA NEVA.

New Brunswick stew, a Canadian casserole, made with string beans, wax beans, new potatoes, onions, green peas, new carrots, cubed smoked ham, cold cubed roast lamb or beef, water, pepper, and salt, all cooked together for about 1 hour in the oven.

New England boiled dinner, a magnificent dish, a speciality of New England, U.S. It consists of corned beef (sometimes a pork shoulder or tongue is used as well), cooked together with onions, carrots, turnips, cabbage, parsnips, potatoes, bay leaf, a little sugar, and water to cover. Extra vegetables are sometimes cooked separately. The meat is served in slices, surrounded by the sliced, variously coloured vegetables, and accompanied by mustard, horseradish, beetroots pickled in vinegar, green tomato pickle, split and buttered corn bread, and, sometimes, a big bowl of cottage cheese sprinkled with caraway seeds.

New England boiled dinner

New England clam chowder, sometimes called Boston clam chowder. A soup made with 2 onions, 2 leeks, and 2 green peppers, all diced, ¼ lb. salt pork and 1 lb. peeled, diced potatoes lightly fried in butter. Then 3 pints (6 cups) fish stock and 3 pints (6 cups) milk, with salt, pepper, sage, and thyme to taste are added, and simmered for 30 minutes. Shortly before serving, 4 cups diced cooked clams, 2 tablespoons parsley and a little worcestershire sauce are added. Salted crackers are served separately. See also CHOWDER.

New England stew, a stew consisting of a shoulder or fore-end of salt pork, sliced turnips, and button onions, all fried lightly to seal, then seasoned, covered with water, and simmered. Diced potatoes are added half-way through cooking, and the stock is thickened before serving.

New England stuffing, a stuffing for poultry. It consists of 4 slices of crustless toasted bread soaked in stock or water, then mixed with 4 oz. diced, fat salt pork, 2 teaspoons chopped sage or thyme, an egg, salt, and pepper.

New Zealand spinach (*Tetragonia expansa*), an annual herb brought to England from New Zealand by Captain Cook. It is also called patent spinach in the London markets. It has pointed leaves and is very creamy when cooked. It may be prepared in any way that is suitable for spinach and is extremely popular in France, where it is called tétragone.

newburg, à la, a method of serving lobster or other seafood. Sliced cooked seafood meat is cut up and sautéed in butter; 2 tablespoons sherry or Madeira and a little paprika is added. Finally ½ pint (1 cup) thick cream with 3 beaten egg yolks is added and heated gently but not boiled. It is also made without the egg yolks.

newburg sauce, an American sauce for shellfish which has been either boiled, baked, or grilled. First 2 tablespoons butter are melted and ½ cup dry sherry added. After simmering slowly for 2–3 minutes, 1 cup thick cream is well mixed in and the mixture is seasoned with salt and paprika. The sauce is poured over well-beaten egg yolks, and the whole placed in the top of a double boiler to cook, being stirred constantly until smooth: dice of lobster coral is sometimes included when lobster is being used. It is served hot.

Newport pound cake, a cake popular in the U.S. First 8 oz. (1 cup) butter is creamed with 6 oz. (1½ cups) flour; then, in a separate bowl, 5 stiffly beaten egg whites are mixed with 10 oz. (1½ cups) powdered sugar and 1 teaspoon vanilla. The 5 egg yolks are beaten until lemon in colour, and then added to the flour mixture. Finally the egg whites and sugar are folded in and 1 teaspoon baking powder is added. The mixture is well beaten and then baked in a greased tin in a moderate oven for 1 hour.

niçoise, à la, I. A French garnish for fish, especially red mullet, consisting of 1 lb. peeled tomatoes and 3 cloves garlic fried in olive oil, with 1 tablespoon capers and 1 tablespoon lemon juice, 1 tablespoon *beurre d'anchois,* and 12 black olives. II. A French garnish for meat, consisting of diced fried tomatoes, garlic, french beans tossed in butter, and *pommes de terre château.* III. A French sauce, consisting of ½ pint (1 cup) mayonnaise to which are added ½ cup pounded pimentos, 1 tablespoon tomato purée, and 2 teaspoons tarragon, all very well blended before mixing. IV. A French salad usually served as an hors d'oeuvre consisting of tunny (tuna) fish, hard-boiled eggs, garlic, tomatoes, anchovies, black olives, capers, other vegetables being added according to season and taste. It is dressed with olive oil and vinegar.

Almost all dishes served à la niçoise contain tomatoes and, usually, garlic; and soups with this title are garnished with cubes of tomato, chervil, and green beans. See also POULET, À LA NIÇOISE.

Nieheimer hopfenkäse, a sour milk cheese from the city of Nieheim in the province of Westphalia, Germany. This cheese is cured between layers of hops. After the cakes of curd have been ripened in a cellar, they are broken up, and salt, caraway seeds, and sometimes beer or milk are added. The mixture is moulded into small cheeses which are covered lightly with straw. When dry, they are packed, with hops, in casks to ripen.

nier, Dutch for kidney. See also KALFSVLEES (GEBAKKEN KALFSNIEREN); KIDNEY.

nierbroodjes, a ragoût of kidneys on bread. First 2 veal kidneys are soaked in water for about 2 hours, during which time the water is changed twice. Then, together with salt, 1 bay leaf, and 1 onion, they are put into boiling water to cover and boiled for about 30 minutes. They are then sliced and added to a sauce consisting of a roux made with 2 tablespoons each of butter and flour, with 1 tablespoon soy sauce, 1 tablespoon parsley, ½ pint (1 cup) stock, and ½ pint (1 cup) cream. Then 6 slices of stale white bread are fried in butter and spread with the kidney mixture. A thick layer of breadcrumbs is placed on top, and each slice is then dotted with butter and browned for about 10 minutes in a moderate oven.

niere, German for kidney. See also KIDNEY.

nierenknödel, an Austrian and German speciality of little balls of minced calf's kidney or liver, beef marrow, eggs, breadcrumbs, and flour, which are poached in soup just before it is served. They make an excellent garnish.

nigger-fish (*Cephalopholis fulvus*), a large grouper found in warm American waters. It is very vivid in colour and ranges from bright yellow to scarlet with blue or black spots, and makes good eating. See also GROUPER.

nimrod, à la, I. A French garnish for game birds, consisting of mushrooms and chestnut purée, french beans, rissoles of marrow bone fat, and *pommes croquettes.* II. A light French game soup, flavoured with sherry or port and garnished with *profiteroles* stuffed with game purée. See also CONSOMMÉ.

niolo, a Corsican goat's milk cheese, at its best from May to December.

nipplewort (*Lapsana communis*), a wild plant of the same order as the sow thistle and the dandelion, which is sometimes used raw in salads, or is cooked as a vegetable and mixed with a leafy and less bitter cultivated vegetable, such as spinach or lettuce.

Nivernais, an ancient French province which, with Morvan, today forms the Nièvre department. It is renowned for the excellence of its root vegetables, and because of the high standard of its turnips, carrots, etc., it has given its name to the classical *nivernaise* garnish. A hot pot with mutton, onions, carrots, and turnips is a speciality of the region, as is an *omelette à la nivernaise.* The smoked hams of Morvan are excellent. The best-known cheese of the region is *fromage sec.*

nivernaise, à la, I. Various French garnishes for entrées. They can be carrots and turnips, cut into olive-shapes, braised lettuce, onions, and plain boiled potatoes; artichoke bottoms stuffed with glazed button onions; small carrots and potatoes cut into olive-shapes. II. Sauce *allemande* garnished with small carrot and turnip balls simmered in butter. III. A French beef consommé flavoured with onion and chervil, garnished with tiny balls of carrot and turnip, and royale garnish. See also CONSOMMÉ. IV. A French thick soup of puréed carrots and turnips garnished with diced root vegetables.

niza, queijo de, a farmhouse-made variety of the Portuguese *serra* cheese.

njure, Swedish for kidney. See also KIDNEY.

njursauté, 2 calf's or 4 pigs' kidneys sliced, dipped in flour and fried in butter. Then ½ lb. diced green bacon is lightly fried in another pan, and 6 mushrooms and 2 onions, chopped and sliced, are added to the bacon and cooked with it. The kidneys are stirred in and seasoned; ½ pint (1 cup) beef stock is poured over, and when this is boiling, 4 tablespoons cream and 1 tablespoon sherry or Madeira are added. It is served with boiled rice or mashed potatoes.

nocciolo, Italian for dogfish, used in *burrida.*

noce, Italian for walnut, used in Italy in many ways, and particularly as the main ingredient of an excellent sauce (*salsa di noci*) made with 4 oz. shelled walnuts pounded, 4 tablespoons chopped parsley, a pinch of salt, 3 tablespoons butter, 4 tablespoons breadcrumbs, and ¼ pint (½ cup) olive oil all mixed together. When the mixture becomes thick, 3 tablespoons milk or cream are included. The sauce should be very green, coloured by the parsley, and well blended, although it need not be too smooth. It is excellent with fish or pasta, or simply spread on bread.

noce moscato, Italian for nutmeg, used especially in *tortelli di erbette,* and *anolini* in Parma, and in *tortellini* in Bologna. It is generally used with spinach and as a flavouring in ricotta cheese.

nockerln, small, oval balls made of flour, butter, and milk, which are traditional in Germany and Austria. They are made with 1 oz. butter and ½ pint (1 cup) milk heated together, but not boiled; then 1 egg is whisked in. This mixture is added slowly to 9 oz. (2½ cups) flour until a thick paste is obtained. The paste is made into little oval shapes which are first poached in boiling salted water for 3 minutes, then drained, and finally turned in hot butter, although not browned. Sometimes 2 oz. semolina or 2 cups breadcrumbs are used in place of flour in some varieties of nockerl. Nockerln are served as an accompaniment to goulash, soups, stews, or roast game. They are also known as *butternockerln* (see *butternockerl-suppe*). A *nockerlbrett* is a thin piece of wood, incorporating a handle, on which the nockerl paste is spread before small pieces of it are cut off and dropped into water or a soup.

lebernockerln, a variation of the above using milk-soaked bread and 4 oz. finely chopped liver, fried very gently in butter with a grated ½ onion and 1 tablespoon chopped parsley. Balls about the size of a hazelnut are formed, and are poached in boiling soup for about 7 minutes, or until they rise to the top.

leberreis, literally "liver-rice," as *lebernockerln,* but instead of being formed into balls the mixture is pressed through the holes of a perforated spoon, so that pieces about the size of grains of rice fall into the boiling soup, where, owing to their size, they are cooked more quickly than the larger *lebernockerln.*

salzburger nockerln, an Austrian delicacy which is a variety of nockerl, but more elaborately made, and served as a pudding. First 3 eggs are separated, and the egg whites whipped until stiff with 1 teaspoon icing (confectioners') sugar. The egg yolks are added, and 1 teaspoon flour. Large heaped spoonfuls of the mixture are fried in hot butter for about 30 seconds, after which the pan is put into a hot oven until the nockerln have browned slightly. (Ideally the centre should be light and creamy, the outside golden brown and frothy.) They are then put on a hot dish and sprinkled with more icing sugar.

noisette, I. A term in French butchery which means a round slice of meat cut from the fillet, rib, or leg of lamb or mutton. Slices should weigh not less than 2 oz. Traditionally, each person is served with two of them. The term is often used loosely to designate a small round fillet of beef or veal. II. A general French culinary term meaning flavoured with, or made from, hazelnuts. III. A French sauce composed of sauce hollandaise with *beurre de noisettes.* IV. Potatoes cut to resemble the size and shape of hazelnuts, then fried in slightly browned butter (*pommes noisette*).

noisettines, small French cakes consisting of 2 layers of short crust pastry sandwiched with hazelnut-flavoured *frangipane* cream, or with cream whipped with ground hazelnuts.

noix, I. French for nut and walnut. Sliced green walnuts, traditionally picked before June 21, St. Jean's Eve, are peeled, skinned, and served as an hors d'oeuvre in Touraine; they are marinated in verjus, shallot, and diluted wine vinegar, and sprinkled with chopped chervil before being served. An oil is also made from walnuts called *huile de noix.* It has a distinctive flavour. See also WALNUT. II. French for the pancreas, the round sweetbread at the top of the breast. See RIS.

noix de veau, one of the three major muscles in a leg of veal. It is almost heart-shaped and is first larded, then cooked by roasting or braising. It is also used for roulades. For garnishes served with this cut, see TENDRONS.

noix patissière, the top rump or thick end of the loin of veal; sometimes called the round in English. In the U.S. it corresponds to what in beef is called the sirloin tip.

nøkkelost, a Norwegian semi-hard, rennetted, salted, and spiced cow's milk cheese. The cheese is made from either whole or skimmed milk, and is spiced with whole cloves and cumin seeds. There are four qualities of nøkkelost, and the law specifies that each cheese be marked accordingly: *helfet* (whole fat), not less than 45% butter-fat; *halvfet* (half fat), not less than 30%; *kvartfet* (quarter fat), not less than 20%; *mager* (fatless), less than 20%. It is the Norwegian version of the Dutch *Leyden* cheese. The city of Leyden has crossed keys as its city arms, and nøkkel is Norwegian for "key," hence nøkkelost. See also OST.

nonat, a tiny Mediterranean fish which is thought to be the fry of the goby. It is a great delicacy, and is prepared like whitebait. Sometimes it is fried and eaten cold with oil and vinegar or mayonnaise. It must be eaten very fresh and is only found on menus of establishments that are near to where they are caught.

nonnette, a commercially made, small, round, iced gingerbread which is a speciality of Dijon and Rheims, France.

nonpareille, I. A variety of French pear, tart in flavour and so used mostly for cooking. II. The French name for small capers pickled in vinegar. III. The French name for very tiny, multicoloured sugar balls used for cake decoration. They are known in England as "hundreds and thousands."

noodles, the English generic name for any ribbon-like pasta, which has many variations, especially in the Italian forms where the variation is also dependent on the local name there. See also MIEN; NUDELN; PASTA.

noques, an Alsatian speciality, similar to *nockerln.* The small oval-shaped balls are made from 6 oz. (1½ cups) flour, ½ lb. (1 cup) butter, a pinch of nutmeg, 2 eggs, and two additional egg yolks. Noques are used in soups and as an entrée, with cheese.

noques à la viennoise, a sweet dish served hot or cold, consisting of noques with sugar added to taste, poached in sweetened milk. The milk is then poured off and made into a custard to be served over the noques.

Norfolk hollow, a small round English roll, crisp and biscuity and not unlike a *Dorset knob.*

Norfolk plover (*Burhinus oedicnemus*), also known as stone curlew, the largest member of the plover family and found all over Europe, North Africa, and India. It visits England in the summer and nests chiefly in Norfolk and Suffolk. It is now protected by law in the British Isles, but in other parts of the world it is killed and cooked by any method that is suitable for plover.

Norfolk pudding, an old English pudding made with sliced, lightly fried apples, sweetened to taste, covered with Yorkshire pudding batter and baked in fat for 30 minutes.

normande, à la, a method of cooking or serving various foods which is common to Normandy in France. This is a very rich cuisine in which cream, butter, and eggs are used extensively. It is noted for the excellence of its seafood (see DIEPPOISE, À LA); the *pré-salé* lamb and mutton; *tripe à la mode de Caen;* Rouen ducks (*caneton à la rouennaise*); and cheeses such as camembert, *pont-l'evêque,* and *livarot.* Many of the foods are cooked in *grasse normande.* There are no vineyards, but extensive apple orchards which produce excellent cider, and the spirit calvados. The famous liqueur *Benedictine* is made at Fécamp, Normandy. I. A method of serving fish, particularly sole, which is braised in white wine to cover and served with a garnish of oysters, mussels, crayfish, and mushrooms poached in white wine, with smelts (2 for each sole) fried in egg and breadcrumbs, sliced truffles, fleurons or small diced croûtons, and sauce *normande.* II. A method of serving small cuts of meat or poultry after they have been cooked, by pouring cider over them and adding calvados to the pan juices to make a sauce. III. A thick soup made from puréed potatoes, dried haricot beans, leeks, turnips, and cream, garnished with chervil. IV. French beans or salsify covered, when cooked, with cream in which egg yolks have been blended. V. A method of serving potatoes. See POMME

DE TERRE (POMMES À LA NORMANDE). VI. A method of cooking pheasant. See PERDREAU, À LA NORMANDE.

normande, sauce, a classical French sauce served with fish, especially sole. The head and bones of the fish to be served are boiled for 30 minutes in equal quantities of white wine and water, with mushroom trimmings, a shallot, and seasoning. This fumet is then strained and used as the basis for the sauce. To prepare, ¼ pint of the fumet is mixed with ½ pint (1 cup) sauce velouté (made with the remainder of the fumet). When this is reduced to half, 2 egg yolks mixed with 2 tablespoons cream are added (though the sauce is not reboiled), and finally 2 tablespoons fresh butter are beaten in, in small pieces as for a sauce béarnaise. The sauce must not boil. After straining, a further 3 tablespoons cream are added and the sauce is poured over the cooked fish. The *normande* garnish is then put round the edges, and the top of the dish is lightly browned under a grill.

Normandy pippins, whole, peeled, cored, and dried apples which are soaked before cooking and then simmered in syrup until tender. These whole, dried apples are nowadays quite rare in Britain, but can be bought at very good grocers from time to time.

nörs, Swedish for smelt, a popular fish in Sweden on the smörgåsbord. See also STRÖMMING.

norvégienne, a French name given to many different preparations in cookery, from soup to sweet. I. A thick puréed potage consisting of cabbage and turnips blended with sauce velouté and garnished with strips of cooked beetroot. II. A method of presenting fish. The whole fish are poached, skinned, then decorated with prawns; cucumber stuffed with a purée of smoked salmon, hard-boiled eggs, marinated tomatoes, and Russian mayonnaise accompany the fish. It is served cold. III. A garnish for meat and poultry, consisting of cooked noodles tossed in butter, with sauce madère. IV. A sauce made from mashed hard-boiled egg yolks seasoned with mustard, vinegar, and olive oil. It is usually served with cold fish. V. *Omelette à la norvégienne* is the French name for baked alaska. (Fruits such as apple or banana, poached or baked and placed on vanilla ice cream, then covered with meringue and grilled quickly, are also called *à la norvégienne*.) *Omelette à la norvégienne* was invented by an American physicist, Sir Benjamin Thompson (1753–1814) whose work earned him the title of Count Rumford.

Norway haddock (*Sebastes norvegicus*), a haddock much prized gastronomically in all Scandinavian countries. It is also found off the Atlantic coasts of the U.S. A bright rose-red when fully grown, it is sometimes known as rosefish. See also HADDOCK; RÖKTFISKPUDDING.

Norway lobster, see DUBLIN BAY PRAWNS.

Norwegian cheeses, see OST.

nostrale or *nostrano*, an Italian word which means "homemade" and is used by the inhabitants of any rural district to describe their own local cheeses. The word is also used for a regional wine or salame which is only consumed in the locality in which it is made.

notch-weed, an alternative name for purslane, which grows in sandy soils by the sea. It can be cooked like spinach, or the young buds can be pickled in vinegar.

Nottingham batter pudding, a regional English pudding made from peeled and cored apples, the core-holes being stuffed with equal quantities of butter and sugar and a pinch of nutmeg. The batter is made by mixing 4 egg yolks with 6 tablespoons flour and a little water or milk and water, and beating them until a thick cream is achieved, which should then be left to stand for 1 hour. Then the stiffly beaten egg whites are added and the mixture is poured over the apples, which are baked for about 45 minutes until cooked.

nouet, a French culinary word for a muslin bag containing spices, herbs, or other flavouring and tied with string, which is cooked with liquids in order to impart flavour to them without leaving solid particles behind. It is removed before the preparation is served, and can be washed and used again. It was formerly called *mignonette*. There is no single word for it in English, although it is used in English cooking. See also MIGNONETTE.

nougat, I. A French sweetmeat (confection) of which there are two chief kinds. White nougat is made commercially at Montélimar in France. It is prepared with ½ lb. sugar fast boiled with ½ lb. honey to 260°F; then 1 stiffly beaten egg white mixed with 1 tablespoon orange flower water and almonds or other nuts is stirred in over a low heat. Glacé cherries are sometimes added. The nougat is set between rice paper. A similar recipe (*turron*) is also a speciality of Spain. A softer variety is made by melting fine sugar to a caramel and stirring in chopped browned almonds. It is turned out onto an oiled marble slab, and is moulded into various shapes for decoration. II. An oil cake made from the residue of walnut oil is called nougat in the south of France.

nougatine cakes, *génoise* cake mixture which, when cool, is cut into 3-inch squares and layered 3 or 4 times. Each layer is spread with praline cream, and the top is iced with chocolate *fondant*.

nudeln, German for noodles. In both Germany and Austria they are invariably homemade. They are served both as an accompaniment to meat, fish, cheese, and eggs, and as a sweet. See also FLECKERLN; NOODLE; NUDELTEIG; SPÄTZLE.

dampfnudeln, sweet noodles, made from 6 oz. (1½ cups) flour, ⅓ oz. yeast, 2 teaspoons butter, 2 egg yolks, 1 heaped tablespoon sugar, and 4 tablespoons milk, all mixed and left to rise, before rolling and cutting into strips. The noodles are poached in milk and butter, in the oven, and served with a custard flavoured with vanilla. See also KÄRNTNER NUDELN; MAULTASCHEN.

nudelteig, plain noodle dough made from 8 oz. (2 generous cups) flour, with a pinch of salt, heaped onto a board. A well is made in the centre, and 2 eggs are beaten with ¼ cup water. This is poured gradually into the well, being worked all the time until a smooth dough is formed. It is rolled to paper-thinness, laid on a towel, and left to dry before cutting into strips. See also NUDELN.

feiner nudelteig, fine noodle dough, made with 3 oz. flour to 2 egg yolks and 1 tablespoon water, then prepared as above.

nuez, Spanish for nut. *Nuez de nogal* is walnut, used extensively in Spain in both sweet and savoury dishes.

nun's beads, an old Scottish savoury made from 4 oz. pounded hard cheese mixed with 2 tablespoons white breadcrumbs and 3 beaten egg yolks. The mixture is formed into walnut-sized shapes, covered in puff pastry, and fried until golden in butter or oil.

Nürnberger eier, an egg dish from Nuremberg, Germany. Shelled, hard-boiled eggs are dipped in batter and fried in deep hot oil. They are redipped and refried 3 or 4 times and then served with a wine sauce.

Nürnberger lebkuchen, German Christmas' cakes from Nuremberg. They are made with 8 oz. (1 cup) sugar and 4 egg whites stirred to a light foam, to which 1 lb. honey, ½ lb. ground almonds, 1 tablespoon mixed spice, 3 oz. chopped candied peel, and 6 oz. (1½ cups) flour are added. The mixture is thickly spread on thin wafers, dried for 2 hours, baked, and then iced. The cakes will keep for months in a tin.

Nürnberger würste, German würst from Nuremberg, made from pounded lean pork and diced fat bacon, flavoured with kirsch and seasoned with thyme, marjoram, nutmeg, salt, and pepper. They are sold in 100-gram (3½ oz.) sections. They are generally served fried in butter. *Nürnberger rostbrat-würste* are smoked sausages grilled over beech charcoal, a speciality of Lower Bavaria. See also WÜRST.

nuss, German for nut.

nussgebäck, small biscuits (cookies) eaten on New Year's Eve, made from ½ lb. sweet melted chocolate mixed with 4 tablespoons cream or milk, 4 tablespoons ginger biscuits crushed to crumbs, 4 tablespoons each of icing (confectioners') sugar, and chopped almonds or walnuts. When the ingredients are well mixed, spoonfuls are dropped onto waxed paper, flattened, and left to get cold and hard.

nuss-strudel, see STRUDEL.

nusstorte, a delicious German cake made by soaking 3 oz. breadcrumbs in a little rum, then beating 1 egg and 2 egg yolks with 1 heaped tablespoon sugar for 20 minutes. The breadcrumbs are then added to the egg mixture with 1 lb. (2 cups) ground walnuts, ¼ pint (½ cup) milk, and finally 2 stiffly beaten egg whites are folded in. The mixture is put into a well-buttered sponge tin and baked in a moderate oven for 1 hour. It can be eaten plain, or layered with cream.

nut, a fruit which consists of a hard or leathery shell enclosing an edible kernel, which is what is usually referred to as the nut. The plants which bear them vary from the large Brazil nut and chestnut trees, to the shrub-like filbert and the almost vine-like herb that bears the peanut. Nuts are extremely nutritious and can be eaten raw or used in cooking. Certain nuts, such as almonds, walnuts, and peanuts, produce valuable oils which are excellent in frying or for salads. The coconut contains a milky liquid used in curries. All nuts can be used in sweet and savoury dishes.

nutmeg (*Myristica fragrans*), a tree which grows wild in the Banda Islands off Indonesia. It is also the commercial name for the fragrant spice that is the kernel of its seed, extracted after a lengthy and complicated drying process. The husks are known as mace. Nutmeg is used, very finely grated, for various culinary purposes, particularly as an ingredient in milk puddings or custards. It is also excellent with vegetables of the cabbage family, and a pinch is often used in beef stews, in sauces, and in cakes. In the Dutch East Indies, the entire fruit of the nutmeg tree is eaten, preserved in syrup.

nymphes, see GRENOUILLES.

nyre, Danish for kidney. See also KIDNEY.

nyreskiver, kidney fritters made from 10 mutton kidneys (previously skinned and soaked for about 3 hours in cold water and 2 teaspoons lemon juice) lightly fried in butter. Then they are dipped in a batter which consists of 4 oz. (1 cup) flour, a pinch of salt and pepper, and a pinch of sugar blended with ½ pint (1 cup) water and 1 tablespoon oil. They are deep fried until crisp and golden brown. The fritters are served with browned butter or tomato sauce, and with watercress as a garnish.

nyre, Norwegian for kidney. *Nyrefett* is the term for the suet from the outside of the kidneys which is rendered down and used for cooking and also in pastry.

oats (*Avena*), the berry of a cultivated grass possibly derived from the wild oat *Avena fatua*. Cultivation is thought to have commenced in Central Europe, but the variety most in use today, and now regarded as the best, was originally obtained from plants found occurring naturally in a potato field in Cumberland in 1788. Oats are hardier in respect of both climate and soil-condition than any of the other cereals. The inner husks of oats are used in Ireland, Scotland, and Wales to make *sowans*. This cereal is also much used as animal fodder, particularly for horses and hens.

oatcake, see BANNOCK; HAVER; HAVRE.

oatmeal, the meal obtained by grinding oats after the husk has been removed. Oatmeal is used for many dishes, especially porridge, but also in cakes, soups, some stews, and for stuffings and dumplings. It is a particularly important ingredient in Scottish cooking. It may be ground into three grades: fine, medium, and coarse. The latter two are used mainly for porridge, but also in soups, haggis, and black and white puddings; the fine oatmeal is the main ingredient of oatcakes and some scones. Oatmeal is also used in Scotland for coating fish such as herring or trout before they are fried. Midlothian oatmeal is said to have the finest flavour of all. In the U.S., oatmeal is used in bread, cookies, and home-made pork sausage. See also BANNOCK; BROONIE; BROSE; BROTCHÁN; CROWDIE (II); FITLESS COCK; GROATS; GRUEL; HODGILS; SKIRLIE; SOWANS.

oatmeal soup, a delicious soup, traditional in the Highlands of Scotland. It is made with 1 heaped tablespoon butter melted in a saucepan to which 1 large peeled and sliced onion is added, and fried until soft but not coloured. Seasoning to taste is added, followed by 2 level tablespoons medium or fine oatmeal. This is cooked for a few minutes, then 1 pint (2 cups) chicken stock is poured in, covered, and simmered gently for 30 minutes. The mixture is sieved or liquidized, returned to the saucepan, and heated up with ¼ pint (½ cup) thin cream or top of the milk. It is garnished with a generous sprinkling of chopped parsley.

oberskren, an Austrian sauce, composed of ½ pint (1 cup) *sauce crème* mixed with 2 tablespoons grated horseradish, 1 teaspoon paprika, 1 teaspoon sugar, salt, and ¼ pint (½ cup) thick cream.

oblade, the French and English name for a Mediterranean fish of the *Sparides* family which is not unlike a grey bream. It may be grilled, fried, or cooked à la meunière, but has not such a good flavour as red bream. It is called *oblada* in Spain. See also SARGO.

obst, German for fruit.

obstessig, a vinegar made from fermented fruit pulp and juice. See also TRAUBEN; VINEGAR.

obstsuppe, German fruit soup, which is eaten a great deal in the Hamburg district and in Berlin. The basic recipe is the same for all such soups. The fruit is cooked, with water, to a pulp, then sieved and slightly thickened with potato flour or corn flour (cornstarch) (1 oz. flour to 1 quart pulp), with sugar to taste. Sometimes a little white wine is added. If the soups are served hot, tiny macaroons or other biscuits accompany them, or little semolina dumplings are floated in them. See also APFEL (APFELBROTSUPPE); HAGEBUTTEN; HOLUNDER-SUPPE; KALTESCHALE.

obuolainis, a Lithuanian yeast cake, topped with apples or plums, which generally accompanies coffee. A yeast sponge is made with 1 lb. (4 cups) flour, 1 oz. yeast, 2 teaspoons sugar, and 3 tablespoons melted butter. Then 2 eggs are blended in, and the sponge is left to rise. The mixture is rolled into oblong shapes which are put into deep pans, brushed with melted butter, topped with slices of apple or plum, and finally sprinkled with sugar and cinnamon. They are again left to rise, then baked for 35 minutes in a moderate oven.

obuolainis tortas, a traditional apple cake. Crustless, dried pumpernickel or malt bread is made into breadcrumbs, and these are cooked in layers with a mixture of apples, sugar, and butter, like apple charlotte. The cake is eaten at *Pabaigtuves,* the Harvest Festival.

oca, occa, or **oka,** a South American tuber resembling a large walnut, with a yellow and red-brown skin, and white, floury flesh. Ocas are best when stale, being rather acid when fresh. They are scraped, not peeled, before being cooked, and are used in all dishes *à la peruvienne,* and also as a separate vegetable. In France they are often served mashed, well-seasoned, and with cream. They may also be dried in the oven and then gently simmered in wine. Oca was introduced into England from Lima, Peru, in 1829 and grows well both there and in Wales. It is also called oxalis.

oca, see GANSO.

ochra, see OKRA.

ochroszka, Polish for the national adaptation of the Russian rye soup, *okroshka,* which is made with fermented rye, hard-boiled eggs, crayfish tails, cold pork, sour cream, mustard, and flour. It is served chilled. See also OKROSHKA.

ochsenfleisch, literally "ox flesh," the German term for beef; see also RINDFLEISCH. *Ochsenmaul* is German for ox cheek; *ochsenschwanz* is oxtail. *Ochsenzunge* is ox tongue, served hot or cold in Germany, often with horseradish. In both Germany and Austria it is also sometimes served with sauerkraut as an accompaniment. See also RIND; TONGUE; ZUNGE.

octopus, a genus of edible marine cephalopod mollusc with eight suckered arms. It is found in the more temperate coastal waters of the Atlantic, and in the Mediterranean, where it is eaten a great deal. It is related to the squid and the cuttlefish. After being beaten for some time, the tentacles or arms are cut in pieces, coated with flour and egg, and fried in hot oil. In Marseilles the pouch is washed and stuffed with a mixture of onions, the finely chopped tentacles, garlic, parsley, and egg yolks; then it is simmered until tender in a mixture of half olive oil and half white wine. In Brittany it is known as *minard* and *pieuvre.* See also CALAMARES; CALAMARETTI CALAMARI; CALAMARY; CHIPIRONES; CHIOCOS; HTAPODI; POLPO; POULPE.

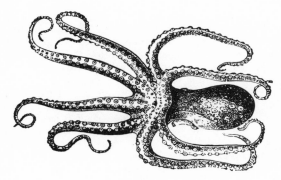

octopus

ocvrti piščaněc, a Slovenian method of cooking chicken by first dipping the bird in egg and breadcrumbs and then roasting it.

oedicnème, French for a type of stone curlew, a bird of medium size. The meat is full of flavour, and it can be prepared in the same way as woodcock.

oester, Dutch for oyster. See also OYSTER. There is an ancient custom in Holland that, when seeing the New Year in, oysters (and nothing else) should be eaten, and champagne drunk. Nevertheless, being extremely expensive, oysters are still regarded there as something of a luxury. The famous Imperiales, oysters from the province of Zeeland, are served in the half shell with pepper and lemon, on ice, accompanied by toast and butter.

oeufs, French for eggs. *Oeufs à la coque* are boiled eggs; *oeufs à la poêle* or *oeufs frits* are fried eggs; *oeufs au four* are baked eggs; *oeufs brouillés* are scrambled eggs; *oeufs durs* are hard-boiled eggs; *oeufs farcis* are stuffed hard-boiled eggs, and *oeufs pochés* are poached eggs. Other methods of preparing eggs in France are described here. See also EGG; OMELETTE.

oeufs en cocotte, eggs cooked in small, flameproof, earthenware moulds, known as cocottes. The moulds are greased and the eggs can either be cooked plain for about 10 minutes in a hot oven, or garnished with cream, herbs, vegetables, mushrooms, ham, poultry, or cheese. In the U.S. this is called shirred eggs. See also VOLTAIRE.

oeufs en gelée, any egg dish cooked en cocotte or moulé, covered with aspic when cold, and served cold.

oeufs mollets, eggs which have been boiled until the whites are solid, but the yolks, although hard on the outside, exude a little liquid in the middle. This method of serving hard-boiled eggs is preferred in France. They are often shelled before use, but not invariably.

oeufs moulés, eggs cooked in a mould lined with herbs, ham, poultry, mushrooms, etc., then cooked in a *bain-marie* with a lid on for 8–10 minutes.

oeufs sur le plat, eggs cooked in a large round metal dish, in the oven or on top of the stove. The method is the same as for *oeufs en cocotte,* but usually means that more than one egg is cooked in the same dish.

French garnishes for eggs are listed below, the eggs to be cooked by soft-boiling or poaching unless otherwise stated. These are only the most common, for there are nearly a thousand of them, but the main classical garnishes described throughout this book will often be found to contain a reference to the fact that they can be served with eggs.

oeufs à l'alsacienne, fried eggs on a layer of sauerkraut and ham, surrounded by demi-glace. The same garnish may be used for poached eggs or *oeufs en cocotte.*

oeufs à l'ancienne, eggs covered with sauce velouté to which Madeira is added.

oeufs à l'antiboise, eggs with *nonats* and Gruyère.

oeufs à l'anversoise, eggs garnished with hop shoots cooked in butter or cream, and masked with sauce *crème.*

oeufs à l'aurore, eggs with sauce *aurore.*

oeufs à la bayonnaise, eggs with Bayonne ham and sautéed cèpes, served on fried bread.

oeufs à la bénédictine, eggs served on top of *brandade de morue,* masked with sauce *crème.*

oeufs à la bordelaise, eggs with cèpes cooked à la bordelaise.

oeufs à la bourguignonne, eggs poached in red wine with herbs, served on fried croûtons with sauce *bourguignonne.*

oeufs à la catalane, eggs with separately fried tomatoes, eggplant, garlic, and parsley.

oeufs à la clamart, eggs in tartlets with cooked green peas and *sauce crème* with pea butter.

oeufs à l'espagnole, fried eggs with fried onions, tomatoes, and sweet peppers.

oeufs à la flamande, eggs with cooked endive or hop shoots and cream.

oeufs à la florentine, eggs with spinach and sauce *mornay.*

oeufs à l'italienne, eggs with ham and sauce *italienne.*

oeufs à la languedocienne, fried eggs with fried eggplant and garlic-flavoured tomato fondue.

oeufs à la lyonnaise, fried eggs, with fried onions and *cervelas.*

oeufs à la milanaise, fried eggs served on a bed of macaroni, with tomato sauce.

oeufs à la nantua, eggs with crayfish and sauce *nantua.*

oeufs à la parisienne, oeufs sur le plat served on a bed of chicken forcemeat mixed with smoked tongue, truffles, mushrooms, and demi-glace.

oeufs à la portugaise, eggs served on cooked tomatoes, sometimes masked with sauce *portugaise.* They are also cooked *sur le plat* with tomato fondue at the bottom.

oeufs à la provençale, eggs with tomatoes and eggplant.

oeufs à la romaine, fried eggs served on spinach mixed with chopped anchovies.

oeufs à la Saint-Hubert, eggs with ground game and sauce *poivrade.*

oeufs à la tripe, see *oeufs soubise.*

oeufs à la villeroi, eggs soft-boiled or poached, coated with sauce *villeroi,* dipped in egg and breadcrumbs, and fried in deep oil. Tomato sauce is served separately.

oeufs à la zingara, poached eggs served on croûtons fried in butter and covered with a slice of lean ham, all masked with sauce *zingara.*

oeufs ambassadrice, I. *Oeufs en cocotte* cooked with foie gras and truffles underneath, and asparagus tips on top. II. Poached eggs in puff pastry cases with *salpicon* of truffles and foie gras, masked with sauce *suprême.*

oeufs Apicius, eggs served on large mushrooms, with braised crayfish tails and sauce *normande.*

oeufs au beurre noir, eggs with *beurre noir* poured over them.

oeufs au beurre noisette, eggs with *beurre noisette* poured over them.

oeufs au chasseur, eggs with chopped mushrooms, sautéed chicken livers, and sauce *chasseur.*

oeufs aux anchois, eggs with anchovies.

oeufs Bagration, eggs with macaroni mixed with truffles, cream, and sauce *crème.*

oeufs bercy, oeufs sur le plat with grilled sausage and tomato sauce.

oeufs Chateaubriand, eggs with artichoke hearts filled with sauce béarnaise.

oeufs choisy, fried eggs with diced cooked potatoes and braised lettuce.

oeufs doria, fried eggs with grated white truffles.

oeufs miroir, poached eggs or *oeufs en cocotte* glazed under a grill or in the oven so that the white over the yolk is shiny.

oeufs mornay, eggs with sauce *mornay.*

oeufs opéra, eggs with chicken livers and asparagus tips, with reduced veal gravy.

oeufs Parmentier, eggs with potatoes. An egg is sometimes put into a large, half-cooked jacket-baked potato, with butter and cream, then baked.

oeufs Rossini, eggs cooked in various ways, but always served with foie gras, truffles, and sauce *madère.*

oeufs soubise or *oeufs à la tripe,* hard-boiled eggs served with onion sauce.

When omelettes are described by any of the titles given above, it means that they are filled with a stuffing containing the ingredients of the appropriate egg garnish.

See also OEUFS MEULEMEESTER; TAPÉNADE, OEUFS DURS EN.

oeufs meulemeester, a traditional Belgian method of serving eggs, from Bruges in the north. First 6 hard-boiled eggs are shredded and mixed with 6 chopped prawns, then covered with a sauce for which 1 tablespoon each of chopped chervil and parsley, ½ pint (1 cup) cream, 1 tablespoon melted butter, 2 teaspoons french mustard, salt, and pepper are mixed well together and lightly heated. Then 1 oz. grated cheese is sprinkled over, and the whole is dotted with butter and browned in a hot oven. See also OEUFS.

offal (*variety meats*), a collective term for all the edible parts of an animal, apart from the main carcase. Tail, head, brains, tongue, and feet are all classed as offal, as are also the entrails—heart, liver, lungs, kidneys, sweetbreads, tripe, and testicles. In certain meats, such as pork, the smaller intestine, called chitterlings, is also offal. In the U.S. offal is known as organ meats, side meats, or variety meats. In Belgium, a special dish called *les choesels* combines several entrails, and it is delicious. In France, the calf's mesentery is also cooked, usually by being first boiled in a court bouillon and then cut into pieces and fried. This is called *fraise de veau.* See also CALF; HEART; KIDNEYS; LIVER; OX; PETTITOES; TONGUE.

ogeechee lime (*Nyssa ogeche*), the fruit of the gum tree which grows in the southern states of the U.S. It is olive-shaped and slightly acid.

ogórki, the Polish word for ridge cucumbers and for salted cucumbers. See also MIZERJA.

ogórki faszerowane, stuffed cucumbers. The cucumbers are first blanched, then slit lengthwise and stuffed with a mixture of minced onion, veal, fish, bread, and eggs. Cucumbers are also sometimes fried in Poland, either stuffed or unstuffed.

ogurtsy, Russian for cucumbers which are eaten extensively in Russia for *zakuski,* and also served stuffed and sautéed with deer. See OLÉN.

svejhie ogurtsy so smetanoy, sliced salted cucumbers, drained and mixed with sour cream, then sprinkled with lemon juice and chopped dill.

ohra, Finnish for barley.

ohrajauhopuuro, barley meal porridge. It is sometimes served with pork.

ohrajauhovelli, barley meal gruel made from 2 tablespoons butter, 3 pints (6 cups) milk, and 1 pint (2 cups) water heated together; then ½ cup barley meal and salt to taste are added. The gruel is cooked gently for about 30 minutes.

ohrarieska, barley meal scones. To prepare, 1 pint (2 cups) skim milk or water is well mixed with 1 tablespoon salt and approximately 1¾ lb. (6 cups) barley meal. The resulting dough is then shaped into rounds which are baked in a hot oven for 15–20 minutes. They are served with butter. See also UUNIPUURO.

ohukaiset, Finnish for small, thin pancakes, served with jam or sugar. They are made with 1¾ pints (3½ cups) milk, ½ pint (1 cup) water, 1 teaspoon salt, 2 tablespoons melted butter, and ½ lb. (2 cups) coarse flour, all well mixed to a batter which is then left for 1 hour. Before using, 2 eggs beaten with 1 teaspoon sugar are added. See also PANNUKAKKU.

oie, French for a fully grown goose; a goose up to six months old is a *oison.* In France, the grey goose, known as *petite,* can weigh up to 10 lb. and is good to roast. The big goose, the *grosse,* can reach almost double that weight. These geese are mainly found in the neighbourhood of Toulouse and are known as Toulouse geese. The Strasbourg goose, used for systematic and intensive fattening or cramming, is bred largely for its liver, which is made into *pâté de foie gras.* Both varieties are used for *confit d'oie,* salted and preserved goose, which is made into dishes with dried beans (*cassoulet*) and rich stews (*alicot*). See also GOOSE.

oie de vise, a Belgian method of cooking goose. It is simmered with onions, cloves, and peppercorns; then a sauce is made from 4 large garlic cloves simmered in 1½ pints (3 cups) milk, to which are added 4 quartered rusks. The sauce is thickened with 6 egg yolks and ½ pint (1 cup) cream, and poured over the jointed goose.

oie en daube, made from cleaned goose, 1 calf's foot, 1 pig's trotter (foot), ¼ lb. diced bacon, 3 cloves, 4 chopped garlic cloves, 6 peeled and sliced shallots, 1 pint (2 cups) red wine, 1 tablespoon mixed parsley, thyme, and basil, 2 bay leaves, water, 1 small glass brandy or rum, salt, and pepper. All the dry ingredients are put into a large pan and the liquid poured over barely to cover. A little more water may be added if necessary. The dish is covered and cooked in a slow oven for about 5 hours. When it has cooled, the goose is lifted out and all the meat removed from the bones and placed in a deep dish. The liquor is strained and any fat spooned off. The stock is then poured over the goose, and the whole is put in a refrigerator or a very cool place until the liquid is set into a soft jelly. It is served hot, or cold and jellied, with potatoes baked in their jackets and an orange salad.

confit d'oie, meat from the goose cut into convenient pieces and rubbed all over, both the skin and the cut side, with about ½ lb. *gros sel.* The pieces of goose are placed in a *terrine,* and the fat is removed from the inside and melted down. The goose meat is now left for 5–6 days if it has been freshly killed, for 2–3 days if bought in a shop; then it is taken out and cooked in the fat. It must be completely covered and cooked very slowly for 2–3 hours, until the juice is pink and not red. It is then drained, and the pieces of meat put in a deep earthenware jar. When the fat has cooled, it is strained and poured over all the meat until it is covered, the jar being then tied down with paper and string. The confit will keep for several months. See also LOU TREBUC.

oignon or *ognon*, French for onion, used a great deal in France, both raw in salads and garnishes, and cooked in stews, soups, sauces, etc. It is also served *à la grecque*, and is the basic ingredient of 3 important French sauces: sauce *bretonne*, sauce *Robert*, and sauce *soubise*. See also ONION.

oignon en fritot, onion sliced in rings and served fried in batter.

oignon farci, onion stuffed with chopped meats and braised in stock.

oignon frit, fried onion rings, sometimes first dipped in flour before frying.

oignon glacé, glazed onion, cooked in stock with 2 oz. (¼ cup) butter for each pint of liquid. It is then sometimes sprinkled with sugar, which gives it a brownish colour.

oignon rôti au four, unpeeled, whole onion baked in the oven until soft (about 1½ hours).

soupe à l'oignon, see SOUPE

soupe à l'oignon gratiné, see SOUPE.

oignonade or *ognonade*, I. A stew containing a very high proportion of onions. II. Finely chopped onion sweated in butter or cooked in white wine.

oil, a form of fat, liquid at room temperature, derived in the main from vegetable and nut products. All oils made from vegetable matter contain polyunsaturated fatty acids, which make them beneficial to health. Animal oils are not generally used for cooking, although the fat melted by the heat when the animal is being cooked, called dripping, is frequently utilised; it is only oily when hot. The most common animal oils are cod liver oil and whale oil. Oil has many uses in the kitchen, primarily for frying and in the composition of sauces and salads, but it makes good pastry and cakes as well. The best-known oils are almond oil, cottonseed oil, peanut oil, olive oil, palm oil, poppyseed oil, sesame seed oil, sunflower seed oil, safflower oil, and walnut oil. See also FAT; HUILE; LARD; OLIO; OLIVE OIL; SOYA BEAN, OIL.

oille, an old French name for a *potée* made from meats, poultry, and vegetables, with herbs. The name is thought to come from the word *oule*, an earthenware cooking pot used in the southwest of France.

oiseaux sans tête, literally "birds without heads," a Belgian speciality. First 16 thin slices of beef are spread with a mixture of 2 cups fresh breadcrumbs, ¼ lb. each of minced pork and veal, 1 chopped onion, 2 beaten eggs, a pinch of nutmeg, ¼ pint (½ cup) cream, 2 tablespoons butter, and seasoning. They are rolled up round the stuffing, and the rolls are then braised in stock to cover, with chopped celery and 1 sliced green pepper, for about 1½ hours. Sometimes mushrooms are added. It is garnished with parsley and lemon slices before serving.

oison, see OIE.

oka, a wholly Canadian cheese which is made by Trappist monks at Oka in Quebec. In appearance and taste it is not unlike the Italian *bel paese*.

oka plant, see OCA.

okra (*Hibiscus esculentus*), a plant of the cotton family and a native of the West Indies. A common English name for it is ladies' fingers. It is a mucilaginous and aromatic plant, bearing sticky, furry fruit-pods that are used in much Balkan, and American, cooking. There are 2 varieties of fruit-pod: the oblong *gomba* and the round *bamya*. Both types are used as an ingredient in soups, curries, and pickles, and the gomba is an essential ingredient in the New Orleans gumbo to which it has

given its name. The young pods are also served as a vegetable dish with chicken, mutton, and shellfish. They are boiled in salted water and drained; then sometimes they are added to onions and tomatoes that have been fried in butter or oil with a seasoning of salt and a little cayenne pepper. The seeds are also occasionally used as a substitute for pearl barley. Extensive canning of okra is carried out in the U.S. and in the Balkans. See also BAMIES.

okrochka, a traditional dish from the Balkans. To prepare it 2 large chopped onions are fried in a little fat. About ¼ pint (½ cup) oil is placed in an oven dish and covered with slices of washed and salted eggplant. On top of these are placed first a layer of minced beef and then a layer of the onions, and this alternate layering is continued until all the ingredients have been used up. The dish is cooked in the oven with 1 pint (2 cups) stock until almost all the liquid has been absorbed (about 1–1½ hours), when a mixture of beaten egg yolk and ¼ pint (½ cup) cream is poured over it. The dish is again placed in the oven and cooked until golden brown.

okroshka, a traditional Russian cold sour soup. A soup tureen is half-filled with ½ pint (1 cup) each of sour cream and sour milk. This is diluted with 2 pints (4 cups) *kvass*, which is a semi-sparkling beverage obtained by fermenting malt, rye flour, and sugar with water. It is seasoned with 1 teaspoon mustard, salt, and pepper. Then ¼ lb. finely chopped roast veal, 2 tablespoons sliced breast of hazel hen (grouse), the same of ox tongue and ham, 4 chopped crayfish tails, and a piece of ice for each serving are added. If the crayfish is omitted, 2 sliced hard-boiled eggs are added instead. It is served sprinkled with chopped dill.

okroshka iz ryby, cold sour fish soup. Small pieces of firm fish, sturgeon or sterlet, are fried in oil, and when cold, are placed in a soup tureen. Diced lobster and crayfish tails are added, and the tureen is filled up with *kvass*, to which are added seasoning, salt, and pepper. The soup is served chilled, sprinkled with chopped chervil and tarragon, and finally garnished with sour cream.

okse, Norwegian and Danish for ox; *oksekjøtt* is beef, which is very popular in Norway, being much used in the preparation of meat cakes, as well as being cooked in joints. See also BEEF; BIFF; KJØTT; MEDISTERKAKER.

okseragu, a rich beef stew, like a goulash.

sprengt oksebryst, boiled and pickled breast of beef. A 5-lb. breast of beef is left for 12 days in a cold pickle consisting of 4 oz. brown sugar, 1 oz. saltpetre, and 2 lb. coarse salt, which have all previously been boiled up together. While in the pickle, the meat should be turned once in 24 hours. It is drained, washed, and covered in boiling water, then simmered until tender (about 3 hours). Then it is served with mustard, swedes (turnips), and potatoes mashed together.

oktapothi, see HTAPODI.

okun, Russian for perch, a fish which is very popular in Russia, and often used for soup such as *uhka*. See also PERCH.

okun so smetanoy, a usual method of preparation. The perch is cut into portions which are rolled in flour, fried in butter, and served with a sauce made from fish stock and sour cream thickened with flour and butter.

oladyi, a Russian yeasted cake resembling a thick pancake. It is made with 1 oz. yeast, dissolved in 2 cups warm milk or water, mixed with 1 lb. (4 cups) flour. The dough is then left to rise. After it has risen, 2 eggs, 2 tablespoons sugar, 1 tablespoon melted butter, and salt are added, and the mixture is fried in spoonfuls in hot oil. Sometimes raisins or slices of apple are mixed in before the little cakes are fried, but usually they are served hot, plain with sugar, honey, jam, or cheese.

Old Heidelberg cheese, an American cheese from Illinois, made from cow's milk. It is a soft, surface-ripened cheese, very similar to *liederkranz*.

olén, Russian for deer. Many varieties are eaten in Russia, particularly elk and roe deer. Deer is always hung for some days and marinated before cooking. A haunch of elk, weighing about 8 lb., is usually roasted, but before this takes place it is larded with 4 oz. (½ cup) butter and 1 teaspoon each parsley, sage, pounded juniper berries, and tarragon, all chopped and creamed together. The haunch is then wrapped in 2 or 3 layers of greaseproof paper or foil, and cooked in a moderate oven for 3–4 hours. About 30 minutes before it is ready, the haunch is taken from the paper and well basted with ½ pint (1 cup) melted butter and ½ pint (1 cup) game stock. Sometimes sour cream and the juice of either pickled cucumbers or lemons are added to the baste. The joint is dusted with flour, and the pan juices are reduced on top of the stove and served with the roast.

Cutlets are sautéed in butter and served on a small baked tart of *kasha* flavoured with cinnamon; they are covered with a pepper sauce (which resembles sauce *poivrade*) mixed with chopped cherries and raisins. Another method is to sauté the cutlets and garnish them with stuffed, sautéed cucumbers and sautéed boletus in sour cream. Alternative garnishes are hard-boiled plover's eggs filled with caviar, or olive-shaped cucumber pieces simmered in butter. In the Caucasus the cutlets are served on a bed of boiled *kasha,* with lightly fried chopped shallots mixed with chopped garlic, crushed coriander seeds and fennel, which are all put into a sauce *poivrade* with a trickle of white wine. The sauce is boiled up and poured over the cutlets.

A Russian sauce for serving with roast venison (olénina) consists of 1 pint (2 cups) game stock reduced with a pinch each of mace, nutmeg, and cayenne pepper, 8 juniper berries, and salt. When half the quantity is left, 3 tablespoons red currant jelly, ½ pint (1 cup) red wine, a large nut of butter rolled in flour, and a little brandy are added. The sauce is allowed to boil for a few minutes and is then served with the venison, but in a separate dish. See also DEER; ELK; REINDEER; SAIGA; VENISON.

olénina, see OLÉN.

oliebollen, Dutch doughnuts, always served on *Sint Nicolaas Avond* with *appelbeignets* and *slemp.* To make them 1½ oz. yeast is dissolved in 3 tablespoons tepid milk. Then ¾ lb. (3 cups) flour is put in a mixing bowl and mixed with 3 eggs, included one by one. Then ¾ pint (1¼ cups) milk is added and well mixed in, followed by 2 tablespoons sugar and 1 tablespoon each chopped candied peel, lemon peel, and raisins. The yeast mixture is put in, and the dough is covered and left in a warm place to rise for 1½–2 hours. Then small balls are formed with floured hands, and are fried in deep, hot oil (370°F or 180°C). These are then drained and sprinkled with sugar.

oliekoeken, a savoury variety of *oliebollen,* made without sugar or fruit, but with cheese, spinach, chopped ham, etc.

olio, Italian for oil. *Olio di oliva,* olive oil, is used extensively for cooking on the Ligurian coast and in Genoa, Tuscany, Piedmont, Naples, and the South. In Rome it is used in varying proportions with *strutto* (pork fat or lard) or butter, and it is used generally throughout Italy for frying. The finest olive oil is thought to come from Lucca, but there is an excellent Ligurian olive oil, as well as a Sardinian variety made from the fruit of the trees in the vicinity of Sassari. See also OIL.

oliva, Italian for olive. See also OLIVE.

oliva ripiene, large stoned olives stuffed with forcemeat as for *anolini,* then coated with egg and breadcrumbs and fried. They are traditional in Ascoli.

olive (*Olea europea*), a plant that yields both a useful, edible fruit and the olive oil of commerce, one of the principal ob-

jects of its cultivation all over the world. It belongs to a section of the natural order *Oleaceae,* of which it has been taken as the type. The genus *Olea* includes about 35 species, scattered widely over the Old World from the basin of the Mediterranean to South Africa and grown nowadays as far east as New Zealand. The earliest record of its cultivation is in an Egyptian inscription of the 17th century B.C. The frequent allusions to the olive by the earliest Greek poets indicate that it was indigenous to Greece; Italy, however, retains its ancient pre-eminence in olive cultivation, and in that country there are many varieties: the *cerignola* is an enormous green olive from Puglie and the oliva spagnuola is rather bitter and has a very large stone. The olives from Castellamare resemble sloes, while those from Rome are small, jet-black, wrinkled, and have a characteristic smoky taste. In Sardinia, the colour varies from yellow to purple and brown. There are many varieties, too, in France, Spain, and other Mediterranean countries. Olives were introduced into Mexico and California by the Jesuits, and are now grown there extensively; they are particularly plentiful in Butte county, northeast of Tulare, California.

The olives of commerce are the green and the black. Green olives are picked before they are fully ripe, and are treated differently from black olives, which are picked ripe and used as a relish or appetizer. Green olives are mostly used, stoned, for garnishing and flavouring, but it is also customary to stuff them with anchovy, pimentos, etc. In Italy they are served fresh, salted, and also stuffed, and are used as part of an antipasto, as a garnish, or are eaten on their own with a glass of wine. In Sicily, the method of preparing green olives is to soak them for several days in cold salted water flavoured with fennel. Greece also makes extensive use of them in cooking, and of the oil. Spain and Portugal also produce a large crop. In the area in Mexico and the U.S. where they are grown, they are used extensively in cooking, being added to salads, Welsh rarebits, meat and poultry casseroles, and pasta dishes. See also ELLIES; OLIVA; OLIVE; OLIVE OIL.

olive, French for olive, used extensively in garnishes in France, and in cooking generally. In the south of France olive oil is generally used for cooking. See also OLIVE.

olives cassées, a speciality of Provence. First 6 lb. green, round olives are cracked on a board, the stones left unbroken. They are put into an earthenware pot filled with water, and allowed to float about. The water is changed every day for a week, and when the olives have lost their bitter taste, the water is changed for the last time and ½ lb. salt and a big

olive

bunch of fresh fennel is added. The olives keep for 2–3 months, and are usually prepared in October, for Christmas. They are used for cooking with small game birds, especially thrush, as well as being eaten raw. (The thrushes are wrapped in bacon, browned in butter, then cooked with onion, tomato, garlic, fennel, parsley, olives cassées, salt, and pepper.)

olive oil, the oil extracted from olives, which is widely used for many culinary purposes, and is considered to be the finest-tasting vegetable oil. There are several grades of olive oil, and the best is extracted from good fresh olives that are simply crushed; the oil smells of the fruit itself, and its colour is greenish. An inferior quality comes from a second crushing, and the colour, taste, and smell are weaker. Both kinds keep well in an airtight container. A second grade olive oil, inferior to that derived through crushing, is extracted by pressure under heat. It is whitish in colour and becomes rancid if exposed to air. See also OLIVE.

olivet (*bleu* and *cendré*), a French cow's milk cheese of the *coulommiers* type. It is a factory-made, soft, whole milk cheese, inoculated with blue mould. *Olivet bleu* is in season from October to June; *olivet cendré* from November to July.

olivette, see HUILE, D'OEILLETTE.

olivette glacate, an Italian stuffed veal roll made from a large thin slice of veal from the top of the leg, on which are placed chopped ham, parsley, and Parmesan cheese. The meat is then rolled up, tied, and braised in white wine, stock, and a little tomato purée.

olla podrida, the old Spanish name for an elaborate soup–stew, called after the pot (*olla*) in which it was cooked. Nowadays it is usually called *cocido* or *puchero*.

øllebrød, a Danish beer porridge. In Denmark, porridge made from dark beer, pumpernickel, and wholemeal bread is a traditional food which can be served as a breakfast or supper dish. In some parts of the country it is served instead of the soup course, and it can also be accompanied by herrings and anchovies as a first course. It is made from 8 oz. each of pumpernickel and stale wholemeal bread soaked for 12 hours in 1½ pints (3 cups) cold water, then cooked over boiling water until a thick paste is formed. Then 2 pints (4 cups) dark beer, together with 3 tablespoons sugar, peel of ½ a lemon, and a small stick of cinnamon are added to the paste, and it is simmered for a few minutes, being constantly stirred. Before being served, and when the pan is off the heat, a beaten egg yolk is stirred in. Whipped cream accompanies this dish.

øllebrød, a Norwegian beer cream. This dessert is served with croûtons fried in butter. To prepare it 2 egg yolks, castor sugar to taste, ¼ pint (½ cup) cream, 1 pint (2 cups) light beer, and ½ pint (1 cup) water are beaten until slightly thick and frothy, in a double saucepan, over water which is just off the boil.

oloron, a French cheese from the Béarn district, made from ewe's milk. It is in season all the year round.

ølsuppe, a Norwegian beer soup, consisting of 4 pints (8 cups) milk, 2 heaped tablespoons ground rice, peel of 1 lemon, and 4 pints mild beer. All are stirred together until boiling, when sugar is added. This soup is served with wheaten biscuits.

omble chevalier, French for char, which is the best fish in the Savoy and Swiss lakes. It is not found in rivers. In Switzerland it is usually poached in red or white wine with shallots and mushrooms. See also CHAR.

ombre commun, French for grayling, gastronomically one of the most highly prized river fish in France. It is prepared in any way as for trout. It is never found in lakes. It is at its prime from October to December. See also GRAYLING.

ombre de mer, French for umbra; also called *ombrine*. See UMBRA.

omelet, see OMELETTE.

omeleta, Portuguese for omelette. A Portuguese omelette does not in the least resemble the classic French omelette. The eggs are beaten and stirred in a pan with a little oil and whatever filling is being used, so that, when cooked, the mixture resembles scrambled eggs. The most popular fillings are cooked meat, shellfish, smoked ham, and tomatoes. See also OMELETTE; OVOS; TORTILHA.

omelette or *omelet,* an egg dish, the name of which is believed to derive from the Romans, who prepared a mixture of eggs and honey known as *ova mellita*. This is no doubt the origin of the sweet omelette, and the savoury one could have evolved from it. The omelette most generally served is savoury, such fillings as ham, mushrooms, tomato, and cheese being the most common. It is not difficult to prepare a good omelette, provided certain basic rules are followed. The pan must be thick (an omelette pan is of course the best, but is not essential); the pan must be hot, and on an easily adjustable heat; butter should be used as a first choice, good olive oil as a second—in either case, not more than 1 oz. (2 tablespoons) should be used for a large omelette, and less for a smaller one. (Too much fat only makes it greasy and less light.) A reasonable-sized omelette is 3 eggs per person but more can be used if desired. They should be beaten in moderation, and seasoned with salt and freshly ground pepper. The butter or oil is melted in the pan, and when it is hot, but not browned or smoking, the eggs are poured in. Some French chefs add the hot butter to the eggs, and this makes a very smooth omelette. It is essential that the eggs should be gently stirred and shaken before they set; small pockets are covered by tilting the pan and letting the uncooked egg run over. If the omelette is to be filled, this should be done while the top is still runny, by placing the filling on one half, then quickly folding over the other half and slipping the omelette onto a warmed plate. The whole operation must be performed rapidly, or the omelette will become overcooked, dry, and leathery. It is ready for eating when the inside is still soft and creamy.

Sweet omelettes can be filled with puréed fruits, jams, or creams, or can be flambéed with rum or a liqueur while being served. Many sweet omelettes are known as "fluffy omelettes" (omelette soufflé). This indicates that the eggs are separated, then the egg yolks beaten and the egg whites stiffly beaten, before they are combined; but the omelette is cooked in the usual manner.

In Spain, most omelettes are not folded. The beaten eggs are poured over various mixtures of fish, meat, or vegetables, and cooked with them. See also BROOD (BROODOMELET); EGG; FRIAR'S OMELETTE; FRITTATA; MUNAKAS; OEUFS; OMELETA; OMELETTE; OMLET; SKINKA (SKINKLÅDA); TORTILHA; TORTILLA; UGNSOMELETT.

omelette, French for omelette. In France, chiffonades, *duxelles,* and *salpicons* are all used to fill omelettes, and many omelettes, as well as containing different fillings, are also garnished with classical garnishes or sauces. (See OEUFS.) Chicken or other poultry, ham, game, kidney, mushroom, seafood, etc., are all cooked before they are added to the eggs, and the name is often taken from the main ingredient, for example, *omelette aux champignons,* etc.

omelette à la Lorraine, sautéed lean bacon, grated Gruyère cheese, and chopped spring onions (scallions) added to the eggs before they are cooked. The omelette is sometimes served flat instead of folded, having been placed under a hot grill for a few minutes at the end.

omelette à la lyonnaise, chopped parsley and finely sliced, lightly sautéed onions added to the eggs. If the omelette is served flat, a few drops of heated vinegar are sprinkled over, and it is garnished with *beurre noisette*.

omelette à la nanceienne. Two omelettes are left flat; the bottom one is covered with 2-inch rounds of lightly fried black pudding, and the second is placed on top and garnished with chopped parsley. Concentrated veal gravy with *beurre noisette* is poured round.

omelette à la nivernaise, an omelette incorporating ham and chives, served flat.

omelette aux fines herbes, chopped parsley, tarragon, chervil, etc., added to the eggs after they have been beaten and before they are cooked.

The following are some French sweet omelettes.

omelette à la dijonnaise, made with a filling of jam, cream, and crushed macaroons.

omelette à la norvégienne, see NORVÉGIENNE.

omelette mousseline, made from separated eggs, the egg yolks mixed with cream before the stiffly beaten egg whites are added.

omenat, Finnish for apples.

paistetut omenat, baked apples, which in Finland are served hot with cream or vanilla sauce.

omlet, Polish for omelette. Typical Polish omelettes are: *omlet z rakami,* crayfish or shrimp omelette; *omlet z szczawiem,* sorrel omelette; *omlet po Serbsku,* a Serbian potato and cheese omelette; *omlet zwijany biszkoptowy,* a rolled sweet biscuit (cookie) omelette. See also OMELETTE.

onglet, a French cut of beef which in English terms would correspond to the top of the skirt. It is very juicy but can be a little tough, so that it is best used for carbonades or sautés. See also diagram, page xxiii.

onion (*Allium cepa*), a native of central Asia, the onion is now probably the most universally used vegetable and flavouring agent. There are innumerable varieties, of which the smallest are grown in boxes, like mustard and cress, and eaten in salads. Spring onions (scallions) are next in size, and these are ordinary onions picked when the beds of seedlings need thinning. When the plant has formed bulbs, these are picked at an early stage as pickling onions. They are also used cooked, as garnishes and for hors d'oeuvre, when they are called button onions. In England, the name Spanish onion is given to any large, mild-flavoured onion, and in the U.S. to the large red variety. The potato or underground onion (var. *aggregatum*) is a particularly early variety. The tree or Egyptian onion (var. *proliferum*) is another variety which produces small bulbs instead of flowers, as well as larger bulbs at the roots. Bermuda onions are large and mild in flavour, like the Spanish onion, and are highly thought of in Bermuda, the West Indies, and the U.S. The Welsh onion or cibol, and the nebuka, are perennials and produce not onions but small leeks with tubular leaves; in fact they are Japanese in origin. The sand-leek or *rochambole* from the Danish *rockenbolle* (onion on rocks) which resembles the Welsh onion, is grown in parts of Ireland, Scotland, England, and the U.S., and has a faintly garlicky flavour. Some members of the onion family, such as chives, are grown not for the bulbs, but only for the leaves, which have a very mild flavour of onion.

The onion was worshipped in ancient Egypt, and it appears in temple decorations. Alexander the Great found onions in Egypt and brought them back to Greece, as he thought they inspired martial ardour. In certain parts of India they are only prepared by men, as it is thought they are an aphrodisiac and might cause infidelity among the womenfolk.

Onions are eaten in innumerable different ways: raw, pickled, boiled, braised, or fried and in soups, stews, and sauces. They have a pungent taste when raw, and the juice affects the eye ducts and produces tears. See also CEBOLLA; CIPOLLA; LØG; LÖK; OIGNON; SHALLOT; SPRING ONION; ZWIEBEL.

onion sauce, a classical English sauce made with ½ lb.

peeled onions boiled in water until soft. They are then cut into fairly large pieces and mixed into 1 pint (2 cups) white sauce, seasoned to taste. The sauce is served hot, with 2 tablespoons cream added at the last moment. It is served with roast or boiled mutton and with goose.

opah (*Lampris regius*), a deep sea fish found in all Atlantic waters and quite highly prized as food. It is also known as moonfish, and sunfish. It has a pinkish flesh not unlike salmon and can be cooked in the same way. In Norway it is known as *laksestørje* (large salmon).

open sandwich, a sandwich without a top layer of bread.

opiekanki z grochu, Polish fritters, made with 1 lb. (2 cups) cooked, puréed split peas mixed with 4 tablespoons breadcrumbs, 2 tablespoons mixed herbs, 1 tablespoon butter, 1 minced onion, egg, and seasoning. This mixture is shaped into small patties which are then dipped in egg and breadcrumbs and fried in deep hot oil.

opletek, a semi-transparent wafer of unleavened dough which has scenes of the Nativity stamped on it. It is eaten on *Wigilia* (Christmas Eve) in Poland.

opossum (*Didelphis virginiana*), a small, ugly nocturnal animal, about the size of a cat, commonly found in the southern and eastern states of America. From this sly little creature, which pretends to be dead when capture is imminent, we get the expression "playing possum."

possum and sweet potatoes, a highly appetizing dish which tastes not unlike rabbit and comes close to taking pride of place in the history of southern cooking. The skinned opossum is simmered in water with red peppers, salt, and pepper for 30 minutes. It is drained, put in the roasting tin with half the reduced stock, and roasted for 1 hour (halfway through cooking, peeled and sliced sweet potatoes are added). Sometimes the opossum is stuffed with breadcrumbs, onion, red pepper, and the chopped liver.

opphengt melk, a Norwegian sour cream dessert. Unpasteurised milk and cream are allowed to curdle in the usual way. The cream is then skimmed from the milk, and the latter is strained through a cloth without being stirred. After several hours, when the whey has drained off, castor sugar and the sour cream to taste are mixed with the curds, and this mixture is served with more sugared cream.

oquassa (*Salvelinus oquassa*), a small char with a delicate flavour, which is found in the lakes of Maine, U.S. See also CHAR.

orach or **orache** (*Atriplex hortensis*), a plant now rather widely cultivated in France, but a native of Tartary. It has broad, arrow-shaped, pliable leaves which are cooked in the same way as spinach. The three main varieties cultivated are *arroche blonde,* with pale green leaves; *arroche rouge,* with dark red stems and leaves; and *arroche verte,* with large, dark green leaves. The wild or mountain orach is an edible weed common in England and Ireland, where it is called "fat hen." In the U.S. it is called French spinach or sea purslane.

orange (*Citrus sinensis; C. aurantium; C. bergamia; C. reticulata*), a familiar fruit of commerce, the produce of a tree closely allied to the citron, lemon, and lime. There are at least 80 different varieties of orange, though all may be traced to one or other of two kinds: the sweet or China orange (*C. sinensis*) and the bitter bigarade or Seville orange (*C. aurantium*). Besides the wide-spread use of the fruit as an agreeable and important article of diet, the sweet orange, with the lemon and lime, is rich in citric acid and possesses to a high degree the antiscorbutic properties that make it also valuable medicinally. The flowers of both sweet and bitter varieties are used in the perfume industry, and the peel is candied and used in baking and confectionery. The bitter orange, cultivated in India from a very early date, was brought to southwest Asia by the Arabs, and thence to Africa and Spain. An orange tree of this variety is said to have been planted by Saint Dominic in the year 1200 in the garden of the monastery of Saint Sabina, Rome, and still to bear fruit. This orange is valuable for the aromatic and tonic properties of the peel. It is used for making marmalade and preserves, for serving fresh in salads, and as an ingredient in sauce *bigarade*. *C. bergamia* has the most highly scented peel of all, which is used largely in perfumery, and for the making of preserves and confectionery. The mandarin orange of China (*C. reticulata*) is a flattened sphere in shape. The peel readily comes off at the slightest pressure, and the pulp has a peculiar and distinctive flavour. The smaller tangerine orange, valued for its fragrance, is derived from the mandarin. Maltese or "blood" oranges, mainly from southern Spain or Italy, are distinguished by their red pulp, and the fact that they have no pips. Jaffa oranges come from Israel, and are large and sweet, with much juice. A popular variety of seedless orange, native to Brazil and now grown in California, is known as the navel. Oranges are grown on a large scale in California, Florida, and many southern states of the U.S., and a thriving industry is engaged in the output of frozen or canned orange juice. See also APPELSIN; BERGAMOT; BIGARADE; MERLIN; ORTANIQUE; SATSUMA; TANGELO; UGLI.

oranges baked with raisins and honey

orange flower water, a fragrant liquid collected from the distillation of neroli, the oil which is obtained from the orange flower. It is used for flavouring cakes, custards, creams, etc., and can be bought at a good chemist's shop. It was immensely popular in 19th-century England, and is still used a great deal in France.

orange sauce, an American sauce served with cold roast duck and galantine of chicken or game. To prepare it 1½ tablespoons sugar, 3 tablespoons red currant jelly, and the grated peel of 1 orange are beaten well together in a basin; then 1 tablespoon orange juice and 1 tablespoon lemon juice are added, with salt and cayenne pepper. Sometimes 1 tablespoon port is added. See also BIGARADE, SAUCE.

orange rockfish (*Rosicola pinniger*), a sea fish commonly found off the coast of California. It is about 2 feet long and makes good eating.

orangine, a French cake made by layering a *génoise* cake which has been flavoured with candied orange peel, and covering each layer with *crème patissière*. The cake is re-formed, and iced with orange *fondant* icing.

oransje, see APPELSIN.

orata, Italian for the daurade of Provence. It is similar to an English sea bream, and is often cooked in *cartoccio*, or with a wine sauce flavoured with sultanas.

oregano, see MARJORAM.

oreiller de la belle aurore, literally "pillow of the beautiful Aurora," a very elaborate game pie said to have been the favourite dish of the famous French chef Brillat-Savarin. It is made from pheasant marinated in fine brandy and Madeira, to which is added a goose liver studded with truffles; ¼ lb. each of rabbit, pork, veal, and bacon are all pounded separately, then mixed together with 2 truffles and seasoning. This mixture is then added to the marinated pheasant, etc. Boned woodcocks, chicken livers, mushroom, and shallot, with herbs, are all arranged very elaborately in a large dish, with the pheasant and forcemeat given above and it is all covered with puff pastry decorated with a variety of fancy shapes. When cooked and still warm, good game stock, which will jelly when cold, is added through the hole in the top of the pastry lid.

oreilles de porc, French for pig's ears, usually served braised with root vegetables and stock, or boiled and then coated with melted butter and breadcrumbs and grilled with a spicy sauce. All pork is especially good from the Sainte Ménéhould district. See also PORC.

oreilles de veau, French for calf's ears, cooked in the same ways as *oreilles de porc*.

orektika, see MEZES.

organ meats, an American term for offal; also called variety meats and side meats.

orientale, à la, I. A French garnish for meat consisting of tomato halves or tartlet cases filled with rice à la *grecque*, and croquettes of sweet potatoes. II. An entrée of eggs or vegetables or fish which are poached in white wine and olive oil, with diced tomatoes, seasoned with fennel, bay leaf, garlic, parsley roots, and saffron, then served cold in the stock, with slices of lemon. III. A French method of serving fish fillets or lobster, in newburg sauce seasoned with curry powder; boiled rice is served separately.

orientale, sauce, a sauce *américaine* flavoured with curry powder and mixed with fresh cream.

origan, see MARJORAM.

origano, Italian for wild marjoram. It has a stronger scent than the English equivalent, and is always used in a good *pizza napoletana*.

original, French for moose, eaten a great deal by French-Canadians. It is prepared in the same way as venison.

Orkney cheese, a cheese from the Orkney Islands, off Scotland. It is a creamy cow's milk cheese of the cheddar type, but more flaky.

Orléans, I. A French consommé of chicken, thickened with tapioca and garnished with three different types of chicken quenelle: one with cream, one with tomato, and one with pistachio nuts or spinach. It is sprinkled with chopped chervil. II. A French beef consommé, garnished with chicory royale, diced french beans, flageolets, and chervil. See also CONSOMMÉ.

orloff, à la, I. A French garnish for meat consisting of braised celery, braised lettuce, tomatoes, and *pommes château*. II. A garnish for saddle of lamb or veal which is braised and sliced, and then has each slice coated with onion purée (*soubise*). The meat is put back into its original shape with a slice of truffle between each slice, and the reconstituted joint is then covered with sauce *soubise* and garnished with asparagus tips, olives, and braised celery. III. A Russian method of preparing sterlet. Fillets of sterlet are poached in a mixture of white wine, fish stock, mushroom essence (extract), and cucumber pickle. They are garnished with small barrel-shaped cucumbers which have been stuffed with fish forcemeat and simmered in butter; also with stuffed olives, stuffed crayfish heads, mushrooms, and *vesiga*.

orly, à la, a French method of preparing fish. The fish is usually filleted, then skinned and dipped in batter, after which it is fried in deep oil. Fresh tomato sauce is served separately. The most common fish prepared in this way is fresh haddock or whiting.

ormer (*Haliotis tuberculata*), a shellfish which is abundant on the rocks of the Channel Islands, where it is highly prized gastronomically. When eaten hot, it is prepared in the same way as scallop, but it may also be pickled. It is also called ear-shell because of its shape.

orphie, French for garfish, used a great deal in France for *cotriade*.

ørred, Danish for trout, a popular fish in Denmark, and usually served poached in salted water with a hot sauce hollandaise.

ørret, Norwegian for trout. Neither river nor sea-trout is washed in Norway, as washing is believed to soften the flesh. When preparing the fish, the entrails and head are removed and the tissue over the backbone and sides is loosened, after which the fish is soaked for 2 hours in a marinade consisting of equal parts of oil, vinegar, and fish stock. It is drained and then lightly coated with a beaten egg and fried. See also FISK; RAKØRRET.

ørret i rømmesaus, trout fried in butter until cooked, when sour cream and chopped chives are added.

orsay, d', a French consommé of chicken, garnished with poached egg yolks and strips of pigeon, pigeon quenelles, and chervil. See also CONSOMMÉ.

orseille, French for a paste made from lichen, used mainly to tint tongue pink.

ortanique, a loose-skinned, sweet, fleshy and juicy fruit of the orange family. It is a seedless hybrid, one parent being the *satsuma*. It is more regular in shape than the *ugli,* which it otherwise resembles. It was introduced into Britain in 1954, and is grown chiefly in the higher and more rainy regions of Jamaica, where the sweet orange does not grow so well. See also ORANGE.

ortolan (*Emberiza hortulana*), a European bunting of exceptional flavour. At one time the ortolan was plentiful, but numbers have decreased, and although highly praised by the gastronome, it is rarely seen today on a menu outside France. Until fairly recently it was netted and kept in captivity on oats and millet, after which it was considered suitable for the domestic market. At least 1 ortolan is allowed for each person, and it should not be drawn, as the trail is esteemed for its delicate flavour. It can be prepared and cooked in the same way as partridge or quail. In 18th-century England, ortolans were wrapped in vine leaves and roasted on a spit; nowadays, the two stages of this method are reproduced, separately, in the preparation of ortolans in the Landes district of France, where they are a speciality. There, they are either cooked on a spit or roasted in their own fat. Another method is to wrap them in vine leaves, brush them with butter, and roast them in a little salted water in a very hot oven for about 5 minutes. This preserves the fat of the little birds, which is greatly esteemed. When they are eaten, the bones are usually crunched up as well, and all recipes for quail can be used. See also GIBIER.

orzechy, Polish for walnuts.

orzechy włoskie z cukrze, glazed walnuts, which are made by simmering peeled walnuts in a thick syrup of sugar and water for a few minutes. They are then removed with a toothpick dipped in iced water and spread out, well spaced, on a greased dish to dry. Chestnuts are also prepared in this way in Poland. See also KASZTANY.

orzo, a Greek pasta used in many main dishes and in soups. See YIOUVETSI.

oseille, French for sorrel, used for chiffonades and to flavour salads, omelettes, sauces, and soups. It is also cooked in the same way as spinach, then puréed and served as a garnish for veal, and particularly for the *alose* (shad) of the Loire.

osetrina, Russian for sturgeon, which is eaten a great deal in Russia, the roe also being much prized, of course, for caviar. The fish itself can be prepared in a number of ways. It is usually cut into steaks or slices which are poached in white wine with mushrooms, butter, and stock, then garnished with lemon slices and strips of salted cucumber. It is also fried, or stuffed with breadcrumbs, onion, and egg and baked in stock or sour cream. Another method is to cut the fish into small chunks, sprinkle them with salt and pepper, then thread them on skewers and grill them evenly, basting with melted butter. The fish is removed from the skewers and served with grilled tomatoes, fried onions, and sprigs of fried parsley. Sturgeon heads are sold separately in Russia and are often stuffed, as described above, and then boiled; or they are used in the preparation of various fish soups such as *okroshka is riba* or *uhka*.

osetrina finlyandskaia, sturgeon cooked in the Finnish manner. It is made with 6 slices of sturgeon simmered in butter, then placed on a bed of buckwheat gruel or *kasha* mixed with chopped mushrooms which have been simmered in butter. All is covered with sauce *smitane,* sprinkled with Parmesan cheese and dotted with nuts of butter. The dish is browned, and decorated with strips of anchovy.

oshàf or *oshàv,* a Bulgarian compote of dried or fresh fruits.

ossenhaas, Dutch for tenderloin or fillet of beef. In Holland, the fillet is more often cooked in a single piece weighing 2—4 lb., than cut into steaks, as is the practice in British and American butchery. The joint is larded with lardoons, rubbed with butter, and baked in a medium oven for 20 minutes to the lb. It is seasoned after cooking, as salt applied beforehand toughens the meat and also makes the blood run out. See also BEEF; RUNDVLEES.

gebraden ossenhaas, roast fillet of beef. The Dutch method is first to rub the joint with butter or other fat, and cover it completely with bay leaves before cooking. It is roasted in a moderate oven for about 20 minutes to the lb. When cooking is completed, the bay leaves are boiled up with the pan juices, with stock added. The flavour is excellent.

ossenhaas à la jardinière, fillet of beef with vegetables. After being trimmed and well pounded, the meat is larded with strips of pork fat. Boiling water is then poured over to seal the meat, and it is baked in butter in a moderately hot oven, allowing about 20 minutes per lb. or according to taste. Basting should be almost continuous throughout the cooking time. The meat is seasoned after cooking and is served arranged in slices, which are surrounded by a selection of cooked vegetables in season, such as small tomatoes, carrots, asparagus, peas, etc. A sauce is made by mixing the pan juices of the meat with 1 tablespoon flour and 1 tablespoon butter, and heating them; when hot, 1 cup stock and 3 tablespoons Madeira are added. Mashed potatoes, sometimes mixed with grated cheese, also accompany this dish. If the dish is served cold, the vegetables are marinated and mayonnaise is served in place of the hot sauce; potato salad is also served, and the fillet slices are garnished with parsley.

ossetong, Dutch for beef or ox tongue. The Dutch method of cooking a fresh tongue is to first trim it, then bring it to the boil in warm water together with salt, onion, parsley, and celery; then simmer it for 3 hours, remove the skin and return the tongue to the stock until it is required for the meal. It is served with *zure saus* and cooked, soaked, dried white beans.

A smoked beef tongue is first soaked overnight; then, together with onion, bay leaves, parsley, and celery, it is brought to the boil in fresh water. Cooking time is the same as that allowed for a fresh tongue, and after cooking it is treated in the same manner, except that it is served with *rozijnen saus*. See also TONG; TONGUE.

ossi buchi alla milanese or *osso bucho,* a famous dish served in many parts of Italy, but perfected in Milan. It consists of shin of veal cut into pieces about 2 inches thick. (Ideally the animal should not be more than 3 months old.) The veal and bone pieces are browned in butter, then arranged upright in a roasting pan, so that the marrow does not fall out. Then ¼ pint (½ cup) white wine is poured over and the veal is cooked for 10 minutes; then ¾ lb. skinned, chopped tomatoes, 1 cup good stock, and seasoning are added, and all are cooked for at least 1½ hours. While the dish is being cooked, a *gremolata,* consisting of a handful of chopped parsley, chopped clove of garlic, and grated peel of ½ lemon, all well mixed, is prepared, and sprinkled on top before serving. *Risotto alla milanese* should accompany this dish.

osso bucco, see OSSI BUCHI ALLA MILANESE.

ost, Czechoslovakian for cheese. See ABERTAM; KOPPEN; OSTEPEK; OSTIEPOK; RIESENGEBIRGE-KÄSE; ZLATO.

ost, Danish for cheese. Denmark is famous for her cheeses, and they are used on the traditional *smørrebrød*. In some parts of the country, as in Aarhus for instance, cheese is served for breakfast. Every Danish cheese that is to be exported must be subjected to state quality-control, and be stamped with the ''*lur*'' trademark. (The *lur* was a beautifully made wind instrument of the Bronze Age; several have been recovered in good condition from Danish bogs in recent years.) See also CASTELLO; DANABLU; DANBO; ELBO; ESROM; FYNBO; HAVARTI; MARIBO; MOLBO; MYCELLA; SAMSØ; TYBO.

ostæg, a recipe for cheese egg balls, consisting of 4 minced hard-boiled eggs, 2 teaspoons minced parsley, 4 oz. grated cheese, 1 egg yolk, and seasoning. After all the ingredients have been well blended, balls are formed, rolled in breadcrumbs, then fried in hot oil until golden brown.

ostekager, cheese cakes. A pastry is made consisting of 8 oz. (2 cups) flour, 8 oz. (1 cup) butter, 8 oz. grated *Samsø* cheese, salt, paprika to taste, and 2 egg yolks. This is rolled out thinly and left for 1 hour before being shaped into small rounds. The cakes are baked in a slow oven. When cool, 2 rounds are placed together with a cream cheese filling in between. A little of the filling is also placed on top, and the cakes are decorated with radishes and cress.

osteklejner, cheese fritters made from *Samsø*. Oblong shapes of the cheese are dabbed with prepared mustard and sprinkled with cayenne. They are then fried in butter until golden. This dish is served with radishes, celery, and wholemeal bread and butter.

ost, Norwegian for cheese. Norwegian cheeses fall into two quite separate categories, according to whether they are made from curd or whey. The three most popular cheeses in Norway, *gammelost, nøkkelost,* and *pultost,* belong to the curd type; *mysost* and *geitost* belong to the whey type. There is also a processed cheese called *primula,* which is made like the caramellised paste of mysost and mixed with butter fat. *Surprim* is a sour milk cheese made from the whey of *Gammelost*. See also GAMMELOST; GEITOST; MYSOST; NØKKELOST; PRIMULA CHEESE; PULTOST; SURPRIM.

ost, Swedish for cheese. Apart from the national cheeses, many imitations of European cheeses are made in Sweden, from cow's milk. Among these are the cheddar and stilton of England (although the taste of the latter is very different from the English one), the camembert and port-du-salut of France, the Swiss emmenthal, the Dutch gouda, and the Russian *steppe*. No Swedish cheese may be sold without the government stamp, which is the *Rune* brand. See also GETOST; HERRGÅRDSOST; MYSOST; PRESTOST; SVECIAOST; VÄSTERBOTTEN-SOST; VÄSTGÖTAOST.

ostpudding, cheese pudding made from 1 pint (2 cups) milk, 1 fillet of anchovy, 1 bay leaf, and a pinch of nutmeg brought to the boil together and then strained. This mixture is added gradually to 3 beaten eggs, 2 oz. grated cheese, pepper, and ½ teaspoon mustard powder. The whole is baked until set in a moderate oven, the dish standing in a tin containing a little warm water.

oštěpek or *oštěpka,* a Czechoslovakian ewe's milk cheese. It is plastic-cured, and resembles the Italian *cacio a cavallo*.

ostiepok, a Czechoslovakian cheese made from ewe's milk and then smoked. It is a speciality of Orava in the Tatras.

ostión, see OSTRAS.

ostras, Portuguese for oysters. Portuguese oysters are long, thin, green, and nearly transparent. Although popular, they do not compare for taste or appearance with *marennes* or Whitstables. They are often served in soups or cooked in batter. See also OYSTER.

ostras, Spanish for oysters. In Spain, as well as being eaten raw, oysters are often rolled in egg and breadcrumbs and then fried in oil, or simply fried with garlic and sweet peppers. This applies particularly in Cádiz, where oyster is called *ostión*. See also OYSTER.

ostreon, Greek for oysters. Oysters are not eaten a great deal in Greece, as the matter they consume is looked upon with disfavour. Mussels are much preferred. When oysters are served, however, they are usually grilled, or baked with onions and tomatoes in olive oil. See also OYSTER.

ostriche, Italian for oysters. It was an Italian, Sergius Orata, in the 5th century B.C., who first had the idea of making artificial oyster beds. As well as being eaten raw, in Venice oysters are sometimes grilled in the halfshell for a few minutes with a mixture of breadcrumbs, herbs, garlic, and olive oil, and served with lemon juice. See also OYSTER.

ostropel, a Rumanian method of cooking duck. It is jointed and sautéed in oil with sliced onions, then sprinkled with flour. When browned, 3 tablespoons water, 1 tablespoon tomato purée, 2 crushed garlic cloves, and a bay leaf are added. The duck is then covered and cooked in a slow oven for 1½ hours. Stock or water is added if the sauce is too thick. Just before it is served, 4 tablespoons wine vinegar are added, and cooking is continued for another 15 minutes. See also DUCK.

oswego tea, see BERGAMOT.

ou, Rumanian for egg, often served poached with *mămăligă,* or fried with *iahnie de cartofi,* as well as being used for baking or omelettes.

ouananiche, the French–Canadian name for a delicious landlocked lake salmon which is cooked as salmon.

oublie, a sweet French wafer made in wafer-irons, for serving with ice creams and other desserts; when rolled up into a cone, it is known as a *plaisir*.

ouillat or *ouliat,* a speciality from the Béarn region of France, consisting of a soup made from 1 large chopped onion which has been fried in oil, crushed garlic, hot water (vegetable water is sometimes used), with a bouquet of herbs, and seasoning. It is strained onto slices of bread. An egg or grated Gruyère is sometimes served with the bread in the plate. When tomatoes are in season, they are fried with the onion. It is also called *tourri,* and in Bigorre, a neighbouring province, it is known as *toulia*.

ouriço, Portuguese for sea-urchins. They are eaten a great deal in Portugal, lightly cooked, drained, then cut open and eaten with a spoon. Sometimes they are eaten raw.

oursins, French for sea-urchins, which are eaten extensively in France. As a first course, they are lightly boiled, then cut like an egg; as a sauce, they are sieved and mixed with mayonnaise. A purée is made of the flesh which is mixed with béchamel sauce and used for *vol-au-vent* or served on fried bread sprinkled with grated cheese and grilled.

outarde, see BASTARDAU; BUSTARD.

ovár, a Hungarian cow's milk cheese with a reddish crust and reddish-yellow paste. It weighs about 10 lb. and the taste is piquant but not too strong.

òvneshki ezìk, a Bulgarian dish of lambs' tongues. To prepare it 6 tongues are boiled for 1 hour, then skinned and fried in oil. Then 1 large onion, 1 sliced carrot, ½ cup white wine, seasoning, and water to cover are added. All are boiled for 20–30 minutes, then covered thickly with sliced raw potatoes and baked in a moderately hot oven until these are cooked and browned.

ovoli, literally "egg shaped," the Italian name given to a very small form of mozzarella cheese.

ovos, Portuguese for eggs, which, apart from being used in many egg dishes in Portugal, also form an important ingredient in soups, sauces, and puddings. They are eaten even with beefsteak (*bifes*). On ceremonial occasions they are often served after the main course. *Ovos duros* or *ovos cozidos* are hard-boiled eggs; *ovos escalfados* are poached eggs; *ovos estredados* are fried eggs; *ovos mexidos* are scrambled eggs; *ovos quenetes* are soft-boiled eggs; and *ovos recheados* are stuffed hard-boiled eggs. An unfolded omelette called a *tortilha* is also frequently made in Portugal, like the Spanish *tortilla*. See also EGG; OMELETA.

ovos à portuguesa, large tomatoes with the pulp scooped out and an egg broken into the cavity of each. They are topped with breadcrumbs and baked in the oven.

ovos nevados, "sweet eggs," which are sold on traditional holidays in Portugal. They are made with stiffly beaten egg whites, which are poached in boiling milk and sugar and then removed. The yolks are added to the milk to make a custard, and the egg-white balls are then put on top of the custard and sprinkled with cinnamon. This dish is a variation of floating islands, and is also called *farófias.*

ox, a domesticated bovine quadruped, much used for food in many parts of the world. In British culinary usage, however, the word ox is only used for inferior cuts of meat, the better meat being known as beef. Ox cheek is the palate and cheek of the animal; very gelatinous, and excellent for soups or pot-au-feu. Ox heart, also called bullock's heart, is good stuffed and braised. Oxtail is classed as offal, but makes an excellent soup or stew. See also OFFAL; TONGUE.

oxtail stew. First trim the oxtail of fat and then brown it in a little oil, with onions. Sprinkle with flour, briefly put back in the oil to brown the flour, then put in a pan and barely cover with water. A bay leaf, ½ teaspoon powdered marjoram, 4 carrots, and plenty of seasoning are added, and all is covered and given long slow cooking (about 4 hours) in the oven. Other flavourings, such as tomato purée, can be added if desired. Ideally, oxtail stew should be allowed to get cold so that the fat can be skimmed from the top, then reheated before serving. When cold, it should be a thick jelly. The same method of cooking is followed for oxtail soup except more water is added.

oxalis, see OCA.

Oxford sauce, an English sauce served with cold venison. It consists of ½ lb. red currant jelly, 1 chopped shallot, the grated peel and juice of 1 orange and 1 lemon, 1 teaspoon made mustard, powdered ginger, and ¼ pint (½ cup) port, all heated up together and then allowed to get cold.

oxkött, Swedish for beef. See also BIFF.

oxbringa, a national speciality, consisting of boiled brisket of beef served with creamed potatoes.

ox-tongue, a country name for *alkanet.*

oyster (*Ostreidae*), a marine bivalve mollusc known to man from very early times. Oysters are of great gastronomic merit and are usually eaten raw, except for the Portuguese or the very large American oysters, which are often cooked. As with all shellfish, they should be eaten only if they live in unpolluted water. All the finest oysters are gathered from special beds where they breed and are husbanded. The finest European oysters are the Native, from Colchester, Whitstable, or other Essex and Kentish beds in England; green *marennes* oysters, which derive their colouring from the algae on which they live; Brittany oysters; Dutch Natives; Galway Bay oysters; Portuguese oysters which, although European, resemble the American type. American oysters, of which bluepoints are the most popular, are sometimes larger than the European varieties and do not have the peculiarly delicate flavour of the latter. They are often cut up and eaten cooked. When oysters are being cooked, they must be allowed only to curl at the edges, otherwise they will be tough. They may be dipped in batter and fried (the batter acting as a protective coating), and are delicious prepared in this way.

Belon oysters

Raw oysters are full of vitamins and contain a high proportion of iodine. (Popular tradition has it that they are an aphrodisiac.) The best way to open them is to insert a small sharp knife at the hinge, break the ligament which attaches the fish to the flat top shell, and serve the oyster in the deep lower shell with its own juice. Oysters are often served as an hors d'oeuvre, both cold and hot. In the latter case, they can be served grilled on skewers, à la *florentine,* or as angels on horseback. Tinned oysters are useful for making soups and sauces and for using as a filling for small *vol-au-vents,* but in flavour they are not to be compared to fresh ones. See also HUITRES; ISTIRIDYÈ; OSTRAS; OSTREON; OSTRICHE.

oyster and noodle casserole (*casserole de nouilles et d'huitres*), a French-Canadian speciality. A casserole is buttered, and a layer of 1½ cups cooked noodles placed on the bottom, followed by 1 pint shelled oysters which have been first heated until they curl, and lemon juice. These ingredients are covered by ½ pint (1 cup) white sauce flavoured with a little worcestershire sauce, salt and pepper, and 2 oz. grated sharp Canadian cheese. Then 1½ cups noodles and ½ pint (1 cup) more of the sauce are added. The dish is covered with breadcrumbs and melted butter, and baked in the oven for about 30 minutes.

oyster chowder, a traditional American soup, for which 2 chopped onions, 2 diced green peppers, and 1 cup okra are simmered in 4 oz. (½ cup) butter. Then 4 pints (8 cups) white stock, salt, and pepper are added, and at a later stage, ½ lb. finely chopped peeled tomatoes. The soup is thickened with 1 tablespoon arrowroot and garnished with 24 bearded oysters. See also CHOWDER.

oyster sauce. Six or more oysters are opened carefully and their liquor collected and strained through fine muslin. The liquor is put into a saucepan with a pinch of powdered mace and a small strip of lemon peel and simmered gently for 10 minutes. Then 1 tablespoon butter and 1 teaspoon flour, which have been rubbed together, are blended in quickly. When the sauce boils, it is seasoned and the bearded oysters are put in to cook gently until their edges curl. The sauce is then served.

oyster soufflé. To a roux prepared with 2 tablespoons butter and 2 tablespoons flour, with 2 egg yolks and ½ pint milk, are added 12 finely chopped oysters and their juice. The 2 stiffly beaten egg whites are then included, and the soufflé is put into a greased 1½-pint dish and cooked in a hot oven for 30 minutes. It is delicious served with oyster sauce.

oyster catcher, a pretty black and white wading bird. See also HUITRIER.

oyster crabs, tiny baby crabs found inside oysters in the U.S. They are stewed in cream, with a little Madeira added before serving, and eaten whole, shell and all. They can also be dipped in milk, turned in flour, and fried in deep oil. See also CRAB.

oyster plant, see SALSIFY.

ozór, Polish for tongue. *Ozór cielęce* is fresh calf's tongue. See also TONGUE.

ozór szpikowany w potrawie, boiled tongue. Salted or smoked tongue is used as well as fresh, but it must first be soaked overnight. It is then cooked in the normal way. In Poland it is then very often served with a sauce made from 1 pint hot tongue stock thickened with a roux, with 2 oz. chopped almonds, 1 tablespoon raisins, 2 teaspoons sugar, and 3 tablespoons white wine added.

ozór z majonez, pickled ox tongue, half-cooked and skinned, then wrapped in 1 lb. minced veal or lean pork (or a mixture of both) well mixed with 2 slices of bread moistened with milk, 5 chopped anchovies, 2 egg yolks, 2 tablespoons parsley, 2 tablespoons sour cream, and seasoning. It is then tied in a cloth, poached in stock for 1½ hours, drained, and served sliced, cold with mayonnaise.

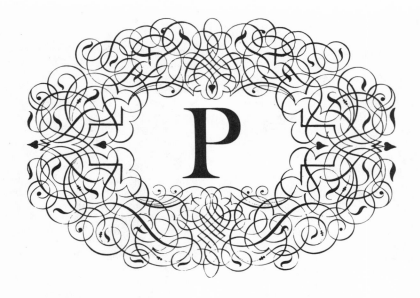

Pabaigtuves, also called *Nuobaigos,* the Lithuanian Harvest Festival holiday, which takes place in late August or early September. A sheaf of the last grain to be cut is dressed with ribbons and flowers and kept until the following year, for it is thought to ensure prosperity; it is called a *boba,* which means "old woman," and is often dressed to represent one. Formerly, the most beautiful girl harvester used to present it to the landowner, who in return gave all his workers a lavish dinner of traditional dishes, such as *koldunai kepta veršiena,* and *obuolainis tortas,* and a traditional drink called *krupnikas,* made of honey and pure alcohol mixed with cinnamon and spices.

pabassinos, small traditional Sardinian cakes made from a dough of 1 lb. (4 cups) flour, 8 oz. (1 cup) sugar, 8 oz. (1 cup) butter, 2 eggs, and 1 tablespoon aniseed, all well mixed and then rolled into small shapes which are baked in a moderate oven for 15–20 minutes. It is sometimes served with grapes soaked in *grappa,* a strong Italian colourless distilled spirit made from grape-husks after the wine has been pressed out.

pača, the Serbo-Croat word for duckling, often baked with garlic and paprika-flavoured sour milk or buttermilk barely to cover, later thickened with 2 beaten egg yolks. See also POD-VARAK.

paça, a Turkish dish of sheep's trotters (feet) stewed with garlic, ½ cup vinegar, 2 lemons, and water to cover; it is served with a sauce made from egg yolks, lemon juice, and the stock, like the Greek *avgolémono.*

Pacific prawn, see PRAWN.

Pacific salmon, a fish of the subgenus *Oncorhynchus,* closely allied to the Atlantic salmon (genus *Salmo*) and much resembling it in appearance and habits, but not thought so highly of as food. There are 6 species of this subgenus, peculiar to the North Pacific and some rivers. *Quinnat* is the largest, bigger than a true salmon but inferior in taste. The others are the dog salmon, cohoe, humpback, sockeye or blue-back or red salmon (known on the eastern seaboard of the U.S. as *redfish*), and the masu, this last being found only in Japanese waters. All are smaller in size than the *quinnat,* but are used extensively for canning as salmon. All are said to die after the first spawning, and only the *quinnat* and red salmon ascend the rivers. Once in the rivers they are of little interest to anglers, as they are reluctant to take a fly or lure in fresh water. However, in tidal river-mouths they give fine sport. See also BLUE-BACK SALMON; QUINNAT SALMON; REDFISH.

packet, a colloquial name for *drisheen* in County Cork, Ireland.

pączki, Polish double doughnuts, made with yeast and containing vanilla and orange flavouring. After the dough has been cooked, 1 teaspoon jam is dropped between two doughnuts, and the sandwich is then fried.

paella, a traditional Spanish rice dish, its name deriving from the flat oval pan with handles in which the rice is served (although this was originally called a *sartén*). About 3 lb. assorted fish and shellfish such as crawfish, cigalas (Dublin Bay prawns), *rape,* and inkfish are cleaned, chopped, and fried with garlic in oil. Then 2 sliced onions are added, and later ½ lb. tomatoes. Lastly 1 lb. rice is stirred in and left for a few moments to absorb the oil, before 2 quarts (8 cups) boiling stock is added, followed by ¼ lb. *chorizo.* The whole is covered and simmered until the rice is tender (about 30 minutes). Chicken and pork are sometimes added as well, and ½ teaspoon saffron, which makes the whole dish a glorious yellow colour. If crawfish are not available, mussels or cockles are substituted. There are many recipes from each province, for this traditional dish, using various available foods, but rice, onions, tomatoes, fish, and sausage always form part of it. The best-known paella is *a la Valenciana.* See also SOCARAT.

paesana, salsa, an Italian sauce served with pasta, made from ½ lb. finely sliced mushrooms and ¼ lb. diced bacon stewed together in 4 oz. (½ cup) butter. When these are cooked, 3 tablespoons grated Parmesan cheese is stirred in so that it amalgamates with the butter, and the sauce is then seasoned. It is often served with *tonnarelle,* when the dish is called *tonnarelle alla paesana.*

pagel, a Provençal name for sea bream.

pagel aux moules à la Provençale, sea bream covered with a purée of tomatoes and garlic and cooked in the oven for 30 minutes, then garnished with parsley and mussels before serving.

paglierino, a regional cheese from Piedmont in Italy, made from cow's milk.

pagotón, Greek for ice cream. Athens is famous for its ice cream, which is made from ewe's milk and is therefore extremely rich.

païdakia, Greek for lamb chops.

païdakia hasapika, 6 lamb chops baked with 2 sliced onions, 1 lb. tomatoes, a pinch of marjoram, salt, and pepper for 1 hour. Then 1 lb. small new potatoes are added, with a cup of water, and the dish is baked for about 45 minutes, or until the potatoes are cooked. This dish may also be made by grilling the chops separately and serving them with the baked vegetables.

paillettes, I. French for little pastry sticks, often flavoured with grated Parmesan cheese (*paillettes au Parmesan*), cayenne pepper, or paprika. They are lightly baked, and served as a garnish for consommé. II. French for fine stick-like slices of vegetable. This method is applied particularly to potatoes in France. Large onions are also made into paillettes, but in this case the onions are sliced into fine rings which are then lightly floured and fried in hot oil. They are drained and then salted. See also POMME DE TERRE (POMMES FRITES PAILLE).

pain, I. French for loaf, or for bread either plain or sweet. *Pain grillé* is toast.

pain de gibier, a forcemeat mould of game meat, used particularly for hare and deer (*pain de gibier à poil*) and for woodcock (*pain de gibier à plume*). To prepare it 1 lb. pounded game meat is mixed thoroughly with seasoning and a panade, made by adding 8 tablespoons flour to 1 cup water boiled with 6 tablespoons butter, and beating well, then mixing in thoroughly 2 eggs and 2 additional egg yolks. The forcemeat is then put into a mould and cooked in a *bain-marie* in the oven for about 1 hour. It is sometimes covered with aspic jelly when cold. *Pain de gibier* can also be made in the same way as *pain de volaille* using game meat instead of chicken.

pain d'épice, a spiced gingerbread, made with honey instead of treacle (molasses), and rye flour in place of white flour. It is a speciality of Dijon.

pain de volaille, a French chicken loaf, made from 1 lb. chicken forcemeat (*mousseline forcemeat*), chopped tarragon, parsley, seasoning, a little brandy to taste (about 2 tablespoons), and 2 egg yolks. It is brushed with butter, covered, and baked in a *bain-marie* in a moderate oven for 1 hour. II. The name is also used for a fruit mould coated with a jelly.

pain perdu, literally, "lost bread." Crustless slices of bread are soaked in a mixture of egg beaten with a little milk, then fried on both sides in butter. They may be served hot, sprinkled with sugar and cinnamon, or used as the basis for a savoury such as *croque monsieur.* This is commonly referred to in the U.S. as "French toast" and is often eaten with maple syrup as a breakfast dish. See also ARME RIDDERE. III. In 18th-century France, pain referred to dishes of forcemeat served hot or cold. The forcemeat was made from meat, fish, shellfish, game, or vegetables, mixed with eggs and stock, and was put into a mould and poached in a *bain-marie.* The word is still used with this meaning in some parts of France, but is gradually being replaced by mousse. The American meat loaf derives from this kind of forcemeat mould.

pain complet, a cake made of almond paste, shaped like a loaf.

pain de gênes, a French almond-flavoured Genoa cake, made from 1 lb. ground almonds mixed with ¾ lb. (1½ cups) granulated sugar and 5 eggs (well stirred in, one at a time). Then 3 oz. corn flour (cornstarch) or potato flour, vanilla, and rum or curaçao to flavour are also added. The mixture is put into small, round, specially designed tins, like shallow cake tins,

and baked in a moderate oven. This cake is also known as *la génoise aux amandes.* See also GÉNOISE.

pain de sucre, French for loaf sugar.

paio, Portuguese smoked mountain ham or pork fillet meat. This is a speciality of Portugal, particularly of Chaves and Melgaço. It is very lean and can be eaten safely without being cooked. The smoked ham of Chaves is prefaced *trás-os-montes,* and that of Melgaço, *minho.* Elsewhere it is called *presunto.* See also HAM; LINGUISA; PRESUNTO.

pak-choy or *bok choy* (*Brassica chinensis*), a Chinese variety of cabbage, now grown in many parts of Europe and North America. It has an oval heart, very tightly closed leaves with white midribs, and is dark green in colour. It is very crisp, and during cooking holds its texture and exudes no odour. It can also be served raw, as a salad green.

pakhtakhor, a salad from Uzbekistan, Russia, made from a mixture of pickled plums (see SLIVA), apples, peaches, cucumbers, olives, and chicken paste. It is served with meats or poultry.

palace bread, see AISH EL SARYA.

palačinke, Yugoslavian pancakes, often served filled with peanuts, cinnamon, and sugar mixed with thick cream.

palacsinta, Hungarian pancakes often spread with minced ham and mushrooms, then sprinkled with grated cheese and sour milk or yogourt, and heated for 10 minutes in a moderate oven.

Palacsinta are also a speciality of Hungarian communities in the U.S. where they may be prepared with a filling of 1 lb. cottage cheese mixed with ½ cup sugar, a few drops of vanilla essence (extract), and 1 well-beaten egg. When filled, they are rolled up, heated in a greased dish, and served topped with sour cream and preserves. They are served as a main course, not a dessert. See also PANCAKE.

paladru, a French cow's milk cheese made in the Savoie. It is at its best from November to May.

palamida or *palamitha,* Greek for the palamid or bonito, a large fish with rich, darkish flesh, which comes from Africa to the Black Sea to spawn. They are surface fish, and they pass through Greek waters in millions on the homeward journey to Africa, during November and December. Palamida can be pickled, served smoked for *meze,* when it tastes not unlike smoked salmon, or prepared in a number of other ways. See also BONITO.

palamida plaki, palamida baked or braised with vegetables, usually celery, tomatoes, onions, and potatoes, with garlic and herbs.

palamida sto harti, palamida rubbed with salt, lemon juice, and olive oil, wrapped in greaseproof paper and baked.

palamut, Turkish for bonito. It is often grilled on a spit in Turkey, and is delicious cooked in this way. See also BONITO.

palate of beef, the palate of the ox, formerly used for soups or stews, or cooked in the same way as calf's head and eaten cold, in slices. It is very gelatinous and can be cooked in the same way as tripe.

palatschinke, an Austrian pancake which has a little brandy in the batter, and is filled with apricot jam mixed with chopped roasted split almonds and 1 teaspoon brandy. See also PANCAKE.

pale, Norwegian for young coalfish. Coalfish belong to the cod family and are especially popular on the west coast of Norway. The fillets are extremely good if simmered slowly in salted water and served with melted butter and parsley or chives. See also COALFISH; FISK; SEI.

paleron, a French cut of beef which has no English equivalent. It is similar to the English and American chuck roast, but is slightly nearer the neck—between that and the bladebone. Its main use in France is for making stock, but it is also used for braising, and particularly for pot-au-feu and similar dishes. See also BOEUF, BOUILLI.

Palestine soup, a 19th-century English name for a soup made from Jerusalem artichokes.

palets de dames, a type of dry petit four flavoured with vanilla, lemon, or orange.

palette, see ÉCHINE DE PORC.

palette-knife, a flexible blunt-bladed knife used in pastry-making for blending, or for picking up the pastry. It is also used to loosen cakes from the baking-tin.

paling, Dutch for eel when cooked in a soup or stew. See also AAL.

paling in groene saus. Fresh eel is washed, cut into pieces, barely covered with white wine and water containing garlic, bay leaf, salt, and pepper, and poached for about 15 minutes, or until tender. Then the fish is removed, skinned, and filleted. A roux is made from 3 tablespoons butter, 3 tablespoons flour, and the fish stock, to which ¼ pint (½ cup) cream and 1 tablespoon chopped parsley are added. Then the fish is added, and it is reheated but not boiled. The dish is eaten hot with boiled potatoes.

palingsoep, a traditional eel soup which is eaten a great deal during Lent in Holland. A cleaned eel is cut into pieces and simmered in 2 quarts (8 cups) boiling water for about 20 minutes, together with salt, peppercorns, and a bay leaf. The fish is then removed, and a roux of 6 tablespoons butter and 6 tablespoons flour is used to thicken the stock, which is cooked for a further 15 minutes and then sieved. Before the soup is reheated, the eel is returned to it, together with chopped parsley. Just before serving, 2 beaten egg yolks are added. See also HOLLANDSE PALINGSOEP.

pallottole d'aranci, an Italian orange sweet. The peels of 6 oranges and 1 lemon are soaked for a day in water containing 1 teaspoon salt. It is then drained and washed, covered with water, and simmered until soft. It is then drained again, chopped very finely, and mixed with its own weight in sugar. This mixture is boiled until a small amount dropped in cold water forms a ball (after about 15 minutes), when it is left to get cold. It is then shaped into balls, which are rolled first in icing sugar and afterwards in finely crushed grilled hazelnuts. The balls are served cold.

palm, a large family of trees, usually subtropical or tropical, which includes the date and the coconut. Sago is derived from the pithy interior of the low palm tree (*Metroxylon sagu*). Young shoots and the terminal ends of branches are cooked in the same way as asparagus. See also CABBAGE PALM; COEUR DE PALMIER.

palmier, I. French for palm. See COEUR DE PALMIER. II. A small Parisian pastry, made from puff pastry rolled 3 times and then sprinkled with icing sugar instead of flour. It is rolled out to ⅛-inch thickness and cut into strips 12 inches long. The ends of the strips are brought to the centre, and the strips then folded in two lengthways. Finally they are cut into pieces ¼-inch thick, and baked on a baking-sheet in a hot oven.

paloise, sauce, a French sauce made like a béarnaise or hollandaise, but flavoured with chopped fresh mint instead of tarragon. It is served with grilled lamb or mutton chops or cutlets.

paloma, Spanish for pigeon. In Spain, pigeons are often split in half and roasted with olive oil, then served on cooked saffron rice garnished with green peas, grilled red peppers, and fried tomatoes. See also PIGEON.

palombacci, Italian for wood pigeons. See also PICCIONE; PIGEON.

palombacci alla perugina. In Perugia pigeons are cooked on a spit, and three-quarters of the way through cooking, the birds are slashed so that the intestines fall into the pan. The intestines are then cooked with olives, sage, juniper berries, and a little red wine. When the birds are cooked, the entrail is ready and is served with them.

palourde, I. The general French term for several varieties of clam. See CLAM; CLOVISSE. II. The name given to vegetable marrow in some districts of France.

palten, a Russian form of black pudding made from ½ lb. creamed butter mixed with 1 quart pig's blood, ½ pint (1 cup) cream, 4 tablespoons flour, and 3 egg yolks. The stiffly beaten egg whites, salt, a pinch of nutmeg, and marjoram are then added. A greased mould is filled with the mixture, which is then cooked in a *bain-marie* in the oven. When turned out, it is covered with browned butter. See also BLACK PUDDING.

pampanito, the Spanish name for a small pompano, a fish found off the California coast.

pamplemousse, see GRAPEFRUIT.

pan, Spanish for bread. *Panecillos* are rolls, *pan moreno* is rye bread, *pan rallado* is breadcrumbs, and *pan tostado* is toast.

pan broil, an American culinary term meaning to cook food in a pan on top of the stove by dry heat, with only enough fat to keep it from sticking. The pan is heated and greased only lightly (if at all) before the food is put in. The food is turned frequently at first, to seal in the juices, then only occasionally, until it is cooked. This method is used mostly for steaks, cutlets, etc.

pan di spagna, Italian for sponge cake. It is made in Italy with 4 eggs separated; the egg yolks beaten with 3 tablespoons castor sugar, then 1 teaspoon grated lemon peel is added. The egg whites are stiffly beaten with 1 tablespoon castor sugar until peaks are formed. Then 4 heaped tablespoons flour are added to the yolk mixture, which is then beaten vigorously. Finally the egg whites are folded in. The mixture is put into a well-greased sponge tin and baked for 30–45 minutes in a moderate oven. It is left to cool before being removed from the tin.

pan dowdy, an American pudding, usually made with 3 cups sliced apples which are placed in a greased baking dish, sprinkled with ½ cup brown sugar or molasses mixed with ¼ teaspoon each of nutmeg, cinnamon, and salt, and baked until they are soft. Then a light sponge mixture is poured over and the pudding is baked until cooked (about 30 minutes). It is served apple side up, with cream or hard sauce. Rhubarb and apricots are also sometimes used instead of apple. It is similar to upsidedown cake.

pan dulce, Spanish for "sweet bread," an egg and flour pudding. It is made from 6 beaten egg yolks added to 8 tablespoons sugar, and the 6 stiffly beaten egg whites are folded in. Then 6 tablespoons flour and 1 tablespoon each of stoned raisins and candied peel are added. This mixture is well beaten and poured into a buttered tin. It is baked in a moderate oven and served hot, sometimes sprinkled with sugar and cinnamon.

pan vis, a Dutch method of making a meal of the leftovers from stock fish or *stokvis.* Extra onions are fried and then mixed with all the leftovers. The dish is topped with butter and then heated. A salad is served with it.

panade, the French term for a binding mixture for fish, meat, and forcemeat, which can take several forms. I. The most common consists of about ½ lb. white crustless bread which is soaked in ½ pint (1 generous cup) boiling water or milk, and allowed to absorb the liquid. It is then left to dry out a little, or is squeezed dry, before use. II. A paste made from 4 oz. (1 cup) flour added to ¾ pint (1½ cups) water and 5 tablespoons butter, boiled and stirred in the same way as chou pastry. When cold, it is used particularly for quenelles. III. A

paste of cooked rice, used in making various forcemeats. IV.
A thick paste of potato, cooked and then mashed with milk
and seasoning. This is used, while still warm, for large quenelles. V. A very thick sauce béchamel, or roux, often used for
mixing with flaked cooked fish for very light fishcakes, and
also as the basis for soufflés. See also FORCEMEAT.

panade à la frangipane, a panade used cold, as a binding
for fish and chicken forcemeats. To prepare, 1 cup flour is
mixed with 4 egg yolks and 6 tablespoons melted butter,
seasoned, and then well stirred while ¾ pint (1½ cups) boiling milk is added. It is cooked for 5 minutes, beating all the
time with a whisk, then allowed to cool.

panage, the French culinary term for the coating of a food
(which is subsequently to be fried or grilled) with breadcrumbs. It is made from bread dried in the oven and pounded.
If the bread is allowed to turn golden, the crumbs are called
chapelure blonde or *chapelure brune,* and if still whitish,
chapelure blanche, or in some cases *panure.* See also PANER;
PANURE.

panais, French for parsnip. In France parsnips are used in
soups, garnishes, and stock, and are served as a vegetable in
the same way as carrots. In the southwest region they are used
in a pastry flan with honey and blackberries. See also PARS-
NIP.

pancake, a thin flat cake made of batter, one of the oldest
forms of cooking. In the Middle Ages it was known by the
Norman-French word *frayse,* and it is thought that the word
had an onomatopoeic origin in the sound made by the batter
as it is poured into the pan. Pancakes are made from a batter
with the consistency of thick, but pouring cream, composed
of 1 egg to 4 oz. flour, ½ pint milk or milk and water, or light
beer, and sometimes a tablespoon of oil or melted butter. A
pinch of salt and/or sugar is sometimes added. The batter is
well beaten and left to stand for at least 30 minutes, to allow
the starch cells to swell and to ensure a smoother pancake.
This is the most basic method; others call for separated eggs,
the stiffly beaten egg white being added last, or for the addition of fruit juices or liqueurs, as in the case of crêpes. The
pan should be thick, very hot, and only lightly greased, as too
much will make the pancakes greasy, and they should in any
case be dry on the outside when cooked. The size of the pancake is a matter of individual preference. Generally, 1 tablespoon thin batter will make a pancake 5–6 inches across. The
pan must be adroitly tilted so that the batter runs evenly and
as thinly as possible. When the pancake becomes mottled
golden and brown on one side, it is turned, either by tossing
or with a spatula, to the other side. When cooked, it is
drained on paper. One pan greasing will cook at least 5 or 6
pancakes. Pancakes are eaten by tradition on Shrove Tuesday,
when they are served rolled with sugar and lemon juice. However, they can also be filled with sweet or savoury mixtures,
according to taste. They keep well in a deep freeze or refrigerator and can be reheated, either by flambéeing in spirit, or by
placing in a sauce in the oven; but they are at their best when
eaten immediately after removal from the pan. In Ireland, buttermilk is sometimes used in the mixture, and the pancakes
are served with warm heather honey. In Wales, too, buttermilk
is used, and in Scotland, oatmeal can be used as well as flour.
In the last century, cream was added to the pancake batter,
and the pancakes were sometimes served unrolled, one on top
of the other, with the filling between them. See also BLINCHKI
S TVOROGOM; BLINTZES; BLINY; CREIER DE VITEL PANE;
CRÊPE; CRESPOLINI; FLENSJES; FRITTATINE IMBOLITTE; PA-
LACINKE; PALACSINTA; PALATSCHINKE; PANNEKAKE; PAN-
NEKOEKE; PANNEQUET; PANNKAKA; PANNUKAKKU; PFANN-
KUCHEN; NALÉSNIKI; NALISNIKI; SCRIPPELLE IMBUSSE.

pancetta, a cured sausage, resembling salami, from Parma in

stuffed pancakes

Italy. It is made from pig's stomach, salted and air-dried, and
can be eaten cooked as well as raw.

pane, Italian for bread. *Pane grattugiato* means breadcrumbs,
used a great deal in Italy for coating foods (*alla milanese*), or
for stuffings and sauces. The stale bread is dried in the oven,
then pounded or grated. *Midolla* or *mollica di pane* is crustless bread soaked in milk or water, then squeezed and used to
thicken soups and sauces or to bind stuffings. *Pane tostato* is
toast.

panedda, an alternative name for *casigiolu,* a Sardinian
cheese.

paner, a French verb meaning to coat a food with breadcrumbs before frying it in oil or butter. Food so prepared is
termed *pané(e).* See also PANAGE.

panetière, I. A French method of cooking by which various
cooked foodstuffs are put into round scooped-out loaves and
"finished" in the oven. See also CROUSTADE. II. A French
method of serving chicken. See POULET, SAUTÉ PANETIÈRE.

panette dolce, a Corsican Easter speciality, consisting of a
bread made with flour, eggs, and sugar and decorated with
raisins.

panettone, a yeast cake which is a speciality of Milan, but
traditionally eaten all over Italy on all main holidays such as
Christmas and Easter. It is made like a large brioche, in many
sizes, but is usually cylindrical in shape. It consists of a
dough made with ¾ lb. (3 cups) sifted flour, 1 oz. yeast, 2
oz. butter, 2 oz. sugar, 3 egg yolks, ¼ pint (½ cup) warm
milk, 3 tablespoons raisins, ½ cup chopped candied peel, peel
of 1 lemon, and salt. It is made in the same way as yeast
dough and left to double its size in a warm place; then the top
is brushed with beaten egg, and it is baked for 35 minutes in a
moderate oven.

panforte, a speciality of Siena in Italy. A honey and fruit cake
which is eaten on all holidays or *festas.* It is made from 4 lb.
honey boiled with 12 oz. (2 cups) chopped blanched almonds
and walnuts mixed, ½ lb. (2 cups) candied peel, 1 teaspoon
allspice, 1 teaspoon cinnamon, and 1 lb. grated bitter chocolate. When it is all well mixed, enough fine rye flour is added
to make a firm paste (about 1½ cups). This paste is formed
into circles about 8 inches across and 1 inch thick, and put
into a cool oven to dry for several hours. They keep well in a
tin, and have a spicy taste, and a chewy consistency not
unlike nougat.

panier, French for basket. A *panier à friture* is a wire
draining-basket used for deep-frying potatoes, fish, etc., and a
panier à salade is a wire salad basket used for shaking lettuce
and other greenstuff after washing.

panierte eier, a German method of preparing eggs in breadcrumbs. First 4 eggs are boiled for 1 minute, then shelled as

quickly as possible, rolled in 1 oz. (1 heaped tablespoon) flour, 1 egg white, and 1 tablespoon breadcrumbs, which makes a thick crust, and cooked immediately in boiling fat or oil. When they attain a golden-brown colour, they are ready to serve on cooked spinach with sauce béchamel, or, if left until cold, on toast with mayonnaise.

pankūkas, a Latvian yeast pancake. See BLINY.

panna, see CREMA.

panne, French for the fat which surrounds pig's kidneys and fillets. It is used in forcemeat and black puddings, and is of excellent quality. It is also called *panne de porc.* See also AXONGE; LARD.

pannekake, a Norwegian pancake made with 5 oz. (1¼ cups) flour, ¼ teaspoon salt, and ¼ teaspoon sugar sifted together, 4 beaten eggs are added and then ¼ pint (½ cup) milk. After further beating, another ¼ pint (½ cup) milk is added, and the mixture is left standing for 3–4 hours, when 3 tablespoons cold water is included. The pancakes are fried in butter in the usual manner and spread with raspberry jam or red currant jelly. See also BLÅBÆR (BLÅBÆRPANNEKAKE); PANCAKE.

pannekoeke, a Dutch pancake, one of the traditional dishes of Holland. They are often baked with bacon and served with molasses, and made in this way, they constitute a meal of their own. Sometimes they are sweet, served filled with *custard saus.* The basic method for making these pancakes uses 2 beaten eggs added to 5 oz. (1½ cups) flour, 1 teaspoon baking powder and a pinch of salt; then 1 cup warm milk mixed with ½ pint (1 cup) water is stirred in gradually to form a batter. A small amount of lard or oil is melted in a large frying pan, and enough batter to cover the base is poured in. The batter is browned on one side, then more oil or lard is added and the pancake turned. A variation called *drie in de pan* ("three in one pan") is often made, using this batter with the addition of raisins. Three smaller pancakes are baked at the same time and are eaten together, either hot or cold, with sugar. See also FLENSJES; PANCAKE.

pannequet, French for pancake; see CRÊPE. The entire surface of the pancake is covered with a filling, then it is folded into four, or rolled, sprinkled with sugar or butter, and glazed in the oven or under a hot grill. Pannequets are frequently served with a savoury filling, as a hot hors d'oeuvre. See also PANCAKE.

pannerone, see GORGONZOLA.

pannfisch, a large German fishcake made from a mixture of cooked white fish and the same amount of cooked mashed potato, both well seasoned; a medium-sized, lightly fried onion is added with a dash of anchovy essence (extract), before frying in a little oil. When lightly browned, it is turned out into a mound-shape, sprinkled with breadcrumbs fried in butter, and garnished with slices of hot beetroot.

pannkaka, a Swedish pancake traditionally served on Thursdays (as is *ärter med fläsk*). They are cooked in a special pan known as a *plättlagg,* which is why they are sometimes called *plättar.* To prepare them ¼ pint (½ cup) milk is stirred into 3 beaten eggs, and 2 tablespoons melted butter are added. Then 5 oz. (1½ cups) sifted flour mixed with salt is gradually beaten in, after which another ¼ pint (½ cup) milk is added. The resulting batter is left standing for 1 hour before the pancake is cooked in butter in the usual manner. It is served with syrup, jam, or spiced cranberries. See also EFTERRÄTER; PANCAKE.

pannkakor, fyllda med räkstuvning, stuffed savoury pancakes. A sauce is made from 2 tablespoons butter, 2 tablespoons flour, ½ pint (1 cup) milk, and the juice from 8 oz. shrimps (a tin of crayfish may also be used). This is seasoned and the drained shrimps are added to it. The pancakes are stuffed with the hot sauce and are then rolled up. They are dabbed with butter, sprinkled with cheese, and browned under the grill.

pannocchie, see CANNOCCHIE.

pannonia, a Hungarian hard cheese made from cow's milk. It has an attractive and distinctive flavour which is hard to describe. Pannonia is a typical and popular cheese, cylindrical in shape and approximately 80 lb. in weight. The paste is a pale yellow colour and full of small eyes.

pannukakku, a thick Finnish pancake. The batter is made with 1 pint (2 cups) milk mixed with 5 oz. (1½ cups) coarse flour, and salt; 2 beaten eggs, 2 tablespoons sugar, and 1 tablespoon melted butter are then added. It is poured into a greased pan and cooked for about 20 minutes. Served cut into wedge-shaped sections, with sugar and jam. See also OHUKAISET; PANCAKE.

panorato alla romana, the Italian version of *pain perdu,* made by soaking the bread slices first in milk and then in beaten egg. The slices are fried on both sides in melted butter, then sprinkled with lemon juice and either vanilla sugar or ground cinnamon.

panoufle, the term in French butchery for the under part of the top of a sirloin of beef.

pansperima, a Greek dish of boiled wheat, dating back to pagan days and symbolically connected with death. It is the forerunner of *kolyva,* which is really an improved version of this earlier dish. It is said to have originated during the reign of Julian the Apostate, who, alarmed at the influence of the early Christian Church, plotted to poison the food of the Greek community of Constantinople during their Lenten fast. According to legend, the head of the Greek Orthodox Church was warned of this in a dream and so instructed his people to eat only their own wheat during Lent. Having been so miraculously saved from death, the Greeks from then on dedicated some Saturdays during each year to the remembrance of the dead. They are known as Soul Sabbaths, and *kolyva* is always eaten. See also KOLYVA.

pantin, I. A French crescent-shaped mould used for making certain pâtés. II. A French pork pâté, sometimes mixed with truffles, made in a small rectangular mould.

panure, a French culinary term for the coating of breadcrumbs pressed onto a foodstuff, melted butter or egg (*panure à l'anglaise*) having been applied first to make the breadcrumbs stick. Afterwards the food is fried until golden. *Panure au beurre* is the term used when the food is first brushed with melted butter; *panure à la milanaise,* the term used when grated Parmesan cheese is mixed with the breadcrumbs. See also PANAGE.

panzanella alla marinna, an Italian bread salad from Tuscany. First 2 slices of bread are soaked in water and, when they have absorbed it, are crumbled finely and mixed with 1 tablespoon chopped basil, 1 tablespoon chopped parsley, 1 tablespoon capers, salt, pepper, and just enough oil and vinegar to moisten them. Then 2 cloves garlic are pounded and mixed with 2 pounded anchovies and 2 chillis, with tarragon vinegar, until the mixture is creamy and fairly thin. The bread mixture is put on a plate and surrounded by sliced hard-boiled egg or tomato, and the garlic dressing is poured over.

panzarotti alla napolitana, small fried ravioli from Naples.

pão, Portuguese for bread, which is often used for puddings in Portugal.

pão constipado is fried bread sprinkled with sugar and cinnamon.

sopa dourada, literally "golden soup," is made from cubes of bread fried in butter. Then put into a syrup mixed with beaten egg yolks and almonds, beaten well together. The top is sprinkled with cinnamon.

pap, Dutch for porridge. In Holland it is usually only the children who eat porridge for breakfast; adults eat a variety of breads, perhaps with cold meat, eggs, or cheese, and jam. Tea is the popular drink at this meal.

papanash, a Bulgarian dish of balls of cheese. A mixture is made of ½ lb. cottage cheese, 1 egg, 1 tablespoon semolina, 1 heaped tablespoon flour, 1 heaped tablespoon butter, and a pinch of salt. The mixture is dropped in spoonfuls into boiling salted water, or formed into small balls, and these are simmered for about 15 minutes. After that, the balls are drained, rolled in sour cream or breadcrumbs fried in butter, and arranged on a dish. If eaten as a dessert, they are served with sugar.

papanaşi, Rumanian cheesecakes made with 1 lb. sieved cottage cheese mixed with 2 oz. (¼ cup) butter, 2 eggs, 1 egg yolk, 3 tablespoons thick cream, with sugar to taste, grated peel of ½ lemon, and a little salt. The mixture is shaped into round flat cakes and fried.

papanaşi cu smantana, as above, served with sour cream.

paparot, a soup which is a speciality of the Istria district of Italy. To prepare it 1 lb. sieved cooked spinach is stirred into a mixture of 2 tablespoons butter and 1 tablespoon flour, with a chopped clove of garlic, salt, pepper, and a pinch of nutmeg. Then 3 pints (6 cups) boiling water are added, and the ingredients simmered for a few minutes, after which the mixture is brought to the boiling point. When the mixture is boiling well, 2 tablespoons fine polenta flour (cornmeal) are shaken in, and the soup is stirred frequently. It should be cooked gently for a further 30 minutes, until well combined. If a blender or *mouli* is used, the spinach can be left on the leaf, and the soup can also be puréed after it has been cooked.

papaw (*Asimina triloba*), a fruit of the same family as the custard apple. It has a purple skin, and should not be confused with the papaya or pawpaw (although the names are sometimes erroneously interchanged). It is served as a dessert fruit, and is popular in the southern states of the U.S.

papaya (*Carica papaya*), the fruit of an American tropical tree, which is large, oblong, and yellow when ripe. The rind is thick and the flesh pulpy, like that of a soft melon. It can be eaten raw, with sugar or lime juice, or may be made into pickles or preserves. Sometimes it is served cooked and sliced with a vinaigrette. The juice is also extracted and canned in America. It is a good digestive and is said to tenderize meat which is placed between two slices of the fruit, and dried papaya is a main ingredient in various commercial tenderisers. It is also called pawpaw.

papaz yahnisi, a Turkish mutton stew. Thick slices of mutton and sliced onion and garlic, seasoned with salt, pepper, and a pinch of cinnamon, with a little vinegar added, are simmered in mutton fat. See also YÀHNI.

paperissa savustettu kala, a Finnish method of smoking fresh fish. The fish is cleaned, rubbed with salt, and after 2 hours, wrapped in greased paper and several layers of newspaper. This package is placed in the embers of the fire, and the newspaper is allowed to smoulder until burnt right down to the greased paper, whereupon the package is removed. The fish is now ready to eat. It may be served either hot or cold.

papillote, en, I. The French culinary term for the method by which food is cooked, and sometimes also served, inside a parchment paper case. The paper is greased and the food is put in whole and seasoned. Then the case is folded up, and the contents are baked. This method preserves the juices of the food, and is particularly good for dry foods such as fish, chicken, or veal. II. A French term which describes a dish such as chop bones, etc., which is decorated with paper frills.

papoutsakia, a Greek dish of stuffed eggplants. To prepare it 6 eggplants are halved lengthwise and the pulp scooped out and chopped, while the cases are first fried before being put in a baking-dish. Then 1 lb. minced meat, 2 onions, and ¼ pint (½ cup) tomato juice are mixed with the pulp, and this mixture is sautéed and then replaced in the cases. The stuffed eggplants are covered with ¾ pint (1½ cups) sauce béchamel

and dotted with butter, then the whole is sprinkled with grated *kasseri* cheese before being baked for about 30 minutes. The dish is served hot. Literally translated papoutsakia means "little shoes," and the stuffed eggplants do resemble them. See also MELITZANES, YEMISTES.

pappardelle, a Tuscan form of *tagliatelle,* made into broad noodles which typically have a crimped or fluted edge.

pappardelle coll' anitra, prepared as for *pappardelle con la lepre,* but using duck intead of hare. It is eaten in Florence on St. Lorenzo's Day, August 10.

pappardelle con la lepre, a Tuscan speciality. The sauce is made from ½ lb. diced hare fried with ¼ lb. chopped bacon, 1 sliced onion, 2 stalks celery, 1 clove garlic, 6 mushrooms, 1 teaspoon marjoram, seasoning, and 1 teaspoon grated lemon peel, 1 heaped tablespoon flour to thicken, ¼ pint (½ cup) red or Marsala wine, and ¾ pint (1½ cups) stock or water all simmered for 1 hour until thick. Before serving, 2 tablespoons grated Parmesan cheese is added, and Parmesan cheese is also served separately.

pappilan hatavara, Finnish for a trifle made with small sweet biscuits (cookies) soaked in fruit juice mixed with a little vanilla and sugar, then decorated with cranberry jam and whipped cream.

paprika, the Hungarian and English name for the dried condiment made from sweet red peppers (*C. frutescens,* var. *grossum;* and var. *tetragonum*). Paprika also means the sweet pepper in Hungary. It is made chiefly in Hungary and widely used there and in Central Europe, but it is also grown and used, to a more limited extent in Spain and Portugal. The two Hungarian districts where these capsicums are grown on a commercial scale are Kalocsa and Szeged. Three distinct grades of paprika are produced: rose or first quality, strong or second quality, commercial or third quality. The very finest qualities of paprika, noble sweet (*nemes édes*) and semi-sweet, are not graded in this way. Paprika is a bright red, aromatic, spicy powder, only hot to the taste in the cheaper qualities; the finest has a concentrated taste of the sweet, smoky peppers from which it is made. It is used extensively in Hungarian cooking, especially in *paprikás, gulyás,* and *pörkölt* both for its pungent flavouring and for its bright colour, which is very decorative in garnishing. Paprika was first brought to Hungary by the Turks and has played an important part in Hungarian cuisine for the past 100 years. As well as being used as an ingredient for paprikás dishes, it is also used for flavouring cheeses, such as *liptauer,* and bacon (*paprikás szalonna*). It is rich in vitamins A and C, and in 1937 Professor Szent-Gyorgi was given the Nobel Prize for finding a new vitamin in paprika, which he called vitamin P. He also proved that it contained more vitamin C than any of the citrus fruits. See also CAPISCUM.

paprika chicken, see CSIRKE PAPRIKÁS; PAPRIKÁS.

paprika-kalbschnitzel, an Austrian dish consisting of 4 thin slices of veal fillet (scallop) which are floured and then fried in butter with 4 medium-sized onions and 1 tablespoon paprika. Then ½ pint (1 cup) sour cream is added 5 minutes before the dish is served. See also SCHNITZEL.

paprikás, a Hungarian stew containing paprika and sour cream, the most famous one being *csirke paprikás* (chicken paprika). Lamb is also cooked in the same manner and is known as *bárány paprikás.* Indeed, there are many fish, meat, and poultry dishes of this kind, all bearing the name paprikás; if the dish contains paprika but does not include sour cream it is known as *pörkölt.* The exception is the paprika stew in which beef is the sole basic ingredient, which is called *gulyás;* nowadays sour cream is sometimes added to *gulyás,* but this is not traditional. See also BORJÚ; GULYÁS.

paprikás borjúszelet, escalopes (scallops) of veal dipped in flour seasoned with salt, pepper, and paprika, and fried with

paprikás of beef

sliced onions in lard. Then 2 cups white stock and 2 shredded green peppers are added, and when they are cooked and the sauce has been reduced, ¼ pint (½ cup) sour cream is poured over and heated. It is served with boiled rice, noodles, or *tarhonya.*

paprikásburgonya, a potato and paprika dish. First 3 finely chopped onions are cooked to a golden colour in fat, and then 2 tablespoons paprika and 1 lb. peeled diced potatoes are added. A little hot water is included barely to cover, and the whole is covered and simmered until the potatoes are cooked. Then ½ pint (1 cup) sour cream is added shortly before the dish is served, and this makes a delicious sauce.

paprikásgomba, a method of cooking mushrooms with paprika. First 2 or 3 small onions are chopped finely and fried until brown. Then 1 lb. peeled mushrooms is added, with 1 tablespoon paprika and salt. They are barely covered with warm water and cooked until the water has evaporated. Then ¾ pint (1½ cups) sour cream is added and stirred well in, and the mushrooms are ready to serve.

paprikásnyúl, a simple but delicious method of preparing hare. First 2 large chopped onions are cooked until golden in hot fat. The hare is cut into thick slices, seasoned with salt and paprika, and added to the onions. A little water is included from time to time until the meat is cooked. Then ½ to ¾ pint (1–1½ cups) sour cream is well mixed in to make a sauce. This dish is traditionally served with dumplings (*csipetke*). See also HARE.

paprikás szalonna, a streaky bacon with a paprika-cured rind. It is used a lot in Hungarian and Balkan cooking, and also in some German dishes. It is quite fat and salty and is often used diced and browned for stews, and with some egg dishes.

paprikásszósz, paprika sauce made from a rich sauce velouté with the addition of cream and a flavouring of paprika.

paragon, one of the best varieties of cultivated chestnut.

parasol mushroom, see MUSHROOM.

parboil, to half boil food before cooking it in another fashion, as for example in the case of sautéed potatoes, which are parboiled before being finished in fat. If there is no refrigeration available, meat is often parboiled to prevent spoilage.

par-cook or *part cook,* to half cook food by roasting or frying, either to increase its keeping properties, or as a preliminary to cooking it in another fashion.

pare, to cut peel from fruit or vegetables.

parfait, an American whipped cream dessert, like a mousse, with a foundation of 1 cup hot syrup cooked in a double-boiler with 4 beaten eggs, both whites and yolks; when cool, 1 pint whipped cream is folded in, and then it is frozen.

Puréed fruit can also be used, and nuts. It can also mean a dessert made from layers of fruit, syrup, ice cream, and whipped cream, served in a tall narrow glass called a parfait glass. See also ICE.

parfait glacé, a French iced sweet, originally flavoured only with coffee. Nowadays it is like a *bombe,* but without the casing of plain ice cream. The cream is made from 6 egg yolks and ½ pint (1 cup) syrup, blended with ½ pint (1 cup) cream and flavoured with rum or brandy; it can also be flavoured with coffee, chocolate, praline, or vanilla.

pargo, Portuguese for the large red bream, also known as porgy, the best of the *Sparidae* family. It is a deep-sea fish with an excellent milky flavour. In Portugal, bream can be poached or fried, in either case being first rubbed with coarse salt, with a few cloves or coriander seeds sometimes added, and left for several hours before being cooked. When served poached, it is usually accompanied by boiled green beans and boiled potatoes. This is called a *cozido.* See also BREAM.

pargo, Spanish for the large red deep-sea bream, also known as porgy, which is cooked as in Portugal (see PARGO), or baked whole with sliced potatoes, onion, lemon slices, tomatoes, and red peppers. See also BREAM.

pargo encebollado, an Andalusian dish, made with 4 chopped tomatoes, 1 tablespoon pounded walnuts, 2 onions, 4 garlic cloves, and a sprig of parsley, all pounded together. Half this mixture is put into a casserole, the base of which is covered with olive oil. A whole pargo, weighing 2–3 lb., is then laid on top, followed by the rest of the pounded mixture and finally 3 sliced green peppers. The whole is seasoned, and ¼ cup oil is poured over. The lid is put on and the contents baked slowly for 45–60 minutes. The lid is removed for the last 15 minutes.

Paris cornichon, see CUCUMBER.

Paris-Brest, a ring-shaped pastry made of chou pastry sprinkled with chopped almonds. After cooking, it is layered with praline butter cream. It is a speciality of Paris.

Paris-gênes, a well-known French cake made with 8 eggs and 8 oz. (1 cup) sugar beaten together for 10 minutes in a double boiler until the mixture has doubled in volume. Away from the heat, it is beaten until cool, when 8 oz. (2 cups) flour, 4 oz. (½ cup) melted butter, and 2 tablespoons rum are added. This mixture is then put into a 9-inch cake tin lined with greased paper and baked for 35 minutes in a moderate oven. When cool, it is split into three and layered with a creamed mixture which is made with 4 egg yolks, 8 oz. (1 cup) castor sugar, and a pinch of salt beaten together until frothy; then 4 oz. plain chocolate is melted with 3 tablespoons rum, and the egg mixture is added to this and heated in a double boiler over a low flame, stirring all the time until it thickens; finally the mixture is removed from the heat and 12 oz. (1½ cups) butter, cut into small pieces, is beaten in. The layered cake is iced with rum-flavoured chocolate icing and decorated with walnut halves.

parisien, a ring-shaped French cake made from sponge mixture. When cooked, it is slit sideways and layered with *frangipane* cream. The centre is filled with crystallised fruits bound with apricot jam, and the sides are covered with meringue which is then set in a very slow oven.

parisienne, à la, I. A French garnish for poultry or entrées, consisting of pommes de terre *à la parisienne* with a variety of vegetables, including artichoke bottoms. See also POULET, À LA PARISIENNE. II. A dish of poached fish garnished with sliced mushrooms and truffles, all covered with white wine sauce and surrounded with crayfish. III. A French chicken consommé with macédoine of vegetables, rounds of royale, and chervil. See also CONSOMMÉ. IV. An alternative name for sauce blonde. Both these names are sometimes incorrectly used for sauce *allemande*. v. A French method of serving potatoes. See POMME DE TERRE (POMMES À LA PARISIENNE).

Parker House croûtons, American croûtons made from bread toasted on one side only, then spread on the untoasted side with a mixture of 4 tablespoons grated Parmesan cheese to 2 tablespoons butter and 1 egg yolk. It is baked in a hot oven until golden brown, and then cut into small cubes.

Parker House rolls, rolls made by scalding 1 cup milk, then adding 2 tablespoons butter, 1 tablespoon sugar, and 1 teaspoon salt. When dissolved and lukewarm, ½ oz. yeast dissolved in 2 tablespoons tepid water is added, also a well-beaten egg. Gradually 2½ cups sifted bread flour is added and kneaded. The dough is then covered and left to rise for about 2 hours (or until double in bulk) before rolling out on a floured surface. It is cut into flouted rounds, and a deep crease is made across the middle with a floured knife handle. The rolls are lightly folded over and pressed together lightly. They are put onto a greased baking sheet and left for ½ hour before baking in a hot oven for about 20 minutes. Both the croûtons and the rolls originated in the Parker House Hotel, Boston.

parkin, a traditional English oatmeal and ginger cake from Yorkshire. In the country round Leeds it is always eaten on Guy Fawkes' Day, November 5. Eggs are not used in traditional parkin recipes, but 1 egg is sometimes added nowadays. Parkin is made with ¾ lb. medium oatmeal mixed with 6 oz. (6 heaped tablespoons) flour, 1 oz. (1 heaped tablespoon) sugar, ¼ teaspoon ground ginger, and a pinch of salt. Then ⅛ pint (¼ cup) milk is warmed to blood heat, when 1 teaspoon baking soda is added, and the liquid is then mixed into the dry ingredients. Next 2 oz. (¼ cup) butter is softened with ¾ lb. (2 cups) black treacle (molasses) and then added to the other ingredients and mixed very well. The mixture is poured into a flat greased baking tin and baked in a moderate oven for 45–60 minutes. Half-way through cooking, the top can be decorated with shredded almonds if desired. When cold, the parkin is cut into squares (a process which is facilitated by leaving it for 2 or 3 days), and in Yorkshire is often eaten with a slice of cheese. See also GINGERBREAD; GRASMERE GINGERBREAD.

párky, Czechoslovakian for frankfurter sausage. The finest kind are a speciality of Prague.

parlies, Scottish ginger cakes, thought to be so called because they were eaten by the members of the Scottish Parliament in the early 19th century. They used to be sold on stalls in the streets of Edinburgh. The following is a Scottish recipe adapted (by Mrs. Fletcher, a well-known 19th-century cook and cookery author) from the Edinburgh *Cook and Housewife's Manual* (1826), also known as *Meg Dod's Manual*. Meg Dod was a famous Scottish innkeeper, a fictitious character created by Sir Walter Scott in his novel *St. Ronan's Well* (1824), and many believe he had a hand in the writing of the Manual, together with Mrs. Isobel Johnstone, who took the name Meg Dod as a pseudonym.

> With 2 pounds of the best dried flour mix thoroughly 1 pound of the best brown sugar and a quarter pound of ground ginger. Melt a pound of fresh butter, add to it one of treacle, boil this, and pour it on the flour. Work up the paste as hot as your hands will bear it and roll out in a rectangular shape, a sixth of an inch, or less in thickness, on a sheet of greased paper to fit a baking sheet. Mark into 4 inch squares. Grease the baking sheet lightly, and draw the paper carefully on to it. Bake in a slow oven for about 40 minutes, when the cakes should be well risen and lightly browned. Separate the squares when soft. They will soon harden.

Half these quantities will make about 30 cakes.

Parma ham, a delicious smoked ham from Parma in Italy. It is eaten raw, cut into very thin slices. See also PROSCIUTTO.

Parmentier, a French word used to describe various dishes which all include potatoes in some form, such as *potage purée Parmentier,* or *boeuf bouilli sauté Parmentier,* or *oeufs Parmentier;* it is also employed when potatoes are used as a garnish. The name is that of the economist, Antoine-Auguste Parmentier (1737–1817), who wrote many books on food and who made the potato popular in France in about 1787. Before his time it was quite rare, and was looked upon with distaste. Sometimes in France a potato is called a parmentière. Parmentier also brought the Jerusalem artichoke into favour, for it was not highly regarded when first introduced into France from Canada in about 1607. See also JERUSALEM ARTICHOKE; POMME DE TERRE (POMMES PARMENTIER).

Parmesan, English and French for *parmigiana,* one of the best-known Italian cheeses; it is also known as *grana* because of its fine graining. Parma cheese is made from skimmed cow's milk mixed with rennet and then cooked for 30 minutes. After many processes of draining and drying over a period of about 6 months, the cheeses are given a black coating, *fumo nero,* which makes them air-tight. At the end of the maturing process the cheese should be a pale yellow, honeycombed with minute holes, and should exude a slight juice. Parma cheese will keep for years. A good one should be at least 2 years old before it is known as *vecchio.* After 3 years it is called *stravecchio,* and after 4 years *stravecchione.* When fresh, it is excellent eaten with bread or on its own. When hard, it grates and cooks better than almost any other cheese, for it does not become sticky or elastic when it melts. It is very often served with pasta. New dishes have been devised to include it, for example *fonduta alla parmigiana.*

parmesane, à la, the French culinary title for foodstuffs or preparations which include grated Parmesan cheese.

parmigiana, one of the best-known Italian cheeses. See PARMESAN.

parnossus, a Greek white cheese made from ewe's milk.

parr, the English name for a young salmon under one year old and still having dark crossed bands on its back. It is protected by law.

parrot fish or ***parrot wrasse,*** the name given to a number of fish of the *Scaridae* family, distinguished by their bright colours and by a mouth which recalls the crossed beak of a parrot. Some varieties are better to eat than others, but, freshly caught and baked or grilled, none is to be despised. See also SCARUS.

parrot wrasse, SEE PARROT FISH.

parsley (*Petroselinum hortense*), an umbelliferous biennial herb, probably the best known and most widely used of all herbs. It is used as a garnish for fish, eggs, meat, and vegetables, or as a flavouring agent in soups and sauces of many kinds. It is an attractive plant with bright green leaves, flat or curly depending on the variety, and with a delicate piquant flavour. Parsley tea was once a popular drink, for it was considered not only refreshing and reviving but good both for indigestion and for rheumatism. Sprigs of parsley fried in hot oil keep their colour, become crisp, and look pretty. See also PERSIL; PERSILJA; PERSILLE.

Turnip-rooted, or Hamburg, parsley is a type which was developed in the 18th century and was used in classical cookery in a *souchet* and in salads. It was much cultivated in England in the Victorian era, but is not seen a great deal nowadays. The fleshy root, which may be lifted and stored, is cooked in the same way as carrot; it has a flavour rather like celeriac. It is used more extensively in Russian cookery, for soups and stews. Turnip-rooted parsley is easy to grow, and a packet of seed produces good results.

parsley honey. Ordinary garden parsley is used, and old plants that have gone to seed will do for this recipe. An enamel saucepan should be packed with washed parsley, which is just covered with water and boiled for 30 minutes, then strained through a muslin. For every pint of juice, 1 lb. sugar is added, and the contents are then boiled up very rapidly until the honey sets. The juice of a lemon may be added with the sugar if desired.

parsnip (*Peucedanum sativum*), a European plant with a long, fleshy, cream-white root which is used as a vegetable. Parsnip has been cultivated for many centuries, and in Elizabethan times was not only served with beef, but was used as a basis for sweet puddings with honey and spice. Indeed the first potatoes, being in fact sweet potatoes, came into favour mainly because they had a sweet taste like parsnips. Parsnip tops make a good green vegetable. Parsnips are never well flavoured unless they have been left in the ground for the first frosts. They may be steamed, boiled, made into fritters, used in soups and stews, and generally cooked in any way that is suitable for Jerusalem artichokes. A dish known as "poor man's lobster salad" is made of cooked parsnip sliced and served with lettuce and a mayonnaise; it has a very vague flavour of lobster. See also PANAIS; PASTINAKE.

candied parsnips, an American method of serving cooked parsnips. They are candied in a mixture of 4 oz. (½ cup) brown sugar, 2 oz. (¼ cup) butter, and 2 tablespoons water, all heated in a frying-pan.

parson's nose, a colloquial English expression for the small fatty joint which holds the tail feathers of poultry. When well crisped after roasting, it is considered a tasty morsel by some people. When the bird concerned is a cooked goose or duck rather than a turkey or a chicken, the joint is called "the pope's nose," although, in a general way, Protestant communities are said to use the latter expression and Catholic communities the former! See also SOT-L'Y-LAISSE.

partan, Scottish for crab, from the Gaelic *partan* (crab).

partan bree, a Scottish soup (bree meaning broth), made from boiled crab, rice, milk, chicken stock, anchovy essence (extract), cream, and seasoning. All the meat is picked from the crab and its claws; meanwhile, 3 tablespoons rice are cooked until soft in 1 pint (2 cups) milk. The rice is then mixed with the meat from the body of the crab, and the mixture is sieved or blended, then heated up in 1 pint (2 cups) chicken stock, flavoured with anchovy essence (extract) and seasoned. The chopped claw meat is then added and, just before serving, ¼ pint (½ cup) cream is added.

partan pie. The flesh of a large boiled and cleaned crab is mixed with salt, pepper, a pinch of nutmeg, 2 tablespoons breadcrumbs, and 1 tablespoon butter. The mixture is then flavoured with ¼ cup vinegar, and 1 teaspoon prepared mustard is stirred in. The mixture is beaten and then put into the crab shell and browned under a grill. This is a Meg Dod recipe, like *parlies.* There seems no obvious reason why it should be called a "pie"; perhaps the word is a corruption of a local dialect term, or possibly this dish was originally made with a pastry crust.

partridge (*Phasianidae*), a game bird of which there are several different species. The common or grey partridge (*Perdix perdix*), found in Europe as far east as the Altai Mountains in west Siberia, is the most common species in Britain, and when partridge is referred to, it is usually grey partridge that is meant. However, in certain parts of the English countryside, particularly in Essex and Hertfordshire, the larger red-legged or French partridge (*Alectoris rufa*) is more common. This bird was introduced from France in about 1660 and is sometimes known as "the Frenchman." In France, it is found mainly in the south. In the U.S. the true partridge is not

found, but some similar birds are called by the name massena quail or ruffed grouse. The Greek or rock partridge (*A. graeca*) is an Alpine variety found in the mountains of France, northern Italy, Switzerland, and other ranges as far east as China. It varies in size and plumage according to the conditions of its habitat.

A young partridge is quite easy to recognize; its first flight feather is pointed at the tip, not rounded as in the older bird, and the feet should be a yellowish-brown (this last does not apply to the red-legged partridge). Birds should be hung in a cool airy place, the young bird for not more than four days, although the older bird may be hung for about a week without spoiling. Gastronomes consider the grey partridge to be the finest to eat, but many regard the red-legged partridge almost as highly. In Britain all young birds are roasted and served with game chips or *pommes de terre frites paille* and a watercress salad; the older birds are casseroled or made into pies. Leftover game is utilised in several ways: potted (see PHEASANT), or made into wafers (see below); other methods are not traditional. In France, many more dishes are served. See also AGERHØNS; ALENTEJO; KUROPATWA; PATRIJZEN; PERDIKES; PERDIZ; PERDREAUX; PERDRIX; PERNICE; RAPPHÖNS; REBHUHN.

partridges (a) grey and (b) red

partridge wafers, a 19th-century English dish for using up leftover partridge; ¼ lb. meat is required. The skin is removed from the birds and the remaining meat cut off. It is minced, and then pounded in a mortar, with the same quantity of butter and breadcrumbs. Then 1 dessertspoon béchamel or another thick white sauce is added. A board is strewn with breadcrumbs, and, with a palette knife dipped in hot water, teaspoons of the pounded meat are spread out on it very thinly. The wafers are trimmed to uniform size and then rolled like small pancakes, hollow inside. They are served as a cold savoury. They can also be made with tongue, ham, or chicken, but if chicken is used, a little ham must be included, otherwise the wafers will be insipid.

pasa makarouna, a Greek dish of Turkish origin made of meat, pasta, and cheese. To prepare it 1 lb. of sheet noodle dough is needed in all. Two sheets are used uncooked as lining and final covering for the baking dish; the rest is cooked and used for intermediate layers. First 2 lb. minced (ground) round steak is sautéed in butter and seasoned. Then the baking dish is lined with a sheet of uncooked pasta, and this is covered with some of the meat, and some grated *kefalotiri* cheese. This is covered in turn with a sheet of cooked pasta, followed by more meat and cheese. The layering is continued in this way until all the meat, all the cooked pasta, and ½ lb. cheese have been used up. Finally a layer of uncooked pasta is put on top and scored with a knife. The dish is baked in a slow oven (300°F) for 30 minutes, when 1 quart (4 cups) chicken stock is added gradually through the slits in the pasta lid. Baking is continued for a further 30 minutes. The name means literally "fit for a pasha, or king."

pashtet, a Russian layered pie, made from fish, shellfish, poultry, or game layered with hard-boiled eggs, potatoes, or forcemeat, moistened with stock, and covered with pastry. However the word has evolved in meaning and is now in common use with the sense of pâté—a dish of pounded fish, shellfish, meat, or poultry.

pashtet iz indeyka, a layered pie made from turkey alternating with forcemeat or veal and bacon. Stock is poured over and a pastry cover put on top. The pie is baked until brown.

pashtet iz rakov, a layered pie made from white fish and crayfish sprinkled thickly with breadcrumbs, with sour cream to cover, and pastry on top.

pashtet iz zaytsa, a layered pie made from young hare, hard-boiled eggs, cream cheese, butter, raw eggs, game stock, and Madeira, with pastry on top.

paskha or *paska,* a flowerpot-shaped cream and cheese dish eaten at Easter in Russia by members of the Russian Orthodox Church. It is made from 2 lb. dry curds (like cottage cheese), ½ pint (1 cup) cream, 1 lb. (2 cups) sugar, 1 lb. (2 cups) butter, 4 egg yolks, 4 oz. sultanas, and ½ teaspoon vanilla. These ingredients are all mixed together and heated gradually, but never boiled. The mixture is then put into a wooden pot specially made for the purpose, which has holes in it for draining. A heavy weight is put on top to drain out any liquid, and it is left overnight. The Russian letters XB are stamped in the mould, meaning "Christ has risen," or these letters are formed on the cake from currants or raisins. In Russia the Easter breakfast (literally the breaking of the Lenten fast) used to go on all day, and paskha or paska was one of the essential dishes. In Imperial Russia, different families had their own private recipes for it, and at Easter they would go from house to house sampling the different kinds. Although the feast of Easter is no longer officially recognized in the U.S.S.R., it is still observed by millions of Russians, and the paskha is indispensable. The dish is also common to Hungary and the Baltic states. The formal title of this dish is *syrnaya paskha.* See also EASTER; KULICH.

paški sir, a soft Yugoslavian cream cheese made from fresh curds.

passa tempo man, a Greek street-vendor who sells nuts and seeds from a small cart, which has a glass-covered tray divided into sections, and at one end a charcoal fire with a

passa tempo man

chimney. The vendor calls at the tavernas where the customers buy his roasted nuts and seeds (for example those of the sunflower and the watermelon), and eat them with a glass of wine or spirits, rather as we eat peanuts or salted almonds with an apéritif.

passarelle, the French term for a dried muscatel grape which is prepared in the Frontignan region of France. The process of turning these grapes into raisins is known as *passarillage.*

passatelli, an Italian soup which is a speciality of the Modena and Bologna districts. It consists of 3 pints (6 cups) of either chicken or beef broth, with a garnish of 4 eggs, 4 tablespoons grated Parmesan cheese and 4 tablespoons fine breadcrumbs, 2 tablespoons butter, a pinch of nutmeg, salt, and pepper, all mixed thoroughly until a paste is formed, which is then forced with a spoon through the holes of a colander, or large sieve into the boiling soup. The small balls of garnish are left to cook for a few minutes before the soup is served with more grated Parmesan cheese. Traditionally this soup used to be a summer dish, the more solid pasta dishes such as lasagne or tagliatelle being provided only until about Easter. See also ZUPPA.

passato, Italian for purée; also purea. *Passato di patate* means mashed potatoes.

passe-crassane, a French variety of pear which is very sweet and fragrant.

passe-pomme, a French apple of which there are three varieties—white, red, and Jerusalem. It ripens early in August.

passe-purée, French for a kitchen utensil used for making purées of meat, fish, fruit, or vegetables.

passion fruit, see GRANADILLA.

passoire, French for a colander or sieve.

Passover, the English word for Pesach, a Jewish holiday which lasts for 8 days, beginning on the evening of the 14th day of Nissan (the 7th month of the Hebrew calendar, corresponding to April in the Christian year), to sunset of the 22nd day. It commemorates the liberation of the Israelites from Egyptian bondage, and commences on the first evening with the traditional Seder table. In all countries except Israel two seders are observed, both having the same ritual, during which many traditional foods are eaten, such as *knaidlach,* grimslich or chremzlach, matzos, beolas, and many dishes which include matzo. Fish and potatoes are also served in various special ways. See also SEDER.

pasta, a farinaceous Italian paste made from flour, salt, water, and frequently eggs. It is the staple diet of millions of Italians, especially in the south. In the north, where rice and maize are grown, risotto and polenta sometimes replace the traditional dish of pasta.

Pasta is believed to have been brought to Italy first by the Ostrogoths, a Teutonic tribe thought to have come from the Vistula area. They first invaded Italy in about 405 A.D. and by 493 A.D. were established all over the north, their leader, Prince Theodoric, having his headquarters at Ravenna. This theory may have some foundation: it is from the Germanic word *nudel* that both English *noodle* and French *nouille* are derived. However, there is no question that the strips of paste were originally Asiatic, for they were known to the Chinese in the Ming dynasty and still figure largely on their menus. It is because of this that other theories credit Marco Polo (1254–1324), the Venetian traveller who went to China, with having introduced pasta into Italy. It is more probable that it was known in Italy well before the 13th century, but was once again made popular by Marco Polo. During the later Middle Ages it was being eaten with tomatoes grown from seeds brought by Fra Serenio from China.

Pasta is the national and traditional Italian food. Served with a wide variety of sauces or with cheese, butter, or olive

several varieties of pasta

oil, it makes a nourishing and filling dish and can be lived on almost exclusively. There are countless varieties of pasta in Italy today, and to make it more confusing, each province has different names for identical kinds.

The first essential distinction to be made is between the homemade pasta not generally found outside Italy, except in Italian stores where it is made freshly, known there as *pasta fatta in casa,* and the mass-produced kind sold in packets, which keeps indefinitely. The best packet pasta comes from Naples and is called *pasta di pura semola, semola* being fine wheat flour, quite distinct from the coarser semolina. The wheat used is the variety called durum, which is harder than British wheats. The best quality pasta, both the homemade and the mass-produced, is made with eggs and is known as *pasta all'uovo.* The basic noodle paste is known in Italy as *taglierini.* Ingredients are 1 lb. (4 cups) flour, 3 eggs, salt, and a little water, all well mixed until the paste becomes elastic. It is rolled out onto a floured table to paper-thinness, left to dry for a short time, and cut into a variety of shapes and sizes. (Homemade pasta needs only half the cooking time of the packaged variety as it is not so dried; it is cooked in plenty of boiling salted water for about 10 minutes.) Any pasta called *verde* is coloured green with puréed spinach.

A further basic distinction is to be made between the pastas served with a sauce, pastas used to enclose stuffing, and pastas used as a garnish for soups.

pasta asciutta, literally "dry" pasta, as opposed to that which is cooked and served in soup. One lb. pasta is cooked in 6 quarts (12 cups) boiling salted water with 1 tablespoon olive oil (the oil prevents the noodles from sticking together) for about 20 minutes, then drained and served straight away, with a sauce. The most important varieties are: bucatini, a thin type of *maccheroni;* alla *chittara,* long thin strips of pasta used in the Abruzzi region; *farfalle,* shaped into bows or butterflies; *fedilini,* long ribbon-like strips; *fettucine,* the Roman name for *tagliatelle* but the width can vary in size; *fusilli,* short spiral-shapes; *maccheroni* (English macaroni), made in long tube-shapes; *pappardelle,* the Tuscan *tagliatelle,* often with fluted or crimped edges; *penne, maccheroni* cut into quill-like shapes and lengths; radiatori, pasta shaped like a motor-car radiator; *rigatoni,* short thick ribbed pieces of *maccheroni;* spaghetti, the most generally known kind of commercially prepared pasta, both in Italy and abroad; *tagliatelle,* the most usual form of homemade or fresh pasta, consisting of

long strips, the width dependent on the type, and known in English-speaking countries as noodles; *tagliolini,* fine matchlike noodles; thin *tonnarelle,* a variety of *tagliolini; tonnellini,* matchstick-like noodles; *trenette,* a Genoese version of *tonnellini; vermicelli,* very fine spaghetti, most frequently served cooked as a garnish for soups but also eaten asciutta. See also MACARONI; MACCHERONI; TORTELLINI.

stuffed pasta, envelopes of pasta filled with a savoury stuffing. They can either be served in clear soup (*in brodo*) or *asciutta* (dry), that is, poached, drained, and served with melted butter and grated cheese. The larger varieties are served *asciutta.* The generic name for almost all kinds of the larger stuffed pasta envelopes is ravioli. They are about 1 inch square. The fillings and the names for these vary from region to region. See RAVIOLI. A variation on spinach-filled ravioli is *tortelli di erbete,* a speciality of Parma. *Cannelloni* is another large ravioli, generally used with similar stuffings. Smaller varieties of ravioli, often served *in brodo,* include *cappelletti* (little hats), much eaten in northern Italy; *cima, malfatti,* and *manicotti,* fresh or homemade versions of *cappelletti,* the first eaten particularly in the south; *panzarotti alla napoletana,* a Neapolitan version of *ravioli alla caprese.*

Other large stuffed pasta are *tufoli,* large, cut *maccheroni* usually stuffed with a meat and cheese filling after boiling, then baked in a sauce (see MACCHERONI, RIPIENI); lasagne (filled rather than stuffed); *calcionetta,* a sweet dish and not a pasta proper. Other small stuffed pasta are *anolini,* stuffed with *stracotto; agnolotti;* gnocchi (originally called ravioli in Tuscany, but not a true stuffed pasta); *tortellini,* small halfmoon coils famous in Bologna, traditional on Christmas Eve and often having a very rich stuffing; tortellini alla panna, as *tortellini,* but served in heated cream. See also AGNOLOTTI; ANOLINI; CANNELLONI; CAPPELLETI; LASAGNA; PASTICCIO, DI RAVIOLI; RAVIOLI.

Many varieties are made in pasta shapes, used as a garnish for clear soups. Acini di pepe, small squares; conchiglia, shells; *crescioni,* crescents; *farfalline,* bows; *maruzze,* larger shells (they may also be served *asciutta*); *pastine* and semini, grain-shapes; *stellete,* stars; and vermicelli. These of course are only a selection; there are innumerable varieties. See also MARUZZE.

pasta asciutta alla marchigiana, a speciality of the Marche province, but not a true pasta. It is made from bread dough (see YEAST, DOUGH) rolled thinly, cut into strips like tagliatelle, left to rise, and then cooked like pasta. It is served with a meat sauce, or any other that is suitable for pasta.

pasta frolla, an Italian sweet short pastry used for pies, flans, and tarts. It is made from ½ lb. flour to ¼ lb. butter, well mixed, to which are added 2 oz. sugar, a little grated lemon peel, salt, and finally 2 egg yolks. If the mixture is too stiff, a little iced water is added to make a firm dough. See also PASTRY.

pasta ke faki, a speciality from the island of Rhodes, which consists of 1 lb. cooked noodles mixed with 1 lb. cooked lentils, the whole garnished with onion rings and fried in butter.

pastas de almendras mallorquinas, a Spanish recipe from Mallorca for almond biscuits. They are prepared with 8 oz. skinned and roasted almonds crushed and mixed with 8 oz. (1 cup) sugar; 2 beaten egg whites are then folded in, and the mixture is dropped, a little at a time, onto an oiled baking sheet. An almond is placed on the centre of each mound, and the biscuits are then baked for 20 minutes. They should be quite small; these quantities make about a dozen.

pastel, Spanish for a sweet or savoury dish in which pastry is used. It can also mean a number of *tortillas* laid one on top of the other with filling in between.

pastel de hornazo, a pasty served traditionally in Salamanca on the Monday following Easter Monday. It contains 2 oz. *chorizo*, 2 oz. each of ham, chicken, or turkey, 2 sliced hard-boiled eggs, and enough stock to moisten, all cooked inside the pastry as for a cornish pasty. It is often eaten on picnics.

pastel de Murcia, a savoury tart traditional in Murcia. It is made of very light puff pastry with a filling of 4 oz. chopped veal, 2 oz. *chorizo*, 2 hard-boiled eggs, 2 oz. chopped brains, 2 oz. minced (ground) meat, and a little stock. The tart is covered with circles of pastry and baked in the oven.

pasteles de almendras, small fried pasties filled with a mixture of 8 oz. ground almonds and 8 oz. sugar mixed with a little water to form a paste.

pastelaria, Portuguese for pastries or pâtisseries. See also SONHOS; SUSPIROS DE FREIRAS; TIJELINHAS DE NATA. Savoury pastries are popular in Portugal. See also EMPADINHAS; PASTELINHOS DE ANCHOVAS; RISSOIS.

pastelinhos de anchovas, Portuguese fingers of pastry served hot and spread with anchovy paste.

pastella, Italian for frying-batter, which consists of ¼ lb. (1 cup) flour mixed with a little tepid water and salt until a smooth thick paste is formed. Then 3 tablespoons olive oil are added and the batter is left to stand for several hours; before it is cooked, a stiffly beaten egg white is added. This mixture makes an excellent light crisp batter which expands a great deal when fried and is ideal for *frittelle*. See also BATTER.

pastelli, a Greek toffee-like sweet made of honey flavoured with sesame. It is popular with children. To prepare it 2 cups sesame seeds to 1¼ cups honey are cooked together very slowly until golden brown (about 15 minutes). When a little of the mixture becomes hard on being dropped into cold water, it is ready to be poured onto a board and cut into pieces like toffees.

pasteurisation, a method of killing a large part of the bacterial content of milk by heating it to a temperature of between 54°C (130°F) and 71°C (160°F), and maintaining it there for some time before cooling. It was devised by the French chemist and bacteriologist Louis Pasteur (1822–1895). It should be noted that this process does not completely sterilize the milk. See also MILK.

pasticciata, a meat stew with herbs and vegetables, a speciality of Verona in Italy.

pasticciata polenta, a Milanese dish, made with ½ lb. polenta cooked in 1½ pints (3 cups) water, which is allowed to cool and then layered in a greased tin with sauce béchamel and cooked mushrooms or truffles. The top is covered with grated Parmesan or Gruyère cheese, and the pasticciata is then baked until golden and bubbling.

pasticcio, Italian for pie. See also ANOLINI; PASTA; RAVIOLI.

pasticcio all' anziana, a flat pastry pie filled with underdone macaroni or spaghetti and a layer of minced (ground) beef or veal mixed with grated orange peel. It is seasoned with salt, pepper, and cinnamon and moistened with a little good beef or veal stock, then covered with more pastry and baked in a slowish oven. It is turned out of the dish and served with a *sugo di carne*.

pasticcio di ravioli, an elaborate dish of ravioli baked with a sauce of chopped chicken livers, bacon, minced (ground) meat, Parmesan cheese, mushrooms, tomato paste, onion, carrot, celery, cream, butter, and stock. Originally it was covered with *pasta frolla*. (It is sometimes made instead with sauce béchamel, a small tomato, peas, bacon, and cheese, all baked for about 15 minutes in a moderate oven.) A similar dish is traditional in Parma for the Sunday luncheon. A dish is lined with *pasta frolla*, filled with about 50 *anolini*, then covered with more pastry, brushed with egg, and cooked in a slow oven for 1½–2 hours.

pastichio or *pastitsio*, a popular Greek dish. It can vary enormously according to the way in which it is prepared, but it is always made with 2 cream sauces: one a thin sauce, consisting of 4 oz. (½ cup) butter, 1 pint (2 cups) hot milk, 1½ oz. (5 level tablespoons) flour, and 2 egg yolks; the other a thick sauce, made by mixing 1 pint (2 cups) cold milk with 4 eggs and 2 oz. (½ cup) flour, heating, and stirring in another pint of milk when hot. The dish itself is prepared by browning 2 lb. chopped beef with 3 onions in butter; then 1 lb. tomatoes, 2 tablespoons tomato purée, a pinch of cinnamon, 3 garlic cloves, a pinch of marjoram and seasoning are added and all simmered for 1 hour. When cool, a few tablespoons of breadcrumbs and 2 unbeaten egg whites are added. Then 1 lb. macaroni is cooked and drained. A pan is spread with breadcrumbs and layers of the macaroni; then the meat mixture and the thin cream sauce are put into it and sprinkled with grated cheese. The thick cream sauce is spread on top and sprinkled with more grated cheese, and the dish is baked for 1 hour in a medium oven. When cool the pastichio is cut into squares, but before being served it is reheated in a hot oven.

pastille, a small round sweetmeat (confection) made from sugar and water, usually with a fruit flavouring.

pastinake, German for parsnip, used in Germany as a vegetable, in stews and soups, and also in a sweet dish. See also PARSNIP.

pastinake-pudding, 3 young parsnips are boiled and mashed, then mixed with 1 tablespoon butter, 3 tablespoons sugar, 2 eggs, 1 cup breadcrumbs, and 2 tablespoons rum. The mixture is put into a buttered mould, sprinkled with a few fresh breadcrumbs and a dot or two of butter, and baked in a moderate oven for 45 minutes. The pudding is served with a sweet white sauce flavoured with orange or lemon.

pastine, small grain-like shapes of pasta. See PASTA.

pastis, a yeast cake which is a speciality of the Béarn district of France. It is made from 12 eggs, 1 spoonful orange flower water, a small glass (4 tablespoons) of brandy, 10 oz. (1¼ cups) castor sugar, a little milk, and 6 tablespoons melted butter, all whisked well together. Then ½ oz. fresh yeast is added and stirred, and enough flour is included to make a good dough. The cake is left, covered, in a warm place overnight, and then baked the next day in a greased tin in a hot oven.

pastitsada kerkireïkïa, a speciality of Corfu. This dish consists of chunks of veal browned with chopped onions, tomatoes, herbs, water, and seasoning. It is served with cooked macaroni stirred into the sauce, the meat being presented on a separate dish.

pastitsio, see PASTICHIO.

pastokydona or *pastokithona*, Greek for quince paste, which may be bought, wrapped in cellophane, in the sweetshops and pastry shops of Athens and other towns. It is extremely good, as well as being a convenient means of using up the pulp left over from the making of quince jam. The following is a recipe from the island of Cephalonia. First 5 lb. pulp is sieved, mixed with 2 lb. (4 cups) strained honey, and cooked slowly for 1½ hours, stirring from time to time. During the last 30 minutes, 6 oz. (1½ cups) toasted or lightly fried almonds are included, together with a 1-inch piece of cinnamon stick (this must be removed when the paste is ready, which is when it starts to come away from the sides of the pan). The paste should be spread out and patted down to a thickness of about 2 inches, and garnished with halved blanched almonds. When cool, it can be cut into shapes which are placed in layers, with bay leaves between each layer (optional), and stored in an airtight tin in a cool place. See also KYDONIA.

pastorella, see BEL PAESE.

pastourmá, a Greek black-rinded smoked bacon, highly flavoured with garlic. It is usually fried until very crisp and it is much favoured by gourmets. It is eaten as an appetizer for *meze,* and is sometimes served with eggs. It is also served very frequently in Turkey.

pastrami, a Rumanian-Jewish cut of meat, usually from breast or shoulder, highly seasoned and smoked. Beef is often used but nowadays turkey pastrami is also popular in the United States. The word comes from the Rumanian *pastra,* to preserve.

pastry, a mixture of flour and fat bound with water. For certain types of pastry, eggs are added. Pastry may be sweet or savoury, and while the usual method is to bake it, there are varieties of pastry that are boiled. The types of pastry that follow are those most used in Britain; their counterparts exist all over the western world. Making pastry is one of the oldest methods of using flour in cooking. See also CIASTO; GERM-BUTTERTEIG; PASTA FROLLA; PÂTE; PHYLLO; PIROZHKI; PIROZHNOYE; PULLATAIKINA; STRUDELTEIG; WIENERBRÖD.

American short crust pastry, a pastry having the same ingredients as short crust pastry, but for which the fat is cut and blended into the flour with a palette-knife instead of being rubbed in. The iced water is sprinkled in, and the pastry chilled before use.

chou pastry, used for eclairs, etc. See CHOU.

flaky pastry, a combination of two ways of making pastry, the short crust method and the puff method. It is used particularly for sausage rolls, jam puffs, Banbury cakes, pies, etc. It is made with 6 oz. (1½ cups) flour to 2 oz. (¼ cup) butter and the same of lard (although some cooks use all butter), a pinch of salt, and 3–4 tablespoons cold water. The flour and salt are sifted into a bowl and the fat is divided into four, one quarter being rubbed into the flour. Water is added, and the whole mixed to a firm dough. The dough is rolled out to a strip about 6 inches wide, and then small lumps of the 2nd quarter of fat are dabbed on to two-thirds of it. The pastry is dusted with flour and folded into 3, left for 15 minutes, then rolled out, away from the cook. This operation is repeated until the remaining 2 quarters of fat are used up. A final rolling is given if the pastry appears streaky. The pastry should be wrapped in paper and chilled before use. See also PASTA FROLLA.

hot-water crust, for raised pies of pork, veal, and ham, etc. This is a completely different method from that used for flaky pastry, and as the pastry is hot it must be worked quickly. It is made with 1 lb. (4 cups) flour and a pinch of salt to ¼ lb. (½ cup) lard and 1½ gills (⅔ cup) water. The lard and water are brought to the boiling point in a saucepan, poured immediately into a basin containing the flour and salt, and mixed with them to a smooth paste. The pastry is quickly rolled, and enough set aside for the pie lid. If no clip mould is available, a stone jar is stood in the middle of the larger rolled piece and the pastry is quickly shaped round it; then pastry and jar are placed in a slow-to-moderate oven. When the pastry is very lightly cooked, so that it is just firm, the jar is removed and the cooked filling is put into the pie, without liquid; the pastry lid, dampened round the edges to make it hold secure, is then placed on top, and the whole brushed lightly with egg to colour it. A small hole is made in the lid to allow the steam to escape, and the pie is again placed in a slow-to-moderate oven. When the pie is cooked and golden, it is slightly cooled, and strong stock that will gel when cold is poured in through the hole. A rosette of pastry is usually made to be put over the hole when the pie is complete.

puff pastry, the finest of all pastries, used for all the best pastries, and containing butter as the only fat. It resembles flaky pastry, but is richer and firmer. Proportions are: equal quantities of butter and flour, a pinch of salt, a little iced water, and a squeeze of lemon juice. It is essential that everything be cold, except the butter which should be firm but not soft, for it will ooze out if the room temperature is very hot. A walnut-sized lump of butter is rubbed into ½ lb. (2 cups) flour, and a firm dough is made by adding the water. The dough is rolled into a rectangle about ½ inch thick, and the whole remaining slab of butter (½ lb. less the nut already used) is put in the centre of one half of it. The other half is folded over, the edges pressed down, and the dough and butter left to stand for 15 minutes. With the sealed edges facing away from the cook, the pastry is rolled outwards until it is about 3 times its original size. Then it is folded into 3, the open edge is turned to face the cook, and the pastry is rolled again. The whole process is then repeated twice more, so that in all the pastry has been rolled and rested 6 times. If the pastry looks fat-streaked, an extra turn should be given. It should be wrapped, and chilled before use.

rich short crust pastry, a pastry used for flans, tarts, or pies, particularly if they are to be eaten cold, for it does not harden. Proportions are ½ lb. (2 cups) flour to 5 oz. (½ cup plus 1 tablespoon) butter, 2 tablespoons water, 1 egg yolk, and sugar if desired. The method is the same as for short crust pastry, and this pastry, too, should be chilled before use. See also PASTA FROLLA.

short crust pastry, the pastry most generally used in Britain for fruit and meat pies, tarts, and flans. It is made by rubbing fat into flour with the finger tips. Proportions are 3 oz. (3 heaped tablespoons) butter, margarine, or a mixture of either with lard, to 6 oz. (1½ cups) flour. A pinch of salt is added, followed by about 3 tablespoons iced water to make a firm pliable dough. A little sugar may be added for a fruit tart or pie. The pastry should be chilled before use. See also PÂTE, BRISÉE.

suet crust, the pastry used for boiled meat puddings, especially beefsteak and kidney puddings, and for sweet boiled puddings. Self-raising flour and plain flour, mixed in equal quantities, should be used, and one third that quantity of chopped or shredded beef suet should be mixed in, with a little salt, followed by a little cold water to make a light and spongy dough. It is lightly rolled into a ball on a floured board, and used immediately after being rolled out.

pastry bag, see FORCING BAG.

pastry cream or **pastry custard,** English renderings of *crème pâtissière.*

pastŭrmà, a dry, garlic-flavoured Bulgarian sausage, served with raw onion rings, and sometimes used in stews.

pasty, a British term for a pastry-enclosed individual dish, not baked in a tin but folded over like a turnover. It is traditional in Cornwall in England. See also CORNISH PASTY.

paszteciki, the Polish name for small pastry cases, usually filled with a savoury mixture of minced poultry, fish, mushrooms, etc. When very small, they accompany hot *barszcz* and other clear soups.

paszteciki z mózgu, Polish calf's brain patties. They are made from 1 set boiled and mashed brains mixed with 1 small minced and sautéed onion, 1 tablespoon flour, 3 tablespoons stock, 1 tablespoon lemon juice, 2 egg yolks, and a pinch of fresh dill. All is seasoned, then put into small shell-like pastry cases and baked for 15 minutes in a moderate oven It is served as a hot hors d'oeuvre, or with clear soups.

pasztet, Polish for pâté, usually made in Poland from 1 lb. goose livers mixed with ¼ lb. salt pork, 1 small onion, 2 tablespoons strong stock, peppercorns, and 1 tablespoon chopped truffle.

pasztet z dziczyny, game pâté, for which 1 lb. each of minced venison and hare are used, mixed with juniper berries and peppercorns to taste, 3 beaten eggs, ¼ pint red wine, herbs, and seasonings. Thrushes or small game birds are also used, with an equal quantity of veal or pork, and ¼ lb. calf's liver (to 1 lb. meat), all minced, and prepared as above.

pata de mulo, see VILLALÓN.

patakukko, a Finnish recipe for fish pie. First 4 lb. fish, together with 12 oz. pork, is chopped up, placed in a dish and covered with pastry made from 1 cup wheat flour, 1 cup rye flour mixed with 1 teaspoon salt, and about 1 cup cold water. The pie is then baked for 4–5 hours in a slow oven, and when the pastry is browned, it is covered with a lid to prevent burning. It may be served either hot or cold, usually with potatoes. See also KALA (KALAKUKKO).

patapaisti, Finnish veal or beef pot roast, garnished with cooked vegetables such as peas, carrots, and onion, and served with a sauce made from the stock thickened with cream.

patáta, Greek for potato. See also POTATO.

patátes keftedes, a Greek speciality of 2 lb. cold boiled mashed potatoes mixed with 4 oz. (½ cup) butter, ¼ cup onion tops, 3 peeled tomatoes, 1 tablespoon parsley, 6 oz. (1½ cups) flour, and seasoning. The mixture is kneaded, rolled out, cut into rounds, and either fried in olive oil or baked on a greased tin in the oven.

patátes kroketes, potato croquettes, a dish often served as an appetizer in Greece. To prepare it 1 lb. potatoes are cooked in their skins, and peeled and mashed as soon as they are cool enough to handle. Then 1 tablespoon finely chopped parsley, 1 small chopped onion, 1 heaped tablespoon butter, seasoning, and an egg are added, and the mixture is formed into small balls which are coated in egg and grated cheese, and fried in deep boiling oil. The croquettes are served very hot.

patátes purée me kreas, a shepherd's pie. Potatoes are cooked as for *patátes kroketes,* and well whipped. Then 1 lb. minced lamb or beef, 2 crushed garlic cloves, and 2 minced onions are gently cooked in butter until the onions are soft, when seasoning is added (tomatoes are also sometimes included in this mixture). A casserole is lined with the potatoes, then the meat mixture is included and finally topped with more potatoes, after which the pie is baked in a moderate oven.

patátes yahni, potatoes mixed with fried onions and tomatoes, all first sautéed in oil, then all braised in water barely to cover.

patátósoupa, potato soup, made from 2 lb. peeled and diced potatoes cooked with 1 onion in 2 pints (4 cups) water and ½ pint (1 cup) milk, with seasoning. When cooked, the soup is sieved and thickened with 2 egg yolks.

patata, Spanish for potato. Boiled and fried potatoes are sometimes served with meat in Spain, but usually potatoes and vegetables constitute a dish on their own, as in the recipe for *patatas y judías verdes* from the Extremadura. Potatoes are often used in place of flour in Spain, owing to the unsuitability of the barren and mountainous terrain for growing grain. In this respect Spain resembles the west of Ireland, where the potato is used in a similar way for bread, cakes, etc. See also BATATAS; POTATO.

patatas y judías verdes, a dish consisting of 2 green sweet peppers which have been roasted, peeled, and cut into rings, 2 peeled and quartered tomatoes, 2 lb. peeled and sliced potatoes, and 2 lb. cooked french beans. The base of a deep saucepan is covered with oil and the ingredients are placed in the pan and seasoned. The pan is then tightly covered and the contents cooked very slowly for 1 hour.

salsa de patatas, a potato sauce, served mainly with fish dishes. First 8 oz. potatoes, 2 tomatoes, 1 red sweet pepper, 2 garlic cloves, 1 bay leaf, and a clove are all chopped finely and simmered in 2 tablespoons oil. When they are soft, 1 pint

(2 cups) boiling water is added and the sauce is simmered for a further 5 minutes, care being taken to stir all the time. It is then sieved, reheated, skimmed, and served with the fish.

patate, French for sweet potato, which is cultivated in France. In the regions where it is grown, the leaves are cooked in the same way as spinach. A delicate jam is also made from sweet potatoes, and when they are preserved or candied in sugar they are not unlike *marrons glacés.* They are also served boiled and sliced, as a salad, with sauce vinaigrette.

pâte, the general French term for pastry (sweet or savoury), bread doughs, pasta, and some batters. Most types of pâte are baked, but some are boiled. The following are the best known. See also PASTRY; PIE.

pâte à baba, à mazarin, à savarin, etc., the term for the particular mixture used for each type of cake. See BABA.

pâte à brioche, pastry made in the same way as plain brioche dough, and used for turnovers or pies shaped by hand. See BRIOCHE.

pâte à chou, see CHOU.

pâte à foncer, see PÂTE, BRISÉE.

pâte à l'eau, simply flour and water well mixed, used for luting.

pâte à pâté, like pâte moulée, but 7 oz. (1 scant cup) butter to 10 oz. (2½ cups) flour is used, as well as 2 egg yolks. The flour and salt are placed in a mound, and a well is made in the middle; all other ingredients are placed in the well and worked into the flour. Enough cold water (2–3 tablespoons) is added to make a pliable dough.

pâte à tartelettes, the pastry used for small flans or tarts. First 4 oz. (1 generous cup) flour is mixed with a pinch of salt and put onto a slab. A hollow is made in the centre, into which are put ½ oz. (1 level tablespoon) sugar, 2½ oz. (⅓ cup) butter, and a very little cold water. The ingredients are blended together and the flour is drawn in to make a pliable paste. The pastry is left in a cold place before being used. It is often preferred for flans and tarts, for it is crisper and more flaky than pâte brisée or pâte sucrée.

pâte au saindoux, the pastry used for large cold pies. It is made from ½ lb. lard, 2 lb. (8 cups) flour, 2 whole eggs, 1 pint (2 cups) warm water, and salt.

pâte brisée, also called pâte à foncer, French short crust pastry. It is usually made with 1 egg added to ½ lb. (2 cups) flour and 4 oz. (½ cup) butter. If used for sweet flans, 1 tablespoon sugar is added. Mixed butter and lard are often used. See also PASTRY, SHORT CRUST.

pâte feuilletée or *feuilletage,* French for flaky or puff pastry, for which butter is the only fat used. The proportion of flour is the same as that of butter. If olive oil is used as well, the pastry is called pâte feuilletée à l'huile.

pâte feuilletée à la viennoise, as above, but two mixtures are made. For the first, 2 egg yolks are mixed with ½ lb. (2 cups) flour, 1 cup water, and a pinch of salt; for the second, ½ lb. more flour is worked with 5 oz. (⅔ cup) butter. The first mixture is rolled out thinly, then 11 oz. (1⅓ cups) butter is enclosed in the flour-and-butter paste, and placed on top. After this the edges are folded over and the rolling procedure followed as described for puff pastry.

pâte frolle, short crust pastry with an egg and ground or pounded almonds added. If a little lemon or orange flavouring is included, this pastry is sometimes used as a basis for petits fours; otherwise flans and sweet pies or tarts are made with it.

pâte levée, yeast pastry, made in the same way as brioche dough.

pâte moulée, pastry used for raised pies or pâtés, made with 10 oz. (2½ cups) flour, half that quantity of fat (butter or butter and lard), water, and 1 egg.

pâte ordinaire, the pastry used for hot or cold pies. It is made with 1 lb. (4 cups) flour to ¼ lb. (½ cup) butter, mixed together; then 2 eggs, salt, and enough cold water to make a stiff dough are added. It is usually left overnight in a cold place before being used.

pâte sucrée, sweet rich short crust pastry, generally used for flans and made of 4 oz. (1 cup) flour to 2 oz. (¼ cup) butter, 2 oz. (¼ cup) castor sugar, 2 egg yolks, and vanilla. The flour is put on a cold slab, and a well is made in the middle; the other ingredients are put in the well and worked into the flour until a ball is formed. The pastry is chilled before being used.

pâté, I. French for a meat, fish, or fruit pie, served hot or cold. This is the original meaning of the word, which is still used for pâté de Paques (and pâté de Noël), an Easter pie, a speciality of the Poitou region of France. It is long, crescent-shaped, and filled with balls of minced or ground meat, slices of pork, chicken, or rabbit (sautéed in butter and left to get cold), and sliced hard-boiled eggs. Pâté de Noël, see TOURTIÈRE. See also PIE. II. The word now in common use for a dish of meat, fish, or fruit, sometimes pounded to a paste, then baked, and in the case of meat or fish, enclosed in either bacon rashers or melted butter. (Strictly speaking, this dish when served cold should be called a *terrine*, after the dish in which it is cooked, but pâté is now commonly used instead.) It may be enclosed in pastry, in which case it is referred to as *pâté en croûte* or *pâté en pantin*. The savoury pâté is made of layers of forcemeat, sautéed strips of the game, fish, poultry, or meat, sometimes truffles, and shallots, herbs, spices, and seasoning, with Madeira wine, red or white wine, brandy, strong stock, or butter. It is usually made in an oval, rectangular, or crescent shape (*pantin*), and is baked in a slow oven for about 1½ hours. If it is to be served cold, a good jellied stock is sometimes added when the pâté is cold, and if it is to be kept, a seal of melted butter is poured over the top. There are many famous pâtés made in France, certain regions being renowned for them. For examples see FOIE GRAS, PITHIVIERS, and TERRINE. See also PASZTET PAVÉ; PETITS PÂTÉS.

pâté de Bruxelles, a Belgian speciality from Brussels. It consists of minced chicken and minced fat bacon, mixed with allspice, brandy, salt, and pepper, all well pounded. The paste is put into a fireproof dish with bay leaves, thyme, and layers of fat bacon rashers, covered, and baked slowly in a *bain-marie* for 2 hours. The pâté is served cold with toast.

pâté de cédrat, a citron preserve, a speciality of Bayonne. It is a thick jam-like paste made in the same way as *cotignac*, *membrillo*, or *marmelade*. See also CITRON.

patelle, the French name for various gastropod molluscs, such as limpets, which are eaten raw like oysters or clams.

patent spinach, see NEW ZEALAND SPINACH.

patervisch, see WATERFISCH.

patience dock, see DOCK.

patinho, Portuguese for duckling. See PATO.

pâtisserie, the French name for small cakes or pastries baked in the oven. A *pâtissier* is a pastry cook.

pâtisson, see COURGES.

patlagele vinete, a Rumanian salad of cold cooked eggplant.

patlican, Turkish for eggplant. See also EGGPLANT; MELISA.

patlıcan ala naz, a Turkish dish adopted by Jewish people from the countries of the Near East. It consists of 2 large eggplants, 1 lb. chopped lamb, 1 large onion, 1 teaspoon paprika, 1 tablespoon tomato purée, 1 tablespoon parsley, salt, and pepper. The eggplants are sliced, then covered in salt and left for at least 1 hour, after which they are drained and dried. The chopped lamb, chopped onions, and parsley are mixed together and spread on top of the eggplant, then covered with tomato purée and baked for 1 hour. The dish is gar-

nished with parsley and served with either boiled rice or mashed potato.

patlidžan, a Serbo-Croat word for eggplant. It is used extensively as a dish on its own, when it is often stuffed and baked and also in stews or in *musaka od plavim patlidzanom*. See also EGGPLANT.

modri patlidžan punjen sirom, stuffed eggplant with cheese. First 1 large peeled eggplant is boiled for 10 minutes in salted water, drained, left to cool, then cut in half lengthways. The inside is scooped out and mixed with ½ lb. (2 cups) grated hard cheese, 2 tablespoons butter, 1 small grated onion, 1 teaspoon chopped parsley, 1 raw beaten egg, and seasoning to taste. This mixture is put back in the skins, dotted with a little butter, and baked in a moderate oven for 20 minutes.

Patna rice, Indian rice with a particularly long thin grain, used for curries, pilafs, etc. See RICE.

pato, Portuguese for duck. Duck is often served smoked in Portugal, and this is a national speciality. See also DUCK.

pato à portuguesa, a duck is first sautéed in hot oil with onions; then ½ lb. peeled tomatoes and 1 chilli are added, followed by 1 tablespoon butter, a bay leaf, 1 tablespoon vinegar, ½ pint (1 cup) red wine, and seasoning. It is covered and cooked in the oven for about 1 hour. Sometimes 1 cup olives is added. It is served with boiled rice, potatoes, or chick peas.

pato, Spanish for duck. See also DUCK.

pato a la sevillana, a traditional recipe from Seville. Wild duck such as a brace of young mallard are best for this dish, and it is expedient to begin preparations a day before it is to be served. The ducks are jointed, lightly floured and seasoned, and browned in oil flavoured with 2 garlic cloves. Then the joints are put in a warm place to drain, and 2 onions are fried in the same oil until soft; 2 lb. peeled tomatoes are added and the whole slowly simmered; later, 1 pint (2 cups) stock from the giblets is included, and the duck returned to the pan together with a bouquet garni. The pan is covered and the contents simmered for 2 hours. In another pan, 2 chopped red sweet peppers and 2 garlic cloves are fried in oil, with 2 oz. (½ cup) breadcrumbs and ½ pint (1 cup) giblet and duck stock. This mixture is then pounded and seasoned and added to the duck. Cooking is continued a little longer, when the duck is again removed and the sauce strained; ½ gill (4 tablespoons) sherry is added to the sauce, which is then reheated. The duck is once more placed in the sauce and cooked for a few minutes longer, after which it is all transferred to a warmed casserole, from which it is served. Then 12 stoned olives are included, and 2 sliced oranges are placed on the pieces of duck. The dish is grilled for a further 5 minutes. Strips of skinned, baked red pepper are used as decoration.

patricieni, spicy Rumanian pork sausages, usually served grilled.

patrijzen, Dutch for partridges, which are popular and plentiful in Holland.

patrijzen met kool, partridges with cabbage. This is a good recipe for elderly partridge which would normally be used for a casserole. Boiling water is poured over 4 birds; then salt is rubbed into the flesh, 3 slices of fat bacon are secured over the breast of each bird, and the birds are roasted in 4 oz. (½ cup) butter in a moderate oven for about 30 minutes, being basted frequently. The bacon is then removed, and the birds are cut lengthwise and placed in a casserole, where they are laid on a bed of boiled shredded cabbage, with more cabbage to cover—using in all 1 large cabbage. Pepper and a pinch of nutmeg are sprinkled over. A sauce is made with 2 medium-sized onions sautéed in a pan, and to them are added the chopped bacon, meat from the breasts, and 1 pint (2 cups) stock. The sauce is poured over the contents of the casserole, the lid is put on, and the dish cooked in a moderate oven for about 2 hours. It is served with boiled potatoes.

patsas, a Greek soup made from 2 lb. tripe, 4 pig's feet, 6 garlic cloves, and peel of 1 lemon, seasoned and cooked in 6 pints (12 cups) water for 2 hours. *Avgolémono sauce* is added to it before serving. Other vegetables, such as onions or celery, can also be included.

patties or **pattys,** I. Small pies, usually made with short crust pastry, although flaky pastry can also be used. Patties contain only savoury fillings such as fish, game, poultry, or meat. Sweet patties are called tarts, tartlets, or pies, as for example mince pies. (In some parts of the country, however, turnovers, which have a sweet filling, are referred to as patties.) Patties are made in individual portions and are best served hot. The filling is cooked before being put in, and is entirely enclosed in the pastry. II. In the U.S. patties are also small cakes of minced meat or poultry, shaped like croquettes, but cooked plain, without first dipping in egg and breadcrumbs.

patum peperium, a 19th-century English anchovy paste, still made commercially, and known popularly as Gentleman's Relish. It consists of pounded anchovies, butter, cereal, spices, and salt, and is usually eaten on hot buttered toast. It is a good tea-time savoury.

pauillac, the most sought-after type of unweaned lamb in France. See AGNEAU.

paupiettes, a French culinary term denoting thin slices of raw meat or fillets of fish (usually sole), filled with forcemeat, rolled up like a pancake, secured, and braised in very little liquid. Sometimes a thin rasher of bacon forms the outer covering. Paupiettes are garnished with various vegetables. See also BEEF OLIVES.

pavé, I. A French culinary term denoting a cold dish, often a pie or mousse, set in a special square or rectangular mould. A pavé may be sweet or savoury; if savoury, salmon, sole, pheasant, or other game is popular. Decorated aspic may be used as a coating. See also PÂTÉ.

pavé aux marrons, a sweet made from 2 lb. cooked, sieved chestnuts mixed with ½ pint (1 cup) syrup and 2 tablespoons butter, put into a rectangular mould, lightly brushed with olive oil, and left in a cold place for a day. It is then removed from the mould with a knife and covered with a mixture of melted chocolate, sugar, water, and a little butter.

pavé du roi, perhaps the grandest pavé of all. A large goose liver, studded with truffles, is enclosed in pastry shaped into a crescent and decorated with pastry fleur-de-lys. The pastry is painted with egg yolk and the pavé is baked. It is left to get cold, and some port-flavoured jelly is then put in through the air-hole which has been made on top. Pavé du roi may also be made in a mould, without the pastry, the liver being cooked first and then set in foie gras mousse.

II. The name for a small square *génoise* or sponge cake, sandwiched with butter icing.

pavé au chocolat, chocolate sponge layered in the mould with chocolate-flavoured butter icing, and iced when cold. Coffee, hazel nut, and fruit sponges are also made.

III. Rice, cooked and sweetened, layered with cooked fruit and then cut into rectangles which are dipped in egg and breadcrumbs and fried. They are served hot with fruit sauce.

pavé de moyeaux, a French cheese made from cow's milk. It comes from Normandy, and is at its best from November to June.

pavezky, the Czech term for thin slices of bread which are moistened with milk, dipped in beaten egg and breadcrumbs, and fried in fat until golden brown all over. They are often served, like croûtons, as an accompaniment to vegetables.

pavie, a firm-fleshed peach, not unlike a clingstone.

pavo, Spanish for turkey. See also TURKEY.

pavo adobado, a Castilian dish of marinated turkey. The marinade is made from white wine, 1 onion, 1 garlic clove, 1 bay leaf, and 12 peppercorns, and the bird is soaked in it for 4 hours. After being dried, the bird is browned in hot olive oil; then 1 lb. peeled tomatoes, 2 onions, 4 garlic cloves, 1 clove, a pinch of cinnamon, the strained marinade, salt, and pepper are all added. The dish is tightly covered and cooked in a slow oven for 2–3 hours.

pavo picante, a Spanish-American dish of small broiling turkeys, jointed and first grilled in butter, then casseroled in 2 pints (4 cups) stock with 1½ tablespoons mole powder. See also PICHE-PACHE.

pavot, graines de, French for poppy seeds, much used in Alsatian cookery.

pawpaw, an alternative name for papaya. It is frequently confused with papaw, but is an entirely different fruit.

pa-y-all, a corruption of *pain à l'ail* (garlic bread), a Catalan peasant breakfast dish. It consists of a piece of fresh bread, sometimes fried first in olive oil or pork fat, then rubbed all over with a peeled garlic clove and sprinkled with coarse salt and perhaps a few drops of olive oil, according to taste.

paysanne, à la, I. A French garnish for entrées, identical to *à la fermière,* but with the addition of *pommes de terre cocotte.* II. The name given to large peas when cooked in a certain way (see POIS). III. A French method of serving potatoes. See POMME DE TERRE (POMMES À LA PAYSANNE).

payusnaya, a coarser, pressed form of caviar, sold all over Russia and eastern Europe. The name comes from *payus,* the term for the adherent skin of the ovaries of the fish.

pea (*Pisum*), a plant of the family *Leguminosae.* The species most commonly used for culinary purposes in the western world is the garden pea (*P. sativum*), also called green pea and shelling pea, which is cultivated in all but tropical and subtropical countries. Its origin is unknown, for efforts to trace its history are complicated by the lack of definition of its ancient name. Such evidence as exists favours western Asia as the original home. Peas of many kinds were known to the ancient Greeks and the Romans, and they have been found in the Bronze Age lake dwellings of Switzerland. Wild peas were used in medieval Britain, and by 1597 the famous herbalist Gerard was able to list 4 varieties grown in British gardens: Rounceval peas (*Pisum majus*) which were cooked in the pod; garden and field peas (*P. minus*); tufted or Scottish peas (*P. umbellatum*); and peas without skins in the pods (*P.*

pea

excorticatum), which were cooked whole like Rounceval. In 1787 Thomas Andrew Knight experimented by crossing different strains, and many of the modern American varieties originated in England as a result of Knight's investigations. Most varieties of pea are grown for the seeds within the pods; successive sowings are made to yield a continuous crop during the summer months, and they are eaten as young and small as possible, freshly picked and shelled. They are the most popular summer vegetable. They are cooked in a minimum of boiling, salted, but also slightly sugared, water, sometimes with a little chopped mint, for not more than 8–10 minutes. They may be served as a separate course, or with any joint or entrée; they are also used for garnishes, in fillings for artichoke bottoms, tartlets, etc., and in salads. Garden peas are also cultivated commercially for deep freezing. Dried peas and split peas are available all the year round. They are used for soups, and are also soaked, boiled, and mashed for purées. Some dried peas are green, others yellow.

Some varieties of garden pea, the sugar peas (*P. sativum*, var. *macrocarpum*), have edible pods which are without the parchment-like lining that is present in the pods of shelling peas. The pods are picked before the seeds, or peas, inside have reached maturity, and are prepared by topping, and tailing, and cooking in any way that is suitable for french beans. See also ÄRT; CAPUCIJNERS; ERWT; GROSZEK; GUISANTES; PISELLI; POIS; SCHOTEN; SPLIT PEA.

pea bean (*Phaseolus vulgaris*), also known as beautiful bean, a variety of climbing french bean cultivated for its seeds, which are round, like peas. It is not very well known, yet is one of the most delicately flavoured of all beans, somewhat resembling the sugar pea. The variety pea bean du pape, offered by English seedsmen, is particularly delicious and of vigourous growth. Another variety, Goliath, produces enormous pods useful for exhibition purposes, but as with most vegetables, the small young ones are the most succulent. Pea beans should be cooked in boiling salted water for not more than 10 minutes, then drained and served with a little butter and freshly ground pepper.

peach (*Prunus persica*), a delicious and universally cultivated fruit, which is a native of China but was introduced into Europe over 2,000 years ago. The Anglo-Saxons called it *perseoc*. There are innumerable varieties, almost all having a rough downy skin. Some are juicy, tender, and aromatic, and are eaten fresh as dessert fruit; others are larger, firmer, and darker of flesh, and are used commercially for canning, bottling, and preserving. Both fresh and preserved peaches are used in confectionery, in the making of jams, jellies, and liqueurs, and as flavouring. Large peaches have not always the best taste; the small greenish yellow and pink ones, particularly the American amsdem grown a great deal in France and Britain, have a finer flavour than the large yellow and red ones. The nectarine is a very juicy, smooth-skinned variety of peach with an excellent flavour. See also BRZOSKWINIE; PÊCHE; PESCA; PFIRSICH.

peacock (*Pavo cristatus*), a beautiful, large blue and green bird, distantly related to the turkey. The female of the species is the peahen. Peacock used to be eaten in Europe at medieval banquets, where it was carved by the most distinguished person present and served by the lady most honoured for her rank or beauty. It was stuffed with herbs and spices and roasted. Sometimes the skin and feathers, having been specially treated, were replaced on the carcase, and the feet and beak were gilded and also put back. Nowadays, but only very occasionally, the young chicks are eaten. Their flesh is inclined to be dry, so they need larding; otherwise they can be prepared in the same way as pheasant. The taste resembles that of turkey.

peacock

peanut (*Arachis hypogea*), also called earthnut or groundnut, in origin a Brazilian plant but now cultivated in many subtropical countries. The pods or fruits are oblong, and cylindrical, with a thin shell. When the flower withers, the stalk bends down, forcing the ovary underground, making the seeds mature some distance underground, hence the name. Its long oily seed provides both peanut oil and peanut butter, the latter made by emulsifying the oil with the nuts. In Europe and the U.S. peanuts make a valuable contribution to vegetarian diets. They are also sold on a large scale, roasted and salted. They are a staple food for millions of people in Africa and in the Far East, where they are made into soup and are also used for stuffing chicken. The oil is used for cooking, and is in fact preferred in many parts of France to other oils.

pear (*Pyrus communis*), a tree native to temperate Europe and to the west of Asia as far as the Himalayas, cultivated for its fruit. A few types of pear are grown in North America, but these are hybrids of the European species. (The parent was no doubt Williams' *bon chrétien*, known as Bartlett pear in the U.S.) The European pear has been cultivated since very early times; Pliny mentions 39 varieties known to the Romans, who were probably responsible for introducing the pear into England. It became a favourite fruit in Italy, and a 16th-century manuscript lists some 232 varieties, 209 of which were served during the course of a year at the table of the Grand Duke Cosmo III. Nowadays there are several thousand varieties, and many French pears are also grown in Britain and the U.S.

Pears vary in shape from the distinctive pear-shaped and calabash, or elongated, to the oval and round. The colour of skin and flesh also varies from one type to another. Some pears are sweet, melting, and juicy, and are eaten as dessert fruit; these include the Williams' (as *bon chrétien* is now called), doyenné de comice, and conference pears. This last was developed at a nursery in Hertfordshire and was first shown to the public at the International Pear Conference held at Chiswick in London in 1885, where it was awarded first prize from among some 10,000 other different varieties, and so was given the name of conference. The harder varieties of pear are used mainly for cooking, canning, and preserving, and in confectionery. One species, the snow pear (*P. nivalis*) is grown solely to make a fermented drink called perry. A small-fruited pear (*P. communis*, var. *cordata*) is found wild in western France, Devonshire, and Cornwall. One of the oldest English pears is *bergamot* (*P. amygdaliformis*, var. *persica*), which is ball-shaped. Another very old English pear is the *warden*. In Shakespeare's *Winter's Tale*, the clown refers to "warden pies" which are to be made with sugar, mace, saffron, nutmeg, ginger, prunes, raisins, and wardens, a variety of pear which was common in the 16th century, and was grown by the monks of Warden Abbey in Bedfordshire. Until the last century warden pies and baked wardens were sold at all local fairs.

pear

If good, pears are eaten raw; they can also be baked, cooked in syrup for a compote, cooked in wine, in flans and tarts, and served with ice cream. See also BIRNE; GRUSZKI; PERA; PEREN; POIRE.

pearl barley, barley with the outer husk removed. It swells a great deal in cooking, and is used for thickening soups and stews, particularly Scotch broth and mutton stew. It has a pleasant nutty flavour. See also BARLEY.

pease pudding, see SPLIT PEAS.

pease-meal bannock, see BANNOCK.

peberrod, Danish for horseradish. See also HORSERADISH.

peberrodssauce, horseradish sauce. This may be made in two ways in Denmark:

Like the English horseradish sauce, then frozen. This sauce is served with hot boiled salmon or with cold ox tongue or alternatively it can be made with a roux of 2 tablespoons each of flour and butter, with ¾ pint (1½ cups) hot milk, 2 teaspoons sugar, and 2 tablespoons fresh grated horseradish. This has the character of an English white sauce, but flavoured with horseradish and sugar. Horseradish is also served with cod. See TORSK.

pebronata, a Corsican speciality of braised beef flavoured with juniper berries. Wild boar is also cooked in this way.

pec, a French word used only in connection with herring. *Hareng pec* is a freshly salted herring which is not smoked before barrelling.

pecan (*Carya oliviformis*), a thin-shelled oblong nut, smooth and reddish, the fruit of a species of hickory tree that grows in the southern states of the U.S. It has a rich nutty flavour, not unlike an extremely good walnut, and is much used in confectionery as well as in cakes and puddings.

pêche, French for peach. The finest varieties grown in France, many of which are of American origin, are *amsdem,* of medium size, round, with juicy greenish-white flesh and a very good flavour, ripening in late June; *croncels,* which ripens in late August, big, oval, amber-coloured, with juicy flesh and a good flavour; *felignies,* of medium size, yellow with crimson flush and a very good flavour, ripe at the end of August;

Hale's early, of medium size, with pink flush and mottled skin, very juicy flesh and a good flavour; *France,* large with very downy skin, yellow and crimson, and very good to eat; *grosse mignonne,* very big, nearly round, with purplish skin and excellent white flesh; *reine des vergers,* large, elongated, with a crimson-purplish flush and good white flesh; *Victoria,* round, of medium size, yellow with a crimson flush, with white melting flesh shading to pink near the stone, and a very good flavour. *Brugnon* and *nectarine* are smooth-skinned varieties. The best peaches are served raw as dessert fruit. They are also made into flans and tarts, crystallised, bottled in brandy, flambéed, and made into compotes, or served with ice cream, etc. See also BELLE-CHEVREUSE; BELLE-GARDE; PEACH.

pêches bourdaloue, peeled, halved peaches poached in vanilla-flavoured syrup, then drained and dried. They are arranged on a layer of *frangipane* which has been mixed with crumbled macaroons, in a lightly baked pastry flan case. Sometimes the top is covered with more *frangipane* and a little melted butter, before glazing in the oven, but this dish can also be served plain, garnished with chopped crystallised fruits and chopped nuts. Other fruits such as pears, apricots, etc., are also served in the same way.

pechenaia kartofel v smetane, a Russian dish of potato and sour cream. To prepare it 1 lb. cold sliced potato is layered in a baking dish with 1 large fried onion, then sprinkled with breadcrumbs mixed with grated cheese, and covered with ½ pint (1 cup) sour cream which has had 2 eggs beaten into it. It is baked in the oven until it is a golden brown.

pecorino, the generic name for all Italian ewe's milk cheeses. The original and best of all is *pecorino romano,* which was mentioned by Pliny. It is a hard-curd, cooked cheese with a yellow crust (except in Siena, where the crust is red). The inside is straw-coloured. It has a strong flavour, and can be eaten with bread or grated for cooking purposes. After pecorino romano, the best-known varieties are *canestrato, cotronese, moliterno, pepato, pietracatella,* pecorino degli abruzzi, pecorino toscano, and *pecorino pugliese.* See also CANESTRATO; COTRONESE; MOLITERNO; PECORINO SARDO; PEPATO.

pecorino sardo, also generally referred to as *sardo,* a hard, white, pungent Sardinian cheese made from ewe's milk, with a sharp salty tang when fresh. It is used in cooking, especially in pesto and for grating over pasta. In the Abruzzi it is served with pears. See also PECORINO.

pecten (*Pectinidae*), a genus of bivalve molluscs with grooved, rounded shells. The most important is the scallop. The scallop shell became the emblem of pilgrims journeying to the shrine of St James at Compostela, and they wore the shell as a badge on the shoulder. This is how the common French name for scallop, *coquille Saint Jacques,* arose. It was first called *peigne Saint Jacques,* as *peigne* is French for pecten. See also COQUILLE SAINT JACQUES; SCALLOP.

pectin, a mucilaginous substance found in certain fruits, for example apples, oranges, lemons, black currants, and red currants, and in certain vegetables such as lentils and peas. Its presence means that, when boiled with sugar, their pulp will set as a jelly; and indeed without pectin the making of jams and jellies is impossible. Some fruits, such as strawberries, contain very little pectin, so that when jams or jellies are to be made with them lemon juice or commercially prepared pectin is often added to ensure that setting takes place.

peel, the outer skin found on some fruits and vegetables, whether hard or soft. In certain fruits it may also be called rind. Peeling is the act of removing peel.

Peggy's leg, an Irish toffee made from 1 lb. (2 cups) brown sugar and the same of molasses and syrup, 1 lb. (2 cups) butter, 1 teaspoon ground ginger, and 4 tablespoons vinegar, all melted and boiled, and well stirred until a small ball of the mixture will set in cold water. One half of the mixture is poured into a greased pan, and the remainder has 1 small teaspoon baking soda added, which makes the mixture froth up and become lighter in colour. This light mixture is then poured onto the dark one, and the double-layered toffee is cut into strips which are twisted and then pulled out into sticks, and cut with greased scissors.

peinirlis, savoury Greek pastries. Pieces of yeast dough, usually boat-shaped, are baked and then packed with one of a variety of possible fillings—fried eggs, eggs and ham, cheese, or sausage. They are served in Greece as a rather special type of appetizer, being more substantial than those usually offered.

peixes, Portuguese for fish. Portugal is particularly famous for her sardines. See SARDINHAS. Sopa de peixes is fish soup. See SOPA DE PESCADOS. Portuguese fish include *atum, bacalhau,* besugo, *lampreia, linguado, lula, pargo, pregado, robalo,* and *salmonete.* See also CALDEIRADA.

pejerrey (*Basilichthys bonariensis*), "the king of fishes," found off the Atlantic coast of South America and also in the Pacific, off Chile. It is also called *pezrey,* and is a member of the silverside family. It resembles a smelt and can be cooked in the same way.

pekmez, a Serbo-Croat word for jam. One of the most popular varieties is made from the native dark blue plum for which Yugoslavia is famous and which forms the basis of *slivovič,* the plum brandy which is a national drink. The jam is usually eaten with hot rolls, particularly in country districts.

pélamide or **pélamyde,** French for bonito. It is also known as bonite, and is called *germon* by Normandy fishermen where it is very highly thought of as food.

pelardou, a French cheese made in the Languedoc region from goat's milk. It is at its best from May to November.

pelle rouge, an alternative French name, with *fer à glacer* and *salamandre,* for the utensil known as a salamander.

pellkartoffeln, German for potatoes cooked in their skins.

pelmeni, a Russian dish of small stuffed envelopes of thin pastry, similar to ravioli. They were originally a Siberian speciality, but are now common in other parts of Russia. The pastry is made from ½ lb. (2 cups) flour mixed with 1 egg, a pinch of salt and approximately 5 tablespoons water to form a stiff dough, which is then rolled out very thinly. Stuffings vary from minced meats to chopped cabbage. The pelmeni can either be poached in boiling salted water or stock and served with melted butter or sour cream, or they can be fried in butter after a preliminary boiling of about 3 minutes. They are often served with borsch polsky.

sibirskie pelmeni, the pastry made as above, the filling consisting of chopped hazel grouse, ham or pork, lemon juice, and meat gravy. Half the pastry area of each envelope is folded over the stuffing, and the edges are pressed together. They are poached for about 20 minutes, then drained, and served hot with melted butter and a little lemon juice, or perhaps with a mustard and vinegar sauce, which the Siberians tend to prefer as an accompaniment.

pelte, an Albanian sweet dish, made from 2 oz. (½ cup) corn flour (cornstarch), 12 oz. (1 cup) molasses, and 3 tablespoons sugar, all boiled with 2¼ pints (4½ cups) water for 30 minutes until it becomes thick and syrupy. Then 1 cup sliced almonds and 3 tablespoons lemon juice are added and cooked for 5 minutes. Finally the dish is baked in the oven for about 10 minutes, to set. This is also eaten in Greece, or used there as a thick syrup.

pelures, a French culinary term for the trimmings or parings of foods such as mushrooms or truffles; they can be used in cooking for flavouring purposes.

pemmican, a name given by North American Indians to strips of air-dried buffalo meat or venison, which were pounded up and then, with the addition of melted fat, mixed into a cake-shape. This used to be taken on exploratory expeditions, for it required no preparation (being eaten raw), kept well, and had great protein value. With the development of dehydration of foods, however, it has been largely superseded by meats dried by modern methods.

penetleu, a Rumanian cheese, which is a type of *caşcaval,* named after the district in which it is made.

pénide, a French confection made of sugar cooked with barley, then poured onto an oiled slab and twisted, like rope, with the hands. The result is a sweetmeat not unlike an opaque barley sugar.

penne, a tube of pasta about 2 inches long and ¼ inch in diameter, with pointed ends, used particularly in *maccheroni alla siciliana.* See also MACCHERONI.

pennyroyal (*Mentha pulegium*), a species of perennial herb with aromatic leaves of a mint-like flavour. See also MINT.

pennyroyal

penoche or **penuche,** a sweetmeat or candy from the southern states of the U.S. It is made from 1½ lb. (3 cups) light brown sugar boiled with ½ pint (1 cup) milk until the consistency of the mixture is such that, when a little of it is dropped into cold water, a soft ball is formed. Then 2 tablespoons butter is added, together with a pinch of salt and flavouring. The mixture is cooked for 10 minutes at 43° C (110° F), without stirring, and then beaten until creamy, when chopped nuts may be added if desired. The penoche is poured into a greased pan and left to harden like fudge; when cold it is cut into cubes.

pentéola, Portuguese for scallop. In Portugal scallops are often cooked with minced pork, tomatoes, and an onion first simmered in olive oil, all thickened with flour, then moistened with milk and grilled until golden on top.

peoci, the name by which mussels are known in Venice. See also COZZE; ZUPPA, DI PEOCI.

pepato, a Sicilian variety of *pecorino* which is highly spiced with pepper.

peperata, salsa, a sauce from Verona in Italy, served with cold cooked meats or poultry. It is made from 2 tablespoons each of beef marrow and butter, 1 cup breadcrumbs, 2 tablespoons grated Parmesan cheese, and seasoning. The ingredients are not cooked, but all just melted until a smooth paste is formed. A little stock or water (about 2 tablespoons) is stirred in to ensure a smooth blending of the ingredients. The sauce is served cold.

pepernoten, a Dutch ginger-nut biscuit (cookie), made from 1 lb. (4 cups) flour, ½ lb. (1 cup) butter, 3 eggs, ½ lb. (1 cup) sugar, 2 tablespoons ginger, 1 tablespoon cinnamon, and the grated peel of 1 orange and 1 lemon. These biscuits are often eaten on *Sint Nicholaas Avond.*

peperonata, an Italian vegetable dish. First, 2 large sliced onions are lightly fried in a mixture of olive oil and butter; then strips of 8 cleaned red peppers are added and simmered until soft, and finally 8 large peeled and chopped tomatoes, salt, and pepper are included. The whole dish is gently simmered until cooked, and when ready it should be fairly dry, not swimming in oil. Garlic is sometimes added but this is optional. It can be served hot or cold, on its own, as a garnish for grilled or roasted meats, or as an omelette filling.

peperoni, Italian for sweet peppers or for the smaller pepper, known as chilli. The sweet variety are often eaten raw in Italy, cut into thin rounds and served as a salad with olive oil and vinegar.

conserva di peperoni, preserved peppers. They are first grilled until the skin is black, then skinned, washed, and the core and seeds removed. They are cut into strips and put into sterilized jars, with salt, and basil leaves are added. The jars are then boiled. Peppers preserved in this way keep for months, but once a jar has been opened the contents must be used up quickly.

peperoni all'aceto, sweet peppers preserved in vinegar.

peperoni fritti, fried peppers. The peppers are cut into rounds, dipped in beaten egg, and fried in oil. They are delicious with the Italian sweet and sour sauce *agrodolce.*

peperoni ripieni, stuffed peppers. Cooked green peppers are stuffed with a mixture of garlic, breadcrumbs, parsley, tomatoes, anchovies, and rice, and are then baked with a little stock. They are excellent hot or cold, as *antipasti.*

pepparkaka, Swedish spice cake. It is made with 6 oz. (1½ cups) flour, 6 oz. (⅔ cup) sugar, 1 heaped tablespoon chopped candied peel, 1 teaspoon ground allspice, and a pinch of natron mixed together. Then 2 eggs are beaten up with ¼ pint (½ cup) buttermilk or sour cream, and this liquid, together with 3 tablespoons melted butter, is poured into a hollow which has been made in the dry ingredients, and well mixed in. The resulting batter is poured into a greased sponge tin, sprinkled with coarsely chopped almonds, and baked in a moderate oven for about 45 minutes. The cake is served cut into wedges.

pepparkakor, Swedish ginger-snaps. First ½ lb. (1 cup) castor sugar is mixed with ¼ cup treacle (molasses) and ¼ cup syrup; then 2 teaspoons ground cinnamon, 2 teaspoons ginger, and 2 teaspoons ground cloves are mixed together. Finally 14 oz. (3½ cups) flour is sifted with 1 teaspoon baking soda. All are mixed gradually into ½ lb. (1 cup) creamed butter. The resulting dough is kneaded and divided into 2 pieces, each of which is shaped into a roll about 1½ inches thick, wrapped in waxed paper, and chilled. The rolls are cut into thin slices which are laid flat on a greased baking-tray; an almond is placed in the centre of each, and they are baked in a moderate oven for about 15 minutes.

pepper, a term covering a variety of seasonings which vary in their degree of pungency. They are made from the dried and finely ground fruits of the plants of 2 different families, the *Piperaceae* (peppers) and the *Solanaceae* (*capsicums*). Next to salt, black and white pepper are the most universal condiments, and two of the first to have been introduced into Europe from the East. Nearly all our foods, except sweets and puddings, are flavoured with them, but they must be used sparingly because when freshly ground they are hot and pungent. Ground pepper should be kept in air-tight receptacles as it contains highly volatile oils. The following are the most important types of pepper, with their sources. See also PFEFFER.

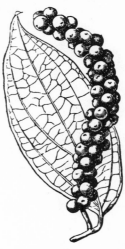

pepper

black pepper, ground from the dried unripe fruit of *Piper nigrum.* The fruit has the form of small berries clustered in a catkin, and it is one of these dried berries which constitutes a peppercorn. The peppercorns of black pepper are usually ground fresh in a mill.

cayenne or *red pepper,* ground from the dried ripe fruit of *Capsicum frutescens,* var. *longum.* See CAYENNE.

paprika, ground from the dried fruit of *Capsicum frutescens,* var. *tetragonum.* Strictly speaking, it is incorrect to call it a pepper, for it is not hot to the taste. See PAPRIKA.

white pepper, ground from the same fruit as black pepper, the *Piper nigrum,* but not until the berries are almost ripe. In England a special grade known as decorticated white pepper can be obtained; it is derived from large berries from which 2 or 3 skins have been removed. Unlike black pepper, which is often ground fresh from the peppercorn by the individual user, white pepper is unfortunately usually sold ready-ground in small cartons. All peppercorns are far superior when freshly ground. It is milder than black pepper.

pepper dulse (*Laurencia pinnatifida*), a red seaweed resembling dulse, to which, however, it is not related. The aromatic plants are dried and used as a spice in Scotland.

peppercorn, the fruit or berry of *Piper nigrum.* See PEPPER.

peppergrass (*Lepidium sativum*), a species of cress which is hot to the taste, also known as peppermint in the U.S.

peppermint (*Mentha piperita*), a plant which is a member of the mint family, with dark green, sharply-toothed leaves. It is mainly cultivated for the oil extracted from the leaves and flowers; this has a strong taste, and is used medicinally and in some confectionery.

pepperpot, see PHILADELPHIA PEPPERPOT.

pepperrot, Norwegian for horseradish, often mixed with cream and frozen, for serving with cold meats, especially tongue, or boiled cod or salmon. It is also a main ingredient in *robin saus.*

peppers, I. The fruits of plants of the genus *Piper.* These include *P. cubeba* and *P. nigrum,* whose finely ground fruits yield black and white pepper (see PEPPER), and the long pepper *P. longum.* II. The fruits of any plant of the genus *Capsicum.* See CAPSICUM; CHILLI; PAPRIKA; SWEET PEPPERS.

pepperwort, see PEPPERGRASS.

pera, Italian for pear. Pears are usually eaten as dessert fruit in Italy. They are also served with cheese, especially *pecorino sardo*. See also PEAR.

pere alla mandorla, pears with almonds. Pears are sliced lengthwise and cored, and their cavities are then filled with a mixture of ground almonds, sugar, and crystallised fruit. They are put in a fireproof dish with a little Marsala, and baked for about 30 minutes in a moderate oven.

pera, Portuguese for pear. Pears are of good quality in Portugal. See also PEAR.

pera, Spanish for pear. Spanish pears generally make good eating. *Peras en almíbar* are pears in syrup, but in restaurants this phrase usually means simply tinned pears. See also PEAR.

pera di vacca, an alternative name for *casigiolu*, a Sardinian cheese.

perçebas, Portuguese for goose-barnacle, a small marine animal rather like the common barnacle. It is grey and scaly and is shaped like a small elephant's foot. Its taste is between that of a shrimp and an oyster, and it is delicious when eaten with a country bread made from maize flour (*broa*). It is available in bars and restaurants in Portugal.

perce-pierre, see SAMPHIRE.

perch (*Perca fluviatilis*), one of the most delicate-tasting of all freshwater fish. Many varieties of it are to be found all over the world. It can reach a length of 14 inches and is olive-green on top and yellow below. It was highly esteemed by Izaak Walton, author of that famous 17th-century celebration of fishing, *The Compleat Angler*, but today it is seldom seen in England, either in shops or restaurants. Finland is a country in which it is popular. The name perch is sometimes given to other species of freshwater fish, especially the black bass and the trout-perch, both of North American origin but now acclimatized in French rivers. "Barse" was in fact the old English name for perch, and the modern word bass is derived from it. Perch is best cooked simply, and all recipes for trout can be used.

The giant perch or pike-perch (*Stizostedion lucioperca*) is found in the rivers Doubs and Saône in France, in the Danube, and in the river Elbe in Germany. It is one of the gastronomic specialities of Dresden, for it has a very white, flaky flesh with a most delicate flavour. It is highly thought of all over northern and eastern Europe, and is often served with a sauce consisting of butter, cream, and crayfish tails. It is also poached in white wine with mushrooms and garnished with small fish dumplings, as well as being fried, grilled, or baked. See also AHVENMUHENNOS; OKUN; PERCHE; RUFFE; SANDACZ; SANDRE; SUDAK; ZANDER.

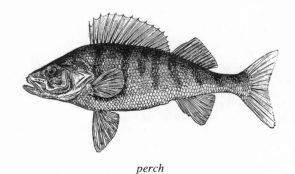

perch

perche, French for perch. *Perchettes* are young perch, which are usually deep fried in oil or served à la meunière. *Perche dorée* is the ruffe; *perche noir* is the black bass. The common or river perch, the trout-perch, and the giant or pike-perch found in the rivers Doubs and Saône, are all valued in French cuisine. One way of preparing pike-perch is to cut it into

fillets which are dipped in flour, fried in butter; and finally covered with fried slices of *calville* apple, lemon juice, and *beurre noir*. See also PERCH.

perdikes or *perthikes*, Greek for partridge, which is fairly easy to obtain in most areas of the Mediterranean. The Greeks do not hang their game for as long as the British, nor do they care for the condition known as "high" in England. See also GAME; PARTRIDGE.

perdikes me ellies ke selino, partridges with olives and celery. First 4 birds are fried in butter, and then 2 heads celery, ½ lb. peeled tomatoes, and 4 oz. (1 cup) stoned olives, all first simmered in water to cover, are added. All ingredients are placed in a pan, topped up with water to which salt has been added, and cooked for about 40 minutes until the birds are tender.

perdiz, Portuguese for partridge, which in Portugal is usually grilled, or prepared in the following ways. See also GAME; PARTRIDGE.

perdizes à alentejana, a national dish of partridges braised in olive oil with onions, parsley, garlic, herbs, bay leaf, white wine, and 1 cup wine vinegar. It is served on slices of fried bread.

perdizes à Lisboeta, Lisbon-style partridge, which is cooked in olive oil with garlic, tomatoes, and pimento.

perdiz, Spanish for partridge, which is very popular in Spain. Each province has its own method of preparation. See also GAME; PARTRIDGE.

perdiz a la mesonera, partridge Segovian style. To prepare it 4 partridges are rolled in flour, then put in a large ovenproof dish with 1 lb. onions, ½ lb. carrots, 3 turnips, ¼ lb. salt ham, all chopped, ½ pint (1 cup) oil and seasoning, and cooked in the oven for 30 minutes. Then 1 pint (2 cups) white wine, ½ pint (1 cup) sherry, and 1 pint (2 cups) fresh tomato sauce are added, and the ingredients are all cooked, uncovered, for 1½ hours or until the birds are tender. Fried potatoes are served with this dish.

perdices en chocolate, 2 partridges are braised in ¼ pint oil and 2 oz. butter, with 1 small onion, 1 tablespoon parsley, and 2 garlic cloves; when browned, 2 tablespoons wine vinegar and ½ pint (1 cup) water are poured over them, and all is simmered for 1 hour. When the birds are cooked, 1 tablespoon grated bitter chocolate and 1 tablespoon breadcrumbs are stirred in and boiled for a few minutes.

perdices escabechadas, 2 partridges are first browned in oil, then stewed until tender in ½ pint (1 cup) oil, ½ pint (1 cup) vinegar, ¼ pint (½ cup) white wine, and ½ pint (1 cup) water, with garlic cloves and herbs. Then they are soused in ¼ pint (½ cup) wine vinegar and enough oil to cover them. The fish dish *escabèches* is prepared in a similar way.

perdices Felipe II, a recipe that was used in El Escorial. First 2 birds are stuffed with a mixture of 2 oz. chopped *salchicha*, 2 shallots, 1 oz. smoked ham, and 20 peeled and pipped grapes, all heated together. Then the birds are roasted quickly for 12 minutes. When cold, they are covered in pastry and cooked for 10 minutes more. They are served on a piece of fried bread spread with liver paste, and a thick sauce madère is poured over them.

salmorejo de perdiz a la Toledana, a recipe from Toledo, a kind of custard surrounded by the partridge breasts in sauce. First 3 partridges are larded with fat bacon and roasted for 20 minutes. A finely chopped shallot is cooked with butter, 1 pint (2 cups) giblet stock, 2 tablespoons red wine, 2 oz. chopped ham, and a bouquet garni. When this is boiling, 2 tablespoons foie gras, or the cooked mashed livers of the birds, are stirred in well, and the mixture is seasoned. The roasted birds are put into this mixture, covered, and allowed to absorb the flavour for 10 minutes over a low heat. They are then drained and cooled, and the breasts and wings are removed and kept on one side. The leg meat is taken off the bones and pounded to a paste with 3 egg yolks, a pinch of nutmeg, ½ pint (1 cup) partridge stock, salt, and pepper. The stiffly beaten egg whites are folded into this, and the "custard" is poured into a buttered dish and baked in a *bain-marie* in a moderate oven for 1 hour. It is turned out, and the reheated breasts, wings, and sauce are arranged round the custard.

perdreau, French for a young partridge hatched the same year it is shot. See also GAME; GÉLINOTTE DES BOIS; GIBIER; PARTRIDGE; PERDRIX.

Partridge can be wrapped in vine leaves and roasted, and made into timbales and *terrines*.

ballottine de perdreau, boned partridge stuffed with truffle, game forcemeat, and foie gras, wrapped in muslin and cooked for 45 minutes in Madeira-flavoured stock made from the bones, herbs, and a knuckle of veal. When cooked, it is drained and, after the muslin has been removed, glazed in the oven. The stock is reduced over a hot flame and is then poured over the partridge. The dish is served hot. All winged game can be prepared in the same way described here.

ballottine de perdreau à la gelée, a cold version of the previous recipe, but having a little aspic added to the stock so that it jellies.

perdreau à la champenoise, partridge stuffed with foie gras which has been moistened with brandy, then pot-roasted in butter. Halfway through cooking, mushrooms are added. A sauce is made from a mixture of pan juices boiled up with a little champagne; 2 tablespoons cream, 1 oz. butter, and ½ truffle cut very fine are added, and the sauce is heated to just below the boiling point, then poured over the bird which has been placed on a fried croûton.

perdreau à la crème, cooked the same way as *faisan en cocotte à la crème.*

perdreau à la financière, partridge cooked in butter and garnished with *financière* garnish.

perdreau à la normande, partridge browned in butter and then baked in a casserole on a bed of peeled, sliced apples sautéed in butter. Cream is used to moisten the dish.

perdreau à la périgueux, partridge stuffed with truffles and cooked in butter, with thick slices of truffle, spices, game stock, Madeira, and brandy.

perdreau à la souvarof, as for the previous recipe, but the partridge is stuffed with foie gras.

perdreau à la vigneronne, partridge cooked in butter in a casserole, after which skinned, pipped grapes, game fumet, and brandy which have been ignited are added. The whole is heated up for 5 minutes and then served.

perdreau au chambertin, roasted partridge covered with sautéed mushrooms and truffles, and served in sauce *chambertin.*

perdreau en chartreuse, partridge roasted, jointed, and put in a mould with braised cabbage which has been cooked in the stock from old poultry or game.

perdreau en crépine, split partridge flattened and seasoned, then sautéed quickly in butter to seal it. It is then coated all over with foie gras forcemeat mixed with sliced truffle, wrapped in a pig's caul and simmered with a lentil purée, with a little Madeira wine and butter added.

perdreau en estouffade, partridge roasted with butter, then put in an ovenproof dish on top of a *mirepoix* of vegetables. The bird is also covered with a *mirepoix,* and butter and brandy which has been ignited are added. The lid is put on firmly and the whole cooked in a hot oven for 30 minutes.

perdreau en estouffade à la cévenole, stuffed partridge, browned, then put in a casserole with chestnuts, mushrooms, veal stock, and breast of pork, moistened with game stock,

Madeira wine, and a little brandy which has been ignited, covered, and cooked in a hot oven for 45 minutes.

suprême de perdreau, a dish made with only the breasts of partridge, sautéed very lightly in butter.

perdrix, French for a partridge over one year old. *Perdrix rouge* is red-legged partridge. In culinary French, young partridge hatched the same year as it is eaten is always called *perdreau,* whether cock or hen, second-year birds of both sexes are known as *perdrix.* Older birds like *perdrix* are generally used for braised dishes. En chartreuse is another method. Older birds also make excellent pâtés, hot or cold, *terrines,* mousses, galantines, *salmis,* soups, stock, and fumet. Birds over two years old should be used only for dishes in which the meat is to be minced, like *crépinettes.* See also GÉLINOTTE DES BOIS; GIBIER; PARTRIDGE; PERDREAU.

perdrix à l'ancienne, partridge cooked in butter, with cock's kidneys, mushrooms, and cream.

perdrix aux choux, second-year birds first browned in butter, the breasts larded. They are placed on half a large cabbage which has been blanched, with ½ lb. lean bacon, 2 sausages, 2 carrots, a bouquet garni, a pinch of mace, and 1 pint (2 cups) giblet stock. The lid is put on and the dish is simmered gently for about 2 hours. Some recipes use the other half of the cabbage by placing it on top of the birds. This is optional, but in either case the cabbage acquires an excellent flavour and the birds are moist and succulent. This method is also used for second-year pheasant, grouse, or guinea fowl.

peren, Dutch for pears. See also PEARS.

stoofperen, stewed pears. The fruit is stewed until tender in equal quantities of water and red wine barely to cover, together with 2 small cinnamon sticks, peel of ½ lemon, and sugar to taste.

périgourdine, à la, I. A French garnish for fillets of beef, consisting of small whole truffles cooked in Madeira wine, with a fine *mirepoix* and sauce *périgueux.* II. A French method of cooking poultry, whereby truffle slices are placed under the skin of the breast, and the bird is then poached and served with sauce suprême with truffle essence (extract). See also POULARDE, TRUFFÉE À LA PÉRIGOURDINE; POULET, FARCI À LA PÉRIGOURDINE. III. A title used for all dishes which have a garnish of truffles and foie gras.

périgourdine, sauce, a classical French sauce consisting of a sauce *périgueux* with the addition of some foie gras.

périgueux, sauce, an important French sauce composed of ½ pint (1 cup) demi-glace reduced with 3 tablespoons truffle essence (extract), 2 tablespoons truffles, and 2 tablespoons madeira wine. Périgueux is the chief city of the French district of the Périgord, and an area famous for truffles. See also PÉRIGOURDINE, SAUCE.

perilla, see TETA.

perişoare cu verdeţuri, a Rumanian national dish, consisting of 2 lb. minced (ground) meat (one part beef and three parts fat pork) mixed with 1 lb. peeled, sliced, and lightly fried onions, seasoned well, then shaped into small balls which are rolled in a mixture of chopped parsley, chervil, dill, spinach, and tarragon. The balls are fried slowly in a little butter and garnished with demi-glace.

periwinkle (*Littorina littorea*), a small, round, black, or sometimes orange, shell, which is inhabited by a sea snail. Periwinkles are plentiful all along the coasts of Europe, and similar species are found in the U.S. and in Australia. They are boiled in salted water for about 20 minutes, then the snail is extracted with a pin. Commonly known as winkles in England, they used to be immensely popular at seaside resorts such as Southend and Clacton, where they were sold cooked and sprinkled with vinegar. In France they are called *bigor-*

neaux, and a large number of those eaten there are imported from the west of Ireland.

periwinkle

perliczki, Polish for guinea hen. *Perliczki pieczone* is roast guinea hen; sometimes the bird is rubbed with ginger before roasting, and this is called *perliczki z imbirem.* See also GUINEA FOWL.

perlot, a name used in the Manche department of France for a small oyster.

pernice, Italian for partridge. In Italy partridge is frequently roasted in olive oil and garnished with glazed button onions, olives, boletus, and garlic-flavoured fresh tomato sauce. See also GAME; PARTRIDGE.

pernice alla zabaglione, roasted partridge served with sugarless *zabaglione,* made with dry Marsala, a traditional dish from the Italian Alps.

pernice arrosto, partridge stuffed with its own chopped liver, 2 oz. ham, 1 large mushroom, and 4 juniper berries, all well mixed, then wrapped in fat bacon and roasted in butter.

pernice in brodo, a Sardinian speciality. Partridge is simmered in stock for 2 hours with onion, celery, and basil. When cooked, it is left to get cold, then removed and served with a sauce of olive oil, lemon juice, and parsley.

pernik, a traditional honey cake from Czechoslovakia, made from 1 lb. (4 cups) flour, 4 oz. (½ cup) sugar, 1 pint (2 cups) honey, 1 tablespoon rum, 4 oz. (½ cup) butter, and 3 eggs. There are many variations of pernik, some with nuts, cinnamon, aniseed, or cloves added, but all containing honey. The cake should be cooked slowly for about 1 hour, as it becomes hard if cooked too fast. It is best to keep it in a tin for a week before eating.

persetorsk, Norwegian salted, boiled, and pressed cod. The head is removed and the fish cut along the length of the backbone. It is cleaned and rinsed well under running water, for all the blood should be removed. Salt is rubbed inside the belly and along the flesh side, then the fish is turned and salt rubbed along the outer side. It is then laid for 2 days between 2 boards. After this period, it is wiped clean of salt, dried, replaced between the boards for a further 2 hours, then washed and cut into steaks 1–2 inches thick. The steaks are covered with boiling water and simmered gently for 5–10 minutes. They are drained, garnished with slices of hard-boiled egg and chopped parsley, and served with melted butter and diced boiled carrots. See also TORSK.

persicata, an Italian peach conserve, made from peeled and stoned peaches cooked with ¾ lb. sugar to 1 lb. prepared fruit. These two ingredients are boiled until they become a paste, which is then turned into a flat greased dish and spread out to an approximate thickness of ¼ inch. The conserve is dried in the sun or in an oven until it is firm enough to be turned over and dried on the other side. It is then cut into squares and stored.

persil, French for parsley. *Persil frisé* is curly parsley; *persil à grosse racine* is Hamburg parsley. *Persillade* is chopped parsley, sometimes mixed with chopped garlic and used as a garnish; the word is also used to describe a dish of leftover meats, particularly beef, fried in butter and sprinkled with chopped parsley (the garlic is optional). *Persiller* means to sprinkle or flavour a dish with chopped parsley. See also PARSLEY.

persilja, Swedish for parsley, used a great deal in Sweden as a garnish for fish, shellfish, and meats. See also PARSLEY.

persille, Danish and Norwegian for parsley, which is often fried in sprigs in Scandinavia and served with fish, as well as being used as a garnish for meats, salads, etc. See also PARSLEY.

persimmon, the name given to the trees and fruit of 2 distinct species of the family *Ebenaceae:* the common or American persimmon (*Diospyros virginiana*), also known as Virginian date; and the Chinese and Japanese persimmon (*D. kaki*). The latter, which has the finer flavour, is cultivated in France, Italy, and Spain as well as China and Japan, and is used in those parts of Europe for making jams and jellies. It is also eaten raw. It is like a large tomato in shape, but the skin is more orange than red. It is soft and pulpy inside, quite pleasant to the taste, but inclined to be cloying. In France it is called kaki.

persimmon pie, made from the American persimmon. A curious feature of this pie is that it must not be baked, for heat causes this variety of persimmon to have an acid, unripe taste. Into a cooked pastry shell is put persimmon purée mixed with a syrup made from sugar, lemon juice, and a little cinnamon. It is topped with whipped cream.

peru, Portuguese for turkey. Turkeys are small in Portugal, and are cooked in any way that is used for chicken (*frango*).

peruna, Finnish for potato. See also POTATO.

perunahaudikkaat, potatoes baked in their skins or jackets, and served with butter.

perunapyöröt, a type of scone, made with the same dough that is used for rye bread. This is cut before cooking into small round pieces, which are covered with a layer of mashed potato, then baked in a hot oven. They are served hot with melted butter poured over the top.

perunarieska, thin potato scones. To prepare them, 1 lb. cooked potatoes, ½ pint (1 cup) potato-water, 2 teaspoons salt, and 6 oz. (1½ cups) barley meal are all rolled into a stiff dough. This is cut into rounds which are baked in a hot oven until brown. They are served hot with butter.

péruvienne, à la, a French garnish for meat, consisting of stuffed *oca* and sauce *allemande.*

pesca, Italian for peach. Peaches are usually eaten raw in Italy, and are also served raw after being marinated in white wine. See also PEACH; PERSICATA.

pesche ripiene, halved, stoned peaches filled with a mixture of crushed macaroons, sugar, butter, and egg yolk, then baked for 30 minutes in a greased dish.

pescada, Portuguese for hake, a common fish in Portugal. It is often cooked well though not imaginatively, boiling being the usual method.

pescadilla, see MERLUZA.

pescadinhas, Portuguese for whiting. Young hake is also often served under this name in Portugal, and is a much better fish to eat.

pescado, Spanish for fish. See ANCHOA; ANGUILA; ATÚN;

BACALAO; BESUGO; ESCOMBRO; GALLINA DEL MAR; MERLUZA; PARGO; PEZ ESPADA; RAPE; RAYA; SALMÓN; SARDINA; SERRANO; TRUCHA; XOUBA.

pescado a la Malaguena, a dish from Málaga, consisting of a mixture of white fish such as bream, bass, pollock or whiting cooked in water with sliced tomatoes, onions, green peppers, garlic, parsley, and a bay leaf. It is served as a soup–stew.

pescado blanco en ajillo, an Andalusian method of cooking any of the above fish, or a mixture of several of them. For 2 lb. fish, 2 thick slices stale brown bread are grated and mixed with 5 chopped garlic cloves, 1 tablespoon olive oil, salt, pepper, and juice of 1 lemon. A layer of this mixture is placed in an oiled casserole, followed by the filleted fish; this is covered with the remainder of the mixture, sprinkled with 2 tablespoons oil and baked for 1 hour.

pescatrice, Italian for the anglerfish, which is used mainly in zuppa di pesce and in *burrida.* In Venice the tails only are sold, and are grilled, or roasted with fennel. It is known on the Adriatic coast as rospo; in Tuscany it is called boldro. See also ANGLERFISH.

pesce, Italian for fish. For *pesce prete,* literally "priest fish," known in England as the common star-gazer, see RATA DEL MAR. *Pesce persico* is perch, fished in Lake Maggiore. *Pesce San Pietro* is john dory, highly thought of in Venice where it is cooked in the same way as sole (*sogliola*). *Pesce spada* is swordfish, which is abundant in Sicilian waters and heavily fished there; it is cooked in the same way as fresh tunny (tuna). Fish soup is served in almost all coastal regions in Italy. Other Italian fish include ACCIUGHE; ANGUILLA; CALAMARETTI; CALAMARI; MURENA; ORATA; SPIGOLA; STORIONE; TONNO; TRIGLIE.

pêssego, Portuguese for peach, usually eaten raw as a dessert fruit in Portugal, but also served cooked in wine or syrup.

pestle, a blunt-headed instrument, used in conjunction with a mortar for pounding foods; it is generally made of porcelain, but can also be of wood or metal.

pesto, an Italian basil and garlic sauce, a speciality of Genoa. It is made with 2 large pounded garlic cloves, 2 oz. (1 cup) chopped fresh basil, 2 oz. (½ cup) grated Parmesan cheese or *pecorino sardo* (or a mixture of equal quantities of both), and 2 oz. pounded pignoli, all beaten in a mortar and thickened gradually with 4 tablespoons olive oil. It should have the consistency of creamed butter. It is delicious with pasta, in minestrone, or on baked potatoes. It is one of the most distinguished of Italian sauces.

pet de nonne, a French soufflé fritter about the size of a walnut, made from chou pastry. When the fritters have been fried and drained, they are filled with various creams or jams. They are also called *soupir de nonne* (nun's sigh).

petit gruyère, a French processed emmenthal cheese. It is sold wrapped in tin foil, in cartons.

petit marmite, see MARMITE.

petit poussin, see POUSSIN.

petit salé, French for salted belly or flank of pork. It is not unlike pickled pork.

petit-carré, the name for fresh *ancien impérial cheese.*

petit-gervais, see PETIT SUISSE.

petit-houx, the French name for a shrub known in English as butcher's-broom (*Ruscus aculeatus*), which has bitter roots which are used in the making of certain aperitifs. The young shoots are prepared in the same way as asparagus.

petit-suisse, a fresh unsalted French cream cheese. It is made of whole milk with the addition of fresh cream. It was first made by a Madame Héroult, who lived near Gournay in the department of Seine-Inférieure. The cheeses were sold at Les Halles in Paris by Monsieur Gervais, her Swiss farm-manager, who subsequently became her partner. Thus the name gervais became connected with the name petit-suisse, and gervais petit-suisse or petit-gervais as it is also called was put on the market.

petits fours, the French name for many kinds of very small cakes and biscuits (cookies). They can be divided into two classes. The first comprises small almond-flavoured cakes such as macaroons, *tuiles,* and *palets de dames;* the second comprises small cakes made from sponge mixtures, elaborately iced. Sometimes marzipan shapes and crystallised fruits are also included in a dish of petits fours. The name derives from the fact that petits fours were baked in the brick ovens (*fours*) after the big cakes had been cooked and when the temperature had been considerably reduced, for most of these small cakes need fairly slow cooking so that they are crisp. See also COPEAUX.

petits pâtés, French for patties, which are served hot in France as hors d'oeuvres and small entrées. They contain fish (usually salmon), game, poultry, or meat forcemeats. See also PÂTÉ.

petits pois, see POIS.

petits-pieds, a French term used on menus to describe small birds such as blackbirds, thrushes, larks, ortolans, finches, etc.

petmèz, a type of treacle (molasses) made in the Balkans by boiling together grape juice and sugar, and storing the resulting syrup in tightly closed jars until the winter. Proportions of 3 lb. sugar to the juice of 2 lb. grapes will produce the right consistency.

pétoncle, an alternative French name, with *coquille saint jacques,* for scallop.

pe-tsai (*Brassica pekinensis*), a Chinese variety of cabbage which looks like a cos (romaine) lettuce and can be eaten raw or cooked. Its great advantage is that it does not give off any odour while being cooked. It is available in the foreign quarters of large cities in the western world, but seeds are also obtainable and it is easily grown.

petti di pollo, Italian for chicken breasts. See also POLLO.

petti di pollo alla bolognese, chicken breasts lightly floured and lightly fried in butter. When they are golden all over, 1 slice lean ham and 1 spoonful grated Parmesan cheese are put on top of each breast. The pan is covered and the contents cooked for 3 minutes, until the cheese has melted.

petti di pollo Cavour, as above, but presented with slices of white truffle cooked in a combination of ¼ pint (½ cup) white wine and ¼ pint (½ cup) chicken stock which is poured over the chicken and reduced before serving.

petticoat tails, a Scottish cake. Its shape resembles that of an outspread bell-hoop crinoline petticoat, and this is said to give the cake its curious name, although it is also claimed that the name is a corruption of *petites gatelles,* small French cakes popular with Mary Queen of Scots, who brought them to Scotland in 1560. To prepare them 6 oz. (1 cup) butter is melted with ¼ pint (½ cup) milk and 6 oz. (1 cup) sugar. These ingredients are then mixed lightly into 1 lb. (4½ cups) flour. The mixture is divided into 2 parts and both of these are rolled out rather thinly to about the size of a dinner plate. A circle 4 inches in diameter is cut in the middle of each round but is left in place. The outer circle of each is then cut into 8 "tails." The cake is sprinkled with fine sugar and baked in a moderate oven for 20 minutes. It is similar in taste and texture to shortbread.

pettitoes, an old English dish made from the feet, heart, liver, and lungs of the pig, boiled together in water to cover and then all but the feet minced very finely. The stock is thickened with flour, and 2 tablespoons lemon juice and a pinch of nutmeg are added, followed by the minced meat. The dish is then heated up, and an egg yolk mixed with ¼ pint (½ cup) milk is stirred in for a moment until it is coated and set. It is served with toast, the feet are split and placed on top.

peynir, Turkish for cheese. See EDIRNE; GRAVYER; KASAR; MIHALIÇ; SALAMURA; TULUM.

pez espada, Spanish for swordfish, one of the finest fish found in Spanish waters. It is sold in steaks, which can be filleted and are usually dipped in egg and breadcrumbs, or batter, fried, and served with *salsa verde.* Swordfish is also grilled, after marinating for 1 hour with chopped onion, garlic, and parsley in olive oil to cover; or it may be baked with sweet peppers, tomato, onion, herbs, and butter, or poached in a court bouillon. See also SWORDFISH.

pez limon, Spanish for the Mediterranean silverfish. It is abundant in Spanish waters and highly thought of as food. It is usually sold in steaks which are grilled or poached.

pfannkuchen, I. German for pancake. Pancakes are often served in Germany with a mixture of currants, candied peel, grated lemon peel, and sour cream. Stuffed pancakes are *gefüllte pfannkuchen.* See also EIERKUCKAS; PALATSCHINKE; PANCAKE; TOMERL. II. A German dialect word for doughnut. III. An Austrian pastry, made from 1 lb. brioche dough cut into pieces about 3 inches in diameter, with 1 tablespoon thick apricot pureé put in the middle. The edges are moistened with water before another round of dough is placed on top. The pastries are left in a warm place to rise, then fried in deep hot oil. After being drained, they are soaked in a hot rum syrup. See also APOSTELKUCHEN.

Berliner pfannkuchen, traditional doughnuts eaten on New Year's Eve. The dough is made with 1 lb. (4 cups) flour, ½ oz. fresh yeast, ¼ pint (½ cup) warm milk, 3 tablespoons melted butter, 2 eggs, 3 tablespoons sugar, and a pinch of salt. Jam is put in the centre of the doughnuts before they are left to rise, then fried in deep hot oil.

pfarvel or **farfel,** a Jewish garnish for soups made from 1 egg beaten with a pinch of salt and enough flour to form a stiff ball, which is then grated on a coarse grater. The shavings are left to dry, and when needed, they are added to boiling soup and cooked in it for 10 minutes.

pfeffer, German for pepper.

pfefferkuchen, a spiced "pepper cake," made from 4 eggs mixed with ½ lb. (2 cups) brown sugar, a good pinch each of ground cinnamon, cloves, cardamom, and black pepper, 1 cup chopped candied peel, and 4 tablespoons rum. When all are well mixed, ½ pint (1½ cups) honey and ¼ lb. (1 cup) butter which have been warmed together are added, with 1 teaspoon baking soda and 1 lb. (4 cups) sifted flour. The mixture is poured into a lined, greased cake tin measuring about 8 inches across and baked in a moderate oven for about 1½ hours. About 15 minutes before it is cooked, the cake is decorated with slices of candied peel and split peeled almonds.

pfeffernüsse, literally "pepper nuts," small cooked balls made of the pfefferkuchen mixture.

pfeffer-potthast, a German stew called "pepperpot." It is made from 3 lb. boned and cubed chuck beef browned with 1 bay leaf, 1 lb. sliced onions and pot herbs, seasoned, covered with water, and cooked slowly for 2–3 hours with a lid on. Then the herbs are removed, and the stock is thickened with 1 cup fresh breadcrumbs and seasoned strongly with pepper.

pfirsich, German for peach. As well as being served as a dessert fruit, it is also made into a fruit cup (*kalteschale*). See also PEACH.

pflaume, German for plum. *Pflaumenkuchen* is plum tart;

pflaumenmus is plum jam. See also PLUM; SCHLOSSERBUBEN; ZWETSCHE.

pflütten, an Alsatian name for *boulettes* of semolina and potato. They consist of 1 lb. puréed boiled potatoes, well-seasoned with a pinch of nutmeg as well as salt and pepper, and ¾ pint (1½ cups) milk, all mixed well and brought to the simmering point. Then 3 tablespoons semolina (for 1 lb. potatoes) is stirred in with a wooden spoon until the mixture is very stiff and leaves the sides of the saucepan, whereupon it is removed from the heat and 2 well-beaten eggs are stirred in. The mixture is then poured into a buttered tin to a depth of 1 inch and left for 12 hours. Squares are cut, and rolled with floured hands into little croquette shapes; then they are fried in a shallow mixture of olive oil and butter until golden all over. They can be served as a first course, or as an accompaniment to meats, particularly *rable de lièvre à la crème.*

pheasant (*Phasianus colchicus*), a game bird which is considered to be the most beautiful in the British Isles. Its Latin name derives from the Ancients, who called it "the bird of Phasis," Phasis being the river which flowed through the land of Colchis, the country which divided Asia from Europe. The pheasant was a native of China, but was imported into Europe at a very early date. Ben Johnson, the Elizabethan poet and dramatist, mentions it in "The Forrest"

> Fertile of wood, ashore, and Sydney's copp's,
> To crowne thy open table doth provide
> The purpled pheasant, with the speckled side:

The pheasant is said to have been imported into the U.S. by George Washington in 1789 for his Mount Vernon estate. However, it was not until 1880 that it became a regular game bird as a result of the large shipments made by Judge Denny, then Consul-General for the United States in Shanghai. He had great numbers of the birds transported direct from China to Oregon, where they were released on the Willamette River. Nowadays they are to be found in almost every state, but are more prolific north of the Mason-Dixon line.

pheasant

Although the cock is the more attractive, the hen is plumper and as a rule more tender. The young bird is best for the table, after a very necessary period of hanging, which varies in length according to the weather and individual taste. The general rule is 4 days in very warm weather, and up to 10 or 12 in winter. The bird should be hung by the neck, and is ready to be cooked when the leading tail-feather can be easily plucked.

The young cock is identifiable by its rounded spurs which, on an older bird, have become sharpened and pointed. The young hen can be identified by its soft feet and light plumage. Although the English shooting season for pheasant is from October to February, the birds are at their best from November to January. In Britain and Ireland, a young pheasant is usually roasted for about 45 minutes and served with bread sauce and game chips; older birds are braised, casseroled, potted, or made into a salmi. Good soup can be made from the carcases, and from the legs of old birds, for example *potage St-Hubert*. See also BAZANT; FAGIANO; FAISAN; FAISÁN; FAISÃO; FASAN; FASANER; FAZANT.

potted pheasant, a recipe which is also suitable for grouse, partridge, pigeon, or goose. The breast-meat only of cold, cooked birds is used. All skin and fat are removed and the meat is minced, then pounded in a mortar until smooth. Then ½ lb. butter is added for every 1 lb. meat, and they are pounded together. The mixture is seasoned with a pinch of mace, salt, and pepper, then passed through a wire sieve, put into pots, and pressed down with a spoon until it is very closely packed. It is set in a low oven to heat through, pressed down again with a spoon, and while still warm, covered with melted butter.

phenomenal berry, see HYBRID BERRIES.

Philadelphia cinnamon buns, a speciality from Philadelphia, U.S., where many old families have their own recipe. The buns are feather-light and deliciously sticky. A traditional recipe consists of ¾ pint (1½ cups) scalded milk, which is then cooled until lukewarm and poured into a basin; 1 oz., or 1 packet dried yeast is dissolved in ¼ cup tepid water and added to the milk. Then ½ lb. (2 cups) flour, 1 teaspoon salt, and 1 tablespoon sugar are sprinkled over, and the whole is covered and set in a warm place to rise. Meanwhile 2 oz. (¼ cup) butter or margarine is creamed with 6 oz. (¾ cup) sugar, then 2 beaten eggs are well mixed in. When the yeast mixture is bubbly, the butter mixture is beaten in with about 12 oz. (3 cups) flour to make a soft dough. This is covered again with a cloth and left to rise until it has doubled its bulk. The dough is then divided in half, and each half is rolled to ¼-inch thickness and spread first with softened butter, then with 4 oz. (½ cup) brown sugar mixed with 2 teaspoons cinnamon. On top is placed a mixture of ½ cup chopped walnuts, the same of raisins or currants, and ½ cup corn syrup. The 2 squares are now rolled up like a swiss roll, and cut into 1½-inch slices which are put into two deep, well-buttered 9-inch tins or pans which have been filled to a depth of ¼ inch with corn syrup. They are covered, and the buns are allowed to rise until they have doubled in size. They are baked in a moderate oven for 45 minutes or until brown, and when cooked, are turned out at once.

Philadelphia ice cream, ice cream made from scalded cream, sugar to taste, salt, and flavouring, all well mixed and frozen. It has no added thickening, and is a speciality of Pennsylvania, U.S.

Philadelphia pepperpot, a traditional soup from the U.S., said to have been created by the head cook of George Washington's Revolutionary Army during the cold winter of the campaign at Valley Forge in 1777. Like chicken Marengo, it was first made with what was available to the army cook. This appears to have been tripe and a veal bone, the gift of a local butcher, and peppercorns given by a Germantown patriot; root vegetables and herbs were also available. Since those days many ingredients have been added, even tomatoes, which at that time were thought to be poisonous. General Washington is reputed to have named the soup pepperpot because of the nature of the ingredients, and Philadelphia after the cook's home town. First ½ lb. tripe is cut into cubes and put into a large saucepan, with a knuckle of veal and water to cover. The tripe and veal are boiled for 10 minutes and the liquid skimmed of any scum. Then chopped parsley, thyme, marjoram, and basil (about ½ teaspoon of each) are added, the lid is put on, and all ingredients are simmered gently for 1 hour. Fresh vegetables such as onion, celery, green peppers, and potato are chopped, lightly fried in 3 tablespoons butter, and then added to the other ingredients. Other vegetables may be included to taste. The soup is seasoned well, principally with a good ½ teaspoon freshly ground black peppercorns, and cooked for a further 30 minutes. Before the soup is served, the veal knuckle is taken out and either cooked rice or cream is stirred in, according to taste.

In Bermuda and the West Indies, a similar soup, called simply "pepperpot," is made. It contains a good deal of tomatoes and red peppers, and is more highly spiced as it contains chilli.

Philadelphia relish, made with the following ingredients mixed in the order given: 2 cups finely shredded cabbage, 2 finely chopped green peppers, 1 teaspoon celery seed, ¼ teaspoon mustard seed, ½ teaspoon salt, 2 tablespoons brown sugar, and ¼ cup vinegar. The ingredients are well mixed and should be left for 1 hour before serving with cold meats, etc.

Philippine spinach (*Talinum triangulare*), the name for a variety of purslane that is cultivated in the U.S. for its green leaves, which are prepared and cooked in the same way as spinach.

pholiota, a genus of fungus. See MUSHROOM.

phyllo, the paper-thin pastry used in most Greek pies, whether savoury or sweet. It requires an expert to make it, and is sold by the pound in Greece, the Balkans, and the Middle East, in shops which sell only pastry. (It can often be found in England in shops owned by Greeks or Cypriots and in the U.S. in some speciality shops.) The dough consists of flour and water only, mixed to a stiff paste. Pieces about the size of a tennis ball are broken off, and with great expertise the professional pastry-cook throws each of these from hand to hand, then rolls it up and down his arms until it resembles a thin circle of parchment-like paper, and finally twirls it round and round in the air so that it becomes ever larger and thinner. Just when it seems that it can get no thinner, it is thrown onto a metal disc and stretched again and again. Finally it is cut to a suitable size for the customer to take home and make into his pastries and pies, which may have a variety of fillings. Almost all Greek pastry used for sweet dishes is soaked in a honey syrup after cooking. When served in Turkey, it is sometimes eaten with a thick cream called *kaimak* (the equivalent of the Greek *kaïmaki*) which is almost solid and can be cut into slices. See also BAKLAVA; KATAIFI; PASTRY.

physalis, a regional French name, with *coqueret* and *alkékenge,* for cape gooseberry, which is made into a preserve.

pianki do zupy nic, a Polish cold soup. The words mean literally "nothing soup" (zupa nic) with a garnish of "kisses." The "kisses" are made from a mixture of 5 heaped tablespoons sugar beaten with 5 egg whites, which is either baked in spoonfuls in a slow oven and cut into squares, or left uncooked and dropped in spoonfuls into the boiling soup. The soup itself, which is cold and sweet, is made by scalding 3 pints milk with 2 inches of vanilla pod which is removed when the milk is hot. The 5 egg yolks are whisked with 6 tablespoons sugar in a double boiler over a low heat, and the milk is added to it gradually until the mixture thickens.

piaz, a Greek salad made from cooked, soaked, dried beans mixed with sliced onion, olive oil, lemon juice, chopped parsley, and seasoning.

picadillo, Spanish for minced meat, or a meat and vegetable hash. *Picado* is Spanish for minced.

picarel, the French name for a small Mediterranean fish which is served like anchovy.

piccalilli, an English mustard pickle, made from 1 large raw chopped cauliflower, 20 small button onions, 6 gherkins, and 1 medium-sized cucumber. All are chopped except the onions, salted overnight, drained, then pickled in a sauce made by boiling up 1 quart vinegar, 2 tablespoons dry mustard and 1 teaspoon pickling spices, all thickened with 2 tablespoons turmeric. It is rather coarse in flavour, but acceptable with certain hard cheeses and bread, or with cold salt beef. It is Anglo-Indian in origin. See also PICKLE.

piccante, salsa, a piquant Italian cold sauce which is served with cold cooked meats, or used as a basting agent for meat or poultry. To make it 1 pint (2 cups) red wine and 1 pint (2 cups) olive oil are mixed with ¾ pint (1½ cups) wine vinegar, 1 sliced onion, 2 cloves garlic, ½ teaspoon red pepper seeds or chilli powder, 1 teaspoon rosemary, and salt. All are beaten well together and then bottled for at least 24 hours.

piccata, Italian for small, thinly sliced squares of veal, also called *scaloppine*. Three or four are served per person; they are seasoned and sprinkled with lemon juice, lightly floured, and then cooked quickly on both sides in butter.

piccata al marsala, as above, but just before serving, 2 tablespoons Marsala wine and 1 tablespoon water or stock are added and allowed to simmer until slightly thickened.

piccione, Italian for pigeon. See also PALOMBACCI; PIGEON.

piccione coi piselli, an Italian dish of 2 pigeons sautéed with 1 large diced onion, 2 oz. chopped tongue, and 2 oz. chopped ham, then seasoned with salt, pepper, and 1 teaspoon basil. A little white wine is added, barely to cover, and the dish is covered and simmered for 1½ hours. Then 1 lb. shelled peas is included and cooked with the birds before serving.

pichelsteiner or **püchelsteiner fleisch,** a German hot pot made with alternative layers of sliced beef, pork, veal, and mutton (all mixed), and sliced ox marrow, onions, carrots, celeriac, cabbage, and potatoes (all sliced). It is seasoned and placed in an earthenware pot which is half-filled with water, then covered and cooked for 2–3 hours. It is served straight from the pot.

piche-pache, a Spanish stew made from turkey giblets. They are first browned in oil or butter with onions, garlic, quartered cabbage, turnips, carrots, potatoes, and ox bone marrow, then 1 pint (2 cups) stock is added, and all are simmered until cooked. It is served with fresh tomato sauce.

picholine, the French name for the large green olive. See OLIVE.

pickerel, I. The English name for a young pike. In France, young pike is used mainly for freshwater fish soups and matelotes. II. The American name for a particular variety of pike (*Esox niger*) which is about 2 feet long and greatly esteemed as food. See also PIKE.

pickle, a condiment which can be made with a variety of vegetables, such as onions, cucumbers, gherkins, cauliflower flowerlets, etc., and green walnuts. These are pickled by being salted or otherwise treated with brine, and then bottled, either in their separate kinds or mixed together, in a liquor based on vinegar, with pickling spices. Pickles are served chiefly with cold meats. See also PICCALILLI; PICKLED ONIONS; PICKLED WALNUTS.

pickle, to, to steep meat, fish, eggs, or vegetables such as onions or gherkins in a solution either of vinegar and spices or of olive oil, vinegar and spices (½ pint olive oil to ¼ pint

vinegar). The ingredients are left in the solution for varying lengths of time, depending on their size and texture. Another pickling-solution is composed of salt, sugar, saltpetre, and spices, but this is generally used only for meat (see CURING). Vegetables pickled with vinegar and spices are known as pickles in English.

pickled butter, a traditional Cornish method of pickling butter in brine. The brine is made by half filling a jar with water and adding salt in sufficient quantity to enable a medium-sized potato to float in it; at this point the brine is of sufficient buoyancy to receive the butter, and amounts of ½ lb. or 1 lb., wrapped in muslin, are then put in. To keep the butter submerged, a plate with a stone on top of it is placed on the jar. The butter can be eaten after a week if required, but it is possible to preserve fresh butter in this way for some considerable time.

pickled eggs, an old English method of serving hard-boiled eggs. When shelled and cool, they are immersed in a mixture of 2 pints white vinegar boiled and cooled with ½ oz. white peppercorns. This solution is enough for 1½ dozen eggs. After 1 month they are ready for use, and are served with drinks, or with cheese, cold meats, etc. Large jars of them are still to be seen in British pubs.

pickled herrings, a Scottish dish, made with fresh herrings baked for 40 minutes with a sliced onion, a little sugar, vinegar and water in equal quantities. This dish is usually served cold. See also HERRING.

pickled onions, small onions, not larger than 1 inch across, peeled and totally immersed in a solution of 1 pint vinegar to 1 oz. sugar and 1 teaspoon pickling spices, all boiled up and then allowed to cool. The top is covered, and the onions should be left for 3 or 4 weeks before eating, until they become brown and impregnated with the pickle. They are eaten in Britain with cold cooked meats and cheese. See also PICKLE.

pickled plums, prepared in the same way as pickled onions, except that wine vinegar is used instead of white vinegar.

pickled pork, pork which has been immersed in a pickle made from 1 lb. common salt, 1 lb. bay or rock salt, ½ lb. sugar, and ½ oz. saltpetre or sal prunella, all stirred into 3 quarts water until dissolved. The pork should be turned daily, and should stay in pickle for about 2 weeks. Generally it is the streaky belly of pork which is referred to when the term pickled pork is used, but shanks are also pickled in this way. Before the pickled pork is used, it is soaked for some hours in water, then boiled in water with the root vegetables that are to be served with it. Traditionally, in Britain, Ireland, and Germany, pease pudding is also served with it; also boiled potatoes. The pork is sweet to the taste, and especially delicious when cold.

pickled walnuts, made with walnuts that have been picked while still green on the outside, before the hard inner shell has formed—that is in mid-June in warm countries and mid-July in more temperate climates. They are pricked all over and put in a brine solution for a week, then drained and allowed to dry, preferably in the sun, until they are quite black. They are then totally immersed in the same vinegar pickle that is used for pickled onions. They will keep for several years, and are excellent with cold meats or cheese. The juice, mixed with honey, is the finest cure there is for an irritating cough. See also PICKLE.

pickling spices, the usual mixture comprises cloves, allspice, blade mace, whole black and white peppercorns, cinnamon, and a few small hot chillies. This is used for making pickles, and small cartons of it can be bought commercially.

picnic, a meal, either hot or cold, eaten in the open air. Originally it also meant a meal, eaten indoors or out-of-doors, to which each guest brought a dish. In 19th-century England it was a popular and elaborate affair, and a Picnic Society was formed in London, the members of which supped at the Pantheon in Oxford Street and drew lots as to what part of the meal each should supply. Picnic is an adaptation of the 18th-century French word *pique-nique* (from *piquer*, to pick, and *nique*, a small coin or any little thing), signifying a small piece of food which could be picked up or picked at. Nowadays most picnics consist of cold food: cooked chickens and hams, Cornish pasties, salads, hard-boiled eggs, cake, fruit, and so on. When food is cooked in the open air, the occasion today is invariably called a barbecue, a word which has been taken from South America and has reached Europe via the U.S.

picnic shoulder, the American term for a hand of pork.

picodon, a goat's milk cheese made in the Dauphiné district of France. It is in season from May to January.

picridie, see SCORZONERA.

picti, see PIHTI HIRINO.

pide, a thin Turkish bread, often served with *kèbābi* (*yòqurtlù pideli kèbāb*) or sliced and put at the bottom of a vegetable or meat casserole. The bread is made from 2½ lb. (10 cups) flour, 1 oz. yeast, 1 tablespoon salt and approximately 1½ pints (3 cups) lukewarm water; the dough is shaped into flat strips about 4 inches wide which are brushed with beaten egg and then baked. The finished bread is only about 1 inch thick.

piddock (*Pholas dactylus*), an edible clam-like mollusc which lodges itself in soft rock or wood by boring a hole, and is remarkable for being phosphorescent. It can be eaten in any way that is suitable for clam.

pie, I. Any food cooked in a deep or shallow dish, known as a pie-dish, and covered with pastry. (If the pastry were put at the bottom and not on top, the correct name of the dish in Britain and Ireland would be tart or flan.) Short crust is the pastry most generally used. With regard to the filling, if the meat, fish, or fruit is not cooked before being put into the dish, it should be cut very small, since otherwise the pastry will be cooked and brown before the filling is ready.

Pies have been made for many centuries all over the world. In 14th-century England, pie-dishes were called "coffins," which suggests that the shape was long and thin like that of a loaf tin. In the 15th and 16th centuries, pies made from globe artichoke bottoms mixed with raisins, currants, butter, herbs, and cream were popular; also lobster pies made with white wine, butter, and cream. Dried fruits such as currants and raisins were almost always included in pork pies.

Meat or game completely enclosed in pastry is known as a raised pie. Special moulds and a special pastry called hot water crust are used for this type of pie. In Britain the most famous raised pies are pork pie, and veal and ham pie (see VEAL). The former originated in Melton Mowbray, Leicestershire, where it is still made commercially on a large scale; the meat inside the pie, instead of being the normal brownish colour of cooked pork, is pink, and this is achieved by adding a very small amount of anchovy sauce or essence (extract) to the chopped meat. In the Nottingham area of England a raised pie is traditionally made with gooseberries, although it is rare nowadays. When cooked, it is filled with melted apple jelly. It is served cold and looks pretty when cut open, with the pink jelly marbling the green berries. Usually soft fruit and stone-fruit is reserved for flans, tarts, or ordinary pies, and not used in raised pies. The most common fruit pie is apple pie, usually flavoured with either a little clove or lemon. Rhubarb is probably next in popularity, followed by blackberry with apple. Gooseberry pie is another favourite.

Another famous English pie is beefsteak and kidney pie, sometimes with a few oysters added. With this pie it is essen-

veal and ham pie

tial that the meat be partly cooked first and a succulent gravy made from the stock. Game pie is made from either furred game such as venison or hare, or winged game such as pheasant, or partridge. Home-made mutton pies used to be made in the Nottingham area from minced meat, and are still made in Scotland. The former were smaller than the Melton Mowbray pork pies and were decorated with sprigs of mint to prevent their being mistaken for pork pies, which had sage sprigs. See also MINCEMEAT (MINCE PIES); PÂTE; PÂTÉ.

II. A dish with a thick crust of mashed potato, for example shepherd's pie and fish pie.

pie plant, an American dialect name for rhubarb.

pie-grièche, French for shrike, a small bird of the *Laniidae* family; in France it is prepared in the same way as lark.

pièce de boeuf, see AIGUILLETTE (DE BOEUF).

pièce de résistance, a French culinary team, originally meaning the largest and most important dish served at a meal, now used for the main course.

pièces montées, the French term for lavish table decorations, sometimes constructed of inedible materials but often made of sugar in various forms. Today they have almost disappeared from the social scene, but do survive in such things as models of castles, ships, etc., made in hard icing or pastry.

pieczarki, Polish for cultivated mushrooms. For wild mushrooms, see GRZYBY.

pieczarki duszone w całości, a dish of 1 lb. large whole cultivated mushrooms baked in a sauce made from ½ pint (1 cup) cream and 1 tablespoon chopped parsley, with 1 beaten egg yolk stirred in just before serving. These very large mushrooms are also served stuffed with chopped veal and breadcrumbs in Poland, or baked in a sauce of cream and Parmesan cheese.

pieczarki faszerowane, stuffed mushrooms. The mushroom stems are used here, together with 1 chopped veal kidney or an equivalent quantity of roast veal, 1 beaten egg, dill, and ½ small onion, chopped, to stuff the caps of 1 lb. large mushrooms. They are then covered with breadcrumbs and baked with butter and served with a sauce made from the pan juices mixed with ¼ pint (½ cup) bouillon.

pieczeń, Polish for roast. *Pieczeń cielęca* is roast veal; *pieczeń sarnia,* roast venison; *pieczeń wieprzowa ze szynki,* roast ham. See BARANINA for roast lamb; INDYK for roast turkey.

pieczeń huzarska (Hussar's roast), a pot roast for which a 5-lb. beef sirloin or round is first scalded with hot vinegar or vodka, and then dredged with flour, salt, and pepper. It is browned in butter, then simmered or casseroled for 2 hours with 1 sliced onion and ½ pint (1 cup) stock; it is kept covered during this time, but is basted frequently and turned at least once. Incisions are then made in the joint, and these are filled with a mixture of 2 tablespoons breadcrumbs, 2 small grated onions, 3 minced mushrooms, a pinch of nutmeg, salt, pepper, 1 egg and 1 tablespoon sour cream. The joint is returned to the stock (a little more of this is added if necessary), covered again and cooked in a moderate oven for 30 minutes.

pied-de-cheval, the French name for a large variety of oyster, not very highly thought of in France.

pieds de mouton, French for sheep's feet or trotters, which are usually cooked in a court bouillon and then fried or served à la *poulette,* à la *vinaigrette,* or à la *sainte-ménéhould.* See also PIEDS DE PORC.

pieds de porc, French for pig's trotters (feet). They are used extensively in stews, daubes, etc., for their flavour and their gelatinous quality. They are often simmered in white stock with onion, carrot, and herbs—once a favourite dish of the porters at Les Halles market in Paris in the early hours of the morning. In the Sainte-Ménéhould district of the Marne, which is renowned for its pig's trotters (feet), they are first cooked as above, then cooled, boned, and cut into strips which are coated with breadcrumbs and melted butter and grilled. Sheep's trotters (feet) are also served in the same way, that is à la *sainte-ménéhould.* See also CRUIBEEN; PIG'S TROTTERS; PORC.

piémontaise, à la, a French garnish for poultry, meat, and entrées, composed of risotto with shredded grey Italian truffles. It is presented either in timbale form, or as a border round the dish it is to garnish.

piens, Latvian for milk. *Rūgušpiens* is soured milk, often drunk with meals in Latvia; *ķērnes piens* is buttermilk which is drunk a lot, and used in cooking.

piernik, a Polish spiced honey cake, made from 1 lb. (4 cups) flour, 2 lb. (4 cups) honey, 1 cup almonds, ½ teaspoon ground cloves, ½ teaspoon ground cinnamon, a pinch of nutmeg, 1 teaspoon baking powder, and 5 separated eggs, the stiffly beaten whites being added last.

piernik łucki, a honey cake made as above, but rye flour is used instead of wheat flour.

pierogi, Polish for "pockets" or envelopes of dough which are stuffed with minced meats, cheese, cabbage, or fruit. They resemble ravioli. The special pierogi dough consists of ½ lb. (2 cups) flour to 2 small eggs, mixed with a few tablespoons of lukewarm water. It is rolled and cut into 2- or 3-inch circles which are filled with chopped Polish sausage, diced cooked pork, or whatever filling is required. The edges of the pockets are then sealed or folded over: if the filling is a savoury one, they are poached in boiling soup or stock; if sweet, they are poached in boiling water, then drained and served with sugar and sour cream. See also PIRUKAS.

pierożki drożdżowe, Polish pierogi made with a yeast dough. First 1 oz. yeast is dissolved in 4 tablespoons warm milk, then added to 1 lb. (4 cups) flour, 4 oz. (½ cup) melted butter, ¼ pint (1½ cups) more milk, and 4 eggs. It is kneaded and left to rise in the same way as yeast dough. Meat, cheese, cabbage, or fruit are the principal fillings. See also PIROZHKI.

pietracatella, see PECORINO.

pig, the animal which is the source of bacon, ham, and pork. It is probably the most useful of all domestic animals and the easiest to rear, for it does not need a large area to graze on and indeed is frequently kept in a sty. To keep a pig has always been an economic proposition, and when a law was passed in England forbidding the keeping of pigs close to a house, owners who had no other land and were thus obliged

to sell their animal, found their diet much impoverished as a consequence. The pig had produced a good supply of meat which was eaten fresh, smoked, or pickled, for many months of the year.

Pigs to be eaten as pork are a different type of animal from those reared for bacon and hams. The latter are much larger, and the finest English example is the large White Yorkshire. It is widely exported for stock breeding, and no strain has done more to raise the standard of pig production all over the world. The Tamworth is another fine strain, and it has done well when crossed with native strains in Canada and the U.S. Having a long body it gives a long side of bacon, and crosses well with the shorter fat-producing types. Of the pigs raised for pork, the Berkshire is a stocky breed which has done well in the U.S. and Australia. It matures quickly and can reach a weight of 120 lb. in 21 weeks; the carcase is very good for small, lean pork joints. Other good breeds are the Essex, a small black and white pig good for pork; the Hampshire, black with a white belt, a breed which crosses well and is popular in the U.S.; the Gloucester Old Spots, a spotted pig which thrives on fallen apples and is good for sucking pig; and the small Welsh, which fattens quickly and forages food for itself on hillsides. Well-known breeds which originated in the U.S. are the Chester white, which was developed in Chester County, Pennsylvania, and is found only in the U.S.; the Duroc-Jersey, a red pig; the Landrace; the Poland-China, which originated in the counties of Butler and Warren in Ohio and from which 3 types have been bred—the large, medium, and small; and the Spotted Poland, similar to the English Gloucester Old Spots which had some influence on its development. All provide good carcase meat. In the Balkans the Mangalitza breed is notable; the fat forms in lumps and is not evenly distributed with the lean, which is often used for sausages.

Almost every part of the pig can be eaten, as pork, bacon, or ham; the blood makes excellent black puddings and white puddings; the intestines (chitterlings) are good as offal (variety meats); even the ears, tail, and feet are utilized and enjoyed. The head used always to be traditional Christmas fare, either as brawn or the traditional boar's head. The fat is rendered down to make lard, which in turn makes excellent pies, pastry, and lardy cakes. See also BATH CHAP; HAM; PIG'S TROTTERS; PORK.

pigeon, a bird of which there are many species and varieties distributed almost all over the world. The three most common varieties in Europe are the wood-pigeon (*Columba palumbus*), which is thought the best to eat; the stockdove (*C. oenas*); and the rock-dove or rock-pigeon (*C. livia*), from which all the other varieties are thought to have evolved. The turtledove (*Streptopelia turtur*) is a summer visitor to England. Pigeon, particularly wood-pigeon, is very good to eat, especially when young, when it is known as squab. Squab is easily recognized by its small pinkish legs and the downy feathers under its wings; it is very good roasted, after larding with bacon. Pigeon's liver contains no gall, so can be left inside the bird during cooking. Older birds are good for pies (pigeon pie is an old English delicacy), casseroles, stews, or soup. Pigeon's eggs are regarded as a great delicacy in China, and after being boiled for 5 minutes are often sliced and added to clear soup. See also GOŁĘBIE; PALOMA; PALOMBACCI; PICCIONE; PIGEON-NEAU; TAUBE; WOOD PIGEON.

pigeonneau, French for young pigeon. Pigeon is cooked en cocotte (see FAISAN), split and grilled with butter, casseroled in wine or with olives, or roasted. See also GIBIER; PIGEON.

pigeon à la Richelieu, pigeon fried in egg and breadcrumbs and garnished with truffle.

pighvarre, Danish for turbot, a popular fish in Denmark. If small, it is often poached with the head left on, as in Scotland, and served with *aurora* sauce. Boiled potatoes accompany the dish. Steaks are also cut from large fish and are poached, grilled, or fried.

pignoli or ***pinoli,*** the Italian and English culinary name for pinenut kernels, used in Italy in rice, sauces, and cakes. They slightly resemble almonds in taste, but are much smaller and have no skin. They are also called pinnochio. They are now imported into England and other European countries. See PESTO; PINENUTS; PINOCCATE.

pig's trotters (*feet*), a favourite old-fashioned dish, in Ireland, where they are known as *cruibeens*. In Ireland only the hind feet are used, as they have particularly succulent bits of meat on them; the front feet lack this and are used only to make a jellied stock. To prepare them 3 pairs of trotters (feet) are cooked in water to cover with 1 large onion stuck with cloves, 1 carrot, parsley, thyme, bay leaf, salt, and pepper for several hours, and are then eaten hot or cold. Sometimes the meat from a cold trotter (foot) is dipped in egg and breadcrumbs and fried in bacon fat. Pig's trotters are better eaten with the fingers than with cutlery, and they go well with a pint of stout; they used to be a favourite dish in public houses in Ireland on a Saturday night. They are excellent for stews with other meats, for they have a good flavour and a gelatinous quality. See also CHISPE; CRUIBEEN; KOŠELIENA; PIEDS DE PORC; PIG; ZAMPONE DI MODENA.

pigwa, Polish for quince. In Poland cooked quince is often eaten with furred game, as well as being made into jam.

pihti hirino, also called *pictí*, Greek for pork brawn, made with a pig's head, bay leaves, and peppercorns. It is very popular in Greece, where it is served with sauce vinaigrette or sauce tartare. See also HIRINO.

piimä, Finnish for clotted milk. See also CLABBERED MILK; KOKKELIPIIMÄ; VIILIPIIMÄ.

piimälimppu, a sour-milk loaf. To prepare it 2 pints (4 cups) warm sour milk is mixed with 1 oz. dissolved yeast and 1 tablespoon caraway seeds, followed by 2 lb. (8 cups) sifted rye meal and 3 lb. (12 cups) wheat flour, all well kneaded; the mixture is then covered and left to rise in a warm place. When doubled in size, the dough is shaped into loaves which are baked in a moderate oven for 1 hour. During this time they are brushed several times with syrup to give them a shine.

piimäjuusto, a Finnish cheese made from skimmed sour milk and eggs. It may also be made with whole sour milk, in which case the eggs are omitted. It consists of 6 pints skimmed milk heated to a temperature of 175°–190°F (79°–88°C). Then 2 eggs are beaten and added to 2 pints sour milk. The warm fresh milk is gradually poured into the egg-and-sour-milk mixture, stirring all the time, and the temperature is then maintained at 180°F (82°C) until the milk curdles. (If the eggs are omitted, as when using whole milk, the temperature of both milk and curd should be about 200°F (93°C). When the whey has separated, the curd is strained into a cheese-muslin and hung up. When dry, the cheese is moulded, salt or sugar is added to taste, and the cheese is then lightly pressed and left for 3–4 hours before serving. In many parts of the country, the cheese is then brushed with melted butter and baked on straw until golden brown. It is served with smörgåsbord.

pike (*Esox lucius*), a large freshwater fish with a voracious appetite for other fishes, even of its own kind. It has a large shark-like jaw with many teeth; it is a greenish colour on the back, white on the belly with reddish fins. Pike can attain a weight of 30 lb., but the best for eating purposes are the young pickerel which do not exceed about 10 lb. Pike abounds in rivers and lakes all over the world, but since the 18th century it has not been esteemed as food in England, al-

though it is highly thought of in France and other European countries. Before cooking, as much salt as possible should be forced down its throat, and it should be left to hang overnight. This makes the flesh more tender and also softens some of the smaller bones so that they will dissolve during cooking. Izaak Walton, writing in *The Compleat Angler* (1653), says that "it is a dish of meat too good for any but anglers, or very honest men." In his recipe, the gutted fish is stuffed with anchovies and the minced fish liver mixed with breadcrumbs, herbs, mace, and butter, before being baked. It is basted with red wine and a clove of garlic. Finally butter, the juice of 3 oranges and some oysters are added to the sauce. See also BROCHET; GÄDDA; PICKEREL; SHCHUKA; SNOEK; SZCZUPAK.

pike

pikelet, a name given in different parts of England to various different yeasted and nonyeasted buns. In Yorkshire, pikelet is the name for a crumpet, while in some parts of England, particularly the south, pikelet is an alternative name for drop scone. This causes confusion, for the 2 are very different in appearance and in texture: the crumpet is nearly 1 inch thick and made with yeast, while the true pikelet is made from drop scone batter, resembles a drop scone, and is cooked on a griddle. In Scotland, pikelets resemble drop scones in appearance but are often yeasted. Proportions for the dough are 1 pint (2 cups) warm milk to 1 lb. (4 cups) flour, 1 oz. yeast, 1 oz. (2 tablespoons) butter, and 2 eggs, all well mixed, beaten, and allowed to rise before being dropped in spoonfuls on a warmed griddle. In Wales, pikelets are made from a similar mixture and are also cooked on a griddle. The word comes in fact from the Welsh *pyglyd* (pitchy), which when pronounced correctly sounds not unlike "pikelet." See also CRUMPET.

pike-perch, see PERCH.

pikkelsagurk, Norwegian for gherkin, used a great deal in garnishes.

pikkulämpimät, Finnish for hors d'oeuvres: these are generally hot, as against the cold *voilepäpyötä*. The literal translation is "hot titbits," but some of the dishes served under this name such as *maksalaatikko,* are quite substantial. See also HORS D'OEUVRE.

pilaf, the name by which pilâv is known in Europe.

pilafi, a Greek rice dish of Turkish origin which has many variations. A basic recipe consists of 1 tablespoon tomato paste diluted with ½ pint (1 cup) boiling meat stock. Then 1 lb. long-grained rice is cooked in 6 tablespoons hot oil (the rice will become almost transparent); and 1½ pints (3 cups) meat stock and the tomato purée are slowly added to the pan, with seasoning. The saucepan is covered and the contents cooked over a low heat for 20 minutes, when all liquid will be absorbed and the rice dry and tender. Greek cooks cover the saucepan lid in a flannel to hasten the drying process. In plain pilafi the tomato purée is omitted and 2 pints stock are used. See also RIZI.

pilafi garides, as above, but with the addition of fresh shrimps or prawns, onion, and herbs.

pilafi me domates, as basic recipe, with 4 large peeled tomatoes added to the rice before simmering.

pilafi midia, as basic recipe, but with the addition of mussels.

pilafi tou fournou, a Græco–American method of baking 1 lb. rice with 2 pints (4 cups) hot stock, covered, in a moderate oven for 45 minutes. The dish is garnished with meat, fish, poultry, or tomatoes, or they can be added during the cooking.

pilâv, a national dish of Turkey, made with rice, oil, and stock or water, to which are added meat, fish, poultry, vegetables, game, or nuts, as well as many herbs. It is the staple diet of the peasants, and in some places *bulgur* is substituted for rice. Proportions are 6 tablespoons hot butter or oil to 1 lb. rice. These are stirred together over a moderate heat until all the grains are lightly cooked. Then 2 pints (4 cups) water or stock are added, followed by the main ingredient of meat, fish, etc., and herbs. The pilâv is covered and simmered gently without stirring, preferably in an oven, for 20–30 minutes or until almost all the liquid is absorbed. In Turkey and Greece, currants and raisins may also be added to the rice. See also PILAW TURECKI; PLOV.

atzem pilâv, meat or poultry cooked with onions, herbs, and rice, as described above. This dish is also eaten in Greece.

yağsiz pilâv, pilâv made with boiled, boned chicken, chicken stock, 2 cinnamon sticks, and the same amount of mastic.

pilaw turecki, a Polish version of *pilâv,* consisting of 1 lb. half-cooked rice and 3 lb. boned chopped lamb, cooked in layers, with 2 tablespoons tomato purée diluted in ½ pint (1 cup) stock, and a pinch of paprika. See also PILÂV.

pilchard (*Sardina pilchardus*), a fish of the herring family. Its name in England in the 16th century was "pylcher" or "pilchar," the origin of which is unknown. Sardine is simply another name for the young pilchard; the sardines that are tinned in France and Portugal are immature fish of the same stock as the pilchards taken off the coast of Cornwall. Pilchards are also called "gypsy herring." Because of their high fat content they travel very badly, which is why, like sardines, they are only to be bought fresh in the neighbourhood of the ports at which they are landed. The shoals appear without warning and only briefly, and often almost the whole catch is tinned. However, in Cornwall it is possible to buy them fresh after a catch, and then they are baked, grilled, or, particularly, prepared as the famous Cornish dish *star gazey* pie. See also SCROWLED PILCHARDS.

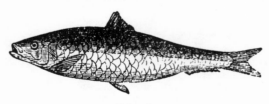

pilchard

Pilchards used to be salted and smoked all over the West Country and were known there as Cornish "fair maids," a corruption of *fumado,* the Spanish word for smoked, which no doubt became current when Spanish fishing fleets used to assemble off the Cornish coast in the 18th century. It is possible that some of the curious sunken pits to be seen in Cornwall were used for the smoking of these fish in very early times. In the 18th century and earlier, oil was extracted from pilchards. The best season for pilchards is the latter half of the year.

They are chiefly obtainable canned in a strong tomato sauce which entirely destroys their original flavour.

pïles, Latvian for duck. See also DUCK.

pïles cepetis ar miežu pildjumu. A large duck is stuffed with 2 slices toasted bread cubed and mixed with 1 cup cooked barley, 1 small onion, and 2 tablespoons chopped green-leaf vegetables. The bird is then roasted until the fat drains out, after which the breast skin is pricked and sprinkled with water to make it crisp. More water is added to the pan juices to make a gravy, but it must only be sprinkled over the breast initially.

pilot fish, I. *Seriola zonata,* a cross-banded amberfish found in the Atlantic. It is quite good to eat. II. A member of the horse mackerel family, *Naucrotes ductor,* which gets its name from its habit of following ships. It is highly thought of in Malta, Greece, and Turkey. It has delicious white flesh which is good grilled with oil or butter, lemon juice and herbs. Maltese fishermen poach it in salt water, and it can be cooked in any way as for mackerel. III. In the eastern states of the U.S., this name is also given to the Menominee whitefish (*Coregonus quadrilaterale*).

piltocks, the Shetland dialect name for saithe, which is also known in other parts of Scotland as cuddy.

pilze, an alternative German name, with champignons, for mushrooms. See also MUSHROOM.

pilze in essig, mushrooms pickled in white wine vinegar, with a blade of mace, peppercorns, and a bay leaf. The pickle is boiled up and, when cool, is poured over small firm mushrooms in a jar. The jar is then tied down.

pilze in essig mit schinken, as above, but the mushrooms are served drained and accompanied by very thin slices of Westphalian or cooked ham.

pilzpudding, 1 lb. chopped mushrooms fried in 4 oz. (½ cup) butter with a sliced onion; 6 tablespoons breadcrumbs are stirred in and turned in the pan, which is then removed from the heat. Then 3 beaten egg yolks mixed with 3 tablespoons cream, salt to taste, 1 tablespoon chopped parsley and, finally, the beaten egg whites are included, and the pudding is put into a greased basin, covered, and steamed for 1 hour. See also SCHWAMMERLSAUCE.

piment basquais, a spicy brick-red pepper used in the Basque country.

pimento, another name for allspice, the dried aromatic berries of the tree *Pimenta officinalis* or *Eugenia pimenta.* It is also called Jamaican pepper and pimenta.

pimentón, Spanish for paprika and for cayenne pepper. In Andalusia paprika is known as pimentón colorado and is used a lot in eggs, and casserole dishes.

pimentos, the name given to the large red and green sweet peppers, particularly those cultivated in Spain, the south of France, Italy, and the U.S. The word is derived from the Spanish *pimentón* and *pimiento.* They are used raw or cooked as an hors d'oeuvre, a vegetable, or a salad, and are also served cooked and stuffed with chopped meats or rice. They are not hot to the taste, but have a pleasant smoky flavour. See also CAPSICUM; PEPERONI; PIMENTOS; PIMIENTOS; PIPERIES; SWEET PEPPERS.

pimentos, Portuguese for sweet peppers. *Pimentos encarnados* are red peppers; *pimentos verdes* are green peppers. In Portugal both varieties are in season in September, and they are used particularly to flavour fish dishes, especially *bacalhau à Portuguesa* and other dishes made from salt cod. Small hot peppers (chillis) are called *piri-piri.* See also CAPSICUM; SWEET PEPPERS.

pimientos, Spanish for peppers, but particularly for sweet peppers. *Pimientos verdes* are green peppers; *pimientos morrones* are red peppers of which there are 2 types in Spain. Both taste alike, but the larger type will be found better to stuff, because they are blunt-ended and stand up well in a pan. If dried red peppers are used, they should be soaked in cold water for a few minutes before cooking. When fresh, they are usually skinned before cooking (being first grilled to make skinning easier), and their stalks and seeds are removed. Green peppers are not usually skinned, although their stalks and seeds are also removed. See also CAPSICUM; PIMENTOS; SWEET PEPPERS.

pimientos rellenos con manos de cerdos, blanched sweet peppers stuffed with chopped, cooked, boned pig's trotters (feet), then baked in a little stock. This is a speciality of Oviedo.

pimientos verdes rellenos, stuffed green peppers. To prepare them 4 chopped garlic cloves are mixed with 2 teaspoons mixed herbs, 2 cups cooked rice, and 1 beaten egg, and the mixture is then slowly fried. This is used to stuff the peppers, which have previously been partially cooked in boiling salted water. Next, 2 small chopped onions are cooked, without browning, in oil; 1 lb. peeled and quartered tomatoes, a bouquet garni, and seasoning are added, and the whole simmered until soft. The stuffed peppers are then placed in a greased dish, the sauce is poured over them, breadcrumbs moistened with oil are sprinkled on top and all is baked in a slow oven for about 30 minutes.

pimprenelle, French for burnet, one of the important herbs used in salads and savoury omelettes. It has a flavour like that of cucumber. Pimprenelle is not to be confused with pimpernel, a tiny scarlet-flowered meadow plant used in the preparation of some medicines.

pinaatti, Finnish for spinach. See also SPINACH.

pinaattikeitto, spinach soup, made with 3 pints (6 cups) milk, 2 tablespoons butter, 1 lb. spinach, 2 tablespoons flour, salt, and a pinch of sugar. The butter and flour is made into a roux, then the milk is added, and finally the puréed spinach. It is usually served garnished with slices of hard-boiled egg, or poached eggs.

pinaattimuhennos, stewed spinach made from 1 lb. (2 cups) cooked spinach added to a sauce made from 3 tablespoons butter, 2 tablespoons flour, and 1 pint (2 cups) milk, then all is seasoned, placed in a dish, and garnished with chopped hard-boiled eggs.

pinaattiohukaiset, thin spinach pancakes which are very popular in Finland. To prepare them ½ lb. fresh chopped spinach is added to the pancake batter, then thin pancakes are fried in a hot pan. They are served hot, with cranberry jam.

pindos or *pinthos,* a Greek cheese similar to *kefalotyri,* but a much improved variety.

pine nuts, the culinary term for these is pignoli or pinoli. They were in common use in medieval England and were known as "pynotys." See also PIGNOLI; POKEROUNCE.

pineapple (*Ananas sativus*), not a fruit in the ordinary sense of the word but a sorosis formed by the union of originally separate flowers, of which the fleshy supporting bracts consolidate the whole into a pulpy, succulent, and fragrant mass. The pineapple is a native of tropical America, and according to one of the issues of the *Illustrated London News* of 1847, it was in that year that the first large consignment of 5,000 pineapples arrived in England from the West Indies. Previously, only small numbers had been received, although pineapples had already been cultivated in Britain under hot-house conditions. The fruit is now cultivated intensively in Hawaii. It is canned, either whole or cut into slices and cubes, for export. The juice is also expressed and canned. Canned pineapple is used in cookery in tarts, puddings, and fritters, in confectionery, and in salads. Both fresh and canned pineapple is used for making preserves and liqueurs. Fresh pineapple makes a

pineapple

delicious dessert fruit. If fresh pineapple is used with gelatine in a pudding, the fruit must first of all be cooked. An excellent dessert is made by filling a hollowed-out pineapple with a mixture of pineapple and other fruits, all chopped, with syrup or ice cream; it is then moistened with brandy or kirsch to taste, and finally chilled. In the Philippines a pineapple vinegar is made which features in chicken *adoho,* a national dish. Also a cloth called *piña* cloth is made on hand-looms from the big mature leaves of the plant. See also ANANASKREM.

pineapple cheese, a cheese first made in about 1845 in Litchfield County, Connecticut, U.S. It gets its name from its shape and the corrugations on its surface, which resemble those of a pineapple. The cheeses are cured for several months, and during this time they are rubbed with oil. Sometimes the outside is shellacked to give a shiny, varnish-like finish to the surface.

pinée, a French name for the best-quality dried cod.

pingiàda, a delicious soup from Sardinia, an island renowned for its abundance of game. Pingiàda is more like a stew than a soup and consists of pigeons and small birds such as snipe and quail (or sometimes larger ones such as hazel grouse and ptarmigan), with beef, tomatoes, celery, sweet basil, onions, rosemary, salt, and black pepper all simmered together with water, stock, or wine for some hours. The aromatic smell alone is sufficient to stimulate the most delicate appetite.

pinion, I. The terminal segment of a bird's wing, also called the tip. The pinions of large birds such as turkey are used for soups, fricassees, and braised dishes, or they are stuffed and either fried in batter or braised. II. A ray-bone in the fin of fish.

pinkelwurst, a German wurst from Bremen, made from groats, smoked pork, and spices. It is known elsewhere in Germany as *grützwurst.*

pinkelwurst mit braunkohl, a dish from the north of Germany consisting of pinkelwurst served with cooked kale. It is especially popular in the region round Bremen. See also BRAUNKOHL, HOLSTEINER ART.

pinoccate, a macaroon made with pignoli instead of almonds. It is a speciality of Perugia in Italy, and traditional fare at Christmas and Epiphany. See also MACAROON.

pinocchio, see PIGNOLI.

pinoli, see PIGNOLI.

pintada, Spanish for guinea fowl, which is cooked like chicken in Spain and is frequently used in paella.

pintade, French for guinea fowl. The young birds are cooked in any way that is used for partridge or pheasant; older birds are cooked in the same way as chicken. See also GUINEA FOWL.

pintail (*Anas acuta*), a migratory wild duck found all over Europe and highly thought of by gastronomes. It is very popular in France, where it is called pilet. It can be cooked in any way that is suitable for wild duck.

pinthos, see PINDOS.

pinto, Portuguese for chicken. See FRANGO.

pinto, see FRIJOLE.

piora cheese, made only in the Swiss canton of Ticino, where 3 kinds are produced: *vero piora,* made only from whole milk of the Piora Alp cows, and fetching the highest price; *tipo piora,* made from cow's milk on other alps in the canton; and *uso piora,* made from a mixture of cow's and goat's milk. The curing process for all three takes from 4 to 6 months, and the cheese is sold mainly in the Ticino, but also in resorts on Lake Lucerne. It is soft to cut and has a delicate flavour.

piparjuuri, Finnish for horseradish. See also HORSERADISH.

piparjuuriliha, Finnish beef with horseradish sauce, made with 3 lb. meat cooked gently in 3 pints (6 cups) boiling salted water for 2–3 hours, then removed and cut into pieces. The stock is thickened with flour; a pinch of sugar, 3 tablespoons vinegar, and 2 tablespoons chopped dill are added, and the whole is poured over the meat. The grated horseradish is served separately in a small bowl. See also BEEF; LIHA.

piparkakut, Finnish for ginger snaps, which are served with coffee at Christmas in Finland.

piper, see CROONER.

pipérade, a speciality of the Basque country, and one which can vary enormously in taste according to how and where it is made. The best and simplest is made with ¼ pint (½ cup) olive oil or goose fat melted in a frying pan, and a large finely sliced onion is fried in it until it turns yellow. Then about 6 green peppers, cored, seeded, and cut into strips, are also fried for about 15 minutes, when 2 lb. peeled and chopped tomatoes, 2 cloves garlic, a pinch of basil, salt, and pepper are added. All are cooked until a pulpy purée is formed. Finally, 4 well-beaten eggs are added and stirred until they begin to thicken, like scrambled eggs; they must not be allowed to dry and harden, for the dish should be fluffy and light. Pipérade is served with grilled or fried ham, or croûtons of fried bread.

piperies, Greek for sweet peppers. Piperies yemistes are stuffed peppers, for which the stuffing for *yemissis me kreas ke rizi* may be used. See also PIMENTO; SWEET PEPPER.

piquage, the French term for the culinary process of interlarding a piece of meat such as veal or saddle of hare with pork fat. It is not the same as larding, a process chiefly designed to provide interior fat, for in piquage the lardoons are sewn through the outer surface of the meat and have the additional function of flavouring and decorating dry meats or game. Nor is it to be confused with *barding,* in which strips of bacon or pork are laid across a chicken breast or other meats before roasting, to protect delicate areas which might dry up in cooking. Piquage is also used for sweetbreads, but these are more generally wrapped in thin rashers of bacon, as in barding. The full title of this process is piquage des viandes. See also BARDING; INTERLARDING; LARDING.

piquante, sauce, a classical French sauce. To prepare it 2 oz. (¼ cup) butter is melted gently in an earthenware pan. When the butter begins to smoke slightly, 4 oz. chopped shallots or onions are stirred in and cooked until evenly browned. Then 1½ oz. (3 tablespoons) flour is added and stirred until the whole mixture attains an even brown colour; ¾ pint (1½ cups) white wine is gradually included, and the mixture is stirred until a thick consistency is obtained. The sauce is seasoned, and gently simmered for about 20 minutes. At this stage it may be passed through a *chinois* or conical metal sieve. Then 1 or 2 chopped pickled gherkins, with chopped parsley, chervil, and tarragon, are added, and the sauce is simmered further. A little good meat essence (extract), or the skimmed gravy from the meat for which the sauce is destined, is stirred in. The addition of a little French mustard is a matter of taste.

sauce piquante à la crème, also called le saupiquet des Amognes. A roux is made as above, with shallots added and stock substituted for wine. This is simmered for 30 minutes, sieved and then reheated with ⅓ pint (¾ cup) cream and 1 tablespoon butter. It is served with thick fried slices of ham. See also SAUPIQUET.

pīrāgs, Latvian pastry turnovers.

kāpostu pīrāgs, cabbage-filled *pīrāgs,* usually made about 6 inches in diameter. The pastry is made with 6 oz. (1½ cups) flour, 1 egg, 1 tablespoon butter, and ¼ pint (½ cup) sour cream, and it is filled with a mixture of chopped cooked cabbage, chopped onion, cooked rice, butter, and seasoning. Pīrāgs are baked in the oven, and are served either as a light luncheon dish or, when made very small, with soup.

piri-piri, Portuguese for small red chillis not more than ¾ inch long. They are very hot and must be used sparingly. A small one is sometimes added to chicken dishes, and especially to *iscas* and *lulas recheadas.* Piri-piri are sold dried, and are also made into a bottled sauce (*molho piri-piri*).

pirog, a Russian yeast dough pastry, which may be fried, baked, or poached. For the dough, see PIROZHKI. Sometimes both pirog and *pirozhki* are made instead with a rich short crust pastry, consisting of 1 lb. (4 cups) flour, ½ pint (1 cup) thick sour cream, 2 tablespoons butter, 1 tablespoon sugar, and ½ teaspoon salt, all mixed to a paste with 2 eggs. The yeast dough pastry is, however, more traditional. See also PIROZHKI.

pirog domashny, roast pork and braised cabbage or sauerkraut are chopped coarsely, then lightly fried chopped onions, seasoning, and a little sour cream are added to them. The yeast dough (*pirozhki*) is rolled out and cut into circles with a round cutter, and the edges of these are moistened. A spoonful of the pork and cabbage mixture is placed in the centre of each circle and is then covered with another circle, and the edges of the two are pressed together. The pasties are cooked in boiling water, drained, and served covered with chopped onions which have been fried in butter.

pirogui, see PIROZHKI.

pirozhki, small Russian pasties not more than 3 inches in diameter, made mainly of yeast dough filled with fish, meat, chopped hard-boiled eggs, cabbage, semolina, kasha, etc., and baked. They are often served hot with soup or for *zakuski,* but in this case they are made not larger than 1 inch in diameter. To make the dough, ½ oz. yeast is dissolved in ½ pint (1 cup) lukewarm milk, then combined with 1 lb. (4 cups) flour, covered, and left to sponge. When risen, the dough is kneaded, and 2 beaten egg yolks, 1 egg, ½ tablespoon sugar, a pinch of salt, and 1 tablespoon melted butter are added and worked in by hand until the dough is smooth. It is covered and left in a warm place for 1½–2 hours, until it is well risen and the surface cracked. It is rolled out on a floured surface to ½-inch thickness and cut into the required shapes, which are filled, folded over (the edges being dampened and well pressed down), placed on a greased baking sheet, and left again in a warm place for 30 minutes to rise. They are then brushed with beaten egg and baked in a hot oven for 30–45 minutes if large, 15–20 minutes if small.

In France, where *pirozhki* are known as pirogui, brioche dough is used for the pastry, and fillings vary from cream cheese to truffles, game, or caviar. A Caucasian variety is made with chou pastry flavoured with cheese and deep-fried. See also PASTRY; PIEROŻKI DRUŻDŻWE; PIROZHNOYE; PIRUKAS.

pirozhki po Finski, small slices of pike-perch fillet poached and, when cold, placed on squares of puff pastry with chopped onions which have been simmered in butter. A tiny piece of pickled herring is placed on top, and the ends of the dough are then folded over to close the pasties. They are brushed with egg white, baked, and finally glazed with crayfish butter.

pirozhki revelskie, small slices of poached fillet of pike-perch are smothered in chopped onions which have been simmered in butter, and placed on round pieces of thinly rolled yeast dough. The half-circle of each is folded over, and the pasties brushed with egg white, then baked. They are served buttered.

pirozhki Russkie, circles of thinly rolled yeast dough filled with a mixture of chopped *vesiga* (marrow of sturgeon), chopped hard-boiled eggs, chopped onions which have been simmered in butter, and chopped herbs. The half-circle of each is folded over and the pasties are bound with thick demi-glace. When baked, they are buttered lavishly.

pirozhki s bekonom, pirozhki with a filling of chopped bacon and lightly fried onions.

pirozhki s kapustoy, pirozhki with cabbage. The centres of squares of thinly rolled yeast dough are filled with a mixture of chopped white cabbage which has been simmered with finely sliced onions, chopped bacon, cream, and seasoning, to which are added hard-boiled egg whites blended with butter. The ends of the dough are folded over and the pasties brushed with egg white and then baked. They are served well buttered.

pirozhki s syomga, small pieces of boiled salmon placed on thinly rolled pieces of yeast dough and covered with chopped onions simmered in butter, chopped hard-boiled eggs, and herbs. When baked, each has a small hole made in the centre, into which a little sauce hollandaise or sour cream is poured.

pirozhnoye, Russian for pastry, often made either with yeast or as a rich short crust pastry with an egg added. See also BELYASHI; CHEBUREKI; PASTRY; PIROZHKI; VATRUSHKI.

pirukas, a small Estonian pasty filled with minced meat, cheese, or vegetables. It is served hot with soups. See also PIEROGI; PIROZHKI.

pisang goreng, a Dutch-Indonesian dish of baked bananas which accompanies *nassi goreng.* After being cut lengthwise, the bananas are sprinkled with salt and lemon juice, dotted with butter, and baked for about 6 minutes in a hot oven.

piselli, Italian for green peas. See also PEA.

piselli al prosciutto, the usual Italian method of serving peas. First 1 small onion is chopped and softened in butter, then 2 lb. young peas and 1 cup water are added and, after 5 minutes, 3 slices of lean chopped cooked ham are included. They are cooked for 7–10 minutes and served. See also RISI E BISI; SFORMATO.

pislicine, a Corsican cake made from chestnut porridge fermented with yeast and flavoured with aniseed, then baked in a moderate oven for 45 minutes.

pissaladière, a traditional dish from the Provençal region of France. Like the pizza which it resembles, it is a savoury tart made with a base of bread dough or yeast pastry which has been left to rise first. Thinly sliced onions lightly fried in olive oil, skinned tomatoes, and sometimes a little garlic, are cooked until the 2 vegetables are amalgamated and almost puréed; then this mixture is spread on the bread dough or yeast pastry. Filleted anchovies are put on top lattice-fashion, interspersed with stoned black olives. The tart is left for about 15 minutes to allow the dough to rise, then baked in a moderate oven for 15–20 minutes. It is better eaten hot, but makes a sizeable snack if cold. In private houses short crust pastry can be used instead of bread dough, which makes the tart far less filling and easier to digest. See also PIZZA; TARTELETTE, À LA PROVENÇALE.

pissenlit, French for dandelion. Many wild dandelions are used, as well as the various cultivated varieties such as très hâtif and plein coeur amélioré. The young leaves are used raw in salads, or are cooked in the same way as spinach. They are also served with a dressing of hot bacon fat.

pistache, en, see MOUTON, EN PISTACHE.

pistachio (*Pistacia vera*), a small tree of southern Europe and Asia Minor with a rather large fruit which contains a stone with a delicious greenish oblong kernel. This pistachio nut is used as a flavouring in confectionery and ice cream, and also with pork. Pistachio trees are now being grown in certain parts of the U.S., but formerly the nuts were not easily obtainable there, so that the word "pistachio" signified only a green colouring and not the presence of the nut itself. So-called pistachio ice creams are sometimes flavoured with almonds, as well as the pistachio nuts, and coloured with a green vegetable dye.

pistachio nut

pisto, a traditional Spanish dish of eggs scrambled in olive oil, like a *pipérade,* with a mixture of red and green peppers and chilli powder. Other vegetables such as artichoke bottoms, courgettes (zucchini), tomatoes, or green beans can also be used, and sometimes a little chopped ham or lean pork is added. It is eaten with toast and a sprinkling of grated cheese.

pistole, see PRUNEAU.

pistou, a French version of the Italian pesto, consisting of 2 cloves garlic pounded with 6 basil leaves, 2 tablespoons oil, 2 tablespoons hot soup, and 4 tablespoons grated Parmesan cheese, which is served with *soupe au pistou.*

pisztráng, Hungarian for trout, which is abundant in the mountain lakes and rivers of Hungary.

pisztráng raston, trout cooked over a charcoal grill, a popular method of serving this fish in Hungary.

pita, a paper-thin pastry like the Greek phyllo, made in Yugoslavia and used for a pie which is often filled with cheese or spinach. Alternate layers of filling and pastry are put into a dish and the pie is baked until golden. *Pita od sira* is cheese pie; *pita od spanaća* is spinach pie. The cooked spinach has cream cheese and eggs beaten into it before it is layered with the pastry. Pita is also used for sweet cakes with walnuts and honey, like phyllo pastry.

Pitcaithly bannock, a traditional Scottish cake, made from 6 oz. (6 heaped tablespoons) flour and 1 oz. (1 heaped table-spoon) rice flour mixed with 3 oz. (3 heaped tablespoons) sugar, then worked into 4 oz. (½ cup) butter. It is worked with the hands, as for shortbread. When mixed, 2 tablespoons chopped almonds and 1 tablespoon chopped candied peel are added. The mixture is then rolled to a flat round cake, the edges are pinched with finger and thumb, and the cake is baked on a greased sheet in a moderate oven for 30 minutes. See also BANNOCK.

pitchy cake, a traditional Cornish cake, so called because it is made by "pitching," or working, fat, currants, and sugar into bread dough after it has risen. Proportions are 2 oz. (¼ cup) fat, 2 oz. (½ cup) currants, and 4 oz. (½ cup) sugar to 1 lb. bread dough. The cake is then allowed to rise again for a short time, before being baked in a moderate oven for about 1 hour.

Pithiviers, I. A lark pâté which has been made for over 200 years in the town of Pithiviers in the Orléanais in France, a district which is also famous for several other gastronomic specialities, particularly *andouille* and other pork products, and a quince paste called *cotignac*. The larks are boned and stuffed with foie gras or forcemeat before being baked in the pie. When the pie has become cold game aspic jelly is poured in through a hole in the top. A thrush pâté is also prepared in the same way, as are excellent wild rabbit pies. II. A cake or tart made from puff pastry, with a filling of 2 oz. (½ cup) ground almonds mixed with 6 tablespoons sugar, 4 table-spoons butter, 3 eggs, and ¼ cup rum (this is sufficient for an 8-inch pastry base). The filling is covered with another layer of puff pastry, the edges are moistened so that it is sealed, and it is brushed with beaten egg and scored on top with a knife before being baked in a hot oven for 25–30 minutes. Just before it is ready, the tart is sprinkled with extra fine sugar and set to glaze for a few minutes in the hottest part of the oven.

Pithiviers au foin, a cow's milk cheese from the Orléanais. It is ripened on hay, and is in season from November to July.

piti, a Russian lamb stew which is very spicy and is served with whole cooked tomatoes floating on top. It is a speciality of Azerbaijan.

pitte con niepita, small Italian turnovers, about 2 inches in diameter, made from short crust pastry filled with a mixture of ½ lb. (1 cup) thick grape jam, 2 oz. (½ cup) ground walnuts, 4 tablespoons grated chocolate, a pinch of ground cinnamon, and 1 tablespoon rum. They are brushed with beaten egg, pricked on top, and baked for 15 minutes in a hot oven. They are a speciality of Calabria.

pitu, Portuguese for baked prawns, left in the shell. Portuguese prawns are of excellent quality.

pitz, a Swiss dish consisting of large raw tomatoes stuffed with minced apples and celeriac marinated in lemon juice and salt, both mixed with equal quantities of olive oil and sour cream. It is a speciality of the lower Valais.

pizza, a traditional Italian savoury tart, usually comprising a case of risen yeast dough which is spread with one of a variety of possible fillings, then baked on a long-handled spade-shaped implement in a hot brick oven. Dough sufficient for one 8-inch pizza is made with ¼ lb. (1 cup) flour, ¼ oz. yeast, about ⅛ pint water, and salt. In Genoa, however, a special kind of bread is used for pizza. In the south of Italy numerous *pizzeria*, cafés for cheap quick meals, have sprung up, at which the pizza is the standard dish. Along the coast, pizza are sometimes made with the addition of mussels to the tomatoes and cheese. This is called a *pizza con cozze*. These described here are the most traditional varieties; apart from *pizza rustica*, all should be eaten hot, straight from the oven.

pizza al tegame. For this pizza a pastry made with 1 tea-spoon baking powder to 4 oz. (1 cup) flour, water, and salt is used. It is rolled out into an 8-inch round which is fried on both sides in hot oil. When cooked, it is filled with cooked tomatoes, anchovies, and marjoram or basil.

pizza alla francescana, made with yeast dough spread with cooked mushrooms, raw or cooked strips of ham, tomatoes, and cheese.

pizza alla genovese, also called *focaccia,* a kind of bread made with flour mixed with olive oil and salt is used for this pizza, and is very good to eat with cheese.

pizza alla Liguria, made with dough spread with anchovies or salted sardines, cooked onion, cooked tomatoes, garlic, marjoram (called *curnieura* in Liguria), and black olives. This pizza is called sardenara in San Remo.

pizza with anchovies and olives

pizza alla napoletana, made with yeast dough spread with cooked tomatoes and mozzarella cheese. Sometimes ancho-vies, marjoram, or basil are added.

pizza alla romana, made with yeast dough spread with cooked onions and olive oil. Many other varieties are also, of course, available in Rome.

pizza rustica, common in the south of Italy. It consists of a short crust pastry case filled with a mixture of 4 oz. chopped ham, 3 oz. each Parmesan cheese and cream cheese, and 2 chopped hard-boiled eggs, all stirred into 1 pint (2 cups) sauce béchamel which has been enriched with 2 egg yolks. Finally the 2 stiffly beaten egg whites are added, and the pizza is baked in a moderate oven for 30 minutes. It is usually eaten cold.

When pizza is made in private houses, a pastry dough like that for pizza al tegame is invariably used. It is spread with twice the quantity of filling usual for an ordinary pizza, and it is called a *pizza alla casalinga.* See also PISSALADIÈRE; PIZZETTE.

pizzaiola, salsa, a Neapolitan sauce, usually served with steak although it can also be used with fish or pasta. It consists of 1 lb. peeled and chopped tomatoes cooked in a very little olive oil with 2 or 3 garlic cloves. The cooking must be quick, and on no account should the tomatoes be allowed to pulp. Just before serving 1 good teaspoon marjoram or fresh basil is added. When preparing *bistecca alla pizzaiola,* the steaks are browned in olive oil, the pizzaiola put on top, the pan covered, and the contents cooked for 5 minutes.

pizzette, a miniature pizza, about the size of a small saucer and very thin. The finest are made in Parma. They are garnished with cooked tomatoes, bel paese, anchovies, and marjoram, and are eaten hot. See also PIZZA.

placek serowy na kruchym spodzie, a Polish and Russian curd cake or cheesecake in a pastry shell. The filling for a 10-inch case consists of 2 lb. (4 cups) sieved curds or cottage cheese, 4 oz. (½ cup) butter, 6 separated eggs (the whites stiffly beaten and added last), 4 oz. (½ cup) sugar, ½ teaspoon vanilla, and sometimes 2 oz. (½ cup) chopped candied orange peel. The filling is whipped for about 1 hour, then, without any cooking, is spread carefully inside the baked pastry case. It is delicious, and can be eaten as a sweet savoury or a dessert. See also CURD CAKE; SER (SERNIK).

plafond, the French culinary term for a tinned copper baking sheet.

plaice (*Pleuronectes platessa*), a salt-water flat fish of the same family as the flounder, easily recognizable by the orange-red spots on its brown upper skin. When it is absolutely fresh, it has quite a delicate milky taste, but it is gastronomically the least good of the flat fish. It can attain a weight of 10 lb., but most of those that are on sale in shops do not weigh more than 2 lb. Plaice is best fried or grilled, served in a good sauce, or it can be prepared in any way that is suitable for sole. In France the method *dugléré* is favoured. Plaice is also sold smoked and marinated. In the U.S., plaice is the name given to the summer flounder (*Paralichthys dentatus*). See also CARRELET; PLATIJA; SCHOLLES.

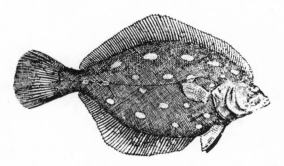

plaice

plaisir, see OUBLIE.

plaki, the Greek method of baking or braising fish with vegetables. See PALAMIDA; PSARI.

plakia, a vegetable dish eaten widely in the Balkans, particularly in Bulgaria. To prepare it 1 lb. peeled sliced onions and 1½ lb. peeled sliced tomatoes are fried in 4 oz. (½ cup) butter, and 1 cup beans (either green or dried) which have been boiled until soft and then drained, are added to them. Next, ½ pint (1 cup) stock or the same quantity of diluted tomato sauce is added, with salt, pepper, and 1 teaspoon sugar, and all are simmered slowly for about 45 minutes. This dish can be served either hot or cold. It is eaten particularly during Lent.

planche à découper, French for a wooden carving-board with channels and a groove for catching the juices that are exuded when the meat is carved.

planche à hacher, French for a chopping board.

planche à pâtisserie, French for a board for making, rolling out, and cutting pastry.

plank, an oak board about 1 inch thick, used for cooking; it must be big enough to take comfortably whatever food is to be prepared on it, such as "planked" chicken, fish, steak, etc. This is a method popular in the U.S. A new plank should be brushed thoroughly with oil or suet and warmed in a slow oven for 1 hour before use. For cooking, it is buttered, and a border of mashed or duchesse potatoes is arranged close to the edge. If any part of the plank is to be left exposed, it must now be well oiled. The food to be cooked is first seared on each side under a grill and, if it is a chicken, split and baked for 40 minutes in a moderate-to-hot oven. Then it is put on the plank with butter, salt, and pepper, garnished with mushrooms, onions, stuffed tomatoes, cauliflower, timbales of peas, etc., and baked in a hot oven until all is cooked. The food is served on the plank. Live shellfish, such as lobster, are split and baked as described above for 15 minutes. After use, the plank is wiped and scraped thoroughly, but never washed.

plantain (*Musa paradisiaca*), generally known as cooking banana, grown in Mexico and Central America. It can be baked, fried, or made into fritters. Although nutritious, it is not recommended for eating raw because it can taste like raw turnip when underripe. However, many of the very large "bananas" sold in shops are in fact plantains. See also BANANA.

plastron, the ventral part of the turtle shell, which, together with the dorsal part, is used for making turtle soup.

plat de côtes, I. A French cut of beef, corresponding to the English forequarter flank and the American short ribs. It is similar to *onglet,* but the forequarter end, and is used for sautés, carbonades, and braises. II. A French cut of pork from the forequarter flank. It is usually left whole and cooked as a joint. There are no equivalent English and American cuts, as this part of the pork carcase is divided up very differently in the different countries. See diagram page xxvi.

plate, an American cut of beef comprising the rear quarter flank.

platija, Spanish for plaice. Plaice is taken off the south coast of Spain, but Spanish plaice is not as good to eat as flounder or sole. It is cooked by frying, baking, or braising.

platine, a shallow French baking tin.

plättar, see PANNKAKA.

pleurotus, see MUSHROOM.

plie, see CARRELET.

pligouri, Greek for bulgur. To prepare it 1 cup bulgur is cooked in ¾ pint (1½ cups) rich stock, with salt, pepper, and a little butter added when serving.

pljeskavica, a Yugoslav sausage, made with minced mutton, pork, and veal flavoured with herbs, spices, and hot red chillis, and shaped round and flat. It is grilled over charcoal and served with cold raw sliced onion. The name is derived from the native word for palate. See also ĆEVAPCIĆI.

plombières, a French ice cream, made from 2 oz. pounded and sieved almonds mixed with ¼ pint (½ cup) milk and 1¾ pints (3½ cups) scalded cream. The mixture is strained and pressed well to remove all liquid. Then 10 egg yolks are mixed first with 5 oz. (⅔ cup) sugar and then with the cream mixture. It is then heated, but not boiled, until it thickens like a custard, whereupon it is vigourously beaten and sieved. It is then frozen, but half-way through the freezing process 1 pint (2 cups) whipped cream is added. When freezing is complete, the ice cream is scooped out into balls which are arranged in pyramid form and covered with apricot jam. Plombières may also be made with a purée of chestnuts, which is sieved but not strained, just as it is when made with almonds. Nowadays the custard would probably be liquidized instead of being beaten and sieved.

plommonspäkad fläskkarré, a Swedish dish of pork stuffed with prunes. One half lb. prunes are soaked overnight, then stoned and halved. They are placed along the centre of a 4-lb. boned loin of pork, which is then tied crosswise and rubbed all over with a mixture of pepper and ginger. The meat is first roasted until browned, then simmered until tender (about 1½ hours) in 1 pint (2 cups) veal stock. The string is removed before serving, and the joint is accompanied by apple sauce and browned potatoes. See also FLÄSK.

plov, the Russian version of *pilâv*. Plov can be eaten with savoury dishes or used as a sweet. In the latter case, it is served with fruits, either cooked or dried. See also PILÂV.

plov gurievsky, a sweet plov, consisting of 1 lb. (2½ cups) cooked rice served with 4 oz. (½ cup) melted butter and a sauce made from ¼ lb. (½ cup) honey and 4 oz. (1 cup) raisins simmered in water to cover for 10 minutes.

plov kavkazky, a Caucasian national dish, made with 1½ lb. sliced leg of mutton fried with 1 onion; 1 pint (2 cups) stock is added, with seasoning, and the meat is simmered until half-cooked. Then ¾ lb. (2 cups) rice is added, with a bay leaf. The dish is covered and cooked until the rice is tender but not mushy. Sometimes tomatoes, potatoes, carrots, and spices are included.

plov uzbek, a dish from Uzbekistan, made from 1 lb. chopped fat lamb or mutton fried with 2 sliced onions and ½ lb. sliced carrots. Next 2 pints (4 cups) water is added, with seasoning, and 1 lb. (2½ cups) rice. It is covered and simmered on a very low heat until the rice is cooked. The plov is served garnished with rings of raw onion.

plover (*Charadriidae*). Three members of this family of birds are excellent to eat and considered game birds. The finest in flavour is the golden plover (*Pluvialis apricarius*), next the grey plover (*P. squatarola*), and finally the green plover (*Vanellus vanellus*), better known as lapwing or peewit. They can be prepared and cooked in the same way as woodcock, and are at their best from October to January. The former delicacy of hard-boiled plover's eggs is to be had no longer, for it is now illegal to take them from the nest. See also GOLDEN PLOVER.

golden plover

pluches, a French term for the leaves of certain herbs such as chervil or parsley. They are generally used raw, but can also be blanched in boiling water.

pluck, the lights (lungs), heart, and entrails of carcase meats. The word does not apply to poultry. Pluck is often used in faggots and haggis.

płucka cielęce, Polish for calf's lights (lungs). In Poland, calf's lights (lungs) are cooked in either a vegetable broth or a dry white wine sauce.

plukkfisk, a Norwegian recipe for fish pie, using 2 lb. filleted hake, halibut, cod, sole, ling, turbot, or whiting. Two lb. pota-

toes are boiled in their skins, then peeled and sliced when cold. The raw fish is skinned, boned, and cut into pieces. Then 4 oz. (½ cup) butter is creamed and the potatoes and fish are added to it, together with seasoning, nutmeg, and grated onion. All are gently simmered until the fish is tender. See also FISK (FISKEPUDDING).

plum, I. The fruit of any tree of the genus *Prunus*, but chiefly that of *Prunus domestica*. This plant has been known through literature for at least 2000 years, although *P. institia,* or the Damascus plum, stones of which have been found in ancient ruins in Asia, possibly pre-dates it. The plum is a true stone-fruit or drupe, and is cultivated all over Europe. Many species are derived from *P. domestica,* including the quetsch or *zwetsch,* the best plum for drying into prunes, and the greengage, which is one of the more delicious dessert fruits. Plums are also used for tarts, pies, jams, jellies, preserves, compotes, confectionery, etc., and for making cordials, wines, and liqueurs. The best-known English varieties are the dessert plums Victoria and Early Rivers, the latter being a small sweet red plum which ripens in late July and is also good for cooking, spicing, and bottling. An important species, *P. salicina,* native to China and cultivated in Japan, was introduced into the U.S. in 1870. In the southern states of the U.S. the best-known species is *P. hortulana,* derived from the large native *P. americana* group, and in the northern states *P. nigra* or the Canada plum is the most popular. However, neither of these is a dessert fruit. See also DAMSON; GREENGAGE; MYROBALAN; PLAUME; SLIVA. II. A word sometimes applied to raisins, and used in this sense in the titles of such English dishes as plum cake and plum duff.

plum duff, the name used in country districts of England, and also familiar among sailors, for spotted dick (see PLUM II).

plum pudding, the name by which the Christmas pudding was originally called. Its innovation at the English court was the occasion for one of the presentations with which William the Conqueror frequently favoured members of his domestic staff, in this case Robert Argyllon, who received a manor at Addington in Surrey. He received it, according to the *Cook's Oracle* (fourth edition, 1822), ". . . by the service of making one mess in an earthen pot in the kitchen of our Lord the King, on the day of his coronation, called De la Groute, i.e. a kind of Plum porridge or Water gruel with plums in it. This dish is still served up at the Royal Table, at Coronations, by the Lord of the said Manor of Addington." The present-day Christmas pudding evolves from the substitution of prunes, and later still dried fruits, for plums, with the addition of spices, eggs, etc.

pluvier, French for plover, highly thought of in France and cooked in the same way as *bécasse.* See also GIBIER; GOLDEN PLOVER.

consommé aux oeufs de pluvier, chicken consommé garnished with poached plovers' eggs. See also CONSOMMÉ.

poach, to, to cook foodstuffs in a clear liquid, plain, spiced or salted, or in a flavoured stock. It is a method applied particularly to eggs, fish, meat, and poultry. Fruit may also be termed poached if it is cooked gently in a syrup. See also SIMMER.

poakan or **poake,** see POKEWEED.

pochard (*Aythyini*), a diving duck which breeds in northern and central Europe as well as in Algeria and western Asia. It has several local names in the British Isles, such as dunbird and red-headed curre. Pochard is much prized by gastronomes and is considered by some to be as good as mallard. It can be prepared in any way that is suitable for wild duck, and the white-eyed pochard braises particularly well and also makes excellent *pâté.* In France pochard is shot during the winter migration, and is much sought after. There is also a closely related American species known in the U.S. as redhead, red-eyed poker, or red-headed widgeon.

pochards

poche, French for forcing (pastry) bag. The various nozzles which can be fitted are called douilles.

pochki, Russian for kidneys. See also KIDNEYS.

pochki v smetanie, kidneys fried in butter with an onion. Just before serving, a little stock and sour cream are added to make a sauce.

pochouse, see MATELOTE.

podkvàsa, the Bulgarian name for the culture used to turn fresh milk into yogourt. Bulgaria is the country in which yogourt was first developed, and it has given its name to *bacillus Bulgaricus* which cultures the milk. Yogourt is drunk extensively in Bulgaria, is used a great deal in cooking, and forms the basis of the chilled soup, *taratòr*.

podre, see BACALHAU, PODRE.

podvarak, a traditional Yugoslavian method of cooking duck. First 2 sliced onions are fried in oil until pale gold, then mixed into ½ lb. sauerkraut with 12 whole black peppercorns. The duck is browned all over, then put in a casserole on top of the onions and sauerkraut. Seasoning and sauerkraut juice are added, and the dish is cooked in a moderate oven for 1½– 2 hours or until the duck is tender. It is served carved, on top of the sauerkraut. See also PAČA.

poêlage, the French method of cooking *à l'étuvée*, that is, in a covered pan with only butter or other fat. It is the equivalent of pot roasting. *La poêle* is a covered shallow casserole in which food can be cooked under closed conditions; *le poêle* is a stove. *Poêlon* is the name for an earthenware pot, and for a long-handled metal pan used for heating and browning sugar.

pofesen, an Austrian version of *pain perdu*, made from 2 crustless slices of bread sandwiched with jam, dipped lightly into a little red or white wine (the bread must not be allowed to get too soggy), then into beaten egg, and finally fried in butter on both sides until golden. It is served hot, sprinkled with sugar, and fruit syrup is served separately.

pogácsa, a Hungarian biscuit (cookie). It is made with 8 oz. (2 cups) flour mixed with a pinch of salt and 5 oz. (⅔ cup) butter. Then 2 small eggs are added and well mixed in, and the dough is rolled out to ½-inch thickness and cut into small rounds. These are brushed with egg, garnished with a salted almond, and baked in a moderate oven until golden.

pogne, a traditional cake or tart from the Dauphiné region of France, which may take one of several forms. The most usual is that of a large pastry flan, filled with fresh cooked fruit in the summer, and sometimes with cooked pumpkin in the autumn and winter. In the Drôme, the pogne is a kind of brioche, but the speciality of this area is the *pogne de romans*.

pogne de romans, first 1½ lb. (6 cups) flour is spread in a circle, and in the centre are put 1 teaspoon salt, 1 tablespoon orange flower water, ½ oz. yeast, ½ lb. (1 cup) soft butter, and 4 eggs. These are all drawn into the flour and worked in

very well. Then 2 more eggs are added one by one, followed by 6 oz. (1½ cups) castor sugar, and both these ingredients are gradually mixed in. The dough is put into a bowl, sprinkled with a little flour, covered, and left in a warm place to rise for 10–12 hours. It is then kneaded, divided into 2 parts, and shaped into balls which are put onto a buttered baking-tin, left to rise for 30 minutes, then brushed with beaten egg and baked in a moderate oven for 30 minutes. The pognes are served with red currant jelly and are eaten hot or cold.

pohjalainen leipäjuusto, a round cheese-curd loaf from Ostrobothnia in Finland, made from 15 pints (30 cups) sweet milk or *beestings* milk, and 2 teaspoons rennet. The milk is heated to 100°F (38°C) and kept at that temperature during the cheese-making. The rennet is mixed with 3 tablespoons water, then poured into the milk and left unstirred for about 20 minutes or until the solution is lightly set. Then it is turned out onto a special wooden slab and left to drain. After the whey has drained away and the curds are firm, they are sprinkled with salt and the outside is browned before an open fire. The loaf is served with *smörgasbord*.

point, à, the French culinary term describing a steak which has been medium cooked.

point steak, the top end of rump steak. It is good, but carries a certain amount of fat or gristle.

pointe de culotte, French for what is termed in Britain a rump steak or roast. In American butchery the equivalent cut is a top of the rump roast. It is also called pièce de boeuf (*aiguillette*), especially on menus in restaurants. See diagram page xxiii.

pointe de filet, a French pork cut, equivalent to the English chump end of pork loin chops.

poire, French for pear. There are very many French varieties of pear, some of which are also grown in other parts of Europe, in Britain, and in the U.S. French pears excel in many ways, for they are cultivated both for use as dessert fruits, and for cooking and canning. They are also preserved by means of crystallisation (*poires glacées*), and one variety of hard pear is preserved by being partly dried in the oven and then flattened on one side (these are known as *poires tapées* and can be bought in grocery shops). The best dessert pears are those which ripen by September or October; the late-ripening varieties are those used for cooking or preserves. The earliest French pear to ripen is the St. Jean, which is ready, as its name implies, about June 25 (the Feast of St. John). It is small and green with an undistinguished taste. The latest pear to ripen is the Bergamotte in November; it will keep very well until the middle of the following June. It is large and round, with a yellowish skin dotted with russet and overlaid with a slight red flush; the flesh is fragrant but often gritty. Another late ripener is Crassane, medium-sized, round, and green with brown dots. It has quite a pleasant, slightly acid taste, and it keeps until April. Other important varieties are *belle-alliance, belle-angevine, belle-de-berry, belle-et-bonne, besi, beurré, bon-chrétien, doyenné, duchesse d'angoulême,* and *louise-bonne.* See also BELLE HÉLÈNE; CONDÉ; MELBA; PEAR.

poireau, French for leek. In France leeks are boiled in salted water for 10 minutes or until tender, and served hot with melted butter or cream. They are also served cold, after boiling, with sauce vinaigrette. See also FLAMICHE; LEEK.

poireaux à la niçoise, leeks cooked in olive oil with tomatoes, garlic, parsley, and seasoning, with a squeeze of lemon added before serving.

poireaux au vin rouge, leeks cooked in olive oil for a few minutes and then salted. A wineglass of red wine and half that quantity of meat stock are added, and all are covered and cooked gently for 7–10 minutes, or until tender but not overcooked.

poirée, French for spinach beet or chard, also called *blette.* The green leaves are cooked in any way that is suitable for spinach, and the white mid-ribs are boiled, drained, and served with melted butter if hot, or à la vinaigrette if cold.

poirée à la crème, spinach beet or chard first blanched in boiling water, then covered in sauce béchamel enriched with cream, dotted with butter, and baked for 30 minutes.

pois, French for peas. Small peas picked before they reach complete maturity are known as *petits pois.* They are delicious and are served a great deal in France, usually scantily cooked in water, then tossed in butter, or mixed with cream and simmered, or served with a white sauce. The most esteemed varieties are the pois de Clamart and the pois michaux. *Pois mange-tout* are sugar peas, cooked whole in the pod. See also PEA.

petits pois à la française, petits pois cooked with chiffonade of lettuce, onions, herbs, sugar, salt, and very little water. Butter is added before serving. If large peas are cooked in the same way, they are called *pois à la paysanne* or *pois à la bonne femme.*

pois chiche, French for chick-pea; in France chick-peas are usually stewed for a long time in a good stock with herbs. This is called *pois chiches en estouffade.* Chick-peas are also used in soups, or puréed as a garnish. See also CHICK-PEA.

poissonnier, the French word for the chef in a large restaurant who cooks all the fish dishes except those that are grilled or fried; those are prepared by either the *rôtisseur* or the *grillardin.* Poissonnier is also the word for fishmonger and fish kettle.

poitrine, French for breast; for example, poitrine d'agneau, is breast of lamb. See diagram page xxvii.

poitrine de boeuf, brisket of beef. When nearer the tail end, it becomes *milieu de tendron,* hampe, and flanchet (flank) in that order, flanchet (flank) adjoining the hind leg. See also BOEUF and diagram page xxiii.

poivrade, I. A French method of serving roebuck cutlets. First 4 cutlets are sautéed in oil or butter on both sides and, when cooked, 1 tablespoon wine vinegar is added, stirred into the pan juices, and boiled up. Then ½ pint (1 cup) sauce *poivrade* is poured in, and the whole heated over a high flame to reduce. The cutlets are served in the shape of a dome, each cutlet alternated with fried croûtons. The sauce is served separately. See also CHEVREUIL. II. A French method of serving cold venison, beef, or lamb in sauce *poivrade,* accompanied by chestnut purée and gooseberry jelly. III. The French name for very young, small cooked globe artichokes which are eaten with salt as the only accompaniment (*à la croque au sel*).

poivrade, sauce, a classical and very popular French sauce. It is made by melting 1 tablespoon butter in a saucepan, and sautéeing 1 sliced carrot, 1 sliced onion, 2 shallots, 1 bay leaf, 1 clove, and 1 sprig of thyme, all seasoned with salt. When these ingredients are lightly coloured, 1 heaped tablespoon flour is stirred in, followed by 1 gill (½ cup) red wine and 1 tablespoon wine vinegar. All are simmered gently for 20–30 minutes, when a good quantity of freshly ground black pepper is added (the sauce should taste quite peppery). If meat jelly is available, 2 tablespoons of it make the sauce full of flavour. The sauce is sieved before serving. It is used with steak, cutlets, liver, and brains. For game, the sauce is boiled up with game trimmings and game essence (extract). The English version of the sauce has a little red currant jelly blended with it, and is sometimes known as roebuck sauce.

poivre, French for pepper.

steak au poivre, steak covered thickly with crushed peppercorns and then fried in butter. It is often flambéed with brandy.

poivre d'âne, the Provençal name for a variety of wild savoury found locally. It has a peppery, slightly bitter taste. Local cheeses of ewe's or goat's milk, resembling *banon* and in season from April to December, are flavoured with this herb.

poivre de guinée, French for guinea pepper or chilli, which is used in some saucissons.

poivre de la Jamaïque, French for allspice; also *toute-épice* or *quatre épices,* used in many dishes such as casseroles of game.

poivre mignonette, the French expression for fresh, rather coarsely ground white peppercorns. In former times, *mignonette* was the name given to a mixture of cayenne pepper, nutmeg, coriander, ginger, cloves, and cinnamon, which was tied in a muslin bag and used to season foods during cooking by dipping it into the saucepan containing them.

pökelfleisch, I. German for pickled pork, one of the most popular meats in Germany. II. German for brawn. See HAUSSULZ.

pokerounce, a curiously named medieval English dish, consisting of hot spiced toast spread with honey and sprinkled with pine nuts. The honey was heated with the sticky pink end of a fir branch in it, and if a strong flavour was required, a pinch of mixed spice was added.

pokeweed (*Phytolacca decandra*), a native shrub of North America, also called poake or poakan, the former meaning ''blood'' in the language of the Indians. It was imported into Europe in the 16th century for the strong red dye that could be made from its blood-red berries, but importation stopped when *cochineal* from Mexico took its place. The root is poisonous, but the young leafy shoots are picked in June, tied into bundles, and cooked in the same way as asparagus, except that the first water is thrown away after 5 minutes, and the pokeweed reboiled in fresh water for a further 15 minutes, then drained and served hot with melted butter. It may also be served cold with oil and vinegar. It is extremely good to eat, and very rich in vitamin C.

Another member of this family (*P. acinosa*) is called *yama gobo.* It can be bought, dried, from Japanese grocers in New York, and is used in soups.

pokhlyobka, a traditional Russian country soup made from dried mushrooms, pearl barley, onions, leeks, carrots, potatoes, dill, salt, and peppercorns, all simmered in water for a few hours. Sour cream is added 5 minutes before serving, and the soup is garnished with chopped dill.

pole flounder, see WITCH FLOUNDER.

polędwica, Polish for fillet or tenderloin steak. *Polędwica z rożna* is fillet or tenderloin steak cooked on a spit. It can also be left overnight in a red wine marinade, then cooked with vegetables in a casserole.

polędwica na dziko, steak first marinated, then larded and grilled. Sour cream is thickened with flour to make a sauce.

polędwica z maderą i truflami, steak either grilled or broiled and served with truffles and sauce madère.

polenta, the name of a traditional porridge made from maize meal in Piedmont, Italy. The meal is boiled in water (1 lb. meal to 2½ pints water) with butter or olive oil, and grated cheese added. The porridge is often further cooked by being spread on a baking tray and baked in the oven, or it can be cut into shapes and fried as fritters, which are afterwards sprinkled with grated cheese. These fritters are a traditional northern Italian garnish for small cooked birds such as thrush and fieldfare, and such dishes were very popular with Napoleon I, who was by birth a Corsican. Sometimes the birds are baked in the oven actually in the polenta, with butter and cheese. This word is also used in Italian for coarsely ground maize or cornmeal. It is the same as the American hominy grits (except polenta is yellow and hominy cream-coloured), and is treated in exactly the same way. It is used in Italy in the dishes described below, and is also used in the southwestern provinces of France in making coarse breads and cakes (for example, *galette* and *miques de maïs*), and in the forcible feeding of geese to enlarge their livers for foie gras. Polenta can also be used to make a sweet dish something like semolina pudding. In Corsica a kind of polenta is made with chestnut flour and eaten with *broccio,* a local cheese.

polenta grassa, a speciality of Piedmont. To prepare it 1 lb. finely ground polenta is cooked for 20 minutes in 2½–3 pints (5–6 cups) salted water, stirring frequently. Into a buttered fireproof dish are put a layer of the polenta, then a layer of slices of *fontina* cheese and small pats of butter, then another layer of polenta, then more cheese and butter. The dish is baked until the top is melted and brown.

polenta pasticciata, a polenta pie which is a speciality of Milan. One-half lb. polenta is cooked in 1½ pints salted water and then left to cool. A layer of the cooked polenta is spread in a buttered fireproof dish, then covered with thick sauce *béchamel* flavoured with nutmeg, and some sliced white truffles. This layering is repeated twice more, ending with a layer of *béchamel.* Grated Gruyère or Parmesan cheese is sprinkled on top, and the pie is baked until golden.

polévka, Czechoslovakian for soup. *Knedlíky* are often served with soups in Czechoslovakia. See also KULAJDA.

bramborová polévka, a traditional vegetable soup. Chopped carrots, celery, and shredded green cabbage are fried in butter, moistened with stock, and cooked. A brown roux is mixed with 2 quarts (8 cups) beef stock, seasoned with garlic, marjoram, salt, and pepper, and then combined with the vegetable mixture and simmered. When the soup is cooked it is strained, then garnished with diced root vegetables, diced mushrooms, diced fried salt pork, and a large amount of diced boiled potato.

hrachová polévka, soup made with dried peas. First 1 lb. dried yellow peas are soaked, then cooked, drained, and sieved. To the purée are added 1 lightly fried onion, 4 tablespoons milk, 1½ tablespoons flour, 1½ pints (3 cups) stock, 1 garlic clove, 1 teaspoon marjoram, and seasoning. All are simmered for 30 minutes, and the soup is garnished with little bread croûtons sprinkled with parsley.

květáková polévka, soup made from 1 medium-sized cooked and sieved cauliflower mixed into 2½ pints (5 cups) veal or chicken stock, with 2 tablespoons cream. When boiling, 2 egg yolks are stirred in, and the soup is garnished with little cauliflowerlets, a pinch of nutmeg, and parsley. It is usually served with *knedlíky.*

ledvinková polévka, a traditional kidney soup. Sliced onions and potatoes are fried in lard and sprinkled with flour, then white stock, salt, pepper to taste, 1 teaspoon each paprika and caraway seeds, and 2 garlic cloves are added. All are cooked slowly and then rubbed through a sieve. The soup is served garnished with very small pieces of calf's kidney which have been stewed in butter.

polewka, traditional Polish rye soup consisting of water thickened with rye flour, seasoned, and mixed with cream. It resembles a thin rye porridge.

polewka z wina, a Polish soup made with 1 pint (2 cups) white wine, ½ pint (1 cup) water, 6 cloves, 1 3-inch cinnamon stick, 2 tablespoons sugar, and 2 egg yolks, all whipped over a low heat until foamy. Beer is sometimes used instead of wine, and the soup is then known as *zupa piwna.* Sweet soups are quite common in Poland.

polipetto, the Genoese name for the most tender and succulent Italian octopus. It is very small and has eight tentacles. In Genoa it is cooked very gently in olive oil and white wine. See also CALAMARI; FRAGOLE DI MARE; POLPO; ZIMINO.

polipo, see POLPO.

poliporo, an edible Italian fungus; see FUNGHI.

Polish cheeses, see SER.

polita, a Greek term derived from polis (city) used in culinary

contexts to describe urbane cookery originating in Byzantium (later Constantinople), or cookery in the style for which Constantinople was renowned. During the era of the Byzantine Empire, Constantinople, or "New Rome," was noted for its culinary achievements. Constantinople is even said to be the place of origin of the chef's white hat. The story runs that after the fall of Constantinople the much-valued imperial chefs took refuge in the monasteries, where they continued to practise their art, greatly to the pleasure of the monks. At first the cooks adopted the black habit and high black hat of the Greek Church, but after a time they felt that their clothes should differ from those of the true monks, and obtained permission to wear the same habit, but in white. Thus the high black hat of the monk became the high white hat of the chef, and it has survived to this day.

pollack or *pollock* (*Pollachius pollachius*), a saltwater fish not unlike cod or rock salmon and of the same family, found from Newfoundland and Greenland to the coasts of Europe. It is sometimes called green cod. There is also a darker species known as coalfish which can be prepared in the same way as cod. See also COALFISH.

pollan or *vendace,* the names given to the whitefish (*Coregonus albula*) found only in the deep Shannon lakes of Ireland, particularly Lough Derg and Lough Ree, in the Castle and Mill Lochs at Lochmaben in Dumfriesshire, Scotland, and in Derwentwater and Bassenthwaite in Cumberland, England. Other types are found in Lough Neagh in Ireland, and there is also a possible link with a similar species found in Siberian lakes. It is certainly closely related to the *gwyniad.* Pollan lives on a type of small shrimp, and being a bottom-feeder is seldom seen, but it is captured in nets at eel-weirs. It is excellent to eat and can be prepared in any way that is suitable for trout. A full account of the pollan is given by W. Thompson in his *Natural History of Ireland* (1849–1856). He was the first to describe it. Its name is derived from pollag, the Irish word for whiting. See also GWYNIAD.

pollo, Italian for chicken. The best chickens are to be found in Tuscany, where they are often grilled over charcoal and basted with butter. *Pollastra* is the fattened, neutered hen which is always the best eating. See also CHICKEN; PETTI DI POLLO.

pollo al latte, as *pollo alla crema,* but using milk.

pollo all' aretina, a jointed and seasoned chicken is added to 2 small chopped onions which have been lightly fried in olive oil, and is browned. Then 1 pint (2 cups) white wine is added and the same amount of stock. When the liquid is boiling, 1 cup shelled green peas and the same amount of rice (½ lb.) are stirred in. It is covered, and cooked over a gentle heat for about 30 minutes or until tender.

pollo alla bolognese arrosto, chicken covered with slices of ham and a sprig of rosemary, seasoned with salt and pepper, then roasted with equal quantities of butter and olive oil. After 30 minutes a large peeled and chopped tomato and 1 crushed garlic clove are added, and the chicken is cooked for a further 30 minutes, or until tender.

pollo alla cacciatora, a jointed and seasoned chicken is fried in oil. When golden, 1 large sliced onion, 1 garlic clove, and ½ pint (1 cup) white or red wine are added, and all simmered for 10 minutes. Then 1 slice diced bacon, 4 peeled and chopped tomatoes, 2 tablespoons chopped parsley, 1 tablespoon basil, seasoning, and about 1 pint (2 cups) stock barely to cover are added. The lid is put on the pan, and the contents are cooked in a moderate oven for about 1 hour or until tender.

pollo alla crema, chicken browned in butter, then sprinkled with flour and set in a pan with sufficient fresh cream to cover. The lid is put on, and the chicken is cooked in a moderate oven until tender. The sauce is thickened with 1 tablespoon potato flour, and flavoured just before serving with 1 tablespoon brandy. If milk is used instead of cream, the dish is called *pollo al latte*.

pollo alla diavolo, a young chicken split in two lengthways, brushed with oil or butter and lightly grilled, preferably over charcoal. In Tuscany the bird is often first marinated in olive oil with parsley, onion, pepper, and ground ginger.

pollo alla Fiorentina, jointed chicken dusted with flour, seasoned, and fried in butter.

pollo alla Livornese, a lemon wedge and a nut of butter are put inside the chicken, and it is then browned all over in 4 tablespoons olive oil. Then ¼ pint (½ cup) chicken stock, juice of 1 lemon, and a sprig of chopped parsley are added, also seasoning. All are covered and cooked on top of the stove for about 2 hours. Cooking is done very slowly, so that the chicken is steamed rather than boiled.

pollo alla montagnuola, a jointed and seasoned chicken is coated in a mixture of 2 eggs beaten with 2 tablespoons water, and left to stand in the mixture for 1 hour. The joints are then rolled in breadcrumbs and put into a well-greased casserole, covered, and baked for 1 hour in a moderate oven. Half-way through cooking, they are basted with 4 oz. (½ cup) melted butter. It is served with lemon wedges.

pollo alla napoletana, chicken casseroled with mushrooms, garlic, bacon, onions, rosemary, tomato purée diluted with water, and a little chicken stock barely to cover. Equal quantities of stock and white wine may be used instead.

pollo alla romana, jointed chicken fried in olive oil until golden, with 2 oz. diced bacon and 1 large garlic clove. It is then sprinkled with chopped rosemary and ¼ pint (1 glass) white wine, and heated. Then 2 tablespoons tomato purée mixed with hot water are added, and all are covered and simmered until the bird is tender.

pollo in padella, chicken jointed and fried in oil with onion, tomatoes, garlic, and pimentos.

pollo in porchetta; chicken stuffed with a mixture of 6 oz. chopped ham, 2 chopped garlic cloves, and 1 tablespoon fennel (either roots or leaves), then cooked in 6 oz. (⅔ cup) butter in a covered casserole in the oven until tender. To soften an older bird, ½ pint (1 cup) stock is included with the butter.

pollo in umido, boiling-fowl browned in oil, floured, then stewed with stock, onions, green peppers, tomatoes, mushrooms, and green olives for 2½ hours. About 30 minutes before serving, 2 cups shelled green peas are added.

pollo marsala, jointed chicken is rolled in seasoned flour and gently fried in oil or butter. Marsala barely to cover is added, and the bird is simmered until tender.

pollo ripieno arrosto, the chicken is stuffed with a mixture of 1 chopped onion, 1½ cups coarse breadcrumbs, and 1 chopped chicken liver and heart, all sautéed in 2 tablespoons each oil and butter, with 2 tablespoons grated Parmesan cheese to taste and ¼ pint (½ cup) stock to moisten. The bird is then roasted with butter in a moderate oven for 20 minutes to the lb.

pollo tonnato, cold boiled chicken, served with ½ pint (1 cup) mayonnaise which is thinned to the consistency of cream with about 3 tablespoons chicken stock, and mixed with 2 oz. puréed tunny (tuna) fish.

pollo, Spanish for chicken, which may be served fried, grilled, or boiled in Spain. If it is boiled and served cold, mayonnaise is served separately. See also CHICKEN.

pollo al ast, spit-roasted chicken.

pollo al Jerez, chicken cooked with sherry, either braised or fried.

pollo Chilindrón. In Aragon, where it is a speciality, this dish comprises the whole meal. Half a bird is allowed per person, and the birds must be young and tender and at least 2½ lb. in weight. To make it, 3 chopped garlic cloves and 1 large onion are cooked slowly in ¼ pint (½ cup) oil; then 2 lb. peeled tomatoes are added, and the resulting tomato sauce is simmered for 1 hour. Three chickens are jointed and lightly browned in oil and garlic; then seasoning and 1 lb. lean sliced ham are added to the pan, and the birds are further browned. Finally the sauce is added, with 6 chopped red sweet peppers and 2 teaspoons parsley, and the whole is covered and simmered until the chickens are cooked. These quantities are sufficient for 6 people.

pollo rélleno, stuffed roasted chicken. The stuffing consists of rice, almonds, ham, chicken livers, and parsley, and the bird is basted with sherry during roasting.

polonaise, à la, I. A Polish and French garnish for vegetables, especially cauliflower or asparagus, consisting of fresh white breadcrumbs fried in butter until crisp, then sprinkled over the cooked vegetables. The dish may then be garnished with sieved hard-boiled egg yolks mixed with chopped parsley. Sometimes the egg whites are chopped and also used as decoration. II. A French method of serving chicken. See POULET, À LA POLONAISE.

polpette, Italian for small flat meat cakes, not much larger than 1–1½ inches in diameter. They are usually made from 2 lb. raw minced (ground) beef or veal, 2 crushed garlic cloves, 1 thick crustless slice of white bread soaked in milk and then squeezed, 1 teaspoon grated lemon peel, 1 tablespoon chopped parsley, 2 eggs, salt and pepper, and a pinch of nutmeg. The ingredients are all well mixed, shaped with floury hands into cakes, and fried quickly on both sides in hot oil. Cold cooked minced meat can also be used, but the flavour is not as fresh. See also POLPETTINE.

polpette di baccalà, as above, but made with cooked salted cod.

polpetti, a traditional Italian cheese soup. To prepare it, 4 tablespoons grated Parmesan cheese is mixed into 1 pint (2 cups) beef broth, and the soup is garnished with pasta.

polpettine, smaller versions of *polpette.* Like *polpette,* these small cakes can be based on other ingredients besides meat. See also POLPETTE.

polpettine di formaggio, hot Italian cheese balls, made from equal quantities of fresh breadcrumbs and grated Parmesan cheese (approximately 2 cups each), 3 eggs, 2 teaspoons chopped parsley, salt, pepper, and a pinch of nutmeg. The mixture is formed into small balls about 1 inch in diameter which are rolled in flour, then sometimes dipped in egg, and finally deep fried in hot oil.

polpettine di spinaci, see SPINACI.

polpettone, Italian for meat roll. It is made with 2 lb. raw minced veal, pork, or beef, 4 eggs, 1 crushed garlic clove, 1 medium-sized onion, 2 tablespoons chopped parsley, salt, and pepper, all well mixed. The mixture is then flattened out on a floured board and 2 chopped hard-boiled eggs are mixed with 2 oz. chopped cooked ham and 2 tablespoons chopped diced *provolone.* This is put in the middle of the meat mixture, which is then gently rolled up, wrapped in greased paper, laid in a greased tin or dish, and covered. It is cooked in a slow oven for 1½–2 hours. It is usually served hot, but it is also excellent cold. Polpettone may also be made with fish, in which case the onion and garlic are omitted, as well as the ham in the stuffing, mushrooms being used instead.

polpo, Italian for octopus; also called polipo. See also OCTOPUS.

polpo affogati, literally "smothered octopus." In the neighbourhood of Naples, small octopus are simmered in small individual casseroles with tomatoes and parsley. No water or other liquid is added.

polvo, Portuguese for octopus. When small, octopus is often cooked in the same way as squid. See also LULA; OCTOPUS.

polynéer, small Swedish pastry tarts filled with a mixture of 4 oz. (1 cup) ground almonds, 4 oz. (1 cup) icing sugar, and 4 egg whites, all beaten until fluffy. The pastry is made from ½ lb. (2 cups) flour, 6 oz. (⅔ cup) butter, sugar to taste, and 2 egg yolks. The tart tins are lined with this, filled three-quarters full with the almond mixture, and topped with lattice strips of pastry. They are baked in a slow-to-moderate oven for about 25 minutes. See also MANDEL (MANDELSKORPER).

polypodium, a species of edible fern, cooked in the same way as bracken.

pomegranate (*Punica granatum*), the fruit of a small tree which is a native of Persia and neighbouring regions. The antiquity of the tree as a cultivated plant is evidenced by the many references to the fruit in the Bible and in Homer's *Odyssey,* and it was introduced into Europe at an early date. Its sweet juice is used for making a refreshing drink, and the flavour of the flesh is both delicious and unique. However, the interior of the fruit is in tiny globular sections, with a small stone in each, and although children are fond of eating pomegranates raw, most adults are discouraged by the labour of disposing of the hundreds of small stones.

pomegranate

pomelo, see GRAPEFRUIT.

pomfret, I. A brown/grey sea fish (*Brama rayi*), also known as Ray's bream and sea bream, found in the North Atlantic, the Pacific, and parts of the Mediterranean. It is cooked in the same way as sea bream. Like all the bream family it is good to eat. See also BREAM. II. *Stromateus fiatole,* a sea fish, which is found in the Atlantic and in parts of the Mediterranean. It is best grilled or fried.

pomidoro, Italian for tomato, which has been used extensively in many forms in Italy since the 15th century, when seeds from China were first brought back and grown by an Italian monk, Fra Serenio. Tomatoes form part of the national diet in the south of Italy, and are used both fresh, and concentrated in a purée which is sold in tins and tubes and forms the basis of sauces for pasta, pizza, etc.

conserva di pomidori, ripe tomatoes packed into sterilized jars with salt and a sprig of fresh basil. These are put in cold water and boiled for about 20 minutes, then screwed down to exclude air. This preserve is used in the winter when fresh tomatoes are scarce.

pomidori ammollicati, large tomatoes cut in half, covered with breadcrumbs mixed with parsley, garlic, and seasoning, then sprinkled with olive oil and baked for 10 minutes.

pomidori col tonno, large raw tomatoes stuffed with tunny (tuna) fish and mayonnaise.

pomidori ripieni alla casalinga, raw tomatoes with their tops cut off, and the pulp removed and mixed with cooked minced (ground) meat, mushrooms, onion, carrot, celery, garlic, parsley, a little sugar, seasoning, and a beaten egg. This mixture is put back in the tomato shells and sprinkled with a mixture of breadcrumbs and grated Parmesan cheese, before being baked in the oven for 20–30 minutes. They are served cold for *antipasti.*

pomidori ripieni di riso, as above, without the meat and mushrooms, but with the addition of cooked rice, mint, and tomato pulp.

salsa di pomidori, often made from *conserva di pomidori.* If fresh tomatoes are used, 2 lb. are cooked with 1 small onion, 1 carrot, 1 piece celery, parsley, salt, pepper, and a pinch of sugar, and simmered until they resemble a purée. The mixture is then sieved, and chopped basil is added. Chopped ham and garlic may also be added to taste.

pomidory, Polish for tomatoes. See also TOMATO.

pomidory pieczone, baked tomatoes. Often the tops are cut off, and the tomatoes are stuffed with a mixture of minced meat or mushrooms and rice, before being cooked in the oven.

pomme, French for apple, of which the finest are grown in the orchards of Normandy and Brittany. The following are the varieties considered the best in France: *calville,* distinguished by a furrowed effect at the base; calville blanche, a large conical apple with a red-flushed, pale yellow skin, delicious and very aromatic, with a faint taste of pineapple; calville rouge, large and conical like calville blanche, with a greenish-yellow skin flushed with dark crimson, and with a flavour reminiscent of raspberry. These are all excellent dessert apples. The following, though dessert apples, are also used for cooking in France: reinette des reinettes, large, with a yellow-flushed, slightly rough-textured skin; reinette du Canada, similar to reine des reinettes; reine franche, a medium-sized, slightly cylindrical apple with a brown-spotted yellowish-green skin, and with very fragrant flesh which keeps well; reine grise, a large apple with crisp fragrant flesh which will keep well into early summer. These apples are baked, boiled with sugar and water, and made into tarts, omelettes, jellies, jams, etc. See also APPLE; RAMBOUR.

pomme de terre, French for potato. New potatoes are *pommes* (de terre) *nouvelles.* There are many excellent varieties of potato grown in France, some of the most notable being the kipfler, a waxy yellow kidney-shaped potato, the jaune langue de Hollande and the rouge langue de Hollande, the shaw, and the quarantine. Lyonnais and Nièvre (the old province of Nivernais and Morvan) are renowned for their good potatoes. The most general ways of serving potatoes in France follow, and the French culinary practise of prefixing the various classical methods by *pommes* rather than *pommes de terre* has been followed. All recipes are for 1 lb. potatoes (after peeling), unless otherwise stated. See also POTATO.

crêpes de pommes de terre, see CRÊPES DE POMMES DE TERRE.

galette de pommes de terre, see GALETTE.

julienne de pommes de terre, alternative name for *pommes frites allumettes.*

pommes à l'alsacienne, new potatoes tossed in butter with some button onions and small pieces of bacon, and a sprinkling of fines herbes or parsley.

pommes à l'anglaise, potatoes steamed or boiled.

pommes à l'auvergnate, peeled potatoes cut into thin slices. To prepare 4 oz. fat bacon or salt pork is cut into small cubes, and 2 or 3 onions are sliced. Some pure lard is heated in a *cocotte* and the sliced potatoes and onions and the cubes of bacon are put in, in alternating layers, and seasoned. The pot is covered and the contents cooked gently for about 1½ hours. They are served from the same pot. (The onions and bacon may be lightly browned before adding to the pot, in which case the fat from the bacon replaces the lard.)

pommes à la basquaise, a Basque method of cooking large potatoes. They are peeled, sliced in half lengthways, and have their centres hollowed out before being parboiled for 5 minutes. They are then drained, dried, and stuffed with tomato fondue mixed with a *salpicon* of sweet peppers cooked in oil or butter, chopped Bayonne ham, parsley, and a little garlic. They are put in a buttered gratin dish with a little oil or butter, and gently cooked in a slow-to-moderate oven. The tops are sprinkled with crisp breadcrumbs before serving.

pommes à la berrichonne, potatoes as cooked in the Berry district of France. They are cut to resemble large olives, and sautéed with a finely chopped onion and diced bacon in a little butter. When the ingredients are lightly browned, enough stock to cover, a bouquet garni, and seasoning are added, the lid is put on, and the whole is gently simmered until the potatoes are cooked. They are served sprinkled with chopped parsley.

pommes à la bordelaise, potatoes cubed and sautéed in butter with a little peeled and chopped garlic.

pommes à la boulangère, a mixture of sliced potatoes and 2 medium-sized sliced fried onions, seasoned, moistened with ½ pint (1 cup) meat stock, and baked in the oven. They are frequently put round and under a shoulder of lamb and roasted in the oven: this is known as *épaule d'agneau à la boulangère.* The phrase can also be used for whole roast potatoes cooked round a joint, but these are more correctly described as *pommes rôties.*

pommes à la Crécy, sliced potatoes layered with carrots à la *Vichy,* and all cooked like *pommes Anna.* They are also called *pommes à la Vichy.*

pommes à la crème, potatoes parboiled in boiling water, peeled, sliced, and finished by being barely covered in milk and then cooked. Then 2 tablespoons fresh cream is added before serving, with a sprinkling of freshly grated nutmeg.

pommes à la hongroise, onions are sautéed in butter with ½ teaspoon paprika and a peeled tomato; thick round slices of potato are added, with salt and enough stock to cover, and the whole is baked in the oven. It is sprinkled with chopped parsley before being served.

pommes à la landaise, 2 onions and 4 oz. Bayonne ham are fried in goose or pork fat until lightly browned; large diced potatoes are added and seasoned, the lid is put on, and the ingredients are fried on all sides until cooked. Before serving, chopped garlic and parsley are added.

pommes à la Lyonnaise, potatoes sliced and tossed in butter, then mixed with 2 medium-sized fried onions and sprinkled with chopped parsley. See also LYONNAISE, À LA.

pommes à la maître d'hôtel, as *pommes à la crème,* but served thickly sprinkled with finely chopped parsley.

pommes à la menthe, new potatoes boiled in salted water with a sprig of fresh mint. They are also garnished with a leaf of mint on each potato when serving.

pommes à la normande, thin round slices of washed, peeled, and dried potato are seasoned with salt and fresh pepper, and then layered in a buttered sauté pan with the shredded white part of leeks, a lot of chopped parsley, a bouquet garni, and enough white stock to cover. Nuts of butter are put on top and the mixture is brought to the boil on top of the stove, then covered and cooked in a moderate oven until done. It is frequently served as a vegetable dish on its own during Lent.

pommes à la parisienne, like *pommes noisette* but smaller in size. When cooked, they should be tossed in dissolved meat jelly and sprinkled with chopped parsley.

pommes à la paysanne, often served alone during Lent, like *pommes à la normande.* Sliced potatoes are put into a buttered sauté pan in alternate layers with 4 oz. sautéed sorrel mixed with 2 tablespoons chervil and 1 garlic clove, then barely cov-

ered with stock, dotted with butter and seasoning, and baked in the oven until cooked (about 1½ hours).

pommes à la provençale, as *pommes sautées,* with the addition of minced garlic. See also PROVENÇALE, À LA.

pommes à la sarladaise, as *pommes Anna,* alternating with layers of sliced truffle.

pommes à la savoyarde, as *pommes dauphinoise,* except that the milk is replaced by stock.

pommes à la toulousaine, peeled potatoes cut into quarters and sautéed in a mixture of ⅔ goose fat and ⅓ olive oil. Seasoning and 1 tablespoon each of chopped parsley, garlic, and flour are added, followed by stock or water to cover, and finally the whole is stirred and brought to the boil. The lid is put on and all are cooked in a moderate oven for 1–1½ hours. They are served sprinkled with fresh chopped parsley.

pommes à la vapeur, French for steamed potatoes, like *pommes à l'anglaise.*

pommes à la Vichy, as *pommes à la Crécy.*

pommes Anna, waxy potatoes are peeled and cut into very thin rings, which are soaked in cold water for 10 minutes and then dried in a cloth. The rings are arranged in layers in a straight-sided fireproof dish which has been well buttered. They are seasoned with salt and pepper and generously dotted with butter. When the dish is full, the top layer is thickly spread with butter, and the lid is put on and made airtight with a flour-and-water paste. The whole is baked in a hot oven for 45 minutes, when the pan is opened and the potato cake turned over and put back inside the pan. The pan is re-covered closely and the cake cooked for another 45 minutes. The butter is finally poured off, leaving the golden cake. When used as a garnish, the potatoes are cooked in small *dariole* moulds.

pommes Annette or *pommes Yvette,* potatoes cut into julienne strips, washed, dried, and seasoned, then put into a buttered casserole and baked with butter as for *pommes Anna.* A variation is to cook them in a heavy frying-pan, like a pancake.

pommes au beurre, another name for *pommes château.*

pommes au four, potatoes baked in their jackets.

pommes bénédictine, potatoes cut to a spiral turban-like shape by a special machine, and then fried in deep fat or oil.

pommes berny, fried croquettes of mashed potato mixed with minced truffle. See also BERNY.

pommes biarritz, mashed potatoes mixed with 2 oz. diced ham, 4 tablespoons finely chopped green peppers, and fines herbes or parsley.

pommes bohémienne, baked potatoes scooped out and filled with a stuffing of sausage meat, then baked again for 15 minutes. See also BOHÉMIENNE.

pommes bonne femme, potatoes cooked with small whole braised onions in stock.

pommes bretonne, large dice of potato, 2 medium-sized chopped onions, 2 cloves garlic, and 4 sliced tomatoes, all cooked in stock to cover.

pommes Byron, small flat cakes made of the mealy part of baked potatoes mixed with 2 oz. grated cheese and ½ pint (1 cup) thick sauce béchamel. They are cooked in hot butter and browned in a hot oven.

pommes cendrillon, whole potatoes baked in their jackets and shaped like sabots. The inside is scooped out, mixed with grated cheese, and replaced in the skins in mounds. The potatoes are browned in a hot oven.

pommes chambéry, boiled potatoes, peeled and sliced, are arranged in layers in a buttered dish, each layer being buttered and sprinkled with grated cheese. They are browned in a hot oven.

pommes château, peeled potatoes cut into shapes like large olives, parboiled, and cooked in butter either in a moderate oven or on top of the stove. This is the traditional garnish for *châteaubriand* steak.

pommes cocotte, as above, but the potatoes are cut much smaller.

pommes crainquebille, large, long, peeled potatoes put onto a foundation of onion fried in butter, with enough stock added to reach half-way up, together with a bouquet garni, a garlic clove, and seasoning: a slice of peeled tomato is placed on each potato. The whole is brought to the boil on top of the stove, then cooked in the oven until tender. It is garnished with breadcrumbs just before serving.

pommes dauphine, mashed potatoes with 2 oz. (¼ cup) butter and 1 beaten egg yolk added. Chou pastry to one third the weight is mixed in, and the whole is formed into large cork-like shapes. These are coated with egg and breadcrumbs or flour, and fried in deep fat or oil.

pommes dauphinoise, an earthenware gratin dish is rubbed over with a cut garlic clove and buttered with softened butter. Peeled and thickly sliced potatoes are laid in the dish with the slices overlapping, and are sprinkled with salt, pepper, and grated Gryuère cheese. This process is repeated, finishing with a layer of the grated cheese. Then 3 tablespoons melted butter are then poured over the mixture, and it is cooked slowly in a moderate oven, the heat being raised later to brown the surface. This dish is sometimes varied by adding a mixture of 2 eggs beaten with a little milk or cream just before the potatoes are done.

pommes duchesse, mashed potatoes with butter, salt, pepper, and egg yolks added. The mixture is shaped, brushed over with beaten egg, and lightly browned in a hot oven. Potatoes prepared in this way are often used for bordering a dish such as *coquille St-Jacques mornay*, when they are put hot into a forcing (pastry) bag and piped round.

pommes Elizabeth, potatoes cooked as *pommes dauphine*, but with a stuffing of creamed spinach.

pommes farcies or *pommes fourrées*, potatoes baked in their jackets, then the pulp scooped out and mixed with a variety of fillings: cooked oysters and mushrooms (*pommes de terre à la cancalaise*); braised chopped cabbage (*à la cantalienne*); sautéed chicken livers and mushrooms (*chasseur*); butter and grated cheese (*au fromage, gratinées*); spinach (*à la florentine*); onion purée (*soubise*); cold minced meat (*farcies à la ménagère*).

pommes fondantes, as *pommes château* but cooked in butter in a covered pan until golden outside and soft inside.

pommes fourrées, another name for *pommes farcies*.

pommes frites, French for fried potatoes or chips.

pommes frites allumettes, potatoes cut into matchstick-shapes and then fried in deep oil. These are also called *julienne de pommes de terre*.

pommes frites chatouillard, potatoes cooked as *pommes soufflées*, but cut into shapes like ribbons with a special cutter. They are served with grilled meat. They are also called *pommes frites collerettes*.

pommes frites chip, game chips.

pommes frites collerettes, another name for *pommes frites chatouillard*.

pommes frites copeaux, potatoes sliced into thin irregular shavings and fried in deep fat or oil.

pommes frites mignonette, fried potatoes, cut to twice the size of *pommes frites allumettes*.

pommes frites paille, long thin straws of potato fried in deep fat or oil, drained, and served with grilled meat. See also PAILLETTES.

pommes frites pont-neuf, rather thick fingers of fried potato.

pommes impériale, potatoes baked in their jackets, halved, and the inside scooped out and mixed with butter, cream, and minced truffles. This mixture is replaced in the skins, to be baked for 10–15 minutes.

pommes lorette, *pommes dauphine* mixture shaped into small crescents and fried in deep oil.

pommes macaire, potatoes baked in their jackets, halved, their insides scooped out and mixed with butter and finely chopped herbs. This mixture is either returned to the skins or spread in a flat cake and fried on both sides until golden.

pommes maire, another name for *pommes à la crème*.

pommes mireille, as *pommes Anna*, but with the addition of artichoke bottoms and slices of truffle.

pommes mirette, potatoes cut into dice and cooked in butter. They are then mixed with 2 tablespoons julienne of truffle and served in a *timbale* with sauce madère over them and a sprinkling of grated cheese. The whole is browned in a quick oven before serving.

pommes monselet, thick rounds of potato cooked in hot butter and served with the centres covered with shredded mushrooms tossed in butter, and chopped truffles.

pommes mont-doré, mashed potatoes mixed with grated cheese, heaped dome-fashion in a buttered ovenproof dish, sprinkled with more cheese and melted butter, then browned in a quick oven.

pommes mousseline, the insides of baked potatoes are removed, mashed with 4 oz. butter, 1 egg yolk, salt, pepper, and nutmeg, and while still hot, ½ pint (1 cup) whipped cream is stirred in. The mixture is piled into a dome-shape, covered with melted butter, and browned in a quick oven. When used as a garnish, it is put into small pastry tartlets baked blind, and served with meats.

pommes nature or *pommes au naturel*, another name for *pommes à l'anglaise*.

pommes noisette, potatoes cut in marble-shapes, tossed in hot butter until cooked, and served with fines herbes or parsley finely chopped. They are often used as a garnish.

pommes Parmentier, cubed potatoes cooked in butter, or with the meat they are to accompany, then sprinkled with chopped parsley before serving. See also PARMENTIER.

pommes persillées, new potatoes which have been simmered in stock and finished in butter. They are served sprinkled with chopped parsley. Unfortunately plain boiled new potatoes with a pat of butter and a little parsley are frequently served under this name.

pommes rissolées, as *pommes château*, but cooked until dark brown.

pommes rôties, potatoes roasted in butter or fat until golden all over.

pommes Saint-Flour, thick round slices of potato layered with sautéed cabbage, lean fried bacon, crushed garlic, and seasoning, covered with stock and sprinkled with grated cheese, then cooked in a slow-to-moderate oven for 1–1½ hours.

pommes sautées, freshly boiled, peeled potatoes fried in fresh hot butter until golden on both sides. They are served sprinkled with chopped parsley.

pommes sautées à cru, as *pommes sautées*, but the potatoes are not boiled before the frying process.

pommes sautées à la Provençale, as *pommes sautées* or *pommes sautées à cru*, but with 1 heaped tablespoon chopped garlic and chopped parsley added at the last minute. In Provence, olive oil is used instead of butter.

pommes soufflées, peeled and regularly sliced potatoes (slices to be not more than ⅛ inch thick), washed and dried, fried in deep, moderately hot fat or oil until they rise to the surface, then drained in a frying basket. Just before serving they are fried again in very hot oil, when they should puff up. They are drained, sprinkled with salt and served on a napkin in a dish. The temperature at the first frying should not exceed 356°F (180°C); at the second, the heat must be at least 10° (6°) higher.

pommes voisin, as *pommes Anna,* except that some grated cheese and a dusting of nutmeg are put on each layer of potato.

pommes Yvette, another name for *pommes Annette.*

purée de pommes au gratin, 1 egg yolk, butter, 2 tablespoons cream, 2 oz. grated cheese, and pepper and salt are all blended into mashed potatoes. The mixture is put into a buttered baking dish, covered with breadcrumbs and grated cheese, and browned in a hot oven.

purée de pommes de terre, mashed potatoes put back on the stove and whipped with 2–3 oz. butter per lb. of purée. A little hot milk is added to lighten the consistency. In purée de pommes à la crème, cream is used instead of milk, and in purée de pommes au gratin, the purée is made as first described but with a little grated cheese added, and it is then put into a fireproof dish, covered with melted butter and more cheese, and browned in a quick oven.

quenelles de pommes de terre, see QUENELLE.

subrics de pommes de terre, see SUBRICS.

pommel, a commercial brand of double-crème French cheese, like *gervais* and *petit-suisse.* It is unsalted and is sold throughout the year.

pommersche suppe, a German soup from Pomerania. It is made with 1 lb. soaked dried white haricot beans cooked with 1 head chopped celery, 1 large onion, 2 quarts (8 cups) stock, and seasoning. When cooked, the mixture is puréed, and a handful of whole beans and chopped parsley is added as a garnish. See also BOHNEN.

pompano (*Trachinotus carolinus*), a salt water fish found in the southern Atlantic, the Gulf of Florida, and the Caribbean. It is about 1½ feet long, and is delicious to eat. It is best served stuffed and baked, poached in white wine or grilled.

pompe, a traditional cake eaten in Provence on Christmas Eve. It is made with 1 lb. yeasted bread dough mixed with 4 lb. (16 cups) flour, 1 lb. (2 cups) brown sugar, ¼ pint (½ cup) olive oil, the finely grated peel of 1 lemon and 1 orange, and 6 eggs. These ingredients are incorporated gradually into the dough, which is then covered and left in a warm place to rise for 5–6 hours. The dough is then kneaded into pieces about ½ lb. in weight, which are shaped into crowns, put on a baking-tin and sprinkled with fine bran. They take a long time to rise, so are left again in a warm place until each is nearly double its original size. They are baked in a hot oven for 45–60 minutes, and when ready, are brushed over with orange flower water diluted with the same quantity of water. Pompe is also called *gibassier.* For other traditional Provençal Christmas dishes, see also PROVENCE.

pomponnettes, small French hors d'oeuvre, made from circles of short crust pastry about 3 inches in diameter on which is placed a filling of meat, fish, shellfish, or vegetable purée. The pastry is folded towards the middle and the edges dampened to secure the filling, producing a pouch-like shape. The pomponnettes are then fried in deep hot oil until crisp and golden-brown, drained, and served hot on a napkin.

ponchiki, Russian fried cakes like non-yeasted doughnuts, made from 8 oz. (2 cups) flour, ½ teaspoon baking soda, 2 tablespoons butter, 2 tablespoons sugar, 1 egg, and ¼ pint (½ cup) milk. The mixture is rolled out to ½-inch thickness and cut in rounds. With a smaller cutter, the middle is cut from each circle, making a ring-doughnut shape. The cakes are fried in hot fat and then sprinkled with sugar. They are also sometimes flavoured with a little ground cinnamon. Ponchiki are very popular in Moscow. See also DOUGHNUTS.

ponebread, a colloquial name used in the southern states of the U.S. for corn bread. See also CORN, PONE.

pönnukökur, traditional Icelandic pancakes. They are large and very thin, and are served for dessert with jelly and whipped cream.

pont l'évêque, a famous French cheese from Normandy, made from unskimmed cow's milk. Rennet is added, and in less than 1 hour after that the curd is placed to drain on a kind of straw matting called a glotte. In the cellars it is affected by the mould *Monilia candida,* a fungoid growth peculiar to the locality, which imparts a distinctive flavour to the cheese. It is in season from October to June. There are many imitations of this cheese. See also AUGELOT.

pontgibaud, a French cow's milk cheese which resembles a roquefort in appearance and texture. It is made in the Auvergne and is in season from August until June.

pont-neuf, I. A French method of preparing potatoes. See POMME DE TERRE (POMMES FRITES PONT-NEUF). II. A French pastry. Tartlet tins are lined with puff pastry and filled with fragipane cream mixed with crushed macaroons. More strips of pastry are put lattice-fashion across the top, and the tartlets are baked in a moderate oven for 15 minutes. When cooked, they are dusted with castor sugar or icing sugar.

pontoise veal, a delicious veal, tender and delicate, sold in Paris. It is also known as river veal.

poona cheese, a comparatively new cheese from New York State, U.S. It is a whole cow's milk soft cheese, and surface-ripened. It resembles a camembert in texture, size, and shape, but it seldom has the ammoniacal taste that taints an over-ripe camembert. It is an excellent cheese and deserves to be better known.

poor knights of Windsor, the English name for *pain perdu.* The bread slices are sometimes sprinkled with a little sherry before being soaked in egg and milk and then fried on both sides in butter. They are served with a sauce made from equal quantities of butter and sugar, with sherry to taste, all boiled up and reduced until syrupy. See also ARME RIDDERE.

poor man of mutton, a Scottish dish consisting of a blade-bone cut of mutton, either grilled or cooked on a spit. A traditional story tells of a noble Scottish lord who fell sick while travelling. When the owner of the inn where he was staying urged him to eat something, he replied, "I think I could tak' a snap o' a Puir Man." The landlord hurried away lest he should be the victim!

popcorn, a type of Indian corn called parch maize, with smaller ears than the white or yellow corn. It has small pointed or rounded kernels with very hard corneous endosperm, which on being exposed to a dry heat "pops" because of the explosion of the moisture within. A white starchy mass, more than twice the size of the original kernel, is produced. Popcorn is eaten with a dusting of salt and melted butter, or with sugar and molasses. A special pan for cooking popcorn called a "popper" is sold in the U.S. However, popcorn can also be "popped" in an ordinary saucepan with a lid, after a thin layer of oil has first been heated in the pan to the boiling point. The same method is used in a popper.

pope, see RUFFE.

popovers, puffy savoury cakes, served in the U.S. at meals in place of rolls or bread. To prepare them, 4 oz. (1 cup) flour is mixed with a good pinch of salt. Then 2 eggs are well beaten with ⅞ cup milk and this is added slowly to the flour. The mixture is beaten well, preferably with an electric blender, and then 1 tablespoon butter is well blended in. At this stage the mixture should have the consistency of heavy cream. It is poured into greased, hissing-hot individual pans to one-third their depth, and baked in the oven for 15–20 minutes. The oven should be very hot to start with, reducing to moderate after 4 minutes. The popovers are served immediately. They can also be made with grated cheese in the middle, by putting a layer of batter in each pan, followed by 1 teaspoon cheese and then a final layer of batter. Another variation is to use half wholemeal flour and half plain flour in the batter, or ²/₃ cup rye flour to ¹/₃ cup plain flour. In the latter case the quantity of milk is increased to ½ pint (1 cup). Popovers are very light and "pop up," mushroom-shaped, over the top of the pans—hence their name.

poppy (*Papaver rhoeas*), an annual plant, chiefly useful in culinary preparations for its dried seeds, which are very tiny and can be blue or white in colour. The blue seeds are preferred by the grocery trade, so that the white seeds, which have an equally good taste, are often coloured artificially. They have a pleasant nutty flavour and are used in or on breads, and in cakes, pastries, etc. They are particularly important in Slav and Balkan cookery, and are often included in *hamantaschen, loksinu su aguonais, and shkūbanky*. An oil is also from the seeds which is used a great deal in France (see HUILE). The young green leaves can be cooked in the same way as spinach if gathered below the poppy blooms. See also MÁKOS.

porc, French for pork. The best-known breeds of pig used for eating in France are the black pig with a white band round the middle, known as Bresse; the Anjou or Craon from the Loire basin, the Lorraine (for bacon), the Normandy (for fresh pork), and the Périgord, the truffle-finding pig from the district of that name. Hams often come from a cross between one of the French breeds and the large English white Yorkshire. As in all countries, the joints most used for roasting are the loin, leg, and fillet.

Some methods of cooking loin of pork are à la *bonne femme* and à la *boulangère*, and usual garnishes are puréed chestnuts or cooked red cabbage and sauerkraut.

Pork chops are also sometimes coated with melted butter, dipped in breadcrumbs and then grilled with either sauce charcutière or sauce Robert, in which case the dish takes the name of the sauce (*côtes de porc sauce Robert*, etc.). In Alsace, sauerkraut is often used as a garnish for pork chops. For cuts see page xxvi. See also ÉCHINE DE PORC; OREILLES DE PORC; PIEDS DE PORC; PORCELET; PORK.

carré de porc à la périgourdine, a recipe from the Périgord. Boned loin of pork is larded with truffles and garlic, rolled up, browned all over in the oven, then braised with 1 pint (2 cups) stock and white wine mixed, and cooked gently for 2–2½ hours. The stock is drained off, the pork defatted, and the remaining jelly chopped and used as a garnish. The pork is served cold.

carré de porc à la Provençale, a 5-lb. loin of pork larded with sage leaves, thyme and garlic, then roasted for 2½ hours with 2 tablespoons oil and ½ pint (1 cup) red or white wine. It is garnished on the skin side with 1 cup breadcrumbs mixed with ½ cup parsley and cooked for a further 30 minutes.

côtes de porc à l'ardennaise, pork chops grilled or fried with a few crushed juniper berries and served with sliced sautéed onion and sautéed potatoes. The pan juices are moistened with white wine.

côtes de porc à la bayonnaise, pork chops larded with slivers of garlic, seasoned, sprinkled with chopped thyme and 1 bay leaf, then brushed with oil and left for 1 hour. They are sautéed in lard, and when browned, sautéed cèpes and browned new potatoes are added. All are covered and cooked in a moderate oven for 45 minutes or until ready. See also BAYONNAISE, À LA.

côtes de porc à la vosgienne, a speciality of the Vosges district. The chops are sautéed with onion and served with stoned sweetened myrobalans. The pan juices are diluted with 1 cup white wine mixed with 1 tablespoon wine vinegar, and reduced by half over a hot flame.

côtes de porc Vallée d'Auge, pork chops seasoned and spread with finely chopped shallots, brushed with oil or

melted butter and then grilled. The pan juices are diluted with 1 cup cider and 2 tablespoons calvados, then reduced over a hot flame for 2 minutes.

noisettes de porc aux pruneaux, a speciality of Tours. First 8 noisettes are sautéed in butter, then braised for 1 hour with 1 lb. prunes (first soaked for 4 hours in ½ bottle white wine), 1 tablespoon flour and seasoning. When the pork is cooked, the stock is mixed with 1 tablespoon red currant jelly and about ½ pint thick cream.

porc salé, salted pork, as well as pickled pork, is often boiled and served with boiled or braised cabbage. Salt pork is also used as a basis for many ragoûts and civets, especially with dry meats such as furred game or poultry, the pork is first diced and then browned before the other meats or vegetables are added.

porceddu, a Sardinian speciality of sucking pig split in 2 lengthways, spit-roasted over wood, and basted with the dripping. When the crackling is golden and well-cooked, the pig is put on a dish covered with fragrant myrtle leaves. More myrtle is put on top, and it is all covered with a second dish so that the meat can absorb the aroma. Another Sardinian speciality involving myrtle is *tàccula*.

porcelet, French for suckling or sucking pig. One method of cooking sucking pig is to season it by sprinkling over salt, pepper, and brandy, and then to stuff it with a forcemeat consisting of ½ lb. cooked pig's liver, ½ lb. cooked calf's liver, and the offal (variety meat) of the piglet, all mixed with 1 sautéed onion, 2 shallots, 2 tablespoons *duxelles*, 1 crushed garlic clove, a few chopped olives, 1 tablespoon chopped parsley, and 2 beaten eggs. The piglet is sewn up, then marinated overnight in 1 pint (2 cups) olive oil with 2 tablespoons brandy, 1 sliced carrot, 1 onion, 2 garlic cloves, and 1 bay leaf. The next day it is drained, and roasted for 30 minutes per lb. with ¾ pint (1½ cups) dry white wine. See also PORC.

porchetta, Italian for roast sucking pig. In Italy it is always cooked with a great deal of rosemary tucked into the belly, and it is basted with white wine.

porco, see MAIALE.

porgand, Estonian for carrot. See also CARROT.

porgandi püree supp, a traditional Estonian soup made from 1 lb. carrots, 1 small root celeriac, and 1 large onion all cooked in salted water and puréed. Then 2 tablespoons flour and 2 tablespoons butter are mixed in a saucepan, and the purée, 2 pints (4 cups) stock, and ¼ pint (½ cup) cream are added. All are heated up, then garnished with parsley and served with hot *pierogs*.

porgy (*Pagrus pagrus*), an Atlantic fish very similar to john dory, found on the American seaboard, and it can be cooked as john dory. It is known as scup in New England. Red porgy is found in the Mediterranean and used in soups and stews.

pork, the culinary word for the flesh of the pig. The best-quality pork is very pale pink in colour, with white fat and a smooth thin rind which, when cut or scored and roasted, is known as crackling. Fresh pork is taken from smaller and leaner animals than those whose flesh is used for smoking or curing, and is used for bacon or ham. When fresh, the most popular methods of cooking larger joints of pork is to roast them. Pork should not be served underdone; if it is cooked for 30 minutes per lb. when roasting (and 30 minutes over all, in addition, when boiling), the flavour will be excellent. It should be cooked slowly, with an oven-temperature not exceeding 350°F (177°C). The best joints for roasting are the leg, loin and spare ribs. Since pork is a rich and fat meat, the usual accompaniment is a sharp fruit sauce, such as apples simmered in very little water with sugar and sometimes a pinch of ground or whole cloves. In earlier days in England, sliced oranges were cooked with pork in both braised and roast dishes, and in the U.S. today tinned fruits are drained of their syrup, dotted with butter, grilled, and served as a garnish. The most popular fruits used in this way are apricots, peaches, and pineapple. Cabbage is a good vegetable to serve with pork, also broad beans, for their mealiness absorbs any fat. In the north of England, and particularly in Yorkshire, pork is layered with peeled apples and onions, and baked with a thick crust of mashed potato. Lima beans are often used in the U.S., and blend well if the joint is very rich. Cold pork should be served with crab apple jelly or Cumberland sauce, and pickled walnuts contrast well with the sweetness of the meat.

roast pork with orange

In Ireland and the U.S. the fillet, or pork tenderloin, is extracted whole from the pig. In Ireland this is known as "pork steak." To prepare these, the fat is pared off and the fillet is cut down the middle, but not through the bottom layer of meat. It is opened out flat by gently pulling the meat until it obtains the shape of a large triangle. The fillet can either be stuffed with a sage and onion stuffing, then rolled up, larded and roasted, or it can be brushed with oil and grilled. (Sage should be used sparingly, for it can have an aggressive flavour; a little rosemary may be used instead to advantage.) Pork steaks also make an excellent casserole with root vegetables. The fillet is a tender part of the pig, but can be dry if overcooked. A sliced and grilled pineapple is sometimes served with it, or a sweet and sour sauce. Another dish popular in the U.S. is pork ribroast, with the breastbone cracked, stuffing inserted, and the joint folded over and then roasted or braised. Either sauerkraut or sweet and sour sauce is served as an accompaniment.

Chops and cutlets are cut from the loin or best end of neck, and are usually grilled or fried. If fried, the fat should be drained off before other ingredients are added or the chops or cutlets are served. Sliced apples and onions are sometimes added, and in the West Country the meat is just covered with draught cider, which is reduced by rapid boiling on the top of the stove until it thickens slightly. Pork chops can also be casseroled with cherries or cranberries and 4 tablespoons honey, for 1–1½ hours in a moderate oven. In the 19th and early 20th centuries sauce robert was served with grilled pork chops, but it is seldom seen today in England. Chestnut purée is also a good garnish.

Young piglets still milking the mother are known as suckling or sucking pigs. They are usually scalded, filled with a sage and onion stuffing, sewn up, roasted whole for 30–35 minutes per lb., and served with crab apple jelly or apple sauce. As a sucking pig ready to be served can still look very lifelike, some people think it more delicate to carve it away from the table. It is succulent, but inclined to be fatty and bland. Sucking pig is a great Russian and Polish speciality, and is used for *porossenok s khrenom i smetanoi,* and *prosie pieczone nadziewane.* A Bulgarian dish using it is *prassentze palneno,* and an Austrian one *spanferkel.*

Salt pork is often used cubed, or in thin slices, as a basis for rich stews or for larding meats. In the U.S., when the fat has been drained off, salt pork is used for clam chowder or is served with scrambled eggs.

Almost all of the pig is used for food or in food making as in brawn, black pudding, chitterlings, crackling, *Bath chap,* cruibeen, lard, and sausage. See also CERDO; GAMMON; HAND; HIRINO; MAIALE; MALÁC; PIG; PORC; SCHAB; SCHWEINEFLEISCH; SIANLIHA; SVINEKJØTT; SVINEKØD; SVINÍNA; SVINJSKO MESO; VARKENSVLEES. For cuts see pork cuts, pages xxv–xxvi.

porker, a young pig over 6 months old, but not more than 1 year.

porkkana, Finnish for carrot. See also CARROT.

porkkanakeitto, a creamed carrot soup, made with 2 tablespoons butter, 2 tablespoons flour, 4 pints (8 cups) milk, 1 lb. carrots, salt, and a pinch of sugar, with 1 tablespoon parsley as a garnish. It is served with small pieces of toast.

porkkanalaatikko, carrot pudding. First 2 oz. (½ cup) pearl barley is simmered in 1 pint (2 cups) milk and 1 pint water until almost cooked. Then 1 lb. grated carrots, 1 beaten egg, salt, and 2 teaspoons sugar, all mixed, are added, and the mixture is placed in a greased pie dish, garnished with breadcrumbs and dabs of butter, and baked for about 1 hour. It is served as an accompaniment to a main course.

pörkölt, a Hungarian stew, very like *gulyás* except that more onions are added, and all meats, poultry, or game can be used. The word means literally "browned" or "scorched." See also BORJÚ; GULYÁS.

pörköltcsirke, a traditional Hungarian method of cooking chicken. The chicken is cut into joints which are sprinkled with salt and allowed to stand. Then 4 large chopped onions are fried in 2 oz. lard and 2 tablespoons tomato purée, to which salt and 2 tablespoons paprika are added. Then the chicken and 1 pint (2 cups) water are included, the pan is covered, and the bird simmered for about 1 hour or until cooked. The chicken is placed on a dish and the sauce is poured over it. It is garnished with cooked pimentos.

puszta pörkölt, a simple meat stew eaten widely in Hungary. Equal quantities of beef, veal, and pork are needed. The meat is cut in lengths, seasoned with salt and paprika, and added to onions which have been cooked in hot lard. When the meat has browned, it is covered with hot water and simmered for 2 hours. About 20 minutes before serving, cubed potatoes should be added.

poron, Finnish for reindeer. Reindeer meat is poronliha. It is prepared in much the same way as beef in Finland, although it is more tender and contains less fat. Reindeer meat does not travel well, and so is only to be had fresh in the north of the country where the reindeer are shot; however, it can always be obtained elsewhere in Finland, either smoked or preserved in various ways. Reindeer tongue is delicious, and the smoked variety (*savustettu poronkieli*) is a delicacy. It is cooked in the same way as ox tongue. Reindeer meat is a staple food throughout much of Finland. See also GAME; LIHA; REINDEER.

poronkaristys, a stew made with 4 lb. sliced reindeer meat, 1 lb. diced bacon, and sliced root vegetables, all barely covered with water and simmered for 1 hour.

poronpaisti, reindeer steak, usually roasted, pot roasted, or grilled.

porossenok a khrenom i smetanoi, a famous Russian dish of sucking pig. The sucking pig is simmered in water with root vegetables; then the fat is removed from the top and the dish served cold with a sauce made from 1 cup horseradish, 3 tablespoons sugar, and 2 cups sour cream. As the stock is jellied, the dish is not unlike a first-class English brawn.

porpoise, the name given to some of the smaller members of the order *Cetacea,* which also includes the whales and the dolphins. Porpoise used to be eaten in France during Lent, and Rabelais mentions it as abstinence fare. The flesh has an oily taste, but is nevertheless cooked in many ways in both Iceland and Newfoundland. It was popular in medieval England, and was served at banquets.

porridge, a traditional Scottish and Irish dish made from oatmeal, salt, and water, now eaten in many parts of the world for breakfast. A similar dish called *brotchan* used to be made in Ireland, but whereas this could be flavoured with vegetables, porridge is usually eaten with salt, milk, or buttermilk. The Gaelic word brochan is still in use in the highlands of Scotland, and also in Ireland. The finest oatmeal is reputed to come from Midlothian in the lowlands of Scotland, but the highland oats are very sweet and nutty. See also BOUILLIE; GRUEL; OATS (OATMEAL).

To make porridge, 1¼ oz. oatmeal is scattered gradually into ½ pint (1 cup) boiling water and stirred in well (2 cups water to 2 heaped tablespoons oatmeal makes enough porridge for 2 persons). Stirring is traditionally done in a clockwise direction, for it is considered unlucky to stir counterclockwise, and in Scotland porridge is stirred with a special wooden stick like the handle of a wooden spoon called a "spurtle" or "theevil." Stirring is continued until all the oatmeal is included, and then quite suddenly the porridge will thicken. It is covered and simmered gently for 10–15 minutes; then the salt is added (it is thought to harden the meal if put in earlier) and the porridge is cooked for a further 5 minutes. In a single bowl of good porridge the texture should vary from creaminess to little nutty bits of oatmeal, and this is why the oats are put in gradually. The porridge is spooned into a separate dish for each person, called a porringer, and in Scotland it is correct to serve separately individual bowls of cold milk, buttermilk, or cream for each person, into which the hot porridge is dipped in spoonfuls by the eater. Tastes regarding accompaniments vary; sugar or treacle (molasses) is liked by children, a knob of butter or honey by others, but these are not traditional. It used to be considered bad manners in Scotland to sit down to eat porridge; it was eaten while walking about the breakfast room, before sitting down for the next course. Horn spoons were traditionally used in preference to metal ones, which could become very hot. Brose and gruel are versions of porridge.

In early Irish literature porridge was often referred to as "stirabout." In the 10th-century *Vision of MacConglinne,* "fair white porridge" made of sheep's milk, and porridge, "the treasure that is the smoothest and sweetest of all food," is mentioned. Another source reads, "The sons of Kings are fed on stirabout made of wheaten meal upon new milk, taken with honey."

In Sweden a form of oatmeal porridge that is boiled up every day for 2 or 3 months is made. It is traditionally eaten in the country districts on St. Lucy's Day or the Day of Light (December 13), by which time it has attained a fine pink colour.

porringer, a round bowl in which porridge or similar foods are served. It is made preferably of birch-wood, but can also be of silver or other metals. In the U.S. porringer refers to a children's bowl or cup with a handle.

porsaansorkat, Finnish for pig's trotters (feet). See also CRUIBEEN; PIED DE PORC.

keitetyt porsaansorkat, boiled pig's trotters, generally served with vinegar and beetroot.

port wine sauce, an English sauce. To prepare it ½ cup gravy from roast mutton or venison, 2 teaspoons red currant jelly, ⅛ pint (1 glass) good port wine, and a dash of lemon juice are brought gently to the boil, beating the jelly to mix it with the gravy. The sauce is then strained and served with mutton or venison. See also WINE JELLY; WINE SAUCE.

port-du-salut, the famous French cow's milk cheese made by the Trappists of the Abbey of Notre-Dame de Port-du-Salut in Entrammes, by the river Mayenne. In 1816, when the monastery was rebuilt after the fall of the Napoleonic regime, the monks first made this cheese for their own consumption. In 1859 they built a fromagerie, bought milk locally, and began to make the cheeses for sale. Port-du-Salut is the trademark, but since it is not protected by law, other port-salut cheeses are made in various parts of France and Belgium by Trappists and others. However, none of these varieties is the genuine Port-du-Salut, and imitations are distinguished by being called port-salut (the "du" omitted). This cheese is eaten all the year round.

porter cake, a traditional Cornish and Irish cake, which used to be made with a dark beer called porter. As this is difficult to obtain nowadays, stout or Guinness is used instead. First ¼ pint Guinness or stout is gently warmed, and then 4 beaten eggs and 1 teaspoon baking soda are added. Next ½ lb. (1 cup) butter is rubbed into 1 lb. (4 cups) flour, and then 1 lb. (2 heaped cups) brown sugar, 1 lb. (2 cups) currants, 1 lb. (2 cups) seedless raisins, 4 oz. (1 cup) almonds, 4 oz. (1 cup) mixed chopped candied peel, 1 teaspoon mixed spice, and finally the Guinness or stout mixture are added. All are well mixed, put into a lined cake tin and baked for 2½–3 hours in a slow-to-moderate oven (for the first 1½ hours it is covered with foil). It is a rich cake and keeps very well in an air-tight tin.

porterhouse steak, a steak about 1½ inches thick cut from the wing-rib of beef. It has a small T-shaped bone in it, and the cut has choice fillet and sirloin included. It is also called a T-bone steak and is usually grilled. See diagram page xxii.

portugaise, à la, I. A French garnish for meat and entrées, consisting of small stuffed tomatoes and *pommes château* with sauce portugaise. II. A French method of serving chicken. See POULET, À LA PORTUGAISE.

portugaise, sauce, a classical French sauce. It is made from 4 or 5 ripe tomatoes peeled, cut up, and placed in a saucepan with 1 minced garlic clove, salt, pepper, and 1 teaspoon olive oil, and cooked until tender. Then 1 tablespoon sauce espagnole and 1 tablespoon tomato sauce are added, and the whole is heated. The sauce is not strained.

Portugal cabbage, see COUVE TRONCHUDA.

Portuguese cheeses, see QUEIJO.

Portuguese oyster, see OSTRAS; OYSTERS.

portulaca, see PURSLANE.

pot barley, barley with the hull or outer husk removed, but not polished to the same extent as pearl barley. Pot barley is nuttier in flavour, but is used in the same way as pearl barley in soups and stews. It should always be used in Scotch broth. See also BARLEY.

pot cheese, a type of cottage cheese made with sour milk and buttermilk. When it has soured, it is drained and a small amount of cream and salt is worked into the curd. It is moulded into small balls before being served.

pot herbs, herbs used in cooking, as against those used for medical purposes. The term is also used in the north of England and Ireland to describe a mixture of sliced root vegetables with parsley and thyme, sold for use in soups and stews.

pot roast, to, to cook foods in a deep pot or saucepan, by first browning the meat or poultry in fat, then adding the vegetables, herbs, and a very little liquid, covering, and simmering the contents together very slowly until they are cooked. For large joints of meat or a bird, ½ pint (1 cup) stock or wine is added, so that more steam is produced. Foods cooked in this way should be so tender that they can be eaten with a fork. Pot roasting is popular in the U.S., particularly for chuck or rump beef, and is also used as a method of cooking in France where it is known as *poêlage*. See also MILCH (MILCHBRATEN); ROSTBRATEN; SAUERBRATEN.

potage, a familiar culinary term which in 17th-century France denoted a large meal of meat or fish, slowly cooked with vegetables in an enormous pot. The pot was made of glazed earthenware, with a lid, and might contain several chickens, ham, meats, etc., as well as a variety of vegetables. When cooked, the meats were drained and then often arranged in elaborate and picturesque structures.

Today, generally speaking, a potage is what is termed a "peasant soup," a thick soup which, with bread, can constitute a substantial meal on its own. There are 3 categories, all coming under the general title of *potages liés*. Other French soups include *aïgo bouïllido*, bouillabaisse, bisque, consommé, *cotriade, garbure*, pot-au-feu, and *potée*. See also SOUPE.

potages crèmes, soups which have a foundation of sauce béchamel, with fish, shellfish, meat, poultry, game, or vegetables added. The ingredients are then sieved, or blended in an electric mixer, and the soup is finished with cream. These soups can be garnished with croûtons, and chiffonade, or small quenelles. Individually, they are known by the principal ingredient used; for example, potage crème de légumes (cream of vegetable soup), potage crème de poissons (cream of fish soup), potage crème de volaille (cream of chicken soup). The basic recipe uses 2 pints (4 cups) sauce béchamel added to about 1 lb. fish, shellfish, meat, game, poultry or vegetables which have been sautéed in butter and seasoned. A little white wine, sherry or brandy is added if shellfish, poultry or game are being used. The whole is sieved or electrically blended, and finished with ½ pint (1 cup) fresh cream. The vegetables most generally used are artichoke, asparagus, chicory, leek, lettuce, mushroom, spinach, and watercress.

potages purées, soups made from fish, meat, game, poultry, or vegetables (including dried vegetables such as dried peas or beans), which are cooked in water with seasoning, herbs, and butter, then puréed. All these soups are finished with a nut of butter for each individual serving, and croûtons are a usual accompaniment. The basic method is to cut 1 lb. fish, meat, poultry, or vegetables into thin slices and cook them in 3 tablespoons butter, with chopped herbs such as parsley, tarragon, basil (for tomatoes), savory, etc., until just soft but not coloured. Then 1 quart (4 cups) stock or water is added, and the whole is covered and simmered gently until cooked. The purée is then rubbed through a fine sieve or electrically blended, and is finished with 2–3 tablespoons butter. If the purée is too thick, a little clear stock or consommé may be added and well amalgamated before the butter is finally included. The best-known potages purées are probably potage purée *saint-germain*, made from fresh or dried peas, and potage purée *Parmentier*, made mainly from potatoes, with a flavouring of leek and a garnish of fresh chopped chervil and small croûtons fried in butter. Others include *lamballe, navarin, nesselrode*, and *nivernaise*.

potages veloutés, soups made from sauce velouté, with fish, shellfish, meat, game, or poultry which is either cooked in the sauce or added to it when cooked and puréed. Velouté soups are always thickened with a liaison of egg yolks and cream. They are garnished with any of the usual soup garnishes, added just before serving. The chief ingredient used is

simmered gently, either in the sauce or in stock, then puréed, and heated; at the last moment the liaison is added. The soup is reheated, but is not allowed to reboil for it would curdle. The quantities are 2 pints (4 cups) sauce velouté and 1 lb. fish, shellfish, poultry, game, or vegetables, to 2 egg yolks mixed with ¼ pint (½ cup) cream. Other potages veloutés include, *bagration, faubonne, lucullus, nelusko, Saint-Hubert*, and *santé*.

potaje, Spanish for soup. See also SOPA.

potaje madrileño, the traditional soup of Madrid. To prepare it, 1 lb. soaked chick-peas are cooked with ½ lb. soaked *bacalao* and seasoning in 3 pints (6 cups) water; then 2 lb. chopped cooked spinach is added; ½ teaspoon saffron and 1 chilli are pounded together in a mortar and added to the soup before serving. See also MADRILEÑO.

potatis, Swedish for potato. See also GRÄSLÖK (GRÄSLÖK-POTATIS); POTATO.

bryní potatis, browned potatoes. First 2 lb. mashed potato is made into small balls which are rolled in breadcrumbs mixed with ½ teaspoon combined sugar and salt. They are browned in hot butter.

potatismos, mashed potatoes with milk, butter, seasoning, and 1 small spoonful castor sugar added. The mixture is then put through a potato ricer.

stekt potatis, potatoes sautéed after boiling.

potato (*Solanum tuberosum*), first found by the Spaniards in 1553, in the neighbourhood of Quito, Ecuador, where it was known by the natives as battato or batata. It is thought that the early English settlers in America traded for it with the Spaniards. It was Sir Walter Raleigh's expedition of 1584 which brought potatoes to the British Isles, and they were planted on his estate at Youghal in County Cork, Ireland, where they grew well although they were not generally used by the whole people until the late 17th or early 18th centuries. (The potatoes brought back by Drake and Hawkins between 1563 and 1565 were sweet potatoes, which are now very rare in Britain, but are grown in the U.S.) By 1558 the potato was well established as a vegetable in Italy and it is mentioned by Gérard in his herbal of 1597; however, its cultivation in England was very slow, and it was still considered a delicacy there in 1666. It was not really until the early 18th century that it became available to all classes, despite the fact that in 1663 the Royal Society urged its cultivation as a precaution against famine—a suggestion which, in the light of our knowledge of the terrible famines brought about by potato blight in Ireland nearly 200 years later, now seems strangely ironical.

The potato is a tuber, and many pounds can be dug from a single root. There are many varieties of potato, some waxy like the kipfler, a Dutch variety, which is excellent for frying, and others floury like the King Edward or the majestic, and good for boiling. The Irish potato kerr's pink is another good variety. Tubers can be oval, round, or kidney-shaped like the golden wonder, which is considered very good as it has a floury texture and almost a chestnut taste. There are also early and late varieties, the early potatoes being dug in May or June and the late from August on through September. Potatoes are an essential element of diet in Britain and Ireland, Belgium, Holland, and other parts of Europe, and in North America, where they are a principal vegetable. They are eaten all the year round, for they keep through the winter and lend themselves to many ways of cooking. Most of the nutritive value of the potato is in, and close to, the skin, and this is the reason for the Irish practice of cooking potatoes in their skins and peeling them at the table. Special "potato rings," large round silver rings like dish-stands, with a napkin placed in the centre, were common in Ireland until early in the 20th century. Potatoes contain 77% water and have two-and-a-half times less carbohydrate than the equivalent amount of bread, which makes them quite acceptable for diets provided that they are not cooked with fat or flour. Countries where the potato is not a staple food use rice, bread, or pasta in its place. Potatoes also form the basis for some *knödel* and quenelles; also *boxty, colcannon,* and *punchep.* See also AARDAPPEL; BATATA; BULYE; BURGONYA; KARTOFEL; KARTOFFEL; PATATA; PERUNA; POMME DE TERRE; POTATIS; POTATO FLAKES; POTET; SWEET POTATO.

baked potatoes, old potatoes baked in their skins or "jackets" for about 1½ hours in a moderate oven, cooking time and temperature depending on their size. To serve, they are cut in half, with seasoning and butter added to taste. Sometimes the cooked inside is mixed with chopped herbs, salt, and pepper, or with sour cream or grated cheese. See also POMME DE TERRE.

boiled potatoes, old potatoes should first be washed, then brought to the boil in cold salted water to cover, with the lid on, and left for about 20 minutes or until tender. Cooking time varies with the different varieties, and they must be tested for tenderness with a fork. New potatoes are treated in the same way, except that they are put straight into boiling salted water, then simmered for 15–20 minutes, drained, peeled, and tossed in melted butter. To make them floury, they should be drained, returned to the saucepan over a very low heat, and covered with a clean napkin or tea-towel.

mashed potato, made by mashing 1 lb. hot cooked potatoes and adding ¼ pint (½ cup) warm milk, a nut of butter, and seasoning. The mixture should be whipped very quickly with a whisk or fork until light and fluffy. When served with pork, 1 chopped celery stalk and a handful of raisins or sultanas are added.

potato cakes or *potato scones,* made in Ireland and the north of England from 2 cups flour mixed with 1 cup cold mashed potato, seasoned with salt, and made into a soft dough with ½ cup milk. This is rolled on a floured board and either shaped into a round flat loaf or cut into small individual rounds. The cake or scones are then baked in a hot oven for 20–30 minutes and eaten hot, split open, with butter or good bacon dripping.

Another method is to mix ½ lb. (2 cups) cooked potato with 2 tablespoons flour, 1 tablespoon melted butter, and salt. The dough is rolled out thinly on a floured board and cut into thin rounds about 5 inches across, which are cooked on both sides, for 3 minutes a side, either on a hot griddle or in a heavy, slightly greased frying-pan. Potato cakes are served with fried bacon, eggs, or sausages in Ireland. See also KNISHES.

potato chowder, an American soup, made with 2 chopped onions, ¼ lb. diced salt pork, 2 leeks, and 2 celery stalks lightly simmered in 2 tablespoons butter. Then 2 quarts (8 cups) white stock is added, followed at a later stage, when the mixture is partly cooked, by 1 lb. diced potatoes. When ready, the soup is blended with cream and seasoned with salt and cayenne pepper. It is served sprinkled with chopped parsley. See also CHOWDER.

potato jowdle, also called tattie fry, a traditional Cornish recipe, said to be an excellent supper dish. A frying pan is filled with sliced raw potatoes, 1 chopped onion, pepper, and salt. Enough water to cover is added, the lid is put on and the ingredients are cooked until soft. Sometimes it is served with eggs poached on top.

potato pastry, made by mixing 1½ lb. (4 cups) cooked potato with 1 tablespoon melted butter, salt, and 4 oz. (1 cup) flour (one quarter the weight of potato used). This mixture is rolled out in the same way as ordinary pastry, and can either be filled with cooked apples and baked, or even a savoury

meat filling. It can also be made into small filled patties which are fried in deep oil.

potato salad, potatoes cooked, sliced, and covered while still hot with a dressing of 3 parts olive oil to 1 part wine vinegar. It is also served with mayonnaise or a sour cream dressing. It is eaten cold. See also KARTOFFEL (KARTOFFEL-SALAT).

potato soup, see POTAGES, PURÉES; VICHYSSOISE.

roast potatoes, potatoes peeled and set in the fat round a roasting joint.

scalloped potatoes, potatoes peeled, sliced, and cooked with an equal quantity of sliced onions in stock, milk, or cream barely to cover in a fireproof dish for about 1½ hours in a moderate oven. The lid is removed for the last 15 minutes to allow the top to brown.

potato flakes, a commercial product made from potatoes cooked by low-pressure steam and then pulped. Heated drums and rollers expel the moisture, leaving a film of crisp potato which is broken into flakes and packaged. It is reconstituted with milk and water, and can be quite good when used for such things as croquettes and fishcakes. However, it is not as good to eat as fresh potato, although useful as a substitute in an emergency. A more pulverised form is known as potato powder and uses only boiling water to reconstitute it. See also POTATO.

potato flour, made from the ground and dried potato tuber. See FECULA; POTETMEL.

potato onion, see ONION.

pot-au-feu, a classical French dish made from boiled fresh beef (preferably a shin, flank or silverside), a beef marrow bone, onions, leeks, carrot, turnip, parsnip, celery, bouquet garni, seasoning, and 2 quarts water (to 2 lb. meat). Other meats, such as knuckle of veal, liver, or giblets, are also added if available. All are cooked for 3–4 hours in a deep pot or *marmite* usually of earthenware or copper and with a lid. The pot-au-feu is two dishes in one, for first the soup is drunk, with the marrow spread on baked bread as a garnish, and then the meat is served afterwards with extra, freshly cooked vegetables, pickled gherkins, capers, horseradish, or mustard. (Both the cooking-utensil and the 2 dishes are known as pot-au-feu.) Any liquid left over is strained and kept for stock, being boiled up once a day. The left-over meat is known as *bouilli,* and can either be minced and made into *boulettes,* or thinly sliced and served with sauce vinaigrette. The latter dish, when garnished with capers, gherkins, cold boiled and sliced potatoes, hard-boiled eggs, chopped shallots, and plenty of parsley, is sometimes called *salade parisienne.*

There are many regional versions of the pot-au-feu, which usually vary with the kind of meat used. In Provence lamb or mutton is often included, but this can sometimes make the dish a little greasy. Oxtail has a similar tendency, and should be watched. In the Béarn a stuffed chicken is added to the ingredients of the pot-au-feu, and this is known as poule-au-pot.

pote, a form of Spanish stew which takes its name from the pot it is cooked in. It is similar to a *cocido,* but white haricot beans are used instead of chick-peas, and beef in place of chicken or pork. It is native to Galicia and is known also as pote Gallego.

potée, a French culinary term, once used simply for foods which had been cooked in an earthenware pot. Nowadays it means a rich meat and vegetable stew which can be eaten as soup, or as a stew for a main course. Pork and cabbage, with other vegetables and herbs are the usual ingredients, but these vary from region to region. It is a meal in itself, especially if eaten with bread and followed by cheese and is good solid

peasant fare like *garbure* and *ouïllade,* meant to sustain people working long hours in the open air. See also AUVERG-
NATE, À LA; BOEUF, SALÉ ET FUMÉ.

potée à la tête de porc, a speciality of the Poitou region
which makes both a soup and a main course. The pig's head
is simmered in water for 4–5 hours with root vegetables,
herbs, leeks, and Vendée cabbage. The soup is served first,
with oven-dried French bread, and then the sliced pig's head
and tongue are eaten sprinkled with sea salt and a dash of
wine vinegar.

potée bourguignonne, a Burgundian potée. Salt pork
knuckle is boiled with cabbage, carrots, turnips, leeks, and potatoes. The soup is served in a special earthenware pot with
thin dried slices of French bread.

potée l'auvergnate, a regional soup from the Auvergne. A
broth is made from a pig's head, and sliced carrots, turnips,
leeks, potatoes, shredded cabbage, and some lentils are cooked
in it. The soup is served in an earthenware pot and is garnished with the diced pig's head. Thin slices of baked French
bread are served separately.

potée Lorraine, a dish from the province of Lorraine. The
earthenware pot is lined with fresh pork or bacon rinds. Fresh
pork fat, a knuckle of pork or ham, chopped carrots, turnips,
chopped leeks, and a whole blanched cabbage are added and
covered with water. The pot is covered, and the contents are
cooked for 3–4 hours. About 30 minutes before serving, potatoes and a large Lorraine sausage, well pricked, are added.

potet, Norwegian for potato, which forms an important part of
the Norwegian diet. Kokte poteter are boiled potatoes. See
also POTATO.

potetboller, potato balls. To prepare them, 2 lb. mashed potatoes are mixed over heat in the order given with 6 chopped
anchovies, 1 teaspoon chopped parsley, a pinch of dry mustard, a pinch of grated nutmeg, salt and pepper, 2 egg yolks
(to 2 lb. cooked potatoes), and a large knob of butter. When
well amalgamated, this is made into small balls which are
dipped first in seasoned flour, then in egg and breadcrumbs,
and are finally fried in deep fat or oil. The anchovies are used
in varying quantities, but about 6 small fillets would be
enough for 2 lb. potatoes.

potetkaker, potato cakes. Flour is well mixed with twice the
quantity of potato, and the mixture is then rolled out and cut
into large plate-sized rounds. The potato cakes are cooked on
both sides on a moderately hot griddle and are eaten in place
of bread, with butter.

potetmel, Norwegian for potato flour.

potetmelstopper, biscuits (cookies) made from potato flour.
First ½ lb. potato flour is added to 4 tablespoons butter which
has been creamed with 4 tablespoons sugar. A beaten egg is
stirred in with 1 teaspoon baking powder. The mixture is
rolled out lightly and made into either balls or rounds which
are baked on a buttered sheet in a moderate oven for 25–30
minutes.

potrawka, the general Polish term for a dish that is
cooked in a casserole in the oven.

potrawka barania z ogórkami, braised lamb cooked with
leek, chopped celery, carrots, onion, and chopped cabbage,
with garlic, Hamburg parsley root and a bay leaf. When half
cooked, the meat is cut into serving pieces, the liquid
strained, and the vegetables discarded. Instead, 2 or 3 sliced
sour or dill pickles are added to the meat, which is then
tightly covered and cooked further until ready.

potrawka z kaczki z ryżem, duck simmered in consommé
for 1 hour with an onion. The stock is strained, and 2 cups
uncooked rice is cooked in it for 10 minutes. Then the boned
duck and rice are arranged in alternate layers in a heavy casserole, each layer being sprinkled with grated Parmesan cheese.

The layering begins and ends with rice. Then ½ pint (1 cup)
sour cream is poured over the top, and the whole is baked in a
hot oven for 30 minutes.

potrawka z kapłona z ryżem, chicken, onion, herbs, and rice
cooked in a casserole as above. See also KACZKA, DUSZONA Z
KAPUSTĄ GERWONĄ.

potrokha, Russian for giblets. See also RASSOLNIK.

potted, a culinary term which, apart from its quite literal
meaning, is also used in connection with certain classes of
foodstuff to indicate various types of preparation which may
or may not be preservative in character, or involve the use of
a pot.

potted char, char cooked in court bouillon, then skinned
and filleted. The drained fillets are put into shallow earthenware pots, covered with clarified butter and cooked for 15
minutes in a slow oven. This is left to get quite cold and then
eaten with toast. It was a breakfast dish in the 19th and early
20th centuries.

potted cheese, cheese, such as Cheshire or double Gloucester, grated and mixed with half its weight of butter and a liberal dash of mace, then put into a pot to be kept until needed,
when it is served cut into slices. Many other English cheeses
were treated in the same way in the 18th century, with the addition of a glass of sack, or sherry.

potted fish and game, this usually means cooked fillets arranged in a shallow dish with enough clarified butter to cover
them. See GROUSE, POTTED.

potted meats, usually meat cooked by simmering, then
pounded into a paste which is put in a pot and covered with
melted butter.

potted shrimps, see SHRIMP.

pouders or **pouldres,** the medieval English spelling for powders, or powdered spices such as ginger, cinnamon, and nutmeg. In *A Proper Newe Booke of Cokerye,* printed at Cambridge in 1573, those described here are mentioned. See also
GALINGALE.

pouder blanche, a white powder made from ginger, cinnamon, and nutmeg all mixed. It is much in use among
cooks.

pouder douce, as above, with sugar added.

pouder fort, a hot mixture of pepper, ginger, cinnamon,
nutmeg, mace, etc. The spices, besides adding flavour, also
had a preservative function. In early books the term "powdered" means pickled, and this was done either by rubbing the food with salt mixed with spices, or by using a
brine. Hence Gabriel Harvey's lines, written in 1620 in a letter to Edmund Spenser:

> He that his joyes would keep
> must weep,
> And in the brine of tears
> and fears
> Must pickle them. That powder will survive.

Powder fort survived in England in an extended form, as a
spiced salt for use in galantines, pies, etc., until W.W.I. It
consisted of 1 lb. salt mixed with 3½ oz. mixed ground spices
such as cinnamon, nutmeg, mace, many different sorts of
pepper, pimento, cayenne, and paprika. A similar mixture is
currently in use in the U.S. and is known as barbecue spice.

pouding, French for pudding. All French puddings are of the
sweet variety and are eaten as a sweet course. In many cases,
especially with milk puddings, they resemble English equivalents, although some are richer and more elaborate, having
cream and eggs added. Although they are still made in the
home, particularly for children or for family meals, they are
seldom eaten nowadays in French restaurants; instead, the
dessert course is usually a fruit flan, an ice cream with a hot

or cold sauce, or fresh fruit. Some authorities believe that the English word pudding is derived not from *pouding* but from *boudin* (black pudding). See also DIPLOMATE PUDDING; NESSELRODE, À LA.

pouding au pain, bread pudding, made by soaking 4 cups breadcrumbs in 1 quart (4 cups) milk, with sugar added to taste. These ingredients are sieved and mixed with 4 egg yolks and the stiffly beaten egg whites, then baked for 1 hour in a buttered mould in a *bain-marie* in a moderate oven. When slightly cooled, the pudding is turned out and served with custard, fruit sauce, or *zabaglione*.

pouding au riz, French rice pudding, made as in England, by cooking ¼ lb. (generous ½ cup) rice with 1 pint (2 cups) boiling milk, except that when the pudding has been cooking in the oven for 30 minutes, 4 egg yolks and the stiffly beaten egg whites are added, and cooking is continued for a further hour in a *bain-marie* in a moderate oven. When ready, the top is sprinkled with sugar and browned under a hot grill. Melted chocolate may be added if desired. A similar pudding is made with sago, semolina, tapioca, or vermicelli.

pouding de fruits, a custard is made with 6 whole eggs and 6 egg yolks for each quart (4 cups) milk, with sugar to taste, and is then mixed with one third of that bulk of fruit purée. Half this mixture is put into a buttered dish and baked in a *bain-marie* in a moderate oven until set (about 45 minutes). It is then covered with more fruit purée and the remainder of the custard, and baked again in a *bain-marie* until the top has set. It is served with a fruit sauce flavoured with a liqueur such as kirsch.

pouding soufflé aux marrons, 2 lb. (6 cups) puréed chestnuts cooked in a sugar water syrup, then sieved and mixed with 6 oz. (⅔ cup) sugar and 6 oz. (6 tablespoons) butter over a gentle heat. The mixture is removed from the heat and 8 beaten egg yolks are added, and finally the 8 stiffly beaten egg whites. The pudding is baked for 30 minutes in a *bain-marie* in a moderate oven. It is served hot with custard or apricot sauce flavoured with kirsch.

pouillard, an alternative French name, with perdreau, for young partridge.

poularde, French for a neutered, fattened hen chicken. These birds are white, firm, and tender, and are a speciality of Bresse, Le Mans, and La Flèche, France. They usually weigh 3½–5½ lb. All recipes suitable for poulet and suprêmes can be used. See also POULET.

poularde à l'allemande, poularde poached in chicken stock, and coated with sauce *allemande* to which 1 cup of the reduced cooking liquor has been added.

poularde à la chivry, as above, with sauce *chivry*, garnished with artichoke bottoms and asparagus tips or *petits pois*.

poularde à la milanaise, poularde stuffed with lamb's sweetbreads, tongue, ham, mushrooms and truffles all bound with brown sauce flavoured with tomato purée, and braised. It is served with *darioles* of macaroni à la *milanaise*.

poularde au gros sel, a speciality of Bresse: poularde poached in white stock with the white part of leeks, onions, and carrots. It is strained, and served with the vegetables and coarse sea salt.

poularde aux huîtres, poularde served with sauce suprême and oysters.

poularde de Madame Filoux, the name given to *poulet à la lyonnaise* in Lyons.

poularde lambertye, a fat hen is poached in chicken stock and left to cool in the liquid. A circular cut is made round the breast, and it is removed. The space is filled with a mousse of foie gras made to resemble the whole bird, and then the sliced breast meat is placed on top. The whole is masked with sauce

chaud-froid, and the breast is garnished with sliced truffle and circles of tongue. It is then glazed with jelly, and served cold on a bed of cooked rice or a large croûton.

poularde souvarov, poularde stuffed with a mixture of chopped foie gras and truffles, which is seasoned and has 1 tablespoon brandy added. The bird is covered and cooked in butter for 45 minutes in the oven. Then 8 medium-sized sautéed ·truffles are added, followed by ½ cup Madeira mixed with 1 cup brown sauce. The dish is again covered, luting paste is put round the lid, and cooking is resumed for 20–25 minutes.

poularde truffée à la périgourdine, poularde stuffed with truffles simmered in a mixture of bacon fat and chicken fat, with a little thyme, ½ bay leaf, and a pinch of nutmeg. The bird is left like this, covered with the peeled skin of the truffles, for 3-4 days. The skins are then removed and sautéed in butter with 1 onion, 1 carrot, and a sprig of parsley. After this, the bird is placed on a spit-roaster, covered with fresh pork fat and the above mixture, then wrapped securely in several thicknesses of oiled paper. It is cooked for 1½ hours, the paper being detached towards the end of that time to allow the bird to brown. The bird is removed and served with sauce *périgueux*. See also PÉRIGOURDINE, À LA.

poule, French for boiling fowl. It is used for poule-au-pot, *purée de volaille*, quenelles, forcemeat, and *terrines*.

poule sultane, French for sultan hen, a web-footed aquatic bird. It is prepared in France in the same way as coot or moorhen.

poule-au-pot, see POT-AU-FEU.

poulet, French for spring chicken, that is, a chicken not more than 3 months old. It is also called poulet de grain and poulet de reine. It should weigh from 2 to 2½ lb., and is usually roasted, sautéed, or split and grilled. Classical French methods for cooking poulet follow, and in many cases they can be adapted for older and younger birds, *poularde* and *poussin*. (When a method includes the word sauté in its title, this automatically means that the bird is first cut up or jointed, and cooked in a sauteuse on top of the stove.) Other classical methods of preparation, sauces, and garnishes include *albuféra, alexandra, algérienne, allemande, ambassadrice, ancienne, andalouse, aurore, demidoff*. See also *côtelettes de volaille; emincé; pain de volaille; pâté; poulet à la wallone*, and suprêmes. See also CHICKEN; POULARDE; POUSSIN; VOLAILLE.

côtelettes de poulet pojarski, chopped raw breast of chicken is mixed with chicken-based velouté and made into cutletshapes which are dipped in egg and breadcrumbs and fried in butter. Sometimes a nut of chilled butter is placed in the middle so that it melts during cooking. It is served with macédoine of vegetables. Alternatively the chicken is prepared with cream and soaked white bread instead of velouté.

poulet à l'anglaise, chicken poached or steamed, served with parsley sauce made from the broth.

poulet à l'Armenonville, chicken first browned in oil, then braised in stock in a casserole, and served with artichoke hearts, tomatoes, french beans, and potatoes, all cooked and tossed in butter.

poulet à la bonne femme, chicken braised in butter with bacon, button onions, and new potatoes. When almost cooked, 4 tablespoons thickened veal gravy is mixed with the pan juices and heated. It is served from the casserole. See also BONNE FEMME.

poulet à la bourgeoise, chicken braised with carrots, onions, bacon, and a little stock. See also BOURGEOISE, À LA.

poulet à la chantilly, chicken stuffed with cooked rice mixed with chopped truffles or foie gras, then covered and cooked in butter in the oven until golden. It is garnished with whole truffles cooked in port wine and foie gras fried in butter. The pan juices are diluted with ½ cup chicken or veal stock and 1 cup sauce velouté, and simmered until reduced to half the original quantity. This mixture is poured over the bird, and at the last moment 2 tablespoons whipped cream is put over the breast.

poulet à la châtelaine, chicken braised in stock with artichoke hearts, truffles, and potatoes.

poulet à la cussy, chicken braised in brown butter and served with *cussy* garnish.

poulet à la derby, chicken stuffed with cooked rice mixed with chopped goose liver and diced truffles, then covered and cooked in the oven with butter. It is garnished with large truffles simmered in port and foie gras sautéed in butter. The pan juices are mixed with a glass (½ cup) of port wine and thickened with brown veal gravy.

poulet à la doria, the bird is poached in white stock; when cooked, the breast fillets are removed and the inside filled with a prepared forcemeat of cock's combs and cock's kidneys, chopped mushrooms, chopped truffles, and very thick sauce velouté made from chicken stock. The breast fillets are sliced and replaced, and the whole is covered with thick sauce *Allemande* and sprinkled with grated Parmesan cheese, then browned in the oven. It is garnished with large chicken quenelles, truffles cooked in champagne, fried cock's combs, and large mushrooms sautéed in butter.

poulet à l'estragon, chicken poached with 3 tablespoons chopped tarragon in water barely to cover, and served with the liquid it has been cooked in, thickened with 2 egg yolks mixed with ¼ pint (½ cup) cream, and more chopped fresh tarragon. This dish can be served hot or cold; in the latter case the sauce will have jellied. See also POULET, SAUTÉ À L'ESTRAGON.

poulet à la financière, braised chicken served with sauce *financière* and *financière* garnish.

poulet à la godard, chicken braised with butter and a little stock, which is thickened. It is all served with *godard* garnish.

poulet à la hongroise, chicken stuffed with paprika-flavoured rice and sautéed in butter; then the pan juices are mixed with white wine and paprika and reduced.

poulet à l'impériale, chicken stuffed with chopped cooked sweetbreads, chopped truffles, and mushrooms, then sautéed in butter. It is garnished with pastry tartlets filled with a mixture of mushrooms, foie gras, and artichoke hearts, and topped with chopped truffles and asparagus tips.

poulet à l'indienne, chicken simmered with curry sauce and served with boiled rice. It is also called cari or kari de poulet.

poulet à la languedocienne, chicken cooked with butter in a covered dish in the oven, and garnished with garlic, tomatoes, and eggplant fried in olive oil. The pan juices are mixed with ½ cup white wine and 1 cup thickened veal gravy, and these are all reduced slightly and poured over the bird. It is sprinkled with chopped parsley. See also LANGUEDOCIENNE, À LA.

poulet à la lyonnaise, another name for poulet demi-deuil, see DEMI-DEUIL, À LA. See also POULET, SAUTÉ À LA LYONNAISE.

poulet à la milanaise, roast chicken served with cooked macaroni mixed with tomato sauce.

poulet à la minute, another name for *poulet au beurre.*

poulet à la nantaise, chicken stuffed with cooked chestnuts, chopped onion, and parsley, then roasted.

poulet à la nantua, chicken (sometimes stuffed with a purée of shrimps mixed with sauce velouté), poached in white stock, then covered with sauce suprême and served with *nantua* garnish.

poulet à la neva, chicken stuffed with chicken forcemeat to which foie gras and truffles have been added, and poached in chicken stock. The bird is served cold, coated with chaud-froid and chicken jelly. It can also be prepared in the same way as *poularde lambertye,* that is, with the breast removed, sliced, put back on the bird again, and then all masked with chaud-froid and jelly. It is garnished with mixed vegetable salad in mayonnaise. See also NEVA, À LA.

poulet à la niçoise, chicken sautéed in oil, seasoned with saffron, garlic, fresh peeled tomatoes and a bouquet garni and cooked in a covered dish in the oven. The pan juices are mixed with 1 cup white wine, 1 garlic clove, and 1 tablespoon tomato purée. It is served with courgettes (zucchini) simmered in butter, new potatoes, and black olives. See also NIÇOISE À LA.

poulet à la parisienne. The chicken is stuffed with a *panade* of 2 cups soaked bread mixed with 4 oz. minced (ground) veal and 3 eggs, and is poached in white stock. When cold, the breast is cut off, and the stuffing is removed and cut into large dice before being used to make *mousseline* forcemeat, with which the chicken is again stuffed. The bird is refashioned to its original shape, and the breast meat is cut into thin slices and then put back over the forcemeat. All this is coated with chaud-froid and set on a long slice of buttered bread. It is garnished with *darioles* of vegetable salad with aspic, and topped with truffle pieces. See also POULET, SAUTÉ PARISIENNE.

poulet à la polonaise, chicken stuffed with forcemeat made from soaked bread, parsley, chicken liver, shallot, thyme, and ½ bay leaf all well seasoned. The bird is then browned in hot butter and roasted in the oven. Just before serving, a little lemon juice is squeezed over and the bird is sprinkled with fresh breadcrumbs browned in butter.

poulet à la portugaise, I. Chicken roasted or sautéed in butter, then the pan juices mixed with ½ cup white wine and 1 cup thickened veal gravy flavoured with tomato and a clove of garlic. It is garnished with stuffed baked tomatoes. II. As above, but cooked in olive oil, with tomatoes (instead of stuffing them separately) and 1 tablespoon chopped onion. It is sprinkled with parsley before serving.

poulet à la régence, chicken larded with fat bacon and braised in brown butter. It is served with calves' sweetbreads sautéed in butter, cock's combs and large prawns cooked in bouillon, truffles cooked in Madeira, and chicken quenelles, all covered with sauce *régence.* See also RÉGENCE.

poulet à la reine, chicken stuffed with 2 cups chopped cooked chicken mixed with ½ cup thick sauce velouté and 1 egg yolk, then poached in the minimum of chicken or veal stock, and drained. It is served surrounded by pastry tartlets filled with chicken purée, a piece of truffle, and sauce *allemande.*

poulet à la renaissance, chicken poached in the minimum of stock, covered with sauce suprême made with mushroom essence (extract), and garnished with *renaissance* garnish. See also RENAISSANCE, À LA.

poulet à la Rossini, chicken cooked in butter in the oven, and garnished with sliced foie gras heated in butter. The pan juices are mixed with Madeira wine and truffle-flavoured sauce espagnole. Sometimes the foie gras is served on croûtons of fried bread.

poulet à la sicilienne, chicken stuffed with half-cooked pasta mixed with pignolis or pistachio nuts and roasted in olive oil.

poulet au riz, chicken poached in chicken stock and served with sauce suprême and boiled rice.

poulet au riz à la basquaise, as above, but three-quarters of the way through cooking, *lou-kenkas* (a spicy Basque sausage) is added, and the dish is spiced with *piment basquais.* It is served with a ragoût of tomatoes and sweet peppers.

poulet au sang, chicken cooked in its own blood. The bird is first jointed and fried in butter, then removed, and 4 oz. chopped bacon, 12 button onions, and 4 oz. mushrooms are lightly sautéed in the same butter. Then 1 tablespoon flour is added, followed by 1 pint (2 cups) red wine and 4 tablespoons beef broth, and all are cooked for 5 minutes. The bird is then put into a casserole with this sauce strained over it, and a bouquet garni is also added. It is covered, and cooked for 45 minutes. Finally the chicken's blood is added, mixed with 2 tablespoons red wine to stop it from coagulating. The sauce is reheated but never reboiled, and just before serving 1 tablespoon warmed brandy is added and ignited.

poulet aux nouilles, chicken stuffed with half-cooked noodles which have been mixed with butter and grated cheese, then covered and cooked with butter in the oven. Sometimes the chicken is simply set on a bed of noodles, dressed as above, instead of being stuffed with them.

poulet belle meunière, chicken stuffed with chopped truffles, mushrooms, and chicken livers, browned in butter, then braised in a mixture of half white wine, half stock.

poulet en aspic, cold boiled chicken coated with sauce béchamel, then glazed with chicken jelly like a chaud-froid.

poulet en barbouille, chicken cooked with its own blood, a speciality of the Berry district of France. It is also called *poulet au sang* in other parts of France.

poulet en capilotade, cold chicken heated up in a sauce crème, sauce *chasseur,* or sauce *Portugaise,* etc.

poulet en cocotte, chicken braised and served in a *cocotte.*

poulet en geleé, poached or boiled chicken, served cold in clear aspic jelly.

poulet farci à la mode de sorges, a speciality of the Périgord. The bird is first stuffed with a forcemeat made from the chopped chicken liver, 2 cups stale breadcrumbs, 2 oz. chopped bacon, 2 tablespoons onion tops or spring onions (scallions), 1 shallot, 1 garlic clove, grated nutmeg, and seasoning all bound with ½ cup of the bird's blood and 1 egg yolk. The bird is next browned all over in goose fat, then put in a deep, ovenproof, earthenware dish and covered with boiling water. It is boiled and the liquid skimmed; then 3 sliced carrots, 2 turnips, the white part of 3 leeks, 1 celery heart, beetroot stalks, and 1 onion stuck with cloves are all added. All are covered and cooked very slowly for 1 hour, or until tender. The chicken is then drained and surrounded with the carrots and the turnips. It is served with sauce *Sorges.* In the Périgord, the broth produced by the cooking of this dish is usually served first, either poured over oven-dried bread or garnished with cut macaroni.

poulet farci à la périgourdine, chicken stuffed with truffles and foie gras, then covered and cooked with butter in the oven. It is served with sauce madère. See also PÉRIGOURDINE, À LA.

poulet Maeterlinck, chicken stuffed with forcemeat made from chopped cock's combs, rognons de coq, lamb's sweetbreads, truffles, and mushrooms, then browned in butter with *couennes de porc,* and carrots and onions cut into rings. The bird is covered and cooked in the oven for 45 minutes, after which it is drained and put into an oval earthenware casserole with truffles and small pieces of foie gras. The pan juices are mixed with 1 cup sherry, 2 cups brown meat gravy, and 4 tablespoons brandy which is ignited. The lid is luted and the contents of the casserole cooked for a further 35 minutes.

poulet poché, chicken poached in stock and usually served with boiled rice and sauce crème.

poulet princesse, chicken poached in chicken stock, then drained and covered with sauce *allemande.* It is garnished with pastry tartlets filled with buttered asparagus tips and sautéed sliced truffles. See also PRINCESSE, À LA.

poulet rosière, chicken stuffed with chicken forcemeat and cream, rubbed with lemon juice, and wrapped entirely in bacon larding fat. An oval casserole is lined with *couennes de porc* cut into strips, rounds of carrot and onion, and a bouquet garni. The chicken is put on top and the whole is covered with white stock. It is cooked in the oven for 1–1½ hours. About 30 minutes before it is ready, calves' sweetbreads are cooked in stock, and then sliced thinly. The chicken is served surrounded by the sliced sweetbreads, and covered with mushroom sauce mixed with cream.

poulet rôti, the breast of the bird is covered with 1 slice fat bacon, and the chicken is roasted with a little butter or chicken fat for 1 hour in a moderate oven. It is served with the pan juices and sprigs of watercress. This method is for a bird about 2½ lb. in weight. It can also be cooked in 2 cups stock.

poulet rôti à l'anglaise, chicken roasted as above, and garnished with grilled rolled-up bacon rashers and grilled *chipolata* sausages. It is served with bread sauce. Before roasting, the chicken may be stuffed with a mixture of 1 cup breadcrumbs, 1 tablespoon finely chopped shallots, a pinch of thyme, and the chopped liver, all bound with an egg yolk.

poulet sauté à la biarrotte, the bird is sautéed in olive oil and browned. The pan juices are mixed with ½ pint (1 cup) white wine and reduced, then ½ cup fresh tomato sauce and 1 crushed garlic clove are added. It is garnished with *cèpes,* eggplant, and 1 onion, all sliced and sautéed in olive oil.

poulet sauté à la bohémienne, the bird is sautéed in olive oil with a sprinkling of paprika. When half-cooked, 4 sweet peppers cut into strips, 2 peeled, coarsely chopped tomatoes, 1 medium-sized sliced onion, 1 crushed garlic clove, and 1 teaspoon chopped fennel are added. The pan juices are mixed with ¼ pint (½ cup) white wine, ½ cup veal gravy, and a squeeze of lemon juice. The dish is served with boiled rice. See also BOHÉMIENNE.

poulet sauté à la bordelaise, chicken sautéed in a mixture of olive oil and butter; ½ pint (1 cup) white wine is added to the pan juices with 1 tablespoon fresh tomato sauce and 1 crushed garlic clove, and all reduced over a hot flame. It is garnished with *pommes sautées,* quartered globe artichokes blanched and cooked in butter, 2 medium-sized onions sliced and fried, and sprigs of fried parsley.

poulet sauté à la bourguignonne, the bird is sautéed in butter and browned. When three-quarters cooked, 12 small sautéed button onions, 12 sautéed mushrooms, and 3 oz. diced lean lightly fried bacon are added. When finally cooked, the pan juices are strained off, mixed with 1 cup red wine and 1 garlic clove, and reduced by rapid boiling; then 1 cup sauce espagnole is added, and when heated, this mixture is poured over the chicken and vegetables. Sometimes it is garnished with heart-shaped croûtons of fried bread.

poulet sauté à la crème, chicken first sautéed in butter without browning, then covered and cooked. The pan juices are diluted with 1½ cups cream, and this is reduced to half the original volume; then 2½ tablespoons butter are added just before serving. Chicken-based sauce velouté can also be added, but not more than 2 tablespoons. The bird is coated with the sauce.

poulet sauté à l'écossaise, chicken sautéed in butter but not browned, then covered and cooked. The pan juices are mixed with 1 wineglass of sherry, and reduced; 1 cup thickened veal gravy is added and the mixture is boiled for a few minutes, then finished with 2 tablespoons butter. The dish is garnished with buttered french beans and thick strips of tongue and truffle heated in sherry.

poulet sauté à l'estragon, the bird is sautéed in butter; then the pan juices are diluted with white wine, chopped tarragon is added, and the mixture is reduced. See also POULET, À L'ESTRAGON.

poulet sauté à l'italienne, chicken sautéed in olive oil and served with a sauce made from the pan juices mixed with ½ pint (1 cup) fresh tomato sauce, 1 lean slice of chopped ham, and mixed chopped herbs.

poulet sauté à la lyonnaise, chicken sautéed in butter with finely chopped onions and served with a thick brown veal gravy. See also LYONNAISE, À LA.

poulet sauté à la marengo, see MARENGO.

poulet sauté à la meunière, chicken sautéed in butter, with chopped parsley, lemon juice, and rich veal gravy added.

poulet sauté à la minute, another name for *poulet sauté au beurre.*

poulet sauté à la nantaise, chicken sautéed in butter with root vegetables and white wine. It is served with onions, carrots, mushrooms, and artichoke hearts, and sauce hollandaise.

poulet sauté à la paysanne, another name for *poulet sauté fermière.*

poulet sauté à la Périgord, another name for *poulet sauté aux truffes.*

poulet sauté à la piemontaise, as for *poulet sauté au vin,* using white wine. Served with a border of risotto mixed with diced white truffles.

poulet sauté à la provençale, the bird is sautéed in olive oil as for *poulet à la portugaise.* It is garnished with stoned black olives, mushrooms sautéed in oil, anchovy fillets, and chopped parsley.

poulet sauté à la romaine, the bird is sautéed in olive oil and browned; then the pan juices are mixed with ½ cup asti wine, and reduced, after which 1 cup thickened veal gravy and ½ cup fresh tomato sauce are added. It is served on leaf spinach which has been cooked in butter and mixed with 2 diced anchovy fillets.

poulet sauté à la zingara, chicken seasoned with paprika, sautéed in olive oil, and browned. When cooked, 4 tablespoons *zingara* garnish is added. The bird is removed, and ¼ cup Madeira is added to the pan juices which are then reduced. Then 1 cup sauce espagnole is poured in and the whole is flavoured with tomato purée. It is served with the garnish arranged in 2 piles, and also some slices of toast with a slice of ham tossed in butter on each. It is all coated with the sauce and sprinkled with chopped parsley.

poulet sauté Angeline, chicken sautéed with truffles, paprika, and grated cheese.

poulet sauté Annette, the bird is sautéed in butter with ½ pint (1 cup) white wine and 4 chopped shallots added; then ½ pint (1 cup) rich brown gravy, 1 tablespoon mixed chopped parsley, chervil, tarragon, 1 tablespoon butter, and a squeeze of lemon juice are also added. The whole is set in a crust of *pommes Annette* and coated with the sauce.

poulet sauté archiduc, the bird is sautéed in butter. Then chopped onion and paprika are added, with ¼ pint (½ cup) white wine, and this is reduced; then 1 cup cream, butter, and a squeeze of lemon juice are added. It is garnished with diced cucumbers simmered in butter.

poulet sauté au basilic, the bird is first sautéed in butter, and the pan juices are diluted with ½ pint (1 cup) white wine and reduced. Then 3 tablespoons butter and 1 tablespoon chopped basil are added, and it is all cooked for 30 minutes.

poulet sauté au beurre, chicken sautéed in butter, then sprinkled with lemon juice and chopped parsley just before serving.

poulet sauté au vin, the bird is sautéed in butter and then browned. The pan juices are diluted with various wines and veal gravy, then all is reduced. The dish takes its name from the particular wine used, for example poulet sauté au madère, etc. When red wine is used, the dish is always entitled poulet sauté à la bourguignonne. See also COQ, AU VIN.

poulet sauté aux artichauts, the bird is sautéed in butter. When half-cooked, globe artichokes are added. The pan juices are mixed with white wine, veal gravy, and chopped parsley, all reduced slightly before serving.

poulet sauté aux cèpes, the bird is sautéed in oil or butter; when three-quarters cooked, ½ lb. chopped *cèpes* are added and 1 small chopped onion. Then ½ cup white wine is added, and 3 tablespoons butter is stirred in. The chicken is sprinkled with chopped parsley, or alternatively *cèpes à la bordelaise* is used as a garnish.

poulet sauté aux champignons, as *poulet sauté aux cèpes,* but champignons replace the *cèpes,* and the dish is served with sauce madère.

poulet sautè aux fines herbes, the bird is sautéed in butter; then the pan juices are mixed with 1 cup white wine, 1 chopped shallot, rich brown gravy, and chopped mixed herbs.

poulet sauté aux jets de houblon, chicken sautéed in butter, then prepared just as for *poulet sauté à la crème.* It is garnished with hop shoots cooked and served in warm cream.

poulet sauté aux morels, as for *poulet sauté aux champignons,* but using *morels* instead of *cèpes.*

poulet sauté aux truffes, the bird is sautéed in butter and browned. When cooked it is covered with thick slices of truffle and returned to the pan for 5 minutes. The pan juices are diluted with ½ cup sauce madère and ½ pint (1 cup) rich thickened veal gravy.

poulet sauté boivin, the bird is sautéed in butter and lightly browned. To it are added about 20 button onions sautéed in butter, 4 small globe artichokes quartered and blanched, and about 20 small new potatoes, and all are covered and put in a moderate oven for 40 minutes with ½ pint (1 cup) stock, 2 tablespoons demi-glace, a squeeze of lemon juice, and a nut of butter. Then the vegetables are taken out and set round the pieces of chicken. The pan juices are boiled up rapidly for 2 minutes, then served over all.

poulet sauté camérani, jointed chicken coated with egg and breadcrumbs mixed with finely chopped truffle, then sautéed in butter. It is served with sauce madère and cooked noodles.

poulet sauté chasseur, chicken sautéed in equal quantities of olive oil and butter. When three-quarters cooked, ¼ lb. raw sliced mushrooms is added. The pan juices are drained off and mixed with 1 sliced shallot, ½ cup white wine, 1 cup veal gravy, and ¼ cup fresh tomato sauce; after boiling up for 2 minutes, 1 tablespoon brandy and 1 tablespoon mixed parsley, chervil, and tarragon are added. See also CHASSEUR, À LA.

poulet sauté Clamart, chicken sautéed in butter in a casserole; then 1 lb. *petits pois à la française* is added and cooked with the bird. See also CLAMART, À LA.

poulet sauté duroc, as *poulet sauté chasseur,* but garnished with small peeled tomatoes and small potatoes cooked in butter. All is sprinkled with parsley. See also DUROC.

poulet sauté en matelote, another name for *poulet sauté à la bourguignonne.*

poulet sauté fermière, the bird is sautéed in butter. When the chicken has browned, 1 cup vegetable fondue is added, also a slice of diced lean ham. The dish is covered and braised in the oven. Just before serving, 1 cup thickened veal gravy is added and heated up. See also FERMIÈRE, À LA.

poulet sauté florentine, chicken sautéed in butter and served with risotto mixed with 2 tablespoons chopped white truffle.

poulet sauté forestière, as for *poulet sauté aux cèpes,* but using *morels* instead of *cèpes,* and served with diced potatoes and small blanched cardoons.

poulet sauté livonienne, the bird is sautéed in butter without being browned. When three-quarters cooked, ½ lb. sautéed *morels* is added. The pan juices are finished as for *poulet sauté à la crème*. All is sprinkled with breadcrumbs fried in butter and chopped parsley.

poulet sauté mireille, the bird is sautéed in butter. The pan juices are then mixed with 1 cup white wine, and reduced; 1 cup rich veal gravy and ¼ cup tomato sauce are added and boiled for a few minutes. It is garnished with chicory hearts braised in cream (see CHICORY) and small peeled tomatoes simmered in butter.

poulet sauté monselet, the bird is sautéed and browned in butter. When three-quarters cooked, artichoke bottoms and truffles are added. The pan juices are mixed with ½ cup white wine and 1 cup thick veal gravy, and all are boiled up and reduced.

poulet sauté panetière, chicken sautéed in butter and cream, and served on a round of bread spread with foie gras. It is garnished with mushrooms cooked in cream.

poulet sauté panurge, jointed chicken is sautéed in butter, then removed from the pan. Next 1½ cups sautéed carrot, onion, and celery are put in the butter, then the chicken is placed on top and 2 cups dry white wine is added. The liquid is reduced by boiling, then 1 cup cream is poured over, and the chicken is covered and simmered gently for 30 minutes. Then 2 dozen stoned green olives are added, together with a knob of butter, and heated up. When served, the finely sliced gizzard, which has been cooked in consommé and turned in butter, and the liver, which has been fried in butter, are added. The dish is garnished with heart-shaped croûtons of bread fried in butter.

poulet sauté parisienne, chicken sautéed and cooked in butter. The pan juices are mixed with 2 cups white wine and butter and reduced. It is served with *purée de pommes de terre* and asparagus tips. See also POULET, À LA PARISIENNE.

poulet sauté petit-duc, the bird is sautéed in butter and browned. The pan juices are mixed with ¼ cup Madeira wine, then boiled up, after which 1 cup sauce espagnole is added and the mixture is boiled again for a few minutes. It is garnished with *morels* and sliced truffle sautéed in butter.

poulet sauté rivoli, the bird is sautéed and browned in butter. When three-quarters cooked, 4 peeled and sliced *pommes sautées* and 2 medium-sized chopped truffles are added. The pan juices are mixed with ¼ cup sherry and reduced; then 1 cup thickened veal gravy is added and boiled up. The mixture is served over the bird.

poulet sauté Stanley, the bird is sautéed in butter; when half-cooked, 2 large finely chopped onions are added. The pan juices and onions are mixed with 1 cup cream and cooked for 10 minutes, then sieved. This purée is seasoned with a pinch of curry powder, and finally 2 tablespoons butter is stirred in. The chicken is coated with this sauce and garnished with thin slices of truffle.

poulet Stanley, chicken poached with onions, and served with the sauce used for *poulet sauté Stanley*.

poulet à la Wallone, a Walloon method of cooking a jointed chicken. A young chicken, a knuckle of veal, and chopped root vegetables are covered with water or stock and simmered for 30 minutes. Then 1 set of cleaned, chopped calf's sweetbreads is added, and all are covered and cooked until tender (about 2 hours). The dish is seasoned well, and just before serving, ½ pint (1 cup) cream, 2 egg yolks, and ½ pint (1 cup) sweet white wine, all beaten together and heated to just below boiling-point, are poured over the jointed chicken, diced sweetbreads, and veal.

poulette, à la, a French method of serving many foods, par-

ticularly sheep's trotters (feet) or sweetbreads, mushrooms, frogs' legs, and mussels. The foods are cooked, usually by poaching, and served in sauce *poulette*.

poulette, sauce, a classical French sauce, a variant of sauce *allemande* which is served with mussels, frog's legs, sheep's trotters (feet), and a ragoût of veal. First 1 pint (2 cups) thick sauce *béchamel* is made, care being taken that the flour does not colour. To this sauce is added ½ pint (1 cup) good white stock, or the liquor from the meat or fish with which the sauce is to be served. When the sauce is smooth and thick, it is removed from the heat and 2 tablespoons thick cream and 2 egg yolks are blended in. Finally a squeeze of lemon juice and seasoning are added. It is sometimes garnished with chopped parsley.

pouligny-Saint-Pierre, a French goat's milk cheese made in and around Pouligny in the Indre department. It is small and pyramid-shaped, and is eaten from April to November.

poulpe, French for octopus, usually stewed for 5 minutes in olive oil with 1 sliced onion, then simmered until tender with ½ bottle white wine, 1 crushed garlic clove, and a bouquet garni. See also OCTOPUS.

poulpe au riz, octopus cooked as above, but ¼ lb. rice is added, with a pinch of saffron, and all is covered and cooked for 30 minutes.

poultry, domestic birds bred for their eggs or for the table. Different varieties are kept for both uses. The word covers chicken, duck, goose, guinea-fowl, and turkey.

pound cake, an old English cake, also popular in the U.S. As the name suggests, it is made from 1 lb. each of (4 cups) flour, (2 cups) sugar, and (2 cups) butter, flavoured with mace or ginger and brandy or some other liqueur, and mixed with 10 egg yolks and 10 stiffly beaten egg whites. It is baked in a slow-to-moderate oven for 1½–2 hours.

poupart, an alternative French name, with *tourteau*, for giant crab. See CRAB.

poupelin, a French cake made by cooking chou pastry in a round mould and filling it when cold with *crème chantilly*, ice cream, or a fruit mousse.

poupeton, a French method of preparing several meats by layering them and then rolling them up. The roll is usually braised, and served cold.

pourgouri, a coarse sort of porridge made from ground wheat, which is used as an alternative to rice in Cyprus.

pourpier, French for purslane, sometimes boiled and eaten as a vegetable, or pickled in vinegar and used as a relish. See also PURSLANE.

poussin, the French name for a young chicken 4–6 weeks old, and weighing approximately 1½ lb. in France and England, but about 2½ lb. in the U.S. where it is known as a broiler. The best type is the Hamburg variety. Although the flesh is tender, poussin has very little flavour compared with *poulet*, and the very small bird known as petit poussin has even less. For this reason poussin must be cooked quickly, to seal in the juices and maintain what flavour there is, and it should be served with a sauce such as sauce béarnaise or the more highly flavoured sauce diable. If it is to be roasted, it should be stuffed with a fine chicken-liver and mushroom forcemeat and cooked for not longer than 30 minutes in a hot oven. One of the best methods of preparing it is to split it in 2 and flatten it, brush it with melted butter or olive oil, and then grill it; otherwise, to coat it in egg and breadcrumbs, or batter, and deep fry it. It is garnished with fried parsley and lemon wedges. It may be marinated first in lemon juice, olive oil, and herbs, in which case the dish is called poussin frit. *Petits pois* are an excellent accompaniment. The methods *à la piémontaise* and *à la polonaise* are also used. See also POULET.

poutine, French for small or undeveloped fish, usually applied to sardines or anchovies. See also NONAT; WHITEBAIT.

pouting (*Gadus luscus*), a species of cod with a copper-coloured body found in the North Atlantic. It is good to eat when very fresh, but quickly goes bad.

powan, the Scottish name for the whitefish *Coregonus lavaretus,* found in Scotland only in Loch Lomond and Loch Eck. See GWYNIAD.

powsowdie, a Scottish stew–soup made from sheep's head and feet, neck of mutton, pearl barley, dried or fresh peas, carrot, turnip, onions, chopped parsley, salt, and pepper, with water to cover. All are covered and cooked very slowly for at least 3 hours. The sheep's head is served separately, as is customary with the meat in a pot-au-feu. Powsowdie used to be eaten as a traditional Sunday dinner dish in Scotland and is mentioned by Sir Walter Scott in his novel *The Antiquary.* The name comes from the Gaelic pow (head), and sowdie (sodden, boiled).

praakes, see HOLISHKES.

praetud vasikaliha hapukoore soustiga, a traditional Estonian stew made from 3 lb. veal cubed and sautéed in 4 oz. (½ cup) butter with 2 large sliced onions; then ½ pint (1 cup) water is added, and seasoning, and the stew is simmered slowly. When almost cooked, ½ pint (1 cup) sour cream is included and allowed to thicken. The stew is served with boiled potatoes, sauerkraut, carrots, and peas or beans. Sometimes a salad of cucumber or beetroot is served with it, or a dish of stewed cranberries.

pragon (*Ruscus aculeatus*), the French name for a small evergreen shrub, a member of the lily family, known in Britain as butcher's broom. The young shoots are eaten in France, prepared in any way that is suitable for hop shoots.

Prague ham, see PRAŽSKÁ ŠUNKA.

praire, see CLAM; PALOURDE.

prairie chicken (*Tympanuchus cupido* and *T. pallidicinctus*), a game bird of the U.S. known as "the grouse of America," and found from the Mississippi to Texas. It is highly thought of as food and can be prepared and cooked in any way that is suitable for grouse, although it needs longer cooking-time as it is much larger.

prairie oyster, a great restorative, usually taken on "the morning after the night before." It is made by breaking a raw egg into a glass and adding 1 teaspoon worcestershire sauce and a measure of brandy. It is swirled round, the egg being left intact, and swallowed in one gulp. Some people omit the brandy and add a pinch of salt, but the true prairie oyster should include the spirit, as it does produce the best results.

pralin, French for a nut and sugar mixture used for adding to creams, ices, cakes, or soufflés. To prepare it 4 oz. (½ cup) sugar and ½ vanilla pod are heated until brown; then 4 oz. (1 cup) almonds, hazelnuts, or walnuts previously browned in the oven, are mixed in. It is turned out to harden on a board or marble and when cool, the mixture is pounded as finely as possible in a mortar or in a blender. The French verb praliner means to add pralin to a dish.

gâteau praliné, a cake made with layers of marzipan, or a *génoese* layered with praline cream, which is made by adding 4 tablespoons powdered pralines to 1 cup butter icing.

pralinate, Italian for pralin, but in the Italian version the pounding process is omitted. The mixture is poured onto a greased slab and, when cold, is cut into small squares. It is served as a sweetmeat or candy.

praline, I. A sweetmeat consisting of a single almond covered, generally, with cooked caramel or a hard icing. It is also known in Britain as sugared almond. II. The English word for *pralin.*

prasa, Turkish and Greek for leeks. See also LEEK.

zeytinli prasa, blanched chopped leeks sautéed in oil, covered with tomato sauce, a little sugar, and lemon juice, then simmered until nearly tender. At this point black olives are added, and cooking is continued for 10 minutes. It is served hot or cold, with meats.

prasèntse pŭlneno, Bulgarian roast stuffed sucking pig. It is stuffed before roasting with the liver, heart, lungs, and kidneys, which are minced and mixed with paprika, herbs, spices, 4 oz. (½ cup) raisins, 2 cups cooked rice, and seasoning. It is basted from time to time with a little hot stock to make the skin crisp, and for festive dinners the skin is also rubbed with 3 tablespoons brandy for the same reason.

pratelle, the French name for the horse mushroom, also known as *boule de neige.* See MUSHROOM.

prawn, a small salt water crustacean. Prawns are delicious, and once the head and the body shell are removed, all the rest is edible, apart from a small black filament which can upset people who are allergic to shellfish, but is otherwise harmless. They should be steamed for 10 minutes before eating or further preparation. Prawns are often made into a paste with mace and butter, and they are eaten in salads, omelettes, and mousse. They are also curried, and used as a garnish. The large American and West Indian prawns (see SHRIMP) can also be fried in batter or grilled. They should not be confused with the Dublin Bay prawn, which is a Norway lobster. See also GAMBA; GAMBERETTI; GARIDES; SCAMPI.

prawn cocktail, a dish served as a first course or appetizer, and usually made in a goblet. A little shredded lettuce is placed in the bottom of the glass, then cooked prawns or scampi (Dublin Bay prawns) are added, and covered with either a cream and wine vinegar dressing, or mayonnaise and lemon juice. Some people add tomato purée and worcestershire sauce, but this entirely destroys the flavour of the prawns.

praz, Rumanian for leek. Leeks are of excellent quality in Rumania, and are often used in *iahnie.* See also LEEK.

prażone, a traditional Polish picnic stew, made with 2 lb. potatoes, 1 lb. onions, *kiełbasa* or *wiankowa* (Polish ring-sausage), ¼ lb. (½ cup) butter, salt, and pepper, all cooked in water for some hours over a wood fire.

Pražská šunka, Prague ham, a very delicately smoked ham from Czechoslovakia, known all over Europe. It is served whole for a main course, either baked or boiled, and cold slices of it are often served as a first course. It is first salted, then left in a mild brine for several months; then it is smoked over beechwood ashes and matured in airy cellars before being sold. See also HAM.

prebkohlsuppe, beef broth with stuffed cabbage, a traditional Austrian soup. Blanched leaves of white cabbage are stuffed with a mixture of 1 lb. pork sausage meat, 2 soaked crustless slices of bread, 2 eggs, 1 tablespoon chopped chives, and seasoning. These rolls are poached in the broth and make a substantial meal. Very small balls of the stuffing may be braised and served as a garnish for the broth.

pregado, Portuguese for turbot; also called *rodovalho.* It is excellent in Portugal, although cooked very simply, usually by poaching.

prêle, the French name for a weed called mare's tail in England. The young shoots are eaten in certain country districts of France, prepared in the same way as asparagus, and they are also pickled in wine vinegar.

pré-salé, French for lamb which has been pastured and fattened on meadowlands, often reclaimed land, near the sea. The aromatic sea plants growing there add a distinctive flavour to the flesh.

present, a French name for edam cheese.

presentoir, the French name for the dish on which a tureen stands.

preserve, another name for jam.

preserving, I. The process by which food is kept from going bad. See CURING; DEEP FREEZING, II. Another name for jam or pickle making.

presnitz, a delicious Italian Easter cake, originally from Castagnevizza but now adopted by Trieste. To prepare it, 3 oz. (scant ½ cup) each of raisins and sultanas are soaked in rum until round and smooth. Then 1 cup stale sponge cake is crumbled, mixed with 3 oz. (½ cup) chopped nuts and 2 oz. (½ cup) chopped candied peel, and added to the fruit mixture, and 2 heaped tablespoons sugar and a squeeze of lemon are added to taste. Next ½ lb. puff pastry is rolled out to a width of 3 inches and a thickness of ½ inch, which is put on a baking-sheet and covered with the rum-soaked mixture. Then 1 egg and 1 tablespoon soft butter are beaten together and brushed over the top, and finally the whole is sprinkled with ground cinnamon and baked in a hot oven until the pastry is cooked and the top is golden brown. See also EASTER; PANETTONE.

pressato, an Italian cheese of the *asiago* type, but much softer and always eaten fresh. It has a sweetish taste, and the inside varies from white to a pale straw-colour.

pressed beef, beef, usually a flank, is rolled and then simmered in water for 3–4 hours with herbs, calf's foot, onion, and seasoning. The beef is sliced when cool, and the strained liquor is reduced and then poured over it. When the meat is quite cool, a weight is put on top which presses it flat. It is served cold, usually with salad.

pressure cooker, a modern version of the digester, and made on the same principle. During cooking in an ordinary saucepan, a considerable amount of steam inevitably escapes and is wasted, but in a pressure cooker, with its hermetically sealed lid, this steam is captured and held inside the vessel. The result is a build up in atmospheric pressure, and this in turn raises the temperature to a heat far greater than that which can be obtained in an ordinary saucepan. For example, boiling water in a saucepan can never produce a temperature above the boiling point 212°F (100°C), whereas in a pressure cooker, with an atmospheric pressure of 15 lb., a temperature of up to 252°F (122°C) can be reached. Under such strong heat, and under an atmospheric pressure sufficient to drive that heat into and through the food, cooking time can be reduced by as much as two-thirds, and this is the great advantage of pressure cooking. In the case of many foods, particularly vegetables, it has also the merit of preserving flavour, colour, and nutritional elements such as vitamins, which may be lost during normal cooking. Precise instructions about the use of the various pressure cookers available are provided by their manufacturers, but there are several general principles which always apply: less liquid will be needed than when cooking in the normal way; the liquid used must be one that will give steam when it boils, such as water, stock, soup, wine, milk, or gravy; the liquid must never under any circumstances be forgotten, and for this reason is best put in first of all.

Of course, pressure cooking is not ideal for all foods. It *is* excellent for dried beans and peas, and foods and dishes which otherwise require long slow cooking—braised oxtail with onions, carrots, herbs, and stock, for example. In a composite dish of this kind, it is better to allow the food to cool after cooking, and then to reheat, either in the cooker or in the casserole from which it will be served; in this way the flavours are amalgamated and the finished result is superior, just as all stews are better for reboiling. Tough meat is made more tender by pressure cooking, and this form of cooking also has the advantage of sterilising fruits and vegetables that are to be used for bottling and pickling. The pressure cooker is indeed a useful, though not a vital, part of kitchen equipment. See also DIGESTER.

prestost, a Swedish cow's milk cheese cured with the traditional national spirit *aquavit.* It has been made since the 18th century. Fresh whole milk is rennetted, and when the curd is firm, it is cut coarsely and put in a sieve to drain off the whey. Then it is put in a cloth and kneaded to make quite sure that all the whey is expelled. Next, *aquavit* is mixed with the curd, which is then put in a basket, sprinkled with salt, and covered with a cloth. The covering is changed daily for 3 days, and after the 3rd day the cheese is washed with *aquavit.* It is cured in a cool moist cellar. Prestost is cylindrical in shape and can weigh anything from 5 to 30 lb. Another name for it is Saaland Pfarr. See also OST.

presunto, Portuguese for cured and smoked ham, often eaten raw, carved in thin slices, like prosciutto crudo. It is also cooked, and a popular method of preparing it is to cook it with soaked, dried white beans, *feijão branco,* garlic, carrots, and herbs. The finest presunto comes from Chaves. See also HAM; PAIO.

prêtre, see ATHERINE.

pretzel, a savoury biscuit from Alsace and Germany, shaped like a loose knot and covered with coarse salt and cumin seed. It is delicious with beer or lager. It is made with ½ pint (1 cup) water to 1 lb. (4 cups) flour, with ½ oz. yeast, salt, and 1 tablespoon pounded caraway seeds, all mixed into a smooth paste and left to rise, covered, for 30 minutes. The dough is shaped into thin loose knots and boiled in a mixture of 1 pint (2 cups) water, 2 teaspoons baking soda, and 1¼ teaspoons carbonate of ammonia. When the knots rise to the surface, they are skimmed off, put on a greased baking sheet, brushed with beaten egg, and sprinkled with coarse salt and crushed cumin seeds, then baked for a few minutes in a hot oven until brown.

prickly pear (*Opuntia ficus-indica*), the fruit of a tropical American cactus. It is generally eaten raw, but may also be cooked.

prim, see MYSOST.

primeur, a French term for fruits, vegetables, or other foods that are used before they are thoroughly ripe or matured, or are brought on to an edible condition before their time by being forced.

primizie, Italian for forced fruit or vegetables. See PRIMEUR.

primrose (*Primula vulgaris*), a plant of which the flower petals can be candied and also used in homemade wines. The whole flowers can be used to decorate salads or roast meats, and are edible. The young leaves are eaten boiled, like sorrel.

primula cheese, a Norwegian processed cheese made from the caramelised whey or *prim* of *gammelost.* See also OST.

princesse, a la, I. A French garnish for tournedos, etc., consisting of artichoke bottoms filled with asparagus tips and *pommes noisette,* with sauce *allemande.* II. A sauce crème flavoured with mushroom and chicken essence (extract), with more cream added before serving. III. A French garnish for poultry consisting of buttered asparagus tips and truffles, sometimes presented in pastry tartlets, served with suprêmes de volaille and poached chicken. See POULET, PRINCESSE. IV. A chicken consommé thickened with tapióca and garnished with chicken quenelles, asparagus tips, and chopped chervil. See also CONSOMMÉ.

prinsefisk, a Norwegian cod dish with an egg sauce. Fillets of cod, each large enough for one person, are gently poached until tender in salted water to cover. After draining, (¼ cup) thick cream (to 1½ cups stock) is stirred into the boiling stock, which is brought back to just under boiling-point and then removed from the heat. Then the sauce is stirred a little at a time into 2 beaten egg yolks, and this mixture is poured over the fish. It is garnished with parsley, lemon, and asparagus tips.

printanière, à la, I. A French garnish for meat and entrées consisting of a variety of seasonable vegetables, cooked, cut up, and arranged in their separate kinds round the dish. II. A ragoût cooked with young root vegetables which are either scooped into small ball-shapes or cut in cubes. III. A consommé with chopped young root vegetables and chopped chervil. See also CONSOMMÉ. IV. A consommé with chopped young root vegetables, and with pearl sago cooked in stock (consommé à la printanière aux perles). See also CONSOMMÉ.

processed cheese, a form of cheese invented in 1910 by two Swiss scientists, Walter Gerber and Fritz Stettler. They had been trying to develop a cheese which would keep longer than emmenthal, and processed cheese was the highly successful result of their endeavours. It is made by blending several kinds of cheese, by heating, stirring, and emulsifying. For many years processed cheese remained the monopoly of Gerber and Co., in Berne, but in 1925 it was exported from Switzerland for the first time, and imitations began to appear almost immediately in all parts of the world. The Swiss variety is still the best, although any processed cheese is a poor substitute for the real thing. It is usually packed in air-tight boxes or polythene, and keeps quite well in a cool place. Most processed cheese tastes nothing like the cheese it is based upon, and some varieties have an unpleasant texture. Several kinds are available, some of which have been smoked.

profiteroles, I. French marble-sized balls of chou pastry piped through a forcing (pastry) bag and either baked for a few minutes, or poached in hot salted water and used as a garnish for clear soup or consommé. II. As above, but larger, about 1–1½ inches in diameter. These are often filled with jams or creams, and brushed with beaten egg before being baked for 5–7 minutes until golden brown. A coating of syrup is added if they are to form part of *croquembouches,* or other small French *gâteaux* of the éclair type. The best-known profiteroles are coated with chocolate sauce after cooking and are called profiteroles au chocolat. Savoury fillings, such as pounded cheese with cream, and game or chicken purée, are also used. These savoury profiteroles are served for hors d'oeuvre or as an entrée. See also CHOU.

pronghorn (*Antilocapra americana*), a horned ruminant found in the western part of the U.S. and Mexico. It is not a true antelope, but the flesh is similar, though drier. It can be prepared and cooked in any way that is suitable for venison or *izard.*

prosciutto, Italian for fresh ham. *Prosciutto cotto* is cooked ham; *prosciutto crudo* is raw salted ham, a delicacy and a speciality of the province of Parma (particularly Langhirano), whose product is known as prosciutto di Parma (Parma ham). For this, the hams are salted with a little saltpetre, which preserves the pink colour, for anywhere between 30 and 60 days depending on their weight. Every week they are moved about, so that the salting is evenly distributed. When ready, they are washed and hung up to dry in a warm current of air for about a week; then they are transferred to a cooler temperature, 68°F (20°C), for one month, to 59°F (15°C) for the second month, and finally to 50°F (10°C) for 3 to 6 months, the air being circulated freely during the whole period. Parma ham is one of the finest cured hams in the

profiteroles au chocolat

.prosciutto di Parma

world. Rump of pork is also cured in the same way in Parma. San Daniele, north of Udine, is another centre where hams are cured in this way, but the output is small. In fact this method of curing is employed in country districts all over Italy, the product being known as *prosciutto di montagna;* but although good, the ham is coarser than either the Parma or San Daniele varieties. Prosciutto crudo is eaten raw, cut in extremely thin slices, and may be served with raw figs (*prosciutto crudo con fichi*), a particularly delicious method; with slices of ripe melon (*prosciutto crudo con melone*); or simply with butter (*prosciutto crudo con burro*). See also CULATELLO DI ZIBELLO; CURING; HAM; PARMA HAM.

prosię, Polish for sucking pig.

prosię pieczone nadziewane, roast stuffed sucking pig. It is basted with warm beer, which makes the skin very crisp and almost orange-coloured.

proso, see MILLET.

prostokvasha, a thick sour milk used for cooking in Russia. It is also served chilled, with sugar, cinnamon, and rye breadcrumbs.

protein, the principal nutritional component in fish, meat, poultry, eggs, vegetables, nuts, and some cheeses. Proteins are all large molecules composed of many amino acids, and in order that they may be digested and assimilated by the body, they must first be broken down, during digestion, into these component amino acids. In addition to the carbon, hydrogen, and oxygen present in many of the other main nutritional substances, proteins contain another element, nitrogen. Some of the more primitive fishes such as shellfish and lampreys contain proteins of a simpler structure than is to be found in most other foods, and these can occasionally produce a condition known as anaphylaxis in very young children. See SHELLFISH.

proti Anástasis, the Greek Easter ceremony of the Resurrection, after which *mayieritsa* is eaten. See also EASTER.

provatura, a Roman cheese made from buffalo milk, which is difficult to obtain nowadays. This cheese is used for *crostini di provatura,* but mozzarella is often substituted.

provençale, à la, I. A French garnish consisting of tomatoes, mushrooms, eggplants, garlic, and sauce provençale. II. A title given to certain dishes which often include both tomatoes and garlic, with olive oil, but sometimes garlic alone. See also POMME DE TERRE (POMMES À LA PROVENÇALE); PROVENCE. III. A French method of serving chicken. See POULET, SAUTÉ À LA PROVENÇALE.

provençale, sauce, a classical French sauce, made with 3 shallots and 1 garlic clove finely chopped and put into 3 tablespoons heated olive oil. They are lightly browned, being stirred frequently, and then sprinkled with 1 tablespoon flour and moistened with ¼ pint (½ cup) meat stock or bouillon. Salt and pepper, 1 small glass (½ cup) white wine, and a small bouquet garni are added, and the saucepan is covered tightly, allowing the contents to simmer gently for 15 minutes, when ¼ lb. chopped mushrooms is added. After further simmering for about 20 minutes, the sauce is strained and lemon juice sprinkled over. It is served cold with cold roast beef, veal, or fish.

sauce provençale aux oeufs, 2 garlic cloves, 4 shallots, 2 stalks fresh tarragon, and 2 stalks chervil are finely chopped and placed in a saucepan with 2 tablespoons wine vinegar, which is then reduced by simmering until it has almost evaporated. It is then replaced by the same quantity of water, heated, then strained and allowed to cool. This liquor is placed in the top of a double boiler, and 4 egg yolks, salt, and pepper are beaten in, after which ½ pint (1 cup) olive oil is slowly added. The sauce is then whipped until thick. It is used hot with grilled fish.

Provence, a region in the south of France well known for many gastronomic specialities, including a garnish (à la provençale) and sauce provençale, also for excellent olive oil. Other dishes include *aïgo bouïllido, aïgo-sau, aïoli, anchoïade, anguilles en catigout, bouillabaisse, bourride, cacalaus, fougasse, pissaladière, pistou, pompe, raito, sartadagnano, sou-fassum, tapénade,* and *terrine d'anguille.*

providence, a French cow's milk cheese made in the monastery of Bricquebec in the Manche department. It resembles port-du-salut.

provola, originally a buffalo milk cheese made from drawn curd in the Campania, Italy, but nowadays made also from cow's milk because of the scarcity of buffaloes. It is sometimes smoked with fresh burning straw. *Provola di pecora* is provola made at San Lazzaro, above Sorrento, with sheep's milk. In Neapolitan dialect, prova denotes the fresh spherical cheese eaten in that part of Italy.

provolone, an Italian cheese made from buffalo or cow's milk. It is made in the same way as *provola* and *cacio a*

cavallo, and the suffix *-one* indicates that it is in fact a larger version of provola. There are two main types of provolone: the *dolce* and the *piccante;* both are strong cheeses, but the flavour of the *piccante* is the more pronounced because the stomachs of young goats are used as a source for the rennet needed in its production. Provolone is made in the Campania, and is produced in many different shapes. It should be eaten fresh, when it is a pale yellow colour and has a soft but firm texture with a thin smooth shiny rind, and a good earthy tang. When stale it is excellent for cooking, and is much used for this purpose in Italy. See also CROSTINI.

pršut, a Yugoslavian smoked and air-dried ham. It is usually served raw, in thin slices, with olives and gherkins. See also HAM.

prugna, Italian for plum. A particularly famous variety is the Gocce d'Oro (drops of gold), a golden plum grown in the region of Venice. See also PLUM.

prugna secca or **pruna,** Italian for prune, used a great deal in Italy for puddings and sauces, and sometimes as the basis of a soufflé or for a pastry tart. See also BUDINO, DI PRUGNE; PRUNE.

salsa di prugne secce, prune sauce served with roast pork and some furred game. It is made with 1 small onion lightly fried in butter or oil; then ¼ pint (½ cup) white wine is added, boiled, and reduced by half. Next 4 oz. soaked stoned prunes are then added, with 2 bay leaves, 1 teaspoon chopped thyme, sugar to taste, salt, and pepper. When the prunes are cooked, the mixture is sieved and beaten until soft. If reheated, a little white wine is added to prevent burning.

prune, a very sweet plum which is picked when fully ripe and then dried. Varieties used for prune production are those grown at Agen in France, and the sweet plums grown in Portugal and elsewhere in southern Europe. Prunes are sometimes eaten as dessert fruit, but more usually they are soaked and stewed, or otherwise used in cookery for stuffings, puddings, compotes, jams, and cakes. Prune production is carried out on a large scale in the U.S. In California the plums are treated mainly by sun drying, but in Washington, Idaho, and Oregon, drying is done in specially built dehydrators under artificial heat. The European variety, Agen, is principally used. Prunes are also canned extensively in these areas, and prune juice is extracted and sold canned or bottled as an appetizer or health drink. See also PRUGNA SECCA; PRUNEAU; SVISKE.

prune, French for plum. A *prune de Damas* is a damson.

prunes au vinaigre, a speciality of Alsace. To prepare them 2 lb. sound ripe plums are first pricked with a needle, then put into a deep dish close together and sprinkled with cinnamon and cloves. A syrup made from 1 lb. sugar boiled for 30 minutes with ¼ pint (½ cup) white wine vinegar is then poured over the plums and they are left for 2 days. On the 3rd day the syrup is strained off, boiled for another 30 minutes, and then poured back. The next day both plums and syrup are boiled for 5 minutes. The plums are then carefully spooned into sterilised jars, the syrup is boiled for another 15 minutes and poured over the plums in the jars, and the jars are sealed and stored. These plums are used for an hors d'oeuvre, and they are thought to have considerable digestive value.

prune jam knaidlach, a traditional Hungarian Jewish Passover dish. It is made with 8 medium-sized potatoes, cooked and mashed, mixed with 4 eggs, 1 cup matzo flour, and 2 tablespoons fat (*schmaltz* is possible), all well mixed and formed into balls the size of a small apple. A depression is made in each ball and filled with prune jam, bringing over the dough to cover the filling. The balls are poached one at a time in a large pan of boiling water. They will float to the top when cooked, and should be skimmed off and kept warm, then rolled in sugar, ground cinnamon, and melted butter, and browned lightly, either in a moderate oven or under a grill. They are served as a dessert. See also KNAIDLACH.

pruneau, French for prune. *Pruneaux à l'Armagnac* are enormously large Agen prunes preserved in Armagnac. *Pruneaux de Tours* are large plums dried on bamboo or slate and sold in wide glass jars. These prunes have an excellent flavour. The Perdrigon plum, when peeled, stoned, dried in the sun, and flattened, is known commercially as *pistole;* however, when left whole and dried in the shade it is called *brignole* or *pruneau fleuri.* Prunes are used widely in French cooking, in both sweet and savoury dishes, such as *noisettes de porc aux pruneaux.* See also PRUNE.

pryaniki, a traditional Russian biscuit (cookie), made in the shape of a pig, a cockerel, or any other farm animal, and sold at village fairs. The biscuits are made from 4 oz. (1 cup) flour, 8 oz. (1 cup) sugar, 3 eggs, and 1 teaspoon crushed cardamom seeds, all well mixed. The required shapes are made about ½ inch thick, and they are baked in a hot oven for about 10 minutes. They are a great favourite with Russian children.

przepiórka, Polish for quail. Quail and coot are often spit-roasted in Poland. The birds are hung for 2 days, then plucked and cleaned. Each one is wrapped in fat bacon or salt pork, threaded onto the spit, and roasted for 15–20 minutes, being basted with butter. They are served on toast. See also QUAIL.

psari, Greek for fish. Fish is both good and plentiful there and constitutes part of the staple diet of the Greeks. It is sold to the housewife still alive, for no Greek would buy a dead fish. A great deal of our present-day knowledge about the preparation and cooking of fish derives from the ancient Greeks. It is said to have been Agres of Rhodes who first thought of filleting fish, and it was Nereus of Corinth who turned the conger eel into a dish "fit for the Gods." Fish is most usually served grilled over charcoal, although it is also baked, simmered, or poached. See also LITHRINI; PALAMIDA; PLAKI.

psari fournou, a Cretan dish of fish baked whole with sliced and peeled tomatoes, 1 cup olive oil, and 2 tablespoons chopped parsley, with potatoes or onion sometimes added. Any white fish can be used.

psari fournou spetsiotiko, baked white fish as prepared on the island of Spetsai. First 4 lb. white fish is covered with 2 tablespoons tomato purée, ¾ pint (1½ cups) olive oil, 2 garlic cloves, 1 tablespoon lemon juice, 2 tablespoons parsley, and seasoning, all mixed together as for a sauce, are put into a dish, covered with a thick crust of breadcrumbs, and baked. Sometimes 4 tablespoons white wine is added if the mixture seems dry.

psari me rigani, grilled white fish sprinkled with marjoram, olive oil, and lemon juice. It is also called *psari riganato.* Fresh sardines, particularly, are cooked in this way.

psari me skordalia, fish poached in stock and served with *skorthalia* sauce.

psari picti, fish poached in stock then set in the jelly and eaten cold.

psari plaki me ellies, fish baked with onions, tomatoes, garlic, olive oil, water, and black olives.

psari psito, grilled fish basted with olive oil and lemon juice. The grilling is often done over charcoal, and the results are extremely good. A variation of this method consists of fish steaks, either grilled or oven baked, spread with mayonnaise and lemon juice.

psari riganato, another name for *psari me rigani.*

psari tighanito, fish dipped in flour and fried in oil.

psari tis skaras, grilled fish.

psari yemisto, fish stuffed with soaked breadcrumbs, minced onion, minced celery, and chopped prawns, then baked in oil or butter. It is basted with butter and lemon juice.

psarosoupa, fish soup, made with 1 cup chopped celery, 2 medium-sized chopped onions, 1 large chopped carrot, and ½

lb. diced potatoes are all cooked until tender in a large saucepan containing 2 quarts water, 3 tablespoons olive oil, salt, and pepper; then 2 lb. mixed fish is added and gently cooked until tender. The stock is then strained and may be served either clear, or with 1 cup cooked rice added. This is a typical Greek fish soup providing another course as well, for the fish itself is served at the same meal, surrounded by the vegetables and accompanied by *avgolémono* sauce if required.

psomi, Greek for bread. See also CHRISTOPSOMO; LAMBROPSOMO.

pstrąg, Polish for trout. See also TROUT.

pstrągi marynowane, marinated trout. A 6-lb. trout is sliced and added, with ½ pint (1¼ cups) dry white wine, 2 tablespoons wine vinegar, 12 peppercorns, and 2 bay leaves, to partly boiled onions and root vegetables, and the whole is then boiled gently for 10–15 minutes. Fish cooked in this way can be preserved for a long period if kept tightly covered and refrigerated.

ptarmigan (*Lagopus mutus*), a member of the grouse family, although it is sometimes referred to as rock partridge. Ptarmigan can be found all over northern Europe and Russia, although like many wild birds are becoming scarcer, and there is also an American variety (*L. rupestris*). In Britain they are now found only in Scotland, and are the only birds in the British Isles which produce white feathers in winter, discarding the grey-brown plumage of spring and summer. They are at their best for eating from September to October. All recipes that are suitable for grouse may be used, and although the ptarmigan is inferior to grouse in taste, it is nevertheless very good. See also RIEKKO; RYPE.

ptarmigan

puant macéré, a French cow's milk cheese made in Flanders. It is in season from October until May. Puant means "stinking," and it gives some indication of the strength of the cheese.

püchelsteiner fleisch, see PICHELSTEINER FLEISCH.

puchero, a Spanish national soup–stew. Raw lean beef and ham or chicken are cooked in water with chick-peas and seasoning. Some *chorizo* is added before the soup is finally cooked. It is served garnished with small dumplings, which are made with a mixture of chopped ham, bacon, eggs, breadcrumbs, and garlic, and are fried in oil. See also COCIDO.

pudding, a somewhat ambiguous term which can refer to several very different things. The etymology of the word pudding is obscure. The Oxford dictionary suggests the French *boudin* (black pudding), but when this word was first in use in Scotland in the 13th century, the word "poding" was already current in England. I. The word pudding is still current in the British Isles as a general description of one particular course of a meal, that is, the sweet or dessert course. The content can vary from a light soufflé to a Christmas pudding. However, when used in this way, pudding does not necessarily imply that the sweet dish is a cooked one, although it often is. There are many traditional English cooked puddings—bread pudding, Canterbury pudding, Cheltenham pudding, Chester pudding, Chichester pudding, diplomate pudding, Exeter pudding, Gotham pudding, hasty pudding, Manchester pudding, Monmouth pudding, muffin pudding, queen of puddings, and summer pudding—but many other dishes are served for the pudding course which do not include the word pudding in their title. II. Sometimes the word pudding denotes a suet crust containing fruit, such as apple or plum, with sugar. This is always boiled or steamed for 2–3 hours, and served with custard or cream. Correctly, it should be called a boiled pudding. It can also consist of short crust pastry entirely enclosing peeled and cored fruit with sugar or jam, which is either baked in the oven or wrapped in a floured cloth and boiled. Suet crust, with raisins, sultanas, sugar, and a pinch of mixed spice either boiled or steamed in a cloth or basin, is called Spotted Dick. III. Another form of steamed pudding is made with a sponge mixture which is steamed in a buttered basin, with the top covered, for 1½ hours. This is called castle pudding, also guards' pudding. IV. Various cereals such as rice, sago, semolina, and tapioca, cooked slowly in the oven with milk, sugar, and flavourings such as vanilla, lemon peel, or bay leaf, are called milk puddings. Proportions are ¼ lb. (½ cup generous) of whatever cereal is used to 1 quart (4 cups) milk, with sugar to taste. A nut of butter and 2 eggs may be added to enrich the pudding, but this is not usual. It should be cooked in a slow oven for 1½–2 hours, when it will be very creamy. It is often served with stewed fruit and given to children and elderly people. Macaroni is also used, and flavoured with grated nutmeg. V. There are also savoury puddings. When properly prepared, these stand as examples of traditional English regional food at its best. The savoury pudding consists of a suet crust lining in a pudding basin, filled, up, popularly, with diced beef and kidney, sometimes 3 or 4 oysters, seasoning, and water or stock to cover, and with more suet crust on top to make a lid. It is tied down with greaseproof paper, foil, or a cloth, and boiled (with boiling water reaching to just under the rim) or steamed for at least 3–4 hours. It is served with more hot water poured into the very concentrated stock, to dilute it a little. The pure essence of the meats is so delicious that no addition of onions or herbs is necessary. Game, both furred and feathered, is also used, and a boiled savoury pudding is an excellent way of using up elderly game birds. It is also made with pickled pork and onion in some parts of Britain, particularly East Anglia. In Kent a similar pudding is made with a jointed chicken (the skin and bone removed), ½ lb. chopped pickled belly of pork, and 1 tablespoon chopped parsley. The basin is filled and the ingredients covered with chicken stock before the pastry lid is put on. The pudding is boiled or steamed for 3 hours and then served with parsley sauce. This is Kentish chicken pudding, and a regular feature on the menu of one of London's most famous old restaurants specialising in British food. Fish puddings are popular in Scandinavia. See FISK. VI. Yorkshire pudding is a batter cooked in the oven in dripping, and served with roast beef. See YORKSHIRE PUDDING. VII. Black and white puddings are not puddings in any of the senses outlined here, but are types of blood sausage. See also BUDINO; BUDYN; POUDING; PUDIM; PUDÍN.

puddinghos a pienu, a Sardinian dish consisting of roast chicken stuffed with the chopped giblets and herbs.

pudim, Portuguese for pudding. The Portuguese make many types of pudding; nuts, eggs, and fruit are the most common ingredients. *Pudim flan* is crème caramel. See also OVOS, NEVADOS; RABANADAS.

pudim de bananas, 6 bananas are simmered for 10 minutes in water to cover, then drained, mashed, and mixed with 2 tablespoons butter, 3 tablespoons white wine, 6 oz. (¾ cup) sugar, and 2 eggs. The mixture is poured into a greased mould and baked in a *bain-marie* for 30 minutes. It is served hot or cold.

pudim de nozes, 8 oz. shelled ground walnuts is mixed with ½ teaspoon mixed spice and beaten with 6 egg yolks and 8 oz. (1 cup) sugar. Finally 3 stiffly beaten egg whites are added, and the mixture is put into a greased mould and steamed for 1 hour. It is served cold.

pudim de ovos à moda de coimbra, 12 oz. (1½ cups) sugar and ¼ pint (½ cup) water are boiled to a syrup; then 9 eggs are beaten in, and the mixture is flavoured with 2 tablespoons port wine. It is poured into a well-greased mould and baked in a bowl of water in the oven for 1 hour. Flavourings vary, and cinnamon, lemon, or orange juice are sometimes added.

pudín, Spanish for pudding. Puddings are not eaten very much in Spain, fresh fruit or ice cream being preferred. The puddings that are served have a milk and egg base, like crème caramel, which is called flan in the south of Spain. See also DULCE DE LECHE.

puff-ball, the popular name for a group of edible fungi, comprising the two genera *Lycoperdon* and *Calvatia,* which resemble snowballs. *C. gigantea,* the giant puff-ball, is the largest British fungus and is often the size of a football; specimens with a 40-inch circumference are not uncommon. *C. caelata,* the mosaic puff-ball, is a much smaller fungus, generally 3–5 inches across, and is very good to eat when young. *L. perlatum,* the common puff-ball, is about the size of a small golf-ball, and also makes very good eating when fresh. Two puff-balls that are often used for drying are *L. pyriforme,* the stump puff-ball, the only one of the group which grows on tree-stumps, and the very small, brownish, spiny puff-ball (*L. echinatum*), which is found in beech woods. All puff-balls must be eaten while young and white. They are delicious sliced, dipped in egg and breadcrumbs, and fried. See also MUSHROOM.

puff pastry, see PASTRY.

pui, Rumanian for chicken. See also CHICKEN.

pui cu ciuperci, a Rumanian recipe for chicken with mushrooms. A young chicken is cut into pieces and fried in butter until it begins to change colour. Then 1 tablespoon flour is added, and when it has browned, about 2 cups stock are included and stirred well. Next 1 lb. chopped mushrooms is added, also a sliced onion, a little chopped dill and parsley, and finally 1 glass (½ cup) white wine. All is covered and simmered until the sauce is quite thick. Sour cream is sometimes served with this dish.

puits d'amour, small French cakes made from *pâte feuilletée* cut in 3-inch rounds, with a small circle cut in the centre as for a *vol-au-vent.* When cooked and cool, they are filled with either thick gooseberry jelly or *crème pâtissière.*

pularda, Polish for fattened, neutered hen. See also KAPŁON.

pularda à la Newa, Polish for chicken à la Neva (see POULET), which is cold chicken set in a jellied white sauce and garnished with truffles. The bird is served on a bed of cold rice with a French dressing. See also KURITSA, NEVSKAYA.

pularda duszona z szynką, chicken simmered with strips of ham in a mixture of broth and white wine.

pulë, Albanian for chicken, which is often served boiled with *kabuní.*

pullataikina or *pulla,* a yeasted dough used in Finland, both as a bread and often as a yeast pastry for tarts, *mustikkapiirakka,* or cheesecake. See also RAHKAPIIRAKKA. To prepare the dough ½ tablespoon yeast is mixed with ½ pint (1 cup) warm milk and 4 tablespoons flour. When this mixture has bubbled, 1 teaspoon salt, 1 beaten egg, 4 tablespoons sugar, 6 oz. (¾ cup) melted butter, and 1 lb. (4 cups) flour (less the small amount used earlier) are added. All are well mixed, and then the dough is covered and left for about 1 hour in a warm place to double its size. It is again kneaded, and left again for 30 minutes to rise before being made into a tart, pie, pasty, etc., and baked in a hot oven. If it is to be used for savoury pasties, or pies, the sugar is omitted. See also YEAST DOUGH.

vehnänen eli pulla, a traditional sweet loaf, made with the pulla dough. It is shaped into a long thick plait, which is brushed with beaten egg and sprinkled with either sugar or chopped almonds, then baked for 20–30 minutes in a moderate-to-hot oven. It is usually served with tea or coffee, like a cake.

pulled bread, originally this was bread taken from the oven about 10 minutes before it was cooked, the crust cut, and the dough pulled out in chunks which were then dried in the oven until golden brown. Nowadays, pulled bread is made by slicing shop bread very thinly, and drying these slices in a low oven until golden brown. Pulled bread has a pleasant rusk-like texture, and is excellent with cheese. It is not unlike melba toast, but the slices are slightly thicker. Pulled bread can also be made by pulling the dough from a very new loaf and drying the chunks in the oven.

pullet, a young female fowl, and, more particularly, a chicken from the time she begins to lay until the first moult. Pullets are often specially fattened, and they make excellent eating. The word is derived from the Latin *pullus,* a young animal.

pulpety, Polish for small balls or croquettes.

pulpety z łoju lub szpiku, marble-sized balls made from ¼ lb. beef marrow sieved with 2 egg yolks, 2 tablespoons breadcrumbs, salt, pepper, and the stiffly beaten egg whites. They are rolled in flour and poached in boiling salted water until they rise to the top, then used as a garnish for soups or tripe (*flaki*).

pulpety z mięsa, as above, but with the addition of ¼ lb. minced beef, pork, veal, or venison, and using unseparated eggs. They are made slightly larger than the standard type, and are served as an entrée.

pulpety z mózgu, as above, but made with calf's brains (1 set), 1 tablespoon minced onion, 4 tablespoons breadcrumbs, 3 tablespoons chopped mushrooms, dill, parsley, 2 eggs, and a pinch of nutmeg. They are served with white sauce.

pulpo, Spanish for octopus. When small, it is cooked like chocos. See also OCTOPUS.

pulse, the seeds of a pod-bearing plant. In culinary usage the name is given to dried vegetables such as beans, peas, split peas, and lentils.

pultost, the best-known soft Norwegian cheese, made from sour skimmed cow's milk. Sometimes sour buttermilk is added to increase the acidity. When the whey has been drained off, the curd is broken up and salted. Sometimes thick cream is added, and also caraway seeds. The cheese is ready to eat after a few days, but it can be stored and ripened for future use. The paste is pale yellow in colour when fresh, but it becomes darker as it matures. In different parts of the country it is also known as *knaost* and *ramost.* See also OST.

pumpernickel, a heavy black bread from Westphalia, Germany. It is made from 1½ lb. (6 cups) unhusked rye flour, 1 oz. yeast, 1 teaspoon salt, 1 pint (2 cups) warm milk, and sometimes 2 tablespoons butter or fat. It is often sold very thinly sliced, in packets or tins, and is very good served with smoked sausages or with cheese or butter. It is also called schwartzbrot (black bread). One story explains the name as a corruption of the phrase "pain pour Nicole." Napoleon I's

horse, Nicole, is said to have been very fond of black bread, and Napoleon therefore frequently demanded "pain pour Nicole," which eventually became "Pumpernickel." See also GÖTTERSPEISE.

pumpkin, the name applied generally in England to all sub-species of the family *Cucurbitaceae,* which in the U.S. are called squashes. Their sweetish orange-coloured flesh is rich in vitamins, and they are used for soups, with a good stock, onion, and a pinch of cinnamon added, and as a vegetable. More specifically, the name is given to the gourd-like fruit of the pumpkin-vine or pompion (*C. pepo*), which is extensively cultivated in the U.S. as a vegetable, and is used for making the pumpkin pies that are traditionally eaten on Thanksgiving Day. It is also used for jam. See also BUNDEVA; DYNIA; TIKVA; VEGETABLE MARROW.

pumpkin

pumpkin pie, a traditional North American dish which consists of 1 lb. (2 cups) cooked mashed pumpkin mixed with 1 lb. (2 cups) brown sugar, 2 teaspoons cinnamon, a pinch of nutmeg, salt, 3 eggs, and ½ pint (1 cup) cream, all baked in a 12-inch pastry shell.

punchnep, a Welsh dish made with root vegetables, nep being the Old English word for root. Equal quantities of potato and turnip are cooked separately in boiling salted water. When drained, they are mashed with butter and pepper, then thoroughly mixed. The mixture is put into a warmed dish and small holes are poked in the top into which cream is poured. It should look like alabaster, with small creamy pools. See also NEEP.

puntarelle, an Italian weed with a thick stalk and spiky leaves which is used a lot in salads, especially in Rome.

puolukkaliemi, a Finnish fruit compote similar to the Russian *kissel,* made from wild cranberries, called lingonberries, thickened with potato flour. Cloudberries are sometimes used.

purée, the French culinary term, now also in general use in English-speaking countries, for a preparation made by mashing and sieving certain foodstuffs, animal or vegetable. The food may be raw or cooked, but a purée is usually made from cooked food, or raw food that is easily mashed, like soft fruit. Nowadays a perfect purée can be made in a matter of seconds with an electric blender or liquidiser; the hand-operated *mouli* (food mill) is also extremely useful for this purpose. Whatever the ingredient to be puréed, the basic principle is always the same; further preparation depends on the nature of the ingredient and the dish for which the purée is destined. Fruit and vegetable purées are sometimes eaten just as they are, though cream may be added to a fruit purée if the recipe calls for it, and butter or *sauce béchamel* are often added to a vegetable purée. Brown sauce is usually blended with any meat purée; and in many cases, purées of such ingredients as meat, shellfish, fish, game, etc., are made in order to be used in the preparation of sauces, soups, garnishes, or quenelles. In France if the word purée is used without a noun, it usually means mashed potatoes. Both tomato purée and chestnut purée are sold commercially in tubes or tins. The tomato purée is very concentrated, and must be diluted with water to the desired strength.

purée chevreuse, see CHERVIL.

purée de cervelles, cooked brains, rubbed through a fine sieve or electrically blended, mixed with 1 cup *sauce béchamel* or velouté to each set of brains, and combined over heat. It is used as a garnish for poached eggs, a filling for pastry cases, or as forcemeat for chicken, mushrooms, artichoke bottoms, etc.

purée de foie, liver turned in butter, sieved and cooked, seasoned, and used for canapés or forcemeat.

purée de volaille, poached chicken, sieved or blended, then mixed with one third its weight of sauce velouté and ½ cup cream. It is used for garnishes or *bouchées,* for *vol-au-vents,* or as a stuffing for vegetables. It is also called purée à la reine.

purée dubarry, a cauliflower is trimmed, steamed, drained, and rubbed through a sieve; one quarter the amount of mashed potato is added, and the 2 ingredients are mixed thoroughly together over a slow heat. Then ¼ cup butter is added, with 1 tablespoon fresh cream. The purée is seasoned with pepper and salt and served with little pieces of fried bread.

Purim, a Jewish feast, also called the feast of Esther, and the feast of dots, which falls on the 14th day of Adar. It commemorates the downfall of Haman, minister of King Ahasuerus of Persia, who intrigued for the extermination of the Jews and was confounded by Esther, the king's wife, and her uncle Mordecai. In some Jewish communities in other coun-

tries the feast also symbolizes deliverance from other disasters.

Purim fritters, traditional Jewish fritters eaten at Purim. They are made from stale rounds of bread dipped in beaten egg and water, and fried on both sides in shallow hot oil. They are served hot, sprinkled with sugar and cinnamon or jam, like *pain perdu.* See also HAMANTASCHEN; NAHIT.

purre, Norwegian for leek. See also GRØNNSAKER; LEEK.

purre i form, a recipe for leek pudding from Bergen. A thin suet crust is made, to line a buttered mould, and this is filled with leeks cut to 1-inch lengths. Seasoning and nutmeg are sprinkled on top, and the basin is covered with a suet crust lid. The pudding is steamed for 2 hours and served immediately.

purslane (*Portulacaceae*), an annual herb which grows in both hemispheres. There are about 40 species, but the 2 principal types are common or winter purslane (*P. oleracea*), and garden purslane or rosemoss (*P. regelii* or *P. rosea*). The flowers vary through purple, pink, and yellow, the latter colour being that of *P. oleracea.* The leaves can be eaten as a salad, or cooked and served with cream and butter. They are also preserved in vinegar and used as a condiment. Purslane can be dried for winter use. In the U.S. it is known as portulaca. See also POURPIER.

puszta pörkölt, see PÖRKÖLT.

pusztadör, a Hungarian cow's milk cheese, semi-hard, and not unlike a *limbürger.*

puter, German for turkey. Turkey is not eaten generally in Germany, since goose is the bird cooked for festive occasions. *Truthahn* is the more common word for turkey-cock.

pytt-i-panna, a Swedish potato and cold meat hash, for which corned beef, veal, or ham are generally used. Sliced onions are browned in butter, then diced boiled potatoes are added, and lastly the chopped cold meat. All are heated up, and a little meat gravy or stock is added. The mixture is garnished with poached or fried eggs on top, and served with pickled beetroot. The dish is possibly the origin of the corned beef hash served in the U.S. See also HASH, CORNED BEEF.

qara baghii m'mimli, a Maltese dish of small marrows or courgettes (zucchini) stuffed with rice, herbs, and minced (ground) meat, then baked for about 30 minutes. Eggplant is also prepared in the same way.

qarita, a Maltese stew made from octopus or cuttlefish. It is first sautéed in olive oil, then simmered with sliced onions, tomatoes, parsley, and mint. See also OCTOPUS.

quaglia, Italian for quail. See also QUAIL.

quaglie alla milanese, quails split down the back and flattened, dipped in egg and breadcrumbs mixed with grated Parmesan cheese, then fried in butter.

quaglie alla piemontese, quails browned in butter, then cooked with ¼ pint (½ cup) white wine, 1 bay leaf per bird, and seasoning. They are served with risotto mixed with diced sautéed quail or chicken livers and white Italian truffles. It is also called risotto con quaglie.

quaglie alla Rossini, boned quails stuffed with goose liver truffé, roasted, and then served on a fried slice of goose liver, covered with sauce madère and garnished with sliced truffle.

quagliette di vitello, an Italian veal dish, meaning literally "little veal quails." Thinly sliced squares of veal are seasoned and sprinkled with lemon juice; a slice of ham of the same size is put on top of each, and each is then rolled up and encased in a thin rasher of bacon. The "quails" are threaded on skewers, alternating with a thin slice of raw onion, a sage leaf, and a small cube of stale bread. The skewers are then put in a fireproof dish, sprinkled with oil or fat, and baked in a very hot oven until cooked. They should be turned over at least once during cooking, and are served on a bed of boiled rice. See also SALTIMBOCCA.

quahog (*Venus mercenaria*), the round American clam found all down the eastern seaboard of the U.S. It has an excellent flavour and can be cooked as clam or scallop. See also CLAM.

quail (*Coturnix coturnix*), a migratory game bird from India and tropical Africa. At one time quails nested in the British Isles, but now they are imported live from Egypt, and fattened before being put on the market. They are rarely, if ever, caught here in their wild state now. The author Norman Douglas recalls that, about 50 years ago, there used to be a wholesale slaughter of these little birds whenever their flocks passed over Capri on the migratory journey from Egypt. He adds that they seem to have learnt of the fate awaiting them,

quail

for nowadays their route does not include Capri. In the U.S., the words "partridge" and "quail" are interchangeable, but the latter is generally used to refer to the bobwhite or the massena quail or partridge.

Quail should be eaten the day after it has been killed, or as soon after as possible. It should be plucked and singed, the head and neck removed, and then the trail drawn from the neck opening. Although a much smaller bird than the partridge, and therefore requiring less cooking time, quail can be prepared and cooked in the same way. In China and Japan quail's eggs are a great delicacy, and they are served either boiled, or hard-boiled and then shelled and set in aspic. See also CAILLE; CODORNIZ; PRZEPIÓRKI; QUAGLIA; WACHTEL.

quamash (*Camassia quamash*), also called camass by the Indians on the west coast of the U.S. The bulbs of this plant are the staple food of the indigenous Indian tribes, for they can be boiled and roasted, and may also be dried and ground into a kind of flour like cassava.

quargel (*käse*), an Austrian cheese made in the western province of Austria from whole sour milk. It is a small cheese weighing about 2 oz., and is covered by a reddish or yellow waxy skin. The paste is smooth, pale yellow outside and white in the centre. It has a pungent smell and a sharp taste.

quark, German for cottage cheese. Two German cheeses that fall into this category are *sauermilchquark,* made with sour milk, and *labquark.*

quarkkoch, a German cheesecake mould, made from 4 oz. (1 cup) cottage cheese, mixed with 3 tablespoons butter which has been beaten with 3 tablespoons fine sugar and 4 egg yolks. Then 1 tablespoon finely chopped almonds, 1 tablespoon currants, and the grated peel of ½ lemon are added, and finally the 4 beaten egg whites are folded in. The mixture is then steamed in a buttered mould for 1½ hours. Quarkkoch is sometimes served with lemon sauce.

quarktorte, cottage cheese is creamed with butter, sugar, and egg yolks, as above, and flavoured with lemon, cinnamon, and a few currants; then the stiffly beaten egg whites are folded in. The mixture is put into a short crust pastry shell, and the torte is baked in a slow oven. It is eaten cold.

quart, le, a French cow's milk cheese of the *maroilles* type. It is square in shape, and has a good flavour.

quartier, the French butchery term for a quarter of a carcase of beef. The front quarter includes the shoulder and sides of the animal, while the hind quarter includes the sirloin and thigh. The inedible parts of a slaughtered animal, such as the hide, hoofs, horns and tallow, are sometimes called the "fifth quarter."

quartirolo, an Italian soft cow's milk cheese made during the autumn in Lombardy. It is a form of *taleggio.*

quasi, a French cut of veal, taken from the chump or rump end of the loin. In American veal butchery it corresponds roughly to the loin steak cut, and is equivalent to the sirloin cut in beef. It is also called cul in French. See diagram page xxiv.

quatre épices, French for allspice and also for the mixture of spices; also *toute-épice,* and *poivre de la Jamaïque.* It is known as *quatre épices* because its flavour is not unlike a mixture of clove, cinnamon, nutmeg, and pepper. In former times, each grocer would make up bags of mixed spices according to his own formula. The usual proportions were 4 oz. ground white pepper to ⅓ oz. powdered cloves, 1 oz. ginger, and 1¼ oz. ground nutmeg. Home cooks should make smaller amounts for flavouring meats or stews, as the volatile oils evaporate quickly, and the flavour is lost.

quatre mendiants, an old-fashioned French dessert, consisting of a plate of dried figs, raisins, filberts, and peeled almonds. The name commemorated the four chief orders of mendicant friars: Franciscans, Dominicans, Augustinians, and Carmelites. It is also called mendiants.

quatre-quarts, a French household cake. The name means "four quarters," and was obviously inspired by the recipe for the cake, which consists of equal quantities of flour, butter, and sugar and the weight of one of these in eggs (the weight of an average egg is 2½ oz.). It is flavoured with orange, lemon, or a liqueur. Pound cake is the English equivalent.

queen of puddings, a 19th-century English pudding, still eaten today. It is made by infusing the peel of 1 lemon in ½ pint (1 cup) warm milk, then straining the milk into a bowl and adding 2 heaped tablespoons white breadcrumbs, 1 tablespoon sugar, and 1 tablespoon butter, stirring well. Then 2 beaten egg yolks are added, and the mixture is poured into a buttered pie-dish, left to stand for 30 minutes, then baked in a moderate oven for 20–25 minutes or until set. When cooked, the pudding is spread first with a red jam, then with meringue, which is made by folding 1 heaped tablespoon sugar into the 2 stiffly beaten egg whites. Finally the meringue is dusted with sugar, and the pudding is put in a slow oven until the meringue is set and lightly browned.

queen scallop, see SCALLOP.
Queensland nut, see MACADAMIA.
queijo, Portuguese for cheese. See ALENTEJO; AZEITÃO; BOLA; CABREIRO; CARDIGA; CASTELO BRANCO; CASTELO DE VIDE; ILHA; RABAÇAL; SALOIO; SERRA; TOMAR.

queijadas de évora, small Portuguese cheesecakes. Shells of short crust pastry are filled with a mixture of ½ lb. cottage cheese, 6 egg yolks, 1 egg white, 4 oz. (½ cup) sugar, ¼ cup melted butter, and 1 heaped tablespoon flour. They are baked in a moderate oven for 25 minutes.

quenelle, the French term, used also in English, for a fine fish or meat dumpling. The origin of the word is obscure, although it is possibly derived from the Anglo-Saxon knyllar (to pound). Since the quenelle has been popular in Scotland for several hundred years, and Quennell is a recognized Scottish surname, it is also possible that the quenelle may originally have been a Franco–Scottish dish, like *howtowdie.*

To call the quenelle a dumpling is almost an insult, for its texture is extremely fine. In order to achieve this, the ingredients are pounded in a mortar (or electrically blended) before sieving. Chicken, fish, game, veal, and potato may all be used for quenelles. Pike is much used in places inland in France, but in Scotland trout is preferred because it produces a far finer texture. See also MOUSSELINE, FORCEMEAT. Quenelles are made in various shapes, in small sausage- or cork-shapes, or in a larger oval which is poached in a special oval mould. They can be served as an entrée, in patties, soups, and *timbales.* When large, they may be decorated with truffles, diced tongue, etc., and used as a garnish for a large braised fish. Small quenelles are used in such garnishes as *financière, godard, lucullus, régence, toulousaine,* etc. Very small nut-sized quenelles used as a garnish for soup are poached only. The following is a general recipe.

First 1 lb. raw chopped chicken, fish, game, or veal, or a mixture of 1½ lb. foie gras and ½ lb. chicken, is rubbed through a fine sieve or put through an electric blender. Half this weight of bread *panade* is added, and all are pounded in a mortar, then sieved or blended again. Gradually 3 beaten egg yolks are added (4 if the eggs are small), together with salt, pepper, and a hint of mace. This mixture should be well beaten, on ice if possible, or in an ice-cold bowl. Then it is made into several small shapes or one large oval one, and these are poached in boiling salted water until they swell and rise to the surface. (The single large quenelle is poached inside a special oval mould.) Finally the quenelles are drained and coated with either a sauce crème or a sauce velouté.

quenelles à la florentine, made from chicken and served with puréed spinach flavoured with a little grated nutmeg.

quenelles de brochet à la lyonnaise, made as described above, using boned, skinned, and pounded pike. They are served either with sauce espagnole, with olives, sliced mushrooms, and truffles added; with sauce *normande;* or put into a buttered baking dish, masked with sauce mornay, sprinkled with grated cheese, and browned under a grill.

quenelles de foie gras, made from ½ lb. raw foie gras, pounded and sieved, mixed with half as much raw, pounded chicken breast and the same of bread *panade.* It is all sieved or blended, then 2 egg yolks are added gradually, also a pinch of nutmeg, and seasoning. Spoonfuls are poached in boiling salted water. They are served with melted butter and sprinkled with breadcrumbs.

quenelles de pommes de terre, 5 or 6 medium-sized potatoes are boiled, mashed, and passed through a sieve. Then 3 well-beaten egg yolks, a dusting of nutmeg, salt and pepper, and 2 tablespoons melted butter are beaten in; then 3 stiffly beaten egg whites are folded lightly in, and the mixture is formed into small sausage-shapes which are poached in boiling bouillon or milk until they rise to the surface. The quenelles are drained, and served with a thick fresh tomato sauce or sauce béchamel.

quenelles de pommes de terre à l'alsacienne or *floutes,* as above, but served with *beurre noisette* mixed with a handful of breadcrumbs. See also FLOUTES.

quenelles de pommes de terre au parmesan, as *quenelles de pommes de terre,* but sprinkled with grated Parmesan cheese and melted butter, then browned under a grill.

quenelles of grouse, a Scottish recipe of ½ lb. raw grouse or other game meat is pounded well with ¼ lb. (½ cup) butter and 2 cups breadcrumbs which have previously been soaked in milk and squeezed dry. Then the whole is passed twice through a sieve or mincer; 1 egg yolk is added and the mixture pounded again; then 2 more egg yolks, salt, pepper, and a little grated nutmeg are added. Finally 2 of the egg whites, stiffly whisked, are folded into the mixture, and it is moulded into little shapes which are laid in a saucepan and covered with buttered paper. Boiling stock or water is poured over, and the quenelles are poached gently for 10 minutes, then served with peas cooked with a few chopped mushrooms. See also GROUSE.

quern, a stone hand-mill for grinding corn. It was made from 2 circular stones, with a hole in the centre of the upper stone through which corn was fed, and it was turned with a wooden handle. The meal came down onto a wide tray, and by means of a wooden spindle was ground coarse or fine, as required. The quern was in common use in the Highlands of Scotland in the 19th century, and is perhaps still used occasionally today in remote areas in various parts of the world. See also FLOUR.

queso, Spanish for cheese. See BURGOS; CABRALES; CEBRERO; CINCHO; QUESO DE BOLA; QUESO DE CABRA; QUESO MANCHEGO; RONCAL; SAN SIMÓN; TETA; ULLOA; VILLALÓN.

queso de bola, a Spanish cheese made from cow's milk. It resembles the red Dutch edam, and is good when fresh, but tends to dry up when kept.

queso de cabra, a Spanish cheese made from goat's milk. It is very good when freshly made.

queso manchego, a Spanish cheese made from ewe's milk. It gets its name from the vast central plateau of La Mancha, where enormous numbers of Churra and Manchego sheep eke out a bare existence. It is a salted, rennetted, pressed, and fermented hard cheese, with a yellow rind at top and bottom. Plaited esparto grass is used to line the cheese moulds, and the imprint of it is left on the sides of the cheese. The paste can be white or yellow, with a lot of small eyes, or with none. This is due to the fact that it is usually farm-made, and as the standards of the farms vary, so does the quality and appearance of the cheese. The best comes from the vicinity of Ciudad Real. It is over 4 feet high and cylindrical in shape. Queso manchego is the most popular Spanish cheese, and has been produced since the 16th century.

quetsche, a member of the plum family, grown extensively in Alsace-Lorraine. See ZWETSCHE.

queue, French for tail. *Queue de boeuf* is oxtail, often braised in France, either à la *jardinière* or à la *printanière,* sometimes with a little red wine added to the stock. Oxtail is also used in some pot-au-feu recipes.

queue de boeuf des vignerons, oxtail as cooked by the vine growers. Chopped and defatted oxtails are first browned in oil, then laid in a pan on a bed of sliced onion, carrot, and 4 oz. chopped salt pork, with 2 bay leaves, parsley, thyme, garlic, salt, pepper, a pinch of mace, and stock to cover. All are simmered for about 20 minutes. Then 2 lb. seeded white grapes are added, the pan is tightly covered, and the contents are cooked in a very slow oven for 4 hours or until the meat is

tender. The vegetables and fruit are puréed and served as a sauce. See also OX (OXTAIL STEW).

queue de porc, pig's tail. The bones are usually removed so that the tail becomes a long bag. This is stuffed with pork forcemeat, tied with string, and braised in a little stock.

queue de porc grillée, as above, but pressed under a weight, brushed with melted butter, rolled in breadcrumbs, and slowly grilled on all sides.

queyras, see CHAMPOLÉON.

quiche, a regional dish of ancient origin from Lorraine, France. Formerly it was an open flan, made from bread dough, with a variety of fillings. Nowadays the dough is replaced by *pâte brisée,* and the most popular quiche is a savoury one known as *quiche lorraine.* All other quiches take their name from the main ingredient of the filling.

quiche à l'oignon, thinly sliced, soft, golden, fried onions replace the bacon and are covered with the cream and egg mixture (as for *quiche lorraine*).

quiche au fromage, thin slices of Gruyère cheese replace the bacon, and are covered with the cream and egg mixture (as for *quiche lorraine*).

quiche au fromage blanc, filled with ¼ pint (½ cup) cream and ½ lb. fresh cream cheese beaten together, then the eggs added.

quiche au jambon, lean ham replaces the bacon, and is covered with the cream and egg mixture (as for *quiche lorraine*).

quiche aux pruneaux, filled with cooked, sweetened *zwetsches,* with a very little of the juice. About 5 minutes before the quiche is removed from the oven, a mixture of 1 egg beaten with 2 tablespoons thick cream is poured over, and this is cooked until the top is golden. Quiche aux pruneaux is also called *féouse, tourte,* or *flan* in different parts of the province of Lorraine.

quiche lorraine, an 8-inch flan tin is lined with *pâte brisée.* Then 6 rashers of streaky bacon are laid in first, followed by a mixture of ½ pint (1 cup) thick cream mixed with 3 egg yolks, plus 1 whole egg well beaten and seasoned. The quiche is baked in a moderate oven for about 30 minutes, or until set, when it should be puffed up and the top golden brown. It can be eaten straight away, or when cold. Sometimes it is garnished with crisp bacon rolls.

quiche lorraine

quignon, French for a big wedge of bread cut from a large French loaf.

quillet, a French cake. To prepare it 15 eggs are whisked over gentle heat with 1 lb. (2 cups) vanilla-flavoured sugar and a pinch of salt. When slightly thickened, this is removed from the heat and beaten until almost cold. Then 1 lb. (4 cups) sieved flour and 1 lb. (2 cups) melted butter are thoroughly blended in. Finally 2 round 8-inch cake tins, well greased, are filled with the mixture, and the cakes are baked in a moderate oven for 35 minutes. When cool they are sandwiched together with a thick almond-flavoured *crème patissière* and decorated on top.

quinad, a vegetable stew traditionally eaten on Good Friday on the island of Ibiza. *Verdura,* the local wild green vegetable, is mixed with the leaves of chard and *guisias* and boiled in salted water until cooked. The vegetables are then drained, and served covered with a mixture of fresh lukewarm water, a little olive oil, salt, and pepper. It is a curious, almost penitential dish.

quince (*Cydonia vulgaris*), the fruit of small trees or shrubs which are native to the Mediterranean region and the Caucasus. The quince was cultivated in parts of Europe before the Christian era and was brought to Rome by the Greeks, who called it the "golden apple" and thought it a symbol of love and happiness. Chaucer referred to it as "coine" from the French *coing.* Quinces were brought to the U.S. by the early Spanish, French, and English settlers.

Quinces cannot be eaten raw, but they have an attractive honey-like flavour when cooked. They make excellent jams and jellies because of their mucilaginous and demulcent properties. One quince added to apple jelly or strawberry jam improves the flavour and the setting quality. Quinces also make good tarts and pies, either alone or with other fruit. In the 18th and 19th centuries in Britain, they were cooked with, and served as an accompaniment to, casseroled partridge, and they are still cooked with beef in Rumania. Unfortunately they are seldom on the market nowadays, but the trees grow freely in temperate climates. See also COTIGNAC; GUTUI; MEMBRILLO; QUITTE.

quinnat salmon (*Oncorhynchus tschawytscha*), the most common species of Pacific salmon. It is used extensively for canning. See also PACIFIC SALMON.

quitte, German for quince. A thick quince jam is also made in

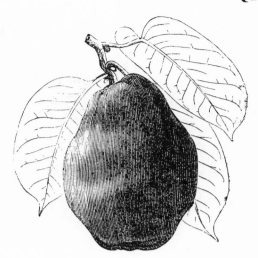

quince

Germany, and a quince paste called *quittenbrot,* which is prepared in the same way as *cotignac.* See also QUINCE.

quitten in kognak, quinces are cooked in water to cover for 15 minutes only, and are then cooled, strained (the liquor being reserved), and peeled. Half the weight of the fruit in sugar is added to the liquor, and just melted; then the fruit is put back in the syrup and left to stand for 24 hours. The syrup is then strained off and the fruit is placed in large preserving jars. The syrup is first boiled up, then mixed with half its quantity of brandy, and this solution is poured over the quinces so that they are well covered. When cool, the jars are tied down. The jars are kept for about three months before being opened.

quofte, Albanian meat balls, usually made from minced mutton.

quofte me mente, a speciality of meat balls flavoured with fresh mint and cinnamon.

R

rabaçal, queijo de, a Portuguese cheese made from ewe's milk, or a mixture of ewe's and goat's milk, in the neighbourhood of Coimbra. It is mild and creamy, about 5 inches in diameter, and cylindrical in shape. See also QUEIJO.

rabanadas, a delicious Portuguese pudding, made with 1 teaspoon cinnamon, ¼ lb. (½ cup) honey, 1 pint (2 cups) milk, 2 tablespoons sugar, peel of 1 lemon, and a pinch of salt are all gently simmered together for 1 hour. Slices of bread about 1½ inches thick are dipped first into this mixture, then into beaten egg, and are then fried slowly in oil on both sides. They are served hot, sprinkled with icing sugar and cinnamon. See also PUDIM.

rabarber, Danish for rhubarb. See also RHUBARB.

rabarberkage, a chilled sweet, consisting of a layer of macaroon biscuits sprinkled with sherry or rum, a layer of steamed and sweetened rhubarb flavoured with vanilla essence, and a layer of sweet rusks also sprinkled with rum or sherry. These layers are repeated until the dish is filled, and the sweet is then topped with whipped cream.

rabarberkompot, chilled cooked rhubarb, served in Denmark with roast chicken or veal. The rhubarb is chopped, and simmered in a double boiler with sugar to taste until the fruit is tender. (As no water is added to the rhubarb, the top saucepan of the boiler must be just rinsed and not dried, to prevent sticking.) Vanilla is used as flavouring, and the kompot is chilled before being used.

rabarber, Dutch for rhubarb. In Holland rhubarb is often used cooked and puréed as a sauce with roast chicken or pork. See also RHUBARB.

rabarber, Swedish for rhubarb. See also RHUBARB.

rabarberkräm, rhubarb cream. To prepare it 1 lb. rhubarb is peeled, and stewed with ½ inch of water, and sweetened to taste. When cooked, it is sieved, and 2 tablespoons corn flour (cornstarch) creamed with ½ pint (1 cup) water is added. The mixture is allowed to cook for several minutes, stirring all the time, and is then poured into a dish and served cold, with cream.

rabbit (*Lepus cuniculus*), a furry rodent, of African origin, formerly known in English as "cony" or "cavy." The rabbit is found all over the world, although the deliberate introduction of myxomatosis into Australia, France, and Britain in the 1950s eliminated much of the rabbit population. Many people are still wary of eating rabbit because of this disease, but fear of infected meat is in fact unfounded, as the disease immunised those rabbits that survived it.

wild rabbit

The flavour of rabbit depends on the age and diet of the animal (a bark-eating rabbit, when eaten in winter, is the most delicious). Rabbit is at its best when shot rather than snared, as prolonged death can cause toughness and loss of flavour. As with hare, a young rabbit can be recognized by the fact that its ears tear easily. Tame rabbits reared in hutches are larger and fatter than wild rabbit, but the flavour is milder. Rabbit pie made with a young jointed rabbit, a piece of diced bacon, a sliced onion, and stock or cider, all covered with pastry, was a succulent English country dish, now, alas, seldom seen. Young rabbit stuffed with bread and herbs and then baked is also excellent, and potted rabbit with layers of bacon or ham is worthy of the same praise as a good *pâté de campagne* in France. Rabbit stew, with onions, root vegetables, herbs, and water or cider to cover, is another English country dish. Rabbit is very gelatinous, and the stock gels well when cold. It therefore makes good cold jellied dishes such as galantine or mousse. Rabbit stock is a good basis for almost any soup. See also COELHO; CONEJO; CONIGLIO; HARE; IEPURE; KANIN; KANINCHEN; KONIJN; KOUNELI; LAPEREAU; LAPIN; LIEBRE.

rabbit-berry, see BUFFALO BERRY.

rabbit-fish (*Promethichthys prometheus*), a sea fish found at great depths in the Mediterranean and the Atlantic. It is rough-scaled, not unlike a mackerel, and related to the *escolar*. It is extremely good to eat.

rabiole, a variety of kohlrabi.

râble, French for saddle, but a word used exclusively for hare. See LIÈVRE.

rabotte, a French baked fruit dumpling, a speciality of Normandy, where it is also called douillon from the word douillette, a priest's overcoat. A peeled apple or pear is wrapped in short crust pastry sweetened with sugar, and then baked in a moderate oven for 45 minutes.

raccoon (*Procyon lotor*), a small mammal about the size of a badger, found throughout the U.S. It chiefly inhabits the vicinity of ponds and streams, and like the otter, washes all its food before eating it. It is a nocturnal animal, sleeping all day, hunting and being hunted only at night. It should be prepared in much the same way as opossum, being simmered for 30 minutes in boiling seasoned water before roasting. A dressed raccoon can weigh between 5 and 14 lb. To improve the flavour of raccoon, it is advisable to wrap the carcase in waxed paper and store it in a refrigerator for about 7 days at a temperature of 35°F (2°C). The age of the animal determines the method of cooking. The young animal is best stuffed with 1 lb. cooked mashed sweet potatoes, 2 peeled apples, 1 cup raisins, and 2 cups breadcrumbs, then roasted for 40 minutes per lb. Older animals must be put in the stewpot.

Rachel, I. A French garnish for tournedos and noisettes, named after the famous French actress of that name (1820–1858). Artichoke bottoms are simmered in butter and the cooked meat is set on top and decorated with ox marrow that has been poached, removed from the bone, and grilled and sliced, with chopped parsley and a red wine sauce. II. A French method of cooking fish. The fish is stuffed with fish forcemeat and sliced truffle, poached in white wine, and garnished with asparagus tips. The stock is thickened and poured over the fish. III. A French chicken consommé, thickened with tapioca and garnished with strips of artichoke bottom. Ox marrow on toast is served separately. See also CONSOMMÉ.

rack, the American term for rib chops in lamb and mutton when they are left in one piece for roasting.

raclette, I. A Swiss dish from the canton of Valais, consisting of *Valais* raclette cheese melted, and served hot with chopped raw white onion in vinegar and boiled potatoes. This is often served as a picnic meal; the large piece of cheese is placed over a wood fire to melt, and the hot creamy part is scraped onto a warm plate to be eaten with the onion and potato. II. A small wooden rake without teeth, like a scraper, used in Brittany to spread the batter for a crêpe while it is being cooked on the hot plate or griddle.

rácponty, a Hungarian fish dish made with a large whole carp, bacon, tomatoes, onions, parsnips, butter, paprika, and salt. The carp is placed on a baking dish, and incisions are made crossways along the back; then the other ingredients are cut into strips and pressed, in alternate rows, into the incisions. Melted butter is poured over, and it is placed in the oven for about 40 minutes, being basted with ½ pint (1 cup) sour cream. See also HAL.

racuszki, Polish potato puffs. They are made with 1 lb. mashed jacket-baked potatoes, 2 tablespoons butter, 2 tablespoons sour cream, 3 separated eggs, 2 tablespoons sugar, and

raclette

salt, all mixed together, the stiffly beaten egg whites being added last. This mixture is fried in spoonfuls in deep hot oil, and the puffs are served with sugar and sour cream. See also ZIEMNIAKI.

radicchie, Italian for radish. It is also called *rapanello*. The leaves are used in salads in Italy as well as the tubers, which are often used for garnish. See also RADISH.

radieschen, German for radish. There are many kinds of radish in Germany, the large black radish is often served as an accompaniment to beer, with bread and salt. See also RADISH.

radikia, a wild plant like a dandelion, but with pink tubers like a radish, found in the mountains of Greece. The plant grows to a height of about 4 inches, and has curly leaves; although these are rather bitter in flavour, they are much esteemed by the Greeks and are used by them for salads, and sometimes for serving with fish. The bulbous radish-like tubers are also eaten, for *mezes,* but they are rather small.

radis, French for radish. In France radishes are sometimes blanched in boiling salted water, then tossed in butter or cream. Radis noirs are black radishes. See also RADISH.

radis beurrés, raw radishes eaten with butter and salt. This is the most common way of serving radishes in France for a first course.

radish (*Raphanus sativus*), an annual or biennial plant, thought to be of oriental origin. There are many varieties, grown chiefly for their pungent peppery root. The shape and size of the root varies from the small nutlike, pink-and-white radish to the larger purple or black radish which can weigh up to 2 lb. or more. The latter is popular in Germany as well as in the East. The wild radish (*R. raphanistrum*) is frequently found along the Mediterranean coast, and sometimes in the British Isles. It is very peppery in taste and is sometimes used in place of horseradish. There is also a rat-tailed radish (*R. caudatus*) which has no edible root, but seed pods 8–12 inches long which are eaten fresh or pickled.

Radishes are usually eaten raw and peeled, with salt and butter or whole, or unpeeled and sliced in salads or for garnish. When cooked, they taste a little like turnips, but it is not usual for radishes to be eaten cooked in Britain. However a delicious soup can be made with scallops, radishes, and milk. It is served garnished with cream and parsley. See also RADICCHIE; RADIESCHEN; RADIS.

rådjurskött, Swedish for venison. The Swedish housewife leaves venison to stand for at least an hour before cooking, in

radish

a marinade composed of equal quantities of lemon juice and olive oil. See also VENISON.

rådjursgryta, stewed venison. First 3 lb. venison is cut in cubes and dipped in seasoned flour; it is then well browned in deep bacon fat. Chopped onion, celery, and parsley are included and fried until golden and tender; then meat and vegetables are transferred to a saucepan. Two pints (4 cups) water is added to the pan, with herbs and a bay leaf, and all are simmered for about 1½ hours, when ½ lb. diced salt pork and 2 cups diced potato are added. Cooking is continued until the potatoes are tender. Finally ¼ pint (½ cup) sour cream is sometimes added to the gravy.

rådjursstek, venison steaks. The steaks are dipped in seasoned flour and brushed with melted fat before being laid on a grilling-rack. Each side is grilled for up to 5 minutes under a moderate heat. They are served with cranberry or red currant jelly.

radolfzeller käse, see MAINAUER KÄSE.

rådyr, Danish for roe-deer which is eaten a good deal in Denmark. See also DYREKØLLE; ROEBUCK.

raekjur, Icelandic for shrimp or prawn. These are usually sold cooked and peeled, and are of good quality.

rafano, Italian for horseradish. See VERDE, SALSA.

raffiné, French for refined; the word does not necessarily imply adulteration.

rafraîchir, French for to refresh, which is commonly done in French restaurants. See also REFRESH, TO.

råg, Swedish for rye. See also RYE.

rågbröd, Swedish rye bread. To make it 2 tablespoons butter is creamed with ½ lb. (1 cup) brown sugar and ½ cup syrup or molasses and syrup mixed. Then 1 teaspoon caraway seeds, 1 teaspoon salt, and 2 pints (4 cups) tepid water are added, and the mixture is simmered in a saucepan for 2 or 3 minutes until the sugar is dissolved, then poured into a basin and left until lukewarm. Next 2 oz. yeast is dissolved in ½ cup tepid water, and this is stirred into the syrup mixture. When all are well blended, ¾ lb. (3 cups) rye flour and 1¼ lb. (5 cups) wheat flour are added. The dough is kneaded well on a floured board, then covered and left in a warm place. When it has doubled its volume, it is kneaded again lightly and shaped into 2 loaves, which are placed on a slightly greased tin and left again until they have doubled in size. The loaves are then baked in a moderate oven for about 1 hour. See also RYE, BREAD.

ragot, the French name for a wild boar which is more than 2 years old.

ragoule, a common French name for the edible fungus, agaric. It is an abbreviation of *barigoule.* See also MUSHROOM.

ragoût, a French word, also used in English, for a dish in which small pieces of meat, fish, or poultry are turned in fat, then cooked slowly with a little stock or water and seasoning. The spelling *ragoo* occurs in medieval English recipes, which would seem to imply that the word was introduced by the Normans. It comes from the French verb *ragoûter* (to revive the taste). In England it denotes a highly seasoned braise, but in France it means correctly a simple stew or braise which, however, can also be incorporated with various elaborate garnishes or sauces and used for filling pastry cases, patties, pies, timbales, and vol-au-vents. There are two types of ragoût, of which the *ragoût à brun* is the better known.

Various garnishes and sauces are added to both kinds of ragoût, the most usual being *banquière, cancalaise, financière, godard, nantua, périgourdine,* and *toulousaine.* In this case the ragoûts are usually cooked in ovenproof dishes, from which they are also served. *Moules à la marinière* is an example of a ragoût of shellfish.

ragoût à blanc or *ragoût à l'anglaise,* the meat, or other basic ingredient, is cubed and put in a sauté pan or ovenproof dish with alternate layers of sliced onion and potato. Herbs and seasoning are added, and enough stock or water barely to cover. The stock is brought to the boiling point, then the lid is put on and the cooking finished either in the oven or over a very low heat. The liquid should be almost absorbed by the time the meat is cooked, and no thickening agent is ever added. Meat cooked à la *boulangère* in France, and the Irish stew of Britain and Ireland, exemplify this method of cooking.

ragoût à brun or *brown ragoût.* The ragoût is thickened with flour, after the meat has been sautéed and before the liquid is added. Garlic, bouquet garni, and sometimes tomato sauce are included. If other vegetables are put in the dish becomes, strictly speaking, a *navarin* (in the case of mutton) or a dish of beef (fish, poultry, etc.) à la *printanière,* and is then best cooked in the oven.

ragoût, the French word is used unchanged in Polish.

ragoût z baraniny, ragoût of lamb. The shoulder and part of the breast are cut into pieces and turned in oil with root vegetables. A little flour is shaken over, then paprika, seasoning, and a spoonful of tomato purée are added, and the ragoût is moistened with equal quantities of red wine and water barely to cover. The ragoût is covered, and cooked gently in a slow-to-moderate oven for 2½ hours or until tender. About 30 minutes before it is ready, some peeled and parboiled potatoes are added.

ragoût z bruściku cielęcego, a dish of 3 lb. of breast of veal and 1 set of calf's brains or sweetbreads turned in butter to which sliced onion, celery, and Hamburg parsley root are added, together with a little water, and all are simmered for 1½ hours. A small cauliflower, mushrooms, and peas are sautéed in butter, sprinkled with flour, and moistened with 2 cups veal stock. These ingredients are mixed with the veal and sweetbreads, and finally 2 beaten egg yolks are stirred in. All are reheated, but not boiled because the ragoût would curdle. It is garnished with dumplings made from beef bone marrow (*pulpety poju lubszpiku*).

ragù, the correct name for salsa bolognese, which is made all over the world, sometimes in very inferior adaptations. In Bologna, where it is usually served in lasagne verdi, it consists of ½ lb. lean minced beef, ¼ lb. chicken livers, 3 oz. (2 slices) bacon or ham, 1 carrot, 1 onion, 1 celery stalk, 1 tablespoon tomato purée, ½ pint (1 cup) stock, a pinch of nutmeg, ¼ pint (½ cup) white wine, and seasoning all simmered until it is thick and succulent. Occasionally ½ pint (1 cup) cream is added for smoothness or, more traditionally, when the hens are laying well in the spring, the unlaid eggs that are found inside the hen are added with the chicken livers, and form golden globules when the sauce is cooked. It is said that this version of the sauce is seldom found outside Bologna; certainly it is not unusual to come across the very worst kind of substitute—left-over cold meat heated in a watered-down tomato purée. *Ragù* may accompany many kinds of pasta. If eaten with spaghetti or *tagliatelli,* it is mixed well with the pasta before serving. See also BOLOGNESE.

ragusano, a hard, whole cow's milk, drawn-curd cheese, which comes from Ragusa, Sicily. It matures in six months and is then eaten fresh. When old, it is used for grating. It is of the same type as *cacio a cavallo.*

rahat lokum or **lokum,** the world-famous Turkish delight. It is made with 1½ lb. (2½ cups) sugar and ½ pint (1 cup) water boiled together; then 4 oz. corn flour (cornstarch) creamed with water is added, followed by ½ teaspoon tartaric acid and 1 tablespoon rose water. All are well mixed, and sometimes chopped pistachio nuts are put in. The mixture is poured into a shallow tin, previously greased with almond oil, and when cool it is dusted with icing sugar. Turkish delight should never be made with gelatine, which imparts a totally spurious texture. See also LOUKOUMI.

rahkapiirakka, Finnish for *viilipiimä* cheesecake. *Pulla-taikina* dough is used for the case. For the filling, 1 lb. *viilipiimä* is baked, the whey strained off, and the curds beaten until smooth. Then 4 tablespoons each of cream and sugar, 2 beaten eggs, ½ cup raisins, and 2 teaspoons vanilla sugar are added and all mixed together. The *pulla* dough is shaped out on a large baking tray and the filling spread over it. The edges of the dough are turned over to make a ¾-inch rim, and the cheesecake is baked in a moderate oven for 40 minutes. It is served with tea or coffee. Small individual cheesecakes, in the shape of round tartlets, are also made.

rahmkäse, an Austrian farmhouse cream cheese seldom found in towns or cities. It is usually salted and slightly soured.

raidir, a French culinary term meaning to seal or sear foods quickly in butter or other hot fats.

raie, French for skate or ray. A *raiton* is a very small skate. See also SKATE.

raie au beurre noir, the classic French skate dish; skate poached in court bouillon, drained, and then covered with butter that has been browned in a saucepan with capers and a little of the caper vinegar. Raie is also served au gratin, deep-fried, or cold, set in its own jellied stock.

raito, a traditional Christmas Eve dish in Provence, of skate baked in red wine with shelled walnuts.

raifort, French for horseradish. See also HORSERADISH.

raifort aux noix, a French sauce made from 2 tablespoons freshly grated horseradish, 2 oz. shelled, peeled, and finely chopped walnuts, juice of ½ lemon, ¼ pint (½ cup) thick cream, salt, and a pinch of sugar. It is served cold with salmon, or freshwater fish such as *omble chevalier.*

raifort, sauce, see HORSERADISH, SAUCE.

rainbow trout, see TROUT.

raised, a word which, when used in the U.S. in conjunction with cakes, doughnuts, muffins, etc., means that yeast is added to the dough.

raised pie, see PIE.

raisin, in the 17th century, this word meant simply a fresh grape or bunch of grapes. Nowadays it is used for a special kind of grape which has been sun-dried, or dried artificially, for later use, to either be eaten plain or for making cakes, pastries, puddings, pies, jams, preserves, sauces, and stuffings. Raisins have been known and used since ancient times. Some

of the choicest varieties such as the Málaga raisins, which are dried Muscat grapes, are eaten as dessert fruit. Grapes are extensively grown for raisin-production in California. See also ROZIJNEN.

raisin sauce, an American sauce served hot with ham. To prepare it ½ tablespoon mustard, ½ tablespoon flour, and ½ cup brown sugar are mixed together. Then ¼ cup chopped, seeded raisins, ¼ cup vinegar, and ⅞ pint (1¾ cups) water are added. All are cooked together until the mixture becomes syrupy.

raisin, French for grape. *Raisin de sec* is raisin, and *raisin de Corinthe* is currant. *Raisin de Málaga,* known in English as a Málaga raisin, is a dried Muscat grape, which is large and very sweet and is eaten as a dessert fruit and also used in cooking. See also CURRANT.

raisiné, a French jam made from unfermented grape juice, or *must,* boiled down without either water or sugar, and stirred continually until it is syrupy. Pears, peaches, apples, lemons, or quinces, peeled and cut into thin slices, are added, and the jam is cooked until it has almost the consistency of glue.

raito, see RAIE.

raiton, French for a small skate. It is usually fried, although sometimes it is used in soup.

rák, Hungarian for crayfish. See also CRAYFISH.

rákpaprikás, 2 dozen crayfish or Norway lobsters are steamed or boiled, shelled, and cooked in ½ cup butter for about 4 minutes. Then they are pounded, and the paste is mixed thoroughly with paprika to taste, 1 tablespoon tomato purée, ½ teaspoon cumin seeds, 1 tablespoon parsley, salt, and 1½ cups sour cream. It is served with boiled rice.

rak, Russian for crayfish. In Russia crayfish are often simmered in *kvass* (a type of beer) or white wine, with parsley, dill, and seasoning; the stock is later thickened with flour and butter. See also CRAYFISH.

raki, Polish for crayfish. The crayfish are at their finest in July and August; the blackish variety are preferable to the green type. In Poland they are usually simmered lightly in boiling salted water, with a handful of dill, then shelled and served with melted butter. They are also cooked in white wine, or blanched in boiling water, simmered in butter, then covered with sour cream, sprinkled with breadcrumbs and dill, and browned under a grill or in a hot oven for 10 minutes. See also CRAYFISH.

potrawa z rakow z kasza, 2 lb. large crayfish are lightly simmered in boiling salted water with a handful of dill. Then the shells are removed and put on one side, and the crayfish are mixed with 2 tablespoons breadcrumbs, 1 tablespoon butter, 2 egg yolks, dill, and salt, the stiffly beaten egg whites being added last. This mixture is put back inside the shells, and they are steamed for 10 minutes.

räkor, Swedish for shrimp or prawn. See also PRAWN; SHRIMP.

räkor sallad, cooked shrimps or prawns are chilled for about 2 hours in tarragon vinegar, with thyme, a bay leaf, peppercorns, and parsley added. The shellfish are drained and served, sometimes on ice, with a mayonnaise or sauce tartare. See also MEDALJONGER (RÄKMEDALJONGER).

rakørret, a Norwegian national dish of half-fermented trout prepared by placing the fish in a jar or barrel and covering it with coarse salt and sugar. A heavy weight is put on top of the fish, and it is left in a cool place for about three months. Not a dish to everyone's taste, but in some parts of Norway it is thought to guard against coronary thrombosis. See also ØRRET.

râle, French for rail. Two species of rail are eaten in France, the *râle de gênet* or *roi de cailles,* known in England as the landrail or corncrake, and the *râle d'eau,* the water rail. The former is the better, and it is prepared in the same way as snipe or quail (*caille*).

rambour, a variety of apple from the Rambour (Somme) district of France, where it was first cultivated. There is a white and a red variety, and the fruit ripens in August. See also POMME.

ramekin, this was originally a term for toasted or baked cheese, but since the 18th century ramekin has taken on two different specialised meanings. In early cookery manuscripts, the word is sometimes spelled "ramkin." See also RAMEQUIN. I. A small pastry or hollowed-out roll, filled with a cheese mixture. A filling for 6 rolls would consist of ½ lb. grated cheese, 2 tablespoons butter, 1 egg, and pepper. In some cases, breadcrumbs can be substituted for half the amount of cheese. The rolls or pastries are baked in a hot oven for about 10 minutes. II. A small earthenware or china baking-dish which may be used for cooking eggs, a small cheese soufflé, or any other individual savoury dish.

ramequin, French for ramekin (the English word is in fact an 18th-century adaptation of the French). It is a word used both for a utensil—a small individual ovenproof container—and for a variety of cheese dishes (*ramequins de fromage*) which resemble the English ramekin. See also RAMEKIN. I. Chou pastry, made without sugar, is piped through a forcing bag with a medium-sized nozzle. Beaten egg is then brushed over it, dice of Gruyère cheese is pressed into it, and it is baked in a moderate oven for 12–15 minutes. II. Another version uses ½ lb. diced cheese melted with 1 chopped onion, 1 tablespoon butter, and pepper, and then the mixture is poured onto toast. III. Chou pastry is mixed with beaten eggs and grated Gruyère to taste, then piped out of a forcing bag and baked.

ramereau, French for young wood pigeon, which is cooked in the same way as *pigeonneau* (see PIGEON).

ramkin, see RAMEKIN.

ramost, see PULTOST.

rampion (*Campanula rapunculus*), a hardy biennial herb, a native of Europe but naturalised in Britain. It is grown both for its leaves and for its roots, which are ready from November onwards, throughout the winter. The leaves are used in winter salads or are prepared and cooked in the same way as spinach; the fleshy roots, after being scraped, are usually eaten raw and grated, or served boiled and chopped with an oil and vinegar dressing, or are prepared and cooked in the same way as salsify.

rampolla, a French consommé of fish, garnished with julienne of eel pout, crayfish, oysters, and mushrooms. The soup is flavoured with hock. See also CONSOMMÉ.

rana, I. An alternative Italian name for *pescatrice*. II. Italian for frog, often made into a soup that is considered a delicacy in Italy. It is also served fried in batter or braised with white wine, garlic, rosemary, and mushrooms. See also FROG.

zuppa di rana, a soup made from 6 pairs frogs' legs seasoned with black pepper and salt. One sliced onion, 1 stalk celery, 1 chopped carrot, and 1 clove garlic are fried lightly in olive oil. The legs are added and fried until golden, then 2 tablespoons chopped parsley and 3 chopped and peeled tomatoes are added, and all are simmered for 30 minutes. Finally 3 pints white stock is poured over, and cooking is continued for another 30 minutes. The soup is sieved or electrically blended, reheated, and served with *crostini*.

rangiport, a French cow's milk cheese made in the Seine-et-Oise department. It is very like port-du-salut.

rangoon bean, a variety of lima bean.

rapanello, see RADICCHIE.

raparperi, Finnish for rhubarb. See also RHUBARB.

raparperikeitto, a dessert, literally "rhubarb soup." It is made from rhubarb cooked with sugar and a little water, and thickened with potato flour.

rape (*Brassica napus*), a small European herb, a member of the cabbage family. The leaves, which are gathered in the spring, may be prepared in the same way as spinach. Some other members of the *Brassica* family, such as *B. campestris*, are also known as rape, and are used instead of turnips for sheep-fodder. Turnips, swedes, and kohlrabi are also members of the rape or cabbage family.

râpe, French for grater. *Râpé* means grated, and is also an abbreviation for *fromage râpé* (grated cheese).

rape, Italian for turnip, usually served boiled, drained, and sprinkled with grated cheese in Italy. See also TURNIP.

rape al burro, peeled turnips, cut into thin rounds, are lightly cooked in salted water for 15 minutes, then drained and fried in butter. Grated Parmesan cheese is sprinkled over them before they are served.

rape, Spanish for anglerfish. It is extremely good when baked whole with slices of lemon, tomato, green pepper, and onion, although it can also be cut into fillets or steaks and fried or grilled. See also ANGLERFISH.

rape al horno, a recipe from Málaga. The fish is cut into thick slices which are baked in a little oil with a sliced onion and 2 peeled tomatoes. A sauce is made from about 12 almonds and peanuts, 3 garlic cloves, 1 teaspoon parsley, and 1 cup breadcrumbs, all fried in oil and pounded in a mortar with ½ teaspoon saffron. The fish stock and tomatoes are mixed with this, and the sauce is poured over the fish.

rapphöns, Swedish for partridge. Most game is served already carved in Sweden, but partridge comes to the table whole. See also PARTRIDGE.

stekt rapphöns, roast partridge. The partridge breasts are covered with strips of bacon, and the birds are roasted in a moderate oven for 35 minutes, being basted with butter. When cooking is nearly completed, 1 cup warm cream is added and reduced with the pan juices, a little lemon juice, and brandy. It is all well stirred and served with the bird. A green salad and *gräslökpotatis* accompany this dish.

rapusalaatti, a Finnish salad of cooked crayfish, lettuce, and hard-boiled eggs, with a dressing of ½ cup olive oil, 3 tablespoons wine vinegar, ½ teaspoon mustard, salt, pepper, a pinch of sugar, and 1 tablespoon chopped dill. See also RAVUT.

rare, an English and American culinary term applied to the cooking of meat, particularly steak, when underdone.

rarebit, also sometimes spelt rabbit, a dish of melted cheese with a variety of flavourings. In the U.S., the name of the secondary ingredient often takes first place, as in oyster rarebit and tomato rarebit. In many of these variations, beaten eggs are added, thus changing the original dish and making it more like scrambled eggs. See also WELSH RAREBIT.

rascasio, Spanish for hogfish, usually baked with chopped garlic, butter, parsley, lemon juice, and a little sherry.

rascasse, French for hogfish, which is always used in bouillabaisse and other French fish soups.

rasher, a single slice of bacon or raw ham. Rashers can be cut thick or thin, and slicing machines have numbered scales which set the knives at the thickness required; numbers up to 4 are classed as thin, 5 and 6 are medium, and 7 is thick. Streaky bacon rashers, from the belly or flank of the pig, are used for barding as well as for frying. Canadian bacon rashers are cut almost exclusively from the belly or flank. They are about half the size of back rashers (loin), or collar rashers (neck), and are almost evenly divided into lean and fat. Back rashers which include part of the belly or flank are known as long back rashers.

rasol, the name for sauerkraut juice in Yugoslavia. It is used there as a seasoning, and also as a mild laxative for children.

raspberry (*Rubus idaeus*), the fruit of the raspberry bush or cane. Cultivated raspberries are red or white and yellow, but there are also black raspberries, produced by the closely related species *Rubus occidentalis*. Raspberries are used for jams, jellies, preserves, confectionery, ice creams, tarts, pies, puddings, and sauces. They are a valuable ingredient of some liqueurs, and a vinegar is also made from them. Together with strawberries, they are the most popular of small dessert fruits. They are ripe from about July to September, depending on the variety.

raspberry

Before 1500, the wild raspberry was known as hindberry in Britain; Gerard and other herbalists are the first to mention the "raspis" bush in the middle of the 16th century. The origin of the word is open to conjecture, but it seems likely that it was derived from *raspie* or *raspeit*, a sweet dark red wine that had been regularly imported from France since the 15th century, and was known in England as "respyce" or "raspis." Its colour must have been reminiscent of crushed raspberries, and it may have been made from a raspberry-flavoured grape, now almost extinct in France as a result of legislation prohibiting its use in wine-making because this strong flavour permeated the wine. Wild raspberries are often called "wood-rasps" by country people in Scotland (who stuff grouse with them), Ireland, and the north of England.

raspberry butter sauce, 1 cup of fresh butter and two of sifted white sugar are thoroughly worked together in a slightly warmed bowl; then sufficient raspberry juice is poured over the mixture to flavour and colour it.

raspberry cream, a private family manuscript dated 1700 gives the following excellent recipe: "When you have whipt your cream, sweeten it, and take two ladlefuls only, and bruise the raspberries into it, season with rosewater, and whip it well, and then put it to your cream, and stirring all together, dish it up." A stiffly beaten egg white added to the whipped cream lightens the consistency and makes the dish less rich and cloying.

raspberry sauce, 1 pint (2 cups) raspberry juice is squeezed out of fresh raspberries and boiled up in a heavy-bottomed saucepan with 3 tablespoons castor sugar and a few drops of lemon juice. It is then strained into a basin, and 1 tablespoon arrowroot is blended in, after which it is returned to the saucepan and brought to the boiling point again, stirring constantly. It is served with vanilla ice cream, etc.

raspberry vinegar, 3 lb. raspberries are packed into a jar and covered with a solution of 1½ pints (3 cups) white or cider vinegar and ½ pint (1 cup) water. The jar is covered tightly and left for at least 1 month. A teaspoonful of the raspberry vinegar is good with fruit salad or with compotes; also with casserole of pork or goose.

rassolnik, the Russian name for various soups of fish or meat which all include salted cucumber. Rassolnik may be made with veal or chicken stock, with strips of the veal or chicken added, or with fish stock, when a piece of boiled fish, usually sturgeon, is served with the soup. Rassolnik is very popular in Moscow.

rassolnik po Moskovsky, 1 lb. trimmed and sliced ox kidney is simmered in water, then drained and put into 4 pints (8 cups) fresh water or stock with seasoning, 2 sliced roots of Hamburg parsley, 1 sliced celeriac heart, 1 large onion, 4 medium potatoes, and 2 salted cucumbers, all of which have first been lightly turned in butter. They are cooked for about 45 minutes, or until tender. About 10 minutes before cooking is completed, 1 cup shredded sorrel or lettuce leaves and 1 tablespoon of juice from the salted cucumbers are added. The soup is served with slices of kidney, and each plate of soup is garnished with 1 tablespoon sour cream and chopped dill.

rassolnik s potrokhami, giblet rassolnik, made from good beef stock and goose giblet stock. It is flavoured with salted cucumber juice, and garnished with small pieces of chopped giblet, chopped herbs such as parsley, fennel, or dill, and sliced salted cucumber. When hot it is thickened with 1 egg yolk mixed with ¼ pint (½ cup) sour cream (to 2 pints liquid), and it is then reheated but not reboiled because it could curdle.

rasstegay, a Russian savoury, consisting of small patties of yeast dough (see PIROZHKI) filled with a mixture of salmon, rice, chopped hard-boiled eggs, butter, and chopped parsley. They are baked in the oven and eaten hot. Sometimes very small *rasstegay* are used as an accompaniment to soup, served on a separate dish as in *solianka s riba.*

rastègne, see ACTINIA.

rat, a rodent regarded as vermin in England and much despised, but eaten in France during the siege of Paris in 1870. According to *Larousse Gastronomique* (1938) they were often eaten by the wine-coopers in the Gironde, who cleaned and skinned them, then grilled them with olive oil and shallots over a fire made from broken wine barrels.

rata del mar, the Spanish name for the common stargazer, an ugly greyish-brown fish with a large mouth. It is about 15 inches long and has a white belly and a black dorsal fin. It is found on the Atlantic coast of Andalusia, and also in Italian waters, where it is known as *pesce prete.* It is eaten in Spain, Italy, and throughout the Mediterranean area, but the flesh is coarse, and it is used only for fish stews and soups, and sometimes for rice dishes.

ratafia, a small macaroon, like a 1-inch button, with a strong flavour of almond. It is used to decorate puddings and also to line moulds filled with custard or creams. Ratafia biscuits (cookies), as they are called, were very popular in Victorian and Edwardian England but are not common nowadays. Ratafia essence (extract), made from oil of almonds, is very strong and is used sparingly for flavouring cakes.

ratatouille, a Provençal vegetable dish, made from a mixture of eggplant, tomatoes, courgettes (zucchini), onion or garlic, and sweet peppers. First 2 large unpeeled eggplants and 3 courgettes are sliced, and left salted for about 1 hour, then drained; then 4 large tomatoes and 1 onion and/or 2 large garlic cloves are peeled, and 3 large sweet peppers are cored and seeded. All are softened in ¾ pint (2 scant cups) olive oil by gentle frying, and are then stewed together, sometimes with a few coriander seeds or a little basil added, until they form a rich mass. Ratatouille may be served hot or cold as an hors d'oeuvre.

rațe, Rumanian for duck. See also DUCK; OSTROPEL.

rațe pe varză, well-browned duck braised on a bed of sauerkraut and golden-brown fried onions, moistened with a little sauerkraut juice. The fat is drained off before the duck is carved and served on the sauerkraut.

rattleran, a term used formerly in the U.S. for the next best cut of corned beef to fancy brisket. It is taken from the end of the brisket, verging on the plate. Although there is some fat and bone on rattleran, it has a thick lean end.

rauchfleisch, German for smoked beef, often sewed in *auschitt,* or with potato salad. It is extremely good to eat.

rauginti kopūstai, Lithuanian for sauerkraut. Sauerkraut is eaten a great deal in Lithuania, with sausage, pork, or *bulvių desroš.*

rautenscholle, see BUTT.

ravani, a Greek cake made with flour, farina (III), butter, sugar, vanilla, baking powder, and eggs. First ½ lb. (1 cup) butter is creamed with 6 oz. (¾ cup) sugar, then 5 eggs are beaten in. Next 4½ oz. (1 cup) farina or semolina, ½ lb. (2 cups) flour, 3 teaspoons baking powder, and 2 teaspoons vanilla are added gradually, and beaten in well. The mixture is poured into a large greased pan and baked for 30 minutes. When cooked it is cut into squares, and a syrup, made from 1 lb. (2 cups) sugar and 1 pint (2 cups) water boiled together for 15 minutes, is poured over. Lemon juice and a pinch of cinnamon are sometimes added to the syrup.

ravier, a flat, boat-shaped china plate, used in France for serving a simple hors d'oeuvre.

raviggiolo, a Tuscan and Umbrian ewe's milk cheese.

ravigote, sauce, one of the most important of the classical French sauces. Basically, ravigote consists of ½ pint (1 cup) sauce velouté with the addition of 1 small chopped shallot or onion, such herbs as tarragon, chervil, chives, and burnet, and a mixture of 2 tablespoons white stock and 2 tablespoons vinegar which has been reduced by two-thirds before being added to the velouté. There are separate recipes for the hot and the cold ravigote. For the cold sauce, 2 raw egg yolks are added to 3 chopped hard-boiled egg yolks, and all blended until a smooth paste has been achieved. Then ½ teaspoon French mustard is added, and at least 2 tablespoons olive oil is beaten in very gradually. Chives, French capers, parsley, tarragon, gherkin, shallots, and an onion are all finely chopped and then stirred into the sauce with 1 tablespoon wine vinegar and fairly strong seasoning. This sauce is served chilled, with fish, calf's head, cold boiled beef, or chicken.

For the hot sauce, first a *beurre ravigote* is made with parsley, chives, chervil, tarragon, 1 shallot, and garlic, all chopped finely and blanched in a little boiling water; they are drained, squeezed to extract surplus water, pounded in a mortar, and passed through a fine sieve, and this purée is then blended with 2–3 tablespoons butter and seasoned. Next, a roux is made with 2 tablespoons butter and 2 tablespoons flour, using ¾ pint (2 scant cups) rich chicken stock to bind the flour mixture; 1 tablespoon wine vinegar, pepper, and a small pinch of nutmeg are added, and when this mixture has simmered for 5 minutes, 1 heaped tablespoon of the *beurre ravigote* is beaten in gently over a low heat. The sauce must on no account boil, or the flavour of the butter will deteriorate. It is served with offal (variety meat) such as sweetbreads, brains, etc., or with poultry.

ravioli, the generic term for almost all stuffed envelopes of pasta eaten asciutti, that is "dry," not in a soup but with a sauce. In Italy the fillings vary from district to district and from cook to cook, but these described here are some of the more usual. Some of the smaller pasta shapes known as *cappelletti, cima, manicotti,* and *malfatti* (a regional name used in Umbria, Italy) are also essentially ravioli, but they are served in broth, or with butter and cheese, not with a sauce. The amounts given fill approximately 1 lb. thinly rolled ravioli paste. For the basic dough, see PASTA. See also MACCHERONI,

RIPIENI ALLA TOSCANA; PASTICCIO, DI RAVIOLI; TORTELLINI.

ravioli alla caprese, Capri ravioli, filled with a mixture of 4 oz. Parmesan cheese, 6 oz. *caciotto* cheese, scant ½ pint (1 cup) milk, 3 eggs, a pinch of nutmeg, pepper, and basil or marjoram to taste. These ravioli are also fried and served with drinks.

ravioli alla genovese, Genoese ravioli, stuffed with 4 blanched and chopped scarole heads, or spinach or chard, 1 lb. minced lean veal, ½ lb. minced calf's udder, ½ calf's brain, 1 sweetbread, 2 tablespoons borage, 4 whole eggs and 2 egg yolks, ½ cup breadcrumbs, and ½ cup grated Parmesan cheese, all pounded to a paste and well mixed.

ravioli di ricotta, ravioli stuffed with a mixture of 1 lb. ricotta, 2 tablespoons chopped parsley, 4 oz. grated Parmesan cheese, 2 egg yolks, and 1 heaped tablespoon butter, all well pounded together.

ravioli di spinachi, ravioli filled with a mixture of ½ lb. spinach purée, 2 egg yolks, 1 heaped tablespoon butter, a pinch of nutmeg, and 2 oz. grated Parmesan cheese. A variation which is a speciality of Parma is called *tortelli di erbette.*

ravut, Finnish for crayfish. See also CRAYFISH.

keitetyt ravut, plain boiled crayfish, usually flavoured with dill. They are generally served with toast and white wine. See also RAPUSALAATTI.

ray, see SKATE.

raya, Spanish for skate. Several types of skate are found in Spanish waters. See also SKATE.

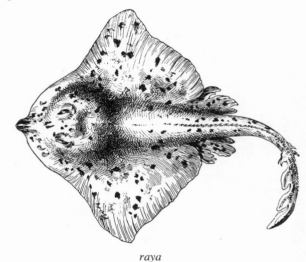

raya

raya en pimentón, an Andalusian method of serving skate in which 4 garlic cloves, 1 teaspoon saffron, 1 teaspoon marjoram, 1 teaspoon parsley, and 1 tablespoon chopped sweet pepper are fried in olive oil, then pounded in a mortar. The fish is put in an oiled dish, the mixture sprinkled over it, and the whole baked for 30 minutes.

rayón, see JABALÍ.

razlevuša, a Yugoslavian cheese pastry. It is made with grated Gruyère mixed with cream cheese and cottage cheese. To 1 lb. mixed cheeses are added 1 scant pint (2 cups) milk and 4 egg yolks. Then ½ lb. (2 cups) flour is gradually worked in, with 2 tablespoons melted butter. Finally, the stiffly beaten egg whites are included, and the pastry is baked for about 1 hour until golden.

raznjići, a Yugoslavian dish similar to shashlyk or *kebab,* made from thin slices or cubes of pork, veal, or lamb rolled up and grilled on a skewer. It is served with rice and chopped raw onion.

razor shell (*Solen siliqua*), a bivalve with a shell 6–8 inches in length, resembling an old-fashioned cut-throat razor. Razor shells are found all over the world, and providing that they can be gathered before gulls or cuttlefish have discovered them, they are very good to eat. They are baked in their shells in the oven for 5 minutes, and then served with pepper and lemon juice. Razor shells can also be cooked as *moules à la marinière*. The Romans knew the razor shell as *aulo*, and esteemed it highly as food.

razza chiodata, Italian for skate or ray. In Italy it is usually cooked in a court bouillon, drained, and then served covered with black butter. It is also fried, but the former method is to be preferred. See also SKATE.

rebhuhn, German for partridge. The classic German way of cooking partridge is to roast it, well larded with bacon, with a few juniper berries, and to serve it with sauerkraut cooked separately. Sour cream may also be mixed with the pan juices, boiled up, and then served with the sauerkraut. Older birds are casseroled and served with hot red cabbage, or are made into pies or stews. See also JÄGERSUPPE; PARTRIDGE.

rebhuhn auf wiener art, a traditional Austrian partridge dish, made with the larded birds wrapped in cabbage leaves and simmered in butter, with onions, and stock barely to cover. When the partridge is cooked, after about 40 minutes, the gravy is strained off and heated up with ½ cup sour cream thickened with 1 tablespoon flour. A variation of this method is to serve the bird with braised lentils and diced fried bacon.

reblochon, a semi-hard French cow's milk cheese. It was first made in the Haute-Savoie near Thômes and Le Grand St. Bernard. In season from September to July.

réchaud, I. A small French portable stove. II. A dish heated by being stood over hot water, used for keeping foods hot at table. The heat is provided by spirit, gas, or electricity.

réchauffé, literally, French for reheated. In culinary terms it means any dish made with previously cooked meats or poultry.

récollet, a French cow's milk cheese from Alsace, in season from October to April.

recuire, I. French for to recook. It has a more specific meaning in the context of biscuit (cracker)-making (*bis cuit* meaning twice cooked), where the whole mixture is first cooked in a single tin at a low temperature, then separated by splitting or putting into special tins or moulds to cook for the second time. Rusks are made by this method. II. A French term used in sweet-making to define the operation of annealing, or bringing to the required temperature, a jelly or syrup which is to be mixed with other ingredients, so that it will hold its texture after the addition of a watery fruit or other foodstuff.

recuite, the French term for cheese made with whey or a skimmed milk cheese.

red cabbage, a purple variety of cabbage, indigenous to China but now cultivated all over the world. It requires much longer cooking than does white or green cabbage, and for this reason it is usually shredded raw before cooking with water, stock, or red wine barely to cover. It is well seasoned, and a variety of additions are used, such as juniper berries, allspice, cloves, caraway seeds, cinnamon, etc. About 2 tablespoons brown sugar to 1 medium-sized cabbage are also advised; also a medium-sized onion and/or apple, diced bacon or ham, and sometimes chestnuts. The addition of 2 tablespoons vinegar or wine will prevent the cabbage turning blue, or, if this has already happened, will restore the original colour. The cabbage is then covered, and can be safely simmered for 2–3 hours without either spoiling or decreasing in bulk; in fact the longer it is cooked, within reason, the better. It is particularly good with game or rich meats such as pork or goose. Cooked red cabbage reheats very well or, left cold, it may be served as a salad.

In Germany red cabbage is served with corned beef. In Britain raw, shredded red cabbage is covered with salt overnight, then drained, packed into jars and covered with cold boiled vinegar and spices. This is called pickled red cabbage, and is traditionally served with Lancashire hot pot, as well as with cold meats. A 19th-century salad consisted of very finely shredded, raw red cabbage mixed with vinegar and 1 tablespoon molasses, salt, and black pepper. This was served with cold ham, goose, pork, or corned beef. See also BLAUKRAUT; KOHL; RØDKAL; ROTKOHL; ROTKRAUT.

red currant (*Ribes sativum*), a hybrid plant, the result of the cross-breeding of three different wild species from Siberia and Eastern Europe, *R. petraeum*, *R. rubrum*, and *R. vulgare*. It was first introduced into England in the 15th century. The white currant is of the same parentage, for it is not a separate variety but an albino strain of red currant. Black currants and gooseberries are of the same genus and family. Red and white currants are used in confectionery and for jellies and jams. They are also delicious eaten raw with cream and sugar, and are essential to summer pudding. See also BAR-LE-DUC; RIPS.

red currant jelly, the fruit is boiled with water to cover for 30 minutes, then strained through muslin. The juice is caught in a bowl underneath, and this is boiled up with 1 lb. sugar to every pint of juice for about 35 minutes, or until a little of it placed in a saucer sets when cold. It is then put into jars, and when cool, is tied down. It is served with mutton, game, and pork, and is also used for tarts or pies.

red deer, see DEER.

red grouse, see GROUSE.

red herring, a herring which has been cleaned but not split, and then heavily salted. The skin retains its original colour, but the eyes turn very red, and it is no doubt this fact which accounts for the name. Unless soaked before cooking, and sometimes even in spite of soaking, red herrings produce a great thirst. Frying or grilling, after soaking, is the best method of cooking them. In the Hebrides they are served with boiled or baked potatoes. Nowadays kippers are far more popular, but red herrings are still enjoyed in the west of England, in Scotland, and in Ireland. See also BLOATER.

red mayonnaise, an old English and American dressing, usually served with lobster salad. It is made by adding the coral of the lobster and a little beetroot juice to ½ pint thick mayonnaise.

red mullet, see MULLET.

red pepper, see CAYENNE.

red salmon, an alternative name for blue-back salmon, a fish which is used mainly for canning.

red snapper (*Lutianidae*), a delicious sea fish found off the coast of the U.S. It is creamy, white-fleshed, and delicate to eat. In Florida it is sometimes turned in butter with a pinch of nutmeg and a sprinkling of grated orange and grapefruit peel, then baked. It can also be grilled or fried, and makes very good soup. There is also a grey snapper, which is good but not as delicate as the red snapper.

red-breasted bream, a member of the *Cyprinidae* family of freshwater fish, found in lakes and rivers in the U.S. and sometimes called flounder. It is considered quite good to eat, and can be cooked as flounder.

red-breasted snipe, see DOWITCHER; SNIPE.

redfin (*Luxilus cornutus*), a small silvery freshwater fish, a member of the carp family, found in lakes all over the U.S. It is known, too, as shiner. The same names are also applied to the *Lythrurus umbratilis* of the Mississippi Valley. It can be cooked as carp.

redfish (*Oncorhynchus nerka*), the American name, on the eastern seaboard, for the fish known on the Pacific side as red or blue-back salmon. It is found off the Atlantic seaboard of the U.S. and plays an important part in creole cookery, especially in New Orleans. See also BLUE-BACK SALMON.

redfish baked and stuffed, the 4- to 5-lb. fish is stuffed with a mixture of 1½ cups breadcrumbs mixed with a little chopped celery, garlic, onion, parsley, cooked shrimp, salt, and pepper. It is put into a baking tin and covered with a sautéed mixture of 2 tablespoons chopped onion, 1 garlic clove, 2 tablespoons chopped green pepper, 1 cup raw shrimp, bay leaf, thyme, 1 stalk celery, ½ cup tomato purée diluted to form a thin sauce, and 1½ cups tomatoes. It is baked in a moderate oven for 10 minutes to the lb., up to a weight of 4 lb. and 5 minutes for each additional lb. It is finally garnished with chopped parsley before serving.

redfish court bouillon, a New Orleans soup, the speciality of well-known restaurants such as Antoine's and Brennan's. It is made by first sautéeing 1 small head celery, 2 medium bell peppers, 1 large onion and green onions, and 4 garlic cloves, in ½ cup oil. Then 3 bay leaves, 1 teaspoon thyme, 3 cups fresh or canned tomatoes, a pinch each of paprika, cayenne, salt, and pepper are added, and it is simmered for about 5 minutes. Then 2 pints (4 cups) fish stock is stirred in. It is covered and cooked very slowly for about ½ hour. Meanwhile 4 lb. fish is lightly sprinkled with seasoned flour and seared on both sides under a hot grill. The heat is then lowered and cooking continued until it is almost done (about 10 minutes). It is then removed and kept warm. Finally 1 cup burgundy and 3 tablespoons lemon juice are added to the soup, and the fish is put in and cooked very gently for about 10 minutes longer. It is all garnished with lemon slices and served with boiled rice. Sometimes the fish is cut into slices and added to the finished soup without the preliminary grilling. It is then gently poached for about 20 minutes.

redhead, see POCHARD.

reduce, to, a culinary term meaning to boil a liquid rapidly, thus reducing its volume by evaporation. In the case of a gravy or sauce, this action not only thickens the liquid, but also concentrates and increases the flavour. Certain dark-coloured sauces are also made more glossy and attractive by this method. Reducing is also the best way of dealing with diluted pan juices, for it avoids the addition of flour or other thickening agent, which in many cases would obliterate the true flavour of the gravy. Reducing is known as "boiling down."

redware (*Porphyra laciniata*), an edible seaweed. It is known in the Orkneys as redware, but in Scotland it is called tangle, and in England, sea-girdle. It is prepared and cooked in the same way as dulse.

reedbird or **bobolink** (*Dolichonyx oryzivorus*), a finch-like bird found in the south of the U.S. It used to be considered a delicacy there, as was the ortolan in Europe, and in fact all recipes for ortolan are suitable for this small bird.

reeve, see RUFF.

Reform Club sauce, an English sauce, first introduced at the Reform Club in London by the chef Alexis Soyer (1809–1858), as an accompaniment to cutlets. It consists of ½ pint sauce *poivrade,* with a julienne of whites of hard-boiled egg, gherkins, mushrooms, truffles, and tongue. Reform Club cutlets were cutlets coated with egg and breadcrumbs before frying, and served with this sauce.

refresh, to, I. A culinary term applied to foods that have been blanched or cooked, meaning to drain them, and then to pour a cup of cold or tepid water over them. In the case of meats, or offal (variety meats) such as brains, this helps to clear away any scum; in the case of vegetables, it sets the colour. It is still a common practice in country districts all over Europe. II. When applied to restaurant and catering practice, this term means to reheat cooked vegetables in boiling, or very hot, water, instead of cooking them freshly for each order.

refrigerator, a regulated machine, run by gas, electricity, or oil, for the purpose of keeping foods cold or frozen and thus preserving them. Deep-freezing will keep foods fresh for a considerable time.

refrigerator biscuits, cakes or cookies, a dough is made from 4 oz. (½ cup) butter creamed with 8 oz. (1 cup) sugar, 1 beaten egg, 6 oz. (1½ cups) flour, a pinch of salt, and baking soda, and any flavouring desired, such as orange, nuts, lemon, vanilla, etc. All are well mixed, and the dough is shaped into a roll which is wrapped in paper and stored in the refrigerator. When needed, slices are cut off and baked on a greased baking-sheet for 8–10 minutes in a hot oven.

régence, I. A French garnish for fish, consisting of oysters and quenelles of fish, with *beurre d'écrevisses,* mushrooms, sliced soft roes, and sauce *normande.* II. A French garnish for poultry, sweetbreads, and *vol-au-vent,* consisting of truffled chicken quenelles, veal quenelles, goose liver, mushrooms, and cock's combs, with sauce *allemande.* This garnish is also sometimes called à la *royale.* See also POULET, À LA RÉGENCE.

régence, sauce, a classical French sauce. I. For fish, a sauce *normande* is prepared with white wine to taste, mushrooms, and truffles. II. For fowl, a sauce suprême, with white wine to taste, mushrooms, and truffles is made. III. For poultry or veal, *mirepoix* and truffle-peelings are reduced in Rhenish wine, demi-glace added, and all is boiled up and strained.

regensburger braten, a German and Austrian meat loaf made from 1½ lb. minced beef and ½ lb. minced pork mixed with 2 oz. grated suet, 4 soaked crustless slices of bread, 2 sautéed onions, 1 clove garlic, a pinch of marjoram, 2 eggs, and seasoning. The mixture is put into a greased tin, melted butter is poured over it, and it is baked for 1½ hours in a moderate oven. It is basted with meat gravy and sour cream. *Kartoffelklösse* are served separately.

regensburger wurst, a spicy, juicy German wurst from Lower Bavaria. See also WÜRST.

reh, German for roe deer, considered in Germany, as in the rest of Europe, to be the finest form of venison. In Germany it is often cooked with juniper berries, the pan juices being rinsed out with sour cream and meat glaze. Braised red cabbage is a usual accompaniment. See also VENISON.

Baden-Badener-reh, saddle of roe deer, well larded, then roasted. It is served slightly undercooked, and garnished with a compote of pears which have been cooked without sugar but with a little cinnamon and lemon peel. Red currant jelly is served as well.

rehbraten mit rahmsauce, an Austrian method of cooking a leg or loin of roe deer. The joint is rubbed with salt, pepper, nutmeg, and crushed juniper berries. Onion, celeriac, and carrot are sautéed in oil or fat, in which the meat is then browned. All are transferred to a casserole, and 1 cup good stock, 1 teaspoon each of French mustard, lemon peel, and thyme, 2 cloves, and 1 bay leaf are added. All are covered and cooked in a slow oven for 30 minutes per lb. Then the meat and vegetables are removed, and the liquid is mixed with ½ pint (1 cup) red wine and ¼ pint (½ cup) sour cream. This mixture is heated up to reduce it, and then poured over the meat and vegetables. Sometimes a few capers are added. It is served with either buttered noodles or rice, and accompanied by cooked cranberries.

rehrücken, the term for a saddle or haunch of roe deer or venison in Austria or Germany. Venison is plentiful, and eaten extensively in Austria and Germany. To avoid toughness, the joint is marinated with root vegetables in wine to cover for about 2 days before cooking. When roasted or stewed, sour cream is often added to the sauce, and red currant jelly is served with the meat.

rehrücken, an Austrian chocolate cake, baked in a special tin, then covered in chocolate icing spiked with blanched almonds to imitate a larded haunch of venison (this is the literal meaning of rehrücken). The tin is oblong (haunch-shaped) and fluted to show the slices the cake should be cut into before being eaten. It is also dented in the middle to simulate the bone.

reibgerstl, an Austrian garnish for soup, made from trimmings of strudel pastry which are left to dry out and are then grated coarsely. These shavings are dried in the oven and then cooked for a few minutes in boiling soup. Alternatively a firm paste is made with 4 oz. (1 cup) flour mixed with a pinch of salt and 1 egg, rolled into a ball and left to dry before grating.

reindeer (*Rangifer tarandus*), a large antlered mammal; the very similar American reindeer is called caribou. The reindeer has been domesticated by the Lapps, who prize it highly for many things including hide, milk, and meat. The meat is finer-grained and more tender than beef, and it can be prepared in the same way as venison or caribou. Smoked tongue of reindeer is considered a great delicacy. Reindeer meat is eaten in northern Finland, Alaska, Russia, and Scandinavia. In Russia it is marinated in a light wine, then larded and roasted, and served with sauce madère and mushrooms in sauce smitane. Sometimes small pastry shells are filled with caviar and used as a garnish. In Norway, reindeer is roasted and served with chestnut purée. Steaks can be cooked in the same way as beef steaks. In Alaska, reindeer and other antlered game are eaten in many ways. The cutlets are rubbed with oil, fennel, salt, pepper, and lemon juice, then marinated in this for a few hours. They are grilled first, then baked with some of the marinade in a roasting tin, and served with red currant jelly and grated horseradish. See also ELK; OLÉN; PORON; REINSDYR; RENSDYR; VENISON.

reindeer

reindlbiftek, an Austrian speciality, consisting of a fillet steak browned in butter, then lightly braised in demi-glace. It is garnished with a fried egg on top, fried potatoes, and sliced gherkins.

reine, I. The French term for a chicken whose size is between *poulet de grain* and *poularde*. II. *Purée à la reine,* a method of preparing chicken. It is poached, then cut up or puréed, and mixed with chicken-based sauce velouté or sauce *allemande* blended with eggs. This mixture is put into moulds, cooked in a *bain-marie,* and then decorated with mushroom and truffle slices. It is used as a garnish, or as a filling for *bouchées,* patties, or *vol-au-vents*. III. Another French method of serving chicken. See POULET, À LA REINE. IV. *Coulis à la reine,* a chicken purée (see II) mixed with cream and served as

a thick soup. V. A French chicken consommé, thickened with tapioca and garnished with plain royale, julienne of chicken, and chopped chervil. See also CONSOMMÉ.

reine-claude, the general French word for greengage, and also the name of a particular well-known horticultural variety.

reine des prés, French for meadowsweet, used to flavour certain vermouths.

reinette, see POMME.

reinsdyr, Norwegian for reindeer. Smoked reindeer tongue is considered to be one of the greatest delicacies. See also REINDEER.

reinsdyrepølse, a Norwegian sausage made from reindeer meat seasoned with sugar, spices, salt, and spirits.

reinsdyrrygg, roasted rib of reindeer, first boned, then flattened and spread with cranberry stuffing, and after that rolled up, seasoned, and larded with bacon dripping. It is cooked in a slow oven for 40 minutes per lb.

reis, German for rice. See also RICE.

reisklösse, small dumplings made with 4 cups cooked rice, 4 oz. finely minced veal or chicken, 1 tablespoon parsley, salt, pepper, a pinch of nutmeg, 1 teaspoon grated lemon peel, and 2 beaten eggs. The mixture is formed into small balls which are cooked in boiling salted water for 5–7 minutes.

reiswürstchen, Austrian rice "sausages," made from 1 lb. cold cooked rice, 1 lb. cooked minced veal, 3 eggs, and seasonings, all well mixed. The minced mixture is wrapped in rice paper to form small sausage shapes, and these are dipped in beaten egg, rolled in breadcrumbs, and fried in hot fat. They are used as a garnish for soups.

Réjane, various preparations named after the famous French actress Gabrielle Réjane (1856–1920). I. A French garnish for entrées. They are tartlets stuffed alternately with foie gras and asparagus tips, covered with sauce madère. For fish, they are rosette-shaped *pommes duchesse,* covered with white wine sauce whipped with demi-glace and *beurre d'écrevisses.* II. A French chicken consommé made from raw beaten eggs strained through a colander into the boiling soup, which is then garnished with carrot royale and hazelnut royale flavoured with chervil. See also CONSOMMÉ.

reje, Danish for shrimp. Shrimps are excellent in Denmark from July until September, and they are eaten extensively.

réjouissance, French for the bones that are weighed in a joint of meat. The proportionate weight of bones allowed to flesh is strictly limited by law in France.

rekling, a Norwegian method of serving thin strips of halibut, usually fried. It is a speciality north of the Arctic Circle.

relâcher, a French culinary term meaning to add liquid to a sauce or purée in order to thin it to a required consistency.

relevé, a French word, now almost obsolete, for the course after the soup or fish and preceding the entrée. The English word is remove.

reliefs, French for the scraps or leavings of a meal.

religieuse, I. A French cake made from filled and iced éclairs which are arranged upright in a pyramid on a base of pastry, and are decorated with cream. See also ÉCLAIR. II. A puff pastry tart of apple and apricot jam, scattered with currants and latticed on top with strips of pastry, then baked.

relish, a culinary term for any spicy or piquant preparation eaten with plainer food to add or enhance flavour. In Britain it usually means a thin pickle or sauce with a vinegar base. In the U.S. the term also embraces finely chopped fruits or vegetables with a dressing of sugar, salt, and vinegar; this is not only served as an adjunct to a main course, but may also constitute the first course of a meal, as apple relish, garden relish, and salad relish.

relleno, Spanish for stuffing or forcemeat. The term is also used adjectivally, to mean stuffed.

remonter, a French culinary term meaning to add a condiment to a sauce or stew to give it more flavour.

remoudou, a Belgian cheese, similar to hervé but twice as large, made chiefly in the Hal country and in the region of Dolhain. It is highly flavoured and slightly salted. Its season is from November to June.

rémoulade, a sauce served with cold eggs, fish, meat, or poultry. To a mayonnaise are added chopped chervil, tarragon, parsley, spring onions (scallions), gherkins, and capers to taste. Sometimes a dash of anchovy essence (extract) is added if the sauce is to be served with cold fish. Rémoulade is also made by gradually adding ¼ pint olive oil to the mashed yolks of 2 hard-boiled eggs and 1 raw yolk; the herbs are included afterwards.

renaissance, à la, I. A French garnish for meat or chicken, consisting of a variety of cooked spring vegetables heaped individually around the dish. The vegetables have usually been boiled and then tossed in butter. See also POULET, À LA RENAISSANCE. II. A French garnish for meats, of artichoke hearts filled with mixed cooked vegetables and cauliflower, then covered with sauce hollandaise.

render down, to, to melt fat in the oven or in a pan until the drippings run freely out and the lumps of fat are brown. The dripping is poured into a jar and left to get cold; then it is clarified by being boiled with a little water until the water has evaporated and the fat is clear. "Rendering down" is a term used particularly in connection with suet. In the U.S. the process is called simply render.

rengha, a Greek dish, used for hors d'oeuvre, which consists of equal quantities of olive oil and lemon juice beaten together, with small pieces of dried smoked and boned herring added.

renklody w spirytusie, Polish for greengages preserved in alcohol, a national speciality.

rennet, a preparation made from the stomach lining of calves, pigs, or sheep, containing a digestive enzyme called rennin which effects the coagulation of milk into curds and whey without souring. As this enzyme is derived from a mammal, it can only act if the temperature of the milk is close to the internal body-temperature of the mammal; and this is why the milk used for junket is warmed to blood heat. It is also used for making cheeses. Some plants, such as the fig and the thistle, produce a substance capable of coagulating milk in a similar way.

rensdyr, Danish for reindeer. In Denmark roast reindeer is served on festive occasions, and joints of reindeer are sold larded and ready for roasting. It is served with red currant jelly, *brunede kartofler,* and a sour cream gravy made by adding 1 cup sour cream to the pan juices and reducing.

repanakia, Greek for radishes, often served for *mezes.*

repère, French for a mixture of egg white and flour which is used to fix elaborate dishes to the serving-plate. Lute is sometimes called repère, but this is incorrect.

restes, French for the leftovers of a meal, which are ample enough to be recooked. For example: *restes de veau* are veal leftovers, usually served reheated in a sauce with mushrooms or something similar. Poultry and meats are often minced (ground) and made into *rissoles.* Cold meats from a pot-au-feu are served in *salade parisienne.* See POT-AU-FEU.

revani me kos, an Albanian cake, made from ½ pint (1 cup) sour milk or buttermilk, 4 eggs, 3 heaped tablespoons butter, melted, 12 oz. (1½ cups) sugar, 2 teaspoons baking powder, and ½ lb. (2 cups) flour all mixed in the order given. The mixture is baked in a flat greased pan for about 30 minutes, and when cool it is covered with a syrup made from 1 lb. (2 cups) sugar and ½ pint (1 cup) water boiled together for 10 minutes. The cool cake is soaked in the hot syrup and served with whipped cream.

réveillon, the French name for both the meal eaten after Midnight Mass on Christmas Eve, and the meal eaten at midnight on St. Silvester's Night (New Year's Eve).

revenir (faire), a French culinary term meaning to brown meat, poultry, fish, or vegetables in hot oil or fat before cooking.

reverdir, a French culinary term meaning to replace green colour in vegetables (usually lost during canning) by using either a pinch of baking soda or spinach water.

revithia, Greek for chick-peas, sometimes roasted and salted, and eaten for hors d'oeuvre. See also CHICK-PEA.

revithia yahni, soaked chick-peas boiled until soft, then flavoured with garlic, chopped onion, tomatoes, mint, parsley, and seasoning, before cooking again for about 15 minutes. This is a popular Greek Lenten dish.

rhubarb (*Rheum rhaponticum; R. undulatum; R. palmatum; R. hybridum*), a plant from Asia, used mainly as a fruit. It has long been cultivated in Europe for its fleshy stalks, which are cooked as the basic ingredient of various puddings, tarts, pies, and preserves. Although it reached British gardens in the 16th century, it was not widely used as food until the early 19th century. In Poland it is served in a savoury dish (see RZEWIEŃ). It is very unwise to eat the leaves of rhubarb as they contain oxalic acid and are poisonous. In the U.S. rhubarb is sometimes known as pie-plant. See also RABARBER; RAPARPERI; RZEWIEŃ.

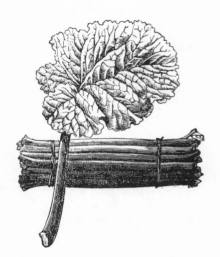

rhubarb

Rhubarb is also the name of a drug made from an oriental variety of rhubarb, which is believed to have been in use in China as early as 2700 B.C. for the relief of bowel disorders.

rhubarb beet, a new variety of chard which has bright red stems, midrib, and veins. It is prepared and cooked in the same way as chard, although its flavour is that of beet rather than chard. Not only is it good to eat, but it is also decorative in flower vases.

rib steak, the name by which entrecôte steak is known in the U.S. See diagram, page xxii.

riba, a Serbo-Croat word for fish. In Yugoslavia fish is plentiful and good, and is served fried, marinated, in risotto, or in thick stews or soups. See also ŠARAN.

riba sa paprikom, 4 lb. fish is put in a casserole with 3 puréed green peppers, 2 tomatoes, 2 small onions, 2 large chopped potatoes, a bay leaf, and 3 pints (6 cups) water. Paprika is sprinkled generously over so that this flavour will predominate as well as a little melted butter. The casserole is tightly covered, and the dish is cooked for about 30 minutes.

riblja čorba, a Slovenian fish soup which has a slightly sour taste. It is made from 2 lb. fish cooked with 1 green pepper, 1 sliced onion, 1 bay leaf, 3 pints (6 cups) water, seasoning, and herbs for 30 minutes. Then the juice of 1 lemon is heated and added, and finally 1 egg yolk mixed with 2 tablespoons cream is included. The soup is served sprinkled with chopped parsley. See also KISELA RIBLJA ČORBA.

ricci, Italian for sea urchins, which were much appreciated by both the Romans and the Greeks. They are eaten raw, served with vinegar, chopped mint, and parsley.

rice (*Oryza sativa*), an annual grass, thought by the botanist Roxburgh to have originated from a wild plant indigenous to India, called *newaree* or *nivara*. However, it was being cultivated in most tropical countries many centuries before Christ; it is mentioned in the Talmud, though not in the Bible. It is said that the Arabs took the plant to Spain, and that its first cultivation in Europe was near Pisa, Italy, in 1468. It was introduced into the U.S. (South Carolina) in 1700. There are many varieties of rice, but the best known are the long-grained Patna, Basmatti, Carolina, and Java; and the short, round-grained Piedmontese rice of Italy.

rice cultivation near Valencia

Rice is the staple diet of many millions of people in the East; in Europe and in the U.S., the long-grained rice is used mainly boiled and drained as an accompaniment to meat, fish, or eggs. It can be served as a vegetable in place of potato, or it can be used for salads and soups. In Italy a special dish of simmered rice with vegetables and sometimes meat is made, called a risotto; in Spain, a similar dish is called paella. Rice should accompany a curry, and it is also served with much Chinese food, with Turkish kebabs, and with many other Oriental dishes. Sweet rice puddings, with milk, eggs, and sugar, are made with the short-grained rice, which cooks quickly and amalgamates more easily than the long-grained variety. See also ARROZ; REIS; RIJSTTAFEL; RIS; RISO; RISOTTO; RIZ; RIZI; RYŻ; RÝZE; WILD RICE.

boiled rice, 1 pint salted water per oz. rice is brought to the boil, and the rice is then added. It is stirred continually until the water boils again, in order to separate the grains, then kept on an even boil. After 12 minutes the first testing should be made; different varieties of rice vary in the amount of time they require, and testing by tasting is the only satisfactory way to tell when it is cooked. Between 15 and 20 minutes should see all varieties of rice properly cooked, that is, soft right through, neither firm nor mushy in the centre of the grain. The rice is then poured into a colander and rinsed with

hot or cold water, after which it is returned to a saucepan with a nut of butter or a little oil, and shaken over a very low heat or put in a low oven to dry out. Rice expands considerably in cooking, and 2 to 3 oz. is considered a reasonable portion for one person. Some cooks wash the rice before cooking, to remove the starch, but this is simply a matter of personal choice and makes little or no difference to the taste.

fried rice, boiled rice that has been left to get cold is best for fried rice. A little oil, butter, or other fat is melted in a frying-pan, and when it is warm but not hot, the rice is put in. A mixture of fried onions, tomatoes, sweet peppers, and chopped herbs can be added and mixed with it. About ½ teaspoon turmeric powder, added to the water before boiling or shaken over the frying rice, imparts a pleasant yellow colour and a spicy taste and smell; saffron is even better, but now almost prohibitively expensive. If used with curry, the fried rice is garnished on top with crisply fried onion rings.

rice flour, rice ground to a very fine powder, even finer than the usual ground rice. It is used for cakes, puddings, and as a thickening agent, and is sometimes incorporated into commercially packed baking powders and custard powders. See also GROUND RICE.

riceys cendré, les, a French cow's milk cheese, sometimes called *champenois.*

riche, à la, the preparations that emanated from the popular Parisienne café Riche in the 19th century. I. A French sauce for fish, consisting of ½ pint (1 cup) sauce *normande,* with 2 tablespoons *beurre homard,* 1 tablespoon brandy, and a pinch of cayenne. It is also called sauce *diplomate.* II. A French dish of fish fillets, particularly sole, cooked with sauce *victoria* and served with a slice of lobster and truffle on each fillet. III. A French garnish for noisettes and tournedos, consisting of médaillons of goose liver, slices of truffle, and artichoke bottoms filled with asparagus tips, all masked with sauce madère.

Richelieu, à la, I. A French garnish for meat, consisting of stuffed tomatoes and mushrooms, braised lettuce, and *pommes château.* II. A French dish of fish dipped in melted butter and white breadcrumbs, fried, then covered with *beurre chivry* and garnished with truffle slices. III. A French sauce, consisting of ½ pint (1 cup) fresh tomato sauce mixed with 2 tablespoons meat glaze and garnished with diced tomatoes. IV. A French sauce consisting of 2 tablespoons demi-glace mixed with ½ pint (1 cup) white wine and reduced to half, with 2 tablespoons fish fumet and 1 tablespoon truffle essence (extract) flavoured with Madeira wine added to it, and all heated together. V. A French cake made from 1 lb. (2½ cups) pounded almonds mixed with 2 egg whites and 2 tablespoons sugar, then mixed with 2 egg yolks and ½ cup maraschino liqueur. Then 6 oz. (⅔ cup) melted butter is added, followed by 1 lb. (4 cups) flour, and finally 10 stiffly beaten egg whites. All are mixed well. The mixture is poured into two buttered flan tins and cooked in a moderate oven for 30 minutes, then sandwiched with apricot jam and *frangipane.*

ricotta, a soft ewe's buttermilk cheese eaten throughout Italy. Usually it is unsalted, although there are peasant versions which are salted and smoked. Ricotta may be pounded and mixed with grated Parmesan, butter, and nutmeg, seasoned, and then stirred into any hot pasta. It may also be used in the filling of ravioli, tarts, flans, and pizza. See also BUDINO, DI RICOTTA; SFOGLIATELLE.

ricotta al caffé, an Italian sweet, literally "coffee cream cheese." It is made with 1 lb. (2 cups) ricotta, 4 heaped tablespoons castor sugar, 2 tablespoons finely ground coffee, and 4 tablespoons rum, all stirred until smooth and thick, then served chilled with fresh cream and wafers.

riddle, a kitchen sieve with large holes, used for separating husk from grain.

riekko, Finnish for ptarmigan, a popular game-bird in Finland. See also GAME; PTARMIGAN.

riekkopaisti, roast ptarmigan. The birds are cleaned in the usual way, and slices of bacon are inserted under the skin of the breast and laid over the outside of the bird. The birds are then placed in a casserole in the oven and browned, then basted with sour cream. When they are cooked, the stock is thickened with ¼ pint (½ cup) thick fresh cream and served as a sauce. Melted cheese of the Danish blue or roquefort variety is sometimes added to taste, for extra flavouring.

riesengebirge-käse, a soft cheese made in the mountains of northern Bohemia from goat's milk. The curd is put into moulds and salted on the surface. It is then dried for 3 or 4 days, and placed afterwards in a cool but moist cellar to cure. The taste is sharp but interesting.

rifaki, Greek for kid. See KATSIKAKI.

rigadelles, the French name on the Atlantic coast for small clams or cockles.

rigani, Greek for wild marjoram, which has a much stronger scent than the cultivated variety. The word comes from *origanon*, which means "joy of the mountains" in English. *Riganato* is a Greek culinary term for a dish that is seasoned with marjoram. See also MARJORAM.

rigatoni, see PASTA.

rigodon, a speciality of Burgundy in France, which used to be made on bread baking day and was cooked after the bread was ready. It was made in sufficient quantity to be served twice, and it has the advantage of being able to be served both as a savoury and as a sweet dish. To prepare it, 1½ pints (3 cups) milk is boiled with 4 oz. (½ cup) sugar, a pinch of salt, half a vanilla pod, and a pinch of cinnamon or 1 teaspoon lemon peel. When it has boiled, it is covered and left on a warm part of the stove to infuse. Then ¼ lb. (2 cups) stale brioche is diced and just moistened with 6 tablespoons milk; then ½ cup chopped walnuts, with a few hazelnuts, are added, together with 7 eggs beaten with 2 tablespoons rice flour. The mixtures are combined and poured into a buttered dish, then dotted with butter and baked in a moderate oven for 45–60 minutes. It is served with fruit purée.

rigodon avec viande, rigodon with meat. This is made exactly as described above, but omitting the brioche, vanilla, cinnamon, lemon peel, and nuts, and adding instead diced, cold cooked streaky bacon or ham. The eggs are mixed with the rice flour, the hot milk is added, and the diced meat put in before baking begins.

rigottes, very small, round French cheeses, produced chiefly in the Rhône Valley, and made from mixed cow's and goat's milk. They are eaten from May to October. *Rigotte de Condrieu* is particularly popular.

rijst, Belgian and Dutch for rice. See also RICE.

rijstepap, a Belgian porridge made from rice flavoured with brown sugar and cinnamon.

rijstsoep met vruchtensaus, rice soup with fruit sauce. To prepare it, ½ lb. (1 cup) rice is simmered for about 30 minutes in 2 pints (4 cups) water with salt and ½ teaspoon grated lemon peel. Then 3 oz. raisins, 6 oz. (¾ cup) sugar and ¾ pint (1½ cups) raspberry or strawberry juice are added, and all are simmered for another 15 minutes. This dessert soup may be eaten either cold or warm.

rijsttafel, a Dutch-Indonesian meal, the name meaning literally "rice table." Innumerable meat, fish, and vegetable dishes, with accompanying sauces, are served with a large bowl of cooked rice. According to taste, these are sometimes curried and mixed with the rice. See also BABI KETJAP; BAHMI; KERRY; NASSI GORENG; PISANG GORENG; SAMBAL OELEK; SATEH.

rillauds, a French potted pork. Breast or belly of pork is cut into very small pieces and gently cooked, but not browned, in lard, sometimes with a bouquet garni and a clove of garlic, and well seasoned. Then ½ pint (1 cup) stock or water is added (for about 6 lb. pork), a cover is put on, and the meat is cooked in a very slow oven for 3–4 hours. It is drained of fat and put into small stone jars; then the fat, having been strained of any sediment, is used to cover it. Paper or foil is put over the jars and they are stored in a cold place for future use, when the potted pork is served with crusty bread or toast. Rillauds are also made with a mixture of goose or rabbit. See also RILLETTES; RILLONS.

rillettes, as *rillauds* and *rillons*, except that after cooking, when the fat has been drained off, the meat is lightly pounded in a mortar, or shredded, before being put into the jars. Rillettes are made commercially almost all over France and are sold in *charcuteries*. The most highly prized come from Le Mans and Tours. See also RILLAUDS.

rillons, as *rillauds* and *rillettes*, except that the pieces of pork are slightly larger, and that rillons are sometimes eaten hot straight from the pan, after straining off the fat. They are also called rillots in some parts of France. See also RILLAUDS.

rim, Portuguese for kidney, usually grilled or fried in Portugal, but also sometimes served like liver, as *iscas*. See also KIDNEY.

rimote, see MILLAS.

rind, the outer skin of some fruits, such as lemon, orange, apple, and pear, and vegetables such as cucumber, marrow (zucchini), etc. The word is also used for the skin of pork (see CRACKLING), bacon, and cheese.

rindfleisch, German for beef. See also OCHSENFLEISCH. *Rinderbrust* is brisket of beef; *rinderleber* is ox liver; and *rinderschmorbraten* is braised steak.

gedämpftes rindfleisch in bier, rigodon with meat. This is beef in beer. A 4-lb. joint of rump beef is pot roasted with 1 large sliced onion, ½ head of celery, 6 carrots, 2 parsnips, seasoning, and 1 pint (2½ cups) beer. It is tightly covered and simmered slowly for about 3 hours. See also BEEF.

rinderhirn, ox brains, usually prepared in Germany by being first blanched, then rolled in egg and breadcrumbs and fried.

rindersuppe mit milzschnitten, a traditional Austrian soup. First 1 lb. cooked milts are minced (ground), seasoned with salt, pepper, and marjoram, and then spread on small pieces of white bread which have been toasted on one side. They are covered with slices of bread similarly toasted on one side, toasted side outwards. These sandwiches are then baked in a dish and served with rich beef broth.

rindfleischwurst, a beef wurst made from a mixture of lean beef, lean pork, bacon, fat, salt, a pinch of saltpetre, ground cloves, garlic, and black pepper. When the skins have been filled with the mixture, the sausages are simmered for about 1 hour, then put into cold water for a few minutes before being hung up to dry. See also WÜRST.

rindsgulasch, beef goulash. See GULASCH.

rindsrouladen, beef olives, generally served with rice and noodles in Germany. See also BRUCKFLEISCH; HAMBURGER RAUCHFLEISCH, MILCH (MILCHBRATEN); PFEFFER-POTHAST; ROSTBRATEN; SAUERBRATEN. For Austrian beef dishes, see G'ROSTL; HUSARENFILET; MAJORAN (MAJORANFLEISCH); MARINEBRATEN; REINDLBIFTEK; TAFELSPITZ AUF ALTWIENER ART; WALDMEISTERBRATEN.

ringneck (*Anas rubripes*), a freshwater duck of the interior of the northeastern section of the U.S. and Canada, also known as black duck. It is excellent to eat, second only to the canvasback. See also WILD DUCK.

riñones, Spanish for kidneys. See also KIDNEY.

riñones al Jerez, kidneys cooked with sherry. First 6 kidneys are split and fried in about 3 tablespoons olive oil, which is then drained off; 1 glass (½ cup) sherry is added and brought to the boil, and the kidneys are cooked in it for 2–3 minutes. They are served at once.

ripa, Swedish for grouse or ptarmigan. In Sweden they are cooked by the methods used in Norway. See RYPE.

ripieno, Italian for stuffing or forcemeat, used a lot for tomatoes, sweet peppers, poultry, and meat.

rippchen, German for pork chops or cutlets from the short rib. This word is used particularly in the Rhineland.

rips, Norwegian for red currant. See also RED CURRANT.

rips iskrem, red currant ice cream. First 2 lb. currants are brought to boiling point in a wet saucepan and the juice is extracted by pressing. One lb. (2 cups) sugar (to 1 pint juice) is dissolved in it, and this is boiled for several minutes before being skimmed. The juice is then mixed with 1 pint whipped cream (for 1 pint [2 cups] juice), and chilled. This mixture is partly frozen, then beaten well before it is returned to the ice tray and freezing is continued.

ris, Danish for rice. See also RICE.

risengrød, Danish rice porridge, which can be very good. The Danes eat it with a sweet malt beer called hvidtøl, which is a non-alcoholic drink. Using a double saucepan, ½ lb. (1 cup) rice is brought to the boiling point in 1½ pints (3 cups) milk, when it is strained, then gradually stirred back into the milk and cooked over water for about 1½ hours. Risengrød is eaten with sugar and cinnamon, and each spoonful of the porridge is dipped into melted butter before eating. If very solid, it is thinned with hot milk or cream. See also GRØD.

risklatter, rice fritters. A mixture is made from 2 beaten eggs, 2 heaped tablespoons flour, grated peel or ½ lemon, 1 tablespoon each of raisins and almonds, and enough cold boiled rice (about 2 tablespoons) to make a thick batter. The fritters are fried in butter and served with a jam sauce. See also FRITTER.

ris, French for sweetbreads. See also SWEETBREADS. Those used for a main course are veal sweetbreads; lamb's sweetbreads are also served, but chiefly as part of a garnish such as *financière* or *toulousaine,* or for filling pastry cases. All sweetbreads should first be blanched by steeping in cold water, which must be changed often, to remove blood and impurities. Then they should be covered in cold water, brought to the boil gently, boiled for 2–3 minutes, drained, and plunged into cold water. They should then be trimmed and skinned before further preparation takes place.

ris de veau à crème aux champignons, 1½ lb. prepared veal sweetbreads are wrapped in a thin slice of larding fat, then put in an ovenproof dish on a bed of sliced onion, carrot, and chopped parsley, covered with equal quantities of water and white wine, or with chicken stock, seasoned, then covered and cooked in a low-to-moderate oven for 45 minutes. Meanwhile 4 oz. mushrooms are sautéed in butter until soft, when ¼ pint (½ cup) thick cream is stirred in. This mixture is heated until it thickens, then combined with the sweetbreads and served with croûtons of bread fried in butter.

Sweetbreads are also braised in stock and served with sorrel or spinach purée; coated with egg and breadcrumbs or batter and fried; or grilled on skewers (en brochette). Garnishes served with lamb's sweetbreads (*ris d'agneau*) include *banquière, Clamart, fermière, financière, jardinière, macédoine, Milanaise, régence,* and *Toulousaine.* Sauces include *allemande, beurres composés, duxelles, financière, madère, périgueux, suprême, velouté,* and *villeroi.*

ris, Norwegian for rice. See also RICE.

risengrynsgrøt, rice porridge. To prepare it, ¼ lb. (½ cup) rice is cooked, tightly covered, in 3 pints (6 cups) boiling milk for about 1 hour, when a little salt is added. It is served hot in individual bowls, sprinkled with castor sugar and cinnamon, and with a pat of butter placed on top of each portion. A glass of raspberry cordial is served with it.

ris, Swedish for rice. See also RICE.

risgrynsgröt, rice porridge. Before cooking, ½ lb. (1 cup) rice is rinsed with boiling water. Then 1 tablespoon butter is melted in a saucepan and the rice is added to it, together with ½ pint (1 cup) boiling water. The rice is cooked until the water evaporates. Then 2 pints (4 cups) milk is gradually stirred in, and simmering is continued for about 45 minutes or until the rice is tender. Salt is included, also 1 tablespoon sugar and a little more butter. The porridge is served sprinkled with equal quantities of cinnamon and castor sugar, and with cream or cold milk.

risi e bisi, a Venetian speciality made from green peas and rice. To prepare, 1 small onion is sliced and softened in 1 tablespoon hot butter. Then 2 slices chopped ham are added, and 12 oz. (3 cups) shelled peas. The pan is shaken so that all the ingredients are coated with butter, then ¾ pint (1½ cups) hot chicken stock is poured in, and when this is boiling 1 lb. (2 cups) raw rice is added, followed by a further pint (2 cups) stock. The contents are covered and cooked very gently for 15 minutes, when they are seasoned and a little more stock is added—just enough to make a trickle of liquid when cooking is completed after a further 10 minutes. The mixture should not be stirred, for the peas should be unbroken, but just before serving 1 tablespoon butter and ½ cup grated Parmesan cheese are added. A bowl of grated Parmesan cheese is also served with this dish. See also RISO, SARTÙ DI.

risi-bisi, a Polish casserole dish of rice and peas. The dish is lined with cooked rice, then cooked peas and a great deal of butter are put in the middle, and the top is sprinkled with grated cheese. It is baked for 20 minutes in a moderate oven.

riso, Italian for rice, used and grown mostly in the north of Italy beside the river Po, and one of the basic foods of Lombardy, Piedmont, and the Veneto. Its origin as an Italian food does not go as far back as that of pasta, and rice probably entered Italy either by way of Sicily or through Arab influence. In medieval Italy it was stocked by chemists and used by doctors in the treatment of stomach disorders. In 1475 Galeazzo Maria Sforza, 5th Duke of Milan, sent 12 sacks to Ercole I to be grown at Ferrara. Piedmontese rice is ideally suited for the making of risotto, because it can stand slow cooking without much liquid, and does not become soggy; the main feature of

riso

a risotto is that the various ingredients are integrated into the cooking of the rice, and (with the exception of *risotto alla milanese* and *ossi buchi*) are not served with it, as they are in many other countries. *Riso in bianco* is boiled rice. See also RICE; RISOTTO.

bomba di riso, pigeons with rice, a speciality of Parma. First 2 pigeons are simmered for 1½ hours in a sauce composed of their giblets, ¼ pint (½ cup) white wine, 1½ pints (3 cups) broth, 2 teaspoons tomato purée, and 1 tablespoon butter. A large round dish is sprinkled thickly with breadcrumbs and half filled with part-cooked plain risotto, then the quartered birds are put on top with their sauce. The remaining rice (½ lb. in all) is put on top of the birds and sprinkled with more breadcrumbs and 2 heaped tablespoons grated Parmesan cheese, and the whole is cooked in a slow oven for 1 hour.

riso al quattro formaggi, rice with four cheeses. The cheeses, bel paese, Gruyère, Parmesan, and provolone, are chopped up with ham or tongue and arranged in layers with parboiled rice. The dish is cooked in the oven until golden brown.

riso alla genovese, Genoese rice. First 1 lb. rice is boiled, strained and then dried over a low flame. It is mixed with a sauce composed of ½ lb. raw minced (ground) meat (beef or veal), 3 chopped carrots, ½ chopped head of celery, 1 large sliced onion, seasoning, herbs, 2 tablespoons butter, 2 tablespoons olive oil, and ¼ pint (½ cup) white wine, all simmered for 1 hour.

riso in bianco con tartufi bianchi, the classic way of eating white truffles raw, grated or finely sliced, with boiled rice, butter, and grated Parmesan cheese to taste.

riso ricco or *riso con la fonduta,* rich rice, or rice with fonduta. To prepare this, 1 lb. boiled and drained rice is cooked in a double boiler with a creamy *fonduta* sauce made of ¼ lb. grated Gruyère, ½ pint (1 cup) milk, 3 egg yolks, salt, and black pepper.

riso verdi, one of the inventions of Marinetti, which he described in his advant-garde cookery book *La Cucina Futurista*. A bed of cooked leaf spinach is placed in a buttered ovenproof dish, followed by a thick layer of boiled rice. This is covered with a purée of cooked green peas, powdered pistachio nuts are sprinkled on top, and the dish is baked in a low oven for 30 minutes. See also MARINETTI.

sartù di riso, one of the few Neapolitan rice dishes, and very elaborate. The bottom of a buttered ovenproof dish is covered first with breadcrumbs, then with a thick layer of boiled rice. On top are put layers of *polpette,* sliced mushrooms cooked in stock, cooked green peas, chopped cooked giblets of chicken or turkey, diced mozzarella, provolone, or Gruyère, and grated Parmesan cheese, with a layer of thick fresh tomato sauce cooked with onion, garlic, herbs, and ham. All are covered with a thick layer of rice and topped with more tomato sauce, grated Parmesan cheese, and finally breadcrumbs. Butter is dotted all over it and the dish is baked in a moderate oven for 30 minutes, or until the top is brown and crusty. See also RISI E BISI; SUPPLÌ.

risotto, a dish which is a speciality of the north of Italy, particularly Piedmont, Lombardy, and the Veneto. It consists of rice cooked slowly in liquid, which is added gradually. The rice grown in Piedmont is the best for making a risotto, and should be used whenever possible. The basic method of preparation will be found under *risotto bianco.* All risottos are served with grated cheese.

risotto alla certosina, risotto served with peas cooked in butter, tomatoes, and Parmesan cheese. Shrimps or prawns cooked in butter and flambéed with brandy are added to the pea mixture and this is put on top of the risotto. More cheese is served separately.

risotto alla finanziera, risotto as above, with the addition of chicken livers.

risotto alla marsala, as for *risotto alla milanese,* but ½ glass Marsala is used instead of the beef marrow.

risotto alla milanese, the most famous risotto. The rice is fried in butter with onion, and with chunks of beef marrow if available; it is then swelled with white wine, as in *risotto bianco,* and chicken stock. When the mixture has been cooked to a creamy consistency, a pinch of saffron is added. Then 1 tablespoon butter and 1 tablespoon grated Parmesan cheese are stirred in. (Parmesan cheese is also served separately.) *Risotto alla milanese* is frequently presented as a dish on its own, but it is traditionally served with *ossi buchi alla milanese.*

risotto alla sbirraglia, risotto with jointed casseroled chicken, ham or bologna sausage, onion, tomatoes, celery, garlic, sweet pepper, mushrooms, and basil or marjoram, all cooked together. The liquid from the casserole is used as stock. About ½ cup rice per person is allowed for the risotto.

risotto alla veronese, a plain risotto with ham. A mushroom sauce is served separately.

risotto bianco, 1 oz. (1 heaped tablespoon) butter is melted in a heavy pan, and 1 small, finely chopped onion is fried in it until soft and golden. Then ½ lb. (1 cup) rice is added and stirred until it is impregnated with the butter but is still white; ⅓ pint (¾ cup) white wine is poured in, and the rice is cooked over a medium flame until the wine has almost all disappeared. Then 1¾ pints (3½ cups) water is added gradually, one cup at a time. The risotto will take 20–30 minutes to cook, and towards the end must be stirred continuously, otherwise it will stick.

risotto con brodo di pesce, risotto made with fish stock and 1 chopped garlic clove, 1 chopped celery stalk, 1 carrot, and 2 tablespoons parsley, all previously fried with 1 small sliced onion in oil or butter.

risotto con funghi, risotto made with mushrooms.

risotto con gamberi, risotto made with celery, onion, garlic, and parsley fried as above, with crayfish or prawns and fish stock.

risotto con quaglie, risotto with quails cooked in wine and bay leaves (1 per bird).

risotto di frutti di mare, risotto made with fish stock and shellfish.

risotto di peoci, risotto made with mussels and a touch of garlic.

risotto di scampi, a typically Venetian risotto, made with scampi cooked in butter and garlic. On special occasions, brandy is poured over the shellfish and set alight before they are added to the risotto.

risotto di secole, a Venetian dish. *Secole* are the scraps left on beef or veal bones after a roast has been boned. To a plain risotto is added a sauce made with this beef or veal (about ½ lb.) cooked in butter and seasoned with salt, pepper, and nutmeg. Then 1 chopped celery stalk and 1 sliced carrot are added, and 1 glass (¼ cup) white wine.

risotto in capro roman, a Venetian dish despite its name, of risotto made with 1 onion, ½ lb. lean chopped mutton or lamb, 2 large tomatoes, ½ pint (1 cup) stock, and ⅛ pint (¼ cup) white wine.

risotto in salto, leftover risotto coated with breadcrumbs and fried like an omelette.

rissois, a Portuguese speciality from the region to the northwest of Lisbon. First ½ pint (1 cup) water is boiled with 1 heaped tablespoon butter; then ½ pint (1 cup) cold water is mixed with 4 oz. (1 cup) flour. The two mixtures are combined, gently heated, and stirred together until thick. When the paste has cooled, it is kneaded and rolled into thin circles.

Half of each circle is filled with shrimps or *bacalhau* in a sauce crème, and the other half of the circle is folded over and the edges dampened. The patties are then dipped in egg and breadcrumbs and fried in deep oil.

rissole, a small round cake about 3 inches in diameter, made of minced (ground) cold meat (sometimes mixed with a little chopped onion and parsley) bound with a beaten egg and fried on both sides in hot fat or oil. It is usually rather uninteresting, and is not at all like the original 13th-century dish or the modern French equivalent (*rissole*). Andrew Boorde, an English physician and author writing in the 16th century, gives the spelling as "Risshe shewes," which might indicate a derivation from "reshow" or *réchauffé*, and the rissole was at that time a batter with cooked chopped meat and herbs mixed in it.

rissole, a French dish of short crust or puff pastry stuffed with chopped, cooked poultry or meats and herbs, folded over like a turnover, with the edges sealed, then fried in deep oil or fat and garnished with fried parsley. Very small rissoles are used as a garnish for joints of meat or for poultry. Sometimes the rissole is dipped in egg and breadcrumbs before being fried. A *rissole de pommes* may be made with apple, and other cooked fruit is also used in the same way. In the 13th century in France the word was *roinsolles,* which referred purely to a batter fried in dripping. Later these pancakes were filled with chopped meat and herbs.

rissoler, a French culinary term meaning to brown slowly in fat or oil.

river veal, see PONTOISE VEAL.

riverbank grape (*Vitis vulpina*), a wild vine that grows in North America and produces a black berry which is too sour to eat raw, but with plenty of sugar makes good tarts, pies, and preserves. The vine is sometimes found along river banks, hence its name.

riz, French for rice. Cooked rice is used in croquettes, *timbales,* and as a filling for tomatoes, *bouchées,* and *vol-au-vents.* It is always served in a ring mould with *blanquette de veau.* Some French sweet dishes are made with rice, as *riz à la crème.* See also RICE.

riz à la crème, 4 oz. (½ cup) rice is boiled with 1½ pints (3 cups) flavoured milk, 5 tablespoons sugar, and a pinch of salt. When soft and cooked, 2 tablespoons butter and 1 cup cream are added. This is used as a basis for hot or cold puddings, when it may be mixed with dessert or crystallised fruits, baked in a pastry case, baked with caramel sauce in a *bain-marie,* or used for *condés.*

riz à la creole, 1 lb. washed Indian rice is put into a thick pan with salt and about 1½ inches water barely to cover. It is covered and cooked over a moderate heat for 30 minutes; then it is pulled to the side of the heat, and left for a further 30 minutes to allow it to dry out. It is usually served with *rougail.*

riz à la grecque, 6 tablespoons butter is melted in a pan; 1 medium-sized sliced onion is added and fried gently, but not browned. Then 1 lb. (2 cups) rice is added and allowed to cook until it has an opaque look. Then 4 pints (8 cups) water or stock is added, followed by seasoning, and the rice is left to cook gently, without stirring, for 20 minutes. When the rice is cooked, 1 cup spicy chopped cooked sausage, ½ cup shredded cooked lettuce, ½ cup cooked green peas, and red sweet peppers sautéed in butter are added, then mixed carefully so as not to break the grains of rice.

riz à l'impératrice, see IMPÉRATRICE, À LA.

rizi, Greek for rice, which is used a good deal in Greece as an accompaniment to fish, meat, and poultry. See also PILAFI; RICE.

rizogalo, Greek rice pudding. Rice pudding is served cold in Greece, and usually on its own, between courses, not at the end of the meal as a dessert. To prepare it, 1 quart (4 cups) milk is boiled with 6 oz. (1 cup) rice, 6 oz. (1 cup) sugar, and 2 teaspoons corn flour (cornstarch). When cooked, cinnamon and lemon peel to taste are sprinkled on top. Sometimes 4 egg yolks are added, and they are beaten into the milk before the rice is cooked.

rizoto, the word for risotto in Yugoslavia. It is often made with shellfish or squid.

rizzared haddock, smoked haddock dried in the sun. See HADDOCK.

roach (*Rutilus rutilus*), a silvery freshwater fish of the carp family, common in England and Europe. It has quite a good taste, but its numerous forked bones make eating difficult and it is therefore usually filleted and fried. In the U.S. the name is given to a different fish, *Leiostomus xanthurus,* sometimes also known as spot or golden shiner. It can be cooked as *carp.*

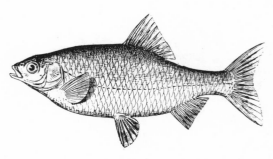

roach

roast, I. The course in a meal now called the main course; in France this was originally served after the *sorbet* and before the *entremets.* After 1900 in Britain it followed the soup, the fish, and the poultry or game, and it always consisted of roast meat. II. The name for the joint of meat, game, or poultry that has been roasted, that is "the roast."

roast, to, originally to cook on a spit over an open fire. This is now known as spit-roasting, as most roasting today is done in an enclosed oven heated by electricity, gas, wood, or coal.

roastit bubbly-jock, a Scottish dish of turkey, stuffed with a mixture of 2 cups breadcrumbs, 6 oysters, 8 chestnuts, chopped turkey liver, 1 chopped celery stalk, 1 tablespoon chopped parsley, and seasoning, then rubbed with butter and roasted for 20–25 minutes per lb. A gravy is made with the liquid from the cooked giblets and 1 tablespoon red currant jelly, and it is reduced on top of the stove. Bread sauce is served separately.

rob, an Old English word for the juice extracted from various fruits, boiled to a syrup with sugar and spice, and stored. In country districts elderberries were often used for this. About ½ lb. sugar is added for every pint of juice, and a stick of cinnamon, then the rob is covered and boiled slowly until thick.

Rob Roy's pleesure, a traditional Scottish dish of a haunch of venison braised with herbs, root vegetables, stock, and claret. It is served with rowan jelly. See also VENISON.

robalo (*Centropomus undecimalis*), a sea fish with a pointed nose, found in tropical American waters. It is highly thought of as food.

robalo, Portuguese for sea bass. See also BASS.

robalo no forno à portuguesa, a whole 2-lb. bass baked for 40 minutes with 4 tablespoons olive oil, juice of 1 lemon, 2 tablespoons tomato juice, 2 tomatoes, 1 garlic clove, 2 small sliced onions, 1 lb. diced potatoes, 1 tablespoon butter, and ½ pint (1 cup) white wine.

robalo, see SERRANO.

Robert, sauce, one of the oldest of the French brown sauces, said to have been invented in France in the early 17th century by Robert Vinot. A roux is made with 2 tablespoons each of butter and flour, and 3 tablespoons finely chopped onions, first softened in butter, is added. It is moistened with ¼ pint (½ cup) white wine and ½ pint (1 cup) strong bouillon, seasoned well, and then simmered for 30 minutes. Before serving a few drops of good wine vinegar and 1 teaspoon French mustard are added. The sauce is served with goose, pork, and venison.

robert saus, a Dutch sauce served with pork, and made with the pan drippings remaining after cooking pork chops or a joint. To the pan drippings are added about 1 pint (2 cups) water, 1 tablespoon chopped onion, ¼ teaspoon ground chilli, 4 cloves, 1 bay leaf, 2 teaspoons sugar, and 1 teaspoon mustard. All are simmered together for about 20 minutes, then strained to make a brown sauce with a *beurre manié*. Finally about 1 tablespoon Madeira is added to taste.

robin saus, a sauce sometimes used in Norway to accompany certain game dishes. Apples are cooked in dry cider or white wine, and puréed. When the purée is cold, mayonnaise or grated horseradish is gradually stirred in.

robiola, one of the best Italian cheeses, runny and soft, but delicate in taste and texture. It is made from cow's milk and comes from Lombardy. In Piedmont, a variety is made with goat's milk.

robiolina, a stronger version of *robiola*.

rocamadour, a French goat's milk cheese produced in Guyenne; it is in season from April to November.

rocambole (*Allium scordoprasum*), one of the milder varieties of garlic which is very popular in Denmark and grown a great deal there. It is also common to central, but not southern, Europe, and is found in the north of England and southern Scotland. It is not very common in the U.S.

rochambeau, à la, a French garnish for meat, consisting of braised carrots, stuffed lettuce, boiled cauliflowers, *pommes Anna*, and demi-glace.

rochen, German for skate or ray. See also SKATE.

rochen mit sauerkraut, skate poached in milk with sliced onion, cloves, and bay leaf for 5 minutes only, then drained, brushed with melted butter and flour, and baked for 20 minutes. It is served with sauerkraut.

rochen mit zwiebelbutter, skate poached as above, but cooked for 30 minutes; it is served with melted butter which has chopped browned onions and lemon juice incorporated in it.

rock cakes, small English cakes made from 12 oz. (2¾ cups) flour mixed with a pinch of salt, 1 teaspoon baking powder, ¼ teaspoon mixed spice, and ¼ teaspoon nutmeg. Then 6 oz. (¾ cup) butter is rubbed in with the fingertips, followed by 6 oz. (¾ cup) sugar. Next 3 oz. (½ cup) currants, 1 beaten egg, and just enough milk to make a stiff mixture are added. This mixture is made into rocky-looking mounds measuring about 2 inches across the base, which are baked on a greased baking sheet in a moderate-to-hot oven for 15–20 minutes.

rock cod (*Epinephelus gigas*), a sea fish, common off the coasts of Spain, which is related to the *Serranidae*. It grows to a length of 6 or 7 feet, has firm white flesh, and is extremely good to eat. The large fish are cut into steaks or fillets which are fried or grilled, while the young ones are often casseroled, whole, with onions, garlic, tomatoes, herbs, and wine. Rock cod is called *mero* in Spain.

rock cornish hen, a breed of poultry resulting from a cross between Plymouth Rock hens and various small game or bantam cocks. It is immensely popular in the U.S. where it is widely available, usually in the frozen state. The birds are small and compact, and in both appearance and flavour resem-

ble a squab rather more than a chicken. Depending on the age and size of the bird it will serve one person, or at most, 2. The birds may be roasted or braised in the same way as chicken or squab, and are sometimes accompanied by cumberland sauce, with wild rice as a vegetable.

rock eel (*Anarrhicas lupus*), a species of catfish with a pinkish tinge on the firm flesh, usually sold skinned. In Great Britain it is often sold, quite erroneously, as rock salmon, especially in fried fish shops. See also ROCK SALMON.

rock hind (*Epinephelus adscenscionis*), a grouper with brown spots found in water off the southern coasts of the U.S.

rock medlar (*Amelanchier ovalis*), also called Savoy medlar, sweet pear, or grape pear, the small fruit of a European shad bush. It is blue-black in colour, about the size and shape of a large black currant; it is used in the same way as rowan berry although it is larger. In the U.S. many varieties are grown, the best being *A. bartramiana, A. canadensis, A. florida, A. laevis*, and *A. oblongifolia*.

rock salmon, I. *Pollachius virens*, also called coalfish, a large saltwater fish found mainly off Icelandic, Norwegian, and Scottish coasts. It is not unlike cod and is marketed fresh, dried, and smoked. In Ireland it is called *glassin*. The name is also used in Britain as a blanket term to cover various white fish of the cheaper variety. See also ROCK EEL. II. In the U.S. the name rock salmon is also given to *Zonichthys falcata* and to amberfish.

rockenbolle, see ONION.

rocket (*Eruca sativa*), an old cottage-garden herb with pleasant peppery leaves which, when gathered young, are good in a green salad. It is not to be confused with the American rocket salad, which is another name for winter cress. In the U.S. it is sometimes called *roquette*.

rockfish, a collective name for any of the numerous seafishes which inhabit rocky coasts or rocky sea-bottoms, especially the red rockfish (*Sebastodes ruberrimus*) and the black rockfish (*S. mystinus*), which are highly thought of as food on the Pacific coast of the U.S. Striped bass and several groupers are also included under this name, although these fish are of different genera.

rock-partridge, SEE PARTRIDGE.

rocksalt, SEE SALT.

Rocky Mountain whitefish (*Coregonus williamsoni*), a species of whitefish found in North America from Vancouver to Colorado. They make good eating and can be cooked as trout. See also WHITEFISH.

rodaballo, Spanish for turbot. Turbot fished from Spanish water makes rather coarse eating.

rødbeter, Norwegian for beetroot. See also BEETROOT.

krydrete rødbeter, Norwegian spiced beetroot, which is much used, chilled and garnished with either chervil or parsley, in the preparation of *smørgåsbord*. Beetroots are baked and then peeled; when cold, they are sliced thinly and left to stand for 30 minutes. The juice is later drained and measured, and three-quarters of that amount of french dressing, together with onion, garlic, bay leaf, and celery seed is mixed with it. The resulting dressing is seasoned, using black pepper and cayenne as well as salt, and left to stand for a period of about 12 hours. Then it is poured over the beetroot, which are left to stand for a further 12 hours before being put into covered jars.

rodding, Swedish for mountain trout, which are of good quality in Sweden. See also TROUT.

stekt rodding, fried trout, popular in the north of Sweden.

rødfisk, Danish for Norway haddock which is eaten a lot in Denmark. See NORWAY HADDOCK.

rødgrød med fløde, Danish fruit mould with cream, an almost traditional summer dessert in Denmark, and also served as a cold soup. Red currants, black currants, and raspberries or strawberries are mashed with a little water and simmered until of a consistency to go through a sieve. Castor sugar is added to the juice and it is brought to the boil. Corn flour (cornstarch) is creamed with water (½ oz. for every pint of juice) and gradually stirred into the juice, which is brought once more to the boil and simmered for a few minutes. During cooling, it should be stirred frequently. It is garnished with fresh red currants and chilled cream.

rødkål, Danish for red cabbage, a very popular vegetable in Denmark, where it is often served with poultry and pork as well as with a number of other meat dishes. The Danes have several ways of serving this vegetable. For each of the three following recipes the red cabbage should be finely grated or shredded. For one recipe a medium-sized red cabbage is simmered for about 2½ hours in water, ¼ cup vinegar, a little castor sugar, and salt. Before serving, about 3 tablespoons red currant jelly or juice is stirred in.

Another method is to stir a medium-sized red cabbage into 3 oz. (scant ½ cup) melted butter and 2 heaped tablespoons sugar, then gently cook for 20 minutes. Juice of ½ lemon and 1½ gills (¾ cup) boiling water are added, and cooking is continued for about 2 hours; red currant juice or jelly, as above, is stirred in before serving.

In another variation red cabbage is sprinkled with salt and left standing for 1½ hours, when it is fried in 4 oz. (½ cup) lard or butter with a chopped onion. A grated apple and sufficient water to cover are then added to the pan, and the contents are simmered for about 2 hours, when 1 level tablespoon corn flour (cornstarch) creamed with 2 tablespoons water and ¼ pint (½ cup) red wine is added, and all allowed to cook for a further few minutes.

In parts of Denmark, when cooking red cabbage, the vinegar from pickled beetroot is substituted for ordinary vinegar or lemon juice, and caraway seeds can also be added to the liquid. See also GRØNSAGER; RED CABBAGE.

rødkål, Norwegian for red cabbage, usually cooked as in Denmark. See RODKÅL.

rodovalho, see PREGADO.

rødspaette, Danish for plaice. Cooking methods are similar to those used in Norway. See RØDSPETTE.

rødspette, Norwegian for plaice. A traditional method of cooking is to skin and fillet the fish, salt it, and then leave for 10 minutes. After this it is first half-fried in oil, then the pan is drained and the frying finished in butter. The dish is garnished with cooked spinach, asparagus tips or mushrooms, and shrimps cooked in cream. Parsley and lemon wedges are served with it. See also FISK; PLAICE.

rødspotta, Swedish for plaice, often used for *fiskgratin* as well as being served fried. See also FISK; PLAICE.

roe, either "hard roe," the mass of fish eggs in the ovarian membrane, which comes usually, though not always, from the female fish; or "soft roe," often known as milt, the gonad of the male fish.

When a rather large fish is bought with a thick roe attached, it is better to remove the roe and cook it separately first, using it later as a garnish; if fish and roe are cooked together, the fish will be ready before the roe, and waiting for the roe to be cooked through would result in overcooking and the loss of the fish's milky texture.

The finest of all the hard roes is caviar, the next *botargo,* followed by salmon roe. These are usually sold already lightly salted and pressed, ready for use. Fresh or smoked cod's roe is also very good, and is served as a savoury or a first course. The smoked roe is sold ready for use; the hard fresh roe is cooked as follows. After being gently poached in water, it is left to cool; when cold, the roe is cut into slices which are dipped in flour or batter, fried, and served with lemon

wedges. Fresh cod's roe is also excellent made into fishcakes with the addition of herbs, soaked bread, and mace. The most common soft roe comes from the herring, and is best gently cooked in butter with lemon juice, seasoning, and sometimes a drop or two of worcestershire sauce, and served with hot toast. Soft roe is also good poached and used as a garnish for, or incorporated with, thick whitefish. In France it is often possible to buy a quantity of soft and hard sole roe, which is very delicate.

roe deer, see DEER; ROEBUCK.

roebuck or **roe deer** (*Caprelous*), the smallest European deer. It can be prepared and cooked in any way that is suitable for *izard* or venison. See also RÅDYR; REH.

roebuck sauce, the English version of sauce *chevreuil.* To prepare it 2 oz. chopped ham and 2 small onions are browned in 2 tablespoons butter; then 1 tablespoon wine vinegar and a bouquet garni are added, followed by a sauce made of 2 tablespoons unreduced demi-glace, 1 gill (½ cup) port wine, and 2 tablespoons red currant jelly, all heated and simmered for 10 minutes.

roesti, see RÖSTI.

røget, Danish for smoked, particularly used for fish, as for example røget aal (smoked eel) and røget laks (smoked salmon), both eaten a great deal in Denmark.

roggenbrot, see PUMPERNICKEL.

rogn, Norwegian for hard fish roe, eaten a great deal in Norway, both fresh and salted; soft roe is *melke.* See also ROE.

rognon, French for kidney. See also KIDNEY.

rognons de veau à la liégeoise, a speciality from Liége in Belgium. To prepare, 4 sliced veal kidneys are browned in butter; then ½ pint (1 cup) white wine and 12 crushed juniper berries are added and the kidneys are simmered until tender. Sometimes quartered parboiled potatoes are included. The whole dish should be cooked in 20 minutes, otherwise the kidneys will be overdone. See also ROGNONS DE COQ.

rognone, Italian for kidney. See also KIDNEYS.

rognoni trifolati, stewed kidneys. Kidneys are first blanched in boiling water, drained, and dried, then fried in oil or butter; ½ pint (1 cup) white wine or Marsala is poured over and reduced by boiling.

rognonnade, French for a cut of veal (the loin) with the kidney left in it. This joint is usually roasted.

rognons de coq, I. Red kidney-shaped dried beans, used in France for soups, salads, and purées. II. The gonads of a male fowl or cock, considered a delicacy in France. They are used poached, and are mixed with a variety of sauces as a garnish (*financière, gauloise*), or are put into pastry cases and served as a hot hors d'oeuvre such as *salpicon à la financière.*

roh, German for raw, crude, or unrefined. It is used to denote, for example, raw sugar (rohzucker) and raw curds (rohkäse), that is curds either before or after cheese making, or when used in the same way as cottage cheese.

rohkost-tomaten, a Swiss recipe for stuffed tomatoes. The tops of 8 large tomatoes are cut off and the pulp removed. This is mixed with 2 large chopped apples, 2 heads of celery, ¼ cup lemon juice and salt; then 3 tablespoons olive oil is mixed with 3 tablespoons thick or sour cream, and all is stirred together and put back into the tomato shells. The tomatoes are garnished with chopped chives, watercress, and radishes.

roi, le, a delicious triple-cream French cheese from the Loire valley and Atlantic provinces. It is small, about 3 inches across, and round, with a creamy, soft, but firm texture. It contains 75 percent cow's milk fat and it is one of the best French cheeses.

rojões à moda do Minho, chopped pork Minho-style, a Portuguese recipe. It is made from 1 lb. chopped leg of pork marinated for 6–8 hours in ½ pint (1 cup) white wine with 6 small sliced onions, parsley, 1 bay leaf, 1 garlic clove, and 1 teaspoon paprika. The meat is drained and fried in oil until brown, when the marinade is added and reduced. The dish is served with diced fried potatoes and slices of lemon or bitter orange.

rokadur, a Yugoslavian cheese made from ewe's milk, and not unlike roquefort.

röktfiskpudding, Swedish for smoked fish pudding. A 3-lb. cooked and smoked haddock is skinned, boned, shredded, and layered in a dish with thinly sliced potatoes and seasoning (the pudding should start with a layer of potatoes). Then 2 beaten eggs are mixed with ½ pint milk and poured over the dish, with additional milk sprinkled over to cover the contents. The pudding is baked in a fairly hot oven for about 45 minutes or until set. See also FISK (FISKPUDDING); HADDOCK; KOLJA; NORWAY HADDOCK.

röktlax, Swedish for smoked salmon (lax), which is prepared in the same way as the Norwegian røyktlaks.

rolé, Italian for roulade, usually made from lean beef or veal. It is a speciality of Parma.

rolé di vitello, 2 lb. boneless lean veal is flattened and then rolled up with a filling of a flat omelette or *frittata* cooked with 2 eggs, 2 slices chopped mortadella, 2 tablespoons grated Parmesan cheese, and chopped parsley. It is then tied with string, browned in butter, and finally simmered in 1 pint (2 cups) milk for 2 hours. It is served hot or cold. Alternatively, it can be stuffed with slices of raw ham and whole hard-boiled eggs with sage, and simmered in white wine.

rolinhos de fígado, a Portuguese dish of baked stuffed liver rolls. Thin good-sized slices of liver are spread with a mixture of chopped onions, cooked rice, parsley, and seasoning, all sautéed in butter. The slices are then wrapped in rashers of bacon and secured with cotton or a stick, and sautéed in hot oil. Cooked tomatoes and salt are added, and the whole is simmered until the liver is cooked. The rolls are removed, and the sauce is thickened with tomato purée and allowed to reduce on a hot flame. The dish is garnished with chopped parsley. See also FIGADO.

rolling pin, a cylindrical utensil with a handle at each end, used for rolling out pastry. It is made of either wood or glass. The glass rolling pins can be filled with iced water, which ensures that the pastry is kept cold.

rollmops, a German method of preparing fresh herrings, known throughout the English-speaking world and in Jewish communities everywhere. The herrings are divested of heads and tails, cleaned, and soaked first in water for 12 hours, then in milk for a further 12. They are then split down the centre and boned. Some onion, gherkin, and peppercorns are put onto each fillet, before they are rolled up and secured with toothpicks. When prepared, the fillets are placed in a large jar. The roes are then beaten until smooth and mixed with enough boiled vinegar to fill the jar. Bay leaves, mustard seed, peppercorns, onion, and sliced gherkin are also added to the jars before securing down the lids. The rollmops should be left for at least 4 days before being used. They are often served with a sauce of sour cream. See also HERRING.

rollot, a French cow's milk cheese from the department of the Somme. It has a reddish crust, and is in season from November to June.

rolls, bread dough shaped into small rounds or oblong forms and baked until the outside is crisp. See YEAST DOUGH.

rolo de ovos, a Portuguese sponge which is rolled like a Swiss roll. It is made with 6 eggs beaten with 12 oz. (1½ cups) sugar and 1 tablespoon flour, mixed and spread on a greased baking sheet and cooked in a moderate oven for 30 minutes. When slightly cooled, it is dredged with icing sugar and rolled up. It is served at the end of a meal, with port.

roly-poly, an old English pudding made from suet crust pastry rolled out to an oblong, spread with jam or golden syrup, (treacle), then rolled up like a Swiss roll. This is usually put into a floured cloth, tied, and boiled in water for 1½–2 hours. It is served hot with melted jam. If baked on a baking sheet in the oven, it is always specified as baked roly-poly. See also PASTRY, SUET CRUST.

romadur käse, a soft-ripened cheese from the southern regions of Austria and Germany, particularly Bavaria. It is made from cow's milk, either unskimmed or partly skimmed, and is made in much the same way as limburger except that it contains less salt and has a milder aroma.

romaine, French for cos lettuce, also called romaine in the U.S. It is said to have been imported into France by Rabelais, the French writer and gourmet (1490–1553). See also LAITUE.

romaine, à la, I. A French garnish for roasted meat, consisting of *timbales* of spinach and individual *dariole* moulds of *pommes Anna,* served with liquid tomato sauce and veal gravy. II. A French method of serving chicken. See POULET, SAUTÉ À LA ROMAINE.

romaine

romana, a Yugoslavian cow's milk cheese eaten with hot peppers and slices of raw onion.

Romanoff or *Romanov,* I. A French garnish for large and small cuts of meat. It consists of rounds of cucumber stuffed with chopped mushrooms (the cucumber is first braised whole, then cut into rounds which are sprinkled with breadcrumbs and browned), and tartlet-shaped *pommes duchesse* filled with *salpicon* of celeriac and mushrooms bound with sauce velouté and sprinkled with grated horseradish, It is served with demi-glace flavoured with Madeira wine. II. A French dessert dish of fruits such as strawberries, peaches, apricots, pears, etc., soaked in orange juice and curaçao, chilled, and decorated with *crème chantilly.*

romans, a French goat's milk cheese produced in the Dauphiné. It is in season from May to July.

Romaria d'Agonia, the most famous folk festival in Portugal. It begins on August 19, the Feast of the Assumption, and lasts for a week. It is a rather noisy festival, beginning at 4 A.M. at Viana do Castelo, the capital of Minho, with the *alvaradas* (awakeners) thundering through the streets playing bagpipes and banging big drums. Soon the streets are crowded and noisy with the music of many bands. Those who are allergic to Portuguese music would be well advised to keep away, for the noisy celebrations continue in full force for seven days, culminating in many bullfights. Open-air meals and picnics are those most favoured, and traditional dishes such as *bacal-*

hau à Portugueza, cestinhos de verduras, and *salada de alface com cebolhas* are eaten.

romarin, French for rosemary, used particularly in France in the cooking of meat and fish.

rømme, Norwegian for sour cream.

rømmegrøt, a traditional sweet, sometimes eaten for breakfast, consisting of semolina pudding made with sour cream. It is called a "porridge" in Norway.

rømmesalat, shredded lettuce served with ½ pint sour cream mixed with 1 teaspoon lemon juice and a pinch of sugar, and garnished with hard-boiled eggs.

rømmevafler, sour cream waffles. To prepare them ½ pint (1 cup) milk and ½ pint (1 cup) water are gradually stirred into 1 pint (2 cups) sour cream. This liquid is beaten into ¾ lb. (3 cups) sifted flour, with sugar and salt to taste, and the mixture is then well beaten before being cooked on a hot buttered waffle iron. See also VAFLER.

Roncal, a hard Spanish cheese which is good for grating, for it keeps well. It takes its name from the Roncal Valley in Navarre, and is the most popular cheese of northern Spain. Roncal is made from cow's milk and rennet. It is hard-pressed, salted, and smoked. The cheese is yellow and close-grained, weighs about 6 lb., and has a rather sharp flavour.

rondin, a French metal cooking-pot, also called a fait-tout. It is round, has two handles and a close-fitting lid, and is used for making stews.

rook (*Corvus frugilegus*), a fairly large, black bird of the crow family. A gregarious bird, it nests in colonies which are known as rookeries. Only the young birds can be eaten; they are quite useful for adding to game soup or stew, and should not be thrown away if there is another game dish to which they can contribute. Rook pie is another dish that can be made with them, but only the breast meat should be used for this as it is the only part of the bird that is completely free from bones. Even so, the flavour scarcely justifies the preparation.

rookworst, a Dutch sausage which has a spiced, smoky flavour and needs slow cooking. It is usually served with kale and potatoes. See also BOERENKOOL; GELDERSE ROOKWORST.

room, Dutch for cream.

roompudding, a blancmange made from 1 pint (2 cups) cream and ¼ pint (½ cup) milk, a few drops of vanilla essence, and sugar or vanilla sugar to taste, brought to the boil, and mixed with 1 tablespoon gelatine which has been dissolved in water. The mixture is allowed to cool until it begins to thicken, when ½ pint (1 cup) whipped cream is stirred in. The pudding is then poured into a mould and chilled. Sometimes, before the mixture thickens, the Dutch housewife adds another ingredient such as sponge (lady) fingers soaked in brandy, ground almonds, chopped dates, figs, or macaroons.

root vegetables, vegetables which are in fact the swollen underground roots of various plants, not the foliage that grows above ground (green vegetables). The most important root vegetables (also known as tubers) include beetroot, carrot, celeriac, kohlrabi, parsnip, potato, radish, salsify, and turnip. Some underground fungi, like the truffle, are tubers, but they are not considered to be root vegetables. Onion, although the bulbous root is partly underground, is of a different formation; it is an interleaved bulb, not solid, and, therefore, not a true root vegetable.

rophos, the Greek name for a large thick reddish-brown grouper. It is excellent to eat, and can be cut into steaks and grilled, fried, or served *plaki.*

Roquefort, the only French cheese that has challenged the right of brie to the title "roi des fromages," calls itself "fromage des rois et des papes." It is the oldest known French cheese and takes its name from a village in the Rouergue country in the Cévennes mountains, one of the poorest agricultural districts in France. It is the sole blue-veined cheese to be made from ewe's milk; it contains a mixture of the unskimmed yields of both morning and evening milkings, and is only made during the lambing season. It is rennetted at a temperature of 90°F (32°C); the curd is rapidly coagulated, drained, and then piled in layers between mouldy breadcrumbs, a selective culture of *Penicillium roqueforti* eventually producing in the cheese the familiar blue veining. After salting and pressing, the cheese curds, in whatever village or district they have been made, is brought for slow and careful maturing in the natural limestone caves of Roquefort, where an underground lake creates a constant humid atmosphere that is uniquely favourable to the ripening process.

roquette, French for rocket, used for flavouring a green salad. See also ROCKET.

roquille, the French culinary term for candied peel (orange) used in cakes and confectionery.

rørt smør, the Danish term for butter beaten well until quite soft. It is used extensively in Denmark, where boiled vegetables are usually tossed in it.

roscón, a Spanish ring-shaped cake, from the word rosca, a twist or coil. To prepare it 1 lb. ground almonds is mixed with ½ lb. (1 cup) sugar, grated peel of ½ lemon, and ½ teaspoon cinnamon. Then 6 beaten egg yolks are gradually added, and finally 6 beaten egg whites are folded in. The mixture is poured into a buttered ring-mould and cooked for 30–45 minutes in a moderate oven. When cool, the cake is turned out, painted with a syrup made from 2 tablespoons sugar to 4 tablespoons water, and finished by being brushed with stiffly beaten egg white. It is put back in the oven for 2–3 minutes to set, and can be eaten hot or cold.

roscón de boniatos, a Spanish dessert of sweet potatoes. First 4 large oven-baked sweet potatoes are skinned, sieved, and mixed with 3 beaten egg yolks and 2 tablespoons ground almonds. This mixture is placed in a ring-mould and painted with a hot sweet syrup (as described for *roscón*). The egg whites are beaten with sugar and brushed over it, and a little cinnamon is sprinkled on top. The dish is baked in a moderate oven for 15–20 minutes until the meringue is slightly browned. It is best eaten cold.

rose, I. A plant of the *Rosaceae* family, now grown almost entirely for decorative purposes but once widely eaten. A sweet pudding was made in China from rose petals, and in Egypt and the Balkan states rose petal jam is still made. See GLYKO; GÜL RECELI. It is believed to have mildly aphrodisiac qualities. In England, candied rose petals were a popular confection until recent times. There are many varieties of roses with different colours, scents, and habits of growth, but the most popular all-round favourite for candying is the province rose (*Rosa provincialis*) which has a red and a white variety, strong growth and an abundance of fragrant blooms. The fresh dry petals are painted singly with 1 teaspoon gum tragacanth dissolved to a smooth paste in water; then equal quantities of castor sugar and glucose are sifted together, and both sides of each petal are covered with it. The petals are then dried slowly in the sun until firm. II. A pastry ornament, usually rose-shaped. It is used to cover the hole made in a pie in order to let the steam escape; it is baked separately from the pie, and put in position when both are cooked.

rose vinegar, a delightfully aromatic vinegar made by macerating about 3 oz. red rose petals in 1 quart wine vinegar for at least 10 days. It is strained, and is then ready for use.

rose water, an important ingredient in Balkan and Oriental cookery, always used in *rahat lokum* and for compotes. It was once also in use in England for cakes and sweets. When used with discretion it imparts a fragrant perfume and flavour. In former times the best rose water came from the famous rose gardens of Bulgaria, where the perfume essence for Attar of Roses also originated.

rose geranium (*Geraniaceae*), a member of the geranium family, with a pretty serrated 7-pointed leaf which has a strong smell of roses. A few crushed leaves add delicacy and aroma to apples, blackberries, or rhubarb when cooked with them. A few leaves mixed with fresh cream and heated, but not boiled, in a double boiler, then left to get cold, impart an exquisite flavour to the cream. The leaves are removed before the cream is served.

rose hips, the fruit of the dog rose (*Rosa canina*). The hips are gathered when ripe and used for making jams, jellies, and preserves. They are rich in vitamin C, and a commercially prepared rose-hip syrup is given to children, or people with a vitamin C deficiency. The jelly is good to eat with roasted meat or game, but it should have a little apple cooked with it since hips are low in pectin. They are used extensively in Germany and Denmark for sauces and preserves. See also HAGE-BUTTEN; HYBEN.

rosefish (*Sebastes marinus*), a variety of Norway haddock found on both the European and American coasts of the North Atlantic. When fully grown it is a bright rose- or orange-red, and it has an excellent flavour. See also NORWAY HADDOCK.

rosemary (*Rosmarinus officinalis*), a perennial aromatic herb which has small blue flowers and grows to a height of about 5 feet. From the Middle Ages onwards, rosemary has been associated with the Virgin Mary, and a wedding used not to be complete unless the bride was followed by someone carrying a bunch of rosemary. The flowers were candied in sugar as a conserve, and the dried leaves were smoked in a pipe as a cure for chest complaints. The flavour of rosemary is strong, and while the addition of a little in cooking is interesting, too much can be quite unpleasant; it is best used discreetly, with beef, lamb, or pork. The Italians, however, use it lavishly with roast young lamb and sucking pig. See also ROSMARINO.

rosemary

rosette, an excellent French sausage made from the shoulder meat of pork. It is a speciality of the Lyons district, and takes its name from the particular kind of sausage skin used, which is thick and fat; it imparts a fresh, moist quality to the meat during the curing process. This sausage is eaten raw.

rosie, Rumanian for tomatoes, which are of exceptional size and quality in Rumania.

rosmarino, Italian for rosemary, always used by cooks in Rome in *abbacchio al forno* and *porchetta*. See also ROSEMARY.

rosół, Polish for broth or consommé. In Poland beef and

chicken broths are mixed together, and this soup is sometimes thickened with buckwheat groats and garnished with diced chicken and bacon, chopped parsley, and fennel. *Rosół czysty* is clear consommé made with beef, veal, and chicken; *rosół z kury lub cielęciny* is chicken or veal consommé.

rosolli, a Finnish herring salad, made with pickled herrings, slices of cooked carrot, pickled cucumber, hard-boiled eggs, sliced beetroot, raw sliced apples, and sliced cooked potatoes. The salad is served with a sauce of ½ pint (1 cup) whipped sour cream, 1 teaspoon mustard, 1 tablespoon vinegar, and 1 teaspoon sugar, and is garnished with strips of egg white.

rospo, see PESCATRICE.

rossel, a traditional Jewish Passover food, consisting of raw beetroot which has been quartered and peeled and put into jars which are filled up with lukewarm boiled water. The beetroot is left for 2–3 weeks to form soured beet juice for the Passover *borsch* soup. Rossel is also added to boiled meats and vegetables. See also BEETROOT.

rossini, à la, I. A French garnish for tournedos and noisettes, consisting of médaillons of foie gras sautéed in butter, slices of truffle, and demi-glace with truffle essence (extract). II. A French method of serving chicken. See POULET, À LA ROSSINI.

rostbraten, I. German for roast beef, which in Germany is cooked in a greased baking dish with 1 large sliced onion and 1 inch of boiling water. It is basted with more water, and just before it is ready a little butter or fat is added. It is usually served well cooked, with a sour cream sauce. II. In Austria, rostbraten may mean a thick sirloin steak, pan-fried. When garnished with anchovies this is called rostbraten mit sardellen. See also RINDFLEISCH.

dampfrostbraten, sirloin steak on a bed of sautéed onions, covered with raw mushrooms, peas, carrots, celery, potatoes, asparagus, and dotted with butter. Then ½ pint (1 cup) stock is added, and the dish is covered and cooked slowly in the oven.

rostélyos, Hungarian for steak.

rostélyos roston köritéssel, grilled steak garnished with mushrooms and other vegetables.

töltött Hunyadi rostélyos, a Hungarian dish of stuffed steaks. See HUNYADI TÖLTÖTT.

rösten, German for to roast or to grill.

rösti, also spelt roesti, a national Swiss potato dish, made from potatoes half baked or boiled in their jackets. The hot potato is cut into slices which are fried on both sides in hot lard, like a cake, until a golden crust has formed. Sometimes a little finely chopped onion is added. Rösti is usually served with cold meat.

rote grütze, a German fruit pudding, made from raspberries and red currants cooked in red wine, puréed, and thickened with sago, semolina, or corn flour (cornstarch). It is served cold.

rotengle, French for a freshwater fish also known as gardon rouge. It has bright-red eyes and fins, and is prepared and cooked like roach.

rôti, French for "the roast," meaning both a dish of roast meat, and the course of a meal for which roast meat is served. Originally this course was served after the *sorbet* and before the *entremets;* in classical French cuisine, however, roast meat was always served as the entrée.

rôtie, French for a slice of bread toasted or baked. It is also the name for a certain type of canapé spread with game forcemeat which is served with roasted game, particularly woodcock.

rôtir, French for to roast. A plaque à rôtir is a tin with a grid for roasting; rôtissage is the roasting process itself. The rôtisserie is the part of the kitchen equipped for roasting or cooking on the spit, and the rôtisseur is the chef in a large French restaurant who prepares only roasts, grills, or fried dishes (in a very high-class restaurant the job would be divided among three chefs: the rôtisseur, the grillardin, and the friturier.

rotkohl, German for red cabbage. It is served all over Germany, usually hot, with bacon, pork, goose, and game dishes. Rotkohl is sometimes cooked with a shoulder of pork or ham. It is also made into a salad, by salting, blanching with boiling water, and leaving for at least 30 minutes; sometimes it is also sprinkled with caraway seeds. It is then drained, squeezed, then dressed with a mixture of 2 parts olive oil to 1 part vinegar, pepper, salt, and 1 teaspoon french mustard. These recipes are also used in Austria. See also BLAUKRAUT; KOHL; RED CABBAGE; ROTKRAUT.

rotkohl auf bayrische art, a Bavarian recipe. A finely shredded medium-sized red cabbage is blanched with boiling water, left for 10 minutes and then drained. Then 2 tablespoons seedless raisins, ¼ lb. (1 cup) diced boiled bacon, 1 teaspoon caraway seeds, 1 glass (½ cup) dry white wine, 3 tablespoons vinegar, and the same of water are added; the pan is covered and the contents are cooked gently for about 1 hour. Next 1 tablespoon sugar, preferably brown sugar, is added, and cooking is continued for 30 minutes. The cabbage is then seasoned and the dish is thickened with 2 teaspoons corn flour (cornstarch) mixed with a little water.

rotkohl auf berliner art, the Berlin method. First 2 tablespoons pork or goose fat is melted in a saucepan, and 1 medium-sized shredded cabbage, 4 peeled, cored, and chopped apples, 1 sliced onion, 1 teaspoon sugar, 3 cloves, 3 tablespoons vinegar, and 3 tablespoons water are added. All are simmered for 2 hours, with a little water added if there is any sign of burning. Then 1 cup or glass of red wine is added, and the cabbage is simmered very gently until all the liquid is reduced.

rotkohl auf westfälische art, the Westphalian method, which follows the Berlin version but contains the addition of fried sliced onion and a ham bone, with 1 tablespoon vinegar sprinkled over the cabbage just before serving.

rotkraut, a Swiss method of serving red cabbage, shredded and cooked for 2–3 hours with ¼ pint (½ cup) cider vinegar, 6 cloves, 4 peeled and sliced tart apples, 4 tablespoons sugar, ¼ pint (½ cup) wine, and water to cover. See also RED CABBAGE.

rotmos, a Swedish dish of turnips and potatoes, literally "mashed roots." The vegetables are boiled (turnips take about 20 minutes longer to cook than potatoes), then mashed together with cream or stock, seasoning, a pinch of castor sugar, and a nut of butter. Pork stock, when available, is used for cooking the vegetables. See also GRÖNSAKER.

roucaou, a Mediterranean fish, a member of the wrasse family, used in bouillabaisse; it is sometimes called *rouquier.*

rouelle, the French butchery term for a fairly thick slice cut across leg of veal.

rouennais, a French cow's milk cheese made in Normandy, and in season from October to May.

rouennais, see AIGUILLETTE; CANARD.

rouennaise, sauce, a classical French sauce served with roast Rouen duck or with poached eggs. It is made with ½ pint (1 cup) sauce *bordelaise,* with the finely mashed raw duck livers and a pinch each of spice, salt, and black pepper added. It is heated up, cooked gently for 7 minutes, then strained and kept hot in a *bain-marie.* See CANARD.

rougail, a hot chutney served with creole dishes and with foods served à la créole, particularly *riz à la créole.* It is usually made from 1 lb. tart apples diced and soaked in salted water, then drained and set on a layer composed of hot pimento and a walnut-sized piece of ginger pounded smoothly and mixed with a little olive oil. Tomatoes, eggplant, and also

shellfish may be used instead of apples, and sometimes a slice of onion is added to the pimento and ginger.

rouge de rivière, French for the shoveller, a duck which, in France, is prized as food and is usually cooked by roasting. See also WILD DUCK.

rouge-queue, French for redstart, a migratory bird much esteemed gastronomically in France, and prepared in the same way as lark.

rouget-barbet, the French generic name for several fish found in the Mediterranean; it includes mullets, surmullets, and gurnards. They are all reddish in colour and have barbels on the lower jaw. Red mullet, the finest among them, is itself known as rouget; this leads to confusion, and means that the inferior fish are sometimes served under the guise of red mullet. See also MULLET.

rouille, sauce, a French sauce from Provence, served with *bourride,* and also with *anguilles en catigout.* It is made from 2 grilled and skinned chillis pounded into 1 pint (2 cups) sauce *aïoli,* with 1 tablespoon each of pounded lobster coral and the pink inside part of sea urchins added. It is quite fiery to the taste, and goes well with the rich dishes it accompanies.

roulade, I. A French culinary term meaning a roll. It is applied to meat, usually veal or pork, or fillets of fish, which are usually stuffed and then rolled up before cooking. A roulade is generally served cold. II. A French term applied to various types of galantine, especially a boned pig's head, stuffed with a forcemeat made from the minced tongue, 2 tablespoons mixed herbs, 2 hard-boiled eggs, 4 oz. chopped bacon, and a pinch of spice, then rolled up and cooked in stock to cover for 2–3 hours.

roulé, the French name for a rolled-out sweet pastry spread with jam and then rolled up, the top sprinkled with praline and toasted almonds before baking.

rouleau, French for rolling pin.

roulette, French for a small-toothed wheel with a handle, used to cut pastry.

rouló, a Greek form of baked beef loaf made with 2 lb. minced (ground) seasoned beef, 1 cup soft breadcrumbs, 2 whole hard-boiled eggs, 1 large minced onion, and 2 tablespoons parsley, all mixed and then baked in ½ pint (1 cup) tomato juice and ¼ pint (½ cup) wine for 45 minutes. It is usually served in thick slices with hot noodles. See also MEAT LOAF.

rouló me makarónia, a Macedonian version of the rouló, made without the hard-boiled eggs and always served with square-shaped cooked pasta.

round, I. A term used in English and American beef butchery for the top part of the leg. This cut is used chiefly for braising or boiling, or for stews; when salted, it is usually known as silverside in Britain. Gîte à la noix is the equivalent French cut. See beef cuts chart, pages xxii–xxiii.

bottom round, an American joint, cut from the leg just under the tail. Also known as round roast when so cooked.

round steak, an Irish and an American cut comprising a slice from the top of the leg, generally used for braising.

top round, an American cut taken from the underpart of the leg, which is often roasted and called round roast.

II. An American cut of veal, the top part of the leg. The meat is obviously younger and more tender than the corresponding beef cut, and is therefore used for roasting or frying. See veal cuts chart, pages xxiii–xxiv.

round roast, as corresponding beef cut (*see above*).

round steaks, as corresponding beef cut (*see above*).

rouquier, see ROUCAOU.

roussette, I. The French name for a kind of fritter made from 1 lb. (3½ cups) flour, 3 eggs, 3 tablespoons milk, ⅛ pint (4 tablespoons) eau-de-vie, and 1 teaspoon orange flower water.

All ingredients are made into a thickish paste and then wrapped in paper and chilled, after which the paste is rolled out into a thin sheet and cut into rounds. The roussettes are dropped into hot oil and browned. Then they are drained, sprinkled with sugar and arranged in a mound on a napkin. II. The French name for a shark-like fish of the *Squatinidae,* sold regularly in French markets. It is known as dogfish in England. See also DOGFISH.

roussir, a French culinary term meaning to turn a piece of meat or poultry (whole) in hot fat in order to colour it lightly.

roux, the general term for a variety of flour bindings. A roux can be brown, white, or blond, according to its ingredients and intended use. To make it 1 tablespoon butter is melted in a small saucepan, and the same amount of flour is then added, stirring well. This amount of roux will require 1 pint (2 cups) of liquid to make a thick sauce; if a thin sauce is required the same amount of liquid is used, but the roux is made with 1 tablespoon flour to 2 of butter. The mixture is allowed to colour gently to the required shade before whatever liquid suggested in the recipe is included. The necessary seasoning is added, and the sauce is mellowed at the side of the stove. To obtain a richer sauce for roast meat, the dripping from the meat is sometimes used instead of butter, particularly for sauce velouté and sauce espagnole. The roux of flour and butter can be mixed, and kept in small quantities in an air-tight jar, for adding to casseroles or sauces.

rova, Swedish for turnip. See ROTMOS.

rowan (*Sorbus aucuparia*), the mountain ash, whose bright red clustered berries are used, either alone or combined with apple, for making a jelly which has a slightly smoky flavour and is delicious served with roast lamb or mutton, venison, or grouse. It is made in the same way as red currant jelly. When rowans are over-ripe they are popular with children. See also JELLY; SERVICE TREE.

royal icing, see ICING.

royale, I. A French garnish, usually served with game soup. To prepare it ½ pint (1 cup) game stock is boiled with 1 tablespoon chopped chervil and seasoning. When cooled a little, 1 whole egg and 3 egg yolks are beaten gently in a basin, and the warm stock is gradually added, being stirred continuously. It is strained into one large or several small buttered moulds and steamed; 30 minutes will be needed for a single large mould, 15 minutes for small moulds. The resulting custard is left until it is quite set and cold, when it is cut into small fancy shapes which are added to the soup just before serving.

royale a l'écarlate, royale garnish with lobster or *langouste purée,* which colours the garnish red.

royale crécy, royale garnish with carrot purée, which colours the garnish orange.

royale vert-pré, royale garnish with a purée of spinach and herbs, which colours the garnish green.

II. A French consommé garnished with plain royale. III. A French dish of poultry poached in very little stock, then coated with reduced sauce velouté with cream and puréed truffles added. IV. A French garnish identical to *régence* II. often used in *vol-au-vent.* V. A sweet dish of hollowed-out pineapple or melon, the pulp being mixed with other chopped fruits and soaked in liqueur.

royale, the French name for a type of cherry, known in England as the Duke cherry. See CHERRY.

royans, French for pilchards. This name is used particularly when they are eaten fresh; when smoked or canned they are called pilchards.

røykt kolje med gulrøtter og eggesmør, a Norwegian dish of poached smoked haddock and boiled carrots served with melted butter and chopped hard-boiled egg.

røyktlaks, Norwegian for smoked salmon, much used for *smørbrød* in Norway. Fresh salmon is frequently cured at home in Norway prior to smoking. The method is as follows. After removal of the head and tail, the fish is cut lengthwise along the back and the backbone and entrails are removed. The belly is cleaned and nearly all the blood taken away. The fish is then laid skin-side down on a mixture of sugar and salt (5 oz. sugar to 4 lb. salt), and a good layer of this is also spread on top of the fish. After 24 hours, it is weighted down and left for a period of 3 days, after which it is wiped clean of salt and washed over with a piece of muslin dipped in a mixture of brandy and saltpetre (½ tablespoon saltpetre is enough for a large salmon). Curing is now completed, and the fish is next smoked for 8 hours (the Norwegian cook sends her fish out for smoking). After this the salmon is kept for at least 7 days, covered, and in a cool place, before it is served.

røykttorsk, Norwegian for smoked cod which is used a lot for fish puddings.

rozbratlę, Polish for either a roasting joint of beef, or a large rib or sirloin steak which can be cooked whole or cut into slices. It is the Polish equivalent of the German *rostbraten.*

rozbratlę duszone, sliced sirloin or rib steak rolled in flour, browned in butter, then simmered for 1 hour with ¼ pint (½ cup) red wine and the same of stock.

rozbratlę duszone z sardelami, as *rozbratlę duszone,* with the addition of 4 chopped anchovies, and using sour cream instead of wine.

rozbratlę po chłopsku, steak peasant-style. Thick slices of steak are pounded, then spread with a mixture of chopped raw potato and chopped ham, rolled up, browned, and then pot roasted for 2 hours with chopped root vegetables, herbs, and ½ pint (1 cup) stock. Usually 4 tablespoons sour cream is added just before serving.

rozbratlę z cebulą, sliced sirloin or rib steak cooked in butter with fried onions.

rozijnen, Dutch for raisins. See also RAISIN.

rozijnen saus, raisin sauce, served in Holland with smoked boiled tongue. It is made from 4 oz. (½ cup) brown sugar dissolved in ½ pint (1 cup) stock from the tongue, and this is then simmered with juice of ½ lemon and ½ cup raisins for about 10 minutes. One-fourth pint (½ cup) white wine and 1 teaspoon grated lemon peel are added, and finally 2 tablespoons butter is stirred in.

rozpeky, Czechoslovakian baked yeast cakes, made from 1 oz. yeast soaked in ¼ pint (½ cup) tepid milk and added to 1 lb. (4 cups) flour, a pinch of salt, and 1 egg yolk. The dough is left to rise, then formed into small rounds which are put on a greased tin to rise again. They are baked in a hot oven. They are usually served with a tomato sauce, and are used in place of dumplings as an accompaniment for meat. They can also be spread with butter and served for tea.

ruacan, see CARPETSHELL.

rubets, Russian for tripe, which is eaten a great deal in Russia. A popular way of serving it is to chop it finely after boiling; it is then mixed with lightly fried onion, cooked buckwheat, and butter. It is sometimes thickened with sour cream.

rubio, Spanish for a variety of red gurnard. It bears a strong resemblance to gurnard, but is not nearly as good to eat.

rudd (*Scardinius erythropthalmus*), a freshwater fish which is allied to the roach and inhabits the same waters.

rudderfish (*Stromateus fiatola*), a delicate-tasting fish found in the Mediterranean. It is cooked in the same way as turbot. See also CHOPA BLANCA.

rue (*Ruta graveolens*), a herb of south European origin which grows into a small shrub. It is an extremely bitter plant, and was originally regarded both as a symbol of repentance and as protection against the evil eye. Rue tea was used medicinally to lower a high temperature, the blue-green serrated leaves being soaked in boiling water and left to infuse for 24 hours. With its greenish-yellow flowers, it makes an attractive garden plant when in bloom. It has a curious scent which does not appeal to everyone, but a few of the leaves, finely chopped, are good in sandwiches of brown bread and fresh butter.

rue

ruff (*Philomochus pugnax*), a bird which migrates in summer to Britain, particularly to Lincolnshire. The cock is called a ruff and the hen a reeve. They were once greatly esteemed as food but are now protected by law. They are prepared and cooked in the same way as woodcock, but unlike woodcock they must be drawn before being cooked.

ruff

ruffe (*Acerina cernua*), a freshwater species of perch found in the south of England, in France, Scandinavia, and Siberia. The flesh is quite delicate and the fish is prepared and cooked in the same way as pike. Also called pope, it is similar to the pike-perches of the Middle West in the U.S. See also PERCH.

ruffed grouse or *ruffed partridge* (*Bonasa umbellus*), one of several American birds with a confusing dual name. It is termed a partridge in the north and a grouse in the south. It is a handsome, ruffed game bird, and can be prepared and cooked in any way that is suitable for partridge or pheasant,

although it requires longer cooking time because it is larger.

rughetta, an Italian weed with leaves not unlike corn salad although the taste is more peppery. It is used a lot in salads in Italy, especially in Rome.

rührei, German for scrambled eggs, sometimes cooked with diced bacon and sprinkled with chopped chives. See also EI.

ruis, Finnish for rye. See also RYE.

ruiskorput, rye rusks. To prepare them 2 tablespoons yeast is dissolved in 2 tablespoons tepid water and then mixed with 1 pint (2 cups) buttermilk; 12 oz. (3 cups) each of rye and graham flour is added, followed by ½ cup melted fat and 2 teaspoons caraway seeds. This mixture is shaped into rounds which are left to rise, then baked in a hot oven. When browned the rusks are split into halves, and these are dried in the oven until crisp. See also RUSK.

ruis-marjapuuro, a rye and berry purée. The berry used is a small wild native cranberry, called *lingonberry* in England. First 1 lb. berries are cooked in 4 pints (8 cups) water and then strained. Then ⅓ lb. (1¾ cups) rye meal is stirred into the boiling juice and it is simmered for 1 hour, being sweetened to taste. If the purée is too thin, 2 tablespoons potato flour is added. It is served either hot or cold.

ruispuuro, rye porridge, made with 3 cups rye flour, 1 tablespoon salt and 4½ pints (9 cups) water, all cooked slowly for 1 hour. It is generally eaten hot with butter and cold milk, but sometimes *laskisoosi* is served with it instead. The Finnish rye harvest in August is always celebrated with ruispuuro.

rukkileiva ja õuna, a sharp-tasting Estonian pudding, made from a mixture of 1 lb. (3 cups) rye breadcrumbs and 3 tablespoons sugar, first turned in 6 tablespoons butter, then layered with 1½ lb. chopped raw cooking apples and baked in the oven. This may be the origin of the American brown betty, brought to the U.S. by Estonian immigrants.

rullepølse, a Danish pressed sausage roll, made from skinned pork belly, minced onions, allspice, cloves, and seasoning. The onion and spices are spread over the flattened belly of pork, then this is rolled up tightly and secured before being rubbed with sugar, salt, and a little saltpetre. The meat is then left for about a week, being turned daily, after which it is washed, and boiled gently until it is tender. It is removed from the liquid, weighted, and put in a cold place. This sausage is a speciality of Ringsted, and can also be made with beef, lamb, or veal. It is eaten for *smørrebrød*.

rum sauce, a sauce served with steamed puddings in Britain. It is made from 2 egg yolks, 2 tablespoons sifted sugar, and a good pinch of grated nutmeg beaten to a smooth cream. The egg whites are beaten to a stiff froth, and just before serving, 2 tablespoons sifted sugar is lightly and quickly mixed with them and the whole is mixed into the creamed yolks. Finally, at least 1 wineglass (½ cup) of the oldest and best Jamaica rum is added.

Rumanian cheeses, see BRÎNZĂ.

rumbledethumps, a Scottish Border dish, made from equal quantities of boiled potatoes and cabbage, cooked separately, then beaten well together with black pepper. Sometimes chopped cooked onion is added.

rump, I. The English hip or buttock cut of beef; also part of the round. It can be roasted if the animal is young, but otherwise should be pot roasted or braised. The same cut does not exist in the U.S.: it is part aitchbone and part rump. The nearest French cut is *pointe de culotte*. II. An American cut of veal, corresponding to the British rump steak cut of beef. It is more tender than the corresponding beef cut, and so can be roasted, grilled, or fried. See meat cuts charts on pages xxii–xxiv.

rump roast, an American joint of beef or veal taken from the end of the loin nearest the hip-bone. It is usually roasted.

rump steak, an English cut of beef, not to be confused with rump. It is cut from the end of the loin nearest the hip bone and can be successfully grilled. It is called sirloin steak in Ireland and the U.S.

rundvlees, Dutch for beef. Runderlapje is Dutch for beef steak for stewing.

runderlappen, a national method of cooking spiced stewing steak. After the seasoned steaks have been browned in fat, they are put in a baking dish with fried onions, water barely to cover, 1 tablespoon vinegar, 1 teaspoon mustard, 2 bay leaves, cloves, and peppercorns. The dish is covered and the contents simmered until tender. Runderlappen is often eaten on December 6, St. Nicholas's Day, a popular holiday in Holland. See also OSSENHAAS.

runner, the name given in the U.S. to two fish of the family *Carangidae,* both good to eat, and both cooked in the same way as grouper. I. The amberfish (*Elegatis bipinnulatus*), found in warm waters. II. The jurel (*Caranx chrysos*), found south of Cape Cod and called the blue runner.

runner bean or **scarlet runner** (string bean) (*Phaseolus multiflorus*), introduced into Europe from Mexico in the early 17th century. Initially it was valued simply as a decorative flowering climber, but later the pods came to be used for food. It is a fast-climbing, free-bearing plant; the pods, if allowed, can reach an enormous size, but they are always picked at the small and medium stages. A stringless semi-runner bean is the Blue Coco, of which the blue pods turn green when cooked. They are tender and of excellent flavour. There are also tender, non-trailing dwarf varieties such as Dwarf Gem, Dwarf Scarlet, Dwarf Bean, and Tenderpod, which is valued for canning and freezing. Runner beans are prepared for cooking by being stringed and thinly sliced; then they are simmered in boiling salted water for about 10 minutes. If small, they are left uncut. See also BEAN; FRENCH BEAN.

rurki z kremem, Polish puff pastry tubes which are cooked and then filled with cream or a syrup of sugar and stiffly beaten egg whites.

rush-nut, see CHUFA.

rusk, a word derived from the Spanish *rosca,* a twist, coil, or roll of bread, It was also thought they were eaten a lot on Russian ships and the word comes from "*russkis.*" Rusk is generally defined as a piece of bread pulled or cut from a loaf and re-baked until dry and crisp throughout. However, rusks are also prepared to a definite recipe. Being very light, they are given to children, invalids, and people on diets. First ½ pint (1 cup) tepid milk is poured over 2 tablespoons yeast; 1 lb. flour is then mixed with ¼ lb. (½ cup) sugar and a pinch of salt, and a well is made in the middle into which the yeast mixture is poured. The flour is then pulled over, and all is covered and set to rise in a warm place. The dough is then beaten and kneaded, shaped into rounds or squares, left to rise again, and baked in a moderate oven. When the rounds are browned they are split sideways with a sharp knife and crisped in a low oven. The French *biscotte* is a rusk, as is the German zwieback, both words meaning "twice cooked." See also RUIS (RUISKORPUT); TEBRØD.

russe, I. A French sauce of Russian origin, made from mayonnaise with one quarter its volume of puréed caviar and lobster coral added, and a pinch of mustard. II. A French garnish containing beetroot and/or sour cream. III. A vegetable salad, with diced beetroot, apple, potato, peas, green beans, cucumber, etc., mixed with mayonnaise. In English it is called Russian salad.

Russian cheeses, see SYR.

Russian dressing, a dressing from the U.S., made with 1 cup mayonnaise, ½ pimento, 1 tablespoon chilli sauce, ½ green pepper, and 1 finely chopped celery stalk. The pimento and green pepper are very finely minced, and then all the ingredients are combined. This dressing is served chilled. It is also sometimes hastily made with only mayonnaise mixed with ketchup.

Russian mayonnaise, a mayonnaise made from ½ pint (1 cup) sauce velouté mixed with ¼ pint (½ cup) sour cream, blended with 2 tablespoons grated horseradish and seasoned with 2 teaspoons tarragon vinegar.

Russian salad, see RUSSE.

Russian turnip, see SWEDE.

rusty dab, see DAB.

rutabaga, see SWEDE.

Rutherglen cream, an excellent sour cream for which Rutherglen in Scotland is famous. New milk is gently heated and left covered until the whey, or "whig" as it is called in Scotland, is visibly separated from the curd. It is drawn off, and the curds are beaten up with moist or Barbados sugar to taste. The whole process takes about 3 days.

Rutherglen sour cakes, traditional cakes eaten at St. Luke's Fair on October 18 in Scotland. About 10 days before the fair, ½ lb. oatmeal is made into a dough with about 1 cup warm water and left to ferment. It is then mixed with a little sugar, and aniseed or cinnamon to taste, and rolled into balls of the required size. These are then rolled out as thin as a piece of paper and toasted on each side on a hot griddle.

ryabchik, Russian for hazel hen (grouse), a bird eaten a great deal in Russia. See also HAZEL HEN; TETERKA.

ryba, Czechoslovakian for fish. The most popular fishes in Bohemia are bream, carp, perch, and pike, also a giant pike-perch. Fish is often fried or baked and served with a sweet-sour sauce of raisins, red currant jelly, almonds, sugar, and vinegar.

marinovaná ryba, fish lightly poached, but not completely cooked in vinegar to cover and salt, which gives it a blue colour. The liquid is strained off and celery, Hamburg parsley roots, onion, garlic, bay leaf, ginger, cloves, allspice, lemon peel, and seasoning are simmered in it. At this stage the fish is added and gently cooked, then removed and placed in a dish. The liquid is strained over the fish, which is then set in a cold place to jelly. It is sprinkled with parsley before serving.

ryba polévka, a traditional fish soup. Carrots, celery, onions, cabbage, parsley, and pieces of cauliflower are cooked in fish stock with salt and nutmeg. The stock and vegetables are then rubbed through a sieve, or blended, milk is added, and finally it is bound with egg yolks mixed with milk. It is garnished with hard carp's roe which has been cooked in fish stock.

ryba, Polish for fish.

bigos z ryby, a fish stew, similar to *ryba polevka* but often containing *harcsa* as well as perch, carp, and pike. It is also popular in Hungary.

ryba, Russian for fish.

ryba zalivniaya, a Russian dish of filleted fish, poached, then set in aspic with cooked vegetables, hard-boiled eggs, and herbs. A sauce made from 1 teaspoon mustard, 1 teaspoon sugar, and 1 cup sour cream is often served with it. Sturgeon is very often used for this dish in Russia.

rye (*Secale cereale*), a genus of grass closely related to wheat and, in parts of Europe, the cereal of next importance. It originated in the region between the Austrian alps and the Caspian Sea, and was introduced from Europe into the U.S., where it is immensely popular, not only for cooking but also for making whisky. Rye flour is grey in colour and rich in nitrogenous content. It is used for breads and cakes, sometimes mixed with what flour; the bread is dark brown when cooked. See also RAG; RUIS.

rye

rye bread, 2½ lb. (10 cups) rye flour is mixed with 2½ lb. (10 cups) wheat flour. Then 1½ oz. yeast is creamed with 1 teaspoon sugar and added to the combined flours, together with 1 quart (4 cups) tepid water. The mixture is left to rise, then kneaded and left to rise again. The dough is formed into 3 loaves which are left to rise once more, then baked for 1–1½ hours in a moderate oven. Bread made with ''whole'' rye flour is called pumpernickel. Sometimes 4 tablespoons of melted butter is added to the dough, and a flavoring of caraway or fennel seeds. See also LIMPA; RAG (RAGBRÖOD).

rype, Danish for ptarmigan. See also PTARMIGAN.

farseret ryper, a recipe for stuffed ptarmigan. The birds are stuffed with hot mashed potatoes, then dipped in seasoned flour and evenly browned in bacon fat. After being basted with ½ pint (1 cup) boiling brown stock, they are gently simmered in a covered pan for about 1 hour, being basted occasionally with fresh stock. This gravy is thickened with flour, before being served separately. The birds are garnished with watercress and served with a lettuce salad and browned potatoes (*brunede kartofler*).

rype, Norwegian for ptarmigan. See also PTARMIGAN.

stekte ryper, a pot roast of ptarmigan. Slices of fat pork are secured over the breasts of the birds, which are placed in a saucepan containing 2 oz. melted butter. Then ¼ pint (½ cup) boiling water is added gradually and the game is simmered for 15 minutes, after which 1 pint (2 cups) boiling milk is slowly added. The heat is reduced and cooking is continued for 3 hours, during which time the steam should be allowed to escape from the pan. When the birds are tender, 2 tablespoons sour cream is stirred in and seasoning added. The birds are re-

moved, and a sauce is made by the addition to the stock of 1 oz. diced cheese and more sour cream (a little butter may be substituted for the second addition of cream). It is served with cranberry jam.

Another pot roast for ptarmigan, dating back to the early 19th century, calls for the birds to be wrapped in slices of fat bacon and are then placed on a bed of sliced carrots and onions, with a pinch of mace and a bouquet garni, in a saucepan. The ingredients are half-covered with milk, the lid is put on, and the contents are simmered for 2–3 hours until tender. More milk is added as necessary. The sauce is made by adding the stock (after the game has been removed) to a roux of 2 tablespoons each of butter and flour; 2 tablespoons demi-glace and seasoning are added to taste, and the sauce is poured over the birds. Either *robin* saus or *viking* saus is served separately. See SAUS.

ryż, Polish for rice. As rice is not indigenous to Poland, most Polish rice dishes are adapted from other rice-growing countries, like *risi-bisi* for example. See also RICE.

ryż po Turecku, Turkish-style rice. To prepare, 1 lb. (2 cups) rice is mixed with salt, pepper, a pinch of saffron, and 3 pints (6 cups) broth made from lamb or mutton. It is stirred once, then covered and baked in a moderate oven for 1 hour. A few minutes before serving, the lid is taken off to allow the rice to dry out.

ryż z bit a śmietan, a sweet dish made with 3 to 4 cups boiled rice mixed with 1 pint (2 cups) sour cream, raisins, and vanilla sugar to taste. It is topped with jam.

ryż z rakami i szampinionami, 1 lb. cooked rice is combined with 24 cooked crayfish, ½ lb. sliced mushrooms, and 1 pint (2 cups) sour cream, and all are heated in a buttered dish for 20 minutes.

rýže, Czechoslovakian for rice. See also RICE.

rýžový nákyp, a rich rice pudding layered with breadcrumbs, often served for luncheon after soup and *halušky.* See also PUDDING (IV).

rzepa, Polish for swede-turnip. The white or small yellow turnips are *brukiew*.

rzepa duszona z kiełbaskami, parboiled swede-turnips covered with sauce béchamel flavoured with caraway seeds and cooked until tender. It is served with *kiełbasa* (Polish sausage), heated in hot water or grilled.

rzewień, Polish for rhubarb. In Poland rhubarb is often combined with potatoes, using it as the vegetable it is, and this makes an excellent mixture. First 2 lb. rhubarb is lightly cooked in broth with 6 dried mushrooms and 1 onion, before being mixed with 1 lb. cooked new potatoes and chopped herbs. Sometimes a cup of the rhubarb broth is thickened with 1 tablespoon corn flour (cornstarch), and this is added to the rhubarb and vegetable mixture. It is very good served with pork or chicken.

saaland pfarr, see PRESTOST.

Saanenkäse, a variety of Gruyère which comes from the Saanen Valley in the Bernese Oberland of Switzerland. However, it has a very much harder texture than Gruyère as a result of the length of the curing process, which takes between 5 and 6 years; this also guarantees that the cheese will keep for about 100 years. Saansen cheese is also called hobelkäse, which means "plane" cheese, because in Saanen a special cheese plane is used to cut it. It is not exported. See also GRUYÈRE.

sábalo, Spanish for shad, a fish which makes good eating. In Cádiz shad is first painted with oil and then baked or lightly grilled. When it has cooled, the scales are scraped off and the fish is boned and lightly poached in seasoned water, then served with lemon juice. It is also called alosa. See also SHAD.

sabayon, French for *zabaglione.* The French version is made with white wine instead of Marsala, and sometimes whole eggs are used. For this reason it is not quite as thick as *zabaglione,* and is frequently used as a warm sauce for hot puddings as well as being served on its own. See also ZABAGLIONE.

sablé, a French biscuit (cookie) or small cake, originally from Normandy. To make it 1 lb. (4 cups) sifted flour is placed in a mound on a pastry board or in a basin. In the middle is put a mixture of the same amount of softened butter, 6 egg yolks, 2 heaped tablespoons sugar, and a pinch of salt. This is mixed in rapidly by hand and well blended, then shaped into a ball and left for 1 hour. It is then rolled out and cut into 4–5-inch rounds which are baked on a greased baking sheet in a moderate oven for 15–20 minutes. Sablés are either eaten plain or sandwiched together with jam or a prepared cream mixture. Savoury sablés can also be made by adding 4 oz. (1 cup) grated cheese to the mixture, together with a little milk if it is too thick; when cooked they are sandwiched with thick cream cheese.

saccharin, the commercial term for a number of related compounds which are derived from coal tar, and are most popularly known to cooks in the form of a white powder not very easily soluble in water. Saccharin is commonly said to be 500 times sweeter than sugar, but it would be more exact to say that it produces a taste of sweetness in concentrations 500 times smaller than sugar; for when saccharin is taken in a concentrated form the effect of sweetness is lost, and a noticeable difference in taste is to be observed.

Sodium saccharin, a related compound, is very much more readily soluble, an important consideration where culinary use is envisaged. However, for excellence of flavour it certainly cannot compare with a well-flavoured sugar such as fructose. The chief use of sodium saccharin is in the preparation of low-calorie diets, where sugar can be replaced and the daily intake of calories thus reduced. It is also of great use in helping to make the sugar-free diets of diabetics more palatable. Saccharin and sodium saccharin are generally obtainable in the form of small tablets, although liquid preparations, more convenient for some culinary operations, are also to be had. Saccharin and its sodium salt have also been used in the adulteration of some jams where, in the absence of sugar, it is necessary to incorporate preservatives. In this way too, jams, preserves, and sweets specially suitable for diabetic and low-calorie diets may quite legitimately be manufactured.

saccharometer, an instrument specially made to measure the specific gravity or density of sugar solutions or syrups. It is essential to the making of certain kinds of confectionery.

Sacher-torte, a famous Austrian cake served on many festive occasions. It was created by the founder of the celebrated Hotel Sacher in Vienna, Franz Sacher, who was then pastry-chef to Prince Metternich. It is eaten in all German-speaking parts of the world, and is made from 4¾ oz. (1¼ cups) fine flour sifted and 6 eggs, separated; then 5 oz. cooking chocolate is chopped and melted in 1 tablespoon water, rum, or Madeira. Next 5 oz. (⅔ cup) butter is creamed with 4 oz. (1 cup) icing sugar, and the egg yolks are added. Then the warm chocolate is well stirred in (it should not be hot). Finally, 1 heaped tablespoon icing sugar is beaten with the egg whites, and when stiff, this mixture is folded into the butter and chocolate mixture alternately with the flour. The whole is poured into a buttered and floured cake tin, about 9½ inches across, and baked in a moderate oven for 50–60 minutes. When cold, the cake is spread with warmed apricot jam and covered with chocolate icing. It is served with whipped cream. Some versions split the cake in two and layer it with the jam, but this is not authentic.

sacristains, French twists of *pâte feuilletée,* rolled and folded with castor sugar and baked in a hot oven until golden brown and slightly caramelised. It is served plain, or with ice cream or compotes.

saddle, a butchery term denoting a joint which consists of the 2 loins of an animal and the connecting backbone. It is applied particularly to lamb or mutton, when the kidneys are also included, as well as to venison. Saddle of hare, however, is the main body of the animal without the hind legs or fore-legs.

saetina, Italian for ground chillis, sometimes used to season soups or pasta, especially in the Abruzzi. See also ABRUZZESE.

safflower, see MEXICAN SAFFRON.

saffran, Swedish for saffron. See also SAFFRON.

saffransbröd, saffron bread. It is made in the same way as *vetebröd,* ½ teaspoon saffron being used instead of cardamom seeds. About 4 oz. sultanas or chopped raisins is sometimes added when half the quantity of flour has been mixed in.

saffron

saffron (*Crocus sativus*), a deep-orange-red powder derived from the dried and powdered stigmas and part of the styles of the saffron crocus. (This should not be confused with the autumn crocus, which it does resemble in producing purple flowers in the autumn in the northern hemisphere.) About 70,000 to 80,000 crocus flowers, each having 3 stigmas, are required to make 1 lb. saffron. The stigmas must be plucked by hand from each flower individually, and must then go through a careful process of drying before they are ready to be powdered. It is thus easy to understand why true saffron is the most expensive spice.

Used from ancient times, as a flavouring substance, a scent, and a yellow dye, saffron was well known to the Greeks and Romans, although not to the Egyptians until a comparatively late date. At first the chief centre of its cultivation was the town of Corycus in Cilicia, Turkey (now the modern Korghoz), and from there it spread eastward into Persia and China and westward into Europe. It was introduced into Cornwall by the Phoenicians at quite an early date, but it did not come into general use in England until after its reintroduction by a crusader returning from Tripoli, who is said to have carried a stolen corm hidden in the hollow of his staff. Saffron Walden in Essex (*walde* is Anglo-Saxon for field) was a centre of cultivation from the reign of Edward III until the latter half of the 18th century, and those who were engaged in the work were known as "crokers." With its honeyed, spicy smell, and its highly characteristic, slightly bitter flavour which stimulates appetite, saffron plays an important part in many culinary preparations and dishes. It figures particularly in the cookery of southern Europe where it is essential to many dishes, especially bouillabaisse, paella, and risotto alla milanese. It is interesting to note that its use continues in Cornwall to this day in saffron cakes.

Since it is an expensive spice, saffron has always been subject to much adulteration, and to this day an inferior substitute is made from the stigmas of Mexican saffron (*Carthamus tinctorius*). For this reason it is advisable to use saffron in stigma or pistil form rather than powder, to make sure it is unadulterated. The stigmas should be pounded up (about 6 is enough for an average portion) and soaked in 2 tablespoons water or stock until the liquid is a vivid, bright orange colour. This liquid is used in cakes, bread, rice, soups, etc. Good saffron has a very strong red-gold colour; if it is too pale or too dark, it is stale. See also SAFFRAN; SAFRAN; ZAFFERANO.

saffron cake, a traditional Cornish recipe, rather more like a sweet bread than a cake. Saffron is believed to have been introduced into Cornwall by the Phoenicians when they came to trade for tin, and was as much a feature of Cornish cookery as the famous Cornish pasty. According to a 17th-century record, it was "a popular crop to grow as it was a great improver of land." First ½ oz. yeast is mixed with 1 gill (½ cup) luke-warm water; 2 heaped tablespoons flour is added, and the basin is covered with a cloth and left in a warm place until a batter has formed and it has doubled in bulk. Then ½ lb. (1¾ cups) flour is mixed with 4 oz. (½ cup) butter, 2 heaped tablespoons sugar, 1 beaten egg, and either ¼ teaspoon powdered saffron or 2 tablespoons water in which 6 saffron stamens have soaked for some hours (only the liquid being used). This is added to the yeast mixture and kneaded well. Finally 3 tablespoons seedless raisins or sultanas, 2 tablespoons currants, 1 tablespoon chopped candied peel or lemon peel, with sometimes a pinch of mixed spice, are well mixed in. A greased baking tin is half-filled with the dough, covered, and left until the dough rises to the top; the cake is then baked in a moderate oven for 1–1½ hours. Small buns are often made from this mixture instead of a single cake. Saffron cakes are traditionally eaten at Easter, like *simnel cake.*

saffron water, hot water in which pounded stamens of saffron are soaked until the water becomes a vivid orange. About ¼ teaspoon saffron will make 2 tablespoons of saffron water. The liquid is strained before use.

safio, Portuguese for conger eel, also known as *congro.* It is used in soups and stews, especially *caldeirada à fragateira.* See also CONGER EEL.

safran, French for saffron, used always in bouillabaisse, as well as in many other Provençal dishes. See also SAFFRON.

saganaki, the Greek name for fried squares of féta cheese, particularly good as an hors d'oeuvre.

sage (*Salvia officinalis*), a perennial herb which comes from the Mediterranean where it is used extensively in cooking. The plant grows to a height of about 2 feet, with silvery-green leaves which have a slightly bitter taste but exude a pleasant fragrance. The leaves should be picked in June and dried. In England sage is used to flavour a variety of dishes, particularly sausages and stuffings for pork and duck, although it is a strong herb and should be used discreetly. Clary (*Salvia sclarea*), another variety of sage, was considered by the herbalist Gerard to be good for the sight; the seeds were soaked in water and then placed in the eye one at a time, in order to relieve inflammation. Clary sage has tall pink, mauve, and white flowering spikes with a scent reminiscent of grapefruit; the flowers are sometimes used in salads and also for a home-made wine. See also SALVIA; SAUGE.

sage

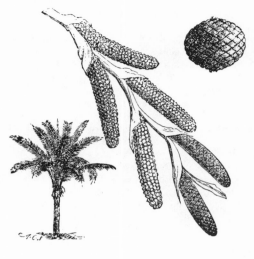

sago

sage and onion sauce, a traditional English sauce for duck or pork. To prepare it 2 tablespoons butter are melted in a pan, and 2 minced onions are cooked in this until a light brown. Then ¾ pint (1½ cups) brown stock is stirred in and the mixture brought to boiling-point, when 1 teaspoon finely chopped sage leaves and 2 tablespoons soft breadcrumbs, with seasoning to taste, are added. As this sauce is usually served with roast pork, 1–2 tablespoons of the meat gravy are added to enrich the flavour.

sage and onion stuffing, see STUFFING.

sage cheese, a cream cheese, with the juice extracted from freshly bruised sage and spinach leaves added to the milk or cream before the cheese is drained, to turn it a faint green colour. It is also known as green cheese. See also AMERICAN SAGE CHEESE.

sage Lancashire, a greenish-coloured cheese made before WW II in very small quantities by adding chopped sage leaves to the curds of Lancashire cheese.

sage grouse (*Centrocercus urophasianus*), a game bird which lives on the sage plains of western North America. In summer, when it has plants other than sage to feed on, it is not unlike a capercaillie in taste and can be prepared as such, but as the sage grouse is a very large bird, double the cooking time is needed.

sago, a starchy product obtained from the pitch of the trunks of certain palm trees. It is bruised in a mortar, washed, strained, then dried into small pellets. It is used mostly in Britain for milk puddings, and in Scandinavia and Germany for a fruit pudding (*rote grütze*) and for soups. In France, it is used as a garnish or thickening agent for certain consommés and soups. German sago is not sago at all, but is made from dried, coloured potato flour.

sagosuppe, a Norwegian dessert. First 5 heaped tablespoons sago is boiled in 3 quarts (12 cups) water for 15 minutes and constantly stirred. Then 5 egg yolks are beaten with ½ cup sugar, and the sago mixture added gradually, whisking all the time. It is flavoured with lemon juice or sherry and served hot with whipped cream.

saibling, German for char, which is popular in Germany and is often prepared by the *blaufisch* method. See also ZUGER RÖTEL.

saiga (*Saiga tatarica*), an antelope of the Capri variety, thickset and bull-necked, with a blunt, trunk-like nose. It inhabits the Siberian steppes, and until the last century was to be found as far west as Poland. The flesh is eaten, and the hides are also valued. See also OLÉN.

saignant, literally "bloody," a French culinary term applied to the cooking of meat, particularly steak, game, and duck, meaning very underdone or rare.

saigneux, a French butchery term for the neck of mutton or veal.

sailor's-choice, a collective name in the U.S. for several different fishes considered good gastronomically. Fishes included are a small porgy found on the eastern seaboard, and grunt and pinfish found in the warmer waters of the south.

Saint-Agathon, a French cow's milk cheese produced in Brittany. It is in season from October to July.

Saint Benoît, a French cheese of the camembert type, from Orléans. It is a soft, cow's milk cheese, and charcoal is added to the salt that is rubbed on the surface during the curing process, giving the cheese an ashen rind.

Saint-Claude, a small French goat's milk cheese from the district of Saint-Claude in the department of the Jura. The milk is rennetted and the curd is put into moulds for several hours. The cheeses are salted on the surface and may be eaten fresh or after ripening.

Saint-Florentin, a French goat's milk cheese made in the Burgundy region; it is in season from November to June.

Saint-Germain, I. A French soup made from fresh green peas cooked in seasoned stock and puréed. II. A French garnish for meat consisting of a purée of green peas bound with egg yolks and poached in *dariole* moulds, with olive-shaped glazed carrots, *pommes fondantes,* and sauce béarnaise. III. A French garnish for sweetbreads of a purée of green peas in artichoke bottoms, with sauce béarnaise. IV. A French method of serving fish. Fillets of the fish are dipped in egg and breadcrumbs, fried with *pommes noisette,* and served with sauce béarnaise.

Saint-Honoré, a French cake which is a Parisian speciality. It is flan-shaped and made with a case of *pâte brisée* filled with *crème pâtissière* with gelatine and stiffly beaten egg whites. The edge is decorated with small balls of chou pastry dipped in syrup and then iced.

Saint-Hubert, a French game soup which can be either a consommé or a potage. The consommé à la Saint-Hubert is a game consommé thickened with tapioca and garnished with game royale and a julienne of mushrooms cooked in butter and sprinkled with Madeira. Mashed or puréed lentils are sometimes added to this consommé, and to the potage. For the potage an old pheasant is simmered with veal and beef bones, a bouquet garni, chopped onion, leeks, carrots, celery, and water to cover, all well seasoned, for about 4 hours. The bird is then removed and the liquid strained. The game meat is taken from the bones and pounded up with 2 tablespoons breadcrumbs, a little stock to moisten, and 1 egg yolk. This mixture is made into small balls which are poached in the boiling soup. Then ¼ pint cream is added before serving. See also CONSOMMÉ.

St. Ivel cheese, a cream cheese made at Yeovil in Somerset.

St. John's Day, June 24, an important day in most fishing districts of County Antrim in the north of Ireland. The salmon fishermen of the river Bush hold a communal dinner known locally as the salmon dinner. It consists of fish soup, freshly caught salmon, new potatoes, and Bushmill's whisky. St. John's wort, a pretty plant with a delicate yellow flower and a fuzzy centre, is used as decoration, and fishermen place bunches of the wild purple orchids in their windows to ward off evil. In most parts of north Antrim and Derry people have a meal of new potatoes on St. John's day, even if enough for only one meal can be dug up and old potatoes have to be eaten again afterwards.

St. Lawrence dressing, a Canadian dressing served with salads consisting of ¼ pint (½ cup) olive oil, 8 chopped green olives, juice of ½ lemon and ½ orange, a pinch of paprika, salt, 1 teaspoon grated onion, 1 teaspoon worcestershire sauce, 1 teaspoon chopped parsley, and ½ teaspoon mustard. All these ingredients are combined, chilled until the oil solidifies slightly, and shaken until the mixture thickens.

Saint-Marcellin, a soft French cream cheese from the village of Saint-Marcellin in the department of Isère. It is usually made from a mixture of goat's and cow's milk. It is in season from April to November.

Saint-Michel, a French cake made from *genoese* mixture, and when cool, cut into three layers. Each layer is spread with butter icing beaten with coffee essence (extract) to taste, and then the three layers are put together. The top and sides are iced with vanilla icing, the top sprinkled with chopped roasted almonds and dots of the coffee-flavoured butter piped through a forcing bag. See also GENOESE.

Saint-Nectaire, a French cheese from the Auvergne. It is made only in the Mont Doré district, from the whole milk of Ferrandaise and Salers cows. The cheese is semi-hard and is matured on rye-straw mats in cool damp cellars, where it acquires a mouldy crust of white, yellow, and red. In season all the year round.

Saint-Paulin, a French semi-hard cow's milk cheese. It is made of unskimmed milk and is slightly salted. It is in season all the year round.

Saint-Rémi, a French cow's milk cheese made mainly in the Franche-Comté and Savoy. It is a whole milk cheese and resembles *géromé.*

Sainte-Anne d'Auray, a French cow's milk cheese produced in Brittany; it is in season from January to December.

Sainte-Maure, a French goat's milk cheese made chiefly in the regions of Sainte-Maure and Loches in the Indre-et-Loire department. It is in season from April to November. Sainte-Maure is also known as *chèvres longs.*

Sainte Ménéhould, a district of the Marne in France, distinguished for its good pork products, especially *pieds de porc;* when these (together with the pig's tails and ears) are boned, dipped in melted butter and breadcrumbs, and then grilled, the dish is called *pieds de porc à la Sainte Ménéhould.*

saithe, the Scottish name for coalfish; the word probably derives from the Norwegian name for the fish, *sei,* or it could come from the Gaelic *sioghean.* Dr. Johnson notes the abundance of these fish in his *Journey to the Western Islands of Scotland* (1775). In the Hebrides, these fish were indispensable: they gave oil for lamps, made a delicious stew with mackerel and assorted shellfish, and were excellent rolled in oatmeal and fried. The livers were mixed with oatmeal and

baked. Even the hens had their share of the fish, as the innards and skin were mixed with their meal. The surplus catch was split, salted, and dried in the sun, and kept as a standby for the winter when stormy weather would prevent fishing boats from going out. The local name for saithe in the northwest of Scotland is *cuddy,* but it is also called *cuith* or *piltock.* The fish is coloured green and white. See also SILLOCKS.

sajt, Hungarian for cheese. See KVARGLI; LIPTO TÚRÓ; PANNONIA; PUSZTADÖR; SZEKELY SAJT. The Hungarians also make a number of cheeses which are imitations of those of other countries, such as emmenthal (called emmenthaler in Hungary), Parmesan, and a blue cheese which resembles roquefort in taste.

sal prunella, a curing agent, not the same as saltpetre, but a form of it in which small quantities of the potassium nitrate are already converted into nitrites, which hasten the salting process in foods. It is much stronger than saltpetre and must be used very cautiously, in the proportion of ¼ oz. to 50 lb. of meat. Too much will turn the pickle or brine green and make the meat hard and dark in colour. See also SALTPETRE.

salad, a word which covers many different kinds of cold food, and derives from the Latin *sal* (salt). Usually it means a dish of raw herbs or vegetables such as lettuce, watercress, chervil, tarragon, endive, cucumber, tomato, etc., with a sauce composed of 3 parts olive oil to 1 part vinegar or lemon juice, with salt and pepper.

If only lettuce, or a similar greenstuff such as escarole or corn salad, is used, this is known as a green salad and is usually served as an accompaniment to cooked meats, game, or poultry in the U.K. and in France. However in the U.S. it is served as a separate course, sometimes to start the meal. If any other vegetable (not including herbs) is added, it becomes a mixed salad, and may consist of lettuce or an equivalent greenstuff, tomatoes, cucumber, beetroot, and, in Britain, slices of hard-boiled egg. However, when a green or a mixed salad is served with cream cheese or cold cooked eggs, fish, meat, poultry, or shellfish, the salad takes its name from the chief nonvegetable ingredient; for example, ham salad, lobster salad.

Salads are also made out of a single raw fruit, or a vegetable that is not a greenstuff. Cucumbers, tomatoes, or sweet peppers are sliced and dressed with oil and vinegar. These salads take their names from their constituent ingredient; for example, cucumber salad, tomato salad, etc. Fruits such as orange (served with roast duck), pineapple, peach, grapefruit, pear, banana, and melon are treated in the same way and also served with a French dressing. These salads are popular in the U.S. (They are not to be confused with fruit salad which is sweet.) Cold cooked vegetables are also made into salads by being sliced or chopped and served with a French dressing or mayonnaise. If a single cooked vegetable is used, such as celeriac, beetroot, peas, beans, potato, cauliflower, etc., the salad is called by its constituent ingredient; for example, potato salad. When several vegetables are mixed together and served with mayonnaise, this is known in Britain as Russian salad (see RUSSE).

In the U.S., a mixture of fresh fruit, cooked fish, meat, or poultry, or cream cheese, cooked shellfish, cooked or raw vegetables, etc., with various additions such as hard-boiled eggs, is chopped and set in an aspic jelly. This is known as a moulded salad.

Salads, originally "sallets" or "salletts," have been popular in Britain since the 14th century. The earliest to be recorded is from Richard II's master-cook and is dated 1390. It reads: "Take parsley, sage, garlic, Welsh onions, leeks, borage, mint, porette, fennel, watercress, rhue, rosemary, and purslane. Lave them clean, pick them and pluck them small with thine hands and munge [mix] them well with raw olive oil. Lay on vinegar and salt, and serve forth.'' A 16th-century salad, made from mixed meats, herbs, and vegetables was called *grand sallett* or salamagundi.

Many salads in Britain, Ireland, and the U.S. are ruined by being dressed with commercially-made bottled salad creams or mayonnaise. The dressing should be freshly made from pure oils and delicate vinegars or lemon juice. See also EN-SALADA; GRAND SALLETT; INSALATA; SALADA; SALADE; SALAT; SALATA; SAŁATA; SALLAD; SALOTAI; SLA.

salad dressings, light dressings for salads of raw or cooked vegetables. These are generally quite simple mixtures of oil and wine vinegar (3 tablespoons oil to 1 tablespoon vinegar), seasoned to taste with salt and pepper. In the U.S. this is called a French dressing, and the term is also gaining popularity in England. However, the American French dressing often has strong flavourings added to it, such as Tabasco, mustard, or ketchup, none of which are recommended, or ever appear in France. The only addition which is permissible in French cuisine is a small amount of fresh, finely chopped herbs, a flavouring of shallot, or a pinch of mustard, and for those who like a very fresh taste, lemon juice may be substituted for the vinegar. If malt vinegar has to be used, it should be diluted by half, with water. Cider vinegar is a much more pleasant alternative. Olive oil is the best and finest oil to use, although nowadays, when price and health reasons often make a special diet necessary, other vegetable oils such as safflower, sunflower, corn, or peanut oil are being more and more used.

This dressing which is used solely for raw or cooked vegetable salads, is known in France as vinaigrette. Eggs, fish, meats, game, or poultry can be served with variations of vinaigrette, or with mayonnaise, sauce *châtelaine*, chiffonade dressing, sauce *rémoulade*, or sauce *vincent*. Some commercially bottled salad creams and mayonnaise may have a strong, coarse taste, which easily destroys the flavour of the delicate foods with which they are served. See also THOUSAND ISLAND DRESSING; RUSSIAN DRESSING.

salad relish, a cooked American relish, made from 1 finely chopped cabbage and 1 lb. green tomatoes cooked with 4 oz. (½ cup) brown sugar, 1 tablespoon white mustard seed, 2 teaspoons celery seed, a pinch of cinnamon and cloves, salt, and 1 quart (4 cups) vinegar for 30 minutes. This would be called a chutney or pickle in Britain.

salada, Portuguese for salad. Green salads are popular in Portugal, dressed with French dressing, as are salads made from mixed raw or cooked vegetables, often with sliced hard-boiled eggs added. Dried white beans are served, cooked and cold, with oil and vinegar. See also SALAD.

salada de alface com cebolhas, a salad of lettuce and onions.

salade, French for salad. There are many varieties of salad in France: the following is a representative selection. See also SALAD.

salade à l'allemande, a salad of cooked chopped potatoes and eating apples, garnished with beetroot, onions, and mayonnaise. Sometimes chopped gherkin and salt herring are added.

salade au chapon, bread rubbed with garlic and sprinkled with olive oil, put in the bowl underneath lettuce or other greenstuff. See CHAPON.

salade composée, a salad containing a number of ingredients, not only vegetables, but also fish, eggs, meats, poultry, shellfish, etc. These salads are usually served as an hors d'oeuvre.

salade demi-deuil, equal quantities of cooked potatoes and truffles cut julienne, seasoned with cream and mustard.

salade doria, celeriac, either raw or cooked, cut julienne,

arranged in a dome shape and masked with mayonnaise. It is garnished with asparagus and beetroot cut julienne and sprinkled with grated hard-boiled egg yolk and parsley.

salade favorite, separate heaps of crayfish, asparagus, and truffles, with sauce vinaigrette.

salade italienne, carrots, peas, potatoes, and green beans, cooked and diced, mixed together with mayonnaise and garnished with anchovy fillets, tomatoes, olives, and capers. Other vegetables according to season can be added to this salad, also herbs.

salade lorette, corn salad mixed with sliced beetroot and sliced celery, with sauce vinaigrette.

salade lyonnaise, chopped meats such as calf's head, *museau* de boeuf, *cervelas,* etc., with chopped shallots, parsley, and sauce vinaigrette.

salade niçoise, chopped tomatoes, green beans, capers, black olives, chopped potatoes, sliced sweet peppers, chopped garlic, anchovy fillets, tunny (tuna) fish, all mixed, dressed with sauce vinaigrette.

salade parisienne, I. Mixed vegetables, chopped crawfish, and truffles, with mayonnaise. It is sometimes set in aspic. II. Thinly sliced *bouilli,* left over from a pot-au-feu, served with sauce vinaigrette and garnished with capers, gherkins, cold boiled and sliced potatoes, hard-boiled eggs, chopped shallots, and parsley.

salade pernollet, mixed chopped crawfish and truffles, set on lettuce leaves coated with mayonnaise.

salade russe, SEE RUSSE.

salade Sarah Bernhardt, chopped artichoke bottoms, asparagus tips, and quartered hard-boiled eggs on lettuce with sauce vinaigrette.

salade simple, a salad consisting of a single variety of vegetable, either raw or cooked, dressed with olive oil, wine vinegar, salt, and pepper. This does not exclude a garnish of freshly chopped herbs. Strictly speaking, raw salads are *salades simples à servir crues,* and cooked salads are *salades simples à servir cuites.*

salade de crudités, see CRUDITÉS.

saladier, French for salad bowl, usually made of white china in France. Wooden bowls, used for mixing ingredients, are known as *sébilles.*

salaison, a French culinary term for the treating of foods with salt in order to preserve them, either by rubbing with salt or by soaking in brine. The foods so treated are called *salaisons.*

salamagundi, see GRAND SALLETT.

salamander, a word covering several genera of lizard-like animals found in Europe and western Asia. A variety called axolotl is considered a delicacy by natives of Mexico and the southern states of the U.S.

salamander, a metal instrument which is made red-hot and used to brown the tops of puddings, especially *crème brûlée.*

salamandre, French for salamander (the cooking utensil). It is also called *fer à glacer* and *pelle rouge.*

salamandre, the French name for breadcrumbs fried in butter until golden and then sprinkled over certain dishes.

salambô, a small French cake made from chou pastry filled with *crème pâtissière* flavoured with kirsch. The top is iced or dipped in hot caramel.

salame (salami), an Italian spiced, salted, and smoked sausage, eaten raw in slices, although it is sometimes added to egg dishes, soups, or stews for flavouring. Some of the larger varieties, which are salted only for a few days, do require cooking, but these are known by their own particular names and not specifically as *salame.* These include *cotechino* and *zampone di modena.* French sausages are *salsiccie.* There are many varieties of salame, for nearly every province in Italy produces its own. It is an essential feature of antipasti (antipasta), which are usually eaten if pasta is not served as a first course. The following are the best known. See also MORTADELLA; SAUSAGE.

salame cacciatori, a small salame (salami) weighing about ½ lb., made from equal quantities of lean pork, pork fat, and beef seasoned with garlic, salt, pepper, and white wine. It is made in the three following shapes and sizes, using the same ingredients: *salame casalinga*—small, with a marbled appearance inside, not unlike *salame Cremona* but more distinctive; *salame Cremona*—larger and coarser-grained than *salame cacciatori; salame crespone*—saltier than salame cacciatori. The fat in this last salame resembles rice grains. It is widely exported, although not particularly highly prized in Italy. It is also called *salame Milano.*

salame di Felino, the most delicate and delicious of all salame, but it does not keep well. It is made at Felino, near Parma, from lean pork flavoured with whole peppercorns, very little garlic, and white wine. It has a handmade, irregular appearance.

salame fabriano, made of equal quantities of pork and young beef. It is a speciality of Ancona and the Marche region.

salame fiorentina, a larger salame (salami) than those described above, made from lean and fat pork, chopped rather coarsely. If flavoured with fennel, it is called *finocchiona.*

salame genovese, made from a mixture which is 50% young beef, 30% fat pork, and 20% lean pork. It is strongly spiced and is eaten in Genoa with raw broad beans and *pecorino sardo* cheese.

salame milano, another name for *salame cacciatori.*

salame napoletano, made from equal proportions of pork and beef, strongly flavoured with black pepper, chilli powder, garlic, and white wine.

salame sardo, Sardinian salame (salami), made from pork strongly flavoured with chilli powder.

salame soppressa, made in Verona, Padua, and the Veneto, from equal parts of pork and young beef.

salame ungherese, literally "Hungarian salame," made from pork, pork fat, and beef, finely chopped and strongly flavoured with garlic, paprika, pepper, and white wine.

salamikäse, an Austrian full cream cheese made in the shape of a salame (salami) sausage and weighing about 4 lb. It is unsalted and has a faintly sour taste and smell.

salamura, a Turkish cheese made from ewe's milk and pickled in brine. It tastes similar to Roquefort and is rather pungent.

salat, Danish for salad. Salads in Denmark are fairly varied, much use being made of cooked vegetables; sometimes these are tossed in a French dressing or, for cucumber (agurkesalat), in a mixture of equal parts of vinegar and water, with a pinch of sugar. Cream is used in the making of mayonnaise in Denmark, in place of olive oil. First 4 beaten egg yolks are heated in a double boiler with ½ pint whipped cream and the mixture is stirred until thick, when it is removed from the heat and 1 oz. butter cut into small pieces is stirred in. When it is cold, juice of ½ lemon is added and seasoning. Salads often take the place of the meat course in Denmark. See also SALAD.

salat, Norwegian for salad. Salads, in season, are popular in Norway, especially lettuce (temme salat) and cucumber salads (agurksalat). All salads are usually served on the koldtbord, and quite often sour cream mixed with a little lemon juice is used as a dressing. See also SALAD.

salat, Russian for salad. Salads are varied in Russia and usually consist of many cooked, raw, and pickled vegetables dressed with oil and vinegar, or sour cream. See also RUSSE; SALAD.

salata, Greek for salad. The traditional Greek salad consists of a mixture of many kinds of greenstuff, including wild vegetables and herbs, often mixed with anchovies, black olives, and féta cheese, and all dressed with olive oil and lemon juice. Sometimes spinaca (*spinaki*) is used. More generally, a salad in Greece is a cooked purée of vegetables served with *skorthalia* sauce. Soaked and cooked dried butter beans or haricot beans are also served as a salad (*fassolia*). See also SALAD.

saláta, Hungarian for salad. See also SALAD.

saláta savanjutéfellel, a method of serving lettuce. It is cooked in salted water for 15 minutes, then drained and put in a dish with sour cream, a little vinegar, and paprika. It is mixed well and served cold.

sałata, Polish for salad. Sorrel leaves are often included in a green salad. Sałata ze śmietaną is salad with a dressing of sour cream flavoured with lemon juice to taste.

sałata zimowa mieszana, a salad of separately cooked green beans, dried beans, red cabbage, potatoes, celeriac, peas, and mushrooms. They are all marinated in equal parts of olive oil and wine vinegar after cooking. Many other vegetables can be included if desired.

salata, Turkish for salad. Greenstuffs are often used, and served either with khıyar tèrètùru or a sauce made from pounded nuts, garlic, and bread, all mixed with mayonnaise made from hard-boiled egg yolks, olive oil, and vinegar or lemon juice (the method being the same as if raw egg yolks were used). Another form of salad is *tarama,* prepared in the same way as the Greek *taramosalata,* with the top sometimes sprinkled with chopped almonds or pistachio nuts. It may be served at all meals even breakfast. A salad is also prepared of cucumber, diced or sliced, salted, and mixed with pounded garlic and curd or yogourt. See also SALAD.

salchicha, Spanish for sausage. Some sausages made from lean beef and red peppers are eaten cooked in soups and stews. Sausages made from a mixture of veal and pork fillet, with nutmeg, white pepper, and rum are particularly good. They are salted and lightly smoked, and eaten raw. See also BUTIFARRA; CHORIZO; LONGANIZA; MORCILLA; MORCILLA BLANCA; MORTADELA; SAUSAGE.

salchicha estremeña, a type of sausage made from equal parts of lean meat, liver, and *tocino* flavoured with marjoram and anis. This sausage is cooked in a *bain marie* before serving. It is a speciality of the Spanish province of Estremadura.

salchichón, a lightly smoked sausage made with minced fillet of pork, fat bacon, and white pepper. This delicious sausage is salted and lightly smoked, and eaten raw.

salé, French for salted and pickled foods. See PETIT SALÉ.

salé aux choux, a speciality of the Périgord which con-

salchichón

sists of pickled pork cooked with cabbage, onion, and herbs. It is usually accompanied by *miques de maïs*.

sale, Italian for salt. The salt used in Italy is sea salt, and most of this comes from the vast salt lagoons on the coast of Sardinia.

salema, see SALPA.

salep or **salop,** the root of *Orchis latifolia,* washed, dried, and ground into powder. It is a gelatinous, floury food which used to be popular in England until the 19th century. One large teaspoonful was mixed with a pint of boiling water, making a drink which was very popular before coffee houses were established. It was sometimes laced with alcohol or mixed with sugar, cream, lemon, cinnamon, or eggs; in Ireland, it was mixed with cream and an egg yolk. It is still drunk a good deal in Greece (see SALEPI). In Persia and Asia Minor it is used for making soups and jellies. The name comes from the Arabic word for it—tha-leb.

salepi, Greek for a drink which looks rather like milk but is in reality a hot, sweet infusion of orchid tubers. It is sold in Greece late at night and in the early hours of the morning. The vendor carries his equipment, which includes a charcoal stove to keep the drink hot, in a brass container. To the English palate salepi tastes somewhat insipid although it was at one time a popular English drink (see SALEP).

sallad, Swedish for salad. Salads of all kinds are very popular on the smörgåsbord. Salads of mixed vegetables, and green salad (grönsallad), are usually served in Sweden with cold meat or cold fish (see SILL). Dressings are usually mayonnaise (often mixed with whipped cream), or a French dressing. See also SALAD.

Sally Lunn, a golden English yeast bun, reputed to have been created by a girl named Sally Lunn who sold them in the streets of Bath in about 1700. Earlier spellings of the name, however, give soleilune (sun-one), which might be West Country French, descriptive of a golden bun. To prepare them ½ oz. yeast is dissolved in ¼ pint (½ cup) lukewarm milk, mixed with ¼ lb. (1 cup) flour, then covered and left to rise. Meanwhile, ¾ lb. (3 cups) flour is mixed with 4 tablespoons sugar and a pinch each of salt and mixed spice. The 2 mixtures are combined, covered, and left in a warm place for several hours or overnight. Small round baking rings are half-filled with the dough and then left until the dough has risen to the top, when it is brushed with beaten egg yolk and baked in a moderate oven for 30 minutes. The baking rings are slipped off, and the buns are served hot, split open and either spread with butter or filled with whipped cream mixed with whipped egg white and sugar.

salmão, Portuguese for salmon. It is caught in Portugal's River Minho, the southernmost salmon limit in Europe. See also SALMON.

salmi, a dish made from game birds which are at least partly cooked. There is doubt about the origin of the word, and the origin of the dish has been placed as far back as the 14th century by some sources, while others ascribe it to the 18th. In Victorian and Edwardian England a salmi was always finished off at the table in a chafing dish. The jointed birds were put in the dish and sautéed with butter, mushrooms, shallots, and herbs. A little flour was sprinkled over, and a cup of game stock and about 4 tablespoons of either red or white wine, port or sherry, was added. It was heated gently and stirred until fairly thick, then served on croûtons of fried bread. Generally snipe, wild duck, partridge, grouse, and woodcock are used, and in the case of the latter the head and beak is left on. Salmis are unlike a stew or ragoût in that the word implies reheating, or both roasting and braising, in the method of cooking. Game birds that have been roasted very rare are often cooked in this way. See also GROUSE.

salmigondis, a French word meaning a ragoût of several reheated meats. When reheated poultry is substituted for meats the dish is called a *capillotade.*

salmon (*Salmo salar*), a migratory fish which lives in the sea but swims up freshwater rivers to spawn. It takes no nourishment while in fresh water, so its condition is least good when it is returning to the sea. In certain Scandinavian lakes and in Canada, the salmon uses the large lakes as ''sea'' and the rivers as spawning grounds. These salmon mature less quickly, however, and the flesh is inferior to that of the sea-going salmon which feed off post-larvae of herrings and other fatty fish. The salmon is in season from February to August, and it usually weighs about 14 lb. although it can be heavier. It is to be found throughout Europe and in the U.S. and Canada. Salmon is considered one of the finest fishes for both food and sport.

salmon

In Europe, Irish and Scottish salmon are thought the best. It is one of the few fishes which can be simply poached in water or a court bouillon and served cold, with no other accompaniment than perhaps a good mayonnaise. Salmon steaks are thick cutlets of the fish, brushed with oil or butter and grilled. A whole fish, either small (when it is called a grilse) or large, can be stuffed with forcement and baked. Cutlets can be baked in white wine. All salmon is equally good eaten hot or cold. Generally speaking, it is better not to serve it with too elaborate a sauce as its own flavour may be disguised and lost. In Russia a delicious pie is made of salmon (see KULEBYAKA). In Sweden it is pickled (see GRAVLAX). In Scotland, Scandinavia, and Ireland, it is smoked whole and then eaten raw in very thin slices, with lemon juice and a little cayenne (see RØYKTLAKS). Salmon roe is exceptionally good, and known as red or salmon caviar. A good deal of what is advertised as tinned ''salmon'' is not true salmon but one of a variety of Pacific salmon, such as blue-back or quinnat. See also DOG SALMON; LAKS; LAX; LOHI; LOSOŚ; SALMÃO; SALMÓN; SAUMON.

salmon hash, a traditional Scottish salmon dish. See TWEED KETTLE.

salmón, Spanish for salmon. See also SALMON.

salmón con aceitunas, salmon cooked in a casserole with stoned green olives, chopped parsley, 1 sliced onion, peppercorns, ¼ cup olive oil, and 1 tablespoon each vinegar and butter. It is baked slowly, sprinkled with hard-boiled egg when cooked, and served with salsa *amarilla.*

salmon trout or **sea trout,** I. *Salmo trutta,* a species of trout, trout themselves being members of the vast salmon family. It lives in both salt and fresh water all over Europe; it is larger than the trout but smaller than the salmon. It has pink flesh which has a very delicate taste. See also BAILA; SJØØRRET. II. The name also given to the Dolly Varden trout of Alaska. It can be cooked by the methods used for both trout and salmon. It is excellent when cured, but is too delicate for smoking. III. The name also given to the weakfish of the Gulf and Atlantic coasts of the U.S. It can be cooked in the same way as salmon or trout.

salmonberry (*Rubus spectabilis*), a wild raspberry found in North America and introduced into England. The berries, large and salmon-coloured, are a pleasant dessert fruit. They can be stewed or made into jam or jelly. They are eaten extensively by the Ten'a Indians and other inhabitants of Alaska.

salmonete, Portuguese for red mullet. It is at its best when cooked en *papillote* with butter and a little port wine. See also MULLET.

salmonete, Spanish for red mullet (also known as *barbo de mar*). In Spain it is often baked whole with lemon juice and sherry. See also MULLET.

salmorejo de perdiz a la toledana, see PERDIZ.

saloio, queijo de, a goat's and ewe's milk cheese made on the farms near Lisbon, Portugal. It weighs only about 4 oz. and is cylindrical in shape. It is quite mild and pleasant to the taste.

salotai, a salad of lettuce, tomatoes, onions, hard-boiled eggs, radishes, and cucumber, all mixed together and served with a sauce of 2 tablespoons lemon juice, 1 teaspoon sugar, a pinch of salt, and ½ pint (1 cup) sour cream or yogourt.

Salotas, Lithuanian for salad. See also SALAD.

salpa, Spanish for gilthead, served fried or poached in Spain, and also cooked in a casserole with tomatoes, sweet peppers, garlic, and parsley. It is also known as *salema* in some parts of Spain.

salpicão, a Portuguese sausage identical to *chouriço,* except that thick slices of pork fillet are used in place of leg. See also SALSICHA; SAUSAGE.

salpicon, a French and English culinary term for food cut into small cubes or dice and bound with a white or brown sauce. It is generally used for garnishing or stuffing eggs, fish, meat, or poultry, or for filling *barquettes, croustades, bouchées,* or *vol-au-vents.* Salpicon can be made from any one vegetable, fish, or meat, etc., or from a mixture.

When these mixtures are formed into cutlet-shapes, coated with egg and breadcrumbs, and then fried, they are called *côtelettes de salpicon.*

salpicon à l'écarlate, chopped pickled tongue bound with demi-glace.

salpicon à la financière, a mixture of quenelles, cock's combs, cock's kidneys, mushrooms, and truffles, bound with sauce *financière.*

salpicon à la montglas, a mixture of foie gras, tongue, truffle, and mushrooms, blended with demi-glace flavoured with Madeira.

salpicon à la périgourdine, a mixture of foie gras and truffles bound with sauce madère.

salpicon à la royale, a mixture of truffles and mushrooms bound with chicken purée.

salpicon à la Saint-Hubert, game bound with demi-glace.

salpicon cancalaise, a hot mixture of poached oysters and cooked mushrooms, bound with sauce *normande* or fish-based sauce velouté.

salpicon cardinal, a mixture of chopped lobster, truffles, and mushrooms, bound with sauce *cardinal.*

salpicon chasseur, a mixture of diced, sautéed chicken livers, mushrooms, and sauce *chasseur.*

salpicon cussy, a mixture of sweetbreads, truffles, and mushrooms, bound with sauce madère.

salsa, Italian for sauce. The word derives from the Latin *salsus* (salted), and sauces have been used in Italy since Roman times. The earliest were not unlike a pickle or relish (see GARUM). Another famous sauce much loved by the Romans was *agrodolce* (sweet-sour), originally made with honey. It survives not only in Italy but, with regional variations, in many other parts of the world. Generally speaking, Italian sauces are quite unlike the classical French sauces;

they do not have a roux as base, they seldom include eggs and cream, and they are stronger and more concentrated than the sauces of other parts of Europe. They are usually made from pounded herbs, fish, cheese, spices, or vegetables, mixed with olive oil and thickened with breadcrumbs. *Maionese* (mayonnaise) and *besciamella* (sauce béchamel) are the exceptions, but these two sauces are not of Italian origin and have entered into the cuisine of almost every European country. Other Italian sauces include *acciughe, alboni, bagna cauda, burro, cappon magro, carne, fegatini, funghi, Genovese, insalata, noce, peperata, pesto, piccante, pizzaiola, pomodoro, prugna secca, ragù, sugo, tartufo, tonno,* and *verde.*

salsa, Portuguese for parsley, which is flat-leaved in Portugal and grows to a height of over a foot.

salsa, Spanish for sauce. Vinaigrette is called *salsa de aceite* in Spain. Other Spanish sauces include *alioli, amarilla, patata,* and *verde.* See also SAUCE.

salsa de almendras con yema, an almond sauce with egg yolks, served with fish. To prepare it 8 oz. almonds are blanched and roasted, then pounded with 3 hard-boiled egg yolks and diluted with a little olive oil or milk.

salsa de nueces para carne de cerdo, a nut sauce served with pork. First 8 oz. scalded walnuts are skinned and ground before being mixed with 1 pint (2 cups) milk, which is then boiled and reduced by half.

salsa para aves (sauce for birds), a sauce for feathered game. A roux of ¼ lb. (½ cup) butter and ¼ lb. (1 cup) flour is removed from the heat, and to it is added a scant ½ pint (1 cup) white wine, which is well beaten in. Then 4 beaten egg yolks are also gradually stirred in with seasoning.

salsa para la fiesta de Navidad, a sauce served at Christmas in Ibiza. A few pistils of saffron, 2 tablespoons sugar, 1 cup biscuit crumbs, and 1 teaspoon cinnamon are pounded together. Then 2 pints (4 cups) hot chicken stock and 8 oz. ground almonds are added gradually; 6 eggs, well beaten, are stirred in, and the mixture is beaten hard with a wooden spoon over a low heat so that the sauce thickens, but does not curdle. It is used to accompany chicken, but is also sometimes served by country people as a hot drink after food.

salsiccie, Italian for fresh sausages (smoked sausage is known as *salame*). Usually made from pure pork and pork fat, they are coarsely minced compared with British or American sausages, and more highly spiced, sometimes having whole peppercorns and coriander or fennel seeds embedded in them. Almost every province has its own variety, but these do not differ greatly from one another. They can be very fatty and gristly if badly made, and for that reason are better grilled than fried. Sage or fennel leaves wrapped round them before cooking impart a good flavour. Sausages made in the north of Italy are the best. See also LUGANEGHE; SAUSAGE.

salsicha, Portuguese for sausage, usually smoked in Portugal. *Salsichas frescas* is the Portuguese name for fresh sausages formed into links. See CHOURIÇO; SALPICÃO; SAUSAGE.

salsifis, French for salsify. In France salsify is usually boiled in a court bouillon and served with a sauce, sauce béchamel, *beurre noisette,* sauce *crème,* sauce mornay, or sauce *provençale.* It is also cooked and served cold with sauce vinaigrette. See also SALSIFY.

salsifis frits, cold, chopped salsify dipped in batter and fried in deep hot oil.

salsify (*Tragopogon porrifolius*), also called salsafy or oyster-plant, the latter name deriving from the vaguely oyster-like flavour of the roots when boiled. Salsify was extremely popular in Britain 100 years ago, but is now thought to be exotic and foreign and is rarely seen in the shops. This is a great pity, for it is a superb winter vegetable. The long, thin white roots are usually scraped, parboiled, drained, and then fried in sizzling butter until tender and served with wedges of lemon. A popular Victorian method of cooking salsify was to parboil the roots, chop them, put them in a white sauce delicately flavoured with a little anchovy essence (extract), and then bake them in a moderate oven for about 30 minutes until the top was golden. See also SALSIFIS; SCHWARZWURZEL; SCORZONERA.

salsify

salt, the chief substance obtained from the evaporation of seawater (seasalt); also found in the earth in crystalline form and obtained by mining (rock salt or bay salt). The chemical name for salt is sodium chloride. Salt is used as a seasoning or preservative of food and is indispensable for cooking, and indeed for health. People on salt-free diets do not do without it entirely, for meat, milk, and certain vegetables have a high salt content. Salted fish, such as herrings or cod, and salt meat, such as salt beef or salt pork, are fresh foods preserved in salt, popular in many parts of the world. Celery salt is fine salt flavoured with dried powdered celery seed, and likewise garlic salt is powdered garlic with salt added. Spiced salt, known in France as *sel épicé,* is a mixture of dry salt, white pepper, and mixed spice. It is used for forcemeat in France. See also SPICED SALT.

salt beef or *corned beef,* a joint of beef which is rubbed with salt to a thickness of ⅛ inch, then with brown sugar (2 tablespoons to 8 lb. meat) mixed with 1 teaspoon saltpetre. It is put in a bowl and turned every day for a week, or left longer if it is not required immediately. This is the method for a joint weighing up to 6 lb.; for larger joints, at least 1 pint water is added to the salt, sugar, and saltpetre to make a liquid brine. Pork is salted in the same way, and in Scotland mutton legs are treated similarly, as are ducks in Wales. The salted joints are always boiled, usually with onions and root vegetables, for 20 minutes per lb. *Pease pudding* is traditionally served with boiled salted joints, also cabbage in Ireland and carrots in England. See also BULLY BEEF; NEW ENGLAND BOILED DINNER; PICKLED PORK.

saltfiskur, Icelandic cured fish. The fish is first cleaned, cut in two, and salted, and then dried, either in the sun or artificially. It is boiled and drained, and served with melted butter and potatoes. See also COD.

šalti barščiai, a Lithuanian national soup, made from 6 large beetroots, 2 teaspoons sugar, and 3 tablespoons vinegar added to 2 quarts (8 cups) water. It should have a slightly acid flavour, and it is served cold with slices of hard-boiled egg, sliced cucumber, thick sour cream, and chopped spring onion (scallion). In winter it is served hot with dried mushrooms added, and is called grybų sriuba.

saltimbocca, an Italian dish which originated in Brescia but is now a speciality of Rome. It means literally "jump into the mouth." Very thin slices of veal are rubbed with lemon and garnished with a leaf of fresh sage. Then a thin slice of ham is placed on top of each veal slice, and each pair of slices is rolled up and secured with a toothpick. These little rolls are browned all over in butter, then Marsala or white wine is poured over them and they are simmered until tender. As frequently happens in Italy, this dish is known by quite different names in different regions: *bocconcini, braciolette, gropetti, involtini, quagliette di vitello,* and *uccelletti scappati,* are all variations on the basic recipe for thin veal slices rolled up with ham or stuffing, and either fried, grilled, or, occasionally, baked. See also QUAGLIETTE DI VITELLO.

saltpetre, known chemically as potassium nitrate, a compound of potassium and nitric acid which forms a salt used in the preserving and curing of meat and other foods. Its preservative power is mainly due to its activity as an oxidising agent, which kills the bacteria of decomposition; it is this oxidising action that produces the pink colour in meats which have been cured in a brine containing saltpetre. However, if saltpetre is used in excess, this same action will also cause it to become a poison or irritant to the human body, for it will have a destructive effect upon the blood. It should therefore be used very sparingly: one-fortieth of the weight of salt used is recommended. Sodium nitrate, sodium nitrite, and potassium nitrite are also used as preservatives in commercially made meat and fish pastes. See also CURING; SAL PRUNELLA.

saltsa, Greek for sauce. Although there are comparatively few Greek sauces, they are quite individual and are not found in other countries. It is said that the Greeks invented sauces, and Orion, the lexicographer of the 5th century A.D., is thought to have been the originator of the white sauce. Lampriades, another innovator, was the inventor of a brown sauce. *Avgolémono* is the national Greek sauce, and it is closely followed in popularity by *skorthalia* and *moustartha.* Others are *ladoxitho* and *maioneza.* See also SAUCE.

salvia, Italian for sage, used mainly with liver in Italy.

Salzburger nockerln, see NOCKERLN.

salzgurke, German for pickled cucumber, usually known in England as gherkin and used extensively in Germany as a garnish, in salads and with sausages.

sambal oelek, a Dutch-Indonesian chilli-flavoured relish, which accompanies all Indonesian dishes, like *rijsstafel.* To prepare it 2 tablespoons finely chopped red chillis are mixed with ½ teaspoon salt, ½ tablespoon olive oil, a squeeze of lemon juice, and ½ teaspoon lemon peel. The resulting paste is kept until required in airtight jars. It is very hot to the palate and should be used sparingly.

samphire (*Crithmum maritimum*), a green, fleshy, perennial plant that grows on cliffs. The succulent leaves were once extensively used raw in salads, or pickled in vinegar. Samphire has a strong, slightly sulphurous smell, much liked by some people. It can be boiled and served with melted butter and eaten either on its own or with mutton, like laver. Shakespeare mentions it in *King Lear:* ". . . one who gathers samphire, dreadful trade . . ."—probably a reference to the perils of collecting it on dangerous cliff faces. A recipe of 1650 mixes it with pickled cucumbers, capers, vinegar, and a little strong broth, a chopped lemon, salt, and nutmeg. The mixture is boiled and thickened with butter and an egg yolk, and sweetened with sugar. This was served over meat on fried bread, and decorated with red barberries—a colourful dish. Original spellings give "sampier," no doubt from the French name for it, "St. Pierre." (Perce Piérre), also called *Christe marine*.

samphire

Samsøe, a popular Danish cheese from the island of Samsøe. It is made from whole cow's milk with a butterfat content of 45%, is shaped like a cartwheel, and weighs about 30 lb. There are rather large holes or eyes in it, and it is a golden colour inside, with a delicate, nutty flavour, and a firm texture. It reaches its full flavour after maturing for 6 months, although it is eaten both younger and older. Other Danish cheeses of the Samsøe type are *danbo, elbo, fynbo, molbo,* and *tybo.* A Samsøe is also made in Ireland. See also OST.

San Simón, a Spanish cheese, called after the parish of San Simón de la Cuesta in the province of Lugo where it is made. It has a shiny, dark-yellow, very thin rind, and is conical in shape, the weight varying from 2 to 10 lb. It has a mild flavour and is similar to *teta.* See also QUESO.

sand cherry (*Prunus pumila*), a small shrub bearing round, sweet, purple-black fruit. It is cultivated in the U.S.

sand dab (*Limanda ferruginea*), a saltwater fish, not unlike plaice in flavour. It is found off North American Atlantic coasts, and is cooked in the same way as plaice or flounder.

sand eel (*Ammodytidae*), also called sand lance, a small, snake-like fish with a long conical snout and a forked tail, common in the North Atlantic. Sand eels are used for bait but also make excellent eating, and they can be cooked in any way that is suitable for smelt. See also LANCES.

sand lance, see LANCES; SAND EEL.

sand leek, see ONION.

sand smelt, see ATHERINE.

sandacz, Polish for perch. Perch is used extensively in Poland, as are many other freshwater fish, for the country has only a small stretch of seacoast. *Sandacz na winie* is perch cooked in white wine and melted butter. Perch is sometimes served stuffed and baked in Poland, or simmered in a sauce of puréed mixed root vegetables and spices. It can also be cooked in any way that is suitable for carp (see KARP). See also PERCH.

sandre, French for giant perch, which resembles a pike but is far finer to eat. See also PERCH; SUDAK; ZANDER.

sandtorte, a German cake. First ½ lb. (1 cup) butter is creamed with ½ lb. (1 cup) sugar. Then 4 egg yolks are added, and the mixture is beaten for 1 hour (or 10 minutes

with an electric beater) with ½ lb. (1¾ cups) potato flour, 1 glass rum, and finally 4 stiffly beaten egg whites, gradually added. The mixture is poured quickly into a greased cake tin and baked for 1 hour in a moderate oven.

sandwich, a composition of two slices of bread with a filling between them. It is reputed to have been named after John Montagu, 4th Earl of Sandwich (1718–1792), who gambled heavily and was so loth to leave the tables for a full meal that he had this concoction served to him while he was still playing. The word has entered into French culinary terminology and is used in many other European countries. Almost anything can be made into the filling for a sandwich, and brown or white bread can be used. Sandwiches are very easy to transport and so are useful on journeys, and under any circumstances that make it difficult to obtain a full meal. There are many variations on the simple sandwich. Double-decker sandwiches are made with two layers (see CLUB SANDWICH). Toasted sandwiches are made by toasting the outer surfaces of the two slices, but leaving the inner surfaces soft, and buttering them, so that the sandwich holds the filling well and is softer to eat. Toasted bread on both sides can also be used. Open sandwiches are simply sandwiches without the top layer of bread. In France and Italy, sandwiches are often composed of a small hollowed-out loaf or roll filled with meat, fish, etc. Bookmaker's sandwich is made from a small French loaf or roll, scooped out, buttered, and filled with a thick grilled steak spread with mustard and seasoned; the top is pressed down, sometimes under a weight, so that the meat juices ooze out into the bread. This is known as steak sandwich in the U.S., and also variously as hunter's or shooter's sandwich.

sangler, a French culinary term meaning to pack ice or ice and salt round a receptacle containing ice cream or a *sorbet* in a mould, in order to freeze it.

sangrante, a Spanish term for meat that is underdone or rare, particularly steak.

sanguinante, an Italian term for meat that is underdone or rare, particularly steak.

sanguine, a dish from the Berry region of France, resembling a fresh blood-pudding pancake. First 1 large sliced onion is cooked lightly in butter until golden; then the blood of 2 chickens is added. The whole is seasoned, shaken, and cooked like an omelette or pancake. It is called a sanquette in the southwest.

sansonnet, I. French for a young mackerel. II. Colloquial French for starling, which is served in the same way as thrush in France.

santé, a French soup made from 3 pints (6 cups) *potage purée parmentier* and 4 tablespoons chiffonade of sorrel thickened with 3 egg yolks mixed with ¼ pint (½ cup) cream and garnished with chopped chervil mixed into butter.

santola, Portuguese for spider crab.

santola recheada, a dish of crab meat served in an oil and vinegar dressing thickened with egg yolk.

sapsago, see SCHABZIEGER.

saracen corn, an alternative name for buckwheat.

saragli, a Greek cake, which consists of nut-filled phyllo pastry rolled in long narrow rolls which are placed side by side in a dish and all covered with syrup after baking. It is similar in taste to baklava.

Sarah Bernhardt, I. A French chicken consommé slightly thickened with tapioca and garnished with quenelles of chicken, julienne of truffles, asparagus tips, sliced poached beef marrow, and *beurre d'écrevisses.* See also CONSOMMÉ. II. A French method of serving eggs. First 6 hard-boiled eggs are sliced lengthways. The yolks are mixed with ½ cup chopped chicken, 1 raw yolk, and 2 tablespoons breadcrumbs, and this mixture is replaced in the egg-white shells, covered with sauce *périgueux* and baked for 30 minutes in a moderate oven.

saramură, a Rumanian broth of vinegar, salt, and garlic in which meat or fish is served.

saramură de stiuca, a traditional dish of yellow pike baked or grilled with cumin seeds, peppers, and oil, then gently simmered for 5 minutes in a *saramură*.

šaran, the Serbo-Croat word for freshwater bream, also called carp bream, a popular fish in Yugoslavia. It is often stuffed with a mixture of chopped celery, garlic, parsley, olive oil, and lemon juice before being baked. See also RIBA.

sarapatel, Portuguese for fried liver and bacon served together.

sarcelle, French for teal, and, inaccurately, culinary French for widgeon, which in formal French is *canard siffleur*. See also GIBIER.

sarde, à la, a French garnish for large and small cuts of meat, particularly steaks, consisting of grilled or fried tomatoes, stuffed cucumber or courgettes (zucchini), and croquettes of saffron-flavoured rice.

sardella, Greek for sardine. See also SARDINE.

sardelles riganato, freshly caught sardines baked with olive oil, lemon, and marjoram.

sardenara, a pizza which is the speciality of San Remo in Liguria. See PIZZA ALLA LIGURIA.

sardina, Spanish for sardine. See also SARDINE.

sardinas rellenas, stuffed sardines. First ½ cup breadcrumbs is soaked in milk and then mashed into 2 tablespoons grated cheese, 1 tablespoon chopped parsley, 1 chopped garlic clove, and seasoning. A beaten egg is used to bind the ingredients. About 24 sardines are split open and the heads, tails, and bones are removed. Then 2 sardines are pressed together with the stuffing spread between them, and the sardine "sandwiches" floured and fried in oil.

sardina, see AGONI.

sardine (*Sardina pilchardus*), the name given to the young pilchard, a migratory fish of the family *Clupeidae*. It is found in great quantities off the coast of Sardinia, where it gets its name. It has a high fat-content, like the adult pilchard, and so can only be eaten fresh in the close neighbourhood of the ports where it is landed, because the flesh deteriorates quickly. Grilled or fried fresh sardines are delicious, and are a popular dish all along the Mediterranean coast. However, sardines are mainly canned, either in oil or brine, and used for hors d'oeuvre. Most of the canning is done with catches made off the coasts of Portugal and Brittany. The word is the same in both French and German.

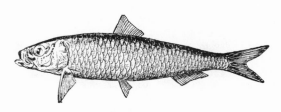

sardine

In the U.S., the name sardine is given to young herrings and anchovies. The true sardine (the young pilchard) is not found there. See also SARDELLA; SARDINA; SARDINHAS.

sardinhas, Portuguese for sardines, which abound off the coast of Portugal; the canning of them is probably the largest Portuguese industry. They are also eaten fresh in Portugal, when they are fried in batter, grilled over small charcoal stoves, or baked with tomatoes and onions in white wine. They are delicious. See also SARDINE.

sardo, see PECORINO SARDO.

sargasso, Spanish for seaweed, eaten in Spain as a salad component.

sargo, Spanish for grey bream, a rather dull fish, unknown in the British Isles. It is also known as *brema*. See also BREAM; OBLADE.

sarladaise, à la, a French garnish for lamb consisting of truffles and sliced potatoes, pan-fried in the oven with thick meat gravy. See POMME DE TERRE (POMMES À LA SARLADAISE).

sarma, stuffed cabbage rolls which are popular in the Serbian part of Yugoslavia. Large blanched cabbage leaves are stuffed with a mixture of 1½ lb. meat (pork, beef, or veal, or a combination), 1 cup rice, 1 teaspoon paprika, 1 clove garlic, 1 large onion, herbs, and seasoning. They are rolled up, packed tightly in a casserole, and baked with a little stock or diluted tomato purée in the oven. These cabbage rolls are a standard feature of cooking throughout the Balkans; the word is the same in Bulgarian, and in Rumania they are called *sarmale*. They are also much favoured by Jewish people from the Balkans, and have become a most popular dish in Israel where they are also known as *holishkes*. Jewish people make them both with and without meat; the meatless rolls often contain bulgur and chopped raisins. Sometimes they are served with yogourt or sour cream. In vine-growing countries vine leaves are used as well as cabbage; see SARMALE, IN FOII DE VIȚĂ.

sarmades, a Greek dish of cabbage leaves stuffed with chopped beef and pork, onions, and raw rice, and rolled up. The rolls are casseroled with lemon slices between the layers and boiling water to cover. They are served with *avgolémono sauce* and are much favoured by the Macedonians and Kastorians.

sarmale, Rumanian stuffed cabbage rolls. See also SARMA.

sarmale in foii de viță, a dish of stuffed vine leaves. A stuffing is made from 2 lb. meat (not necessarily all one single variety), 2 chopped onions, rice, a little each of chopped parsley and dill, and seasoning. A spoonful of this mixture is placed on each washed vine leaf, which is then rolled up into a small parcel. These parcels are placed tightly together in a deep pan, and a sauce made from 1 tablespoon butter, 1 tablespoon flour, 4 cups stock, and 3 cups white wine is poured over them. They are cooked for about 2 hours. Another cup of boiled white wine is then poured over, and they are cooked for a further 30 minutes. Diluted tomato purée can also be used if the wine is omitted. The dish is usually served with sour cream and yogourt. It can also be made with spinach instead of vine leaves, when it is known as sarmale in foii de spanac.

Sometimes the vine leaves are salted. Young tender leaves are placed in a stone jar with alternate layers of salt, ending with a layer of salt. No water is added, as the salt itself produces moisture which colours the leaves and prevents them from drying out. The salted leaves may be kept for months. For stuffing, they are blanched with boiling water, drained, and rolled up with the filling described above. See also DOLMADES.

sarnina, Polish for venison, also called *jelenina*. Venison is nearly always marinated in a mixture of vinegar or wine, water, herbs, and root vegetables before cooking is begun; if this is not done, the meat is rubbed with vodka instead and wrapped in a vodka-saturated cloth for 2 to 3 days. Recipes usually include juniper berries, and sour cream is used to dilute the pan juices. See also VENISON.

sarrasin, French for buckwheat, also called blé noir. It is used in France for *galettes,* pancakes, and porridge.

sarsaparilla (*Smilax officinalis*), a South American plant with cord-like roots which are dried and used to make mineral waters, and a wine which is thought to have tonic qualities and which was frequently drunk by Victorian ladies in England.

sarsaparilla

sassafras

sartadagnano, a speciality of Provence. It is a mass of very small fish (*poutine* and *nonat*) cooked in olive oil in a frying-pan, and pressed together when cooking so that it can be turned like a pancake. It is served sprinkled with hot vinegar. This is also an excellent way of cooking whitebait.

sartén, a flat, heavy, two-handled Spanish pot, used for cooking paella. Sometimes the pot itself is known today as a paella.

sartù, see RISO, SARTÙ DI.

sås, Swedish for sauce. Sauces play an important part in Swedish cookery, although many of the recipes have a French origin. Cream, herbs such as chervil, dill, and tarragon, and wines such as sherry and Madeira, are extensively used as flavouring. Swedish sauces include *fänkålsås, fisk, hummer, korint, krogvärdens sås, skarpsås,* and *vanilj.* See also SAUCE.

sassafras (*Sassafras albidum*), a tree of the laurel family, with aromatic bark and leaves. It is also called ague-tree, and is found in the U.S. The root is used for root beer and also yields an oil used in perfumery. The sassafras is most important, however, for its leaves, which are dried and powdered to make filé powder, an essential ingredient of gumbo, the famous Creole stew. The powder was originally made by Choctaw Indian squaws, but it is now produced commercially. Dried sassafras leaves were also once sold in the French market in New Orleans for use in teas and tisanes.

sassenage, a French blue-veined cow's milk cheese produced in the Dauphiné. It is in season from September to June.

sateh, a popular Dutch-Indonesian dish of meat or poultry prepared on skewers. It is often served as part of the *rijsstafel.*

  sateh ajam, chicken sateh. The chicken is cut into small chunks which are rubbed with seasoning and left to stand for 15 minutes. They are then threaded onto a skewer (about half a dozen to each skewer), basted with oil, and either roasted in a slow oven, turning often, or grilled over a barbecue. They are served with *sateh saus.* Lamb sateh (*sateh kambing*) and pork sateh (*sateh babi*) are prepared in the same way.

  sateh saus. Each sateh dish has an individual sauce requiring a wide variety of Indonesian ingredients. Countess von Limburg Stirum, however, in her book *The Art of Dutch Cooking,* gives this shortcut sauce as being suitable for all three sateh dishes mentioned above. First 4 tablespoons peanut butter is mixed with 8 tablespoons hot water; then ½ teaspoon crushed red chilli, 2 teaspoons molasses, 1 table-

spoon soy sauce, 1 crushed clove garlic, and lemon juice are all stirred in, and the mixture is simmered for about 5 minutes. Just before serving, the sateh is covered with this sauce.

satsuma (*Citrus reticulata*), a large juicy Spanish tangerine which ripens in late October and November and appears in the shops in Britain in time for Christmas.

sauce, a liquid or semi-liquid preparation served as an accompaniment to other foods to make them taste and look better. The word comes from the Latin *salsus* (salted), but nowadays there are sweet as well as savoury sauces. The word "saucer" comes from sauce. In Norman times the sauce was poured into individual saucers, and each person dipped his food, according to personal taste, in the sauce. In medieval England sauces had more the character of a relish, hence the meaning of the now colloquial "saucy," that is, sharp or pert.

  There are four kinds of British sauce: uncooked vinegar-based sauces, such as mint sauce and horseradish sauce; cooked sauces based on a roux diluted with milk or stock, such as white sauce, caper or parsley sauce, or bread sauce, in which breadcrumbs are used instead of flour; cooked sweet sauces, made either with a roux, or with eggs and milk like the true custard; and sweetened purées of cooked fruit, such as apple or gooseberry sauce, which are served with meat or poultry.

  Other sauces such as Harvey, Tabasco, tomato, and worcestershire sauce, which are sold commercially in bottles, should really be classed as either condiments or relishes and should be used sparingly. Crab apple, red currant, and rowan jelly, and cumberland sauce, which are served with game or mutton, should not strictly be classed as sauces but rather as accompaniments.

  Recipes for individual English sauces will be found under the entry for their main ingredient, for example onion sauce, under onion, etc. See also MOLHO; SALSA; SALTSA; SÅS; SAUCE; SAUS; SOS; SÓUS; SUGO, DICARNE.

sauce, Danish for sauce. See CHAMPIGNON SOUS; KAPER (KAPERSOUS); LOG; PEBERROD; SENNEP, SAUCE.

sauce, French for sauce. The French have produced more classical sauces than any other nation, and in France almost every food has its accompanying sauce and garnish. Five of the great classical sauces were evolved there in the 18th century, and it is from these that many other sauces are derived; they are known in France as *les grandes sauces* or *les sauces mères,* and are sauce béchamel, sauce brune or espagnole, sauce tomate, mayonnaise, and sauce velouté. Other sauces derived from these are called *sauces composées* (compound sauces) and will be found under their respective names throughout this book. See also DEMI-GLACE; FONDS DE CUI-SINE; SAUCE.

sauce, German for sauce. Most German sauces are similar to either French or English sauces; that is, they can be made with a roux base, or with a vinegar base like a relish. The latter are often made from salted cucumbers, onions, beetroot, or horseradish, all sprinkled with a little sugar and salt and covered with vinegar. Caraway seeds are used in sauce béchamel and also in onion sauce in Germany. Other German sauces include *karottensauce, kümmelsauce, meerettichsauce, oberskren, sauerampfersauce, schwammerlsauce, wienerzwiebelsauce,* and *zwiebelsauce.* See also SAUCE.

sauce alone (*Alliaria petiolata*), a local name for garlic mustard, a common pot herb which grows wild in England.

sauciaux, the local name for pancakes in the Bourbonnais, the old French province which now forms the department of Allier and a small part of Puy-de-Dôme, Creuse, and Cher.

saucisse, French for small sausage, of which there are many varieties in France. They are all made from pork, both fat and lean, and are delicately flavoured and sometimes smoked or very highly salted. They are made both round and long, and short and flat, the latter being called *crépinettes* and, in the Ardèche where they are a speciality, *cayettes.* The most common of the long sausages, and the least good, is *cervelas* which, apart from being poached and served with hot potato salad, is also used in *cassoulets.* Other French sausages are the *saucisse aux herbes,* a sausage flavoured with herbs which is a speciality of the Rhône district; the *saucisse de Strasbourg,* a fine-flavoured Alsatian sausage, lightly smoked like a frankfurter, and served with sauerkraut; and the *saucisse de Toulouse,* a hand-made sausage with a simple but good taste, usually grilled or fried. Sausages of foreign origin are also used in France—*chipolatas, chorizos* (*saucisses rouges*), frankfurters, and Vienna sausages. Homemade sausages are called *saucisses de ménage.* See also CERVELAS; JUDRU; ROSETTE; SAUCISSON; SAUSAGE.

saucisse en brioche, cervelas cooked in brioche pastry.

saucisses au vin blanc, sausages cooked in the oven, the pan juices diluted with white wine, demi-glace, and a little butter.

saucisson, French for a large sausage weighing between 12 and 16 oz., which is always made from pure pork, lean and fat, to which veal, beef, or mutton may be added in the various regional specialities. Any adulteration such as flour, bread, horsemeat, or donkey meat is stated on the label. A proportion of saucissons are salted and smoked. The most famous are the saucissons of Lorraine, Luchon, Lyons, Mortagne, and Strasbourg, the *saucisson de Bretagne* and the *saucisson d'Arles.* All the smoked sausages are eaten sliced and raw, but they can also be cooked by poaching very slowly for about 1 hour, then served with hot potato salad—a method which applies particularly to the saucissons of Lyons and Strasbourg. See also ARLES, D', SAUCISSON; CERVELAS; SAUCISSE; SAUSAGE.

saucisson en brioche, saucisson de Lyons cured with cubes of fat embedded in it, cut into thick slices and interlarded with more fat, then wrapped in brioche dough, and baked. It can also be made with *cervelas* or *cervelas truffé* wrapped in brioche dough and baked.

sauerampfer, German for sorrel. See also SORREL.

sauerampfersauce, an Austrian sauce which consists of a white drawn-butter sauce garnished with shredded sorrel. It is often served with roast goose. See also SORREL, SAUCE.

sauerbraten, an Austrian and German dish of beef, which is first marinated for 4 days in equal quantities of wine vinegar and water with onion, bay leaf, cloves, and thyme and then braised with the marinade and fried onions, carrots, and a

saucissons épices

little sugar until the meat is tender. One cup sour cream is stirred in just before serving.

sauerkraut, a German speciality of salted, finely shredded, white cabbage. A particular kind of large tub is filled with layers of cabbage, a thick sprinkling of salt, and a few caraway seeds. A little water is added (1 cup for each large cabbage), then a cloth is put over the cabbage before a heavy lid with a weight on top is placed over it. It is kept for at least 3 weeks, but each week the lid and cloth are lifted, any scum that has come up is taken off, and a little more salted water (1 tablespoon salt to 1 pint water) is added. Sauerkraut is a traditional German speciality and is used extensively as a vegetable and as a garnish. In France it is known as *choucroute.*

sauge, French for sage. There are 3 varieties commonly used in France: *grande sauge,* which has a thick square stem and grey-green leaves; *petite sauge de Provence,* which has small, pale leaves, and is the most highly prized; and *sauge de catalogne,* which is even smaller than the Provençal variety. Sage is used in France in salads, for flavouring green vegetables such as beans and peas, for encasing and flavouring small birds such as blackbird or thrush, for forcemeats, and for making sage-flavoured vinegar. See also SAGE.

saumon, French for salmon. It is served grilled, baked, or poached in court bouillon. Sauce velouté, prepared with the fish stock, is the most usual accompaniment when the poached fish is served hot, and sauce hollandaise is also much used; when served cold, *chantilly, gribiche,* mayonnaise, *ravigote,* rémoulade, tartare, or sauce *verte* are the sauces most often served; and both hot and cold salmon are sometimes garnished with crayfish tails, chopped lobster, or a macédoine of vegetables. A small whole salmon is sometimes stuffed with fish forcemeat, rubbed with butter, wrapped in *pâte brisée,* and baked in a slow-to-moderate oven for 1–1½ hours. This was a speciality of the famous Mère Catherine restaurant in Paris before WW II. Cutlets of salmon, called côtelettes *darnes* or *tranches de saumon,* are grilled, poached, braised, or served à la *meunière.* Cold cooked salmon is often used for forcemeat, mousse, mousseline, mayonnaise, and soufflés. See also SALMON.

saumon glacé bellevue en aspic, salmon poached in court bouillon and served cold in its jelly. A wine such as Chambertin or a Bordeaux can also be used for this dish.

saumonette, the French generic name for a number of sea fish which are shark-like in appearance. It includes the *chien de mer,* the *roussette,* and other types of dogfish.

saumure, French for brine. See also BRINE.

grande saumure, a brine made from 10 gallons water, 20 lb. rock-salt, 2 lb. saltpetre, and 2½ lb. (4 cups) brown sugar, all boiled until a raw potato will float more or less in the middle. It is used for pickling large joints of meat which have first been rubbed with salt mixed with a very little saltpetre (1 teaspoon saltpetre to 1 lb. salt).

saumure liquide, a brine made from 1 gallon water, 4 lb. rock-salt, ¾ lb. (1⅔ cups) brown sugar, 3 oz. saltpetre, 20 peppercorns, 20 juniper berries, a sprig of thyme, and 1 bay leaf all boiled for 30 minutes, then cooled. This is used in France for pickling tongue and beef. The saltpetre turns the meat a reddish-brown colour.

saupiquet, a medieval French wine sauce, thickened with grilled bread and containing spices such as cinnamon and ginger, which used to be served with roasted rabbit. A similar sauce, called *sauce piquante à la crème,* is served today with hare in southwest France, and also with slices of Morvan ham fried in butter. See also PIQUANTE, SAUCE, À LA CRÈME.

saur, French for a herring which has been both salted and smoked. The word was originally *sauret* or *soret.*

saurel, the name given to two allied species of a long sea fish, *Trachurus trachurus* and *T. symmetricus.* They resemble the mackerel and are known in England as horse mackerel. The first inhabits European waters, the second only the North Pacific. The flesh of both makes good eating, but is not as rich as that of the true mackerel. In France saurel is usually served in fillets. It is spelled *sawrell* in Malta.

saus, Dutch for sauce. The world-famous Dutch sauce is of course hollandaise, which has entered into classical French cooking. Other Dutch sauces include *robert saus, rozijnen saus, sambal oelek, sateh saus,* and *zure saus.* See also SAUCE.

saus, Norwegian for sauce. Sauces and gravies are popular in Norway, and butter and cream are essential ingredients. In certain regions fresh and sour cream are used together to make gravies for game and poultry as well as for some fish dishes, although in the latter case the most usual accompaniment is melted butter and lemon juice. White and cream sauces are served with vegetables. Sweet sauces served with fruit desserts are not unlike custard or *zabaglione.* Norwegian sauces include *robin saus, skum saus,* and *viking saus.* See also SAUCE.

sausage, minced pork or other meat often mixed with a proportion of bread or rusk and lightly seasoned, then inserted into long cylindrical cases made of gut which are twisted into regular lengths when full. The quality of the sausage can vary enormously, depending on the quality of the meat used, and the proportion of meat included in relation to carbohydrate. Sausages are always sold raw in Britain, and are usually either grilled or fried and served with mashed potatoes, a dish known popularly as "sausages and mash." They are also used for toad-in-the-hole, and small sausages, called *chipolatas,* are served hot on cocktail-sticks with drinks or used as a garnish for roast poultry. Various other named types of sausage are also eaten. Breakfast sausage is cooked and lightly smoked and tastes mostly of preservative; it is served cold in slices. The name of the saveloy sausage is a corruption of the French *cervelas* and was originally made from brains. Now it is made from various extremities of the pig such as the head and tail, flavoured with herbs and spices, and lightly smoked. It is eaten cold, just as it is bought, in slices with salad. Italian saveloys are sold in Britain and can be quite good. Compared to continental sausages, the British commercially made varieties are very disappointing. See also FRANKFURTER WÜRSTCHEN; KIEŁBASA; KOLBASA; KOLBÁSZ; LOUKANIKA; MAKKARA; REINSDYR (REINSDYREPØLSE); ROOKWORST; RULLEPØLSE; SALAME; SALCHICHA; SALPICÃO; SALSICCIE; SALSICHA; SAUCISSE; SAUCISSON; SAUSSISKA; SOSISKI; SOUDZOUKAKIA; WÜRST.

sausage roll, an English snack consisting of a sausage (or sausage meat rolled into a sausage-shape) enclosed in short crust or puff pastry and baked.

saussiska or *sassiska,* Russian smoked sausage, often served for *zakuski* in Russia. A popular recipe is *saucissiski v tomate,* in which sausages are cut into pieces and cooked in a hot tomato sauce for about 10 minutes. See also SAUSAGE.

saussoun, a French sauce which is a speciality of the Var district of France. It is spread on bread as an hors d'oeuvre or used as a filling for sandwiches. First 6 fresh mint leaves are pounded in a mortar with the same number of anchovy fillets. Then 3½ oz. (½ cup) ground almonds, 3½ oz. (½ cup) olive oil, and slightly less of water are added in turn. The sauce is mixed well until it has the texture of a thick mayonnaise. A squeeze of lemon juice can be added if the sauce is too thick.

sauter, a French verb meaning to cook over a brisk heat in a fat such as oil or butter. The literal translation is "to jump" and the word has become part of culinary terminology because the food must be tossed in the fat, either by being shaken in the pan or by being turned with a fork, so that it does not stick and burn. Sauté is the corresponding case of poultry—and cooked on top of the stove in butter or oil, with stock, wine, or a thickened liquid added to the pan juices (see POULET, SAUTÉ). In a finished sauté, the sauce should be just sufficient barely to cover or coat the food, neither too thick nor too liquid. If too concentrated, more stock, water, or wine should be added to prevent the flavour being impaired. In France a special pan with a thick base and low, outward-sloping sides is used when fish, meat, poultry, and vegetables are sautéed. It has a lid and is known as a *sautoir.* Another pan, called a *sauteuse,* is also used for sautéeing; it has a handle and is heavy and shallow like the *sautoir,* but its sides are straight.

savarin, I. A type of *baba,* baked in a special ring-mould with a rounded top. When cooked, the middle is filled with various mixtures such as *crème chantilly,* cherries (savarin montmorency), or fruits puréed and mixed with rum. See also BABA. II. A French consommé of beef garnished with sweetbread and onion purée, and quenelles. See also CONSOMMÉ.

savarin with apple

sável, Portuguese for shad, an excellent fish, but treated rather unimaginatively in Portugal where it is either poached or fried and served with a simple garnish of lemon. See also SHAD.

saveloy, see SAUSAGE.

Savoie, a sponge cake which originated in the Savoy region of France. To prepare it 7 egg yolks are beaten with ½ lb. (1 cup) castor sugar, with ½ tablespoon vanilla sugar or vanilla essence (extract) added. Then 3½ oz. (1 scant cup) fine flour and the same of potato flour are added. The 7 egg whites are beaten stiffly and added to the sponge mixture, which is then poured into buttered and floured Savoie sponge tins (often fluted) to two-thirds their depth, and baked in a slow-to-moderate oven for 30 minutes.

The Savoy region of France is also noted for its dairy produce, its game, from which excellent *civets* are made, and its fish, particularly the char (*omble chevalier*) and the *féra*. Its honey is also highly thought of. All dishes served à la *savoyarde* derive from this region, and usually include eggs, milk, cream, Gruyère cheese, or potatoes among their ingredients.

savory, a useful herb of which there are 2 species. The summer savory (*Satureia hortensis*) is a half-hardy annual herb which tastes not unlike marjoram and is extremely good when mixed with cooked broad beans. In France it is used in sausages and in stuffing veal. The winter savory (*S. montana*) is a hardy perennial sub-shrub herb which has green spicy leaves and will withstand the severest weather. It has a flavour between that of marjoram and thyme, but more delicate than either, and retains this flavour even in the depths of winter. It is best grown from cuttings, for seed germination is slow. It can be used with almost all meats and vegetables.

savoury, an English culinary term denoting a course following the dessert. A savoury is a small dish which is salty and piquant instead of sweet, so that it clears the palate after the sweet course, in preparation for the port and liqueurs which follow. Cooked cheese, devilled soft roes, or any foods cooked with spices or relishes are suitable. Others include things like angels on horseback, devils on horseback, golden buck, ramekins, Scotch woodcock, and Welsh rarebit. The word is also an adjective and may be applied to any food that is highly seasoned. In the U.S. it is spelt savory.

savoury ducks, see FAGGOTS.

savoy (*Brassica oleraceai,* var. *capitata*), one of the oldest and most popular members of the cabbage family. The name savoy includes a wide variety of cabbages whose common feature is their crimped leaves. They are pulled after the first frosts, and have a more delicate and nutty flavour than the common cabbage. They are cooked in the same way as cabbage, but require less cooking time than the straight-leaved variety.

savoy medlar, see ROCK MEDLAR.

savoyarde, à la, I. Potatoes sliced and cooked with grated Gruyère cheese and stock; they are like *pommes dauphinoise,* but use stock instead of milk. II. An omelette filled with rounds of sautéed potato and coarsely grated Gruyère cheese. Sometimes the filling is added to the raw eggs, and the dish is cooked like a pancake. III. A French garnish for meat consisting of pommes à la savoyarde (see above) with thickened meat gravy flavoured with tomato purée. IV. A French method of cooking escalopes. They are first browned in butter, then 5 tablespoons dry vermouth (Chambéry or Savoy), ¼ pint (½ cup) cream, and seasoning are added, and all simmered for 5 minutes or until the mixture has thickened.

savusilakat, see SILAKAT.

savustetto poronkieli, see PORON.

sawrell, Maltese for saurel, often baked in Malta with onions, tomatoes, mint, and parsley.

sbrinz-käse, perhaps one of the oldest Swiss hard cheeses. The name is thought to come from Brienz, a small town in the Bernese Oberland. It is similar to Gruyère, but is cured for 2 or 3 years and is therefore hard and good for grating. It has very small eyes about the size of a pinhead, and the weight is about half that of a Gruyère. It is exported mainly to France and Italy. Immature sbrinz cheeses, which do not grate, are called spalen and are sold only locally. Sbrinz is also made in Italy, but the cheese of the same name which is made in the Argentine and sold in the U.S. is not a true sbrinz at all, but a variety of whole-milk Parmesan.

scad, an alternative name for horse mackerel.

scald, to, I. To immerse food in boiling water in order to make it easier to peel. II. To bring a liquid such as milk just to the point of boil and cooking at that temperature (about 180°F) to hasten the cooking process.

scale, to, to remove the scales of a fish with the back of a knife before cooking, so that it is more pleasant to eat. This applies particularly to herring and salmon, which have rather horny scales.

scallion, see SPRING ONION.

scallop (*Pectinidae*), a genus of bivalve mollusc. The most familiar species in British waters is the great scallop (P. *maximus*), which has radially ribbed shells with an undulated edge the top shell being curved and the bottom one flat. It is commonly found on the coasts of the English Channel and the Atlantic. There are also several other varieties, from the small bay scallop to the larger deepwater scallop (see below). The flesh is extremely delicate, and this includes the coral "tongue" which is in fact the scallop reproductive gland or roe; indeed all but the little black bag which constitutes the stomach can be eaten. Scallops should be washed, then placed in a very low oven, with the rounded part downwards; this makes them open very easily. There are many ways of cooking them. They can be fried in batter or baked in white wine, sauce mornay, or sauce crème, but the simpler methods are best for preserving the delicacy of the flesh. They are particularly good poached in a little sherry and water, then drained (the liquid being reserved) and turned in butter; then the stock and butter are poured over and reduced over a hot flame, and the scallops are seared in the sauce. Scallops served in a sauce mornay have come to be known in English-speaking countries as *coquilles-St.-Jacques,* which in France is simply the common general name for all scallops. The deeper, rounded scallop shells, well scrubbed, may sometimes be used as a container for the scallop dish, which can then be cooked in the shell and served from it, if it is large enough.

The queen scallop (*Chlamys opercularis*) is smaller than *P. maximus,* easily identifiable in that it has 2 convex or curved shells instead of 1 curved and 1 flat; it seldom exceeds a diameter of 1¼ inches. It has a sweet flavour and requires less cooking than the great scallop as it is more tender. Large quantities of queen scallop have recently been located in the Irish Sea off County Wicklow, and a large proportion of these are being exported to Europe and the U.S. where there is an increasing demand for them. They resemble the American New Bedford (Massachusetts) scallop (*P. tenvicostata*), and the *tanrogan* of the Isle of Man. Off the north-west coast of Spain (Compostela) they are known locally as zamboriña; in the north of Scotland they are sometimes called clams. As with all varieties of scallop they are at their fattest and best from January to June, although there is no closed season since they are hermaphroditic and can be eaten throughout the year.

In the U.S. scallops are smaller than those found off British coasts; they also have no coral but only a small bluish-white roe, and they do not have as good a flavour. See also PECTEN; PENTÉOLA; VIERAS.

scalloped, a culinary term originally used to describe creamed dishes cooked in a scallop shell. In the U.S., however, it is now used particularly to describe sliced vegetables, fish, poultry, fruit, etc., cooked in a sauce or liquid in the oven and served from the dish in which they were cooked.

scaloppe, Italian for large escalopes (scallops) of veal.

scaloppe farcite, thin slices of veal sandwiched with a slice of ham, mushrooms or truffles, and grated cheese. They are fried in butter, with a thin slice of Gruyère on top, and served with the pan juices which have been diluted with meat glaze.

scaloppe milanese, escalopes (scallops) coated with egg and breadcrumbs, seasoned, and fried in butter. They are served with lemon and chopped parsley.

scaloppine, an alternative name for *piccate* or small *scaloppe.*

scamorza, an Italian soft cheese made from cow's milk, similar in texture to *fior di latte* and *provola,* and used for the same dishes. It is sometimes smoked.

scampi (*Nephrops norvegicus*), the Italian name for what we know as Dublin Bay prawns. However, although zoologically identical, the Italian scampi are taken only from the deep waters of the Adriatic and are at least twice the size of our Dublin Bay prawns, so the Italian word has been naturalized into English as descriptive of these particularly large specimens. Authentic scampi should be prepared in the same way as crayfish. In Italian restaurants, ordinary prawns are sometimes called scampi. It is quite a normal procedure in Italy for a customer to ask to see the scampi before ordering, to confirm that the scampi advertised on the menu are in fact the real thing. See also LOBSTER; MAZZANCOLLE; SHRIMP.

Scanno, an Italian ewe's milk cheese of the *pecorino* type made in the town of Scanno in the Abruzzi.

scappati, a variation of *saltimbocca*—thin slices of veal rolled up with a slice of ham or some kind of stuffing, and then fried, grilled, or baked.

scarlet runner, see RUNNER BEAN.

scarola, Italian for escarole or Batavian endive. See also ESCAROLE.

scarola ripiene, escarole stuffed with a mixture of 1 cup breadcrumbs, 12 chopped, stoned black olives, 4 anchovy fillets, 20 capers, 2 tablespoons each of pignoli and sultanas, 2 garlic cloves, and 2 tablespoons chopped parsley, all mixed together with ⅛ pint (2 tablespoons) olive oil and seasoned with pepper. This stuffing is placed in the leaves, and the whole escarole is tied with string to keep it firm, and then cooked with a little olive oil, ½ cup water and a *battuto* for about 1 hour, very slowly. About 15 minutes before it is ready, a glass of white wine is added.

scarus, a Mediterranean species of parrot fish, of which there are many varieties. It was particularly highly prized by the Romans and the Greeks. It can be cooked in a court bouillon or à la meunière, or it can be fried. This fish is possibly the skaros declared by Pliny to be the most savoury of all fish, referred to by Norman Douglas in his *Birds and Beasts of the Greek Anthology* (Chapman and Hall, 1928) as the parrot wrasse. See also PARROT FISH.

scaup duck (*Nyroca marila*), a wild duck common in northern and central Europe. It closely resembles the pochard in habit and appearance. A smaller species, the lesser scaup (*Nyroca affinis*), is found in the U.S. Opinions vary about the food value of the scaup; the flavour depends upon the diet of the individual bird. Scaup is cooked in the same way as wild duck.

schab, Polish for roast loin of pork (with the fillet left in). See also PORK.

schab po wiedeńsku, boiling vinegar is poured over the loin 2 hours before cooking. The meat is then dried, and sprinkled with salt and caraway seeds before roasting. A little minced onion is added to the pan juices, with a few tablespoons of water with which to baste the meat. It is served with cooked red cabbage and potatoes.

schabzieger or **green cheese,** a rindless Swiss cheese that has been made for the past 500 years. It comes from the Swiss canton of Glarus and is sometimes known simply by the name of the canton. It is made from skimmed cow's milk to which buttermilk and whey are added. After heating to 198°F (92°C), the albumen is left to ferment naturally; then it is

scaup duck

dried, milled, and mixed with blue melilot, which gives the cheese a very pungent flavour. It is then shaped into flat-topped cones called stöckli which are mostly used for grating. It is also sold in powder form, to be mixed with butter and used as a spread for sandwiches. About half the yearly output is exported to Germany, Holland, and Denmark, where it is known variously as glarnerkäse, grünerkäse, grünerkrauterkäse, and krauterkäse, and to the U.S. where it is known as Swiss Green Cheese, or *sapsago,* which is also its name in France.

schaleth, a Jewish dish, made from noodle paste which is prepared in the usual way (see PASTA). When it has dried in thin sheets, it is cut to line a large, well-greased ovenproof dish. Then 1½ lb. (4 cups) apple purée, 2 tablespoons each of raisins, currants, and sultanas, a little grated orange and lemon peel, sugar to taste, and a pinch of grated nutmeg are well mixed with 5 whole eggs and 3 egg yolks. A wineglass of Málaga wine is added, and the mixture is stirred thoroughly and turned into the noodle-lined dish. The top is covered with another layer of noodle paste, and a little hole is made to allow the steam to escape. The dish is baked for 45 minutes in a moderate oven, and is allowed to cool for a few minutes before being served. It is a popular dish in France where it is called *schaleth à la Juive.* In France it is also sometimes made without the top layer of noodle paste. See also CHARLOTTE.

schelly or **skelly,** see GWYNIAD.

schiacciala, an Italian Easter cake eaten at Leghorn, Tuscany. It is made by mixing 2 oz. yeast, dissolved in a little warm water, with 1 lb. (4 cups) flour. This mixture is covered and left for 3 hours to rise. Then 3 eggs and a little sugar are kneaded in, and 1 lb. (scant) flour is added. After the mixture has been left for a further 3 hours, 16 egg yolks, 8 egg whites, ¾ lb. (1½ cups) sugar, and a little more flour are added. The whole is left to stand for 30 minutes and then ¼ lb. (½ cup) butter, ½ teaspoon aniseed, 2 tablespoons rose-water, and a further ¾ lb. (1½ cups) sugar are well worked in to make a very firm paste. This is formed into large shapes which are left to rise for 30 minutes, then painted with egg yolk and baked in a moderate oven. These quantities will make enough for about 20 people.

schinken, German for ham. There are several world-famous German varieties. Westphalian ham is probably the finest; it is cured and smoked, and can be cooked, or eaten raw in very thin slices. Other well-known and succulent hams are made in Mainz, Hamburg, Stuttgart, Holstein (*Katenschinken*), and Oldenburg (Ammerlander). See also HAM.

schinken auf mecklenburger art, ham cooked in the Mecklenburg manner. The ham is boiled, skinned, and thickly coated with rye breadcrumbs mixed with half their quantity of sugar and a good pinch each of ground cinnamon and cloves. Melted butter is dripped over, and the ham is browned in the oven.

schinken auf schwäbischer art, ham cooked in the Swabian manner, braised in equal quantities of light beer and good stock with sliced onions. The stock is thickened with arrowroot.

schinken mit bohnen und birnen, a Westphalian dish of sliced raw ham simmered with soaked haricot beans; green vegetables, sliced pears, and either apples or potatoes are added during cooking, so that when the dish is ready they are cooked but not mushy.

schinkenfleckerln, see FLECKERLN.

schlagober, the Viennese term for whipped cream, quantities of which are served in coffee and with cakes. It is sometimes abbreviated to *schlag*.

schleie, German for tench, which is eaten quite often in Germany, and cooked as *kabeljau in biersauce*. It is also served au *bleu*, with sauce hollandaise mixed with chopped dill. In Silesia it is poached in fish stock and a little white wine, with a julienne of root vegetables; the stock is thickened with egg yolks mixed with cream, and it is garnished with parsley and lemon slices. In the Tyrol, tench is rolled in flour and fried in butter, then served on a bed of skinned, coarsely chopped tomatoes, covered with sauce *tyrolienne* and garnished with fried onion rings. See also TENCH.

schlesisches himmelreich, literally "Silesian heaven," a German dish of pork chops, first simmered for 30 minutes, then fried in butter with cooked, soaked, mixed dried fruits such as apricots, pears, apples, and prunes, and a cup of the fruit liquid. It is served with dumplings (*knödel*) made from semolina or potato.

schlosserbuben, a traditional Austrian sweet consisting of soaked prunes stuffed with almonds, then dipped in a batter made from 4 oz. (1 cup) flour, 1 tablespoon sugar, 1 tablespoon oil, ¼ pint (½ cup) beer, and a separated egg (the stiffly beaten white added last). They are fried in hot fat, drained, and sprinkled with grated chocolate.

schlosskäse, an Austrian soft cheese made in both the north and the south. It is very like both limburger käse and *romadur-käse*, but much smaller. It is shaped like a minute sandcastle and weighs under 2 oz. This tiny "castle" cheese is very popular.

schmaltz, Jewish rendered-down chicken or goose fat. The fatty skin and clusters are cut into small pieces, then covered with cold water and boiled, without a lid on the pan, until almost all the liquid has evaporated. Then either chopped onions or a few cloves of garlic are added and cooked until brown. Sometimes potato is added as well. The schmaltz is ready when the onion is crisp. The fat is allowed to cool slightly and is then strained. The animal skin with the onion and potato that have been cooked with it are called *grebenes*, and are used to flavour some liver dishes and plain vegetables. Both schmaltz and *grebenes* are used in dishes eaten at Passover. See also GREBEN.

schmarrn, an Austrian pudding quite unlike any other. The name means "a mere nothing," a trifle, but schmarrn is far from trifling. Essentially farinaceous, it can be made from flour, semolina, rolls, or croissants. Norman Douglas, in his book *Together* (Chapman and Hall, 1923), mentions schmarrn with delight as being a speciality of his childhood home, Bludenz, Austria.

griessschmarrn, schmarrn made with semolina. One pint (2 cups) milk, a vanilla pod, 1 tablespoon sugar, and a nut of butter are boiled together. Then 6 oz. (6 heaped tablespoons)

coarse semolina are added and stirred constantly until cooked; 1 heaped tablespoon raisins is added, and the mixture is left to stand for 5 minutes. It is then put into a buttered dish, and the same procedure is followed as for kaiserschmarrn.

kaiserschmarrn, perhaps the best-known kind of schmarrn. It is made with 3 oz. (⅔ cup) flour sifted with ½ tablespoon sugar; then ¼ pint (½ cup) milk is added gradually, and 2 beaten egg yolks are blended in so that the mixture is very smooth. Finally the stiffly beaten egg whites are folded in. Then 1 tablespoon butter is melted in a baking dish, and when hot, the batter is poured in and 1 heaped tablespoon seedless raisins is scattered over the top. (The batter should be about 1 inch deep in the tin.) If the schmarrn is preferred soft, it is baked in the oven until golden brown; when crisp schmarrn is wanted, it is turned over to crisp in the baking dish. It is then torn into small pieces with two forks, returned to the oven for a few minutes, and served with icing sugar flavoured with vanilla.

kipfelschmarrn, schmarrn made in the same way as *semmelschmarrn*, but using the crescent-shaped rolls that are popular in Austria instead of bread slices.

semmelschmarrn, schmarrn made from 6 stale, crustless slices of bread cut into dice. Then ½ pint (1 cup) milk, 2 eggs, and a pinch of salt are beaten and poured over the bread, which is left to stand until soft. Next 4 tablespoons butter is heated, and the mixture is fried in it until golden on both sides. Using two forks, it is torn into pieces, then cooked quickly again until it is golden brown on all sides.

schnecken, I. German for snails. II. Rectangular Austrian pastries made from puff pastry which is filled with chopped raisins, walnuts, bitter chocolate, and sugar sprinkled with melted butter. The puff pastry is spread with the filling, then rolled up like a Swiss roll, and cut into ½-inch slices which are baked in a moderate-to-hot oven for 20–30 minutes. The tops are glased with icing sugar mixed with a little rum. The rolls resemble snails, hence the name.

schnittkäse, the collective term for German and Austrian semi-hard cheeses. These include *edamer käse, edelpilzkäse, tilsiter käse, trappistenkäse,* and *wilstermarsch-käse*. Others are geheimratskäse, schafkäse, and steinbuscher-käse. There are also German versions of gouda and gorgonzola which fall into this category.

schnitzel, German for a cutlet or escalope (scallop) of meat, usually veal. If fillet of veal only is used it is correctly a kalbsschnitzel. See also KALB.

Bismarck schnitzel, schnitzel coated in egg and breadcrumbs and fried in butter. It is garnished with halved, hard-boiled plover's eggs, sautéed mushrooms, and truffles and covered with fresh tomato sauce.

Holsteiner schnitzel, as above, but garnished with a poached (or fried) egg, diced gherkins, beetroot, capers, olives, anchovies, and lemon slices, and sprinkled with chopped parsley.

Leipziger schnitzel, schnitzel coated with egg and breadcrumbs and fried in butter. It is served with sauce béarnaise and *Leipziger allerlei*.

naturschnitzel, schnitzel rubbed with salt, pepper, and a little flour and fried in butter. The pan juices are diluted with a little stock and a nut of butter.

rahmschnitzel, schnitzel floured and fried in butter. The pan juices are boiled with a dash of french mustard, paprika to taste, capers, pepper, and ¼ pint (½ cup) water. Then ¼ pint (½ cup) cream is heated in this sauce, and the whole is poured over the meat.

schwäbisches schnitzel, schnitzel floured and fried in butter, with lemon juice and ¼ pint (½ cup) cream added. It is served with *spätzle* covered with breadcrumbs and fried in butter.

zigeuner schnitzel, schnitzel browned in butter, then simmered in ½ pint (1 cup) fresh tomato sauce mixed with mushrooms and strips of smoked ox tongue.

naturschnitzel and *rahmschnitzel* are specialities of both Germany and Austria.

The following are Austrian schnitzel specialities.

kaiserschnitzel, schnitzel larded and fried in butter, then braised in equal quantities of veal stock and sour cream which is slightly thickened with flour and seasoned with lemon juice and capers.

paprika schnitzel, schnitzel floured and fried in butter with onions and 1 tablespoon paprika. Before serving ½ pint (1 cup) sour cream is added.

paradies schnitzel, schnitzel floured and turned in butter, then braised in tomato sauce. It is served with noodles or rice.

pariser schnitzel, schnitzel floured and seasoned lightly, then dipped in beaten egg to which 1 tablespoon milk has been added, and fried on both sides in butter.

wiener schnitzel, a Viennese method in which the schnitzel are beaten, flattened, and rolled in seasoned flour. They are then dipped in egg and breadcrumbs and fried on both sides in hot butter. In Vienna, they are generally garnished only with lemon slices sprinkled with parsley, but in other countries where this dish has become famous, chopped olives, capers, anchovy fillets, chopped hard-boiled eggs, or sliced gherkins also form part of the garnish.

schöberl, an Austrian garnish for clear soups made from 1 egg white whisked with salt until stiff and then mixed with the beaten egg yolk. Then 1 oz. (1 heaped tablespoon) flour is added, and the mixture is spread on a buttered and floured baking tin. It is cooked in a moderate oven for 10–15 minutes, cooled, and cut into small squares which are reheated and served as an accompaniment to the hot soup. See also BIS-KUITSCHÖBERI-SUPPE.

scholle, German for plaice. Fresh plaice is generally termed *maischolle,* and smoked plaice as *flunder.*

scholles, a Belgian speciality of plaice dried in the sun. *Moules et frites* is another national speciality.

schöps, German for mutton when taken from a castrated ram, or wether. The term schöpsen is used mainly in Austria for mutton or third-year lamb. Young lamb is lamm. The general term for mutton is hammel. See also HAMMEL.

schöpsenschlegel, an Austrian dish of larded leg of mutton or lamb, pot-roasted on a bed of onions, carrots, parsnips, turnips, and celery, with 1 pint (2 cups) stock and seasoning. All are covered and cooked gently for 1½ hours, when the meat is turned; 2 glasses (1 cup) white wine is added, and cooking is continued for a further 1½ hours.

steirisches schöpsernes, a mutton stew from the Styrian province of Austria. First 3 lb. cubed mutton is blanched with boiling water for 10 minutes. Then 2 carrots, 2 Hamburg parsley sprigs and their roots, 1 celeriac stalk, and 1 onion are chopped and fried very lightly in oil or fat. The fat is poured off, water to cover is added and boiled, and then the drained meat, with seasoning, bay leaf, thyme, and 2 tablespoons vinegar per 1½ pints water, are added. When the meat is almost cooked, 1 lb. quartered potatoes is added and cooked until tender. It is served with grated horseradish sprinkled on top.

schoten, German for green peas. Schotensuppe is green pea soup. See also PEA.

schoten mit reis und tomaten, a dish made from ½ lb. (1 cup) rice cooked in 2 pints (4 cups) stock with a little butter; It is strained, and green peas are cooked in the same liquid. Then 1 lb. tomatoes are skinned and fried in butter with a very little chopped onion and parsley, and rubbed through a sieve. The rice and peas are then mixed together, garnished with the tomato mixture, and served with *frankfurter wurstchen.*

schusterpfanne, literally "shoemaker's pot," a German dish which is a type of stew made from 2 lb. chopped loin of pork with 2 lb. peeled and sliced pears, 1½ lb. sliced carrots, 2 lb. chopped potatoes, and 1 teaspoon each of sugar and salt, all cooked in a covered pot in ¼ pint (½ cup) water for about 1 hour.

Schwäbische würste, German würste from Swabia. They consist of chopped lean and fat pork (2 parts lean to 1 part fat) sprinkled with salt, saltpetre, and pepper, and left for some hours, then minced and pounded. Pounded garlic and a little water are added, and the mixture is again minced, after which it is put into skins. The resulting sausages can be boiled and served plain, or may be lightly smoked.

schwammerlsauce, an Austrian mushroom sauce often served with *knödel.* It is made from ½ lb. mushrooms sweated in butter with a pinch of caraway seeds, salt, pepper, and the juice of ½ lemon. When the mushrooms are soft, 1 tablespoon flour is sprinkled over and 1 cup broth added. The sauce is simmered for 7–10 minutes, when enough sour cream is added to thicken. It must not be reboiled.

schwarzbrot, see PUMPERNICKEL.

schwarzfisch, an original and delicious Austrian method of cooking carp or other river fish. Although the traditional recipe uses freshwater fish because Austria is many miles from the sea, any white fish, such as cod, hake, haddock, or *hecht.* (pike) can be used without deterioration of the recipe. A fish weighing about 4 lb. is cleaned, boned, cut into convenient pieces, and sprinkled with salt. Equal quantities of water and dark beer, sufficient barely to cover the fish (about ¾ pint of each) are placed in a large saucepan, followed by 1 sliced celeriac, 1 sliced lemon with its peel, 1 sliced onion, 5 lumps sugar, 5 peppercorns, 1 blade of mace, and 1 piece of root ginger. The contents of the saucepan are brought to the boil and simmered for about 20 minutes, then the fish pieces are put in and cooked. When the fish is removed, about 5 tablespoons crumbled honey cake, 2 tablespoons each of butter, and either red currant jelly or plum jam, with 1 tablespoon each of raisins, sultanas, almonds, and walnuts are added to the liquid in the pan. This is slightly reduced by boiling, and then the fish is served with the sauce poured over it. See also KARPFEN.

schwarzwürste, black sausages. These German würste are made with a mixture of pork and one-quarter its weight in pork fat, cooked in very little water and then finely chopped. This is mixed with one-eighth its weight in fine breadcrumbs, garlic, a pinch of ground cloves, allspice, salt, and pepper, all moistened with pig's blood mixed with salt to keep it liquid (1 pint blood is enough for 4 lb. meat). This mixture is put into skins and simmered for 30 minutes. When cold, the sausages can be hung for 2 days to dry or lightly smoked for the same time. See also WÜRST.

schwarzwurzel, German for salsify. A favourite German method of preparing it is to dip pieces of boiled salsify into batter, deep fry them, and serve them with fried parsley. See also SALSIFY.

schwein, German for pig. See SCHWEINEFLEISCH.

schweinefleisch, German for pork, probably the most popular meat in Germany. All parts of the pig are used, fresh, salted, or smoked. Pork is often accompanied by sauerkraut and root vegetables, and fruit such as apple and pear is sometimes cooked with it. *Schweinsfüsse* are pig's trotters (feet); *schweinsrippen* are pork chops. See also GESELCHTES; PÖKEL-FLEISCH; PORK; SCHINKEN; WÜRST.

schweinebauch mit birnen, belly of pork with pears. To prepare this, 4 lb. chopped meat, 1 lb. onions, 1 teaspoon sage, 12 peppercorns, salt, water to cover, and a dash of vinegar are brought to the boil, skimmed, and then simmered until tender. The liquid is strained off, and peeled, cored, and quartered pears are cooked in it. Then the stock is thickened and 1 teaspoon dry mustard added. It is also cooked with potato and sauerkraut.

schweinebraten, roast pork, sometimes basted with beer or white wine and Madeira. The meat is rubbed with flour, a pinch of mustard, and a chopped bay leaf before the liquid is poured round it. Onions stuffed with prunes can be cooked with the meat.

schweinskarree, a delicacy of cured and smoked pork fillet. It is cooked in stock with kale or sauerkraut and served with potatoes.

schweinskotelette, pork cutlets, which can be served with a variety of sauces made from the pan juices by using sour cream, or tomato and stock, or all 3. They may also be rolled in egg and breadcrumbs and fried, then garnished with braised red cabbage, sautéed apples, and sautéed potatoes. This dish is known as schweinskotelette auf berliner art.

schweinsohren, pig's ears, which are eaten extensively in Germany. They are soaked and simmered for 2 hours, then rolled in egg and breadcrumbs, and fried. They are served with caper sauce and sauerkraut.

schweinsrücken, chine of pork, which is often roasted, being basted with hot water. When cooked the pork is dredged with breadcrumbs mixed with cinnamon and sugar, and crisped. It is served with purée of cherries.

schweinesulz, an Austrian dish of lean pork cooked for 2 hours with ½ pint (1 cup) wine vinegar, 2 pints (4 cups) water, pork bones, root vegetables, bay leaf, thyme, parsley, and seasoning. It is strained, and the meat is sliced and set in its own jelly with slices of hard-boiled egg. It is served cold.

Other German pork recipes, include *eisbein, fleischkuchen, kasseler rippenspeer, schlesisches himmelreich, schusterpfanne, sulperknochen.* Further Austrian pork recipes are *bauernschmaus, haussulz, jungfernbraten, jungschweinskaree, kaiserfleisch, spanferkel.*

schweizer käse, see SWISS CHEESE.

schweizer kraut, German for marigold leaves cooked in salted water, drained, then washed by having fresh boiling water poured over them. They are then chopped, mixed with butter and pepper, and served like spinach.

scifers, a local Cornish name for the Welsh onion. The tops are used for the traditional Cornish soup, *kiddley broth.*

sciule piene, Piedmontese dialect for *cipolle ripiene,* a dish of stuffed onions which is a speciality of Piedmont. To prepare them 4 large unpeeled onions are boiled for 15 minutes. When they are cool, the skins are removed and the core taken out and kept. The stuffing is made from 3 crumbled macaroons pounded with a small slice of crustless bread which has been soaked in milk, a handful of sultanas, a pinch each of nutmeg, cloves, cinnamon, salt, pepper, 1 egg, and 3 heaped tablespoons grated Parmesan cheese all mixed with the chopped core of the onion. The cored onions are then filled with this mixture, put into a greased baking dish, and baked in a slow-to-moderate oven for 35 minutes. They can be eaten hot or cold.

scolymus, see GOLDEN THISTLE.

scone, a small, soft Scottish and Irish bread–cake, made from wheat or barley flour, white or brown. (Oatmeal or potato flour may also be used.) The dough is usually mixed with buttermilk or sour milk. Traditionally, a scone should be triangular in shape, made by cutting a circle of dough 8–9 inches across into triangular sections from the centre. Originally, too, scones were baked on a griddle. Nowadays they are usually oven baked, and they are also cut into small rounds instead of the three-cornered *farl.*

There are many slightly varying ways of making scones,

but, generally 1 lb. (4 cups) flour is mixed with ½ teaspoon salt, 1 teaspoon baking soda, and 2 teaspoons cream of tartar; then about ½ pint (1 cup) tepid buttermilk or fresh milk is added, to form a soft dough. The dough should be handled as little as possible, being rolled out lightly to ½-inch thickness and cut into shapes which are either griddle-cooked or baked in a medium oven. Nowadays a little fat or butter (3 tablespoons to 1 lb. flour) is often added; also sugar, and sometimes dried fruits such as sultanas. Scones are served hot, split open and buttered. Wholemeal or brown scones are made with equal quantities of brown and white flour.

The etymology of the word is dubious. The *Scottish National Dictionary* derives it from the Middle Dutch *schoonbrot* (fine bread); *Chambers Dictionary* gives the Gaelic *sgonn* (block) and *sgonn aran* (a block of bread). It is pronounced ''skonn.'' See also BANNOCK; DROP SCONES; POTATO CAKES.

scorfano, the Genoese name for hogfish, used in Italian fish stews and soups, especially the Genoese *burrida* and *cacciucco Livornese.* Chapon, used in bouillabaisse, is called *scorfano rosso.*

scorza di noce moscata, Italian for mace, used in Italy in savoury dishes as well as sweet ones.

scorzonera or *black salsify* (*Scorzonera hispanica*), a vegetable resembling salsify, with black cylindrical roots of very good flavour which are used in any of the ways that are suitable for salsify. It has been known in Britain for over 200 years, and in earlier times it was called ''viper grass'' because it was used as a remedy for snake bites. If left in the ground the roots will produce green shoots early in the following spring, which, when cooked, are tender and delicately flavoured, like chard or asparagus shoots. The related French variety, *picridie,* is grown for its leaves rather than its roots. They are used in green salads, and taste like chicory, but without its bitterness. See also SALSIFY.

Scotch blue hare or *mountain hare,* a hare which chiefly inhabits mountain districts, slightly smaller than the variety found on the plains, but they have a more delicate flavour. It is a bluish colour in summer, but in winter turns almost white. This hare is found all over Europe and an allied species is found in the U.S.

Scotch broth, also called barley broth, the national soup of Scotland. It is made with 2 oz. pearl barley, 1 lb. chopped mutton, 3 large onions, 4 carrots, 4 turnips, 2 leeks, peas, and a small cabbage or available greenstuff such as kale, all well seasoned and simmered in rich mutton broth until quite thick. A good soup, providing the meat used is not fatty. It was one of the first soups based on mutton to achieve fame. Fanjas de St. Fond, Commissioner for Wines for the King of France, remarked on it when visiting Scotland in the 1780s, as did Dr. Johnson during his tour of the Hebrides: '' 'You never ate it before?' Johnson was asked, and he replied, 'No, sir; but I don't care how soon I eat it again.' '' Boswell's *Journal of a Tour to the Hebrides with Samuel Johnson* (1785).

Scotch currant bun or *black bun,* a delicious Scottish cake traditionally eaten at Hogmanay and on other festive occasions. In an old Scottish dialect the word bun meant plum cake. It is made in a loaf tin about 12 inches long. This is greased and lined with short crust pastry, keeping enough back for the lid. Inside is placed the filling of 2 lb. seedless raisins, 3 lb. currants, ½ lb. chopped blanched almonds, ½ lb. (1 cup) sugar, ¾ lb. (2¾ cups) flour, 2 teaspoons allspice, 1 teaspoon each of ground ginger, cinnamon, cream of tartar, and baking powder, and ¼ teaspoon black pepper all well mixed and moistened with about ¼ pint (½ cup) milk. The edges of the pastry are dampened and the pastry lid securely pressed down. The top is pricked all over with a fork, brushed with beaten egg, and cooked in a slow over for 2½–3 hours.

Brandy or whiskey can be added to taste. This cake keeps well in a tin. See also HOGMANAY.

ingredients for a Scottish black bun

Scotch eggs, a Scottish egg dish made from hard-boiled eggs (slightly undercooked—7–10 minutes is enough), which are shelled, dipped in beaten egg, and entirely covered with well-seasoned pork sausage meat. They are coated with egg and breadcrumbs before being fried in deep hot oil. Scotch eggs are served cold with salad or, in Scotland, eaten hot for breakfast.

Scotch eggs

Scotch grouse, see GROUSE.

Scotch woodcock, a Scottish savoury made from 4 egg yolks beaten with ½ pint (1 cup) single (light) cream and a pinch of cayenne, cooked in a double boiler, stirring all the time, until thick. This mixture is poured over buttered toast, spread with anchovy fillets, then garnished with chopped parsley and served hot.

scoter (*Melanitta nigra*), a common black duck found in Europe and in North America. It breeds in the north of the U.S. and migrates to the south for the winter. Only the young birds are fit to eat, and opinions vary about their quality. They should be cooked very slowly with plenty of fat. Braising, or cooking them wrapped in oven-foil in a very slow oven, produces the best results. They are easy to shoot and so are quite a popular game bird. See also DUCK.

scoubri, Greek for mackerel. It is often cooked by sprinkling

with lemon juice, grilling over charcoal, and garnishing with chopped parsley and raw onion rings.

scoubri plaki, mackerel poached with onion, tomatoes, parsley, white wine, and seasoning.

scoubri yemista, mackerel stuffed with chopped raisins, pignoli, soaked bread, parsley, and seasonings, then baked with a little olive oil and lemon juice for about 30 minutes.

scrapple, formerly a breakfast speciality of Philadelphia, U.S., but now eaten as a brunch dish all over the eastern U.S. It originated in the German (Deutsch) community in Pennsylvania about 200 years ago. It used to be made at pig-killing time and was first called *pawn-haus*. Then it was a mush made from cornmeal mixed with pork trimmings, like a very thick porridge with meat added. It the early 19th century herbs such as sage, thyme, or marjoram were added and still remain. It used to be a winter dish, but now scrapple is canned and so is available all year round, although it is too heavy for a warm-weather dish. In a traditional recipe 3 quarts (12 cups) strong pork broth made from pork shoulder or neck meat, until it falls apart, together with 2 cups of the meat finely cut, is simmered with 3 cups cornmeal, chopped onion, herbs, and seasoning for about 1 hour, then it is poured into large loaf pans to get cold. When cold it is cut into ½-inch slices, sometimes sprinkled with flour, and sautéed, preferably in bacon drippings, or butter. It should not be turned more than once because it breaks up easily. It may be eaten hot or cold and served with various accompaniments such as tomato ketchup, or brown sugar syrup, poached eggs, fried bananas, apple sauce, or casseroled cabbage.

scrippelle imbusse, Italian pancakes filled with grated pecorino or Parmesan cheese mixed with chopped ham, rolled up, and placed side by side in a greased baking dish. They are half-covered with boiling chicken stock, the lid is placed on the dish, and they are left to stand in a warm place for 5–7 minutes before being served. See also PANCAKE.

scrod, the American name for a young cod or haddock which is split down the back and has the backbone removed. It is usually brushed with melted butter or oil, then sprinkled with seasoned breadcrumbs before broiling. It is served with melted butter or *beurre maître d'hôtel* and creamed or hashed potatoes.

scrowled pilchards, a traditional Cornish dish. Fresh pilchards are cleaned and split open, then sprinkled generously with a mixture of salt, sugar, and pepper and left to stand overnight. They are then "scrowled," or grilled, on a gridiron over a bright glowing fire. See also PILCHARD.

scum, the froth which forms on the top of boiling liquids. Usually it contains impurities and is removed with a perforated spoon known as a skimmer.

scup (*Stenotomus versicolor*), one of the porgies, or American sea breams. It is used in soups and stews.

sea anemones (*Actiniaria*), edible sea creatures which are found off the coasts of France, particularly the Mediterranean coasts. They are known as *anémones de mer* in France.

sea bass, see BASS.

sea beef, the name used in the Western Isles of Scotland for the flesh of the young whale.

sea bream, see BREAM.

sea burbot, see LING.

sea cat, a sailor's name for catfish.

sea cow, an alternative name for a sea mammal called the manatee. It tastes somewhat like pork and is a very popular dish in the West Indies.

sea cuckoo, a sailor's name for red gurnard.

sea date, see DATTERI DI MARE.

sea devil, a sailor's name for anglerfish.

sea eagle, a sailor's name for a large ray or skate.

sea hen, a sailor's name for the crooner.

sea hog, a sailor's name for porpoise.

sea kale, sea kail, or *sea cole* (*Crambe maritima*), a plant which grows in most of the coastal districts of western Europe. It is cultivated for its leaf stalks, which are usually bleached and forced for sale early in the year. (If grown near the sea it is often bleached by piling seaweed over the leaves; in Donegal, Ireland, the local name for it is "strand cabbage.") It is a most delicious winter vegetable and was particularly popular in Britain in the 17th and 18th centuries. It can be eaten raw, when it is served in salads or with cheese, like celery. If cooked, it is best simply boiled and served with hot melted butter, when it constitutes a course on its own, like asparagus.

sea kale beet, see CHARD.

sea kale cabbage, see COUVE TRONCHUDA.

sea lark, see ALOUETTE DE MER.

sea moss, see CARRAGEEN.

sea needle, see GARFISH.

sea owl, a sailor's name for lumpfish.

sea oxeye (*Borrichia arborescens*), a fleshy European weed which grows near the sea. It used to be pickled in vinegar as a condiment like samphire, but it is not widely known nowadays.

sea perch (*Serranidae*), a relative of the sea bass family, as is the American grouper. It has firm white flesh with a very good flavour. It inhabits Atlantic waters off both European and American coasts.

sea purslane, see ORACH.

sea quinces, small shellfish found in the Mediterranean. They make excellent eating.

sea robin, an American name for certain gurnards.

sea rocket (*Cakile edentula*), a plant which grows beside the sea in Great Britain. When the leaves are young they may be used in salads.

sea slug or *sea cucumber* (*Holothuroidea*), a marine gastropod without a shell, highly prized as food in the Far East.

sea trout, see SALMON TROUT.

sea truffle (*Venus verrucosa*), a mollusc with a ridged shell. In Italy, where they are called *tartufi di mare,* they are eaten extensively, usually raw. They are identical to the French *praire* (clam) and similar to the *clovisse,* which are both members of the *Venus* family.

sea urchin (*Echinoidea*), a spiny marine animal in a hard round shell, found off the coasts of Europe, America, and Asia. The best for eating are the green and the black sea urchins; they should only be taken from unpolluted waters and should be eaten very fresh. They are cut open through the middle and can be eaten raw with bread, like an egg (for which reason they are sometimes known as "sea eggs"), or

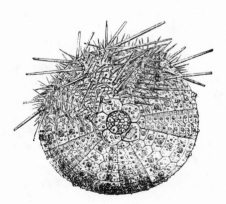

sea urchin

cooked and made into a purée or a sauce with mayonnaise. They taste strongly of iodine and salt, and are definitely an acquired taste—though well worth trying. They are extremely popular in France where they are known as *oursins.* See also OURIÇO; OURSINS.

sea wife (*Labrus vetula*), a wrasse found off the European coast of the Atlantic, used mostly for making soups.

sea wolf, see CATFISH.

sea wrack (*Fucus*), an edible seaweed of the membranous or filment type. It is eaten in Scandinavian countries and in Iceland and Scotland, but is now out of fashion generally. It is also called sea lettuce in Scotland and is used in salads.

seafood, assorted shellfish and crustacea, both raw and cooked.

seal, a large, carnivorous, marine mammal of the *Phocidae* family. The flesh is said to be dark but not unpleasant to eat. The brains, heart, liver, and tongue are greatly esteemed by the Eskimos, who also make a kind of sausage from the offal (variety meats).

seal, to, to brown meats quickly in a hot pan with very little fat so that the juices are sealed in. This is a means of preserving meats for a short time in the absence of refrigeration; the surface is sealed to prevent decomposition, but the meats are not in any sense cooked. This process is also known as searing.

seasoning, a general term for salt, pepper, and sometimes other spices, added to food to enhance its flavour.

seaweed, marine plants, of which algae are the most numerous. Many are edible, such as agar-agar, carrageen, dulse, laver, pepper dulse, *redware,* sea-wrack, *sloke.*

sebadas, a traditional Sardinian dish which, although made with cheese, is eaten as a sweet course. First 1 lb. hard cheese is cut into small pieces and simmered in water barely to cover until melted. The solution is poured onto a cold wet surface and cut into rounds 2 inches across and ¼-inch thick. A pastry is made from 1 lb. (4 cups) flour, ½ lb. (1 cup) butter, salt, 3 tablespoons olive oil, and 6 tablespoons tepid water, and this is rolled out in rounds. There must be twice as many pastry rounds as there are cheese rounds, and the pastry rounds must be slightly larger. Each round of cheese is then placed on a pastry round and sprinkled liberally with orange and lemon juice, then covered with another round of pastry. The edges of each pair of pastry circles are moistened to seal them, and the rounds are then fried in deep oil. They are served hot, sprinkled with more orange and lemon juice, and sugar and honey.

sébille, the French name for a bowl made of wood, used especially for beating eggs or mixing chopped ingredients. Most French salad bowls are made of white china and are called *saladier.*

Sechseläuten, a Swiss spring festival which takes place in Zurich and lasts for 2 days. Great feasting and drinking accompany it. On the first day children dress in historical costumes and form a procession. The centre of attraction is however Böogg, a vast snowman figure made from cotton wool and filled with fireworks. He symbolizes the end of winter, and at the climax of the festivities, he is exploded over a pyre. People dressed as Arabs or Africans gallop round on Arab horses, and sometimes animals from the zoo are also paraded. After this a huge feast takes place, with such foods as *Zürcher leberspiessli, bindenfleisch,* and *apfelwahe.*

secole, a Venetian name for the scraps of meat taken from the bones of a joint of beef or veal after boning by the butcher. In Italy these scraps are sold to form the basis for *risotto di secole.*

sedano, Italian for celery. In Italy celery is green all the way down, and rather stunted compared with the blanched British and American heads. It has an excellent flavour, but is seldom eaten raw. Both leaves and stalks are used for soups and stews.

sedano rapo, is celeriac, often served cut into strips and dressed with mayonnaise for *antipasto.* It is also cooked, chopped, and used as a vegetable or for salads.

Seder, a Jewish home festival which begins at sundown on the evening preceding the first day of Passover week. For the Seder service it is customary to have specially prepared matzoh called *shemura matzoh,* and 3 of these are placed in a large napkin folded in four; one matzoh in each fold, so that none is actually touching another. These represent the Sabbath loaves and symbolize the "bread of affliction" and slavery. A roasted shank bone of lamb is put on a plate, to represent the Paschal lamb and one egg roasted in its shell is placed next to the bone to symbolize sacrificial offerings at the Temple and rebirth. On the same plate are put some pieces of raw horseradish, with leaf, symbolizing the bitterness of Israel's bondage in Egypt. These are the "bitter herbs," and it is possible that the custom of serving mint sauce with lamb derives from this. These 3 items are placed next to the 3 matzohs. *Charoseth* which represents the clay from which Jews made bricks while slaving for the pharoahs; parsley, lettuce, or other available herbs, represent the spring crops. These are accompanied by a small bowl of salt water and placed in front of the man conducting the service. The salted water is a reminder of the tears shed during slavery. Sliced hard-boiled eggs with salted water are passed to everyone at the table, and sufficient wine for 4 full glasses for each person, symbolizing the fourfold promise of redemption. "Elijah's cup" is a spare goblet of wine on the table, not used during the ceremony, but set aside for the prophet Elijah. At this time the door is left ajar for "the coming of Elijah," and of a world of justice and joy for all mankind.

seed cake, see MADEIRA CAKE.

seedless raisin, the term used in the U.S. for sultana, especially the Thompson raisin produced by Mr. W. Thompson in 1878. In Britain the name is also given to a particular variety of seedless grape when dried.

sei, Norwegian for coalfish or coley. The Scottish name for coalfish is *saithe,* and the Scottish and Norwegian names are doubtless linked. See also PALE.

seibiff, a Norwegian speciality made with fillets of coalfish tossed in flour and fried in oil and butter. Crisply fried onions are spread thickly on top before serving.

sekahedelmäkeitto, Finnish for stewed dried fruit flavoured with cinnamon.

seledka, Russian for herring. A popular Russian dish consists of sliced salted herrings garnished with sliced raw onions, hard-boiled eggs, and salted cucumbers.

seledka rublennaya, chopped and filleted salted herrings, mashed to a paste with butter, grated raw apple, and a pinch of nutmeg.

selery, Polish for celery. In Poland celery is often cooked in bouillon with Madeira added. Alternatively, it is boiled, drained, and served with sauce hollandaise.

selery faszerowane, celery stuffed with mushrooms and minced (ground) veal, then simmered in stock.

self-raising flour, a commercially blended wheat flour, containing a raising agent such as baking powder. It is used mainly for cake or pastry making, but is not suitable for breads where yeast is incorporated in the dough. In the U.S. it is called "self-rising" flour. It is made from selected winter wheats and is used for some cakes.

selinon, Greek for celery and celeriac.

selinorrizes avgolémono, celeriac with *avgolémono sauce.* The peeled, chopped root is lightly fried in butter; seasoning

and just enough stock or water to cover are added, and it is simmered until tender. It is strained, and the stock is used in the sauce, which is then poured over the cooked celeriac. Celery is also cooked in the same way.

seljankakeitto, a Finnish fish soup usually made with 2 kinds of fish such as whitefish and bass. A stock is first made with the bones, heads, and skins. Then flour, chopped onion, tomato purée, and sliced mushrooms are added, and all are allowed to cook. Finally the chopped fish, capers, cucumber, and a paste made from pounded crayfish meat are all added. It is served very hot, garnished with dill and lemon slices.

Selkirk bannock, a Scottish yeasted fruit loaf made from 2 oz. (¼ cup) melted butter added to ¼ pint (½ cup) tepid milk and ½ oz. yeast mixed with ½ teaspoon sugar which, when creamy, is added to the milk. Next, 1 lb. (3½ cups) flour is put into a warmed bowl; a well is made in the centre and the yeast mixture poured into it, a little flour being brought down from the sides to cover the yeast. The bowl is then covered and left for 30 minutes in a warm place. When the yeast has broken through, another ¼ pint (½ cup) milk is added and the mixture is kneaded to make a soft dough. It is again covered, and left until it has doubled in size. Then 2 tablespoons sugar, 2 tablespoons sultanas, 1 tablespoon currants, and 1 tablespoon candied rind are added, all having been slightly warmed first. The mixture is lightly kneaded again, shaped into a large flat round, and left once more in a warm place for 30 minutes. It is brushed with milk in which a little sugar has been dissolved, and baked for about 40 minutes in a moderate-to-hot oven. It should be tested with a skewer before being removed from the oven. In Scotland it is not unusual for this bread to be eaten at almost every meal, with butter. It was a great favourite with Queen Victoria. See also BANNOCK.

selles-sur-cher, a French cheese made with goat's milk. It comes from the Berry district and is in season from May to October.

semi di finocchio, Italian for fennel seeds, used in Italy in various sausages and also for flavouring dried figs.

semmelknödel, see KNÖDEL.

semmelschmarrn, see SCHMARRN.

semolina, a product of wheat-flour milling, and derived particularly from the hard or Durum wheat. After the outer skins, or bran, have been removed from the wheat berry, but before it is ground into flour, the largest particles of the enclosed endosperm may be separated and detached. These are known as semolina. Semolina is used for making gnocchi and various cakes and milk puddings and for thickening soups. In Russia a similar milling product made from buckwheat is known as *kasha.*

semolina pudding, a plain milk pudding made by adding 2½ oz. (½ cup) semolina, with sugar to taste, to 1 pint (2 cups) milk. Flavourings are added as desired, and sometimes an egg is included. The pudding is either cooked in a double boiler until thick, or baked in a moderate oven for 40 minutes.

semoule, French for semolina. In culinary parlance the word is often wrongly used as the name for fine forms of various flours.

sennep, Danish for mustard.

sennep sauce, mustard sauce made with 1 pint (2 cups) fish stock and ¼ cup cream added to a roux of 2 tablespoons each flour and butter, with 1 tablespoon mustard. It is gently simmered, stirring all the time until thick and smooth. It is served with fish.

sepolini, see FRAGOLE DI MARE.

seppie, see FRAGOLE DI MARE.

septmoncel, a French blue-veined cheese from the Jura mountains. It is semi-hard and is made from a mixture of cow's and goat's milk fermented and ripened in the same way as *gex.*

sept-oeil, the French name for the spawn on the lampern or river lamprey, and also for the lamprey itself. It means literally "seven-eye."

sequillo, a small Spanish cake, similar to a macaroon, but made with hazelnuts. First 3 egg whites are beaten with 8 oz. (1 cup) sugar, and grated peel of 1 lemon and ½ cut pounded roasted hazelnuts are worked in. Small ovals of the mixture are put onto ricepaper and baked very quickly in a moderate oven.

ser, Polish for cheese. Most cheeses made in Poland today are imitations of more popular foreign cheeses such as *tilsiter käse, Edam, trappisten-käse, salamikäse,* emmenthal, and Gruyère. Processed cheese has also become more popular in Poland lately, and a great deal is made. No doubt some farms produce homemade cream cheeses, but these are not for sale in the shops.

sernik, Polish curd cake or cheesecake. A pastry case is made of rich short crust with 1 added teaspoon grated lemon peel, and is baked blind. Then 3 egg yolks are mixed with 2 heaped tablespoons castor sugar, 2 tablespoons melted butter, ½ lb. curds or cottage cheese and finally 3 stiffly beaten egg whites, and all are put into the pastry case. Three eggs and 1 tablespoon each of flour, sugar, and melted butter are then beaten together and spread over the top. The cake is baked in a moderate oven for 20–30 minutes until golden brown. See also CHEESECAKE; CURD, CAKE; PLACEK SEROWY NA KRUCHYM SPODZIE.

serpa, queijo de, a regional farmhouse-made variety of the Portuguese *serra* cheese.

serpentaria, see DRAGONCELLE.

serra, the generic name for the most typical Portuguese cheese. Many Serra cheeses bear the additional name of the region they come from, the finest being Serra da Estrella from the north. Serra means "mountain" and these cheeses are all made in the highlands of Portugal from ewe's milk or a mixture of ewe's and goat's milk. Occasionally they are made only from goat's milk. Serra is a flat cheese about 6 inches in diameter. The paste has very small oval "eyes" and is yellowish and soft—at its best when runny in the centre. Perhaps the most popular Portuguese cheese, it has a pleasant, sharp taste, and is at its best from November to May although it is good all year round. Serra da Estrella is a soft, oily cheese with a pleasant taste. Local varieties are made at Alcobaça, Alverde, Évora, Niza, and Serpa. See also AZEITÃO; CASTELO DE VIDE; TOMAR.

serrano, Spanish for sea bass. In Spain it is often grilled or used in soups, stews, or rice dishes. It is also poached, skinned, and boned, and then served cold with mayonnaise or sauce vinaigrette. Other Spanish names for sea bass are *labina* and *robalo.* See also BASS; VAQUITO.

serré or *seray,* a cheese made from whey, where curdling takes place by scalding. In the Glaris district of France it is curdled a second time with rennet, and the serré is then pounded with herbs (particularly wild celery), dried, and made into hard slabs called schabzigger. These are then grated and mixed with butter to make a soft cheese called *crème de Glaris.* It is sold ready-mixed and packed and is extremely aromatic. A similar cheese called *schabzieger* is made in Switzerland.

serviceberry, I. The fruit of the service tree. II. An alternative name for the shad bush.

service tree (*Sorbus domestica*), a tree closely related to the rowan tree, which grows in southern Europe, North Africa, and western Asia. Its berries, known as serviceberries or sorbapples, can be eaten raw or made into wine. The tree itself is sometimes called the sorbapple. See also ROWAN.

serviettenknödel, see KNÖDEL.

sesame (*Sesamum indicum*), a small annual plant of the *Peda-*

liaceae family, grown extensively in the Balkans, India, and the Far East. The seeds are small and vary in colour from honey-brown to black; they give a rich, toasted flavour to breads, biscuits, and cakes, and sesame is the main flavouring used in the commercially made *halvas.* Oil is made from the sesame plant which is used in India and China for the same purposes as olive oil. See also SUM-SUM.

sesos, Spanish for brains. See also BRAINS.

sesos fritos, fried brains. The brains are first blanched, then marinated for 30 minutes, with a lid on, in boiling water with a dash of vinegar and a sliced onion. Then they are dried, dipped in flour and egg, and fried in hot oil.

sévigné, à la, a French garnish for tournedos and entrées consisting of lettuce stuffed with fine forcemeat and *duxelles,* grilled mushrooms, *pommes château,* and sauce madère.

Seville orange, see ORANGE.

sfenci di San Giuseppe, a St. Joseph's Day speciality in Italy. Small buns of chou pastry flavoured with orange and lemon peel are baked and filled with cottage cheese beaten with sugar, grated chocolate, preserved chopped fruit, and a little maraschino. See also FESTA DI SAN GIUSEPPE.

sfogato, a Greek dish from the island of Rhodes. It is a sort of meat and vegetable custard or soufflé and is an excellent way of using tough meat. To prepare this dish 2 large minced onions are lightly fried in ¼ cup oil or butter, then added to 2 lb. minced (ground) meat (usually lamb, but any kind can be used), 1 lb. peeled and cubed courgettes (zucchini) or squashes, ½ pint (1 cup) stock, 2 tablespoons parsley, and seasoning. The whole is gently cooked until the meat is tender and the gravy thickens. When cool, 4 beaten eggs are folded in, and the dish is baked in a pan of water in a moderate oven for about 35 minutes or until firm. It is served with fresh tomato sauce and either green vegetables or a green salad.

sfogliatelle, Neapolitan pastry shells, baked in the shape of a fan or scallop shell and filled with a mixture of sweetened ricotta cheese and diced candied fruit.

sformato, an Italian dish somewhere between a soufflé and a pudding, which can be made from meats or poultry, cheese, or vegetables. The vegetables most frequently used are spinach, beans, or peas.

sformato di asparagi, the tips from 2 lb. asparagus (approximately 3 cups) are cooked, drained, and chopped. A roux is made from 3 tablespoons melted butter and 4 tablespoons flour, with ¾ pint (1½ cups) warm milk; it is seasoned, a pinch of nutmeg is added, and it is cooled. Then 3 well-beaten eggs, 2 oz. (¼ cup) grated Parmesan cheese, and the asparagus tips are folded in, and the whole is poured into a buttered dish, covered, and cooked in a *bain-marie* in a moderate oven for 45–60 minutes. Sometimes it is served with a sauce béchamel with cream added, and *crostini* of fried bread. The eggs can be separated as for a soufflé, but the method given here is the more usual.

shad, a migratory fish of the same family as the herring, but much larger and having a deeper body. It is found off all coasts of western Europe, in the North Sea, and in the Mediterranean. In spring the shad go up the rivers to spawn in

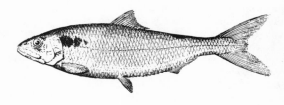

shad

fresh water, and the female, if caught soon after spawning, is most delicious to eat with a very delicate flavour. Although all shad have innumerable small bones which can be irritating when the fish is eaten, shad is gastronomically the finest of all whitefish. The roe is also much esteemed, especially the soft roe or milt of the male fish. Of the two distinct European species, the Allis or Allice shad (*Alosa alosa*) is the more prized, the elongated Twaite shad (*A. finta*) is generally less delicate in flavour. In certain French rivers, however, conditions seem to suit the Twaite shad admirably, and in France *finte* is considered a delicacy. In France, shad is called alose.

In the U.S. another species of shad is found (*A. menhaden*), which is highly prized gastronomically, especially for its roe. The fish can be baked whole, fried, or grilled, with the roe as garnish. See also SÁBALO.

shad roe, generally parboiled in salted water with a little vinegar, and when cold, cut into slices which are dipped in flour or breadcrumbs before frying. It is also cooked in cream with a little brandy or sherry (after first parboiling), or fried and served with spinach and sauce crème.

shad bush (*Amelanchier canadensis*), a small tree native to North America. Its red fruits are used for pies and are also canned for winter use. It is also known as serviceberry.

shaddock, the largest of the citrus fruits, imported from the East Indies to Barbados in 1696 by Captain Shaddock. It is a coarse, dry fruit, now superseded by the grapefruit, which resembles it but is smaller. The shaddock was originally called pompelmous, which survives in pamplemousse, the French word for grapefruit. See also GRAPEFRUIT.

shallot (*Allium ascalonicum*), one of the most important members of the onion family, a small brown-cased vegetable, slightly tinged with purple on the inside. It has a slight taste of garlic and is thought by some people to be more easily digested than the onion. It can be used in any way that is suitable for onion, but the flavour is not as pungent. A very good powdered shallot is prepared commercially in France, which is excellent for sprinkling in stews, sauces, or soups. In the north of England shallots are sometimes misleadingly called scallions. They came originally from the Ascalon district of Palestine and are mentioned in the Book of Judges in the Old Testament. They were brought to Britain by the crusaders in the early part of the 13th century, and were called Ascalonian onions. They were planted extensively in private gardens. Traditionally, they are planted on the shortest day of the year and lifted on the longest. See also CEBULKA; ÉCHALOTE; ONION.

shallot

shallot sauce, 2 tablespoons finely chopped shallots with 5 tablespoons vinegar are cooked in an enamel or earthenware saucepan over a strong heat and constantly stirred until practically all the vinegar has evaporated. Then 2 cups bouillon,

salt, pepper, and a bouquet garni are added, and all cooked gently over a low heat for 15 minutes. Before serving, the bouquet garni is removed and a beurre manié added. The sauce is not strained.

shank and *shank end,* English butchery terms for the lower part of the leg in pork, lamb, and mutton—shank is the word used for the foreleg, shank end for the hind leg. In Britain and Ireland pork shank is also called hand when it comprises the foreleg, with or without the trotter (foot), and a small part of the shoulder just round the bone. It is often salted, as for pickled pork. Lamb shanks are delicious if braised with very little stock or water, chopped herbs, and a little garlic or onion. They can also be rubbed with butter, seasoning, and herbs, wrapped in oven foil and cooked slowly for 1–1½ hours. The corresponding part of leg of veal and of beef is termed shin, not shank.

In the U.S. the term shank is used for foreleg of beef, veal, and lamb, and foreleg and hind leg of pork; the term shank end is used for hind leg of lamb and mutton. See Table of Cuts of Meats, pages xxi–xxvii.

sharàn sŭs orèhi, a Bulgarian dish consisting of a large whole carp stuffed with a mixture of grated walnuts, fried onions, and cayenne pepper. It is first browned in oil, then cooked either in the oven or on top of the stove, being basted with ½ cup hot water. This is a famous national dish, eaten particularly on St. Nicholas's Day. See also CARP.

shark, a fish belonging to the order *Pleurotremata*. There are many species, and several of these are eaten generally, both in Europe and the Far East. The most common is the tope, a firm whitefish, good to eat and often sold as halibut by unscrupulous fishmongers. It is found in European waters and off the Pacific coast of the U.S. Dogfish, anglefish or monkfish, and sunfish are other species which are frequently eaten. In the Orkney Islands, shark flesh is dried for eating during the winter. Shark steaks, taken chiefly from fish caught in the Pacific, appeared in a number of markets in the U.S. in the early 1950s. They were found to be meaty and were compared to halibut. Kippered or lightly smoked shark is like a dry, inferior smoked salmon. Shark fins are highly thought of by the Chinese, who make from them a strong gelatinous consommé which is excellent and is sold canned and bottled all over the world. The livers of all sharks are rich in oil, and as much as 1½ tons have been extracted from a single basking shark found on the west coast of Ireland.

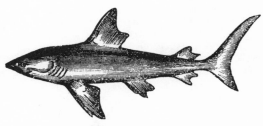

shark

sharp-tailed grouse (*Padioeces phasianellus*), a North American bird, found on the West Coast. It is similar to the prairie chicken and can be cooked in the same way.

shashlyk, a Russian method of grilling lamb or mutton. The dish originated in the Caucasus and is said to stem from the Caucasian warriors' practice of grilling lamb on their swords over campfires during campaigns. The lamb, with skin, fat, and gristle removed, is cut into 1- or 2-inch pieces wich are marinated in olive oil, lemon juice, onion, salt, and pepper for some hours. Then they are drained and threaded on skewers alternately with sliced onion and bay leaves. The lamb is grilled on all sides and served on a bed of rice, the marinade being reduced over a hot flame and served as gravy. Small mushrooms, chopped bacon, chopped tomatoes, or chopped eggplants are sometimes added in the other parts of Europe where this dish is also served. It is known in Turkey as *shish kébábi*. See also KÈBĀB.

shchi, a traditional Russian green vegetable soup—in fact it is often loosely called Russian cabbage soup in English-speaking countries. Diced onions, carrots, celeriac, parsley root, and leeks are simmered in beef and pork stock, to which are added shredded, blanched cabbage, salt, peppercorns, and bay leaves. On special occasions the soup is strained and then boiled with a piece of brisket; or, if there is no stock immediately available, the soup is made by boiling the meat first and adding the vegetables to it. Sour cream and the sliced brisket are served separately. Shchi is also made with spinach or nettles as the green vegetable, and can have either fish or meat stock as a base. It often forms the main course in a country meal, like the pot-au-feu of France.

shchi nikolayevskie, prepared as basic recipe, except that the stock is made with pork bones roasted in fat, and the vegetables are grated rather than diced. Tomato purée is added to taste.

shchi russkie, made with chopped white cabbage and sliced onions fried in lard, with stock made from pork bones added to them. Chopped vegetables, a piece of bacon, a piece of brisket, and salt, peppercorns, and bay leaves are also added, and all the ingredients are then boiled together. The soup is served with kasha.

shchi soldatskie, prepared as basic recipe, but sauerkraut is used instead of cabbage.

shchi zelenye, "green" shchi, prepared as basic recipe, but shredded sorrel, spinach, or lettuce are used instead of cabbage, and slices of hard-boiled egg are sometimes added.

shchuka, Russian for pike. Pike is used extensively in Russian cooking, often in fish soups such as ukha. It is also stuffed with a mixture of soaked bread, 1 tablespoon sugar, 1 tablespoon olive oil, salt, and pepper, all bound with an egg, and then laid on a bed of sliced onions, beetroots, and carrots, covered with water, and baked for 1½–2 hours with the lid on. Kasha is an alternative stuffing. See also PIKE.

sheep, see LAMB; MUTTON.

sheepshead, an English name for the grey and the red bream.

sheldrake or **shelduck** (*Tadorna tadorna*), a common wild duck found all over Europe. It is larger than a mallard, but does not compare with it for flavour. However, the natives of the Friesian Islands eat both the ducks and their eggs. The sheldrake is black, white, and light brown—very striking to look at.

sheldrake

shellfish, a term which, in culinary usage, denotes all edible marine and freshwater organisms without backbone or notochord and having an external chitinised or calcified protective shell. There are 3 categories: the crustaceans, to which belong all lobsters, crawfish, crabs, hermit-crabs, spider-crabs, crayfish, scampi, Dublin Bay prawns, prawns, shrimps, and barnacles; the molluscs, to which belong all oysters, clams, scallops, abalones, mussels, cockles, razor shells, sea truffles, sea dates, whelks, periwinkles, and limpets; and the echinoderms, to which belong the sea urchins and sea slugs.

All shellfish, without exception, should be eaten only when very fresh or immediately after unfreezing, and many are best cooked alive, especially crustaceans, oysters, and mussels. Both oysters and mussels have, together with other molluscs, a tendency to concentrate in their bodies harmful bacteria and algae; this means that when water is even only slightly polluted they may be dangerous to health, and if there has been contact with such poisonous algae as give rise to algal blooms and "red tide," this danger will not be removed by cooking.

Shellfish, and also lampreys, can also be dangerous in that they contain proteins of a simpler structure than is to be found in the higher fishes, and these proteins are sometimes absorbed into the bodies of very young children without being broken down. This can produce a condition known as anaphylaxis, in which the child's body develops, and retains over many years, a heightened sensitivity to that particular protein, so that he may react with severe sickness if he eats the shellfish again. The effect may be eradicated by giving the child or adult minute quantities (a tiny fragment only) of the shellfish in question, and increasing the amount very gradually over a long period—diminishing it at once if any symptoms of sickness recur. A troublesome procedure, but considering the gastronomic delights of fine shellfish, well worth while. Obviously the wisest course of action, however, is not to give shellfish or lampreys of any description to very young children. See also MOLLUSC; OYSTER.

shemis (*Ligusticum scothicum*), an aromatic plant which grows on the rocky shores of the Hebrides and the western seaboard of Scotland. It is used locally as a green vegetable, both raw and after boiling in water.

shepherd's pie, an old English dish consisting of minced meat, usually beef or mutton, mixed with minced onion to taste, herbs, seasoning, and a little gravy. It is put into an ovenproof dish and covered with a thick layer of mashed potato before being baked in the oven until the top is lightly browned. In earlier times it would be taken by shepherds to the hillsides and heated over a wood fire as they watched their flocks. It can be quite good if made with fresh, rather than cooked, meat. It is also called cottage pie.

sherbet, the name given to water ice by the Arabs, who first made it. See ICES.

shin, an English butchery term for the lower part of the leg in beef and veal. In lamb and pork the cut is generally known as shank or shank end. It is very lean, but sometimes sinewy. However, slow cooking reduces the sinews to jelly, and the flavour of the meat is far superior to that of many other stewing or braising cuts. Shin of beef is excellent for stews, pies, or casseroled dishes. Shin of veal (more generally called knuckle of veal) is usually cut into sections and braised; in Italy it is used for *ossi buchi,* as well as for making a gelatinous stock. See Table of Cuts of Meats, page xxi.

shiner, see REDFIN.

shirred eggs, the culinary term in the U.S. for *oeufs en cocotte*.

shish kebab, see KÈBĀB; SHASHLYK.

shkubánky, a traditional potato cake from Czechoslovakia. To prepare it 2 lb. potatoes are cooked, drained, and mashed well, and small holes are made reaching right to the bottom of the purée. These holes are filled with approximately 4 oz. (1 cup) rye flour, and then a little boiling water is poured over. The purée is left to stand, covered, for 30 minutes, any excess liquid being drained off; then it is beaten to a stiff smooth dough. Spoonfuls are placed on a plate and sprinkled with a combination of 2 heaped tablespoons sugar and 3 oz. (⅓ cup) lard, which has been mixed either with 2 heaped tablespoons poppy seeds or with crumbled gingerbread. Another alternative is to sprinkle the cakes with grated cheese and to pour melted butter over. Sometimes shkubánky cakes are dipped in egg and breadcrumbs and fried. These potato cakes are used to accompany spinach or peas.

shoo-fly pie, a speciality of the Pennsylvania Dutch, U.S., consisting of a pastry shell which can have several fillings, some more moist than others. Amounts given for the following fillings will be sufficient for an 8- or 9-inch shell. For one filling a liquid mixture of ¼ oz. (⅓ cup) molasses, 3 fluid oz. (⅓ cup) boiling water, and a pinch of baking soda is put into the shell first, then topped with a mixture consisting of 5 oz. (1¼ cups) flour, 2 oz. (¼ cup) lard, and 2 oz. (⅓ cup) brown sugar, all mixed with the hands. The pie is then baked in a moderate oven for 20–25 minutes.

For another filling a liquid mixture of 6 oz. (½ cup) molasses, 1½ gills (¾ cup) boiling water, ½ teaspoon baking soda, and 1 well-beaten egg yolk is put into the shell first, then topped with a mixture of 3 oz. (¾ cup) flour, ½ teaspoon each of cinnamon and ginger, a pinch each of nutmeg and cloves, 2 tablespoons butter, and 4 oz. (½ cup) brown sugar, all mixed with the hands. The pie is then baked in a moderate oven for 20–25 minutes.

In another variation the dry, cake-like shoo-fly is made with 4 oz. (½ cup) brown and white sugar mixed, 1 teaspoon baking powder, 2 tablespoons butter, and 6 oz. (1½ cups) flour. The liquid mixture consists of 6 oz. (½ cup) molasses, ¼ pint (½ cup) boiling water, and 1 small teaspoon baking soda. One-third of the liquid mixture is put into the shell first, then the remaining two-thirds is alternated with the dry mixture (ending with the dry), so that the resulting texture is more like that of a cake.

short crust pastry, SEE PASTRY.

short ribs, or rolled ribs, an English joint of beef taken from the lower ribs, always sold boned and rolled. It roasts quite well, but has a large proportion of fat. It is sometimes known as forequarter flank.

The American short ribs cut is taken from between the brisket and the flank of the animal, just below the shoulder on the belly side. It is usually used for pot roasting or braising. See diagrams, page xxii.

shortbread, a Scottish cake which is eaten all the year round, but particularly at Christmas and *Hogmanay*. Originally it was a large round cake, notched at the edge, probably a descendant of the Yule bannock which was notched to symbolize the sun's rays. Nowadays shortbread is often cut, before baking, into triangular or even round pieces. The best shortbread is made from equal parts of flour and rice flour; the same amount of butter as flour is worked in with the fingertips, together with half the amount of sugar, and all well mixed. Generally no liquid is used, but if the dough is too crumbly it can be barely moistened with a little milk. It is rolled to about ¾-inch thickness, cut as desired, and pricked all over with a fork. The edges are fluted and the shortbread is then baked in a moderate oven for 45–60 minutes, depending on the size. For festive occasions it can be decorated with chopped almonds, candied peel, caraway seeds (a Shetland speciality), or small sweets with a hard sugar coating called comfits. In the Shetland Islands, shortbread is served at weddings; a comfit the size of a sixpence is set in the middle of it, and each unmarried guest has to break off a piece of cake; it is said that whoever touches the comfit will remain unmarried. The cake is known as the "bride's bonn(ach)."

shortening, the American term for vegetable fat or lard, used a great deal in the U.S. for pastry-making. Unlike butter it contains no liquid, and so gives a crisp "short" texture to the pastry.

shoulder, the top of the front leg of quadruped mammals. Depending on the age of the animal, the shoulder can be cooked in almost any way; shoulder of lamb roasts particularly well, either whole or boned and stuffed. See also HAND.

shoveller (*Anas glypeata*), a common wild duck of the northern hemisphere. It breeds in the northern parts of the British Isles and the temperate parts of North America, where it is also called spoonbill and river duck. If its diet has been a good one, it can make very good eating, and it is much esteemed by gastronomes. It is prepared and cooked in the same way as wild duck.

shred, to, to scrape with a grater into very small pieces, as in the case of carrot, or to tear with the fingers. It applies particularly to vegetables, such as carrots or lettuce, especially the latter, which should not be cut with a knife because the metal may darken the edges of the leaves.

shredded suet, SEE SUET.

Shrewsbury cakes, English cakes or biscuits not unlike shortbread, originally from the town of Shrewsbury. They are made from ½ lb. each flour, butter, and sugar, and 1 egg white. The mixture is rolled out and cut into rounds which are baked in a moderate-to-hot oven. See also SIMNEL CAKE.

shrimp, like the prawn, a name given to some of the smaller relatives of the lobster, crayfish, etc., of the order *Decapoda*. They are not zoological terms, but indicative of size only; in Britain a prawn must be over 2–3 inches long, and anything smaller than that is a shrimp. Thus all members of the *Palaemonidae, Pandalidae,* and *Penaeidae* can be classed as either shrimps or prawns, depending entirely on the size of the specimens being considered. All members of the genus *Crangon* are classed as shrimps because they do not reach a length of more than 2–3 inches. The common shrimp (*Crangon crangon*) is found all over Europe and is referred to as the "brown shrimp," or *crevette grise* in French, because it becomes a brownish-grey colour when boiled. The "pink shrimp" or *crevette rose* (*Pandalus montagui*) turns pink when boiled, and is a little larger than the brown shrimp, with a better flavour.

shrimp

In the U.S. all crustaceans of this type are generally known as "shrimps," although by British standards they would certainly be regarded as prawns, and are indeed much larger than any prawns caught in British waters. Several large members of the *Penaeidae* are caught in American waters, also a large river prawn of the genus *Macrobrachium*. In the West Indies and the Pacific, a large prawn almost as big as a lobster is caught (*Macrobrachium carcinus*). European prawns tend to be rather smaller, but a very large and delicious prawn (*Penaeus caramote*) is caught in Italian waters and called locally *mazzancolle*. The prawn most commonly taken in Britain is the *Palaemon serratus*.

Shrimps are marketed fresh, frozen, and canned. If fresh, they are cooked alive in salt water for not more than 10 minutes, then drained. They are laborious to shell, and the amount of flesh on a single shrimp is minute, but they have a good flavour. They are used in soups, garnishes, sauces, butters, and potted pastes, and are added to various dishes such as risotto and paella. See also CAMARÂO; GAMBA; GARIDES; GARNAAL; PRAWN; SCAMPI.

potted shrimps, the most famous British way of serving shrimps. Shelled cooked shrimps are pressed into warm butter flavoured with mace and pepper and put into a small earthenware container; melted butter is poured over them when they are cold. They are eaten cold with hot toast, and make an excellent appetizer or first course.

shrimp sauce, ½ pint (1½ cups) freshly boiled brown shrimps are peeled, then all the soft part of the heads, with about 6 of the shrimp bodies, are pounded to a paste and pressed through a fine sieve. This shrimp paste is thoroughly stirred into ¾ pint (1½ cups) rich white sauce to which a generous amount of good fresh butter and 1 tablespoon thick cream have been added. When the sauce is ready to be served the rest of the shrimps are added to it, and the whole is allowed to heat through, though not to boil.

Shropshire damsons, see DAMASCENES.

Shrove Tuesday, the day preceding Ash Wednesday (the first day of Lent), so called because it is the day set aside by the Church for the shriving of sins in preparation for the Lenten fast. It is characterized in English-speaking countries by the serving of pancakes, and for this reason it is often called Pancake Day. This custom probably arose out of the necessity for using up all the lard, fat, and dripping in the larder before Lent, when these foods were forbidden. In European Catholic countries, the day is celebrated with a carnival and great feasting; the French Mardi Gras, or "Fat Tuesday," when a fat ox was ceremonially paraded through the streets, is the most generally known. Mardi Gras is also celebrated in South America and the French-settled city of New Orleans.

shunis, see LOVAGE.

shurpa, a Russian soup from Uzbekistan, made with 6 pints (12 cups) beef or mutton stock into which are put 3 medium-sized fried onions, 1½ lb. chopped potatoes, and 1 lb. tomatoes. All are simmered until cooked. A large raw onion is crushed with a wooden spoon and sprinkled with black pepper, and a portion of this is put into each soup plate. The hot soup is poured over it and is garnished with dill.

sianliha, Finnish for pork.

sianlihakastike, a Finnish method of preparing fat pork. The pork is cut into cubes, sprinkled with flour, and browned in a pan with chopped onions. It is covered with boiling water and allowed to simmer. A little cream or tomato purée to taste may be added to the gravy. This dish is often served for lunch with rice or barley porridge, boiled potatoes, or *viliipiimä*. It is known colloquially as *läskisoosi*.

sibirskie pelmeni, see PELMENI.

sidemeats, an American term for offal, also called organ meats and variety meats.

sienet, Finnish for mushrooms, of which there is a very great variety in Finland. The most popular types are *maitosienet* and *korvasienet*. They are preserved by salting, and are also used for various dishes. See also MUSHROOM.

paistetut sienet, fried mushrooms. They are fried with chopped onion, then breadcrumbs, boiling milk, and sour cream are added and simmered until thickish, about 5 minutes.

sienikastike, mushroom sauce, made with a mixture of mushrooms, milk, and onions, thickened with flour. It is prepared in the same way as *sienimuhennos*, but with more milk so that the consistency is thinner.

sienimuhennos, stewed mushrooms. First 1 lb. salted mushrooms are soaked, then drained and fried in ½ cup butter with 1 medium-sized chopped onion. Then 4 tablespoons flour is stirred in, with seasoning, and finally 1 pint (2 cups) creamy milk. All is simmered, stirring well, for 30 minutes.

sienisalaatti, mushroom salad, made from fresh or salted mushrooms boiled in water for 2 minutes, drained, then finely sliced and mixed with a small quantity of grated onion, covered with cream mixed with a little sugar and white pepper, and served cold.

sieva bean, a bean similar to the lima bean and grown extensively in Florida and California.

sieve, a utensil with a circular frame covered with coarse wire or nylon which is fixed rigidly to the sides, and through which foods can be poured or pressed for the purpose of making purées, soups, sauces, etc. Nowadays food mills and electric blenders take the place of the older utensils. Some sieves can also be used as fine strainers for clarifying liquids.

sig, Russian for whitefish, found in certain Russian lakes. Whitefish is highly thought of in Russia, and is smoked, pickled with alcohol, and frozen, as well as being eaten fresh. See also WHITEFISH.

sikotakia, Greek for liver. See also LIVER.

sikotakia me saltsa, a recipe from the island of Rhodes. First 1 lb. sliced or chopped liver is marinated for about 1 hour in red wine to cover. Next, 2 small onions are sliced and lightly browned in 4 tablespoons olive oil. The liver is then removed from the marinade, dried, coated with seasoned flour, and browned in the same oil (a little more may need to be added) with a pinch of marjoram or rosemary. The wine marinade is added gradually to the liver, which is covered and cooked very gently until the sauce has thickened. Kidneys are also cooked in the same way.

sikotakia tiganita, liver cut in small pieces which are threaded on skewers, sprinkled with chopped herbs, and fried on all sides in olive oil.

sikotakia tis kottas me saltsa, a speciality of Corfu. To prepare it 1 lb. chicken livers and 6 lamb's kidneys (chopped to the same size as the chicken livers) are cooked in butter, to which are added ½ pint (1 cup) consommé, 1 small grated onion, 2 cloves garlic, parsley, and 4 tablespoons white wine. The dish is seasoned to taste, and is cooked quickly so that the sauce thickens and the livers and kidneys are not overdone.

silakat, Finnish for sprats. Suolasilakat are salted sprats; see also SPRAT; SUUTARINLOHI.

hiillostetut silakat, grilled sprats, with which mashed potatoes are generally served. A sauce is not usual.

keitetyt suolasilakat, salted sprats cooked together with parboiled potatoes. The sprats are garnished with dill and butter, and the boiled potatoes are served with a white sauce. See also SUUTARINLOHI.

muhennetut silakat, stewed sprats. The sprats are placed in layers in a pan with chopped chives, dill, parsley, pepper, and salt. They are covered with boiling water and cooked for 10 minutes, then covered with more chopped herbs. It is the dill which gives the characteristic flavour to this dish.

paistetut silakat, fried sprats. The sprats are cleaned, rolled in rye flour, and fried in butter.

savusilakat, a Finnish method of smoking fresh sprats. The fish are rubbed with salt and put in an iron pot which is placed on green juniper and alder shoots, then covered with greased paper and a tight-fitting lid. They are cooked for about 10 minutes until they are lightly browned, then left to get cold in the covered pot. The sprats are served cold for smörgåsbord.

silakat ja munakokkelia, a dish of fried sprats served with scrambled eggs. Tiny whitebait are also used as well as small sprats.

silakkahyytelö, a way of preparing filleted, rolled sprats in aspic, similar to *silakkakääryleet.* When cooked, the fish are allowed to cool in the stock, which is used to make a jelly by boiling up with 1 tablespoon aspic to 1 pint (2 cups) stock. The fish are covered with the jelly and the dish is often garnished with beetroot slices.

silakkakääryleet, 1 lb. fresh boned sprats are sprinkled with 1 medium-sized finely chopped onion, and dill, then rolled up, placed in a pan, and braised in ½ pint (1 cup) vinegar mixed with 1 heaped teaspoon sugar. They are seasoned with salt and pepper and cooked in a moderate oven for about 20 minutes.

silakkakaviaari, sprat caviar, a dish of salted or smoked sprats. First 1 lb. fish is skinned, boned, chopped very finely, and made into a paste with ¼ pint (½ cup) whipped cream, 1 finely chopped onion, and white pepper, all well pounded and beaten until creamy. This dish can be served as a component of smörgåsbord. Needless to say, it bears no relation to caviar.

silakkalaatikko, sprats au gratin, using fresh or salted fish. To prepare it 1 lb. sprats are cleaned and placed in alternate layers in a dish with sliced potato and finely chopped onion, finishing off with very thin slices of pork and dabs of butter. A mixture of 1 beaten egg and 2 cups milk is then poured over this, and breadcrumbs are sprinkled on top. The dish is baked for 1 hour.

silakkapihvit, a method of preparing sprat fillets. First 1 lb. fish are cleaned, and the heads, backbones, and tails are removed. Half the number of fillets available are spread out and sprinkled with salt, pepper, and herbs; then the remaining halves are placed on top to form a kind of fish-and-herb sandwich. They are sprinkled with rye flour and fried in butter, and usually served with mashed potatoes.

sild, I. Danish for herring, which are of exceptionally good quality in Denmark. They are eaten in many different ways when fresh, and can be grilled, baked, or fried. They are also extensively treated by curing and smoking, and many of these cured and smoked varieties are canned for export. See also BÖCKLING; GAFFELBIDDER; FISK; HERRING. II. Danish for the young of the herring, which are also known as *brisling.* They are canned and smoked, and exported from Denmark all over the world under the names of both sild and *brisling.* They are frequently sold in the U.S., Great Britain, and Ireland in place of sardines, although they are nothing like as good, being smaller and less succulent. See also BRISLING.

stegt sild med brun sauce, filleted fresh herrings rolled in seasoned flour and fried on both sides in butter. They are served with fried onions (cooked in a separate pan), chopped parsley, and brun sauce, which is made by adding 1 tablespoon flour to the pan juices, stirring well, then pouring in ½ pint (1 cup) hot milk.

stegt sild med løgsauce, as above, but served with onion sauce and boiled potatoes.

sild, Norwegian for herring. Herring are an important item of diet in all Scandinavian countries. They are eaten fresh, salted, or smoked, and are served hot or cold for the smörgåsbord. See also BRISLING; FISK; HERRING.

innbakt fylt sild, baked stuffed herring. Fresh herrings are filleted and prepared for cooking in the usual manner, then spread with a filling composed of breadcrumbs, shredded suet, chopped fried mushrooms, chopped parsley, crushed herbs, and milk. The fish are then rolled up, brushed with beaten egg, lightly sprinkled with sieved breadcrumbs and dabbed with butter, before being baked in a moderate oven for about 30 minutes. They are served hot.

innbakt sild i form, herring pie. First 1 pint (2 cups) boiling milk is poured over 4 beaten eggs, then seasoning and a pinch nutmeg are added and the mixture is sieved or liquidised. This forms the sauce. A baking dish is lined with pastry, and chopped herrings, either fresh or canned, are placed in it (if canned fish are being used, the oil must be drained off). The sauce is poured over them and the pie baked in a moderate oven for about 30 minutes or until golden brown. It should be served at once.

sildesalat, herring salad. There are two chief variations: in one, filleted, salted herrings are served with lettuce, onion, cucumber, and chopped tomatoes, with sprigs of parsley and lemon wedges. Mayonnaise is served separately; in another, the herrings are boiled, then boned and skinned. Then they are cut into small pieces which are mixed with diced boiled potato and diced peeled apple, with a mixture of parsley, chervil, fennel, and tarragon sprinkled on top. A French dressing is made with olive oil and either claret or a wine vinegar.

sursild, sour pickled herring, a national dish in Norway. It is served for *smørbrød,* often with sour cream and cooked beetroot.

sill, Swedish for herring. Herrings are extremely popular throughout Sweden and are eaten fresh, pickled, and smoked. See also BÖCKLING; FISK; HERRING; STRÖMMING.

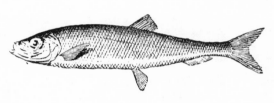

sill

inlagd sill, pickled salted herring. The head is removed from a pickled salted herring, and after cleaning the fish is soaked overnight in cold water. It is then divided into fillets which are cut crosswise into small slices. These are rearranged in the shape of the herring and covered with a dressing consisting of 2 heaped tablespoons sugar dissolved in 1½ gills (¾ cup) white vinegar, with 1 small minced onion, white peppercorns, allspice, and 2 tablespoons water added. Chopped chives, dill, or onion rings are used as a garnish.

sillbullar, herring croquettes. After overnight soaking in cold water, 2 salted herrings are filleted and chopped, then mixed with 1½ lbs. cold mashed potato and 1½ cups chopped cooked beef. Then 1 beaten egg and pepper are added, and the mixture is shaped into croquettes which are rolled in brown breadcrumbs and then fried on both sides in butter or oil. *Korintsås* is served separately.

sillsallad, Swedish herring salad. The head is removed from a salted herring, and the fish is well cleaned and soaked overnight in cold water. Then it is skinned, filleted, and diced. The pieces are mixed with 1 cup each of boiled potatoes, pickled beets, pickled gherkins, and dessert apple, all diced. Then 1 small minced onion, 4 tablespoons vinegar, 2 tablespoons water, 2 tablespoons sugar, and pepper, are beaten together (—with ¼ pint (½ cup) whipped cream folded in at the end if desired—), and this mixture is added to the salad. The whole is then chilled in a mould and served with a sour cream dressing. It is garnished with hard-boiled eggs sprinkled with chopped fennel or parsley.

sillabub, see SYLLABUB.

silli, Finnish for herrings. See also HERRING.

hillostettu tuoretta sillia, a Finnish speciality of fresh herring cooked on a grill over charcoal.

sillilaatikko, fish and potato casserole. Herring would generally be the fish used, but this dish is also made with perch, pike, burbot, salmon, or whitefish. If salted fish is to be used, it is first soaked for 6 hours. The fish is placed in a baking-dish in alternate layers with potatoes and onions, then all is seasoned, covered with 1 cup melted butter, sprinkled thickly with breadcrumbs, and baked for 1½ hours in a moderate oven. It is served hot, as *pikkulämpimät.*

sillipyörykät, a method of preparing fishballs from salted herring. First 2 salted herrings, after overnight soaking in cold water, are minced with 2 cups mashed potato and 1 cup cooked meat, mixed with 1 chopped onion and 1 tablespoon potato flour, then formed into balls which are rolled in breadcrumbs and fried in butter. These fishballs are usually served with boiled potatoes, beetroot, and a brown sauce.

suolasilli, a method of serving salted herrings. They are soaked overnight in water, cold tea, or skimmed milk, before skinning and filleting. Then they are arranged on a flat dish and garnished with onion slices, chives, dill, and hard-boiled eggs. They can be served alone or with boiled potatoes. See also ROSOLLI.

sillocks, the fry of coalfish. According to a traditional Scottish fisherman's recipe, the tiny fish, with the heads removed, are rolled in salted oatmeal and then fried in butter. When cooked, they are eaten with the fingers; the tail is pulled off and the backbone removed by pressure on the sides, and the savoury morsel is eaten with the fingers as a single mouthful. Brown scones or bannocks are eaten as an accompaniment. The fish are also salted and dried in bunches until quite hard, and eaten uncooked with buttered bannocks; schoolchildren used to eat them like this at their morning break. See also SAITHE.

silungur, Icelandic for trout, which is of excellent quality in Iceland. It is served fresh, when it is grilled, baked, or fried, and is also smoked, pickled, and salted.

silure (*Silurus glanis*), one of the largest freshwater fish of Europe, found chiefly in the rivers Danube, Oder, Vistula, and Elbe. In the river Doubs, France, it can attain a length of 6 feet and a weight of 50 lb. It makes extremely good eating and is excellent fried, or cut into steaks, grilled, and served with *beurre maître d'hôtel* or *beurre anchois* and served with caper sauce. It is also known as *wels.*

Dwarf silure, also called freshwater catfish, were imported from America to stock French rivers, but they do not grow to more than 24 inches in length. The flesh is delicate and well thought of, and it can be fried in egg and breadcrumbs, or painted with oil, grilled and served with *beurre maître d'hôtel,* or poached and served with caper sauce, shrimp sauce, sauce *robert,* or melted butter and lemon juice. See also CATFISH.

silver beet, see CHARD.

silver fish (*Seriola dumerili*), a fish of the family *Carangidae,* found in the Mediterranean, and in tropical and subtropical waters where it is called amber fish. It grows to a length of 6–7 feet, and is silver-grey in colour with an iridescent yellow streak running the whole length of its body. It has firm white flesh with an excellent flavour, and is usually sold in steaks which are poached or grilled. It is found particularly off the coasts of Spain and Morocco, where it is called *pez di limón.*

silver hake (*Merluccius bilinearis*), a sea fish which is abundant off the northern coast of New England in the U.S. It is superior in taste and texture to the European hake. In the U.S. it is also called whiting.

silver onion, also called silver-skin onion, a very small onion not more than ½ inch across, with a silvery skin and pure white flesh. It is generally used for pickling but some French garnishes, such as *batelière,* also incorporate it.

silver sild, a small sea fish related to the herring which is found in the Atlantic waters off the eastern coast of the U.S. It has a very delicate flavour, and when the fish is young, its bones are very soft and delicate. For this reason it is often fried whole in breadcrumbs, for the bones can be eaten as well.

silverside, an English cut of beef which comprises the best side of the round. It is also known as the half-round. Although it can be casseroled or stewed when fresh, silverside is usually salted and boiled, and the term is generally used to describe a lean cut of salt beef.

silverside, another name, much used in the U.S., for the *atherine* or sand smelt. American silversides are larger than those found in Europe, and many freshwater forms are to be found in the lakes of North America, from Lake Ontario to Texas.

silverweed (*Potentilla anserina*), a weed with starchy roots which in the Hebrides are eaten like parsnips. In a time of food shortage they could be ground into a kind of flour.

simmer, to, to cook foods in liquid (this includes sauces) at just below boiling point—approximately 195°F (91°C), depending on the density of the liquid so that the surface just ripples but does not bubble. Poached foods, and stews such as pot-au-feu, are cooked entirely by simmering. See also POACH.

simnel cake, a traditional English Easter cake. The name comes from the Latin *siminellus,* a Roman festival bread made from a fine wheaten flour known as *simila,* which was eaten during the spring fertility rites. In England this cake was originally made for the 4th Sunday in Lent, known as Mothering Sunday and now called Mother's Day. Mothering Sunday grew out of an old pre-Christian tradition which was deliberately adapted and fostered by the early Church to uplift the devout during the Lenten fast. It was a day devoted to celebrating "Mother Church," when small gifts were presented to parents, especially the mother, cakes were made, processions took place, and there was a general relaxation of the abstinence rules. Much later it became the day when servants were given a holiday to visit their parents, taking with them a simnel cake, the ingredients of which were donated by the servants' employers.

Simnel cake is a rich fruit cake with layers of marzipan, and there are at least three well-known varieties: the shrewsbury, with a thick crust of saffron bread; the devizes, made in the shape of a star; and the bury, which is a flattish cake with fluted edges. The cake is made with 6 oz. (1½ cups) flour, 4 oz. (½ cup) butter, 4 oz. (½ cup) sugar, 4 oz. (1 cup) sultanas, 2 oz. (½ cup) currants, 2 oz. (½ cup) raisins, ½ cup candied peel, 1 teaspoon spice, 3 eggs, and 2 tablespoons brandy or rum—not unlike the mixture for a Christmas cake. A paste is also made with ½ lb. ground almonds beaten with the same amount of icing sugar, with 2 eggs, juice of ½ lemon, and 1 tablespoon sherry added. Half the cake mixture is put into a cake tin and covered with half the almond paste, then the rest of the mixture is put on top and the cake is baked in a slow-to-moderate oven for 2–3 hours. It is cooled, and the top is spread with warm apricot jam and then covered with the remaining half of the marzipan. It is often decorated with small marzipan "eggs" round the edges, and even little "nests" of stiffly beaten egg white are sometimes to be seen, with the marzipan eggs inside them and Easter chickens, also of marzipan, placed close by. Originally there were thirteen such decorations, symbolizing Christ and the Twelve Disciples. When ready, the cake should be put in a very cool oven for 30 minutes to set the marzipan. Simnel cake keeps very well and can be delicious.

singing hinny, a griddle cake from Northumberland, England, said to get its name from the sound the dough makes when put on the hot griddle. To prepare the dough ¾ lb. (3 cups) flour is mixed with 2 oz. (2 heaped tablespoons) ground rice, 1 teaspoon salt, and 2 teaspoons baking powder. Then, 1 heaped tablespoon lard is rubbed in, and 3 oz. (¾ cup) currants is included. Then 1 gill (½ cup) composed half of cream and half of milk, is added, and all the ingredients are mixed to a fairly soft dough. This is rolled out to ¼-inch thickness, pricked over with a fork, and cooked on a fairly hot griddle until golden brown on both sides. It is cut into quarters and served hot with butter.

Sint Nicolaas Avond, the eve of St. Nicholas's Day, December 5–6, a popular festival in Holland. Many traditional dishes such as *apfelbeignets, sprits, borstplaat, olie bollen, slemp,* and *speculaas* are eaten. There is a great party given on the eve, and presents, chosen for fun rather than for value, are hidden throughout the house. On the eve of the day, people dressed to represent St. Nicholas arrive in Amsterdam and elsewhere, seated on a white horse, wearing a red cloak and bishop's mitre and carrying a mace. St. Nicholas is accompanied by his servant Black Peter, who according to tradition would put naughty children in a bag and take them away to Spain—at one time Holland's worst enemy. The arrival of St. Nicholas marks the beginning of the festival, which seldom finishes until Christmas is over. See also CHRISTMAS.

sippets, a 19th-century English name for triangular pieces of toast served with some melted cheese dishes and with cooked minced beef. Originally it meant toasted bread soaked in gravy, sauce, or wine; the name was also given to soup with sippets in it. Sippets were also called soppes.

sir, the Serbo-Croat word for cheese. See BELI SIR; DOMAĆI BELI SIR; EVARGLICE; KAČKAVALJ; KEFALOTIR; LIPSKI SIR; PASKI SIR; ROKADUR; ROMANA; SOMBORSKI SIR; VIZE.

siréné, one of the two most important national cheeses of Bulgaria, the other being *kashkavàl.* It is made from ewe's milk, is a little sour in taste and faintly salty, but a mild cheese nevertheless and very good. It is an unusual 6-sided shape with a smaller square base, and weighs between 1½ and 2¼ lb. The paste is semi-hard, smooth, pale cream in colour, and shiny. It is kept for not less than 7 weeks at a temperature of 59°F (15°C) before it is mature enough to be ready for eating.

sirloin, an English butchery term for a joint of beef which extends from the last rib down to the sacrum. It comprises the upper part of the loin, and the undercut or fillet. A whole sirloin can weigh up to 14 lb., and it is usually subdivided into separate joints weighing from 4 lb. upwards. Fillet, T-bone, and rump steak are taken from this part. The joint can be boned and rolled, but this is only advised for small sirloin joints which would otherwise be difficult to carve. The T-shaped bone in fact keeps the meat moist inside and increases its succulence. Sirloin is the finest roasting joint of beef there is, and should not be overcooked—16 minutes per lb., and 16 minutes in addition, is enough to make the outside brown but leave the middle still pink and juicy. In Britain sirloin is traditionally served with Yorkshire pudding, parsnips, and horseradish sauce. The name is reputed to have been created by an English king (various monarchs are mentioned), who so delighted in the joint (loin) that he knighted it at table. It is much more probable that it comes from the French sur longe (on [the] loin), as in 1554 it was being spelled ''surloin'' in England.

In the U.S. a joint cut from this part is called eye of sirloin.

In France sirloin is aloyau, and when cut as a joint, *contre-filet.* See diagram, pages xxii–xxiii.

sirloin steak, an English cut of steak, taken from the end of the loin, before it becomes rump steak. However, many butchers and restaurateurs often offer the latter for the former.

šiškevap, a Yugoslavian dish of beef or lamb rolled in paprika, then grilled on skewers with potato and onion slices.

sjokolade, Norwegian for chocolate. See also CHOCOLATE.

sjokolade knask, small chocolate cakes made with crispbread. First 1 oz. chocolate and 1 tablespoon butter are melted together, and 1 tablespoon golden syrup and 2 cups very thin crushed crispbread flakes are stirred in. The mixture is cooled, then formed into cakes which are decorated with chopped nuts, raisins, ginger, etc., and left overnight to harden.

sjøørret, Norwegian for salmon trout, which is eaten a great deal in Norway. See also SALMON TROUT.

kokt sjøørret, poached salmon trout with cucumber salad, a popular dish in Norway.

sjøørret med smelter smør, the Norwegian version of *truite au bleu.*

sjøtunge or *tunge,* Norwegian for sole, which is of excellent quality in Norway. See also SOLE.

sjøtunge Stavanger, devilled sole, a speciality of Stavanger. A large sole is put in a marinade of 2 parts olive oil to 1 part wine vinegar, with a pinch of mace, cloves, and parsley, a bay leaf, onion, and seasoning, for at least 1 hour. It is then baked with some of the marinade for 30 minutes in a hot oven, and served with a devil sauce made from ½ teaspoon curry paste, 1 tablespoon chopped chutney, and juice of ½ lemon mixed into a white sauce flavoured with anchovy. It is garnished with sliced beetroot and lemon. This recipe is also good for flounder.

skabu kapostu supa, traditional Latvian sauerkraut soup made with 1 lb. smoked pork, 1 large onion, 2 lb. sauerkraut, and 4 oz. pearl barley, and garnished with ½ pint (1 cup) sour cream. The ingredients are cooked with 3 quarts (12 cups) water and salt, and during the last half-hour ½ lb. each of sliced tomatoes and apples can be added. One variation has fresh meat in it and no barley. It is a substantial dish which is usually served after the main course.

skaltsounia, a popular Cretan pastry like a turnover, filled with a mixture of *féta* cheese and beaten eggs, then fried in hot oil and sprinkled with honey. Sometimes chopped nuts, cinnamon, clove, masticha (a liqueur made from *mastic*), and honey are used as a filling instead.

skarp saus, a Norwegian sauce, not unlike worcestershire sauce.

skarpsås, a Swedish cold sauce which has a sharp but creamy flavour and is served with boiled or poached fish. It is made with 1 hard-boiled egg yolk sieved and mixed with 1 raw yolk. The mixture is seasoned, 1 tablespoon wine vinegar is blended in, and ½ pint (1 cup) whipped cream is gradually folded in. The sauce must be served immediately as it curdles quickly.

skate (Raiidae), the name given to a number of different kinds of ray. *Raja laevis* and *R. batis* are usually found in European and Atlantic waters; *R. binoculata* and *R. erinacea* are allied species found in the Pacific and off the eastern coasts of the U.S. *R. erinacea* is a small skate, whereas some specimens of the other varieties reach a weight of 125–150 lb. The skate is a flat wide scaleless fish, with fins in the form of wings and a thick tail. Skate is coarse in texture but has a good, creamy flavour. The flat cartilaginous bones, in regular formation with the flesh on either side, make the skate easy to eat and therefore a particularly good fish for children. The wings are the most appetizing part. Skate is also very gelatinous. In Great Britain it is often sold skinned, for the skin tends to be tough. Skate can be kept for 2–3 days in a cool place, and in fact becomes more tender with keeping. For cooking, it is usually cut into thick pieces about 6 inches long which can be fried, poached, or boiled. The most famous method is au *beurre noir*. Skate liver is a delicacy, and should be poached with the fish, then pounded with an equal quantity of butter, lemon juice to taste, a pinch of mixed spice, salt, and pepper; it should then be shaped into a largish pat and served on top of the hot fish. Cooked skate makes excellent fishcakes. In Scotland, skate is often put on damp grass and covered with sods for a day or two to make it tender. The Scots also make it into a good soup with onion, potato, and herbs, and also into a good breakfast dish by cutting it up small and frying it in bacon fat. In the U.S. skate is only recently becoming accepted on the East coast. See also RAIE; RAYA; RAZZA CHIODATA; ROCHEN.

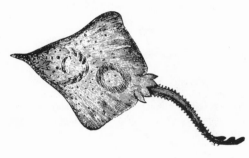

skate

skembe, Greek for tripe which is often made into a soup in Greece.

skewer, a pointed instrument which may be of varying length and thickness, on which pieces of meat or fish are threaded for cooking. This method of cooking is popular in Russia (*shashlik*), France (*brochettes*), Turkey (*kèbābi*), and Greece (*souvlakia*). Wooden skewers are used by butchers to hold a joint together, and small metal skewers hardly bigger than a darning-needle are used to secure stuffing or to hold garnishes in place. See also SPIT.

skillet, an American term for a frying pan.

skim, to, to take the fat from liquids, especially the cream from milk. It also means to remove the scum or other impurities from sauces, soups, or stock. Jams and jellies are also skimmed to remove the sugar which collects in a froth on the top. A skimmer is a perforated spoon made especially for this process.

skink, a word that occurs in both Scots and Irish, meaning formally essence (extract), but in more general culinary usage a stew–soup. This can be made from any meat and a variety of green or root vegetables, with herbs and seasoning. See also BALNAMOON SKINK; CULLEN SKINK.

skinka, Swedish for ham. See also HAM; JULSKINKA.

skinklåda, ham omelette made from 6 eggs, 6 oz. diced ham, and ¾ pint (1½ cups) milk beaten together, seasoned, and baked in a greased dish in the oven for 30 minutes or until set.

skinke, Danish for ham. *Tivoli skinke* is ham from the district of Tivoli, which is of excellent quality. It can be boiled, baked, or grilled. See also HAM.

kogt skinke med ostecreme, 1 lb. boiled ham cut into slices which are rolled round a creamed cheese filling. Then ½ pint (1 cup) white sauce is made, to which are added 2 egg yolks, 4 oz. (1 cup) grated *samsoe* cheese, and seasoning. This filling, which should be very thick, is spooned onto the ham slices, which are then rolled up and placed in a baking-dish. They are covered with fresh tomato sauce and sprinkled with

more grated cheese, before being baked in a slow oven for 20 minutes.

tivoli skinke og æggeanretning, 12 slices boiled Tivoli ham (green or smoked) are lightly spread with a purée of foie gras and rolled up. The yolks are then removed from 6 hard-boiled eggs and mixed with 1 tablespoon chopped chives or parsley, 2 tablespoons mayonnaise and seasoning, and the egg whites are stuffed with this mixture and garnished with anchovies. Next, tomatoes are hollowed out, and the pulp is mixed with mayonnaise and reinserted as a filling for the tomatoes, which are garnished with asparagus tips. The stuffed tomatoes, stuffed eggs, and ham rolls are finally served together on a bed of lettuce.

skinke, Norwegian for ham. *Spekeskinke* is cured ham, eaten raw and carved in very thin slices. See also HAM.

skinke og egg, thin slices of raw cured ham served with cold scrambled eggs.

skirlie, a Scottish dish made from 4 oz. oatmeal added to sliced onion that has been fried in pork dripping, cooked for 10 minutes, and seasoned to taste. It is used as an accompaniment for fish, poultry, and meat, and as a stuffing for poultry and meat. It is sold commercially in a skin, and is also known as mealie pudding. See also WHITE PUDDING.

skirret (*Sium sisarum*), a perennial plant grown in England and Europe for its rather large white roots, which are composed of fleshy tuberous prongs. Their taste is similar to that of a sweet potato, and they are cooked and served in the same way as salsify.

skirret pie, an 18-century Irish dish of cooked skirret seasoned with cinnamon, nutmeg, and salt, sprinkled with sugar, dotted with bone marrow and butter, and then covered with preserved gooseberries, grapes, and barberries. Finally the top is covered with a layer of flaky pastry and the pie is baked for 30 minutes.

skirt, an old English name for flank of beef. It was often stuffed, rolled, and tied, then casseroled slowly with onions and stock. It was served either hot or cold; if cold, it was usually pressed overnight.

skirts and bodices, a local name in County Cork, Ireland, for fluted trimmings of pork and pickled spareribs of bacon, which look like old-fashioned boned bodices. They are often stewed with pork and pork kidneys, root vegetables, and herbs. Traditionally, they are eaten with potatoes boiled in their skins and mashed turnips or parsnips.

skiver pan, a special pan sold in Scandinavian stores in the U.S. for cooking a round fried cake, especially *ebleskiver*. It has about seven rounded hollows in it, which are greased before the cake batter is dropped into them.

skordalia, a Bulgarian sauce, like the Greek *skorthalia,* usually served with fried eggplant. First 1 medium-sized eggplant per person should be washed, salted, and left to drain; they are then dried and sliced, dipped in flour and fried. A sauce is made by mixing 2 cups mashed potato with 6 crushed garlic cloves, then adding a mixture of 3 cups oil (preferably the oil used for first frying the eggplants) and ½ cup vinegar, stirring constantly. The sauce is served as a separate accompaniment to the eggplants. It is also served with courgettes (zucchini).

skórka, Polish for peel. *Skórka Pomarańczowa w Cukrze* is candied orange peel which is used a lot in cakes and puddings.

skorthalia or **skordalia,** one of the classical Greek sauces, eaten with many meat, vegetable, and fish dishes, particularly with salted fish. There are several variations of the basic sauce, but its essential ingredients are garlic, lemon, and usually nuts such as walnuts, almonds, pistachios, pignoli, etc. It derives from *skortho,* Greek for garlic.

skorthalia me amygdalia, skorthalia with almonds. First 1 medium-sized cooked potato is crushed and added while still hot to a mixture of 8 garlic cloves pounded with 1 cup ground almonds. When well blended, 1½ gills (¾ cup) olive oil and the juice of 1 lemon are added alternately, drop by drop, until a stiff sauce is obtained. This can be done in a blender.

skorthalia me fystikia, a variation which includes 1 cup soaked white bread instead of the potato, and pistachio nuts instead of almonds, but which is otherwise prepared as above. Pignoli can be used instead of pistachio nuts.

skorthalia me karidia, skorthalia with walnuts. A mixture of 6 garlic cloves pounded with 1 lb. walnuts is added to 10 slices crustless bread which have first been soaked in water and squeezed. This mixture is again well pounded. Then ½ pint (1 cup) olive oil is gradually added, alternately with ¼ pint (½ cup) lemon juice, the sauce being beaten well after each addition. Finally ½ pint (1 cup) tepid-to-warm water is beaten in.

skorthalia me patates, skorthalia with potatoes. As *skorthalia me amygdalia,* but with 6 medium-sized cooked potatoes pounded with 6 garlic cloves, then 1½ gills (¾ cup) oil and juice of 2 lemons added in the typical manner. Finally the sauce is diluted with a little fish or meat stock, depending on the kind of dish it is to accompany.

skorthalia me yaletta, as *skorthalia me amygdalia,* but using 2 cups soft breadcrumbs (or 1 cup flour) moistened with water and squeezed, instead of potatoes or bread. This is pounded with 8 garlic cloves, and 1½ gills (¾ cup) olive oil and juice of 1 lemon are added in the usual manner. Nuts are added if desired.

skrei, a very large cod from Lofoten in Norway, which is excellent when eaten between February and the end of April. It is usually poached and served with mustard sauce.

skum saus (froth or foam sauce), a Norwegian sauce which is served hot with steamed puddings, and cold with various fruit desserts. First ½ pint (1 cup) cream is stirred into 6 beaten egg yolks, and the mixture is heated in a double-boiler. Then 1 heaped tablespoon castor sugar is added, and when this is dissolved, grated peel of ½ lemon and 2 tablespoons sherry are stirred in. The mixture is whipped until it is thick and foamy. It is sometimes coloured pink with a few drops of cochineal.

sky, a Danish meat and vegetable jelly or aspic, used for garnishing a meat *smørrebrød.* A knuckle of beef, onion, root vegetables, parsley, thyme, bay leaf, and seasoning are all simmered for 4–5 hours, then strained, clarified, and chilled until jellied.

sky-blue and sinkers, a traditional Cornish recipe. Water was boiled in the three-legged "crock" over a brush fire of gorse and turf. Barley meal and scalded milk were mixed together and poured into the boiling water, then all boiled for a couple of minutes before being poured into basins in which sops of barley bread had been placed. These rose, and then immediately sank to the bottom of the light-blue liquid; hence the picturesque name of "sky blue and sinkers." The dish was always eaten with an iron spoon.

skyr, a traditional Icelandic dish made from soured skimmed milk. It is similar to a thin cottage cheese or yogourt and is served with sugar and cream or bilberries as a dessert.

Skyros, a Greek island cheese made from ewe's milk. It is of the Gruyère type, but inferior in quality. However, it is considered better than the Greek *kefalotyri.* See also TYRI.

sla, Dutch for lettuce, and for salad. When in season, salads are usually served for the *Hollandse koffietafel;* cucumber, lettuce, radish, and tomato are all popular. See also SALAD.

slasaus, a Dutch dressing for a green salad. Seasoning and a pinch each of sugar and mustard are added to a mashed

hard-boiled egg. Then 4 tablespoons oil and 1½ tablespoons vinegar (or juice of ½ lemon) are blended in gradually, together with a little shredded leek or 1 spring onion (scallion). The dressing is then mixed with the lettuce, and the salad is served immediately.

slake, to, a former English culinary term meaning to liquefy corn flour (cornstarch) or arrowroot with a little water (2 tablespoons are enough for 2 teaspoons corn flour). In this way, when corn flour (cornstarch) is needed to thicken a sauce, soup, or stew, it can be added to the liquid without the risk of lumps forming, and will amalgamate easily with it after a little gentle stirring. In modern culinary works this action is referred to as "creaming" or "dissolving." These terms describe the process well, for the corn flour (cornstarch) and water blend to a cream-like consistency.

slatko, a Serbian jam or preserve made from raspberries or strawberries or watermelon rind, which is served in all Balkan countries, especially Yugoslavia, with a glass of water. Later black coffee is offered to the guest, and if he overstays his welcome a second cup is proffered, which is considered the signal to leave.

slaw, see COLE SLAW.

śledzie, Polish for salted herring. See also HERRING.

śledzie nadziewane, 4 salted herrings stuffed with the chopped roes, chopped milts and 1 small onion, rolled in breadcrumbs and then fried in hot butter.

śledzie z śmietanie, salted herrings first soaked in water, drained, and then marinated in cream to cover mixed with wine vinegar to taste. They are then served raw.

sleeve-fish, an English name for *calamary.*

slemp, a Dutch spiced drink made for children in Holland on St. Nicholas's Night, when it is served with *appelbeignets* and *oliebollen.* (See also SINT NICOLAAS AVOND.) A pinch each of cloves, saffron, and mace, and a cinnamon stick, are tied in a bag, placed in a pan of 2 pints (4 cups) scalded milk and simmered for about 30 minutes. Sugar is then added to taste, and also 2 tablespoons corn flour (cornstarch) which have been dissolved in a little water. The drink is cooked for about 5 minutes longer, when the bag of spices is removed.

slim cake, a traditional plain Manx fruit cake, made from 1 lb. (4 cups) plain flour, 4 oz. (½ cup) lard, 2 oz. (½ cup) currants, 2 oz. (¼ cup) sugar, 2 teaspoons baking powder, a pinch of salt, and ¼ pint (½ cup) milk. The fat is rubbed into the flour and then the other ingredients are added. All is well mixed, then rolled out thinly to 1-inch thickness and cooked on a griddle or in a large heavy pan.

ślimaki, Polish for snails. See also SNAILS.

ślimaki smażone, snails first boiled, then drained, rolled in egg and breadcrumbs and fried in butter.

slip sole, a common English name for a small sole weighing under ½ lb.

slipcote or **slipcoat,** the name given to a stilton cheese that bursts its shape and spills down in a soft mass after moulding. These cheeses are eaten straight away. See also CREAM CHEESE.

slipper, a wedge-shaped English cut of pork or ham from the corner of the fillet.

sliva, Russian for plum. See also PLUM.

marinnovanye slivi i vishni, pickled ripe plums. They are cooked first in an earthenware pot with very little water, then the juice is strained off, mixed with 2 tablespoons vinegar (to 1 pint juice) and sugar to taste, then boiled until the sugar has dissolved. When cool, the solution is poured over the plums and the pot is covered tightly and stored. These plums are served with cooked game.

sloe (*Prunus spinosa*), the small purplish fruit of the blackthorn. It is extremely bitter and is mainly used in the British

Isles to flavour the excellent liqueur known as sloe gin. In the Haute-Saône region of France there is a cultivated sloe which makes excellent jam.

sloke, an Irish and Scottish word for laver. After simmering with water for 3–4 hours, the laver becomes soft and jelly-like, and can be stored in jars. Fishermen used to take a supply to sea with them, to eat with oatcakes or bannocks. It has a delicate taste, not unlike a very mild anchovy.

slokan, a traditional recipe from the Isle of Barra. The sloke is washed well and simmered with water until it becomes jelly-like. This jelly is beaten (but not cooked again) over heat with a very little seawater, pepper, and butter, then served hot with mashed potatoes.

sloke sauce, also known in fashionable circles as marine sauce. The laver jelly is seasoned well and flavoured with Seville orange juice. It is heated and served with roast mutton.

slot, Shetland Island fish liver dumplings, made from skinned cod's roe and ¼ of a ling liver. They are beaten together, with barley meal to bind, salt, and pepper. Spoonfuls are dropped into boiling fish stock and cooked for 30 minutes. These little dumplings are served with fresh boiled fish.

sly cakes, a traditional Cornish recipe. Flaky pastry is rolled out thinly, then half of it is covered with a mixture of currants and chopped candied peel, and the other half is folded over this and lightly rolled. The top is sprinkled with sugar, and then the pasty is cut into different shapes which are baked in a moderate-to-hot oven for 20 minutes or until golden.

små köttbullar, very small Swedish pork meat balls, used for smörgåsbord. See also KÖTT (KÖTTBULLAR).

småkager, Danish for small cakes or biscuits.

småkaker, see KJEKS.

small salad, an old-fashioned American name given to watercress and white mustard when they are used as a salad or for a sandwich.

smallage, an old English name for wild celery.

smelt (Osmeridae), a small silvery fish, called éperlan in France because of the pearly sheen of its skin. It is found in both salt and fresh water, as it is a migratory fish which goes to fresh water to spawn. Freshly caught smelts have a lovely smell reminiscent of violets and cucumber, and they are delicious gutted, rolled in flour, quickly fried, and served with lemon. In France they are sometimes skewered first through the head (about 6 to a skewer) before frying. They can also be pickled, and in Spain are used in *escabèches.* In Scotland they are known as sparling or sperling. They are found in the Atlantic and the Pacific as well as in European waters, and on these coasts the very small young smelts are cooked like whitebait. See also KORYUSHKI.

smelt

smetana, Russian for sour cream, used extensively in Russia both for cooking and for sauces and garnishes. See also SOUR CREAM.

smetanik, a sweet pie. A mixture of ½ lb. pounded almonds combined with a few spoonfuls of cherry and raspberry jam, 1 egg yolk, 1 cup sour cream, and a pinch of cinnamon is put into a pastry case, covered with more pastry and baked until brown.

smetane, sauce, see SMITANE.

śmietana, Polish for sour cream, often used in Poland for sauces to accompany meat, game, poultry, fish, and vegetables. See also SOUR CREAM.

smitane, sauce, a classical French sauce of Russian origin. It is made with 1 finely chopped onion lightly browned in butter, and a full glass (½ cup) of dry white wine is added. This mixture is reduced by simmering to half the original volume, when 1 pint (2 cups) sour cream is stirred in and the sauce is boiled for a few moments. It is then passed through a fine sieve (*chinois*), and juice of 1 lemon is added. In Russia it would then be seasoned with *kabul* sauce, a piquant, commercially bottled Russian sauce which is used for flavouring sauces and salads. See also KABUL SAUCE.

smoke, to, to treat a food with salt and then put it into a chamber over wood-smoke. Small, portable smoking cabinets are now available for home smoking. Bacon and ham are so treated, *prosciutto.* Many fish are smoked, particularly haddock (finnan haddie), salmon, trout, and sometimes turkey. See TURKEY, SMOKED.

smolt, the name for a salmon when it is about two years old and first goes to the sea. It is no longer a parr but not yet a grilse. At this stage it is 4–8 inches long and is protected by law. See SALMON.

smör, Swedish for butter. Butter is used extensively in Swedish cooking. Margarine is rarely, if ever, used as a substitute, except for those margarines that are specially prepared from vegetable oils for people susceptible to coronary attack or arterial disease.

smørbrød (buttered bread), Norwegian for the open sandwiches which are an integral part of eating in Norway. Bread spread with *gjeitost* or pickled fish, jam, or marmalade is eaten at breakfast. Bread and butter covered with a variety of cold meats is served at luncheon, and the same, although more elaborately prepared and frequently set in aspic, can sometimes appear at the supper table.

smörgåsar, Swedish for sandwiches, which are very popular in Sweden. Almost all savoury foods are used for fillings. Sometimes the sandwiches are open, sometimes toasted. Much care goes into their garnishing.

smörgåsbord, the Swedish "cold table," or hors d'oeuvre. In time past, it was customary in the country districts of Sweden for guests to bring some food with them as a contribution to the cold table or smörgåsbord. The tradition of smörgåsbord is still carried on, although now the guests are no longer expected to contribute. Luncheons and dinners in Sweden are usually preceded by herring salad and cheese, or open sandwiches, or perhaps pickled herrings with bread and butter. On festive occasions such as Christmas, the smörgåsbord is laid out in greater variety and includes preserved and pickled meat or fish, and sometimes a choice of hot foods as well (see *julskinka*). The Swedes give a great deal of care and thought to the presentation of the food, often garnishing it most elaborately. See also BÖCKLING; HORS D'OEUVRE; KOLDTBORD.

smørrebrød, Danish for open sandwiches. The word means "butter on bread," and rye bread, pumpernickel, or wheat bread is buttered or spread with *krydderfedt,* then topped with fish, meat, eggs, and cheeses of all varieties. There are nearly 1,000 different kinds of smørrebrød, and it differs from hors d'oeuvre in that it is not only eaten at home, but is also taken to work for lunch, or on a picnic. *Smørrebrød* is an essential part of any meal in Denmark, served either as first course or as a whole meal, depending on the number of variations prepared.

snack, something cooked simply and eaten quickly in place of a meal, such as a sandwich, a sausage roll, or eggs cooked in a plain fashion. A snack can be hot or cold and may not necessarily be cooked at all. The word comes from the Middle Dutch "snacken," to snap up or snap at.

smørrebrød

snail (*Helix pomatia; H. aspersa*), an edible mollusc which lives on dry land. Snails were immensely popular as food with the Romans, who introduced *H. pomatia* into Great Britain. They are still traditional food in the west of England, especially in the area round the Mendip hills, where they are known as "wallfish." They used to be roasted over braziers by workmen, and were also sold in the public-houses. Until early in this century, the glassmen of Newcastle-on-Tyne had an annual snail feast, collecting the snails on the Sunday beforehand. *H. pomatia* is the snail most commonly eaten, but *H. aspersa* is in fact more succulent, although smaller. In the 17th and 18th centuries snails were thought in England to be good for people suffering from a "decline" and for backward children, and a snail soup was administered to them. Until a few years ago snail soup was drunk by some Somerset miners as a precaution against silicosis. In the London Gazette of March 23, 1739, there was a long account of a £5,000 award being made to a Mrs. Joanna Stephens for her tried and approved pills made from calcined snail- and egg-shells mixed with fat and honey. However, snails are far more popular on the continent of Europe, especially France, than in Britain. They have the advantage of being permitted food on abstinence days in Catholic countries. See also ESCARGOT; LUMACHE; SCHNECKEN; ŚLIMAKI.

Mendip snails. The snails are immersed for 36 hours in salt water, then drained and put into boiling water for 5 minutes, then into fresh boiling water for the same time. This serves to wash and rinse the snails. They are now ready to be simmered slowly for 4 hours in a court bouillon of 2 pints water, 1 pint cider or white wine, bay leaves, tarragon, onions, carrots, cloves, salt, and pepper. They are then cooled on a wire rack, mouth down. A sauce is then made. Proportions for 3 dozen snails are ½ lb. (1 cup) butter, 2 tablespoons grated cheddar cheese, 2 tablespoons cream, and herbs—usually 1 teaspoon each of dill, fennel, chervil, chives, and balm, all finely chopped. This mixture is gently warmed and beaten, although it is not allowed to become oily. The snails are nearly, but not quite, pulled out of their shells, and the sauce is forced in with a small spoon; then the stuffed snails are either grilled or put into a hot oven for a few minutes. They are served in their shells. An excellent snail consommé is also made from the court bouillon with more vegetables and herbs added. These recipes are constantly used at the "Miner's Arms" restaurant, Priddy, Somerset. See also ESCARGOT.

snake root (*Aristolochia serpentaria*), an alpine grass with intertwining snake-like roots. The young leaves can be used in the same way as spinach.

snap bean, see FRENCH BEAN.

snapper, I. The English name for different varieties of the same genus (*Mesoprion*) of a sea fish found in the Atlantic. It makes very good eating, and can be cooked in the same way as bass. II. The name given in the U.S. to several varieties of a popular sea fish (*Lutianidae*). See RED SNAPPER. III. The name given in the U.S. to a freshwater turtle (*Chelydra serpentina*). See also SOFT SHELL TURTLE; TERRAPIN.

snapper soup, made in the same way as a good beef soup, with diced, assorted fresh vegetables and herbs added to the snapper (turtle) meat, and thickened with either cream or egg yolk.

snapper stew. The turtle is first plunged into boiling water, so that the horny skin can be peeled off. It is simmered with water, butter, and herbs until tender, then sherry is added to taste, and cream and egg yolks to thicken. If the snapper is bearing eggs, they are added last and just heated through.

sneboller (*snowballs*), Danish cakes which are deep fried, like doughnuts. First 2 oz. (¼ cup) butter is melted in a saucepan, and 4½ oz. (1¼ cups) flour is added gradually to it until frothy. Then ½ pint (1 cup) water is added. When the mixture leaves the sides of the pan, it is removed from the heat and 3 eggs are added to give a dough-like consistency. The mixture is then shaped into balls which are fried in deep fat and then dredged with icing sugar.

šnicle, a word derived from German *schnitzel,* and used generally in Yugoslavia for any thin fillet of meat.

teleče šnicle sa belim lukom, veal escalopes (scallops) fried in oil with garlic.

uvijene svinjske šnicle s miselim kupusom, pork fillets stuffed with sauerkraut, rolled up, and secured before being fried in oil.

snipe (*Scolopacidae*), the name given to a large family of small game birds which includes the common snipe, great snipe, jack snipe, and dowitcher or red-breasted snipe. The common snipe (*Capella gallinago*) is found all over the world and is considered a delicacy in Great Britain and Europe. It has a delicious flavour and weighs between 2 oz. and 10 oz. A young tender bird is recognizable by its soft feet (they thicken with age), downy feathers under the wing, and pointed flight feathers. If the bill is moist and the throat muddy, the bird has been dead for some time. Snipe must be handled carefully because of their delicate flesh. They should be skinned by having the wings and head cut off and the skin rubbed gently away from the breast—the feathers and skin should come away easily, like a jacket. Snipe are not drawn, the tail being secured with skewers before cooking.

snipe

Perhaps snipe is most delicious when cooked straight after it has been shot. The skinned birds are rubbed with butter and grilled, either under a grill or over an open fire of peat or charcoal. Snipe is always served rare. It can be roasted, when cooking time is 15 minutes in a hot oven, or made into a *salmi,* or prepared in any way that is suitable for woodcock or corncrake. See also BÉCASSINE; BEKASY; BEKKASIN.

snittebønner, Norwegian for green beans, both runner beans and french beans.

snitter (*titbits*), a Danish word for small snacks, like hors d'oeuvre, eaten at buffet parties.

snöbollar, Swedish biscuits (cookies) rather like macaroons. First 2 oz. (¼ cup) melted butter, 8 oz. (1 cup) fine sugar, 4 oz. (1 cup) flour, and 4 oz. (1 cup) ground almonds are mixed with vanilla essence (extract), and 3 stiffly beaten egg whites. The mixture is formed into balls which are rolled in icing sugar before being dried out in a slow oven for 30 minutes.

snoek, Dutch for pike. The Dutch cook has a way of dealing with the many small bones which are always present in this fish. After cutting the fish lengthwise and cleaning it, she lets it stand overnight, covered with a mixture of vinegar and water. By morning most of the small bones have dissolved. See also PIKE.

snoek balletjs, pike dumplings, made from 3 cups pounded or minced cooked pike, mixed with 2 thick slices of crustless bread moistened in milk, ½ cup minced smoked eel or salmon, 2 eggs, salt, and pepper, all well blended and formed into 1-inch balls. These are poached in boiling water for 10 minutes, drained, and served sprinkled with chopped parsley and covered with melted butter. Boiled potatoes are served separately.

snoek in witte wijn saus, pike with a white wine sauce. The fish is cut into serving pieces which are arranged in the original shape of the fish in a casserole. To prepare it 1 large sliced onion, 1 tablespoon parsley, 1 head chopped celery, and a pinch of nutmeg and mace are seasoned and gently fried in butter, then added to the casserole. White wine and water are added barely to cover, and the contents of the casserole are topped with breadcrumbs and slices of lemon. The fish is baked in a moderate oven for about 30 minutes or until tender. A white sauce is made, consisting of 1 tablespoon butter, 2 tablespoons flour, and 1 pint (2 cups) of the fish liquid; then 2 tablespoons capers are added, the sauce is removed from the heat, and 2 beaten egg yolks are stirred in. The sauce is either served separately or poured over the pike.

snow partridge, the English name for *arbenne.*

snowshoe rabbit, see HARE.

sobronade, a country soup from the Périgord region of France. It is made from ½ lb. diced pork, both salt and fresh, cooked until the fat runs out and the cubes are golden. Then ½ lb. soaked dried beans, 6 carrots, 2 onions, 1 lb. potatoes, 3 leeks, and 1 head celery (all chopped except the beans) are added, together with several quarts of water, and the soup is simmered until it is quite thick. See also SOUPE.

socarat, the Catalan word for any lumps of rice found sticking to the bottom of the paella pan after the paella has been dished up. These are considered a delicacy, and are usually given to the most honoured guest.

socca, coarse thick pancakes from Nice, made from chick-pea flour. They are fried in oil and vendors sell them hot, from street barrows.

sočivo salata, a Yugoslavian salad of cooked lentils, covered with a dressing of olive oil, vinegar, garlic, salt, and paprika.

socker, Swedish for sugar.

sockerstruvor, a kind of Swedish waffle, cooked on a special iron waffle-mould in the shape of a rosette. The batter is made from 2 whole eggs and 1 yolk beaten with ¼ pint (½ cup) thick double cream, into which 4 oz. (1 cup) flour mixed with 2½ oz. (¼ cup) sugar is gradually beaten. The batter is covered and left to stand for 2 hours. The waffle-iron is heated in hot oil, drained, then quickly dipped in the batter and gently lowered into the oil again. The waffles are cooked until golden, then drained and filled with jam or cream.

sockeye, see PACIFIC SALMON.

socle, a solid shape of cooked and pounded rice, used as a base or pediment for elaborate cold foods so that they were raised up above the dish in which they stood and formed an attractive centrepiece. These pediments were made in various shapes and were sometimes covered with silver paper. They were not intended to be eaten. They are seldom seen nowadays, except at very formal banquets, but were in frequent use before WW I.

soda, see BICARBONATE OF SODA.

soda bread, the traditional bread of Ireland, still baked in many farmhouses all over the country and also made by commercial bakeries. It is simple to make and delicious to eat. Every housewife has her own recipe, and no two agree on exact quantities; nevertheless, it is universally good all over the country. In remote country districts, particularly in County Cork, it is baked in a *bastable oven* and for this reason is also called bastable cake. The leaven used is bicarbonate of soda or baking soda, and buttermilk or soured milk is generally used for mixing. Fresh milk can also be used, but in this case a pinch of cream of tartar should be added to the ingredients. Soda bread can be made from wholemeal or white flour, or a mixture of the two. All soda bread must be baked within about 13 minutes of mixing the dough, otherwise the baking soda loses its effect. If an oven is not available, the mixture can be rolled to a thickness of 1 inch and cooked on a griddle, allowing 10–15 minutes for each side.

For one loaf measuring about 10 inches across, 1 oz. (2 tablespoons) butter is rubbed into 1 lb. 3 oz. (4¼ cups) flour, with 1 teaspoon each of salt and baking soda; then about ½ pint (1 cup) buttermilk or sour milk is added, and well mixed in with a wooden spoon to form a soft dough. This is turned onto a floured board or table, kneaded lightly, and formed into a flat circle about 1½ inches thick. A cross is cut on top, to ensure even cooking. The dough is baked in a moderate-to-hot oven for about 35 minutes. When taken from the oven the bread is cooled a little, then wrapped in a damp tea-cloth and left standing upright for 6–8 hours until it has set. (The dough may be formed into small squares instead of a single large loaf, in which case these are baked for about 20 minutes and are served hot, split, with butter. They are called "white cakes.") A variation of the recipe given above includes a handful of washed sultanas, or, for special occasions, chopped glacé cherries. See also BREAD; DOUGH; YEAST DOUGH.

brown soda bread, made with twice the quantity of wholemeal flour to white flour—that is, 1 lb. 3 oz. (4¼ cups) wholemeal to 9½ oz. (2½ cups) white flour—and 1 oz. (2 tablespoons) butter (this can be omitted, but it makes the bread "short" or crisp), 1½ teaspoons baking soda and salt, and 1 pint (2 cups) buttermilk or sour milk. It is cooked in the same way as the white loaf (above).

golden drop, a soda bread made with 9½ oz. (2½ cups) corn meal and 9½ oz. (2½ cups) white flour mixed with 1 teaspoon salt and 1 teaspoon baking soda. The ingredients are made into a dough with ½ pint (1 cup) buttermilk or sour milk, and it is baked in the same way as the other varieties of soda bread.

treacle soda bread, a soda bread made for children, using fresh milk, and heating 2 tablespoons treacle (molasses) in it with the cream of tartar.

soep, Dutch for soup. Many Dutch soups are garnished with meat balls and vegetables. Chopped smoked sausage such as *rookworst* is also used as a garnish, especially with dried pea soup. Vegetable water is used as a basis for many soups made from fresh and dried vegetables, some of which are flavoured with curry powder. Herbs, especially chervil and parsley, are used a great deal. The most traditional Dutch soup is made from eel. Some soups are considered to constitute a whole meal, as they are extremely substantial, such as *erwtensoep, bruine bonensoep, palingsoep*. See also SOUP.

soep balletjes, meat balls for garnishing soup, made with 2 slices of crustless bread soaked in a little milk, then mixed with ½ lb. finely minced beef or veal, 1 egg, and seasoning of salt, pepper, and a pinch of nutmeg. The mixture is rolled into tiny balls which are poached in the hot soup. If desired, 2 teaspoons curry powder can be added.

soffritto, another name for *battuto*.

sofrito, Greek for steak cooked in a garlic sauce, a speciality of Corfu, and an excellent way of using slightly tough meat. Rump steak is beaten and flattened, and then slits are made on the surface. The steak is rolled in flour and fried in butter, then more flour is sprinkled over it, followed by a generous amount of chopped garlic. When the garlic becomes golden, either red or white wine, with a dash of vinegar, is poured over barely to cover and is brought to the boil. It is seasoned, and a little hot water is added if the sauce is too thick; then the whole is simmered or casseroled slowly until the meat is tender. See also KREAS.

soft roe, the milt or sperm of the male fish. See ROE.

soft shell crabs, see CRAB.

soft shell turtle (*Trionychidae*), a turtle which lives in slow-running rivers and in lakes and ponds in the Mississippi Valley, in the region of the Great Lakes, and in Africa and Asia. The carapace and plastron are covered with a soft skin, and it has paddle-shaped forelimbs. These turtles feed on fish and molluscs, which gives them strong jaws. The meat is of excellent flavour, and can be prepared in the same way as snapper, and also cooked with noodles. The eggs are particularly sought after as food. See also SNAPPER; TERRAPIN; TURTLE.

sogan dolma, a dish of stuffed onions from Bosnia and Hercegovina. The centres of large onions are removed, the cavities filled with minced (ground) meat and rice, and the stuffed onions are then braised in stock for 1½ hours.

sogliola, Italian for sole. In southern Italy it is called solua or solva. See also SOLE.

sogliole alla veneziana, a famous Venetian dish of sole. Fillets of sole are grilled with a mixture of 4 oz. (½ cup) butter, 1 tablespoon chopped mint and parsley, with a little garlic pressed into incisions made along the fish. They are served with a sauce made from 1 large sliced onion sautéed in butter, with ¼ pint (½ cup) white wine, ¼ pint (½ cup) water, and seasoning, all reduced and poured over the fillets. Marsala wine is sometimes cooked with sautéed sole in Italy.

soir, a famous Estonian cheese made from sour milk curd and flavoured with caraway seeds.

soissonnaise, à la, I. A French garnish for mutton, consisting of large cooked white haricot beans mixed with tomato sauce with a little garlic. II. A purée of haricot beans mixed with cream, butter, and thin tomato sauce. See also SOLE.

sola, Polish for sole. See also SOLE.

sola na białem winie, sole braised in white wine. The fish is first cooked for 20 to 30 minutes with ½ pint (1 cup) white wine, 1 tablespoon butter, ½ pint (1 cup) broth, and 6 sliced mushrooms; when cooked, the sole is put onto a warmed dish and kept hot. Then 2 tablespoons more butter is melted, and 1 heaped tablespoon flour is added; the fish stock, first gently heated, is stirred in gradually, and finally 2 lightly beaten egg yolks are added, heated, but not allowed to boil. This sauce is poured over the fish before serving.

sola zapiekanka, the fish is barely covered in sour cream which has been mixed with 1 teaspoon flour, then sprinkled with breadcrumbs and grated Parmesan cheese, dotted with butter, and baked for 30 minutes.

solan goose, see GANNET.

soldaatjes (little soldiers), fingers of fried bread served in Holland with spinach and various other dishes.

sole (*Solea solea*), a flat fish found off all coasts of Europe. It can weigh up to several pounds, but 1–2 lb. is the usual weight. Soles caught in the English Channel are considered the best, and are known as Dover soles. The same fish is called "black sole" in Ireland, to distinguish it from lemon sole, Torbay sole, witch sole, and megrim, which are more inferior flat fish. Sole keeps quite well, and in fact is sometimes more tasty if it is kept for a few days before cooking. The flesh is firm and white, and has a definite and pleasant flavour. It is excellent brushed with oil or butter, plainly grilled on the bone, and served with *beurre maître d'hôtel*. The side bones are easily detached, and the backbone is firm and strong so that flesh can be scraped from it without difficulty. Sole is often filleted, poached in white wine, and served with sauce mornay, mushrooms, or spinach. Sometimes the fillets are stuffed with forcemeat before cooking. It can also be prepared in many other ways. It is one of the most important fishes used as food, and can be served with almost all the classical French sauces for fish. Sole roes are very deli-

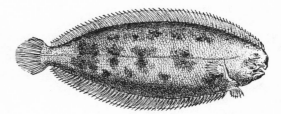

black sole

cate in flavour, and should be cooked and used as a garnish. The true sole is not to be found in North American waters and is not sold in the U.S., but flounder is often used in its place. See also SJØTUNGE; SOGLIOLA; SOLA; SOLE; SOTUNGE; TONG.

sole, the same word in French as in English. Classical French garnishes and sauces which are ideal for sole are américaine, *ancienne, bercy, cancalaise, colbert, daumont, dauphine, dieppoise, florentine,* meunière, mornay, *nantua, normande, véronique, walewska*.

paupiettes de sole, fillets of sole spread with forcemeat made from whiting or some other fish, then rolled up and poached very gently in fish stock with white wine.

sole sur le plat, sole left on the bone, but with the fillets slightly loosened, seasoned with butter, salt, and pepper, and then baked with ½ cup fish stock or fumet, dots of butter, and lemon juice. The fish is basted frequently so that it develops a golden glaze.

solilem, see SOLIMEME.

solimeme or *solilem,* an Alsatian cake made with yeast. First ½ oz. yeast is made into a batter with 4 tablespoons tepid water and 4 oz. (1 cup) flour, then covered and left in a warm place to prove. To this are added 2 eggs, ½ gill (¼ cup) cream, and 12 oz. (3 cups) flour, and all are kneaded well. Then gradually 4 oz. (½ cup) soft butter, 2 more eggs, and ½ gill (¼ cup) more cream are mixed in, and the dough is beaten. It should be fairly soft; if still stiff, a little more cream should be added. It is poured into a round greased tin to halfway up its sides, covered, and left to rise for 1 hour. The cake is then baked in a moderate oven for 1 hour, turned out, and cut horizontally into two halves which are spread with warm salted butter and then sandwiched together. It is served hot or warm.

solomon's seal (*Polygonatum officinale*), a favourite garden plant of the lily family. The young shoots may be eaten in the same way as asparagus.

soltetees or *soltys,* a medieval cake with a surprise filling. It was an edible joke, and the lines from the old nursery rhyme:

". . . four-and-twenty blackbirds baked in a pie;
When the pie was opened, the birds began to sing . . ."

describe a dish of this kind. It was part of the fun of a banquet, and was paraded about before being carved up. Soltetees comes from the Latin *saltare,* to jump, and ingenuity on the part of the cooks was of greater importance than the excellence of the food.

solua, see SOGLIOLA.

solyanka, a Russian stew. Its name comes from the Russian word for salt, and it is made from approximately 2 lb. fish, game, or meat with various vegetables—perhaps 1 lb. sauerkraut, ¼ lb. mushrooms, 1 large onion, dill pickle, or 1 large sliced salted cucumber—and at least ½ lb. (1 cup) butter. The ingredients are all put in layers in a casserole and baked until golden brown. This version is called solyanka po Moskovsky (Moscow solyanka), but different variations exist in many parts of Russia. See also KAPUSTA.

solyanka ribnaya, a traditional Russian fish soup–stew, made with 2 sliced onions fried in oil, then 2 pints (4 cups) fish stock and ¼ pint (½ cup) juice from pickled cucumbers is added. The soup is garnished with small pieces of sterlet or sturgeon which have been poached in the stock, strips of pickled cucumber, marinated mushrooms, capers, and peeled sliced lemons, and is sprinkled with chopped dill. Black olives and *rastegai* are served separately.

somborski sir, a local Yugoslavian cheese, eaten with slices of raw onion or gherkins.

sonhos, a national Portuguese sweet dough. To prepare it ½ pint (1 cup) water is heated with 4 oz. (½ cup) butter and 2 oz. sugar, and when boiling, 5 oz. (1¼ cups) flour is quickly mixed in, and the whole removed from the heat and beaten until cold. Then 4 eggs are added one by one, and spoonfuls of the mixture are dropped into hot oil and fried until puffy and golden. They are eaten hot with sugar and cinnamon sprinkled over them. The name means "dreams."

sopa, Portuguese for soup. See also AÇORDA; CALDO; SOUP.

sopa de agriões, watercress soup thickened with potato purée.

sopa de hortaliça, mixed vegetable soup.

sopa de mariscos, a soup of shellfish, tomatoes, pimentos, and rice.

sopa, Spanish for soup. Spanish soups are very varied, many constituting almost a meal in themselves. The hot fish soups are particularly good, and many cold soups are also made. See also CALDO; POTAJE; SOUP.

gazpacho andaluz, an iced purée made with 1 lb. very finely chopped raw tomatoes, 1 small cucumber, 2 green or red sweet peppers, and 2 cloves garlic, mixed with 4 tablespoons olive oil and 1 tablespoon wine vinegar. It is particularly good on a hot day. Sometimes shrimps or diced *chorizo* are added; also 1 cup fresh breadcrumbs—but this depends on the ripeness of the tomatoes. Croûtons of fried bread are served separately. If served hot, this soup is called *gazpacho colorado* (red *gazpacho*). This soup is also common to Portugal, but is spelt *gaspacho* in Portuguese.

sopa de ajo, see AJO, SOPA DE.

sopa de pescados, a fish soup made from about 2 lb. bream, whiting, hake, etc. The fish is fried in oil with 1 lb. tomatoes, 4 onions, 2 red sweet peppers, 2 garlic cloves, and parsley. All are covered with boiling water and sprinkled with breadcrumbs, then 2 tablespoons chopped almonds and hazelnuts are stirred in. The soup is simmered until reduced by two-thirds.

sopa wilfredo, a traditional soup, made from ½ lb. chopped onions and 3 green peppers fried in olive oil, then crushed garlic and 1 tablespoon tomato purée are stirred in, followed by 3 pints (6 cups) white stock, salt, and a pinch of cinnamon. The soup is bound with 2 egg yolks and garnished with slices of *morcilla* and croûtons.

soppa, Swedish for soup, which is very popular in Sweden. Many soups have pork or fish stock as a base and much use is made of fresh herbs, spices, and cream. Clear soups often have dumplings or meat balls as a garnish. Traditional soups include *ärter och fläsk* and *nässelkål.* See also SOUP.

tisdagssoppa, Tuesday soup, made from 2 tablespoons pearl barley simmered in 2 pints (4 cups) pork stock until tender, when diced root vegetables—2 carrots, 1 turnip, 1 parsnip, ½ celeriac, and 4 potatoes—are added. When all are cooked, 1 pint (2 cups) milk is added, with seasoning to taste. Finally ¼ pint (½ cup) cream is stirred in gradually just before serving, but the soup is not reboiled.

soppes, see SIPPETS.

soppresso, a pork and beef salame (salami), sold in Padua, Verona, and the Veneto. See SALAME.

sorbais, le, a French cow's milk cheese of the *maroilles* type, from the Ardennes. In season from September to May.

sorbapple, I. The fruit of the service tree. II. An alternative name for the service tree itself.

sorbet, see GRANITA; ICES.

sorges, sauce, a sauce from the Périgord region of France, served with *poulet farci à la mode de sorges.* It consists of 1 pint (2 cups) highly seasoned sauce vinaigrette with 3 chopped spring onions (scallions), 2 shallots, and parsley added, bound with the yolks of 2 soft-boiled eggs. The egg whites are recooked, diced, and added last of all.

sorrel (*Rumex acetosa*), a perennial herb with many varieties. The leaves of all contain oxalate of potash in varying amounts, which imparts the characteristic acid taste. Wood sorrel (*Oxalis acetosella*) and mountain sorrel (*Oxyria digyna*) are the sharpest-tasting; the French sorrel (*Rumex scutatus*) is the mildest. The latter is eaten uncooked in salads. Other varieties are best cooked and puréed and are served particularly with veal fricandeau, sweetbreads, or fish. The purée is made by cooking 2 lb. washed damp sorrel without water (like spinach, it reduces enormously in cooking). Then a roux blond is added, with about ½ cup stock, pepper, salt, and a pinch of sugar. This is covered and put in a moderate oven for 30 minutes, then sieved, and after that reheated on top of the stove. Then 2 egg yolks mixed with ½ cup cream are stirred in during the final stage. Sorrel is also made into a chiffonade. See also OSEILLE; SAURAMPFER; SZCZAW; ZURING.

sorrel sauce, an old English sauce for serving with goose, 1 lb. fresh sorrel leaves is boiled rapidly for about 7 minutes in plenty of salted water. They are drained, cooled, drained again, and then rubbed through a sieve. This purée is put into a saucepan with a good knob of fresh butter, a little sifted sugar, juice of 1 lemon, and sufficient brown gravy from the dripping of a roast goose to produce the necessary consistency. It is served very hot. Another method is to chop 2 cups fresh sorrel leaves. Then 1 oz. fresh butter and 1 tablespoon flour are put into a saucepan and stirred over the fire until well mixed, when ½ pint (1 cup) fresh cream and 2 tablespoons stock are stirred in. The sauce is brought to the boil, the chopped sorrel added, and the sauce reheated. It is seasoned with salt, pepper, and a dusting of nutmeg. See also SAUERAMPFERSAUCE; SOS, SZCZAWIOWY.

sort gryde, a Danish dish of pork or veal cut into pieces of equal size and fried with mushrooms. It is served with a sauce made from 4 thin chopped rashers of bacon, 1 fried onion, 1 tomato, and a little flour to thicken, then seasoned with 1 tablespoon tomato purée, diluted with 1 cup water, paprika, and salt. Finally 2 tablespoons cream are stirred in. It is garnished with fried tomatoes and crisp curls of bacon.

sos, Polish for sauce. Sour cream is often used to make sauces in Poland, and dill and sorrel are popular flavourings. For Polish sweet sauces, see CHAUDEAU. See also SAUCE.

sos głogowy, bouillon thickened with flour and hawthorn berry jam (głogowy), with white wine added. It is used as an accompaniment to game.

sos gorący do dziczyzny, a hot sauce for game and venison, consisting of herbs, spices, and root vegetables, all cooked, then sieved and mixed with sour cream, soy sauce, and pepper.

sos koperkowy, dill sauce, made from 2 tablespoons chopped fresh dill added to ¾ pint (1½ cups) sauce béchamel made from equal quantities of chicken stock and sour cream. It is served with boiled beef, poached fish such as sturgeon, or chicken. See also ZUPA, KOPERKOWA.

sos ogórkowy, 2 pickled cucumbers (known as dill pickles in Britain and the U.S. because they are pickled with dill) are sliced and simmered in ½ pint (1 cup) broth. A roux made with 1 tablespoon each of flour and butter is combined with ¼ pint (½ cup) cream, and then added to the mixture, with sugar to taste. This sauce is served with boiled beef or boiled fish.

sos Polski szary, Polish "grey" sauce. To prepare it 1 cup stock is added to a roux made as above, followed by 1 tablespoon each of chopped almonds and raisins, ¼ pint (½ cup) red wine, 1 tablespoon lemon juice, and a pinch of sugar. It is served with tongue or carp.

sos szczawiowy, sorrel sauce, made from 1 cup sorrel sautéed in butter, with 1½ tablespoons flour, ¼ pint (½ cup) stock, ½ pint (1 cup) sour cream, and seasoning added. The sauce is brought to the boil and should be quite thick. It is good with eggs, fish, or meat, particularly veal. See also JAJA; SORREL, SAUCE.

sos zimny do dziczyzny, a cold sauce for venison or game, made from 2 raw egg yolks and ½ pint (1 cup) olive oil, as for a mayonnaise, well mixed with 2 chopped hard-boiled eggs, 4 chopped shallots, 6 crushed juniper berries, and grated peel and juice of 1 lemon.

sosiski, Polish for sausages of all kinds, both smoked and fresh. They resemble frankfurters. See also KIELBASA; SAUSAGE.

sosiski à la sierzputowski, sausages served with a mustard sauce.

sot-l'y-laisse, a French phrase meaning "a fool leaves it," and the name given to the small piece of meat above the parson's nose (Pope's nose) in a chicken or other bird, which was considered a delicacy many years ago. See also PARSON'S NOSE.

søtunge or *tunge,* Danish for sole, which like all fish in Denmark is of excellent quality. It may be grilled or fried, and many other European methods are also employed, such as à la *véronique.* In one method, small fillets are rolled up, poached in white wine, then put into open pastry cases, covered with *hummersaus,* and baked in the oven. Sole is also poached and served with melted butter. See also FISK; SOLE.

soubise, purée, 2 lb. blanched and sautéed onions are puréed and beaten with ½ lb. cooked rice. This is sieved, mixed with ½ cup butter, bound with 2 egg yolks, and finally mixed with either ¼ pint (½ cup) double cream or 1 pint (2 cups) thick sauce béchamel. It is served with *côtes de veau orloff* and grilled meats, or used as a stuffing. All dishes bearing the title soubise include onions in their preparation. See also ORLOFF.

soubise, sauce, a classical French sauce, which can be described as a purée of onions diluted with a sauce béchamel. To prepare it—2 pints (4 cups) béchamel is reduced to half by simmering very gently over a slow heat. Meanwhile, about 20 small peeled onions, 2 tablespoons butter, salt, pepper, and a dusting of nutmeg are put into a small saucepan, covered closely and allowed to cook slowly until the onions are tender but not browned. They are pressed through a sieve, and the béchamel is blended well in. A little fresh butter is added before serving.

souchet, a 19th-century English method of cooking fish, particularly trout. The fish are poached in the oven with fish stock well flavoured with onions and sliced Hamburg parsley roots. Either the stock is thickened, or else the dish is served with steamed potatoes. It is sometimes spelt "souchy."

souchet, see GALINGALE. Also French for shoveller. See DUCK.

souchet, sauce, a classical French sauce, consisting of a white wine sauce with a julienne of potatoes, carrots, leeks, and celery cooked in butter and moistened with fish stock. It has obvious affinities with the English *souchet,* the same basic method seems here to have been refined into a classical sauce.

soudzoukakia, a spiced sausage made from minced veal or pork, garlic, eggs, parsley, cumin seeds, breadcrumbs, flour, and seasoning. It is a speciality of Smyrna. The sausages are fried in hot olive oil and are served with tomato sauce. See also SAUSAGE.

sou-fassum, a local speciality from Nice, France, of cabbage stuffed with chopped bacon, sausage meat, onion, beet leaves, peas, tomatoes, rice, garlic, and parsley, all sautéed in oil and seasoned. It is wrapped in muslin and simmered for 3–4 hours in a mutton pot-au-feu. It is served with fresh tomato sauce.

soufflé, a very light French dish, made basically from butter, flour, and eggs. A puréed or finely chopped flavouring gives the soufflé its name: lobster flavouring makes a lobster soufflé, apricot flavouring, an apricot soufflé, and so on. The true soufflé is baked, usually in a china dish (although metal was used formerly) called a soufflé dish. However, the word is also used for very light steamed puddings, whether sweet or savoury (such would be the English and American versions of *fiskebudding*), and for mousse and mousseline preparations, which vary in their making and in the ingredients required, and which are often no more than a mixture of puréed foods and cream, beaten with gelatine to give them a light, soufflé-like appearance.

basic soufflé method, a roux is made by melting 1 oz. (1 heaped tablespoon) butter in a strong saucepan, then mixing 1 oz. (1 heaped tablespoon) flour well in. Gradually a little under ½ pint (1 cup) milk is stirred in until the mixture is quite smooth, when it is cooked very gently for 8–10 minutes, stirring all the time. Then the main flavouring is added: if cheese, 2 oz. (1 cup) grated Parmesan cheese, or if preferred, a softer cheese such as Gruyère or cheddar; for ham, game, fish, spinach, etc., about 1½ cups of the dry puréed ingredient is added. The mixture is now taken from the stove, and 4 beaten egg yolks are stirred well in, together with seasoning, and it is left to cool. The 4 egg whites remaining, with 1 extra egg white if a heavy filling such as meat is being used, are stiffly beaten and then folded into the mixture with a palette knife. It should now look foamy and spongy. The soufflé is then turned into a buttered dish. It should reach only to halfway up the sides, to allow for rising, and a deep circle is marked on the surface an inch from the edge with the palette knife, to give the characteristic "lid" look. It is then immediately placed in an oven preheated to 400°F (204°C). A soufflé of this size takes about 25–30 minutes to cook, and is an adequate light course for two people. If cooked in small individual moulds, these will take 8–12 minutes.

A special mystique has gathered about the making of a soufflé, but if the method is carefully followed it is less trouble to make than a pancake. All soufflés owe their lightness to

asparagus soufflé

the fact that the air introduced into the mixture by the beating expands when it is hot, and is caught in the beaten egg white, making the soufflé rise. This is also the reason why a soufflé falls when cool, because the air is reduced and the egg white contracts. A true baked soufflé must be served directly from the oven, but there need be no alarm if it does fall a little; indeed it is bound to do so as soon as a serving-spoon is put into it. Falling does not alter the taste in any way, although, considered aesthetically, a soufflé certainly looks better when it is puffed up. However, any major disaster will be avoided if the following simple rules are remembered: a) The egg whites to be used must be scrupulously separated from the yolks, so that there is no trace of yolk in the white. b) It is best to use eggs which have been kept at cool room temperature; eggs that have been stored in the refrigerator for some days will prove hard to whip, although a single hour at a low temperature will not affect them. c) The bowl and whisk used for whipping the egg whites must be clean and dry, otherwise they will not rise. d) The egg whites must not be overbeaten. When they stand in creamy peaks, they are ready. e) They should be beaten only just before they are to be folded into the mixture and the soufflé is to be cooked. If beaten early on in the cooking process, water will collect at the bottom and they will not produce the desired effect, so it is essential to make the roux first. f) The roux must be left to cool before the egg whites are added, as they will coagulate if the roux is too warm. In fact the roux can be made well in advance without this having any deleterious effect on the finished result. It is also extremely useful to know that if the roux is made with corn flour instead of flour, the soufflé can be successfully reheated, and will re-puff. Reheating should be done in a moderate oven, and the soufflé should be left in the dish in which it was cooked, and the dish placed in a tin containing water to reach half-way up its sides.

Steamed soufflés are made exactly as described above, but require 1 hour's steaming in a buttered mould.

methods for sweet soufflés (soufflés d'entremets). There are two principal types of sweet soufflé—a cream base and a fruit base. The majority of sweet soufflés have the cream base, which varies very little from the basic recipe given above except that less butter is used and the sugar is dissolved with the milk before being added to the roux. First ½ tablespoon butter is melted and 2 tablespoons flour added to it, followed by ¼ pint (½ cup) warm milk which has had 2 tablespoons sugar dissolved in it. (If vanilla sugar is used, this becomes a vanilla soufflé.) It is cooked gently for about 5 minutes, stirring all the time until it is smooth. (In France, arrowroot or potato flour is used instead of ordinary flour, the former often for invalid cookery.) The mixture is taken off the heat, as in the basic method, while the yolks of 2 eggs are added. Then 3 tablespoons of the required flavouring is now included—roasted chopped almonds, apple or apricot or cherry purée (all cooked with the minimum of liquid), chestnut, grated orange or lemon peel, or a liqueur. (For all liqueur soufflés, 2 sponge (lady) fingers or macaroons can be soaked in liqueur, crumbled, and added to the basic mixture.) When needed, the 2 egg whites remaining, and 1 extra egg white, are beaten and folded in as described for the basic method. The soufflé is baked in a buttered mould for 20–25 minutes. It is impossible to give an exact timing, so the soufflé should be looked at during the last 5 minutes of cooking to make sure that it will not overcook.

Puréed dried fruits do not need a basic mixture at all. For ½ lb. cooked, drained, and puréed dried apricots, sweetened to taste, 2 beaten egg yolks and 2 tablespoons thick cream are required. For this mixture 5 egg whites are needed and the baking time is approximately 25 minutes in a moderate oven. Dried apple can be used in the same way. A simple method uses cooked, puréed, dried fruits folded into slightly beaten egg whites.

soufflé à la chartreuse, a vanilla cream base, flavoured with chartreuse.

soufflé à la maltaise, a cream base flavoured with Curaçao and juice of blood oranges instead of milk.

soufflé à la royale, a cream base with sponge (lady) fingers soaked in kirsch and fruit *salpicon.*

soufflé à la sicilienne, a cream base flavoured with orange, crushed praline, and diced oranges.

soufflé ambassadrice, a vanilla cream base, flavoured with 2 macaroons soaked in rum and 3 tablespoons chopped blanched almonds.

soufflé au chocolat, a soufflé which does not need a basic mixture, as the melted chocolate is thick enough on its own and has a better flavour if it is not mixed with flour. First 4 oz. bitter chocolate is melted with 3 tablespoons brandy, rum, or water, and stirred until smooth. Then 2 tablespoons sugar and 4 well-beaten egg yolks are added, and when cool, the stiffly beaten whites of 6 eggs. The soufflé cooks more quickly because there is no flour present, and 18 minutes in a hot oven, about 400°F (204°C), is sufficient. It may become dry if cooked longer.

soufflé camargo, a cream base flavoured with half hazelnut and half tangerine, with tangerine juice and zest instead of milk. Also 2 sponge (lady) fingers soaked in Curaçao.

soufflé mercedes, a cream base flavoured with fruit *salpicon* soaked in kirsch and maraschino.

soufflé mont-bry, a cream base mixed with one third its volume of chestnuts cooked in vanilla syrup.

soufflé palmyre, a vanilla cream base, flavoured with sponge (lady) fingers soaked in anisette.

soufflé Rothschild, a vanilla cream base, flavoured with 3 tablespoons chopped crystallised fruits soaked in Danziger goldwasser, kirsch, or brandy.

For the fruit-base soufflé, 1 cup sugar, cooked to light- or small-crack degree 264°F (129°C) (see SUGAR BOILING), is added to 2 cups puréed fruit and boiled for 1 minute. It is then quickly mixed with 6 stiffly beaten egg whites, and cooked as in the other methods described above.

soufflé glacé, iced soufflé, which is a frozen mousse made from a meringue italienne mixture with thick whipped cream added. If fruit is to be included, an equal amount of puréed fruit is added to the meringue and cream mixture.

soul food, the modern name for dishes of Negro cuisine in the U.S. Most of the dishes came originally from the ''deep South,'' but at present this cuisine is also popular in the north. Some of the staples of soul food include the cheaper cuts of pork, such as ham hocks, spareribs, chitterlings, pig's trotters (feet) etc. Chicken, deep-fried in batter or made into pies is also used. Catfish, shrimps (the large American varieties), often deep-fried, and crab are often served, with corn bread and sweet potatoes or sweet potato pie. Cornmeal dishes such as hominy grits, cornmeal mush, corn griddle cakes, and hush puppies are very common. Dried beans of many kinds are used, baked, or boiled with onion, pig's tail, sweet peppers, herbs, and seasonings. The vegetables used are the cheaper turnip tops (turnip greens), dandelion leaves, collard greens— also often cooked with pork jowl or other pork pieces—okra, onions, and sweet peppers. It is a simple yet spicy cookery, lacking in pretension but full of taste.

soumaintrain, a French cow's milk cheese from the Aube and Yonne departments. It is a whole-milk cheese, with a yellow, rather soft paste, and an orange-yellow rind. The finest is made in the Armance valley, and it is at its best from November to June.

soup, a liquid preparation usually made from fish, game, meat, poultry, shellfish, or vegetables, with water or stock, herbs, often an onion, and seasoning. In parts of Europe such as Scandinavia, Finland, and Germany, soups are also made of fruit, such as *frugtsuppe; kalteschale.* Soup may be clear or thick, the former being usually called broth. In Britain and the U.S., thick soups are generally thickened with a roux of flour and butter or, less generally, with cream and egg yolks. If the soup is made with vegetables which have been puréed or sieved after cooking, thickening is unnecessary, just as it is with soups made from dried beans or peas.

Most English soups take their name from the predominating ingredient, for example potato soup, tomato soup, etc. A general recipe which can be used for many soups uses 1 lb. chopped vegetables, meat or fish gently sweated, not browned, in butter or fat, then sprinkled with flour, seasoning, and herbs to taste, and covered with 2 pints (4 cups) water, milk and water, or stock. When in doubt it is always better to use too little liquid rather than too much; a good, strong concentrated soup can always be thinned down, but it is difficult to give flavour to a weak soup. Butter, cream, or croûtons can be added after cooking as a garnish if required. Some British and Irish soups not named after their main ingredient, and French soups which have been anglicised and are widely served in the United Kingdom, include bisque, brewis, brotchán, broth, cock-a-leeky, feather fowlie, lorraine, mock turtle, mulligatawny, partan bree, powsowdie, Scotch broth, skink, Welsh cawl, and Windsor. American soups not named after their main ingredient, include chowder, gumbo, Philadelphia pepperpot, southern bisque, and vichyssoise. See also BROTH; CALDO; CHORBÀ; CIORBÁ; ÇORBA; ČORBA; ELZEKARIA; POLÉVKA; POTAGE; SOEP; SOPA; SOPPA; SOUPA; SOUPE; SUP; SUPA; SUPP; SUPPE; ZUPA; ZUPPA.

soup ladle, a utensil consisting of a deep spoon with a long handle, used to serve soup. Soup ladles are of various sizes, the capacity of the largest being between ¼ pint and ½ pint. Silver ladles of great beauty were made in the 18th and 19th centuries, for serving soup at the table from a silver tureen.

soupa, Greek for soup. Greek soups include *avgolémono, fasolada, kaccavia, lahana, mayieritsa, patsa,* and *psari.* See also SOUP.

apo aravosito soupa, a Cretan village soup made from dried sweet corn. The corn is pounded and mixed with dried milk, and kept for use in the winter. When needed, the dried corn and milk is mixed with water and simmered.

soupe, the word used in modern France for a substantial country-style soup, usually made from vegetables and served with large croûtons or slices of dried bread, sometimes with cheese on them. Originally, soupe was the word for the ingredients that were put into a broth, such as meat, fish, or croûtons of bread. See also POTAGE; SOBRONADE; SOUP.

soupe à l'ail, a traditional French garlic soup. Four sliced garlic cloves, a sprig of sage, 2 bay leaves, salt, and pepper added to 3 pints (6 cups) water are boiled for 15 minutes. Slices of French bread are sprinkled with grated cheese and browned in the oven, then placed in an earthenware soup-pot and sprinkled on top with a few drops of oil. The hot strained soup is then poured over them amd allowed to stand for 2 minutes before being served.

soupe à la bonne femme, the white parts of 4 leeks are sweated until soft but not coloured in 3 tablespoons butter, then added to 1 lb. (2 cups) sliced potato, seasoning, and 2 quarts (8 cups) bouillon or consommé. All are simmered gently, and when the potatoes and leeks are cooked after about 30 minutes, 4 tablespoons butter and 1 tablespoon chopped chervil are added.

soupe à l'eau de boudin, a speciality of the Périgord when the black puddings (boudins) are being made. First 1 chopped savoy cabbage, carrots, leeks, turnips, celery, and 1 onion, all sliced, are simmered for 45 minutes in 2½ quarts (10 cups) of the water in which the puddings have been cooked. Then ½ lb. (2 cups) thickly sliced potato is added and cooked. About 15 minutes before the soup is ready, 4 tablespoons of the root vegetables are removed and fried in pork fat, sprinkled with flour which is allowed to brown lightly, then put back into the soup. This is called a fricassée in the Périgord, and it is used in the preparation of many vegetable soups. The tureen is lined with thin slices of bread, and the soup is poured over them.

soupe à l'oignon, onion soup. First ½ lb. chopped onions are fried in butter until soft and opaque, but not browned, and then sprinkled with flour. Then 1 quart (4 cups) white stock or water is added with seasoning, and the mixture is boiled for 30 minutes. French bread is cut into thin slices which are arranged in layers in a special earthenware soup pot, and the soup is poured over them.

soupe à l'oignon gratinée or *soupe au fromage,* a traditional French soup. As in the preceding recipe, chopped onions are fried in butter, white stock and seasoning are added, and the whole is simmered and poured into an earthenware soup pot. Slices of French bread are sprinkled with grated cheese and placed on top, then browned in a hot oven or under the grill. This soup is a speciality of Paris, and used to be a great favourite with market porters in the early hours of the morning.

soupe au cresson, potato soup with a pinch of nutmeg and a bunch of finely chopped watercress leaves. Cream is added just before serving. If electrically blended, the watercress stalks can be used as well.

soupe au pistou, a speciality of Nice, and the French version of the Italian *zuppa di pesto.* There are several variations, but generally it is a vegetable soup using onion, tomatoes, french beans, soaked dried haricot beans, courgettes (zucchini), potatoes, celery, leek, etc., all first sliced and sweated in olive oil, seasoned, and then covered with water to a depth double that of the vegetables. When it has been cooking for about 20 minutes, a handful of chopped vermicelli is added. When all are cooked, the soup is served with a pistou. Grated Parmesan or Gruyère cheese is handed round separately, and sometimes skinned and grilled tomatoes, mashed and mixed with a little olive oil, are added as a garnish. See also PISTOU.

soupe de poissons, fish soup made like bouillabaisse. The fish is strained and pounded, then put back into the liquid with a handful of pasta. When cooked, it is served with grated cheese. It is a speciality of Marseilles. See also BOUILLA-BAISSE.

soupir de nonne, see PET DE NONNE.

sour cream, cream which has been allowed to sour by being cultured with a bacillus similar to the yogourt bacillus. The cream used should be unpasteurised, otherwise it simply becomes stale tasting and bad, not soured. However in the U.S. all milk products are pasteurised. In taste and texture sour cream resembles beaten cottage cheese, but is slightly thinner. It is used for sauces and dressings, and plays a very important part in Russian and Polish cooking, and also in Scandinavian cuisine. It is excellent with salted fish such as herring, as well as with meats. Beaten sour cream is often coloured and flavoured with beetroot juice. See also CREAM; CRÈME FRAICHE; SMETANA; ŚMIETANĄ; TEJFEL.

sourire, a French culinary term meaning to simmer very gently. Literally translated the word means "to smile."

soursop (*Annona muricata*), a variety of custard apple which bears a large succulent pear-shaped fruit. The pulp is rather acid, but tastes not unlike black currants. It is popular in the West Indies and is sometimes known as West Indian custard apple. It is also exported to France, where it is eaten raw. See also ANNONA.

sous, Danish for sauce. See SAUCE.

sóus, Russian for sauce. Undoubtedly the most popular sauces in Russia are those made with sour cream, and this can be made into a simple sauce which will accompany almost anything, by mixing it with flour in the pan juices of the main dish. Sauces used with chicken include *tkemali sous.* See also KÚRITSA. Dill, mushroom, tomato, onion, and white sauces are also served. Other popular Russian sauces are as follows. See also SAUCE.

sóus iz ikrá, caviar sauce. First 2 tablespoons caviar is beaten well with 2 tablespoons hot water and 2 teaspoons butter. When well blended, 2 teaspoons lemon juice is added. It is served with roast veal or baked fish.

sóus iz khrena s korinkoy, 1 cup grated horseradish mixed with ½ cup cooked currants. This is served with boiled beef. It may also be made with cooked grated beetroot instead of currants, when it can be served with meats or fish.

sóus iz seliodki, 2 filleted salted herrings are chopped with 1 onion, fried in butter, and sprinkled with flour. Then 1½ pints (3 cups) stock is added, and all is simmered for 30 minutes before being strained. Just before serving, ½ cup sour cream and lemon juice to taste are added and well mixed in.

sóus iz solonisenikh ogurkov, sliced salted cucumbers are simmered in stock and strained; then flour and mushrooms are added, and the sauce is further simmered until thick.

sóus orekhovy, 4 oz. pounded walnuts mixed with 1 teaspoon mustard, 2 hard-boiled egg yolks, 4 tablespoons brown breadcrumbs, ¼ pint (½ cup) oil, and ½ gill (¼ cup) vinegar. This sauce is served with boiled or fried fish, and also with boiled french beans or runner beans, or soaked and dried beans, when 1 medium-sized finely chopped onion, or the equivalent volume of spring onions (scallions) is added.

sóus tkemali, a sauce from the Caucasus, usually served with *kúritsa tabaka* (see KÚRITSA). It is made from plums simmered until soft in a little water, then strained, stoned, and sieved. A little plum liquid is added, also a few crushed garlic cloves, chopped dill, salt, and pepper. The sauce should be of a creamy consistency, and is served cold. Tkemali is the

Georgian name for the wild plums that grow in the Caucasus; in regions where these are not available, bullace, damsons, or prunes may be used for the sauce instead.

sóus yaichniy, egg sauce, popular in Russia and often served with vegetables. There are several versions of varying richness. The plainest sauce is made by adding ¾ pint (1½ cups) vegetable stock to 1 tablespoon butter mixed with 1 heaped tablespoon flour (which is allowed to brown slightly), stirring until the sauce is thick and smooth. Then ¼ pint (½ cup) stock is then beaten with 1 egg yolk, and added. The sauce is reheated but not reboiled. Another version: 2 tablespoons water are boiled with a pinch of salt; then 2 egg yolks are stirred into this in a double boiler over boiling water. Then 6 oz. (⅔ cup) butter is cut into small pieces and added, stirring all the time until the sauce is thick. When thick, a squeeze of lemon juice is added. The sauce must not boil while it is cooking. A third method uses 2 hard-boiled eggs chopped, and heated in 4 oz. (½ cup) butter; then 1 tablespoon chopped parsley is added, followed by juice of 1 lemon and seasonings. The sauce is served hot with boiled fish, or shellfish such as crab.

sous-noix, a French butchery term for the under part of a leg of veal. It corresponds to the British silverside cut in beef.

souse, to, to steep or cook food in vinegar or white wine, sometimes diluted with water.

soused herrings or *mackerel,* the most common English soused dish. The fish are cleaned, sometimes filleted, and laid in an ovenproof dish. Bay leaf, sliced onion, peppercorns, and a little of a herb such as dill or fennel are added. The fish is barely covered with vinegar (if a strong variety is used, it should be half diluted with water), covered, baked for 30 minutes in a moderate oven, and served cold. It is also called pickled herrings or mackerel. See also BRATHERINGE.

South American marrow or **squash,** see ZAPPALLITO DE TRONCO.

southern bisque, a traditional soup from the U.S. made from 2 diced onions, 1 head celery, 3 carrots, and 2 leeks first fried in butter, then sprinkled with flour. Next 2 bay leaves, 10 peppercorns, 2 cloves, and 2 chopped garlic cloves are added, and the whole is well stirred. Next 2 tablespoons tomato purée, 2 cups stewed corn, and a ham bone are added with 3 quarts (12 cups) white stock. The soup is simmered for 2 hours and is then strained and seasoned. It is garnished with whole corn kernels and diced green peppers.

souvarov, a French petit four made from 1 lb. (4 cups) flour mixed to a thick paste with 8 oz. (1 cup) butter, 4 oz. (½ cup) sugar, and cream to moisten. It is left for 2 hours, then rolled out thinly and cut into small rounds which are baked in a moderate-to-hot oven. The rounds are sandwiched together with thick apricot jam.

souvarov, à la, a French method of cooking feathered game or poultry. The birds are first cooked in an earthenware casserole with foie gras and butter; when little more than half-cooked, truffles, partly cooked in Madeira are added, with the stock, and the casserole is then luted and the birds cooked for a further 15–20 minutes. This is a method which is used particularly for pheasant.

souvlakia, a Greek speciality consisting of small pieces of lamb threaded on a skewer with vegetables, and grilled over charcoal. These are often sold at wayside stalls and are similar to Turkish *kèbābi.*

sow thistle (*Sonchus oleraceus*), a weed with leaves that can be blanched and used in salads like those of the dandelion, although they are rather bitter. The ancient Greeks boiled sow thistle like spinach, and thought it beneficial. In Lapland the young shoots of the mountain sow thistle (*S. alpinus*) are considered a delicacy.

sowans or *sowens,* an old Scottish and Irish oatmeal dish, not unlike a fermented gruel. It is made from the inner husks of oat grain, known as "sids," with twice their bulk of luke-warm water poured over them. When they rise to the surface, they are pressed down until all are wet. This solution is left in a warm place for several days, up to a week, until acetous fermentation ("serf," or *searbh* in Gaelic) takes place, and the husks are quite sour. All is then poured through a sieve, and the liquid is allowed to stand for 2 days until the starch goes to the bottom. (The sids can be given to the hens.) When required for use, the liquid is put into a saucepan, 1 gill (½ cup) for each person, with 2 gills (1 cup) water and a pinch of salt. It is boiled, stirring all the time, and simmered for about 10 minutes until thick and creamy, then served in a deep plate with cream or milk. It has a curious, slightly sour taste, which needs to be acquired. It was traditionally eaten on Halloween, and this practice still survives in remoter country districts. Soaked sids, not fermented, are made into pancakes and eaten on Halloween in Scotland; and in Aberdeenshire the evening of Christmas Eve was called Sowans-Nicht, and sowans was eaten laced with whisky.

soya bean or **soybean** (*Glycine max*), the most nutritious and the most easily digested of all the bean family—in fact it contains a digestive enzyme. It grows easily in arid countries and, although a native of China, is now cultivated generally. It is almost immune from attack by insects. There are several varieties of soya bean, and these are coloured variously green, yellow, and black. The soya bean is one of the richest and cheapest sources of vegetable protein and has a low starch content.

soya bean flour, flour made from soya beans, which is used extensively in cakes, confectionery, and vegetarian products. In the latter case it is often mixed with yeast extract, and the resulting product tastes and looks not unlike ham.

soya bean oil, an oil obtained from the seeds which is used in the manufacture of margarine and shortening and in the production of vegetarian "cheeses." Although the soya bean plant was not introduced into the U.S. until 1804, that country is the leading producer of soya bean oil, followed by Germany and Manchuria.

soy sauce, a bottled sauce made from a fungoid growth on soya beans. This is used extensively in China and the Far East as a condiment, in place of salt. It is used in Britain as a base for many commercially bottled sauces such as Harvey sauce and worcestershire sauce and has been extremely popular ever since the 17th century, when anything connected with the new East India Company was automatically fashionable. Small silver collars were made, with "soy" written on them, to hang round the necks of attractive bottles containing the sauce; some can still be found in curio shops. The sauce was used first as a condiment, then as a flavouring for stews, soups, etc. It is a very dark brown and fairly sweet, and only a few drops of it are needed; it is excellent with chicken or rice. A thick soy paste called Hoisin sauce is also made; if it is mixed with brown sugar and rubbed on duck skin, or the outside of a ham before baking; it gives an original and delicious flavour to the meat. It is also used for making sauces for meats and as a dip.

spada or **pesce spada,** Italian for swordfish. See also SWORDFISH.

spada alla graticola, skinned and chopped swordfish marinated in olive oil, lemon juice, parsley, salt, and pepper for 1 hour. It is then grilled for 5 minutes, removed from the heat, brushed with the marinade and grilled again on both sides. It is served with lemon and parsley.

spagheto, Greek for spaghetti. See also FIDES; MAKARONADA; PASTA.

spagheto me kima saltsa, a dish popular in Rhodes and throughout Greece, consisting of boiled spaghetti served with a meat sauce. For this sauce, ½ lb. minced beef is sautéed in oil and added to 2 fried onions, 2 tomatoes, and 1 crushed garlic clove; this is moistened with ¾ pint (1½ cups) diluted tomato purée and flavoured with a pinch of cinnamon, bay leaf, salt, and pepper. The sauce is simmered gently until the meat and vegetables form a thickish purée, and it is then served over the spaghetti. It may also be served with macaroni.

spaghetti, the most generally known form of pasta, eaten with many different kinds of sauce. Almost all sauces served with spaghetti can be served also with other kinds of pasta asciutta (see PASTA). See also FIDEOS; SPAGHETO.

spaghetti al burro, spaghetti with melted butter and grated Parmesan cheese stirred into the hot pasta before serving. Fettucine is often served in this way in Rome.

spaghetti all' aglio e olio, spaghetti served with olive oil, and garlic cloves previously browned in oil, mixed into the drained pasta. In the Abruzzi a pinch of ground hot chilli is added, and this is called spaghetti all' aglio, olio e saetini.

spaghetti alla bolognese, spaghetti served with *ragù bolognese,* butter, and grated Parmesan cheese.

spaghetti alla marinara (con le acciughe), spaghetti served with a sauce made from 1 lb. cooked tomatoes, 2 onions, 2 garlic cloves, 4 tablespoons olive oil, marjoram or basil, seasoning, and 6 boned anchovies. Cheese is not served with this dish.

spaghetti alla matriciana, see MACCHERONI, ALLA MATRICIANA.

spaghetti alla napoletana, spaghetti served with a sauce made with ½ lb. chopped meat or ham, 1 large onion, 1 garlic clove, 2 celery stalks, 1 pint (2 cups) tomato purée diluted with stock or water, and a sprig of fresh basil. The cooked and drained spaghetti is turned in olive oil before the sauce is added. Grated cheese is also served. See also NAPOLETANA.

spaghetti all' olio e all' uovo, spaghetti mixed with olive oil, and with a raw egg stirred into the hot pasta, which partly cooks it. Previously browned garlic can also be added, as in *spaghetti all' aglio e olio.*

spaghetti alla paesana, spaghetti served with a sauce made from ½ lb. finely sliced mushrooms and 2 oz. diced bacon, seasoned and stewed together in butter. When these are cooked, 4 tablespoons grated Parmesan cheese is stirred in to amalgamate with the butter.

spaghetti alla spoletina, spaghetti served with a sauce made from 1 cup chopped white truffles, 4 anchovy fillets, 1 garlic clove, 2 tablespoons tomato purée, ¼ cup olive oil, ¾ pint (1½ cups) water, and seasoning, all gently simmered. No cheese is served. This dish is a speciality of Spoleto in Umbria.

spaghetti alla torinese, cooked spaghetti mixed with chopped fresh basil, butter, raw egg, and grated cheese, all stirred in when hot. It is a speciality of Turin.

spaghetti alle vongole, spaghetti served with a sauce made from 2 garlic cloves, 1½ lb. tomatoes, ¼ cup olive oil, 2 tablespoons parsley, and seasoning, with 2 cups chopped clams added. All are simmered, but once the clams have been added, the sauce must only be heated gently through, for boiling would make them rubbery. No cheese is served.

spaghetti col tonno, spaghetti served with a sauce made from 6 oz. tunny fish (tuna) pounded with 2 tablespoons olive oil, 1 tablespoon parsley, and ½ pint (1 cup) white wine, all cooked gently for 5 minutes.

spaghetti con carne, spaghetti served with a puréed sauce of ½ lb. minced meat, ½ lb. tomatoes, 2 carrots, 1 celery stalk, 1 onion, herbs, and grated Parmesan cheese.

spaghetti con salsa di zucchine, a dish from the Sorrentine peninsula. The sauce is made from 2 lb. salted, unpeeled, chopped zucchini, fried until soft in ½ cup olive oil and ½ cup butter mixed.

spaghetti con salsiccia, spaghetti served with a sauce made from Italian pork sausage cooked in olive oil, with onion, and tomato purée diluted with stock and white wine. No cheese is served.

spaghetti e finocchi alla siciliana (con le sarde), a Sicilian method of serving spaghetti with a sauce made from Florence fennel boiled and mixed with fried onions, fresh boned sardines, raisins, pignoli, stock, and seasoning. Half the sauce is mixed into the cooked pasta, which is sprinkled with breadcrumbs and well stirred before being put on the individual plates. The rest of the sauce is handed round separately. No cheese is served, as this dish is a St. Joseph's Day speciality and cheese is not eaten on that day. See also FESTA DI SAN GIUSEPPE.

spaghetti sauce, one of the many Italian-American sauces made with 6 large, ripe tomatoes plunged in boiling water, then in cold water, then peeled, cored, and seeded. They are finely chopped with 1 cup chopped pork or ham, garlic, bay leaves, salt, and pepper, then simmered in olive oil for 1 hour. The sauce should be thick and rather highly seasoned; it is poured over the spaghetti and sprinkled with grated Parmesan cheese. Sometimes a chopped onion or shallots are included with the ham mixture. There are a large variety of spaghetti sauces available commercially in the U.S.

spalen, see SBRINZ-KÄSE.

spanaki, Greek for spinach, a popular vegetable in Greece. See also LAHANIKA; SPINACH.

spanaki salata, spinach salad. The spinach is washed, cooked, and drained, then dressed with olive oil, lemon juice, salt, and pepper. It is eaten hot or cold.

spanakopita, a traditional spinach pie. In earlier days, wild spinach would be used, with wild mountain herbs and dandelion. Nowadays the pie is made with cooked spinach, herbs, aniseed, sliced onions, and seasoning, baked between layers of phyllo pastry. Feta cheese is sometimes added.

spanakorizo, a dish of spinach and rice. First 2 lb. chopped spinach, 2 medium-sized onions, and 2 leeks (optional) are browned in ¼ pint (½ cup) olive oil with seasoning. When the mixture is soft, 1 pint (2 cups) water is added and brought to the boil, at which point 4 oz. (½ cup) rice is put in and cooked until tender. If leeks are used, as much of the green part as possible is included.

spanferkel, an Austrian dish of sucking pig which is roasted with slices of lemon laid along the back for about 2 hours. It is served with a sauce made from ½ pint (1 cup) cream and 1 tablespoon capers, heated gently but not boiled. This is poured over the piglet, which is garnished with more lemon slices and with a whole lemon in the mouth.

Spanish mackerel (*Scomberomorus maculatus*), a sea fish found off the coasts of America during the warmer months, closely related to the mackerel. It can weigh between 6 and 10 lb., and is at least 4 times bigger than the European mackerel. Another American mackerel is the Monterey Spanish mackerel which is found off the Californian coast. See also MACKEREL.

Spanish onion, see ONION.

Spanish oyster plant, see GOLDEN THISTLE.

Spanish potato, a large, reddish-brown variety of sweet potato used in Spain for both sweet and savoury dishes. See BATATAS.

Spanish sauce, see SAUCE ESPAGNOLE.

spare ribs, an English pork cut comprising the first 4 ribs. It is the equivalent of the American shoulder butt. See also BOCZEK; SPARERIBS.

spareribs, an American and Irish butchery term for the ribs nearest the loin in pork and in Ireland it can also refer to beef. These are sold with a certain amount of meat left on the bones, and are sometimes sawn in half if they are from a large animal. They are generally roasted or grilled and served with a sharp sauce such as sweet and sour sauce or barbecue sauce.

Pork spareribs are very popular in the U.S.; sometimes they are stuffed (the stuffing put between 2 sections) with a breadcrumb, apple, onion, celery, and herb mixture, before roasting in a moderate-to-hot oven for 1 hour. Sauerkraut is also used as a stuffing. Spareribs can also be quickly sealed in hot fat and then braised with root vegetables, cabbage, potatoes, herbs, and spices.

barbecued spareribs, spareribs preferably cooked over charcoal, but they can also be cooked in a roasting pan, meaty side up, with a slice of onion and lemon on each rib. They are roasted in a hot oven for 30 minutes, when the temperature is lowered to moderate, and the meat is basted with a hot mixture of ketchup diluted with 3 times the amount of water, and a large dash each of Tabasco sauce, chilli powder, and worcestershire sauce. If the sauce becomes too reduced, more water is added. Depending on the size of the ribs, cooking time varies from 1½ to 2 hours. Another baste for spareribs consists of 1 cup honey mixed with soy sauce to taste, ketchup, garlic, and white wine mixed with water, but there are many tastes to please the individual cook.

spargel, German for asparagus. In Austria and Germany asparagus tips are sometimes boiled and drained, then sprinkled with breadcrumbs, browned in the oven in butter, and served with more melted butter poured over them. German asparagus is usually of the variety that has a thick white or purplish-white stalk. See also ASPARAGUS.

sparkakor, Swedish pastries. Rich short crust pastry with sugar added is put into a forcing-bag and piped into 2- or 3-inch strips which are baked in a moderate oven until golden. When cool, they are sandwiched together with red currant jelly.

sparling or *sperling,* the Scottish name for smelt.

sparrow (*Passer domesticus*), a member of the finch family and a very common bird in the British Isles and Europe. Less than 100 years ago it was a known, if not common, practice in country districts to net sparrows for sparrow pie. Small as they were, they were plucked, drawn, and decapitated. They made an excellent rich gravy, and the small soft bones were eaten as well as the flesh.

spatchcock, an old English method of cooking young or small birds, and eels, by splitting them down the back, flattening them slightly, rubbing them with butter, and grilling or cooking them over charcoal. The breast side of the bird is often brushed with a thin English mustard mixture made with milk, then sprinkled with breadcrumbs and basted with melted butter. It is a good way of serving a very young chicken, which loses its juices and flavour if roasted; it is accompanied by watercress salad. Spatchcock can also be served with a devil sauce. The name derives from "dispatch-cock," meaning a fowl killed and cooked in a hurry. It is sometimes called "spitchcock," which is the Welsh rendering of the word.

spatula, a long metal or wooden strip with a handle, used for mixing pastry, for stirring sauces or other mixtures, and for folding beaten egg whites into other ingredients. When made of metal, it bends easily and is useful for removing pastry or cakes from tins. It can also mean a long-handled implement with a flat rubber head, and sometimes they are made entirely of plastic, but the latter are not to be recommended for general use.

spätzle, the word used in Austria and Germany for tiny noodles. The batter is made from 3 oz. (⅔ cup) flour, 1 egg, ⅔ cup warm water or milk, water, and salt, all well mixed. It should be stiff enough just to run from a spoon. It is left to stand for 30 minutes; then a special colander (spätzle colander) is placed over a saucepan of boiling water and the batter poured gradually through the holes. The spätzle rise to the surface when cooked, and they can resemble a tiny dumpling. They are drained and put into a warmed dish, and melted butter and warmed cream are poured over them. They are served with chicken, game, and meats. Sometimes they are added to stews, the liquid being used for the poaching.

spearmint, see MINT.

speckknödel, see KNÖDEL.

speculaas, traditional Dutch biscuits (cookies). To make them 1 lb. (4 cups) flour, ½ lb. (1 cup) butter, ½ lb. (1½ cups) brown sugar, 1 teaspoon salt, 4 teaspoons baking powder, 1 teaspoon cinnamon, and a pinch each of cloves, nutmeg, anise or ginger, and pepper are all mixed to a stiff paste with milk. The dough is rolled and cut into large pieces, and blanched almonds and chopped candied peel are pressed into them before they are baked in a moderate oven for 25–30 minutes, or until brown. They are eaten on St. Nicholas' Eve, December 5. See also SINT NICOLAAS AVOND.

spek, Dutch for bacon. Bacon is often boiled and served with sauerkraut in Holland.

 spekkie sla, a bacon and potato dish from Gelderland, consisting of 2 lb. hot puréed potatoes with ½ lb. finely chopped escarole in them, served with 1 lb. hot, fried, and diced smoked fat bacon. The golden bacon cubes are served on top of the potato mixture, with vinegar and pepper sprinkled over them.

spekepølse, a Norwegian sausage made from minced mutton and lightly smoked. See also FÅR.

spekesild, Norwegian salted herrings which are prepared for use by being marinated in milk and water for 7 hours, then drained. They are often dressed with vinegar, sugar, and chopped onion, with boiled potatoes, beetroot salad, and crisp bread served separately.

 spekesild salat, salted herrings prepared as above and served with the same ingredients, but herrings, onion, beetroot, and boiled potatoes are all cut into small dice and combined.

spekeskinke, see SKINKE.

spelta, see WHEAT.

spenat, Swedish for spinach. See also SPINACH.

 spenat soppa, spinach soup made from 1½ lb. (2 cups) chopped cooked spinach added to 1 pint (2 cups) sauce béchamel, ¼ pint (½ cup) cream, seasoning, and chives. The soup is often garnished with slices of hard-boiled egg or frankfurters. It may be diluted with ¼ pint (½ cup) milk, when it is served with a poached egg.

 stuvad spenat, chopped cooked spinach served in a sauce béchamel, with a pinch of sugar, salt, and pepper.

spet (*Sphyraena sphyraena*), a small barracuda found in European waters, but not used much for food.

spezzatino di vitello, an Italian veal stew made from cubed veal lightly fried in butter with an onion. Pan juices diluted with white wine, chopped tomatoes, sweet peppers, and seasoning are added, and the whole is simmered slowly for 2 hours.

spiced beef, a medieval method of preserving beef through the winter, and one which still persists in Ireland, where spiced beef is traditional at Christmas, and in parts of the U.S., mainly the eastern seaboard. It is basically salt beef rubbed with spices. Lean cuts such as brisket, rump, round, or tail-end should be used. For a 6-lb. joint, 3 bay leaves, 1 teaspoon cloves, 2 chopped shallots, 1 teaspoon each mace and allspice, ½ teaspoon crushed peppercorns, 3 tablespoons brown sugar, and chopped thyme and rosemary are all well mixed in a mortar. Then 1 lb. coarse salt and 1 teaspoon saltpetre are added and well mixed in. This mixture is rubbed all over the meat, which is then laid on a bed of the same mixture. The meat is left for 2 days, more of the spiced mixture already in the bowl being rubbed in each day. Then 2 tablespoons treacle (molasses) is poured over and rubbed with the spiced salt mixture, into the joint. The meat is left for a week, being turned and rubbed each day. At the end of this time, it is tied up, covered with water, and simmered very gently with root vegetables for 5–6 hours. Then it is pressed between 2 dishes and weighted. Spiced beef is nearly always served cold. In country districts the joint is sometimes placed on a bed of bones and a bottle of Guinness is added to the water in which it is cooked half an hour before it is ready to be served.

spiced cheese, a salted version of the Dutch *friesian* cheese, but only cumin seeds are mixed with the curd. It weighs between 12 and 18 lb. See also LEYDEN.

spiced salt, salt with added spices. There are several varieties of spiced salt in use in the U.S., popular ones being barbecue spice and hickory-smoked salt. They are bottled and sold commercially for seasoning steaks, cutlets, pies, galantines, etc. The English variety, *pouder fort,* did not survive WWI. The closest English versions are celery and garlic salt, but these are not spiced. See also HICKORY; POUDERS; SALT.

spices, aromatic and pungent vegetable substances, used to flavour food both sweet and savoury. The most commonly used spices are allspice, cayenne, cinnamon (ground or in sticks), chillis, cloves, coriander, cumin, ginger, mace, caraway seeds, cardamom, nutmeg, paprika, and pepper (black and white, whole or ground). See also HERBS.

spickgans, a German delicacy of breast of goose, cured and smoked.

spider crab (*Majidae*), the name given to a type of crab with a rough shell, larger than the common crab, with a coarser flavour. It is known in France as *araignée de mer,* and is prepared and cooked in the same way as crab. The claws are all the same size, with very little meat in them. See also CARANGUEJO; CRAB; ESQUINADO.

spiedini, Italian for skewers on which small meat balls and other foods, are fried or grilled. The meat mixture consists of 1 lb. raw minced (ground) beef, 2 tablespoons grated Parmesan cheese, 4 tablespoons breadcrumbs or 2 thick slices of bread moistened with water or milk, chopped garlic, salt, and pepper. It is bound with 2 beaten eggs and shaped into small balls, which are put in a cold place to harden. These are then threaded on skewers, with a cube of bread and a piece of bacon between each meat ball, and each filled skewer is either fried in deep oil, or brushed with olive oil and grilled on all sides. They are usually served with a plain risotto. Spiedini can also be made with raw scampi, brushed with oil, grilled or fried on skewers with bacon, also mozzarella cheese squares interspersed with cubes of bread.

spiegeleier, Dutch for fried egg. See also EIEREN.

 spiegeleieren met kaas, fried eggs with cheese. In Holland edam cheese is used for this dish. Thick slices of the cheese are gently fried on each side in butter, then an egg is placed on top and sprinkled with paprika or pepper. This dish is often accompanied by fresh radishes and a lettuce salad.

spigola, the Italian name for a fine-flavoured sea bass, found in the Mediterranean and in the Adriatic, where it is also called *branzino.* It is usually baked or grilled, but if large, can be poached whole and served cold with mayonnaise. See also BASS.

spiked rampion (*Phyteuma spicatum*), an herb which is commonly found growing wild in Great Britain and was once an essential feature of any country herb garden. As with all herbs, it can be used raw, or it may be cooked in stews, soups, etc. In Switzerland, where it is called *clochette,* it is used for salads. It is a member of the *campanula* family.

spinach (*Spinacea oleracea*), one of the most useful and delicious vegetables. It is thought to be of Persian origin and was introduced into Europe in the 16th century by both the Moors and the Dutch. It was unknown to the Romans. There are 2 main varieties of cultivated spinach, the common winter spinach, and the round-leaved spinach, which is best for spring and summer use. Orach, or mountain spinach, is a coarser variety only occasionally cultivated. There is also a giant Mexican spinach which reaches a height of more than 7 feet. The so-called New Zealand spinach, brought to England by Captain Cook, is not a true spinach although it is prepared in the same way and tastes very similar. Spinach is a nourishing vegetable for it contains potassium oxalate and a certain amount of iron.

spinach

When used as a vegetable, spinach is cooked in very little water, then drained and either puréed, or mixed with butter, pepper, and salt, or with cream. However, it also has a variety of other uses, as a filling for soufflés, pancakes, and croquettes, in soups, with various forms of pasta (which are then called "green" pastas), and in *tarte niçoise,* where the spinach is mixed with eggs, breadcrumbs, and either sardines or olives, and baked in a pastry crust. It is also essential to lasagne verdi and cannelloni, and to some *subrics.* It is used for a number of garnishes, and any dish with the title *fiorentina* or *florentine* must include spinach. In Great Britain, poached eggs on spinach is a popular dish. See also ÉPINARD; PINAATTI; SPANAKI; SPENAT; SPINACI; SPINAZIE; SZPINAK.

spinach beet or **perpetual spinach,** see CHARD.

spinaci, Italian for spinach, eaten extensively in Italy and used not only as a vegetable, but also to flavour and colour pasta such as lasagne, for savoury flans, and as a filling for cannelloni and ravioli. See also SPINACH; ZUPPA, DI SPINACI.

flan di spinaci, a 12-inch pastry case baked blind and then filled with a mixture of 1 large sliced fried onion sprinkled with 2 tablespoons flour, and moistened with ½ pint (1 cup) cream or milk, stirred, and simmered until smooth; after seasoning, 3 cups cooked, drained, and chopped or puréed spinach is added and heated. The mixture is then removed from the heat and ½ cup grated Parmesan cheese and 2 beaten eggs are added. Finally it is flavoured with nutmeg and poured into the pastry case, and the flan is baked in a moderate oven for 20 minutes.

polpettine di spinaci, spinach dumplings. Two tablespoons melted butter and 1 tablespoon flour are made into a roux and then moistened with 1 tablespoon cream. After that, 1 lb. (about 2 cups) cooked spinach, 1½ cups ricotta or cottage cheese, ½ cup grated Parmesan, a pinch of sugar, nutmeg, seasoning, and 2 egg yolks are added. The mixture is shaped into small dumplings which are poached in boiling water, drained, and served with melted butter or fresh tomato sauce, and grated Parmesan. This mixture can also be shaped into croquettes and fried.

spinaci all' acciughe, spinach cooked (unsalted), drained, chopped, and heated in butter with lemon juice, garlic, and chopped anchovies. It is served on triangles of fried bread.

spinaci alla parmigiana, cooked spinach served with seasoning, nutmeg, and grated Parmesan cheese.

spinaci alla romana, a Roman method of preparing spinach. It is cooked, drained, chopped, and turned in bacon fat with a few raisins, pignoli, onion, seasoning, and nutmeg.

spinaci con uvetta, cooked spinach heated in butter or olive oil, then mixed with chopped garlic, pepper, and a handful of sultanas and pignoli.

spinazie, Dutch for spinach, which in Holland is often cooked with very little water, drained, chopped, and then reheated in butter and served with fingers of fried bread, quarters of hard-boiled egg, and lemon quarters. See also GROENTE; SPINACH.

spiny lobster, see CRAWFISH.

spit, a thin metal bar on which meat, poultry, or game is roasted before an open fire. Most modern spits are of steel, but early examples were made of iron. In fact this method of cooking pre-dates the Iron Age, when spits of hardened wood were employed. Until comparatively recent times, it was more common to roast a large portion of an animal's carcase than the small joints we are familiar with today, and it was not unusual for an ox to be roasted whole during festivities. On the horizontal spit, the earliest form, the piece of meat to be roasted is pierced through lengthways, one end of the spit being pointed to make this easier. The ends of the spit projecting beyond the roast are then used to suspend the whole on two hook-shaped brackets which are fixed on either side of the fireplace. Originally, the end of the spit was turned slowly by hand to ensure even cooking of the roast, first by means of a handle and later with a hand crank. Still later, simple reduction gearing was introduced, and the mechanical appliance, called a spit jack, was usually turned by a boy known as a turn spit. A small squirrel-cage treadmill containing a dog was also used to impart motion to the reduction gearing. At about the time of the Renaissance, rotating vanes, fitted in the chimney and connected by an axle, pulleys, and chain to the gearing of the jack, introduced into this process what would now be regarded as an early form of automation. These improved jacks, known as smoke jacks, drew their motive power from the hot ascending air in the chimney, so that, when skilfully constructed, they had the advantage of accommodating, to some extent, the rate of rotation of the spit to the heat of the fire.

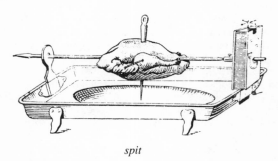

spit

Later, in the search for an even more reliable method of control, weight-driven clockwork was applied to the spit. In its most developed form in the late 18th and early 19th centuries, when the size of joints to be roasted had begun to assume dimensions similar to those met with today, this led to the production of a vertical spit, driven by clockwork whose speed was controlled by an adjustable governor. Beneath the spit was placed a dish to catch the drippings so that these might be used for basting, and on the far side from the fire a

convex metal shell reflected back onto the roast a further portion of the fire's heat, and also shielded the joint from the
draughts necessarily blowing towards the fireplace. Change in
eating and cooking habits, and the greater economy resulting
from the introduction of oven roasting, led to the abandon-
ment of this exceedingly effective method which, for certain
meats and birds, produced the most succulent results.

Fortunately, the introduction in this century of efficient
electrical appliances, such as the electric motor and the 3-
micron heater, has enabled modern roasting spits to be made
which have all the good qualities of the old ones, while dem-
onstrating a much greater economy of use and effort. See also
SKEWERS; TURNSPIT.

spitzkäse, a German spiced cheese made from soured
skimmed cow's milk. It is similar to limburger, except that
caraway seeds are added to the curd.

spleen, an organ situated at the left of the stomach in mammals. The spleen of the ox is sometimes used in stews or pot-
au-feu.

split peas, dried peas which are split in half. There are 2
kinds, green and yellow, although there is little difference in
taste; perhaps the green ones taste more like peas, the yellow
more like chick-peas. When cooked, yellow split peas can in
fact be used as a substitute for puréed chick-peas. Split peas
should be soaked for at least a few hours, before being cooked
in salted water (2 quarts to 1 lb. split peas) with 1 onion and a
bouquet garni. Depending on the amount of water used, this
will make either a soup or a purée. This purée constitutes the
very old English and Irish dish known as *pease pudding* and is
particularly good with boiled salt beef or pickled pork. If it is
to be served with meat, it is better to put the peas in a muslin
bag and to cook the "pudding" with the meat and stock. In
Ireland, an egg is often beaten into the *pease pudding* after
cooking to make it more creamy. The green variety make the
finest pea soup and, if cooked long enough, naturally form a
purée without having to be mashed. A ham bone boiled with
them adds flavour. Split peas can also be cooked with
chopped vegetables, but they must have plenty of water in
which to swell, or they will burn.

sponge, a light mixture made from flour, eggs, sugar, and
water, beaten for a long time to incorporate air, then baked.
First 3 eggs are beaten; then 3 oz. (scant ½ cup) sugar is dissolved in 2 tablespoons boiling water and added to the eggs.
The mixture should be beaten for 20–30 minutes, or put in an
electric blender for 2–3 minutes. Gradually 4 oz. (1 cup) flour
is added, and the mixture is baked in a greased tin in a moderate oven for 15 minutes. This method makes a soft sponge,
good for a Swiss roll or a sponge sandwich. With butter or
other fat added, it becomes a Victoria sponge.

sponge (lady) fingers, small fingers of sponge mixture, used
in trifles and other puddings. In the last century in Britain they
were served with wine, and they were known commonly as
"funeral fingers" because of the practice of giving 4 or 5 of
these fingers, neatly tied with black tape, to children to eat on
a long carriage drive to a funeral. To make them with a crust
on top, the eggs are separated, the yolks beaten into the dissolved sugar, and the stiffly beaten whites added alternately
with the flour.

sponge pudding, an English baked or steamed pudding made
from 2 eggs and the same of their equivalent weight in butter,
in castor sugar, and in self-raising flour (the average weight of
a whole, shelled egg is approximately 2 oz.). Various flavourings, such as ginger, treacle (molasses), dates, vanilla, candied peel, raisins, lemon, orange, etc., can be added to taste.
The mixture is well beaten, put into a greased basin, and
steamed or baked for 1½–2 hours.

sponging, see YEAST DOUGH.

spoom, a water ice with a sugar density of 20° Baumé. It is
made with half the quantity of syrup necessary for an ordinary
water ice, that is 3 oz. (⅓ cup) sugar to ½ pint (1 cup) water.
When the ice is half frozen, an equal amount of meringue
mixture is beaten in. The syrup can also be made from fruit
juices or wines, in the same proportions as above. Spoom is
served very cold, in a glass.

spoon bread, see COUNTRY SPOON BREAD.

spoonbill (*Threskiornithidae*), a wading bird distantly related
to the herons and the storks. It is sometimes wrongly called
shoveller. It may be prepared in the same way as heron.

spoonbill

spoon-shell, see GAPER.

spoonwort, see COCHLEARIA.

spot (*Leiostomus xanthurus*), a small sea fish found off American coasts and used for food. This name is also commonly
given to both the red drum fish (*Sciaenops ocellata*), which is
a much larger game fish, and to the spottail pinfish (*Diplodus
holbrooki*).

spotted Dick, see PUDDING.

sprat (*Sprattus sprattus*), a small sea fish about 4 inches long,
related to the herring and resembling it, though much smaller.
Sprats are quite good grilled and served with mustard sauce
or, if very small, dipped in batter and fried like whitebait.
They are also quite good to eat when salted, but are perhaps
best of all when smoked, as the bones are softer. Smoked
sprats make an excellent appetizer. See also SILAKAT.

spring onion or *scallion,* names applied in different parts of
the British Isles and Ireland to various different members of
the onion family. In parts of England and Wales these names
are given to the Welsh onion, and scallion also used to be
synonymous with shallot, although it is now used with this
meaning only in dialect. Generally speaking, however, these
names are used for onion seedlings that have been thinned out
before they have begun to bulb; in Ireland particularly these
are known as scallions. They are mainly eaten raw and often
chopped, in salads, like chives, and are also used in many
Irish potato dishes such as *champ*. See also ONION.

sprits, traditional Dutch biscuits (cookies), often produced in
the form of dolls, animals, and particularly bishops, in mem-
ory of St. Nicholas, on whose feast day eve, December 5, the
biscuits are eaten. They may also be made in the form of people's initials by putting the dough through a forcing (pastry)
bag. Sprits are made like *speculas,* but with the addition of a
little grated lemon peel and 1 egg. They are served with
mulled claret, which is often called bishop's wine (bisschop)
and also has strong connections with St. Nicholas's Eve (*Sint
Nicolaas avond*).

spritsar, Swedish almond ring-cakes. First 4 oz. (½ cup) butter is creamed with 3 oz. (¾ cup) icing (confectioners') sugar;
then 5 oz. (1¼ cups) flour, 1 tablespoon chopped almonds, and

sprits and boter moppen

1 egg yolk are added. The dough should be sticky, and piped from a forcing (pastry) bag in the shape of a ring. The biscuits are baked for 10 minutes in a hot oven. See also MANDEL.

sprouting broccoli, the English name for broccoli with flowerlets.

sprue, a fern used in England. They are asparagus seedlings, or the thin stalks of wild asparagus, which are excellent for making soup or for garnish. See also ASPARAGUS.

spruitjes, Dutch for brussels sprouts, sometimes simply boiled, drained, and turned in butter with a pinch of nutmeg. See also BRUSSELS SPROUTS; GROENTE.

spruiten purée, Dutch brussels sprout purée. Two lb. sprouts are boiled in the usual manner, drained, and put through a sieve. Then the resulting purée is flavoured with salt and nutmeg and mixed with ½ pint (1 cup) cream. This makes an extremely good vegetable accompaniment for pork or duck.

spruitjes met kaas, brussels sprouts and cheese. One lb. cooked and drained sprouts is put into a fireproof dish with ½ pint (1 cup) stock, then sprinkled with 2 tablespoons grated parmesan cheese mixed with ½ teaspoon nutmeg or mace, dotted with butter, and baked until the cheese is melted.

spuds and herring, a traditional dish from the Isle of Man. Scrubbed but unpeeled potatoes are put in a saucepan and covered with cold water, and salted herrings are placed on top. The water is boiled, and all is simmered gently until the potatoes are cooked, when the herrings are removed and the potatoes drained. The potatoes are then peeled, a knob of butter is added to them, and they are served with the herrings. Buttermilk is drunk with this dish.

spun sugar, see SUGAR BOILING.

spurs of Bacchus, the English translation of *éperons bachiques.*

spurtle, a wooden stick traditionally used in Scotland for stirring porridge. It is also called a theevil.

squab, a term used in the U.S. and in Britain for a young pigeon. It is at its best at the age of about 4 weeks, when, by means of special feeding, a dozen birds together will average 8–12 lb. or more, and the individual squab will sometimes weigh as much as the mature bird. The flesh of the squab damages very easily, and it needs great care in handling. When buying the birds, points to be looked for are size, plumpness, and light-coloured flesh; one squab is allowed for each person. See also CORMORANT; PIGEON.

squab pie, an old Cornish recipe. (Young cormorants were also popular for this pie, but had to be skinned before use.) In one method of preparation the young squabs are cleaned and placed in a pie dish with a little mutton, sliced onions, and

apples. The dish is covered with short crust pastry and the pie baked in a hot oven. Another method is a variant of the traditional pie still made in parts of Cornwall. It uses most of the ingredients described above, but although it is still called squab pie, it does not include squabs. It is said to have been brought over by the Phoenicians when they came to Cornwall to mine tin, but this story probably owes more to legend than to fact. The ingredients are mutton chops (all fat removed and bones boiled separately for stock), apples, onions, currants, honey, a little spice, and salt. A layer of mutton chops is arranged in the bottom of an earthenware dish, then covered with a thick layer of sliced apples spread with honey, followed by a thin layer of onions and salt; then currants sprinkled with spice are added, then more mutton, and lastly another layer of apples and a little stock. A dish is placed on top, and the pie is boiled for 1½ hours on a slow heat. It is then removed, covered with a light thin short crust pastry, and baked in a moderate oven for 30 minutes.

squash, the general American term for gourds which are members of the genus *Cucurbita.* The most important species are: the autumn and winter squash (*C. maxima*), a group which includes the Hubbard and the turban squashes; the Cushaw squash (*C. moschata*); the summer squash (*C. Pepo*), known in England as pumpkin (this group also includes the crookneck squashes, and the marrow squashes known in England as vegetable marrow. These 3 species differ from each other chiefly in respect of shape, and of colour of interior flesh. All have a very similar flavour, rather resembling that of a cooked melon, and are all cooked and served in similar ways. After peel and seeds have been removed, they may be steamed or lightly boiled, well drained, and served with white sauce or cheese sauce; or they may be dipped in batter and deep fried, or stuffed like vegetable marrow (summer squash). See also VEGETABLE MARROW.

squash soup, a soup from the U.S. of 2 chopped onions, 2 diced leeks, and 1 head celery fried in ½ cup butter and moistened with 4 tablespoons white stock. Then 1 diced green squash is added, with salt, pepper, and 2 pints (4 cups) more stock. When these are all cooked, 1 cup cream is added and the soup is garnished with boiled rice.

squeteague, an Indian name for weakfish originating in Narragansett, Rhode Island.

squid, see CALAMARY; CUTTLEFISH.

squill fish (*Squillidae*), a small shellfish which resembles a marine grasshopper. It is found off the coasts of Spain, Italy, and England, and is prepared in the same way as prawn. See also CANNOCCHIE.

squirrel, a small rodent of which there are many species. Although not hunted very widely in Great Britain, the squirrel is popular game all over the U.S. and is the main ingredient of the famous Brunswick stew. Squirrel meat, especially that of the grey squirrel (*Sciurus carolinensis*), is delicious if properly cooked. The flesh is light-red or pink, and the flavour is only slightly gamey. The young animal is best fried or grilled, and only the oldest and toughest squirrel requires stewing.

srpske čufte na luku, Yugoslav meat balls, similar to the Turkish köfte. They are usually shaped out of a mixture of 1 lb. minced (ground) pork, ½ lb. beef, 4 slices soaked bread, 1 large fried onion, and seasoning, and are then rolled in breadcrumbs. More onions are fried, paprika is sprinkled over them, and they are then placed in a casserole with the meat balls on top of them and tomatoes forming the final layer. A little water is added, and the contents are baked for 1 hour.

stabburpølse, a Norwegian blood sausage made with a mixture of meats and blood. It means literally "stone house sausage."

stachys, see JAPANESE ARTICHOKE.

stamna, an earthenware pot used in Greece for *klephtes* cooking.

stamppot, a vegetable hot pot which is one of the national dishes of Holland. It is eaten a great deal in the winter, and can be made with carrots, kale, or soaked dried beans, as well as cabbage.

witte kool stamppot, white cabbage stamppot. A large white cabbage is chopped and cooked for 30 minutes in boiling salted water, then drained and chopped finely. It is sautéed in ¼ lb. (½ cup) butter or lard, with salt and ¼ pint (½ cup) milk added. Then 1 lb. (4 cups) peeled and quartered potatoes are cooked in 1 pint (2 cups) water, salt, and 4 tablespoons pork, bacon, or veal fat, and when cooked these are mixed with the cabbage and the mixture is shaped into a mound. This dish makes an entire meal, and it is often served with smoked sausages such as frankfurters, or pork chops, although this is not traditional.

stangenkäse, an Austrian cream cheese, made with sour milk in the Steiermark and in Salzburg. It is brick-shaped, weighing about 7 lb., and of a soft, creamy consistency. It is also called bierkäse.

stanley, a French method of serving chicken. See POULET, SAUTÉ STANLEY.

stap, a traditional Shetland Island dish of washed haddock livers cooked slowly over water until they dissolve. Flakes of cooked haddock from the head and top of the fish are added, and the dish is eaten with bannocks.

star anise (*Illicium verum*), a small aromatic shrub, the fruit of which can be used in the same way as aniseed. The seeds' heads are much larger than aniseed.

star gazer (*Zaleoscopus tosae*), a species of hogfish, found only in warm seas. It is quite common in the Mediterranean, where it is used in bouillabaisse.

star gazey pasty, a variant of the traditional Cornish pasty made from cleaned and boned herrings or pilchards stuffed with a mixture of breadcrumbs, grated onion, and herbs, rolled up, and encased in a suet crust. The heads and tails are left on the fish, and these protrude from the dough. The pasties are baked in a moderate over for 30 minutes.

star gazey pie, a traditional Cornish pie made from filleted pilchards with the heads left on. The fish are stuffed with a mixture of sliced onion, lemon peel, parsley, bacon, and breadcrumbs, and are then arranged in a circle on a flat pie dish, with the heads at the edge so that they will protrude from the pastry. The fish are covered with slices of hard-boiled egg, a little cider is poured over to moisten them, and the whole is covered with short crust pastry (sometimes a thin layer is also put underneath), brushed with milk, and baked in a moderate oven for about 1 hour. Sprigs of parsley are often put into the fishes' mouths as a garnish after cooking. (It is not unusual for a thick layer of breadcrumbs to be used instead of the bottom layer of pastry, and for the top crust to be made of mashed potato.)

star of Bethlehem (*Ornithogalum umbellatum*), a small plant with a pretty green and white flower found in many cottage gardens. The roots are edible and can be cooked in the same way as salsify.

star of the earth, see HARTSHORN.

starling (*Sturnus vulgaris*), a small black bird with iridescent plumage, common in the British Isles, in France, and to a lesser degree in Ireland. It is a slightly gamey bird, but without a great deal of flavour. It was highly thought of by the Romans, and starling pie is occasionally made today. In France starling is cooked in the same way as thrush.

steak, a common English, Irish, and American term for a slice of meat or fish. In fish, the word denotes a slice of cod, salmon, etc., which is cut across the width of the fish. In meat, the word has particular meanings when used in connection with particular meats.

I. In beef, the word "steak" used alone almost always implies "beef steak," and is further defined by the cut from which the steak is taken (fillet, rump, sirloin, etc.). Stewing steak is beef that is suitable for stewing. See also BEEF; BOEUF.

steak and kidney pie, a thick beefsteak and kidney stew covered with short crust or puff pastry. The meat must be cooked first, otherwise it will still be tough and underdone when the pastry is cooked.

steak and kidney pudding, a traditional English dish. A basin is lined with suet crust (keeping enough back to form the lid), filled with lean, cubed, and floured stewing beef, chopped ox kidney (¼ lb. kidney to 2 lb. beef), and seasoning, then topped up with stock or water. Originally 2 or 3 oysters were included to enrich the liquor. The edges of the pudding are dampened, and the pastry lid put on and pressed down at the edges to secure the juice. A sheet of greaseproof or buttered paper is put over first, then a cloth; both are tied round with string; and the four corners of the cloth are knotted on top to facilitate handling. The pudding is put into a saucepan of boiling water so that the water reaches to just under the basin rim, then the saucepan lid is put on and the pudding is boiled for 3–4 hours. The boiling water should be topped up with more when the level sinks. It is served hot with a green vegetable and potatoes, and the gravy will be so concentrated that it will need thinning down with hot water. The pudding has a pure, strong flavour, and when well made, is a good example of the finest English country cooking. However, it is important that it should be cooked long enough; fortunately it is a dish that it is almost impossible to overcook.

steak tartare, see BIFTECK À L'AMÉRICAINE.

II. In pork, ork steak is a term used only in Ireland, and it describes the long pork fillet. This cut is known as tenderloin in the U.S. It can be grilled, casseroled, or roasted. See also PORK.

III. In ham, a ham steak is a thick slice of gammon. It is usually fried or grilled, and may be served with a variety of garnishes; pineapple rings are particularly popular.

steam, to, to cook a food by steam alone. It is done preferably in a utensil called a steamer, which consists of 2 containers that fit one on top of the other: the top one has a lid, and the base of the container is perforated with holes which allow the steam to pass through; the lower container is a saucepan which, for the purpose of steaming, is half filled with boiling water. The food to be cooked is put into the top section, while the water in the lower section is kept at a steady boil and topped up when necessary if the steaming is to be lengthy. One way of improvising, if a steamer is not available, is to place the food in a basin, and to stand this on a grid or piece of wood placed inside a saucepan of boiling water, so that the water reaches halfway up the basin's sides. The saucepan lid should not be removed during steaming as this causes condensation and loss of heat.

Most foods can be cooked by this method, for example fish, meat, vegetables, and especially such things as suet puddings, steak and kidney pudding, Christmas pudding, etc. Puddings are usually put into a basin and securely covered or tied down for steaming; other foods need not be covered with more than a piece of waxed or greaseproof paper. Generally speaking, food that is to be cooked by steaming is given a longer cooking time than would be allowed if it was to be boiled. This does not apply, of course, when the steaming process is being used only to soften or to blanch such foods as green or red peppers, or vegetable marrows, as a preparation for stuffing or baking them. Steaming is an excellent way of cooking delicate foods like fish, as the water does not come into contact with it; disintegration is avoided, and the flavour is retained. It is a method especially recommended for invalids.

steelhead (*Salmo gairdneri*), a rainbow trout found in rivers and lakes in the west of the U.S.

steep, to, see MACÉRER.

stefado, see STIPHÁDO.

stegt forskank, Danish roasted forehock or shank of bacon. The bacon is soaked overnight, then boiled in fresh water for 30–45 minutes. In Denmark this joint is usually boned and rolled. A paste is made from flour and water, and rolled out to 1-inch thickness. The bacon is skinned and wrapped entirely in the paste, then roasted in a moderate oven for 1 hour, or 25 minutes per lb. The joint is removed from the oven and the paste taken off. The fat is spread with brown sugar moistened with a little fruit juice, and studded with cloves; it is then browned in a moderate oven for 15–20 minutes.

steierisches schöpsernes, see SCHÖPS.

stelk, an old Irish potato dish often eaten with bacon. Old potatoes are boiled, and a bunch of chopped spring onions (scallions), with the green part left on, is covered in milk and simmered. The potatoes are mashed with the milk from the onions, and the onions are worked in with a little butter; then the mixture is seasoned well and beaten until it is a light green fluff. The dish is also called thump in parts of Ireland.

stellete, very small star-shaped pasta, used for garnishing soups.

steppe, a Russian cheese of the Dutch gouda type.

sterlet (*Acipenser ruthenus*), a small sturgeon found in rivers in the U.S. and Europe, and especially in the Caspian and Black Seas. It is a migratory fish, coming up the rivers to spawn. Sterlet is the most exquisite fish, and its flesh is more delicate than that of the larger sturgeon; its roe produces the finest caviar. It is eaten grilled, baked, or poached in white wine, and it may also be dried, salted, and smoked. The Russians have many delicious ways of preparing sterlet. See also STERLYAD; STURGEON.

sterlyad, Russian for sterlet. See also STERLET; STURGEON.

sterlyad demidoff, sterlet poached in white wine with fennel, celeriac, and pickled cucumber, then garnished with poached crayfish tails and sliced truffles. This is a Russian dish which also forms part of French classical cuisine.

sterlyad orloff, fillets of sterlet poached in a mixture of white wine, fish stock, mushroom essence (extract), and cucumber pickle. They are garnished with small barrel-shaped cucumbers which have been stuffed with fish forcemeat and simmered in butter; they are also garnished with stuffed olives, stuffed crayfish heads, mushrooms, and *vesiga.*

sterlyad po monastyrski, fillets of sterlet lightly fried in butter, then arranged in an ovenproof dish, covered with sliced mushrooms and surrounded by a border of sliced boiled potatoes. Sour cream is poured over, and the dish is sprinkled with breadcrumbs and grated Parmesan cheese, and dotted with butter before being baked in the oven.

sterlyad po Russki, fillets of sterlet poached in white wine, fish stock, and mushroom essence (extract). Tomato purée and gravy are added to the stock, which is then reduced, thickened with *beurre manié,* and poured over the fish. The dish is garnished with slices of decoratively shaped carrot, parsley root and knob celery, sliced mushrooms and pickled cucumbers, and peeled slices of lemon and olives, with grated horseradish sprinkled over.

sterlyad provi, fillets of sterlet poached in white wine, fish stock, and mushroom essence (extract). The stock is thickened with creamed butter and seasoned with lemon juice and

cayenne pepper. The dish is garnished with crayfish tails and mushrooms. Grated horseradish is served separately.

sterlyad s ikroy i smetanoy, sterlet rolled in flour and lightly fried, then baked in sour cream and butter for 1 hour. It is garnished with caviar.

sterlyad v rassole, fillets of sterlet poached in a mixture of white wine, fish stock, and cucumber pickle. The stock is thickened with *beurre manié.* The dish is garnished with stuffed cucumbers (see, *sterlyad orloff*), mushrooms, stuffed crayfish heads, and *vesiga.*

stew, I. The name for a dish of foods cooked with liquid in an enclosed pan. Stews often take the name of the main ingredient, for example beef stew. Two basic types of stew are made in Britain: a white stew and a brown stew. For a brown stew, the meat, usually beef, is browned in fat before the vegetables and liquid are added. A white stew is made with mutton, chicken, or fish; the classic example of a white stew is Irish stew. Foreign stews include *bigos, boeuf, casoeula, cocido, cozido, cuisada, djuvec, gulyas, miezu putra, mish me bamje, navarin, New Brunswick stew, porkölt, pot au feu, pote, praetud, ragoût, sauerbraten, stiphádo, stracotto, stufatino, tocana, turlü, and yahni.* II. The word for an artificial oyster bed or a fish tank.

stew, to, to cook food with liquid in an enclosed pot or saucepan. The temperature is the same as that used in simmering, 190°F (88°C). The authentic stew pan is made in various sizes and resembles a shallow saucepan with a lid and handles. The word comes from Old French *estuier*—to shut up or enclose.

stikkelsbaer, Norwegian for gooseberry. Stikkelsbærkrem is gooseberry fool. See also GOOSEBERRY.

stikkelsbærgrøt, gooseberry and raspberry fruit soup dessert. The fruits are simmered together until of a mushy consistency, then strained through a bag or muslin. When the resulting juice is cold, it is thickened with corn flour (cornstarch) (1 heaped tablespoon to 1 pint juice) and then brought to the boil. Sugar to taste is stirred in until dissolved. The soup is chilled in individual moulds and served with cream.

Stilton, an English double-cream, blue-veined, mould-ripened cheese made from cow's milk. There is also a white variety, which does not approach the mellow taste of the blue stilton but is quite a pleasant sharp cheese. There is no evidence that Stilton was ever made at Stilton in Huntingdonshire; although some Stilton is made in this county, the best comes from Leicestershire and Rutland. It is thought to have been first made in about 1730 at Little Dalby in Leicestershire, by a Mrs. Orton. It soon achieved great popularity through the activities of an inn-keeper at Stilton, who retailed it to travellers calling at his inn. Very few banquets or festive occasions in the British Isles are considered complete unless there is a stilton, wrapped in a napkin, on the side table. Some people add a glass of port to it when it has been opened, but this is purely a matter of taste and experts do not approve of the practice. It certainly combines excellently with a glass of port after dinner. Stilton is best when nine months old; the rind should be well wrinkled, free from cracks, and of a drab brown colour; the veining should be evenly distributed throughout. All attempts at imitating it have been unsuccessful.

stint, the English name for the smaller species of sandpiper, which is prepared like snipe.

stiphádo vothinó, also spelt stefado, a Greek stew of beef, onions, garlic, bay leaf, tomato purée, a little red or white wine, and seasoning. It is cooked slowly for about 4 hours, and the eventual consistency should be thick and jam-like.

kotopoulo or *kouneli stiphádo,* as above, but made with

chicken or rabbit. When almost cooked, 1 cup walnuts and ½ cup cubed féta cheese is often added to all forms of stiphádo.

stirabout, see PORRIDGE.

stirred curd cheese, see CANADIAN COLBY.

stocaficada, a Niçoise method of cooking stockfish, a thick stew made from the soaked fish cooked with onions, tomatoes, leeks, garlic, sweet peppers, potatoes, herbs, and black olives. The potatoes and olives are added after the other ingredients have been simmering for about 1 hour, and the dish is ready when these are cooked. See also STOCKFISH.

stock, the equivalent English term for the French *fond de cuisine.* The word covers many culinary preparations, but generally speaking a stock is the liquid extracted from fish, meat, poultry, or vegetables by slow cooking with water, or wine and water. The liquid is strained, and subsequently used in such preparations as casseroles, sautées, sauces, gravies, and soups. A stock should contain all the juices and goodness from bones, gristle, giblets, etc., and when boiled down, should be used as a flavouring, essence (extract), or glaze. Certain foods such as young chicken, veal, oxtail, pork chine bones, pig's trotters (feet), calf's foot, and fish heads, bones, and skin produce a stock which jellies when cold. This is far superior in flavour to gelatine or aspic and should be used whenever possible for cold dishes served in jelly. The jelly obtained from calf's foot can be flavoured with lemon or orange and used for sweet dishes. Game stock is made with the carcases, etc., of mixed furred and feathered game, with a bouquet garni and 1 part white wine to 3 parts water.

To obtain stock, long slow cooking of the basic ingredient is needed, and in the initial stages care should be taken not to include too much water, the solid ingredients being just covered with liquid. If very condensed it can always be watered down, whereas it is difficult to add strength to a weak stock. For savoury dishes, herbs and seasoning should be added. The contents should be simmered gently or the liquid will become cloudy, and it should reduce in volume by at least one-third. Then it is strained and when cold, defatted. If boiled up every day, it will keep for some time; if deep frozen, indefinitely. See also ESSENCE; EXTRACT; FONDS DE CUISINE; FUMET.

stock duck, the Orkney Island name for mallard.

stockfish, the name given to air-dried Norwegian cod. It should be soaked for a day before being used. It is popular in Germany, Belgium, Holland, and the south of France, where *brandade de morue* is made with it. The same word is used in Germany for this fish. See also STOKVIS; STOCAFICADA.

stokvis, Dutch for stockfish, a popular winter dish in Holland. The dried cod is soaked overnight. After cleaning, the fish is cut into long strips which are rolled up and secured. The rolls are simmered in boiling water until tender but not soft (about 1 hour), and then they are untied. Each piece is served with boiled potatoes, fried onions, boiled rice, and melted butter. Sometimes mustard sauce is also served. Each helping is topped with a fried egg. The Dutch mix all these together on their plates and eat it with a spoon; it tastes excellent. See also COD; PAN VIS; STOCKFISH.

stollen, a traditional German Christmas and holiday bread, consisting of fruit-filled loaves of yeast dough. Each province has its own recipe, but dresdner stollen is popular all over the country. When eaten at Christmas it is called weihnachts-stollen.

dresdner stollen, 2 oz. yeast is dissolved in 4 tablespoons lukewarm water; then 8 oz. (1 cup) butter, 1 pint (2 cups) warm milk, 2 eggs, 8 oz. (1 cup) sugar, 1 teaspoon salt, and 1 lb. (4 cups) sifted flour are worked to a smooth batter with the yeast. The batter is turned out onto a floured board, and ½ lb. (2 cups) more flour is kneaded in. The mixture is put into a

greased bowl, covered, and left to double its bulk in a warm place. It is then punched down, and left to rise again for 1 hour. Then ¾ lb. (1½ cups) raisins and ½ cup candied peel are shaken with ¼ cup flour and worked in, with 1 cup chopped blanched almonds and grated peel of 1 lemon. The dough is divided into 4, and each part is patted into an oval shape, brushed with melted butter, then folded over in half. It is brushed again with butter and left to rise for 30 minutes on a greased baking sheet, before being baked in a moderate oven for about 30 minutes. When cool, these loaves are either sprinkled with icing sugar or iced with white icing. This yeast dough forms the basis for many German cakes and sweet breads. It stores well.

stone curlew, see NORFOLK PLOVER.

stonecrop (Sedum), a decorative rock garden plant, with several species that are useful in cooking. The tender young leaves of the white stonecrop, the crooked yellow stonecrop, and the orpine stonecrop may be eaten in green salads and are also very good pickled. Their taste resembles that of purslane.

stoof, the popular diminutive of the Dutch word gestoofde, meaning braised or stewed. For example *stoofperen* are stewed pears.

stoofsla, a Dutch dish of braised lettuce. Lettuce hearts are cooked for 15 minutes in boiling salted water, then dotted with butter, topped with breadcrumbs, and braised in meat gravy in a moderate oven for another 15 minutes. See also GROENTE; SLA.

gevulde stoofsla, stuffed cooked lettuce. To make this 1 crustless slice white bread softened in water is mixed with 1 lb. ground or minced veal, a pinch of nutmeg, and salt. The resulting mixture is divided into small balls. Then 12 lettuce hearts are boiled as above and, when tender and drained, a ball of the meat mixture is placed in the middle of each. The stuffed hearts are then braised as for stoofsla (water may be used instead of meat stock or gravy).

stoofvlees, a Dutch dish of braised stewing beef (chuck steak is often used). About 4 lb. meat is first marinated for 2 days in red wine with onion, bay leaf, carrot, cloves, herbs, peppercorns, and salt, being turned each day. It is then drained, dried, and sautéed in butter and 2 tablespoons flour and half the marinade are added, and the whole is simmered for 2–3 hours, more marinade being added if required. The gravy is strained, seasoned with a peppery sauce, and served over the sliced meat.

stør, Danish for sturgeon. In Denmark, sturgeon is usually served in steaks larded with anchovies and bacon strips. Before being cooked it is marinated in olive oil, vinegar, onion, herbs, and seasoning for several hours, then poached or baked in white wine barely to cover. The liquid is drained off when the fish is cooked, thickened to taste with a *beurre manie,* and sometimes flavoured with a few drops of anchovy essence (extract). See also FISK; STURGEON.

store cheese, the Canadian slang name for the popular Canadian cheddar, a cheese which is found in all food stores throughout Canada.

storione, Italian for sturgeon, which is sometimes found in rivers near the Adriatic coast. It is often roasted whole, or cut into steaks and grilled, or poached and served cold with mayonnaise.

storioni, Greek for sturgeon, which is either grilled or served *plaki.*

stracchino, an Italian cheese of which there are several varieties. It is similar to *taleggio* but varying in quality. It has a pungent flavour and is often used to flavour pasta. See also CRESCENZA.

stracciatella, an Italian soup, made all over Italy although it originated in Rome. It is made from 3 pints (6 cups) good strong broth, either beef or chicken. Three eggs, 2 tablespoons chopped parsley, 3 oz. (½ cup) Parmesan cheese, and 1 tablespoon fine semolina (optional) are all mixed with a little of the broth. The remainder of the broth is heated, and when nearly boiling, the egg mixture is gradually added, while beating continuously with a fork for 3 or 4 minutes. The egg mixture forms curls or strands, and the soup is served hot. See also CONSOMMÉ ALL'UOVO; ZUPPA.

stracotto, a rich Italian beef and pork sausage stew made from 1 onion, 2 carrots, and celery browned in butter or olive oil; then a 2-lb. piece of lean beef and an Italian pork sausage weighing about 6 oz. are added to them. They are gently cooked for 10 minutes on all sides, when 1 pint (2 cups) meat stock, 2 tablespoons tomato purée, and 1 cup white wine are included. All are boiled up, then seasoned with salt, pepper, and 2 cloves. The lid is tightly sealed or luted, and the stew is cooked in a very low oven for 3 hours. The beef should be tender enough to cut with a fork and the sauce thick. If 6 whole cloves and a ½-inch stick of cinnamon is added, and red wine used, it is called *il garafolato.* Stracotto is also used as a filling for *anolini* and other ravioli.

strainer, a kitchen utensil used for straining sauces and occasionally soups. Originally a *tammy* cloth was used for this purpose. Nowadays strainers are made of aluminium or stainless steel, of varying mesh. Plastic strainers are also available, but are not recommended because very strong heat causes them to shrivel up. Different shapes are made for different purposes; round strainers are generally used for puréeing fruit or vegetables for sauces, and conical strainers for other preparations. The latter is called a Chinese strainer or, in French, a *chinois.*

Strasbourgeoise, à la, a French consommé flavoured with juniper berries and thickened slightly with *fecula.* It is garnished with julienne of red cabbage and poached *saucisse de Strasbourg.* It is served with fresh grated horseradish. See also CONSOMMÉ.

straw potatoes, potatoes cut into match-like strips and deep fried in oil. *Pommes frites allumettes* is the French equivalent.

strawberry (Rosaceae), a fruit which grows wild over vastly extended areas and under enormously varied climatic conditions. It belongs to the genus *Fragaria,* and there are indigenous species in every continent. Although known since early times, it received little attention from gardeners until the late Middle Ages. Wild strawberries are smaller than cultivated varieties, but are often superior in flavour and fragrance. Alpine or perpetual strawberries are small, round, and firm, and their flesh is white or golden, and fragrant; they also have the advantage of not being liked by birds and so are not spoiled by them. The common garden strawberry is larger, conical in shape, with a hollow core; when ripe, the exterior is dark red and the flesh white. The modern large-fruited varieties owe their origin to American species, the Virginian strawberry (*F. virginiana*), and *F. chiloensis* which was brought from Chile to Europe in 1714 by a French naval officer. The name strawberry is derived from the Anglo-Saxon streawberige, and is in no way connected with the practice of laying straw under the fruits.

Strawberries are eaten fresh with sugar or sometimes, surprisingly, black pepper, and with or without cream. They are used on a large scale commercially for bottling, canning, freezing, and jam-making. They are also used in compotes, tarts, mousse, soufflés, fruit salad, ice cream, jellies, and in many kinds of confectionery. See also CAPSUNĂ; ERDBEER; FRAGOLE; JORDBAER; MANSIKKA.

strawberry condé, strawberries are first soaked in kirsch. Cooked rice is put into a mould, then steamed in a *bain-marie*

fresh strawberries in meringue

for 30 minutes, cooled, and turned out. The strawberries are arranged on the bed of rice, and the condé is served with a purée of mixed strawberries and raspberries.

strawberry shortcake, a round sponge cake layered with sliced, sugared strawberries, and whipped cream. Whole strawberries are placed on top.

strawberry tomato (Physalis alkekengi), a perennial plant which grows in central and southern Europe, the Balkans, and North and South America. The tiny yellow tomato-like fruit is edible, but it must be carefully separated from the leafy calyx which encloses it. Its taste is a cross between the tomato and strawberry. The fruits of several species of *Physalis* are edible. Some are known as tomato or winter cherry. See also ALKÉKENGE; CAPE GOOSEBERRY.

straws, strips of puff pastry, often cooked with grated cheese and known then as cheese straws. See also ALLUMETTES.

streaky bacon, see BACON.

streickwürst, German for sausage made to be used as a spread. These sausages are usually smoked and are composed of meat so finely ground and pounded that it has to be dug out of the casing before it can be spread on bread. There are many varieties of streichwurst, the best known being *cervelatwurst, mettwurst,* and *teewurst.* The latter is made solely from pork fillet and is expensive. Some *leberwürst* also come under this heading. See also METTWURST; WURST.

string beans, the American name for french beans.

striped bass (Roccus saxatilis), a fish native to the Atlantic coastal waters of North America, but now found also in the Pacific. It is olive-green above, with silver-yellow sides marked with black stripes. It is a good game fish and can be prepared in the same way as salmon. Although not a true rockfish, it is often called by this name.

strisciule, a Corsican stew made with goat's meat which has been sun-dried, onions, herbs, and stock.

stroganoff, I. A Russian method of serving beef, named after the general who is said to have invented it. It is, however, common to nearly all the Baltic countries, and indeed to Europe. See also BEEF STROGANOFF. II. A Russian method of serving fresh herrings. They are rolled in flour, laid in a greased baking dish, and layered with slices of boiled potato and sautéed onions or shallots. The top is covered with sour cream mixed with *kabul sauce* to flavour, and sprinkled with grated cheese, and the dish is then baked in the oven.

strömming, the Swedish name for fresh young herring, caught off the Baltic coast. When smoked, these fish are known as *böckling.* Both strömming and *böckling* are served on the smörgåsbord, and in sandwiches. Strömming is also the name used for smelt in Sweden. See also FISK; NÖRS; SILL.

inkokt strömming, small pickled herrings, split, boned, and rolled up with dill, then cooked for a few minutes in a mixture of half water and half white vinegar flavoured with a bay leaf, allspice, a little sugar, peppercorns, and salt. The fish are served cold with a little of the sauce, and are garnished with chopped dill or fennel.

strömmingslada, a dish made of fillets of fresh young herring, salted, then baked with butter, grated cheese, and breadcrumbs.

struan Micheil (St. Michael's cake), a large traditional bannock eaten at harvest time in the Hebrides. It is baked on September 29 in honour of St. Michael, and consists of a mixture of 1 lb. each of oats, barley, and rye (representing the fruits of the harvest) mixed with ½ lb. butter and 3 teaspoons baking soda combined with approximately 2 pints (4 cups) buttermilk. During the cooking it is painted with three successive layers of batter made from 2 eggs, ½ pint cream, and ½ lb. butter. When small individual cakes are made of this mixture, wild cranberries, blaeberries or blackberries, caraway seeds, or wild honey are often added, according to availability and taste. See also BANNOCK.

strudel, an Austrian and German pastry, which may have either a sweet or a savoury filling. It is made from paper-thin strudel dough (*strudelteig*) with the filling placed on top; it is rolled up like a long Swiss roll, brushed with melted butter, baked in a moderate oven for about 1 hour, and while still warm dusted with fine sugar (if containing a sweet filling). It can be eaten hot or cold, but this type of pastry, which resembles noodle dough, is at its best when warm. The most common varieties are as follows. See also STRUDELTEIG.

apfelstrudel, the sheet of pastry first thinly spread with a layer of fried white breadcrumbs, then with a layer of thinly sliced apples, with a few raisins and a pinch of cinnamon added.

käsestrudel, strudel with a filling of cream cheese mixed with beaten egg yolks (1 lb. cheese to 2 egg yolks), a few sultanas, and the beaten egg whites.

kirschstrudel, strudel with a filling of stoned cherries, sugar, and a pinch of cinnamon, placed on a layer of breadcrumbs.

marillenstrudel, as above, but using apricots.

milchrahmstrudel, as *käsestrudel* using sour cream instead of cream cheese.

mohnstrudel, strudel with a filling of 2 oz. crushed poppy seeds mixed with sugar and red wine and left to macerate for 1 hour. It is then mixed with 4 egg yolks, 1 cup honey, 1 grated lemon peel, 1 cup apricot jam, 1 cup chopped raisins, and ½ cup melted butter.

nuss-strudel, strudel with a filling of ground hazelnuts mixed with sugar, cinnamon, eggs, and butter.

topfenstrudel, as *käsestrudel* using cottage cheese instead of cream cheese.

strudelteig, strudel dough, used in Austria and Germany for making *strudeln.* In Austria, strudelteig is made with a fine flour known as *glattes mehl,* but ordinary plain flour is quite acceptable. Contrary to most methods of pastry making, the ingredients used for strudelteig should be fairly warm. One lb. (3½ cups) flour is sifted, and a well is made in the centre into which 2 teaspoons of either lemon juice or mild vinegar is poured. Then 1 tablespoon melted butter is added and mixed in (some recipes also include 1 egg), and finally enough tepid water is added (about ½ pint or 1 cup) to make a soft dough.

This is well kneaded, taking care that the dough does not touch the sides of the bowl, until little "blisters" or airpockets form. Then it is covered and left in a warm place for 30–60 minutes, during which time the filling can be prepared. For the next stage, a cloth a little larger than a big table napkin is spread on the working surface and sprinkled with flour. The floured side of the dough is put on the cloth and rolled out to its extent. Now begins the most difficult operation. The hands are lightly brushed with melted butter and slipped underneath the dough; then, using the ball of the thumbs and working from the middle outwards, the sheet of dough is pulled very gently until it has been stretched as far as it will go without tearing. If it is torn, it must be "patched" with odd pieces from the edges. When it is of paper thinness, it is brushed with melted butter and left to dry for 15 minutes. The filling is spread evenly over the pastry, which is then rolled up very carefully and its edges trimmed and pressed together to close it up. It is put on a buttered baking sheet, shaped like a horseshoe, brushed with melted butter, covered with oiled paper, and baked for 45–60 minutes, the paper being removed for the last 10 minutes.

The above quantities will make 1 large *strudel* or 2 smaller ones. Yeast is occasionally used, and in this case a quantity of 1 oz. would be added to the quantities given above. (For a German yeast dough, see STOLLEN.) Strudeln can be boiled or poached as well as baked. In this case they are put into a buttered dish, sprinkled with melted butter, and just browned; then a little milk is added to reach halfway up the sides, the dish is covered, and when the milk is absorbed the strudeln are ready. See also PASTRY; STRUDEL.

štrukli, a sweet Yugoslavian pudding made from homemade boiled noodles mixed with cream cheese and cream.

studen, a Russian dish of calf's feet simmered for several hours with carrots, onions, parsley, bay leaves, and seasoning. It is left to get cold, and then the fat is taken off and the liquid strained. The meat is taken off the bones, which are put back in the stock with juice of 1 lemon, and cooked until the liquid is reduced to one quarter the original volume. The sliced meat is put into a mould with sliced hard-boiled eggs, and the jelly, which should be cool but not set, is poured over. The dish is put into a cool place to set and is served with beetroot and horseradish sauce.

stufatino, an Italian meat stew, served particularly in Rome.

stufatino alla romana, 3 lb. of lean beef (shin is good) is trimmed and chopped, then sautéed in butter with 1 small onion and a few garlic cloves. When lightly browned, 1 slice chopped bacon, marjoram, salt, and pepper are added, and all are stirred. Then 1 cup red wine is added, and reduced, then 1 tablespoon tomato purée or 4 large peeled fresh tomatoes. When this has amalgamated with the other ingredients, the meat is just covered with hot water. The lid is put on and the contents are simmered slowly for 2–3 hours.

stufatino di vitello, as above, except that leg of veal is used instead of beef, and rosemary and basil are added. White wine is used instead of red.

stufato, an Italian meat stew. A 4-lb. joint of beef or other meat is first marinated for about 4 hours in red wine, with garlic, bay leaf, and marjoram. It is drained and then browned in olive oil with a thick slice of bacon, which is taken out when crisp. Flour is sprinkled over, and 1 sliced onion and the strained marinade are added. The meat is covered and cooked in a slow-to-moderate oven for 2½–3 hours.

stuffatu, a Corsican stew, made with mutton, herbs, onions, and other vegetables.

stuffing, the name given in England to combinations of a variety of foods which are inserted into meats, poultry, fish, eggs, or vegetables. In the U.S., stuffing is also called dressing. A stuffing can consist of almost anything from breadcrumbs and herbs to fruits, nuts, rice, or vegetables. These ingredients are usually sliced or chopped, and sometimes bound with an egg. If chopped or minced meats, fish, game, poultry, or offal (variety meat) are themselves being used as stuffing, this is then properly known as forcemeat. No stuffing should be so piquant or aggressive that it overwhelms the flavour of the food that contains it. See also FORCEMEAT.

The most common stuffing for meat, poultry, or fish consists of milk-soaked breadcrumbs, chopped herbs, a little grated onion, and seasoning all bound with an egg. Some more elaborate English and American stuffings are described here.

apple stuffing, for roast pork, goose, and duck. An American recipe uses ¼ cup diced salt pork browned in fat until crisp, then removed from the pan. Next ½ cup chopped celery, ½ cup chopped onion, and ¼ cup chopped parsley are cooked in the fat for 3 minutes, then removed. Then, 4 peeled and diced cooking apples are put into the same pan, sprinkled with sugar (optional), covered, and cooked until tender, when they are uncovered and further cooked until brown and glazed. To them are added 1 cup fine dry breadcrumbs and all the other ingredients, and the stuffing is seasoned with salt and pepper. Prunes can be used instead of apples, or substituted for half their amount.

chestnut stuffing, for turkey. About 2 lb. chestnuts are slit, and baked, boiled, or roasted for 20 minutes. The outer and inner skins are removed, and the chestnuts are placed in a saucepan with enough good meat stock to cover them. They are cooked until tender and almost dry, and are then rubbed through a fine sieve. Butter, salt, sugar, and pepper are added, and if possible a truffle or truffle peelings to enrich the flavour. Sometimes ½ cup fresh breadcrumbs and 1 beaten egg to bind are added to this stuffing.

mushroom stuffing, for small feathered game or pigeons. About 6 oz. fresh mushrooms, including the stalks if firm and white, are washed, dried, and finely chopped. They are then fried with a small chopped rasher of bacon, stirring constantly. This mixture is added to 6 oz. fresh breadcrumbs and seasoned well. It is bound with 1 oz. butter and 1 beaten egg.

mushroom stuffing, for poultry. This consists of ½ lb. peeled mushrooms or truffles mixed with 1 pint (2 cups) sour cream, salt, and pepper.

potato stuffing, for goose, used in both Ireland and Poland. Depending on the size of the bird, 2 lb. mashed potatoes are mixed with 1 chopped celery heart, 1 small minced onion, herbs, and the chopped heart and liver of the bird.

sage and onion stuffing, for goose. First 1 large peeled onion and 2 sage leaves are finely chopped and mixed into ½ cup fresh breadcrumbs; all are seasoned with salt and pepper and blended with butter.

sausage stuffing, for poultry. First ½ lb. pork sausage meat is mixed with 4 oz. fresh breadcrumbs. Then 2 tablespoons butter, chopped parsley, salt, and pepper are added, and the mixture is lightly fried for a few minutes. It is cooled, and 1 beaten egg is blended in.

stuffing for fish, 2 oz. veal suet, very finely chopped, is mixed with 2 oz. chopped bacon. If desired, 2 teaspoons mixed herbs and some chopped parsley are added. If oysters are included, as they often are in this stuffing, they are opened and if large, chopped, before being added. All these ingredients are mixed with ¼ lb. fresh breadcrumbs and 4 tablespoons melted butter. The mixture is seasoned and bound with 2 beaten eggs. A light grating of lemon peel is sometimes added for flavour. Milk is added if the stuffing is too dry.

stuffing for hare or rabbit. Three oz. chopped fat pork or bacon is fried to a light brown, then removed while the liver of the hare or rabbit is fried in the fat. When cooked, this is chopped and mixed with the pork or bacon, 3 oz. veal suet, marjoram, thyme, parsley, and 1 minced shallot. The mixture is highly seasoned. Then 8 oz. fresh breadcrumbs and 1 anchovy are added, and the whole is thoroughly pounded in a mortar. It is bound with a beaten egg. A little milk is added if the stuffing is not moist enough.

stuffing for poultry. The giblets are boiled in just enough water to cover, with salt, some onion, and a small bouquet garni. When tender, the giblets are removed, the neck bones are taken out of them and they are finely chopped. Then 4 cups rather coarse fresh breadcrumbs or 3 crustless slices of bread are soaked in the stock and mixed with the giblets. The mixture is seasoned and bound with ½ cup just-melted butter and 1 beaten egg.

stuffing for vegetables, often used for vegetable marrow (zucchini), eggplant, cucumber, sweet peppers, large tomatoes, or cabbage. To prepare, 1 lb. minced (ground) meats or ham are mixed with 1 onion, herbs, 1 cup cooked rice, salt, pepper, and 2 peeled and chopped tomatoes, and all are then bound with 1 egg.

sturgeon, I. The common sturgeon (*Acipenser sturio*), a saltwater and a freshwater fish found in almost all seas and rivers in the Northern Hemisphere. It is particularly abundant in the Vistula, Rhine, Weser, Elbe, Oder, and Garonne, and certain American rivers, but nowhere is it found in such numbers as in the Black and Caspian Seas. It is a migratory fish and comes up the rivers to spawn. Its roe is caviar. The flesh is inclined to be hard unless the fish is hung for a few days, when it is white and delicious. It is often grilled or fried in butter, when it tastes not unlike veal. It is also good poached in white wine, with mushrooms, fennel, and cucumber. In France it is often braised like a *fricandeau*. See also OSYETRINA; STERLET; STERLAD; STØR; STORIONE. II. The Beluga or great sturgeon (*A. huro*), the largest member of the family. It is found mostly in the Caspian and Black Seas, also in the Volga, the Ural, and the Danube. It is also a migratory fish, like the common sturgeon. From this fish comes the famous Beluga caviar, and the spinal marrow is specially dried, when it is called *vesiga*. A deluxe method of cooking this fish in France is to poach it in champagne and stock with a *mirepoix;* the champagne stock is then mixed with sauce espagnole and reduced before serving, and the dish can be garnished with braised cucumbers, turtle meat, truffles, or mushrooms. It is also cooked in cream, onion, wine, and butter.

sturgeon

subrics, a French dish which is a variant of croquettes, differing from them in that subrics are never coated ,with egg and breadcrumbs, and that they are sautéed in butter, not fried in deep oil. The basic ingredient may be spinach, potato, foie gras, veal, beef, chicken, pork, brains, sweetbreads, tongue, or ham, all minced, mixed with eggs, a little flour, grated cheese, salt, and pepper. Sometimes cream is added, or a little sauce béchamel. They are formed into small portions with a spoon, and fried on all sides in butter. Various sauces, such as tomato sauce or sauce *piquante*, can be served with them, and they are either eaten as an hors d'oeuvre or entrée, or, when made from vegetables, are used as a garnish. The name is thought to derive from the phrase sur briques, for subrics used to be cooked on the hot bricks of the open range.

subrics de boeuf, beef subrics. Made with ½ lb. (1½ cups) cold minced boiled beef mixed with 2 beaten eggs, 1 tablespoon flour, 2 oz. (½ cup) grated Gruyère, salt, and pepper, and spooned into rounds which are sautéed in hot butter, or a mixture of oil and butter.

subrics de pommes de terre, potato subrics. First 6 large potatoes are baked in their skins; the pulp is then mixed with 2 tablespoons thick sauce béchamel, 2 oz. (½ cup) grated cheese, 1 egg, salt, and pepper. They are cooked as above.

suc, French for the juice obtained from meats or vegetables when squeezed, and for juice which has been reduced by boiling. *Suc de viande* is the juice from raw or cooked meat, and it is also the term for a very reduced consommé.

succotash, a dish from the U.S., consisting usually of equal quantities of sweet corn and lima beans mixed together and seasoned to taste. Each ingredient is boiled separately. Succotash is served well buttered, and sometimes has cream added. The dish and its name are taken directly from the Algonquin Indians.

succoth or *sukkoth,* the Feast of Booths, a Jewish festival of thanksgiving celebrated originally as a harvest festival, and commemorating the temporary shelter of the Jews during their wanderings. A booth (called a sukkah) is made of green branches, arranged so that the stars can be seen through it, and it is decorated inside with fruits of the harvest, such as corn, apples, grapes, cranberries, pumpkin, and so on. It is traditional to eat in the booth. East European Jews include one meal of *holishkes* (chopped meat in cabbage leaves), which is called *galuptze* in Russia. In Rumania *sarmali* are eaten, and strudel is usually the dessert.

sucées, French petits fours made from 8 oz. (1 cup) sugar, 8 oz. (1 cup) butter, 5 oz. (1¼ cups) flour, 5 egg yolks, and 1 cup chopped crystallised fruits, all well mixed. Finally 5 stiffly beaten egg whites are added. The mixture is shaped as desired, and baked in a hot oven for 15 minutes on a buttered baking sheet.

suck cream, a traditional Cornish dish from Boscastle. To prepare it 1 pint (2 cups) cream is boiled and mixed with 1 beaten egg yolk, 3 tablespoons white wine, sugar to taste, and grated peel of 1 lemon. The mixture is stirred over a gentle heat until it thickens to the consistency of thick cream. It is served cold, in glasses, with long fingers of dry toast. The name is a corruption of "sack cream," "sack" being an old word for Spanish white wine.

sucking or suckling pig, a piglet not older than 5–6 weeks; it is often stuffed and roasted whole. See PORK.

sudak, the Russian name for the pike-perch, or giant perch. It is very plentiful in most Russian rivers, and is also found in the Elbe and the Danube, Germany. See also PERCH.

sudak po Russki, the fish is first scored, then poached in white wine, fish stock, and mushroom essence (extract). It is removed and arranged in a baking dish with long thick strips of cucumber, sliced mushrooms, crayfish tails, and oysters. A little of the stock is added, then a covering of browned breadcrumbs dotted with butter, and it is baked in the oven. The remainder of the stock in which the fish has been cooked is reduced, blended with butter, and served separately.

sudak po Russki na skovorodke, fillets of sudak are arranged in a baking dish and covered with thin slices of boiled potato and pickled cucumber. The top is dusted with flour and a little fish stock is added, then a layer of grated cheese and breadcrumbs. Finally it is dotted with butter and baked in the oven.

suédoise, a French fruit purée, usually made from stone fruit such as apricots or plums, set with gelatine or a fruit- or liqueur-flavoured jelly.

suet, the hard, firm, dry fat surrounding the kidneys and loins of beef and mutton. It is highly thought of for cooking, especially when rendered down, and is used for pastry making or frying. Ready-grated suet, known as shredded suet, is sold in packets. The word comes from the old French *seu* and from the Latin *sebum* (tallow).

suet crust pastry, see PASTRY.

Suffolk cheese, a cheese which came from Suffolk but is now no longer made. It was renowned for its hardness and seems to have been similar to the Essex cheese. Dean Swift referred to these cheeses as "cartwheels" and the local names for it were "Suffolk bank" or "Suffolk bang." It was made after selling the butter off the milk, so that only the casein or hard protein was left, and this no doubt accounts for its hardness.

suflet, Polish for soufflé. *Suflet kawowy* is coffee soufflé; *suflet z kasztanów* is chestnut soufflé.

suflet owocowy, fruit soufflé. Apples, apricots, and hawthorn berries are among the fruits used in Poland.

sugar, the name given to a class of carbohydrates of great nutritional and culinary importance. The words for sugar in modern European languages derive ultimately from the Sanskrit *sarkara* (gravel) via the Persian *shakar*. Crude, unrefined sugar has been known from very ancient times, being derived from the sugarcane (*Saccharum officinarum*) of eastern tropical Asia and Bengal, where its cultivation was first begun. In classical times it was known to the Greeks as *sakkharen* and to the Romans as *saccarum*. It was a dark sticky paste, semi-crystallised, and often used in medicine in the form of a syrup (see TREACLE). During this period it was also known in India, but did not reach China until the early 7th century, still in its crude form. The first steps towards the production of refined sugar were made by the Persians at the time of the Arab conquests and consisted of the removal of acidic impurities by the action of lye made from wood ash; the sugar made at Ashkar-Mokram, Iran, was particularly famous for both quality and quantity. The Arabs adapted these techniques, spreading them widely through the Mediterranean basin; Egypt, Jordan, and Morocco became the chief centres of cultivation, and from there it spread outwards to Cyprus, Sicily, and Spain. In 1420 the Portuguese prince Dom Enrique, Infante de Sagres, better known to English readers as Henry the Navigator and in fact a grandson of John of Gaunt, began the cultivation of sugar in Portugal with stocks from Cyprus and Sicily. In the same year Portuguese mariners brought the sugarcane to Madeira; from there it was taken to the Canaries, and then to Brazil and Haiti—although the Spaniards had brought limited supplies of cane to San Domingos in Guinea in 1494. By 1641 it had been introduced into Barbados and other islands of the West Indies. The rapid growth of sugar production at this time meant that sugar began to replace honey as a sweetening agent in western Europe, and trading became so remunerative that the major part of the money for building Charles V's palaces at Madrid and Toledo could be provided from import dues levied on the sugar produced in San Domingos. However, it was Venice that became the main centre of the European sugar trade at the end of the 15th century, and it was a Venetian who invented the method of preparing loaf sugar, the form chiefly used in Europe for domestic purposes for the next 200 years. By the early 18th century the West Indies had become the chief centre of production; the growing popularity of chocolate, coffee, and tea drinking in this century vastly increased the demand for sugar, and thus developed the great slave trade with Africa, not eradicated until more than 100 years later, and having social consequences which are still affecting society today. The use of slave labour, and the speed and quality of cultivation that the tropical sunlight of Africa made possible, reduced the price of sugar considerably, so that it gradually came within the reach of all classes. This in turn led to the establishment of the great sugar companies and to important developments in maritime transportation.

Serious scientific investigation of sugar began in the 17th century, and in 1615 the Italian Bartolletti discovered the existence of sugar in milk. In the succeeding century the presence of sugar in various root vegetables such as carrots, parsnips, and especially beetroot, was chemically proved for the first time. In 1747 the German scientist Margraf obtained identified sugars from the juices of carrot and beetroot, as well as from other roots in lesser quantities, and by the end of 1760 he had succeeded in obtaining as much as 6.2% by weight of sugar from the juice of a white variety of beetroot. These were exceedingly important discoveries. Parsnips and beetroots had been used for sweetening in England since Saxon times, and almost certainly in other parts of Europe too; the wild carrot of the Scottish Hebrides had been known as a source of sweetness from a very early date:

Is e mil fe'n talmah a th' anns a'churran gheamhraidh,
E' adar Latha an Naoimh Aindreadh agus An Nollaig.

Honey underground is the winter carrot,
Between Saint Andrew's Day and Christmas.

9th century anonymous
(*from* F. MARIAN MCNEILL, *The Scots Kitchen*)

But now the way was prepared for the extraction of sugar from these vegetables on a commercial basis. Sugar, which had already become a dietary staple of Europe, could now be produced on a large scale from a source other than sugarcane, and actually within the countries that provided the chief consumer markets. Sugar beet, the name by which the white *Beta maritima* came to be called (later developed as *B. vulgaris*), was first cultivated in England for industrial purposes in 1868. However, it was not until the last years of the 19th century and the early years of the 20th that the production of sugar from sugar beet became a serious rival of the cane sugar industry. The two world wars of the first half of the century gave a considerable impetus to its production, so that since the 1950s many European countries have relied to a considerable extent, some exclusively, upon native production from *Beta maritima*. Sugar is also prepared from the sap of certain palms. The sap of the Canadian maple is rich in sugar, and makes an excellent flavoured candy. See also SOCKER.

sugar cane

Chemically speaking, there are a great variety of sugars with widely differing properties. Glucose is one of the most common; fructose is one of the most deliciously flavoured, although it has recently been implicated in the development of athero-sclerotic conditions. Beet sugar is generally very much less sweet than cane sugar, the latter being best for culinary purposes.

The types of sugar in current culinary use are classified either as white sugar, that is to say, fully refined sugar composed of clear colourless or crystal fragments; or brown sugar, which is less fully refined and contains a greater amount of treacle residue, which gives it its colour.

Sugar can be flavoured for future use by adding flavouring to a jar of sugar and keeping it well-stoppered. For example 1 oz. aniseed (wrapped in paper) to 1 lb. sugar, or 1 chopped stick of cinnamon, cloves, lemon or orange peel, vanilla pods, etc., give a delicate aroma. This avoids the need to use synthetic preparations.

The main varieties of white sugar are as follows:

castor or *caster sugar,* very fine crystals, about 0.5 mm in size. It is used at the table in a sugar castor and in the kitchen for the preparation of puddings and cakes. Commonly referred to as superfine sugar in the U.S.

granulated sugar, clear, white, dry crystals, up to 0.05 cm in length. It is used in the kitchen for the preparation of foods.

icing (confectioners') sugar, very finely powdered white sugar, sometimes mixed with a small quantity of cornstarch to prevent lumping. It has the appearance of flour, and is used for making icing for cakes and in confectionery.

lump sugar, refined white sugar compressed into lumps, in England generally of cuboid form, in other parts of the world often elongated. It is intended for use at the table and is sometimes known as loaf sugar, though this description is rarely used now, for it referred to the time when the lumps were made by breaking pieces from a sugarloaf (a mass of crystallised sugar formed in a mould) with a sugar cutter (an implement which is now a collector's item).

preserving sugar, large, clear, white, dry crystals, of irregular shape (chippings of cane sugar) up to 1 cm in length; it is used in the making of jams and jellies.

The main varieties of brown sugar are as follows:

Barbados sugar, a less coarse-grained sugar than foot sugar, but in other respects resembling it; used in cooking for the making of honey breads, gingerbread, and dark spicy cakes in general. It is also known as moist sugar, and as dark brown sugar in the U.S.

demerara sugar, sugar in a similar stage of refinement to soft sugar, but less moist and having much larger, light, amber crystals.

foot sugar, the most unrefined form of cane sugar available; a very moist, almost black, treacly sugar, with coarse grains, having a very high proportion of molasses in its composition.

soft sugar, also known as sand sugar, more refined than Barbados sugar, having the colour and texture of slightly damp, pale sand. It is used chiefly in confectionery. It is referred to as light brown sugar in the U.S.

sugar candy, also known as coffee sugar, a sugar with large clear crystals, sometimes as much as an inch (2.54 cm) across, often formed upon a length of string. The colours of the crystals vary from a deep brown to a pale amber; sometimes edible dyes are incorporated to vary the colours. Sugar candy is chiefly used in coffee or as decoration. This is called rock candy in the U.S.

sugar beet (*Beta vulgaris*), the variety of beetroot with the highest sugar content, cultivated mainly for the sugar-making industry. The usual type is white both inside and outside, but some varieties have black or yellow skins. Sugar beet may be eaten cooked as a vegetable, like garden beet.

sugar boiling, one of the most complicated kitchen processes, which is in the main only practised by confectioners. Apart from the making of a stock syrup, other processes require a copper pan of the right size, a sugar boiling thermometer, and a saccharometer for measuring the density of a syrup.

The usual proportions for making syrups of varying degrees of density are 2 lb. (4 cups) sugar to ¾ pint (1¼ cups) water. This is brought to the boil, then skimmed of any impurities; the addition of 1 teaspoon liquid glucose per lb. of sugar will avoid graining caused by scum. Before becoming caramel, the sugar (cane, loaf, or granulated sugar are best) passes through 6 stages: short or small thread at 215°–220°F (102°–104°C), used for butter creams (see CRÈME, AU BEURRE) and water ices; long thread, large thread, or feather, at 225°–230°F (107°–110°C); soft or small ball at 240°F (115°C), used for *fondant icing* and frosting; hard ball or large ball at 245°–250°F (118°–121°C); small crack 310°F (154°C); hard crack at 325°F (163°C), used for dipping fruits into so that they are crystallised. Beyond these degrees the syrup becomes caramel at 380°–390°F (193°–199°C), and at 400°F (204°C), black jack, which is burnt caramel used for colouring gravy browning, etc. When the right degree has been reached, the syrup must be removed from the heat and the base of the saucepan stood in cold water. It will then be ready for use. See also CRYSTALLISED FRUIT.

To identify these stages more accurately professional confectioners generally use a saccharometer marked according to the Baumé scale (named after its inventor Antoine Baumé, 1728–1804). It is graduated from 0° to 44° Baumé.

spun sugar or *candy floss,* fine web-like sugar used mostly to decorate ice creams or iced soufflés, and very difficult to make. It can be made without a sugar thermometer, but it will be a failure unless boiled to the right degree. The syrup is made with 5 oz. (⅔ cup) granulated or lump sugar, ½ gill (¼ cup) water, and 1 tablespoon liquid glucose all boiled, without stirring or shaking, to 325°F (163°C), or hard crack. (At this point it is advisable to put paper on the floor, for the process becomes rather messy.) The base of the saucepan is plunged into cold water, and then put onto a board. The complicated "spinning" procedure is then begun, using either a sugar spinner—an implement rather like a biscuit pricker—or, if this is not available, two forks. These are dipped lightly into the syrup and stretched apart until a thread forms. Too much syrup must not be taken at one time, or it will form into drops instead of a thread. Now the "throwing" begins. The thread of syrup is placed on an oiled rolling pin, held in the hand at arm's length, and the throwing is done with a loose, dexterous movement of the wrist, to and fro, like playing Diabolo. This process is continued until the syrup is used up. The sugar, which will be like floss, and should be white in colour, is then drawn off the utensil and either used or stored. It used to be an essential garnish for peach melba, and large sticks of it, like flares, can still be bought at country fairs. Nowadays spun sugar can be made with an electric machine with a spinning hub; this extrudes thin filaments of sugar syrup which solidify on cooling, and which can then be wound on a stick into the familiar fluffy mass.

sugar pea (*Pisum sativum,* var. *macrocarpum, excorticatum*), also known in England and France as the *mange-tout* pea because the pods have no parchment or hard skin in them, so that the whole pod can be eaten. They are picked when quite young and small, being topped and tailed like french beans, boiled, drained, and eaten whole. The sugar pea grows easily in temperate regions and has an excellent flavour.

These peas were known and appreciated in the 16th century, for the herbalist Gerard refers to them in 1597. A hundred years later they became wildly popular and were considered "a dainty dish for ladyes" (*sic*). Madame de Maintenon, mis-

tress, and later second wife, of Louis XIV of France, wrote that they were esteemed a great luxury, and that the eating of them was so much a fashion that it could almost be described as a mania.

sugar cane (*Saccharum officinarum*), a thick, tall, perennial grass, cultivated for the sweet sap in its stalks or canes, which ultimately becomes sugar. It flourishes only in tropical or subtropical regions.

sugared almond, see PRALINE.

sugherello (*Trachurus*), the name in the north of Italy for a kind of mackerel, used in *burrida* and other fish stews.

suglhupf, see KUGELHUPF.

sugo, I. Italian for juice, for example, *sugo di limone* is lemon juice. II. Italian for sauce, with the sense of the French *jus*. The word is generally used for a meat juice sauce. The more usual Italian word for sauce is *salsa,* from salso (salty).

sugo di carne, a meat juice sauce which is a variation of *ragù*. It is made with ½ lb. minced (ground) lean beef, 1 onion, 1 carrot, ½ oz. dried mushrooms, 1 tablespoon butter, ½ pint (1 cup) meat stock, 1 teaspoon tomato purée, ¼ cup white wine, and seasoning. It is served with all kinds of pasta and with potato gnocchi.

sulperknochen, a German dish from Hesse, consisting of boiled pickled pork leg, tail, ears, and snout, served with sauerkraut and *pease pudding.*

sultan hen (*Porphyrio porphyrio*), also called purple waterhen because of its beautiful violet plumage. It is a member of the *Rallidae* family, which also includes rails, coots, and moorhens, and it is prepared in the same way as coot. It is found on both sides of the Mediterranean and in the Antipodes and is often eaten there. It is also frequently served in France, where it is known as *poule sultane.*

sultana, the dried fruit of a white seedless grape. Sultanas are light brown in colour, quite juicy and sweet; they are used a great deal in cakes and puddings. The finest come from Turkey and used to be shipped from Smyrna, hence the name "Smyrna raisins," by which they were known several hundred years ago. Two separate varieties of grape are grown for sultana production in California, a true sultana grape and the Thompson seedless grape. The latter was first cultivated by W. Thompson in 1878, but it does not have the flavour of the true sultana. Nowadays grapes for sultana production are grown in many countries of the Near East, and also in Australia and South Africa. In the U.S. sultanas are known as "seedless raisins."

sultana, Italian for sultana. In the south of Italy a dessert dish is eaten which consists of sultanas soaked in brandy and then wrapped up like small parcels in lemon leaves.

sultane, a large French *millefeuille pastry* set in a cage of latticed sugar and decorated with feathers made from spun sugar.

sultane, à la, I. A French garnish which accompanies chicken breasts that have been dipped in egg and breadcrumbs mixed with chopped truffles, then fried in butter or oil. It consists of poached cutlet shapes of chicken forcemeat, and tartlets filled with puréed truffle and topped with chopped cock's combs and pistachio nuts; all is covered with a curry-flavoured sauce suprême. II. A title which indicates that pistachio nuts, often in the form of *beurre pistache,* have been included in a dish; such would be a *potage velouté à la sultane,* for example. Various sweets and pastries incorporating pistachio nuts also take this title.

sulugun, a Georgian (U.S.S.R.) cheese. A speciality of this region is a dish made by frying slices of the cheese (sometimes first dipped in batter), and serving them with sour cream.

summer pudding, an English pudding often called hydropathic pudding in 19th-century England because it was served in nursing-homes, spas, and other places where patients were not allowed to eat pastry. A pudding basin is lined with crustless slices of bread, then filled with a mixture of cooked and raw soft fruit such as raspberries, strawberries, and red, black, or white currants, and their sweetened juice. The top is covered with more slices of bread, and it is then weighted and left overnight. The next day it is turned out, and is served with cream. It can be surprisingly good when well made.

summer snipe, another English name for the sea lark. See ALOUETTE DE MER.

summer teal, see GARGANEY.

sum-sum, an alternative name for sesame.

sum-sum squares, a traditional Jewish holiday sweetmeat made from 1 cup sesame seeds, ½ cup each of honey, chopped nuts, and sugar, ¼ cup hot water, and salt all boiled in a double boiler until golden brown. The mixture is then tipped out onto a wet board and worked quickly before being shaped into small squares or diamonds to harden. They are eaten cold.

şuncǎ, Rumanian for unsmoked bacon. *Şuncǎ afumatǎ* is smoked ham, often served boiled or baked with quince in Rumania.

sundae, an American ice cream dish. The ice cream is served in a glass called a sundae cup and is decorated with fruit, crystallised fruit, nuts, and *crème chantilly* or whipped cream. Several different-flavoured ice creams are sometimes used together. See also COUPE GLACÉES.

sundew (*Drosera rotundifolia*), an insect-eating plant, common all over the British Isles, Ireland (where it is known as oil-plant), and Europe. It has dew-like secretion on its leaves, which no doubt gives the plant its name. In the 16th century it was used as an aphrodisiac, and Gerard says that cattle pastured on land where sundew grew were thought to be "stirred up to lust by eating even of a small quantitie." For this reason it was known as youth grass, and potions and foods which incorporated sundew mixed with sugar, mace, ginger, nutmeg, cinnamon, aniseed, liquorice, and dates are mentioned in Thomas Cogan's *Haven of Health* (1548). It was also mixed with ale and many garden herbs. In France, where the plant is called rossolis, a liqueur used to be made from it, and the leaves are still used, both raw and cooked, either as a salad or as a vegetable served with meats or poultry.

sunfish, I. *Eupomotis gibbosus,* a brightly coloured freshwater fish of the *Centrarchidae* family, found in the north of the U.S. It is similar to perch. II. A marine fish of the *Molidae* family, curious, tailless, large, and deep-bodied, inhabiting warm seas and usually resting at the surface. Sunfish may attain a length of 8 ft., and can weigh up to 2 tons. The truncated sunfish (*Ranzania truncata*) is about 2 feet long and has a smooth skin. Both these fish are tough and rather tasteless to eat. They are best made into soups, or served with a strong spiced sauce.

sunflower (*Helianthus annus*), a plant whose seeds are dried and roasted in Greece, Turkey, and Russia, as are those of the watermelon, and eaten with wines and spirits in Greece. They are also sold roasted by a nut vendor called the *passa tempo* man. Sunflower seeds are also used to make an excellent oil.

suomalainen pannukakku, Finnish for pancakes, which are baked in the oven instead of being cooked in a pan on top of the stove. They are served with fruit, usually cooked and puréed.

suomalaiset puikot, a Finnish biscuit made in the shape of a short stick about the thickness of a finger, and sprinkled with chopped almonds and sugar. To prepare them 6 oz. (¾ cup) butter is creamed with 2½ oz. (⅓ cup) sugar, then mixed with 1 teaspoon almond essence (extract) and ½ lb. (2 cups) flour. This paste is shaped into short sticks which are brushed with

sunfish II

sunflower

beaten egg, sprinkled with a mixture of ¼ cup finely chopped almonds and 2 teaspoons sugar, and then baked on a greased tray in a moderate oven for about 10 minutes.

suomi gruyère, a Finnish processed cheese with a faint taste of gruyère.

sup, Russian for soup. Russian soups include *borshch, borshchok, botvinya, bozbash, chikhirtma, kharcho, krapiva, okroshka, pokhlebka, rassolnik, shchi, shurpa, sjeloni, solianka s riba,* and *ukha.* See also SOUP.

sup iz rakov, crayfish soup. A rich fish stock is garnished with sliced carrots, parsley root, leeks, chopped fried onions, crayfish tails, and fish quenelles. Each portion of soup is served with a little crayfish butter on top. Rasstegay and peeled lemon slices sprinkled with chopped dill are served separately.

sup malorossiysky, a traditional Russian hare soup made by mixing a purée of hare with cooked barley, stock, a little beetroot juice, and sour cream. It is garnished with strips of hare meat.

sup meshchansky, citizens' soup, consisting of beef broth garnished with strips of cooked carrot, leek, and celery. Small balls of stuffed cabbage are served separately, made by stuffing cabbage leaves with veal forcemeat, shaping them into balls, and braising them. They are then sprinkled with Parmesan cheese and browned on top.

sup moskovskaya, Muscovite soup, consisting of rich beef

broth with small dumplings made with 1 lb. (2 cups) cottage cheese mixed with 1 tablespoon butter, ½ lb. (2 cups) flour, 3 egg yolks, ¼ pint (½ cup) buttermilk or sour milk, salt, 1 tablespoon sugar, and grated peel of 1 lemon; then 3 stiffly beaten egg whites are folded in. The dumplings are first poached, then drained and sprinkled with grated cheese, and finally browned on top. They are served separately. They can also constitue a meal on their own.

supă, Rumanian for fruit or vegetable soup. The fruit soup is sweet, and is made from puréed cherries, apples, raspberries, strawberries, etc., sweetened to taste. It is usually served cold, often with sour cream. See also CIORBĂ; SOUP.

supă ţărănească, a vegetable soup made with 2–3 lb. mixed vegetables, 2 chopped onions, 1 oz. (2 tablespoons) butter, salt, and pepper. The vegetables and butter are placed in a pan with enough water to cover, then boiled for 1 hour, when a further 1 pint (2 cups) water is added and the soup simmered for 10 minutes. Just before serving, 1 egg yolk is mixed with a little sour milk or cream and added to the soup.

supp, Estonian for soup. One of the traditional soups served in Estonia on many occasions is carrot soup, *porgand.* Fish soup (kala supp) is also popular. See also SOUP.

suppe, Danish for soup. Soups are extremely varied in Denmark and a lot of trouble is gone to in their preparation. Sweet soups such as *kærnemælkskoldskal* are served hot, chilled, or even tepid, and sometimes form the first course of a meal, or are sometimes eaten after the main course. Soups are also of course made from meat, chicken, and vegetables. In cream soups *boller, melboller,* and also rusks are often included, and in country districts such soups often form the main course of a meal. Danish soups include *frugtsuppe, hvidkål, kørvel,* and *kraasesuppe.* See also SOUP.

suppe, German for soup. In Germany soups are made with fruit and beer, as well as with fish, meat, and vegetables, and in the north, fruit soups, beer soups, and thick vegetable soups are particularly favoured. German soups include *bierkaltsuppe, biersuppe, braunesuppe mit leberpurée, frankfurter bohnensuppe, hamburger aalsuppe, holundersuppe, kaltschale, pommersche suppe, warmbier, westfälische bohnensuppe.* See also *aal, apfel, brot, erdbeere, gans, geflügel, gerste, hagebutten, krebs, mehl, obst, wurst.* In the south, and in Austria, the preference is for clear soup with noodles and additional garnishes. See also BISKUITSCHÖBERICESUPPE; BISMARCKSUPPE; BRANDKRAPFERLSUPPE; BRIESSUPPE; BUTTERNOCKERLSUPPE; KRAFTBRUEHE; PREBKOHLSUPPE; TIROLER KNÖDLSUPPE; ULMER GERSTLSUPPE.

suppe, Norwegian for soup, which is served throughout Norway. Dinner often starts with a fish soup garnished with fishballs. Meat soups are also eaten. Sometimes these Norwegian soups are so filling that they are a meal in themselves. As in other Scandinavian countries, the sweet soup is important. Norwegian soups include *blabærsuppe, fisksuppe, ølsuppe, viltsuppe.* See also SOUP.

suppevisk, a Danish bouquet garni, made from 2 trimmed leeks and a bunch of parsley tied together. It is included in soups and stews and removed after they are cooked.

suppion, the French name for a small member of the *Cephalopodiae,* a tiny squid. Suppions are crisply fried in olive oil and served with lemon.

supplì, Italian rice croquettes often made with leftover risotto. The rice is bound with eggs (2 cups cooked rice require 2 eggs), and made into balls sometimes containing a small piece of ham or sausage and a small slice of bel paese or mozzarella cheese. In the latter case they are called supplì al telefono, as the cheese becomes stringy, resembling telephone wires. These are rolled in breadcrumbs and fried in oil until golden, when the cheese will have melted into threads.

suprême, a French word used to mean a dish of fine quality presented in a particular way, as in *suprême de volaille.*

suprême, sauce, a classical French sauce consisting of 1 pint (2 cups) sauce *velouté* with ½ pint (1 cup) fresh cream and 1 teaspoon mushroom essence (extract) added just before serving.

suprêmes, the French term for the breast and wings of a chicken or game bird such as partridge when they are removed, raw, in one piece from each side of the bird. For cooking, they are then skinned and cut into two or three slices, depending on the size of the bird. Suprêmes are also known as *côtelettes* or fillets (*de volaille,* etc.), when they are served as entrées. There are two basic ways of serving suprêmes: either seasoned, coated with flour or egg and breadcrumbs, then fried or sautéed in butter (''brown'' suprêmes); or poached with a little stock and butter (''white'' suprêmes). White suprêmes are sometimes lightly sautéed before poaching, but they are never allowed to brown. Recipes are as follows, with a designation of either white or brown, or variations of these methods, and with the appropriate garnishes and sauces. Where stuffing is mentioned, this is inserted into a pocket cut in the breast, and the suprême is seared before further cooking takes place, in order to seal the aperture.

suprêmes à l'andalouse (white), stuffed with chicken forcemeat, and covered with sauce suprême to which diced and sweated sweet peppers have been added.

suprêmes à l'arlésienne (brown), garnished with eggplant and onion sliced and fried in olive oil with chopped tomatoes. Demi-glace flavoured with tomatoes is served separately.

suprêmes à la bordelaise (white), garnished with artichoke bottoms.

suprêmes à la crème (white, first lightly sautéed in butter), deglacéed with 1 tablespoon cognac and ½ pint (1 cup) cream mixed and reduced with the pan juices; all covered with sauce crème.

suprêmes à la cussy (white), set on artichoke bottoms, with sauce suprême and truffles. Breadcrumbs instead of truffles are favoured by Escoffier.

suprêmes à la d'albuféra (white), stuffed with chicken mousseline forcemeat and set on a tartlet filled with *albuféra* garnish; all covered with sauce *albuféra.*

suprêmes à la doria (brown), garnished with oval shapes of simmered cucumber sprinkled with lemon juice; they are all covered with *beurre noisette.*

suprêmes à la favorite (brown), served on slices of foie gras; it is garnished with asparagus tips.

suprêmes à la financière (white), served on a croûton, with *financière* garnish and sauce *financière.*

suprêmes à la florentine (white), set on spinach, covered with sauce mornay with chicken essence (jelly) added, and glazed.

suprêmes à la hongroise (white), served on rice, with sauce crême flavoured with paprika.

suprêmes à l'impériale (white), studded with truffles and pickled tongue, then cooked in chicken stock; set in pastry *barquettes* which are then filled with a purée of truffles with cream; they are lightly covered with sauce suprême.

suprêmes à l'indienne (white), served with boiled rice and curry sauce.

suprêmes à l'italienne (brown), served with sauce *Italienne,* garnished with artichoke hearts.

suprêmes à la japonaise (white), served on moulded rice; they are garnished with tartlets filled with creamed Japanese artichoke. Thick veal gravy is served separately.

suprêmes à la jardinière (brown or white), served with spring vegetables.

suprêmes à la maréchale (brown), coated with breadcrumbs

mixed with truffles; a slice of truffle coated with demi-glace is placed on top. They are garnished with asparagus tips.

suprêmes à la mascotte (brown), served on foie gras slices and garnished with crescents of pickled ox tongue, truffles, and chicken quenelles flavoured with tongue and truffles.

suprêmes à la périgueux (white), served on croûtons of fried bread; garnished with sliced truffles and served with sauce *périgueux*.

suprêmes à la provençale (brown), as for *poulet à la provençale*.

suprêmes à la régence (white), with sauce *régence* and *régence* garnish.

suprêmes à la valois (brown), garnished with stuffed olives. Sauce *valois* is served separately.

suprêmes Adelina Patti (white), stuffed with chicken forcemeat and goose liver and covered with sauce suprême flavoured with paprika; garnished with artichoke bottoms filled with small glazed truffle balls.

suprêmes Agnes Sorel (white), poached in lemon juice and butter, mounted on a tartlet of chicken mousseline filled with sliced sautéed mushrooms, covered with sauce suprême, and garnished with a ring of ox tongue with a circle of truffle.

suprêmes ambassadrice (brown), garnished with chicken livers, cock's combs, *rognons de coq,* and rounds of truffles, all sautéed; they are served with the pan juices mixed with veal demi-glace, flavoured with Madeira and reduced.

suprêmes archiduc (white), mounted on a croûton, covered with sauce *archiduc,* and garnished with truffle slices.

suprêmes boistelle (brown), stuffed with chicken forcemeat and served with sautéed mushrooms.

suprêmes camérani (brown), set on cooked noodles and served with pan juices diluted with brown veal gravy flavoured with Madeira, and with a julienne of sweated celery and truffles added.

suprêmes Carême (white), stuffed with mushroom purée mixed with julienne of cock's combs and truffles, then sautéed in butter. Set on croûtons, garnished with chicken quenelles, and mushrooms, and served with the pan juices reduced with thickened veal gravy, with tomato and butter.

suprêmes chimay (white), served with *morilles* and asparagus tips.

suprêmes Gabrielle (brown), covered with sweated *mirepoix,* and garnished with shredded lettuce mixed with cream and *beurre noisette*.

suprêmes grand-duc (white), with a large truffle on top, covered with sauce mornay blended with *beurre d'écrevisses* and glazed; they are garnished with asparagus tips and crayfish tails.

suprêmes judic (white), served on braised lettuce, truffle, and peas, with a braised cock's comb on each suprême; they are covered with thick veal gravy.

suprêmes Marie-Louise (brown), served on artichoke bottoms filled with mushroom purée mixed with purée soubise; they are covered with *beurre noire*.

supremês marquise (white), garnished with tartlets filled with salpicon of cock's combs, *rognons de coq,* and truffles, mixed with cream; they are served with the pan juices diluted with cream, butter, and a little chopped truffle, then reduced.

suprêmes montpensier (brown), garnished with asparagus tips sautéed in butter and truffles, all covered with thickened veal gravy and sprinkled with *beurre noisette*.

suprêmes pojarski (not a true suprême, and a dish in which twice-cooked chicken must not be used). First 1 lb. cooked chicken meat is chopped and mixed with ¼ lb. (4 crustless slices) bread soaked in cream; then the mixture is seasoned with a pinch of nutmeg and shaped into ovals which are fried

in butter; they are garnished by sprinkling with *beurre noisette.*

suprêmes polignac (white), coated with sauce suprême mixed with a julienne of mushrooms and truffles.

suprêmes princesse (white), served on croûtons of fried bread and covered with sauce *allemande*.

suprêmes Richelieu (brown), served with *beurre maître d'hôtel* and slices of truffle.

suprêmes Rossini (white, first lightly sautéed in butter), served on croûtons of fried bread with foie gras, and covered with sauce madère mixed with sliced truffles.

suprêmes Saint Germain (white, first lightly fried in butter), served with a purée of green peas and, separately, sauce béarnaise.

suprêmes Talleyrand (white), stuffed with foie gras and served with timbale of macaroni, chopped truffles, and sauce madère.

suprêmes tsarina (white), coated with sauce suprême mixed with julienne of fennel, and garnished with ovals of cucumber cooked in sour cream.

suprêmes Verdi (white, first lightly sautéed in butter), served in a pastry shell filled with cooked macaroni mixed with a purée of foie gras; truffle slices are put on top of each suprême, and all is coated lightly with demi-glace flavoured with Marsala.

suprêmes verneuil (brown), marinated in olive oil and lemon juice with chopped shallot and parsley, dipped in egg and breadcrumbs and fried in butter; then covered with sauce *colbert* and garnished with artichoke purée.

suprêmes villeroi (white and brown), first poached lightly, then coated with egg and breadcrumbs and fried quickly in deep oil; sauce *périgueux* is served separately.

surkål, Norwegian for sour cabbage and sauerkraut. For the Norwegian method, chopped cabbage is gently simmered in butter and very little water, with a sprinkling of flour, salt, caraway seeds, and pepper. When the cabbage is tender and all the water has been absorbed, 1 tablespoon castor sugar and 1 tablespoon malt vinegar are stirred in. It is served hot. See also GRØNNSAKER; KÅL.

surmullet, a saltwater fish found mainly in the Mediterranean; it is related to the mullet. The flesh is fine and delicate, and it is prepared like sea bass.

surprim, a Norwegian sour milk cheese made from the whey of *gammelost.* See also OST.

sursild, see SILD.

suspiros de freiras, literally "nun's sighs," a Portuguese sweet flaky pastry, poached in a syrup made like the syrup used for *sonhos.*

sutlyàsh or **sutliyàsh,** a Bulgarian pudding made with rice and served with the rosepetal jam (*glyko*) for which Bulgaria is famous. First ½ lb. rice is cooked in 1 pint (2 cups) milk, with sugar and vanilla to taste. It is drained and left to get cold, then mixed with ½ pint (1 cup) yogourt or sour cream. Served cold with 1 teaspoon rose petal jam on each portion.

suutarinlohi, a Finnish way of preparing salted sprats. The fish are soaked overnight, then gutted and filleted. The fillets are placed in layers with pepper and sliced onion, then covered with a sauce made from 4 tablespoons sweetened vinegar and ½ teaspoon ground allspice. They should be eaten within a couple of hours, and are generally served with boiled potatoes. See also SILAKAT, KEITSETYT SUOLASILAKAT.

svamp, Danish and Swedish for mushrooms and edible fungi in general. See also CHAMPIGNON; CHAMPINJON; MUSHROOM.

sveciaost, svecia cheese, a typical Swedish cheese made from whole cow's milk, similar to *herrgårdsost* in appearance except that the holes are irregular in shape, but made quite differently. It is dry-salted and has a fresh and distinctive flavour. Sometimes caraway seeds and cloves are added to the paste. It is usually matured for 2–4 months, and it weighs from 25 to 30 lb. If it is stored for too long, the taste becomes very aggressive and pungent. See also OST.

svekla, Russian for beetroot, used extensively in Russia for salads, soups, stews, and as a vegetable. It is often served cooked, with sour cream. It is, in fact, perhaps the most popular Russian vegetable after cabbage. See also BEETROOT; BORSCH.

sveske, Danish for prune.

svestkové knedliky, see KNEDLIKY.

svid, a typical Icelandic dish, made from prepared lamb's head split in 2 and the brains removed. The head is simmered, and the meat is taken from the bones and served either hot or cold with mashed turnips.

svinekjøtt, Norwegian for pork, which is traditionally eaten at Christmas and served with sauerkraut. Svinekotelett is pork chop. In Norway lamb and mutton are the two most popular meats, but minced pork is often used for meat loaves or cakes, sometimes set in aspic. See also KJØTT; PORK.

svinekød, Danish for pork; *svinekotelet* is pork cutlet. See also FLÆSKE; KØD; PORK.

svinekød med grønsager og kartofler, stewed pork and carrots served with potatoes. Fillet of pork is cut up and gently fried with 1 sliced onion, after which boiling water is added to cover, and the meat is simmered for about 30 minutes. Then carrots, ½ lb. chopped celery, and ½ lb. peeled and sliced pears, with salt and pepper, are added, and the whole is then simmered for about 1 hour. The gravy is thickened by adding creamed corn flour (cornstarch), also a little browning. Boiled new potatoes accompany the dish.

svinemørbrad med æbler og svesker, pork stuffed with apples and prunes. Fillets of pork are slit lengthwise and filled with diced apples and scalded, stoned prunes. Then they are browned in butter. About 1 cup water is added to the pan, and the meat is simmered for about 1½ hours or until tender. The gravy is thickened with slaked corn flour (cornstarch). It is served with red cabbage and *brunede kartofler.*

svinina, Russian for pork. See also PORK.

svinaya grudinka s gribami, a popular joint of pork, roughly corresponding to shoulder or brisket of beef, roasted with mushrooms inserted in the fat. It is served with *kasha.*

svinaya grudinka s sladkim sousom, grudinka (shoulder or brisket) of pork cut into strips and boiled until tender, then drained, rolled in flour, coated with egg and rye breadcrumbs, and browned in the oven. It is served with a sauce made from the stock simmered with 2 tablespoons each of apple, cherry, and plum jam, honey and red wine, grated peel of 1 lemon, and a pinch each of cinnamon and cloves.

svinjsko meso, the Serbo-Croat term for pork. See also PORK.

svinjsko meso duvec, a pork and vegetable casserole, made from lean pork, onions, sweet peppers, garlic, zucchini, carrots, tomatoes, potatoes, parsley, and celery leaves, all sautéed in oil and cooked with a little stock and half-boiled rice for 1½–2 hours.

sviske, Norwegian for prune, used in a great variety of ways in Norway. See also PRUNE.

sviskeblancmange, an excellent cold pudding made from 2 cups finely chopped, stewed prunes, and 1 cup of the water in which they are cooked, brought to the boil with ¼ lb. (½ cup) sugar. Then 4 level tablespoons corn flour (cornstarch) is slaked with the same amount of water and stirred in. The mixture is simmered for 15–20 minutes, stirring from time to time. The prune stones are cracked, and the kernels taken out, chopped, and added to the mixture with 1 teaspoon cinnamon

and juice of ½ lemon. The mixture is poured into damp moulds and chilled. It is usually served with cream.

sviskefylling, Norwegian prune stuffing for duck or goose. One lb. prunes are soaked in water for several hours, then strained and stoned. The fruit is mixed with 4 large chopped cooked apples, ½ cup chopped cooked pork, 1 small minced onion, ½ cup breadcrumbs soaked in 2 tablespoons milk, 1 egg yolk, and salt and pepper to taste. These quantities will be sufficient for a large duck; at least twice as much will be required for a goose.

swan (*Cygninae*), a large white bird, once consumed in great quantities. In the Middle Ages no banquet was complete without roast swan, and it was customarily served to the guests by either the lady of highest rank or the lady of greatest beauty. It is an extremely rare item on modern menus, but it is still traditionally served, once a year, by the Swan Warden of the Vintners' Company at the Vintners' Hall in the City of London, after the Thames swans (owned by Her Majesty) have been marked and counted. Only the young bird or cygnet is worth eating; it is well fleshed and carves well. When dressed it looks rather like a dark-coloured goose, although the flavour is quite different. It is stuffed with chestnuts, sausage meat, onion, and herbs, and the breast is larded with bacon before roasting as the meat is inclined to be dry. The bird is basted with warm red wine.

sweat, to, a cooking term which means to draw the juices from foods before cooking, by gently heating in fat or butter. The foods must become soft, but not brown, before the other ingredients are added. The lid is kept on, and the saucepan is shaken during the sweating time, usually 5–7 minutes. The process is applied particularly to white meats such as chicken and veal, and to chopped vegetables that are to be used for braising.

swede or **Swedish turnip** (*Brassica napo-brassica*), a plant whose large round roots, with their yellow or white flesh, resemble turnips. They are used mainly for cattle food in northern Europe, except in the British Isles where they are a well-known vegetable. Swede may be cooked in any way that is suitable for turnip.

Swede is known by several names: Russian turnip, rutabaga, and turnip-rooted cabbage. In Ireland, however, it is called turnip, the true turnip being known there as "white" turnip, and it is prepared by first boiling it, then mashing with butter, pepper, and a pinch of cinnamon or mace. See also LANTTU.

sweet and sour sauce, a Chinese sauce now popular in Britain and America. There are two American versions: For one, 2 tablespoons butter is browned in a small pan, when 2 tablespoons flour is stirred in and well browned. After that, 2 cups vegetable water or stock, 2 tablespoons vinegar, 2 tablespoons sugar, salt, and pepper are added. The mixture is beaten until smooth, then cooked, a dash of french mustard being sometimes added. It is served with boiled beef, grilled spareribs of pork, or with cooked vegetables served as a separate course. In another method 1 cup honey or sugar and 1 cup vinegar are combined and then boiled up until sticky. The sauce is seasoned with a little soy sauce and may be slightly thickened with corn flour (cornstarch). It is very good with fish as well as with pork or ham. See also AGRODOLCE.

sweet cicely (*Myrrhis odorata*), an aromatic perennial plant with a bracken-like leaf which smells a little like myrrh. The leaves are used, finely chopped, in salads and stews. All the acidity is removed from rhubarb or other acid fruits when a leaf of sweet cicely is cooked with them.

sweet corn, see CORN.

sweet gale (*Myrica gale*), also known as bog myrtle or Dutch myrtle, but not in fact related to the true myrtle. It has been used from very early times to flavour beer. See also MYRTLE.

sweet javril (*Osmorhiza claytoni*), an American perennial herb with aromatic roots and leaves. It is often called sweet cicely in the U.S., and can be used in the same way.

sweet pear, see ROCK MEDLAR.

sweet peppers or *bell peppers* (*Capsicum frutescens*, var. *grossum*), the large fruits of a species of capsicum in which the hot-flavoured oleoresin, capsaicin, is present only in very small amounts, so that their chief flavour is mild, pleasant, and distinctly smoky. These savoury fruits have the distinction of containing a percentage of vitamin C higher even than those of any of the citrus fruits. Until just before they reach maturation they are a very fine bright green, but when fully ripened they turn a beautiful clear yellow or red. Some varieties, when dried and powdered, become paprika. They are an essential ingredient of many of the stew-like dishes of southern France, Italy, Spain, Portugal, Rumania, Yugoslavia, Greece, and Turkey. They may be eaten either raw or cooked. Raw, de-seeded, thinly sliced sweet peppers make a very good salad when combined with raw peeled tomatoes and served with sauce vinaigrette. The core and seeds are removed from peppers before cooking or serving, as they have an acrid taste. Some cooks burn off the skin by fierce grilling, but when fresh, the skin does not spoil the flavour. See also CAPISCUM; PIMIENTOS; PIMENTOS.

stuffed peppers, peppers which are de-seeded and then steamed or blanched for 5–7 minutes. Fillings vary, but chopped meats or poultry, cold rice, herbs, and a little onion or garlic are usually included. The peppers are baked for 35–40 minutes in a moderate oven with 1 inch of tomato purée diluted in water. If small, they can be served cold with sauce vinaigrette as an hors d'oeuvre, but the large ones, served hot, make an excellent light meal.

sweet potato (*Ipomoea batatas*), sometimes known as long potato in the U.S., and as Virginia potato in early English cookery books. The plant, found first in Central America, is cultivated for its tubers, which are faintly scented, sweet, and yellowish in colour. It is not quite as hardy as the true potato. Sweet potatoes were introduced into Spain in the 16th century, and are used extensively there today for both sweet and savoury dishes. It was in the latter part of the same century, between 1563 and 1565, that they were brought to England by Drake and Hawkins. Sir Francis Drake said this of them: "These potatoes be the most delicate rootes that may be eaten, and doe farre exceed our passenpes or carets. Their pines be of the bignes of two fists, the outside whereof is of the making of a pine-apple, but it is soft like the rinde of a cucomber, and the inside eateth like an apple but it is more delicious than any sweet apple sugred." They quickly superseded the parsnip as an accompaniment to roast beef.

American cookery, particularly dishes made in the southern states, and creole cookery, include sweet potatoes prepared in many ways, both as a vegetable, and as a stuffing for poultry when they are combined with sausage meat, onion, celery, and breadcrumbs. Sweet potatoes may also be cooked in the same way as true potatoes. An attractive and popular way of preparing them is to serve them mashed, in scooped-out half shells of orange peel. The orange juice can be used to moisten the sweet potatoes, which are placed in the shells, sprinkled with brown sugar, and then baked or grilled. For another method, cooked sliced sweet potatoes are layered with peeled and sliced apples, sprinkled with brown sugar mixed with a pinch of cinnamon, dotted with butter, moistened with a little water or orange juice, and baked for 45–60 minutes in a moderate oven. They are served with ham. The same dish is made using bacon rashers instead of apple, onion instead of cin-

sweet potato

namon, and milk instead of orange juice or water. See also POTATO; YEMAS.

candied sweet potatoes, sweet potatoes first cooked, then peeled, sliced, and simmered in butter and plenty of brown sugar or syrup so that they become sticky. They are delicious with ham steaks, and corn bread, or chicken.

sweet potato pone, a sweet potato dish that is also served with ham. To prepare it, 6 medium-sized, cooked, sliced sweet potatoes are put in a single layer in a casserole. Then 1 lb. (2 cups) sugar is mixed with 2 oz. (¼ cup) butter, 1 teaspoon each of allspice, cinnamon, cloves, and ground nutmeg, 12 oz. pale raisins, and 3 beaten eggs. This mixture is poured on top of the sweet potatoes, and the dish is baked in a slow oven for 1 hour. A cake may be made with the same ingredients as above, but with 2 cups flour added and with only 1 cup sugar; the raisins are soaked in rum or bourbon whisky before being included.

sweet sauces, generally served with steamed puddings or rice in England, or incorporated into other puddings such as trifle, etc. Jams or golden syrup (molasses), heated, are often served over steamed or baked puddings, and would be called jam sauce or golden syrup sauce.

apricot sauce, made from ¼ lb. (½ cup) fine apricot jam, 1 wineglass (½ cup) white wine, and sugar to taste, boiled up and served warm. Other sauces may be made by substituting different jams or marmalade for apricot.

brandy or *rum butter*, see BRANDY BUTTER.

brandy sauce, often served with Christmas pudding. First ½ pint (1 cup) milk is thickened with 2 teaspoons creamed corn flour (cornstarch), then boiled up, sweetened to taste, and flavoured with 4 tablespoons brandy. It is further enriched with 2 egg yolks beaten with 2 tablespoons cream, and is heated but not reboiled.

chocolate sauce, served with steamed puddings or ice cream. To prepare it 1 egg yolk is beaten with 2 tablespoons sugar and 2 tablespoons grated bitter chocolate, all gently heated in a double boiler; when the chocolate has melted, the stiffly beaten egg white is whisked in. It is served hot.

creamed sauce, served with steamed puddings. To make it 4 oz. (½ cup) butter, 1 tablespoon ground almonds, 2 tablespoons castor sugar, and 4 tablespoons brandy are all beaten together. It is served chilled.

custard sauce, see CUSTARD.

hard sauce, the American name for brandy or rum butter.

sweet sauce, served with sweet puddings. Using a wooden spoon, 4 oz. (½ cup) sifted sugar is stirred with 4 egg yolks in a saucepan or double boiler until well mixed. Then 2 gills (½ cup) fresh cream is added very gradually with constant beating, and the peel of 1 orange is finely grated in. The mixture is stirred for about 5 minutes over a gentle heat; it must not boil. It is then strained through a sieve and served at once.

sweet whipped sauce, served with a light steamed pudding. To prepare it 2 egg yolks, 1 level tablespoon castor sugar, and 2 tablespoons cold water are placed in the top of a double boiler over the heat, and whisked together until the mixture begins to thicken. Then 1 glass sherry (½ cup) is added slowly. The whole preparation of this sauce takes not more than 10 minutes; it should be served at once.

sweetbreads, the culinary term for the pancreas and the thymus gland of mammals; the former is large and oval in shape, the latter, the throat sweetbread, smaller, elongated, and irregular. Calf's sweetbreads are considered the best, followed by lamb's and then pig's. Sweetbreads are very gelatinous and contain a lot of albumen; the flesh is white and, if properly cooked, should be soft. Sweetbreads require a certain amount of preparation before cooking. First they are soaked in cold, lightly salted water for 3–4 hours, the water being changed at least once; they are then blanched in fresh water with a dash of vinegar or a slice of lemon, and when they are cool, any skin, membrane, or gristle should be removed. When cold, they are ready for further cooking. If they are of uneven size, it is advisable to cut them to a regular pattern. The most general method of cooking in Britain is to coat each piece in egg and breadcrumbs, fry the pieces in butter, and serve them with lemon. However, sweetbreads are also excellent braised, or served in a sauce béchamel enlivened with chopped herbs and a little white wine, and finished with cream, with a sprinkling of chopped parsley and croûtons of fried bread. See also ANIMELLE; KALVKÖTT (KALVBRÄSS); MLECZKO; RIS; ZWEZERIK.

braised sweetbreads, an 18th-century recipe. First 1 lb. blanched sweetbreads is seasoned, rolled in flour, and put into a casserole with sherry-flavoured stock to cover. Several mushrooms, sweated in butter, are added, and the whole is covered and cooked in a hot oven for 30 minutes. The liquid is then drained off, and 8 large stoned prunes are simmered in it for 15–20 minutes, then removed and put with the sweetbreads. The stock is reduced, and the prunes and sweetbreads added; the mixture is then thickened with 1 egg yolk mixed with 2 tablespoons cream and reheated, but not reboiled or it will curdle. It is served with wedges of lemon.

More often in England, sweetbreads are braised in a thickened brown sauce or gravy, with onion, peas, chopped carrots, etc. This tends to destroy their delicate flavour.

sweetsop, see CUSTARD APPLE.

sweitzer käse, see SWISS CHEESE.

Swiss chard, see CHARD.

Swiss cheese, also known as schweizer käse or sweitzer käse, a hard cow's milk cheese first made in about 1850 by Swiss immigrants in the U.S., and still made, mainly in Wisconsin, Illinois, Ohio, and Wyoming, by their descendants. It is based on emmenthal cheese.

Swiss cheese plant, see MONSTERA.

Swiss cheeses. See APPENZELL CHEESE; APPENZELL RÄSS CHEESE; BATTELMATT CHEESE; BELLELAY; EMMENTHAL; FRIBOURG VACHERIN; GRUYÈRE; PIORA; SAANENKÄSE; SBRINZKÄSE; SCHABZIEGER; SWISS TILSITER CHEESE; TOGGENBURGER KÄSE; VACHERIN, DU MONT D'OR; VALAIS RACLETTE. See also KÄSE.

Swiss roll, a sponge mixture baked in a shallow tin, then spread with a jam or cream filling, and rolled up while still warm. It is served cold, cut into circles.

Swiss steaks, slices of rump or round beef, floured and cas-

Swiss cheeses (clockwise from top: appenzeller, tilsiter, emmenthal, Gruyère, tilsiter. Inner circle: brie and gervais)

seroled in a moderate oven for 1½ hours with tomatoes, onion, sweet peppers, and tomato juice to cover, sometimes they are braised without the vegetables.

Swiss tilsiter cheese, an entirely different type of *tilsiter käse* from the German cheese, made in the Swiss cantons of Thurgovia, St. Gallen, and Zurich and sold only in Switzerland. It was introduced into the country in 1896 by the Swiss cheesemaker Wegmüller, who brought the method of making it from East Prussia. It is softer and sweeter than the German tilsiter käse.

swordfish (*Xiphius gladius*), an enormous saltwater fish found in the Atlantic and Pacific Oceans and in the Mediterranean. It can weigh up to 600 lb., and is sold both fresh and salted. The flesh is white and quite delicate, and grilled swordfish steaks are a popular and delicious American dish. It may also be baked with plenty of butter or strips of salt pork, fried, poached, or treated in any way that is suitable for tunny fish (tuna). See also ESPADA; ESPADON; SPADA.

swordfish

syllabub or *sillabub,* an English sweet dating back to Elizabethan days. The name comes from "Sille" (Silléry), the part of the Champagne country from which the wine came, and "bub," which was an Elizabethan slang term for a bubbling drink. Originally, milk and cream fresh from the cow were poured from a height into the glasses, to make the drink frothy. Some early books suggest that the cow was milked into the glass, and a servant was sent out for this purpose, with a warmed bowl.

A sprig of rosemary is put into a long glass, with a pinch of nutmeg, a little lemon peel, a red fruit juice such as raspberry, sugar to taste, and white wine. The syllabub should reach to halfway up the glass, which is then covered and the contents left for some hours, preferably overnight, to infuse. The rosemary and lemon peel are then removed, and each glass is filled up with lightly whipped cream. The cream should not be

syllabub

too stiff, but firm and frothy. Syllabub is served chilled, and as it is rather rich, is accompanied by sponge (lady) fingers or wafers. Brandy or sherry can be added to the wine. It is also called whipped or whipt syllabub.

syltekjøtti, Norwegian jellied mutton chops. Chump chops are boned and trimmed of all fat, before being simmered in water with seasoning and a bouquet garni until tender. The liquid is drained, strained, and measured. Then 2 tablespoons garlic or tarragon vinegar, and 3 sheets of gelatine to 2 pints (4 cups) stock, are added, boiled up, and then cooled before being poured over the chops in a deep dish. Served cold, with beet-root salad dressed with sour cream or fresh cream.

syltetøy, Norwegian for jam, which in Norway is often made from several fruits together. The most popular mixture is white, red, or black currants, gooseberries, loganberries, and raspberries, or cloudberries.

synagrida, Greek for dentex, which is cooked like mackerel in Greece.

syr, Czechoslovakian for cheese. See ABERTAM; KOPPEN; OŠTĚPEK; RIESENGEBIRGE-KÄSE; ZLATO.

syr, Russian for cheese. Very little information concerning the content of individual Russian cheeses is available, but the following is a list of some of the more common varieties (generally speaking, they are named after the area in which they are made): Altaysky, Brynza, Dorogobuzhsky, Gollandsky, Gorny Altay, Kobiysky, Kostromskoy, Latviysy, Moldavsky (a smoked cheese), Moskovsky, Motal, Sovetsky, Stepnoy, Tushinsky, Volzhsky, Yaroslavsky, Yartsevsky. See also SU-LUGUN; TVOROG.

syrnaya paskha, see PASKHA.

syrniki, traditional Russian cheese dumplings. They are made by mixing 2 cups flour, 4 eggs, and 4 tablespoons melted butter with 1 lb. (2 cups) pressed curds or cottage cheese, and seasoning with salt, pepper, and a pinch of nutmeg. This dough is formed into round flat cakes which are poached in boiling water. They are served covered with melted butter.

syrup, a solution of sugar and water, or sugar and fruit juice, boiled until it is of a sticky consistency. The usual proportions for a stock syrup are 2 lb. sugar (lump or granulated) to ½ pint (1 cup) water; if the syrup is to be kept, 1 teaspoon liquid glucose or cream of tartar is added to prevent graining. The syrup is boiled to 215°–220°F (102°–104°C) and skimmed while boiling, then cooled slightly and strained through muslin. It is of a thick consistency and can be stored and used for *fondants* and water ices, or for cooking fruits. The container into which it is put should not be tightly stoppered, but covered with foil.

Syttende Mai, Norwegian Independence Day, May 17, a national holiday during which many traditional dishes are eaten. People hold open house and serve *eggedosis* (see EGG) and *mandelkaker.* See also BLØTKAKE.

szczaw, Polish for sorrel, which is used extensively in Poland as a vegetable, for sauces, and also for soups. Both the wild and the cultivated varieties are used, but the wild is preferred, and large quantities are brought into the markets daily from the surrounding countryside. Sorrel is cooked in the same way as spinach, then it is drained, and a little sugar and sour cream are added. If served as a vegetable course it is garnished with slices of hard-boiled egg. Sometimes it is enriched with 2–3 egg yolks beaten into the hot purée, and served with veal and fried croûtons. See also SORREL; SOS, SZCZAWIOWY; ZUPA, SZCZAWIOWA.

szczupak, Polish for pike, a fish which is eaten a great deal in Poland. A whole pike, weighing 3–4 lb., is salted for 2–3 hours and either simmered in stock or baked in butter. It is usually served with horseradish sauce and lemon. It can also be stuffed with soaked breadcrumbs, sour cream, and chopped anchovies. If the fish is large, it may be cut into steaks or fillets to be grilled or fried. See also PIKE.

szczupak duszony, pike placed on a bed of root vegetables with a little water, butter, bay leaf, and thyme, covered, and simmered or casseroled for about 1 hour. It is served with cooked noodles.

szczupak po polsku, whole salted pike baked and basted with sour cream. It can be stuffed with veal forcemeat.

szczupak po żydowsku, a Jewish-Polish method of preparing pike. The fish is skinned and filleted, then stuffed with soaked bread mixed with onion, nutmeg, and butter, and bound with 1 egg. It is then sewn up and placed on a bed of diced carrots, celeriac, parsnip, and Hamburg parsley root, with butter and a cup of water. It is covered and steamed slowly for about 1 hour. The sauce is sometimes thickened, and the fish is served with horseradish sauce.

székely sajt, a Hungarian soft cheese made from ewe's milk and sold in skins or bladders. There is also a smoked variety.

Szent István Király Nap, St. Stephen's Day, August 20, a great Hungarian religious and national holiday. Many traditional dishes such as *húsleves májgombócal* and *borjúpörkölt* are eaten. Today it is still a holiday, celebrating the declaration of the new People's Constitution.

szilváslepény, a Hungarian plum pie, excellent eaten hot. A yeast dough is made from 1 oz. yeast, ¼ pint (½ cup) tepid milk, 9 oz. (2 heaped cups) flour, 2 egg yolks, 1 oz. (1 heaped tablespoon) butter, and a pinch of salt. The dough is well kneaded, then covered and left in a warm place for 1 hour. When it has doubled in size, it is spread on a greased baking sheet and covered with stoned plums. The plums are sprinkled with sugar and cinnamon; then 3 oz. (3 heaped tablespoons) butter, 3 oz. (3 heaped tablespoons) sugar, and 2 heaped tablespoons flour, are all well mixed and placed on top. The pie is baked for 30–40 minutes and served warm, with cream.

sznycle, Polish for escalopes (scallops). See CIELĘCINA.

szparag, Polish for asparagus, sometimes served in Poland with a sauce béchamel which has crayfish or shrimp added. See also ASPARAGUS.

szpinak, Polish for spinach. See also SPINACH.

szpinak z czosnkiem, washed and chopped spinach simmered in a sauce made from a roux moistened with strong brown stock, with crushed garlic, salt, and pepper. About ½ pint (1 cup) stock is sufficient for 2 lb. spinach.

szpinak ze śmietanką, as above, but the spinach is simmered in a sauce béchamel with cream added. The garlic is omitted.

kotlety ze szpinaki, croquettes made from 1 cup cooked spinach to which 1 cup breadcrumbs, 1 tablespoon butter, and 1 egg are added. A small fried and diced croûton is put in the middle of each croquette, which is then rolled in breadcrumbs and fried on both sides in butter or oil.

sztuka mięsa, Polish for boiled beef served with root vegetables and hot horseradish sauce.

szynka, Polish for ham, often smoked in Poland, and soaked before cooking. See also HAM.

szynka duszona na czerwonym winie, ham casseroled with root vegetables, juniper berries, cloves, bay leaf, and Hamburg parsley (root and leaf), with equal quantities of red wine and stock barely to cover. When cooked, the vegetables are sieved and returned to the stock, which is then flavoured with a little Madeira, and if too thin, thickened with a little flour. The stock and sieved vegetables are heated up and served with the ham.

szynka z ryzem zapiekana. One lb. cooked sliced ham is placed at the bottom of a greased fireproof dish and covered with 2 cups cooked rice mixed with grated Parmesan cheese and 2 egg yolks, followed by ½ pint (1 cup) sauce béchamel which has been mixed with 2 oz. chopped mushrooms. The dish is baked in a moderate oven for 30 minutes.

Tabasco sauce, a liquid seasoning of American origin, made commercially since 1868. It is prepared from chillis, salt, and spirit vinegar, is extremely hot to the tongue and is therefore used sparingly. A few drops of Tabasco adds great piquancy to eggs, shellfish, various fish soups, cooked cheese dishes, and some ragoûts.

tacaud, a common French name for a variety of young Atlantic cod. It is quite good to eat, but inclined to be bony.

tacchino, Italian for turkey. Compared with turkeys in the U.S., Italian birds are quite small, the average weight being 9–12 lb. They are often eaten on feast-days, and are sometimes sold cut into joints. The breast fillets are especially popular, cooked separately like *petti di pollo*. The legs and wings are often casseroled with root vegetables, herbs, and white wine. When cooked whole, turkey is invariably stuffed and roasted. See also TURKEY.

filetti di tacchino al marsala, turkey fillets dredged with flour and cooked in butter, with a glass of Marsala and stock.

filetti di tacchino alla bolognese, turkey fillets flattened, seasoned, dredged with flour, and gently browned in butter for 10–15 minutes. Then a slice of cooked ham, white truffle, and a layer of grated Parmesan cheese are placed on each fillet, with 1 tablespoon stock for each fillet. The pan is covered, and the contents simmered gently for 10–12 minutes.

filetti di tacchino alla modenese, turkey fillets sliced very thinly, dipped in egg and breadcrumbs, fried in butter until golden, then transferred to a casserole and put on a layer of sliced ham or bacon and Gruyère, and covered with another layer. They are baked in a hot oven until the cheese is melted.

tacchino arrosto ripieno (alla Lombarda), roast stuffed turkey from Lombardy. The stuffing contains 1 lb. minced (ground) veal or pork, 1 lb. cooked chestnuts, ¼ lb. chopped prunes, the liver of the bird, 4 raw, peeled, and cored pears, a pinch of rosemary, 1 small onion, 2 tablespoons grated Parmesan cheese, 2 beaten eggs, and seasoning. Sometimes apple is used instead of pear. The turkey is thickly rubbed with butter, and cooked for 15 minutes per lb. During the last hour of cooking it is basted with ½ pint (1 cup) white wine.

tàccula, a Sardinian method of cooking small birds of various kinds. They are simmered in a little stock until tender; then, while still hot, they are put into a sack filled with myrtle and allowed to get cold among the fragrant leaves. This gives them a piquant taste. See also BECCAFICO; FIELDFARE; FIG-EATER; GAME; LARK.

taco, a Mexican speciality eaten in many parts of the U.S. A taco is a *tortilla* fried in hot olive oil or lard and given a filling. Each taco is filled with a mixture made from 1 lb. ground beef, chicken, or pork, and eaten with a sauce made from 2 mashed avocado pears, 2 peeled and pounded tomatoes, chilli to taste, a pinch of coriander, and *mole* powder. The *tortilla* is folded over the filling like an envelope. When served hot in the street, it is topped with shredded lettuce; in the U.S. a sprinkling of grated white Mexican cheese and hot chilli sauce is added.

Tadcaster pudding, a baked suet pudding which is a speciality of Tadcaster in Yorkshire. To prepare it ½ lb. grated suet, 4 oz. (1 cup) flour, 4 oz. chopped dried fruits, 2 teaspoons baking powder, and a pinch of salt are mixed with 1 tablespoon golden (or corn) syrup and ¾ pint (1½ cups) milk. The mixture is poured into a shallow greased baking dish and cooked in a moderate oven for 45–60 minutes. The pudding is turned out upside-down and covered with 2 tablespoons hot treacle (molasses) boiled up with 1 cup cider, a squeeze of lemon juice and a pinch of mixed spices.

taetei cu nuci, a Rumanian speciality of broad, cooked noodles served hot, mixed with butter, sugar, and chopped hazelnuts or walnuts.

tafelspitz auf alt wiener art, a Viennese speciality, which is a particular Austrian cut of lean beef from the rump end, simmered very slowly in stock and herbs. It is usually served with chive and horseradish sauce and beetroot salad, or with horseradish mixed with breadcrumbs (semmelkren).

taffelost, see MYSOST. See also OST.

tagliatelle, the most usual form of homemade pasta, consisting of long, ribbon-like strips about ¼–½ inch wide, although the size can vary, known as fettucine in Rome and as noodles in English-speaking countries. When coloured green with spinach, it is called tagliatelle verdi. A Bolognese speciality is to serve it col prosciutto, that is with strips of ham sautéed in butter mixed into the cooked pasta, and with grated cheese. Extra cheese is served separately.

taglierini, the Italian name for the basic noodle dough. See PASTA.

taglioline, Italian fine, thin noodles. See PASTA.

468

tahina, a Middle Eastern paste made either from crushed sesame seeds and olive oil, or from ½ pint (1 cup) sesame oil mixed with 4 tablespoons iced water (the cold water solidifies the oil). Then a little salt and ¼ pint (½ cup) lemon juice are stirred in, and the paste is served with bread for *mezes.* It can also be mixed with 1 crushed garlic clove and ½ lb. cooked lentils or chick-peas mixed with a little olive oil. See also HUMMUS.

tail, in shellfish such as shrimps, prawns, crayfish, and lobsters, the tail is the largest edible part and highly prized. Certain mammal tails are used as food, namely those of lamb, pig, and ox, which are eaten throughout Europe. The tail of the beaver is considered a delicacy in Germany (see BIBERSCHWANZ). See also QUEUE.

tailloir, French for a wooden board on which meat is cut up. Much earlier, before plates had become common, this was the word for a thick slice of bread on which food was served. These slices were given to the poor after use. They were also called tranchoirs, thus the English "trencher."

tăitei cu nuci, see TAETEI CU NUCI.

talatourri, a Cyprian salad consisting of sliced cucumber garnished with yogourt mixed with chopped garlic and mint. It is sometimes served with fried mullet or with cheese.

taleggino, a stronger version of *taleggio.*

taleggio, an Italian cream cheese made from cow's milk. It is soft and creamy, delicate in flavour, and comes from Lombardy.

talkkuna, a traditional Finnish dish consisting of 2 tablespoons rye flour mixed with 1 lb. cooked peas, spices, and seasoning. *Viilipiimä* is usually served with it.

Talleyrand, I. A French sauce made from ½ pint (1 cup) chicken-based sauce velouté, with 1 pint (2 cups) white stock added to it and then reduced. The sauce is removed from the heat, and 4 tablespoons cream and 2 tablespoons Madeira are added and well blended in. It is garnished with a *mirepoix* of vegetables, chopped truffles, and diced pickled tongue. II. A French garnish for meat and poultry of cooked elbow macaroni bound with butter and grated Parmesan cheese, then mixed with diced goose liver, julienne of truffle, and sauce *périgourdine.* III. A sherry-flavoured French chicken consommé garnished with truffles cooked in sherry. See also CONSOMMÉ.

tallow wood or *ximenia* (*Ximenia americana*), a tree that grows in Mexico and the warmer parts of the U.S. It is also known in the U.S. as the mountain or seaside plum, as it bears an edible fruit with a sweet aromatic flavour, although it is a little rough to the palate. The plant is named after Francisco Ximenez, a Spanish monk who wrote about Mexican plants in the early 17th century.

talmouses, small French tartlets with a variety of fillings which always have cheese as a base. The baking tins are lined with a *pâte brisée* or chou pastry and are usually filled with a cheese soufflé mixture, or spinach mixed with cheese, then baked in a slow oven. They are served for hors d'oeuvre.

tamal(es), a flat Mexican cornmeal pancake similar to *tortilla.* The name comes from the Aztec name for the cornmeal *mixtamal.* They are made with 2 cups finely ground white corn kernels, 2 tablespoons soft lard, 1 teaspoon salt, and about 1½ to 2 cups of boiling water, enough to make the batter of a spreading consistency. Sometimes a beaten egg is added, but this is not essential. The salt is added to the cornmeal and the softened lard rubbed in. Then the boiling water is poured in and well mixed, and finally the beaten egg if used. Traditionally tamales are cooked in the soft insides of corn husks, which are prepared by removing the corncob, soaking the husk in boiling water to clean and soften. While hot the inside surfaces are rubbed with a piece of pork fat.

The tamale batter is spread over about 5 inches by 3 inches and ⅛ inch thick. Then any filling used is put on top, the husks are shaped into cylinders, and the ends tied. They are then steamed for 15 to 20 minutes. Sometimes they are fried after that, having been removed from the husks, in a heavy pan rubbed over with a piece of pork fat, or on a griddle. Fillings can vary enormously, from a spicy meat sauce, to fish, game, chicken, pumpkin, or fruit. A simpler version is to make the tamale batter into a pie.

tamales de cazuela, first make a spicy sauce from 1 lb. ground beef, fried with a sliced onion and tomatoes and seasoned with chilli powder, salt, and pepper. Then make the tamale batter as above. Grease a baking dish; then spread over a layer of tamale batter, then a layer of the meat mixture, then the tamale batter, meat, and so on, ending with a layer of the batter. Spoon over a tablespoon of oil and bake in a moderate oven for about 1 hour. It can be served with a tomato sauce as well.

tamarind (*Tamarindus indica*), a tree which is the sole representative of its genus, a native of Asia but now cultivated in many tropical countries. The name is derived from the Arabic *tamr* (a ripe date) and *hind* (India). In India the leaves are used in curries, as are the flowers, but in the West Indies, Asia, and Europe, tamarind is chiefly important for the aromatic pulp surrounding the seeds in the long fruit pods, which is used for making spicy relishes, chutneys, and sauces, such as worcestershire sauce.

tamboril, Portuguese for the anglerfish, also called frogfish. It is used a great deal in *caldeirada à fragateira.*

tamie, a French cheese made with cow's milk, produced in Savoy almost all the year round.

tamis de crin, French for a drum hair sieve of very fine mesh on a wooden frame.

tammy or *tammy bag,* a piece of cloth, known as tammy cloth and similar to rough flannel, used to press and strain a sauce or soup through. It was used a great deal before the arrival of the blender, to ensure smoothness, and also by gloss, emulsification. In Scotland it is the name for a jelly bag.

tanag, a hard-pressed, skimmed-milk cheese which used to be made in Ireland several centuries ago from cow's milk. In old manuscripts tanag is glossed with *gruth* (curd), and with the Latin *formellas* (small forms), which implies that it was pressed in small pots or moulds.

tangelo, a fruit of hybrid origin, the result of a cross between the mandarin orange (some varieties of which are known as tangerines) and grapefruit. The most favoured of these hybrids was produced in Florida in 1897 by W. T. Swingle and is known as the Sampson tangelo. The tangelo is a very sweet and juicy fruit, irregular in shape with a greenish-orange skin, not at all attractive to look at but good to eat. It is generally known in Britain as ugli or *ortanique,* although the latter is a similar but technically different hybrid.

tangerine, see ORANGE.

tangleberry (*Gaylussacia frondosa*), a dark-blue berry of the huckleberry variety, which grows on all peaty soils in the U.S. Tangleberries are very sweet and can be eaten fresh or cooked. It was originally called dangleberry because of its very long pedicels.

tanrogan, the Manx name for scallops, large quantities of which are regularly exported to France from the Isle of Man. They are of excellent quality.

tansy (*Tanacetum vulgare*), an attractive perennial plant which blooms in about September. It has delicate bright-green leaves, and yellow button-like umbelliferous flowers which have a warm spicy fragrance. Tansy is associated with Easter, and small, yellow, bittersweet custard cakes called tansies, made from milk, eggs, sugar, flour, and tansy leaves, used to be eaten on Easter Sunday. It is also one of the "bitter herbs" eaten by the Jews at the feast of the Passover. In Ireland the leaves are used to flavour *drisheen*.

tapénade, a Provençal purée. The name comes from the Provençal word for caper, *tapeno*. To prepare it 2 dozen stoned black olives, 8 anchovy fillets, 2 heaped tablespoons tunny (tuna) fish, and 2 heaped tablespoons capers are all pounded together in a mortar to form a thick purée. About ½ cup olive oil is gradually added and worked in, followed by juice of ½ lemon and ½ tablespoon brandy or other spirit. All ingredients must be thoroughly blended. This purée can be served as part of an hors d'oeuvre, but a very common method is to serve it with hard-boiled eggs, as follows.

oeufs durs en tapénade, the purée is spread in a dish, then hard-boiled eggs, halved lengthways, are placed on top. If preferred, the egg yolks can be removed and mixed with a little of the purée, then replaced in the cooked shells of egg white. See also OEUFS.

tapioca, a farinaceous starch-like substance extracted from the roots of the cassava or manioc plant. The juice contains a large amount of starchy matter. This is roasted, dried, and then sifted into various grades of tapioca, such as flake, medium, and pearl. When simmered in milk, these rough granules become transparent and jelly-like. Tapioca is used mostly for milk puddings in the proportions of 1½ oz. (¼ cup) tapioca to 1 pint (2 cups) milk, with sugar to taste. It is also used to thicken soups and broths, and when cooked in consommé gives added nourishment to invalids.

cassava plant

tara, a comparatively recent Irish cow's milk cheese, which has a good flavour not unlike a port-salut. It is yellowish in colour, with small holes, and has a red outer casing.

tarak, Turkish for scallops, usually served as *kebabs,* or in *piláv.* They are also grilled over charcoal, sprinkled with olive oil and fennel, and seasoned.

tarama, Greek and Turkish for fish roes. It is also the Turkish name for the pounded mullet roe, called *taramosalata* in Greek. See also CAVIAR.

taramo keftedes, a Greek dish, often eaten during Lent, of rissoles made of ½ lb. pounded fish roe, 1½ lb. mashed potatoes, 1 chopped onion, parsley, mint, and seasoning, rolled in flour, and fried in hot olive oil.

taramosalata, a delicious Greek purée of the roe of the female grey mullet. See also AVGOTARAHO; BOTARGO.

taratòr, a cold soup originally from Bulgaria, but now eaten throughout the Balkans. It is made with 1 pint (2 cups) yogourt, 1 small cucumber cut into pieces, chopped nuts (preferably walnuts), 1 clove garlic, olive oil, salt, pepper, and

some vinegar. The ingredients are well beaten, and chilled. A spoonful of cream is sometimes placed on top of each plateful. See also CHORBÀ.

taratouri, the Greek version of the Bulgarian *taratòr.* See also TSATSIKI.

tarhonya, the staple food, like bread or pasta, of the Alföld (lowland plain) of Hungary. It is a paste made with 2 lb. flour, 4 eggs, and just enough water to make it very stiff. This is well kneaded and broken up into tiny balls the size of peas, which are browned in lard with minced onions and paprika. Then they are simmered in boiling water, which is absorbed into them. Tarhonya serves as an accompaniment for meats, but it is also eaten on its own, like pasta, by the poor. In country districts it is dried and stored, sometimes with dried strips of meat, and used through the winter.

tarragon (*Artemisia dracunculus*), a perennial herb which is a native of southern Europe. It is used extensively in French cooking. It grows to a height of 3 or 4 feet, and has long, delicate, polished green leaves. The herb owes most of its fame to the flavour it imparts to vinegar. A sauce crème with tarragon is a classical French sauce for chicken (see POULET, À L'ESTRAGON); it has a slight flavour of aniseed. In the 16th century tarragon was credited with healing powers and was used to cure the bites of venomous creatures. See also DRAGONCELLE.

tarragon

tarragon purée, ½ cup tarragon leaves pounded and added to 2 cups thick sauce béchamel. It is used for *vol-au-vents,* or for cold vegetable, chicken, or fish dishes.

tarragon sauce, made by the addition of blanched chopped tarragon leaves to the many white sauces and veloutés which lend themselves naturally to this. Brown tarragon sauce is made by simmering chopped shallots in white wine, mixing in demi-glace, and garnishing with chopped tarragon.

tarragon vinegar, made by putting a handful of fresh tarragon leaves into a ½-gallon earthenware jar, which is then filled up with white or red wine vinegar. The jar, well corked, is left to stand for about a fortnight in the sun, being turned over occasionally. The vinegar is then filtered and bottled for future use.

tart, 1. In Britain, as in France, a tart is the same as a flan, that is a case of pastry, usually short crust or rich short crust, sometimes baked blind, and with either a sweet filling of cooked fruit, jam, golden syrup, or custard, or with a savoury mixture of beaten eggs, milk, cheese, ham, chicken, or shellfish, or a thick sauce béchamel incorporating chopped herbs, cheese, etc. Savoury tarts are browned in the oven and are eaten hot or cold, for example *quiche,* and *tarte.* II. In Britain, a tart can also be a flat, double-crusted fruit-filled pastry dish, or a bottom crust containing a filling and having strips of pastry put lattice-fashion across the top. III. In the U.S. the word pie would apply to all the descriptions in I and II. (Sometimes, but not always, a pie denotes a pastry-covered ingredient cooked in a pie dish, which is sometimes a bit deeper than a tart or flan tin.)

A tart or flan dish is usually 8–9 inches across. Jam tarts, however, although they may be as big as this, are usually much smaller, not more than 2–3 inches across, and should strictly speaking be called jam tartlets. Tartlets can also have other sweet or savoury fillings. However, the word tartlet is seldom used in English, and tart is the generally accepted name for all sizes. See also FLAN; TARTE.

tartan purry, an old Scottish dish, consisting of finely chopped, cooked kale mixed with oatmeal. The name comes from the French *tarte-en-purée,* which indicates that originally it may have been served in a pastry case.

tartar, see CREAM OF TARTAR.

tartare, sauce, I. A classical French sauce usually made with ½ pint thick mayonnaise, which is thinned to the required consistency with 1 teaspoon dry white wine and 1 teaspoon red wine vinegar; then 1 teaspoon dijon mustard, finely chopped parsley and tarragon, salt, pepper, 3 minced shallots, and 2 or 3 coarsely chopped gherkins are added. It is served with fried fish, croquettes, fried brains, etc. II. An English variation of the French classical sauce. To prepare it 2 teaspoons each of chopped gherkins, chopped capers, and chopped parsley is mixed carefully with 1 cup mayonnaise and seasoned well.

tarte, French for tart, consisting generally of a pastry case with filling, as in England. The filling may be sweet or savoury, although many French savoury tarts are known as *quiches.* Some French cheesecakes are also called tartes, like *tarte bourbonnaise;* no doubt this was originally presented in a pastry case like the Polish and American cheesecakes. See also TART.

tarte à l'oignon, an Alsatian speciality, also known as *zewelwaï.* The dish is lined with *pâte brisée* which has had an egg added to it. The filling is made with 1 lb. peeled and finely sliced onions, softened in butter until pale golden and seasoned with a pinch of nutmeg, salt, and pepper; then 3 egg yolks are mixed with ¼ pint (½ cup) cream and added gently. This filling is then poured into the pastry case, and the tart is baked in a moderate-to-hot oven for 30 minutes. It is served hot.

tarte Alsacienne, the tin is lined with *pâte frolle;* then strips cut from the remainder of the pastry are put lattice-fashion across the top of the tart, to form sections, and are dampened at the edges to secure them. Each square or diamond is filled with a different kind of jam or marmalade, each kept separate from the others by the pastry strips. The pastry is then brushed with egg yolk, and the tart is baked for 20–30 minutes in a moderately hot oven.

tarte Alsacienne aux abricots, a *pâte brisée* lining filled with apricots soaked in kirsch and covered with custard before baking.

tarte Alsacienne des pommes, as for *tarte Alsacienne aux abricots,* but with apples. The custard is flavoured with cinnamon.

tarte bourbonnaise, 1½ lb. (3 cups) thick fresh cream cheese or cottage cheese is pounded in a bowl with 4 tablespoons butter, 4 tablespoons flour, and 4 eggs. When well mixed, this mixture is put into a flat buttered pie dish, and small holes are made on top (about 8 of them), into each of

which is put a nut of butter. The tarte is then baked in a slow oven for 30–40 minutes, and is served hot or cold, sprinkled with sugar.

tarte des demoiselles tatin, a 9-inch tin, 2½ inches deep, is well greased with butter; then a layer of sugar ⅓ inch deep is added, followed by peeled and quartered apples. Then the tart is covered with *pâte brisée* and baked for 20–30 minutes until the bottom is well caramellised. (If preferred, the sugar and fruit can be cooked a little before the pastry is added.) It is served hot and is turned out so that the caramellised fruit is on top. It is also called *tarte tatin.*

tarte niçoise, a savoury tart from the vicinity of Nice, made from 2 cups puréed spinach mixed with either 3 sardines or 12 black olives, and ½ cup breadcrumbs, 2 raw eggs, salt, and pepper, all baked in a case of *pâte brisée.* Spinach beet or chard, both the green leaves and the white stalk, are often used instead of spinach.

tarte au suif, a Canadian tart or pie consisting of a suet crust filled with 1 cup chopped nuts mixed with 3 beaten eggs and 1 cup maple syrup. It is baked for 45 minutes in a slow-to-moderate oven and served cold.

tartelette, French for a small tart or tartlet. In the 16th century the word was *flannet,* from flan. Tartelettes are often given savoury fillings as well as fruit fillings, and these are used as a garnish for meats, poultry, or fish, or for hors d'oeuvre.

tartelettes à la provençale, small open pastry cases, each with a different savoury filling. Examples of fillings used are mushroom and tomato, olives, onion and anchovy, and cooked prawns with green olives. One tartlet of each filling is served to each person as a course. See also PISSALADIÈRE.

tartine, French and Italian for a slice of bread spread with butter, jam, honey, etc.

tartines suisses, puff pastry cut into 4-inch rectangles which are brushed with egg, baked, and then sprinkled with sugar. When cold, these are split in half and filled with a vanilla custard which, when cooked and cooled, has had stiffly beaten egg whites added to it.

tartufi de cioccolata, chocolate truffles, Italian sweetmeats, so called because of their resemblance to small truffles. To make them ½ lb. bitter chocolate is melted with 2 tablespoons black coffee or milk, and when a smooth mixture has been achieved, it is removed from the heat and 3 oz. (3 tablespoons) butter and 2 egg yolks are worked into it. It is left to harden for 4 hours, when it is formed into walnut-sized shapes which are rolled in cocoa.

tartufi di mare, Italian for sea truffles. In Genoa they are called *tartufoli di mare.* They are eaten raw in Italy, and have an excellent flavour.

tartufo, Italian for truffle. *Tartufo bianco* is the white truffle. See also TRUFFLE.

salsa di tartufi, a white truffle sauce served with roasted meats. It is prepared with 1 grated onion and 1 garlic clove lightly fried in butter; then 1 tablespoon flour is stirred in, with ½ glass (¼ cup) Marsala, and all is beaten until smooth. The garlic is removed, the sauce is seasoned, and 1 cup sliced truffles is added. It is simmered very slowly for a further 5 minutes.

tas kebab, a type of Greek stew with a thick sauce, containing small pieces of meat, usually lamb, cooked in an earthenware pot (*tas*).

táth, an early Irish cheese, no longer produced. It was made from sour milk curds which were unpressed. The curds were heated and stirred, in a way similar to that used in the making of many continental cooked cheeses, until they coalesced in a single mass.

tattari, Finnish for buckwheat.

tattaripuuro, a boiled buckwheat porridge.

tattariuunipuuro, a baked buckwheat porridge, made from 1½ cups buckwheat soaked overnight in 2 pints (4 cups) water, then boiled in the same water the next day. When the water has been absorbed, 3 pints (6 cups) boiling milk is gradually added and the pudding is cooked for 30 minutes. It is then put into a greased dish and baked in a low oven for 2 hours, or until golden. It is served with hot milk.

tatties an' herrin', a traditional dish from the Scottish islands. New potatoes are half-boiled in their jackets, then the water is drained off and the potatoes are covered with fresh herrings. A cloth is pushed down on top, and the whole cooked gently for a further 15–20 minutes in the steam.

taube, German for pigeon or dove. See also DOVE; PIGEON.

tauben in specksauce, quartered pigeons browned in butter, with diced bacon and the pigeon livers then added to them. The whole is dredged with flour and browned; then shredded lemon peel and lemon juice, shallot, stock to cover, salt, and pepper are put in, and all covered and simmered gently for several hours.

tautog, see BLACKFISH.

tavuk, Turkish for chicken. *Tavuk kebabi* is spit-roasted chicken; *tavuk yahni* is braised chicken; *tavuk yahnissi* is braised chicken. See also CHICKEN.

çerkez tavugu, Circassian chicken, a Turkish chicken dish ''borrowed'' from Circassia (an area in the northern Caucasus). A chicken is boiled with slices of garlic fried brown in oil. Then the meat is taken from the bones and served with a sauce made of 2 thick, crustless slices of white bread soaked in water, then squeezed dry, 1 lb. (4 cups) shelled walnuts, finely minced, twice, in a grinder, seasoned well, and minced twice more with the bread. Finally ½ pint (1 cup) clear, skimmed chicken stock is stirred in well until a thick sauce is obtained. This sauce is spread over the cold chicken, and all is sprinkled with paprika.

tayglach or *taiglach,* a Jewish holiday confection, eaten at Rosh Hashanah, made, as is usual with Jewish holiday foods, with honey, nuts, and spices. First 1 cup honey, 1 cup sugar, ½ cup chopped nuts, and 1 teaspoon spices are boiled together, and a dough mixture is made from ½ lb. (2 cups) flour, 3 eggs, salt, and ½ teaspoon nutmeg or ginger. The dough is made into small balls which are cooked in the boiling-hot honey and sugar mixture for about 8 minutes, then drained and sprinkled with chopped nuts. When cold, the tayglach balls are stored, and they are eaten like sweets. They can also be shaped like a pyramid with honey, nuts, and candied fruits embedded to keep it together. Small balls of the dough mixture are also poached in boiling soup, and then served with the soup as a garnish.

T-bone steak, the American cut of beef including in it the tail of both the fillet and the sirloin.

tchorbà, see CHORBÀ.

tea, I. *Camellia sinensis,* a small evergreen tree or shrub of the camellia family, whose dried and processed leaves are used to make the hot beverage, tea. The plant was originally native to China, and it has been used there since very early times. Only in the early 19th century was the shrub introduced into India and Ceylon, and it was in the middle of that century that Indian tea began to be imported into England.

China and Indian teas are those most generally drunk in Europe. Some of the important Indian teas are Darjeeling, Assam, Cachar, Sylhet, Terai, etc., and Ceylon tea. Indian teas are classified, according to their method of preparation, as green, black, or oolong. In the case of China teas, the gradations in order of quality are: flowery orange pekoe, broken orange pekoe, orange pekoe, pekoe, pekoe souchong, and souchong. The pekoes are made from small leaves, souchong from the larger and coarser leaves. See also AGRIMONY.

II. A meal, consisting of scones, tea cakes, sandwiches, biscuits, etc., which is taken at about 4 or 5 P.M. in Britain and sometimes Ireland. In Ireland, ''tea'' is more generally a cooked meal consisting of fried foods such as steak, chops, bacon, and eggs, etc., or a meat salad served with brown bread, with tea as the beverage. This is eaten between 6 and 7 P.M., and is known in the north of England and Scotland as ''high tea.''

tea

tea cake, a speciality of Yorkshire, and often known as Yorkshire tea cake. There are many individual recipes, but the following is traditional. First ½ oz. yeast is dissolved in ¼ pint (½ cup) tepid milk and water mixed, and a sprinkling of flour is shaken over to make a batter. The batter is then covered with the remainder of 1 lb. flour, salt is added, and it is set in a warm place for about 20 minutes with a cloth over the top. It is not mixed at this stage, and the yeast mixture will break through the dry flour. Then 3 oz. (½ cup) butter is melted and 1 heaped tablespoon sugar is added to it; the mixture is poured into the flour and yeast, and stirred in. Finally 1 beaten egg is added, and a dash more warm milk, if needed, to make a soft dough. The dough is covered and left for about 1 hour to rise, then turned onto marble or a cold table and kneaded very lightly. It is stamped out into small rounds which are put on a greased baking sheet, then left to rise again for 15 minutes. They are baked in a moderate oven for 30 minutes. When cooked, the rounds are broken open, each half is dipped in hot melted butter, and then they are put together again and served hot. Any tea cakes left over and likely to be stale can be toasted and served with butter.

teal, I. The European teal (*Anas crecca*) is a small species of wild duck with a beautiful colouring, highly esteemed by gourmets. A full-sized bird offers a meal for only one person, and so it has never become very popular. The teal is considered at its best after the frost has set in, from October to January. All recipes for wild duck are suitable for teal, though less time will be required for cooking, not more than 15 minutes in a hot oven. Like all wild duck, it is usually served underdone. It is generally grilled or roasted with port wine added to the pan juices, which are boiled up and reduced. Watercress is served as a garnish. In France, teal is permitted food on fast and abstinence days. See also GARGANEY. II. *A. carolinensis; A. discors* are the teals of America and Canada, of which there are many varieties. They are highly thought of as food and can be cooked in any way that is suitable for wild duck, or as described for the European teal.

tębaliki z jaja, see JAJA.

tebrød, Norwegian rusks. To prepare them 8 oz. (1 cup) butter is beaten with 6½ oz. (¾ cup) sugar; then 2 beaten eggs

teal

are added, alternately with 1 lb. 6 oz. (5 cups) flour mixed with 2 teaspoons baking powder. The dough is lightly kneaded, and then divided into small balls which are flattened and baked in a moderate over for 15–20 minutes until pale gold in colour. They are split in half and dried out in a very low oven, then stored. See also RUSK.

teewurst, a very fine German wurst made from finely pounded pork fillet, and smoked. It is one of the spreading sausages, or *streichwürste.* See also WÜRST.

tefteli or *teftely,* Russian meat balls. The minced (ground) meat is mixed with onion; the balls are shaped and then rolled in flour and lightly fried in butter. They are then put into a flat pan with tomato sauce, meat stock, bay leaves, garlic, and black peppercorns, and simmered for about 15 minutes. Sometimes a little sharp chutney is added before serving. Tefteli are eaten with boiled rice, *kasha,* or potatoes.

tegamini, small Italian utensils made from either metal or fireproof china, and having two handles. They are used for cooking eggs, usually individually, as for *uova al tegame.*

tejfel, Hungarian for sour cream, which is used in many Hungarian dishes, and also figures largely as a garnish for soups and stews.

tejfeles galuska, a soup garnish made in the same way as *csurgatott teszta,* but with the addition of chopped parsley.

tejfeles hal, see HAL.

teleća janija od spanaća, a popular Yugoslavian dish of veal simmered with spinach, onions, green peppers, and stock barely to cover.

telemes, a Greek cheese of the *féta* type, and sometimes confused with it, although it is more heavily salted and matures more quickly. It is produced in squares weighing about 2 lb. each, which are packed in layers with a good deal of salt between each layer. It is made from both ewe's and goat's milk, depending on what is available. See also TYRI.

tèleshko (mesò), Bulgarian for veal. See also VEAL.

tèleshko sŭs sìni domati, 2 lb. chopped veal is sautéed in oil, then casseroled with 2 fried onions, 1 teaspoon paprika, and 1 pint (2 cups) water for 1 hour. Halfway through cooking, 2 large peeled and sliced tomatoes, and 2 medium-sized eggplants which have first been dipped in egg and flour and then fried, are added. The whole is then cooked for a further 30 minutes.

telli kadayif, a Turkish pudding made with 8 oz. noodles boiled in 2 pints (4 cups) milk, with sugar to taste. A syrup is made by boiling 4 oz. (1 cup) raisins with an equal quantity of sugar, and this is poured over the pudding before serving.

Teltower rübchen, see WEISSE RÜBE.

telyatina, Russian for veal, sometimes served in Russia with a caviar sauce. See also VEAL.

telyatina s sousom iz ikry, fillet of veal simmered with stock, lemon juice, bay leaf, cloves, and a little white wine. When cooked, it is sliced and covered with a sauce made from the skimmed stock, caviar, butter, and lemon juice.

tenax, see WHEAT.

tench (*Tinca tinca*), a small freshwater fish related to the carp. It is found in many English and European rivers, but not at all in the U.S. In Europe it is used a great deal for *matelotes,* but it is also good to eat grilled or *au bleu,* especially if it has been caught in fairly fast-running waters. See also LIN; SCHLEIE.

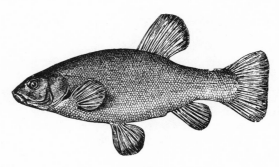

tench

tende de tranche, a French cut of beef equivalent to the English topside.

tenderising, the culinary operation of making meat more tender before cooking is commenced. There are 3 chief ways of doing this. One is by beating the meat, either with a specially designed flat-surfaced iron or wooden mallet known as a cutlet bat, a method usually employed in the preparation of escalopes (scallops), or by wrapping the meat in a napkin and swinging it forcefully against a smooth stone or wood surface, a method generally used in the preparation of a filet mignon. Another is to subject the meat to the influence of papaya juice, either by adding the juice to the meat and rubbing it on, or by placing the meat between two thick slices of the fruit for several hours. A similar effect is produced by using slices of pineapple and some vegetables. Papaya powder is sold commercially in the U.S. as a tenderiser. However, all methods using vegetable enzymes do reduce the flavour of the meat by drawing out the blood. A third method is subjecting the meat to the influence of bacterial enzymes, by marinating. The most commonly used are those to be found in yogourt or in sour milk. This method also reduces the flavour of the meat, but not to quite such a marked degree as the use of vegetable enzymes. See also MARINADE.

tenderloin, the American name for fillet of pork or beef.

tendrons, I. A French cut of veal extending from the extremities of the ribs to the sternum or breast bone; it must include the full width of the breast. It is an economical cut, corresponding to a middle-cut of breast in England, or riblets in the U.S. It is cartilaginous, and is usually braised. It is also known as *côtelettes parisiennes.* It may be served with all garnishes used for *fricandeau* or *noix de veau,* that is *bouquetière, bourgeoise, clamart, florentine, jardinière, macédoine, milanaise,* or *Piémontaise,* or with various vegetables such as braised celery, chicory, lettuce, mushrooms, etc. II. French for gristle.

tepary bean (*Phaseolus acutifolius*), a Mexican haricot bean grown in the southwestern states of the U.S. It is able to withstand great heat, and continues growth during drought. Mexican names for it, also used in Texas, are frijole and pinto.

terbiye, a Turkish sauce served with stuffed vine leaves, egg-plants, and courgettes (zucchini). To prepare it 2 beaten eggs are mixed with 1 heaped tablespoon corn flour (cornstarch) which has been dissolved in 2 tablespoons cold water and the juice of 1 lemon. This mixture is beaten vigorously with about 1 pint (2 cups) hot vegetable stock until it is frothy and thickened.

tern (*Sterno hirundo*), a common sea bird of the North Atlantic. It is not eaten, but the eggs are highly thought of and can be served hard-boiled.

ternera, Spanish for veal. In Spain this is generally baby beef (that is, cattle about 1 or 2 years old), for calves are not killed there until almost mature. It is far superior, however, to Spanish beef. *Ternera asada* is roast veal. See also MORROS DE TERNERA; VEAL.

lomo de ternera, veal escalopes (scallops) from the rump end of the loin are dipped in egg and breadcrumbs mixed with grated cheese, covered with melted butter, and baked in a greased dish. Fresh tomato sauce is poured round them when they are cooked.

ternera a la Sevillana, a recipe from Seville. First 1 lb. veal is browned in oil; then garlic, onions, and carrots are browned and removed. Next 2 teaspoons flour is stirred into the remaining oil and cooked slightly, then 1 pint (2 cups) stock, ¼ pint (½ cup) sherry, and seasoning are added. The meat and vegetables are returned to the pan, covered, and cooked slowly for 1–1½ hours. Just before serving, 12 stoned olives are added.

ternera con alcachofas a la cordobesa, a Cordoban method of preparing veal. Veal cutlets are browned with onions in oil, then blanched globe artichokes, 1 cup stock, ½ cup Montilla wine, salt, and pepper are added. All are covered and cooked slowly for 2 hours.

terrapin, the name given to several varieties of edible turtle found in fresh or estuary water in the U.S. The finest of all is the diamondback terrapin of which there are five varieties. It gets its name from the faceted scales that cover its shell. Two other varieties of terrapin are the red-bellied and the yellow-bellied, but these are inferior gastronomically, although the eggs are a delicacy. Terrapin is made into soup and a delicious stew. It is also served in a sauce crème. Recipes are the same as those for snapper. See also SNAPPER; SOFT SHELL TURTLE; TURTLE.

terrine, I. An oval French ovenproof dish in earthenware or china, which has a lid with a hole in it through which the steam can escape during cooking. This is necessary, as the lid is often luted. They vary in size, but the most common terrines are about 8 inches long, 6 inches wide, and 4 inches deep. A terrine has no handles, but there are often small projections at each end. It is used for the making of terrines of fish, game, meat, or poultry, or of foie gras from the livers of game or poultry. II. Food cooked in a terrine. A terrine is not unlike a pâté, that is a pie, but cooked without the pastry crust; the meats used, however, are often more coarsely cut in a terrine. In restaurants the word has become loosely interchangeable with pâté. To be correct, however, a terrine when cooked in a terrine dish should be called a pâté en terrine. All terrines are eaten cold in slices, sometimes with fresh bread or toast. Salad is not necessary and often detracts from the flavour. See also PÂTÉ.

terrine d'anguille, a traditional Christmas Eve dish in Provence. Finely sliced leeks, chopped parsley, and black olives are all laid in a terrine dish to form a thick bed which is moistened with white wine. A skinned eel is placed on top and covered with breadcrumbs, and the terrine is baked for 1½–2 hours.

terrine de campagne, also called *pâté maison* or *terrine du*

chef in restaurants. It generally consists of 1 lb. streaky (belly) pork, 1 lb. veal, ½ lb. pork liver, 1 garlic clove, ½ teaspoon black peppercorns, ½ teaspoon juniper berries, a pinch of mace, salt, 1 glass (½ cup) dry white or red wine, 2 tablespoons brandy, and some fat bacon rashers for covering the top. (The garlic, mace, and juniper berries are optional and the proportion of liver to meat used is adjustable.) The pork, veal, and liver are minced (ground), but a little of the pork is kept back and cut into small dice. All the ingredients are well mixed and left to stand for 1½ hours before cooking. The small pork dice are then added, so that they stud the minced mixture irregularly (this is characteristic of a terrine). The mixture is put into the terrine and covered with the rashers of bacon; the lid is put on, and the terrine is cooked in a *bain-marie* for about 1½ hours in a slow-to-moderate oven. It should be left to cool naturally, weighted when cold if desired. If the terrine is to be kept for several days, it should be covered with melted lard or butter.

terrine de gibier, game terrine, made as above but with the veal replaced by half-roasted game, either furred or feathered.

terrine de porc et de canard, pork and duck terrine, for which the ingredients are 1 lb. fillet of pork, ½ lb. domestic duck (the meat being taken from the legs and wings), the chopped duck's liver, 4 truffle slices, ¼ cup brandy, 2 egg yolks, and seasoning. The procedure is the same as that for *terrine de campagne.* Sometimes the whole duckskin is preserved raw, the minced ingredients being wrapped in it before they are put into the terrine. If price is no object, the breast of the duck is used as well as the joints.

teta, a mild pear-shaped Spanish cheese made in parts of the provinces of Lugo and Coruña, from cow's milk. It is also called perilla.

tête d'aloyau, a French butchery term denoting the end of a rump of beef.

tête de maure, see EDAM.

tête de moine, see BELLELAY CHEESE.

teterka, Russian for hazel grouse, which in parts of Russia is perhaps the most popular game bird. See also GAME; HAZEL GROUSE; RYABCHIK.

kholodnaya teterka, a dish of cold potted hazel grouse or grey hens (the female of the blackcock). It is made with 4 birds jointed, the breasts filleted, sliced, and placed in a pan with layers of fat bacon, 1 onion, 3 bay leaves, 5 cloves, 1 teaspoon cinnamon, and 1 pint (2 cups) red wine. All are covered with reduced stock made from the giblets, the remaining joints and the bones. The lid is put on and the ingredients are baked in a slow oven for 3–4 hours. When the meat has been allowed to cool, a weight is placed on top and it is chilled.

teterka s smetanym sousom, hazel grouse roasted and served with a sour cream sauce, the most usual way of cooking them.

tetine, French for calf's or cow's udder. In France it is soaked in cold water, blanched, and then allowed to cool, whereupon it is flattened under a weight. Then it is sometimes studded with fat bacon, braised in stock, and served accompanied by such garnishes as *bourgeoise, clamart, jardinière,* macédoine, *milanaise,* or *piémontaise.* It may also be salted and smoked.

tétragone, see ÉPINARD.

tétras, French for grouse, which is rare in France. Blackcock or black grouse, known as *coq de bruyère,* is widely distributed.

Tewkesbury saucer batters, a traditional dish made in areas all along the Welsh border and cooked there by fruit pickers. A batter is made from 1 egg yolk, 1 cup milk, and 1 cup flour, with 1 stiff egg white folded in last; it is poured into two thick, hot buttered saucers and cooked in a hot oven for 10–15 minutes. Hot cooked and sweetened fruit is poured onto one "batter saucer," and covered with the other. Sometimes young green peas or beans are used instead of fruit.

Thanksgiving Day, the fourth Thursday in November, which is a holiday in the U.S., commemorating the arrival of the Pilgrim fathers in Plymouth, Massachusetts in 1620, and their thanksgiving to God for their safe deliverance from the many hardships they had endured. It is said that the first edible game the Pilgrim fathers found was the wild turkey, so thenceforth turkey was always eaten on Thanksgiving Day. Pumpkin pie is also traditional, and in Massachusetts Marlborough pie is the speciality.

theevil, see SPURTLE.

thenay, a type of camembert, a soft French whole-milk cheese.

thermidor, a method of serving lobster. A sauce is made, consisting of sauce *bercy* mixed with a little English mustard and grated Parmesan cheese. The flesh of the lobster is diced and put back in the shell with this sauce, then sprinkled with more grated Parmesan cheese and lightly browned under the grill.

thermometer, an instrument for measuring temperature. There are 4 types used for culinary purposes. An ordinary clinical thermometer can be used for the making of yogourt, since it will only need to register temperatures between 105°F (41°C) and 108°F (42°C) Bottling thermometers are used for bottling fruit, etc., and register up to 212°F (100°C). Frying thermometers are used for testing the heat of fat and register up to 500°F (260°C). Oven thermometers register up to 500°F (260°C). Sugar thermometers are used for registering the different degrees of sugar boiling, between 220°F (105°C) and 400°F (204°C).

thicken, see LIAISON.

thimbleberry (*Rubus occidentalis*), a wild American raspberry with light red berries and a good flavour.

thiples, see DIPLES.

thon, French for tunny (tuna) fish, eaten both fresh and canned in France. Thonine is a species of tunny. See also TUNNY-FISH.

thon à la grècque, slices of fresh tunny (tuna) poached in court bouillon with sliced onion, garlic, carrot, seasoning, salt, olive oil, and lemon juice. The fish is cooled and served in the stock.

thon à la Provençale, fresh tunny (tuna) fillets larded with anchovy fillets, then baked with sliced onion, garlic, tomatoes, herbs, white wine barely to cover, and ½ pint (1 cup) sauce espagnole.

thonné, a French method of preparing veal by marinating in olive oil for 24 hours, then cooking with lemon slices, thyme, bay leaf, allspice, and pepper.

thornback (*Raia clavata*), a European skate or ray with spines along its back. It can be cooked in the same way as skate, and in 16th-century England, it was cooked and served with a mustard sauce mixed with the fish liver.

thourins or ***tourin,*** a white onion soup made in the south of France. To prepare it 3 large onions are peeled, sliced, and cooked in butter until a pale gold colour, then sprinkled with 2 tablespoons flour and seasoned with salt and freshly ground pepper, stirring all the time. Next 2 quarts (8 cups) warm milk is poured over, mixed well, and simmered slowly for 30 minutes. Just before serving, 4 egg yolks beaten with 1½ cups cream and 2 tablespoons butter are added. The soup is not reboiled. It is served with croûtons.

thourins à la Provençale, as above, but before the egg yolks and cream are added, 1 cup vermicelli is poached in the soup. It is served with grated cheese.

Thousand Island dressing, equal parts of mayonnaise and Russian dressing mixed together, with one quarter the quantity of stiffly whipped cream added and the whole thoroughly blended. Sometimes chopped chives, tarragon, and parsley are included.

Thracian cress (*Barbarea longirostris*), a type of cress common in the Balkans but fairly new to England. Like all other varieties, it has a high vitamin content and a delicate flavour, combining the mustard-oil flavour of mustard with that of raw cabbage. It is useful in green salads and in all vegetable salads.

thread herring, see HERRING.

thrush (*Turdidae*), a beautiful brown song bird with a speckled breast found in many parts of the world. It used to be eaten in England and is still enjoyed a great deal in many parts of France, Italy, and Corsica. It can be cooked in many ways, but is best roasted or grilled over charcoal and served on a croûton fried in butter. In France it is often boned and stuffed, then reshaped and wrapped in a pig's caul before being cooked in butter in the oven. It is also prepared en caisse (see CAILLE). In Liège it is roasted with juniper berries. *Pâtés, terrines,* and chaud-froid are also made with thrush. In Italy it is grilled on a skewer (see UCCELLETTI) and in Sardinia it is used for *tàccula*.

thump, see STELK.

thunder and lightning, see CORNISH SPLITS.

thyme (*Thymus*), the general name for a genus of plants with aromatic leaves. Garden thyme (*T. vulgaris*) is upright in form. It is a small shrub-like perennial, with tiny leaves which are used in the flavouring of soups and stews, and for stuffings of delicate meats. The twigs of the shrub are gathered in June and dried for winter use. *T. serpyllum,* wild thyme, known as "mother of time," grows all over the world. It has a creeping, prostrate habit of growth, and for hundreds of years the leaves have been combined with other scented herbs in the making of perfumes. The Greeks and

thyme

Romans flavoured their wines with wild thyme, and, nearer our own times, the great herbalist Culpeper remarked: "It is a certain remedy for that troublesome complaint, the nightmare." (This was probably by virtue of its digestive properties.) It grows wild on chalk and limestone all over Europe, and the meat from sheep which graze on such pasturage has an excellent flavour. Lemon thyme has a delightful fragrance and a rich lemon flavour. It is an ideal herb to accompany fish dishes of all kinds, and is also excellent with chicken and veal. Its flavour is more delicate and generally more pleasant than that of garden thyme.

tian, a traditional Provençal dish which is eaten in almost all Provençal homes and often served cold on picnics, but is seldom found on the menu of a restaurant. It consists of green vegetables, such as spinach, chard, and sometimes baby marrows (zucchini), all chopped and lightly sautéed in olive oil. A little garlic, rice, or dried peas may be included, and eggs may be beaten in. Tian is topped with breadcrumbs and grated Parmesan cheese, then baked in a moderate oven for 1½–2 hours. It can be accompanied by fresh sardines and anchovies. The dish takes its name from the large heavy earthenware pot in which it is cooked. In country districts near Vallauris it is sent to the local bakery to be cooked over a wood fire.

Tibetan partridge, see ARBENNE.

tiganites, a Greek fritter, similar to *loukoumades* but made with baking powder instead of yeast. The procedures are the same, and the quantities are 1 lb. (4 cups) flour to 2 teaspoons baking powder, 1 small glass brandy or *ouzo,* salt, and juice of 1 lemon, with enough cold water to make a smooth, fairly thick batter. See also FRITTER; LOUKOUMADES.

tigiega mimlica, a Maltese method of roasting chicken which has been stuffed with equal quantities of minced beef and pork, chopped hard-boiled egg, and ½ cup breadcrumbs.

tignard, a hard French blue-veined cheese from the Tigne Valley in Savoy. It is similar to *gex* and *sassenage* and is made from either goat's or ewe's milk.

tijelinhas de nata, small Portuguese cakes consisting of puff pastry cases filled with a rich custard made with cream.

tikva, Bulgarian for pumpkin. See also BUNDEVA.

tikvenik, pumpkin pie, made with 2 lb. cooked pumpkin, ½ lb. (1 cup) sugar, 1 teaspoon cinnamon, and 1 cup nuts all topped with a pastry crust.

tile fish (*Lopholatilus chamaeleonticeps*), a large saltwater fish found in deep waters off the eastern seaboard of the U.S. The flesh is coarse but edible.

tilliliha, a Finnish dish of mutton with dill sauce. The mutton is placed in boiling water with salt and dill and cooked slowly. It is then removed from the stock, cut into pieces, and placed on a platter. Flour is blended with the stock to make the sauce, which is then seasoned with vinegar and sugar and poured over the meat. It is garnished with chopped dill. See also LAMMAS.

tilsiter käse, a German semi-hard cow's milk cheese, which may be made from either whole or skimmed milk. It is a faintly yellow cheese with a flavour ranging from mild to medium-sharp piquancy, depending on the milk used. Caraway seed is sometimes added to skim-milk tilsiter. It was introduced by immigrants from the Netherlands to the district around Tilsit in East Prussia. It is also made in Austria.

tilslørte bondepiker, Norwegian apple charlotte, a traditional pudding in Norway. To prepare it 2 lb. peeled and cored apples and ½ lb. (1 cup) sugar are simmered to a purée with 6 tablespoons water; then 2 cups cold breadcrumbs, which have previously been sprinkled with sugar and lightly fried in butter, are spread between layers of the cold purée. The dish is topped with whipped cream. Alternatively, this pudding may be baked and served hot, when dried breadcrumbs are used.

timbale, I. A round mould made from metal or china, with straight or slightly sloping drumlike sides, sometimes fluted. It can be quite small, about 3 inches across, or large and high. The word comes from the Arabic "thabal" (drum). In early days a timbale was a drinking cup. *Timbale à soufflé* is a fireproof or metal dish shaped like a timbale mould, used for cooking *soufflés.* II. A dish that is cooked or served in a timbale mould. Originally this meant a preparation cooked or served in a pastry crust, a usage which is rarely met with today. Nowadays the timbale mould is more generally lined with cooked macaroni or rice. Timbales can be made from al-

most any foods, even fruits. Many garnishes, such as *financière, joinville,* or *toulousaine* are cooked in these moulds, often layered with macaroni or noodles. Mixed cooked vegetables are set in aspic in small timbales and turned out to garnish various dishes, or used for hors d'oeuvre. In modern culinary usage timbale frequently refers, in addition, to foods served pyramid-fashion, often garnished.

timbale de macaroni, a timbale mould lined with cooked macaroni, and the middle is filled with a variety of forcemeat, often of the quenelle kind. It is poached in a *bain-marie,* then turned out and served hot with demi-glace or sauce madère.

timbale van ham, ham timbale, a Dutch dish. To prepare it 1 thick stale slice of white bread (without crust, and previously softened in a little milk), 1 lb. chopped boiled ham, 3 egg yolks, 1 tablespoon combined chopped onion and parsley, seasoning, ¼ pint (½ cup) bouillon, and 1 tablespoon Madeira are all mixed together and then folded into 3 beaten egg whites. All are steamed for about 1¼ hours in a covered timbale mould, standing in a pan of water, in a fairly hot oven. It is turned out of the mould and served.

timpana, one of the most popular Maltese dishes. It consists of 1 lb. macaroni, boiled, drained, and then combined with a mixture of diced sautéed liver, onions, and cream cheese, 2 eggs, and sliced eggplant. The mixture is then put into a greased pie dish with a pastry crust and baked, or it can be wrapped in pastry and baked like a turnover.

tinamou (*Tinamidae*), a game bird not unlike a partridge, native to South America and Mexico. It has been successfully introduced into France and may now be counted there as a game bird.

tioro or **ttoro,** a Basque fish stew containing as many pounds of onions as there are of fish. The onions and fish are first softened in olive oil before being simmered for 1 hour with double the volume of water or fish stock.

tipo piora, see PIORA CHEESE.

tipsy cake, an alternative English name for trifle. Originally tipsy cake was a sponge cake soaked in sherry, covered with whipped cream and decorated with chopped nuts and preserved fruit.

tiri tiganismeno or **saganaki,** a Greek dish of squares of fried *féta* cheese, often served for *mezes.*

tiroler g'röestl, see G'RÖSTL.

tiroler knödlsuppe, an Austrian regional soup from the Tyrol, consisting of rich beef broth garnished with large dumplings (*knödel*) which are made by soaking diced bread in milk, adding to it flour, eggs, chopped onions, and diced salt pork, and boiling in water.

tiroler leber, a liver recipe from the Austrian Tyrol. Sliced liver is cooked with a small sliced onion and served with a sauce made from the pan juices mixed with 2 tablespoons flour, ½ pint (1 cup) sour cream, 3 tablespoons capers, salt, and pepper. It is served with cooked rice or *nockerln.*

tiropeta, a Greek dish made with phyllo pastry, cheese, and eggs, and baked as a pie or folded into rolls or small triangles. It is often served for *mezes.*

tisane, a word deriving from the Latin *ptisana* (barley water), a drink which was also familiar to the Greeks and is mentioned by Hippocrates. Nowadays it means an infusion of herbs, either dried or fresh, which is drunk in the same way as tea. In Greece today many people cultivate herbs especially in order to make tisanes. They are also drunk in France, the most usual being made with chamomile or lime. The same word is used in English, French, and Greek for this beverage.

tisdagssoppa, see SOPPA.

Tiverton batter pudding, a speciality of Tiverton in Devonshire. To prepare it 4 eggs are separated, and the yolks and whites are beaten separately. To the yolks are added 1½ heaped tablespoons flour, 1 tablespoon sugar, a pinch of cinnamon and ginger, and 2 tablespoons finely chopped candied lemon peel. Then 1 pint (2 cups) milk is mixed in and, finally, the beaten egg whites. The mixture is poured into a greased basin and steamed for 1 hour, then turned out and served with melted butter and fine sugar.

tjur, Danish for *capercaillie.*

stegt tjur, roasted capercaillie. The bird should be well hung, then trussed before cooking and its breastbone broken down. It is then well larded and browned in butter. Next 1 pint (2 cups) cream is added, and cooking is continued for about 2 hours in a covered pan, with frequent basting. More cream is added during cooking if required, and any sauce remaining is served with the bird. During the last 15 minutes the bird is dredged with seasoned flour, and the lid of the pan left off. It is served with cranberry jelly, pickled gherkins, and roast potatoes.

tkemali, the Georgian name for the wild plums that grow in the Caucasus. See SOUS.

toad-in-the-hole, an English dish which consisted originally of chopped beef steak, and sometimes kidney, put into batter and then baked in good beef fat in the oven until set and puffed up. Nowadays it is made with sausages put into batter and then baked in the oven. It is advisable to grill or fry the sausages lightly first, so that they are pale brown; this gives them a more pleasing appearance in the batter. Toad-in-the-hole should be eaten as soon as it is ready.

toadstools, the common name for cap fungi. Many of these, such as the edible species of *Agaricus,* are called mushrooms. See MUSHROOM.

toast, a slice of bread browned on both sides, either under a grill, in an electric toaster, or in front of an open fire. If required crisp, it is put in a metal holder called a toast rack to allow the moisture or steam to escape; if preferred soft, the toast is kept warm in a napkin. See also MELBA.

tocana, a traditional Rumanian onion and vegetable stew. About 1 lb. of any kind of fresh meat is chopped and then fried in butter until browned. About 2 lb. sliced onions are added, and simmered with ¾ pint (1½ cups) water until cooked; 2 green peppers are included, with seasoning, and then 4 peeled sliced tomatoes and 2 tablespoons vinegar. The contents of the pan are stirred gently all the time, and when cooked, the stew can be kept in a moderate oven. Sour cucumbers and *mămăligă* are usually served with tocana, and most pickles combine well with it. This is a delicious stew, with a subtle flavour all its own.

tocino, Spanish for bacon, also the term for the skin and fat from any part of the pig. Crackling is unknown in Spain, for all joints have the skin and fat removed before they are sold. Tocino is used for rendering down to make lard, for barding, and in sausage making (see SALCHICHA).

toffee, the generic name for many kinds of hard sweetmeat (confection) made from sugar, butter, and milk or water. Nuts, dried fruits, and any one of a variety of flavourings such as vanilla, coffee, etc., may also be added. In the U.S. toffee is generally known as candy or taffy. A mixture of 1 lb. sugar (preferably brown), ¼ pint (½ cup) water or milk, and 4 oz. (½ cup) butter must be boiled rapidly until a small ball of it, dropped into cold water, hardens immediately. The sugar can also be mixed with one quarter its quantity of syrup—golden syrup, corn syrup, or maple syrup—this makes a very smooth, shiny toffee. Other well-known varieties of toffee include butterscotch, glessie, peggy's leg, vinegar candy, and yellowman.

toffee apples, one of the earliest treats for children, once popular at all country fairs but now not seen very often in the British Isles. A mixture of ½ lb. boiled treacle (molasses), 1

lb. brown sugar, and 1 tablespoon vinegar is made and boiled for 20–30 minutes. Small ripe apples, impaled on short sticks inserted in place of the stalk, are dipped into the hot syrup and then set bottom-down, the stick standing upright, to get cold and hard. Also known as caramel apples in the U.S.

toggenburger käse, also known as bloder käse, a Swiss cheese made mainly in the alps of the St. Gall, Toggenburg, in the Werdenberg district; a little is also made in the principality of Liechtenstein. It is the only Swiss cheese made from sour milk. The curing period takes from 6–9 months, and the cheese does not develop a true rind, but what is called a speckschicht or layer of fat. The cured curd is white and the texture granular. Toggenburger is only sold locally.

toheroa (*Amphidesma ventricosum*), a marine bivalve found off the northwest coast of New Zealand. It is about the size of a large scallop, is canned for export, and'makes a very fine, thick bisque. The name is Maori and means "long-tongued"; it has a long tongue-like roe similar to that of a scallop.

tökfözelék, a Hungarian method of preparing vegetable marrow (zucchini) with sour cream which is quite simple and makes an interesting first course for any meal. The marrow is peeled and cut into thin slices, seasoned with salt, and left to drain. It is then put in a pan with a little hot fat and paprika and cooked for a few minutes. A little flour and sour cream are then added, and the marrow (zucchini) is simmered in this sauce for a further 10 minutes.

tollo, Spanish for a dogfish which is eaten a good deal in Spain. This type is spotted, and can be cooked in the same way as bar.

tomar, a smoky-tasting farmhouse variety of *serra* cheese from the Arrábida, Portugal. The cheeses are small, about 1 inch in diameter. See also SERRA.

tomaat, Dutch for tomato. *Tomaatensla* is tomato salad.

gevulde tomaaten, stuffed tomatoes. The stuffing consists of a mixture of meat (pork, beef, veal, or a mixture of all 3), grated onion and parsley, bread which has previously been soaked in milk, nutmeg, and seasoning. The tops and insides of the tomatoes are sieved and the resulting purée, together with butter, is put over the stuffed tomatoes which are then baked for 30 minutes in a moderate oven.

tomatada à portuguesa, a fresh Portuguese tomato sauce mixed with freshly cooked vegetables such as peas, beans, carrots, potatoes, etc., and served hot with scrambled eggs.

tomate, French for tomato, served extensively in France, especially raw for salads and hors d'oeuvre. Tomatoes form an essential ingredient of many dishes in the south, particularly in garnishes or sauces, such as *catalane, helder, languedocienne, marseillaise, mexicaine, niçoise, portugaise, provençale* and *tyrolienne.* See also TOMATO.

tomate, Portuguese for tomato. Tomatoes are large and sweet in Portugal and of excellent quality. See also TOMATADA À PORTUGUESA; TOMATO.

tomates recheados, tomatoes stuffed with a cheese and breadcrumb mixture, sprinkled with olive oil, and baked. This is a common dish in Portugal.

tomate, Spanish for tomato. Spanish tomatoes often have a large amount of fibrous tissue and are not very juicy; this is especially true of tomatoes grown in the south, because of drought. They are usually peeled and seeded before cooking for this reason. All over Spain, tomatoes are stewed in oil with garlic and chopped onion, the resulting thick paste being used as an accompaniment to meat, fish, etc., as a sauce or flavouring.

tomato (*Lycopersicum esculentum*), a native of tropical America, botanically speaking a fruit, but regarded as a vegetable because of the way in which it is served. It is a perennial only in warm countries, and in Europe and North America it is cultivated as an annual. It was introduced into Europe in the 16th century, when it was known as "love apple" or "pomme d'amour." Curiously enough, it was not eaten generally in the U.S. until about 1835, for during the early 19th century many people thought it poisonous. One superstition which still persists in remote districts is that the pips can cause appendicitis. It is, however, an excellent source of vitamins A and C, and nowadays is eaten extensively, both raw and cooked. There are many varieties, but usually it is the round or oval red tomato that is most used for cooking and canning. The round or oval yellow tomato is quite superior to it for eating raw, because it has a finer flavour and its skin is less tough; that it is not more common can only be due to the fact that the general public expects a tomato to be red, and considers yellow tomatoes as unripe specimens.

Uncooked tomatoes should be skinned before use by being immersed in boiling water for 2 minutes; the skin will then come away very easily. They are used, either by themselves or mixed with other vegetables, in hors d'oeuvre, salads, sandwiches, and garnishes. Cooked tomatoes are stuffed and baked, made into chutneys and pickles, and used in soups, stews, soufflés, omelettes, sauces, and purées. Concentrated tomato purée (paste) is sold in tins and tubes; it should be used sparingly for sauces, as it has a metallic flavour and is not to be compared with a homemade purée. Tomatoes can be bottled at home and, as long as the jars are hermetically sealed, will last some months. Very occasionally tomatoes are prepared as a fruit and are delicious first peeled and sliced, then served with sugar and cream. Italian cooking relies very heavily on the tomato, which is prominent in all dishes entitled *napoletana*. Both in the U.S. and in Italy, tomato juice is canned on a very large scale and is used as a drink; it is also mixed into soups and stews. Tomatoes are an essential ingredient in many Provençal dishes, especially *ratatouille*. Basil is the herb which most enhances a tomato dish, and a sprinkling of it either fresh or dried brings out the flavour. See also DOMATES; POMIDORO; POMIDORY; TOMATE.

tomato fritters, slices of tomato dipped in batter, then fried in deep hot fat or oil until just browned.

tomato mayonnaise, 2 tomatoes are peeled and the seeds removed. They are rubbed through a coarse sieve, and the liquid is drained off. Then 2 hard-boiled egg yolks are mashed in a bowl which has been rubbed with garlic; 1 raw egg yolk is then blended in and, when a smooth paste has been achieved, 6 tablespoons olive oil is added, drop by drop, and some lemon juice. When the mixture is thick and smooth, the tomato pulp and seasoning are mixed in. A few drops of Tabasco sauce is sometimes added.

tomato purée, see PURÉE.

tomato sauce, much used throughout Europe and the U.S., and made by many different methods. (In all the recipes here the sauce can be electrically blended instead of sieved.) In one method 4 lb. fresh tomatoes are boiled to a pulp in ½ pint (1 cup) stock with basil, then sieved and seasoned and served hot. This is considered by many to make the lightest and best tomato sauce. For another method flour is added to an equal amount of butter, as in the first stage of preparing a roux for white sauce. When the mixture bubbles, it is moistened with water or white stock, and when it is boiling, the peeled tomatoes are added, with salt and pepper, and the cooking is continued in the thickened sauce. A third method uses 2 lb. ripe, chopped and peeled tomatoes and 1 onion, with bouquet garni, salt, and pepper. They are boiled together in ½ pint (1 cup) stock or water until the tomatoes are cooked. The mixture is strained through a fine sieve and all pulp removed. The liquor is then heated gradually to the boiling point, and a mixture of flour and milk or water is gradually stirred in as bind-

ing. A few minutes are allowed for the flour to cook and the sauce to thicken. Before serving, a large lump of fresh butter is added.

In Austria, tomato sauce is made with chopped onion and a *mirepoix* sautéed in butter, with sliced tomatoes and white stock added. The sauce is boiled, thickened with butter and flour, and seasoned with salt, sugar, and vinegar. It is called *paradeis sauce.*

See also POMIDORO, SALSA DI; TOMATADA À PORTUGUESA.

tomber à glace, faire, a French culinary term used when a food, particularly a vegetable, is cooked in a little liquid which, by boiling, is reduced to nothing.

tomber, faire, a French culinary term, meaning to cook meat in a saucepan without any liquid other than that produced by the meat itself. When cooking is finished, the juices should have the consistency of syrup.

tomcod (*Microgadus tomcod*), a small saltwater fish resembling a cod which inhabits the eastern seaboard of the U.S. It is prepared in the same way as cod.

tomerl, an Austrian pancake made from 1 cup cornmeal mixed to a medium-thick batter with 2 eggs and ½ pint (1 cup) milk. Before frying, a little salt and chopped fried onions are added to the mixture.

tomini del talucco, an Italian goat's milk cheese, made at Pinado, in Piedmont.

tomme, I. The name given to a number of small French cheeses made mostly in Savoy during the summer months, usually from cow's milk, often skimmed. Generally speaking, the whole-milk cheeses take longer to ripen, whereas the skim-milk cheeses are ready more quickly. This means that there is a tomme ready at almost all times of the year. If goat's milk is used, the cheese must be sold as *tomme de chèvre.* The various regions use different methods and flavourings for their cheeses. II. The name of a specific cheese of the group described above, made from fermented buttermilk and a speciality of the Dauphiné region.

tomme au fenouil, a cow's milk cheese flavoured with fennel, from Savoy. It matures around September.

tomme au marc, a cow's milk cheese produced in Savoy; it is another form of *fromage au raisin* but ripened in the grape pomace after the marc has been distilled. It is in season from November to May.

tomme au raisin, a type of *tomme de Savoie.*

tomme de bellay (*tomme de chèvre*), a goat's milk cheese produced in Burgundy; it is in season from May to October.

tomme de cantal, a fresh, soft, unfermented cow's milk cheese from the Auvergne district of France. It should not be confused with *cantal.*

tomme de praslin (*tomme de chèvre*), a cheese made from goat's milk and produced in Savoy; it is in season from June to September.

tomme de Savoie, a cow's milk cheese made during the summer months from skimmed milk. Some tommes de Savoie are made from goat's milk. A favourite cheese of this group is *tomme au raisin,* commonly called *fromage au raisin,* which is ripened in a dry mixture of grape skins, pips, and stalks. It is popular in England.

tomme grise, a cow's milk cheese from the Savoy district; it is in season from January to December.

tomtate (*Bathystoma rimator*), another name for the grunt. It belongs to a large family of small fish (*Haemulidae*) which inhabit the waters off Florida and the West Indies. It can be cooked in the same way as smelt.

Tonbridge brawn, a speciality of Tonbridge in Kent. This was, and still is, a great fruit-growing area, and during the 18th and 19th centuries, large numbers of pigs were kept very cheaply by leaving them to feed on the fallen fruit in the numerous cherry and apple orchards, so that large quantities of cured pork and allied products were always available in the district. Tonbridge was also a posting stage for coaches, and dishes such as brawn, cold ham, pies, and cheese (see STILTON) were kept by the inn keepers for travellers. The brawn is made from pickled pig's head boiled with herbs, mace, onion, and celery, boned and chopped when cooked, and then set in its liquid with a weight on top. It is left in a cold place until jellied, and sprinkled with breadcrumbs before being served in slices.

tong, Dutch for sole. Fried sole is *gebakken tong*. See also SOLE.

tong filets in witte wijn, fillets of sole in white wine. The fish is salted and baked in white wine barely to cover with dabs of butter. After about 20 minutes in a moderate oven, the fish is drained and the liquid is strained and made into a white sauce with flour and more butter. The fish is served in the sauce.

tong, Dutch for tongue, whether of ox, calf, lamb, or pig, cooked both fresh and smoked in Holland. The name of the animal prefixes the word, i.e., ox tongue is *ossetong*. Freshly boiled tongue of all kinds is often served hot with cooked, dried white haricot beans and *zure saus*. Smoked ox tongue is soaked overnight, then boiled in water with onion, bay leaves, celery, and parsley and eaten with *rozijnen saus*. See also OSSETONG; TONGUE.

tongue, classed as offal (variety meats), from whatever mammal it is taken. The largest and best known is the ox tongue, which can weigh between 3 and 6 lb. Although fresh tongues are available, they are usually sold pickled or salted, the slight amount of saltpetre used in the process giving them a characteristic pink colour. Pickled or salted tongue should be soaked for several hours, or overnight, before cooking. After trimming, which is essential, it is cooked in water with peppercorns, herbs, onion, and root vegetables for 30 minutes per lb. or 45–60 minutes in a pressure cooker for a whole tongue. When the tongue has been cooked, all horny parts must be cut away, and it is then skinned. The easiest way to do this is to plunge the tongue, still hot, into cold water, which cools it enough to make skinning simple. The skin should come off without any meat adhering to it if the tongue has been cooked correctly. In Britain tongue is usually served cold. It is skinned, then curled round inside a basin, and some of the stock (if not too salty), mixed with aspic powder, is poured over. When cold, paper and a weight are placed on top of it to make pressed tongue; this is served cut into rounds, with a salad and mustard. Early this century in England, a good dish was often made by heating up thick slices of cold tongue in sauce madère and serving them in a border of cooked spinach. When tongue is served hot, the most usual English sauce to accompany it is a white sauce with chopped parsley added.

Lambs' and pigs' tongues are treated in the same way as ox tongue, but as they are much smaller, require only 1–1½ hours, cooking time. Calve's tongues are smaller versions of ox tongues. Smoked reindeer tongues are a delicacy in all countries where the reindeer lives, as is elk tongue in North America.

See also LANGUE DE BOEUF; LENGUA; LINGUA DE VACA; LINGUA DI BUE; OCHSENFLEISCH; OFFAL; OSSETONG; OX; OZÓR; TONG; ZUNGE.

tongue cress (*Cruciferae*), a species of cress of which there are several varieties: common cress, curly cress, golden cress with pale green leaves, and large-leaf cress. The larger leaved variety of tongue cress is used for soups, salads, and garnishes, particularly in France. See also ALÉNOIS.

tonillo, traditional Spanish egg soup. Salt and thyme are added to 2 pints (4 cups) water, and a few drops of olive oil

are sprinkled in. Then 1 cup white breadcrumbs is added and the soup is bound with 2 raw eggs. It is served hot.

tonka bean (*Dipteryx odorata*), the seed of a tree native to tropical South America. It has a strong, sweet, pungent scent, and it can be used for flavouring, like a vanilla pod.

tonnarelle, the regional name for a variety of pasta, matchstick-fine noodles which can be served in any way that is suitable for *maccheroni* or spaghetti, but are usually prepared alla *paesana*, with grated cheese, or col *pesto*. It is called *trenette* in Genoa and *taglione* in Florence. See also PASTA.

tonnellini, Italian for fine noodles. See also PASTA.

tonnellini con funghi e piselli, tonnellini with a sauce made from ½ lb. sliced mushrooms, 2 oz. diced bacon, 1 onion, 1 lb. (2 cups) shelled green peas, and 4 tablespoons water. Cheese is served separately.

tonnetto, a sea fish found in Italian waters. It is a fat fish with pale pink flesh and a dark-blue and silver skin. Tonnetto is at its best at the end of August and is delicious fried or grilled. In Capri and other southern areas tonnetto is used in soup (*zuppa*).

tonno, Italian for tunny (tuna) fish. See also TUNNY-FISH.

salsa di tonno, an Italian sauce served with risotto or spaghetti, made from 1 cup tinned tunny (tuna) fish mixed with 1 tablespoon chopped parsley and tossed in hot olive oil or butter. After 5 minutes, 1 cup chicken or veal stock is added. The sauce is well seasoned and simmered for 5 minutes.

uova di tonno, a speciality of Sardinia. Fried and salted tunny (tuna) fish roe is cut into thin slices and served with olive oil and lemon juice.

tonnos, Greek for tunny (tuna) fish, served *plaki*, fried, or grilled with olive oil and lemon. See also TUNNY-FISH.

top round, see ROUND.

tope (*Galeus vulgaris*), a small bottom-living shark with small serrated teeth. It is found in British and Irish waters as well as in tropical seas. The flesh is firm and white, usually sold skinned to disguise its origin. However it can be recognized by a secondary slimy transparent skin which should be cut away before cooking. It has a good flavour and is particularly suitable for baking, as its firmness prevents it from disintegrating under long slow cooking.

topfen, a German word which, when used as a prefix, means that the dish concerned contains curd or cottage cheese.

topfengolatschen, an Austrian recipe. Squares of puff pastry are given a filling of a mixture of 2 oz. (¼ cup) butter creamed with 2 oz. (¼ cup) sugar, 1 lb. (2 cups) cottage cheese, 2 eggs, grated peel of ½ lemon, and 3 tablespoons currants. The edges are folded over on top and secured by damping the edges, and the pastry is brushed with egg and baked in a moderate oven.

topfenknödel, knödel made with 2 cups cottage cheese to ¼ cup butter, 5 eggs, 2 cups flour, and 1 cup breadcrumbs all well mixed and shaped into small rounds which are first poached in boiling water, then drained, rolled in breadcrumbs, and browned in butter. They are served separately with plum compote; or if very small they can be used to garnish soups. See also KNÖDEL.

topfenpalatschinken, a Hungarian speciality, consisting of large pancakes which are filled with a mixture of 1 lb. cottage cheese, 2 egg yolks, 4 oz. (½ cup) sugar, grated peel of 1 lemon, 3 tablespoons currants, and 3 beaten egg whites. They are then packed into a soufflé dish, covered with custard and baked. Before being served, the pancakes are sprinkled with icing sugar and glazed.

topfentorte, an Austrian cheesecake made from rich short crust pastry baked blind, then filled with a mixture of ½ lb. (1 cup) cream cheese beaten with 3 oz. (3 heaped tablespoons) sugar, 3 egg yolks, grated peel of ½ lemon, 1½ gills (¾ cup) milk, 4 oz. (1 cup) flour, and 3 stiffly beaten egg whites. The top is sprinkled with raisins, and the cake is baked in a slow-to-moderate oven for 45–60 minutes.

topinambours, French for Jerusalem artichokes. In France they may be simmered in boiling salted water and served cold with sauce vinaigrette or mayonnaise, or put hot into a sauce crème or sauce mornay, or used for soup. See also JERUSALEM ARTICHOKE.

topknot, a rather rare fish of the North Atlantic. Three species are known: the common topknot (*Zeugopterus punctatus*), Block's topknot (*Z. unimaculatus*), and the Norwegian topknot (*Z. norvegicus*). It is good to eat.

topside, an English butchery term for a joint of beef cut from above the shin and round, and below the silverside. It comes from the hind quarters, is lean, and roasts reasonably well. See charts of meat cuts, page xxii.

Torbay sole, the name used for lemon sole on the West Country coast of England.

tordo de mar, see LABRO.

toro, Spanish for bull. See also CARNE DE VACA.

cadero de toro, topside of beef cooked whole in a casserole with garlic, onion, cloves, peppercorns, bay leaf, ¼ pint (½ cup) olive oil, ½ pint (1 cup) water, 1 gill (½ cup) white wine, and 1 teaspoon wine vinegar. It is allowed to braise slowly for about 4 hours, in the same way as a pot roast.

lomo de toro, loin fillet of beef. Thin steaks are left for 6 hours in a marinade of oil, vinegar, garlic, and salt before being fried in butter.

torpille, the French name for a large fish resembling a skate, found in the Mediterranean. The flesh, however, is not as good as that of skate. It is called torpedo fish in English.

torrijas, a sweet Spanish dish consisting of small squares of white bread without crusts, soaked in milk, then dipped in egg, and fried in butter. The squares are then placed in a buttered ovenproof dish, covered with equal amounts of honey and water, and slowly baked.

torrijas de nata, a Portuguese sweet dish which is a fritter formed out of a very thick custard made with cream.

torrone, Italian for nougat, traditionally eaten at Christmas and Easter in Italy. A hard nougat which is a speciality of Cremona (*torrone di Cremona*), is made with ½ lb. (1 cup) sugar heated for just 2 minutes, or until light brown, being stirred constantly; then ½ lb. (1 cup) honey is heated in a double-boiler, 3 stiffly beaten egg whites are folded in, and both are mixed with the sugar and cooked over a low heat for 10 minutes, being stirred constantly. The mixture is taken from the heat and 1½ lb. assorted chopped nuts (almonds, hazelnuts, and pistachios) are added. The whole is poured into a shallow greased pan and evened off, then cut through into small squares or rectangles. When cold, each piece is wrapped in rice paper (which can be eaten). If put into an airtight container, the nougat keeps for some weeks.

torrone molle, soft nougat made from ½ lb. (1 cup) each cocoa, butter, sugar, and ground almonds, 1 egg, and 1 egg yolk. The butter and cocoa are well mixed, then the almonds are added, followed by the sugar, which has been melted with 2 tablespoons water, the beaten egg and yolk, and finally, 1 cup small dice of plain sweet biscuit (cookie), mixed in gently so that they do not break up. The mixture is put into an oiled mould and chilled.

torrons de xixona, an Andorran sweetmeat (confection) like a nougat made from a mixture of ground almonds, sugar, egg whites, and honey rolled into little balls which are left overnight to harden. Torrons de xixona is eaten traditionally in Andorra on the day *La Morratxa* is danced in the village of San-Julià-de-Lória, that is the second day of the saint's feast,

the last Sunday of July. This is a traditional dance symbolizing the Acte de Paréage of 1278 by which Andorra was assured its freedom.

torsk, Danish for cod, which is of truly exceptional quality in Denmark, having a milkiness and flavour usually found only in turbot. It is said that one does not know what cod really tastes like until one eats it in Denmark. The liver is also prized, as is the roe. There are 2 traditional ways of cooking cod on its own, although it can also be made into *fiskebudding, fiskefrikadeller,* and *fiskegratin.* When salted, it is known as *klipfisk.* See also FISK.

kogt torsk med sennepsauce, large fillets of cod poached in stock and served with mustard sauce made from the thickened fish stock, with dry mustard to taste, and cream—2 tablespoons cream to ½ pint (1 cup) stock. Sometimes this dish is garnished with grated horseradish and chopped parsley, when it is known as torsk med sennepssauce, peberrod og persilla. This is a speciality of the winter months after Christmas.

kogt torsk med smør, cod steaks poached as above. Served separately are a jug of melted butter with a squeeze of lemon juice, and a small jug of the fish stock.

torsk, Norwegian for cod. In Norway, large cod are eaten very fresh, small ones are smoked. The giant Lofoten cod, called *skrei,* is only eaten between February and April. Cod is eaten throughout the country and is highly esteemed. It is baked, fried, and grilled. *Torskerogn* is cod's roe, which is served fresh and also smoked. The liver is a delicacy, fresh or smoked, and both roe and liver are smoked and then canned or bottled for use as appetizers with bread or toast. See also FISK; PERSETORSK.

torskerogn på ristibrød, smoked cod's roe soaked in milk for 5 hours, then cut into even slices. A large onion is sliced and cooked in butter, then 1 teaspoon curry powder, 1 tablespoon chutney, and juice of ½ lemon are added, and all is stirred until boiling. The roe is added and heated through, then served on fried bread with the sauce on top. It is garnished with chopped gherkins, dill, or parsley.

torsk, Swedish for cod. Boiled cod is *kokt torsk.* See also COD; FISK; KABELJO.

torskrompastej, 1 lb. mashed boiled cod's roe is mixed to a paste with a roux made from 1 oz. flour and 1 oz. butter, and 3 tablespoons fish roe stock. This mixture is flavoured with anchovy essence (extract) and cayenne pepper, then put into scallop shells which have been buttered and lined with breadcrumbs, and baked for 15 minutes in a hot oven.

tort, Polish for cake, more especially a rich, light sponge, often layered with a variety of fillings such as icing, jam, or creams mixed with chopped nuts, chocolate, coffee, or cinnamon.

tort czekoladowy niepieczony, a chocolate cake which requires no cooking. First, ½ lb. (1 cup) butter is creamed with ½ lb. (1 cup) sugar and ½ lb. finely grated bitter chocolate. All must be thoroughly blended, and the mixture is then chilled until set in a layer tin with a removable base. A topping of ½ lb. (2 cups) ground walnuts, ½ lb. (1 cup) sugar, and 4 tablespoons thick cream is spread on top, and the whole is covered with chocolate icing.

tort kawowy z kremem, 10 oz. (1¼ cups) butter is beaten with 2 eggs, then 10 oz. (1¼ cups) sugar and 10 oz. (2½ cups) ground almonds are added. Next 12 oz. (2½ cups) flour is stirred in gradually, and a pinch of salt is added. The mixture is divided into 3, and each layer is baked separately in a moderate oven for 30 minutes. The layers are spread with a creamed filling flavoured with coffee or chocolate, etc., and the cake is iced the next day.

torta, Italian for tart or cake which, as is usual in many countries, may be sweet or savoury. The pastry most generally used is *pasta frolla*. Torta is in fact one of those ambiguous words which can be applied to a variety of preparations.

torta di patate, a crust made of 2 lb. cooked mashed potatoes is filled with 2 oz. cubed ham, 4 oz. grated bel paese or Gruyère cheese, 2 sliced hard-boiled eggs, and 2 oz. diced *mortadella*, then all is covered with mashed potato, sprinkled with breadcrumbs and melted butter, and baked in a hot oven for 20 minutes.

torta di ricotta, a pastry crust filled with 1 lb. (2 cups) ricotta, 2 beaten eggs, 4 oz. (½ cup) sugar, ¼ cup currants, and ¼ cup chopped candied peel to taste, all well mixed, then baked.

torta di riso, rice pudding cooked with ground almonds and decorated when cold with chopped crystallised fruit.

torta paradiso, a cake, not a tart, made from 5 egg yolks beaten with 1 tablespoon lemon juice and 5 oz. (¾ cup) sugar. This mixture is heated over boiling water and stirred until it thickens, then cooled. The 5 stiffly beaten egg whites are now added, alternately with 3 heaped tablespoons flour. Then the mixture is poured into a greased sponge tin and baked in a moderate oven for 30 minutes. It is left to get quite cold in the tin before it is turned out.

torta pasqualina, a curious Easter cake made from 1 lb. (4 cups) flour to 1 tablespoon olive oil and enough water to make a pliable dough. This is divided into 30 pieces which are rolled into balls and left covered with a damp cloth for about 1 hour. The white stalks and spines are stripped from 1 lb. spinach beet and the leaves are chopped coarsely, then fried lightly in butter with a little sliced onion, parsley, marjoram, seasoning, and 3 heaped tablespoons grated Parmesan cheese. A second mixture is made by whipping ½ lb. (1 cup) curd or cottage cheese with 3 oz. (3 tablespoons) flour, then adding ½ pint (1 cup) cream and a few drops of olive oil. Half the pastry balls are now rolled out as thinly as possible to rounds of uniform size. Then a flat baking tin is oiled, and on it are placed the rounds of dough, one on top of the other, each oiled before the next is added. The top one is spread with the spinach beet mixture, and this is covered with the curd or cottage cheese mixture; 6 small "wells" are made in this, to hold 6 raw eggs that are then dropped in and dotted with little curls of butter. The remaining balls of dough are rolled out as before and placed on top, each one oiled as above. The top layer is pricked with a fork, and the whole cake is then baked in a moderate oven for 1 hour.

torta, Portuguese for a tart, or a light spongy cake.

torta amêndoim, almond cake, served as a pudding. It is made from 8 oz. ground almonds beaten with 8 oz. (1 cup) sugar; then 5 egg yolks are added 1 at a time, followed by 2 tablespoons softened butter. Finally the 5 stiffly beaten egg whites are added, and the mixture is put into a greased and floured mould and baked in a moderate oven for 30 minutes. It is served cold, dredged with sugar.

torta, Spanish for pie or tart or a dish containing pastry, although, like the German *torte*, this word can also mean a light round cake or biscuit (cookie). See also CONEJO, PASTEL DE; TORTERA DE SEVILLA.

tortas de aceite, a kind of Spanish olive oil biscuit (cookie) from Seville. To prepare it 8 oz. (2 cups) flour, 4 oz. (½ cup) sugar, salt, and grated peel of 1 lemon are beaten together; a well is made in the middle of the mixture, and into this are gradually poured 1 beaten egg, 2 tablespoons olive oil, and 1 glass (4 oz.) anis. The mixture is rolled out thinly and formed into small circles which are baked on a greased baking sheet in a hot oven for about 10 minutes.

törtchen, German for a tartlet or small tart made from rich

short crust pastry or puff pastry, baked blind and filled with assorted fruits, cream, curd cheese, custard, etc. See also TORTE.

torte, a German word which is extremely difficult to translate, for, according to context, it may have one of several meanings. Basically it means a tart or flan with a filling, such as *linzer torte*, or *topfen*. However, the more general image conjured up by the word torte is that of an extremely light cake, sometimes layered with a rich filling, often iced, and frequently served with whipped cream. It is impossible to give a more precise definition, for the word covers many kinds of cake, some with a cream cheese filling, and so on. Many are not unlike a French *gâteau;* others resemble the orthodox cake. There are many varieties made all over Germany, Austria, and Hungary, including *dobosh torta, nuss torte, Sacher torte*, and *sandtorte*. See also TÖRTCHEN.

tortelli di erbette, a speciality of Parma made from ½ lb. ravioli filled with 6 oz. (2 cups) chopped cooked spinach, chard, or green leaves of beetroot, mixed with 6 oz. (1½ cups) ricotta cheese, a pinch of nutmeg, 2 eggs, and salt. The tortelli are poached in water and served with melted butter and grated Parmesan cheese.

tortellini, small half-moon coils of stuffed pasta, famous in Bologna. Tortellini is a great Christmas Eve dish, either eaten in broth, or served poached and drained with grated cheese and butter and sometimes sliced white truffles. A typical Christmas filling for tortellini consists of 4 oz. minced (ground) lean pork, 2 oz. veal, 2 oz. turkey or chicken, 2 oz. ham, 1 oz. chopped mortadella cheese, 2 oz. calf's brains, ½ teaspoon nutmeg, 2 eggs, 1 oz. butter, and 3 oz. grated Parmesan cheese. See also MACCHERONI, RIPIENI ALLA TÓSCANA; RAVIOLI.

tortera de Sevilla, a special Spanish sweet tart eaten at Christmas, especially in Seville. A sweet pastry crust is filled with *cabello de angel* and cooked in the oven 30 minutes. See also TORTA.

tortiglione, Italian almond cakes resembling coiled snakes. To prepare them 1 lb. ground almonds is mixed with 1 lb. (2 cups) sugar and 1 heaped tablespoon flour. Then 4 stiffly beaten egg whites are stirred in and the mixture is piped into coiled shapes. Sometimes coffee beans are added for eyes, and sliced glacé cherries for tongues. They are cooked in a very low oven until dried out, like meringues, and are not allowed to brown. See also MANDORLA.

tortilha, Portuguese for omelette, although the word *omelletta* is also used. The Portuguese omelette is served unfolded, with chopped brains, meat, or tomatoes, etc., cooked with the eggs. In the south it resembles scrambled eggs with the additional ingredient mixed in. See also OMELETTE.

tortilla, a large, thin, pancake-wafer, used instead of bread in Mexico, also eaten in the southwest U.S. Tortillas date back to Aztec times. They are made with a specially ground cornmeal called *mixtamal*, a word derived from the Aztec *maza*, and known now as masa, meaning wet corn mixed into flour, and *tamalina*, the name given to the corn when it was dried and finely ground. Tamalina is also the source of the modern *tamal*, the name of the flat Mexican cornmeal pancake. To make tortillas 1½ cup cornmeal (masa) and 1 teaspoon salt are mixed with about ½ cup lukewarm water until a light batter is formed. This is then rolled out into paper-thin circles measuring 5–6 inches across, which are cooked for a few seconds only on each side, on an ungreased griddle. When first cooked, the tortilla is known as a *blandita;* when a little stale, and fried in olive oil, it becomes a *tostada;* when fried with a filling it becomes a *taco*. Tortillas are sold canned or frozen in the U.S. The customary way of eating them is to break off a triangular-shaped piece which is used as a natural fork for scooping up food. Large piles of tortillas are put at each end of the table, and in well-to-do houses a special maid is employed, whose sole duty is to keep fresh, hot tortillas ready for the family.

pastel de tortillas

tortilla, Spanish for omelette. Spanish omelettes are usually made by stirring the eggs into cooked fish, shellfish, or vegetables, and are served flat, not folded over. They are very filling, and make a satisfying meal with a salad. They are eaten hot or cold.

tortilla al sacromonte, a famous dish from Granada. Chopped blanched calve's brain is fried in oil, then mixed with chopped cooked sweetbreads, cooked peas, and fried potatoes. All are mixed with beaten eggs and cooked flat in the pan, the top being browned under the grill.

tortini, Italian for small round cakes or croquettes of food, not usually sweet.

tortini di ricotta, cheese croquettes, made from 6 oz. (1 cup) ricotta or white cheese, 2 heaped tablespoons grated Parmesan cheese, 1 tablespoon flour, 1 egg, herbs, and seasoning to taste, all well mixed and formed into croquettes. They are dipped in egg and breadcrumbs, then fried in a mixture of olive oil and butter. They are sometimes served with chicken or veal.

tortini d'uova nella neve, eggs baked with mashed potatoes and thin slices of mozzarella, sprinkled with grated Parmesan cheese, and dotted with butter. It means literally "eggs baked in snow." See also UOVA, CON PURÉ DI PATATE.

tortoni, a frozen dessert, named after the celebrated Italian owner of the Paris café of the same name in the latter part of the 18th century. To prepare this, ½ pint (1 cup) cream is whipped to a foam, and 6 tablespoons icing sugar is gradually added to the cream and whipped until very stiff, when 2 tablespoons rum is beaten in. Finally, 1 stiffly beaten egg white is folded in, and all is put into one large chilled mould or small individual ones, sprinkled with chopped roasted almonds, and frozen hard. See also ICES.

tortue, I. A French sauce served with calf's head and other offal (variety meats). It is made from ½ pint (1 cup) white wine boiled with thyme, bay leaf, parsley, sage, basil, and rosemary, with a pinch of cayenne, 4 tablespoons demi-glace, 3 tablespoons fresh tomato sauce, and 12 mushroom stalks, all boiled down, and having (¼ cup) Madeira wine added at the last moment. II. French for turtle. See NAGEOIRES DE TORTUE.

herbes à tortue, a mixture of basil, thyme, bay, and marjoram sold commercially in France, ready-prepared, to season appropriate sauces and soups.

toscanello, see PECORINO.

tostada, see TORTILLA.

totani, see FRAGOLE DI MARE.

tôt-fait, a French cake made from 8 oz. (2 cups) sifted flour, 8 oz. (1 cup) sugar, 1 tablespoon grated lemon peel, and 3 eggs, all well beaten until smooth, when ½ lb. (1 cup) melted butter is blended in. The mixture is poured into a buttered mould and baked in a moderate oven for 45 minutes.

totuava (*Eriscion macdonaldi*), a variety of weakfish weighing 150 lb. or more, found in the Gulf of California. It is much esteemed as food.

Tou Sotiros, St. Sotiros' feast day in Greece, August 6, but also one of the 12 most important feast-days of the Orthodox Church since it is the Day of Transfiguration, when Christ manifested his divinity to 3 of his disciples. In the Greek Orthodox Church the period between August 1 and 15 is called Sarakosti Dikapendavgoustou, the Fast of the Virgin Mary, and it is a time of abstinence from meat, fish, eggs, and cheese. However, the people are allowed to break their fast on August 6, and they first of all celebrate by swimming in the sea—after 5 P.M., for it is forbidden earlier in the day on account of the treacherous tides at this time of the year, which subside in the evening. A race is popular, to see who can pass 40 waves, dip his hands in and sprinkle his head with water, and arrive first at the finishing line. Afterwards there is a big feast which always includes a fish soup called *kaccavia* and a sweetmeat (confection), *halvahs.* One of the customs is for a young virgin to prepare a dish called *esperinudia* (from the word *esperas* meaning "evening") on the night before *Tou Sotiros,* consisting of wheat boiled with spices and sugar. This dish is taken to the church to be blessed, and the following day it is presented to the namesakes of Saint Sotiros.

toucinhos, a Portuguese sweet consisting of small light cakes or custards. To prepare it 1 lb. (2 cups) sugar is boiled with ¾ pint (1½ cups) water until dissolved, and then the mixture is cooled before 8 egg yolks and 3 egg whites, which have been beaten with 1 heaped tablespoon flour, are added. Small greased moulds are filled with this mixture, and they are then cooked in a *bain-marie* for 30 minutes. The custards are sometimes flavoured with ½ lb. ground almonds.

touffe, a French word for herbs or vegetables, with their stalks, tied in a bundle.

toulia, see OUILLAT.

toulon, a la, a French regional method of preparing whole whitefish by stuffing it with whiting forcemeat and then poaching it in fish stock with mussels. It is served with fish velouté with added butter.

touloumotyri, a variety of the Greek *féta* cheese. It is packed in goat skins and weighs between 60 and 70 lb. When a cheese is opened, the contrast between the dark, coarse goat skin and the pure white of the cheese inside is quite spectacular. See also TYRI.

Toulousaine, à la, I. A French garnish for chicken, sweetbreads, and *vol-au-vent* consisting of chicken quenelles, braised diced sweetbreads, white mushroom caps, cock's combs, and truffle slices in sauce *allemande* flavoured with mushroom essence (extract). II. A ragoût à blanc bound with sauce béchamel. It is served with poached or roasted poultry, or used as a filling for *croustades, tartes,* or *vol-au-vent.* III. A French method of serving potatoes. See POMME DE TERRE (POMMES À LA TOULOUSAINE).

toupin, a curiously shaped earthenware pot, bulbous at the bottom and narrowing at the top, used in the Béarn district of France for cooking the traditional beef and wine stew known as *daube.* See also DAUBIÈRE.

tour de feuilletage, a French culinary term for the "turns" or series of rollings given to puff pastry.

tourd, the French name for a type of wrasse found in the

Mediterranean. The fish has an insipid taste, but is used for soups.

tourin, see THOURINS.

tourlou, a Greek word used to denote a stew of meat, usually lamb, and various vegetables such as okra, eggplant, green beans, green peppers, zucchini, tomatoes, and onions, all cooked in stock or water.

tournedos, the French name for thick slices of meat taken from the heart or middle of a whole fillet of beef. Tournedos should be 3–4 inches thick and should weigh not less than 4 oz. In many good restaurants, this piece of meat is tightly wrapped in a wet cloth and banged on a wooden table until it has acquired the slightly conical shape characteristic of the tournedos. Tournedos should be fried in a mixture of butter and olive oil, fairly quickly, so that although the outside is brown, the inside is pink and juicy. After cooking it can be served on a croûton of fried bread with sauces or garnishes such as *algérienne, archiduc, Arlésienne, béarnaise, bordelaise, chasseur, clamart, helder, Henri IV, Maguéry, Marie-Jeanne, Marie-Louise, marquise, mascotte, masséna, périgourdine, princesse, Rossini, Sévigné,* and *valenciennes.* Tournedos garni are tournedos garnished with an unspecified number of cooked vegetables arranged round the meat. See also BEEF; FILET.

tournée, an old French name for sauce *allemande,* referring to the constant whisking involved in the making of this sauce.

tourner, a French verb which means literally "to turn." In culinary terminology, it means specifically to shape certain vegetables, for instance potatoes or carrots, while preparing them. In other words, to cut them into ovals, diamonds, or whatever shape the recipe requires, at the same time as they are being scrubbed and peeled to make them ready for cooking. In the case of mushrooms, truffles, etc., it can also mean "to trim."

touron, French for the Spanish sweetmeat (confection) *turrón,* which is also made in France but by a slightly different method, and is served there in the same way as petits fours. First ½ lb. (2 cups) ground almonds is mixed with 2 egg whites, then 12 oz. (1½ cups) castor sugar is added. The mixture is sprinkled with more sugar and rolled out to ½-inch thickness. Then 3 cups chopped pistachio nuts is mixed with 12 oz. (1½ cups) sugar, grated peel of 1 orange, and ½ cup royal icing. This second mixture is spread on top of the first, and then the whole is cut into shapes which are dried in a very low oven.

tourri, see OUILLAT.

toursi, Greek for pickled. It is used particularly as a term for pickled vegetables and fruits, such as celery, peppers, cauliflower, tomatoes, and olives, prepared either in brine or in oil and vinegar and served as a relish. It is also used for squid pickled by sousing in vinegar, olive oil, and pickling spices. Toursi is often eaten with sliced raw onion and lentil or bean soup on fast days.

tourte, I. French for a savoury pastry tart. There are certain sweet tourtes, but they are usually referred to as *tartes.* The word comes from the Latin *tortus,* meaning round, and the tourte is round in shape. A *quiche* is very like a tourte, and in parts of France is called by this name.

tourte à la Lorraine, a speciality of Lorraine, this delicious tart is made with ½ lb. each chopped veal and pork marinated in herbs and white wine, then put in a pastry case with some of the marinade (about ½ pint) beaten with 4 eggs and ¼ pint (½ cup) cream. It is baked for about 30 minutes, until golden on top.

II. A Corsican chestnut porridge, to which pignoli, aniseed, and raisins are added before it is baked in the oven.

tourteau fromagé, a speciality of the Poitou region of France,

consisting of 1 lb. cream cheese or goat cheese pounded into a fine paste, then mixed with one quarter its weight in flour, sugar to taste, 1 oz. butter, 2 egg yolks, and the stiffly beaten egg whites. This mixture is put into a mould, allowed to ferment slightly, then baked in a slow-to-moderate oven for 30 minutes. It is eaten cold.

tourterelle, French for turtle dove, which is eaten in France, and is prepared in the same way as pigeon.

tourtière, I. A Christmas pie eaten in Canada, made with 1 lb. chopped pork, ½ lb. chopped veal or chicken, 6 medium-sized minced onions, allspice, seasoning, and 1 pint (2 cups) consommé. The top and sides of the dish are covered with pastry and the pie is baked in a slow oven for 1½ hours, then eaten either hot or cold. It is also known as *pâté de Noël.* See also CHRISTMAS. II. French for a pie dish in which *tourtes* are made. Originally these dishes were made of earthenware, but are nowadays more frequently cast in metal. Some have fluted sides.

trahana, a Greek dough made by peasants from goat's milk or yogourt and ground wheat. The mixture is made firm enough to break into small, nutlike pieces which, when dried and rubbed between the hands, become like oatmeal. This is dropped into broth or stock to make a soup which resembles porridge. Trahana is a speciality of Asia Minor and is best made in August or September, when the harvest is brought in and the goat's milk is at its best.

trail, the intestines of small game birds. That of the woodcock is particularly esteemed and is cooked with the bird, not drawn. Thrush, blackbird, rail, and warbler are also left undrawn; only the gizzard is removed and cleaned for use in making stock with the neck, etc.

train de côtes, see CÔTES DE BOEUF.

train de lièvre, see LIÈVRE.

tranbär, Swedish for cranberry, which grows wild in Scandinavia and is used for sweet soups, puddings, pies, etc.

tranche au petit os, a French cut of beef, taken from the middle of what is known in England as silverside, in the U.S. as rump. See chart of meat cuts, pages xxii–xxiii.

tranche grasse, the French butchery term for a wedge-shaped cut taken from a leg of beef. It extends the whole length of the English topside, as far as the rump. It is known as top rump or sirloin tip in the U.S., and the term top rump is also used in Britain, although it is not a true English cut. See chart of meat cuts, pages xxii–xxiii.

tranchoir, see TAILLOIR.

trappisten käse, a cheese made in both Upper and Lower Austria. It is a copy of the French port-du-salut.

traquet, French for wheatear, classed as game in France and cooked in the same way as lark.

trás-os-montes, a famous Portuguese smoked ham. See PAIO.

trauben, German for grapes.

traubenessig, grape vinegar made with unripe grapes, or grapes that do not ripen for dessert fruit. They are crushed and left covered for 24 hours, then the juice is strained off, put into bottles or a cask, and left in a warm place to ferment. When fermentation stops, any scum is removed with a spoon and cork. If the weather is not warm, it is advisable to rinse out the bottles with a good malt vinegar before bottling.

traut, Danish for trout, a popular fish in Denmark. It is usually poached in salted water and served with a hot sauce *hollandaise.*

travailler, a French culinary term meaning to beat, especially with a wooden spoon or spatula. It applies particularly in the making of batters, forcemeats, and sauces.

treacle, a thick semi-liquid syrup obtained during the early processes of refining cane sugar. The word was first used for a medicinal compound of several ingredients used against poison, particularly snake bites, and is ultimately derived from the Greek Θηριακά, literally, drugs used as an antidote against the bite of wild beasts (Θήρ). It appears in Latin as *theriaca* and in Old French as *triacle,* meaning the composition of electuaries with honey, and the same word was quite naturally taken over as the name for the similar syrup obtained from the drainings of sugar. There are several grades of treacle. The darkest in colour and strongest in taste is called molasses in the U.S. and black treacle in Britain; it is made from the drainings of crude sugar and is used a good deal in cooking in the southern states of the U.S. There are 3 kinds of molasses in the U.S., sulphered, unsulphered, and blackstrap. When molasses is refined a thinner syrup is produced, brown in colour but not as dark or thick as molasses; in Britain this is called simply, treacle, and is the form most generally used in Britain and Europe. A third type of treacle is obtained in the process of making refined crystallised sugar, an uncrystallised fluid known as golden syrup which is similar in texture and colour to the American corn syrup. Golden syrup is not made in the U.S. Confusingly, this is also sometimes referred to as treacle, but usually when treacle is specified for cakes, puddings, or bread, it is the brown syrup obtained from refined molasses that is meant. See also GOLDEN SYRUP.

treacle soda bread, see SODA BREAD.

treacle tart, an English tart made with a 9-inch short crust pastry case filled with a mixture of 1 lb. golden syrup (originally treacle was used), 6 oz. (4 cups) fresh white breadcrumbs, and a squeeze of lemon juice (optional). Strips of pastry are placed lattice-fashion across the top and dampened at the edges where they meet the main crust. All is brushed with beaten egg or milk to colour the pastry, and the tart is baked for 20 minutes in a moderate oven. It is eaten hot or cold.

treccia, an Italian plaited mozzarella cheese.

tree onion, see ONION.

trefoil, French for melilot, which is also called trefoil in parts of England.

treipen, a dish from Luxembourg consisting of black pudding, sausages, and mashed potatoes, all served hot with horseradish sauce.

tremper, a French culinary term meaning to soak a slice of bread in liquid, for instance in soup. Trempette is the word for the slice of bread thus treated.

trenette, a Genoese form of *tonnarelle* pasta. See PASTA.

tresse, French for a plaited bread or cake.

triantafillo, Greek for rose petal, often used to make a jam in Greece, called *glyko.*

trifle, a traditional English pudding, the excellence of which depends entirely on the quality of the custard used and the amount of sherry or brandy poured over the sponge cakes. To prepare it 6 sponge cakes are split and spread with good jam, then arranged in the bowl from which they will be served, and soaked with at least ¼ pint (½ cup) sherry or brandy. A rich custard is made with 4 egg yolks to 1 pint (2 cups) milk and 2 tablespoons vanilla sugar or a flavouring of almond essence (extract). It is well beaten and poured over the cakes. The trifle is then left until well chilled, when the top is covered with whipped cream and decorated with chopped almonds or crystallised fruits. Trifle is also called tipsy cake.

triggerfish (*Balistes capriscus*), a brightly coloured sea fish with a spine in the dorsal fin which is stuck up at any sign of danger. The species found in the Mediterranean makes a grunting sound when caught and so is sometimes called pigfish. The flesh is quite good to eat and can be cooked in the same way as tunny (tuna) fish or sturgeon.

trigla, see GALLINA DEL MAR.

triglia, Italian for red mullet. In Venice it is cooked with fresh mint and a garlic clove put inside the fish, which is then rolled in flour and fried in olive oil. A sauce composed of 1 fried onion, ½ pint (1 cup) white wine, and 1 tablespoon wine vinegar is boiled up and poured over. It is usually served cold, but may be eaten hot. See also MULLET.

triglie col pesto, a Genoese recipe. Grilled mullet is served hot with a *pesto* sauce.

tripa, a Corsican speciality resembling a black pudding. It consists of a sheep's belly stuffed with a mixture of beetroot, spinach, herbs, and sheep's blood, all tied up like a pudding and boiled in salted water.

tripas, Portuguese for tripe in the Oporto region; it is called *dobrada* in the Lisbon area. It is eaten a great deal in Portugal. See also DOBRADA; TRIPE.

tripas à moda do porto, a dish of calf's tripe, smoked ham or *chouriço,* and pig's trotters (feet), stewed with dried beans, herbs, and fresh vegetables, and served with boiled rice.

tripas à portuguesa, a casserole of tripe and soaked, dried white beans. First 1 lb. beans is half-cooked, and then 4 oz. *chouriço,* 4 oz. *salpicão,* 1 sliced calf's foot, and 2 lb. tripe, all cut very small, are added to them. The dish is seasoned with garlic, paprika, salt, and pepper.

tripe, the lining or walls of the stomachs of herbivorous ruminant mammals. That most generally used in England comes from the calf or bullock, although pig's and sheep's tripe is also edible. Ruminants like the ox have two stomachs, the first smooth and regularly marked, the second, which is considered the best for consumption, honeycombed. In Britain and Ireland tripe may only be sold for human consumption if it has first been cleaned and washed, when it is known as dressed tripe. Tripe is rich in gelatine and, when slowly cooked, is good for invalids.

Tripe can also be rolled in egg and breadcrumbs, fried in oil, and served with lemon or sauce vinaigrette. It is eaten a lot in Russia. See KISHKA. See also CALLOS; FLAKI; GRAS-DOUBLE; INDVOLDE; KALLUN; TRIPAS; TRIPES; TRIPES; TRIPPA; TUZLAMA; ZADĚLÁVANÉ DRŠKY.

Balmoral tripe, a Scottish way of serving tripe. It is rolled with thin slices of ham, packed into a saucepan on top of 2 large broken bay leaves, scattered with chopped onion and mushrooms, covered with stock, and cooked gently for 2 hours. Before serving, ¼ cup cream and some chopped parsley are added.

tripe and onions, the most famous English dish of tripe, and extremely popular in the north. Onions, to the same weight as the tripe being used, are peeled and sliced. Then 2 tablespoons butter is melted in a saucepan and the onions fried until soft but definitely not coloured. The tripe, cut into squares, is added, together with a bay leaf, a pinch of mace, seasoning, and milk or milk and water to cover well. The tripe is cooked very slowly for at least 2 hours, preferably in a double boiler or in a low oven. When it is quite soft, the bay leaf is removed and the gravy is thickened with 1 tablespoon corn flour (cornstarch) dissolved in a little cold water. When this bubbles up and thickens, the dish is ready to be served.

tripes, French for the intestines of ruminants; sometimes the word means what we know as tripe, sometimes intestines, sometimes chitterlings. A *tripière* is a flat, oval, earthenware dish with a lid, used in Normandy for cooking *tripes à la mode de Caen* (see GRAS-DOUBLE). See also TRIPE.

tripette, a Corsican dish, made from the small intestines of sheep cut into squares and sautéed in lard with tomatoes, herbs, and seasoning.

triple-crème, a superior grade of *Fontainebleau* cheese. Triple means a high fat content.

tripletail (*Lobotes surinamensis*), a large sea fish found in the warmer waters off the North Atlantic seaboard of the U.S. The flesh is coarse but quite acceptable.

trippa, Italian for tripe. The tripe used in Italy comes from the calf's stomach and is very delicate. Trippa is used in *busecca,* a soup-stew traditional in Milan, Rome, and Turin. See also TRIPE.

trippa alla fiorentina, tripe boiled for 1 hour, then cut into strips and simmered in fresh tomato sauce containing 1 tablespoon marjoram. It is served with a thick layer of grated Parmesan cheese on top.

trippa alla parmigiana, tripe boiled for 1 hour, then cut into strips and fried in butter. Grated Parmesan cheese is added and allowed to melt before the dish is served.

trippa alla romana, tripe boiled for 2 hours, then cut into strips and simmered with an onion sautéed in oil, garlic, carrots, and celery leaf, with 1 cup white wine for 3 lb. tripe, 1 tablespoon chopped mint, and 1 lb. peeled tomatoes for a further hour. It is sprinkled with grated Parmesan or *pecorino* cheese before serving.

trognon, French for the edible heart of a vegetable, especially of cabbage, lettuce, or chicory, or of certain fruits such as fresh figs.

trois frères, I. A special tin or mould (*moule à trois frères*) used for cooking the French cake called *bonvalet* or *beauvilliers.* It is round with diagonally fluted sides and base, and has a well in the centre. II. The cake baked in the mould described above. Generally this is known as a *bonvalet* or *beauvilliers,* but it sometimes takes the name of the mould.

tronçon, a French culinary term for a "chunk" of food cut so that its length is greater than its width. It is often used for middle cuts of fish, when it is correctly called *tronçon de milieu* (middle cut). *Darne* is possibly the more popular word for cuts of fish on restaurant menus.

trôo, a French goat's milk cheese made in Touraine, and matured in ashes. It is in season from May to June.

tropique, a French word used to describe the hottest part of the oven.

trota, Italian for trout, usually boiled (*in bianco*), fried, or grilled, and served with melted butter and lemon wedges. The quality of the trout found in the lakes and rivers of northern Italy is excellent.

trout (*Salmonidae*), a fish closely related to the salmon. There are many varieties, some living solely in fresh water, some migratory. See also FOREL; FORELLE; ØRRED; ØRRET; PSTRĄG; TRAUT; TRUCHA; TRUITE; TRUTA.

brown trout, by far the best of the freshwater trout. Its flesh is white and the taste very delicate and good, which is why plainer methods of cooking should be used in order to preserve the flavour. Trout is excellent simply grilled, or cooked *au bleu.* An old English method is to fry it in butter and almond oil, and serve it with fried split almonds on top, and lemon. In Scotland it is split and boned, then rolled in fine oatmeal before being fried in butter. The rainbow trout is an inferior fish, though good. In both Britain and the U.S., brown and rainbow trout are often smoked and then eaten just as they are, with fresh horseradish sauce and lemon juice, as a first course. Smoked trout is moist and white in appearance, subtle and excellent in flavour. It is not in the least like smoked salmon, which is rich and oily by comparison. (Char is a member of the same family as trout, and may be cooked in the same way.)

European trout (Salmo fario), also known in England as brook trout or brown trout, and in France as truite de rivière. The U.S. brook trout is the same family. There are several different varieties to be found in the various freshwater lakes of Europe such as Lake Geneva and Lake Garda, in the Caspian Sea, and in the rivers and lakes of Dalmatia and Hungary, but they are all very much alike. The fish vary in size according to the depth of water in which they live.

rainbow trout (S. irideus), an American trout imported into England and Europe from California at the turn of this cen-

tury. The prevalence of this fish in England is now unfortunately making it difficult to obtain the delicious, but less hardy, brook trout, for rainbow trout is able to adapt itself to life in almost stagnant water hitherto regarded as suitable only for coarse fish. It is also artificially bred in fish "farms." It is good to eat, but not nearly as good as a brown trout from fast-running waters. Rainbow trout will go to the sea, and in many cases have never returned to fresh water.

stuffed rainbow trout

sea trout (Salmo trutta), see SALMON TROUT.

steelhead (Salmo gairdneri), found in the western states of the U.S. and called trout. In the eastern states trout is the term used for char (*Salvelinus fontinalis*). Both of these fish are members of the salmon family. Midwestern restaurants sometimes serve catfish as trout.

trout, cured, an Irish method perfected by Mrs. Monica Sheridan of Dublin. A salmon trout about 4 lb. in weight is cleaned, filleted, and opened at the belly, but the skin is left on. The flesh is rubbed with ½ tablespoon salt, and left in a cool, but not cold, place for 24 hours. On the second day it is patted dry with a cloth and rubbed all over with olive oil, massaging well. The processes of the first and second days are repeated on the third and fourth, and the process of the first day is again repeated on the fifth. On the sixth day the fish is rubbed with oil and 1 tablespoon brown sugar, and on the seventh day it is hung by the neck in a steady, but not gusty, current of air to become firm. On the eighth day it is ready, and is served in thin slices like smoked salmon. It should be consumed within one week of first slicing for, not being smoked, the keeping properties are not as powerful once it has been cut. See also CURING.

trout-perch, see PERCH.

Troyes, see BARBEREY.

trucha, Spanish for trout. See also TROUT.

trucha a la Navarre, trout marinated for 1 hour in red wine with peppercorns, mint, thyme, rosemary, chopped onion, and parsley, then cooked in the marinade. The marinade is reduced and strained, and 1 egg yolk per trout is beaten into it. It is heated until it thickens and is then poured over the fish.

truckles, an English country name, given in different parts of the country to different kinds of cheese. In Wiltshire it refers to a blue, skimmed-milk cheese not unlike blue dorset, but in the west of England, it can also mean a full-cream cheddar shaped like a round loaf.

truffado, la, a traditional French potato dish from the Auvergne. The potatoes are thinly sliced, placed in a heavy frying pan in such a way that the slices overlap and form a pancake, and then cooked in a mixture of butter and oil, with 1 chopped garlic clove and a little diced ham or bacon. As soon as they start to cook the heat is lowered, and when half cooked, small cubes of fresh *tomme de cantal* cheese are added. The potatoes are lifted so that the cheese melts around them. Finally a lid is put on, the heat turned out, and the dish left for about 5 minutes before being served.

truffe, French for truffle, used extensively in France in fritters, in foie gras, and for garnishes and sauces, such as *périgourdine, périgueux,* or *Rossini.* See also TRUFFLE.

truffes au champagne, one lb. large, regular-shaped, unpeeled truffles are cooked with ½ lb. (1 cup) butter and 2 tablespoons *mirepoix* of vegetables until soft; then ¾ pint (1½ cups) champagne is added, the lid put on, and all gently simmered for 15 minutes. The truffles are removed to a warm dish, and the liquid is reduced to half, then mixed with 4 tablespoons veal demi-glace. Madeira wine can be used instead of champagne, or cream in place of either; the latter dish is called *truffes à la crème.*

truffiat, a homemade potato scone traditional in the Berry province of France.

trufflage, a French culinary term for the addition of slices or pieces of truffle to foods, particularly to poultry or game.

truffle (*Eutuberaceae* and *Terfeziaceae*), a subterranean tuber-like fungus which is a valuable food. The most common are the following:

English truffle (*Tuber aestivum*) is smaller than the French truffle and far inferior to it. It is also known as the Bath or red truffle. Although it used to be found on the South Downs and in Epping Forest, where it was sought out by terriers, it is seldom seen nowadays.

French truffle (*Tuber melanosporum*), the best and therefore the most expensive, which means that it is generally used only sparingly, as a garnish. It is brownish-black, round, and covered with many-sided warts. The flesh of the young truffle is white, then turns grey, and when fully ripe becomes a violet-black with white veins. It has little flavour, but a wonderful aroma which permeates any food it comes into contact with. The finest truffles in France come from the Lot and the Périgord regions, and they are used in pâté de foie gras, especially that made of goose liver; for larding chicken or game; sautéed with champagne or Madeira (see TRUFFE, AU CHAMPAGNE); and made into a tart or pie with foie gras. In the days of open hearths, truffles were often larded with bacon and baked in a dish in the hot embers.

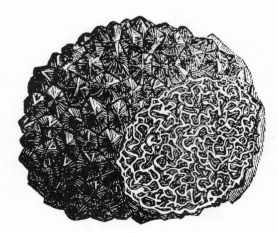

truffle

Italian truffle (*Tuber magnatum*), also called the grey or white truffle of Piedmont, has a slightly peppery, garlicky taste. It is seldom cooked and is chiefly used for grating, raw,

over risotto; this dish is particularly a speciality of Turin, and is called *riso in bianco con tartufi bianchi.*

terfezia leonis is of a different family from the other truffles mentioned. It looks rather like a potato, and flourishes in Algeria, Sardinia, and parts of Italy. It is mainly eaten raw, sometimes dipped in olive oil or raw egg. It has little scent.

truffe violette (*Tuber brumale*) is a good-quality truffle found in France, northern Italy, Switzerland, and southern Germany.

The truffle has been known since Greek and Roman times, and there are references to it in the writings of Theophrastus (*c.* 300 B.C.) and Pliny. Truffles grow underground, usually below oak, beech, or birch trees, or in calcareous clay soil. The odour of many truffles is extremely strong, and pigs and dogs, especially trained to distinguish the scent, have long been used to detect their presence. The animals are always given a small reward of meat or cheese to stop them devouring the valuable truffle. Generally truffles develop at about a foot below ground, but if they are less deep, they can crack the surface when mature. Their whereabouts is also sometimes indicated by a swarm of small yellow flies which often hovers over a spot where truffles are present. Goats are also said to be trained to find them in Sardinia, and very occasionally a man has the ability to detect them, rather as a water-diviner has the power to detect the presence of water. It is a great pity that truffles are now so vastly expensive; they have become a symbol of all that is most rare and delicate in the realm of food, but few people ever taste more than the merest flavouring. They are preserved in cans or jars, commercially, and are available all over the western world. See also TARTUFO; TRUFFE; TRUFLE.

trufle, Polish for truffle, found in many Polish forests. In Poland truffles are usually canned or preserved, when they are called *trufle w konserwach.* This is done by heating the truffles in equal quantities of broth and red wine, and putting them into jars which are steamed for 30 minutes and then covered with airtight caps. They are kept in a cool place for use as necessary. See also TRUFFLE.

truite, French for trout. *Truite arc-en-ciel* is rainbow trout; *truite de lac* is lake trout; *truite de rivière* and *truite de ruisseau* are river trout; *truite saumonée* is salmon trout, often found in land-locked lakes; *truite de mer* is sea trout. Trout is plentiful in French lakes and rivers, and the most usual ways of serving it in France are à la bourguignonne, à la *colbert,* à la *meunière,* à la *normande,* en *papillote,* en matelote, fried, grilled, or baked in red or white wine. It is also smoked (*truite fumée*). Salmon trout is often served poached in white wine with mushrooms and herbs, then drained and coated with sauce *normande.* It is sometimes stuffed first with fish forcemeat. See also TROUT.

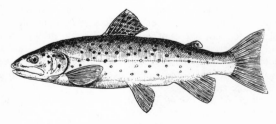

truite de rivière

truite au bleu, freshly killed trout rubbed with wine vinegar, then poached very quickly in a court bouillon containing a lot of vinegar. It is served hot with melted butter or sauce hollandaise, or cold with sauce *ravigote.*

truss, to tie or secure with string or skewers the legs and wings of poultry or game in order to make the bird easier to manage during cooking. Methods of trussing can vary with different birds and for different dishes, but for roasting, the wing tips are generally tucked under the bird and the legs left outside. Woodcock and sometimes snipe have their heads left on and the bill tucked into the skin of the wing. Needles are sometimes used to make the operation easier; they are 6–8 inches long, with a large eye to take the string. Joints which have been fastened with string or skewers to make them easier to carve can also be said to be "trussed," but strictly speaking this is not correct, for in culinary contexts the term is used only for poultry or game. In the case of meat, the phrase used is "prepared for the oven."

truta, Portuguese for trout, usually fried or grilled in Portugal. Small trout are often prepared like *escabèches.* See also TROUT.

truthahn, see PUTER.

tsargana, a small swordfish found in Greek waters, usually served brushed with oil and grilled, or *plaki.*

tsatsiki, a Greek salad made from goat's milk yogourt with peeled and cubed cucumber, chopped mint leaves, salt, and paprika. In Turkey, where it is also served, it is known as *cacik.* In Macedonia it is chilled and served as a soup called *taratouri,* which resembles the Bulgarian *tarator.*

tsipoura, Greek for snapper, one of the best fish to be found in Greek waters. It is usually rubbed with oil and lemon and then grilled on both sides.

tsiros, a silver fish about 6 inches long, not unlike a smelt, found in Greek waters. It is dried, and resembles a Bombay duck.

tsiri salata, a dish served as an appetizer. Tsiri are first dried and salted, then held over burning paper until the outer skin blisters and breaks, when they are filleted. The pieces are marinated for 30 minutes in oil and vinegar, and drained before being served. They are often grilled over charcoal out-of-doors as they have an unpleasant smell while cooking; this evaporates quickly however, and the tsiri make a tasty appetizer.

tsourekia, traditional Greek bread buns with a plaited shape, which are eaten on Easter morning in Greece. They are prepared with 2½ lb. (10 cups) flour mixed with 1 lb. (2 cups) sugar, 1 teaspoon salt, and 3 teaspoons *mahleb* (or alternatively grated lemon or orange peel); into a well in the middle of this are poured 5 well-beaten eggs, 1 cup melted butter, and 1 oz. or 1 package yeast dissolved in 1 cup lukewarm water. All are blended in gradually, first with a wooden spoon and then with the hands. Next, the mixture is turned out and kneaded, covered, and set in a warm place for 4–5 hours to rise. Then plaits are formed from it, and these are brushed with beaten egg and sprinkled with sesame seeds, then baked in a moderate oven for 30–40 minutes. These quantities make about 4 twists, although a single large plaited shape can be formed if preferred. Sometimes the mixture is shaped into dolls or animals for children, with a red-painted, hard-boiled egg for a face (*kokkina avga*). In the Greek Orthodox Church red eggs represent the blood of Christ and are a traditional feature of Easter festivities. See also HALVA; LAMBROPSOMO.

ttoro, see TIORO.

tufoli, large, thick-cut *maccheroni,* usually first boiled and drained, then stuffed with a meat and cheese filling, and then baked in a sauce. It is best in *maccheroni ripieni alla toscana.* See also PASTA.

tuiles, French biscuits (cookies) shaped like curved tiles (tuile being French for tile). They are made from ½ lb. (1 cup) butter creamed with 8 oz. (1 cup) sugar, 5 eggs, added singly, and 8 oz. (2 cups) flour. This mixture is spooned or piped into round flat cakes which are baked for 10–15 minutes in a moderate oven. As soon as the biscuits (cookies) are brought out of the oven, and while they are still warm, they are folded round one side of a rolling pin so that they take on a curved tile shape. They can be flavoured with almonds, vanilla, lemon, etc.

tulum, a popular Turkish cheese made from ewe's milk. It is semi-hard, pressed, and ripened in skins. When it is of good quality, its taste resembles that of Roquefort.

tumbada, a Sardinian pudding consisting of a lemon-flavoured custard mixed with crushed macaroons. It is served cold.

tumbet, a speciality of Mallorca. Sliced potatoes, eggplant (sliced but unpeeled), sliced green peppers, and garlic are all fried separately in olive oil, then drained and layered in a fireproof dish, with seasoning. Fresh tomato sauce is poured over, then the dish is sprinkled with breadcrumbs and baked for 15 minutes.

tuna, see TUNNY-FISH.

Tunbridge cherry batter, a batter fritter which is a speciality of Tunbridge Wells in Kent. To prepare it 1 pint (2 cups) milk is boiled, and as much flour as it will take is stirred in to make a thick batter. The mixture is well beaten and, when tepid, 3 eggs, 2 tablespoons sugar, and flavouring are stirred in. The batter is left to get quite cold in a flat dish, when it is cut into slices, dipped in egg and breadcrumbs, and fried on all sides in butter or oil. These fritters are served on a mound of hot, cooked, stoned cherries.

tunge, see SJØTUNGE.

tunny-fish (*Thunnidae*), called tuna in the U.S., a giant relative of the mackerel, found in temperate seas and especially in the Mediterranean. Many related varieties of tunny, sometimes called horse mackerel, are also found off both the Atlantic and the Pacific coasts of the U.S., but these are coarser-tasting fish. Tunny is seldom to be bought fresh in Britain, but in the neighbourhood of the ports where it is caught in Italy and Sardinia, in other Mediterranean harbours, and in the U.S., fresh tunny is plentiful at certain times when a large shoal has just been netted. Fresh tunny can be somewhat dry, and in Italy and Sardinia the stomach (*ventresca*) should be particularly asked for as it is tender and delicate. Tunny cans remarkably well, and as it is an immense fish which varies in degree of flavour according to the cut, the great majority of it is in fact tinned. It may also be salted and smoked.

Thonine, called "little tunny" in English and "thouna" at Nice in the south of France, is a species of tunny-fish found only in the Mediterranean. It is never more than about 3 feet in length, and the flesh is firm and tasty, somewhat resembling veal when grilled or fried. It is also cooked in white wine with tomatoes, garlic, and herbs. In Italy, and particularly in Sardinia, the roes are dried and salted whole, like *botargo,* and resemble dark, rusty red sausages. See also ALBACORE; ATUM; ATUN; BONITO; THON; TONNO; TONNOS.

tuoni e lampo, an Italian country dish made from broken pieces of mixed pasta, cooked and mixed with cooked chickpeas, Parmesan cheese and olive oil, butter, or tomato sauce. The name means "thunder and lightning," no doubt because of the condition of the smashed pasta fragments, sold cheaply to clear out the bottom of the sacks the pasta is stored in.

turban, a type of edible gourd.

turban, I. A general French culinary term used to describe any circular arrangement of food on a dish. II. A French term for certain preparations, particularly forcemeats, which are cooked in circular border-moulds; for example, turbans of fish, poultry, game, etc.

turbot (*Scopthalmus maximus*), a large European flat fish which can weigh up to 60 lb., and is most delicious and delicate in flavour. The main fishing areas are the Baltic Sea, the English Channel and the Atlantic coastal waters of France. Turbot is not found in American waters, although the name is given in the U.S. to a large flounder which is nearly as delicate a fish. The American fish which most nearly resembles the turbot in taste is the halibut.

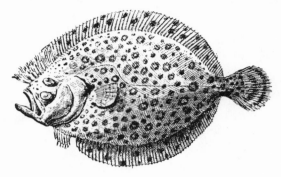

turbot

The scales of the turbot are so minute that the fish seems to be scaleless, and to have simply a rough skin. The flesh is so good that the most common way of cooking it is simply to poach it in either water or a court bouillon, then to serve it with shrimp or lobster sauce, or sauce hollandaise; but it can also be fried, grilled with or without herbs, or baked. See also PIGHVARRE; TURBOT.

turbot, French for turbot. *Turbot double* is a species which has a coloured skin on both sides. It is to be avoided, for the flesh is very inferior to true turbot, but it is at its prime from March to August. *Turbotin* is a small-sized or baby turbot, known in English as "chicken" turbot. Turbot may be cooked by any of the classical French fish methods, particularly *bonne femme, bercy,* and *dugléré,* or it may be served cold with a mayonnaise, rémoulade, sauce *gribiche,* or sauce *verte.* In Normandy it is called *caillebot.*

A turbotière is a square fish-kettle with a removable grid, used for cooking turbot and other large flat fish. See also TURBOT.

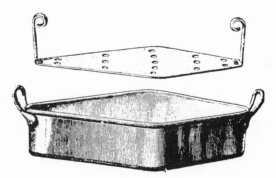

turbotière

tureen, a deep, wide dish, often with a lid, from which soup is served. It can be made from china or metal, and is large enough to hold sufficient liquid for all at table. The tureen dates back to the 18th century; before that time, soup was served to each person separately in individual covered bowls. The word is thought to derive from the French *terrine,* as early English spellings render it "terreen."

turfjes met bessensap, a Dutch bread pudding with raspberry sauce. Twelve slices of stale, crustless bread are fried until golden on both sides in hot butter. They are put in layers in a

large dish, each layer being sprinkled with ground cinnamon, sugar, and puréed raspberries, ending with a layer of fried bread. The dish is left for several hours in a cold place, and covered with whipped cream before serving.

turkey (*Meleagrididae*), originally a wild game bird of North and Central America. There are 2 main species, the ocellated turkey of Mexico, and the common turkey (*Meleagris galloporo*) occurring throughout North America. It is from the latter that domesticated breeds are descended, and there is evidence that these birds had already been partially domesticated by the Indians before the discovery of America in 1492. Domesticated birds were first imported into Spain in 1498, and from there became distributed throughout Europe, being introduced into England between 1524 and 1540. A 17th-century proverb states,

"Turkeys, carps, hops, pickerel, and beer
Came to England all in one year."

The name of turkey had first been given to the guinea-fowl when it was imported from West Africa, but it was transferred to the American bird and has stuck for over 400 years. Turkeys are still found wild in remoter parts of the U.S. and Canada, where they are hunted by pointer or setter dogs, especially in the Tidewater and Piedmont sections of Virginia, though "turkey dogs" are seldom found west of the Blue Ridge Mountains. Wild turkeys do not attain the gigantic weights of the domesticated birds, and 10–12 lb. is a good average. Curiously, a variety bred in England, called Norfolk Black and Norfolk Fawn, was taken back to America by early English colonists and served as a foundation strain for the long-established and famous North American varieties: Bronze (average weight 35–40 lb.); White Holland (28 lb.), known as White Austrian in Europe; Bourbon Red, Black, and Slate (30 lb.); and Narragansett (25–30 lb.). The American Government has also developed a Small White turkey, weighing 12–14 lb. when cleaned and dressed. In Britain, smaller birds are preferred, and the 2 best-known breeds are the Norfolk Black and the Cambridge, neither of which achieves more than about 20 lb. In Italy and Spain turkeys are seldom much bigger than a large capon.

turkey

Turkey makes good eating, but requires plenty of basting during cooking to keep the breast moist. A hen turkey is more tender than a cock, and has more flesh per bone than the larger-framed cock. It is essential to stuff turkey (see STUFFING), for this also bastes the meat from inside. Chestnuts are complementary and should be included in the stuffing, which is put both in the empty crop and in the interior. Sausage meat is also good, and should be used either in the crop or inside the bird. The bird must be cooked quite slowly: 3–3½ hours for a 12-lb. turkey, at 325°F (163°C), is ideal. The bird should be rubbed with butter before cooking, and covered with buttered paper or foil. It is usually roasted, and it is served in England with bread sauce, in the U.S. with cranberry sauce or jelly. Occasionally it is braised or boiled (see YORKSHIRE BOILED TURKEY). It is traditionally served in the U.S. on Thanksgiving Day, as well as at Christmas, as in Britain and Ireland. Cold turkey lends itself well to recooking. It can be put into a sauce béchamel or sauce velouté, with mushrooms; it can be curried; or it can be mixed with cooked pasta, mushrooms, Parmesan cheese, and sauce béchamel and baked in the oven for 30 minutes (this is called turkey Tettrazzini after the famous opera singer). It can also be fricasséed, braised in stock with vegetables, used in pilaf or risotto, devilled, minced, and used for croquettes, rissoles, or *kromeskies,* or made into pies or *terrines* with pork or ham. See also DIN-DONNEAU; GALLOPOULO; INDEYKA; INDYK; KALKON; PAVO; TACCHINO.

smoked turkey, a popular delicacy in the U.S. The best wood to use when smoking turkey is peach; the next best, apple; and the third, hickory. When the turkey has been cleaned, the neck skin is brought over the neck opening and secured with skewers on the back of the bird, and the wingtips are bent backwards. This is to ensure that any fat which oozes out during smoking is caught. For a 15-lb. turkey (which is a good, medium size for smoking), a flat ovenproof plate is filled with refined salt and heated well in a slow oven. The bird is put into boiling water to cover and boiled for 5 minutes, then quickly drained, put onto a board or table, and rubbed with ½ oz. ground saltpetre and as much of the heated salt as the meat will absorb. This operation, which is continued until the bird is lukewarm (about 15–20 minutes), must be carried out very rapidly, so that the maximum amount of salt is rubbed in during the time. Next, 4 oz. more salt is dissolved in 1 pint boiling water and injected into the wing and leg joints and the flat parts of the breast bones. The inside of the bird is stuffed with a large bunch of mixed herbs such as tarragon, marjoram, and lemon thyme, and the whole is wrapped in muslin and tied. The turkey is then smoked (at once, or the meat will toughen) for 48 hours continuously, then for 12 hours a day for 4 days, exposing the bird to the air during the other 12 hours. Chicken and duck can be smoked in the same way, but need only 4 days and 7 days, respectively. See also CURING.

Turk's cap

turlu, a Turkish mutton stew. Mutton is cut into cubes and simmered in butter with chopped garlic or onions, sliced tomatoes, pumpkin, and red peppers. Sliced eggplants and green beans are added with seasoning and a very little water, and the whole is stewed.

turlu gyuvèch or **gyuvèch,** a Bulgarian mutton and vegetable stew. The meat is half-cooked by boiling until tender enough for the bones to be removed, when it is layered in a casserole with sliced carrots, turnips, celeriac, fennel root or leaf, onions, peas, beans, potatoes, and tomatoes, covered with the stock and juice of ½ lemon, and cooked in the oven until the vegetables are ready. If young lamb is used, it is boned, cubed, and first sautéed in oil before layering; it is not boiled. Sometimes several meats are used together, such as veal with bacon, and pork or ham with beef. See also GYUVÈCH.

turmeric (*Curcuma longa*), a plant of the order *Zingiberaceae* and related to ginger. Its roots are dried and powdered to make the familiar spice. Turmeric made from the ovate central tubers is known as round turmeric, while that made from the more cylindrical lateral tubers is called finger turmeric. The powder has a characteristic sweet, spicy smell and an appetizing, slightly bitter taste. It also has a fine, rich gold colour, not quite as orange as saffron, and so is used for colouring as well as for flavouring. Turmeric grown in China is more greenish in colour than that grown in India or the East Indies, and both the roots and the ground spice are used in Chinese cooking and pickles. Turmeric is always used in curries and for certain pickles, especially *piccalilli;* it colours and

stuffed roast turkey for Thanksgiving

Turkish cheeses, see PEYNIRI.
Turkish delight, see LOUKOUMI; RAHAT LOKUM.
Turk's cap, an edible gourd.

turmeric

flavours rice; it is an important ingredient in *mulligatawny soup;* and it is also sweet enough to be used in cakes instead of saffron. Many prepared mustards owe their colour and taste to the inclusion of turmeric powder. Turmeric also has the capacity to slightly thicken the liquid in certain dishes.

turnip (*Brassica rapa*), a plant which is chiefly cultivated for its root. It originated in Asia, and there are now many varieties all belonging to 1 of the 2 main classes of turnip: the long rooted and the flat or round rooted. The latter is superior in flavour and sweetness. Turnips are useful in stews and ragoûts, for they have remarkable powers of absorption and become richer and more succulent by association with the meats in these dishes. It is for this reason that they are often served with fatty meats such as mutton, duck, and goose. Young turnips are always used in a *navarin,* and also in soups. When used as a vegetable they are usually peeled and then boiled and served with butter, salt, and pepper, or else they are puréed.

The green tops of turnip are also eaten boiled in salted water, then strained and chopped. They are not very popular in Britain but are used a great deal in Portugal, where they are tossed in olive oil after boiling, and served with many dishes, especially *chouriço de sangue.* In the U.S., especially in the South, turnip greens are cooked with diced salt pork, salt, a dried pod of chilli, or a pinch of cayenne, and water, all boiled for 15–20 minutes or until tender. Garden relish is served separately. See also BRUKIEW; RAPE; WEISSE RÜBE.

turnip pasty, a variant of the traditional Cornish pasty. The filling consists of turnip and potato, or sometimes all turnip mixed with butter or cream or flavoured with fat bacon.

turnip-rooted cabbage, see SWEDE.

turnip-rooted chervil, see CHERVIL.

turnip-rooted parsley, see PARSLEY.

turnover, an old English pastry made from either short crust pastry or puff pastry, the best-known example being the Cornish pasty. The pastry is cut in the shape of a circle, half of which is covered with fruit, jam, meat, or vegetables; then the edges are moistened with water, and the plain half is folded over the filling, pressed down, and crimped at the edges. The turnover is then baked in a moderate oven for about 30 minutes. It can be eaten hot or cold. Some turnover-like pastries include *chausson, checky pig,* and *Lancashire foot.*

turnspit, originally the name for the dog who worked the old spits by walking a treadmill, and later given also to the boy who turned it by hand. Later, spits were worked by clockwork, and nowadays they are powered by electricity or gas. See also SPIT.

turrón, a Spanish sweetmeat (confection) not unlike nougat, which is traditionally eaten at all fiestas. It varies slightly from region to region: that of Jijona is soft whereas that of Alicante is hard. A certain amount is exported in wooden boxes. In Spain it is served as a dessert or eaten with soft curd cheese. It is always eaten at the *Falla de San Chusep.* See also TOURON.

turrón de Alicante, made with 12 egg yolks beaten with 2 lb. powdered almonds and the same amount of sugar. After being well blended, the mixture is put into a flat greased tin, covered with a cloth and weighted for 2–3 days, after which it is cut into slices.

turrón Jijona, as above, with the final addition of 2 stiffly beaten egg whites. The mixture is put into greased paper and wrapped up before weighting and leaving for 2–3 days. Sometimes chopped roasted almonds, honey, and grated orange peel are added.

turshìya, Bulgarian mixed pickles.

turtle (*Testudines*), an aquatic reptile of the same order as the tortoise. It feeds on marine vegetation and is found in many of

green turtle

the warmer parts of the world. Edible turtles, of which there are many varieties (*Chelydra serpentina,* the green turtle *Chelonia mydas,* and turtles of the genera *Chrysemys* and *Malaclemys*), are particularly excellent in the form of turtle soup. True turtle soup is made from green turtles freshly killed for the purpose, but in most countries where live turtle is not readily available, dried turtle is used, and turtle flesh, dried in the air and sun, is imported from South America, Africa, Australia, and from the West Indies, which produces the finest of all. Turtle eggs are soft shelled, and are highly prized as food. They are laid in warm sand, covered by the turtle, and abandoned. When hatched, the young turtles make for the sea and fend for themselves. The laying of the eggs is watched for by collectors who scoop them out as soon as they have been deposited. This has led to a very serious decline in the number of turtles. Of the flesh, turtle flippers are the true delicacy, and they are served in many ways, for example *nageoires de tortue.* See also SOFT SHELL TURTLE; TERRAPIN.

turtle soup (dried). One-half lb. dried turtle flesh is soaked overnight, then simmered in stock for 6–8 hours. It is chopped, then put back into the stock with chopped basil, seasoning, lemon juice, and 1 glass sherry, and simmered gently until the turtle flesh is quite soft.

turtle soup (fresh). The live turtle is put in straw and given water every 2–3 hours. It is beheaded when required, the shell is stripped off, and it is left hanging neck downwards overnight. About 3–4 lb. chopped turtle, a knuckle of veal, and 4 oz. cubed lean ham are covered with cold water to 4 times the quantity of meat, and this is brought slowly to the boil, then seasoned and simmered for 4 hours. Mushrooms and basil are added for the last 30 minutes, and a glass (½ cup) of white wine or Madeira, then all are brought just to boiling point. The soup is strained and served, but small pieces of turtle meat are sliced as a garnish. It is usually served clear, but may be slightly thickened with a *beurre manié.*

turtle herbs, a mixture of basil, thyme, and marjoram, sold commercially to flavour soups such as strong beef consommé, which is then called à la *tortue.*

tusk, an alternative name for cusk.

tutti-frutti, a mixture of soft fruits bottled in brandy. For each pound of fruit, 1 lb. (2 cups) sugar is added, and the container is filled with brandy. This delicious mixture can be served over ice cream, used with parfaits, trifles, etc., and also served with cold ham, pork, or chicken.

tuzlama, a Rumanian way of cooking tripe. First 3 lb. tripe is simmered with a calf's foot and peppercorns, salt, sliced onion, root vegetables, and 2 quarts (8 cups) water for about 2 hours. Then 2 large carrots are grated and lightly fried in butter; 1 teaspoon flour is sprinkled over them, and 1 pint (2 cups) of the tripe stock is added. After boiling this for 15 minutes, the liquid is drained off but the carrot pulp reserved. The meat of the calf's foot is then cut into cubes and the tripe cut into 2-inch squares, and this is put into a saucepan. Next 1 egg yolk and 1 tablespoon lemon juice are mixed into the carrot mixture, and this is heated but not boiled and served over the tripe and the meat.

tvorog, Russian for cottage cheese, which is used for almost all Russian cheesecakes. It is used rather dry, and if it is still moist after straining through muslin, it should be pressed between two boards to squeeze the moisture out. *Tvorozhniki,* another name for syrniki (see SYR). See also COTTAGE CHEESE.

zapekanka iz tvoroga, a cheese dish made from 1 lb. dry tvorog mixed with 3 tablespoons melted butter, 1 egg, 2 tablespoons sugar, 2 tablespoons semolina, vanilla, and salt. When well mixed, 1 cup sultanas or raisins is added (sometimes spinach, nuts, and candied peel are used instead). All is put into a buttered dish and sprinkled with breadcrumbs and sour cream, before baking for 30 minutes. This dish may be served with hot fruit syrup or more sour cream.

twaite shad, see SHAD.

tweed kettle, also called salmon hash, a traditional Scottish dish of salmon which was popular in Edinburgh in the 19th century. First 1 lb. fresh salmon is boned and skinned, then cut into 1-inch cubes. It is seasoned with a pinch of mace, salt, and pepper before being poached in a mixture of water, wine vinegar or white wine, minced shallot, chives, and parsley. It is cooked very gently for about 30 minutes. It is served hot with either girdle scones or mashed potatoes, or cold, garnished with cress and cucumber.

twins, see AMERICAN CHEDDAR.

tybo, a brick-shaped Danish cheese belonging to the samsøe family. It is golden with a red skin, and weighs between 4½ lb. and 6½ lb. It comes from Ty, where in bygone days it was the custom on Midsummer Day (when the trolls and witches are hunted and when the grass is at its best) for farmers to bring a gift of milk to the parson and other important people, including the midwife, who made it into cheese. To this day it is sometimes said to be made of "magic" milk. See also OST.

tyri, Greek for cheese. Although some of the commercially made Greek cheeses are exported to Greek communities abroad, the cheeses of Greece are not world-famous. Most are soft cheeses, made from ewe's or goat's milk. They are made by the shepherds and peasants, so that their quality depends on local skill. The most popular of all Greek cheeses is *féta.* See also AGRAFA; ANARI; ANTHOLYTI; ANTHOTYRO; GRAVIERI; GRUYÈRE; HALORINI; KASSERI; KEFALOTYRI; KOPANISTI; MANOURI; MITZITHRA; PARNOSSUS; PINDOS; SKYROS; TELEMES; TOULOUMOTYRI.

tyropita, a cheese pie, eaten during *Tyrini* or *Apokries.* It is made from 10 sheets of phyllo pastry, each one brushed with melted butter, then all placed one on top of the other in a large, shallow, greased baking tin. They are spread with a mixture of 1 lb. *féta* cheese, 1 lb. *mitzithra* cheese, and 4 eggs beaten in one by one, and 2 heaped tablespoons flour stirred into ½ cup cream. The mixture is covered with 10 more buttered sheets of phyllo pastry, then the edges are pressed down to stop the filling oozing out. The top sheet is sprinkled lightly with cold water to prevent curling, and the top 4 layers are then scored through to indicate serving pieces, either diamonds or squares. It is baked in a moderate oven for 45 minutes and served warm.

tyrini, Greek "cheese week," the last week of the pre-Lenten carnival. See also APOKREO.

tyrolienne, I. A sauce béarnaise made with olive oil instead of butter, served with hot meats (usually grills) or fish. II. A French method of cooking fish. It is fried and then served on pulped tomatoes, garnished with fried onion rings. III. A method of serving meat. It is grilled and served on pulped tomatoes garnished with onion rings, as above, but sauce *tyrolienne* is added.

tyrolienne, sauce, a classical French sauce for cold fish or cold meat, consisting of a mayonnaise lightly flavoured with tomato purée.

tyttebaer, Norwegian for cranberry. It grows extensively in Norway and is much used there as a dessert fruit and also for making jams and jellies to accompany turkey and some game dishes. See also CRANBERRY.

tyttebær og ris, a dish of cranberries and rice. Rinsed cranberries are sprinkled with sugar and left to stand for an hour or more, during which time they are frequently stirred. When a syrup has formed, it is strained off and served with boiled rice and cream. Alternatively, the syrup may be preserved for future use.

tzatziki, see TSATSIKI.

tzenios, the Greek name for the collecting grounds of the roe of the grey mullet, used for *botargo* and *taramosalata.*

tzimmes, a traditional Jewish Sabbath and holiday dish of which there are many varieties. It can be made with or without meat, and with fruit such as prunes, or with vegetables. The method of preparing it is always the same, however, and although the following recipe is for a prune, beef, and potato tzimmes, the same instructions may be adapted for use with different ingredients.

Sauté 2 lb. brisket of beef and 1 lb. onions in oil, then add 1 lb. small potatoes and ¾ lb. prunes. Cover the whole with cold water and cook, uncovered, for 1 hour. Then seasoning, a pinch of nutmeg or cinnamon, and ½ cup honey, syrup, or brown sugar are added. The whole is covered and simmered gently for a further hour. The consistency must not be soupy; on the other hand, if there is a tendency for the mixture to run dry a little more water should be added. Just before serving, 2 tablespoons flour is lightly browned in chicken fat and shaken into the stew. This tzimmes is served either as a main dish, or as a garnish for cooked, boiled or baked chicken. Rice may also be used, either with, or instead of potato, as may other root vegetables. Sometimes *farfel* is added instead of flour, thus making a *farfel* tzimmes. There is also a tzimmes dumpling (tzimmes, *knaidle*), which is made of 4 oz. (1 cup) flour mixed with 2 oz. (½ cup) suet, a little sugar, and parsley, all moistened with water and then made into small balls which are put into the tzimmes mixture to poach about 20 minutes before it will be ready. In Rumania and other Balkan countries, a compote of dried fruits cooked with honey and rice is called tzimmes, as are beans cooked with honey. When the tzimmes is meatless, it is qualified by the word *milchig.*

Tzimmes is particularly associated with Rosh Hashanah, the Jewish New Year's Day, because it is sweet and succulent and symbolizes a sweet and happy New Year. In the vernacular, the word has also come to mean making a fuss of someone or something, on account of the complications of the preparations.

U

uccelletti, a collective Italian word covering all kinds of small edible birds such as larks, thrushes, fieldfares, and blackbirds. They are usually roasted or grilled, threaded on a very large skewer with a bay leaf and a piece of bread between each bird until the skewer is full. In the north of Italy they are served on a bed of polenta or rice. In the case of very small birds, the bones are crunched up with the flesh. See also BECCAFICO; FIELDFARE; FIGEATER; GAME; LARK.

udder, the mammary gland of cattle; it is eaten in France (see TÉTINE). In Italy, calf's udder is used in the stuffing of *ravioli alla genovese*.

ugli, the name used in Great Britain for the hybrid citrus fruit that is called tangelo in the U.S., its country of origin. It has a loose skin and looks like a large irregularly shaped tangerine. It is not good to look at, but the taste and juice of the fruit are excellent. It is generally eaten raw, but the English who live in the West Indies bake it in hot cinders and eat it sprinkled with sugar.

ugnsomelett, a Swedish baked omelette. Made from 4 eggs, seasoned and beaten with 1 cup cream. Then 1 tablespoon butter is melted in a shallow ovenproof dish, and the mixture is poured in and baked in a moderate oven for 15–20 minutes. When cooked, the omelette is slid out onto a warmed plate, half covered with a warm, cooked filling of mushrooms, shrimps, chicken, etc., and then folded over and eaten at once. See also OMELETTE.

uitsmijter, a fried egg and meat sandwich, a traditional Dutch dish which is eaten all over Holland by people such as businessmen who have only a short time for a meal. Meat or ham is laid on buttered bread or bread which has been fried in butter, a couple of fried eggs are placed on the meat, and the sandwich is topped with dill pickle.

Ujházi leves, a soup that was first made by one of Hungary's most famous chefs, Ujházi, and is only one of the many dishes named after him. A boiling fowl is cut into 8 pieces which are simmered in water with 1 carrot, 1 parsnip, 1 onion, 1 turnip, 1 tomato, salt, and peppercorns until tender. A *májgombóc* is added shortly before the soup is to be served.

ukha, a Russian clear fish soup, usually made from the stock of freshwater fish such as perch, bream, or sturgeon, although other small freshwater fish are also added to give the proper consistency and typical flavour. Perch scales are scraped off

uitsmijter

first, for they give a bitter taste. The soup is garnished with pieces of fish.

ukha iz sterlyadey, ukha with sterlet, which consists of fish stock made from bass, perch, ruff, and possibly gudgeon, with sliced onions, celery, peppercorns, and bay leaves. It is strained and clarified with pressed caviar (see below) and pounded with ice and egg whites, then garnished with small pieces of sterlet which have been boiled in fish stock, Madeira, and lemon juice; it is served with slices of peeled lemon and small pirozhki or rasstegay. Ukha may also be garnished with burbot, carp, eel, salmon, sturgeon, or whitebait, and sometimes sorrel is added.

Clarification by means of caviar is performed by pounding a few ounces of caviar in a mortar with a little cold water, then diluting it with 1 cup very hot fish stock. Half this mixture is poured into the soup, stirring all the time until it boils. This is left to stand for 15 minutes, when the other half of the caviar mixture is mixed in, and the soup is again boiled for a few minutes. After this it is left until the caviar settles in the bottom, when it is strained and reheated.

Ukrainskaya galushki, see GALUSHKI.

Ukrainskaya kolbasa, see KOLBASA.

ulloa, a Spanish cheese from Galicia. It has a softish creamy paste, not unlike a ripe camembert.

ulmer gerstlsuppe, a traditional Austrian barley soup, consisting of 3 pints (6 cups) rich beef broth, thickened with 2 egg yolks which have been beaten with ½ pint (1 cup) milk, and garnished with pearl barley. See also GERSTENSUPPE.

umbles, the edible entrails of deer. They used to be made into a pie which was usually given to the lower orders of the domestic staff in a large household, and this is no doubt the origin of the expression "to eat [h]umble pie." The entrails were cooked in stock with ginger, nutmeg, dates, raisins, and currants, then given a pastry crust and baked in the oven. In hunting communities this used also to be called lumber pie.

umbra, I. A kind of minnow, also called mud minnow, found in freshwater in Europe and North America. It is not usually marketed in Britain, but is sometimes found in France where it is called *ombre*. II. *Umbrina cirrhosa* and *U. leccia*, a Mediterranean fish resembling perch or a very large sea bass. It is also called umbrine. It can weigh about 30 lb., and has firm white flesh which is good to eat. In Italy, where it is known as *ombrina*, it is usually cooked *in bianco* (boiled) and served cold with mayonnaise. In France, where it is called *ombre de mer*, it is cooked like bass.

under roast, a traditional Cornish dish. Good grilling steak is cut into fairly small strips, then each piece is seasoned with pepper and salt, rolled up, placed in a roasting tin, sprinkled with flour, and covered with cold water. A layer of peeled potatoes is placed on top, and the dish is baked in a moderate oven for 1½ hours.

undercut, an alternative English name for fillet of beef.

underground onion, an alternative name for potato onion (see ONION).

unleavened bread, bread made without yeast or any raising agent. The best-known examples are the Scottish oatcake (see BANNOCK), and the Jewish *matzoh*. In the Middle Ages, in pre-Reformation days, the finest *manchet bread* was unleavened when used for the Mass.

unrefined sugar, see SUGAR.

uova, Italian for egg. Eggs are also used to garnish soups such as zuppa *Parese*, or *stracciatella* in Italy. *Tuorlo d'uovo* is egg yolk. See also EGG.

uova affogate, poached eggs.

uova affogate sui crostina, poached eggs on toast.

uova al burro, eggs cooked on top of the stove in a buttered dish.

uova al piatto, eggs cooked in a buttered dish on top of the stove, as above, but they can also be cooked or garnished with anchovies, grated cheese, tomatoes, or peas.

uova al tegame, eggs cooked in individual buttered dishes which are made of china or metal and called *tegamini*. They are often cooked with a layer of ham or cheese such as mozzarella or bel paese underneath.

uova alla cacciatora, eggs hunter's-style. They are cooked in a sauce of fried chicken livers, onion, tomato purée, basil, rosemary, white wine, and seasoning.

uova alla casalinga, eggs baked in large scooped-out tomatoes.

uova all' Emiliana, eggs cooked *al piatto* with chicken livers, or garnished with chicken livers.

uova bazzotte, soft-boiled eggs.

uova col riso, eggs baked in cooked rice with grated cheese on top. This is also done with poached eggs or *uova mollette*.

uova con acciughe, or *con alice,* eggs cooked *al piatto* with anchovies, or garnished with anchovies.

uova con puré di patate, poached eggs served on mashed potatoes, with grated cheese. See also TORTINI D'UOVA NELLA NEVE.

uova divorziate, a garnish rather than a dish in itself. Eggs are hard-boiled and the yolks and whites separated; the yolks are crumbled and served as a garnish to puréed potatoes, the whites are finely shredded to garnish puréed carrots.

uova fiorentina, eggs baked in cooked spinach in the oven, garnished with chopped anchovies and grated cheese.

uova fritte, fried eggs.

uova mollette, see OEUFS MOLLETS.

uova mollette con funghi e formaggio, boiled eggs shelled and served with mushrooms fried in butter, with grated Parmesan cheese melted on top.

uova mollette in salsa agrodolce, uova mollette served in *agrodolce* sauce.

uova ripiene, stuffed eggs.

uova sode, hard-boiled eggs.

uova stracciate, or *strapazzate,* scrambled eggs.

uova stracciate con tartufi fanchi, scrambled eggs served with grated white truffles on top.

uova tonnate, hard-boiled eggs sliced lengthways and covered with *maionese tonnata*.

uova di bufalo, an egg-shaped mozzarella cheese.

uova di pesce, Italian for hard fish roe. A fish with a hard roe is described as *pieno d'uova* (full of eggs). Tunny (tuna) roe is *uova di tonno*. Soft roe is *latte di pesce*.

upland cress, a plant similar to American cress.

Upsala, a Swedish method of cooking fish from the university town of the same name. It is poached in white wine sauce with coarsely chopped fennel bulbs simmered in butter.

upside-down cake, an American cake, also served as a pudding, which is baked in the oven and turned out upside-down for serving. Almost any fruit can be used, but the most popular are apricot or pineapple (canned). First 2–4 oz. (¼–½ cup) butter is melted in a cake tin with ¼ lb. (½ cup) brown sugar; then 15 oz. drained fruit slices is put in, sometimes with a scattering of chopped nuts, and all are heated in the oven. Next 2 oz. (¼ cup) butter is creamed with 4 oz. (½ cup) sugar, and 1 egg is added; then 6 oz. (1½ cups) flour is stirred in, alternately with ¼ pint (½ cup) milk, 1½ teaspoons baking powder, and a pinch of salt. When well blended, this sponge mixture is poured over the fruit, and the pudding is baked in a moderate oven for 40 minutes. It is cooled slightly before being turned out and is served hot or cold.

Urbain-Dubois, à l', I. A French method of serving fish. It is poached and boned; first a sauce *aurore* mixed with diced crayfish tails and truffles is poured over it, then on top of that is poured 1 pint crayfish soufflé. The whole is then baked for 35 minutes in a hot oven. II. Another French method of serving fish. It is poached, boned, then covered with lobster soufflé, garnished with sliced truffles, small quenelles of whiting and sauce *normande,* and baked as above. III. A French dish of scrambled eggs mixed with diced lobster and served in opened lobster claws, with lobster sauce. They are all named after the 19th century gourmet and cookery writer.

ursuline, à l', a French method of serving *oeufs mollets,* dressed on slightly hollowed rounds of salmon forcemeat filled with a white purée of mushrooms. Sliced truffle is placed on top and the whole is coated with sauce mornay, sprinkled with grated Parmesan cheese, and glazed under a grill. See also OEUFS.

uso piora, see PIORA.

ùsskùmrù, Turkish for mackerel. See also MACKEREL.

firinda ùskùmrù, mackerel baked with 1 sliced onion, a large tomato, 1 tablespoon parsley, and 1 bay leaf. It is served with 4 tablespoons olive oil mixed with 2 tablespoons lemon juice.

ùsskùmrù kebabı, chopped and skewered mackerel rubbed and marinated in salt, pepper, chopped parsley, and fennel for 1 hour, then brushed with oil, and grilled with a bay leaf between each chunk of fish. Eel, mullet, and other fish may be cooked in the same way.

ùsskùmrù külbastısı, mackerel marinated as above, then

grilled over charcoal and served with chopped parsley mixed with finely chopped raw onion and lemon juice.

ùsskùmrù yahnisi, mackerel fillets stewed with lightly fried onions, parsley, fennel, olive oil, ¼ pint (½ cup) wine vinegar, 1½ pints (3 cups) water, salt, and pepper. Sometimes tomatoes are added. The dish is sprinkled with cinnamon before serving.

usturoi, Rumanian for garlic, used a great deal in Rumanian cooking, particularly for the much-used sauce, *mujdei de usturoi*.

uszka do barszczu, Polish for small ravioli made from a paste of ½ lb. (2 cups) flour mixed with 1 large egg and 1 tablespoon water, well worked, rolled out paper thin, and cut into 3-inch squares. The filling, which consists of finely ground meats and herbs, is placed on one half of each square, and the other half is folded over and pressed down. The ravioli are cooked in boiling salted water and used to garnish soups.

uszka postne, as above, but filled with a mixture of breadcrumbs, butter, and mushrooms.

utka, Russian for duck. See also DUCK.

utka farshirovannaya gribami, duck stuffed with 2 oz. salted mushrooms, ½ lb. chopped veal, 1 cup breadcrumbs, 2 tablespoons sour cream, and 1 egg, then roasted with butter. Sour cream is often added to the pan juices and reduced.

uunijuusto pihkamaidosta, Finnish for cheese that is made in the oven from beestings (the milk taken from a cow 3–5 days after calving). The milk is poured into an ovenproof dish, seasoned with salt, and cooked very slowly. It is usually served hot with milk and sugar as a dessert, but it can also be served cold, cut into pieces, with jam.

uunipuuro, a Finnish barley pudding, perhaps better described as a barley oven porridge. The barley (1¼ cups) is soaked overnight in cold water. The next day 6 cups boiling milk is added (the water is not changed), and the mixture is cooked for 30 minutes. It is poured into an ovenproof dish and baked slowly for several hours.

uva, Italian for grape. *Uva di corinto* is a currant; *uva passa* is a raisin; *uva sultane* is a sultana. *Sorta d'uva passa* is a term also used for sultana.

uva passolina, a dessert dish eaten in the south of Italy, which consists of sultanas soaked in brandy, then wrapped up like little parcels in lemon leaves.

uzbek plov, see PLOV.

Uzès, sauce, a French sauce consisting of sauce hollandaise beaten with anchovy essence (extract) and flavoured lightly with Madeira wine. It comes from Uzès, an ancient episcopal seat, in France.

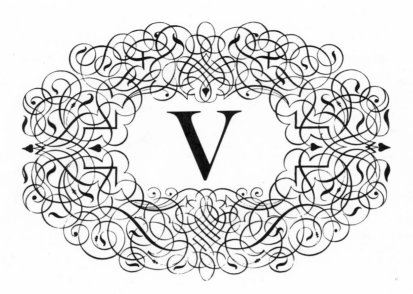

V

vacherin, a French sweet dish or dessert which can be made in several ways. One way is to bake large flat rounds of meringue mixture in a very low oven and layer them with *crème chantilly*. Alternatively, almond paste may be used in place of the meringue. Another method is to set small ovals or rounds of meringue in a ring or crown shape and fill the centres with fresh soft fruit and cream. Again, almond paste may be used in place of meringue for this method.

vacherin, the name of several cheeses made in the French Savoy and Franche-Comté districts, and in Switzerland. They have a firm crust with a soft inside similar to camembert. See also COMTÉ.

vacherin

vacherin d'abondance, a French cow's milk cheese produced in the Savoy; it is in season from April to October.

vacherin de joux, a French cow's milk cheese produced in the Franche-Comté; it is in season from October to April.

vacherin des beauges, a French cow's milk cheese with a leathery crust and a very soft paste inside produced in the Savoy; it is in season from April to June.

vacherin du mont d'or, the only original soft Swiss cheese, made only in 12 mountain dairies in the Joux valley. It is made in the autumn. It has a mild taste and a creamy texture, and the cheese tends to run when it is mature; it also develops a red grease. It is sold in the Lausanne area, but only during the cold weather as it does not travel well.

văcuță, Rumanian for beef. See also BEEF.

văcuță cu gutui, a dish of beef and quinces. To make it 2 lb. diced brisket of beef is simmered with 1 onion in water to cover until half cooked; then it is removed and fried in fat to which 4 peeled and chopped quinces, 2 tablespoons brown sugar, 2 sliced onions, and 1 pint (2 cups) beef stock mixed with 1 tablespoon flour and a dash of vinegar are added. It is all gently simmered until the meat is tender and the liquid reduced to about ½ pint. Sometimes prunes or dried apricots are also added. It is served with *mămăligă* or *rice*. See also GUTUI, CA CARNE.

våfflor, see GRÄDDVÅFFLOR.

vafler, Norwegian for waffles, often served for breakfast in Norway. First 4 well-beaten eggs are beaten into a mixture of 8 oz. (2 cups) flour, 1½ oz. (2 tablespoons) sugar, and a pinch of salt. Very gradually 1 pint (2 cups) sour cream is beaten in, and the mixture is cooked in heated waffle irons. Fresh milk may be used instead of sour cream. See also RØMMEVAFLER.

väiksed heeringad piimä saustiga, an Estonian national dish of small salted herrings fried lightly in butter. Milk is then added and the fish are cooked for about 15 minutes, when finely chopped dill is put in. They are served with cooked potatoes, pickled cucumber, or dill pickles. See also HERRING; KALA.

Valais raclette cheese, a Swiss cheese made only in the canton of Valais and used mainly for preparing a local dish called *raclette*. It weighs 15–20 lb. and takes three months to cure. It is not exported. See also RACLETTE.

Valençay, a French goat's milk cheese made in and around Valençay in the Indre department. It is rather like *levroux* and is eaten from April to November.

Valenciennes, à la, I. A French garnish for tournedos, noisettes, and poultry consisting of pilaf mixed with chopped ham and sweet peppers. For meat it is served with the pan juices diluted with tomato purée, then boiled up with veal gravy and reduced; for poultry, it is served with sauce suprême flavoured with tomato purée. II. A French chicken consommé garnished with chicken quenelles and chopped chervil. See also CONSOMMÉ.

valois, à la, I. A French garnish for fish consisting of soft roes sautéed in butter, crayfish, boiled potato balls, and *sauce valois* (see FOYOT). II. A French garnish for small pieces of meat or poultry consisting of sliced raw potatoes and artichoke bottoms sautéed in butter. It is served with the pan juices boiled up with white wine and veal gravy and reduced and then whipped with butter.

valois, sauce, a French sauce, also called *foyot,* which is sauce béarnaise which has a little meat jelly added to it.

Vandyke, an old English culinary title for a dish that was circled with a border of toast, pastry, or potato cut into pointed shapes or triangles. They were reminiscent of the pointed Vandyke beard, so named from the many portraits of the English royal family and aristocracy by the Flemish painter Van Dyke (1599–1641), in which all the male subjects are portrayed with triangular pointed cavalier beards.

vanilj, Swedish for vanilla. See also VANILLA.

vaniljkräm, vanilla cream, sometimes used in Sweden as a filling for cakes and pastries (see LINSER). The cream is made in a double boiler. First 2 tablespoons castor sugar is sifted with 1 tablespoon potato flour and added to 2 egg yolks; then ½ pint (1 cup) cream is added. The mixture is cooked until thick over water which is just off the boil, then flavoured with vanilla essence (extract). It is served cold and should be stirred occasionally during the cooking process.

vaniljsås, vanilla sauce. A double saucepan is needed to make this sauce. First 3 egg yolks and 2 tablespoons sugar are beaten over hot water; then ½ pint (1 cup) warm cream is stirred in. Stirring is continued until the mixture thickens, when it is removed from the heat and vanilla essence (extract) is added to taste. When cold, 1 cup whipped cream is folded in.

vanilla, a member of the orchid family (*Orchidaceae*); there are about seventy species of the genus *Vanilla* scattered over tropical regions of both hemispheres. The pods of this climbing plant are used for flavouring cakes, sweets, and many sweet dishes, and are gathered before they are completely ripe, plunged into boiling water, then put, still damp, into air tight containers. The finest vanilla is obtained from *V. fragrans,* syn. *planifolia,* which has pods 8–12 inches long with a smooth black skin and a frosted surface when dried. Another variety is *V. fragrans variegata* which has greenish pods with cream stripes, but this has not the fine aroma of *planifolia.* Nowadays, unfortunately, a great deal of vanilla essence (extract) is not obtained from the vanilla pod but is made from vanilline, a synthetic product. True vanilla has an extraordinarily pungent and sweet aroma, and must be used sparingly if it is not to be mawkish. The name is derived from the Spanish word *vainilla* (little sheath), an allusion to the shape of the fruit.

vanilla sauce, 1 vanilla pod is boiled in 1 pint (2 cups) milk with sugar to taste, when the saucepan is removed from the heat. Then 3 egg yolks are beaten with 2 tablespoons flour, and the warm, flavoured milk is added to them. The mixture is stirred over a gentle heat until thick, but it must not boil. The 3 egg whites are then beaten to a stiff froth with castor sugar, and added to the sauce before serving. It is served with steamed puddings, or can be eaten alone as a kind of frothy custard.

vanilla sugar, perhaps the best way of using the pods so that the flavour does not obtrude. About 6 pods are placed upright in a deep jar or bottle, which is then filled up with sugar and a lid screwed on. Within a few days the sugar will be impregnated with the vanilla and may be used in the making of cakes, puddings, and custards where a vanilla flavour is

required. If the pods are kept covered with the sugar they will remain pungent for several years. The pods can also be used boiled up in syrup; if this is being prepared for a fruit that is already sweet, the pods are removed when cooking is completed, washed, dried, and replaced in the sugar.

vanilla pods

vanner, a French culinary term meaning to stir a sauce constantly in order to make it smooth and to prevent a skin from forming.

vannkarse, see BRØNNKARSE.

vánočka, a sweet Czechoslovakian bread traditionally eaten at Christmas. It is made from 1 lb. (4 cups) flour, 2 oz. yeast, 8 oz. (1 cup) sugar, 8 oz. (1 cup) butter, 1 pint (2 cups) milk, 1 teaspoon vanilla, ½ lb. (1 cup) sultanas, 4 oz. (1 cup) almonds, grated peel of 1 lemon, and 2 eggs. The dough is left to rise for a couple of hours, when it is divided into eight equal portions which are formed into long thin rolls. Then 4 of the rolls are plaited to form the base of the vánočka, then a plait made from three more rolls is put on top. Finally the last roll is divided into two, and these are plaited and placed on top of that. The vánočka is kept in shape by slivers of wood, and is left to rise again; then it is brushed with beaten egg, sprinkled with chopped almonds and baked in a hot oven for 45 minutes. Sugar is sprinkled on top while the vánočka is still warm.

vaquito, a fish from Spanish waters whose unusual markings are very similar to those of the serrano, although, unlike the latter, this fish is tasteless. It is also known as *cabrilla.* There is no English name for this fish.

varenetzs, a traditional Russian country dish. To prepare it 2 quarts (8 cups) creamy milk is put into a wide earthenware pan and heated in a slow oven until a skin forms, which is then pushed down to the bottom. This procedure is repeated about six times until the milk becomes a peach colour, when it is taken from the oven and left to cool. Then ½ pint (1 cup) sour cream is added and mixed in well, and the mixture is left in a warm place for a day, after which it is chilled and served in bowls, sprinkled with sugar, cinnamon, and rye breadcrumbs.

vareniki, a type of Russian ravioli made of noodle dough with various kinds of stuffing such as meat, curds or cottage cheese, cabbage, etc. Thin rounds of the dough are heaped with small mounds of the stuffing, and then covered with similar rounds. The edges are moistened with water and pressed firmly together, and the vareniki are then poached in salted water. They are usually served covered with melted butter and sour cream. If a curd filling is used, fruit syrup is the accompaniment. See also VIRTINIAI.

vareniki litovskie, see VIRTINIAI.

vareniki malorussiysky, vareniki filled with a mixture of 1 lb. (2 cups) butter creamed with 2 egg yolks, 4 oz. (½ cup) sugar, 1 lb. strained curds or cottage cheese, and grated peel of 1 lemon. After being poached in salted water and drained, they are served covered with melted butter and sugar. Sour cream is served separately.

vareniki s kapustoy, vareniki with a stuffing of sauerkraut. The sauerkraut is boiled in stock, drained, chopped, and mixed with chopped fried onions and seasoning before being used as the filling. After poaching, these vareniki are arranged in a dish and served covered with sliced onions which have been fried in butter.

varenne, la, a French sauce made from mayonnaise to which dry *duxelles,* chopped chervil, and parsley are added to taste.

vareschaga, a Russian national dish. A 4–5-lb. loin of lean pork is cut into thin strips about 3 inches long, which are fried in hot fat, then put into a saucepan with ½ pint (1 cup) pickled beetroot juice and water to cover. Next 1 large sliced onion, salt, and pepper are added and the whole brought to the boil, when several tablespoons of rye breadcrumbs are added and mixed in well. The vareschaga is boiled once more and served hot.

variety meats, the American term for offal; they are also called organ meats and side meats.

varkensvlees, Dutch for pork. *Varkenscarbonaden* are pork chops. See also PORK.

varkenscarbonaden met purée en robert saus, pork chops with potato purée and robert saus. The chops are seasoned, rubbed with butter, and seared in a hot pan. More butter is added, and the chops are cooked over a reduced heat until tender (about 20 minutes). They are then laid round the potato purée and served with robert saus.

varkensschiff, rolled rib of pork. In Holland this is boned, rolled, and tied, and then cooked in the following way. A kettleful of boiling water is first poured over the meat, and it is then baked for about 2 hours (30 minutes per lb.) in 4 oz. (½ cup) butter or fat in a fairly hot oven. Then 1 apple, seasoning, and 1 teaspoon marjoram or sage are added after the first hour. About ½ pint (1 cup) water may be added during cooking if the meat gets too brown, and frequent basting is required.

varme osteboller, Danish hot cheese balls. To prepare them ¼ lb. (½ cup) butter, ½ pint (1 cup) milk, and salt are brought to the boil. Then 4½ oz. (1¼ cups) flour is added quickly and the mixture is stirred until smooth; then it is gently cooked until it leaves the sides of the pan. It is cooled slightly, and 4–5 eggs are beaten in one at a time. This paste is then shaped into small balls. The rind is removed from a camembert and the cheese is blended with whipped cream until it is of a consistency to go through a forcing bag. The balls are fried in deep hot oil and served hot with the cheese mixture piped on top.

vasilopita, a Greek New Year's cake. New Year's Eve is one of the most important dates in the Greek calendar, and New Year's Day is also the feast of St. Basil, the patron saint of Greece. On New Year's Eve all Greeks gamble in an effort to assess their luck for the coming year, and in this evaluation the vasilopita plays an important part. At midnight it is dramatically set on the gaming table, and if the first 3 pieces reveal the lucky coin hidden in the cake, good fortune is assured for all present. The head of the family cuts the cake, first making the sign of the cross over it with the knife. Traditionally the first piece is set aside for Jesus Christ, the second for Our Lady Theotokos, and the third for St. Basil. The fam-

ily are then served in order of seniority. What is left over is given to the poor the next day, and there is always the chance that the lucky coin will be in that portion. After the cake has been distributed, 1 portion to each person, the table is cleared, champagne is served, and the gambling continues, sometimes until dawn, when a 21-gun salute is sounded from Mount Lycabettus. Contrary to the English superstition that in order to bring luck on New Year's Day, the first caller to cross the threshold must be a dark handsome man, in Greece it is a handsome blond young man who will signify good fortune for the household. *Kourabiethes* and *glyka koutaliou* are often served to guests and carol singers.

A traditional vasilopita is very large, and each family has its own recipe. The basic ingredients are flour, sugar, eggs, butter, milk, mahlefi, sesame, and salt. Sometimes yeast, and almonds, brandy, and orange peel and juice are also added, according to the family recipe. The cakes differ from region to region; some are a sweet bread, others a flat cake. The finest is a rich yeast cake which is made with ¼ pint (½ cup) milk scalded, then mixed with 2 oz. (2 tablespoons) sugar, 6 oz. (¾ cup) butter, and 1 teaspoon salt, and left until lukewarm. Then ¼ cup tepid water and 2 tablespoons sugar are mixed together, and 2 oz. (2 packages) yeast are added and left for 10 minutes, when the cool milk mixture and 3 beaten eggs are stirred in. Next 13 oz. (3 cups) flour is gradually added and beaten until smooth. One tablespoon ground mahleb and 12 oz. (3 scant cups) more flour is stirred in, then the dough is turned out onto a floured board and kneaded until smooth. It is put into a greased bowl, brushed with melted butter, covered with a cloth, and left to rise for 1½–2 hours until it has doubled in bulk. It is kneaded lightly once more and formed into two 9-inch cakes which are put into greased tins, covered, and again left, this time for 1 hour, until they have risen. The tops are brushed with egg and sprinkled with sesame seeds and chopped almonds, before the cakes are baked in a moderate oven for 45–60 minutes. Baking powder may be used instead of yeast, in which case 6 eggs are used instead of 3. Flavourings such as orange, lemon, or a liqueur are used according to taste.

vasque, the French name for a shallow round bowl, usually of crystal, china, or silver, used for the elegant preservation of all kinds of cold foods such as fruit, ices, mousses, etc.

västerbottensost, a slow-maturing hard cheese, first made in the northernmost part of Sweden from cow's milk. It takes 8–12 months to mature, and weighs between 35 and 40 lb. It is highly flavoured and pungent, and inclined to become bitter if stored for too long. See also OST.

västgötaost, a semi-hard pressed Swedish cheese from West Götland. It is similar to *sveciaost,* but the paste is looser and the flavour more pungent. It takes 4–6 months to ripen and weighs between 20 and 30 lb. See also OST.

västkustsallad, literally "west coast salad" in Swedish, the name of a fish and vegetable salad. Cold cooked filleted and skinned fish is added to a mixture of sliced mushrooms, boiled peas, asparagus tips, mussels, and cooked shrimps. Shredded lettuce is tossed in a French dressing in a salad bowl which has previously been rubbed with garlic, and the fish and vegetable mixture is stirred in. It is decorated with slices of hard-boiled egg.

vatkattu karpalohyytelö, Finnish for whipped jelly made with cranberries or other berries, which in Finland is served with cream as a dessert.

vatkattu marjapurro, a Finnish dessert made with berries (cranberries, cloudberries, red currants, bilberries, etc.), semolina, sugar, and water. First 1½ lb. berries are cooked in 4 pints (8 cups) water for 15 minutes; then the liquid is strained, 4 oz. (1 cup) semolina and sugar to taste are added to it, and the whole is cooked until creamy. It is then beaten until stiff, poured into the serving dish, sprinkled with sugar, and served with milk.

vatrachopsaro, Greek for anglerfish or frog-fish, used in *kakkavia.*

vatrushki s tvorogom, Russian cheesecakes. To prepare them 1 lb. fresh curds or cottage cheese is strained and mixed with 4 oz. (½ cup) creamed butter, 2 eggs, and salt, and this is spooned onto large rounds of thinly rolled, unsweetened yeast dough. The cakes are pinched together at the top, leaving a small gap, and are left to rise; then they are brushed with egg yolk and baked in a hot oven for 15 minutes. They are served with sour cream. They resemble pirozhki, but are left open. They are also made in France, where the pastry used is either unsweetened brioche dough or *pâte brisée.* Vatrushki tartlets are sometimes used to garnish *borsch.*

vautes, the Middle English word for a kind of fritter made with veal kidney, bone marrow, plums, eggs, ginger, cinnamon, saffron, and salt. The word comes from the French volter, to turn, referring to the way the fritter has to be turned, like a pancake. It is also spelt "voutes" or "vowtes."

växt, see GRÖNSAKER.

veado, Portuguese for venison, usually served braised with onions and herbs in Portugal.

veal, the culinary name for the meat of a calf. The best meat, which should be greeny-pink, comes from animals up to three months old which have been fed only on milk; if the meat is reddish, it means that solid food has been given. In England veal has never been as popular as it is on the continent, and for many years a country superstition held that only the weak calves were killed off; this of course did not encourage the sale of veal. During the Middle Ages it was known as "froth" meat, as it was usually boiled, and was considered very light and "frothy," being used principally for invalid food such as calve's foot jelly. The original *blancmange* consisted of this pale meat cooked in milk. After the French Revolution many émigrés came to England, and anything and everything that was French quickly became fashionable. One result of this was that veal gained in popularity, and to this day most of the ways of serving veal that are familiar in Britain are of French origin. Almost the only traditional English dish made from veal is veal and ham pie. All calf offal (variety meat) is highly thought of, especially the liver, heart, kidneys and sweetbreads. See also BORJÚ; CALF; CIELĘCINA; FRICANDEAU; KALB; KALFVLEES; KALV; KALVE; MOSCHARI; SCHNITZEL; TELESHKO; TELYATINA; TERNERA; VEAU; VITELA; VITELLO.

veal and ham pie, an English pie consisting of chopped veal and ham, well seasoned, and sliced hard-boiled eggs, all enclosed in hot water crust pastry. The top of the pie is slit to about 2 inches before cooking, so that afterwards, while it is still hot, strong stock that will gel can be poured in. The pie is baked, then served cold when the stock round the contents has become a thick flavoursome jelly. See also PASTRY, HOT WATER CRUST.

veal birds, an American cut of veal taken from the top of the knuckle where it joins the leg. It is boned and rolled for sale.

veal gravy or *stock,* see FONDS BLANC; STOCK.

veau, French for veal, which is eaten extensively in France. The meat most highly esteemed is from animals 2½–3 months old, when the flesh is pink-white with a slightly greenish tinge. All veal offal (variety meat) is used in France, even the spinal marrow (*amourette de veau*), which is prepared in the same way as brains. French veal butchery differs markedly from that of Britain or the U.S. (see meat cut charts, pages xxiii–xxiv). See also VEAL.

ballottine de veau, shoulder or loin of veal, boned, stuffed and shaped like a bundle, then braised. Served hot or cold with such garnishes as *bouquetière, bretonne, bruxelloise, chipolata, jardinière, macédoine,* or *nivernaise.*

blanquette de veau, see BLANQUETTE.

brézolles de veau, see BRÉZOLLES.

brochettes de veau, chunks of veal skewered with bacon and mushrooms, brushed with oil, and grilled.

carré de veau, rib-joint or rack of veal, roasted and served accompanied by one or other of garnishes such as *bouquetière, bourgeoise, chasseur, clamart, jardinière, macédoine, milanaise, piémontaise,* or *Talleyrand.*

côtelettes de veau, veal cutlets, which may be served by the methods described below for *côtes de veau.*

côtes de veau, veal chops, usually grilled or fried in butter (*au naturel*) and served with the pan juices; also braised and served with any sauce or garnish suitable for meat, or with *beurre maître d'hôtel.*

côtes de veau à l'ancienne, veal chops fried in butter and garnished with cock's combs, cock's kidneys, and sweetbreads, and truffles and mushrooms heated in Madeira, all bound with sauce velouté and cream.

côtes de veau à l'ardennaise, veal chops baked with 3 juniper berries per chop, onion, carrots, and butter, with a slice of ham on each chop; they are sprinkled with breadcrumbs and chopped parsley and moistened with 1 glass (½ cup) white wine.

côtes de veau à la bonne femme, veal chops larded with lean bacon, sautéed in butter, and then baked with fried button onions, and potatoes cut to look like olives. Thickened brown gravy is added just before serving.

côtes de veau à la bordelaise, veal chops fried and served with sauce bordelaise.

côtes de veau à la crème, veal chops sautéed in butter, then the pan juices diluted with Madeira or white wine and cream, and all reduced. Sauce velouté may be added to thicken.

côtes de veau à la duxelles, veal chops sautéed in butter, then the pan juices mixed with duxelles, white wine, and demi-glace slightly flavoured with tomato.

côtes de veau à la hongroise, veal chops sautéed in butter, then the pan juices seasoned with paprika, mixed with fried onion and sour cream, and reduced.

côtes de veau à la lyonnaise, veal chops sautéed in butter, to which half-cooked, chopped onion is then added; finally 2 tablespoons wine vinegar, chopped parsley, and 4 tablespoons demi-glace are added to the pan juices.

côtes de veau à la milanaise, veal chops coated with egg and breadcrumbs mixed with grated Parmesan cheese, then cooked in butter. They are served with macaroni à la milanaise.

côtes de veau à la provençale, veal chops sautéed in butter, then the pan juices mixed with tomato fondue, white wine, garlic, and chopped parsley.

côtes de veau au basilic, veal chops sautéed in butter, then the pan juices diluted with white wine and stock, with chopped basil and butter added.

côtes de veau aux truffes, veal chops sautéed in butter, with truffles, then the pan juices diluted with Madeira and demi-glace.

côtes de veau bourguignonne, veal chops sautéed in butter with button onions, button mushrooms, and bacon, then the pan juices diluted with red wine and demi-glace and thickened with *beurre manié.*

côtes de veau clamart, veal chops fried and served with *clamart* garnish.

côtes de veau cussy, veal chops lightly sautéed, slit open and stuffed with salpicon of mushrooms, ham, and carrot mixed with sauce béchamel, then coated with egg and bread-crumbs and fried in butter. It is served with risotto with grated cheese and sliced truffle, and *beurre noisette* (I) on each chop.

côtes de veau en papillote, veal chops sautéed in butter, then each chop overlaid with a slice of cooked ham and covered with sauce duxelles. Each chop is wrapped individually in oiled paper and baked in the oven. The chops are served in the paper.

côtes de veau en portefeuille, veal chops slit open, seasoned, and stuffed with forcemeat, then wrapped in pork fat or pig's caul and grilled.

côtes de veau marchand, veal chops fried on one side only, then this side thickly coated with artichoke purée, grated Parmesan cheese, and butter, and the chops baked in the oven. They are served with small croûtons, beef marrow, and *pommes de terre noisettes.*

côtes de veau orloff, veal chops lightly sautéed, then slit open lengthwise to form a pocket which is stuffed with thick white onion purée mixed with chopped truffle. The tops are coated with more plain onion purée, then all is covered with sauce mornay, sprinkled with breadcrumbs, and browned under a hot grill.

côtes de veau pojarski, the meat of veal chops minced and mixed with breadcrumbs soaked in milk, seasoned, reconstituted in shape, floured, and fried in butter. It is served with *beurre noisette* (I) and lemon.

côtes de veau vert-pré, grilled veal chops served with *vert-pré* garnish.

côtes de veau vichy, veal chops sautéed in butter and served with carrots.

côtes de veau zingara, veal chops sautéed in butter and served with sauce *zingara.*

épaule de veau, shoulder of veal, usually boned and rolled in France. It is sometimes stuffed with forcemeat or herbs, or it may be cut up for ragoûts, sautés, or fricassées.

épaule de veau à la boulangère, shoulder of veal, boned, then seasoned inside and out, rolled lengthways, tied, and roasted for 30 minutes in a hot oven. Meanwhile 2 large onions or several small ones are sliced and sautéed lightly in butter, and well seasoned. They are added to the veal with the butter and cooking is continued for 25 minutes per lb., basting frequently. About 10 minutes before it is ready, 4 tablespoons thickened brown veal stock is added, or the pan juices are diluted with stock and reduced on the top of the stove.

escalopes de veau. Escalopes (scallops) are usually rolled in egg and breadcrumbs, fried in butter, and served with slices of lemon or *beurre noisette* (I). They are also coated with flour, fried in oil or butter, and served with various garnishes such as *Holstein, hongroise, milanaise, parisienne,* and *viennoise.*

jarret de veau à l'italienne, knuckle of veal served in the same way as *ossi buchi alla Milanese.*

jarret de veau à la printanière, knuckle of veal braised with green beans, carrots, and turnips.

jarret de veau à la provençale, knuckle of veal braised with onion, tomatoes, garlic, white wine, bouquet garni, and veal gravy.

matelote de veau, veal braised with button onions, mushrooms, and red wine, all thickened with beurre manié.

médaillons de veau, médaillons of veal, served in the same way as escalopes (scallops).

noisettes de veau, noisettes of veal, usually sautéed in butter (en cocotte), and served with braised lettuce, purée of sorrel, *petits pois,* or a macédoine.

noix pâtissière, and *sous-noix de veau,* cuts usually studded with bacon fat, then braised or pot roasted. See also FRICAN-DEAU. Garnishes used are *bordelaise, bouquetière,*

bourgeoise, clamart, jardinière, macédoine, milanaise, *oseille, piémontaise, renaissance,* and risotto. Another method is to braise the meat and then leave it to get cold in the braising stock, which will become jellied. The meat is garnished with the chopped defatted jelly.

paupiettes de veau, paupiettes of veal, usually stuffed with a forcemeat which includes either mushrooms, truffles, duxelles, sweet peppers, or herbs. Then they are rolled and secured, and braised slowly in stock. They are served with various sauces or garnishes such as *bourgeoise, bourguignonne, capucine, chipolata, Marie-Jeanne,* or *Marie-Louise.*

poitrine de veau, breast of veal, usually braised or stewed.

poitrine de veau à l'allemande, breast of veal stuffed with pork forcemeat, onion, and parsley mixed with raw egg, then braised with mixed vegetables (carrot, leek, turnip, etc.). The vegetables are served with the meat, together with hot horseradish sauce.

poitrine de veau à l'alsacienne, breast of veal braised and served with sauerkraut mixed with goose liver.

poitrine de veau à la sauce aux groseilles vertes, breast of veal braised with white wine, lemon peel, green gooseberries, cinnamon, and a pinch of sugar. Then the sauce is sieved and thickened with egg yolk.

poitrine de veau à la sauce soubise, breast of veal stuffed with breadcrumbs and onion, then braised. It is served with sauce *soubise.*

ris de veau, see RIS.

rognons de veau, see ROGNONS.

sauté de veau, meat taken from the shoulder, breast, neck, etc., of veal, chopped, lightly fried, then cooked slowly on top of the stove, the pan juices being diluted with wine, gravy, or demi-glace, or cream or tomato sauce. Various vegetables such as *cèpes,* mushrooms, peas, or cucumber, or a macédoine are served with it. It may also be served *Parmentier,* or with a *Portugaise* garnish. See also MARENGO.

sauté de veau à la minute, boned shoulder chops of veal, cubed, and seasoned, then sautéed quickly in hot butter. Next ½ pint (1 cup) white wine, 1 tablespoon meat glaze, 2 tablespoons butter, juice of ½ lemon, and 1 tablespoon chopped parsley are added to the pan juices. Cooking is finished in the oven.

sous-noix de veau, see SOUS-NOIX; NOIX PTISSIÂÈRE, VEAU.

tendrons de veau, see TENDRONS.

tête de veau, calf's head, usually simmered in a court bouillon, and the meat then taken from the bones. If the calve's head is served cold, the stock is poured over and jellied; a sauce vinaigrette accompanies this dish. If the calf's head is served hot, it may be accompanied by a variety of cold sauces such as *aïoli, gribiche,* rémoulade, tartare, or Vincent.

tête de veau en tortue, calf's head served hot or cold in a *timbale,* garnished with quenelles of minced veal, mushrooms, olives, truffles, and sauce *tortue.*

veau saumoné, boned and rolled leg of veal, rubbed with salt and saltpetre, and marinated for 4 days before cooking. It is then simmered gently, and served cold, thinly sliced, with sauce *ravigote.*

vegetable marrow (summer squash) (*Cucurbita pepo*), an edible gourd indigenous to North and South America. In the U.S. many other gourds of the same family are also eaten extensively, and they are all known generally as squashes, but in Britain the vegetable marrow has always been the most popular. It was introduced into Britain in the early 19th century, and was immediately acclaimed as a substitute for mango (a snob fruit of the time) for making chutneys, pickles, and relishes. Much later it was served as a vegetable, usually boiled or steamed and served with white sauce or cheese sauce. Courgettes, zucchini, cocozelle, *avocadella,* and vegetable spaghetti are some of the best-known varieties of marrow, but they differ from each other in size and shape rather than in taste. Summer squash is used as soon as it is formed; winter squash is usually stored when fully ripe, to be used as needed over the winter. Only well-ripened and matured marrows, stored until the end of October or later, should be used for chutney or pickle making, otherwise the result is like porridge; conversely, only young fresh marrows should be used as vegetables. Most marrows belong to either the trailing-marrow or the bush-marrow class.

vegetable marrow

Young marrows are excellent fried, steamed, or stuffed and baked. Hollowed-out young marrow, steamed with a bunch of herbs inside, makes an excellent salad when filled with young, chopped, cooked or raw vegetables mixed with mayonnaise. Large, old marrows should only be used for jam (with ginger and lemon) or pickles. They are excellent for pickles because of the absence in them of any strong flavour, and because of their texture, which allows them to absorb the stronger vegetables pickled with them. The golden flowers of the vegetable marrow used to be stuffed with sausage meat, dipped in batter, and fried in deep hot oil. They were known as "golden pockets." See also CALABACINES; KOLOKITHAKIA; KUERBISKRAUT; SQUASH; ZAPPALITO DE TRONCO.

stuffed marrow, an excellent dish. A medium-sized marrow is peeled, the top is cut off, and the inner seeds are removed with a long spoon. Then it is steamed for 7–10 minutes. The stuffing, which should be quite highly seasoned, consists of minced meat with herbs and a little minced onion. The stuffed marrow is baked with stock or diluted tomato purée for about 1 hour in a moderate oven, then served in thick slices.

vegetable pear, an alternative name for the custard marrow.

vegetable spaghetti, a trailing vegetable marrow (summer squash) about 8 inches long. It is boiled whole for 20–30 minutes, and when cut in half the inside will be found to be full of long strands like spaghetti. It is served hot with butter, or cold with mayonnaise or sauce vinaigrette. It must be eaten fresh, not stored.

vegetables, plants used for culinary purposes or for feeding cattle. Herbaceous vegetables are those in which the leaves only are used, while root vegetables are those in which the roots or tubers are used. Many languages distinguish between the 2 types by having completely different words for green vegetables and for leguminous vegetables. They can be eaten cooked and raw, and in many cases both the leaves and the roots or tubers are edible. Some of the items we term vegeta-

bles are, botanically speaking, fruits, since they contain seeds. The most notable example is the tomato, which is regarded as a vegetable because of the way in which it is served, that is, as an accompaniment to meat and other savoury dishes. Nowadays, however, many other fruits are also served as vegetables, particularly in salads. See also GROENTE; GRONNSAKER; GRONSAGER; GRÖNSAKER; LAHANIKA.

vehnänen eli pulla, see PULLA.

veitchberry, see HYBRID BERRIES.

velös leves, traditional Hungarian brain soup. To prepare it ½ lb. sliced mushrooms, chopped parsley, and 2 sets calves' brains are fried in butter, then sprinkled well with flour and allowed to brown slightly. Then 2 pints (4 cups) beef stock is added, with salt, pepper, and mace. When it has boiled, the soup is strained and the purée of calves' brains is blended in. It is garnished with croûtons.

velouté, sauce, originally called *sauce blonde,* one of the basic French classical sauces. Velouté is the general term applied to the sauce, which is almost identical to *béchamel grasse* and is made with a blond roux and stock from veal, chicken, or fish; according to the type of stock used, the sauce is called *velouté de veau* (veal velouté), *velouté de volaille* (chicken velouté), etc. The stock should be of very fine quality, and the sauce, as the name implies, should be of a velvety texture. Once the sauce is made no other seasonings or flavourings are necessary, except perhaps a liaison of cream or egg yolks added just before serving.

The quantities given here are enough for a small household, but if a large quantity is required, a whole fowl or fish, or joint of veal of equivalent weight, is used. First the stock is made, using a 2-lb. knuckle of veal, with the bones. Then 2 tablespoons butter is melted in a heavy saucepan, then 2 carrots and 2 medium-sized onions are sliced and added, followed by scraps of ham and the raw knuckle (or lean white meat or fish mentioned above), and finally a bouquet garni. The meat is lightly sautéed, and then all are sweated gently over a low heat, taking care that the ingredients do not colour; to prevent this, 1 pint (2 cups) water is added and the simmering continued until the gravy is much reduced. At this point, the meat or fish is pricked all over with a fork to allow the juices to flow into the gravy and 3 or 4 freshly peeled mushrooms, 2 cloves, salt, and pepper are added. The pan is filled up with cold water, it is tightly covered, and the ingredients are simmered for 4 hours—after carefully skimming when the stock starts to boil. When it is ready the contents are all strained through a fine sieve, the liquid is cooled, the fat removed from the top, and the resulting stock brought to boiling point again in another saucepan. Then ½ pint (1 cup) white sauce is now carefully blended in, stirring constantly. The whole is allowed to simmer gently over a low heat to improve the flavour, before it is cooled and stored (it will keep in a refrigerator for 2–3 days).

Velouté is quite frequently used as a base for other sauces, notably *allemande,* which is sometimes called *velouté lié* (thick velouté), *aurore,* chaud-froid, *Normande,* poulette, royale, suprême, *Talleyrand,* and white wine sauce. On its own, it is always used for *blanquette de veau.* The word velouté is also applied to certain thickened soups, or soups with a velouté base, such as *potage velouté.*

venaison, French for venison. Formerly the word covered all game but nowadays it refers only to deer. See also CHEVREUIL. Basse venaison is the term for the meat of hare or wild rabbit.

vendace, another name for pollan, used only in Scotland.

Vendée, a department of France in the Poitou region, well-known for many local specialities, such as *Vendée fressure, Vendée pâté, véritable Nantais dit du curé.*

Vendée fressure, a dish made from pig's pluck (—lights (lungs), liver, heart, and melts (spleen)—)chopped and mixed with congealed pig's blood. It is cooked slowly for 4–5 hours with chopped fat bacon, and eaten cold like a terrine.

Vendée pâté, a pâté made from fillets of wild rabbit and rabbit forcemeat mixed with an equal quantity of chopped half-cooked belly of pork.

vendôme, a cheese like a coulommier made in France from cow's milk. It is in season from June to October.

vendôme bleu, a French cow's milk cheese from Touraine; it is in season from September to July.

vendôme cendré, vendôme cheese ripened in charcoal.

veneto, an Italian cow's milk cheese, also known as *venezza*. It resembles a superior *asiago* and can be eaten fresh, or when old can be grated. The inside is granular and greenish-yellow in colour, although when made in the spring it is sometimes straw-coloured. Veneto has a rather bitter, sharp flavour.

venison, the name now used for the flesh of any kind of deer, particularly fallow deer, roebuck, red deer, elk, antelope, or reindeer. Formerly, in both French and English, the word was used for the meat of any game animal, but in French the fallow deer is called *daim*. The meat of the buck or male deer has more flavour than that of the female or doe, and is at its best when taken from an animal between 18 months and 2 years old; venison is inclined to be dry if the animal is over 3 years. All venison should be hung for at least a week, and unless the animal is definitely known to be young, it should be either larded, or marinated overnight or longer (see below). The best parts of the deer are the fillets, the haunch (the top of the hind leg), the loin (for chops), and the liver (see DEER). Other parts of the animal can be used for making a galantine, pie, or terrine. Cumberland sauce is excellent with all furred game, although it is not a traditional accompaniment.

Fillet of young venison should be cut into thick steaks and banged with a wooden mallet to tenderize. They are sautéed in butter, after which a little red wine is added to the pan juices and all is boiled up and allowed to thicken. Sauce poivrade should be served with the steaks, or lemon wedges and red currant or cranberry jelly.

Haunch of venison is usually roasted with fat in England and Scotland, and served with red currant jelly and sauce *poivrade*. A little of the marinade used should be heated, and the joint basted with it during cooking time (25 minutes per lb.). In French the haunch is called cuissot or cimier.

Shoulder of venison is generally casseroled after marinating, and the method is the same as for jugged hare, although the blood is not used to thicken the gravy.

Venison cutlets or chops should be pounded with a wooden mallet, brushed with olive oil, then fried or grilled.

Excellent sausages can be made by mixing minced venison with one quarter of its amount of minced pork or veal, a little pinch of allspice and nutmeg, some chopped marjoram, salt, and black pepper. The mixture should be formed into sausage shapes and either put into skins or rolled in flour, before frying. Leftover venison can also be minced and mixed with half its quantity of minced pork, onion, mace, seasoning to taste, and 2 eggs to each 1½ lb. meat, and then made into small cakes which are rolled in flour and fried in oil. *Beurre maître d'hôtel* and lemon are served with them.

See also CERVO; CHEVREUIL; DEER; DOE; DYREJØTT; DYRE-KØLLE; ELK; IZARD; JELENIA; OLÉN; RÅDJURS KÖTT; REH; REIN-DEER; ROEBUCK; SARNIA.

venison pie, the meat is first simmered with chopped onion, parsley, mace, and a little red wine. When cooked, it is transferred to a pie dish, the pastry lid is put on top, and the pie is then baked in a moderate oven for 30 minutes. A venison pastry can be made in the same way.

galantine of venison, for which the thick end of the breast is ideal. The meat is first boned and any gristle removed, and the venison bones are boiled up in water with marjoram, thyme, and seasoning. The boned meat is then placed on a board and half of it spread with sausage meat with a little diced ham in it, followed by a layer of 2 sliced hard-boiled eggs. Then it is covered with more sausage meat mixture, rolled up carefully, and tied up in a floured cloth. It is put into the boiling venison stock and simmered for 3–4 hours, then left to cool in the liquid. When cold, it is removed from the stock and the cloth untied. The galantine is placed in a close-fitting dish and covered. A weight is put on the top and it is left overnight. The stock can be used, with herbs and root vegetables added, as the basis for a good soup.

marinade for venison, prepared with a mixture of 1 pint (2 cups) red or white wine, 1 cup wine vinegar and water mixed, 1 sliced onion, garlic, cloves, bay leaf, rosemary, peeled shallots, mixed herbs, and whole peppercorns. The better the wine, the more the meat will be flavoured. Some cooks prefer to leave out the wine vinegar and water, and add instead a little olive oil. The venison is soaked in the marinade for at least 24 hours, being turned so that the whole of the meat is impregnated with it.

method of preparing venison (Duc de Coigny, 1822, quoted by Lady Clark of Tilliepronie, 1909). A roebuck is first cleaned thoroughly and left in its skin, for 3 days in summer and for 5 days in winter. It is then skinned, the body divided into equal parts, the two haunches cut off, and the shoulders cut from the breast. The shoulders are eaten fresh, either in stews, or made into excellent pies. The breast, when pickled, can be made into cutlets. The deer is cut up and the pieces washed thoroughly, taking care that none of the hair remains on the flesh. Then a pickle is prepared by boiling about ½ gallon good vinegar and an equal amount of water for 15 minutes with 1 bay leaf, parsley, thyme, sweet basil, salt, and pepper. This is poured hot into a large earthenware dish. Before the joints are put into the pickle they must be larded with fat bacon. Two days is a long enough time to pickle the cutlets, but very large joints must remain 6, 8, or even 10 days in the pickle. The haunches will keep for 6 weeks in the marinade, if kept in a cool place and turned every day. When a joint is required, it is taken out of the liquor and, if the vinegar is not liked, the joint is rolled in a clean linen cloth and pressed until all the pickle is squeezed out. If the joint is a haunch, it should be roasted very slowly for 1½–2 hours in a paste of bran or oatmeal and water, and served with red currant or cranberry jelly.

tained venison, making it suitable for use (it may become tainted if it is a long time in transit). A mixture of half strong ale and half vinegar, with salt, is boiled up, then any scum that has collected is removed and the liquid left to get cool. The venison is then steeped in it for 12 hours, after which it is taken out, pressed and dried, then parboiled with salt and pepper. The venison will then be fit for use in any way that is required.

ventagli, an Italian pastry made in the shape of a horseshoe or fan. Strips of puff pastry are formed into these shapes, which are brushed with melted butter, dredged with sugar, and baked in a moderate oven until a fairly dark gold colour. While still hot they are sprinkled with vanilla sugar. Ventagli are eaten cold.

ventresca, a Sardinian speciality, the stomach of fresh tunny (tuna) fish, which is served cut in thin slices, brushed with oil, and grilled. The stomach is the best part of tunny, and should be especially asked for in Italy or Sardinia as it is tender and delicious.

venus, another name for cockle.

veprovy ovar s krenem, a traditional Czechoslovakian dish of boiled pig's head served with horse radish sauce.

verbena (*Verbena officinalis*), also called lemon verbena because of its delicate lemony taste. It was originally a "holy herb," used in sacrifice by the Druids. It is used nowadays for herb-tea infusions, in fruit salads and jellies, and in wine punch, the fresh, narrow, pale green leaves being crushed to release their aromatic oils before they are added to the preparation. A plant of the same family, called junellia in honour of the Swedish botanist Sven Junell, is indigenous to Chile and Argentina and is generally used in the same way as verbena in the U.S. and in its country of origin.

verde, salsa, Italian "green" sauce, made from 1 part lemon juice to 2 parts olive oil, with a good deal of parsley to make it thick and green, capers, chopped garlic, salt, and pepper, all well mixed as for a sauce vinaigrette. Chopped anchovy fillets may also be added.

salsa verde al rafano, green sauce with horseradish. To prepare it 2 large peeled tomatoes are chopped and mixed with ½ cup chopped parsley and 2 chopped sprigs of mint, 1 tablespoon fresh grated horseradish, and 2 heaped tablespoons fresh white breadcrumbs, and all are well pounded together. Then 3–4 tablespoons olive oil is added gradually until the sauce is quite thick, when it is seasoned. It is served with cold meats and dishes which are specialities of Liguria. See also MAIONESE VERDE.

verde, salsa, a Spanish "green" sauce made from parsley, seasoning, and olive oil. The parsley is ground down in a mortar and oil is beaten in drop by drop, followed by seasoning. A good bunch of parsley will take about 1 cup olive oil. It is served with cold fish, meat, or poultry.

verdel, see ALMEJAS.

verdura, I. Spanish for green vegetables; root vegetables are *legumbres.* In Spain vegetable dishes often constitute a course in themselves. This is especially true of the north, where delicious plates of mixed vegetables are served. Vegetables are also often used in stews, but they are rarely eaten as an accompaniment to meat. II. The Spanish name for a green plant that grows wild on the island of Ibiza. It is a member of the celery family and can be eaten either cooked or raw. See also QUINAD.

veriohukaiset, Finnish for blood pancakes. To prepare them 2 cups pig's or cow's blood, ½ cup rye flour, ½ cup barley flour, 1 beaten egg, 1 cup kalja (a non-alcoholic beer), 1 medium-sized onion, ¼ teaspoon marjoram, salt, and pepper are all mixed well together, and the resulting batter is cooked in a hot pan. The pancakes are served hot with melted butter and cranberry jam. They are very popular all over Finland.

veripalttu, Finnish for black pudding, made from 2 cups cow's or pig's blood, 1½ cups coarse rye flour, ¾ cup barley flour, ½ chopped onion, ½ teaspoon marjoram, and seasoning. It is prepared in the same way as *veriohukaiset,* but is then poured into a well-greased tin or bowl, sprinkled with breadcrumbs and steamed for 2 hours. It is eaten with melted butter and cranberry jam. See also BLACK PUDDING.

véritable Nantais dit du curé, a small, soft, cow's milk cheese, first made in 1890 by a Breton priest in the Vendée region of France. At that time it was called Petit-Breton. It is now made commercially in the Loire Inférieure department and is available throughout the year.

verjuice, literally "green juice," also spelled "vergis" and, in old manuscripts, "veriuyce." It comes from the Latin *jus viride,* and originally referred to the juice extracted from crab apples, which was in constant use in cooking up to the last century, when its place was taken by the "squeeze of lemon juice." It was used particularly in meat, fish, or game pies, and resembled a sharp cider rather than vinegar. A

manuscript note (*c.* 1791), made by the Reverend R. Warner in the British Museum copy of *The Babee's Book (c.* 1475) reads: "Our ancestors made verjuice of crabs (apples) as cyder is made of Apples. They used much of it in Cookery." Something akin to it may also have been made from sour grapes, but in Britain this was not used for the same purpose (see VERJUS).

verjus, French for verjuice, but extracted from the verjus grape. It is still used in the preparation of certain commercially made mustards sold in France.

vermicelli, very fine spaghetti, frequently served cooked as a garnish in soups, but also served alla *vongole,* or a Venetian speciality, cooked with pounded anchovies, garlic, oil, and butter, when it is called *bigoli in salsa.*

vermicelli alla siracusana, a Sicilian dish, from Syracuse, consisting of cooked vermicelli served with a sauce of chopped garlic, tomatoes, eggplants, yellow sweet peppers, anchovy fillets, chopped basil, white wine, salt, and black pepper, all sweated together in olive oil for about 20 minutes. The sauce is then mixed with the vermicelli.

vero piora, see PIORA CHEESE.

véron, a French consommé of beef, garnished with strips of sweet pepper and cubes of flageolet royale and flavoured with truffle essence and port wine. See also CONSOMMÉ.

véronique, à la, I, A French garnish in which white grapes play a prominent part. II. A method of baking or poaching sole fillets in fish stock and white wine, then garnishing with seeded white grapes, after which the stock is reduced and beaten with butter, and the whole glazed under a grill or in the oven. This dish should never be presented as sole in a thickened white sauce with added grapes.

verte, sauce, a classical French sauce served with fish, poultry, and hard-boiled eggs. It can be made in two ways. In one method 1 cup each parsley, chervil, and tarragon leaves are finely minced and pounded in a mortar. A drop of onion juice or 1 teaspoon chopped chives is sometimes also added. A little cold water is included, and the mixture is passed through a fine sieve lined with muslin. Puréed spinach and watercress are sometimes included for colour and taste. Finally the mixture is added to ½ pint (1 cup) seasoned mayonnaise. In a second method purée of chervil, spinach, and tarragon is added to a mayonnaise and blended with whipped aspic to taste.

vert-pré, au, I. A French garnish for grilled meats, consisting of *pommes allumettes* and watercress, with *beurre maître d'hôtel.* II. A French method of serving fish or poultry coated with sauce *verte.* III. A French beef consommé thickened with tapioca and garnished with asparagus tips, french beans, and shredded lettuce. See also CONSOMMÉ.

verza, Italian for green cabbage.

verze ripiene, stuffed cabbage. The cabbage is blanced in boiling water for 5 minutes, then the leaves are detached, filled with a stuffing of meat, herbs, breadcrumbs, etc., rolled up, and simmered for 1 hour in broth or olive oil.

vesiga, the marrow from the backbone of the great sturgeon, the largest member of the sturgeon family, found in the Caspian and Black Seas and also in the rivers Volga and Danube. This cartilage is gelatinous, and is often dried for sale, like turtle meat. After soaking it is added to various dishes such as *kulebyaka.*

vesirinkelit, literally "water rings," Finnish biscuits (crackers) made from 2 cups water, salt, 1 oz. yeast, and 2½ lb. flour. The ingredients are mixed to a stiff dough which is allowed to rise, then shaped into small rings which are dropped into boiling water. When they rise to the surface after a few minutes, they are removed, put onto a baking tray and baked in a hot oven for 15–20 minutes. They should be brown outside and soft inside. They are served cold, split, and buttered, with tea or coffee.

vessie, French for bladder. In *charcuterie* products the bladders of some mammals are used to enclose certain meats before cooking. This is also done in the case of some poultry dishes, particularly duck, as in *caneton rouennais en chemise.*

vetebröd, a sweet Swedish bread made with 1 pint (2 cups) milk boiled with ¼ lb. (½ cup) butter, 5 oz. (²/₃ cup) sugar, 1 teaspoon freshly ground cardamom seeds, and a pinch of salt. All is left to get lukewarm and 1 oz. (1 package) years which has been dissolved in ¼ cup tepid water is mixed in. Then 2 beaten eggs are added and well blended before stirring in 1½ lb. (6 cups) flour. The whole is well mixed with a wooden spoon, covered, and left to double its bulk. The dough is made into a plaited shape, sprinkled with ground cinnamon mixed with chopped blanched almonds, and left on a buttered baking sheet to rise again. It is then baked in a moderate-to-hot oven for about 30 minutes. It can also be made without the eggs.

vetekrans, similar to *vetebröd,* but shaped into a ring.

vézelay, a French goat's milk cheese produced in Burgundy from May to September.

vic-en-bigorre, a soft cow's milk cheese from the Béarn in France. It is in season from October to May.

Vichy, à la, i. A French method of cooking carrots in Vichy water, named after the town of Vichy which is famous for its medicinal waters and for the carrots grown there. ii. A French garnish for meat, consisting of *carottes à la Vichy* and *pommes château.* iii. A French method of serving potatoes, see POMME DE TERRE (POMMES À LA VICHY).

vichyssoise, a delicious cold soup created by Louis Diat, late chef of the old Ritz Carlton Hotel of New York. There are many imitations of this excellent soup, but in M. Diat's original recipe 1½ cups of the white part of leeks and ½ cup onion are both chopped and then sweated gently (so they do not colour) in 1 tablespoon butter. Then 1 quart boiling water, 5 medium-sized peeled and chopped potatoes and 1 tablespoon salt are added, and all cooked for 30 minutes or until tender. The soup is puréed or blended, mixed with 2 cups milk and the same of thin cream, heated, and carefully sieved. When cold, it is sieved again and mixed well with 1 cup double or heavy cream. It is served chilled, sometimes with the bowl set in a bed of ice, and is sprinkled with chopped chives.

Victoria, à la, i. A French sauce served particularly with sole or other fish. It consists of a sauce *allemande* to which has been added one third the quantity of good white wine. Chopped cooked mushrooms are added, and the sauce is thoroughly heated but not allowed to boil. Then lobster coral, well pounded and mixed with fresh butter, is added. The sauce is stirred until ready to serve. ii. A French garnish for sole and other Fish consisting of sliced crawfish and truffles, covered with sauce *Victoria* (i) and glazed. iii. A French method of serving tournedos, noisettes, or chicken breasts, with tomatoes stuffed with mushroom purée and gratinéed, and artichokes quartered and cooked in butter; port and gravy are added to the pan juices and reduced. iv. A French iced bombe lined with strawberry ice cream and filled with *plombières* mixture; or lined as before but filled with ice cream mixed with crushed glacé chestnuts and crystallised fruit; or lined with vanilla ice cream and filled with *crème chantilly* and red currants. v. A French salad made from diced crawfish, cucumbers, truffles, and asparagus tips, all bound with mayonnaise mixed with the creamy substance adhering to the crawfish shell. The crawfish coral is scattered on top.

Victoria cheese, a cream cheese made at Guildford in Surrey.

Victoria sponge, an English sponge mixture used for jam sponge sandwich, spongecakes, castle puddings, and Swiss

rolls. It is made from 3 eggs, and their weight in butter, in castor sugar, and in self-raising flour (an average egg weighs 2½ oz.). The butter is creamed with the sugar, and the eggs are then added alternately with the self-raising flour. The whole is well beaten and, for a sandwich cake, the mixture is put into two flat greased tins and baked for 20–30 minutes in a moderate oven. The two halves are sandwiched together when cool with jam or cream. See also JAM SAUCE.

videlle, i. A wheel-shaped French pastry cutter. ii. A small French tool for removing stones from fruit.

Vienna bread, a long loaf made from a yeasted dough mixed with milk and water, to which a little butter has been added. It is made with Vienna flour, which gives it a light texture.

Vienna flour, the English name for *glattes mehl.*

Vienna sausage, an Austrian sausage not unlike a frankfurter, and served in the same way.

Vienna steaks, finely minced (ground) beefsteak mixed with 1 medium-sized minced onion, parsley, marjoram, and a dash of mushroom or tomato ketchup, then shaped into small flattish cakes. These are fried on both sides in hot fat or oil, and served with rolls of crisp bacon and fried or braised onions.

Viennoise, à la, a French garnish for escalopes (scallops) of veal, cutlets, chicken joints, or fish which have been rolled in egg and breadcrumbs and fried. They are garnished with capers, hard-boiled eggs (white and yolk chopped separately), olives, parsley, *beurre noir,* and lemon slices. When a garnish of this name is presented in Vienna, only lemon is served; the detailed garnish described above is definitely a French one.

vieras, Spanish for scallops, which in Spain are served fried in batter, poached in wine, or used with fish and other shellfish in *zarzuela.* Other Spanish names for scallop are *almejón, marisco liso,* and *morcillón* (the latter two are applied particularly to the small smooth-shelled variety).

vierge, the French name for a mixture of 4 oz. (½ cup) butter beaten well with juice of 1 lemon, salt, and pepper until it becomes creamy and frothy. It is served with vegetables which have been plainly boiled, such as asparagus or sea kale.

vifter, literally "fans," Danish pastries of the *wienerbrød* variety. (For the dough, see WIENERBRØD iii). After rolling out to a square of ¼ inch thickness, the dough is cut into smaller 6-inch squares. Each square is brushed on top with melted butter and sprinkled with chopped roasted almonds, together with cinnamon-flavoured sugar. The two adjoining sides are folded in to the centre, and each is coated with the above mixture as before, after which the pastries are folded in half lengthwise and lightly rolled. Slits about ½ inch deep and ½ inch apart are made along 1 edge. The pastries are then put on a greased baking-tin, gashed side outside, and coated with a mixture of 1 egg yolk and 1 tablespoon water beaten together, to glaze them. Then they are baked in a fairly hot oven for 20 minutes.

vignettes, the name for winkles in Brittany.

viilipiimä or *piimä,* Finnish for clotted milk made from fresh milk and sour cream or sour milk. It is a national beverage. It may also be served as a sauce for fish or potatoes, or as a separate course. First 1 saltspoon sour cream is put into a small bowl or jug, which is then filled up with fresh milk. The mixture is brought to blood heat and then left to stand at room-temperature until it has set, after which it is chilled. It is drunk with many meals, but especially with the Finnish national dish of *talkkuna.* When served as a separate course, sugar and ginger or cinnamon accompany it. Viilipiimä resembles yogourt but, unlike yogourt, the form in which it appears owes more to *Lactobacillus acidophilus* than to *Bacillus bulgaricus.* See also KOKKELIPHMÄ; PIMÄ.

viipurin rinkeli, a type of Finnish biscuit (cookie), translatable as viipuri twists. A dough is made with 4 eggs, 14 oz. (1¾ cups) sugar, 4 oz. (½ cup) butter, 1½ pints (3 cups) milk, nutmeg, 4 lb. (16 cups) flour, 2 oz. yeast, salt, and 1 teaspoon ground cardamom. The dough is allowed to rise, is well kneaded, and then divided into 4 parts, each of which will make one "twist." Each length is rolled into a long finger-shape, thicker in the middle than at the ends; the roll is curled round in the form of a circle, and the thin ends of the roll are twined round each other and turned inwards to stretch across the diameter of the circle. Finally the very ends of the twined strand are separated and attached one on either side of the thick part of the roll at the far side of the circle, thus forming a small triangle. The biscuits (cookies) are then sprinkled with boiling water and baked for 30 minutes in a moderate oven. Viipuri twists are an old traditional recipe and it is said that they were first baked for Christmas in a Finnish monastery in 1433. See also JOULUTORTUT.

viking saus, a Norwegian sauce sometimes served with game. The recipe is the same as that for *robin saus,* except that whipped cream is used instead of mayonnaise or horseradish.

vildfågel, literally "wild birds," Swedish for feathered game. In Sweden game birds are often cooked on top of the stove with cream and butter, and are served carved in portions or slices. Game such as *rapphöns* and *ripa* is plentiful in the south of Sweden.

vildt, Danish for game, of which there is an excellent variety in Denmark; pheasant, partridge, snipe, and hare are plentiful. Roebuck and wild boar are also hunted. See also GAME.

villalón, a soft ewe's milk cheese which is made in Spain in the central provinces of León, Valladolid, Zamora, and Palencia. The milk for this cheese is rennetted in 2–3 hours, and then the curd is put in a little bag called a fardel to drain, before being pressed into wooden moulds; it is salted and washed, and is then ready to eat. The cheese is shaped like a long cylinder and is also known as *pata de mulo* or "mule's leg." After *manchego,* it is one of the most popular Spanish cheeses.

villand, Norwegian for wild duck, often served roasted, or cooked in the same way as ptarmigan (*rype*) or grouse.

villedieu, a French cow's milk cheese produced in Normandy almost all the year round.

villeroi, à la, French sauce used to coat foods before they are fried; the dish is then described as *à la villeroi.* It is made from ½ pint (1 cup) sauce *allemande* boiled down with 4 tablespoons stock (fish stock for a fish dish) and 1 tablespoon mushroom or truffle fumet, until thick enough to coat the back of a spoon. When this mixture is cold, the food is coated with it before being dipped in beaten egg and breadcrumbs and fried in hot oil.

purée villeroi soubisée, villeroi mixed with onion purée.

purée villeroi tomatée, with tomato purée.

vilt, Norwegian for game. Included are *ryper dyrekjøtt, hjortekjøtt, elgbiff,* and *rensdyr.* See also GAME.

viltsuppe, game soup. A roux is made of 2 oz. (¼ cup) butter and 2 oz. (½ cup) flour, to which is added 2 quarts (8 cups) game stock (it must be almost at boiling-point when it is added), 4 oz. stewed prunes, 4 cooked and sliced apples, 2 sliced boiled carrots, 1 parsnip, 1 tablespoon vinegar, 2 teaspoons sugar, salt, and a pinch of either cloves or mace. The resulting soup is garnished with boller.

vin blanc, sauce. See WHITE WINE SAUCE.

vinaigre, French for vinegar, usually made from wine in France.

vinaigrette, sauce, a French sauce served chiefly with cold vegetables, raw or cooked, but also sometimes with cooked meats. The basic recipe is simple, but there are many variations. For vegetables, 3–4 tablespoons olive oil to 1 tablespoon wine vinegar is seasoned with salt and pepper to taste.

These quantities will be enough for 2–3 servings. For meats such as calf's head and cold boeuf bouilli, 1 tablespoon mixed chopped parsley, chervil, tarragon, and chives is added to the seasoned oil and vinegar, and also 1 tablespoon capers. If accompanying calf's head, the brains can be included as a thickening agent; if accompanying beef, ½ teaspoon prepared mustard is mixed thoroughly with the oil before the vinegar is beaten in, and the whole is well shaken. For another variation 6 shallots are peeled and finely chopped, then squeezed dry and pulped with ½ cup chopped parsley. Then 1 teaspoon mustard is worked in, followed by 2 tablespoons capers, 2 chopped gherkins, salt, and pepper. Then ½ pint (1 cup) olive oil is trickled in and the sauce well stirred. Finally 2 tablespoons tarragon vinegar is added and mixed well in. The sauce should be quite thick, and green with the parsley.

vinaigrette à la crème, seasoned oil and vinegar (proportions are 3–4 parts oil to 1 part vinegar), with the addition of 2 tablespoons cream, either plain or whipped.

vinaigrette à la crème moutardée, as *vinaigrette à la crème,* with the addition of 1 teaspoon mustard.

vinaigrette au lard, seasoned oil and vinegar, as above, with the addition of 2 tablespoons finely diced cooked bacon.

vinaigrette aux oeufs, seasoned oil and vinegar as above, with 2 quartered hard-boiled eggs added.

vincent, sauce, a French sauce made from mayonnaise to which a purée of blanched green herbs, chopped hard-boiled egg yolks, and egg whites are added.

Vincisgras, an Italian dish made from lasagne and named after an Austrian general who is said to have invented it. It consists of cooked lasagne with sauce. First, half a boned sautéed chicken and 4 oz. sautéed chicken livers are cut into strips; then 1 small onion and 2 oz. soaked dried mushrooms are simmered for 10 minutes in ½ pint (1 cup) strong meat broth, with 1 tablespoon tomato purée diluted with ¼ pint (½ cup) stock, and seasoning. These two mixtures are combined, and 1 pint (2 cups) thick sauce béchamel flavoured with cinnamon and Marsala wine is added. The sauce is then layered with the *lasagne* each layer being sprinkled with grated parmesan cheese and a little sliced truffle, and the dish is left overnight. The next day, another 2 cups sauce béchamel, with Parmesan cheese added, is poured over, and the dish is baked for 30 minutes in a moderate oven.

vine (*Vitis vinifera*), the plant of which grapes are the fruit. The vine has been known since earliest times and is mentioned in the Book of Genesis, as well as in ancient Greek and Egyptian manuscripts. There are an immense number of varieties grown all over the world, and there are also many wild vines.

vine leaves, used when young in the cookery of Greece and many Mediterranean countries. In France certain cheeses, such as *chevrotins,* are wrapped in vine leaves. Game, especially ortolan, quail, and partridge, is barded with pork fat and cooked wrapped in vine leaves. Very young, tender vine leaves are dipped in batter and made into fritters. They can also be shredded and used in salads. In Greece and some Balkan states they are used to wrap up a mixture of cooked rice, onions, spices, lemon, and olive oil and for such dishes as *cailles aux raisins, dolma, dolmadakia, dolmades, sarmale in foii de vita.* Vine leaves can also be salted, and they are often sold canned in brine for use as required.

vinegar, a dilute solution of acetic acid, usually containing other substances in very small quantities which give character to the different vinegars. There are 3 principal varieties of vinegar. Only crystal or white vinegar is sometimes made today by the simple operation of diluting pure acetic acid with water. This method is used to produce a cheap but flavourless vinegar which has a purely acid taste and pungency, and is devoid of all the aromas that are present in superior culinary vinegars. A better form of crystal vinegar is made by de-colourising malt vinegar. Malt vinegar is produced by oxidizing a fermented malt wash in which the sugar has already been turned into alcohol by yeast. This oxidation is accomplished by the action of *mycoderma aceti* which, together with various other organisms, forms a growing mass or zoogloea in the liquor and converts the alcohol into acetic acid. Malt vinegar is often coloured brown by the addition of caramel. Vinegars are also made from fermented fruit juices, the most usual being wine, though cider, perry, and white currant juice are also used. Wine vinegar is usually of 2 kinds: one made from white wine, which should be a very pale golden colour, and the other from red wine, which should be a rose colour. The finest wine vinegar is made in Orléans, France.

While there are a few culinary uses which are best served by correctly diluted, flavourless crystal vinegars (for example the production of raspberry vinegar and the pickling of fruit, vegetables, and nuts), the cider, the perry, and most particularly the wine vinegars are greatly to be preferred because of their superior aromas. Wine vinegars are also extremely important because they form the base for vinegars flavoured by a few particularly aromatic vegetables and herbs. Such are, for example, tarragon vinegar, garlic vinegar, rosemary vinegar, rose vinegar, and violet vinegar, and they are usually made by macerating the flavouring agent in an appropriate wine vinegar. The simple unaromatised vinegar made from fermented white currant juice has a particularly delicate flavour, and it is an especially good accompaniment to crayfish, lobster, prawns, and sole. An excellently-flavoured vinegar is also made, particularly in Germany where it is called *Traubenessig* from green unripened grapes, usually by inoculation with the "vinegar plant." The vinegar from pickled walnuts is also useful in flavouring, and one of its remarkable properties is that, when mixed with twice its volume of honey, a few sips of the mixture will often stop a persistent cough in a matter of moments.

The so-called vinegar plant often referred to in the context of vinegar, is a zoogloea or living mat, composed chiefly of *mycoderma aceti* and other micro-organisms having a similar action; these form in the liquors containing alcohol during the course of their oxidation into acetic acid, thus giving rise to vinegar. A small quantity of this zoogloea, added to a dilute solution of ethyl alcohol such as wine, will greatly reduce the time taken for it to become vinegar. Some forms of this zoogloea contain yeast, and these symbiotic aggregates can perform the whole operation of converting a dilute solution of sugar into vinegar, and may be kept for considerable periods in the dry state as long as they are periodically allowed a few days in a weak sugar solution and are not, either in the wet or the dry state, subjected to extremes of temperature.

vinegar cake, an Irish cake, also eaten in the U.S., for which vinegar is used instead of eggs. To prepare, 6 oz. (¾ cup) butter is rubbed into 12 oz. (3 cups) flour. Then 6 oz. (1 cup) brown sugar and 1 teaspoon mixed spice are added. Next 2 tablespoons vinegar is mixed with 1 teaspoon baking soda and ½ pint (1 cup) milk. When frothy, the second mixture is added to the first. Finally ½ lb. mixed dried fruit is added, and the mixture is poured into a greased, lined cake tin and baked in a moderate oven for 1½ hours.

vinegar candy, an American toffee made by boiling 2 tablespoons butter with ½ cup vinegar and 2 cups sugar. The mixture is boiled to 256°F (124°C) or until brittle, when a small ball will set if put in cold water. It can be pulled and stretched when cool.

vinete, Rumanian for eggplant. A popular Rumanian method of cooking it is to bake it whole in the oven with onions, oil, and tomato sauce for about 35 minutes or until cooked, when an incision is made on one side and the eggplant is stuffed with crisp fried onion slices. See also EGGPLANT.

salată de vinete, eggplant baked, skinned, mashed, then mixed with grated raw onion and lemon juice, and beaten with olive oil like a mayonnaise. It is served cold as an hors d'oeuvre garnished with quartered tomatoes.

violet (Viola odorata), a plant bearing scented purple flowers which were much used in the past for making conserves, syrups, and pastes. The leaves and flowers were also used in salads (see NASTURTIUM) and soups, and in the 18th and 19th centuries in England, violets were used to decorate a roast of veal. A violet vinegar is still made today.

Virginia potato, see SWEET POTATO.

virgouleuse, a variety of French pear which keeps throughout the winter. It comes from Virgoulée near Limoges.

virtiniai, a type of Lithuanian ravioli filled with equal amounts of chopped *steak* and finely chopped *veal suet* mixed with chopped onions, fried in butter, and seasoned with salt, pepper and nutmeg to taste. Chopped parsley and a little béchamel are added. The mixture is spread between two sheets of thinly rolled noodle dough and stamped out into rounds. These are boiled in salted water, well drained, covered with melted butter, and served.

vis, Dutch for fish. Generally speaking, it is only fresh fish that is eaten in Holland, although in winter there are times when this is scarce and dried cod (*kabeljauw*) is much relied upon. When in season, haddock, cod, sole, pike (*snoek*), and eel (*aal, paling*) all feature extensively on the Dutch menu. Shrimps (*garnal*) are a popular seafood, and oysters (*oester*) are also obtainable. The Dutch herring (*haring*) is exceptionally good.

viskoejes, fishcakes. Any kind of fish or fish leftovers may be used, provided they have previously been cooked and minced and had all skin and bones removed. First, 1 cup fish is mixed with 1 thick slice of crustless bread softened in milk, 1 egg, parsley, and salt. This mixture is formed into cakes which are rolled in breadcrumbs and then fried in butter.

vişne, Turkish for morello cherry. Vişne reçeli is morello cherry jam.

vişne şurubu, a syrup made from morello cherry juice and sugar. It is used for making sherbets (*hoşaflar*).

visniski, Russian pasties, which are also served in France. Walnut-sized rounds of yeasted pastry are filled with cooked chopped fish mixed with chopped fennel and plain sauce velouté. Another round of pastry is put on top and the edges dampened and pressed down, before the visniski are set in a warm place to rise. When needed, they are fried in very hot oil and used in soups as a garnish, or for hot *zakuski*.

vissino, Greek for sour or morello cherry. See GLYKO.

vitela, Portuguese for veal. See also VEAL.

vitela assada, veal covered with ham slices, chopped tomatoes, and onions, moistened with port, and roasted.

vitela assada no espeto, veal rubbed with olive oil and spit roasted. See also BIFINHOS DE VITELA; LINGUA DE VACA; VEAL.

vitello, Italian for veal. In Italy this always means the meat from an animal which has been killed when only weeks or months old and which has been fed solely on milk. It is sometimes roasted with butter and herbs, but more generally braised; or it is cut into chops, cutlets, or escalopes (scallops) and served in any one of a great number of ways. See also SCALLOPE; VEAL.

vitello alla genovese, veal cut into small thin slices and fried gently in butter with previously cooked globe artichokes.

The pan juices are diluted with a glass (½ cup) of white wine and reduced on top of the stove.

vitello tonnato. A 4-lb. leg of veal is boned, studded with small pieces of anchovy, and rolled up. It is then simmered in water to cover with 1 onion stuck with cloves, celery, carrot, bay leaf, parsley, and seasoning. When cold, it is cut into thin slices and either served with maionese tonnata or put into a mixture composed of 6 oz. tunny (tuna) fish in oil, 2 anchovy fillets, juice of 2 lemons, 2 cups olive oil, and capers, all pounded together.

vitellone, Italian for beef from an animal between 1 and 3 years old. This is the meat that is used for steaks (see BISTECCA), and it is usually from an ox bred only to be eaten and not worked in the fields. *Bistecchine* means baby beef (or veal) fillets and is an alternative name, with scallopine, for *piccate.* Bue, used as well, means ox. *Manzo* is also a word for beef, sometimes from an older animal or a heifer and generally used for boiling or braising, although if young enough it can be roasted. Vitellone is "older" than *vitello* and "younger" than *manzo.* See also MANZO.

vive, French for weever. See also DRAGONFISH.

vive en matelote vierge, cleaned weever cut in 3 pieces and cooked with bouquet garni, onions, garlic, cloves, nutmeg, and white wine to cover. The sauce is cooked with mushroom pieces, then reduced and thickened with egg yolks.

viveurs, a French culinary term used to describe a dish that is strongly seasoned with cayenne pepper or paprika, for example *potage des viveurs.*

vize, a popular Yugoslavian cheese made from cow's milk. See also SIR.

vladimir, a French sauce consisting of ½ pint (1 cup) sauce suprême blended with 2 tablespoons liquid demi-glace.

vlees, Dutch for meat. The Dutch usually eat meat as the main course at their evening meal. Beef, particularly steak (see BIEFSTUK), is extremely popular as is veal and pork. Lamb is not eaten very much; nevertheless, there are some very good, if rather complicated, Dutch recipes for it.

vodino or *vothino,* Greek for beef. See also BEEF; KREAS.

vodino me lahanika, beef cut into cubes and browned in butter; then potatoes and other root vegetables are added, with seasoning and water to cover. The dish is cooked for several hours in the oven. Sometimes the vegetables are drained and puréed, then returned to the meat.

vodino stifado, a thick beef stew with onions, tomatoes, bay leaf, a little vinegar, and seasoning. It is also sometimes made with wine.

voileipäpyötä, Finnish cold hors d'oeuvre, which usually consist of smoked or pickled fish. Hot hors d'oeuvres are known as *pikkulämpimät* (hot tidbits). See also HORS D'OEUVRE.

volaille, French for poultry or fowl. See also POULET.

côtellettes de volaille, usually a minced chicken mixture made into the shape of a cutlet, dipped in egg and breadcrumbs, and fried; it can also mean breast of chicken sautéed or fried (see SUPRÊMES). See also POULET, CÔTELETTES DE.

vol-au-vent, a French entrée made from *pâte feuilletée* shaped into a large oval or round 6–8 inches across, or into several smaller shapes (correctly, these should be called *bouchées*). A small circle is marked out in the centre of the pastry shape and

is removed after cooking, leaving a hollow case to be filled with purée of chicken, mushrooms, or shellfish bound with velouté or sauce béchamel; the small pastry "lid" is placed on top. Various other French garnishes are used to fill vol-au-vents, the most usual being *financière,* marinière, *normande, parisienne,* royale, *salpicons* of meat or poultry, *Talleyrand, toulousaine,* or veal sweetbreads (see RIS). Vol-au-vents should be served warm but they can be eaten cold.

vol-au-vents with crabmeat filling

volière, en, a very elaborate old-fashioned French method of serving game birds, now seldom seen. It involved reconstituting the birds with their feathers, head, tail, and wings, all held in place by little wooden pegs or clips, and was used chiefly for peacocks, pheasants, and woodcock.

Voltaire, a French method of serving *oeufs en cocotte.* The eggs are placed on a base of chicken purée, covered with sauce crème, sprinkled with grated Parmesan cheese, and browned under a grill. See also OEUFS EN COCOTTE.

vongole, the word for little clams in Rome and southern Italy, where they are cooked like mussels, and are often used for soup and as a sauce for pasta (see SPAGHETTI ALLE VONGOLE). Each region of Italy has its own local name for them: in Venice they are known as capperozzoli, in Genoa and Sardinia as arselle, and in Florence as telline.

vothino, see VODINO.

vredne unger, a Danish pastry, which resembles twisted coils and is filled with vanilla cream. For this recipe any kind of yeasted Danish pastry can be used (see WIENERBRØD). The dough is rolled out and spread with melted butter and castor sugar flavoured with cinnamon, then folded lengthways in two, and cut into strips ½ inch wide and 8 inches long. These strips are twisted and shaped like a coil, then brushed with a mixture of beaten egg and water, and left in a warm place until they have doubled in size. Then they are baked for about 20 minutes in a moderately hot oven.

Vuzkresènie (Resurrection Day), the biggest Easter Festival in Bulgaria. After the severe Lenten fast, the most elaborate meals of the year are planned and eaten. These always include Easter lamb (see *àgne*), *kozunàk,* and *chervèni yaytsà.* See also AGNESHKA CHURBA; AGNESHKA SOUP.

wachtel, German for quail. In Germany quail is usually wrapped in bacon and sautéed in butter, then braised with sauerkraut. See also QUAIL.

wachtel auf berliner art, a method from Berlin. The bird is stuffed with goose liver forcemeat and, if it has been boned, is shaped like a ball, wrapped in a cloth, and poached in veal stock. When cooked it is unwrapped and served on an artichoke bottom; it is covered with sauce *allemande* made from the stock, and garnished with grated truffle.

wafers, very thin biscuits (cookies) made into various shapes, sometimes curled, and used mainly as an accompaniment to ices, ice creams, and iced puddings. They are made from a paste of 1 lb. (4 cups) flour, 1 lb. (2 cups) fine sugar, 6 oz. (⅔ cup) butter, and ½ pint (1 cup) milk, rolled extremely thin and usually stamped with a device. They are served cold. They vary enormously in texture and taste, and are nearly always made commercially.

Wafers have been made in England since the 12th century and were probably in use even earlier; their use was reinforced in the 14th century by the mass immigration of Flemish weavers, with whom the wafer was an important article of diet. Wafers were used both as ordinary fare and for the celebration of Mass. The Mass wafer of pre-Reformation days was made from the finest-textured flour and was quite small, being only a little larger than the Communion wafer of today. The ordinary everyday wafer was the size of a large bread-plate, and was served hot as an "extra," rather as we serve hot buttered toast or scones for tea today. The poet Geoffrey Chaucer (1340–1400) wrote of "Wafers piping hot out of the Gleed," and Thomas Tusser (*c.* 1524–1580), poet and farmer, wrote:

Wife, make us a feast, spare fleshe neither corne,

Make wafers and cakes, for our shepe must be shorne.

At sheep-shearing neighbours no other thing crave

But good chere and welcome like neighbours to have.

An early English wafer recipe from a manuscript in the British Museum reads as follows: "Take fine wheaten flour, mix with cream yolks of eyroun [eggs], spice it and beat it, then warming your irons on a fire, anoint well with butter, lay on your batture [batter], press it, and bake it white or brown [light or dark]." A 12th-century manuscript drawing of the type of wafer iron referred to in this recipe can be seen in the Bod-leian Library at Oxford. They were usually round, though sometimes square, and had a long handle like a toasting fork so that the batter-filled iron could be held well over the fire without burning the fingers. Designs were cut on the irons which would be imprinted in the batter of each wafer. (It was these wafer irons that went to America with the Elizabethan settlers and came back to us much later as waffle irons.)

The word wafer comes from the Norman-French *wafre,* but wafers were first called "gaufres" in England, from the French *gofer,* to flute or crisp. *Gauffres* are still popular in Belgium and parts of France, and are served hot, straight from the gaufre iron. The sole survivor of the homemade wafer in Britain today is the brandy snap, which is served warm or cold. See also BRANDY SNAP; GAUFRE; WAFFLE.

waffle, a hot wafer or biscuit (cookie) made from a light batter poured onto a special mould or iron. First 6 oz. (1½ cups) flour, 3 teaspoons baking powder, 2 teaspoons sugar, and a pinch of salt are mixed well with 2 well-beaten egg yolks, 1 cup milk, and 6 tablespoons melted butter. The ingredients are mixed quickly, then the 2 well-beaten egg whites are added last. If necessary a little more milk may be added to make the batter of a pouring consistency. If very crisp waffles are required, the sugar is omitted. About 1 tablespoon of batter is enough for each compartment in the heated waffle iron, which, after being filled, is covered and left closed until the waffles are well puffed up and light brown in colour.

Waffles may be made with yeast instead of baking powder. Half a yeast cake, dissolved in ¼ cup lukewarm water, is added to the above mixture just before the eggs are included, and the mixture is left to rise for 4 hours. These are known as raised waffles in the U.S., where they are often served as a breakfast dish with maple syrup, sausages, bacon, etc. Cornmeal waffles, in which half the quantity of flour is replaced by cornmeal, are also made. See also GAUFRE; WAFERS.

wähen, a Swiss pastry pie filled with fruits or vegetables, cheese, or mushrooms.

waldmeister, German for woodruff, also called mariengras. In Austria this herb is used for flavouring braised dishes and stews, such as *waldmeisterbraten.* See also WOODRUFF.

waldmeisterbowle, a well-known German wine cup, made by putting the young blossoms of woodruff in a muslin bag and steeping them in Moselle wine.

507

waldmeisterbraten, an Austrian dish of braised beef. Rump steak is first marinated for at least 4 hours in dilute wine vinegar with a bunch of woodruff, then drained, browned on all sides in butter with sliced carrots and onions, and finally braised with 1 pint (2 cups) of the marinade and seasoning until tender. The stock is thickened with flour mixed with red wine and reduced. Finally ½ pint (1 cup) sour cream is added.

waldorf salad, a salad which originated in the U.S. It consists of equa amounts od diced, peeled, and cored apple and celery, mixed with mayonnaise and chopped pecan nuts or walnuts.

waldorf sweetbreads, an American dish of previously blanched sweetbreads, which are sautéed in butter, and then placed on artichoke bottoms, the whole being covered with sauce *allemande*.

Walewska, à la, a French method of preparing fish, particularly sole. The fish fillets are poached in fish fumet, then put on a hot dish and garnished with slices of crawfish and truffle. The whole is coated with sauce mornay and butter pounded with puréed lobster or crawfish.

wall-eyed herring, see HERRING.

wall-eyed pike (*Stirostedion vitreum*), a freshwater fish of the pike-perch family, found in American lakes and rivers. It is also called yellow or blue pike. It is a delicious fish, not unlike an excellent sole in taste, and is prepared in any way that is suitable for sole.

wall-eyed pollack (*Theragra chalcogramma*), a large black pollack which makes fairly good eating, found off the Pacific coast of the U.S.

walnut (*Juglans regia*), a tree which produces nuts that are of considerable culinary importance and have great protein value. They are eaten fresh as a dessert and are used in confectionery, cake, and sweetmeat (confection) making. In England they are pickled whole when green and eaten with cold meats and sometimes with cheese (see PICKLED WALNUTS), and in parts of France they are crushed to produce *huile de noix,* which for some purposes is preferred to olive oil because of its strong distinctive flavour. See also NOCE; NOIX; ORZECHY.

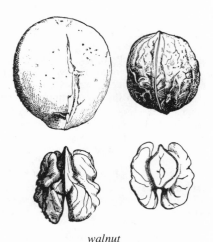

walnut

walnut ketchup, 4 lb. green walnuts are steeped in 2½ lb. rock salt for 6 days, the skins being crushed from time to time and the juice poured off daily until only the pulp remains. The juice is then boiled and skimmed, after which it is reboiled for 30 minutes with 2 oz. (½ cup) ground ginger and the same of mixed spice and cayenne. The ketchup is bottled and kept for several months before being used as a condiment.

walnut tart, 3 eggs are beaten and added to ½ pint (1 cup) golden or corn syrup, 4 oz. (1 cup) shelled chopped walnuts,

4 oz. (½ cup) sugar, ½ teaspoon vanilla, and ½ teaspoon salt. This filling is poured into a short crust pastry case, and the tart is baked in a slow-to-moderate oven for 45 minutes. It is served cold, to allow it to set, with a layer of whipped cream and walnut halves.

wälschkorn, a German pickle made from young unripe corncobs no bigger than a finger, packed into jars with 1 bay leaf and peppercorns, then covered with cooled boiled white vinegar.

wapiti (*Cervus canadensis*), a deer found chiefly in Canada but also in the U.S. It is similar to the red deer, but larger. It is quite good to eat and can be prepared and cooked in any way that is suitable for venison.

warden, see PEAR.

warmbier, a German hot beer soup made with raw eggs beaten into warm beer and flavoured with lemon.

washed curd cheese, a type of Canadian cheddar, but made softer and more moist than standard cheddar by a process in which cold water is run over the curd after it has been milled.

wasserteig, German for raised crust or hot water crust pastry. For cold pies a richer version is sometimes used, in which 2 egg yolks are added before the hot water is poured in. See PASTRY, HOT WATER CRUST.

water biscuits, very thin, round biscuits (crackers), served with cheese. They are made with 1 lb. (4 cups) flour, 1 heaped tablespoon butter, and enough milk to make a stiff dough. This is rolled very thin and cut into rounds which are pricked all over before being baked quickly in a hot oven. The biscuits should be white with brown patches.

water chestnut, the edible, nut-like fruit of several water plants of the genus *Trapa. T. natans,* known as "the Jesuits' nut" because the seeds were often used in making rosaries, is grown in southern Europe as well as Asia, and has also been introduced into the U.S. The seeds of the Chinese *T. bicornis* are eaten all over the Far East and are served a great deal in Chinese dishes; they are white in colour, measuring about 1 inch across, and have a delicate flavour. In the West they are available peeled, in cans, and do not need further cooking. They can be sliced into soups or rice dishes.

water hen, see MOORHEN.

water ice, see ICES.

water parsnip (*Sium aquaticum*), an aquatic plant with edible leaves that taste of celery and are used for salads; the roots are poisonous. It is also called water smallage, water parsley, and creeping watercress.

water rail (*Rallus aquaticus*), an excellent game bird which abounds in the British Isles and is very good either roasted or casseroled. The young bird, of course, is always preferable to the old, and can be recognized by its small pinkish legs and the downy feathers under the wings. One bird should be allowed for each person. Water rail is at its best from September to November and can be prepared in the same way as partridge.

watercress (*Nasturtium officinale*), a European water plant which grows freely on the banks of streams and in damp meadows, as well as being cultivated commercially. It is rich in mineral salts and has a strong peppery taste. It is used in salads, as a garnish, and for a very good soup (see SOUPE AU CRESSON). In Cornwall it used to be stewed, chopped, dressed with butter, and served with freshwater fish. In County Sligo in Ireland it is frequently cooked with boiled bacon or ham in place of cabbage, especially in spring before the young cabbages are ready. See also AMERICAN CRESS; WINTER CRESS.

waterfisch or **patervisch,** I. A Dutch word used in France as a general term for freshwater fish. II. A French sauce served with freshwater fish, usually perch. For a hot sauce, julienne of carrot, leek, celery, and parsley root are all cooked in butter until soft; then ½ pint (1 cup) fish stock is added and reduced to almost nothing. Finally ¾ pint (1½ cups) white wine sauce is added and slightly reduced. For a cold sauce, the same preparation as for the hot sauce is used, but with gelatine added to the fish stock, and no white wine sauce. This sauce is used to coat the fish after it has been cooked, and the fish is left to set in the jelly.

watermelon, an edible gourd the seeds of which in Greece, are dried and roasted, and often served with drinks (see PASSA TEMPO MAN). See KARPOUZI; MELON.

waterzooi or **waterzootje,** a famous Belgian speciality which can be made with either chicken or fish. For chicken *waterzooi* the bird is rubbed with lemon and then simmered with onions, leeks, celery, carrot, cloves, herbs, water, and white wine to cover; it is then cut into pieces and served with the vegetables and stock. Fish *waterzooi* is usually made in the same way as the chicken dish, using freshwater fish of all kinds such as bream, pike, eel, or carp and including butter in the cooking; slices of toast are put into soup plates and covered with the fish, vegetables, and stock.

wątróbka, Polish for liver. See also LIVER. One way of cooking calf's liver in Poland is to casserole it with mushrooms and parboiled potatoes in bouillon and Madeira wine.

wątróbka cielęca z jałowcem, calf's liver stuffed with crushed juniper berries. The liver is partially sliced to allow for the stuffing, and is served with a sauce *smitane*.

wątróbki z drobiu duszony w maderze, a dish of poultry livers. About 1 lb. poultry livers are first sautéed in butter with a small sliced onion, then sprinkled with flour and boiled up for 8 minutes with 4 tablespoons stock and the same of Madeira wine.

wax caps, fungi of the genus *Hygrophorus,* some of which are prized as esculents. None are poisonous. They are subdivided into 3 groups which some authorities consider separate genera, *Limacium, Camarophyllus,* and *Hygrocybe.* The most esteemed by gourmets are the ivory wax cap (*L. eburneus*) and the meadow wax cap (*C. pratensis*).

wax pod beans, see FRENCH BEANS.

weakfish (*Cynoscion regalis*), a sea fish found all along the eastern seaboard of the U.S. It is highly prized gastronomically. It can be cooked in the same way as trout, and is also sometimes called sea trout. The American Indian name for it is squeteage.

wędlina, the Polish term for a plate of cold cooked meats or sausage, similar to the French *assiette anglaise* or the German aufschnitt (cold meats).

weenie, an American diminutive for a *wienerwurst*.

weever, the general name for fish of the genus *Trachinus*. Two species are found chiefly in the waters of northwest Europe, the greater weever or dragonfish (*T. draco*) and the weever (*T. vipera*); two more are found mainly in the Mediterranean (*T. radiatus, T. araneus*). All have poisonous

weever

glands at the base of the large dorsal fin, and these remain poisonous even after the fish is dead. The greater weever is highly prized as food and has firm white flesh. It can be prepared in any way that is suitable for whiting. On Mediterranean coasts all species of weever are eaten and are used particularly in soups and bouillabaisse. See also DRAGONFISH; DRAKENA; VIVE.·

węgorz, Polish for eel. See also EEL.

rolada z węgorza, roulade of eel. The eel is boned and stuffed with chopped hard-boiled eggs, gherkins, and mushrooms; then it is wrapped in a cheesecloth and poached in vegetable broth and a little vinegar. When cold, it is garnished with lemon slices and mushrooms and served either with a mustard sauce or with mayonnaise.

węgorz duszony, eel simmered in a bouillon and white wine sauce to which shrimps or lobster paste, egg yolks, and mushrooms are added. Cooked crayfish and fish quenelles may also be included.

Eel is also baked in Poland, or served in aspic.

weichkäse, German for cream cheese. German cream cheeses include briekäse, camembertkäse, deutscher weichkäse mit schimmelbildung, kümmelkäse, münster-käse, weinkäse, and ziegenkäse. See FRÜHSTÜCKSKÄSE; LIMBURGER KÄSE; MAINAUER KÄSE; ROMADUR-KÄSE; WEISSLACKER-KÄSE.

weichseltorte, an Austrian tart made with morello cherries.

weihnachtsbäckerei, see BÄCKEREI.

weinachtsstollen, see STOLLEN.

weisse rübe, German for turnip. See also TURNIP.

Teltower rübchen, Teltow turnips, grown in the vicinity of Berlin. They are very small but quite delicious. They are sometimes cooked by simmering in a syrup of sugar, butter, and stock until they are browned and glazed and the liquid has almost evaporated.

weissfisch, German for dace; the name is also sometimes loosely applied to other silver-scaled freshwater fish.

weisslackerkäse, a soft ripened cow's milk cheese made in Bavaria. It takes its name from its white, smeary, lustrous surface. It is usually made by mixing skimmed evening milk with morning whole milk. Sufficient rennet is added, at a temperature of 82°–86°F (28°–30°C), to form curd firm enough to cut in the space of 60 or 80 minutes. The curd is then transferred to large moulds divided into sections, to form the individual cheeses. The moulds are turned frequently. When the cheeses are removed they are salted on the surface and cured at a temperature of about 55°F (13°C). Cool moist conditions are essential for the development of the surface smear. During the first few days of the curing process, the cheeses are in contact with one another in the curing-room; afterwards they are separated. After 3 months they are wrapped in parchment, and they are fully mature after another month.

weisswürste, German "white" würste which are a speciality of Munich and the surrounding district. They are extremely light and delicate in both flavour and texture. They are made from minced lean pork, veal, soaked white bread, nutmeg, a trace of lemon peel, salt, and white pepper (4 lb. pork to 1 lb. veal and 1 lb. white bread). The mixture is put into skins 4–5 inches long. The sausages are plainly boiled and are served hot or cold with sauerkraut and potato salad. See also WURST.

Wellington steak, an English and Irish method of serving a fillet steak weighing anywhere between 2 and 6 lb. It is first sautéed very rare, then wrapped entirely in puff pastry and baked in a hot oven until the pastry is golden; sometimes mushrooms or pâté are laid along the top of the steak before the pastry envelope is put on. This dish is said to have been a favourite with the Duke of Wellington. It is also eaten in France, where it is known as *filet de boeuf en croûte,* and in the U.S., where it is known as beef Wellington.

wels, an alternative English name for silure.

Welsh cakes, small cakes made in Wales. They resemble rock cakes in all respects except that mixed fats are used, lard being substituted for half the usual quantity of butter.

Welsh cawl, a Welsh national soup (cawl is the Welsh word for soup) made from mutton, root vegetables, onions, and leeks. It is sometimes served in the same way as a pot-au-feu—the boiled meat eaten first, with the vegetables, and the broth afterwards (or the other way round, as preferred).

Welsh cheese pudding, a cheese pudding, made with 4 slices of bread toasted on one side only and buttered on the un-toasted side. Then 2 slices are laid at the bottom of a dish, buttered side up, and ¾ lb. grated Gloucester Cheddar, or *Caerphilly* cheese is placed on top, followed by the remaining 2 slices of toast buttered side down, and then another ¼ lb. grated cheese. Next 1 pint milk is heated until lukewarm, then 1 egg is beaten in, and this mixture is poured over the contents of the dish. The pudding is left for 20 minutes, then baked for 20 minutes in a moderate-to-hot oven. Cream can be substituted for half the quantity of milk, and a pinch of cayenne pepper can be added, to taste.

Welsh onion (*Allium cepa perutile*), a species of onion which has a bunching, leek-like, interleaved bulb and tubular leaves. It is a perennial evergreen and has a delicate flavour. A leaf or two is broken off as required leaving the main plant undisturbed. In spite of its name the Welsh onion is Siberian in origin and was not introduced into England until the early 17th century. Other names for it are everlasting onion, cibol, and in Cornwall, *scifers.* It is often confused with a similar onion called the Japanese bunching onion, which it resembles, but the Welsh onion is smaller. See also ONION.

Welsh rarebit, an extremely good savoury, eaten all over the British Isles. Methods of preparing it vary, but essentially it should be made with ½ lb. strongly flavoured crumbly cheese such as Cheddar, Gloucester, or Lancashire, broken up into small pieces and mixed with 1 teaspoon dry English mustard powder and 2 tablespoons dark beer. (If the cheese is dry a nut of butter should be added.) These are gently heated and stirred until all is melted and amalgamated. The mixture is then spread over fresh toast and gently browned under the grill. These quantities will make enough for at least 4 large rounds of toast. See also BUCK RAREBIT; RAREBIT.

Wensleydale cheese, one of the oldest and best English cheeses. Legend has it that it has been made in Wensleydale, Yorkshire, in the valley of the river Ure, for the past thousand years. It was probably made first at the abbeys of Jervaulx, Kirkstall, and Bolton in that part of the country. Originally it was a blue cheese, but during WW II the Ministry of Food declared that it had to be sold white and unripe. It is a tragedy that only the white Wensleydale now survives, and no doubt the people who remember the deliciousness of the blue variety are rapidly dying out. Before the turn of the century, it was a farm-made cheese, but in 1897 a Mr. Edward Chapman opened a small factory for its production at Hawes, Yorkshire, which was highly successful. Mr. Alfred Rowntree followed suit by opening 3 more in the neighbouring districts of Masham, Coverham, and Thoralby. Nowadays Wensleydale is a very popular English cheese and is made in many sizes from 1 lb. upwards. It has a good flavour and a soft texture, and it well deserves its popularity in England and Ireland.

wentelteefjes, a Dutch form of pain perdu. Two eggs are beaten and mixed with sugar, grated lemon peel, cinnamon, vanilla, and ½ pint (1 cup) tepid milk. Six slices of stale bread are soaked in this mixture for about 30 minutes. Then each slice is fried separately in butter and sprinkled with icing sugar.

Westfälische bohnensuppe, a regional Westphalian German soup made from a purée of soaked and cooked dried kidney beans, with enough white stock added to achieve the required consistency. The soup is garnished with diced cooked celeriac, carrots, leeks, and potatoes, and slices of smoked sausage.

Westphalian ham, see SCHINKEN.

wet devil, see DEVIL.

Wexford cheese, a recent Irish cheese, made in County Wexford, from full-cream milk. In colour and texture it is not unlike the English Cheshire cheese, being a pale orange, and soft and crumbly; however its flavour is creamy, and closer to the double Gloucester. It has little or no rind, and is an excellent cheese both for eating and cooking.

whale, a large aquatic mammal of the *Cetacae* family. There are a great number of species and varieties found in warm waters all over the world. Many people consider whale meat good to eat, and during WW II it was on sale in England. Only the meat of young whale should be used. It can make a rich stew with good gravy, and is quite tender when baked in the oven, though a little fishy in taste. It can be prepared and cooked in the same way as beef. In the Middle Ages in France it was sold as *crapois* on meatless days during Lent.

whaup, see CURLEW.

wheat (*Triticum*), a cereal grass which, together with rice, is the chief source of the food grains eaten by humanity. Wheat indeed is more widely distributed than rice and has adapted itself to a very much greater range of climates and soils. It has been cultivated since very early times, and there is some evidence to indicate that cultivation first took place in Mesopotamia. The 3 wild forms, commonly known as wild emmer, spelt, and wild einkorn, were the plants then used, and these have played an important part in the development of the wheats grown today. Modern wheats are divided into 3 botanical groups, according to the number and the nature of the grains each plant bears, and the most important species within these groups are as follows.

In one group is *T. monococcum,* einkorn. This plant still grows wild in Greece and Mesopotamia. It was cultivated by the prehistoric Swiss lake dwellers and is still grown today in Yugoslavia, Asia Minor, and North Africa.

Included in another group is *T. durum,* durum, macaroni, or pasta wheat. This is believed to be a descendant of emmer. It is second in importance to the bread wheats of *T. aestivum.* It is a hard wheat with a high proportion of gluten and makes a flour with very good keeping properties, and one suitable for the production of high protein bread, and of pasta. It is grown in all countries bordering on the Mediterranean, in the U.S.S.R., Iraq, Iran, Pakistan, India, China, Canada, the U.S., Mexico, Argentina, Uruguay, and Chile. In the same group is also *T. turgidum,* English wheat, grown in western Europe, Mediterranean countries, Asia Minor, and China. It was also at one time the chief wheat in southern England until it was supplanted by bread wheats.

A third group includes *T. aestivum,* bread wheat, incomparably the most important species from an economic and culinary point of view. Its distribution is universal in lands of suitable climate, and it has many thousands of varieties, mostly developed through breeding. Varieties of *T. aestivum* produce the flours of the highest quality for bread making. *T. dicoccum,* emmer, also in this group, was the main wheat grown in prehistoric times. It is still grown today in southern Europe, Iran, Pakistan, India, and the U.S. *T. compactum,* club wheat, another member of this group, is used in the manufacture of biscuits (cookies), cakes, and pastry. It is grown in the Pacific states of the U.S., Chile, Asia Minor, etc. It is known in the U.S. as cake flour. Another member *T. spelta,* is a very hardy wheat, well adapted to mountainous regions and poor soil. It is grown in parts of Germany, Spain, France, Italy, and Switzerland. See also FLOUR.

wheat germ, the embryo plant in the wheat "berry" or grain. It is separated out in the production of ordinary white flour, but is present in wholemeal or graham flour. It contains a high proportion of protein and of vitamin E, an important nutritional element which promotes fertility and is generally beneficial to health. Wheat germ can be sprinkled raw into soups and stews, providing a thickening without bulk or great calorie increase. It is therefore useful for diets where nutritional value is important. Small quantities can also be added to white flour for cake or bread making; approximately 4 tablespoons wheat germ added to 1 lb. flour improves flavour and nutritional value without making the mixture or dough turn brown. Wheat germ can be bought loose, as it is, or further enriched with vitamins and minerals, and packaged commercially. See also FLOUR.

wheatear (*Oenathe oenanthe*), a small migratory bird which used to be trapped in considerable numbers on the Downs in England when it arrived from Africa early in the year. The young birds made quite good eating and could be cooked in the same way as quail, but they are now protected by law. They are much prized in France, where they are classed as game and prepared in the same way as lark.

wheatear

whelk, the name given to a large number of spiral-shelled marine molluscs. The common whelk (*Buccinum undatum*) is popular as food in Europe. Whelks are boiled in salted water for 15 minutes, then taken from the shell and eaten cold with lemon juice or vinegar. Another common whelk (*Fusus antiquus*) is found off the Cheshire coast, in England, and sold mostly in Liverpool.

whey, the liquid surrounding sour milk, buttermilk, curds, and junket. It has several important culinary uses, and in the past was particularly valued as an excellent cooling drink. It was much appreciated in 16th-century England, as the rhyme of "Little Miss Muffet" testifies, and in the 18th century, Alexander Pope wrote:

Water and whey, of drinks are first,
They cool, dilute, and quench the thirst.

In Ireland it was called *medgg* (modern Irish meadhgg), and was used instead of milk on fast-days in strict monastic communities, sometimes being diluted with water when it was known as *modgusci* (whey water). St. Patrick is said to have sent bowls of it to reapers of his household. Goat's milk whey, especially, was believed to have great medicinal value,

whelk

and as late as the 19th century was much used in County Down and Dublin for invalids who went there specifically in order to drink it. It is also drunk in the Scottish Islands, particularly the Shetlands, where it is allowed to ferment in oak casks until it is sparkling. It is known as bland.

Whey also plays an important part in cheese making. Generally, it has simply to be drained off after natural souring and rennetting of the milk, so that the cheese can be made from the curd. However certain cheeses, notably the *gjeitost* and *mysost* of Norway and Sweden, and the *schabzieger* of Switzerland, are actually made from whey or, in the latter case, from a mixture of skim milk and whey. This is done in the following manner. Since whey is 90–95% water, and the small percentage of solid matter is difficult to coagulate, the water is evaporated by cooking the whey very slowly for many hours in large copper pans. As evaporation gradually takes place, a kind of brown caramelised paste is obtained. This is then emulsified, and either eaten as it is, but with added flavouring, or mixed with small amounts of fat solids. Whey butter and whey cream are also manufactured in small quantities by a similar method of evaporation and emulsification, before other solid matter is added. Whey cheeses have a very individual flavour, not liked by everyone; but the flavour of whey butter or whey cream is almost indistinguishable from that made from full-cream milk. See also WHIG.

whig, a word used variously in Scotland for the whey from sour cream or buttermilk, and for a beverage consisting of whey fermented and flavoured with herbs. The origin of the word is obscure, but some authorities believe this word to be the source of the political term "Whig"—possibly implying "sourness"—which was first applied by Scottish Episcopalians to Presbyterians, and by Presbyterians of the Established Church to those other dissenting bodies (see F. N. McNeill, *The Scots Kitchen*). However, other sources state that there is no connection between the culinary and the political term, the political title being in fact an abbreviation of the earlier "Whiggamore," a nickname given to Scots Covenanters who came to Leith to buy corn, and derived from the Gaelic whig, meaning "mare," or "to jog or drive." See also WHEY.

whig or wig biscuits (cookies), small cakes or biscuits (cookies) which were called "whigs" after 1825. They are made in the same way as rock cakes, but with 1 tablespoon finely chopped candied peel, angelica, and a few glacé cherries added. The tops are brushed with beaten egg and milk, and then the cakes are baked for 20–30 minutes in saucers.

They are sprinkled with sugar when cooked, and split in 2 and buttered while still hot.

whim-wham, a Scottish pudding mentioned by Sir Walter Scott in his novel *The Bride of Lammermoor*. It is not unlike a *syllabub* and consists of 1 pint (2 cups) sweetened cream mixed with 1 glass (½ cup) white wine and grated peel of 1 lemon, all whisked to a froth. This is layered in a dish with thin slices of sponge (lady) finger and red currant jelly, the last layer being of the sweetened cream, then decorated on top with match-like strips of candied peel.

whip, to, to beat one or several ingredients with a whisk, egg beater, or fork until they either thicken, as in the case of cream, or become very smooth, as in the case of sauces, and vegetables that are being whipped to make a purée.

white basil (*Basella alba*), a climbing plant with edible stems and leaves which can be cooked in the same way as spinach or chard. It is indigenous to India, but is now grown in Europe.

white beet, an alternative name for chard.

white cakes, see SODA BREAD.

white cheese in brine, the English name for the Bulgarian cheese, *siréné*.

white currant, see RED CURRANT.

white devil, see DEVIL.

white perch (*Roccus chrysops*), a small migratory fish found in the East of the U.S. It is related to the American sea bass.

white pudding, a traditional Irish sausage which used always to be made in the shape of a horseshoe, but which nowadays, when plastic casings are used, is sometimes straight like the ordinary sausage. It consists of leaf or flaked lard mixed with an equal quantity of toasted oatmeal, cloves to taste, black pepper, and salt all put into a skin, and it is served fried or grilled with bacon either for supper or for Sunday morning breakfast. It should be eaten fresh and can be very good if properly made. It is the Irish equivalent of the Scottish *skirlie*. See also SKIRLIE.

white sauce, a term which in fact covers several different sauces, all called by the same name because of their colour. In Britain and the U.S. the term is also often used for *béchamel maigre*. White sauce with milk and flour is made with ½ pint (1 cup) milk and 1 pint (2 cups) cream put into a double boiler over the heat. Then 4 tablespoons flour is combined with ½ pint (1 cup) milk to form a paste, and mixed into the milk and cream mixture when it boils. The sauce is stirred for 2 minutes, then covered and cooked for 8 minutes. Next 2 egg yolks are beaten with ¼ pint (½ cup) cream, and this is mixed into the sauce, which is immediately removed from the heat. Chopped parsley and pepper and salt are added before serving.

For white sauce without flour, sliced mushrooms are boiled in 1 pint (2 cups) good white stock until the stock is reduced by one third. The saucepan is then removed from the heat, and 4 beaten egg yolks and ½ pint (1 cup) cream are stirred in, with salt, pepper, a dusting of grated nutmeg, and a few drops of lemon juice. The sauce is stirred over the heat until it reaches boiling point, when it is instantly removed. It is then ready to serve.

A white sauce without milk or cream is made from 1 pint (2 cups) of the liquor in which the poultry or fish has been cooked and is boiled until reduced by half; then 1 tablespoon flour or corn flour (cornstarch) mixed with 2 tablespoons water is stirred in, and the stirring continued until the flour is cooked. The saucepan is removed from the heat, and 2 eggs beaten in a little water are well mixed in. It is seasoned to taste, and stirring is continued over a very low heat until the sauce is thick. If the sauce is to be served with sweetbreads or poultry, 3 tablespoons concentrated veal gravy is added for every ½ pint (1 cup) sauce.

The usual English method of making white sauce is with 2 tablespoons butter melted in a saucepan; then 2 tablespoons flour is stirred in, followed by 1 pint (2 cups) warm milk. The sauce is stirred continuously until it thickens, to avoid lumps. When smooth, it is seasoned. It is sometimes served plain with vegetables such as cauliflower, celery, or marrow (squash), or it can be flavoured with grated cheese, parsley, or whatever is suitable for the dish it is to accompany. It is a basic English sauce, in the same way as the sauce béchamel is basic to French cuisine.

For French white sauce, see IVOIRE, SAUCE.

white wine sauce, I. One pint (2 cups) fish fumet or chicken stock and ¼ pint (½ cup) white wine are boiled down, bound with 2 egg yolks, and beaten with 2 oz. (¼ cup) butter, according to the method described for sauce hollandaise. II. One pint (2 cups) sauce *allemande* is simmered with ¼ pint (½ cup) reduced fish fumet or chicken stock and ¼ pint (½ cup) white wine. III. Fish fumet or chicken stock and white wine are boiled down to glaze and beaten with butter. See also WINE SAUCE.

whitebait, the fry of the common herring and the sprat. They should not exceed 2 inches in length, and after washing they are rolled in flour and fried in deep oil. These immature fish are consumed whole, heads and tails as well, and no bones are noticeable. Whitebait are a delicious dish when served with lemon juice and salt. If they are served with cayenne pepper or Tabasco sauce, the dish is called devilled whitebait.

white-eyed duck or **white-eyed pochard,** see POCHARD.

whitefish, the name given to all members of the family *Coregonidae*. These fish are rather like freshwater herrings, and there are species widely distributed over the world. Many are highly prized as food. See also FÉRA; GREAT LAKE HERRING; GWYNIAD; LAVARET; PILOT FISH; POLLAN-ROCKY MOUNTAIN WHITEFISH; SIG.

white-headed duck (*Oxyura leucocephala*), a duck found from the Mediterranean through Turkestan as far as India. It is not highly thought of as food, but the natives of the Kirgiz Steppe are fond of its eggs. The bird can be cooked in the same way as wild duck.

white-leaf beet, another name for the true chard.

whiting, I. A very common European sea fish, *Gadus merlangus*, about 12 inches long. It is in season all the year round but is best when bought in the winter. The flesh is white and insipid, but is easily digested and is frequently served to invalids. When very fresh, or caught in very deep water, whiting has some merit, but on the whole it is the dullest of the usual fish to be found in shops. It may be fried, grilled, or poached, and a good sauce such as sauce mornay is indicated. It is sometimes fried with its tail in its mouth; in France this is called *merlan en colère*. See also MERLANGO; MERLANO; MERLUZZO. II. Another American name for silver

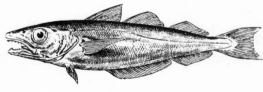

whiting

hake. III. *Gadus poutassou* is the blue whiting, a deep-water fish which reaches a length of about 18 inches. During February and April it appears in massive shoals off Norway, the west coast of Ireland, and northern Scotland. When skinned and boned, it is ideal for commercially frozen fish fingers, fish cakes, etc.

Whitley goose, a traditional English dish from Whitley Bay in Northumberland, and not made from goose at all. To prepare the dish 4 medium-sized peeled onions are boiled until tender in salted water, then drained, chopped, and mixed with 2 oz. (½ cup) grated hard cheese such as cheddar or *Wensleydale,* and pepper. An ovenproof dish is lightly buttered, and ¼ pint (½ cup) light cream or top of the milk is poured in; the onion mixture is put into it, the top sprinkled with 2 more table-spoons grated cheese, and the dish baked in a hot oven for 10 minutes or until the top is browned. It is served either alone, as a supper dish, or with hot or cold roast meats.

wholemeal, a word applied to flour which contains a certain proportion of bran (this flour is stone ground, and unsifted or unbolted), or to flour which is a mixture of wheat and rye flours. It is also applied to bread made with wholemeal flour, and this is light or dark brown in colour (instead of white), depending on how much rye flour is used. See also FLOUR.

whortleberry, see BILBERRY.

widgeon (*Anas penelope*), a wild duck, larger than the teal, but smaller than the mallard. It is found almost all over Europe and Asia, and there is a related species in the U.S. Widgeon does not like saltwater, and it is a very clean feeder generally. It is very good to eat and would be more popular if it were not for its small size, for while a mallard provides a

widgeon

very good meal for 2 and sometimes 3 people, 1 widgeon must be allowed for each person. Another factor is that the price of widgeon is not much lower than that of mallard. Widgeon can be prepared in any way that is suitable for wild duck, allowing a slightly shorter cooking time.

wiener knödelsuppe, a traditional Austrian soup consisting of rich beef broth garnished with dumplings. The dumplings are made by soaking equal quantities of toast and plain bread in milk (about 4 thick slices), then mixing it with 2 eggs, salt, nutmeg, and enough flour to make a firm dough. This mixture is shaped into small dumplings which are then poached for 5–8 minutes either in salted water or in the broth. Many cooks prefer to poach them separately and add them to the broth af-terwards, thus preserving the clearness of the soup.

wiener koch, a Viennese pudding rather like a soufflé. To prepare it 3 eggs are separated, and the yolks blended with 1 tablespoon flour and 1 tablespoon milk. Then ⅔ pint (¾ cup) milk is heated with 2 tablespoons butter and stirred into the yolk mixture, which is then cooked in a double boiler, stirring constantly, until thick. It is removed from the stove and stirred until cool, and finally the stiffly beaten egg whites are

folded in. The pudding is baked in a moderate oven for 10–12 minutes.

wiener krapfen, Viennese doughnuts, made from a rich yeast dough with grated lemon peel added. They are very similar to *Faschings krapfen* (See also FASCHINGS KRAPFEN).

wiener schlagobers, a Viennese whipped cream made from chilled ice cold cream whipped with 2 tablespoons vanilla sugar for every pint (2 cups) of cream. It is used with cakes, fruit, coffee, chocolate, or puddings. The common name for it is *schlag.*

wiener schnitzel, see SCHNITZEL.

wiener wurst, a small Austrian wurst which resembles a frankfurter.

wiener zwiebelsauce, Viennese onion sauce. To make it 4 chopped onions and 2 cloves garlic are first browned in lard; then a roux of 2 tablespoons flour and the same of butter is added, followed by 1 pint (2 cups) beef stock. The sauce is seasoned with salt and a pinch of sugar.

wienerbrød, Danish yeast puff pastry, a speciality of Den-mark. The word is used both for this particular type of pastry, and for the individual pastries that are baked from it. These pastries are made in various shapes and with different flavour-ings, and recipes vary, but the sweet varieties all share the same basic ingredients of flour, sugar, yeast, milk, salt, and eggs, and may take the form of cakes, tarts, twists, filled pas-tries, etc. Savoury kinds are frequently made with mashed po-tato.

In one recipe 2 oz. fresh yeast is dissolved in ½ pint (1 cup) tepid milk, then stirred into 1 well-beaten egg. Then 1 lb. (4 cups) flour is mixed with 2 tablespoons castor sugar and 1 teaspoon salt. The yeast and egg mixture is then beaten well into the flour mixture with a wooden spoon, and the dough is turned out onto a floured board and rolled out to ¹/₃-inch thick-ness. Then ¾ lb. (1½ cups) butter is softened, but not melted, and this is dotted onto ⅔ of the dough. The ⅓ without butter is folded over, and the remaining buttered ⅓ of dough folded over that, envelope fashion. The edges are pressed down, and the "envelope" is half turned, before rolling thinly. This folding and rolling is repeated 3 or 4 times, as for puff pastry. The dough is chilled before use.

In another method the basic dough is prepared as above and rolled out, but instead of being dotted with softened butter it is sprinkled with 2 teaspoons grated lemon peel, a pinch of nutmeg, and ½ teaspoon almond essence (extract). It is then covered with a cloth and left in a warm place to double its bulk. Then it is rolled out again, to ½-inch thickness, and a 6-oz. (²/₃ cup) oblong of butter is put in the centre; the dough is divided into 3, folded envelope fashion, and rolled, just as above, and this process is repeated 3 or 4 times. It is then baked for 20 minutes in a hot oven, being sometimes brushed with beaten egg beforehand. When cold, it is sometimes iced and covered with nuts to taste.

Another method calls for 2 oz. fresh yeast dissolved in ¼ cup tepid water, then added to ¾ cup tepid milk, and ¼ lb. (4 heaped tablespoons) flour, and beaten until smooth. Then 2 beaten eggs and 1 egg yolk are blended in together, with 3 heaped tablespoons castor sugar, ½ teaspoon salt, a pinch of ground cardamom seeds or mace, 1 teaspoon grated lemon peel, and ¾ lb. (3 cups) flour. This time the dough is lightly rolled into a large square about ¼ inch thick, ¾ lb. (1½ cups) pounded butter is put in the centre, and the edges of the dough are folded over it. The dough is rolled into a large square and folded into 3, and 3 again, giving 9 layers, then covered with a damp towel and left in a cool place (not a refrigerator) for 1 hour. When firm it is rolled again into a large square and folded, as before, into a small one. The process of folding and rolling is carried out 3 or 4 times as before, but before the process is repeated for the last time the pastry is left to stand for 20 minutes. After the final folding and rolling, it is shaped into individual portions, as desired, and baked in a fairly hot oven for about 25 minutes. It is decorated to taste.

For savoury wienerbrød, ½ lb. (2 cups) flour is sifted with ½ teaspoon salt; then ¼ lb. (½ cup) butter is rubbed in, and another ¼ lb. cut into small dots and mixed in. Next ¼ cup cold water is added gradually, and finally 1 cup cold riced potato (potato sieved in a coarse vegetable mill) is gently pressed in. The mixture is chilled in greased paper, then rolled out for use on a lightly floured board. This pastry is used for pies or patty cases, and the quantities given will make enough to line a 9-inch flan tin. See also PASTRY.

Wigilia, the Polish Christmas Eve, a fast day in the Roman Catholic Church until quite recently. Meat was forbidden, and the day was marked in Poland by many traditional meatless dishes such as *barszcz z uszkami* and *karp*, with a *baba* to follow. Wigilia was traditionally started with a slice of unleavened bread.

wild, the collective German term for all wild animals that are hunted for food, but particularly deer, elk, antelope, and reindeer; venison is the equivalent English word. In Germany, as elsewhere in Europe, roebuck is considered the finest.

Fillet of venison is generally cut into individual steaks or cutlets in Germany, and these are beaten and then cooked in butter on both sides until medium-cooked. Lemon wedges and apple sauce, or red currant jelly are served with the meat, and sometimes a little white or red wine is stirred into the pan juices and boiled up to make a gravy. Steaks and cutlets can also be dipped in egg and breadcrumbs and fried, but in this case the wine is not added as it would make the coating soggy. A haunch is often marinated and then jugged, being cooked in the same way as jugged hare. See also GAME; REH.

wild boar, see BOAR; WILDSCHWEIN.

wild duck, a general term applied to several species of duck including mallard, pochard, widgeon, and teal, but also applied in particular to the mallard, which is the largest of the wild ducks and very good to eat. Contrary to some belief, wild duck does not taste fishy; indeed its diet consists of seeds and marsh plants. It is only in freezing weather that it is forced to find unfrozen foods in brackish or estuary waters, and is driven to eat molluscs and other fishy food.

Before cooking, wild duck should be hung for at least 2–3 days, after which a greenish tinge will be seen on the skin of the belly. A well-known method of preparing it is to cook it with orange. The bird is half-roasted with butter; then orange juice and peel are added and the duck is cooked for a further 15 minutes. A glass (½ cup) of port and 1 cup giblet stock are then included. The sauce is allowed to reduce on a hot stove, and is then served separately.

A famous French method of cooking wild duck is to braise it with turnips, as these absorb any fat. The bird is casseroled with onions, turnips, bouquet garni, and a little giblet stock for about 2 hours or until it is tender. The sauce may be thickened with a *beurre manié* or a little cream.

Wild duck is often made into *pâtés* and *terrines*, and *salmi* of wild duck is also popular in both Britain and France. A classical French sauce often served with wild duck is sauce *bigarade*. See also ANITRA SELVATICA; CANARD SAUVAGE; MALLARD; WILDENTE.

pressed wild duck, a very special and elaborate dish for which a press is necessary. The duck is roasted on a spit or in a hot oven for about 20 minutes, then removed and placed on a carving dish. The breast is carved in long fillets and the wings and legs are taken off. All are put into a chafing dish. The carcase, and the meat left on it, are now put into the press, which is a circular dish with a tight-fitting metal lid that can be raised and pressed down by a screw. The screw is tightened, and all the juices are squeezed out and collected in the rim of the press, which has a spout through which they can be poured off. The juices are then poured over the bird in the chafing dish, and the juice of a small orange is added, followed by a small glass (¼ cup) of brandy. The brandy is lit. When the flames have died down, the dish is ready. Pressed wild duck is sometimes served with an orange salad. See also CANETON.

wild goose (*Anser*), a name applied particularly to the barnacle goose and to the greylag, from which the modern domestic goose is descended, but used more generally to cover a great many different varieties of the same family. Wild geese are much loved by sportsmen all over the world as it requires a good deal of skill to shoot them. Unfortunately, as far as food is concerned, a wild goose will not bear comparison with a domestic one, for it is a lean bird with little of the succulence of the latter; however, if the bird is young it can be prepared and cooked by exactly the same methods. It should be hung for at least a week before eating. See also GOOSE.

wild rice (*Graminaceae*), an annual water-grass of which there are several species, growing chiefly in North America (*Zizania aquatica*) and parts of Asia (*Z. caducifolia*). It belongs to the same family as rice, but its grey and brown grains which are both delicious and nutritious, are at least twice the length of ordinary rice grains and have a flavour all their own. Harvesting is still done in a very primitive way, and in the U.S. is carried out almost exclusively by the Chipewa Indians, who call wild rice the "good berry" and believe that the "Great Spirit" provided it specifically to make them fit and strong. The harvest takes place once a year, in September, the time of the "Rice Moon"; Indians come from miles around in their canoes to help gather it. It is a delicate operation, for the wind and rain can very easily damage the ripened grains or blow them into the water. These circumstances, together with the exceedingly small amount that is grown, make wild rice expensive even in its country of origin. However, it is economical to use, and has a unique, almost nutty taste. The wildfowl that feed on it are much prized by gourmets for their excellent flavour.

Wild rice is cooked by being first brought to the boil in water which is then strained off, then cooked in a very little fresh water for 30 minutes or so until the long greyish-brown seeds open slightly. It is excellent for stuffing game or poultry, or served as a dish on its own with onion, tomatoes, and sweet peppers. See also RICE.

wildente, German for wild duck. In Germany it is often roasted with crushed juniper berries and butter, after which stock and sour cream are added to the pan juices and reduced. The duck is served on large croûtons covered with a paste of the cooked liver and heart, bacon, and herbs. See also WILD DUCK.

wildschwein, German for wild boar, which is eaten in a variety of ways in Germany. When young it is known as *frischling*. Wild boar can be roasted, stewed, or made into a delicious *pâté;* its taste resembles that of a strong bacon. If the animal is over six months old the joints should be marinated for several days before cooking. See also BOAR.

wildschweinsrücken, cutlets of wild boar, marinated in buttermilk overnight and then dried, before cooking with juniper berries and other herbs.

William, a variety of English pear which is very juicy and sweet. It is known as the Bartlett pear in the U.S.

wilstermarschkäse, a German semi-hard cheese made in Schleswig-Holstein from cow's milk. It is rather similar to *tilsiter käse*, but it is made by a different process and the period of curing is shorter. It is somewhat acidic in flavour.

wilted cucumber, an American term for peeled cucumber soaked in salted water or sprinkled with salt before serving.

wilted lettuce, an American speciality consisting of a cos (romaine) lettuce, washed and crisp, served with a sauce made from 1 fried sliced onion, 2 diced bacon rashers, 1 teaspoon sugar, and ½ cup vinegar, all heated and well stirred and poured hot over the lettuce.

Wiltshire cheese, a cheese of which there are 2 varieties, both having some resemblance to Gloucester. The first is shaped like a Gloucester, but the curd is heated twice and this increases the fermentation and alters the teyture and flavour; it is better than a single Gloucester in taste. The second variety is made in small cylindrical cheeses known as "Wiltshire loaves"; the curd is heated only once and the cheese tastes very like a Gloucester.

Wiltshire loaves, see WILTSHIRE CHEESE.

Windsor soup, I. A rich beef consommé slightly thickened with arrowroot, flavoured with turtle herbs and sherry, and garnished with strips of calf's foot. II. A veal stock thickened with ground rice, flavoured with turtle herbs, and garnished with strips of calf's foot. Sometimes egg yolks are used instead of ground rice.

windy pasty, a favourite method of using up pastry left over after making a batch of Cornish pasties. The pastry is rolled into a round, folded over, and crimped as for an ordinary pasty, then baked in the oven. While still hot the pasty is opened out, both sides of it are filled with ham, and it is eaten warm, just as it is.

wine jelly, an old English and Scottish dessert dish which was often served to convalescents. It makes a delicious sweet course, with restorative qualities. First 1 lemon is washed and peeled, and the juice is squeezed out and heated up with ½ pint (1 cup) water, 2 teaspoons red currant jelly, 2 oz. (¼ cup) powdered glucose, and ½ oz. (1 heaped tablespoon) gelatine. The mixture is stirred until the gelatine has dissolved, then it is drawn to the side of the stove and allowed to infuse for 15 minutes. Finally ½ pint (1 cup) port wine is added, and the jelly is strained and poured into individual bowls. Red wine may be used instead of port wine, but the latter is more usual.

wine sauce, I. A sweet sauce for serving with hot, usually steamed, puddings. A roux of 2 oz. (¼ cup) butter and 2 oz. (½ cup) flour is thinned with 1 pint (2 cups) sweet white wine, heated and stirred well. When it has thickened and become smooth, sugar and grated lemon peel are added. It is served hot. See also WHITE WINE SAUCE. II. A savoury sauce made in the same way as white wine sauce, but omitting the sugar and lemon, and using either red wine or port. See also MARCHAND DE VIN.

wineberry or **wine raspberry** (*Rubus phœnicolasius*), the fruit of a Chinese and Japanese wild raspberry, first brought to Britain in 1876 and to the U.S., where it is now cultivated, in 1889. Two species, *R. kuntzeanus* and *R. biflorus,* have been hybridized with the Cuthbert and Latham raspberries, respectively; these yield a delicious fruit and also have extremely decorative foliage. The berries are about half the size of a raspberry, coloured orange-red and yellow to begin with but turning a deep blood-red when fully ripe. They are eaten raw with cream, or cooked. All species are easily grown from seed, which is available in Britain and Europe as well as in the U.S. See also HYBRID BERRIES.

winkle, a common English name for the periwinkle.

winter berry, I. The fruit of the evergreen shrub *Gaultheria procumbens,* grown in the U.S. It is also called checkerberry or spicy wintergreen. It is red in colour, with a spicy flavour, and like the cranberry, is used mainly for pies, puddings, stuffings, and sauces. II. *Ilex laevigata,* a deciduous shrub from the eastern U.S., a member of the ilex family and related to the holly. It has an orange-red fruit, globose and rather flattened, with an acid taste when raw, but edible when cooked with sugar.

winter cress (*Barbarea vulgaris*), an herb which is a member of the same family as watercress, and has smooth, shining dark-green leaves and an erect angular stem bearing yellow flowers. It grows freely in moist places. It is known in the U.S. as rocket salad. See also WATERCRESS.

winter greens, a name given to kale and turnip tops.

winterthur, à la, a French method of serving lobster or crawfish. It is cooked in a court bouillon, drained, then covered with shrimp sauce and stuffed with a salpicon of peeled shrimps and crawfish.

wishbone, the popular name for the merrythought bone, and also for the cut of chicken containing it. When broken between 2 people, the person who secures the longer forked part of the bone is supposed to be granted his or her wish. Other birds have a similar bone, but it is not called a wishbone, and magical properties are not attributed to it.

witch flounder (*Glyptocephalus cynoglossus*), a large deep-sea flounder found in the North Atlantic. It is also called pole flounder, or fluke.

witloof, a Belgian chicory, the name meaning literally "white leaf." It can be eaten raw or cooked, and the slightly bitter white leaves with their pale green tips are now popular all over the world. It is also called chicorée de Bruxelles and barbe de bouc in Belgium and France. See also CHICORY.

witloof cultivation in Belgium

witte bonen, Dutch for dried white beans of the haricot variety, served in stews, soups, and salads in Holland.

witte saus, a white sauce used in Holland to accompany braised sweetbreads. A roux is made with 2 oz. (¼ cup) butter and 2 oz. (½ cup) flour, then 1 pint (2 cups) stock from the sweetbreads is added and the sauce is heated and stirred until smooth. Finally, 1 tablespoon brandy is added. This sauce can also be served with poultry or brains.

wolf fish (*Anarrhichas*), a sea fish found in the deep waters of the Arctic Ocean and other northern seas. When approaching the shore to breed, wolf fish is often caught, and after head and skin have been removed, it is frequently sold in England as rock salmon. It is also sold a great deal in Germany, where it is called seewolf. Wolf fish makes quite good eating and can be baked, fried, poached, or grilled. In France it is called *loup marin.*

wolf fish

wood grouse, an alternative name for *capercaillie.*

wood pigeon (*Columba palumbus*), the commonest form of

wild pigeon in the British Isles, and also one of the largest. It can be cooked in any way that is suitable for pigeon, and should be hung for a few days before being used. Only squabs, young pigeons under 6 months old, should be roasted, but older birds can be casseroled with either stock or dark beer, or, with a little chopped steak added, made into pigeon pie. See also PIGEON.

wood pigeon casserole, 4 chopped leeks are turned in butter, and 4 split pigeons are browned in the same way and placed on top; they are covered with a small rasher of bacon, seasoned, and three-quarters covered with stock. The pan is tightly covered and the birds are cooked in a moderate oven for 45–60 minutes or until tender.

wood sorrel (*Oxalis acetosella*), an herbaceous plant common in both Europe and North America. Its leaves resemble those of a four-leaf clover and have a pleasantly bitter taste. They are used in green salads and can also be prepared in the same way as sorrel.

woodchuck (*Marmota monax*), a North American rodent, also called groundhog and, popularly, prairie dog. It is in fact a marmot or ground squirrel, and is ardently hunted in the U.S. It is herbivorous, and although only about 20 inches long it can weigh from 6 to 10 lb. When young, woodchuck makes very good eating and tastes like a cross between duck and squirrel; however, the small red glands situated high up in each foreleg near the body must be cut out before cooking. It should be prepared for cooking by being soaked overnight in a marinade, or in water if no marinade is at hand; then it can be pot roasted with root vegetables, or simmered and then made into a pie. If young it can be stuffed with prunes, apples, and onions, and roasted.

woodcock (*Scolopax rusticola*), a game bird related to the snipe, but unlike snipe not restricted to marshes for its habitat. It is found almost all over the world. Woodcock is usually hung for a day or so, but not drawn as the trail is considered a great delicacy by gastronomes everywhere. However, it can also be eaten when freshly shot. Like almost all small game birds, it does not need long cooking; it should be pink but not bloody. When grilling woodcock, whether the bird is freshly shot or has been hung, a time of approximately 7 minutes for each side, over a good but not blazing fire, is enough. A touch of the fire enhances the delicious flavour, but care must be taken that the flesh does not char.

woodcock

Woodcock is trussed by crossing the legs and bringing the head down towards the flanks, then pushing the beak side-

ways through the leg-flesh to keep the legs in position. Gourmets say that for a ragoût, the best part is the wing, but that in a roast the leg is best. All recipes for quail can be used for woodcock. See also BÉCASSE.

salmi of woodcock, a recipe also suitable for partridge or grouse. A brace of woodcock is half-cooked by roasting or braising very lightly for about 15 minutes. The birds are then jointed and all the pieces are put into a saucepan with stock to cover and simmered for 10–15 minutes. They are then piled on a dish, and the heads are added, with their bills, so that the identity of the birds is plain. (This part of the method is not followed in the case of grouse or partridge.) A sauce is then made with 1 glass (½ cup) port or claret, and seasoning and is added to the stock in which the birds have been cooked. This is reduced for 10 minutes on a gentle heat; a *beurre manié* is added and allowed to thicken the sauce slightly, and the sauce is then poured over the birds.

woodcock flambée, 2 woodcock are allowed for each person, and the undrawn birds are roasted in a few ounces of butter in a hot oven for about 15 minutes. They are then cut into pieces—first they are cut in half, then the legs and wings are cut off—and all the separate pieces are put into a warm dish. The intestines are finely chopped and the blood squeezed out, and both are mixed together well with the juices in the baking tin. Seasoning is added to taste, and a glass of brandy is poured over and set alight. The whole is reduced on a good heat on top of the stove (or, preferably, the whole operation is carried out in a chafing-dish), and a squeeze of lemon juice, 2 tablespoons red wine, and some black pepper are added. The sauce is boiled up and further reduced just a little, then poured over the hot pieces of woodcock. It is served at once.

For those who find the taste of the trail too strong, the following alternative method of preparation is ideal as it separates the trail from the carcase so that only those who like it need eat it. The birds are drawn, then roasted as before, but the trail is fried separately in butter with a little marjoram or basil, salt, and pepper, then mashed well and spread on crustless slices of fried bread. The pieces of woodcock are served on these. It is a good idea to fry the pieces of bread in the butter in which the woodcock have been roasted, for the resulting flavour is quite unique.

woodruff (*Asperula odorata*), an old English and European herb with pretty china-blue flowers and pale green leaves. It develops a sweet, hay-like smell as it dries, and used to be made into a medicinal tea. It is now an important ingredient in a German wine cup and is also used in Austrian cooking. See also WALDMEISTER.

worcester berry, see HYBRID BERRIES.

worcestershire sauce, one of the most popular commercially bottled English sauces. Some of its ingredients are soya beans, garlic, old and matured anchovies, West Indian tamarinds, onion, limes, spices, and vinegar.

worst, see ROOKWORST.

wortleberry, an alternative name for bilberry.

wrasse (*Labridae*), the collective name for a number of sea fish found on the European coasts of the Atlantic. The one most used for food is the *girella* or rainbow wrasse, which is often used as an ingredient of bouillabaisse. See also LABRUS.

würst, German for sausage. Sausage is a country-wide speciality in Germany, and wurst is made in many farmhouses, in private homes, and commercially, and is eaten extensively. It is served plainly boiled, hot or cold, or fried; if smoked, it is eaten raw or spread on bread. The most usual accompaniments are *kartoffelsalat* and sauerkraut. The sausages vary slightly in different localities, and many imitations are made all over the world. Good German beer should be drunk with them, and a dish of *weisswürste* accompanied by the dark or light beer made by the nuns at Andechs in Bavaria makes a memorable meal. A würstchen is a small sausage, for example frankfurter würstchen. Beutwürst is a black pudding wurst. See also: AUGSBURGER WURST; BRATWURST; BUNDNERWURST; CERVELATWURST; FRANKFURTER WÜRSTCHEN; GEHIRNWURST; GERÄUCHERTE BRATWÜRSTE; HAMMELWÜRSTE; JÄGERWURST; KNACKWÜRSTE; KNOBLAUCHWÜRST; KÖNIGSWURST; LEBERWURST; MECKLENBURGER BRATWURST; METTWURST; NÜRNBERGERWÜRSTE; PINKELWÜRST; REGENSBURGERWURST; RINDFLEISCHWURST; RINDHEISCHWURST; SAUSAGE; SCHWÄBISCHE WÜRSTE; SCHWARZWÜRSTE; STREICHWURST; TEEWURST; WEISSWÜRSTE; WÜRSTE VON KALBSGEKRÖSE.

würstelbraten, an original Austrian method of larding a lean joint of beef with whole frankfurter sausages. A hole is made in the meat with a large skewer and the sausage is pushed through. The larded meat is then dusted with salt, pepper, paprika, and flour and fried on all sides in fat with a sliced onion. It is then transferred to a casserole, a large glass of water is added, and the meat is slowly cooked until tender.

Sometimes sour cream or yogourt is added to the gravy. The meat is served sliced, so that each round has small pieces of sausage in it.

wurstsuppe, a peasant soup made in the south of Germany from the stock in which freshly made sausages have been cooked.

würste von kalbsgekröse, German würst made from calf's mesentery. The mesentery is blanched and finely chopped, seasoned with nutmeg, salt, and pepper, and mixed with eggs and cream (2 eggs and ¾ cup cream for every 2 lb. meat). This mixture is put into pork gut casings and poached. When cool, the sausages are fried in butter. See also WURST.

wurstkraut, the German term for herbs such as sweet marjoram and savory that are used to flavour certain *würste.*

würz, German for spice or seasoning.

würzfleisch, a spicy stew or ragoût. The term also means spiced meat.

würzkräuter, a general German term for aromatic herbs with a very pungent smell.

xavier, I. A classical French soup consisting of beef consommé thickened with arrowroot, flavoured with Madeira and garnished with fine strips of unsweetened pancake. See also CONSOMMÉ. II. A French *potage* velouté, made from chicken-based sauce velouté blended with rice flour and garnished with diced chicken and royale garnish.

xerotiyana, see DIPLES.

ximenia, see TALLOW WOOD.

xiphios, Greek for swordfish, usually cut into steaks in Greece, then brushed with oil and grilled or served *plaki*.

xouba, a small Spanish fish not unlike a sardine in size and taste. It is usually served grilled over charcoal.

xouba

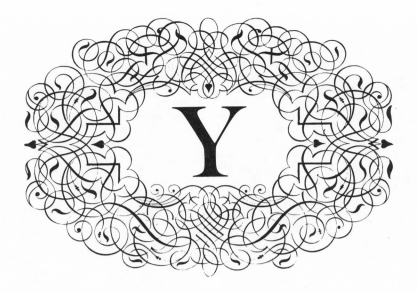

Y

yabloko, Russian for apple. Apples are used in many ways in Russia: for stuffing goose or duck, fried in rings as an accompaniment for fried or poached chicken or fish, in *kissel,* and for making jam. They are also preserved. See also APPLE.

sup iz yablok, a cold apple soup which is of Polish origin but also very popular in Russia. It is made with 2 lb. apples, 1 pint (2 cups) red wine, juice of 1 lemon, 8 oz. (1 cup) sugar, 4 tablespoons black currant jelly, a 1-inch stick of cinnamon, and 4 oz. (1½ cups) breadcrumbs. The apples are first cooked with the sugar and a little water until soft; then they are rubbed through a sieve, and all the other ingredients are added. Sometimes dumplings of grated apple mixed with breadcrumbs and egg are poached, drained, and added to the soup.

yabloki mochenye, preserved cooking-apples. Sound, whole apples are layered in a deep earthenware pot or barrel with black currant or *kizil* leaves. The apples are arranged stalks upwards, and the final layer is one of leaves. They are then covered with either a sweet or a non-sweet liquid, depending on whether the apples are wanted sweet or sour. For a sweet liquid, 1 lb. (2 cups) sugar and 3 tablespoons salt are boiled with 20 (40 cups) pints water. The liquid is cooled, then poured over the apples so that it reaches 3 inches above the top layer. After 4 days it is topped with plain cold water since the apples absorb a lot of liquid. The apples are ready for use in a month's time, but they will keep indefinitely if stored in a cold place. For a non-sweet liquid, ½ lb. (1¾ cups) rye flour and 2 tablespoons salt are mixed with 20 pints (40 cups) boiling water. The mixture is not boiled again but allowed to cool, then strained and used as for the sweet liquid.

yahni, a Greek method of cooking. The food is braised with onions in olive oil, then a little water and sometimes tomatoes are added, and all are simmered until cooked.

yahni, the Turkish term for a meat stew, usually made of mutton in Turkey but occasionally of lamb or even hare. See also PAPAZ YAHNISSI.

bèyaz yahni, a white stew made with a thick cut from leg of mutton which includes part of the bone and weighs about 3 lb. It is cut into pieces which are first fried in mutton fat, then simmered for 20 minutes in water to cover, and then skimmed. Next 3 sliced onions, ½ lb. soaked chick-peas, and seasoning are added, and all are cooked until tender. This stew is usually served with rice or toasted bread.

mayandozlu yahni, a mutton stew, cooked as above until after the liquid has been skimmed. Then 3 lightly fried onions are added and simmered until nearly cooked, when 2 handfuls chopped parsley are included and the stew is cooked for a further 15 minutes. The juice of 2 lemons beaten up with 4 egg yolks is then added to chicken, and the stew is stirred constantly but not allowed to boil.

tavşan yahni, a hare stew. Chopped hare is stewed with water to cover, 6 thinly sliced onions, salt, and pepper, until the onions are half cooked. The stock is strained into a basin and then boiled in a saucepan with ¾ pint (1½ cups) wine vinegar and 10 peeled garlic cloves until reduced by half. The half-cooked onions are fried in butter, and both these and the stock are poured over the hare, and cooking is resumed until the hare is tender and a thick gravy has formed.

yàlàndji-dòlmàs, see DÒLMÀ.

yam (Dioscorea), a climbing plant of which there are many species. It has an edible root, large and bulbous with white flesh and a pinkish-brown skin. It tastes not unlike a sweet potato, and can be prepared in the same way. A starch product called Guiana arrowroot is extracted from the species *Dioscorea alata.* Yams are grown in South and Central America,

yam

in the East, and in the West Indies, and are imported into Europe. They are particularly popular in the southern states of the U.S. and are a common ingredient in soul food. They are often prepared by being boiled or baked until tender and then candied with 4 oz. (½ cup) butter and ½ cup molasses (to about 2 lb. yams), or they may be cooked in butter, mixed with chopped pecan nuts and sprinkled with cinnamon. They can also be boiled, drained, and made into fritters.

yaourti, Greek for yogourt, usually made of ewe's milk in Greece. Greek yogourt is of excellent quality and is used in many recipes, both sweet and savoury. See also TSATSIKI; YOGOURT.

yaourtopita, I. An extremely light and moist cake made with yogourt. First 4 oz. (½ cup) butter is creamed with 1 lb. (2 cups) sugar; 10 oz. (2½ cups) flour which has been mixed with ½ teaspoon baking soda and the same of salt is added, alternately with 2 beaten eggs and 1 cup yogourt, to the butter and sugar mixture. The mixture is poured into a greased tin and baked in a moderate oven for 40 minutes. Sometimes the eggs are separated and the stiffly beaten whites added last. When cooked, and while still warm, the cake is covered with either a sugar and water syrup or icing sugar. II. A tart made with ½ lb. cream cheese beaten with 1 cup yogourt until smooth; then 3 tablespoons honey and 1 teaspoon vanilla are added, and the mixture is poured into a baked pastry shell to be chilled for 24 hours before serving.

Yarmouth bloater, see BLOATER.

yarrow (*Achillea millefolium*), sometimes called milfoil, a European herb with strongly scented leaves rather like chervil, and very good in salad or with cottage cheese. There are about 100 species of the genus *Achillea,* many of them alpine plants which grow especially well in Switzerland. Yarrow is now grown also in the U.S. See also ACHILLÉE.

yaytsa or *jajtza,* Russian for eggs. A popular egg dish in Russia is *zapekanka,* often served on its own without meat. Hard-boiled eggs are used in a variety of ways. They are served in salads with pickled cucumbers, lettuce, and sour cream, and they are also stuffed with breadcrumbs, mushrooms, ham, onion, and herbs, then covered with melted butter and grated cheese, and baked; sometimes the baked stuffed eggs are set on a layer of mashed potato. Hard-boiled eggs are also used as a garnish for salted herrings; chopped filleted salt herrings and cooked spinach are also served mixed into scrambled eggs. Hard-boiled eggs are served as an accompaniment to caviar; or the whites are stuffed with caviar and the yolks are sieved, mixed with mayonnaise, and spread over the caviar-stuffed whites. For Russian egg sauce, see sous. See also EGG; KRASHENIE YAYTSA.

yeast (*Saccharomyces cerevisiae*), a single-celled fungus used in the production of alcohol by fermentation. The fermentative process, however, as well as converting sugar solutions into alcohol converts a part of the sugar into carbon dioxide gas, and it is this latter effect—a mere by-product in brewing—that makes yeast indispensable as leaven in bread and cake making. (Alcohol is still inevitably produced during the proving of a yeast dough, but, it is driven off in the course of the subsequent baking operation.)

By a process of continuous selection and propagation, 2 chief varieties of yeast have been developed, brewer's yeast and baker's yeast, each being especially well adapted to its particular purpose. Good baker's yeast is obtainable in most European countries and in Canada and the U.S. In the U.S. active yeast is also sold dried and compressed in airtight packages, and in Britain this dehydrated form is available in airtight tins. It is treated as ordinary fresh baker's yeast, but only half the usual amount is required (instructions are given on the containers).

yeast dough, the first thing to remember in the preparation of any dough is that when using yeast, the flour, water, and utensils must be warm, but not hot, as strong heat would destroy the living organisms in the yeast. The amount of yeast required varies considerably with the quantity and quality of flour to be used in the dough, the liquid and fat content of the dough, the amount of time to be allowed for rising, and the general temperature of the surroundings.

A larger proportion of yeast to flour is needed for a small quantity of flour than for a large quantity. Unless otherwise stated in a specified recipe, these are the amounts:

½ oz. yeast for up to 1½ lb. (6 cups) flour

1 oz. yeast for over 1½ lb. (6 cups) and up to 3½ lb. (14 cups) flour

1½ oz. yeast for over 3½ lb. (14 cups) and up to 7 lb. (28 cups) flour

2 oz. yeast for over 7 lb. (28 cups) and up to 14 lb. (56 cups) flour

Wholemeal flour requires more yeast than white flour; if proportions suitable for a white loaf are used for a wholemeal loaf, the wholemeal loaf will be too solid. About 3 lb. (12 cups) wholemeal flour needs 1¼ oz. yeast and about 1½ pints (3 cups) warm milk and water mixed. If white flour is added to ⅓ the above proportion of wholemeal, 1 oz. yeast will be enough. Both these quantities will need at least 2 hours' rising time.

The less yeast is used, the longer the dough is to be left to rise. Thus, for a recipe using 1 pint (2 cups) liquid, proportions would be as follows: if the dough is to be left overnight in a warm place, such as an airing-cupboard or a room temperature of 68°F (20°C), only ¼ oz. yeast will rise well; if it is to be left to rise for 5 hours, 1 oz. yeast will be needed; if it is to be left to rise for 3 hours, 2 oz. yeast will be needed. Thus, 1 oz. yeast will rise 6 lb. (24 cups) flour if the dough is to be left overnight; but a more convenient equation would be 1 oz. yeast for 4 lb. (16 cups) flour, with 2–3 hours to rise in a warm place. (It is also possible for yeast dough to rise in a cold place if it is wrapped in greased polythene bags or in stout, covered plastic containers, but in this event rising takes at least 12 hours, and the dough must be allowed to stand in a warm room temperature for 20–30 minutes before it is shaped into rolls or loaves.)

Mixtures containing eggs, or a larger amount of fat than 2 tablespoons, require more yeast or a longer time to rise. Light, spongy open-textured rolls or buns can take as much as 1 oz. yeast to raise 1 lb. (4 cups) flour. The addition of butter or other fat to the dough produces a soft crust and keeps the roll or bun fresh and soft for a longer time. A crisp crust is achieved if no fat is used, and the baked bread is brushed with cold water and put back for a few minutes in the oven.

Kneading is very important in the preparation of yeast dough, for it produces a finely textured loaf. See also BREAD; DOUGH; FLOUR; SODA BREAD.

white household bread, 4 lb. (16 cups) flour is mixed with 1 tablespoon salt in a basin and a well is made in the middle. Then 1 oz. (1 package) yeast is creamed with 1 teaspoon sugar and 2 pints (4 cups) lukewarm water, and poured into the well in the flour. The whole is gently stirred so that the flour from the sides falls into the liquid, until a liquid batter is formed. The top of the batter is thickly sprinkled with the flour remaining on the sides. The dough is covered with a cloth and left in a warm, even temperature for about 30 minutes, or until the batter has broken through the surface of the flour—a process which takes place fairly quickly and is called "sponging." The dough is then beaten and kneaded by hand (or on a kneading-hook supplied with some electric blenders), first in the bowl and then on a floured table. It is then put back in the bowl, cut with a cross on top to allow even air distribution, covered, and left in a warm place for at least 2 hours. It is then shaped into loaves (this amount will make 4 small or 2 large loaves), which are covered again and left for 20–30 minutes until they have risen well; this action is known as "proving" the dough. If the loaves are put into tins, the tins must be lightly greased, and only half-filled so that the dough can rise to the top in the last 30 minutes of proving. The loaves are baked in a hot oven for the first 15 minutes, then temperature is reduced to moderate and cooking continued for 45 minutes, when the loaves draw slightly away from the sides of the tins. A properly cooked loaf has a hollow sound when tapped on the bottom. Rolls are made from the same mixture, but are shaped into rolls or twists and baked in a hot oven for 15–20 minutes. Wholemeal bread is made in the same way, proportions being 3 lb. (12 cups) wholemeal flour to 1 lb. (4 cups) white flour and 1 oz. yeast, with sugar and liquid as above.

yeast dough with butter and eggs, dough that can be used for a variety of breads, rolls, and pastries. Pastries made with the puff pastry *germbutterteig* are usually filled with jam, fruit, nuts, and a cream or cream cheese mixture. See GERM-BUTTERTEIG.

yeast soup, a soup which is popular in Czechoslovakia and is rich in vitamin B2. To prepare it 1 sliced onion and 3 oz. fresh yeast are fried in 2 oz. (¼ cup) butter, and when the yeast browns at the edges, 2 oz. (½ cup) plain flour is sprinkled over and mixed well in. Then 3 pints (6 cups) water is added, together with 1 finely chopped carrot, ½ celeriac root, Hamburg parsley root, and 1 small turnip, and all is seasoned, whisked well, and simmered for 20 minutes. Then 1 egg is beaten into a paste with 3 tablespoons milk and 3 oz. semolina, and small pieces of this are dropped into the boiling soup and cooked for 5 minutes.

yellow berry, the name by which the fruit of the cloudberry is known in Quebec.

yellow tail (*Lutianus chrysurus*), a long, beautiful, golden sea fish found in the warmer waters of the Atlantic. It is a member of the snapper family, and the flesh is firm, delicate, and good to eat. It is excellent stuffed and baked in the oven.

yellow tomato, see TOMATO.

yellowman, a traditional toffee made in Northern Ireland, and still eaten at the *Lammas* Day Fair at Ballycastle in County Antrim. It is made from 3 lb. golden syrup to 1 lb. treacle (molasses), ½ tablespoon vinegar, ½ cup (¼ pint) water and 1 teaspoon cream of tartar, all boiled for about 20 minutes or until the toffee is brittle. It is then put onto a greased slab and pulled with the hands so that a honeycomb effect is produced. Then it is cut into lengths with scissors. This toffee can also be made with brown sugar and butter, with a little water added; or it can be made all of treacle, in which case it is called "blackman."

yemas, literally "yolks" (*yema de huevo* is Spanish for egg yolk), but also the name of a Spanish sweetmeat (confection), the main ingredients of which are sugar and eggs. There are many recipes, some using cooked potatoes—ordinary white potatoes, and sweet potatoes (see BATATAS). First 1 lb. cooked and sieved sweet potatoes is beaten with 3 eggs which have been whipped with 1 lb. (2 cups) sugar; then 1 lb. ground almonds is worked in, and the paste is formed into small balls. These are rolled in icing sugar and left to dry for 24 hours, then wrapped individually in paper. When made with ordinary potatoes they are called yemas economicas. See also PATATA.

yemas de Santa Teresa, a speciality of Ávila. A thick syrup is made with 2 tablespoons sugar, 1 tablespoon water, ½ teaspoon powdered cinnamon, and 1 teaspoon grated lemon peel. This syrup is mixed rapidly with 6 beaten egg yolks in a double boiler until thickened and blended. It is beaten until cold, then poured onto a greased dish, shaped into a long roll, and when cold, cut into pieces.

yemas variadas, 12 egg yolks are beaten with ½ lb. (1 cup) sugar in a double boiler over gentle heat until thickened. The mixture is poured onto a slab covered with powdered sugar and formed into shapes. Chopped nuts, dates, prunes, cherries, candied fruits, etc., can be added as desired. The yemas can also be dipped in syrup after they have been made.

yemissis, Greek for stuffing, used for *dolmades* and other dishes.

yemissis horis kreas, literally "stuffing without meat," a stuffing for eggplants, courgettes (zucchini), or tomatoes consisting of onions, rice, pignoli, and parsley fried in olive oil.

yemissis me kreas ke rizi, a stuffing of meat and rice for hot *dolmades*. Minced lamb, onions, parsley, and seasoning are fried in hot olive oil; then rice is added, followed by stock and sage, and all is cooked until the rice is ready and the liquid is absorbed. It is left to cool before being used.

yemissis me kreas ke selinor, a stuffing for eggplants, courgettes (zucchini), or tomatoes consisting of minced meat, onion, celery, cinnamon, rice, and parsley fried in olive oil.

yemissis me rizi, a meatless stuffing for cold *dolmades* of onions, rice, tomato purée, currants, pignoli, sage, mint, and sugar.

yemista, the Greek term for vegetables stuffed with minced meat and rice, and either simmered or baked until cooked.

yermades, the name of an excellent peach grown in Greece.

yialandji, the Greek word for a dish that has no meat in it, such as *dolmades, imam bayeldi, kolokithaki yahni,* or *spanakopita*. Such dishes are usually served cold.

yiouvetsi, a speciality of Athens. Cubed lamb is braised in tomato sauce or soup. When cooked, the meat is removed to a hot dish, and noodles or macaroni are cooked in the sauce. The meat is put back before serving, and the dish is garnished with *kasseri* cheese. Yiouvetsi can also be made with veal. See also DUVEČ; GHIVECI.

yogourt, milk which has been inoculated with *Lactobacillus bulgaricus,* which thickens the milk until it is like a creamy curd. It is most popular all over the Balkans, in Russia, Persia, and Turkey. It is said to have many health-giving properties, and elderly Balkans claim it is the secret to their longevity. It is also good for stomach ailments. There are many stories concerning the origin of yogourt. One claims that it was discovered by nomadic Turks who carried their milk in gourds slung over the backs of camels, where the sun and the constant movement encouraged the development of the bacillus. Another story tells that early Greeks who left their goat and sheep milk exposed to bacteria in the open air, found that it developed a new character which was liked so much that yogourt became a staple part of Greek diet. According to another legend, the 16th-century French king Francis I was the first man in western Europe to realize the beneficial effect yogourt could have on intestinal disorders. It is reputed that his ambassador in Turkey first recommended it to him, and that an aged Jewish doctor from Constantinople walked with a herd of sheep and goats across Bulgaria, Serbia, Hungary, Austria, and Germany to the French court, where he then proceeded to supply the king daily with yogourt, which vastly improved his health. But the old man refused to divulge the secret of its preparation, and after some months he departed with his flock the way he had come. It is said that the king's bad health returned, and that he died sorely lamenting the loss of the daily yogourt which had so alleviated his suffering. Scientifically speaking, however, it was Professor Massal at Geneva who, in about 1870, isolated the *Lactobacillus bulgari-*

cus in yogourt, and passed his information on to Professor Mechnikov (1845–1916) in Russia, where yogourt has become almost as popular as it is in the Balkans.

It is important to note that the ordinary souring of milk produced by *Lactobacillus acidophilus* is altogether inferior, both in flavour and effect, to the product of *L. bulgaricus*. It is therefore essential to use only fresh milk or cream for yogourt making. This is brought to boiling point for a few minutes, then cooled to a temperature of about 105°F–107°F (40°C). About 1 teaspoon yogourt per pint (1 cup) of milk is stirred well in, and the mixture is then kept in a warm place overnight. In cold climates a wide-necked vacuum flask makes perfect yogourt if securely corked and left to stand for a minimum of 8 hours. A teaspoonful of the culture must be reserved for the next time yogourt is to be made.

Yogourt can be eaten plain, with or without sugar. It also makes excellent sauces and soups, and is essential in the making of certain dishes and cakes, such as *yaourtopeta*. It can be stabilised so that it does not curdle when boiled by first whipping the yogourt until liquid, then adding 1 tablespoon of corn flour (cornstarch) to 2 pints yogourt and bringing it to the boil. It must be stirred constantly, in one direction only, and when boiling, simmered slowly for 10 minutes or until thick. It should then be left, uncovered, until cold. Yogourt can also be used to tenderize meat if the meat is soaked in it for some hours before cooking, as the lactic acid breaks down the tough fibres and tissues.

There are many alternative spellings of the word—yagourt, yogort, yoghourt, yoghurt, and yogurt. See also YAOURTI; YOĞURT.

yoğurt, Turkish for yogourt. See also YOGOURT.

yoğurtlu biber, a hors d'oeuvre made with chopped fried green peppers mixed with cold yogourt and salt.

yoğurtlu havuç kizartması, an hors d'oeuvre made with boiled carrots mixed with breadcrumbs and eggs, then sautéed in oil. It is served cold with yogourt and garlic mixed. This dish is similar to yoğurtlu biber.

yoğurtlu pideli kebab, a casserole is lined with *pide* and then filled with fried skinned tomatoes and grilled *keuftés*. It is covered with yogourt and baked in a hot oven for several minutes.

yoğurtlu şhalgm, or *kizartmasl,* parboiled turnips or carrots chopped into slices which are rolled in flour and fried in butter, then half covered with borth and simmered for 10 minutes. This dish is served with yogourt on top, and melted butter with a pinch of pepper.

York cheese, a soft fresh English farmhouse cheese, made from unskimmed cow's milk. It does not keep and is rarely seen for sale in shops. Cambridge cheese is identical, but is made during the summer months in and around the Isle of Ely instead of in the region of York, and is sold a few days after making. Together York and Cambridge may be classed as the most important English soft cheese after cream cheese.

York Club cutlets, a 19th-century English method of serving lamb cutlets, called after a London club of that name. A sauce is made from 4 large onions which are peeled, sliced, and boiled in a little water for 10 minutes, then drained (the stock being retained); they are then fried with 1 teaspoon sugar in a little butter until soft but not brown, when 1 tablespoon flour is added, followed by the warm onion stock, 1 cup warm milk, and finally 2 tablespoons cream. The cutlets are trimmed, and grilled on 1 side only, then put in a baking tin, raw side down, and covered with the onion sauce. The whole is sprinkled with breadcrumbs, dotted with butter, and cooked in a hot oven for 15–20 minutes until the top is browned.

York ham, a world-famous English ham. The original York

hams were said to have got their flavour by being smoked with the oak sawdust used in the building of York Minster. York ham comes from large white Yorkshires (see PIG), and is cured with salt, saltpetre, and coarse brown sugar for at least 3 weeks before being smoked. It is always eaten cooked, either hot or cold, and is very moist and succulent. See also HAM.

Yorkshire apple pudding, made in exactly the same way as Yorkshire pudding (I), but with 2 large peeled, cored, grated cooking apples mixed into the batter. The pudding is baked in 2 tablespoons butter or lard for 30–40 minutes and dredged with sugar when cooked. It is eaten hot. An identical dish is eaten in County Armagh, Ireland, on Halloween, but it is cooked by steaming in a basin; it is called simply, apple pudding.

Yorkshire boiled turkey, a traditional Yorkshire method of cooking turkey. Originally this dish was made with a boned turkey which was stuffed and sewn up to resemble its original shape, just like the "cockatrice" (the name for a chicken prepared in this way). It was usually eaten cold, carved across so that stuffing and turkey were served together.

The bird is stuffed with 1 lb. minced (ground) veal and 4 tablespoons grated suet, well seasoned, with a cooked and skinned pig's tongue put in the middle. Then ½ lb. diced salt pork is melted in a saucepan large enough to take the turkey, and when the cubes are browned, 2 sliced carrots and 1 celery heart, cut in half, are cooked until soft but not brown. The turkey is boned and stuffed as described above, and a large onion stuck with cloves is added, followed by giblet stock, water to reach half-way up the saucepan, and seasoning. The whole is covered and simmered very slowly for 4–5 hours, depending on the age and size of the bird. The turkey should be turned over at least once during cooking. When it is nearly ready, a sauce is made by melting 2 oz. (2 heaped tablespoons) butter in a small saucepan, adding 1½ heaped tablespoons flour and mixing in well, following it gradually with 1 pint (2 cups) hot turkey stock, stirring all the time. It is seasoned to taste and finally ¼ cup cream is mixed in. If the bird is served hot, the sauce is served separately; if cold, the turkey is skinned, and the sauce is poured over it.

Yorkshire herring pie, a traditional Yorkshire dish consisting of filleted herrings layered with sliced potatoes, sour apples, and butter. The pie is baked in the oven for about 1 hour.

Yorkshire pudding, a traditional English batter pudding served with roast beef. It was originally cooked in a pan under the roasting spit so that it was basted by all the juices from the beef. It was served hot from the fire, cut into pieces, before the meat course. Nowadays it is served with the meat, and although it is sometimes cooked under the joint of beef if the meat is being cooked on a trivet, it is more usually cooked in a separate baking tin. Sometimes it is baked in several small tins, but these individual puddings do not have quite the flavour of a large one. The batter should be made when the meat is first put in the oven, and left to stand so that the air gets into it. There are 2 methods of making Yorkshire pudding, the first one being an authentic Yorkshire recipe In this recipe 2 eggs are separated and both whites and yolks are beaten. Then 4 heaped tablespoons flour are mixed into the egg yolks, and this mixture is thinned down to the consistency of thick cream with about ¼ pint (½ cup) milk and water mixed; it is seasoned, and finally the stiff egg whites are added. The batter is then poured into about ½ inch sizzling-hot beef dripping and baked in a moderate oven for about 20 minutes, or until it is puffed up and cooked through. It will drop a little as it cools, like a soufflé, but it will be very light and crisp.

The other recipe uses 4 heaped tablespoons flour and a pinch of salt, mixed together; then a well is made in the centre and 2 eggs are mixed in; 1 pint (2 cups) milk is added gradually, beating all the time until a thick smooth batter is achieved. Lastly 1 teaspoon olive oil is mixed in, and the batter is beaten again, then covered and left to stand for 1 hour. It is cooked in the same way as the first recipe. It is essential that the fat should be sizzling-hot before the batter is poured in.

Yorkshire teacake, see TEACAKE.

Young America, a type of American cheddar.

youngberry, see HYBRID BERRIES.

youvarlakia, see GIOUVARLAKIA.

ysa, Icelandic for fresh haddock, which is of excellent quality in Iceland. It is often served hot with melted butter, or cold with mustard sauce. It is also smoked. See also HADDOCK.

yufka böreği, a Turkish pie. A pastry is made from 1 lb. (4 cups) flour and about 1 gill (½ cup) water, and this is rolled very thinly and cut into sheets which are baked on both sides on a baking sheet. They are then brushed with 2 beaten eggs, 2 oz. melted butter, and ¼ cup broth, and layered in a baking tin with fried minced meat and fried chopped onions. The top layer of pastry is brushed with egg and butter, and the pie is baked until golden brown. Cheese may be used instead of meat. In Turkey baking tins are circular, 1–2 feet in diameter and about 3 inches high, and are made of copper; baking sheets are often made of iron and are circular and slightly domed—these are used only for layers of flour and water paste, as described above.

yufkalı kadayif, a Turkish pudding. Three very thin slices of raw puff pastry are laid one on top of the other in a well-buttered baking tin, then covered with a 1-inch layer of boiled vermicelli sprinkled with 6 tablespoons melted butter, followed by 3 more slices of pastry. The pudding is pricked with a fork and baked until risen and golden, then covered with warm syrup. A lid is put on and the pudding is left for 15 minutes, then cut into squares or diamond shapes. It is eaten lukewarm.

Yugoslavian cheeses, see SIR.

Yule, an alternative word for Christmas from the Old English *géol.*

Yule-log cake, a cake shaped like a log, very popular at children's Christmas parties. It is usually made from a sponge mixture, or is rolled up like a Swiss roll; the top and sides are covered with melted chocolate and the top is then roughly iced with royal icing to represent snow, with glacé cherries and angelica strips to look like holly.

yuyo, the Spanish culinary word for a sauce flavoured with herbs, or greenstuff, such as spinach.

Yvette, I. A French method of cooking fish. The fish is poached with herbs and stock barely to cover, then thickened with *beurre manié,* glazed, and garnished with small tomatoes stuffed with sole purée. II. A French method of serving poached eggs, presented on corn fritters coated with sauce *archiduc.* III. A French method of serving scrambled eggs. They are mixed with crayfish tails, garnished with asparagus tips, and surrounded with shrimp sauce. IV. A French method of serving potatoes. See POMME YVETTE. V. A French soup made from lobster purée blended with fish velouté, garnished with tiny fish quenelles, chopped lobster, and truffles. VI. A French consommé of chicken flavoured with turtle herbs and garnished with tiny chicken quenelles and spinach. See also CONSOMMÉ.

zabaglione or zabaione, one of the best-known Italian sweet puddings. The true zabaglione is made solely from egg yolks, sugar, and Marsala (quantities per person are 2 egg yolks to 2 teaspoons fine white sugar and 1 gill (¼ cup) Marsala. The egg yolks and sugar are beaten until frothy, then the wine is added and the whole mixture stirred over a gentle heat (or in a

zabaglione

double-boiler) until it thickens. It must not boil, and it must be whisked all the time. It is served in warmed glasses. It can also be served frozen hard, when it is known as *zabaglione gelato*. In the U.S. it is served as a custard, and is also served iced, when it is beaten over ice and either dissolved gelatin is added, and then it is all beaten, or stiffly whipped cream is added to make it keep its shape. The hot zabaglione can also be served as a sauce with hot puddings, and in the Italian Alps it is made with dry Marsala and served with partridge. See also SABAYON.

żabki, Polish for frog's legs. Zabki smażone are fried frog's legs. See also FROG.

żabki w potrawce, frog's legs dusted with flour, sautéed in butter, and then simmered for 30 minutes with mushrooms,

sweetbreads, stock, and white wine, all seasoned. Finally the stock is thickened with egg yolks.

zacierka, a very dry Polish dough which is grated into soups as a garnish. It is made from 1 cup flour to 1 egg. It is best if no water is used, but a little may be added if the egg is small. The dough is grated into the boiling soup 5 minutes before serving. Zacierki may be stored in a cold place for use when required. See also KLUSKI FRANCUSKI; KNELKI; LANE CIASTO.

zadělávané dršky, tripe cooked in traditional Czechoslovak style. First 2 lb. tripe is partially cooked by boiling in water for 30 minutes, drained, then cut into thin strips and simmered in 4 oz. (½ cup) butter with 1 chopped onion and garlic. Then 2 tablespoons flour is sprinkled over and 1 pint (2 cups) stock is added. When it is simmering, ½ lb. chopped ham and 2 tablespoons chopped parsley are mixed in, and the whole is gently simmered for a further 2 hours or until tender. See also TRIPE.

zafferano, Italian for saffron, used especially in Italy for risotto alla Milanese and for *zuppa di pesce.* See also SAFFRON.

zährte, German for *zarthe.* See also ZARTHE.

zährte in gelee, zarthe poached in stock with dill and seasoning, and left to gel. *Zährte in gelee* is also sold commercially.

zając, Polish for hare, which is eaten a great deal in Poland, generally stewed as a civet, or jugged or casseroled. It is also cooked in the Russian manner with root vegetables and sour cream. See also GAME; HARE; ZAYATS.

zając do zimnej zastawy, an impressive-looking and excellent-tasting cold dish, made from the saddles and hind legs of 2 hares. First the saddles are roasted, and when cold they are boned and put on one side. Next a *pâté* is made from the liver, salt pork, and the front legs of the hares, which have been simmered with onion, celery, leek, carrot, parsley, juniper berries, bay leaf, peppercorns, salt, and a little water. The meat is strained and finely pounded or minced (ground) twice, then mixed with 4 anchovy fillets, 4 hard-boiled egg yolks, and 4 tablespoons olive oil. Finally 1 tablespoon French mustard, lemon juice, and pepper are added. The saddle fillets are spread with this mixture, and all is covered with aspic jelly, allowed to get cold and set, and then served with salad with a mayonnaise dressing.

zając duszony po myśliwsku, hare cooked hunter's-style. It is casseroled for 2½ hours with ½ lb. diced salt pork, 12 shallots, 2 teaspoons paprika, 6 juniper berries, 1 pint (2 cups) red wine, seasonings, and chopped herbs, then served with cooked red cabbage.

zajęczy pasztet, pâté made from the front legs, neck, and giblets of a hare simmered for 45 minutes in 1 pint (2 cups) stock with 4 slices of bacon or salt pork, 1 carrot, 1 onion, 1 bay leaf, a sprig each of thyme, marjoram, and parsley, and 4 juniper berries all seasoned to taste. The meat is removed from the bones and chopped or minced finely, as are the bacon and hare liver. Then 2 tablespoons cream, 2 egg yolks, salt, and pepper are added and beaten well until the pâté is creamy. It is served on croutons. See also GRZANKI FAS-ZEROWANE ZAJĄCEM.

zakuski, Russian for hors d'oeuvre, which in Russia may include stuffed eggs, radishes, anchovy fillets, oysters, caviar, smoked sturgeon or smoked salmon, sardines, small marinated fish of various kinds, sausages, cheese, or *pirozhki* filled with fish or meat. They are served with vodka or other spirits, in glass or china dishes, in a room adjoining the dining room. See also HORS D'OEUVRE.

zalatina, a unique Cypriot brawn made from pig's head or lean pork or veal, the jelly flavoured with bitter orange or lemon juice, chilli, rosemary, cinnamon, and cloves.

zalivnoe, a cold jellied Russian dish which may be made from fish, meat, poultry, game, or eggs, with vegetables cooked with them. The stock, if not gelatinous enough, is set with aspic.

zalivnoe iz ryabchikov, as above, made with cooked stuffed hazel grouse usually garnished with cooked beetroot, capers, and potatoes. Sometimes mayonnaise is served separately.

zalivnoe s solonine, as above, but made with layers of cooked salt beef, root vegetables, and hard-boiled eggs. It is served with a mustard sauce.

zamboriña, a local name used by fishermen off the northwest coast of Spain for the queen scallop. See SCALLOP.

zampone di Modena, an Italian speciality of a stuffed pig's trotter (foot) and part of the leg. All the meat is carefully removed and boned, the tough skin being left intact to contain the stuffing. This forcemeat is made from the pork removed from the leg skin, bacon, truffles (all finely minced), and seasoning; it is reinserted in the pig's leg skin and the whole is then cured and smoked. The stuffed trotter (foot) is prepared for cooking by being soaked overnight in cold water, the skin being incised with a fine skewer to allow for swelling. It is then boiled in water, lying flat, for 3–4 hours. It is served very hot, usually with cooked black lentils or dried white beans, and is a traditional New Year's Day dish. Zampone are also sold commercially.

zander, the German name for a giant perch or pike-perch found mainly in the rivers Elbe and Danube. It is a gastronomic delicacy and is served baked, cut into steaks and grilled, or stuffed (sometimes with crayfish tails) and simmered in wine. It is immensely popular in Russia where it is called *sudak.* See also FISCH; PERCH; SANDRE.

zanzarelle, an Italian soup not unlike *stracciatella.* To prepare it 3 beaten eggs are mixed with 6 tablespoons flour in a double-boiler until a smooth paste of pouring consistency is obtained. If the eggs are small, a little milk may be added. Flavouring of nutmeg, salt, and pepper is included. The mixture is then poured into boiling hot stock so that it falls like strings of thin pasta (a colander is useful to pour it through). Finally a little grated Parmesan cheese is added to the stock, and the soup is cooked rapidly for 5 minutes.

zapallito de tronco, a variety of small vegetable marrow (summer squash) or squash, also known as *avocadella* and Argentine or South American marrow or squash. The plant is of the bush-type, and the large fruits cluster round the base of the main stem. The flesh of the fruit is pink and the taste resembles that of avocado pear. Zapallito de tronco is easily grown from seed in temperate climates with the aid of cloches or a cold greenhouse. It has long been popular in France and is rapidly gaining success in Britain and Iceland.

The fruits are prepared by being boiled whole for 10 minutes only, then cut in half when cool, and the pips removed. They can be served in a number of ways similar to those used for the avocado. The flesh may be scooped out, diced, given a dressing of mayonnaise, or olive or vegetable oil and vinegar, then chilled and left to stand for several hours; or the flesh may be scooped out, diced, and mixed with chopped mushrooms, peas or beans, fish, prawns, cold chicken, ham, etc., and bound with mayonnaise. Many people prefer *avocadella* to avocado as it tastes less rich. See also VEGETABLE MARROW.

zapekanka, a Russian vegetable dish, made from a mixture of 2 lb. potatoes mashed with ½ pint (1 cup) milk, 2 eggs, and 3 tablespoons melted butter layered in a casserole with 3 large fried onions. It is finished with a layer of the potato mixture, and then either melted butter or sour cream is poured over before baking for about 30 minutes. Mushroom sauce is often served with zapekanka. See also KARTOFEL.

zaprażka biała, Polish for a white roux made from equal amounts of flour and butter, heated, and stirred well together. A brown roux is zaprażka rumiana; zaprażka na surowo is *beurre manié.*

zarthe (*Abramis vimba*), a freshwater fish found in most European rivers, though not in the Rhine. It is a species of bream and can be cooked in the same way as bream. It is particularly popular in Poland, where it is canned extensively. See also ZÄHRTE.

zarzuela de mariscos, a Spanish fish stew which is a speciality of Catalonia, especially Barcelona. The fish used is likely to be sea bass, the large red bream, bonito, angler fish, flounder, or sole. To prepare it 1 lb. fish, with 2 lb. shrimps or prawns, mussels, scallops, or clams, is sautéed in olive oil, sprinkled with flour, and flambéed with brandy. The fish and shellfish are removed, and 1 sliced onion, 1 sweet pepper, 2 garlic cloves, 2 tomatoes, and 3 tablespoons chopped almonds are cooked in the same oil until tender. Then 1 wineglass (½ cup) white wine is added, and the whole is boiled up until it thickens. The fish and shellfish are replaced and reheated, then the stew is sprinkled with parsley and served in soup plates.

zayats, Russian for young hare or leveret, which is popular in Russia. It is either roasted, after first marinating in ½ pint (1 cup) wine vinegar and 2 pints (4 cups) water and served with a sauce made from onions, beetroot, and demi-glace; or it is turned in butter, sprinkled with flour, and then casseroled with root vegetables, onions, 1 pint (2 cups) sour cream, ½ pint (1 cup) giblet stock, 2 Hamburg parsley roots and leaf, and seasonings. See also GAME; HARE; ZAJĄC.

zébrine, a variety of eggplant which has violet and white stripes. It is grown in many parts of Europe, especially France.

Zeeland oysters, extremely good oysters from the Dutch province of Zeeland, which is situated at the mouth of the river Scheldt.

zelèn fasùl, Bulgarian for runner (string) bean.

zelèn fasùl sŭs yaytsà, runner (string) beans with eggs. First 1 lb. beans is chopped and fried with onions, sprinkled with flour, and seasoned with a little paprika and parsley. Then 2 eggs beaten with ½ pint (1 cup) milk is poured over the vegetables. The whole is then baked in a moderate oven for 20 minutes.

zelèn hayvèr, a typical Bulgarian salad made from baked,

skinned, pulped eggplants beaten with vinegar, olive oil, garlic, tomatoes, sometimes a small hot green chilli, and seasoning, before being put through a sieve. Zelèn hayvèr means ''green roes''—the eggplants constituting the mock roes. This salad mixture is sometimes roasted with poultry, when it is called *purée zelenchùk*.

zeli, Czechoslovakian for cabbage.

zelná polévka, a traditional cabbage soup. A white roux is made and mixed with chopped blanched cabbage. Then beef stock is added to the required amount, followed by salt, pepper, and nutmeg. The soup is thickened with egg yolks blended with milk.

zelný guláš, a cabbage and beef goulash. This is made as for beef goulash, with a seasoning of paprika and caraway seeds; then white wine mixed with 1 tablespoon vinegar is added to cover, followed by the shredded cabbage.

zéphir, I. The French name for any light or frothy dish. II. A French mousseline forcemeat made of game, poultry, or white meat mixed with stiffly beaten egg whites and baked in small soufflé dishes.

zeppole alla napoletana, also called *zeppole di San Giuseppe,* small fried pastries which are a St. Joseph's Day speciality in Naples. They are made from 8 oz. (2 cups) flour mixed gradually with 1 pint (2 cups) water until smooth. Then ¼ pint (½ cup) brandy and a pinch of salt are added. The mixture is cooked over a low heat, stirring constantly, until it leaves the sides of the saucepan. When cool, the mixture is kneaded, rolled into a long sausage shape, and cut into slices which are formed into balls and fried in deep hot oil. When drained, they are rolled in icing sugar and eaten hot. See also FESTA DI SAN GIUSEPPE.

zest, the outer layer containing the essential oils of the skin of lemon, orange, and other citrus fruits. A fine grater or a lump of sugar rubbed on the outside is used to detach it. See also ZESTE.

zeste, French for zest. Zester is the verb meaning to detach the zest, and a zesteur is a special implement rather like a fine potato peeler which is used for this process. See also ZEST.

zewelwaï, see TARTE À L'OIGNON.

zeytinli prasa, see PRASA.

ziemniaki, a Polish potato dish. It consists of mashed potatoes mixed with herring fillets, layered with sliced, hard-boiled eggs, melted butter, and sour cream. It is baked for ½ hour. See also RACUSZKL.

zillertalerkrapfen, see KRAPFEN.

zimino, a Genoese fish stew using olive oil and no other liquid. It is often made with cuttlefish and squid as well as with other fish, and sometimes even with snails (lumache). The fish is cooked with oil, onion, fennel, celery, parsley, and spinach or chard leaves. Tomatoes, too, can be added according to taste.

ziminù, the Sardinian name for *zimino,* which is eaten extensively in Sardinia.

zimt, German for cinnamon.

zimtsterne, star-shaped cinnamon biscuits or cookies, which are also popular in the U.S. To prepare them 8 oz. (1 cup) sugar, 1 teaspoon cinnamon, and 1 teaspoon grated lemon peel are mixed together. Then 3 egg whites and a pinch of salt are beaten until stiff, then the sugar mixture is gradually added, beating all the time. Next 1½ cups grated unblanched almonds are included and the mixture is chilled. It is then rolled out on a sugared and floured board, and the biscuits (cookies) are cut out with a star cutter, brushed with beaten egg yolk, and baked on a greased baking sheet in a slow-to-moderate oven for 15–20 minutes.

zingara, à la, I. A French sauce for small cuts of meat, poultry, or eggs. It consists of demi-glace flavoured with tomato purée, cayenne pepper, and Madeira, and garnished with a julienne of mushrooms, truffles, ham, and ox tongue, seasoned with a little paprika. II. A French garnish for poultry and small cuts of meat. It is composed of finely chopped lean ham, tongue, mushrooms, and truffles, all sautéed in butter and bound with demi-glace flavoured with tomato purée and tarragon. III. A method of preparing chicken. See POULET À LA ZINGARA.

žirniai, a Lithuanian method of cooking peas with butter and very little water.

ziste, the French word for the acrid white pith found between the peel and the fruit in citrus fruits.

zlato, a Czechoslovakian cheese made from goat's or ewe's milk. It has a good flavour and a soft consistency.

znojemský gulás, a Czechoslovakian stew made by simmering diced beef with onion and very little water, then thickening with flour. Sliced pickled cucumbers are added to the sauce. It is served with *knedlíky* or potatoes.

zola, a French consommé of beef garnished with tiny cheese dumplings mixed with chopped white truffles. Grated cheese is served separately. See also CONSOMMÉ.

zorilla, a French chicken consommé garnished with cooked chick-peas and rice and flavoured with tomato juice. See also CONSOMMÉ.

zouave, a French sauce consisting of demi-glace flavoured with tomato purée and seasoned with garlic, mustard, and chopped fresh tarragon.

zrazy, a dish of Polish origin, but one which, for a long time now, has also been a national dish in Russia. It resembles beef olives but can be made with other meats and also with fish. It consists of rolls of fish or meat stuffed with a mixture of savoury breadcrumbs or kasha, fried onion, chopped cooked mushrooms (usually dried), chopped bacon, herbs, etc., covered with stock, and baked for about 1 hour in the oven. The stock is thickened with sour cream, and potatoes or buckwheat are served as an accompaniment.

zrazy wołowe z kaszą i grzybami, beef slices stuffed and rolled with minced field mushrooms, onions, roast chicken, and *kasha,* all bound with raw eggs.

zrazy z kapustą kwaśną, beef slices with sauerkraut. The slices are arranged in a casserole, each slice being covered, or rolled up, with sauerkraut. Soup stock is poured over all and the dish is baked.

zübdei hünkâri, ''Imperial cream,'' a Turkish sweet dish made from 6 oz. (⅔ cup) castor sugar, ¾ cup rose water, ¼ pint (½ cup) maraschino, and 1½ oz. gelatine. The gelatine and sugar are dissolved, and the other ingredients added. When cool, 1 pint (2 cups) whipped cream is mixed in well and the dish is chilled and then served.

zucchetti, see ZUCCHINI.

zucchini or **zucchetti,** Italian for baby marrow (zucchini), also called courgettes in France and Britain. When slicing, cut from the flower end to avoid bitterness.

pasta con salsa di zucchine, a dish popular in Naples and particularly in Positano. It consists of pasta served with a sauce made from *zucchini* which have been salted and then fried until they are soft. Another method is to serve thin slices, crisply fried with pasta. This is a speciality of the Grand Hotel, Rome. The male flowers of zucchini are eaten in Italy. They are usually dipped in batter (*pastella*) and fried, but in some country areas they are stuffed with rice, then fried, and served cold.

zucchine alla milanese, a Milanese method of cooking baby marrow (zucchini), used for antipasti (antipasto). They are skinned and sliced, dipped in beaten egg and breadcrumbs, and then fried.

zucchine in salmi, another way of cooking baby marrows

(zucchini), also used for antipasti (antipasto). They are fried, then marinated in water containing vinegar, bay leaves, cloves, pepper, onion, carrot, and seasoning.

zucchine ripiene, baby marrows (zucchini) stuffed with meat, rice, breadcrumbs, and herbs or cheese, then baked in oil or butter.

zuger rötel, a small red freshwater fish of the char family, common in Switzerland. It is cooked by frying in oil, and in Basel is served with an onion sauce, elsewhere with an egg sauce.

zunge, German for tongue. Tongue is served hot or cold in Germany, often with horseradish; in both Germany and Austria it is frequently served with sauerkraut as an accompaniment. See also TONGUE.

zunge mit kapernsauce, a popular German method of serving tongue. The tongue is cooked with 2 sliced onions in equal quantities of white wine and stock for about 2 hours. When the tongue is tender, it is skinned, the stock is thickened with flour, and capers and sour cream are added.

zupa, Polish for soup. Herbs such as sorrel are used extensively for soups in Poland, as well as dried mushrooms and sour cream. In the summer, cold soups, often with a sweet flavour and made from berries and fruits, or beer, are popular. Other Polish soups are *barszcz, chłodnik gotowany, kalteszal, kapusniak,* and *krupnik.* See also ROSÓL; SOUP.

The most popular soups follow here:

zupa chelbowa, 3 pints (6 cups) vegetable broth is simmered with 2 cups stale, soaked rye or wholemeal bread, then sieved; ½ pint (1 cup) milk and a pinch of nutmeg are added, and all is heated but not boiled. Then 3 beaten eggs are mixed with a little of the hot soup and then blended with the whole, taking care that it does not curdle. It is served with slices of hard-boiled egg. This soup can also be made with thickened beef stock instead of vegetable stock, and served with slices of toasted rye bread with a poached egg on top as a garnish. In this case the 3 eggs are omitted. This soup is also sometimes garnished with sliced sausage.

zupa grzybowa czysta, vegetable and dried mushroom soup, to which sour cream may be added.

zupa jagodowa czysta, a soup made from puréed blackberries, blueberries, etc., with sugar to taste and potato flour added to thicken, sometimes topped with sour cream and usually served cold. All fruits can be treated in this way.

zupa kalafiorowa, cauliflower soup, thickened with egg yolk and cream.

zupa kminkowa, beef broth simmered with caraway seeds, thickened with a *beurre manié,* and garnished with diced sausage and croûtons.

zupa koperkowa, fresh chopped dill mixed with raw egg yolks and sour cream, and whisked into hot, but not boiling, stock.

zupa 'nic,' see PIANKI DO ZUPY NIC.

zupa pieczarkowa, fresh mushroom soup.

zupa piwna, a soup made with 3 pints (6 cups) beer, 6 egg yolks, and 1 tablespoon sugar. The raw egg yolks are beaten with the sugar, then the hot beer is gradually added, beating all the time as for an egg nog.

zupa pomidorowa czysta, clear tomato soup.

zupa rakowa, crayfish soup.

zupa szczawiowa, sorrel soup. Chopped raw sorrel is sautéed in butter, sprinkled with flour, and mixed with sour cream. It is then stirred into hot stock and garnished with hard-boiled eggs cut in quarters.

zupa szczawiowa na rosole, chopped sorrel cooked in beef stock, served with 1 poached egg for each person.

zupa watrobiana, liver soup. Calf's liver is cut into strips, sautéed, and added to vegetable soup. It is sometimes thickened with egg yolks.

zuppa, Italian for soup. See also BOMBOLINE DI RICOTTA IN BRODO; BRODO; MINESTRA; MINESTRONE; PAPAROT; PASSATELLI; SOUP; STRACCIATELLA; ZANZARELLE.

zuppa alla Genoese, a regional soup from Genoa. Two lb. chopped fish, 1 onion, and parsley are simmered in butter, then 2 quarts (8 cups) water or fish stock is added and boiled gently for 30 minutes. The soup is seasoned, and grated nutmeg is added, before all is put through a sieve. It is thickened with egg yolks, and then served with little fish dumplings fried in olive oil.

zuppa alla Palermitana, a regional soup from Palermo. Diced veal, beef, ham, calf's liver, and salt pork are simmered in butter with carrots, celery, and leeks. Water is added, with a seasoning of peppercorns, marjoram, bay leaves, and salt. When cooked, the soup is rubbed through a sieve and white wine is added. It is garnished with veal quenelles, and grated Parmesan cheese is served separately.

zuppa alla pavese, a regional soup from Pavia. Slices of toasted bread are placed in an earthenware soup pot. A raw egg is broken over them, and then a thick layer of grated Parmesan cheese is sprinkled on top. The soup pot is then filled with rich beef or vegetable broth, and the floating bread slices are browned in a very hot oven. This is the traditional method. More often, the egg is broken into the hot soup in the plate and is cooked lightly by the heat.

zuppa alla pavese

zuppa dei pescatore (fishermen's soup), for this traditional Italian soup a quantity of about 3 lb. assorted small sea fish are cooked in a stock made with chopped onions, carrots, celery, and leeks in water seasoned with salt, pepper, allspice, thyme, and bay leaves. When cooked (after about 15 minutes) the fish are carefully removed. Slices of bread are fried in oil and then arranged in a soup tureen with the fish on top of them. Then the soup, which has been strained and kept hot, is poured over. Grated Parmesan cheese is served separately.

zuppa di castagne, soup made from chestnuts, onion, celery, seasoning, and stock (vegetable, chicken, or veal). When cooked it is sieved and served with croûtons.

zuppa di ceci, traditional eel soup, eaten on All Souls' Night in Lombardy. See also ANGUILLA.

zuppa di cozze, a rich soup made with mussels in their shells, onions, olive oil, tomatoes, celery, parsley, garlic, marjoram or basil, lemon peel, white wine, and seasoning. See also COZZE.

zuppa di fave, an excellent soup made from dried broad beans. First 1 lb. beans is soaked overnight, then cooked slowly with 1 large sliced onion, 1 chopped garlic clove, ½ teaspoon each chopped rosemary and parsley, salt, and pepper to taste, and water covering the ingredients by 2 inches. When the beans are soft, after about 2 hours, 2 tablespoons olive oil is stirred in. This thick nourishing soup is eaten hot in winter; in summer it is served almost cold, particularly on the Sorrentine peninsula and in Capri, and is surprisingly good. With cold meat, salami, or cheese to follow, it makes a simple, filling lunch.

zuppa di peoci, a Venetian soup containing mussels, olive oil, garlic, and parsley. In Venice mussels are known as peoci.

zuppa di pesce, fish soup. Many different varieties of fish soup are made in Italy (see below). See also BRODETTO; BURRIDA; CACCIUCCO.

zuppa di pesce alla caprese, Capri fish soup. A broth is made by sautéeing 2 lb. tomatoes in ¼ pint (½ cup) olive oil, then adding ¼ pint (½ cup) white wine. Sliced octopus, *mazzancolle,* mussels, *tonnetto,* and several other fish are added and cooked in the oily tomato soup for about 30 minutes or until tender. The soup is served with fried bread.

zuppa di pesce alla romana, first a fish stock is made with the heads, tails, and skins of *cappone,* hogfish, angler fish, and *morena;* next a chopped octopus and an inkfish are cooked to make a second stock (the pieces of octopus and inkfish being put on one side), and the 2 stocks are strained. In another pan, celery, garlic, parsley, and tomatoes are sautéed in olive oil for 5 minutes; then to them are added the chunks of cooked fish, and scrubbed mussels, clams, scampi, or whatever else is available, in their shells. Finally the strained stock is included, and when the fish is tender and the shellfish are open, the soup is ready. It is served with fried bread.

zuppa di pesto, vegetable soup, using cabbage, zucchini, beans, peas, tomatoes, potatoes, etc. It is served with 1 teaspoon *pesto* in each plate.

zuppa di pomidoro, tomato soup. Onion and tomatoes are sweated in butter with a little sugar, salt, basil, and parsley; then stock is added, after which the soup is sieved. Sometimes cream is added as a garnish.

zuppa di spinaci, spinach simmered in butter until soft, when seasoning and a pinch of nutmeg are added, followed by 1 quart (4 cups) stock (to 2 lb. spinach). When all is puréed, 2 tablespoons cream is added. It is served with fried croûtons, sometimes spread with *pâté* or anchovy paste.

zuppa di verdure, vegetable soup, using onion, carrots, celery, potatoes, tomato purée, and garlic, and served with grated Parmesan cheese. When green beans, zucchini, cucumber, watercress, mint, and a lot of parsley is used, it is called zuppa di vercolor.

zuppa di vongole, clam soup. The clams are scrubbed and cooked in white wine until they open, when they are removed and the stock put on one side. Leek, onion, garlic, tomato, and celery leaves are lightly sautéed in olive oil with basil or marjoram; then the clam stock and 1½ pints (3 cups) fish stock are added and simmered for 10 minutes. The clams, their shells removed, are just heated in the soup, and it is served with croûtons of bread fried in oil.

zuppa inglese, not a soup at all but a lavish Italian cake like a trifle. Its name certainly confuses tourists with a scanty knowledge of Italy, and must have originated in some kind of joke. It resembles an English tipsy cake (which is like a trifle), consisting of layers of sponge cake, fruit preserves, rum, and custard, all covered with rum-flavoured whipped cream and diced candied fruits. Some sources suggest *zuppa* is derived from "sop," a moistened bread, and that *inglese* is a distortion of *angelica.*

zürcher leberspiessli, see LEBER.

zürcher topf, a Swiss dish consisting of boiled brisket of beef with root vegetables.

zure saus, a Dutch sour sauce often served with boiled fresh tongue. A roux is made from equal amounts of butter and flour, diluted with hot tongue stock so that it is fairly thin. The juice of 1 lemon is added, and 1 beaten egg yolk per pint of liquid is folded into the hot, but not boiling, sauce. Just before serving, small dots of butter are added and allowed to melt. The sauce is then poured over the sliced tongue.

zuring, Dutch for sorrel. A traditional method is to cook about 2 lb. sorrel with very little water, drain, and then simmer with 3 tablespoons butter and 3 tablespoons sugar. About 10 minutes before serving, 2 tablespoons raisins is added. See also SORREL.

zuurkool, Dutch for sauerkraut. Sauerkraut is often served with bacon in Holland (zuurkool met spek).

zwetsch, a member of the plum family, grown extensively in Germany, and also in Alsace-Lorraine where it is called *quetsche* and forms the base of a local spirit, *quetsch.* It is chiefly used for drying into prunes. See also QUICHE AUX PRUNEAUX.

zwetschken-bavesen, plum jam fritters, traditionally eaten in Bavaria on the feast-day known as *Kirchweih.* Stale crustless rolls are cut in half and plum jam is spread between; then they are soaked in cold milk, dipped in beaten egg, and fried in hot fat until golden brown. They are sprinkled with sugar and cinnamon and served hot.

zwetschkenknödel, see KNÖDEL.

zwetschkenkuchen, a cake of yeasted dough made with sugar, lemon peel, melted butter, egg yolk, and halved fresh plums. See STOLLEN for dough.

zwezerik, Dutch for sweetbreads. See also SWEETBREADS.

zwezerik pudding, ½ lb. sweetbreads is first rinsed three times in warm water and then once in cold, after which the fat and membrane are removed and the sweetbreads are simmered with parsley, celery, a pinch of mace, and salt. After the sweetbreads have been drained and rinsed once more, and their skins have been removed, they are cut up and mixed with 2 crustless slices of stale white bread soaked in a little cream, 3 egg yolks, 2 tablespoons butter, seasoning, and 1 tablespoon chopped parsley. This mixture is folded into beaten egg whites, and is then steamed for 30 minutes in a greased, covered basin, or dish standing in a pan of hot water in a moderate oven. The dish is served with *witte saus.*

zwieback, a German rusk sold commercially. The name comes from *zwei* (twice) and *backen* (to bake). The rusks are made from 1 lb. (3½ cups) flour, ¼ lb. (½ cup) sugar, ¼ lb. (½ cup) butter, ½ pint (1 cup) tepid milk, and 2 tablespoons yeast. First the yeast is dissolved in the lukewarm milk. The dry ingredients are mixed together and the melted butter added to them, then a well is made in the centre into which the yeast is poured. When the yeast has been combined with the other ingredients (using the same method as for making a batter), the mixture is covered and left to rise in a warm place for 2 hours; then it is shaped into rounds which are put to rise again, then brushed with milk and baked in a hot oven. The next day the rusks are split in half and laid crust-side down in a cool oven until the top is crisp and a pale yellow colour. Zwieback is also popular in France, and in Holland where it forms a main ingredient of *appelschoteltje.*

zwiebel, German for onion which are often cooked in stock in Germany. See also ONION.

zwiebelfleisch, an Austrian dish consisting of 1 lb. thinly sliced beef browned in fat with 1½ lb. sliced onions. The ingredients are seasoned, moistened with beef stock, and simmered in a moderate oven for 1½–2 hours or until the meat is tender.

zwiebelkuchen, an Austrian savoury flan. A 9-inch flan tin is lined with a pastry case, which is given a filling of 6 sautéed onions, 2 tomatoes, and 4 chopped bacon rashers, all seasoned, and bound with a mixture of 1 egg and 1 egg yolk beaten up with ¼ pint (½ cup) thin cream and seasoned with a pinch each of paprika and nutmeg. The flan is baked in a moderate oven for 30 minutes and is served hot. An almost identical dish, called zwiebeltorte, is made in Germany, but the bacon and tomatoes are omitted.

zwiebelsauce, Austrian and German onion sauce, made from onions sautéed until golden, a pinch of sugar, salt, stock, paprika, lemon juice, and a thick slice of crustless rye bread, all boiled up, then sieved. It is served hot with meat. See also WIENER ZWIEBELSAUCE.